THE PSYCHOLOGY OF LANGUAGE

Now in full color, this fully revised edition of the best-selling textbook provides an up-to-date and comprehensive introduction to the psychology of language for undergraduates, postgraduates, and researchers. It contains everything the student needs to know about how we acquire, understand, produce, and store language.

Whilst maintaining both the structure of the previous editions and the emphasis on cognitive processing, this fourth edition has been thoroughly updated to include:

- the latest research, including recent results from the fast-moving field of brain imaging and studies
- updated coverage of key ideas and models
- an expanded glossary
- more real-life examples and illustrations.

The Psychology of Language, Fourth Edition is praised for describing complex ideas in a clear and approachable style, and assumes no prior knowledge other than a grounding in the basic concepts of cognitive psychology. It will be essential reading for advanced undergraduate and graduate students of cognition, psycholinguistics, or the psychology of language. It will also be useful for those on speech and language therapy courses.

The book is supported by a companion website featuring a range of helpful supplementary resources for both students and lecturers.

Trevor A. Harley is Dean of Psychology and Chair of Cognitive Psychology at the University of Dundee, Scotland. He was an undergraduate at the University of Cambridge, where he was also a PhD student, completing a thesis on slips of the tongue and what they tell us about speech production. He moved to Dundee from the University of Warwick in 1996. His research interests include speech production, how we represent meaning, and the effects of aging on language.

THE PSYCHOLOGY OF LANGUAGE

FROM DATA TO THEORY

FOURTH EDITION

TREVOR A. HARLEY

Ψ Psychology Press
Taylor & Francis Group

LONDON AND NEW YORK

Fourth edition published 2014
by Psychology Press
27 Church Road, Hove, East Sussex BN3 2FA

and by Psychology Press
711 Third Avenue, New York, NY 10017

Psychology Press is an imprint of the Taylor & Francis Group, an informa business

First edition published by Psychology Press 1995
Third edition published by Psychology Press 2008

British Library Cataloguing in Publication Data
A catalogue record for this book is available from the British Library

Library of Congress Cataloging-in-Publication Data
Harley, Trevor A.
The psychology of language: from data to theory / Trevor A. Harley.—Fourth edition.
pages cm
Includes bibliographical references and index.
1. Psycholinguistics. I. Title.
BF455.H2713 2014
401′.9—dc23
2013022343

ISBN: 978-1-84872-088-6 (hbk)
ISBN: 978-1-84872-089-3 (pbk)
ISBN: 978-1-315-85901-9 (ebk)

Typeset in Times
by Book Now Ltd, London

Printed in Great Britain by Bell & Bain Ltd, Glasgow

CONTENTS

PREFACE TO THE FOURTH EDITION

I started writing this fourth edition with mixed feelings. On the positive side, it is an honor and a delight to be able to write the fourth edition of something. It must also mean that someone is reading it. I also welcomed the chance to make the book better in every way. On the less positive side, it is a huge amount of work.

Apart from updating references and key ideas and models, I have two main aims in this new edition.

Students often find cognition in general difficult and say it is the part of their psychology degree that they like least, but the psychology of language in particular is feared and disliked. I have, I'm almost ashamed to say, only really come to appreciate how much many students dislike it over the last few years. I can't help feeling a bit responsible for this fear: one fair criticism of previous editions of this book is that students find it difficult. It contains a lot of material, perhaps too much. (For those struggling I am biased, but I recommend reading my own book *Talking the Talk* (Harley, 2010) first.) What is more there is a balance to be had between making texts informative with respect to sources (and of course avoiding plagiarism and giving due credit) but making them so reference dense it puts the student off. I fear earlier editions have been reference dense, so I've tried to be lighter in this edition. (This strategy is not without its risk, so if any author or researcher feels I have slighted them, please let me know.)

Therefore my first aim is to make this edition easier and more approachable, and to try to stimulate students into finding psycholinguistics interesting and important. I try to do this explicitly in the first chapter, but you can't persuade someone something is good just by telling them; you have to show it. The resulting book is a compromise between making the subject fun and relevant and depth and perhaps even rigor of coverage. I have learned that you can't please all reviewers, so though some teachers will approve the easier approach, others might bemoan the lack of detail that was in the earlier editions.

Why do students dislike the subject and find it difficult? I think there are several reasons. First, it seems very abstract. I have tried to point out as many applications of the subject as possible, and to give as many concrete examples as I can. Second, they think the subject is full of jargon—which it is. I am surprised to discover how many students are unclear what a noun is, so no wonder they find parsing difficult. I have therefore tried to reduce the jargon and make sure all terms are explained. There is a glossary that should help. Third, perhaps most oddly, they don't like or see the point in models, and psycholinguistics has more models per square page than any other discipline I know. Fourth, psycholinguists rarely come to definitive conclusions—usually at any one time in any one area there are two opposing models out there battling it out. I've tried to stress why models are important, and point out that in cutting-edge science we sometimes have to live with uncertainty.

The field has changed a great deal over the last few years as a result of results from brain imaging, particularly fMRI studies. My second aim therefore is to incorporate as much as is possible of this exciting new research into the book where relevant. Some might know that I am skeptical about what brain imaging can offer cognitive psychology; I have tried not to let this skepticism affect this revision. Most researchers believe that brain imaging has greatly advanced our understanding of psycholinguistics over the last decade.

Technology has changed for the better, too, making writing books much easier. Writing the first edition involved constant trips to the library and much photocopying. In this edition I could read every reference I wanted at the luxury of my desk thanks to Google and electronic journals. I wrote the first draft of this book using the wonderful Scrivener 2.0 on a Mac, and then finished it in Pages.

There is a website associated with this book. It contains links to other pages, details of important recent work, and a "hot link" to contact me. It is to be found at: http://www.psypress.com/cw/harley. I still welcome any corrections, suggestions for the next edition, or discussion on any topic. My email address is now: t.a.harley@dundee.ac.uk. Suggestions on topics I have omitted or under-represented would be particularly welcome. The hardest bit of writing this book has been deciding in what to leave out. I am sure that people running other courses will cover some material in much more detail than has been possible to provide here. I would be interested to hear, however, of any major differences of emphasis. If the new edition is as successful as the third, I will be looking forward (in a strange sort of way) to producing the fifth edition in five years' time.

I would like to thank all those who have made suggestions about one or more of the previous editions, particularly Jeanette Altarriba, Gerry Altmann, Elizabeth Bates, Paul Bloom, Helen Bown, Peer Broeder, Gordon Brown, Hugh Buckingham, Annette de Groot, Lynne Duncan, the Dundee Psycholinguistics Discussion Group, Andy Ellis, Gerry Griffin, Zenzi Griffin, Francois Grosjean, Evan Heit, Laorag Hunter, Lesley Jessiman, Barbara Kaup, Alan Kennedy, Kathryn Kohnert, Annukka Lindell, Nick Lund, Siobhan MacAndrew, Nadine Martin, Randi Martin, Elizabeth Maylor, Don Mitchell, Wayne Murray, Lyndsey Nickels, Jane Oakhill, Padraig O'Seaghdha, Shirley-Anne Paul, Martin Pickering, Julian Pine, Ursula Pool, Eleanor Saffran, Lynn Santelmann, Marcus Taft, Jeremy Tree, Roger van Gompel, Carel van Wijk, Alan Wilkes, Beth Wilson, Suzanne Zeedyk, and Pienie Zwitserlood. I would also like to thank several anonymous reviewers for their comments; hopefully you know who you are. Numerous people pointed out minor errors and asked questions: I thank them all. George Dunbar created the sound spectrogram for Figure 2.1 using MacSpeechLab. Lila Gleitman gave me the very first line; thanks! Katie Edwards, Pam Miller, and Denise Jackson helped me to obtain a great deal of material, often at very short notice. This book would be much worse without the help of all these people. I am of course responsible for any errors or omissions that remain. If there is anyone else I have forgotten, please accept my apologies. Many people have suggested things that I have thought about and decided not to implement, and many people have suggested things (more connectionism, less connectionism, leave that in, take that out, move that bit there, leave it there) that are the opposite of what others have suggested.

In particular the writing of this edition was made immeasurably easier by spending time in the glorious environment of the University of California, San Diego. I wish to thank everyone there from the bottom of my heart, particularly my hosts Tamar Gollan and Vic Ferreira.

I would also like to thank Psychology Press for all their help and enthusiasm for this project. Finally, I would like to thank Brian Butterworth, who supervised my PhD. He probably doesn't realize how much I appreciated his help; without him, this book might never have existed.

Finally, I hope that any bias there is in this book will appear to be the consequence of the consideration of evidence rather than of prejudice.

Professor Trevor A. Harley
School of Psychology
University of Dundee
Dundee DD1 4HN
Scotland
t.a.harley@dundee.ac.uk
February 2013

ILLUSTRATION CREDITS

Chapter 10

Page 290: © Claudia Steininger/Shutterstock.com. Page 316: From Friederici (2002). Copyright © 2002 Elsevier. Reprinted with permission.

Chapter 11

Page 327: © Anton_Ivanov/Shutterstock.com. Page 330: © Bozena Fulawka/Shutterstock.com. Page 337: © Mogens Trolle/Shutterstock.com. Page 339: © PR Michel Zanca/ISM/Science Photo Library. Page 343: From Sitton, Mozer, and Farah (2000). Copyright © 2000 by the American Psychological Association. Reprinted with permission. Page 344: From Snodgrass and Vanderwart (1980). Copyright © 1980 by the American Psychological Association. Reprinted with permission. Page 348: © Alfred Pasieka/Science Photo Library.

Chapter 12

Page 361: © Tomasz Trojanowski/Shutterstock.com. Page 362: © Bettmann/Corbis. Page 365: From Bransford and Johnson (1973). Copyright © 1973 Academic Press. Reproduced by permission of Elsevier. Page 372: © Tim Pannell/Corbis. Page 379: © Roy McMahon/Corbis.

Chapter 13

Page 397: © Bettmann/Corbis. Page 413 (top): From Indefrey and Levelt (2004). Copyright © 2004. Reproduced by permission of Elsevier. Page 413 (bottom): © Wellcome Dept. of Cognitive Neurology/Science Photo Library. Page 414: © image100/Corbis. Page 416: From Caramazza (1997). Copyright © 1997 Psychology Press. Page 419: From Levelt et al. (1991). Copyright © 1991 by the American Psychological Association. Reprinted with permission. Page 424: From Dell (1986). Copyright © by the American Psychological Association. Reprinted with permission. Page 436: Reprinted from Grodzinsky and Friederici (2006). Copyright © 2006, with permission from Elsevier. Page 439: © Bsip, Mendil/Science Photo Library. Page 441: From Martin et al. (1994). Copyright © 1994 by Academic Press. Reproduced by permission of Elsevier.

Chapter 14

Page 450 (top): © Mike Watson Images/Corbis. Page 454: © Don Hammond/Design Pics/Corbis. Page 456: Adapted from Ferreira et al. (2005). Copyright © 2005, with permission from Elsevier.

Chapter 15

Page 463: © Wellcome Dept. of Cognitive Neurology/Science Photo Library.

Chapter 16

Page 476: © Geoff Tompkinson/Science Photo Library. Page 478: © James King-Holmes/Science Photo Library.

HOW TO USE THIS BOOK

This book is intended to be a stand-alone introduction to the psychology of language. It is my hope that anyone could pick it up and finish reading it with a rich understanding of how humans use language. Nevertheless, it would probably be advantageous to have some knowledge of basic cognitive psychology. (Some suggestions for books to read are given in the "Further reading" section at the end of Chapter 1.) For example, you should be aware that psychologists have distinguished between short-term memory (which has limited capacity and can store material for only short durations) and long-term memory (which is virtually unlimited). I have tried to assume that the reader has no knowledge of linguistics, although I hope that most readers will be familiar with such concepts as nouns and verbs. The psychology of language is quite a technical area full of rather daunting terminology. I have defined technical terms and italicized them when they first appear. There is also a glossary with short definitions of the technical terms.

Connectionist modeling is now central to modern cognitive psychology. Unfortunately, it is also a topic that most people find extremely difficult to follow. It is impossible to understand the details of connectionism without some mathematical sophistication. I have provided an appendix that covers the basics of connectionism in more mathematical detail than is generally necessary to understand the main text. The general principles of connectionism can, however, probably be appreciated without this extra depth, although it is probably a good idea to look at the appendix.

In my opinion and experience, the material in some chapters is more difficult than others.

I do not think that there is anything much that can be done about this, but to persevere. Sometimes comprehension might be assisted by later material, and sometimes a number of readings might be necessary to comprehend the material fully. Fortunately, the study of the psychology of language gives us clues about how to facilitate understanding. Chapters 7 and 11 will be particularly useful in this respect. It should also be remembered that in some areas researchers do not agree on the conclusions or on what should be the appropriate method to investigate a problem. Therefore it is sometimes difficult to say what the "right answer," or the correct explanation of a phenomenon, might be. In this respect the psychology of language is still a very young subject.

The book is divided into sections, each covering an important aspect of language. Section A is an introduction. It describes what language is, and provides essential background for describing language. It should not be skipped. Section B is about the biological basis of language, the relationship of language to other cognitive processes, and language development. Section C is about how we recognize words. Section D is about comprehension: how we understand sentences and discourse. Section E is about language production, and also about how language interacts with memory. It also examines the grand design or architecture of the language system. This final section concludes with a brief look at some possible new directions in the psychology of language.

Each chapter begins with an introduction outlining what the chapter is about and the main problems faced in each area. Each introduction ends with a summary of what you should know by the end of the chapter. Each chapter concludes with a list of bullet points that gives a one-sentence summary of each section in that chapter. This is followed by questions that you can think about either to test your understanding of the material, or to go beyond what is covered, usually with an emphasis on applying the material. If you want to follow a topic up in more detail than is covered in the text (which I think is quite richly referenced, and should be the first place to look), then there are suggestions for further reading at the very end of each chapter.

One way of reading this book is like a novel: start here and go to the end. Section A should certainly be read before the others because it introduces many important terms, without which later going would be very difficult. I certainly recommend starting with Chapter 1. After that, alternative orders are possible, however. I have tried to make each chapter as self-contained as possible, so there is no reason why the chapters cannot be read in a different order. Similarly, you might choose to omit some chapters altogether. In each case you might find you have to refer to the glossary more often than if you just begin at the beginning. Unless you are interested in just a few topics, however, I advise reading the whole book through at least once. Each chapter looks at a major chunk of the study of the psychology of language.

OVERVIEW

Chapter 1 tells you about the subject of the psychology of language. It covers its history and methods. Chapter 2 provides some important background on language, telling you how we can describe sounds and the structure of sentences. In essence it is a primer on phonology and syntax.

Chapter 3 is about how language is related to biological and cognitive processes. It looks at the extent to which language depends on the presence and operation of certain biological, cognitive, and social precursors in order to be able to develop normally. We will also look at whether animals use language, or whether they can be taught to do so. This will also help clarify what we mean by language. We will look at how language is founded in the brain, and how damage to the brain can lead to distinct types of impairment in language. We will look in detail at the more general role of language, by examining the relation between language and thought. We will also look at what can be learned from language acquisition in exceptional circumstances, including the effects of linguistic deprivation.

Chapter 4 examines how children acquire language, and how language develops throughout childhood. Chapter 5 examines how bilingual children learn to use two languages.

We will then look in Chapter 6 at what appear to be the simplest or lowest level processes and work towards more complex ones. Hence we will first look at how we recognize and understand single words. Although these chapters are largely about recognizing words in isolation in the sense that in most of the experiments we discuss only one word is present at a time, the influence of the context in which they are found is an important consideration, and we will look at this also.

Chapter 7 looks at how we recognize words and how we access their meanings. Although the emphasis is upon visually presented word recognition, many of the findings described in this chapter are applicable to recognizing spoken words as well. Chapter 8 examines how we read and pronounce words, and looks at disorders of reading (the dyslexias). It also looks at how we learn to read. Chapter 9 looks at the speech system and how we process speech and identify spoken words.

We then move on to how words are ordered to form sentences. Chapter 10 looks at how we make use of word order information in understanding sentences. These are issues to do with syntax and parsing. Chapter 11 examines how we represent the meaning of words. Chapter 12 examines how we comprehend and represent beyond the sentence level; these are the larger units of discourse or text. In particular, how do we integrate new information with old to create a coherent representation? How do we store what we have heard and read?

In Chapter 13 we consider the process in reverse, and examine language production and its disorders. By this stage we will have an understanding of the processes involved in understanding language, and these processes must be looked at in a wider context (Chapter 14).

In Chapter 15 we will look at the structure of the language system as a whole, and the relation between the parts. Finally, Chapter 16 looks at some possible new directions in psycholinguistics.

SECTION A

INTRODUCTION

This section describes what the rest of the book is about, discusses some important themes in the psychology of language, and examines some important concepts used to describe language. You should read this section before the others.

Chapter 1, The study of language, looks at the functions of language and how the study of language plays a major role in helping to understand human behavior. We look at what language is and what it is used for. After a brief look at the history and methods of psycholinguistics, the chapter covers some current themes and controversies in modern psycholinguistics, including modularity, innateness, and the usefulness of brain imaging, and studies involving people with brain damage, for looking at language.

Chapter 2, Describing language, looks at the building blocks of language—sounds, words, and sentences. The chapter then examines Chomsky's approaches to syntax and how these have evolved over the years.

CHAPTER ❶

THE STUDY OF LANGUAGE

INTRODUCTION

What's the best joke you've heard? I find it difficult to remember any (and very few that can be put into print), but a search through Google of "best joke in the world" throws up this gem:

A couple of New Jersey hunters are out in the woods when one of them falls to the ground. He doesn't seem to be breathing, his eyes are rolled back in his head. The other guy whips out his cell phone and calls the emergency services. He gasps to the operator: "My friend is dead! What can I do?" The operator, in a calm soothing voice, says: "Just take it easy. I can help. First, let's make sure he's dead." There is a silence, then a shot is heard. The guy's voice comes back on the line. He says: "OK, now what?"

Well, I must admit that one did make me laugh. Why is it funny? Notice how much the joke depends on language, in every way.

What was the last thing you said? The last thing you heard? The last thing you read? And the last thing you wrote? How did your brain do these things?

Think of the steps involved in communicating with other people. We obviously must have the necessary biological hardware: We need an articulatory apparatus that enables us to make the right sort of sounds, and of course we also need a brain to decide what to say, how to say it, and

to make the components of the articulatory apparatus move at just the right time. We also need a language complex enough to convey any possible message. We need to know the words and how to put the words in the right order. Young children somehow acquire this language. Finally, we have to be aware of the social setting in which we produce and understand these messages: We need to be aware of the knowledge and beliefs of other people, and have some idea of how they will interpret our utterances. The subject matter of this book is the psychological processing involved in this sort of behavior.

Although we usually take language for granted, a moment's reflection will show how important it is in our lives. In some form or another it so dominates our social and cognitive activity that it would be difficult to imagine what life would be like without it. Indeed, most of us consider language to be an essential part of what it means to be human, and it is largely what sets us apart from other animals. Our culture and technology depends on it. Crystal (2010) describes several functions of language. The primary purpose of language is of course to communicate, but we can also use it simply to express emotion (e.g., by swearing), for social interaction (e.g., by saying "bless you!" when someone sneezes), to make use of its sounds (e.g., in various children's games), to attempt to control the environment (e.g., magical spells), to record facts, to think with, and to express identity (e.g., chanting in demonstrations). We even play with language. Much humor—particularly punning—depends on being able to manipulate language (Crystal, 1998).

It is not surprising then that understanding language is an important part of understanding human behavior, with different areas of scientific study emphasizing different aspects of language processing. The study of the *anatomy* of language emphasizes the components of the articulatory tract, such as the tongue and voice box. Neuroscience examines the role of different parts of the brain in behavior. *Linguistics* examines language itself. **Psycholinguistics** is the study of the psychological processes involved in language. **Psycholinguists** study understanding, producing, and remembering language, and hence are concerned with listening, reading, speaking, writing, and memory for language. They are also interested in how we acquire language, and the way in which it interacts with other psychological systems. Many people think that "psycholinguistics" has a rather dated feel, emphasizing the role of linguistics too much. Although the area might once have been about the psychology of linguistic theory, it is now much more. Still, there is currently no better term, so it will have to do.

One reason why we take language for granted is that we usually use it so effortlessly, and most of the time, so accurately. Indeed, when you listen to someone speaking, or look at this page, you normally cannot help but understand what has been said or what is printed on the page in front of you. It is only in exceptional circumstances that we might become aware of the complexity involved: if for example we are searching for a word but cannot remember it; if a relative or colleague has had a stroke that has affected their language; if we observe a child acquiring language; if we try to learn a second language ourselves as an adult; or if we are visually impaired or hearing impaired, or if we meet someone else who is. And, of course, if you find this book so difficult to understand that you have to keep reading and rereading it to make any sense of it. As we shall see, all of these examples of what might be called "language in exceptional circumstances" reveal much about the processes involved in speaking, listening, writing, and reading. But given that language processes are normally so automatic, we also need to carry out careful experiments to understand what is happening. Modern psycholinguistics is therefore closely related to other areas of cognitive psychology, and relies to a large extent on the same

sort of experimental methods. We construct **model**s of what we think is going on from our experimental results; we use observational and experimental data to construct theories. This book will examine some of the experimental findings in psycholinguistics, and the theories that have been proposed to account for them. Generally the phenomena and data to be explained will precede discussion of the models, but it is not always possible to neatly separate data and theories, particularly when experiments are tests of particular theories. I'll be talking a bit more about models and theories later.

This book has a cognitive emphasis. It is concerned with understanding the *processes* involved in using and acquiring language. This is not just my personal bias; I believe that all our past experience has shown that the problems of studying human behavior have yielded, and will continue to yield, to investigation by the methods of cognitive psychology and neuroscience.

WHY STUDY LANGUAGE AND WHY IS IT SO DIFFICULT?

Even before I get on to saying what language is, I want to ask why we should study it. Some people (mostly psycholinguists) think the answer is obvious, but in practice many students are often perplexed as to why so much of their psychology course is devoted to the subject. What's more I've noticed that students often find the psychology of language the most difficult part of psychology. It's often the part they like least (and often actively dislike). So why should we study language?

Well, you're reading this book right now, aren't you? Reading words and sentences and making sense of them (or trying to); that's part of psycholinguistics, for starters. It's a good bet that you're pretty good at reading, but you probably know someone who has had some difficulty in learning to read, or even now finds reading and spelling difficult (that is, they have dyslexia). Perhaps you know someone who has had a stroke and now finds reading difficult. More psycholinguistics!

But I bet you've listened to the radio or TV today, or listened to music with words (talking, more psycholinguistics). I'll be a little surprised if you've not talked to anyone at all (speaking, listening; even yet more psycholinguistics). You've probably written something too (you get the idea).

But even if by some miracle you haven't, I bet you've heard a voice in your head. The voice in your head probably uses words. In fact it's hard (I find impossible) to think about human thought without thinking about language. So thinking, the essence of being human, is completely intertwined with language.

What is more we transmit our learning and culture by language. The major reason civilization has reached its heights, that we live in centrally heated houses with thin computers and cell phones, using social networking sites, is because we have built up a culture and a technology that would have been completely impossible without language. For this reason the evolutionary biologist Martin Nowak (2006) says that language is "the most interesting invention of the last 600 million years" (p. 250). He says that the impact of language is comparable with only a few other events in biological history, such as the evolution of life and the evolution of multi-celled animals.

So here is my list of reasons of why the study of the psychology of language is so important:

1. We use language nearly all the time; technology and our cultures would be impossible without it.
2. We usually think in language.
3. Some people have difficulty learning spoken or written language (developmental disorders), or have difficulty with language as a consequence of brain damage (acquired disorders).

We can agree then that studying language is important; but why do so many students find it hard? I think there are several reasons. First, the importance and applications of language are not always made as clear as they might be. If I told you that I could teach you to read a textbook in a way that would guarantee you'd remember it and understand it and get an A in an exam, you'd probably pay attention. (Sadly I can't, otherwise I would be very rich, although later I will give you some tips.) So in this book I've tried to emphasize the importance

of the applications of the psychology of language. Second, the subject seems to have a lot of jargon in it, and teachers sometimes forget this or underestimate their students' knowledge. How can you be expected to understand what a reduced relative clause is when you don't know what a clause is? Or even aren't that clear what a noun is? I've tried to make life as easy as possible by defining all technical terms, trying to keep jargon to a minimum, and providing a glossary which contains a simple definition of every technical term I can think of. Third, psycholinguists are an argumentative bunch, and rarely seem to agree on anything. Sometimes they can't even agree whether they agree or not. So there are few situations when we can say "now THAT's the answer." And people like answers. They don't like to be left with the conclusion "it could be this or it could be that and it all depends," and that's going to be my conclusion most of the time. But life is full of uncertainties, so get over it and live with it. And the final reason that people find psycholinguistics difficult is because it's full of models. A colleague once told me that she overheard some students talking in front of her (yes, we love to eavesdrop) and one said to the other "language—it's just all these models." Models are the most important thing in science; they're the closest we get to an explanation. I'll talk about models below.

WHAT IS LANGUAGE?

It might seem natural at this point to say exactly what is meant by "language," but to do so is much harder than it first appears. We all have some intuitive notion of what language is; a simple definition might be that it is "a system of symbols and rules that enable us to communicate." Symbols are things that stand for other things: Words, either written or spoken, are symbols. The rules specify how words are ordered to form sentences. However, providing a strict definition of language is not straightforward. Consider other systems that many think are related to human spoken language. Are the communication systems of monkeys a language? What about the "language" of dolphins, or the "dance" of honey bees that communicates the location of sources of nectar to other bees in the hive? How

Are these elephants communicating using a language?

does the signing of people with hearing impairment resemble or differ from spoken language? Because of these sorts of complications, many psychologists and linguists think that providing a formal definition of language is a waste of time. We look at whether animals have language and at the characteristics of language in more detail in Chapter 2.

We can describe language in a variety of ways: for example, we can talk about the sounds of the language, or the meaning of words, or the grammar that determines which sentences of a language are legitimate. These types of distinctions are fundamental in linguistics, and these different aspects of language have been given special names. We can distinguish between **semantics** (the study of meaning), **syntax** (the study of word order), **morphology** (the study of words and word formation), **pragmatics** (the study of language use), **phonetics** (the study of raw sounds), and **phonology** (the study of how sounds are used within a language) (see Figure 1.1).

Syntax will be described in detail in the next chapter, and semantics in Chapter 11. Morphology is concerned with the way that complex words are made up of simpler units, called **morpheme**s. There are two types of morphology: **inflectional morphology**, which is concerned with changes to a word that do not alter its underlying meaning or syntactic category, and **derivational morphology**, which is concerned with changes that do. Examples of inflectional changes are pluralization (e.g., "house" becoming "houses," and "mouse" becoming "mice") and verb tense changes (e.g., "kiss" becoming "kissed," and "run" becoming "ran"). Examples of derivational changes are "develop" becoming "development," "developmental," or "redevelop." The distinction between phonetics and phonology, which are both ways of studying sounds, will also be examined in more detail in Chapter 2.

The idea of "a **word**" also merits consideration. Like the word "language," the word "word" turns out on closer examination to be a somewhat slippery customer. The dictionary definition of a word is "a unit of language," but in fact there

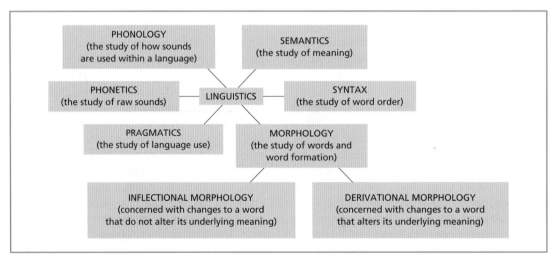

FIGURE 1.1

are many other language units (e.g., sounds and sentences). Crystal (2010, p. 461) defines a word as "the smallest unit of grammar that can stand on its own as a complete utterance, separated with spaces in written language." Hence "pigs" is a word, but the word ending "-ing" by itself is not. A word can in turn be analyzed at a number of levels. At the lowest level, it is made up of sounds, or letters if written down. Sounds combine together to form syllables. Hence the word "cat" has three sounds and one syllable; "houses" has two syllables; "syllable" has three syllables.

Words can also be analyzed in terms of the morphemes they contain. Consider a word like "ghosts." This is made up of two units of meaning: the idea of "ghost," and then the plural ending or **inflection** ("-s"), which conveys the idea of number: in this case that there is more than one ghost. Therefore we say that "ghosts" is made up of two morphemes, the "ghost" morpheme and plural morpheme "s." The same can be said of past tense endings or inflections: "Kissed" is also made up of two morphemes, "kiss" plus the "-ed" past tense inflection which signifies that the event happened in the past. There are two sorts of inflection, regular forms that follow some rule, and irregular forms that do not. Irregular plurals that do not obey the general rule of forming plurals by adding an "-s" to the end of a noun, or forming the past tense by adding a "-d" or "-ed" to the end of a verb, also contain at least two morphemes. Hence "house," "mouse," and "do" are made up of one morpheme, but "houses," "mice," and "does" are made up of two. "Rehoused" is made up of three morphemes: "house" plus "re-" added through mechanisms of derivational morphology, and "-ed" added by inflection. Every child's favorite word "antidisestablishmentarianism" is made up of six morphemes.

Psychologists believe that we store representations of words in a mental dictionary. We call this mental dictionary the **lexicon**. The lexicon contains all the information (or at least pointers to all of the information) that we know about a word, including its sounds (phonology), meaning (semantics), written appearance (orthography), and the syntactic roles the word can adopt. The lexicon must be huge: estimates vary greatly, but a reasonable estimate is that an adult knows about 70,000 words (Nagy & Anderson, 1984; but by "greatly" I mean that the estimates range between 15,000 and 150,000—see Bryson, 1990). Recognizing a word is rather like looking it up in a dictionary; when we know what the word is, we have access to all the information about it, such as what it means and how to spell it. So when we see or hear a word, how do we access its representation within the lexicon? How do we know whether an item is stored there or not? What are the differences between understanding speech and understanding visually presented words? Psycholinguists are particularly interested in the processes of lexical access and how things are represented.

HOW HAS LANGUAGE CHANGED OVER TIME?

Language must have changed enormously over time, and one obvious consequence of these changes is that there are now many different languages in the world. Depending on exactly how something counts as a separate language, there are now thought to be around 5,000–6,000 (but the number is getting smaller as languages, like species, become extinct), although estimates vary between 2,700 and 10,000. We do not even know whether all human languages are descended from one common ancestor, or whether they are derived from a number of ancestors (my bet is on one). However, it is apparent that many languages are related to each other. This relation is apparent in the similarity of many of the words of some languages (e.g., "mother" in English is "Mutter" in German, "moeder" in Dutch, "mère" in French, "maht" in Russian, and "mata" in Sanskrit). More detailed analyses like this have shown that most of the languages of Europe, and parts of west Asia, derive from a common source called proto-Indo-European. All the languages that are derived from this common source are called Indo-European. We can gather ideas about where the speakers of the ancestral language came from, by looking at the words that are shared in the descendant languages. For example, all Indo-European languages have similar words for horses and sheep, but not for palm tree or vine. Hence the original language must have been spoken somewhere where it was easy to find horses and sheep, but where palms and vines could not be found. Such observations suggest that the speakers of proto-Indo-European probably spread out from Anatolia (approximately modern-day Turkey) with the expansion of agriculture about 9,000 years ago (Bouckaert et al., 2012). Indo-European has a number of main branches: the Romance (such as French, Italian, and Spanish), the Germanic (such as German, English, and Dutch), and the Indian languages (see Figure 1.2). There are some languages that are European but that are not part of the Indo-European family. Finnish and Hungarian are from the Finno-Ugric branch of the Uralic family of languages. There are many other language families in addition to Indo-European, including Afro-Asiatic (covering north Africa and the Arabian peninsula), Niger-Congo, Japanese, Sino-Tibetan, and families of languages spoken in and around the Pacific and in north and south America. Altogether linguists have identified over 100 language families, although a few languages, such as Basque, do not seem to be part of any family. The extent to which these large families may be related further back in time is unknown.

Languages also change over relatively short time spans. Chaucerian and Elizabethan English are obviously different from modern English, and even Victorian speakers would sound decidedly archaic to us today, my dear old bean. Even listening to 1970s sitcoms can be disconcerting at times. We coin new words or new uses of old words when necessary (e.g., "computer," "television," "internet," "rap"). Whole words drop out of usage ("thee" and "thou"), and we lose the meanings of some words, sometimes over short time spans—rather sadly I can't remember the last time I had to give a measurement in rods or chains. We borrow (or perhaps steal is a better word) words from other languages ("café" from French, "potato" from Haiti, and "shampoo" from India). Sounds change in words ("sweetard" becomes "sweetheart"). Words are sometimes even created by error: "pea" was back-formed from "pease" as people started to think (incorrectly) that "pease" was plural (Bryson, 1990).

We most definitely should not gloss over differences between languages. Although they have arisen over a relatively short time compared with the evolution of humans, we cannot assume that speakers of different languages process them in the same basic way. Whereas it is likely that most of the mechanisms involved are the same, there might be some differences, particularly in the processing of written or printed words. Writing is a recent development compared with speech, and as we shall see in Chapters 7 and 8, there

Chaucerian language seems archaic and verbose in comparison to modern English.

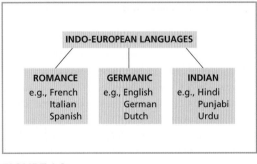

INDO-EUROPEAN LANGUAGES

ROMANCE	GERMANIC	INDIAN
e.g., French	e.g., English	e.g., Hindi
Italian	German	Punjabi
Spanish	Dutch	Urdu

FIGURE 1.2

are important differences in the way that different written languages turn written symbols into sounds. Nevertheless, there is an important core of psychological mechanisms that appear to be common to the processing of all languages.

WHAT IS LANGUAGE FOR?

The question of what language is used for now is intimately linked with its origin and evolution. It is a reasonable assumption that the factors that prompted its origin in humans are still of fundamental importance. Primary among these is the fact that language is used for communication. Although this might seem obvious, we can sometimes lose sight of this point, particularly when we consider some of the more complicated experiments described later in this book. Nevertheless, language is a social activity, and as such is a form of joint action where people collaborate to achieve a common aim (Clark, 1996). We do not speak or write in a vacuum; we speak to communicate, and to ensure that we succeed in communicating we take the point of view of others into account. We look at this idea in detail in Chapter 14.

Although the primary function of language is communication, it might have acquired (or even originated from) other functions. In particular, language might have come to play a role in other, originally non-linguistic, cognitive processes. The extreme version of this idea is that the form of our language shapes our perception and cognition, a view known as the Sapir–Whorf hypothesis. Indeed, some have argued that language evolved to allow us to think, and communication turned out to be a useful side effect. As I noted above, technology and culture would be impossible without language. I examine these ideas in more detail in Chapter 3.

THE HISTORY AND METHODS OF PSYCHOLINGUISTICS

Now we know something about what language is, let us look at how modern psycholinguistics studies it. We will begin by looking briefly at the history of the subject.

Spoken words can have a powerful influence on the listener's state of mind.

A brief history of psycholinguistics

Given the importance of language, it is surprising that the history of psycholinguistics is a relatively recent one. The beginning of the scientific study of the psychology of language is often traced to a conference held at Cornell University, USA, in the summer of 1951, and the word "psycholinguistics" was first used in Osgood and Sebeok's (1954) book describing that conference. Nevertheless, the psychology of language had been studied before then. For example, in 1879 Francis Galton studied how people form associations between words. In Germany at the end of the nineteenth century, Meringer and Mayer (1895) analyzed slips of the tongue in a remarkably modern way, and Freud (1901/1975) tried to explain the origin of speech errors in terms of his psychodynamic theory (see Chapter 13). If we place the infancy of modern psycholinguistics sometime around the American linguist Noam Chomsky's (1959) review of Skinner's book *Verbal Behavior*, its adolescence would correspond to the period in the early and mid-1960s when psycholinguists tried to relate language processing to Chomsky's transformational grammar. Since then psycholinguistics has left its linguistic home and achieved independence, flourishing on all fronts.

As its name implies, psycholinguistics has its roots in the two disciplines of psychology and linguistics, and particularly in Chomsky's approach to linguistics. Linguistics is the study of language itself, the rules that describe it, and our knowledge about the rules of language. The primary concerns of early linguistics were rather different from what they are now. Comparative linguistics was concerned with comparing and tracing the origins of different languages. In particular, the American tradition of the linguist Leonard Bloomfield (1887–1949) emphasized comparative studies of indigenous North American Indian languages, leading to an emphasis on what is called structuralism: A primary goal of linguistics was taken to be providing an analysis of the appropriate categories of description of the units of language (Harris, 1951).

In modern linguistics the primary data used by linguists are intuitions about what is and is not an acceptable sentence. For example, we know that the string of words in (1) is acceptable, and we know that (2) is ungrammatical. How do we make these decisions? Can we formulate general rules to account for our intuitions? (An asterisk conventionally marks an ungrammatical construction.)

(1) What did the pig give to the donkey?
(2) *What did the pig sleep to donkey?

This emphasis on our knowledge led to greater emphasis on what humans do with language, rather than just on its structure.

Early psychological approaches to language saw the language processor as a simple device that could generate and understand sentences by moving from one state to another. There are two strands in this early work, derived from information theory and behaviorism. Information theory (Shannon & Weaver, 1949) emphasized the role of probability and redundancy in language, and developed out of the demands of the fledgling telecommunications industry. Working out what was the most likely continuation of a sentence from a particular point onwards was central to this approach. Information theory was also important because of its influence in the development of cognitive psychology. In the middle part of the twentieth century, the dominant tradition in psychology was behaviorism, which emphasized the relation between an input (or stimulus) and output (response), and how conditioning and reinforcement formed these associations. Intermediate constructs (such as the mind) were considered unnecessary to provide a full account of behavior. For behaviorists, the only valid subject matter for psychology was behavior, and language was behavior just like any other sort. Its acquisition and use could therefore be explained by standard techniques of reinforcement and conditioning. This approach perhaps reached its acme in 1957 with the publication of B. F. Skinner's famous (or to linguists, infamous) book *Verbal Behavior*.

Psycholinguistic tests of Chomsky's linguistic theory

Attitudes changed very quickly: in part this change was due to a devastating review of Skinner's book by Chomsky (1959). The American linguist Noam Chomsky (b. 1928) has had more influence on how we understand language than any other person. Unusually, the book review came to be more influential than the book it reviewed. Chomsky showed that behaviorism was incapable of dealing with natural language. He argued that a new type of linguistic theory called transformational grammar provided both an account of the underlying structure of language and also of people's knowledge of their language (see Chapter 2 for more details).

Psycholinguistics blossomed in attempting to test the psychological implications of this linguistic theory, and the influence of linguistics peaked in the late 1960s and early 1970s. The enterprise was not wholly successful, and experimental results suggested that, although linguistics might tell us a great deal about our knowledge of our language and about the constraints on children's acquisition of language, it is limited in what it can tell us about the processes involved in speaking and understanding.

The rest of this section is rather technical and can be skipped on the first reading. You might like to return to it before or after reading Chapter 10 on parsing.

What can the linguistic approach contribute to our understanding of the processes involved in producing and understanding syntactic structures? When Chomsky's work first appeared, there was great optimism that it would also provide an account of these processes. Two ideas attracted particular interest and were considered easily testable: these were the *derivational theory of complexity* (DTC), and the *autonomy of syntax*. The idea of the derivational theory of complexity is that the more complex the formal syntactic derivation of a sentence—that is, the more transformations that are necessary to form it—the more complex the psychological processing necessary to understand or produce it, meaning that transformationally complex sentences should be harder to process than less complex sentences. This additional processing complexity should be detectable by an appropriate measure such as reaction times. The psychological principle of the autonomy of syntax takes Chomsky's assertion that syntactic rules should be specified independently of other constraints further, to mean that syntactic processes operate independently of other ones. In practice this means that syntactic processes should be autonomous with respect to semantic processes.

Chomsky (1957) distinguished between optional and obligatory transformations. Obligatory transformations were those without which the sentence would be ungrammatical. Examples include transformations introduced to cope with number agreement between nouns and verbs, and the introduction of "do" into negatives and questions. Other transformations were optional. For example, the passivization transformation takes the active form of a sentence and turns it into a passive form, for instance turning (3) into (4):

(3) Boris applauded Agnes.
(4) Agnes was applauded by Boris.

Chomsky defined a subset of sentences that he called kernel sentences. Kernel sentences are those to which only obligatory transformations have been applied. They are therefore the active, affirmative, declarative forms of English sentences.

Miller and McKean (1964) tested the idea that the more transformations there are in a sentence, the more difficult it is to process. They looked at detransformation reaction times to sentences such as (5) to (9). Participants were told that they would have to make a particular transformation on a sentence, and then press a button when they found this transformed sentence in a list of sentences through which they had to search. Miller and McKean measured these times.

(5) The robot shoots the ghost. (0 transformations: active affirmative form)
(6) The ghost is shot by the robot. (1 transformation: passive)
(7) The robot does not shoot the ghost. (1 transformation: negative)
(8) The ghost is not shot by the robot. (2 transformations: passive + negative)
(9) Is the ghost not shot by the robot? (3 transformations: passive + negative + question)

We can derive increasingly complex sentences from the kernel (5). For example, (9) is derived from (5) by the application of three transformations: passivization, negativization, and question formation. Miller and McKean found that the time it took to detransform sentences with transformations back to the kernel was linearly related to the number of transformations in them. That is, the more transformations a participant has to make, the longer it takes them to do it. This was interpreted as supporting the psychological reality of transformational grammar.

Other experiments around the same time supported this idea. Savin and Perchonock (1965) found that sentences with more transformations in them took up more memory space. The more transformationally complex a sentence was, the fewer items participants could simultaneously remember from a list of unrelated words. Mehler (1963) found that when participants made errors in remembering sentences, they tended to do it in the direction of forgetting transformational tags, rather than adding them. It was as though participants remembered sentences in the form of "kernel plus transformation."

Problems with the psychological interpretation of transformational grammar

The tasks that supported the psychological reality of transformational grammar all used indirect measures of language processing. If we ask participants explicitly to detransform sentences, it is not surprising that the time it takes to do this reflects the number of transformations involved. However, this is not a task that we necessarily routinely do in language comprehension. Memory measures are not an on-line measure of what is happening in sentence processing; at best they are reflecting a side effect. What we remember of a sentence need have no relation with how we actually processed that sentence. Indeed, other findings that were difficult to fit into this framework soon emerged.

Slobin (1966a) performed an experiment similar to the original detransformation experiment of Miller and McKean. Slobin examined the processing of what are called reversible and irreversible passive sentences. A reversible passive is one where the subject and object of the sentence can be reversed and the sentence still makes pragmatic sense. An irreversible passive is one that does not make sense after this reversal. If you swap the subject and object in (10) you get (12), which makes perfect sense, whereas if you do this to (11) you get (13), which, although not ungrammatical, is rather odd—it is semantically anomalous:

(10)   The ghost was chased by the robot.
(11)   The flowers were watered by the robot.
(12)   The robot was chased by the ghost.
(13)   ? The robot was watered by the flowers.

In the case of an irreversible passive, you can work out what is the subject of the sentence and what is the object by semantic clues alone. With a reversible passive, you have to do some syntactic work. Slobin found that Miller and McKean's results could only be obtained for reversible passives. Hence detransformational parsing only appears to be necessary when there are not sufficient semantic cues to the meaning of the sentence from elsewhere. This result means that the derivational theory of complexity does not always

obtain. Slobin's finding that the depth of syntactic processing is affected by semantic considerations such as reversibility is also counter to the idea of the autonomy of syntax, although this proved more controversial. Using different materials and a different task (judging whether the sentence was grammatical or not), Forster and Olbrei (1973) found no effect of reversibility, and more recently Ferreira (2003) found that there was always some cost to processing a passive sentence, even irreversible ones. Taken together, these results mean that what we observe depends on the details of the tasks used, but both syntactic and semantic factors have an effect on the difficulty of sentences.

Wason (1965) examined the relation between the structure of a sentence and its meaning. He measured how long it took participants to complete sentences describing an array of eight colored circles, seven of which were red and one of which was blue. It is more natural to use a negative in a context of "plausible denial"—that is, it is more appropriate to say "this circle is not red" of the exception than of each of the others "this circle is not blue." In other words, the time it takes to process a syntactic construction such as negative-formation depends on the semantic context.

In summary, early claims supporting the ideas of derivational complexity in linguistic performance that were derived from Chomsky's formulation of grammar were at best premature, and perhaps just wrong. As we shall see in later chapters, the degree to which syntactic and semantic processes are independent turns out to be one of the most important and controversial topics in psycholinguistics.

Linguistic approaches have given us a useful terminology for talking about syntax. They also illuminate how powerful the grammar that underlies human language must be. Chomsky's theory of transformational grammar also had a major influence on the way in which psychological syntactic processing was thought to take place. In spite of their initial promise, later experiments provided little support for the psychological reality of transformational grammar. Chomsky had a retreat available: Linguistic theories describe our linguistic *competence*, our abstract knowledge of language, rather than our linguistic *performance*, what we actually do. That is, transformational grammar is a description of our knowledge of our linguistic competence, and the constraints on language acquisition, rather than an account of the processes involved in parsing on a moment-to-moment basis. This has effectively led to a separation of linguistics and psycholinguistics, with each pursuing these different goals. Miller, who first provided apparent empirical support for the psychological reality of transformational grammar, later came to believe that all the time taken up in sentence processing was used in semantic operations.

Psycholinguistics and information processing

Psycholinguistics was largely absorbed into mainstream cognitive psychology in the 1970s. In this approach, the information processing or computational metaphor reigned supreme. Information processing approaches to cognition view the mind as rather like a computer. The mind uses rules to translate an input such as speech or vision into a symbolic representation: cognition is symbolic processing. This approach can perhaps be seen at its clearest in a computational account of vision, such as that of Marr (1982), where the representation of the visual scene becomes more and more abstract from the retinal level through increasingly sophisticated representations. Processing could be represented as flow diagrams, in the same way that complex tasks could be represented as flow diagrams before being turned into a computer program. Flow diagrams illustrate levels of processing, and much work during this time attempted to show how one level of representation of language is transformed into another. The computational metaphor is clearly influential in modern psycholinguistics, as most models are phrased in terms of the description of levels of processing, and the rules or processes that determine what happens in between. We will see this type of approach throughout this book. Many traditional psycholinguistic models are specified as "box-and-arrow" diagrams, with boxes referring to processing levels, and the arrows being the means of getting from one box to another (see Chapters 7 and 13 in

particular for examples). This approach is sometimes called, rather derogatorily, "boxology." It is certainly not unique to psycholinguistics, and such an approach is not as bad as is sometimes hinted. It at least gives rise to an understanding of the architecture of the language system—what the "boxes" of the language system are, and how they are related to others.

As a consequence of the influence of the computational metaphor, and with the development of suitable experimental techniques, psycholinguistics gained an identity independent of linguistics. Modern psycholinguistics is primarily an experimental science, and as in much of cognitive psychology, experiments measuring reaction times have been particularly important (especially in word recognition and comprehension; see Chapters 6 through 12). Psychologists try to break language processing down into its components, and show how those components relate to each other.

The "cognitive science" approach

The term "cognitive science" is used to cover the multidisciplinary approach to the study of the mind, with the disciplines including adult and developmental psychology, philosophy, linguistics, anthropology, neuroscience, and artificial intelligence (AI). We have already seen how linguistics influenced early psycholinguistics, particularly early work on syntax. Philosophy has played an important role in our understanding of meaning. AI involves getting computers to do things that appear to need intelligence, such as understanding a story, or understanding speech. Apart from the obvious technological uses of AI, the hope has been that it will increase our understanding of how humans do such tasks. AI involves computer modeling of human behavior emphasizing rules, plans, and goals. Implementing a model in a computer program has the great advantage that you have to be explicit about everything. There are no hidden assumptions in models that are implemented as programs. On the other hand, this compulsory explicitness has a significant disadvantage: Because modelers have to be explicit about everything, they often have to make unwarranted assumptions about processes and representations, and simplify the context or the scope of the model to a degree where its usefulness becomes debatable. Nevertheless, computational models have many advantages and have become increasingly important.

If you have seen Kubrick's film *2001: A Space Odyssey*, you will probably remember HAL, the talking, listening, all-seeing, thinking computer. AI researchers hope someday to emulate HAL's linguistic abilities. Some early successes made researchers optimistic that this goal might soon be realized. Among the earliest of these successes was Weizenbaum's (1966) program, called ELIZA. The program simulated a non-directive, Rogerian therapist. In the following example, the output of the computer—the ELIZA program—is in capitals.

Men are all alike.

IN WHAT WAY

They're always bugging us about something or other.

CAN YOU THINK OF A SPECIFIC EXAMPLE

Well, my boyfriend made me come here.

YOUR BOYFRIEND MADE YOU COME HERE

He says I'm depressed much of the time.

I AM SORRY TO HEAR THAT YOU ARE DEPRESSED

It's true that I am unhappy.

DO YOU THINK COMING HERE WILL HELP YOU NOT TO BE UNHAPPY

I need some help, that much seems certain.

WHAT WOULD IT MEAN IF YOU GOT SOME HELP

Perhaps I could learn to get along with my mother.

TELL ME MORE ABOUT YOUR FAMILY

The program worked in a very simple way, using a few techniques such as matching sentences to pre-stored structures or templates, producing predetermined responses to a few keywords (such as "mother"), and repeating what was input to it back with a few appropriate changes in word order. Nevertheless, people who used the program became very attached to it, even if they knew it was only a machine producing the output. Although some people even wanted to consult regularly with ELIZA in private, this perhaps says more about human concerns than it does about how language is produced. There were a number of variants of ELIZA, such as PARRY (Colby, 1975), which "simulated" the output of a paranoid schizophrenic.

The next influential program was called SHRDLU (Winograd, 1972; the name came from the letters of one row of a typesetting machine and was often used by typesetters to flag a mistake). This program could answer questions about an imaginary world called "blocksworld." Blocksworlds are occupied by objects such as small red pyramids sitting on top of big blue cubes. SHRDLU's success in being able to "understand" sentences such as "move the small red pyramid on top of the blue cube" was much hailed at the time.

The concept of a computer that thinks and talks like a human has existed in science fiction for some time. The smooth-talking HAL from *2001: A Space Odyssey*, a scene from which is depicted here, is one of the more ominous and disturbing creations. The name HAL stands for "Heuristically programmed ALgorithmic computer."

However, SHRDLU could only "understand" in as much as it could give an appropriate response to an instruction, and most people would say that there is much more to understanding than this. Furthermore, these early demonstrations worked only for very simple, limited domains. SHRDLU could not answer questions about elephants, or even say what "block" means. Its knowledge was limited to the role of blocks within blocksworld.

These early attempts did have the virtue of demonstrating the enormity of the task in understanding language. They also revealed the main problems that have to be solved before we can talk of computers truly understanding language. There are an infinite number of sentences, of varying degrees of complexity. We can talk about and understand potentially anything. The roles that context and world knowledge play in understanding are very important: potentially any piece of information we know could be necessary to understand a particular sentence. The conventional AI approach has had some influence on psycholinguistic theorizing, particularly on how we understand syntax and how we make inferences in story comprehension.

ELIZA and SHRDLU had extremely primitive syntactic processing abilities. ELIZA used templates for sentence recognition, and did not compute the underlying syntactic structure of sentences (a process known as parsing). SHRDLU was a little more sophisticated, and did contain a syntactic processor, but the processor was dedicated to the extraction of the limited semantic information necessary to move around "blocksworld." Early AI parsers lacked the computational power necessary to analyze human language.

The influence of AI on psycholinguistics peaked in the 1970s. More recently an approach called **connectionism** (but also known as parallel distributed processing, or neural networks) has become influential in all areas of psycholinguistics. Connectionist networks involve many very simple, richly interconnected neuron-like units working together without an explicit governing plan. Instead, rules and behavior emerge from the interactions between these many simple units. The principles of connectionist models are described more fully in the Appendix.

One concept that is central in many types of model, including connectionist models, is the idea of **activation**. The idea has been around for a long time. Activation is a continuously varying quantity, and can be thought of as a property rather like heat. We talk of how activation can spread from one unit or word or point in a network to another, rather like electricity flowing around a circuit board. Suppose we hear a word such as "ghost." If we assume there is a unit corresponding to that word, it will have a very high level of activation. But a word related in meaning (e.g., "vampire") or sound (e.g., "goal") might also have a small amount of activation, whereas a completely unrelated word (e.g., "pamphlet") will have a very low level of activation. The idea that the mind uses something like activation, and that the activation level of units—such as those representing words—can influence the activation levels of similar items, is an important one.

The methods of modern psycholinguistics

Psycholinguistics uses many types of evidence. We will use examples of observational studies and linguistic intuitions, and make use of the errors people make. Much has been learned from computer modeling. Recently, neuroscience has contributed greatly to our understanding. But the bulk of our data, as you will see if you just quickly skim through the rest of this book, comes from traditional psychology experiments, particularly those that generate reaction times. For example, how long does it take to read out a word? What can we do to make the process faster or slower? Do words differ in the speed with which we can read them out depending on their properties? The advantage of this type of experiment is that it is now very easy to run on modern computers. In many experiments, the collection of data can be completely automated. There are a number of commercial (and free) experimental packages available for both PC and Macintosh computers that will help run your experiments for you, or you can program the computer yourself.

One of the most popular experimental techniques is called **priming**. Priming has been used in almost all areas of psycholinguistics. The general idea is that if two things are similar to each other and involved together in processing, they will either assist with or interfere with each other, but if they are unrelated, they will have no effect. For example, it is easier to recognize a word (e.g., BREAD) if you have just seen a word that is related in meaning (e.g., BUTTER). This effect is called **semantic priming**. If priming causes processing to be speeded up, we talk about **facilitation**; if priming causes it to be slowed down, we talk of **inhibition**.

Most psycholinguistic research has been carried out on healthy monolingual English-speaking college students, in the visual modality (i.e., with printed words). Psycholinguistic research does not differ from other types of psychology in this bias, but it does have consequences: for example, it has meant that there has been a great deal of research on reading when, for most people, speaking and listening are the main language activities in their lives. Fortunately, in recent years this situation has changed dramatically, and we are now seeing the fruits of research on speech recognition, on language production, on speakers of different languages, on bilingual speakers, on people with brain damage, and on people across the full range of the lifespan. A lot of this work has been spurred by recent developments in **brain imaging**, which over the last few years has revolutionized how we understand language.

MODELS IN PSYCHOLINGUISTICS

What do we do when we have a lot of data? We have to explain it. We do this by constructing a model of the data. A good model is an account of the data that provides an explanation of why the data are as they are and that makes novel, testable predictions. Psycholinguistics is full of models, and they're very important.

At this point it is useful to explain what is meant by the words "data," "theory," "model," and "hypothesis." Data are the pieces of evidence that have to be explained. Types of data include experimental results, case studies of people with brain damage, brain scans, and observations of people using language correctly or incorrectly. A theory is a general explanation of how something works. A model is rather more specific: For example, computer simulations are models of processes that are particular instances or parts of more abstract theories. The distinction between a model and a theory is a bit fuzzy though, so don't worry about it too much. A hypothesis is a very specific idea that can be tested. An experimental test that confirms the hypothesis is support for the particular theory from which the hypothesis was derived. If the hypothesis is not confirmed, then some change to the theory is necessary. It need not be necessary to reject the theory completely, but as long as the hypothesis is derived fairly from the theory, then some modification will be necessary. Testing theories by making predictions and trying to falsify them is a fundamental part of science. And that's why psycholinguistics is a part of science.

What's an explanation then? An explanation simplifies. If you carry out an experiment and make one hundred observations, an explanation of those observations is something simpler than those hundred data points. Suppose you could summarize why you got those observations in a sentence or one mathematical equation; that would be a good explanation (and the equation would also serve as a model). Explanations should also avoid being circular. A circular explanation is one that explains itself in terms of itself; for example, we could say children learn language because they have a language acquisition module, and define the language acquisition module as what enables children to learn languages. Good explanations transcend levels; complex phenomena are explained in terms of simpler descriptions, and may involve different areas.

Good models also make use of converging evidence; evidence from different sources that come together. A model of some behavior that is expressed as a computer model and makes novel, falsifiable predictions about real human behavior is a good one, particularly if it is supported by evidence from other areas such as the study of the brain.

LANGUAGE AND THE BRAIN

Cognitive neuroscience studies how the brain and behavior are related. For a long time we were restricted to exploring how language and the brain were related by looking at the effects of brain damage on language. More recently advances in neuroimaging have enabled us to look at the brain in action during normal processing.

Lesion studies

The brain is very vulnerable to damage (which is why this precious organ is encased in a thick padded skull). Sites of damage to the brain are called **lesion**s. Some unfortunate individuals suffer brain damage in a variety of ways, including strokes, brain surgery, and trauma from accidents (e.g., car crashes) or poisoning.

Lesion studies involve examining the effects of brain damage on performance, and have made enormous contributions to understanding how psychological processes are related to the brain. A particular approach to using lesion studies, called cognitive neuropsychology, has led to great advances in our understanding of psycholinguistics over the last 30 years or so. Traditional neurology and neuropsychology have been concerned primarily with questions about which parts of the brain control different sorts of behavior (i.e., with the localization of function), and with working out how complex behaviors map onto the flow of information through brain structures (see Figure 1.3). In one of the best-known traditional neuropsychological models of language, the Wernicke–Geschwind model, language processes basically flow from the back of the left hemisphere to the front, with high-level planning and semantic processes towards the back, in what is called Wernicke's area, and low-level sound retrieval and articulation towards the front, in what is called Broca's area, with the two regions connected by a tract of fibers called the arcuate fasciculus (see Figure 1.4). The emphasis of cognitive neuropsychology is rather different: the goal is to relate brain-damaged behavior to models of normal processing.

Shallice (1988) argued that cognitive neuropsychology can be distinguished from traditional neuropsychology in three crucial respects. First, it has made a theoretical advance in relating neuropsychological disorders to cognitive models. Second, it has made a methodological advance in

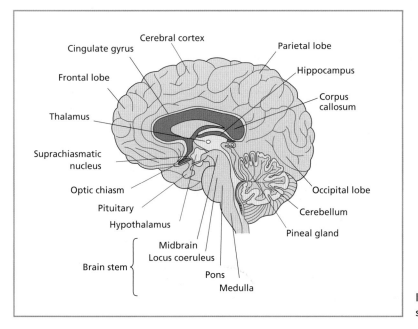

FIGURE 1.3 A cross-sectional view of the brain.

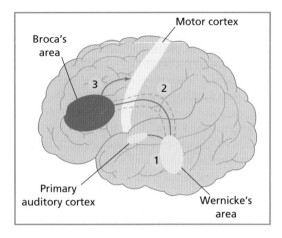

FIGURE 1.4 The location of Wernicke's area (1) and Broca's area (3). When someone speaks a word, activation proceeds from Wernicke's area through the arcuate fasciculus (2) to Broca's area.

emphasizing the importance of single-case studies, rather than group studies of neuropsychological impairment. That is, the emphasis is on providing a detailed description and explanation of individual patients, rather than on comparing groups of patients who might not have the same underlying deficit. Third, it has contributed a research program, in that it emphasizes how models of normal processing can be informed by studying brain-damaged behavior. Cognitive neuropsychology has contributed a great deal to our understanding of language.

Shallice went on to argue that sometimes this approach has been taken too far, and called this extreme position ultra-cognitive neuropsychology. First, it has gone too far in arguing that group studies cannot provide any information appropriate for constructing cognitive models. This proposal led to heated controversy (e.g., Bates, McDonald, MacWhinney, & Appelbaum, 1991; Caramazza, 1986, 1991; McCloskey & Caramazza, 1988). Second, it has gone too far in claiming that information about the localization of function is irrelevant to our understanding of behavior (e.g., Morton, 1984). Third, it has undervalued clinical information about patients. Seidenberg (1988) pointed to another problem, which is that cognitive neuropsychology places too much emphasis on uncovering the functional

architecture of the systems involved. That is, the organization of the components—specifying levels of processing and how they are connected to each other—involved is emphasized at the cost of exploring the processes actually involved, leading to the construction of box-and-arrow diagrams with little advance in our understanding of what goes on inside the boxes, or how we get from one box to another. More emphasis is now being placed on what happens inside the components, particularly since connectionist modeling has been applied to cognitive neuropsychology.

A concept important in both traditional and cognitive neuropsychology is that of the **double dissociation**. Consider two patients, A and B, given two tasks, I and II. Patient A performs normally on task I but cannot perform task II. Patient B displays the reverse pattern of behavior, in performing normally on task II but not on task I (see Figure 1.5). In such a situation the two tasks are said to be doubly dissociated. The traditional interpretation of a double dissociation is that different processes underlie each task. If we then find that patients A and B have lesions to different parts of the brain, we will be further tempted to draw a conclusion about where these processes are localized. To anticipate an example of a double dissociation, we will see in Chapter 7 that some patients are unable to read nonwords (e.g., SPUKE), but they can read words with irregular spelling (e.g., STEAK). Other patients can read nonwords, but are unable to read irregular words.

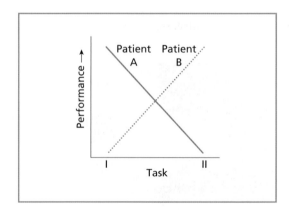

FIGURE 1.5 Illustration of a hypothetical double dissociation.

Although the traditional interpretation of a double dissociation is that two separate routes are involved in a process, connectionist modeling has shown that this might not always be the case. Apparent double dissociations can emerge in complex, distributed, single-route systems (e.g., Plaut & Shallice, 1993a; Seidenberg & McClelland, 1989; both are described in Chapter 7). At the very least, we should be cautious about inferring that the routes involved are truly distinct and do not interact (Ellis & Humphreys, 1999).

Some more general care is necessary when making inferences from neuropsychological data. Some researchers have questioned the whole enterprise of trying to understand normal processing by studying brain-damaged behavior. Gregory (1961) made an analogy of attempting to discover how a radio set works by removing its components. If we did this, we might conclude that the function of a capacitor (an electrical component) was to inhibit loud wailing sounds! Furthermore, the categories of disorder that we will discuss are not always clearly recognizable in the clinical setting. There is often much overlap between patients, with the more pure cases usually associated with smaller amounts of brain damage. Finally, things are not usually in a fixed state as a result of brain damage; intact processes reorganize, and some recovery of function often occurs, even in adults.

Neuroimaging

Reaction times enable us to infer how the mind works; lesion studies enable us to infer which part of the brain does what; suppose we could look directly at how the brain works? New techniques of brain imaging are gradually becoming more accurate and more accessible. As a consequence brain imaging has been one of the most widely used and important techniques in psycholinguistics in the last few years.

Traditional X-rays are of limited use to us because the skull blocks the view of the brain and, in any case, there is little variation in the density of the brain. Hence neuroscientists have had to use even more ingenious techniques. These are based on measuring the brain's electrical activity, or creating images of brain activity. Ideally, we would like both good temporal (being able to separate and time events very accurately) and spatial (being able to localize very accurately in space in the brain) resolution.

EEGs (electroencephalograms) and **ERP**s (event-related potentials) both measure the electrical activity of the brain by putting electrodes on the scalp. ERPs measure voltage changes on the scalp associated with the presentation of a stimulus (see Figure 1.6). The peaks of an ERP are labeled according to their polarity (positive or negative voltage) and latency in milliseconds (thousandths of a second) after the stimulus begins (Kutas & van Petten, 1994). The N400 is a much-studied peak occurring after a semantically incongruent sentence dog (Kutas & Hillyard, 1980). Of course, that previous sentence should have ended with "sentence completion," and "dog" should therefore have generated a large N400 in you. P300 peaks are elicited by any stimuli requiring a binary decision (yes/no). The contingent negative variation (CNV) is a slow negative potential that develops on the scalp when a person is preparing to make a motor action or to process sensory stimuli.

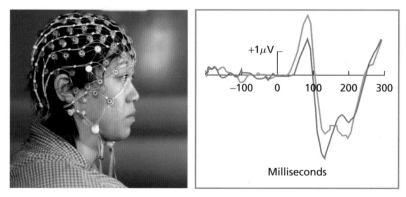

FIGURE 1.6 An EEG (left) measures electrical potentials in the brain by means of electrodes placed across the scalp. An ERP (example on the right) is a complex electrical waveform related in time to a specific event.

EEG and ERP have very good temporal resolution—they can currently resolve the timing of events to within a millisecond or so. Their spatial resolution, however, is very poor. **MEG** (magnetoencephalography) is a recent development that measures the magnetic activity of the brain. MEG has the advantage of both very good temporal and spatial (within 3 mm) resolution, but is more difficult to carry out and much more expensive to run, needing superconducting devices called SQUIDS, extreme cooling using liquid helium, and magnetic shielding.

CAT (computerized axial tomography) produces medium-resolution images from integrating large numbers of X-ray pictures taken from many different angles around the head (see Figure 1.7). MRI (magnetic resonance imaging) uses radio-frequency waves rather than X-rays and produces higher resolution images than CAT. These techniques enable neuroscientists to study the structure of the brain. PET (positron emission tomography) scans produce pictures of the brain's activity. A radioactive form of glucose, the metabolic fuel that the brain uses, is injected into the blood, and detectors around the head measure where the glucose is being used up. In this way we can find out which parts of the brain are most active when it is carrying out a particular task.

In recent years **fMRI** (functional magnetic resonance imaging) has become widely accessible, and "brain scans" derived from fMRI have become one of the most important sources of data in psychology. fMRI was developed in the 1990s. It measures the energy released by hemoglobin molecules in the blood, and then works out the areas of the brain receiving the greatest amounts of blood and oxygen. It therefore tells us which parts of the brain are most active at any time. It provides much better temporal (about 1–5 seconds) and spatial (within 1 mm) resolution than PET, although the temporal resolution is still clearly inferior to EEG. fMRI is now the most widely used imaging technique used in psycholinguistics, and its importance to the field has grown dramatically in the last few years.

Another recently developed tool is **TMS** (transcranical magnetic stimulation). TMS is in some ways the reverse of imaging: rather than observing the brain, we make part of it do something. A very powerful set of magnets is used to directly stimulate part of the cortex of a participant, and we then record what that participant does or experiences.

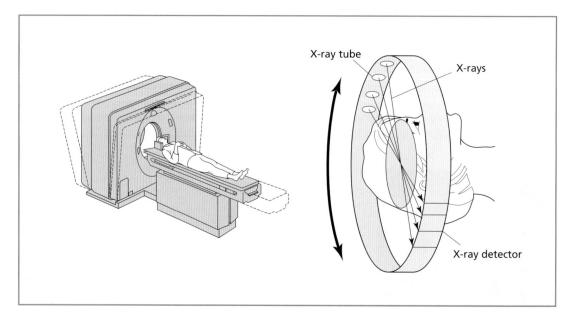

FIGURE 1.7 In a CAT scanner, X-rays pass through the brain in a narrow beam. X-ray detectors are arranged in an arc and feed information to a computer that generates the scan image.

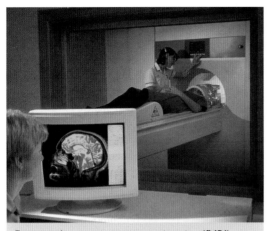

Functional magnetic resonance imaging (fMRI) scans have become an important source of data in psychology.

These techniques could potentially tell us a number of things. They could tell us a great deal about the time course of processes, and when different sources of information are used. Imaging could be particularly revealing about the extent to which mental processes interact with other processes. Suppose that in a brain scan taken during the production of a single word, we find that the area responsible for processing the meaning of words becomes active, and then some time after

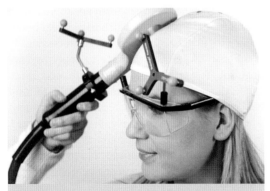

This participant is undergoing transcranial magnetic stimulation (TMS), which is used to map brain function. A figure-of-eight coil is placed over the participant's skull and an electric current is passed through it, producing a magnetic field that induces an electric current within a discrete area of the brain.

this a different area responsible for processing the sound of words becomes active. This would suggest that, when speaking, processes involving meaning and sound do not overlap. On the other hand, we might find that the meaning and sound areas overlap and become almost immediately simultaneously active. This result would suggest that meaning and sound processing interact. In effect, we could plot the graphs of the time course of processing and how different types of information interact.

Brain imaging is still relatively expensive, and the spatial and particularly temporal resolution of even fMRI still leave something to be desired, although they are improving rapidly all the time. A more significant problem with current brain imaging is that the results are often difficult to interpret. It is hard to be sure exactly what is causing any activity. Imaging will tell us where something is happening, but in itself it does not tell us how, what, or why. Looking at how the brain works is not the same thing as looking at how the mind works. In the context of a theory of language processing and brain structure, however, imaging might provide us with important clues as to what is going on. The main method used in brain imaging is called subtraction: the participant carries out one task (e.g., reading aloud) and then a variant of that task (e.g., reading silently), and the images of one are subtracted from the images of the other. You then identify where the critical difference between the two is located (in this case the vocalizing component of reading aloud). The subtraction method may sound straightforward, but in practice it is often difficult to find suitable comparison conditions. Quite often the difference between the two conditions is a subtle one that needs theoretical interpretation (Bub, 2000). Furthermore, imaging techniques often show activation of non-overlapping cortical areas for similar tasks, which again is difficult to interpret (Poeppel, 1996). Imaging studies also suggest that cognitive processes are more localized than is indicated by other sorts of methods (such as the study of people with brain damage), because imaging techniques reveal the many areas that are active in a task, regardless of whether or not those areas are carrying out an important role (Howard,

1997). Also, group studies using imaging techniques average brain images across people, when functions might be localized inconsistently in different parts of their brains (Howard, 1997). It is also easy to get carried away with focusing on where in the brain things happen, rather than on the underlying processes (see Harley, 2004a, 2004b; Loosemore & Harley, 2010).

In general, imaging techniques do not tell us in any straightforward way what high activity in different parts of the brain means in processing terms. Suppose we see during sentence processing that the parsing and semantic areas are active at the same time. This could be a result of interaction between these processes, or it could reflect the parsing of one part of the sentence and the semantic integration of earlier material. It might even reflect the participant parsing a sentence and thinking dimly about what's for dinner that night. It might be possible to tease them apart, but we need clever experiments to do this. Imaging data now play an important role as part of the converging evidence for a particular model, or even distinguishing between competing accounts. Imaging already plays an important diagnostic role in investigating the effects of brain damage and brain disease. More optimistically, in the more distant future, imaging will play a more important role in treatment and therapy.

THEMES AND CONTROVERSIES

Ten themes recur throughout this book (see Figure 1.8). The first theme is to discover the actual processes involved in producing and understanding language. The second theme is the question of whether apparently different language processes are related to one another. For example, to what extent are the processes involved in reading also involved in speaking? The third theme is whether or not processes in language operate independently of one another, or whether they interact. This is the issue of **modularity**, and we look at it in more detail below. Fourth, what is innate about language? Fifth, do we need to refer to explicit rules when considering language processing? Sixth, are

the processes we examine specific to language, or are they aspects of general cognitive processing sometimes recruited for language? Seventh, how sensitive are the results of our experiments to the particular techniques employed? That is, do we get different answers to the same question if we do our experiments in slightly different ways? To anticipate, the answers we get sometimes do depend on the way we get those answers, which obviously can make the interpretation of findings quite complex. One consequence is that we find that the experimental techniques themselves come under close scrutiny. In this respect, the distinction between data and theory can become very blurred. Eighth, what can be learned from looking at the language of people with damage to the parts of the brain that control language? Ninth, what difference does it make speaking a different language? We have already seen that there are many thousands of languages in the world. Many countries have more than one language, and some (e.g., Papua New Guinea) have hundreds. Some languages have hundreds of millions of speakers; some just a few hundred. There are important differences between languages that may have significant implications for the way in which speakers process language. It is sometimes easy to forget this, given the domination of English in experimental psycholinguistics. Some people speak more than one language. How they do this, how they learn the two languages, and how they translate between them are all important questions, the answers to which have wider implications for understanding cognitive processing.

Finally, we should be able to apply psycholinguistic research to everyday life and problems. Although language comes naturally to most humans most of the time, there are many occasions when it does not: for example, in learning to read, in overcoming language disabilities, in rehabilitating patients with brain damage, and in developing computer systems that can understand and produce language. Advances in the theory of any subject such as psycholinguistics should have practical applications. For example, in Chapters 6 and 7 we will examine research on visual word recognition and reading. Learning to read is a remarkably difficult task. A good theory of reading should cast light on how it should best be taught. It should indicate

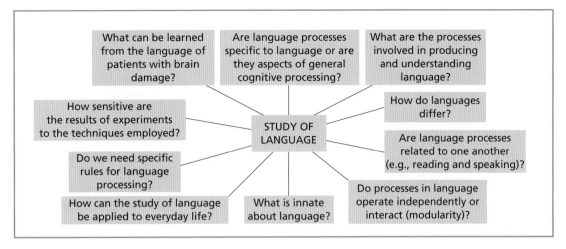

FIGURE 1.8

the best strategies that can be used to overcome difficulties in learning to read, and thereby help children who find learning to read particularly difficult. A good theory should specify the best methods of dealing with adult illiteracy. Furthermore, it should help in the rehabilitation of adults who have difficulty in reading as a consequence of brain damage, showing what remedial treatment would be most useful and which strategies would maximize any preserved reading skills.

Let us look at some of these themes in more detail.

How modular is the language system?

The concept of modularity is an important one in psycholinguistics. Most researchers agree that psychological processing can be best described in terms of a number of levels. Processing begins with an input that is acted on by one or more intervening levels of processing to produce an output. For example, when we name a word, we have to identify and process the visual form of the word, and access the sounds of the word. There is much less agreement on the way in which these levels of processing are connected to each other. For a particular process, at what stage does any kind of context have an influence? When do different types of information have their effects? For

example, does the meaning of a sentence help in recognizing the sounds of a word or in making decisions about the sentence structure?

A module is a self-contained set of processes: it converts an input to an output, without any outside help for what goes on in between—we say that the processes inside a module are **independent** of processes outside the module. Yet another way of describing it is to say that processing is purely data-driven. Models in which processing occurs in this way are called autonomous.

The opposing view is that processing is **interactive**. Interaction involves the influence of one level of processing on the operation of another, but there are two intertwined notions involved. First, there is the question of overlap of processing between stages. Are the processing stages temporally discrete or do they overlap? In a **discrete stage model**, a level of processing can only begin its work when the previous one has finished its own work. In a **cascade model**, information is allowed to flow from one level to the following level before it has completed its processing (McClelland, 1979). If the stages overlap, then multiple candidates might become activated at the lower level of processing. An analogy should make this clear. Discrete models are like those water wheels made up of a series of tipping buckets; each bucket only tips up when it is full of water. Cascading models on the other hand are like a series of waterfalls.

The second aspect of interaction is whether there is a reverse flow of information, or feedback, when information from a lower level feeds back to the prior level. For example, does knowledge about what a word might be influence the recognition of its component sounds or letters? Does the context of the sentence help to make identifying the constituent words easier? A natural waterfall is purely **top-down**; water doesn't flow from the bottom back up to the top. But suppose we introduce a pump. Then we can pump water back up to earlier levels. There is scope for confusion with the terms "**bottom-up**" and "top-down," as they depend on the direction of processing. So a non-**interactive model** of word recognition would be one that is purely bottom-up—from the perceptual representation of the word to the mental representation—but a non-interactive model of word production would be one that is purely top-down—from the mental representation to the sound of the word. "Data-driven" is a better term than "bottom-up," but the latter is in common use. The important point is that models that permit feedback have both bottom-up and top-down information flow.

Fodor (1983) argued that many psychological processes are modular. To what extent are the processes of language self-contained, or do they interact with one another? According to many researchers, we should start with the assumption that processes are modular or non-interactive unless there is a very good reason to think otherwise. There are two main reasons for this assumption. First, modular models are generally simpler—they involve fewer processes and connections between systems. Second, it is widely believed that evolution favors a modular system. On the other hand, there is no consensus on how good a "very good reason" has to be before we dump the modularity hypothesis. It is always possible to come up with a saving or auxiliary hypothesis that can be used to modify and hence save the modularity hypothesis (Lakatos, 1970). We will observe many instances of auxiliary hypotheses introduced to save the main hypothesis that processing is modular. In theories of word recognition researchers have introduced the idea of post-access processes; in syntax and parsing they have proposed parallel processing with deferred

decision making; and in word production they have proposed an editor, or emphasized the role of **working memory**, or claimed that some kinds of data (e.g., picture-naming times) are more fundamental than others (e.g., speech errors). Researchers can get very hot under the collar about the role of interaction. Both Fodor (1983, 1985) and Pinker (1994), who are leading exponents of the view that language is highly modular and has a significant innate basis, give a broader philosophical view: modularity is inconsistent with relativism, the idea that everything is relative to everything else and that anything goes (particularly in the social sciences). Modules provide a fixed framework in which to study the mind.

The existence of a neuropsychological dissociation between two processes is often taken as evidence of the modularity of the processes involved. When we consider the neuroscience of modularity, we can talk both about physical modularity (are psychological processes localized in one part of the brain?) and processing modularity (in principle a set of processes might be distributed across the brain yet have a modular role in the processing model). It is plausible that the two types of modularity are related, so that cognitive modules correspond to neuropsychological modules. However, Farah (1994) criticized this "locality" assumption, and argued that neuropsychological dissociations were explicable in terms of distributed, connectionist systems.

To what extent is the whole language system a big, self-contained module (or set of modules)? Is it just a special module for interfacing between social processes and cognition? Or does it provide a true window onto wider cognitive processes? On the one hand, Chomsky (1975) argued that language is a special faculty that cannot be reduced to cognitive processes. On the other, Piaget (1923) argued that language is a cognitive process just like any other, and that linguistic development depends on general cognitive development. We will return to this question in Chapter 3 when we consider the relation between language and thought. In addition to there being a separate module for language, there are some obvious candidates for subsystems being modules, such as the syntax module, the speech processing module, and the word recognition module. But even if language is a big, self-contained module, it has to interact with the rest of the cognitive system. We talk about what we think about, our thoughts are often in verbal form (what we call **inner speech**), and we integrate what we hear with the rest of the information in our long-term memory. As we will see (particularly in Chapters 12 and 15), language plays a central role in our working memory, the short-term repository of information.

In each case where modularity arises as an issue, you need to examine the data, and ask whether the auxiliary hypothesis is more plausible than the non-modular alternative. You also need to think about whether data *converges* from experimental and imaging sources. Often, with existing data, it is impossible to decide.

Is any part of language innate?

There are broader implications of modularity, too. Generally, those researchers most committed to the claim that language processes are highly modular also argue that a significant amount of our language abilities are innate. The argument is essentially that nice, clean-cut modules must be built into the brain, or hard-wired, and therefore innately programmed, and that complex, messy systems reflect the effects of learning.

Obviously there are some prerequisites to the acquisition of language, if only a general learning ability. The question is, how much has to be innate? Are we just talking about general learning principles, or language-specific knowledge—to what extent is the innate information specifically linguistic? A related issue is the extent to which the innate components are only found in humans. We will look at these questions in more detail in Chapters 3 and 4. Connectionist modeling (discussed below) suggests ways in which general properties of the learning system can serve the role of innate, language-specific knowledge, and shows how behavior emerges from the interaction of nature and nurture at all levels (Elman et al., 1996).

Does the language system make use of rules?

To what extent does the language-processing system make use of linguistic rules? In traditional linguistics, much knowledge is encapsulated in the form of explicit rules. For example, we will see in Chapter 2 that we can describe the syntax of language in terms of rules such as "a sentence can comprise a noun phrase followed by a verb phrase." Similarly, we can formulate a rule that the plural of a noun is formed by adding an "-s" to its end, except in a limited number of irregular forms, which we would need to store separately. Clearly then we can describe language with a system of rules, but do we actually make use of such rules when speaking and listening?

Until quite recently, the answer was thought to be "yes." Many researchers, particularly those with a more linguistic orientation, still believe this. For many other researchers, connectionist modeling has provided an alternative view.

Connectionism has revolutionized psycholinguistics over the last 25 years. In connectionist models, processing takes place in the interaction of many simple, massively interconnected units. Connectionist models that can learn are particularly important. In these models, information is learned by repeated presentation; the connections between units change to encode regularities in the environment. The general idea underlying learning can be summarized in the aphorism, based on the work of Donald Hebb (1949), that "cells that fire together, wire together": the simultaneous activation of cells (or units) leads to an increase in synaptic (or connection) strength.

What does the "model" part of "connectionist model" mean? A few years ago I built a model rocket. It was only a foot high, and made out of plastic, but it did take off (eventually), and went a few hundred feet in the air. It differed from a "real" rocket in many ways other than scale; the rocket propellant was very different from that used in real rockets, and many aspects of it were decorative rather than functional. It was also, needless to say, greatly simplified. Yet it did illustrate many important principles of rocket flight, and you can learn a lot about real rocketry by playing with such models. Computational models of mind are very similar. They are scaled-down models of the mind, or parts of it, made from different materials, but which illustrate important principles of how the mind works. What is more, we can learn from them. Their behavior is not always totally predictable, in the same way as it is difficult to predict exactly how the model rocket is going to behave in different conditions on the basis of limited knowledge about its raw materials. Modeling then is a very important idea in modern psycholinguistics.

What makes connectionist models so attractive? First, unlike traditional AI, at first sight they are more neurally plausible. They are loosely based on a metaphor of the brain, which is a structure made up out of many massively interconnected neurons, each one of which is relatively simple. It is important not to get too carried away with this metaphor, but at least we have the feeling that we are starting off with the right sorts of models. Second, connectionist modelers usually try to minimize the amount of information hard-wired into the system, emphasizing looking at what emerges from the model. Third, just like traditional AI, connectionism has the virtue that writing a computer program forces you to be explicit about your assumptions.

There have been three major consequences from the success of connectionist modeling. First, it has led to a focus on the processes that take place inside the boxes of our models. In some cases (e.g., the acquisition of the past tense), this new focus has led to a detailed re-examination of the evidence motivating the models. The second consequence is that connectionism has forced us to consider in detail the representations used by the language system. In particular, connectionist approaches can be contrasted with rule-based approaches. In connectionist models rules are not explicitly encoded, but instead emerge as a consequence of statistical generalizations in the input data. Examples of this include the grapheme–phoneme correspondence rules of the dual-route model of reading (see Chapter 7), and the acquisition of the past tense (see Chapter 4). It is important to realize that this point is controversial, and we shall see throughout the book that the role of explicit rules is still a matter of substantial debate among psycholinguists. Third, the shift of emphasis from learning rules to learning through many repeated specific instances has led to an increase in probabilistic models of language acquisition and processing (Chater & Manning, 2006). Probabilistic models

have proved particularly influential in language acquisition, where children are thought to learn language by statistical or distributional analysis of what they hear rather than learning explicit rules (see Chapter 4).

Are language processes specific to language?

Does language depend on very specific processes that have evolved to do nothing else, or does it make use of more general cognitive processes? For example, when we understand sentences, do we make use of a general-purpose working memory store, or do we have dedicated stores that can store only information about language? Do children learn language using general-purpose learning rules, or do they make use of information restricted to the linguistic domain?

The ideas of innateness, modularity, rules, and language-specific processing are related. There is a divide in psycholinguistics between those who argue for innate language-specific modules that make extensive use of rules, and those who argue that much or all of language processing is the adaptation of more general cognitive processes.

Are we certain of anything in psycholinguistics?

One important point to note is that there are very few topics in psycholinguistics where we can say that we know the answer to questions with complete certainty. Time after time you will notice that even when there is consensus, or when we appear to agree on what happens, there are dissenting voices. Uncertainty is a fact of life when trying to understand the psychology of language.

The discipline is still relatively quite young, and we have a lot to learn. It's not like physics which has hundreds of years of solid research to stand on. Imagine being a physicist debating experiments and models in seventeenth-century Europe. That's a bit like where we're at now.

So I'm sorry; as I said earlier, sometimes I'll just have to throw my hands up and say "sorry, we don't know," and you'll have to leave it at that.

SUMMARY

- Language is a communication system that enables us to talk about anything, irrespective of time and space.
- Psycholinguistics arose after the Second World War as a result of interaction between the disciplines of information theory and linguistics, and as a reaction against behaviorism.
- Later experiments revealed a number of problems with a purely linguistic approach to understanding language.
- Two ideas from Chomsky's original work that were picked up by early psycholinguists were the derivational theory of complexity and the autonomy of syntax.
- The earliest experiments supported the idea that the more transformationally complex a sentence, the longer it took to process; however, experiments using psychologically more realistic tasks failed to replicate these findings.
- Although linguistic theory influenced early accounts of parsing, linguistics and psycholinguistics soon parted ways.
- Modern psycholinguistics uses a number of approaches, including experiments, computer simulation, linguistic analysis, brain imaging, and neuropsychology.
- Early artificial intelligence (AI) approaches to language such as ELIZA and SHRDLU gave the impression of comprehending language, but had no real understanding of language and were limited to specific domains.
- Language processes can be broken down into a number of levels of processing.
- Psychologists have different views on the extent to which the mind can be divided into discrete modules.
- The use of brain imaging is becoming particularly important in the study of language.
- There is considerable debate about whether language processing is interactive or autonomous.
- An important question, particularly for the study of how we acquire language, is the extent to which language is innate.
- Whereas traditional approaches, based on linguistics, state that much of our knowledge of language is encoded in terms of explicit rules, more recent approaches based on connectionist modeling state that our knowledge arises from the statistical properties of language.
- Double dissociations are important in the neuropsychological study of language.

QUESTIONS TO THINK ABOUT

1. What are the methodological difficulties involved for linguists who study people's intuitions about language?
2. What are the advantages and disadvantages of using brain imaging to study language?
3. What are the advantages of a modular system? Are there any disadvantages that you can think of?
4. What are the disadvantages of group experiments in neuropsychology?
5. Are there any limits to what single-case studies of the effects of brain damage on language might tell us?

(Continued)

(Continued)

6. What is the difference between neuropsychology and neuroscience?
7. How would you define language? What do you think are its most important characteristics?
8. Which do you think is going to tell us more about how humans use language: experiments or computational modeling? Which would you prefer to do, and why?
9. What does knowing where something happens in the brain tell us about what is happening?
10. What is the difference between linguistics and psycholinguistics, and does the distinction matter?

FURTHER READING

There are many textbooks that offer an introduction to cognitive psychology. Any introductory text on psychology will provide you with rich material. If you want more detail, try Anderson (2010), Eysenck and Keane (2010), or Quinlan and Dyson (2008).

For a summary of the early history of psycholinguistics, see Fodor, Bever, and Garrett (1974), and of linguistics, Lyons (1977a). If you wish to find out more about linguistics, you might try Fromkin, Rodman, and Hyams (2011). Crystal (2010) is a complete reference work on language. Clark's (1996) book is about language as communication. For an amusing read on the history of English, and much more besides, see Bryson (1990).

Thagard (2005) provides a general survey of cognitive science. There are many introductory textbooks on traditional AI, including Negnevitsky (2004). Introductions to connectionism include Bechtel and Abrahamsen (2001) and Ellis and Humphreys (1999)—the latter emphasizes the impact of connectionism on cognitive psychology.

Kolb and Whishaw (2009) describe traditional neuropsychology and the Wernicke–Geschwind model in detail; see also Andrewes (2001), Banich (2004), or Stirling (2002) for recent introductions to neuropsychology. For a more advanced source on neuropsychology and language, try Hillis (2002). Notice that these references are now getting rather dated; that's because the emphasis has switched from pure neuropsychology to neuroscience. Gazzaniga, Ivry, and Mangun (2008) and Ward (2010) are good general introductions to imaging and cognitive neuroscience.

Chalmers (1999) is a good introduction to the methods and philosophy of science.

Altmann (1997) and Pinker (1994) are introductions to the psychology of language that take the same general approach as this book. There are some recent handbooks and encyclopedias of psycholinguistics that will provide you with more detailed coverage of the topics in this book, including Gaskell (2007), Spivey, McRae, and Joanisse (2012), and Traxler and Gernsbacher's (2006) second edition of the *Handbook of Psycholinguistics*. As already mentioned, Crystal (2010) is a very good reference for linguistics.

A number of journals cover the field of psycholinguistics. Many relevant experimental articles can be found in journals such as the *Journal of Experimental Psychology* (particularly the sections entitled General; Learning, Memory, and Cognition; and, for lower level processes such as speech perception and aspects of visual word recognition, Human Perception and Performance), the *Quarterly Journal of Experimental Psychology*, *Cognition*, *Cognitive Psychology*, *Cognitive Science*, and *Memory and Cognition*. Three journals with a particularly strong language bias are the *Journal of Memory and Language* (formerly called the *Journal of Verbal Learning and Verbal Behavior*),

Language and Cognitive Processes, and the *Journal of Psycholinguistic Research*. Theoretical and review papers can often be found in *Psychological Review*, *Psychological Bulletin*, and *Behavioral and Brain Sciences*. The latter includes critical commentaries on the target article, plus a reply to those commentaries, which can be most revealing. Articles on connectionist and AI approaches to language are often found in *Cognitive Science* again, and sometimes in *Artificial Intelligence*. Many relevant neuroscience papers can be found in *Brain and Language*, *Cognitive Neuropsychology*, the *Journal of Cognitive Neuroscience*, *Neurocase*, and sometimes in journals such as *Brain* and *Cortex*. Papers with a biological or connectionist angle on language can sometimes also be found in the *Journal of Cognitive Neuroscience*. Journals rich in good papers on language acquisition are the *Journal of Experimental Child Psychology*, *Journal of Child Language*, and *First Language*; see also *Child Development*.

As we will see, designing psycholinguistics experiments can be a tricky business. It is vital to control for a number of variables that affect language processing (see Chapter 6 for more detail). For example, more familiar words are recognized more quickly than less familiar ones. We therefore need easy access to measures of variables such as familiarity. There are a number of databases that provide this information, including the Oxford Psycholinguistic Database (Quinlan, 1992) and the Nijmegen CELEX lexical database for several languages on CD-ROM (Baayen, Piepenbrock, & Gulikers, 1995).

There is a website for this book. It contains links to other pages, details of important recent work, and a means of contacting me electronically. The URL is http://www.psypress.com/cw/harley.

CHAPTER (2)

DESCRIBING LANGUAGE

INTRODUCTION

This chapter introduces the building blocks of language: sounds, words, and **sentence**s. It describes how we make sounds and form words, and how we order words to form sentences. The chapter also provides means of describing sounds and sentence structure.

The study of syntax often comes across as being rather technical, with what appears at first sight to be a lot of jargon and some daunting symbols. However, it is worth persevering, because linguistics provides us with a valuable means of describing sentence structure and a way of showing how sentences are related to each other. By the end of this chapter you should:

- Know how the sounds of language can be categorized.
- Understand how we make different sounds.
- Understand how syntactic rules describe the structure of a language.
- Be able to construct parse trees of simple sentences.
- Understand the importance of the work of the linguist Chomsky.

HOW TO DESCRIBE SPEECH SOUNDS

Acoustics is the name of the study of the physical properties of sounds. Acoustic information about sounds can be depicted in a number of ways. One of the most commonly used is a sound spectrogram (see Figure 2.1). A spectro-gram shows the amount of energy present in a sound when frequency is plotted against time. The peaks of energy at particular frequencies are called **formant**s. Formant structure is an important characteristic of speech sounds. All **vowel**s and some **consonant**s have formants, but the pattern of formants is particularly important in distinguishing vowels.

We can describe the sounds of speech at two levels. **Phonetics** describes the acoustic detail of speech sounds (their physical properties) and how they are articulated, while **phonology** describes the sound categories each language uses to divide up the space of possible sounds. An example should make this clear. Consider the sound "p" in the English words "pin" vs "spin." The actual sounds are different; you can tell this by putting your hand up to your mouth as you say them. You should be able to feel a breath of air going out as you say "pin," but not as you say "spin." The "p" sound in "pin" is said to be **aspirated**, and that in "spin" **unaspirated**. In English, even though the sounds are different, it does not make any difference to the meaning of the word that you use. If you could manage to say "pin" with an unaspirated "p" it might sound a little odd, but to your listeners it would still have the same meaning as "pin" when said normally. But in some languages aspiration does make a difference to the meaning of words. In Thai, "paa" (unaspirated) means "forest," while "paa" (aspirated) means "to split."

A **phoneme** is a basic unit of sound in a particular language. In English the two sorts of "p"

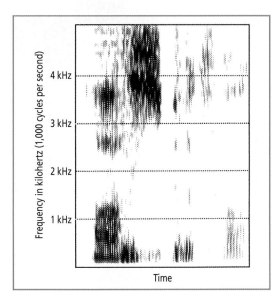

FIGURE 2.1 Sound spectrogram for the word hospital. The burst of noise across a wide range of frequencies corresponds to /s/; the noticeable gaps are the stop consonants /p/ and /t/. In normal speech the final vowel is barely represented.

are the same phoneme, whereas in Thai they are different phonemes. The two "p" sounds are phonetically different—they are said to be different phones. Two phones are said to be an instance of the same phoneme in a particular language if the difference between them never makes a difference to the meaning of words. Different phones that are understood as the same phoneme in a language are called **allophones**. Hence in English the aspirated "p" sounds are allophones: Whether or not a "p" is aspirated never makes a difference to the meaning of a word. To take another example, the sounds "l" and "r" are clearly different phones, and in English they are also different phonemes. In Japanese they are just allophones of the same phoneme. On the other hand the sounds at the beginning of "game," "dame," "fame," and "same" are different phonemes in English—switch them around and you change the meaning of the words. A special notation is used for distinguishing between phones and phonemes. Square brackets are used to designate [phones], whereas slanting lines are used for /phonemes/. Broadly speaking

phonetics is the study of phones, and phonology is the study of phonemes. There are three types of phonetics depending on what is emphasized: articulatory (which emphasizes how sounds are made), auditory or perceptual (which emphasizes how sounds are perceived), and acoustic (which emphasizes the sound waveform and physical properties).

Two words in a language that differ by just one sound are called **minimal pair**s. Examples of minimal pairs are "dog" and "cog," "bat" and "pat," "fog" and "fop." We can also talk about minimal sets of words (e.g., "pat," "bat," "cat," "hat"), all of which differ by only one phoneme, in the same position. As we have just seen, substituting one phoneme for another by definition leads to a change in the meaning, whereas just changing one phone for another (e.g., aspirated for unaspirated [p]) need not necessarily lead to a change in meaning.

In many languages, such as English, there is not a perfect correspondence between letters and sounds. The letter "o" represents a number of different sounds (such as in the words "mock," "moon," and "mow"). The sound "ee" can be spelled by an "i" or a "y." It is convenient to have a system of representing individual sounds with specific symbols, but letters are not suitable because of these ambiguities. The International Phonetic Alphabet (or IPA for short) is the standard method of representing sounds. The symbols of the IPA and examples of words containing the English phonemes they represent are shown in Box 2.1.

Note that the ways in which these words are pronounced can vary greatly, both between and within countries speaking the same language. These examples are based on "Received Pronunciation" in English. Received Pronunciation (RP) is the supposedly high-prestige, educated accent that gives no clue to the regional origin of the speaker within Britain; examples of RP can often be found by listening to national news broadcasts—particularly from 50 years ago! (It is important to note that these examples do not mean that these are the correct ways of pronouncing these words.) Vowel sounds are often very different between British English and American English.

Box 2.1 The International Phonetic Alphabet (IPA)

Consonants

p	*pat*	*pie*
b	*bat*	*babble*
t	*tie*	*tot*
k	*kid*	*kick*
d	*did*	*deed*
g	*get*	*keg*
s	*sun*	*psychology*
z	*razor*	*peas*
f	*field*	*laugh*
v	*vole*	*drove*
m	*mole*	*mum*
n	*not*	*nun*
ŋ	*sing*	*think*
θ	*thigh*	*moth*
ð	*the*	*then*
∫ (š)	*she*	*shield*
ʒ (ž)	*vision*	*measure*
l	*lie*	*lead*
w	*we*	*witch*
ʍ	*when*	*whale*
r	*rat*	*ran*
j	*you*	*young*
h	*hit*	*him*
t∫ (č, tš)	*cheese*	*church*
dʒ (ǰ, dž)	*judge*	*religion*
x	*loch*	(Scottish pronunciation)
ʔ	*bottle*	(glottal pronunciation)

Vowels

British English		American English	
i	*reed*	*beat*	i
ɛ	*bed*	*said*	ɛ
I (I)	*did*	*bit*	I
æ	*rat*	*anger*	æ
ɔ	*saw*	*author*	ɔ (in *saw*)
a (ɑ)	*hard*	*car*	ɑr
ɒ	*pot*	*got*	ɑ
u	*who*	*boot*	u
U (ω)	*could*	*foot*	ω
ə	*above*	*sofa**	ər
ʌ	*hut*	*tough*	ʌ

Diphthongs (vowel–vowel combinations)

aI (ay)	*rise*	*bite*	aI
aω (æω)	*cow*	*about*	aω
ɔI (ɔy)	*boy*	*coy*	ɔI
eI (e)	*may*	*bait*	eI
oU (oω)	*go*	*boat*	ou
Iə	*here*	*mere*	Ir
ɛə	*mare*	*rare*	er
aɪɔ	*hire*	*fire*	aIr
ju	*new*	French	tu

Frequently used alternative symbols shown in parentheses. Main examples are for most speakers of British English; the far right symbols for vowels and diphthongs are for most speakers of American English.

*This is the *schwa*, a weak, neutral vowel often used to replace unstressed vowels.

There are also many specific differences between British and American pronunciations; for example, American English tends to drop the initial /h/ in "herbs." (There are also different words for the same thing, of course, such as "sidewalk" for "pavement," and "trash" for "rubbish.") Different systems of pronunciations within a language are known as *dialects*. Dialects mostly differ in their vowel sounds. One advantage of the IPA is that it is possible to represent these different ways of pronouncing the same thing.

We produce speech by moving parts of the vocal tract, including the lips, teeth, tongue, mouth, and voice box or larynx (see Figure 2.2). The basic source of sounds is the larynx, which modifies the flow of air from the lungs and produces a range of higher frequencies called harmonics. Different sounds are then made by changing the shape of the vocal tract. There are two different major types of sounds. Vowels (such as a, e, i, o, and u) are made by modifying the shape of the vocal tract, which remains more or less open

Received Pronunciation (RP) has long been perceived as the most prestigious spoken form of the English language. RP belies the origins of its speaker, and is sometimes referred to as the "Queen's English," as it is spoken by the monarch.

sounds is to look at their **place of articulation**—that is, the place where the vocal tract is closed or restricted. The contrasting features needed to describe sounds are known as distinctive features.

CONSONANTS

Consonants are made by closing or restricting some part of the vocal tract as air flows through it. We classify consonants according to their place of articulation, whether or not they are voiced, and their **manner of articulation** (see Table 2.1).

The place of articulation is the part of the vocal tract that is closed or constricted during articulation. For example, /p/ and /b/ are called bilabial sounds and are made by closing the mouth at the lips, whereas /t/ and /d/ are made by putting the tongue to the back of the teeth. To understand the difference between /b/ and /p/, we need to introduce a concept called **voicing**. In one case (/b/), the vocal cords are closed and vibrating from the moment the lips are released; the consonants are said to be pronounced with voice, or just voiced. In the other case (/p/), there is a short delay, as the vocal cords are spread apart as air is first passed between them; hence they take some time to start vibrating. These

while the sound is being produced. The position of the tongue modifies the range of harmonics produced by the larynx. Consonants (such as p, b, t, d, k, g) are made by closing or restricting some part of the vocal tract at the beginning or end of a vowel. Most consonants cannot be produced without some sort of vowel. This description suggests that one way to examine the relation between

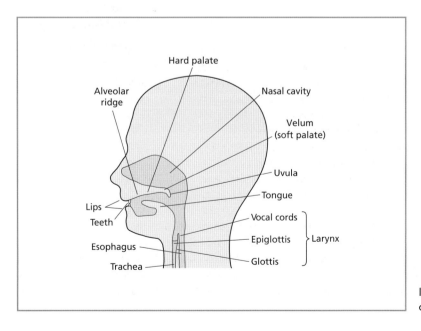

FIGURE 2.2 The structure of the human vocal tract.

consonants are said to be voiceless (also produced without voice or **unvoiced**). The time between the release of the constriction of the airstream when we produce a consonant, and when the vocal cords start to vibrate, is called the **voice onset time (VOT)**. Voicing also distinguishes between the consonants /d/ (voiced) and /t/ (voiceless). The sounds /d/ and /t/ are made by putting the front of the tongue on the alveolar ridge (the bony ridge behind the upper teeth). Hence these are called alveolars. Dentals such as /θ/ and /ð/ are formed by putting the tongue tip behind the upper front teeth. Labiodentals such as /f/ and /v/ are formed by putting the lower lip to the upper teeth. Postalveolar sounds (e.g., /ʃ/, /ʒ/, formerly called alveopalatals) are made by putting the tongue towards the front of the hard part of the roof of the mouth, the palate, near the alveolar ridge. Palatal sounds (e.g., /j/, /y/) are made by putting the tongue to the middle of the palate. Further back in the mouth is a soft area called the soft palate or velum, and velars (e.g., /k/, /g/) are produced by putting the tongue to the velum. Finally, some sounds are produced without the involvement of the tongue. The glottis is the name of the space between the vocal cords in the larynx. Constriction of the larynx at the glottis produces a voiceless glottal fricative (/h/).

When the glottis is completely closed and then released, a **glottal stop** (/ʔ/) is made. Glottal stops do not occur in the Received Pronunciation of English, but are found in some dialects and in other languages. (The glottal stop can be heard, for example, in some dialects of the south-east of England in the middle of words like "bottle," replacing the /t/ sound.)

The other important dimension used to describe consonants is the manner of articulation. Stops are formed when the airflow is completely interrupted for a short time (e.g., /p/, /b/, /t/, /d/). Not all consonants are made by completely closing the vocal tract at some point; in some it is merely constricted. Fricatives are formed by constricting the airstream so that air rushes through with a hissing sound (e.g., /f/, /v/, /s/). Affricatives are a combination of a brief stopping of the airstream followed by a constriction (e.g., /dʒ/, /tʃ/). Liquids are produced by allowing air to flow around the tongue as it touches the alveolar ridge (e.g., /l/, /r/). Most sounds are produced orally, with the velum raised to prevent airflow from entering the nasal cavity. If it does and air is allowed to flow out through the nose we get nasal sounds (e.g., /m/, /n/). Glides or semi-vowels are transition sounds produced as the tongue moves from one vowel position to another (e.g., /w/, /y/).

TABLE 2.1 English consonants as combinations of distinguishing phonological features.

PLACE OF ARTICULATION	stop +V	stop –V	fricative +V	fricative –V	affricative +V	affricative –V	nasal +V	nasal –V	lateral approximant +V	lateral approximant –V	approximant +V	approximant –V
bilabial	b	p					m				w	
labiodental			v	f								
dental			ð	θ								
alveolar	d	t	z	s			n		l			
postalveolar			ʒ	ʃ	dʒ	tʃ					r	
velar	g	k					ŋ					
glottal		ʔ		h								

TABLE 2.2 Vowels as combinations of distinguishing phonological features.

	Front	Central	Back
High	i		u
	I		ω
Mid	e	ə	o
	ε		ɔ
Low	æ	ʌ	ɑ

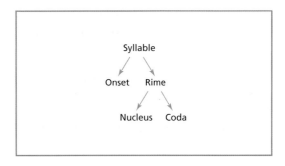

FIGURE 2.3 Hierarchical structure of syllables.

So we can describe consonants in terms of the articulatory distinctive features, place of articulation, manner of articulation, and voicing. It should be noted that some languages produce consonants (such as clicks) that are not found in European languages.

VOWELS

Vowels are made with a relatively free flow of air. The nature of the vowel is determined by the way in which the shape of the tongue modifies the airflow. Table 2.2 shows how vowels can be classified depending on the position (which can be raised, medium, or lower) of the front, central, or rear portions of the tongue. For example, the /i/ sound in "meat" is an example of a high front vowel because the air flows through the mouth with the front part of the tongue in a raised (high) position.

Two vowel sounds can be combined to form a **diphthong**. Examples are the sounds in "my," "cow," "go," and "boy."

Whereas the pronunciation of consonants is relatively constant across dialects, that of vowels can differ greatly.

SYLLABLES

Words are divided into rhythmic units called **syllable**s. One way of determining the number of syllables in a word is to try singing it—each syllable will need a different note (Radford, Atkinson, Britain, Clahsen, & Spencer, 1999). For example, the word syl–la–ble has three syllables. Many

words are **monosyllabic**—they only have one syllable. Syllables can be analyzed in terms of a hierarchical structure (see Figure 2.3). The syllable **onset** is an initial consonant or cluster (e.g., /cl/); the **rime** consists of a *nucleus*, which is the central vowel, and a *coda*, which comprises the final consonants. Hence in the word "clumps," "cl-" is the onset and "-umps" the rime, which in turn can be analyzed into a nucleus, which is the central vowel ("u"), and coda ("mps"). In English, all of these components are optional, apart from the nucleus (all words have to have at least a central vowel). The rules that describe how component syllables combine with each other differ across languages—for example, Japanese words do not have codas, and in Cantonese only nasal sounds and glottal stops are possible codas.

Features of words and syllables that may span more than one phoneme, such as pitch, stress, and the rate of speech, are called suprasegmental features. For example, a falling pitch pattern indicates a statement, whereas a rising pitch pattern indicates that the speaker is asking a question. Try saying "it's raining" as a statement, "it's raining?" as a question, and "it's raining!" as a statement of surprise. Stress varies within a word, as some syllables receive more stress than others, and within a sentence, as some words are emphasized more than others. Taken together, pitch and stress determine the rhythm of the language. Languages differ in their use of rhythm. In English, stressed syllables are produced at approximately equal periods of time—English is said to be a stressed-timed language. In French, syllables are produced in a steady flow—it is said to be a syllable-timed language.

In English, although we can use pitch to draw attention to a particular word, or convey additional information about it, different pitches do not change the meaning of the word ("mouse" spoken with a high or low pitch still means mouse). In some languages pitch is more important. In the Nigerian language Nupe, [ba] spoken with a high pitch means "to be sour," but [ba] spoken with a low pitch means "to count." Languages that use pitch to contrast meanings are called *tone languages*.

LINGUISTIC APPROACHES TO SYNTAX

Linguistics provides us with a language for describing syntax. In particular, the work of the American linguist Noam Chomsky (b. 1928) has been influential in indicating constraints on how powerful human language must be, and how it should best be described. We looked at his influence on the development of psycholinguistics in Chapter 1.

The linguistic theory of Chomsky

Chomsky's work is based on two related ideas: first, the relations between language and the brain, and how children acquire language, and second, a technical description of the structure of language.

The American linguist Noam Chomsky argued that language is innate, species-specific, and biologically pre-programmed.

I examine his views on the relation between language and thought and on language acquisition in Chapters 3 and 4. Chomsky argued that language is a special feature that is innate, species-specific, and biologically pre-programmed, and that is a faculty independent of other cognitive structures. Here we are primarily concerned with the more technical aspect of his theory.

For Chomsky, the goal of the study of syntax is to describe the set of rules, or **grammar**, that enables us to produce and understand language. Chomsky (1968) argued that it is important to distinguish between our idealized linguistic **competence**, and our actual linguistic **performance**. Our linguistic competence is what is tapped by our intuitions about which are acceptable sentences of our language, and which are ungrammatical strings of words. We know that the sentence "The vampire the ghost loved ran away" is grammatical, even if we have never heard it before, while we also know that the string of words "The vampire sleep the ghost ran away" is ungrammatical. Competence concerns our abstract knowledge of our language. It is about the judgments we would make about language if we had sufficient time and memory capacity. In practice, of course, our actual linguistic performance—the sentences that we actually produce—is greatly limited by these factors. Furthermore, the sentences we actually produce often use the more simple grammatical constructions. Our speech is full of false starts, hesitations, speech errors, and corrections. The actual ways in which we produce and understand sentences are also in the domain of performance.

In his more recent work, Chomsky (1986) distinguished between externalized language (E-language) and internalized language (I-language). For Chomsky, E-language linguistics is about collecting samples of language and understanding their properties; in particular it is about describing the regularities of a language in the form of a grammar. I-language linguistics is about what speakers know about their language. For Chomsky, the primary aim of modern linguistics should be to specify I-language: it is to produce a grammar that describes our knowledge of the language, not the sentences we actually produce. Another way of putting this is that I-language is about mental phenomena, whereas E-language is about social phenomena (Cook & Newson, 2007). Competence is an aspect of I-language.

As a crude generalization, we can say that psycholinguists are more interested in our linguistic performance, and linguists in our competence. Nevertheless, many of the issues of competence are relevant to psychologists. In particular, linguistics provides a framework for describing and thinking about syntax, and its theories place possible constraints on language acquisition.

Let us look at the notion of a grammar in more detail. A grammar uses a finite number of rules that in combination can generate all the sentences of a language—hence we talk of **generative grammar**. Obviously we could produce a device that could emit words randomly, and although this might, like monkeys typing away with infinite time to spare, produce the occasional sentence, it will mainly produce garbage. For example, "dog vampire cat chase" is a non-sentence in English. It is an important constraint that although our grammar must be capable of generating all the sentences of a language, it should also never generate non-sentences. (Of course, from time to time we erroneously produce non-sentences, but this is an aspect of performance; remember we are concerned only with linguistic competence here.) Chomsky further argued that a grammar must give an account of the underlying syntactic structure of sentences. The sentence structures that the grammar creates should capture our intuitions about how sentences and fragments of sentences are related. We know that "the vampire kissed the ghost" and "the ghost was kissed by the vampire" are related in some way. Finally, linguistic theory should also explain how children acquire these rules.

Chomsky's linguistic theory has evolved greatly over the years. The first version was described in a book called *Syntactic Structures* (1957). The 1965 version became known as the "standard theory"; this was followed in turn by the "extended standard theory," "revised extended standard theory," and then "government and binding (or GB) theory" (Chomsky, 1981). The latest version is called minimalism (Chomsky, 1995). Nevertheless, the central theme is that language is rule-based, and that our knowledge of syntax can

be captured in a finite number of syntactic rules. A moment's reflection should show that language involves rules, even if we are not always aware of them. How else would we know that "Vlad bought himself a new toothbrush" is acceptable English but "Vlad bought himself toothbrush new a" is not?

Describing syntax and phrase-structure grammar

How should we describe the rules of grammar? Chomsky proposed that phrase-structure rules are an essential component of our grammar, although he went on to argue that they are not the only component. An important aspect of language is that we can construct sentences by combining words according to rules. Phrase-structure rules describe how words can be combined, and provide a method of describing the structure of a sentence. The central idea is that sentences are built up hierarchically from smaller units using rewrite rules. The set of rewrite rules constitute a phrase-structure grammar. Rewrite rules are simply rules that translate a symbol on the left-hand side of the rule into those on the right-hand side. For example, (1) is a rewrite rule that says "a sentence (S) can be rewritten as a noun phrase (NP) followed by a verb phrase (VP)":

(1) S → NP + VP

In a phrase-structure grammar, there are two main types of symbol: terminal elements (consisting of vocabulary items or words) and non-terminal elements (everything else). It is important to realize that the rules of grammar do not deal with particular words, but with categories of words that share grammatical properties. Words fall into **class**es such as **noun**s (words used to name objects and ideas, both concrete and abstract, such as "pig," or "truth"), **adjective**s (words used to describe, such as "pink," or "lovely"), **verb**s (words describing actions or states, or an assertion, such as "kiss," or "modify"), **adverb**s (words qualifying verbs, such as "quickly"), **determiner**s (words determining the number of nouns they modify, such as "the," "a," and "some"), **preposition**s (words such as "in," "to," and "at"), **conjunction**s (words such as "and," "because," and "so"), **pronoun**s ("he,"

Box 2.2 A grammar for a fragment of English

S	→	NP + VP (A)
NP	→	DET + N (B)
NP	→	N (C)
VP	→	V + NP (D)
VP	→	V (E)
N	→	Vlad, Boris, poltergeist, vampire, werewolf, ghost …
V	→	loves, hates, likes, bites, is …
DET	→	the, a, an …

Abbreviations

S	sentence		N	noun
NP	noun phrase		V	verb
VP	verb phrase		DET	determiner

"she," "it"), and so on. Box 2.2 is an example of a phrase-structure grammar that accounts for a fragment of English.

We can distinguish two types of word. **Content word**s do most of the semantic work of the language, and **function word**s do most of the grammatical work. Content words include nouns, adjectives, verbs, and most adverbs. Function words include determiners, conjunctions, prepositions, and pronouns. Function words tend to be short and used very frequently. Whereas the number of content words is very large and changing (we often coin new content words, such as "television" and "computer"), the number of function words is small and fixed (at about 360). For this reason, content words are sometimes called **open-class word**s, and function words **closed-class item**s.

Words combine to make **phrase**s, which express a single idea. For instance, "Vlad," "the vampire," "the old vampire," and "the grouchy old vampire" are all examples of **noun phrases**— they can all take the part of nouns in sentences. They all make acceptable beginnings to the sentence fragment "__ bought a new toothbrush." Phrases are **constituent**s that can generally be systematically replaced by a single word while maintaining the same sentence structure. Hence in the sentence "The nasty vampire laughed at the poor ghost," "The nasty vampire" is a phrase (as it can be replaced by, for example, "Vlad"), whereas "The nasty" is not; "laughed at the poor ghost" is a phrase (for example, it can be replaced by just "laughed"), but "at the" is not.

Phrases combine to make **clause**s. Clauses contain a **subject** (used to mention something), and a **predicate** (the element of the clause that gives information about the subject). Every clause has a verb. Sentences contain at least one clause but may contain many more. The essential idea of a phrase-structure grammar is the analysis of the sentence into its lower level constituents, such as noun phrases, verb phrases, nouns, and verbs. Indeed, this approach is sometimes called constituent analysis. Constituents are components of larger constructions.

Two other important syntactic notions are the subject and the **object** of a sentence. The subject of a sentence is the noun phrase that is immediately dominated by the highest-level element, the sentence node. An easy test to discover the subject of a sentence is to turn the sentence into a question that can be answered by "yes" or "no" (Burton-Roberts, 1997). The phrase that functions as the subject is the one required to change its position in forming the question. So from (2) "the vampire" is forced to change position (relative to "is") to form the question in (3); hence "the vampire" is the subject:

(2) The vampire is kissing the witch.
(3) Is the vampire kissing the witch?

There are different types of verbs, each requiring different syntactic roles to create acceptable structures. **Transitive verb**s require a single noun phrase called a direct object. "Kisses" is a transitive verb. In (4) "the vampire" is the subject and "the witch" is the object. **Intransitive verb**s do not require any further noun phrase; in (5) "laughs" is an intransitive verb. Ditransitive verbs require two noun phrases called the direct object and the indirect object; in (6) "the vampire" is the subject, "the ring" is the direct object, and "the witch" is the indirect object.

(4) The vampire kisses the witch.
(5) The vampire laughs.
(6) The vampire gives the ring to the witch.

Because each sentence must contain at least one clause, and each clause must have a subject, it follows that every sentence must have a subject. Not all sentences have an object, however. Sentences containing just intransitive verbs, such as (5), contain only a subject.

You might think by now that the subject is that which is doing the action, and the object is having something done to it. This type of description is a semantic analysis in terms of semantic roles or **theme**s. While this generalization is true for many sentences (called active sentences), it is not always true. Consider sentence (7):

(7) The vampire is being kicked by the witch.
(8) S → The vampire + verb phrase + prepositional phrase.

Now which is the grammatical subject of this sentence and which is the grammatical object? If we apply the yes–no question test, we form "Is the vampire being kicked by the witch?," with "the vampire" moving position. "The witch" stays where it is. In addition, the structure of (7) is outlined in (8). Clearly "the vampire" is immediately dominated by the sentence node. Hence "the vampire" is the subject of this sentence, even though "the witch" is doing the action and "the vampire" is having the action done to him. This type of sentence structure is called a passive. The object in the active form of the sentence has become the grammatical subject of the passive form. We will examine passives in more detail later.

The simple grammar in Box 2.2 can be used to generate a number of simple sentences. Let us start by applying some of these rewrite rules to show how we can generate a sentence (9). The goal is to show how a sentence can be made up from terminal elements:

(9) Starting with S, rule (A) from Box 2.2 gives us NP + VP.
     Rule (B) gives us DET + N + VP.
     Rule (D) gives us DET + N + V + NP.
     Rule (C) gives us DET + N + V + N.

Then the substitution of words gives us, for example, the following sentence: "The vampire loves Boris."

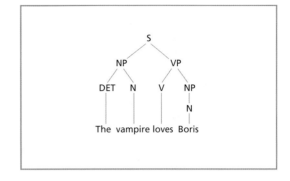

FIGURE 2.4 Parse tree for the sentence "The vampire loves Boris."

We desire more of a grammar than that it should merely be able to generate sentences: we need a way to describe the underlying syntactic structure of sentences. This is particularly useful for syntactically ambiguous sentences. These are sentences that have more than one interpretation, such as the sentence "I saw the witches flying to America." This could be paraphrased as either "When I was flying to America, I saw the witches," or "There I was standing on the ground when I looked up and there were the witches flying off to America." A phrase-structure grammar also enables us to describe the syntactic structure of a sentence by means of a tree diagram, as shown for the sentence "The vampire loves Boris" in Figure 2.4. The points on the tree corresponding to constituents are called nodes. The node at the top of the tree is the sentence or S node; at the bottom are terminal nodes corresponding to words; in between are non-terminal nodes corresponding to constituents such as NP and VP.

Tree diagrams are very important in the analysis of syntax, and it is important to be clear about what they mean. The underlying structure of a sentence or a phrase is sometimes called its phrase structure or phrase marker. It should be reiterated that the important idea is capturing the underlying syntactic structure of sentences; it is not our goal here to explain how we actually produce or understand them. Furthermore, at this stage directionality is not important; the directions of the arrows in Box 2.2 do not mean that we are limited to talking about sentence production. Our discussion at present applies equally to production and comprehension.

Phrase-structure rules provide us with the underlying syntactic structure of sentences we both produce and comprehend.

Clearly, this is an extremely limited grammar. One obvious omission is that we cannot construct more complex sentences with more than one clause in them. However, we could do this by introducing conjunctions. A slightly more complex example would be using a relative clause with a relative pronoun (such as "which," "who," or "that") to produce sentences such as (10):

(10) The vampire who loves Boris is laughing.

Natural language could only be described by a much more complex phrase-structure grammar that contained many more rules. We would also need to specify detailed restrictions on when particular rules could and could not be applied. We would then have a description of a grammar that could generate all of the sentences of a language and none of the non-sentences. Obviously another language, such as French or German, would have a different set of phrase-structure rules.

Although these grammars might be very large, they will still contain a finite number of rules. In real languages there are potentially an infinite number of sentences. How can we get an infinite number of sentences from a finite number of rules and words? We can do this because of special rules based on what are known as recursion and iteration. Recursion occurs when a rule uses a version of itself in its definition. Recursive rules enable phrases to contain examples of the same sort of phrase, such as in the old song "Little does she know that I know that she knows that I know …" (Kursaal Flyers, 1976). One of the most important uses of recursion is to embed a sentence within another sentence, producing center-embedded sentences. Examples (12) and (13) are based on (11):

(11) The vampire loved the ghoul.
(12) The vampire the werewolf hated loved the ghoul.
(13) The vampire the werewolf the ghost scared hated loved the ghoul.
(14) *The vampire who the werewolf who the ghost had scared loved the ghoul.

This process of center-embedding could potentially continue forever, and most linguists would argue that the sentence would still be perfectly well-formed; that is, it would still be grammatical. Of course, we would soon have difficulty in understanding such sentences, for we would lose track of who scared whom and who loved what. Many people have difficulty with sentence (13), and many people find constructions such as (14) grammatically acceptable, although it is missing a verb (Gibson & Thomas, 1999). Although we might rarely or never produce center-embedded sentences, our grammar must be capable of producing them, or at least of deciding that they are grammatical. Given a piece of paper and sufficient time, you could still understand sentences of this type. This observation reflects the distinction between competence and performance mentioned earlier: We have the competence to understand these sentences, even if we never produce them in actual performance. (Remember that judgments of grammatical acceptability are based on intuitions, and these might vary. Not everyone would agree that sentences with a large number of center-embeddings are grammatical. Indeed, there is some controversy in linguistics about their status; see Hawkins, 1990.) Nevertheless, most people think that recursion is a central property of language and perhaps human thought (Fitch, Hauser, & Chomsky, 2005).

Iteration enables us to carry on repeating the same rule, potentially for ever. For example, we can use iteration to produce sentences such as (15).

(15) The nice vampire loves the ghost and the ghost loves the vampire and the friendly ghost loves the vampire and …

There are different types of phrase-structure grammar. Context-free grammars contain only rules that are not specified for particular contexts, whereas context-sensitive grammars can have rules that can only be applied in certain circumstances. In a context-free rule, the left-hand symbol can always be rewritten by the right-hand one regardless of the context in which it occurs. For example, the writing of a verb in its singular or plural form depends on the context of the preceding noun phrase.

Transformations

Chomsky argued that a phrase-structure grammar is not capable of capturing our linguistic competence. Although it can produce any sentence of the language while not producing any non-sentences, and although it can provide an account of the structure of sentences, it cannot explain the relation between related sentences. Consider sentences (16) and (17):

(16)   The vampire chases the ghost.
(17)   The ghost is chased by the vampire.

Clearly our linguistic intuitions tell us that sentence (16) is related to sentence (17), but how can we capture this relation in our grammar? Phrase-structure grammars are not capable of capturing some relations. Chomsky (1957) showed that knowledge of such relations could be flagged by the introduction of special rewrite rules known as **transformation**s. Transformations are so central to the theory that the whole approach became known as **transformational grammar**. A normal rewrite rule takes a single symbol on the left-hand side (e.g., S, NP, or VP), and rewrites it as something else more complex. A transformation is a special type of rewrite rule that takes a string of symbols (i.e., more than one symbol) on the left-hand side, and rewrites this string as another string on the right-hand side. Sentences (16) and (17) are related to each other by what is called the passivization transformation; (17) is the passive form of the active form (16). The transformation that achieves this change looks like (18):

(18) $NP_1 + V + NP_2 \rightarrow NP_2$ + auxiliary + V* + by + NP_1

An **auxiliary verb** is a special verb (here, "is"), and the asterisk indicates that it is necessary to change the form of the main verb, here by changing the "-s" ending to an "-ed" ending.

Chomsky postulated many other types of transformations. For example, we can turn the affirmative declarative form of a sentence (16) into an interrogative or question form (19), or into a negative form (20). We can also combine

transformations—for example, to form a negative question, as in (21). The sentence that formed the basis of all the transformed versions (here 16) was called the kernel sentence.

(19)   Does the vampire chase the ghost?
(20)   The vampire does not chase the ghost.
(21)   Does the vampire not chase the ghost?

Not only do transformations capture our intuitions about how sentences are related, but they also enable the grammar to be simplified, primarily because rules that enable us to rewrite strings as other strings capture many of the aspects of the dependencies between words (particularly the context-sensitive aspect described earlier).

Of course, in a fully fledged grammar the rules would be much more numerous and much more complex. For example, we have not looked at the details of changes to the form of the verb, or specified the types of sentences to which passivization can be applied.

Surface and deep structure

Chomsky (1965) presented a major revision of the theory, usually called the standard theory. The changes were primarily concerned with the structure of the linguistic system and the nature of the syntactic rules. In the new model, there were now three main components. First, a semantic system (which had no real counterpart in the earlier model) assigned meaning to the syntactic strings; second, a phonological component turned syntactic strings into phonological strings; and third, a syntactic component was concerned with word ordering. The syntactic component in turn had two components, a set of base rules (roughly equivalent to the earlier phrase-structure rules), and transformational rules.

Perhaps the most important extension of this later theory was the introduction of the distinction between deep structure and surface structure (now called d-structure and s-structure). To some extent this distinction was implicit in the earlier model with the concept of kernel sentences, but the revised model went further, in that every sentence was stipulated to have a deep structure and a surface structure. Furthermore, there was no longer a distinction between optional and obligatory transformations. In a sense all transformations became obligatory, in that markers for them are represented in the deep structure.

In the standard theory, the syntactic component generated a deep structure and a surface structure for every sentence. The deep structure was the output of the base rules and the input to the semantic component; the surface structure was the output of the transformational rules and the input to the phonological rules. Describing sentences in terms of their deep structure has two main advantages. First, some surface structures are ambiguous in that they have two different deep structures. Second, what is the subject and what is the object of the sentence is often unclear in the surface structure. Sentence (22) is ambiguous in its surface structure. However, there is no ambiguity in the corresponding deep structures, which can be paraphrased as (23) and (24):

(22) The hunting of the vampires was terrible.
(23) The way in which the vampires hunted was terrible.
(24) It was terrible that the vampires were hunted.

Sentences (25) and (26) have the same surface structure, yet completely different deep structures:

(25) Vlad is easy to please.
(26) Vlad is eager to please.

In (25), Vlad is the deep structure object of please; in (26), Vlad is the deep structure subject of please. This difference can be made apparent in that we can build a deep structure corresponding to (27) of the form of (25), but cannot do so for (26), as (28) is clearly ungrammatical. (The ungrammaticality is conventionally indicated by an asterisk.)

(27) It is easy to please Vlad.
(28) *It is eager to please Vlad.

Principles and parameters theory, and minimalism

As Chomsky's theory continued to develop, many of the features of the grammars changed, although the basic goals of linguistics remained the same.

The new "standard version of the theory" was originally known as Government and Binding (GB) theory (Chomsky, 1981), but the term principles and **parameter**s theory is now more widely used. This name emphasizes the central idea that there are principles that are common to all languages and parameters that vary from language to language (see Chapter 4).

There have been a number of important changes in the more recent versions of the theory. First, with time, the number of transformations steadily dwindled. Second, related to this, the importance of deep structure has also dwindled (Chomsky, 1991). Third, when constituents are moved from one place to another, they are hypothesized as leaving a trace in their original position. (This has nothing to do with the TRACE model of spoken word recognition that will be described in Chapter 9.) Fourth, special emphasis is given to the most important word in each phrase. For example, in the noun phrase "the vampire with the garlic," the most important noun is clearly "vampire," not "garlic." (This should be made clear by the observation that the whole noun phrase is about the vampire, not about the garlic.) The noun "vampire" is said to be the head of the noun phrase.

Fifth, the revised theory permits units intermediate in size between nouns and noun phrases, and verbs and verb phrases. The rules are phrased in terms of what is called $\bar{X}$ (pronounced "X-bar") syntax (Jackendoff, 1977; Kornai & Pullum, 1990). The intermediate units are called $\bar{N}$ (pronounced noun-bar) and $\bar{V}$ (verb-bar), and are made up of the head of a phrase plus any essential arguments or role players. Consider the phrase "the king of Transylvania with a lisp." Hence "king" is an N and the head of the phrase; "the king of Transylvania" an $\bar{N}$ (because Transylvania is the argument of "king," the place that the king is king of); and "the king of Transylvania with a lisp" an NP. This approach distinguishes between essential arguments (such as "of Transylvania") and optional adjuncts or **modifier**s (such as "with a lisp"). The same type of argument applies to verbs, which also have obligatory arguments (even if they are not always stated) and optional modifiers. The advantage of this description is that it captures new generalizations, such as if a noun phrase contains both argument and adjunct, the argument must always be closer to the head than the adjunct: "The king with a lisp of Transylvania" is distinctly odd. It is an important task of linguistics to capture and explain such generalizations. This method of description also enables the specification of a very general rule such as (29):

(29) $\bar{X} \to X, ZP*$

That is, any phrase (X-bar) contains a head with any number of modifiers (ZP*). Such an abstract rule is an elegant blueprint for the treatment of both noun phrases and verb phrases, and captures the underlying similarity between them.

English is a head-first language. Japanese, on the other hand, is a head-last language. Nevertheless, both languages distinguish between heads and modifiers; this is an example of a very general rule that Chomsky argues must be innate. This general rule is an example of a parameter. The setting of the parameter that specifies head-first or head-last is acquired through exposure to a particular language (Pinker, 1994). I examine parameters and their role in language acquisition in Chapter 4.

In the most recent reworking of his ideas, the minimalist program aims to simplify the grammar as much as possible (Chomsky, 1995). The Principle of Economy requires that all linguistic representations and processes should be as economical as possible; the theoretical and descriptive apparatus necessary to describe language should be minimized (Radford, 1997). The less complex a grammar, the easier it should be to learn. Although this principle sounds simple, its implications for the detailed form of the theory are vast. In minimalism, the role of abstract, general grammatical rules is virtually abolished. Instead, the lexicon incorporates many aspects of the grammar. For example, information about how transitive verbs take on syntactic roles is stored with the verbs in the lexicon, rather than stored as an abstract grammatical rule. Instead of phrase-structure rules, categories are merged to form larger categories. The lexical representations of words specify grammatical features that control the merging of categories. These ideas are echoed by modern accounts of parsing.

Chomsky is the most influential figure in the history of linguistics, with his central idea being that the goal of linguistics is to specify the rules of a grammar that captures our linguistic competence. Later I look at the implications of this idea for psycholinguistics.

Optimality Theory and Cognitive Linguistics

Although Chomsky's earlier work had great influence on the psycholinguistics of the time, this influence has waned. Minimalism, although important for linguists, has had no impact on psycholinguistics. Many of the key ideas of modern psycholinguistics are reflected in other branches of linguistics, particularly Optimality Theory (McCarthy, 2001). Optimality Theory has been applied to phonology, morphology, semantics, and syntax; its main idea is that the surface form of an expression results from the resolution of conflicts between underlying representations. It shares much with connectionist approaches to language. As we shall see in Chapter 10, one important approach to understanding sentences is that of constraint satisfaction; we try to satisfy as many constraints as possible, and make sure that we satisfy all the important ones. We choose the best interpretation available in the context on the basis of all data.

Cognitive Linguistics is the name given to the general approach that emphasizes language as one aspect of general cognition. In contrast with Chomsky's generative grammar approach, cognitive linguists do not believe there is a separate faculty of language, and argue that we process language using the same sorts of cognitive process as we use in every other aspect of cognition. We learn language using general cognitive processes, rather than language-specific ones. These ideas are reflected in psycholinguistic approaches to language acquisition that emphasize the importance of general learning mechanisms (see Chapter 4).

The formal power of grammars

This part is relatively technical and can be skipped, but the ideas discussed in it are useful for understanding how powerful a grammar must be if it is to be able to describe natural language. The study of different types of grammar and the devices that are necessary to produce them is part of the branch of mathematical linguistics or computational theory (a subject that combines logic, linguistics, and computer science) called automata theory. Automata theory also reveals something of the difficulty of the task confronting the child who is trying to learn language. An automaton is a device that embodies a grammar and that can produce sentences that are in accordance with that grammar. It takes an input and performs some elementary operations, according to some previously specified instructions, to produce an output. The topic is of some importance because if we know how complex natural language is, we might expect this to place some constraints on the power of the grammar necessary to cope with it.

We have already defined a grammar as a device that can generate all the sentences of a language, but no non-sentences. A language is not restricted to natural language: it can be an artificial language (such as a programming language), or a formal language such as mathematics. In fact, there are many possible grammars that fall into a small number of distinct categories, each with different power. Each grammar corresponds to a particular type of automaton, and each type produces languages of different complexity.

We cannot produce all the sentences of natural language simply by listing them, because there are an infinite number of grammatically acceptable sentences. To be able to produce all these sentences, our grammar must incorporate recursive and iterative rules. Some rules need to be sensitive with respect to the context in which the symbols they manipulate occur. Context-free and context-sensitive languages differ in whether they need rules that can be specified independently of the context in which the elements occur. How complex is natural language, and how powerful must the grammar be that produces it?

The simplest type of automaton is known as a finite-state device. This is a simple device that moves from one state to another depending on only its current state and current input, and produces what is known as a Type 3 language. The current state of a finite-state device is determined by some finite number of previous symbols (words). Type 3 grammars are also known as right-linear grammars, because every rewrite rule can only be of the form A → B or A → x B, where x is a terminal element. This produces right-branching tree structures. For example, if you use the rules in (30) you can produce sentences such as in (31). Just substitute the appropriate letters; the vertical separator | separates alternatives.

(30) S → the A | a A
      A → green A | vicious A
      A → ghost B | vampire B
      B → chased C | loved C | kissed C
      C → the D | a D
      D → witch | werewolf

(31) The vicious vampire chased the witch. A green vicious ghost kissed the werewolf.

The corresponding finite-state device is depicted in Figure 2.5. The finite-state device always starts in the S state, and then reads words from the appropriate category to move on to the next state, before moving onto the next state. It finishes producing sentences when it reaches the end state. We can produce even longer sentences if we allow iteration with a rule such as (32), which will enable us to produce sentences of the form (33).

(32) D → and S
(33) The vicious vampire chased the witch and a green vicious ghost kissed the werewolf.

Next up in power from a finite-state device is a push-down automaton. This is more powerful than a finite-state device because it has a memory; the memory is limited, however, in that it is only a push-down stack. A push-down stack is a special type of memory where only the last item stored on the stack can be retrieved; if you want to get at something stored before the last thing, everything stored since will be lost. It is like a pile of plates. It produces Type 2 grammars that can parse context-free languages. Next in power is a linear-bounded automaton, which has a limited memory, but can retrieve anything from this memory. It produces Type 1 grammars, parsing context-sensitive languages. Finally, the most powerful automaton, a

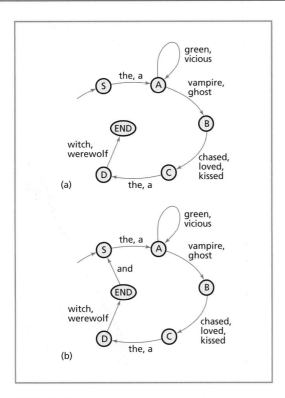

FIGURE 2.5 An example of a finite-state device.

Turing machine, has no limitations, and produces a Type 0 grammar.

Chomsky (1957) showed that natural language cannot be characterized by a finite-state device. In particular, a finite-state device cannot produce arbitrarily long sequences of multiple center-embedded structures, where the sequence of embedding could carry on for ever. You can only produce these sorts of sentences if the automaton has a memory to keep track of what it has produced so far. Recursion is necessary to account for this type of complexity, and recursion is beyond the scope of finite-state devices. At the time this conclusion was surprising: Theories of language were dominated by behaviorism and information theory, and it was thought that knowledge of the previous states was all that was necessary to account for human language. In effect, Chomsky showed that no matter how many previous words were taken into account, a finite-state device cannot produce or understand natural language. An important extension of this argument is that children cannot learn language simply by conditioning.

Chomsky went further and argued that neither context-free nor context-sensitive grammars provided an account of human language. He argued that it is necessary to add transformations to a phrase-structure grammar; the resulting grammar is then a Type 0 grammar, and can only be produced by a Turing machine. Chomsky thought that transformations were needed to show how sentences are related to each other. They also simplify the phrase-structure rules necessary and provide a more elegant treatment of the language. Finally, there is some linguistic evidence that appeared to show that no context-free or context-sensitive grammar can account for certain constructions found in natural language. For example, Postal (1964) argued that the Mohawk language contains intercalated dependencies, in which words are cross-related (such as a1 a2 . . . an b1 b2 bn, where a1 relates to b1, and so on). Hence it seems that natural human language can only be produced by the most powerful of all types of grammar.

Although this conclusion was accepted for a long time, it has been disproved. First, it is not clear that all the complex dependencies between words described by Chomsky and Postal are necessarily grammatical. Second, there is a surprising formal demonstration by Peters and Ritchie (1973) that context can be taken into account without exceeding the power of a context-free grammar. Third, Gazdar, Klein, Pullum, and Sag (1985) showed that context-free languages can account for the phenomena of natural language thought to necessitate context sensitivity if more complex syntactic categories are incorporated into the grammar. So while a finite-state device is too weak to describe human language, a Turing machine might be unnecessarily powerful.

Finally, it is worth reiterating that, although most of the examples in this chapter are in English, the same basic principles will apply to other languages. The rules and descriptions will differ from language to language, but we can use the same underlying approaches (e.g., describing sounds by their method of articulation, or grammars in terms of phrase-structure rules) to describe all languages.

SUMMARY

- The basic sounds of a language are called phonemes.
- Different languages use different phonemes, and languages vary in the differences in sounds that are important.
- Phonetics describes the acoustic detail of speech sounds and how they are articulated; phonology describes the sound categories each language uses to divide up the space of possible sounds.
- The IPA (International Phonetic Alphabet) provides a notation for sounds and a way of classifying them.
- Consonants are made by almost closing the vocal tract, whereas vowels are made by modifying its shape; in both cases the place of constriction determines the sound we make.
- Consonants further depend on the manner of articulation and whether voicing is present.
- Words can be divided into syllables, and syllables into onset and rimes.
- Syntactic rules specify the permissible orders of words in a language.
- Parsing is the process of computing the syntactic structure of language.
- Sentences can be analyzed by parse trees.
- The most influential work on linguistic theories of syntax has been that of Noam Chomsky.
- Chomsky distinguished between actual linguistic performance and idealized linguistic competence; the goal of linguistics is to provide a theory of competence.
- According to Chomsky, a complete linguistic theory will be able to generate all of the sentences of a language and none of the non-sentences, will provide an account of people's intuitions about the knowledge of their language, and will explain how children can acquire language.
- The generative power of language is given by recursion and iteration.
- In his early work, Chomsky argued that sentences are generated by the operation of transformational rules on a deep structure representation generated by phrase-structure rules, resulting in a surface structure representation.
- Chomsky later argued that important generalizations about language are best explained by a set of principles and parameters; language acquisition involves setting these parameters to the appropriate value given exposure to particular languages.
- In his more recent minimalist work Chomsky has attempted to simplify the grammar by incorporating many of its aspects into the lexicon.
- Automata theory provides a formal account of the power of artificial and natural languages; Chomsky argued that only the most powerful automaton (the Turing machine) could cope with natural language.

QUESTIONS TO THINK ABOUT

1. To what extent have linguistics and psycholinguistics converged or diverged?
2. What might psycholinguistics have to offer people trying to develop computer systems that understand natural language?
3. Think about the different languages you know. What are their similarities and dissimilarities?
4. How would you describe samples of different dialects of your language (e.g., regions of Britain or the USA) in terms of the IPA?

FURTHER READING

Crystal (2010) and Fromkin et al. (2011) provide excellent detailed introductions to phonetics and phonology, and in particular give much more detail about languages other than English.

Fabb (1994) is a workbook of basic linguistic and syntactic concepts, and makes the meaning of grammatical terms very clear, although most of the book avoids using the notion of a verb phrase, on the controversial grounds that verb phrases are not as fundamental as other types of phrases. For a more detailed account see Burton-Roberts (1997). Also try Tarshis (1992) for a friendly introduction to grammatical rules in English. For a more advanced review, see Crocker (1999).

Pinker (1994) gives a brief and accessible description of Chomsky's theory of syntax. Borsley (1991) provides excellent coverage of contemporary linguistic approaches to syntax, and Radford (1981) provides detailed coverage of the linguistic aspects of Chomsky's extended theory. Radford (1997) provides an excellent introduction to the minimalist approach; be warned, however, that this is a very technical topic. An excellent, detailed yet approachable coverage of Chomsky's theory, which emphasizes principles and parameters theory, is Cook and Newson (2007). See also references to his ideas on the development of language at the end of Chapter 3.

If you want to find out more about the relation between linguistics and psycholinguistics, read the debate between Berwick and Weinberg (1983a, 1983b), Garnham (1983a), Johnson-Laird (1983), and the articles by Stabler (1983) and Jackendoff (2003), with the subsequent peer commentaries. An introduction to automata theory is provided in Johnson-Laird (1983) and Sanford (1985); a more detailed and highly mathematical treatment can be found in Wall (1972).

See Fauconnier and Turner (2003) for a general account of cognition and language in the cognitive linguistics vein.

SECTION B

THE BIOLOGICAL AND DEVELOPMENTAL BASES OF LANGUAGE

Chapter 3, The foundations of language, asks where language came from, whether language is unique to humans, and what we can learn from attempts to teach human language to animals. Next we examine the biological basis of language and what mechanisms are necessary for its development. We look at the cognitive and social basis of human language development. Finally, we examine the relation between language and thought.

Chapter 4, Language development, is concerned with how language develops from infancy to adolescence. Do children have an innate device that enables them to acquire language from input that is often impoverished? How do infants learn to associate words with the objects they see in the world around them? How do they learn the rules that govern word order?

Chapter 5, Bilingualism and second language acquisition, asks what cognitive processes are involved when a child is brought up using two languages, and whether these differ from the situation of an adult learning a second language. How should languages be taught?

CHAPTER ⬤ 3

THE FOUNDATIONS OF LANGUAGE

INTRODUCTION

Children acquire language without apparent effort. This chapter examines the requirements for language acquisition. What biological, cognitive, and social precursors are necessary for us to acquire language normally? How are language processes related to structures in the brain? Is language unique to humans? What mechanisms need to be in place before language development can begin? What affects the rate of linguistic development? What are the consequences of different types of impairment or deprivation for language? The chapter also examines how language is related to other cognitive processes. By the end of this chapter, you should:

- Know how language might have evolved.
- Know about animal communication systems and be able to say how they differ from human language.
- Be able to describe attempts to teach languages to apes and to evaluate how successful these have been.
- Know to what extent language functions are localized in the human brain.
- Know how lateralization develops.
- Understand what is meant by a critical period for language development.
- Understand the effects of different types of deprivation on linguistic development.
- Understand the relation between language and thought.

WHERE DID LANGUAGE COME FROM?

There is a rich archeological record available to help us understand the evolution of the hands and the development of the use of tools. There is no such record available when examining the evolution of language, so at first sight it might seem to be a wholly speculative undertaking. Indeed, in 1866 the Linguistic Society of Paris famously banned all debate on the origins of language.

We have no idea what the first language was like. Some words might have been onomatopoeic— that is, they sound like the things to which they refer. For example, "cuckoo" sounds like the call of the bird, "hiss" sounds like the noise a snake makes, and "ouch" sounds like the exclamation we make when there is a sudden pain. The idea that language evolved from mimicry or imitation has been called the "ding-dong," "heave-ho," or "bow-wow" theory. However, such similarities can only be attributed to a very few words, and many words take very different forms in different languages.

Perhaps the most obvious idea about how language came into being is that it evolved as a beneficial adaptation shaped by natural selection. However, even this hypothesis is controversial. The alternative is that language arose as a side effect of the evolution of something else, such as an increase in overall brain size and an increase in general intelligence (e.g., Chomsky, 1988; Hauser, Chomsky, & Fitch, 2002; Piattelli-Palmarini, 1989). Several arguments have been proposed in favor of the side-effect theory. First, many researchers believe that there has not been enough time for something so complex as language to evolve since the evolution of humans diverged from that of other primates. Second, a grammar cannot exist in any intermediate form (we either have a grammar or we don't). Third, as possessing a complex grammar confers no obvious selective advantage, evolution could not have selected for it.

In recent years, however, the hypothesis that language evolved by Darwinian natural selection as an advantageous adaptation has largely won, partly because it provides a well-understood general mechanism—indeed, the only mechanism understood—for how language could have arisen (natural selection), and partly because the objections do not hold much water. It is now apparent that there was indeed sufficient time for grammar to evolve, that it evolved to communicate existing cognitive representations, and that the ability to communicate using a grammar-based system confers a big evolutionary advantage. For example, it obviously makes a big difference to your survival if an area has animals that you can eat, or animals that can eat you, and if you are able to communicate this distinction to someone else (Fitch, Hauser, & Chomsky, 2005; Jackendoff & Pinker, 2005; Pinker, 2003; Pinker & Bloom, 1990; Pinker & Jackendoff, 2005).

The capacity for language and symbol manipulation must have arisen as the human brain increased in size and complexity when *Homo sapiens* became differentiated from other species, between 2 million and 300,000 years ago. Study of the fossil evidence suggests that a structure corresponding to Broca's area, a region of the brain clearly associated with language in modern humans, was present in the brains of early hominids as long as 2 million years ago. The shape of the human skull has changed significantly over time, enabling better control of speech: Neanderthals would not have been capable of controlling their tongues sufficiently to be able to articulate as clearly as we do. The articulatory apparatus has not changed significantly over the last 60,000 years. The evolution of language has come at a cost: the structures in the throat that enable us to control the production of sounds also make us more likely than other primates to choke on our food. Obviously the evolutionary advantages conferred by language must outweigh the disadvantage of this increased risk.

We do not know whether language existed in some intermediate form—although it seems unlikely that early humans went from communicating through a few grunts to a rich language that used grammar. Bickerton (1990, 2003) has controversially championed the idea of a protolanguage that was intermediate between primate communication systems and human language. Protolanguage arose with the evolution of *Homo erectus* about 1.6 million years ago. Protolanguage has vocal labels attached to concepts, but does not

This picture illustrates the stages in human evolution that have occurred over the last 35 million years. As the physical form and the brain changed, language also developed.

have a proper syntax; it is distinguished from language by the power of syntax (Chapter 2). The idea of a protolanguage is a powerful one: primates taught sign language (this chapter), very young children (Chapter 4), children deprived of early linguistic input (this chapter), and speakers of pidgin language (this chapter) could all be said to use a protolanguage rather than language.

What pressures selected for language? The social set-up of early humans must have played a role in the evolution of language, but many other animals, particularly primates, have complex social organizations, and although primates also have a rich repertoire of alarm calls and gestures, they did not develop language. In a rich social environment an adaptation that enables rich communication confers a huge evolutionary advantage on that species.

It is unlikely that language evolved in one step, or depends on a single gene. However, recent evidence suggests that important aspects of language, especially grammar, may be associated with a specific gene, called the FOXP2 gene. In animals, the FOXP2 gene seems to be involved in coordinating sensory and motor information, and skilled complex movements (Fisher & Marcus, 2006). Damage to the FOXP2 gene in humans leads to difficulty in acquiring language normally. The evidence suggests that the current structure of the FOXP2 gene in humans arose through a mutation within the last 100,000 years (Corballis, 2004), leading to greater development of Broca's region and an enhanced ability to coordinate complex sequences of movement (Fisher & Marcus, 2006). Corballis argues that the flowering of human culture, art, and technology, and the expansion of *Homo sapiens* about 40,000 years ago, were all associated with the FOXP2 mutation and the development of language. The mutation meant that speech could become fully autonomous in the sense that it no longer relied on gestures; this autonomy at once freed the hands and enabled better communication. A hundred thousand years is a long time in evolution: A mutation giving a 1% gain in fitness would increase in frequency in the population from 0.1% to 99.9% in just 4,000 generations (Haldane, 1927). However, it is likely that the Neanderthals—a branch of the genus

Homo that became extinct about 30,000 years ago—also carried the FOXP2 mutation and used some form of language, although these results are controversial because they might just reflect interbreeding between *Homo sapiens* and *Homo neanderthalensis*. We examine what the FOXP2 gene may control in more detail in Chapter 4.

The extent to which the evolution of language depended on the hands, and whether grammar arose from the use of manual gestures, is still controversial. Paget (1930) was the first to propose that language evolved in intimate connection with the use of hand gestures, so that vocal gestures developed to expand the available repertoire. Corballis (1992, 2003, 2004) argued that the evolution of language freed the hands from having to make gestures to communicate, so that tools could be made and used simultaneously with communication. Corballis argues that language arose not from primate calls, but from primate gestures. Additional evidence that language evolved from gestures comes from imaging studies that show that the brains of great apes are specialized in a very similar way to humans (Cantalupo & Hopkins, 2001). Chimpanzees and gorillas, like humans, show an asymmetry between the left and right hemispheres of the brain, with what is called Brodmann's area 44 being particularly enlarged on the left. This area is probably involved with the production of gestures; furthermore, it corresponds to Broca's region in humans, a key part of the brain involved in producing speech. One plausible explanation of this finding is that the brains of great apes became specialized to enable the production of sophisticated gestures, but this specialization continued in humans with speech arising from these gestures. Mirror neurons in this region play a particular role in imitating gestures; they fire when an animal performs a specific action or sees another animal performing the same action (Rizzolatti, Fadiga, Fogassi, & Gallese, 1996). They have been argued to play a particular role in the evolution of language (Stamenov & Gallese, 2002), with manual gestures rather than vocal communication driving evolution. The mirror neuron system for grasping enabled imitation, which in turn allowed early manual signs to develop (Arbib, 2005). Although many species (including birds and frogs) show left-hemisphere dominance for producing sounds, only humans show very strong right-handedness dominance; in other animals gesture production is bilateral across the population. (Although individual nonhuman primates, dogs, cats, and even rats tend to favor one paw, there is no systematic preference for left or right within these species.) As the gesture-based language evolved, vocalizations became incorporated into the gesture system, leading to the specialization and lateralization of the language and gesture systems and the right-handed preference in humans.

Of course, the relation between evolution and language might have been more complex than this. Elman (1999) argued that language arose from a communication system through many interacting "tweaks and twiddles." Deacon (1997) proposed that language and the brain co-evolved in an interactive way, converging towards a common solution for the cognitive and sensorimotor problems facing the organism. Symbolic gestures and vocalization preceded fully blown language. As the frontal cortex of humans grew larger, symbolic processing became more important, and linguistic skills became necessary to manage symbol processing, leading to the development of speech apparatus to implement these skills, which in turn would demand and enable further symbolic processing abilities. Fisher and Marcus (2006) propose that language was not a single wholesale innovation, but a complex reconfiguration of several systems that became adapted to form language. Such a conclusion is similar to that of Christiansen and Chater (2008), who see language itself as an evolving system that has made use of pre-existing brain structures.

DO ANIMALS HAVE LANGUAGE?

Is language an ability that is uniquely human? I examine both naturally occurring animal communication systems, and attempts to teach a human-like language to animals, particularly chimpanzees. There are a number of reasons why this topic is important. First, it provides a focus for the issue of what we mean by the term language. Second, it informs debate about the extent to which aspects

of language might be innate in humans and have a genetic basis. Third, it might tell us about which other social and cognitive processes are necessary for a language to develop. Finally, of course, the question is of great intellectual interest. The idea of being able to "talk to the animals" like the fictional Dr. Dolittle fascinates both adults and children alike. It can become an emotive subject, as it touches on the issue of animal rights, and the extent to which humans are distinct from other animals.

Animal communication systems

Many animals possess rich communication systems—even insects communicate. Communication is much easier to define than language: it is the transmission of a signal that conveys information, often such that the sender benefits from the recipient's response (Pearce, 2008). The signal is the means that conveys the information (e.g., a sound or a smell). It is useful to distinguish between communicative and informative signals: communicative signals have an element of design or intentionality in them, whereas signals that are merely informative do not. If I cough, this might inform you that I have a cold, but it is not a communication; but telling you that I have a cold is.

A wide range of methods is used to convey information. Ants rely on chemical messengers called pheromones. Honey bees produce a complex "waggle dance" (see Figure 3.1) in a figure-of-eight shape to other members of the hive (von Frisch, 1950, 1974). The direction of the straight part of the dance (or the axis of the figure-of-eight) represents the direction of the nectar relative to the sun, and the rate at which the bee waggles during the dance represents distance.

Primates use visual, auditory, tactile, and olfactory signals to communicate with each other. They use a wide variety of calls to symbolize a range of features of the environment and their emotional states. For example, a vervet monkey produces one particular "chutter" to warn others that a snake is nearby, a different call when an eagle is overhead, and yet another distinct call

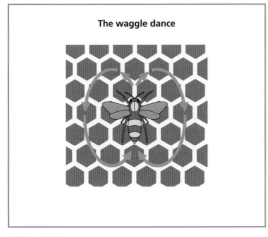

The waggle dance

FIGURE 3.1

Research shows that dolphins do not possess a language in terms of the intentional structuring of sub-units to deliver intelligible communications. However, this prompts the question; at what juncture do we decide that communication can be classed as a language?

to warn of approaching leopards. Each type of call elicits different responses from other nearby vervets (Demers, 1988). However, the signals are linked to particular stimuli and are only produced in their presence. Primates communicate about stimuli for which they do not already possess signals, suggesting that their communicative system has an element of creativity.

It is a widespread belief that whales and dolphins possess a language. However, the research does not support this belief. There is currently no evidence to suggest that dolphins employ sequences of sub-units that convey particular messages, in the same way as we combine words to form sentences to convey messages. Early research suggesting that dolphins were communicating with each other to carry out cooperative tasks to obtain fish turned out to be explicable in terms of conditioning; the dolphins carried on making sounds in the obvious absence of other dolphins (Evans & Bastian, 1969). Hump-backed whale song consists of ordered sub-parts, but their function is unknown (Demers, 1988).

How would we decide if an animal communication system had crossed the boundary to be counted as a language?

Defining language

"Language" is a difficult word to define. The dictionary defines language as "human speech … an artificial system of signs and symbols, with rules for forming intelligible communications for use, e.g., in a computer" (*Chambers Twentieth Century Dictionary*, 1998). Many introductions to the study of language avoid giving a definition, or consider it to be so obvious that it does not need to be defined. To some extent the aim of modern theoretical linguistics is to offer an answer to this question (Lyons, 1977a). Perhaps the difference between an animal communication system and a language is just a matter of degree?

Design features

Hockett (1960) attempted to sidestep the thorny issue of defining language by listing 16 general properties or design features of spoken human language (see Box 3.1). The emphasis of his design features is very much on the physical characteristics of spoken languages. Clearly, these are not all necessary defining characteristics—human written language does not display "rapid fading," yet clearly written language is a form of language. Nevertheless, design features provide a useful framework for thinking about how animal communication systems differ from human language.

Box 3.1 Hockett's (1960) "design features" of human spoken language

1. Vocal-auditory channel (communication occurs by the producer speaking and the receiver hearing)
2. Broadcast transmission and directional reception (a signal travels out in all directions from the speaker but can be localized in space by the hearer)
3. Rapid fading (once spoken, the signal rapidly disappears and is no longer available for inspection)
4. Interchangeability (adults can be both receivers and transmitters)
5. Complete feedback (speakers can access everything about their productions)
6. Specialization (the amount of energy in the signal is unimportant; a word means the same whether it is whispered or shouted)
7. Semanticity (signals mean something: they relate to the features of the world)
8. Arbitrariness (these symbols are abstract; except with a few onomatopoeic exceptions, they do not resemble what they stand for)
9. Discreteness (the vocabulary is made of discrete units)
10. Displacement (the communication system can be used to refer to things remote in time and space)
11. Openness (the ability to invent new messages)
12. Tradition (the language can be taught and learned)
13. Duality of patterning (only combinations of otherwise meaningless units are meaningful—this can be seen as applying both at the level of sounds and words, and words and sentences)
14. Prevarication (language provides us with the ability to lie and deceive)
15. Reflectiveness (we can communicate about the communication system itself, just as this book is doing)
16. Learnability (the speaker of one language can learn another)

Which features do animal communication systems possess? All communication systems possess some of the features. For example, the red belly of a breeding stickleback is an arbitrary sign. Some of the characteristics are more important than others; we might single out semanticity, arbitrariness, displacement, openness, tradition, duality of patterning, prevarication, and reflectiveness. These features all relate to the fact that language is about meaning, and provide us with the ability to communicate about anything. We might add other features to this list that emphasize the creativity and meaning-related aspects of language. Marshall (1970) pointed out the important fact that language is under our voluntary control; we intend to convey a particular message. The creativity of language stems from our ability to use syntactic rules to generate a potentially infinite number of messages from a finite number of words using iteration and recursion (see Chapter 2).

Syntax has five important properties (Kako, 1999a; Pinker, 2002). First, language is a discrete combinatorial system. When words are combined, we create a new meaning: the meanings of the words do not just blend into each other, but retain their identity. Second, well-ordered sentences depend on ordering syntactic categories of words (such as nouns and verbs) in correct sequences. Third, sentences are built round verbs, which specify what goes with what (e.g., you give something to someone). Fourth, we can distinguish words that do the semantic work of the language (content words—see Chapter 2) from words that assist in the syntactic work of the language (function words). Fifth, recursion—phrases containing examples of themselves—enables us to construct an infinite number of sentences from a finite number of rules. No animal communication system has these properties.

We can use language to communicate about anything, however remote in time and space.

Hence, although a parrot uses the vocal-auditory channel and the noises it makes satisfy most of the design characteristics up to number 13, it cannot lie, or reflect about its communication system, or talk about the past. Whereas monkeys are limited to chattering and squeaking about immediate threats such as snakes in the grass and eagles overhead, we can express novel thoughts; we can make up sentences that convey new ideas. This cannot be said of other animal communication systems. Bees will never dance a book about the psychology of the bee dance. We can talk about anything and effortlessly construct sentences that have never been produced before.

In summary, many animals possess rich symbolic communication systems that enable them to convey messages to other members of the species, that affect their behavior, that serve an extremely useful purpose, and that possess many of Hockett's design features. On the other hand, these communication systems lack the richness of human language. This richness is manifested in our limitless ability to talk about anything using a finite number of words and rules to combine those words. However difficult "language" may be to define, the difference between animal communication systems and human language is not just one of degree. All nonhuman communication systems are quite different from language (Deacon, 1997).

Can we teach language to animals?

Perhaps some animals have the biological and cognitive apparatus to acquire language, but have not needed to do so in their evolutionary niche. The alternative view is that only humans possess the necessary capabilities: that other animals are in principle incapable of learning language.

Most people think that dogs and parrots "know" some aspects of language. Dogs respond to instructions. One border collie called Rico knew the labels of over 200 items (Kaminski, Call, & Fischer, 2004), being able to fetch items with different names from around the house, even when he could not see the owner (thereby eliminating the possibility of the "Clever Hans" effect, which is that animals that appear to know language are in fact just picking up cues from their owner). When faced with a new name, he would infer that the name applied to a novel object, rather than being another name for an object with which he was familiar—this "novel name equals nameless category" principle is one that children use to learn some new words. However, unlike children, Rico's knowledge was restricted to the names of physical objects, and he showed no understanding of how the meanings of words might be related (e.g., that doll and ball are both types of toy). Nevertheless, this performance is impressive, and also suggests that general (rather than language-specific) learning mechanisms might go some way to explaining early word learning in children.

Everyone knows that parrots can be taught to mimic human speech. Pepperberg (1981, 1983, 1987, 2009) took this idea further and embarked on an elaborate formal program of training of her African grey parrot (*Psittacus erithacus*) called Alex. After 13 years, Alex had a vocabulary of about 80 words, including object names, adjectives, and some verbs. He could even produce and understand short sequences of words. Alex could classify 40 objects according to their color and what they were made of, understand the concepts of same and different, and count up to six. Alex showed evidence of being able to combine discrete categories and use syntactic categories appropriately. However,

Pepperberg's (1981) African grey parrot, Alex, showed evidence of being able to combine discrete categories and possibly to use syntactic categories appropriately.

he knew few verbs, showed little evidence of being able to relate objects to verbs, and knew very few function words (Kako, 1999a). Hence Alex's linguistic abilities are extremely limited.

Herman, Richards, and Wolz (1984) taught two bottle-nosed dolphins, Phoenix and Akeakamai, artificial languages. One language was visually based, using gestures of the trainer's arms and legs (see Figure 3.2), and the other was acoustically based, using computer-generated sounds transmitted through underwater speakers. However, this research tested only the animals' comprehension of the artificial language, not their ability to produce it. From the point of view of answering our questions on language and animals it is clearly important to examine both comprehension and production. Even so, the dolphins' syntactic ability was limited, and they showed no evidence of being able to use function words (Kako, 1999a).

Most of the work on teaching language to animals involves other primates, particularly chimpanzees, as they are highly intelligent, social animals and are our closest genetic neighbors. In the following discussion it is useful to bear in mind the distinction between teaching word meaning and syntax. Remember that an essential feature of human language is that it involves both associating a finite number of words with particular meanings or concepts, and using a finite number of rules to combine those words into a potentially infinite number of sentences. Before we can conclude that apes have learned a language we need to show that they can do both of these things.

What are the other cognitive abilities of chimpanzees?

We have seen that primates have a rich communication system that they use in the wild. The cognitive abilities of a chimpanzee named Viki aged 3½ years were generally comparable to those of a child of a similar age on a range of perceptual tasks such as discriminating and matching similar items, but broke down on tasks involving counting (Hayes & Nissen, 1971). Experiments on another chimp

FIGURE 3.2 Some of the gestures used to communicate with Akeakamai the dolphin. Adapted from Herman et al. (1984).

named Sarah also suggested that she performed at levels close to that of a young child on tasks such as conserving quantity, as long she could see the transformation occurring. For example, she understood that pouring water from a tall, thin glass into a short, fat glass did not change the amount of water. Hence the cognitive abilities of apes are broadly similar to those of young children, apart from the latter's linguistic abilities. This decoupling of linguistic and other cognitive abilities in children and apes has important implications. First, it suggests that for many basic cognitive tasks language is not essential. Second, it suggests that there are some non-cognitive prerequisites to linguistic development. Third, it suggests that cognitive limitations in themselves might not be able to account for the failure of apes to acquire language.

Talking chimps

The earliest attempt to teach apes language was that of Kellogg and Kellogg (1933), who raised a female chimpanzee named Gua along with their own son. (This type of rearing is called cross-fostering or cross-nurturing.) Gua only understood a few words, and never produced any that were recognizable. Hayes (1951) reared a chimp named Viki as a human child and attempted to teach her to speak. This attempt was also unsuccessful, as after 6 years the chimpanzee could produce just four poorly articulated words ("mama," "papa," "up," and "cup") using her lips. Even then, Viki could only produce these in a guttural croak, and only the Hayes family could understand them easily. With a great deal of training she understood more words, and some combinations of words.

These early studies have a fundamental limitation. The vocal tracts of chimps are physiologically unsuited to producing speech, and this difference alone could account for their lack of progress (see Figure 3.3). Nothing can be concluded about the general language abilities of primates from these early failures.

Washoe

Although the design of the vocal tracts of chimps is unsuited to speaking, chimps are manually very dexterous. Later attempts at teaching apes language were based on systems using either a type of sign language, or involving manipulating artificially created symbols. Perhaps the most famous example of trying to teach language to an ape is that of Washoe. Washoe is a female chimpanzee who was caught in the wild when she was approximately 1 year old. She was then brought up as a human child, doing things such as eating, toilet training, playing, and other social activities

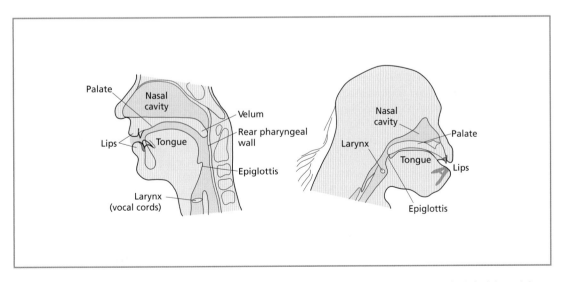

FIGURE 3.3 Compare the adult vocal tract of a human (left) with that of a chimpanzee (right). Adapted from Lieberman (1975).

(Gardner & Gardner, 1969, 1975). In this context, she was taught **American Sign Language** (ASL, sometimes called AMESLAN). ASL is the standard sign language used by people with hearing impairment in North America. Just like spoken language, it has words and syntax.

At the age of 4, Washoe could produce about 85 signs, and comprehend more; a few years later her vocabulary had increased to approximately 150–200 signs (Fouts, Shapiro, & O'Neil, 1978). These signs came from many syntactic categories, including nouns, verbs, adjectives, negatives, and pronouns. Her carers argued that she made over-generalization errors similar to those of young children (for example, in using the sign for "flower" to stand for flower-like smells, or "hurt" to refer to a tattoo). It was further claimed that when she did not know a sign, she could create a new one. When she first saw a duck and had not learned a sign for it, she coined a phrase combining two signs she did have, producing "water bird." Furthermore, she combined signs and used them correctly in strings up to five items long. Examples of Washoe's signing include: "Washoe sorry," "Baby down," "Go in," "Hug hurry," and "Out open please hurry." She could answer some questions that use what are called WH-words (so called because in English most of the words that are used to start questions begin with "wh," such as "what," "where," "when," or "who"). She displayed some sensitivity to word order in that she could distinguish between "You tickle me" and "I tickle you."

Do chimps who have been taught language go on to teach their offspring, or can the offspring learn language by observing their parents? These are important questions, because there is little evidence that human children are explicitly taught language by their parents. Researchers observed that Washoe's adopted son Loulis both spontaneously acquired signs from Washoe and was also seen to be taught by Washoe. Although this is a clear indication of what is known as cultural transmission, it is unclear whether it is a language that has been transmitted, or just a sophisticated communication system (Fouts, Fouts, & van Cantfort, 1989; Fouts, Hirsch, & Fouts, 1982).

At first sight Washoe appears to have acquired the use of words and their meanings, and at least some sensitivity to word order in both production and comprehension.

Sarah

A different approach was taken by Premack (1971, 1976a, 1976b, 1985, 1986a). Sarah was a chimpanzee trained in a laboratory setting to manipulate small plastic symbols that varied in shape, size, and texture. The symbols could be ordered in certain ways according to rules. Together, the symbols and the rules form a language called Premackese. One advantage of this set-up is that less memory load is required, as the array is always in front of the animal. Sarah produced mainly simple lexical concepts (strings of items together describing simple objects or actions), and could produce novel strings of symbols. These, however, were generally only at the level of substituting one word for another. For example (with the Premackese translated into English), "Randy give apple Sarah" was used as the basis of producing "Randy give banana Sarah." She produced sentences that were syntactically quite complex (for example, producing logical connectives such as "if … then"), and showed metalinguistic awareness (reflectiveness) in that she could talk about the language system itself using symbols that meant "… is the name of." However, there was little evidence that Sarah was grouping strings of symbols together to form proper syntactic units. (Also see Figure 3.4.)

FIGURE 3.4 Here we see another of Premack's chimpanzees, Elizabeth. The message on the board says "Elizabeth give apple Amy." Adapted from Premack (1976a).

Nim and others

Terrace, Petitto, Sanders, and Bever (1979) described the linguistic progress of a chimpanzee named Nim Chimpsky (a pun on Noam Chomsky). They taught Nim Chimpsky a language based on ASL. Nim learned about 125 signs, and the researchers recorded over 20,000 utterances in 2 years, many of them of two or more signs in combination. They found that there was regularity of order in two-word utterances—for example, place was usually the second thing mentioned—but that this broke down with longer utterances. Longer utterances were largely characterized by more repetition ("banana me eat banana eat"), rather than displaying real syntactic structure. Terrace et al. were far more pessimistic about the linguistic abilities of apes than were either the Gardners or Premack. Unlike children, Nim rarely signed spontaneously; about 90% of his utterances were in reply to his trainers and concerned immediate activities such as eating, drinking, and playing, and 40% of his utterances were simply repetitions of signs that had just been made by his trainers. However, O'Sullivan and Yeager (1989) pointed out that the type of training Nim received might have limited his linguistic skills. They found that he performed better in a conversational setting than in a formal training session.

There have been other famous attempts to teach language to primates. Savage-Rumbaugh, Rumbaugh, and Boysen (1978) reported attempts to teach the chimpanzees Lana, Sherman, and Austin language, using a computer-controlled display of symbols structured according to an invented syntax called Yerkish. The symbols that serve as words are called lexigrams (see Figure 3.5). The linguistic abilities of other primates such as gorillas have also been studied (e.g., Koko, reported by Patterson, 1981).

Evaluation of early attempts to teach language to apes

At first sight, these attempts to teach chimps language might look quite convincing. The important design features of Hockett all appear to be present. Specific signs are used to represent particular words (discreteness), and apes can refer to objects that are not in view (displacement). The issue of semanticity, whether or not the signs have meaning for the apes, is a controversial one to which we shall return. At the very least we can say that they have learned associations between objects and events and responses. Sarah could discuss the symbol system itself (reflectiveness). Signs could be combined in novel ways (openness). The reports of apes passing sign language on to their young satisfy the feature of tradition. Most importantly, it is claimed that the signs are combined according to specified syntactic rules of ordering: that is, they have apparently acquired

Student teacher Joyce Butler with Nim Chimpsky the chimpanzee, named after American linguist, philosopher, cognitive scientist, and political activist Noam Chomsky. Joyce is showing Nim the sign configuration for "drink" and Nim is imitating her. Photographed during project Nim, an extended study of animal language acquisition conducted in the 1970s.

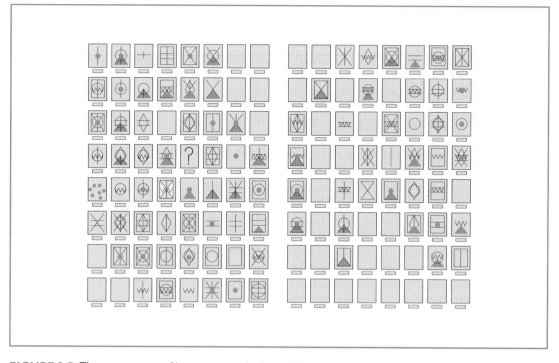

FIGURE 3.5 The arrangement of lexigrams on a keyboard. Blank spaces were non-functioning keys, or displayed photographs of trainers. From Savage-Rumbaugh, Pate, Lawson, Smith, and Rosenbaum (1983).

a grammar. Maybe, then, these animals can learn language, and the difference between apes and humans is only a matter of degree?

Unfortunately, there are many problems with some of this research, particularly the early, pioneering work. The literature is full of argument and counter-argument, making it difficult to arrive at a definite conclusion. There have been two sources of debate: methodological criticisms of the training methods and the testing procedures used, and argument over how the results should be interpreted.

What are the methodological criticisms? First, one criticism was that ASL is not truly symbolic, in that many of the signs are icons standing for what is represented in a non-arbitrary way (Savage-Rumbaugh et al., 1978; Seidenberg & Petitto, 1979). For example, the symbol for "give" looks like a motion of the hand towards the body reminiscent of receiving a gift, and "drive" is a motion rather like turning a steering wheel. If this were true, then this research could be dismissed as irrelevant because the chimps are not learning a symbolic language. Clearly

it is not true; not all the attempts mentioned earlier used ASL—Premack's plastic symbols, for example, are very different. In addition, the force of this objection can be largely dismissed on the grounds that although some ASL signs are iconic, many of them are not, and that deaf people clearly use ASL in a symbolic way. No one would say that deaf people using ASL are not using a language (Petitto, 1987). Nevertheless, ASL is different from spoken language in that it is more condensed—articles such as "the" and "a" are omitted—and this clearly might affect the way in which animals use the language. And in Washoe's case at least, a great proportion of her signing seemed to be based on signs that resemble natural gestures. It is also possible that her trainers over-interpreted her gestures, first incorrectly identifying some gestures as signs, or thinking that a particular movement was indeed an appropriate sign. Deaf native signers observed a marked discrepancy between what they thought Washoe had produced (which was very little), and what the trainers claimed (Pinker, 1994). Again, these criticisms are hard to justify against the lexigram-based studies, although Brown (1973) noted that Sarah's performance deteriorated with a different trainer.

In these early studies, reporting of signing behavior was anecdotal, or limited to cumulative vocabulary counts and lists. No one ever produced a complete corpus of all the signs of a signing ape in a predetermined period of time, with details of the context in which the signs occurred (Seidenberg & Petitto, 1979). The limited reporting has a number of consequences that make interpretation difficult. For example, the "water bird" example would be less interesting if Washoe had spent all day randomly making signs such as "water shoe," "water banana," "water refrigerator," and so on. In addition, the data presented are reduced so as to eliminate the repetition of signs, thus producing summary data. Repetition in signing is quite common, leading to long sequences such as "me banana you banana me give," which is a less impressive syntactic accomplishment than "you banana me give," and not at all like the early sequences produced by human children. The chimps produced many imitations of the signs that had just been produced by the humans, while truly creative signing in the absence of something to imitate is rare. Thompson and Church (1980) produced a computer program to simulate Lana's acquisition of Yerkish. They concluded that all she had done was to learn to associate objects and events with lexigrams, and to use one of a few stock sentences depending on situational cues. There was no evidence of real

understanding of word meaning or syntactic structure. (For details of these methodological problems, see Bronowski & Bellugi, 1970; Fromkin et al., 2011; Gardner, 1990; Pinker, 1994; Seidenberg & Petitto, 1979; and Thompson & Church, 1980.)

There are also a number of differences between the behavior of apes using language and of children of about the same age, or with the same vocabulary size (see Table 3.1). The utterances made by chimps are tied to the here-and-now, with those involving temporal displacement (talking about things remote in time) particularly rare. There is a lack of syntactic structure and the word order used is inconsistent, particularly with longer utterances. Fodor et al. (1974) pointed out that there appeared to be little comprehension of the syntactic relations between units, and that it was difficult to produce a syntactic analysis of their utterances. There was little evidence that "acquiring" a sentence structure as in the string of words "Insert apple dish" would help, or transfer to, producing the new sentence "Insert apple red dish." Unlike humans, these chimpanzees could not reject ill-formed sentences. They rarely asked questions—an obvious characteristic of the speech of young children. Children use language to find out more about language; chimpanzees do not. Chimps do not spontaneously use symbols referentially—that is, they need explicit training to go beyond merely associating a particular symbol or word in a particular context; young children behave quite differently. Finally, it

TABLE 3.1 Differences between apes' and children's language behavior.

Apes	Children
Utterances are mainly in the here-and-now	Utterances can involve temporal displacement
Lack of syntactic structure	Clear syntactic structure and consistency
Little comprehension of syntactic relationships between units	Ability to pick up syntactic relationships between units
Need explicit training to use symbols	Do not need explicit training to use symbols
Cannot reject ill-formed sentences	Can reject ill-formed sentences
Rarely ask questions	Frequently ask questions
No spontaneous referential use of symbols	Spontaneous referential use of symbols

is not clear that these chimps used language to help them to reason.

These criticisms have not gone unchallenged (e.g., Premack, 1976a, 1976b). Savage-Rumbaugh (1987) pointed out that it is important not to generalize from the failure of one ape to the behavior of others. Furthermore, many of these early studies were pioneering and later studies learned from their failures and difficulties. Broadly, however, much of the early work is of limited value because it is not clear that it tells us anything about the linguistic abilities of apes; if anything, it suggests that they are rather limited.

Kanzi

The major challenge to the critical point of view comes from more recent studies involving pygmy chimpanzees. Strong claims have been made about the performance of Kanzi (Greenfield & Savage-Rumbaugh, 1990; Savage-Rumbaugh & Lewin, 1994; Savage-Rumbaugh, McDonald, Sevcik, Hopkins, & Rupert, 1986). Whereas earlier studies used the common chimpanzee (*Pan troglodytes*), comparative studies of animals suggest that the bonobo or pygmy chimpanzee (*Pan paniscus*) is more intelligent, has a richer social life, and a more extensive natural communicative repertoire. Kanzi is a pygmy chimpanzee, and many believe he has made a vital step in spontaneously acquiring the understanding that symbols refer to things in the world, behaving like a child. Unlike other apes, Kanzi did not receive formal training by reinforcement with food on production of the correct symbol. He first acquired symbols by observing the training of his mother (called Matata) on the Yerkish system of lexigrams. He then interacted with people in normal daily activities, and was exposed to English. His ability to comprehend English as well as Yerkish was studied and compared with the ability of young children (Savage-Rumbaugh, Murphy, Sevcik, Brakke, Williams, & Rumbaugh, 1993). Kanzi performed as well as or better on a number of measures than a 2-year-old child. By the age of 30 months, Kanzi had learned at least seven symbols (orange, peanut, banana, apple, bedroom, chase, and

Sue Savage-Rumbaugh holds a board displaying some of the lexigrams with which she and Kanzi communicate. From Savage-Rumbaugh and Lewin (1994).

Austin); by the age of 46 months he had learned just under 50 symbols and had produced about 800 combinations of them. He was sensitive to word order, and understood verb meanings—for example, he could distinguish between "get the rock" and "take the rock," and between "put the hat on your ball" and "put the ball on your hat." Spontaneous utterances—rather than those that were prompted or imitations—formed more than 80% of his output.

Both Kanzi's semantic and syntactic abilities have been questioned. Seidenberg and Petitto (1987) argued that Kanzi understands names in a different way from humans. Take Kanzi's use of the word "strawberry." He uses "strawberry" as a name, as a request to travel to where the strawberries grow, as a request to eat strawberries, and so on. Furthermore, Kanzi's acquisition of apparent grammatical skills was much slower than that of humans, and his sentences did not approach the complexity displayed by a 3-year-old child. In reply, Savage-Rumbaugh (1987) and Nelson (1987) argued that the critics underestimated the abilities of the chimpanzees, and overestimated the appropriate linguistic abilities of very young children. Kako (1999a) argued that Kanzi shows no signs of possessing any function words. He does not appear to be able to use morphology: he does not modify his language according to number, as we do when we form plurals. And there is no clear evidence that Kanzi uses recursive grammatical structures.

Kanzi is by far the best case for language-like abilities in apes. Why is Kanzi so successful? Although bonobos might be better linguistic students, another possibility is that he was very young when first exposed to language (Deacon, 1997). Perhaps early exposure to language is as important for apes as it appears to be for humans.

Evaluation of work on teaching apes language

Most people would agree that in these studies researchers have taught some apes something, but what exactly? Clearly apes can learn to associate names with actions and objects, but there is more to language than this. In a recent analysis of a large (3,448) corpus of signs made to humans by five chimpanzees (*Pan troglodytes*) with a long history of sign use, Rivas (2005) found that the chimpanzees used mainly signs for actions and objects. Furthermore, they showed little evidence of either syntactic or semantic structure in their signing, showing instead much repetition and simple concatenation of signs, mostly with the goal of acquiring food or some other object. Rivas concluded that the signing of apes showed many differences from the early language of children.

Let us consider word meaning in more detail. How do we use names—in what way is language different from simple association? Pigeons can be taught to respond differentially to pictures of trees and water (Herrnstein, Loveland, & Cable, 1977), so it is an easy step to imagine that we could condition pigeons to respond in one way (e.g., pecking once) to one printed word, and in another way (e.g., pecking twice) to a different word, and so on. We could go so far as to suggest that these pigeons would be "naming" the words. So in what way is this "naming" behavior different from ours? One obvious difference is that we do more than name words: we also know their meaning. We know that a tree has leaves and roots, that an oak is a tree, that a tree is a plant, and that they need soil to grow in. We know that the word "leaf" goes with the word "tree" more than the word "pyramid." That is, we know how the word "tree" is conceptually related to other words (see Chapter 11 for more detail). We also know what a tree looks like. Consider what might happen if we present the printed word "tree" to a pigeon. By examining its pecking behavior, we might infer that the best a trained pigeon could manage is to indicate that the word "tree" looks more like the word "tee" than the word "horse."

Is the use of signs by chimpanzees more like that of pigeons or of humans? There are two key questions that would clearly have to be answered "yes" before most psycholinguists would agree that these primates are using words like us. First, can apes spontaneously learn that names refer to objects in a way that is constant across contexts? We know that a strawberry is a strawberry whether it's in front of us in a bowl covered in cream and sugar, or in a field attached to a strawberry plant half covered in soil. We do not need different words for each, or restrict our usage to just one context. Second, do these primates have the same understanding of word meaning as we do? Despite the promising work with

Kanzi, there are no unequivocal answers to these questions. For example, Nim could sign "apple" or "banana" correctly if these fruits were presented to him one at a time, but was unable to respond correctly if they were presented together. This suggests that he did not understand the meaning of the signs in the same way that humans do. On the other hand, Sherman and Austin could group lexigrams into the proper superordinate categories even when the objects to which they referred were absent. For example, they could group "apple," "banana," and "strawberry" together as "fruit," although this claim is controversial (Savage-Rumbaugh, 1987; Seidenberg & Petitto, 1987).

In summary, whereas chimpanzees have clearly learned associations between symbols and the world, and between symbols, it is debatable whether they have learned the meaning of the symbols in the way that we know the meanings of words. Nevertheless, they can sometimes learn very effectively, in a manner akin to children (Lyn & Savage-Rumbaugh, 2000). Kanzi and another bonobo chimpanzee (called Panbanisha), also reared in a naturalistic environment, could learn new words naming objects very quickly, with only a few exposures to novel items (at a rate similar to that of language-delayed children). In addition, the chimpanzees could sometimes learn by observation, rather than having to have the object pointed out to them each time its name was presented.

Let us now look at chimps' syntactic abilities. Has it been demonstrated that apes can combine symbols in a rule-governed way to form sentences? In as much as they might appear to do so, it has been proposed that the "sentences" are simply generated by "frames." That is, it is nothing more than a sophisticated version of conditioning, and does not show the creative use of word-ordering rules. It is as though we have now trained our pigeons to respond to whole sentences rather than just individual words. Such pigeons would not be able to recognize that the sentence "The cat chased the dog" is related in meaning to "The dog is chased by the cat," or has the same structure as "A vampire loved a ghost." We have a finite number of grammatical rules and a finite number of words, but combine them to produce an infinite number of sentences (Chomsky, 1957). We have seen that recursion—where phrases can include phrases of the same type—is an essential feature of human language. There is no evidence that apes can use recursion. More recent research reinforces this view. Monkeys can learn very simple grammars, but they cannot learn more sophisticated, human-like grammars that use hierarchical structures where there are long-distance dependencies between words (e.g., the word "if" is usually followed by "then," but any number of words can intervene; we can embed sentences within others, such as in "the cat the rat bit died"). Cotton-top tamarins perform well at a range of language-like tasks. They can, for example, like young children (see Chapter 4), learn which sequences of sounds tend to occur often together (essentially, they can discriminate words from nonwords; see Hauser, Newport, & Aslin, 2001). We can study their abilities to learn grammars by their ability to discriminate instances of strings of sounds that follow a syntactic rule from strings that violate that rule; essentially, we are asking them to make what we call grammaticality judgments. When the monkeys hear a string that violates the rules they tend to look at the loudspeaker; we could say that they "look surprised." The monkeys can be taught simple invented grammars (e.g., that produce a string of sounds corresponding to an ABABAB syllable structure), but are unable to learn more sophisticated artificial grammars that use hierarchical structure (e.g., that produce a string

The cotton-top tamarin performs well on a range of language-like tasks; for example, they can learn which sequences of sounds tend to occur often together.

of sounds corresponding to AAABBB; Fitch & Hauser, 2004). The generation of hierarchical structures such as these depends on the ability to use recursion, and only humans can use recursion.

Hauser et al. (2002) and Fitch et al. (2005) go so far as to claim that recursion is the only uniquely human component of language—yet an immensely powerful one. Pinker and Jackendoff (2005) and Jackendoff and Pinker (2005) take issue with this extreme claim, arguing that there are many more aspects of language, including properties of words and grammar, and the anatomy and control of the vocal tract, that are unique to humans. In addition, the FOXP2 gene (see Chapters 1 and 4) is unique to humans and is involved in the control of speech and language, but does not seem to involve recursion. And furthermore, the Piraha language of the Amazon does not seem to use any recursion, yet is clearly a human language (Everett, 2005).

In summary, some higher animals can learn the names of objects and simple syntactic rules. However, they do not develop sophisticated representations of meaning as do humans, and they cannot learn complex, more human-like grammars.

There is disagreement on how well apes come out of a comparison of chimps and children. One problem is that it is unclear with which age group of children the chimpanzees should be compared. When there is more work on linguistic apes bringing up their own offspring, the picture should be clearer. However, this research is difficult to carry out, expensive, and difficult to obtain funding for, so we might have to wait some time for these answers.

At present we can conclude that chimps can learn some symbols and some ways of combining them, but they cannot acquire a human-like syntax. At best, they have acquired a protolanguage.

Why is the issue so important?

As we saw earlier, there is more to the issue of a possible animal language than simple intellectual interest. First, the debate has led to a deeper insight into the nature of language and what is important about it. We can see what makes human language so very different from vervets "chattering" when they see a snake. Second, it is worth noting that although the cognitive abilities of young children and chimpanzees are not very different, their linguistic abilities are. This suggests that language processes are to some degree independent of other cognitive processes. Third, following on from this, Chomsky claimed that human language is a special faculty, which is independent of other cognitive processes, has a specific biological basis, and has evolved only in humans (e.g., Chomsky, 1968). Language arose because the brain passed a threshold in size, and only human children can learn language because only they have the special innate equipment necessary to do so. This hypothesis is summed up by the phrase "language is species-specific and has an innate basis." (Although as Kako, 1999a, observes, a better statement might be, "some components of language are species-specific.") In particular, Chomsky argued that only humans possess a language acquisition device (LAD) that enables us to acquire language; without this device we would be stuck forever at the level of a protolanguage (see Chapter 1). In particular, the ability to use recursive syntactic rules, which is what gives human language its full power, is unique to humans (Hauser et al., 2002). Even Premack (1985, 1986a, 1990) has become far less committed to the claim that apes can learn language just like human children. Indeed, he also has come to the conclusion that there is a major discontinuity between the linguistic and cognitive abilities of children and chimpanzees, with children possessing innate, "hard-wired" abilities that other animals lack. At the very least we can say that whereas children acquire language, apes have to be taught it.

THE BIOLOGICAL BASIS OF LANGUAGE

What are the biological precursors of language? How is language development related to the development of brain functions? How do biological processes interact with social factors?

Are language functions localized?

The brain is not a homogeneous mass; parts of it are specialized for specific tasks. How do we know this? In the past most of our knowledge about how brain and behavior are related came from lesion studies combined with an autopsy: neuropsychologists would discover which part of the brain had been damaged, and relate that information to behavior. Now we have brain-imaging techniques available, particularly fMRI (see Chapter 1), which can also be used with non-brain-damaged speakers. These techniques indicate which parts of the brain are active when we do tasks such as reading or speaking.

Most people know that the brain is divided into two hemispheres (see Kolb & Whishaw, 2009). The two hemispheres of the brain are partly specialized for different tasks: broadly speaking, in most right-handed people the left hemisphere is particularly concerned with analytic, time-based processing, while the right hemisphere is particularly concerned with holistic, spatially based processing. For the great majority (96%) of right-handed people, language functions are predominately localized in the left hemisphere. We say that this hemisphere is dominant. According to Rasmussen and Milner (1977), even 70% of left-handed people are left-hemisphere dominant. This localization of function is not tied to the speech modality; imaging studies show that just the same left-hemisphere brain regions are activated in people producing sign language with both hands (Corina, Jose-Robertson, Guillermin, High, & Braun, 2003).

Early work on the localization of language

How do we know which bits of the brain do what? In the 1950s, Penfield and Roberts (1959) studied the effects of electrical stimulation directly on the brains of patients undergoing surgical treatment for epilepsy. More recently, a number of techniques for brain imaging have become available, including PET and CAT scans (see Chapter 1). These techniques all show that there are specific parts of the brain responsible for specific language processes.

Most of the evidence on the localization of language functions comes from studies of the effects of brain damage. An impairment in language production or comprehension as a result of brain damage is called **aphasia**. The French neurologist Paul Broca carried out some of the earliest and most famous work on the effects of brain damage on behavior in the 1860s. Broca observed several patients where damage to the cortex of the left frontal lobes resulted in an impairment in the ability to speak, despite the vocal apparatus remaining intact and the ability to understand language apparently remaining unaffected. (We look at this again in Chapter 13.) This pattern of behavior, or **syndrome**, has become known as **Broca's aphasia**, and the part of the brain that Broca identified as responsible for speech production has become known as Broca's area (see Figure 3.6).

A few years later, in 1874, the German neurologist Carl Wernicke identified another area of the brain involved in language, this time further back in the left hemisphere, in the part of the temporal lobe known as the temporal gyrus. Damage to Wernicke's area (Figure 3.7) results in **Wernicke's aphasia**, characterized by fluent language that makes little sense, and a great impairment in the ability to comprehend language, although hearing is unaffected.

The Wernicke–Geschwind model

Wernicke also advanced one of the first models of how language is organized in the brain. He argued that the "sound images" of object names are stored in Wernicke's area of the left upper temporal cortex of the brain. When we speak, this information is sent along a pathway of fibers known as the arcuate fasciculus to Broca's

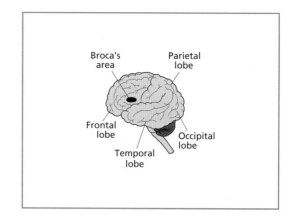

FIGURE 3.6 Location of Broca's area.

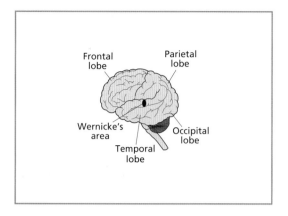

FIGURE 3.7 Location of Wernicke's area.

area, in the left lower frontal cortex, where these sound images are translated into movements for controlling speech. Although modern models are more detailed, they essentially still follow Wernicke's scheme. The Wernicke–Geschwind model (Figure 3.8; sometimes called the Wernicke–Lichtheim–Geschwind model) is an elaboration of Wernicke's scheme. Geschwind (1972) described how language generation flows from areas at the back to the front of the left hemisphere. When we hear a word, information is transmitted from the part of the cortex responsible for processing auditory information to Wernicke's area. If we then speak that word, information flows to Broca's area where articulatory information is activated, and is then passed on to the motor area responsible for speech. If the word is to be spelled out, the auditory pattern is transmitted to a structure known as the angular gyrus. If we read a word, the visual area of the cortex activates the angular gyrus and then Wernicke's area. Wernicke's area plays a central role in language comprehension. Damage to the arcuate fasciculus results in difficulties repeating language, while comprehension and production remain otherwise unimpaired. This pattern is an example of a disconnection syndrome. Disconnection occurs when the connection between two areas of the brain is damaged without damage to the areas themselves. The angular gyrus plays a central role in mediating between visual and auditory language.

This model is now known to be too simple for several reasons (Kolb & Whishaw, 2009; Poeppel & Hickok, 2004). First, although for most people language functions are predominantly localized in the left hemisphere, they are not restricted to it. Some important language functions take place in the right hemisphere. Some researchers have suggested that the right hemisphere plays an important role in an acquired disorder known as deep dyslexia (see Chapter 7), that it carries out important aspects of visual word recognition, and that it is involved with aspects of speech production, particularly prosody (regarding the loudness, rhythm, pitch, and intonation of speech); see Lindell (2006) for a review. Subcortical regions of the brain might play a role in language. For example, Ullman et al. (1997) found that although people with Parkinson's disease (which affects subcortical regions of the brain) could successfully inflect irregular verbs (presumably because these are stored as specific instances rather than generated by a rule), they had difficulty with regular verbs, suggesting that subcortical regions play some role in rule-based aspects of language. However, subcortical damage is usually also accompanied by cortical damage (e.g., see Olsen, Bruhn, & Öberg, 1986), and diseases such as Parkinson's leads to damage to the cortical regions of the brain to which these subcortical regions project, so claims that subcortical regions play a critical role in language need to be treated with some caution. The right cerebellum becomes significantly activated when we process the meaning of words (Marien, Enggelborghs, Fabbro, & De Deyn, 2001; Noppeny & Price, 2002; Paquier & Marien, 2005; Petersen, van Mier, Fiez, & Raichle, 1998). Second, even within the left cortex it is clear that brain regions outside the traditional Wernicke–Broca areas play an important role in language. In particular, the whole of the superior temporal gyrus (of which Wernicke's region is just part) is important. Third, brain damage does not have such a clear-cut effect as the model predicts. Complete destruction of areas central to the model rarely results in permanent aphasias of the expected types. Furthermore, we rarely find the expected clear-cut distinction between expressive (production) and receptive

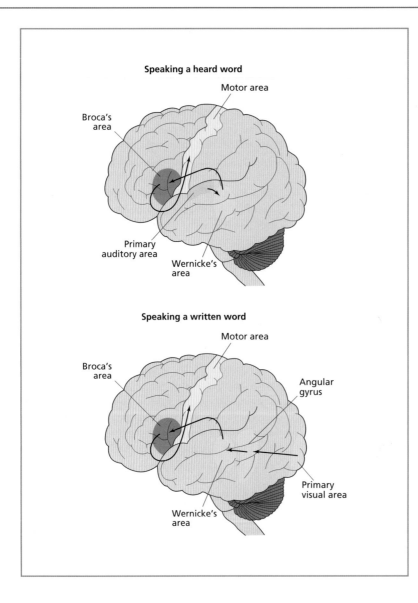

FIGURE 3.8 The top diagram shows the sequence of events when a spoken word is presented and the individual repeats the word in spoken form. The bottom diagram shows the sequence of events when a written word is presented and the individual repeats the word in spoken form.

(comprehension) disorders. For example, people with damage to Broca's region often have difficulty understanding sentences. Different types of aphasia have variable clusters of symptoms that tend to go together, and that are not as clearly related to regions such as Broca's or Wernicke's as the model predicts. Fourth, virtually all people with aphasia have some anomia (difficulty in finding the names of things) regardless of the site of damage. Finally, electrical stimulation of different regions of the brain often has the same effect, and selective stimulation of Broca's and Wernicke's areas does not produce the simple, different effects that we might expect.

More recent models of how language is related to the brain

Ullman (2004) proposed a model, called the D/P (declarative/procedural) model, of how language relates to the brain. He argued that language depends on two brain systems. The mental dictionary, or lexicon, depends on a declarative memory system based mainly in the left temporal lobe. The mental grammar, which depends primarily on procedural

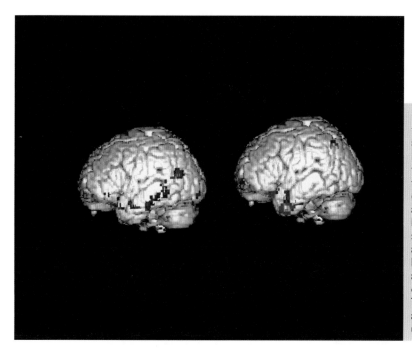

Colored PET scans of the areas of the brain active while understanding language. (The fronts of these human brains are to the left.) Active parts of the cerebral left hemispheres are red/orange. Various language areas of the extra sylvian temporal region are active in the scan on the left, which shows activity associated with working out the meaning of words. The scan on the right shows activity associated with understanding sentences.

memory, is based on a distinct neural system involving the frontal lobes, basal ganglia, cerebellum, and regions of the left parietal lobe. Essentially this distinction is one between linguistic rules, or syntax, and words. The distinction will recur throughout this book, so it is important to remember that there is some anatomical justification for this distinction. Another important idea here is that language processing makes some use of cognitive processes and brain structures that are not just dedicated to language.

Recent work has used imaging to explore the exact role of Broca's area in language, and one result is that its precise role has become much more controversial. The fact that damage to Broca's area leads to aphasia shows that it plays an important role, but is it dedicated to language specifically, or does it just involve more general processes that underpin language? Are other regions of the brain involved in processing syntax? The answer to the latter question is almost certainly yes, and to the former, maybe. Imaging suggests that Broca's area may play a role in general phonological working memory rather than syntactic manipulation as such (Rogalsky & Hickok, 2011; but see also Fedorenko & Kanwisher, 2011). There is even debate as to the exact language-related processes

that Broca's area computes, including phonological short-term memory (Rogalsky & Hickok, 2011), building a hierarchical structure (Friederici, 2002; Friederici, Bahlmann, Heim, Schubotz, & Anwander, 2006), linearizing a hierarchical structure (Bornkessel-Schlesewsky, Schlesewsky, & von Cramon, 2009), and unifying concepts into a planned sentence (Hagoort, 2008). Quite a list!

Some portions of the brain are more important for language functions than others, but it is difficult to localize specific processes in specific brain structures or areas. It is likely that multiple routes in the brain are involved in language production and comprehension. Modern brain-imaging techniques show that much larger regions of the brain may be involved in language processing than were once thought. For example, the temporal gyrus seems to play an important role in language comprehension (Dronkers, Wilkins, van Valin, Redfern, & Jaeger, 2004). A wide-ranging account of the relation between language and the brain is provided by Hickok and Poeppel (2004), who, drawing on data from brain imaging and lesion studies, focus on auditory comprehension. They argue that early stages of speech perception involve the superior temporal gyrus bilaterally (on both sides, although more on the left). The cortical processing system then diverges into dorsal (towards the back and top of the brain) and ventral (towards the front and bottom of the brain) streams (see Figure 3.9). The ventral stream is mainly concerned with turning sound into meaning. The dorsal stream is concerned with mapping sound onto a representation involving articulation, and relates speech perception to speech production. Most of what we traditionally think of as "speech perception" takes place in the ventral stream. The output of the dorsal stream is an integration of auditory and motor information, and the stream is important when we focus on the sounds of the words involved (e.g., in learning to make speech sounds, or in analyzing the sounds of words, or repeating back nonwords).

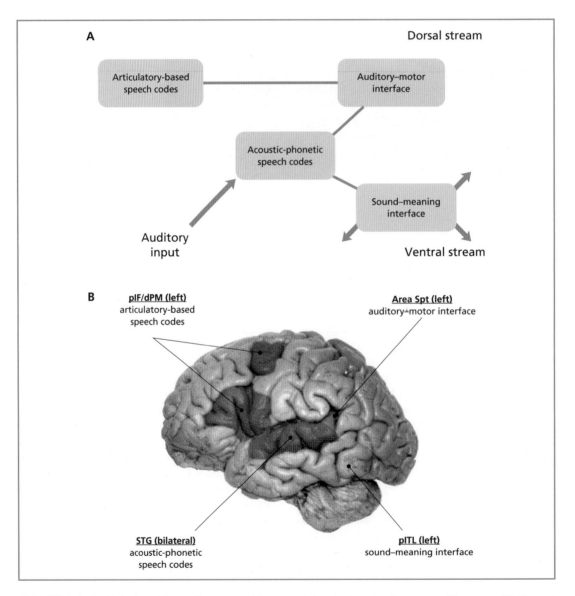

FIGURE 3.9 (A) Hickok and Poeppel's proposed framework for the functional anatomy of language. (B) General locations of the model components shown on a lateral view of the brain. From Hickok and Poeppel (2004).

In summary, although we can point to specific regions of the brain—particularly in the left frontal and temporal lobes—that play particularly important roles in language, lesion and imaging studies show that the neural systems underlying language are variable, flexible, and distributed over many brain regions (Corina et al., 2003).

In a recent synthesis, Friederici (2012) describes how the cortical regions of the brain involved in language are connected by ventral and dorsal pathways. The ventral pathway is involved in auditory-to-meaning mapping, and the dorsal pathway is involved in auditory-to-motor mapping. The dorsal pathway might also be involved in syntactic processing, particularly with syntactically complex sentences. She argues that these two functions are so dissimilar that we distinguish two dorsal streams on the basis of function and structure. The ventral pathway supports sound-to-meaning mapping and local syntactic structure building.

Sex differences and language

Girls appear to have greater verbal ability than boys, while boys appear to be better than girls at mathematical and spatial tasks (Kolb & Whishaw, 2009; Maccoby & Jacklin, 1974). It is probably too simplistic, however, to characterize this difference as simply "verbal versus visual," as this summary does not capture all the differences involved: females tend to have superior visual memory, for example. It is also difficult to establish the direction of causality for findings in this area, as some differences may be attributable to cultural rather than biological causes. Nevertheless, there is plenty of evidence that from an early age girls are superior to boys on at least some verbal tasks (Baron-Cohen, 2003). Girls start talking before boys by about an average of 1 month. They have better verbal memories, and are better readers and spellers.

Some researchers have found that males show greater lateralization than females (Baron-Cohen, 2003; Kolb & Whishaw, 2009). Males show a greater right-ear left-hemisphere advantage for perceiving speech sounds, while females suffer relatively less aphasia after damage to the left hemisphere, and they recover faster. Brain imaging has shown that Broca's area is activated differently in boys and girls when they carry out the language task of deciding whether two nonwords rhyme or not. Girls tend to show activation in both the left and right pre-frontal cortex, while with boys activation is limited to the left hemisphere (Shaywitz et al., 1995). It seems that the less lateralized brain leads to an advantage for language processing—perhaps because both hemispheres can be used.

There are also sex differences in language use in later life. Doubtless there are some cultural factors. Anderson and Leaper (1998) report a meta-analysis of gender differences in the use of interruptions. They found that men are significantly more likely to interrupt than women, and women are more likely to be interrupted than men. However, women also tend to be fluent, producing more words, longer sentences, and fewer errors in a given time, and men are much more likely to suffer from clinical disorders such as stuttering.

IS THERE A CRITICAL PERIOD FOR LANGUAGE DEVELOPMENT?

It is widely believed that the ability to acquire language declines with increasing age, with very young children particularly well-adapted for language acquisition. The *critical period* hypothesis of Lenneberg (1967) comprises two related ideas. The first idea is that certain biological events related to language development can only happen in an early critical period. In particular, hemispheric specialization takes place during the critical period, and during this time children possess a degree of flexibility that is lost when the critical period ends. The second component of the critical period hypothesis is that certain linguistic events must happen to the child during this period for development to proceed normally. Proponents of this hypothesis argue that language is acquired most efficiently during the critical period.

The idea of a critical period for the development of particular processes is not unique to humans. Songbirds display hemispheric specialization in that only one hemisphere controls singing (Demers, 1988). Many birds such as the chaffinch

Many songbirds, such as the chaffinch, are born with the rudiments of a song, but must be exposed to the male song of their species between the ages of 10 and 15 days in order to acquire it normally.

are born with the rudiments of a song, but must be exposed to the male song of their species between the ages of 10 and 15 days in order to acquire it normally. Evidence for a critical period for human linguistic development comes from many sources.

Evidence from the development of lateralization

The structure of the brain is not completely fixed at birth. A considerable amount of development continues after birth and throughout childhood (and indeed perhaps in adolescence); this process of development is called **maturation**. Furthermore, the brain (primarily the cortex) shows some degree of plasticity, in the sense that after damage it can to some extent recover and reorganize, or can adapt in response to pronounced changes in input, even in adulthood. It is now known that the brain is much more flexible even in adulthood than was once thought (Begley, 2007).

We are not born with our two hemispheres completely lateralized in function; instead, lateralization emerges throughout childhood. The most striking evidence for this claim is that damage to the left hemisphere in childhood does not always lead to the permanent disruption of language abilities.

There are three accounts of how lateralization takes place (Bates & Roe, 2001; Thomas, 2003). The *equipotentiality* hypothesis states that the two hemispheres are similar at birth with respect to language capability, each able in principle to acquire the processes responsible for language, with the left hemisphere maturing to become specialized for language functions. The irreversible determinism (or *invariance*) hypothesis states that the left hemisphere is specialized for language at birth and the right hemisphere only takes over language functions if the left is damaged over a wide area, involving both the anterior and posterior regions (Rasmussen & Milner, 1975; Woods & Carey, 1979). Irreversible determinism says that language has an affinity for the left hemisphere because of innate anatomical organization, and will not abandon it unless an entire center is destroyed. The critical difference between the equipotentiality and irreversible determinism hypotheses is that in the former either hemisphere can become specialized for language, but in the latter the left hemisphere becomes specialized for language unless there is a very good reason otherwise. The *emergentist* account brings together these two extremes, saying that the two hemispheres of the brain are characterized at birth by innate biases in types of information processing that are not specific to language processing (e.g., the left hemisphere is better at processing complex sequences), such that the left hemisphere is better suited to being dominant, although both hemispheres play a role in acquiring language (Lidzha & Krageloh-Mann, 2005).

The critical period hypothesis is the best known version of the equipotentiality hypothesis. Lenneberg (1967) argued that at birth the left and right hemispheres of the brain are equipotential. There is no cerebral asymmetry at birth; instead lateralization occurs as a result of maturation. The process of lateralization develops rapidly between the ages of 2 and 5 years, then slows down, being complete by puberty. Lenneberg argued that the brain possesses a degree of flexibility early on, in that, if necessary, brain functions can develop in alternative locations.

Lenneberg examined how a child's age affected recovery after brain damage. Damage to the left hemisphere of the adult brain leads to significant and usually permanent language impairment. Lenneberg's key finding was that the linguistic abilities of young children recover much better after brain damage than those of adults after brain damage, and the younger the child, the better the chances of a complete recovery. Indeed, the entire function of the left hemisphere can be taken over by the right if the child is young enough. There are a number of cases of complete **hemidecortication**, where an entire hemisphere is removed as a drastic treatment for exceptionally severe epilepsy. Such an operation on an adult would almost totally destroy language abilities. If performed on children who are young enough—that is, during their critical periods—they seem able to recover almost completely. Another piece of evidence supporting the critical period hypothesis is that crossed aphasia, where damage to the right hemisphere leads to a language deficit, appears to be more common in children (Woods & Teuber, 1973). These findings suggest that the brain is not lateralized at birth, but that lateralization emerges gradually throughout childhood as a consequence of maturation. This period of maturation is the critical period.

On the other hand, Dennis and Whitaker (1976, 1977) found that children who had had the whole left cortex removed subsequently had particular difficulties in understanding complex syntax, compared with children who had had the whole right cortex removed. One explanation of this finding is that the right hemisphere cannot completely accommodate all the language functions of the left hemisphere, although Bishop (1983) in turn presented methodological criticisms of this work. She observed that the number of participants was very small, and that it is important to match for IQ to ensure that any observed differences are truly attributable to the effects of hemidecortication. When IQ is controlled for, there is a large overlap with normal performance. It is not clear that non-decorticated individuals of the same age would have performed any better.

Evidence from studies of lateralization in very young children

Contrary to the critical period hypothesis, there is evidence that some lateralization is present at a very early age, if not from birth. Entus (1977) studied 3-week-old infants using a **sucking**

habituation paradigm. Exploring the cognitive and perceptual abilities of very young infants is obviously difficult, so we need to use clever experimental paradigms. In this task, the experimenter monitors changes in the infant's sucking rate as stimuli are presented. Rapid sucking is an innate response to stimulation; when the infant gets bored, or habituated, to the stimulus, the sucking rate drops. If a new stimulus is presented, and if the infant can detect the change, the sucking rate increases again. Hence monitoring sucking rate is a very useful way of being able to tell if an infant can detect change. Entus found a more marked change in the sucking rate when speech stimuli were presented to the right ear (and therefore a left-hemisphere advantage, as the right ear projects on to the left hemisphere), and an advantage for non-speech stimuli when presented to the left ear (indicating a right-hemisphere advantage). Molfese (1977) measured evoked potentials (a measure of the brain's electrical activity) and found hemispheric differences to speech and non-speech in infants as young as 1 week, with a left-hemisphere preference for speech. Very young children also show a sensitive period for phonetic perception that is more or less over by 10–12 months (B. Harley & Wang, 1997; Werker & Tees, 1983).

Mills, Coffrey-Corina, and Neville (1993, 1997) examined changes in patterns of ERPs (event-related potentials) in the electrical activity of the brain in infants aged between 13 and 20 months. They compared the ERPs as children listened to words whose meanings they knew with ERPs for words whose meanings they did not know. These two types of word elicited different patterns of ERP, but whereas at 13–17 months the differences were spread all over the brain, by 20 months the differences were restricted to the more central regions of the left hemisphere. Clearly some specialization is occurring here—but still considerably before the window of the critical period originally hypothesized by Lenneberg. These data also suggest that the right hemisphere plays an important role in early language acquisition. In particular, unknown words elicit electrical activity across the right hemisphere, perhaps reflecting the processing of novel but meaningful stimuli. The same idea could explain the observation that focal brain injury to the right hemisphere of very young children (10–17 months) is more likely to result in a delay in the development of word comprehension skills than damage to the left hemisphere (Goldberg & Costa, 1981; Thal et al., 1991).

Differences in early asymmetry may be linked with later language abilities. Infants who show early left-hemisphere processing of phonological stimuli show better language abilities several years later (Mills et al., 1997; Molfese & Molfese, 1994).

Hence there does seem to be a critical period in which lateralization occurs, but the period starts earlier than Lenneberg envisaged. As there is considerable evidence for some lateralization from birth, the data also support the idea that the left hemisphere has a special affinity for language, rather than the view that the two hemispheres are truly equipotential.

Evidence from second language acquisition

The critical period hypothesis has traditionally been used to explain why second language acquisition is difficult for older children and adults. Johnson and Newport (1989) examined the way in which the critical period hypothesis might account for second language acquisition. They distinguished two hypotheses, both of which assume that humans have a superior capacity for learning language early in life. According to the maturational state hypothesis, this capacity disappears or declines as maturation progresses, regardless of other factors. The exercise hypothesis further states that unless this capacity is exercised early, it is lost. Both hypotheses predict that children will be better than adults in acquiring the first language. The exercise hypothesis predicts that as long as a child has acquired a first language during childhood, the ability to acquire other languages will remain intact and can be used at any age. The maturational hypothesis predicts that children will be superior at second language learning, because the capacity to acquire language diminishes with age. However, it is possible under the exercise hypothesis that, all other things

being equal, adults might be better than children because of their better learning skills. Research has addressed the issue of whether there is an age-related block on second language learning.

Are children in fact better than adults at learning language? The evidence is not as clear-cut as is usually thought. Snow (1983) concluded that, contrary to popular opinion, adults are in fact no worse than young children at learning a second language, and indeed might even be better. We often think children are better at learning the first and second languages, but they spend much more time being exposed to and learning language than adults, which makes a comparison very difficult. Snow and Hoefnagel-Hohle (1978) compared English children with English adults in their first year of living in the Netherlands learning to speak Dutch. The young children (3–4 years old) performed worst of all. In addition, a great deal of the advantage for young children usually attributed to the critical period may be explicable in terms of differences in the type and amount of information available to learners (Bialystock & Hakuta, 1994). There is also a great deal of variation: Some adults are capable of near-native performance on a second language, whereas some children are less successful (B. Harley & Wang, 1997). Although ability in conversational syntax correlates with duration of exposure to the second language, this just suggests that total time spent learning the second language is important—and the younger you start the more time you tend to have (Cummins, 1991). The conclusion is that there is little evidence for a dramatic cut-off in language-learning abilities at the end of puberty.

Adults learning a language have a persistent foreign accent, and hence phonological (sound) development might be one area for which there is a critical period (Flege & Hillenbrand, 1984). And, although adults seem to have an initial advantage in learning a second language, the eventual attainment level of children appears to be better (see Krashen, Long, & Scarcella, 1982, for a review).

Johnson and Newport (1989) carried out one of the most detailed studies of the possible effects of a critical period on syntactic development. They found some evidence for a critical period for the acquisition of the syntax of a second language. They examined native Korean and Chinese immigrants to the USA, and found a large advantage in making judgments about whether a sentence was grammatically correct for immigrants who arrived at a younger age. In adults who had arrived in the USA when they were aged between 0 and 16 years of age, there was a large negative linear correlation between age of arrival and language ability (on this measure). Adults who arrived between the ages of 16 and 40 showed no significant relation between age of arrival and ability, although later arrivers generally performed slightly less well than early arrivers. The variance in the language ability of the later arrivers was very high. Johnson and Newport concluded that different factors operate on language acquisition before and after 16 years of age. They proposed that there is a change in maturational state, from plasticity to a steady state, at about age 16. Other researchers place the age of discontinuity much earlier, at around 5 (see Birdsong & Molis, 2001).

There is some controversy about whether Johnson and Newport's data really represent a change at 16 from plastic to fixed state. Is there a real discontinuity? Elman et al. (1996) showed that the distribution of performance scores can also be fitted by a curvilinear function nearly as well as two linear ones, suggesting that there is a gradual decline in performance rather than a strong discontinuity. Nevertheless, the younger a person is, the better they seem to acquire a second language. Furthermore, Birdsong and Molis (2001) replicated the original Johnson and Newport (1989) study, using Spanish speakers learning English. Contrary to the original findings, and contrary to the critical period hypothesis, Birdsong and Molis found no learning discontinuity around 16. Furthermore, some late learners (starting to learn the second language after the presumed end of the critical period) achieved near-native performance on it—something that should not be possible if the critical period hypothesis is correct.

In summary, there is evidence for a critical period for some aspects of syntactic development and, even more strongly, for phonological development. However, rather than any dramatic discontinuity, decline seems to be gradual. Second language acquisition is not a perfect test of the hypothesis, however, because the speakers have usually acquired at least some of a first language.

What happens if we cannot acquire a first language during the critical period?

Evidence from hearing children of hearing-impaired parents

In principle, the language of hearing children of deaf parents should provide a test of the critical period hypothesis. However, linguistic deprivation is never total. Sachs, Bard, and Johnson (1981) described the case of "Jim," a hearing child of deaf parents whose only exposure to spoken language until he entered nursery at the age of 3 was the television. Although his parents signed to each other, they did not sign towards him. They believed that as he had normal hearing it would be inappropriate for him to learn signing. Jim's intonation was abnormally flat, his articulation very poor, with some utterances being unintelligible, and his grammar very idiosyncratic. For example, Jim produced utterances such as "House. Two house. Not one house. That two house." This example shows that Jim acquired the concept of plurality but not that it is usually marked by an "-s" inflection, although normally this is one of the earliest grammatical morphemes a child learns. Utterances such as "Going house a fire truck" suggest that Jim constructed his own syntactic rules based on stating a phrase followed by specifying the topic of that phrase—the opposite of the usual word order in English. Although this is an incorrect rule, it does emphasize the drive to create syntactic rules (see Chapter 4). Jim's comprehension of language was also very poor. After intervention, within a few months Jim's language use was almost normal. Jim's case suggests that exposure to language alone is not sufficient to acquire language normally: it must be in an appropriate social, interactional context. It also emphasizes humans' powerful urge to use language.

People exposed to sign language (e.g., ASL) early achieve a better level of ultimate competence (Newport, 1990). In particular, late learners have particular difficulty using signs to represent complex verbs. These observations also support the critical period hypothesis.

What happens if children are deprived of linguistic input during the critical period?

In a very early psycholinguistic experiment, King James IV of Scotland reputedly abandoned two children in the wild (around the year 1500). Later he claimed that they grew up spontaneously learning to speak "very good Hebrew." What really happens to children who grow up in the absence of linguistic stimulation?

The other important idea of the critical period hypothesis is that unless children receive linguistic input during the critical period, they will be unable to acquire language normally. The strongest version of the hypothesis is of course that without input during this period children cannot acquire language at all. Supporting evidence comes from reports of wild or feral children who have been abandoned at birth and deprived of language in childhood. Feral children often have no language at all when found, but more surprisingly, appear to find language difficult to acquire despite intensive training. "Wolf children" receive their name from when children are reputedly cross-fostered by wolves as wolf cubs (such as the Romulus and Remus of Roman legend). One of the most famous of these cases was the "Wild Boy of Aveyron," a child found in isolated woods in the south of France in 1800. Despite attempts by an educationalist named Dr. Itard to socialize the boy, given the name Victor, and to teach him language, he never learned more than two words. (This story was subsequently turned into a film by François Truffaut, called *L'enfant sauvage*, and is described by Shattuck, 1980.) More recent reports of feral children involving apparent cross-fostering include the wolf children of India (Singh & Zingg, 1942) and the monkey boy of Burundi (Lane & Pillard, 1978). In each case, attempts to teach the children language and social skills were almost complete failures. These cases describe events that happened some time ago, and what actually happened is usually unclear. Furthermore, we do not know why these children were originally abandoned. It is certainly conceivable that they were developmentally delayed before

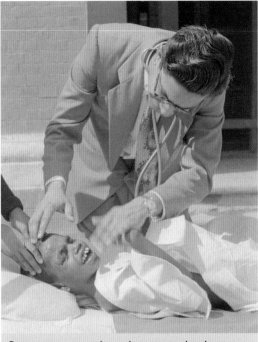

Ramu was a young boy who appeared to have been reared by wolves. He was discovered in India in 1960. At the time of his death, aged about 10, he had still not learned to speak. The above picture shows Ramu being examined by a doctor.

abandonment, and therefore might have been language-impaired, whatever the circumstances.

It is less easy to apply this argument to the unfortunate child known as "Genie" (Curtiss, 1977; Fromkin, Krashen, Curtiss, Rigler, & Rigler, 1974). Genie was a child who was apparently normal at birth, but suffered severe linguistic deprivation. From the age of 20 months, until she was taken into protective custody by the Los Angeles police when she was 13 years 9 months, she had been isolated in a small room, most of the time strapped into a potty chair. Her father was extraordinarily intolerant of noise, so there was virtually no speech in the house—not even overheard from a radio or television. Genie was punished if she made any sounds. The only contact she had with other people was a few minutes each day when her mother fed her baby food, and occasionally when her father and older brother barked at her like dogs—clearly this is extreme social, physical, nutritional, and linguistic deprivation. Not surprisingly, Genie's linguistic abilities were virtually non-existent. At the age of nearly 14 the critical period should be finished or almost finished, so could Genie learn language? With training, Genie learned some language skills. However, her syntactic development was always impaired relative to her vocabulary. She used few question words, far fewer grammatical words, and tended to form negatives only by adding negatives to the start of sentences. She failed to acquire the use of inflectional morphology (the ability to use word endings to modify the number of nouns and the tense of verbs), the ability to transform active syntactic constructions into passive ones (e.g., turning "the vampire chased the ghost" into "the ghost was chased by the vampire"), and the use of auxiliary verbs (e.g., "be"). Furthermore, unlike most right-handed children, she showed a left-ear, right-hemisphere advantage for speech sounds. There could be a number of reasons for this, such as left-hemisphere degeneration, the inhibition of the left hemisphere by the right, or the left hemisphere taking over some other function.

Because of financial and legal difficulties, research on Genie did not continue for as long as might have been hoped, and hence many questions remain unanswered. (Genie is now in an adult foster home.) In summary, Genie's case shows that it is possible to learn some language outside the critical period, but also that syntax appears to have some privileged role. The amount of language that can be learned after the critical period seems very limited.

Of course, the other types of deprivation (such as malnutrition and social deprivation) to which Genie was subjected might have played a part in her later linguistic difficulties. Indeed, Lenneberg discounted the case because of the extreme emotional trauma Genie had suffered. Furthermore, there has been no agreement over whether Genie was developmentally delayed before her period of confinement. Indeed, her father locked her away precisely because he considered her to be severely developmentally delayed, in the belief that he was protecting her. Contrary to this, there is some evidence that aspects of Genie's non-linguistic development proceeded normally following her rescue (Rymer, 1993).

Some children might be able to recover completely from early linguistic deprivation as long as they are given exposure to language and training at an early enough age. "Isabelle" was kept from infancy, with minimum attention, in seclusion with her deaf-mute mother until the age of 6½ (Davis, 1947; Mason, 1942). Her measured intelligence was about that of a 2-year-old and she possessed no spoken language. But with exposure to spoken language she passed through the normal phases of language development at a greatly accelerated rate, and after 18 months her intelligence was in the normal range and she was highly linguistically competent.

In summary, the evidence from linguistic deprivation is not as clear-cut as we might expect. Children appear able to recover from it as long as they receive input early enough. If deprivation continues, language development, particularly syntactic development, is impaired. A major problem is that linguistic deprivation is invariably accompanied by other sorts of deprivation, and it is difficult to disentangle the effects of these.

Evaluation of the critical period hypothesis

There are two reasons for rejecting a strong version of the critical period hypothesis. Children can acquire some language outside of it, and lateralization does not occur wholly within it. In particular, some lateralization is present from birth or before. Nevertheless, it is possible to defend a weakened version of the hypothesis. A critical period appears to be involved in early phonological development and the development of syntax. The weakened version is often called a sensitive period hypothesis. The evidence supports the weaker version. There is a sensitive period for language acquisition, but it seems confined to complex aspects of syntactic processing (Bialystok & Hakuta, 1994).

The critical period does not apply only to spoken language. Newport (1990) found evidence of a critical period for congenitally deaf people learning ASL, particularly concerning the use of morphologically inflected signs. She also found a continuous linear decline in learning ability rather than a sudden drop-off at puberty. Of course adults can learn sign language, but it is argued they learn it less efficiently.

Why should there be a critical period for language? There are three types of explanation. The **nativist** explanation is that there is a critical period because the brain is pre-programmed to acquire language early in development. Bever (1981) argued that it is a normal property of growth, arising from a loss of plasticity as brain cells and processes become more specialized and more independent. Along similar lines, Locke (1997) argues that a sensitive period arises because of the interplay of developing specialized neural systems, early perceptual experience, and discontinuities in linguistic development. Lack of appropriate activation during development acts like physical damage to some areas of the brain.

The maturational explanation is that certain advantages are lost as the child's cognitive and neurological system matures. In particular, what might first appear to be a limitation of the immature cognitive system might turn out to be an advantage for the child learning language. For example, it might be advantageous to be able to hold only a limited number of items in short-term memory, to be unable to remember many specific word associations, and to remember only the most global correspondences. That is, there might be an advantage to "starting small," because it enables the children to see the wood for the trees (Deacon, 1997; Elman, 1993; Kersten & Earles, 2001; Newport, 1990). It is possible that the limited cognitive resources of the child are actually advantageous to children (an idea called "less is more"), as it means they can only process limited amounts of language at any one time. They can then get the small segments right before they start on the larger and more complex units, without being overwhelmed from the beginning. A related variant of the maturational answer is that, as the brain develops, it uses up its learning capacity by dedicating specialist circuits to particular tasks. Connectionist modeling of the acquisition of the past tense of verbs suggests that networks do indeed become less plastic the more they learn (Marchman, 1993).

The main differences between these answers are the extent to which the constraints underlying the critical period are linguistic or more general, and the extent to which the timing of the acquisition process is genetically controlled (Elman et al., 1996). With insights from connectionist modeling, the maturational answer has recently received the most attention. However, perhaps the two approaches are not really contradictory. A system that matures and is more efficient for learning language will have an evolutionary advantage.

THE COGNITIVE BASIS OF LANGUAGE

Jean Piaget is one of the most influential figures in developmental psychology. According to Piaget, development takes place in a sequence of well-defined stages. In order to reach a certain stage of development, the child must have gone through all the preceding stages. Piaget identified four principal stages of cognitive development (see Figure 3.10). At birth, he argued that the child possesses only innate reflexes. In the first stage of development, which Piaget called the sensorimotor period, behavior is organized around sensory and motor processes. This stage lasts through infancy until the child is about 2 years old. A primary development in this period is the attainment of the concept of object permanence—that is, realizing that objects have continual existence and do not disappear as soon as they go out of view. Indeed, Piaget divided the sensorimotor period into six sub-stages depending on the progress made towards object permanence. Next comes the pre-operational stage, which lasts until the age of about 6 or 7. This stage is characterized by egocentric thought, which means that these children are unable to adopt alternative viewpoints to their own and are unable to change their point of view. The concrete operations stage lasts until the age of about 12. The child is now able to adopt alternative viewpoints, as shown by the conservation task. In this task water is poured from a short wide glass to a tall thin glass, and the child is asked if the amounts of water are the same. A pre-operational child will reply that the tall glass has more water in it; a concrete operational child will correctly say that they both contain the same amount. Nevertheless the child is still limited to reasoning about concrete objects. In the formal operations stage, the adolescent is not limited to concrete thinking, and is able to reason abstractly and logically. Piaget proposed that the main mechanisms of cognitive development are assimilation and accommodation. Assimilation is the way in which information is abstracted from the world to fit existing cognitive structures; accommodation is the way in which cognitive structures are adjusted in order to accommodate otherwise incompatible information.

According to Piaget, there is nothing special about language. Unlike Chomsky, he did not see it as a special faculty, but as a social and cognitive process just like any other. It therefore clearly has cognitive prerequisites; it is dependent on other cognitive, motor, and perceptual processes, and its development clearly follows the cognitive stages of development. Adult speech is socialized and has communicative intent, whereas early language is egocentric. Piaget (1923/1955) went on to distinguish three different types of early egocentric speech: repetition or echolalia (where children simply repeat their own or others' utterances); monologues (when children talk to themselves, apparently just speaking their thoughts out loud); and group or collective monologues (where two or more children appear to be taking appropriate turns in a conversation but actually just produce monologues). For Piaget, cognitive and social egocentrism were related.

The cognition hypothesis is a statement of Piaget's ideas about language, and says that language needs certain cognitive precursors in order to develop

(Sinclair-de-Zwart, 1973). For example, the child has to attain the stage of object permanence in order to be able to acquire concepts of objects and names. Hence an observed explosion in vocabulary size at around 18 months is related to the attainment of object permanence. However, Corrigan (1978) showed that there was no correlation between the development of object permanence and linguistic development once the child's age was taken into account. Furthermore, infants comprehend names as much as 6 months before the stage of object permanence is complete. Indeed, having unique names available for objects may help children acquire object permanence. Xu (2002) found that having two distinct labels available for two distinct objects (e.g., a toy duck and a ball) facilitated the discrimination abilities of 9-month-old children, but having one label, or two distinct tones, or two facial expressions, did not.

There is some evidence that language acquisition is related to the development of object permanence in a more complex way. An important, though at first small, class of early words are relational words (e.g., "no," "up," "more," "gone"). The first relational words should depend on the emergence of knowledge about how objects can be transformed from one state to another, at the end of the

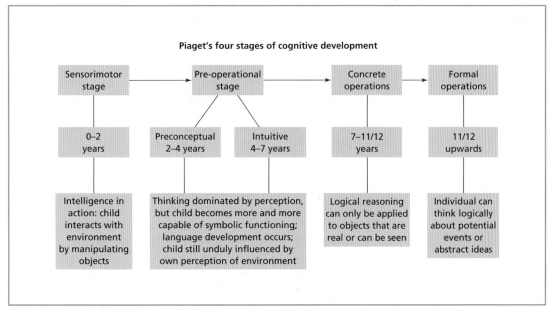

FIGURE 3.10

sensorimotor period. These words do indeed tend to enter as a group near the end of the sensorimotor period (McCune-Nicolich, 1981). Words that relate to changes in the state of objects still present in the visual field (e.g., "up," "move") emerge before those (e.g., "all gone") that relate to absent objects (Tomasello & Farrar, 1984, 1986).

Language development in children with learning difficulties

An obvious test of the cognition hypothesis is to examine the linguistic abilities of children with learning difficulties. If cognitive development drives linguistic development, then impaired cognitive development should be reflected in slow linguistic development. The evidence is mixed but suggests that language and cognition are to some extent decoupled.

Although some children with Down's syndrome become fully competent in their language, most do not (Fowler, Gelman, & Gleitman, 1994). At first, these children's language development is simply delayed. Up to the age of 4, their language age is consistent with their mental age (although it is obviously behind their chronological age). After this, language age starts to lag behind mental age. Lexical development is slow, and grammatical development is especially slow (Hoff-Ginsberg, 1997). Most people with Down's syndrome never become fully competent with complex syntax and morphology.

On the other hand, there are several types of impaired cognitive development that do not lead to such clear-cut linguistic impairments. Laura was a girl who showed severe and widespread cognitive impairments (her IQ was estimated at 41), yet appeared unimpaired at complex syntactic constructions (Yamada, 1990). Furthermore, factors that caused problems for Laura in cognitive tasks did not do so in linguistic tasks; for example, while non-linguistic tasks involving reasoning about hierarchies were very difficult for Laura, her ability to produce sentences with grammatical hierarchies was intact. Although her short-term memory was very poor, she could still produce complex syntactic constructions. Yamada concluded that cognitive

Some people with Down's syndrome may have impaired linguistic abilities, whereas others become fully competent. It seems that cognitive and linguistic abilities are distinct, and a person with Down's syndrome may show greater abilities in their cognition than in linguistic ability, or vice versa.

and linguistic processes are distinct, and that as normal language could develop when there is severe general cognitive impairment, cognitive precursors are not essential for linguistic development. The situation is not straightforward, however, as not all Laura's linguistic abilities were spared. For example, she had difficulty with complex morphological forms. In another case study, Smith and Tsimpli (1995) described a man who had a non-verbal IQ beneath 70, and was unable to live independently, yet who had a normal verbal IQ and could speak several foreign languages.

Williams syndrome is a rare genetic disorder that leads to physical abnormalities (affected children have an "elfin-faced" appearance) and a very low IQ, typically around 50. However, the speech of such people is very fluent and grammatically correct (Bellugi, Bihrle, Jernigan, Trauner, & Doherty, 1991). Indeed, they are particularly fond of unusual words. Their ability to acquire new words and to repeat nonwords is also good (Barisnikov, van der Linden, & Poncelet, 1996). This dissociation between severe cognitive impairment and normal (in some respects, better than normal) language skills makes Williams syndrome particularly interesting and important for thinking about how language and cognition are related.

Finally, children with autism find social communication difficult, and their language use is often idiosyncratic. The things they talk about are different, for example, and they use some words in unusual ways (Tager-Flusberg, 1999). Their peculiarities of language use probably arise from their lack of a "theory of mind" about how other people think and feel, and is unlikely to be attributable to straightforward deficits in linguistic processing (Bishop, 1997). Their grammatical skills are relatively unimpaired.

Cases such as these pose difficulty for any position that argues either for interaction between cognitive and linguistic development, or for the primacy of cognitive factors. The evidence favors a partial, but not complete, separation of language skills and general cognitive abilities such as reasoning and judgment.

Evaluation of the cognition hypothesis

The cognition hypothesis says that cognitive development drives linguistic development. However, there is no clear evidence for a strong version of the cognition hypothesis. Children acquire some language abilities before they obtain object permanence. Indeed, Bruner (1964) argued that aspects of cognitive performance are facilitated by language. The possibility that linguistic training would improve performance of the conservation task was tested by Sinclair-de-Zwart (1969), who found that language training only had a small effect. Linguistic training does not affect basic cognitive processes, but helps in description and in focusing on the relevant aspects of the task.

Cognitive processes obviously continue to develop beyond infancy. For example, working memory capacity increases through childhood from about 2 items at age 2–3, to the adult span of 7 plus or minus 2 in late childhood, and there might also be changes in the structure of memory (McShane,

1991). Young children also rehearse less than older children do. It is possible that changes in working memory might have consequences for some linguistic processes, particularly comprehension and learning vocabulary (see Chapter 15).

There is currently little active research on the Piagetian approach to language. The emphasis has instead shifted to the communicative precursors of language and the social interactionist account (see below). However, to be effective communicators children need to develop the ability to adopt others' point of view. An essential component of this development is the acquisition of a "theory of mind." Although this might be driven by cognitive development, it might also be driven linguistically. The acquisition of verbs such as "know," "believe," "think," and "want," and the development of linguistic structures that enable us to express complex statements about beliefs, truth, and falsehood in a relatively simple way, are almost certainly driving forces as well (de Villiers & de Villiers, 2000; Shatz, Diesendruck, Martinez-Beck, & Akar, 2003).

THE SOCIAL BASIS OF LANGUAGE

We noted earlier that it is difficult to disentangle the specific effects of linguistic deprivation in feral children from the effects of social deprivation. Cases such as that of Jim, the hearing child of deaf parents, suggest that children need to be exposed to language in a socially meaningful situation (Sachs et al., 1981). It is clearly not enough to be exposed to language; something more is necessary. Adults tend to talk to children about objects that are in view and about events that have just happened: the "here-and-now." The usefulness of this is obvious (for example, in associating names with objects), and it is clear that learning language just by watching television is going to be very limited in this respect. Furthermore, such situations involve the child having to both comprehend and produce language. To be effective, early language learning must involve interaction; it must take place in a social setting. Social interactionists emphasize the importance of the development of language through interaction with other people (Bruner, 1983; Durkin, 1987; Farrar, 1990; Gleason,

Hay, & Crain, 1989). According to social interactionists, although biological and cognitive processes may be necessary for language development, they are not sufficient. Language development must occur in the context of meaningful social interaction.

Bruner (1975, 1983) emphasized the importance of the social setting in acquiring language. In many respects his views are similar to those of Piaget, but Bruner placed more emphasis on social development than on cognitive development. Bruner stressed the importance of the social setting of the mother–child dyad in helping children to work out the meaning of utterances to which they are exposed. Although child-directed speech is an important mechanism, the social dyad achieves much more than a particular way of talking. For example, the important distinction between agents (who are performing actions) and objects (who are having actions carried out on them) is first made clear in turn-taking (and games based on turn-taking) with the mother. As its name implies, turn-taking is rather like a conversation; participants appear to take it in turns to do things, although obviously the conscious intent on the part of the infant in this may be limited. Processes such as mutual gaze, when the adult and child look at the same thing, and joint attention to objects and actions, are important in enabling the child to discover the referents of words. Bruner suggested that some of these social skills, or the way in which they are used in learning language, may be innate. Bruner described language development as taking place within the context of a LASS (language acquisition socialization system).

Other aspects of the social setting are important for linguistic development. Feedback from adults about children's communicative efficiency plays a vital role in development. For example, the social-communicative setting can be central to acquiring word meanings by restricting the domain of discourse of what is being talked about (Tomasello, 1992b). Along the same lines, the social-communicative setting may also facilitate the task of learning the grammar of the language. There has been a great deal of debate about the role of negative evidence—for example, whether children have to be told that certain strings of words are ungrammatical—in language acquisition, and its limitations have been used to justify the existence of innate principles. Although parents might

Bruner emphasized the importance of the mother–child dyad in acquiring language. For example, processes such as mutual gaze and joint attention to objects are important in enabling the child to discover the referents of words.

not provide explicit negative evidence (in the form of explicit correction), they do provide implicit negative evidence (Sokolov & Snow, 1994). For example, parents tend to repeat more ill-formed utterances than well-formed ones, and tend to follow ill-formed utterances with a question rather than a continuation of the topic. There are also regional and class differences: rural southern working-class mothers in the USA provide more explicit corrections than do middle-class mothers (Sokolov & Snow, 1994). Clearly the development of communicative competence is an essential prerequisite of language acquisition.

Turn-taking in early conversation

There is more to learning to use language than just learning the meanings of words and a grammar: we also have to learn how to use language. Conversations have a structure (see Chapter 14). Clearly we do not always talk all at once; we appear to take turns in conversations. At the very least children have to learn to listen and to pay some attention when they are spoken to. How does this ability to interact in conversational settings develop? There is some evidence that it appears at a very early age. Schaeffer (1975) proposed that the origins of turn-taking lie in feeding. In feeding, sucking occurs in bursts interspersed with pauses that appear to act as a signal to mothers to play with the baby, to cuddle it, or to talk to it. He also noted that mothers and babies rarely vocalize simultaneously. Snow (1977) observed that mothers respond to their babies' vocalizations as if their yawns and burps were utterances. Hence the precursors of conversation are present at an early age and might emerge from other activities. The gaze of mother and child also seems to be correlated; in particular, the mother quickly turns her gaze to whatever the baby is looking at. Hence again cooperation emerges at an early age. Although in these cases it is the mother who is apparently sensitive to the pauses of the child, there is further evidence that babies of just a few weeks old are differentially sensitive to features of their environment. Trevarthen (1975) found that babies visually track and try to grab inanimate objects, but they make other responses to people, including waving and what he called pre-speech— small movements of the mouth, rather like a precursor of talking. The exact role of this pre-speech is unclear, but certainly by the end of the first 6 months the precursors of social and conversational skills are apparent, and infants have developed the ability to elicit communicative responses.

Evaluation of social interactionist accounts

Few would argue with the central theme of the social interactionist approach: To be effective, language acquisition must take place in a meaningful social setting. But can this approach by itself account for all features of language acquisition? We will see in Chapter 4 that there is considerable evidence that language development relies on some innate knowledge. One particular disadvantage of the social interactionist approach is that until recently these accounts were often vague

about the details of how social interactions influence development. Cognitive processes mediate social interactions, and the key to a sophisticated theory is in detailing this relation.

Disorders of the social use of language

There are several developmental disorders of using language in a social context. Bishop (1997) describes semantic-pragmatic disorder, which is a language impairment that looks like a very mild version of autism. Children with semantic-pragmatic disorder often have difficulty in conversations where they have to draw inferences. They give very literal answers to questions, failing to take the preceding conversational and social context into account, as in the following (from Bishop, 1997, p. 221):

Adult: Can you tell me about your party?
Child: Yes.

Although semantic-pragmatic disorder is poorly understood, it is clear that its origins are complex. Whereas related disorders might be explicable in terms of memory limitations or social neglect, semantic-pragmatic disorder is probably best explained in terms of these children having difficulty in representing other people's mental states. This in turn is probably the result of an innate or developmental brain abnormality. This deficit illustrates how difficult it can be to disentangle biological, cognitive, and social factors from each other.

THE LANGUAGE DEVELOPMENT OF VISUALLY AND HEARING-IMPAIRED CHILDREN

One way of attempting to disentangle the development of language and cognition is to examine language development in special circumstances. If cognition drives language development, then visually impaired children, who are likely to show some differences in cognitive development compared with sighted children, should also show differences in linguistic development. If language drives cognitive development, then hearing-impaired and non-hearing-impaired children should differ in their cognitive development.

The cognitive development of blind or visually impaired children is slower than that of sighted children. The smaller range of experiences available to the child, the relative lack of mobility, the decreased opportunity for social contact, and the decreased control of the child's own body and environment all take their toll (Lowenfeld, 1948). The reliance of the development of the concept of object permanence on the senses of hearing and touch leads to a delay in attaining it, and necessarily leads to a different type of concept.

Early studies suggested that the language development of blind children differed from that of sighted

There is a difference in the rate of development of linguistic abilities in blind and visually impaired children compared with non-impaired children, due to their different experience of the world.

children in that their speech was more egocentric, stereotypic, and less creative. Cutsford (1951) went so far as to claim that blind children's words were meaningless. It is now known that these are overgeneralizations, and are probably totally wrong.

Some (but not all) blind children may take longer to say their first words, although this is controversial (Lewis, 1987). Bigelow (1987) found that blind children acquired the first 50 words between the mean ages of 1 year 4 months and 1 year 9 months, compared with the 1 year 3 months to 1 year 8 months Nelson (1973) observed for sighted children. The earliest words seem to be similar to those first used by sighted children, although there appears to be a general reduction in the use of object names (Bigelow, 1987). Not surprisingly, unlike with sighted children, names do not refer to objects that are salient in the visual world, particularly those that cannot be touched (e.g., "moon"). Blind children use far fewer animal names in early speech than sighted children (8% compared with 20%; see Mulford, 1988). Instead, they refer to objects salient in the auditory and tactile domains (e.g., "drum," "dirt," and "powder"). Blind children also use more action words than sighted children do, and tend to refer to their own actions rather than the actions of others.

The earliest words also seem to be used rather differently. They appear to be used to comment on the child's own actions, in play or in imitation, rather than for communication or referring to objects or events. Indeed, Dunlea (1984) argued that as blind children were not using words beyond the context in which they were first learned, the symbolic use of words was delayed. Furthermore, vocabulary acquisition is generally slower. The understanding of particular words is bound to be different: Landau and Gleitman (1985) described the case of a 3-year-old child who, when asked to look up, reached her arms over her head. Nevertheless, Landau and Gleitman demonstrated that blind children can come to learn the meanings of words such as "look" and "see" without direct sensory experience. It is possible that children infer the meanings of these words by observing their positions in sentences and the words that occur with them.

There is considerable controversy about the use of pronouns by blind children. Whereas some researchers have found late acquisition of pronouns and many errors with them (e.g., using "you" for "me"; Dunlea, 1989), better controlled studies have found no such difference (Pérez-Pereira, 1999).

There are differences in phonological development: Blind children make more errors than sighted children in producing sounds that have highly visible movements of the lips (e.g., /b/), suggesting that visual information about the movement of lips normally contributes to phonological development (Mills, 1987). Nevertheless, older blind children show normal use of speech sounds, suggesting that acoustic information can eventually be used in isolation to achieve the correct pronunciation (Pérez-Pereira & Conti-Ramsden, 1999).

Syntactic development is marked by far more repetition than is normally found, and the use of repeated phrases carries over into later development. Furthermore, blind children do not ask so many questions of the type "what's that?" or "what?," or use modifiers such as "quite" or "very" (which account for the earliest function words of sighted children). This observation might reflect the fact that their parents adapt their own language to the needs of the children, providing more spontaneous labeling. There is also a delay in the acquisition of auxiliary verbs such as "will" and "can" (Landau & Gleitman, 1985). Again this is probably because of differences in the speech of the caregivers. Mothers of blind children use more direct commands ("Take the doll") than questions involving auxiliaries ("Can you take the doll?") when speaking to their children. The other curious finding is that the children's use of function words (which do the grammatical work of the language) is much less common early on (Bigelow, 1987).

Hence the linguistic development of blind children is different from that of sighted children, but the differences are mostly the obvious ones that one would expect given the nature of the disability. There is little clear evidence to support the idea that an impairment of cognitive processing causes an impairment of syntactic processing, and therefore we cannot conclude that cognitive processes precede linguistic ones. Neither is there much evidence to support the idea that blind children's early language is deficient relative to that of sighted children. Indeed, behavior that was once thought to be maladaptive in some way may in fact provide blind

children with alternative communicative strategies (Pérez-Pereira & Conti-Ramsden, 1999). For example, repetition and stereotypic speech are used to serve a social function of keeping in contact with people. Blind children use verbal play to a greater extent than sighted children, and may have better verbal memory. It should also be noted that work on blind children is methodologically complex and tends to involve small numbers of participants; many studies might have underestimated their linguistic abilities (Pérez-Pereira & Conti-Ramsden, 1999).

In any case, even if blind children were to show an unambiguous linguistic deficit, it would be very difficult to attribute any deficit just to differences in cognitive development. For example, the development of mutual gaze and the social precursors of language will necessarily be different; and sighted parents of blind children still tend to talk about objects that are visually prominent. However, caregivers try to adapt their speech to the needs of their children, resulting in subtle differences in linguistic development.

On the other hand, it is obvious that the development of spoken language is impaired in deaf or hearing-impaired children. There is some evidence that deaf children spontaneously start using and combining increasingly complex gestures in the absence of sign language (e.g., Mohay, 1982). This finding shows that there is a strong need for humans to attempt to communicate in some way. However, given adequate tuition, the time course of the acquisition of sign language runs remarkably parallel to that of normal spoken language development. Meier (1991) argued that deaf children using sign language pass the same linguistic "milestones" at about the same ages as hearing children (and some milestones perhaps before hearing children).

Research on the cognitive consequences of deafness has given mixed results. In one early experiment, Conrad and Rush (1965) found differences in coding in memory tasks between hearing and deaf children. This result is not surprising given the involvement of acoustic or phonological processing in short-term or working memory (Baddeley, 1990). If rigorous enough controls are used, it can be demonstrated that these indeed reflect differences in the memory systems rather than inferiority of the hearing-impaired systems (Conrad, 1979). Furth

(1966, 1971) found that compared with hearing children, deaf children's performance on Piagetian tasks was relatively normal. A review of results on tasks such as conservation gave a range of results, from no impairment to 1–2 years' delay; the evidence was mixed. Furth (1973) found that deaf adolescents had more difficulty with symbolic logic reasoning tasks than did hearing children. Furth interpreted these data as evidence for the Piagetian hypothesis that language is not necessary for normal cognitive development. Any differences between deaf and hearing children arise out of the lack of experiences and training of the deaf children.

However, most deaf children learn some kind of sign language at a very early age, so it is difficult to reach any strong conclusions about the effects of lack of language. Deaf children with deaf parents acquire sign language at the same rate as other children acquire spoken language (Messer, 2000). Best (1973) found that the more exposure to sign language that deaf children had, the better their performance on the Piagetian tasks.

Evaluation of evidence from deaf and blind children

There are clearly differences in cognitive development between hearing-impaired and non-hearing-impaired children, but it is not obviously the case that the linguistic performance of one group is superior to that of the other. The cognitive development of deaf children generally proceeds better than it should if language were primary, and the linguistic development of blind children generally proceeds better than it should if cognition were primary. Deaf children learn a sign language, and blind children acquire excellent coping strategies and acquire spoken language remarkably well. Indeed, the linguistic development of deaf children and the cognitive development of blind children both proceed better than we would expect if one were driving the other. There is little supporting evidence for the cognition hypothesis from an examination of children with learning difficulties or a comparison of deaf and blind children. If anything, these findings support Chomsky's position that language is an independent faculty. Nevertheless, social factors are clearly important. Biological, cognitive, and social factors work together in language development, and deficits in one of these areas can often be compensated for by the others.

WHAT IS THE RELATION BETWEEN LANGUAGE AND THOUGHT?

In this section we examine the relation between language and other cognitive and biological processes. Does the form of our language influence the way in which we think, or is the form of our language dependent on general cognitive factors?

Many animals are clearly able to solve some problems without language, suggesting that language cannot be essential for problem solving and thought. Although this may seem obvious, it has not always been considered so. Among the early approaches to examining the relation between language and thought, the behaviorists believed that thought was nothing more than speech. Young children speak their thoughts aloud; this becomes internalized, with the result that thought is covert speech—thought is just small motor movements of the vocal apparatus. Watson (1913) argued that thought processes are nothing more than motor habits in the larynx. Jacobsen (1932) found some evidence for this belief because thinking often is

According to Messer (2000), deaf children with deaf parents acquire sign language at the same rate as other children acquire spoken language.

accompanied by covert speech. He detected electrical activity in the throat muscles when participants were asked to think. But is thought possible without these small motor movements? Smith, Brown, Thomas, and Goodman (1947) used curare to temporarily paralyze all the voluntary muscles of a volunteer (Smith, who clearly deserved to be first author on this paper). Despite being unable to make any motor movement of the speech apparatus, Smith later reported that he had been able to think and solve problems. Hence there is more to thought than moving the vocal apparatus.

Perhaps language sets us apart from animals because it enables new and more advanced forms of thought? We need to distinguish how language and thought might affect each other developmentally, and in the fully developed adult state.

We can list the possible alternatives; each of them has been championed at some time. First, cognitive development determines the course of language development. This viewpoint was adopted by Piaget and his followers. Second, language and cognition are independent faculties (Chomsky's position). Third, language and cognition originate independently but become interdependent; the relation is complex (Vygotsky's position). Fourth, the idea that language determines cognition is known as the Sapir–Whorf hypothesis. The final two of these approaches both emphasize the influence of language in cognition.

The interdependence of language and thought

The Russian psychologist Vygotsky (1934/1962) argued that the relation between language and thought was a complex one. He studied inner speech, egocentric speech, and child monologues. He proposed that speech and thought have different ontogenetic roots (that is, different origins within an individual). Early on, in particular, speech has a pre-intellectual stage. In this stage, words are not symbols for the objects they denote, but actual properties of the objects. Speech sounds are not attached to thought. At the same time early thought is non-verbal, so up

to some point in development, when the child is about 3 years of age, speech and thought are independent; after this, they become connected. At this point speech and thought become interdependent: thought becomes verbal, and speech becomes representational. When this happens, children's monologues are internalized to become inner speech.

Vygotsky contrasted his theory with that of Piaget, using experiments that manipulated the strength of social constraints (see Figure 3.11). Unlike Piaget, Vygotsky considered that later cognitive development was determined in part by language. Piaget argued that egocentric speech arises because the child has not yet become fully socialized, and withers away as the child learns to communicate by taking into account the point of view of the listener. For Vygotsky the reverse was the case. Egocentric speech serves the function of self-guidance that eventually becomes internalized as inner speech, and is only vocalized because the child has not yet learned how to internalize it. The boundaries between child and listener are confused, so that self-guiding speech can only be produced in a social context. Vygotsky found that the amount of egocentric speech decreased when the child's feeling of being understood lessened (such as when the listener was at another table). He claimed that this was the reverse of what Piaget would predict. However, these experiments are difficult to evaluate because Vygotsky omitted many procedural details and measurements from his reports that are necessary for a full evaluation. It is surprising that the studies have not been repeated under more stringent conditions. Until then, and until this type of theory is more fully specified, it is difficult to evaluate the significance of Vygotsky's ideas.

The Sapir–Whorf hypothesis

In George Orwell's novel *Nineteen Eighty-Four*, language restricted the way in which people thought. The rulers of the state deliberately used "Newspeak," the official language of Oceania, so that the people thought what they were required to think. "This statement ... could not have been sustained by reasoned argument, because the

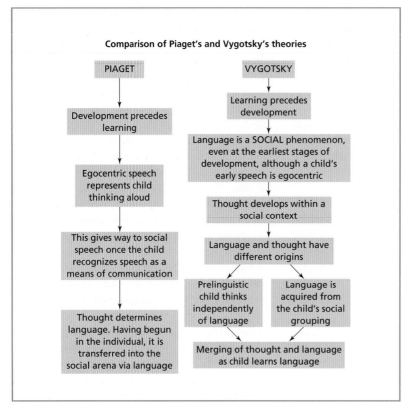

FIGURE 3.11

necessary words were not available" (Orwell, 1949, p. 249, in the appendix, "The principles of Newspeak"). Orwell's idea is a version of the Sapir–Whorf hypothesis.

The central idea of the Sapir–Whorf hypothesis is that the form of our language determines the structure of our thought processes. Language affects the way we remember things and the way in which we perceive the world. It was originally proposed by a linguist, Edward Sapir, and a fire insurance engineer and amateur linguist, Benjamin Lee Whorf (see Whorf, 1956a, 1956b). Although Whorf is most closely associated with anthropological evidence based on the study of American Indian languages, the idea came to him from his work in fire insurance. He noted that accidents sometimes happened because, he thought, people were misled by words—as in the case of a worker who threw a cigarette end into what he considered to be an "empty" drum of petrol. Far from being empty, the drum was full of petrol vapor, with explosive results.

The Sapir–Whorf hypothesis comprises two related ideas. First, linguistic determinism is the idea that the form and characteristics of our language determine the way in which we think, remember, and perceive. Second, linguistic relativism is the idea that as different languages map onto the world in different ways, different languages will generate different cognitive structures.

Miller and McNeill (1969) distinguished between three versions of the Sapir–Whorf hypothesis. In the strong version, language determines thought. In a weaker version, language affects only perception. In the weakest version, language differences affect processing on certain tasks where linguistic encoding is important. It is the weakest version that has proved easiest to test, and for which there is the most support. It is important to consider what is meant by "perception" here. It is often unclear whether what is being talked about is low-level sensory processing or classification.

Anthropological evidence

The anthropological evidence concerns the inter-translatability of languages. Whorf analyzed Native American Indian languages such as Hopi, Nootka, Apache, and Aztec. He argued that each language imposes its own "world view" on its speakers. For example, he concluded that as Hopi contains no words or grammatical constructions that refer to time, Hopi speakers must have a different conception of time from us. Whorf's data are now considered highly unreliable (Malotki, 1983). Furthermore, translation can be very misleading. Take as an example Whorf's (1940/1956b, p. 214) analysis of "clear dripping spring" in the following quote:

We might isolate something in nature by saying "It is a dripping spring." Apache erects the statement on a verb ga: "be white (including clear, uncolored, and so on)." With a prefix no—the meaning of downward motion enters: "whiteness moves downward." Then to, meaning both "water" and "spring," is prefixed. The result corresponds to our "dripping spring," but synthetically it is "as water, or springs, whiteness moves downward." How utterly unlike our way of thinking!

In fact, Whorf's translation was very idiosyncratic, so it is far from clear that speakers of Apache actually dissect the world in different ways (Clark & Clark, 1977; Pinker, 1994). For example, both languages have separate elements for "clear," "spring," and "moving downwards." Why should the expression not have been translated "It is a clear dripping spring"? The appeal of such translations is further diminished when it is realized that Whorf based his claim not on interviews with Apache speakers, but on an analysis of their recorded grammar. Lenneberg and Roberts (1956) pointed out the circularity in the reasoning that, because languages differ, thought patterns differ because of the differences in the languages. An independent measure of thought patterns is necessary before a causal conclusion can be drawn.

Vocabulary differentiation

The way in which different languages have different vocabularies has been used to support the Whorfian hypothesis, in that researchers believe that cultures must view the world differently because some cultures have single words available for concepts that others may take many words to describe. For example, Boas (1911) reported that Eskimo (or Inuit) language has four different words for snow; there are 13 Filipino words for rice. An amusing debunking of some of these claims can be found in Pullum (1989): Whorf (1940/1956b) inflated the number of words for snow to seven, and drew a comparison with English, which he said has only one word for snow regardless of whether it is falling, on the ground, slushy, dry or wet, and so on. The number of types of snow the Inuit were supposed to have then varied with subsequent indirect reporting, apparently reaching its maximum in an editorial in the *New York Times* on February 9, 1984, with "one hundred" to "two hundred" in a Cleveland television weather forecast. In fact, it is unclear how many words Inuit has for snow, but it is certainly not that many. It probably only has two words or roots for types of snow: "qanik" for "snow in the air" or "snowflake"; and "aput" for "snow on the ground." It is unclear whether you should count the words derived from these roots as separate. This story reinforces the importance of knowing how you define a "word," and also of always checking sources! Speakers of English also in fact have several words for different types of snow (snow, slush, sleet, and blizzard).

Vocabulary differences are unlikely to have any significant effects on perception—although again it is important to bear in mind what perception might cover. We can learn new words for snow: people learning to ski readily do so, and while this does not apparently change the quality of the skiers' perception of the world, it certainly changes the way in which they classify snow types and respond to them. For example, you might choose not to go skiing on certain types of snow. Vocabulary differences reflect differences in experience and expertise. They do not seem to cause significant differences in

Opinion on the exact number of Inuit words for "snow" has varied wildly, depending on the source of the figure, and on the parameters that have been adopted in determining what does and does not constitute another word for "snow." This illustrates the need for clarity when deciding how to define a "word."

perception, but do aid classification and other cognitive processes. Not having words available for certain concepts does seem to have a detrimental effect. Members of the Piraha tribe from the Amazon basin have words for the numbers "one" and "two," and then just "many." Their performance on a range of numerical tasks was very poor for quantities greater than three (Gordon, 2004). Whereas we can count above two and assign precise numbers to quantities, members of the Piraha tribe just seem to be able to estimate. Not having a word available for a concept does appear to limit their cognitive abilities.

Grammatical differences between languages

Carroll and Casagrande (1958) examined the cognitive consequences of grammatical differences in the English and Navaho languages. The form of the class of verbs concerning handling used in Navaho depends on the shape and rigidity of the object being handled. Endings for the verb corresponding to "carry," for example, vary depending on whether a rope or a stick is being carried. Carroll and Casagrande therefore argued that speakers of Navaho should pay more attention to the properties of objects

that determine the endings than do English speakers, and in particular they should group instances of objects according to their form. As all the children in the study were bilingual, the comparison was made between more Navaho-dominant and more English-dominant Navaho children. The more Navaho-dominant children did indeed group objects more by form than by color, compared to the English-dominant group. However, a control group of non-Native American English-speaking children grouped even more strongly according to form, behaving as the Navaho children were predicted to behave! It is therefore not clear what conclusions about the relation between language and thought can be drawn from this study.

A second example is that English speakers use the subjunctive mood to easily encode counter-factuals such as "If I had gone to the library, I would have met Dirk." Chinese does not have a subjunctive mood. Bloom (1981, 1984) found that Chinese speakers find it harder to reason counter-factually, and attributed this to their lack of a subjunctive construction. Their memories are more easily overloaded than those of speakers of languages that support these forms. There has been some dispute about the extent to which sentences used by Bloom were good idiomatic Chinese. It is also possible to argue counter-factually in Chinese using more complex constructions, such as (translated into English) "Mrs. Wong does not know English; if Mrs. Wong knew English, she would be able to read the *New York Times*" (Au, 1983, 1984; Liu, 1985). Nevertheless, Chinese speakers do seem to find counter-factual reasoning more difficult than English speakers. If this is because the form of the construction needed for counter-factual reasoning is longer than the English subjunctive, then this is evidence of a subtle effect of linguistic form on reasoning abilities.

A third example is that of grammatical gender. Although English does not mark grammatical gender, many languages do. Italian, for example, marks nouns as masculine or feminine, and German marks them as masculine, feminine, or neuter. Vigliocco, Vinson,

Paganelli, and Dworzynski (2005) found that effects of gender on thought were highly constrained. They were found in Italian (a two-gender language), but only with tasks that require verbalization and only with certain semantic categories (animals) and not others (artifacts). For example, when participants are asked to judge which two of three words are most similar (e.g., donkey–elephant–giraffe), grammatical gender affected similarity judgments for animals but not for artifacts. There were no effects at all in German, a language with an additional neuter gender. The likely reason for this difference is that in two-gender languages gender is a reliable cue to sex—but of course this rule is inapplicable with artifacts. The conclusion is consistent with a weak version of the Sapir–Whorf hypothesis—language can affect performance on some tasks that use language.

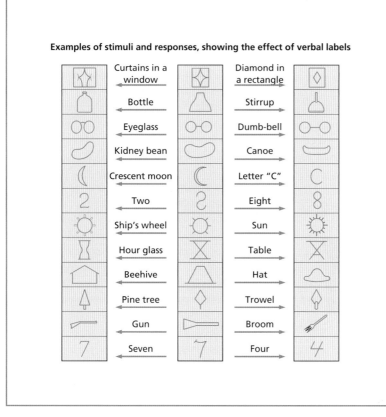

Examples of stimuli and responses, showing the effect of verbal labels

	Curtains in a window		Diamond in a rectangle	
	Bottle		Stirrup	
	Eyeglass		Dumb-bell	
	Kidney bean		Canoe	
	Crescent moon		Letter "C"	
	Two		Eight	
	Ship's wheel		Sun	
	Hour glass		Table	
	Beehive		Hat	
	Pine tree		Trowel	
	Gun		Broom	
	Seven		Four	

FIGURE 3.12 Carmichael et al.'s study involved two groups of participants who were shown the drawings in the central column. One group were given the description on the left, and the other group were given the description on the right. For example, one group were told an object was a gun and the other that it was a broom. Later the participants were asked to reproduce the drawings from memory. Their sketches matched the description they were given, not the original drawings, demonstrating that perceptual recall is not influenced solely by the stimulus, but is also affected by knowledge.

Indirect effects of language on cognition

There is more evidence that language can have an indirect effect on cognition, particularly on tasks where linguistic encoding is important. Carmichael, Hogan, and Walter (1932) looked at the effects of learning a verbal label on participants' memory for nonsense pictures (see Figure 3.12). They found that the label that the participants associated with the pictures affected the recall of the pictures. Santa and Ranken (1972) showed that having an arbitrary verbal label available aided the recall of nonsense shapes.

Duncker (1945) explored the phenomenon known as functional fixedness, using the "box and candle" problem (see Figure 3.13) where participants have to construct a device using a collection of commonplace materials so that a candle can burn down to its bottom while attached to the wall. The easiest solution is to use the box containing the materials as a support; however, participants take a long time to think of this, because they fixate on the box's function as container. Glucksberg and Weisberg (1966) showed that the explicit labeling of objects could strengthen or weaken the functional fixedness effect depending on the appropriateness of the label. This demonstrates a linguistic influence on reasoning.

In an experiment by Hoffman, Lau, and Johnson (1986), Chinese–English bilinguals read descriptions of people, and were later asked to provide descriptions of the people they'd read about. The descriptions had been prepared so as to conform to Chinese or English personality stereotypes. Bilingual people thinking in Chinese used the Chinese stereotype, whereas bilingual people thinking in English used the English stereotype. The language used influenced the stereotypes used, and therefore the inferences made and what was remembered.

Hence work on memory and problem solving supports the weakest version of the Whorfian hypothesis. Language can facilitate or hinder performance on some cognitive tasks, particularly those where linguistic encoding is routinely important.

Number systems

Hunt and Agnoli (1991) examined how different languages impose different memory burdens on their speakers. English has a complex system for naming numbers: we have 13 primitive terms (0–12), then special complex names for the "teens," then more general rule-based names for the numbers between 20 and 100, and then more special names beyond that. On the other hand, the number naming system in Chinese is much more simple, necessitating only that the child has to remember 11 basic terms (0–10), and three special terms for 100, 1,000, and 10,000. For example, "eleven" is simply "ten plus one." English-speaking children have difficulty learning to count in the teen range, whereas Chinese-speaking children do not (Miller & Stigler, 1987). Hence the form of the language has subtle influences on arithmetical ability, a clear example of language influencing cognition.

Although Welsh numbers have the same number of syllables as their English counterparts, the vowel sounds are longer and so they take longer to say (Ellis & Hennelly, 1980). Hence bilingual participants had worse performance on digit-span tests in Welsh compared with English digit names, and also slightly worse performance and higher error rates in mental arithmetic tasks when using Welsh digit names.

Key evidence comes from the Piraha people of the Amazon (Everett & Madora, 2011; Gordon, 2004). The Piraha lack precise numerical terms, and seem to have great difficulty on

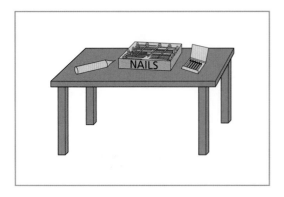

FIGURE 3.13 The objects presented to participants in the "box and candle" problem.

tasks involving numbers greater than three. It appears that in order to count accurately we need to have linguistic number terms available.

Color coding and memory for color

The most fruitful way of investigating the strong version of the Sapir–Whorf hypothesis has proved to be analysis of the way in which we name and remember colors. Brown and Lenneberg (1954) examined memory for "color chips" differing in hue, brightness, and saturation. Codable colors, which correspond to simple color names, are remembered more easily (e.g., an ideal red is remembered more easily than a poor example of red). Lantz and Stefflre (1964) argued that the similar notion of communication accuracy best determines success: People best remember colors that are easy to describe.

This early work seemed to support the Sapir–Whorf hypothesis, but there is a basic assumption that the division of the color spectrum into labeled colors is completely arbitrary. This means that, but for historical accident, we might have developed other color names, like "bled" for a name of a color between red and blue, and "grue" for a name of a color between green and blue, rather than red, blue, and green. Is this assumption correct?

Berlin and Kay (1969) compared the basic color terms used by different languages. Basic color terms are defined by being made up from only one morpheme (so "red," but not "blood red"), not being contained within another color (so "red," but not "scarlet"), not having restricted usage (hence "blond" is excluded), and being common and generally known and not usually derived from the name of an object (hence "yellow" but not "saffron"). Languages differ in the number of color terms they have available. For example, Gleason (1961) compared the division of color hues by speakers of English with that of the languages Shona and Bassa (see Figure 3.14). Berlin and Kay found that across languages basic color terms were present in a hierarchy (see Figure 3.15). If a language only has two basic color terms available, they must correspond to "black" and "white"; if they have three then they must be these two plus "red"; if they have four then they must be the first three plus one of the next group, and so on. English has names for all 11 basic color terms (black, white, red, yellow, green, blue, brown, purple, pink, orange, and gray). Berlin and Kay also showed that the typical colors referred to by the basic color terms, called the focal colors, tend to be constant across languages.

Heider (1972) examined people's memory for focal colors in more detail. Focal colors are the best examples of colors corresponding to basic color terms: they can be thought of as the best example of a color such as red, green, or blue. The Dani tribe of New Guinea have just two basic color terms, "mili" (for black and dark colors) and "mola" (for white and light colors), although subsequently there has been some doubt as to whether this really is the case. Heider taught the Dani made-up names for other colors. They learned names more easily for other focal colors than for non-focal colors, even though they had no name for those focal colors. They could also

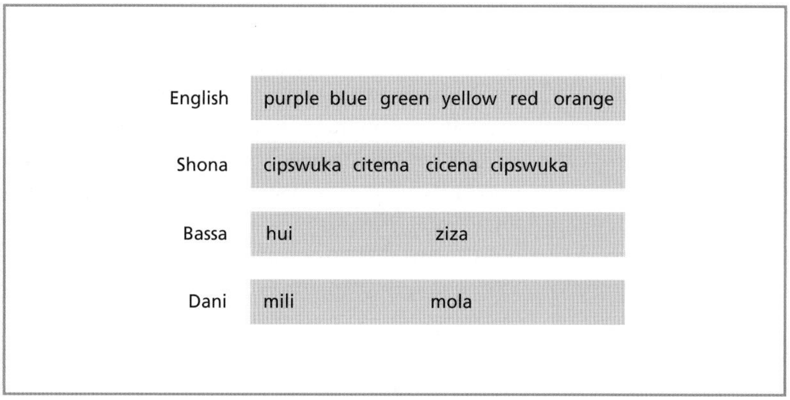

FIGURE 3.14
Comparison of color hue division in English, Shona, Bassa, and Dani (based on Gleason, 1961).

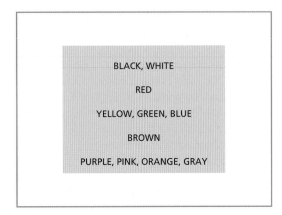

FIGURE 3.15 Hierarchy of color names (based on Berlin & Kay, 1969).

remember focal colors more easily than non-focal colors, again even those for which they did not have a name. Three-year-old children also prefer focal colors: they match them more accurately, attend to them more, and are more likely to choose them as exemplars of a color than non-focal colors (Heider, 1971). In a similar way, English speakers attend to differences between light and dark blue in exactly the same way as Russian speakers, even though the latter have names for these regions of the color spectrum while English speakers do not (Davies et al., 1991; Laws, Davies, & Andrews, 1995; note that there has been considerable debate about whether these are basic color names).

At first sight then, the division of the color spectrum is not arbitrary, but is based on the physiology of the color vision system. The six most sensitive points of the visual system correspond to the first six focal colors of the Berlin and Kay hierarchy. Further evidence that differences are biological and have nothing to do with language comes from work on prelinguistic children by Bornstein (1985). Children aged 4 months habituate more readily to colors that lie centrally in the red and blue categories than to colors that lie at the boundaries.

Bornstein (1973) found an environmental influence on the take-up of these color terms. He noted that with increasing proximities of societies to the equator, color names for short wavelengths (blue and green) become increasingly identified with each other and, in the extreme, with black.

He argued that the eyes of peoples in equatorial regions have evolved to have protection from excessive ultraviolet light. In particular, there is greater yellow pigmentation in the eyes, which protects the eye from short-wave radiation, at a cost of decreased sensitivity to blue and green.

Brown (1976) discussed the revised interpretation of these color-naming data and their consequences for the Sapir–Whorf hypothesis. He concluded that these later studies show that color naming does not tell us very much about the Sapir–Whorf hypothesis. If anything, it appeared to emphasize the importance of biological factors in language development. There are some problems with some of these studies, however. Of the 20 languages originally described in the Berlin and Kay (1969) study, 19 were in fact obtained from bilingual speakers living in San Francisco, and the use of color categories by bilingual speakers differs systematically from that of monolingual speakers. In particular, the color categorization of bilingual people comes to resemble that of monolingual speakers of their second language, whatever their first language. This in itself would give rise to an artifactual universality in color categorization. There are also methodological problems with the expanded set of 98 languages studied later by Berlin and Kay (Cromer, 1991; Hickerson, 1971). The criteria Berlin and Kay (1969) used for naming basic color terms are suspect (Michaels, 1977). The criteria seem to have been inconsistently applied, and it is possible that the basic color terms of many languages were omitted (Hickerson, 1971).

There were also problems with the materials used in the original studies by Heider. The focal colors are perceptually more discriminable than the non-focal colors used in Berlin and Kay's array in that they were perceptually more distant from their neighbors. When the materials are corrected for this artifact, Lucy and Shweder (1979) found that focal colors were not remembered any better than non-focal colors. On the other hand, a measure of communication accuracy did predict memory performance. This finding suggests that having a convenient color label can indeed assist color memory. Kay and Kempton (1984) showed that although English speakers display categorical perception of colors that lie on either side of a color name boundary, such as blue and green, speakers of the Mexican Indian language Tarahumara, who do not have names for blue and green, do not. Hence having an available name can at least accentuate the difference between two categories. These more recent findings suggest that there are indeed linguistic effects on color perception.

There are limitations on the extent to which biological factors constrain color categorization, and it is likely that there is some linguistic influence. The Berinmo, a hunter-gatherer tribe also from New Guinea, have five basic color terms. The Berinmo do not mark the distinction between blue and green, but instead have a color boundary between the colors they call "nol" and "wor," which does not have any correspondence in the English color-naming scheme. English speakers show a memory advantage across the blue–green category boundary but not across the nol–wor one, whereas Berinmo speakers showed the reverse pattern (Davidoff, Davies, & Roberson, 1999a, 1999b). In a further series of experiments using more sensitive statistical techniques, Roberson, Davies, and Davidoff (2000) were unable to replicate Heider's earlier results with the Dani with the Berinmo. They found no recognition advantage for focal stimuli, no facilitation of learning focal colors, and a relation between color recognition was affected by color vocabulary.

It is now also apparent that even within English not all basic color terms are equal. "Brown" and "gray" are acquired later than other basic color terms, are the two least preferred colors, and are used less frequently in adult speech to children than other color terms (Pitchford & Mullen, 2005).

In summary there appear to be effects of biological and linguistic constraints on memory for colors. Perhaps color naming is not such a good test of the Sapir–Whorf hypothesis after all. First, the task is clearly very sensitive to the details of the experimental procedures and materials used. Second, the more basic the cognitive or perceptual process, the less scope there is likely to be for the top-down influence of language, and color perception, a mechanism shared with many nonhuman species, is pretty

low level. As Pinker (1994) observes, no matter how influential language might be, it is preposterous to think that it could rewire the ganglion cells. Third, in any case, there do appear to be effects of language on color perception: Roberson et al. found effects of categorical perception for colors, but aligned with linguistic categories rather than more biologically based categories.

Linguistic differences in the coding of space and time

In a recent review, Boroditsky (2003) concludes that there are several instances where encoding differences between languages leads to differences in performance by speakers of those languages. For example, different languages encode spatial languages in different ways. Most languages (such as English) use relative terms (e.g., front of, back of, left of, right of) to encode relative spatial terms. Languages such as Tzeltal (a Mayan language) use an absolute system (similar to our system of describing compass points, e.g., to the north). Speakers of Dutch (which uses the relative system) and Tzeltal interpret and perform very differently on a non-linguistic orientation task. In this task, people see an arrow pointing in one direction, to the left or right. The viewpoint is then rotated 180 degrees, and people are asked which is most like the one they had originally seen—an arrow pointing in relatively the same way, or absolutely the same way. Preferences depend on whether the language uses an absolute or a relative coding system, with the Dutch speakers preferring the right-pointing arrow if they had seen that previously, but the Tzeltal speakers preferring the left-pointing arrow (Levinson, 1996a). This is because "what is north" does not vary with rotation, but "what is left" does. Different spatial frames of references are acquired with ease by children from different cultures using different languages—the absolute and relative systems are acquired equally easily (Majid, Bowerman, Kita, Haun, & Levinson, 2004). Different languages encode time in different ways: in English we mainly use a front–back metaphor (look ahead, falling behind, move meetings forward), while Mandarin speakers systematically use vertical metaphors (with up corresponding roughly to last and down to next). Mandarin speakers are more likely to construct vertical timelines to think about time, while English speakers are more likely to construct horizontal ones. For example, Mandarin speakers are faster to confirm that March comes before April if they have just seen a vertical array of objects than if they had seen a horizontal one. English speakers showed the reverse pattern (Boroditsky, 2001). Similar differences in performance can be found for the way in which languages encode object shape and grammatical gender (Boroditsky, 2003).

Languages differ in the way in which they encode movement—do these linguistic differences lead to cognitive differences? English encodes the direction of motion with a modifier ("to," "from") and the manner of motion in the verb ("walk," "run"), whereas in Greek the opposite is the case: the verb encodes the direction of motion, while the manner is encoded by a modifier. Papafragou, Massey, and Gleitman (2002) tested Greek and English children on two types of task involving motion: one involving non-linguistic tasks (remembering and categorizing motion in pictures of animals moving around), the other involving linguistic description. They only found a difference in performance on the linguistic tasks.

There has recently been debate about whether these linguistic differences reflect the presence or absence of external cues, and whether they affect performance on all tasks, or just linguistic tasks. Li and Gleitman (2002) argued that the results of the studies by Levinson and colleagues on spatial frames of reference described above were artifactual. Li and Gleitman suggested that the results depend on the presence of environmental cues. They tested a group of native English speakers, and found that they could make them perform using relative or absolute frames of reference depending on the presence of landmark cues in the environment. When participants could not see the outside world (the blinds of the testing room were down), the speakers tended to use a relative frame; when they could see the outside world (the blinds were up), they were more likely to use an absolute frame of reference. On the other hand, Levinson, Kita, Haun, and Rasch (2002) were unable to replicate these

results, arguing that the purpose of the task was too apparent to Li and Gleitman's participants. They also pointed out that their groups were tested with equal amounts of environmental cues available, being tested equally indoors and out.

In summary, there is evidence that the way in which different languages encode distinctions such as time, space, motion, shape, and gender influence the way in which speakers of those languages think. These differences suggest that our language may determine how we perform on tasks that at first sight do not seem to involve language at all, although this claim remains controversial.

Evaluation of the Sapir–Whorf hypothesis

The weak version of the Sapir–Whorf hypothesis has enjoyed a resurgence. There is now a considerable amount of evidence suggesting that linguistic factors can affect cognitive processes. Even color perception and memory, once thought to be completely biologically determined, show some influence of language. Furthermore, research on perception and categorization has shown that high-level cognitive processes can influence the creation of low-level visual features early in visual processing (Schyns, Goldstone, & Thibaut, 1998). This is entirely consistent with the idea that, in at least some circumstances, language might be able to influence perception.

Indeed, it is hardly surprising that if a thought expressible in one language cannot be expressed so easily in another, then that difference will have consequences for the ease with which cognitive processes can be acquired and carried out. Having one word for a concept instead of having to use a whole sentence might reduce memory load. The differences in number systems between languages form one example of how linguistic differences can lead to slight differences in cognitive style.

We will see in later chapters that different languages exemplify different properties that are bound to have cognitive consequences. For example, the complete absence of words with irregular pronunciations in languages such as Serbo-Croat and Italian is reflected in differences between their reading systems and those of speakers of languages such as English. Furthermore, differences between languages can lead to differences in the effects of brain damage.

The extent to which people find the Sapir–Whorf hypothesis plausible depends on the extent to which they view language as an evolutionarily late mechanism that merely translates our thoughts into a format suitable for communication, rather than a rich symbolic system that underlies most of cognition (Lucy, 1996). It is also more plausible in a cognitive system with extensive feedback from later to earlier levels of processing.

Language and thought: Conclusion

Perhaps the main conclusion about how language and thought are related is that there is a relationship, but it is a complex one. Environment and biology jointly determine our basic cognitive architecture. Within the constraints set by this architecture, languages are free to vary in how they dissect the world and in what they emphasize. These differences can then feed back to affect aspects of perception and cognition.

We noted above that paralyzing overt speech does not stop us being able to think. Clearly language is an important medium of thought and conceptualization. Although there is a great deal of individual variation, a significant proportion of our mental life is conducted in language (Carruthers, 2002); we hear "inner speech," which often seems to be expressing or guiding our thoughts, or which sometimes is the product of reading. The extent to which inner speech or language plays a real role in thinking is unclear and controversial (Carruthers, 2002). A strong view is that language is essential for conceptual thought and is the medium in which it is conducted; a weaker view is that language is the medium of conscious propositional (as opposed to visual) thought; an even weaker view is that language is necessary to acquire many concepts, and influences cognition in ways that we have seen above; yet another view is that there is essentially no relation at all (although language can clearly express thoughts). Carruthers presents evidence from a range of sources to justify his claim that inner speech is the glue that sticks cognition together, and enables the modules of the mind to communicate: that is, language is the medium of conscious thought.

Even here we must note that there might be cultural differences. In the West, it is assumed that language and inner speech assist thinking; in the East, it is assumed that talking interferes with thinking. These cultural differences affect performance: thinking out loud helped European Americans to solve reasoning problems, but hindered Asian Americans (Kim, 2002; Nisbett, 2003).

The influence of language on thought has some important consequences. For example, does sexist language really influence the way in which people think? Spender (1980) proposed some of the strongest arguments for non-sexist language. For example, that using the word "man" to refer to all humanity has the association that males are more important than females; or that using a word like "chairman" (rather than a more gender-neutral term such as "chair" or "chairperson") encourages the expectation that the person will be a man. These expectations do have real effects. Gender-stereotyped nouns (e.g., "surgeon," "nurse") are those to which many people have a strong initial expectation of the gender of the person (surgeon as male, nurse as female). Readers take longer to read a subsequent pronoun referring to the noun if the pronoun is in conflict with the stereotyping (such as using "she" to refer to a surgeon rather than "he"; e.g., Kennison & Trofe, 2004). Such a theory is a form of the Sapir–Whorf hypothesis, although there has been surprisingly little empirical work in this area.

As Gleitman and Papafragou (2005) conclude, clearly we can have thought without language—some animals clearly reason and solve problems; prelinguistic infants have rich cognitive abilities; people with brain damage destroying most of their language abilities display rich cognitive abilities. Yet there is also much evidence that language and culture can affect our ways of thinking. Language and thought are related, but in a complex way.

SUMMARY

- Language must have conferred an evolutionary advantage on early humans.
- Many animals, including even insects, have surprisingly rich communication systems.
- Animal communication systems in the wild are nevertheless tied to the here-and-now, and animals can only communicate about a very limited number of topics (mainly food, threat, and sex).
- Hockett described "16 design features" that he thought characterized human spoken language.
- Early attempts to teach apes to talk failed because the apes lack the necessary articulatory apparatus.
- Later attempts to teach apes to communicate using signs (e.g., Washoe and Kanzi) show at least that apes can use combinations of signs in the appropriate circumstances, although it is unclear whether they are using words and grammatical rules in the same way as we do.
- Some language processes are localized in specific parts of the brain, particularly the left cortex.
- Broca's area is particularly important for producing speech, while Wernicke's area is particularly important for dealing with the meaning of words.
- Damage to particular areas of the brain leads to identifiable types of disrupted language.
- We are not born with functions fully lateralized in the two cortical hemispheres; instead, much specialization takes place in the early years of life.
- There are sex differences in language use and lateralization from an early age; females tend to have better linguistic skills.
- There is a sensitive period for language development during which we need exposure to socially meaningful linguistic input.
- The stronger notion of a critical period for language acquisition between the ages of 2 and 7 cannot be correct because there is clear evidence that lateralization is present from birth, and that older children and adults are surprisingly good at acquiring language.
- The acquisition of syntax by the left hemisphere is particularly susceptible to disruption during the sensitive period.
- The relation between language and cognitive processes in development is complex.
- Infants do not need to attain object permanence before they can start naming objects.
- The cognitive development of deaf children proceeds better than it should if language underlies cognition, and the linguistic development of blind children proceeds better than it should if cognition underlies language.
- Language use has important social precursors; in particular, parents appear to have "conversations" with infants well before the infants start to use language.
- Parents adapt their language to the needs of their children, and the way that caregivers speak to blind children leads to differences in their grammatical development compared with sighted children.
- The Sapir–Whorf hypothesis states that differences in languages between cultures will lead to their speakers perceiving the world in different ways and having different cognitive structures.
- The most important sources of evidence in evaluating the Sapir–Whorf hypothesis are studies of color naming.
- Color naming and memory studies show that although biological factors play the most important role in dividing up the color spectrum, there is some linguistic influence on memory for colors.
- There is evidence that language can affect performance on some perceptual, memory, and conceptual tasks.

QUESTIONS TO THINK ABOUT

1. Why might early humans have needed language while chimpanzees did not?
2. What do you think is the most important way in which human language can be differentiated from the way in which Washoe used language?
3. What would convince you that a chimpanzee was using a language like humans?
4. How easy is it to separate features that are universal to language from features that are universal to our environment?
5. One reason why second language acquisition might be so difficult for adults is that it is not "taught" in the way that children acquire their first language. How then could the teaching of a second language be facilitated?
6. How might individual differences play a part in the extent to which people use language to "think to themselves"?
7. Compare and contrast the language of Genie with the "language" of Washoe.
8. What ethical issues are involved in trying to teach animals language?
9. Clearly the alleged experiment on creating wild children reputed to have been carried out by King James IV was extremely unethical. What ethical issues do you think might be involved in cases such as Genie's?
10. How could you tell whether sex differences in language use result from biological or cultural factors (or both)?
11. Can you find any examples of sexist language in magazines, newspapers, or official documents? Has it influenced your understanding of the roles people play?
12. Can you think of any examples of when your cognition has been affected by the words you use?

FURTHER READING

For more on the origins and evolution of language, see Aitchison (1996), Deacon (1997), Harley (2010), and Jackendoff (1999). Christiansen and Kirby (2003) is a more advanced but still approachable recent edited collection about language evolution; start with the chapter by Pinker for an overview. Dennett (1991) discusses the evolution of language, and its possible relation to consciousness.

For a more detailed review of animal communication systems and their cognitive abilities, see Pearce (2008). A detailed summary of early attempts to teach apes language is provided by Premack (1986a). Gardner, van Cantfort, and Gardner (1992) report more recent analyses of Washoe's signs. Premack's later stance is critically discussed in reviews by Carston (1987) and Walker (1987); see also the debate between Premack (1986b) and Bickerton (1986) in the journal *Cognition*. A popular and contemporary account of Kanzi is given by Savage-Rumbaugh and Lewin (1994). See also Deacon (1997) for more on animal communication systems and the evolution of language. See Klima and Bellugi (1979) for more on sign language in humans. Aitchison (1998) is a good description of attempts to teach language to animals and the biological basis of language. There

(Continued)

(Continued)

is a special issue of the journal *Cognitive Science* on primate cognition (2000, volume 24, part 3, July–September). See Pepperberg (1999) and Shanker, Savage-Rumbaugh, and Taylor (1999) for replies to Kako's (1999a) criticisms; and Kako (1999b) for replies to them.

Most textbooks on neuropsychology and neuroscience have at least one chapter on language and the brain (e.g., Gazzaniga et al., 2008; Kolb & Whishaw, 2009). See Poeppel and Hickok (2004) and the rest of the special issue of the journal *Cognition* for a recent review of work on the biology and anatomy of language.

Muller (1997) is an article with commentaries about the innateness of language, species-specificity, and brain development. He argues that the brain is less localized for language and that language is less precisely genetically determined than many people think. The article is also a good source of further references on these topics.

An excellent source of readings on the critical period and how language develops in exceptional circumstances is Bishop and Mogford (1993). Bishop (1997) provides a comprehensive review of how comprehension skills develop in unusual circumstances. For a more detailed review of the critical period and second language hypothesis see McLaughlin (1984). Bishop also describes specific language impairment (SLI) and semantic-pragmatic disorder in detail; see also Bishop (1989). Gopnik (1992) also reviews SLI, emphasizing the role genetics plays in its occurrence. A popular account of Genie and other attic children plus an outline of their importance is given by Rymer (1993). See Shattuck (1980) for a detailed description of the "Wild Boy of Aveyron" and Curtiss (1989) for a description of another linguistically deprived person called "Chelsea." Description of the neurology of hemispheric specialization can be found in Kolb and Whishaw (2009). Skuse (1993) discusses other cases of linguistic deprivation. Cases of hearing children of deaf parents and their implications are reviewed by Schiff-Myers (1993). See Harris (1982) for a full review of cognitive prerequisites to language. Social precursors of language are discussed in more detail in Harris and Coltheart (1986).

Gleason and Ratner (1993) give an overview of language development covering many of the topics in this and the next chapter. See Cottingham (1984) for a discussion of rationalism and empiricism. A general overview of cognitive development is provided by Flavell, Miller, and Miller (1993) and by McShane (1991). Piattelli-Palmarini (1980) edited a collection of papers that arose from the famous debate between Chomsky and Piaget on the relation between language and thought, and the contributions of nativism versus experience, at the Royaumont Abbey near Paris in 1975. Piattelli-Palmarini (1994) summarized and updated this debate. Lewis (1987) discusses general issues concerning the effects of different types of disability on linguistic and cognitive development. For more on language acquisition in the blind, see the collection of papers in Mills (1983). Kyle and Woll (1985) is a textbook on sign language and the consequences of its use on cognitive development. Cromer's (1991) book provides a good critical overview of this area, and indeed of many of the topics in this chapter. Gallaway and Richards (1994) is a collection of papers covering research on child-directed speech and the role of the environment; the final chapter by Richards and Gallaway (1994) provides an overview.

For more on the early language of blind children, see Dunlea (1989) and Pérez-Pereira and Conti-Ramsden (1999), and for more on language in deaf, blind, and handicapped children, Cromer (1991). For the effects of linguistic training on cognitive performance, see Dale (1976). Leonard (2000) is a review of work on SLI. For a good review of the critical period hypothesis, see B. Harley and Wang (1997). For a review of the biology of sex differences see Baron-Cohen (2003).

See Gleitman and Papafragou (2005) for an overview of the relation between language and thought. Gumperz and Levinson (1996) is an edited volume about linguistic relativity. Dale (1976) also discusses the Sapir–Whorf hypothesis in detail. See Levinson (1996b) for cross-cultural work on differences in the use of spatial terms, and how they might affect cognition. Fodor (1972) and Newman and Holzman (1993) review the work of Vygotsky and its impact. For a detailed review of the Sapir–Whorf hypothesis in general and the experiments on color coding in particular, see Lucy (1992). Clark and Clark (1977) provide an extensive review of the relation between language and thought, with particular emphasis on developmental issues. Nisbett (2003) discusses cultural differences in language and cognition.

CHAPTER 4

LANGUAGE DEVELOPMENT

INTRODUCTION

This chapter examines how language develops from infancy to adolescence. How do children acquire language? What is the time course of development? Although there is a clear progression in the course of language development, it is contentious whether or not discrete stages are involved. Are there stages in development?

Children are not born silent: they make vegetative sounds from birth: they cry, burp, and make sucking noises. Around 6 weeks of age they start cooing, and from about 16 weeks old they start to laugh. Between 16 weeks and 6 months they engage in vocal play (Stark, 1986). This involves making speech-like sounds. Vowels emerge before consonants. From about the age of 6–9 months, infants start **babbling**. Babbling is distinguished from vocal play by the presence of true syllables (consonants plus vowels), often repeated. Around 9 months the infant starts noticing that particular strings of sounds co-occur with particular situations (Jusczyk, 1982; MacKain, 1982). For example, whenever the sounds "ball" are heard, a ball is there. Infants might even understand some words as early as 6 months if they refer to very salient, animated figures, such as parents (Tincoff & Jusczyk, 1999). Children start producing their first words around the age of 10 or 11 months. The single words are sometimes thought of as forming single-word utterances. Around the age of 18 months, there is a rapid explosion in vocabulary size, and around this time two-word sentences emerge. This vocabulary explosion and the onset of two-word speech are strongly correlated (Bates, Bretherton, & Snyder, 1988; Nelson, 1973). At this point children may be learning 40 new words a week. Before children produce utterances that are grammatically correct by adult standards, they produce what is called **telegraphic speech**. Telegraphic speech contains a number of words but with many grammatical elements absent (Brown & Bellugi, 1964). As grammatical elements appear, they do so in a relatively fixed order for any particular language. From the age of approximately 2 years 6 months, the child produces increasingly complex sentences (see Figure 4.1). Grammatical development carries on throughout childhood, and we never stop learning new words. It has been estimated that the average young teenager is still learning over 10 new words a day (Landauer & Dumais, 1997).

Carrying out controlled experiments on large numbers of young children to examine their linguistic development can be quite difficult to do. One commonly used technique is known as the **sucking habituation paradigm**. In this procedure, experimenters measure the sucking rate of infants on an artificial teat. Babies prefer novel stimuli, and as they become habituated to the stimulus presented, their rate of sucking declines. If they then detect a change in the stimulus, their sucking rate will increase again. In this way it is possible to measure whether the infants can detect differences between pairs of stimuli. In the preferential-looking technique, researchers examine what children look at when they see scenes depicting sentences they are hearing; children spend longer looking

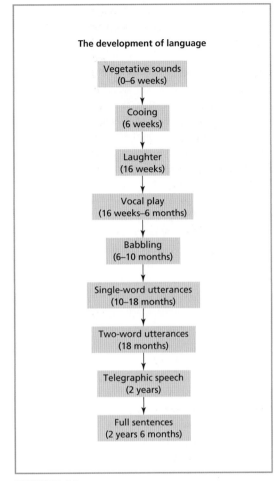

The development of language

Vegetative sounds
(0–6 weeks)

Cooing
(6 weeks)

Laughter
(16 weeks)

Vocal play
(16 weeks–6 months)

Babbling
(6–10 months)

Single-word utterances
(10–18 months)

Two-word utterances
(18 months)

Telegraphic speech
(2 years)

Full sentences
(2 years 6 months)

FIGURE 4.1

at scenes that are consistent with what they hear. In the conditioned head turn technique, infants are taught to turn their heads (by reinforcing them with visual reinforcement of, for example, a brightly lit toy bunny playing drums) whenever there is a change in the stimulus; the conditioning phase is followed by a testing phase that tests what distinctions these infants are capable of making. Cross-sectional studies look at the performance of a group of children at particular ages. One problem with the cross-sectional methodology is that there is enormous linguistic variation between children of the same age. Not only are some children linguistically more advanced, there are also differences in linguistic style between children. Because of this, observational and diary studies have also been important methodologies. Longitudinal studies of individual children, often the experimenters' own, have been particularly influential. One consequence of this is that most of the literature concerns a surprisingly small number of children, and one possible consequence of this is that variation between individuals in development may have been underestimated.

In Chapter 2 we saw that Chomsky distinguished between a speaker's competence, their knowledge of their language, and their actual linguistic performance. For linguists such as Chomsky, the most interesting question about development is how children acquire competence—the ability to judge what is and what is not grammatical. For psycholinguistics, the most interesting question is about how children acquire performance—how they acquire the ability to produce and understand words and sentences. These are different goals, and might be influenced by different factors; our main interest is how children acquire performance.

By the end of this chapter you should:

- Know the time course of language development.
- Understand the difference between rationalism and empiricism.
- Know what drives language development.
- Understand what is meant by a Language Acquisition Device and by Universal Grammar.
- Understand the nature and importance of child-directed speech.
- Know how babbling develops.
- Understand how children learn names for things.
- Understand how children come to learn syntactic categories.
- Know how syntax develops.

WHAT DRIVES LANGUAGE DEVELOPMENT?

What makes language development happen? What transforms a non-speaking, non-comprehending infant into a linguistically competent individual?

One of the most important issues in the study of language development is the extent to which our language abilities are innate. There are two contrasting philosophical views on how humans obtain knowledge. The rationalists (such as Plato and Descartes) maintained that certain fundamental ideas are innate—that is, they are present from birth. The empiricists (such as Locke and Hume) rejected this doctrine of innate ideas, maintaining that all knowledge is derived from experience. Locke (1690/1975) was one of the most influential empiricists. He argued that all knowledge held by the rationalists to be innate could be acquired through experience. According to Locke, the mind at birth is a *tabula rasa*—a "blank sheet of paper"—on which sensations write and determine future behavior. The rationalist–empiricist controversy is alive today: it is often called the nature–nurture debate. Chomsky's work in general and his views on language acquisition are in the rationalist camp, and there are strong empiricist threads in Piaget. (Piaget argued that cognitive structures themselves are not innate, but can arise from innate dispositions.) Behaviorists, who argued that language was entirely learned, are clearly empiricists. Although we must be wary of simplifying the debate by trying to label contrasting views as rationalist or empiricist, the questions of which processes are innate, and which processes must be in place for language to develop, are of fundamental importance. Nevertheless, we must not forget that behavior ultimately results from the interaction of nature and nurture. Work in connectionism has focused attention on the nature of nurture and the way in which learning systems change with experience (Elman et al., 1996).

We should be wary of seeking any simple answer to the question "what drives language development?" The answer is almost certainly that many factors do. It should also be remembered that language development is a complex process that involves the development of many skills, and processes that may be important for syntactic development, for example, might be of less importance in phonological, morphological, or semantic development. Nevertheless, we can tease apart some likely important contributions.

Imitation

The simplest theory of language development is that children learn language by imitating adult language. Although children clearly imitate some aspects of adult behavior, it is clear that imitation cannot by itself be a primary driving force of early language development, and particularly of syntactic development. A cursory examination of the sentences produced by younger children shows that they do not often imitate adults. Children make types of mistakes that adults do not. Furthermore, when children try to imitate what they hear, they are unable to do so unless they already have the appropriate grammatical construction (see examples that follow). Nevertheless, imitation of adult speech (and that of other children) plays an important role in acquiring accent, in the manner of speech, and in the choice of particular vocabulary items. It might also be more important in older children, as we will see below.

Box 4.1 How do humans obtain language?

Rationalist perspective

- originated from the ideas of Plato and Descartes
- based on the premise that certain fundamental ideas are innate
- language capacity is present from birth
- favors nature in the nature–nurture debate
- developed into Chomskian viewpoint

Empiricist perspective

- originated from the ideas of Locke and Hume
- based on the premise that all knowledge is derived from experience
- the newborn is a "*tabula rasa*"—a blank slate
- favors nurture in the nature–nurture debate
- developed into the behaviorist viewpoints and plays an important role in the Piagetian perspective

Conditioning

To what extent can language development be explained by learning alone, using just the processes of reinforcement and conditioning? Skinner's (1957) book *Verbal Behavior* was the classic statement of the behaviorist approach to language. Skinner argued that language was acquired by the same mechanisms of conditioning and reinforcement that were thought at the time to govern all other aspects of animal and human behavior (see Chapter 1). However, there is much evidence against this position.

First, adults (generally) correct only the truth and meaning of children's utterances, not the syntax (Brown & Hanlon, 1970; see Example 1). Indeed, attempts by adults to correct incorrect syntax and phonology usually make no difference. Examples (2) and (3) are from the work of de Villiers and de Villiers (1979). At the age of 18 months their son Nicholas went from correctly producing the word "turtle" to pronouncing it "kurka," in spite of all attempts at correction and clearly being able to produce the constituent sounds. In Example 3 the mother does not correct a blatant grammatical solecism because the meaning is apparent and correct. Parents rarely correct grammar, and if they try to do so the corrections have little effect (see Example 4, from Cazden, 1972). Finally, Example 5 (Fromkin et al., 2011) shows that in some circumstances children are unable to imitate adult language unless they already possess the necessary grammatical constructions.

(1) Child: Doggie [pointing at a horse].
     Adult: No, that's a horsie [stressed].
(2) Adult: Say "Tur."
     Child: Tur.
     Adult: Say "Tle."
     Child: Tle.
     Adult: Say "Turtle."
     Child: Kurka.
(3) Child: Mama isn't boy, he a girl.
     Adult: That's right.
(4) Child: My teacher holded the rabbits and we patted them.
     Adult: Did you say teacher held the baby rabbits?
     Child: Yes.
     Adult: What did you say she did?

Child: She holded the baby rabbits and we patted them.
Adult: Did you say she held them tightly?
Child: No, she holded them loosely.
(5) Adult: He's going out.
     Child: He go out.
     Adult: Adam, say what I say: Where can I put them?
     Child: Where I can put them?

Parents do not always completely ignore grammatically incorrect utterances. They may provide some sort of feedback, in that certain parent–child discourse patterns vary in frequency depending on the grammaticality of the child's utterances (Bohannon, MacWhinney, & Snow, 1990; Bohannon & Stanowicz, 1988; Demetras, Post, & Snow, 1986;

Parents will sometimes correct grammatical errors, particularly by repeating the child's utterance in a grammatically correct form, or by asking a follow-up question that helps the child to rephrase.

Hirsh-Pasek, Treiman, & Schneiderman, 1984; Moerk, 1991; Morgan & Travis, 1989). For example, parents are more likely to repeat the child's incorrect utterance in a grammatically correct form, or to ask a follow-up question (Saxton, 1997). Example (4) exemplifies this. On the other hand, if the child's utterance is grammatically correct, the adults just continue the conversation (Messer, 2000). People from different cultures also respond differently to grammatically incorrect utterances, with some appearing to place more emphasis on correctness (Ochs & Schieffelin, 1995).

Whether this type of feedback is strong enough to have any effect on the course of acquisition is controversial (Marcus, 1993; Morgan & Travis, 1989; Pinker, 1989). Such feedback is probably too infrequent to be effective, although others argue that occasional contrast between the child's own incorrect speech and the correct adult version does enable developmental change (Saxton, 1997). Evidence in favor of this argument is that children are more likely to repeat adults' expansions of their utterances than other utterances, suggesting that they pay particular attention to them (Farrar, 1992). The debate about whether or not children receive sufficient negative evidence (sometimes called the no negative evidence problem), such as information about which strings of words are not grammatical, is important because without negative feedback it is a challenge to specify how children learn to produce only correct utterances. One possible solution is that they rely on mechanisms such as innate principles to help them learn the grammar.

Second, the pattern of acquisition of irregular past verb tenses and irregular plural nouns cannot be predicted by learning theory. Some examples of irregular forms given by children are "gived" for "gave," and "mouses" for "mice." The sequence observed is: correct production, followed by incorrect production, and then later correct production again (Brown, 1973; Kuczaj, 1977). The original explanation for this pattern (but see later) is that the children begin by learning specific instances. They then learn a general rule (e.g., "form past tenses by adding '-ed'"; "form plurals by adding '-s'") but apply it incorrectly by using it in all instances. Only later do they learn the exceptions to the rule. This is an example of what

is called U-shaped development: performance starts off at a good level, but then becomes worse, before improving again. U-shaped development is suggestive of a developing system that has to learn both rules and exceptions to those rules. We examine this type of development in detail later.

The third piece of evidence against a conditioning theory of language learning is that some words (such as "no!") are clearly understood before they are ever produced. Fourth, Chomsky (1959) argued that theoretical considerations of the power and structure of language mean that it cannot be acquired simply by conditioning (see Chapter 2). Finally, in phonological production, babbling is not random, and imitation is not important: The hearing babies of hearing-impaired parents babble normally. In general, language development appears to be strongly based on learning rules rather than simply on learning associations and instances.

Poverty of the stimulus

Can children learn language from what they hear? Chomsky showed that children acquire a set of linguistic rules or grammar. He further argued that they could not learn these rules by environmental exposure alone (Chomsky, 1965). The language children hear was thought to be inadequate in two ways. First, they hear what has been called a degenerate input. The speech children hear is full of

---

Box 4.2 Arguments against the learning theory of language development

- Adults correct mainly the truth and meaning of a child's utterances, rarely the syntax
- Some words are understood before they are produced
- The pattern of acquisition of irregular past tense verbs and irregular plural nouns is U-shaped
- Aspects of the structure of language mean it cannot be acquired simply by conditioning
- In phonological production, babbling is not random and imitation is not important

slips of the tongue, false starts, and hesitations, and sounds run into one another so that the words are not clearly separated. Second, there does not seem to be enough information in the language that children hear for them to be able to learn the grammar. They are not normally exposed to a sufficient number of examples of grammatical constructions that would enable them to deduce the grammar. In particular, they do not hear grammatically defective sentences that are labeled as defective (e.g., "listen, Boris, this is wrong: 'the witch chased to a cave'"). These obstacles to learning language constitute the poverty of the stimulus argument (Berwick, Pietroski, Yankama, & Chomsky, 2011).

Child-directed speech

Adults (particularly mothers) have a special way of talking to children (Snow, 1972, 1994). This special way of talking to children was originally called motherese, but is now called **child-directed speech** (CDS for short), because its use is clearly not limited to mothers. It is commonly known as "baby talk." Adults talk in a simplified way to children, taking care to make their speech easily recognizable. The sentences are to do with the "here-and-now"; they are phonologically simplified (baby words such as "moo-moo" and "gee-gee"); there are more pauses, the utterances are shorter, there is more redundancy, the speech is slower, and it is clearly segmented. There are fewer word endings than in normal speech, the vocabulary is restricted, sentences are shorter, and prosody is exaggerated (Dockrell & Messer, 1999). There is a great deal of repetition in the speech of mothers to their children, and they focus on shared activities (Messer, 1980). Carers are more likely to use nouns at the most common or **basic level** of description (e.g., "dog" rather than "animal"; Hall, 1994). They are also more likely to use words that refer to whole objects (Masur, 1997; Ninio, 1980). Speech is specifically directed towards the child and marked by a high pitch (Garnica, 1977). Furthermore, these differences are more marked the younger the child; hence adults reliably speak in a higher pitch to 2-year-olds than to 5-year-olds. The most important words in sentences receive special emphasis. Although mothers use CDS more, fathers use it too (Hladik & Edwards, 1984). Mothers using sign language also use a form of CDS when signing to their infants, repeating signs, exaggerating them, and presenting them at a slower rate (Masataka, 1996). Even 4-year-old children use CDS when speaking to infants (Shatz & Gelman, 1973). In turn, infants prefer to listen to CDS rather than to normal speech (Fernald, 1991). There appears to be some feedback between the language of the adult carer and that of the child: the vocabulary of carers becomes modified by exposure to the language of the child. The same is not true of syntax, however, suggesting that the adult's CDS directly and causally influences the syntactic development of the child (Huttenlocher, Waterfall, Vasilyeva, Vevea, & Hedges, 2010).

What determines the level of simplification used in CDS? Cross (1977) proposed a linguistic feedback hypothesis, which states that mothers tailor the amount of simplification they provide depending on how much the child appears to need. Counter to this, Snow (1977) pointed out that mothers produce child-directed speech before infants are old enough to produce any feedback on the level of simplification. Instead, she proposed a conversational hypothesis in which what is important is the mother's expectation of what the child needs to know and can understand. Cross, Johnson-Morris, and Nienhuys (1980) found that the form of CDS used to hearing-impaired children suggested that a number of factors might be operating, and that elements of both the feedback and the conversational hypothesis are correct. The form of CDS also interacts in a complex way with the social setting: Maternal speech contains more nouns during toy play, but more verbs during non-toy play (Goldfield, 1993). The nature of CDS also varies with the socioeconomic status of the family, with higher status mothers saying more, using more variety in their language, and using longer utterances. These differences in CDS correlate with subsequent vocabulary development in the child (Hoff, 2003), and might be one reason why the vocabulary and language skills of children from high-status families grow more quickly than those of children from low-status families. (Of course, we cannot rule out genetic factors, as mother and child are genetically very similar.)

According to Goldfield (1993), motherese, or child-directed speech (CDS), tends to contain more nouns during toy play, but more verbs during non-toy play.

The use of child-directed speech gradually fades as the child gets older. It is sensitive to the child's comprehension level rather than production level (Clarke-Stewart, Vanderstoep, & Killian, 1979). Hence speech intended for children is specially marked in order to make it stand out from background noise, and is simplified so that the task of discovering the referents of words and understanding the syntactic structure is easier than it would otherwise be. In this respect Chomsky's claim about children only being exposed to an inadequate input does not hold up to scrutiny.

However, there is some controversy about the difference that CDS actually makes to development. Do children require a syntactically and phonologically simplified input in order to be able to acquire language? The evidence suggests not, although the data are not entirely consistent. Although the use of CDS is widespread, it is not universal across all cultures (Heath, 1983; Ochs & Schieffelin, 1995; Pye, 1986). Furthermore, there is great variation in the styles of social interaction and the form of CDS across different cultures (Lieven, 1994). On the other hand, it is possible that these cultures compensate for the lack of CDS by simplifying language development in other ways, such as emphasizing everyday communal life (Ochs & Schieffelin, 1995; Snow, 1995). Another problem is that the rate of linguistic development is not correlated with the complexity of the children's input (Ellis & Wells, 1980). What seems to be important about CDS is not merely the form of what is said to the children but, perhaps not surprisingly, the content. In particular, the children who learn fastest are those who receive most encouragement and acknowledgment of their utterances. Questioning and directing children's attention to the environment, and particularly to features of the environment that are salient to the child (such as repeated household activities), are also good facilitators of language development. Cross (1978) demonstrated the value of extended replies by adults that amplify the comments of the children. The children who showed the most rapid linguistic development were those whose mothers both asked their children more questions and gave more extensive replies to their children's questions (Howe, 1980).

If the form of CDS makes little difference to linguistic development, why is CDS so widespread? One possibility is that it serves some other function, such as creating and maintaining a bond between the adult and child. Child-directed speech helps establish joint focus. Harris and Coltheart (1986) proposed that the syntactic simplification of CDS is just a side effect of simplifying and restricting content. Needless to say, all these factors might be operative.

In summary, even though CDS might not be necessary for language development, it might nevertheless facilitate it (Pine, 1994b). A child acquiring language on the basis of CDS is going to have a less impoverished input than one not exposed to CDS. If CDS is not necessary, then how do children learn a language on the basis of a degenerate and impoverished input? Chomsky considered it to be impossible that a child could deduce the structure of the grammar solely on the basis of hearing normal language. Something additional is necessary. He argued that the additional factor is that the design of the grammar is innate: Some aspects of syntax must be built into the mind.

THE LANGUAGE ACQUISITION DEVICE

What might be innate in language? Chomsky (1965, 1968, 1986) argued that language acquisition must be guided by innate constraints, and that language is a special faculty not dependent on other cognitive or perceptual processes. It is acquired, he argued, at a time when the child is incapable of complex intellectual achievements, and therefore could not be dependent on intelligence, cognition, or experience. Because the language they hear is impoverished and degenerate, children cannot acquire a grammar by exposure to language alone. Assistance is provided by the innate structure called the **language acquisition device (LAD)**. In Chomsky's later work the LAD is replaced by the idea of **universal grammar**. This is a theory of the primitives and rules of inferences that enable the child to learn any natural grammar. In Chomsky's terminology, it is the set of principles and **parameter**s that constrain language acquisition (see Chapter 2). For Chomsky, language is not learned, but grows.

Obviously languages vary, and children are faced with the task of acquiring the particular details of their language. For Chomsky (1981), this is the process of parameter setting. A parameter is a universal aspect of language that can take on one of a small number of positions, rather like a switch. The parameters are set by the child's exposure to a particular language. Another way of looking at it is that the LAD does not prescribe details of particular languages, but rather sets boundaries on what acquired languages can look like; languages are not free to vary in every possible way, but are restricted. For example, no language yet discovered forms questions by inverting the order of words from the primary (declarative) form of the sentence. The LAD can be thought of as a set of switches that constrain the possible shape of the grammars the child can acquire; exposure to a particular language sets these switches to a particular position. If exposure to the language does not cause these switches to go to a particular position, they stay in the neutral one. Parameters set the core features of

languages. Thus this approach sees language acquisition as parameter setting.

Let us look at a simple example. In languages like Italian, it is possible to drop the pronoun of sentences. For example, it is possible just to say "parla" (speaks). In languages such as English and French, it is not grammatical just to say "speaks"; you must use the pronoun, and say "he speaks." Whether or not you can drop the pronoun in a particular language is an example of a parameter; it is called the pro-drop parameter. English and French are non-pro-drop languages, whereas Italian and Arabic are pro-drop languages. But once the pro-drop parameter is specified, other aspects of the language fall into place. For example, in a pro-drop language such as Italian you can construct subjectless sentences such as "cade la notte" ("falls the night"); in non-pro-drop sentences, you cannot. Instead, you must use the standard word order with an explicit subject ("the rain falls"). Pro-drop languages always permit subjectless sentences, so pro-drop is a generalization about languages (Cook & Newson, 2007).

Is language learning parameter setting?

Is learning language setting parameters? For Chomsky and others who view language acquisition as a process of acquiring a grammar, the basis of which is innate, acquiring a language involves putting the built-in switches (parameters) into the correct positions. One obvious problem with this view is that language development is a slow process, full of errors. Why does it take so long to set these switches? There are two explanations. The continuity hypothesis says that all the principles and parameters are available from birth, but they cannot all be used immediately because of other factors. For example, the child has first to identify words as belonging to particular categories, and be able to hold long sentences in memory for long enough to process them (Clahsen, 1992). The second explanation is that the children do not have immediate access to all their innate knowledge. Instead, it only becomes gradually available over time as a consequence of maturation (Felix, 1992) (see Figure 4.2). There is little agreement about which of these provides the best account of language development.

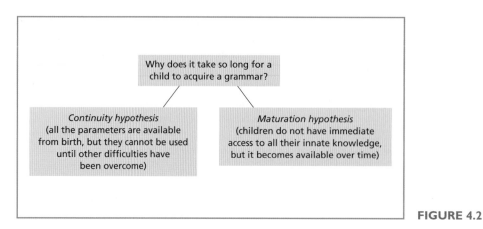

FIGURE 4.2

Another problem is that it has proved difficult to find examples of particular parameters clearly being set in different languages (Maratsos, 1998). In telegraphic speech, English-speaking children often omit pronouns. One possible explanation for this is that they have incorrectly set the parameter for whether or not pronouns should be included in their utterances. At first sight this makes the language look like Italian, but this comparison fails because Italian verbs specify the subject, whereas English ones provide much less information.

Other problems for the parameter-setting theory include how deaf children manage to acquire sign language. There are some indications that similar processes underlie both sign language and spoken language. First, all the milestones in both types of language occur at about the same sort of time. Originally it was thought that because the manual system matures more quickly than the language system, the first signs appeared before the first spoken words (Newport & Meier, 1985; Schlesinger & Meadow, 1972). However, it is possible that people tend to over-interpret gestures by young children, and that in fact signed and spoken words emerge at about the same time (Petitto, 1988). Second, signing children make the same sorts of systematic errors as speaking children at the same time (Petitto, 1987). Hence, although spoken and signed language develop in very similar ways, it is unclear how sign language gestures can be matched to the innate principles and parameters of verbal language. It is also problematic how bilingual children manage to acquire

two languages at the same time, when the languages involved might need to have parameters set to different positions (Messer, 2000).

These are difficult problems for the theory of principles and parameters. To counter them, Chomsky toned down the idea that grammatical rules are abstract, and generally reduced their importance in language acquisition (e.g., Chomsky, 1995).

Linguistic universals

Constraints must be general enough to apply across all languages: clearly innate constraints cannot be specific to a particular language. Instead, there must be aspects of language that are universal. Chomsky argued that there are substantial similarities between languages, and the differences between them are actually quite superficial. Pinker (1994, p. 232), perhaps controversially, suggested that "a visiting Martian would surely conclude that aside their mutually unintelligible vocabularies, Earthlings speak a single language." Although there are 6,000 languages in the world, they all share the same basic structure—and this basic structure is universal grammar.

Linguistic universals are features that can be found in most languages. Chomsky (1968) distinguished between substantive and formal universals. Substantive universals include the categories of syntax, semantics, and phonology that are common to all languages. The presence of the noun and verb categories is an example of a substantive universal, as all languages make this distinction. It is so fundamental that it can arise in the absence of linguistic input. "David," a deaf child with no exposure to sign language, used one type of gesture corresponding to nouns, and another type for verbs (Goldin-Meadow, Butcher, Mylander, & Dodge, 1994). A formal universal concerns the general form of syntactic rules that manipulate these categories. These are universal constraints on the form of syntactic rules. One of the goals of universal grammar is to specify these universals.

An interesting example of a linguistic universal relates to word order. Greenberg (1963) examined word order and morphology in 30 very different languages and found 45 universals, focusing on the normal order of subject, object, and verb (English is a SVO language: its dominant order is subject–verb–object). He noted that we do not appear to find all possible combinations; in particular, there seems to be an aversion to placing the object first. The proportions found are shown in Table 4.1. (Note that in general OVS and VOS languages are very rare, comprising less than 1% of all languages, and although some linguists believe that there are a few OSV languages, there is no consensus; see Pullum, 1981.) Even more striking is the way in which the primary word order has implications for other aspects of a language: it is an example of a parameter. Once primary word order is fixed, other aspects of the language are also fixed. For example, if a language is SVO it will put question words at the beginning of the sentence ("Where is … ?"); if it is SOV, it will put them at the end. SVO languages put prepositions before nouns ("to the dog"), while SOV languages use postpositions after the noun.

TABLE 4.1 Different word orders, as percentages of languages (based on Clark & Clark, 1977).

subject	object	verb	44%
subject	verb	object	35%
verb	subject	object	19%
verb	object	subject	2%
object	verb	subject	0%
object	subject	verb	0%

There are four possible reasons why universals might exist. First, some universals might be part of the innate component of the grammar. There is some evidence for this claim in the way in which parameters set apparently unrelated features of language. For example, at first sight there is no obvious reason why all SVO languages must also put question words at the beginning of a sentence. Second, some universals might be part of an innate component of cognition, which then makes them more likely to be incorporated in some or all languages. For example, 5-month-old infants are sensitive to the conceptual distinction between things that fit tightly and things that fit loosely. Using the standard dishabituation paradigm, infants start to pay attention when there is a change from cylinders in a narrow container to cylinders in a wider container (Bloom, 2004; Hespos & Spelke, 2004). That is, they are sensitive to the conceptual contrast. Some languages (e.g., Korean, which uses different verbs when referring to things fitting tightly compared with things fitting loosely) mark this contrast linguistically, and some (e.g., English) do not. Hurford (2003) argues that the predicate-argument distinction has a neural basis, reflecting distinctions such as that between the "what" and "where" visual processing pathways. Of course, the wider view is that neural systems have evolved to interact with the physical laws of the universal, such as a distinction between mass and movement. Language learning is a process of linking words to universal, pre-existing concepts that enable animals to navigate the world. Third, constraints on syntactic processing make some word orders easier to process than others (Hawkins, 1990). Languages evolve so that they are easy to understand. Fourth, universals might result from strong features of the environment that are imposed on us from birth, and make their presence felt in all languages. Languages make use of important distinctions in the environment. Different languages might pick up on some differences rather than others. In practice it might be very difficult to distinguish between these alternatives. Finally, it should be noted that the notion that there are true universals common to all languages has recently been criticized; instead, it has been argued, there is variation across languages in all ways in which variation is possible (Evans & Levinson, 2009).

The commonly accepted view is that innate mechanisms make themselves apparent very early in development, whereas aspects of grammar that have to be learned develop slowly. Wexler (1998) argued that this does not have to be so. Some parameters are set by exposure to language at a very early age, whereas some innate, universal properties of language can emerge quite late, as a consequence of genetically driven maturation. As evidence for early parameter setting, Wexler observed that children know a great deal about the inflectional structure of their language when they enter the two-word stage (around 18 months). Furthermore, the parameter of word order—whether or not the verb precedes or follows the object, and all that follows from it—is set from the earliest observable stage.

Pidgins and creoles

Further evidence that there is a strong biological drive to learn syntax comes from the study of pidgin and creole languages. **Pidgins** are simplified languages that were created for communication between speakers of different languages who were forced into prolonged contact, such as the result of slavery in places like the Caribbean, the South Pacific, and Hawaii. A **creole** is a pidgin language that has become the native tongue of the children of the pidgin speakers. Whereas pidgins are highly simplified syntactically, creole languages are syntactically rich. They are the spontaneous creation of the first generation of children born into mixed linguistic communities (Bickerton, 1981, 1984). Creoles are not restricted to spoken language: hearing-impaired children develop a creole sign language if exposed to a signing pidgin. A community of deaf children in Nicaragua developed their own sign language from scratch (Kegl, Senghas, & Coppola, 1999). Furthermore, the grammars that different creoles develop are very similar. Deaf children who are not exposed to sign language (because they have non-signing hearing parents) nevertheless spontaneously develop a gesture system that seems to have its own syntax (Goldin-Meadow, Mylander, & Butcher, 1995). They also develop within-gesture structures analogous to characteristics of word morphology. It is as though there is a biological drive to develop syntax, even if it is not present in the adult form of communication to which a child is exposed. Bickerton calls this idea the language bioprogram hypothesis: children have an innate drive to create a grammar that will make a language even in the absence of environmental input.

Genetic linguistics

More evidence that aspects of language are innate comes from studies of the genetic basis of language, genetic linguistics. **Specific language impairment**, or SLI, is a disorder that affects about 5% of the population. SLI is marked by significant problems with spoken language without any obvious accompanying brain damage or problems with hearing, and those affected have IQs in the normal range. Importantly, it runs in families (Gopnik, 1990a, 1990b; Gopnik & Crago, 1991; Leonard, 1989, 2000; Pinker, 2001; Vargha-Khadem, Watkins, Alcock, Fletcher, & Passingham, 1995). For example, the "KE" family of London is a large family spanning three generations where about half the members have some speech or language disorder. Affected members have difficulty controlling their tongues and making speech sounds, but they also have trouble identifying speech sounds, understanding speech, and making judgments about the grammatical acceptability. They have particular difficulty with regular inflections (e.g., forming the plural of nouns by adding an "s" at the end), and a study of the heritability of the disorder suggests that a single dominant gene is involved (Hurst, Baraitser, Auger, Graham, & Norell, 1990). Their language is replete with grammatical errors, particularly involving pronouns. They have difficulty in learning new vocabulary. The speech of the affected people is slow and effortful, and they have difficulty in controlling their facial muscles. Contrary to the earlier reports that were based on quite a small number of items, affected members of the family also have difficulty with irregular inflections. SLI can also cause severe difficulties in language comprehension (Bishop, 1997).

The distribution of the disorder in the family suggests it is caused by a dominant gene (or a set of linked genes) on a non-sex chromosome; the most likely candidate is a segment of chromosome 7 labeled SPCH1 (Fisher, Vargha-Khadem, Watkins, Monaco, & Pembrey, 1998). Study of another person with SLI enabled the disorder to be tied to a specific gene, called FOXP2 (Lai, Fisher, Hurst, Vargha-Khadem, & Monaco, 2001—see also Chapter 3). The FOXP2 seems to play some causal role in the brain circuitry underlying normal language development, including Broca's area; in particular, it seems to be involved in controlling fine movements of the face and articulatory system (Fisher & Marcus, 2006).

Clearly, then, genetic factors affect language proficiency, although there is considerable disagreement about just how specific the grammatical impairment in the KE family actually is. As noted above, Vargha-Khadem and colleagues showed that in fact affected members of the KE family performed poorly on many other language tasks in addition to regular inflection formation (Leonard, 1989; Vargha-Khadem & Passingham, 1990; Vargha-Khadem et al., 1995). Furthermore, systems other than language might also be involved. For example, Tallal, Townsend, Curtiss, and Wulfeck (1991) proposed that children who tended to neglect word endings and other morphological elements did so because of difficulties in temporal processing. There is also debate about whether people with SLI have near-normal IQ on tests of non-verbal performance. Affected members of the KE family scored 18 points lower on performance IQ tests than unaffected members (Vargha-Khadem et al., 1995). Although SLI might have a genetic basis, it is nevertheless to some extent treatable. Members of the KE family learned to compensate for their difficulty in generating syntactically complex sentences by memorizing structures, and by consciously applying rules most of us apply unconsciously.

An alternative view is that SLI is not primarily a disorder of grammar, but arises from impaired sound processing (Joanisse & Seidenberg, 1998). Children with SLI who have syntactic deficits also have difficulty in tasks such as repeating nonwords (such as "slint"), and tasks of phonological awareness, such as recognizing the sound in common in words ("b" in "ball" and "bat"). Joanisse and Seidenberg argued that normal syntactic development has an important phonological component. For example, in order to be able to form the past tense of verbs correctly, you have to be able to accurately identify the final sound of the word. If the final sound of a present tense verb is a voiceless consonant, then you form the past by adding a /t/ sound ("rip" becomes "ripped"). But if it is a voiced consonant then you must add a /d/ sound ("file" becomes "filed"), and if it is an alveolar stop you must add an unstressed vowel as well as a /d/ ("seed" becomes "seeded"). Hence these morphological rules have an important phonological component. Watkins, Dronkers, and Vargha-Khadem (2002) argued that the core deficit in SLI is sequencing sounds, with the problems with inflections and syntactic sequencing secondary to that of sequencing sounds.

The argument about the theoretical importance of SLI hinges on the extent to which these impairments are truly specific to language or to knowledge of grammar. On balance, the evidence suggests that language difficulties can "run in families," but that these difficulties are quite general and not limited to innate knowledge about linguistic rules. The mapping between genes and language is a complex one, but the FOXP2 gene clearly plays an important role.

Formal approaches to language learning

How do children learn the rules of grammar? Most accounts stress the importance of induction in learning rules: Induction is the process of forming a rule by generalizing from specific instances. One aspect of the poverty of the stimulus argument is that children come to learn rules that could not be learned from the input they receive (Lightfoot, 1982). Gold (1967) showed that the mechanism of induction is not sufficiently powerful to enable a language to be learned by itself; the proof of this is known as Gold's theorem. If language learners are presented only with positive data, they can only learn a very limited type of language (known as a Type 3 language—see Chapter 2). They would then not be able to construct sentences with an unlimited number of center embeddings. Human language is substantially more powerful than a Type 3 language. This observation means that, in principle, human language cannot be acquired by induction only from positive exemplars of sentences of the language.

If children cannot learn a language as powerful as human language from positive exemplars of sentences alone, what else do they need? One possibility might be that language learners use negative evidence. This means that the child must generate ungrammatical sentences that must then be explicitly corrected by the parent, or that the parent provides the child with utterances such as "The following sentence is not grammatical: 'The frog kiss the princess.'" As we have seen, the extent to which children use negative data is questionable, and few parents spontaneously produce this type of utterance. Hence Gold's theorem seems to suggest that induction cannot be the only mechanism of language acquisition. The explanation given most frequently is that it is supplemented with innate information. The area of research that examines the processes of how language learning might occur is known as learnability theory or formal learning theory.

Pinker (1984) attempted to apply learnability theory to language development. He placed a number of constraints on acquisition. First, the acquisition mechanisms must begin with no specific knowledge of the child's native language—that is, the particular language to be learned. Pinker emphasized the continuity between the grammar of the child and the adult grammar. He argued that the child is innately equipped with a large number of the components of the grammar, including parameters that are set by exposure to a particular language. He also argued that the categories "noun" and "verb" are innate, as is a predisposition to induce rules. Even though children are supplied with these categories, they still have to assign words to them, which is not a trivial problem. Pinker argued that the linking rule that links a syntactic category such as "noun" to a thematic role—the role the word is playing in the meaning of the sentence—must be innate.

More general innate accounts

Other researchers agree that the child must come to language learning with innate help, but this assistance need not be the language-specific information incorporated in universal grammar. Slobin (1970, 1973, 1985) argued that children are not born with structural constraints such as particular categories, but with a system of processing strategies that guide their inductions. He emphasized the role of general cognitive development. Slobin examined a great deal of cross-cultural evidence, and proposed a number of processing strategies that could account for this acquisition process (see Box 4.3). For Slobin, certain cognitive functions are privileged; for example, the child tries to map speech first onto objects and events. In a similar vein, Taylor and Taylor (1990) listed a number of factors that characterize language acquisition (Box 4.4). These principles apply to learning other skills as well. Of course, other factors (albeit biological, cognitive, or social) may in turn underlie these principles.

Problems with innate accounts of language acquisition

The controversy about innateness is how much of language is innate, and how language-specific the innate information has to be. A study of a large

---

Box 4.3 Some general principles of acquisition (based on Slobin, 1973)

1. Pay attention to the ends of words
2. The phonological form of words can be systematically modified
3. Pay attention to the order of morphemes and words
4. Avoid interruption or rearrangement of units
5. Underlying semantic relations should be clearly marked
6. Avoid exceptions
7. The use of grammatical markers should make semantic sense

Box 4.4 Pragmatic factors affecting acquisition (based on Taylor & Taylor, 1990)

- Simple and short before complex and long
- Gross before subtle distinctions
- Perceptually salient (in terms of size, color, etc.) first
- Personal before non-personal
- Here and now before those displaced in time and space
- Concrete before abstract
- Frequent and familiar before less frequent and unfamiliar
- Regular before irregular forms (though interacts with frequency)
- Items in isolation before capturing relationships
- Whole first, then analyzed into parts, then mature whole

where the principles come from and how they work: for example, by showing which genes control language development and how. As Braine (1992) asked, exactly how do we get from genes laid down at conception to syntactic categories 2½ years later? We are a long way away from being able to answer this question.

Nativist accounts tend not to give enough emphasis to the importance of the social precursors of language. It is possible that social factors can do a great deal of the work for which innate principles have been proposed. Researchers who are opposed to nativist theories argue that the learning environment is much richer than the nativists suppose: in particular, children are presented with feedback. Deacon (1997) argues that the structure of language itself facilitates learning it: Language has evolved so that it has become easy to learn.

An alternative to innate knowledge: Distributional information

The alternative to innate knowledge about language is that there is sufficient information in the input for children to be able to learn language. Connectionist modeling provides an alternative account of these phenomena, showing how complex behavior can emerge from the interaction of many simpler processes without the need to specify innate language-specific knowledge (e.g., Elman, 1999; Elman et al., 1996). Modeling emphasizes the role of the actual linguistic input to which children are exposed. In addition, as we will see, there is now a considerable amount of evidence that infants make use of information about the distribution of sounds and words in what they hear. The central idea is that children make use of general-purpose associative learning mechanisms (Gomez & Gerken, 2000). Often they seem able to learn a great deal about linguistic form without knowing the meaning of what they are listening to. (This idea is particularly apparent in the studies that show children can learn patterns and rules in artificial languages that do not have meaning.) This finding suggests that meaning need not precede form.

number of same-sex twins found that vocabulary and grammatical abilities are correlated at the ages of 2 and 3, suggesting that the same genetic factors influence both abilities (Dionne, Dale, Boivin, & Plomin, 2003). Such results suggest that the innate basis of language is very general. To some extent the debate is no longer simply about whether nature or nurture is more important, but about the precise mechanisms involved, and the extent to which general cognitive or biological constraints determine the course of language development.

Many people consider there is something unsatisfactory about specific innate principles. Having to resort to saying that something is innate is rather negative, because it is easy to fall back on a nativist explanation if it is not easy to see a non-nativist alternative. This is not always a fair criticism, but it is important to be explicit about which principles are innate and how they operate. Innate principles are also difficult to prove. The best way of countering those researchers who see this as a negative approach would be to show

Elman (1993) showed that networks could learn grammars with some of the complexities of English. In particular, the networks could learn to analyze embedded sentences, but only if they were first trained on non-embedded sentences, or were given a limited initial working memory that was gradually increased. This modeling shows the importance of starting on small problems that reflect the types of sentences to which young children are in practice exposed. It also provides support for Newport's (1990) idea, called the less-is-more theory, that initially limited cognitive resources might actually help children to acquire language, rather than hinder them. In a study involving how easily adults learned an artificial language, Kersten and Earles (2001) found that adults learned the artificial language better when they were initially presented with only small segments of the language than when they were exposed to the full complexity of the language from the beginning. On the other hand, making the task more realistic by introducing semantic information into the modeling suggests that starting small provides less of an advantage than when syntactic information alone is considered. Indeed "starting small," or "less is more," might actually hinder development with more naturalistic inputs to the learning system (Rohde & Plaut, 1999). In any case, connectionist modeling shows that explicit negative syntactic information might not be needed to acquire a grammar in the absence of innate information—there might after all be sufficient information in the sentences children actually hear.

It should be pointed out, however, that these connectionist networks have only modeled grammars approaching the complexity of natural language. In general, it is debatable whether the constraints necessary to acquire language in the face of Gold's theorem need to arise from innate language-specific information, or can be satisfied by more general constraints on the developing brain, or by the social and linguistic environment (Elman et al., 1996).

Nevertheless, adults and children are able to extract at least some syntactic structure on the basis of exposure to statistical information alone. Saffran (2001, 2002) tested adults and 6–9-year-old children on an artificial language and then asked them to decide whether test items followed the rules of the language or not. Both groups learned the structure of the language (e.g., that an A phrase consists of an A-type word plus a B-type word) by extracting predictive dependencies—that some things consistently go with other things. Interestingly, similar results were found with non-linguistic sounds and even in the visual modality, suggesting that these learning mechanisms are not specific to language. Very young children are also able to extract structure from what they hear. Seven-month-old infants attend longer to sentences with unfamiliar structures than to sentences with familiar structures (Marcus, Vijayan, Rao, & Vishton, 1999). Marcus et al. tested children on sequences in an artificial language where simple counting or statistical mechanisms would not suffice to learn the rule generating the sequence because they heard new items. For example, suppose you hear items like "ga ti ga" and "li na li" repeated several times. You then hear the new item "wo fe wo"; this item does not generate surprise, because it conforms to the rule you have inducted (sequences must be of the form ABA). If, however, you hear "wo fe fe" you might be surprised, and pay more attention, because this stimulus does not conform to the rule. Marcus et al. found that the 7-month-olds behaved in the same way. So very young children are able to extract abstract rules from very little input. There is, however, some debate as to what counts as a "rule," and the extent to which connectionist networks can model this behavior using only simple statistical mechanisms (Christiansen & Curtin, 1999; Seidenberg & Elman, 1999; see Marcus, 1999, for a reply).

HOW CHILDREN DEVELOP LANGUAGE

Many things drive language development: genes, the environment, and particularly social interaction. The main issue is the extent to which children need genetically encoded language-specific information, rather than general-purpose learning mechanisms. We should note that learning mechanisms change as the child grows: Connectionist modeling has focused attention on the way in which learning systems change with experience. Finally, we should remember that the balance of the driving forces for phonological, syntactic, semantic, and pragmatic development might be very different.

Do children learn any language in the womb?

Children do not start speaking at birth because they need some exposure to language before they can start using it, and because other processes (e.g., sound perception, vision, brain maturation, and social interaction) have to reach some level of ability first. But children do start learning language before birth. The mother's womb provides shelter, but it does not exclude all stimuli from the outside world. Sounds including language penetrate the uterus, and the baby in the womb can hear those sounds, although speech sounds different; in particular, the amniotic fluid prevents the higher frequencies from reaching the baby. Indeed, only sounds up to 1,000 Hz (cycles per second) will get through to the baby. In comparison, people with normal hearing can hear frequencies up to 20,000 Hz; speech contains sounds in the range of 100 to 4,000 Hz; and telephones only convey sounds up to 3,000 Hz: so the speech the fetus hears will sound very muffled (Altmann, 1997).

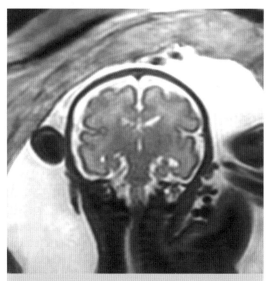

Fetus' brain. Colored magnetic resonance imaging (MRI) scan of a coronal section through the brain (center) of a 25-week-old fetus in its mother's womb. At 25 weeks the connections within the fetus' brain are developing, especially in the areas responsible for emotions, perception, and conscious thought. The fetus is also able to hear at this stage.

In spite of the impoverished nature of the sounds that reach the baby in the womb, there is a substantial amount of evidence that there is still sufficient information for the baby to be able to learn something from those sounds (Gomez & Gerken, 2000). DeCasper and Spence (1986) asked a group of pregnant women to read aloud a short story every day for the final 6 weeks of their pregnancies. After the babies were born, DeCasper and Spence tested the babies to see if they could distinguish the story that they had heard in the womb from another story. Discovering what very young infants can and cannot do, and what they want and do not want to do, is obviously very difficult. You cannot just ask a newborn baby "have you heard this story before?" One of the most commonly used techniques to investigate the preferences of young infants is called non-nutritive sucking. In this technique, the infant sucks on a teat that controls the presentation of a stimulus. Babies learn very quickly to adapt their rate of sucking to control the presentation of the stimulus. They might have to suck quickly to obtain one stimulus, and slowly to obtain another. DeCasper and Spence showed that the infants preferred to listen to the story to which they had been exposed in the womb, rather than a new story. Importantly, they preferred the story that they had heard before even if it was spoken by someone other than their mother. So in the womb they must have learned some characteristic of the language, rather than just having become familiar with a particular voice.

Another study by DeCasper, Lecanuet, Maugais, Granier-Deferre, and Busnel (1994) supports the same conclusion. The mothers read aloud a story every day between the 34th and 38th weeks of pregnancy. The experimenters then played a story to the fetus directly through the mother's abdomen (so the mother was unaware of what was played). They monitored changes in the heart rate of the fetus, and found that it decreased when the familiar story was played, but not when an unfamiliar story was played.

These experiments show that infants in the womb learn something about the spoken language around them. Given the muffled nature of what they hear, it is unlikely to be anything very specific. So what might it be? One possibility is suggested by a study by Mehler et al. (1988). These researchers played tapes of French speech to 4-day-old babies. They used a variant of the sucking habituation technique, and found that the babies sucked until the novelty wore off. When the sucking rate fell, they switched to playing Russian speech. The speech was recorded from a bilingual French–Russian speaker, so there were no differences in voice. The sucking rate increased again. The same result was found if the tapes were played the other way round. Hence the newborn babies could detect the change of language.

What characteristics of the languages do babies pay attention to such that they can detect changes? In another experiment, Mehler et al. (1988) played the babies tapes of language that had been filtered to remove high frequencies. We depend on the high-frequency sounds to be able to recognize individual sounds. The babies still detected the change. So it is unlikely that they were distinguishing the languages just on the basis of the repertoire of sounds. Instead, the babies must have detected the different prosodies of the two languages. Prosody is the collective name given to all the information about languages that span individual sounds. One important aspect of prosody is stress, which determines the rhythm and emphasis of speech. Another important aspect is intonation, the way in which the pitch of speech rises and falls, which determines the melody of language. When we ask a question, we use a different intonation than when we make a statement—the pitch rises at the end of questions. These studies show that babies in the womb, and at birth, can detect changes in prosody. Sensitivity to prosody is important because it later helps children distinguish and identify the sounds of language.

PHONOLOGICAL DEVELOPMENT

Infants appear to be sensitive to speech sounds from a very early age. As we saw in Chapter 3, there is some evidence that the infant brain is lateralized to some degree from birth. How does the child's ability to hear and produce language sounds develop?

Early speech perception

Even though they have not yet started to talk, babies have surprisingly sophisticated speech-recognition abilities. Prelinguistic infants have complex perceptual systems that can make subtle phonetic distinctions. Using the techniques described at the start of the chapter, it has been shown that from birth children are sensitive to speech sounds, as distinct from non-speech sounds. Indeed, it has been argued that infants between 1 and 4 months of age, and perhaps even younger, are sensitive to all the acoustic differences later used to signal phonetic distinctions (Eimas, Miller, & Jusczyk, 1987). For example, they are capable of the categorical perception of voicing, place, and manner of articulation (see Chapter 2). Cross-linguistic studies, which compare the abilities of infants growing up with different linguistic backgrounds, show common categorizations by infants, even when there are differences in the phonologies of the adult language. Eimas, Siqueland, Jusczyk, and Vigorito (1971) showed that infants as young as 1 month old could distinguish between two syllables that differed in only one distinctive phonological feature (e.g., whether or not the vocal cords vibrate, as in the sound [ba] compared with the sound [pa]). Eimas et al. played the different sounds and found they could elicit changes in sucking rate. Furthermore they found that perception was categorical, as the infants were only sensitive to changes in voice onset time that straddled the adult boundaries: that is, the categories used by the babies were the same as those used by adults. This suggests that these perceptual mechanisms might be innate.

From an early age, infants discriminate sounds from each other regardless of whether or not these sounds are to be found in the surrounding adult language. The innate perceptual abilities are then modified by exposure to the adult language. For example, Werker and Tees (1984) showed that infants born into English-speaking families in Canada could make phonetic distinctions present in Hindi at the age of 6 months, but this ability declined rapidly over the next 2 months. A second example is that 2-month-old Kikuyu infants in Africa can distinguish between [p] and [b]. If not used in the language into which they are growing up, this ability is lost by about the age of 1 year or even less (Werker & Tees, 1984). (Adults can learn to make these distinctions again, so these findings are more likely to reflect a reorganization of processes rather than complete loss of ability.)

Infants are sensitive to features of speech other than phonetic discriminations. Neonates (newborn infants) aged 3 days prefer the mother's voice to that of others (DeCasper & Fifer, 1980; see above). From an early age, infants can distinguish languages as long as they are rhythmically distinct enough; newborn French infants can distinguish British English from Japanese, but not from Dutch (Nazzi, Bertoncini, & Mehler, 1998). The sensitivity of babies to language extends beyond simple sound perception. Infants aged 8 months are sensitive to cues such as the location of important syntactic boundaries in speech (Hirsh-Pasek et al., 1987). Hirsh-Pasek et al. inserted pauses into speech recorded from a mother speaking to her child. Infants oriented longer to speech where the pauses had been inserted at important syntactic boundaries than when the pauses had been inserted within the syntactic units. The infant appears early on to be identifying acoustic correlates of clauses (such as their prosodic form—the way in which intonation rises and falls, and stress is distributed).

One of the major difficulties facing children learning language is how to segment fluent speech they hear into words. Words run together in speech; they are rarely delineated from each other by pauses. Young children probably make use of several strategies in order to be able to segment the speech stream. Child-directed speech may help the child learn how to segment speech. For example, carers put more pauses in between words in speech to young children than in speech to other adults. Children are further aided by the great deal of information present in the speech stream. **Distributional information** about phonetic segments is an important cue in learning to segment speech (Cairns, Shillcock, Chater, & Levy, 1997; Christiansen, Allen, & Seidenberg, 1998). Distributional information concerns the way in which sounds co-occur in a language. For example, we do not segment speech so that a word

begins with a sequence like /mp/ because this is not a legitimate string of sounds at the start of English words. Similarly the sounds within words such as "laughing" and "loudly" frequently co-occur by virtue of these being words; the sounds "ingloud" occur much less frequently together— only when words like "laughing loudly" are spoken adjacently. This type of low co-occurrence information provides a way of dividing the speech stream. On the other hand, the sounds making up "mother" co-occur very frequently; hence the way in which sounds cluster together is another important cue. Cairns et al. (1997) and Batchelder (2002) showed that it is relatively straightforward to construct a computational model that learns to segment English and other languages using distributional information. Of course, once a child has successfully segmented a few words, it becomes progressively easier to segment the rest of the speech stream. This idea of using a little information to uncover more of the same is known as **bootstrapping**—by analogy to the idea of trying to pull yourself up by your own bootstraps. Bootstrapping is an important theme in language acquisition. Batchelder's computational model (called BootLex) shows how useful bootstrapping is. Furthermore, infants do seem to be sensitive to this sort of distributional information. Saffran, Aslin, and Newport (1996) found that 8-month-old infants very quickly learn to discriminate words in a stream of syllables on the basis of which sounds tend to occur together regularly. Once they have learned the words, they then listen longer to novel stimuli than to the words presented in the stream of syllables. Children probably use both divisional and clustering distributional information at some time.

Although children can segment speech on the basis of statistical information alone, their performance is much better if they can make use of other types of information. Eight-month-old babies also make use of speech-specific information, including phonotactic cues such as co-articulation—the way in which sounds change in the presence of other sounds (Johnson & Jusczyk, 2001; Mattys & Jusczyk, 2001). For example, Mattys and Jusczyk found that 9-month-old infants turned and looked longer at the source of a sound producing consonant–vowel–consonant triplets with good phonotactic cues to a word boundary than triplets without these cues. For example, the triplet "gaffe" stands out more if it is preceded by "bean" (the good phonotactic cue) than "fang" (the neutral cue). A single, isolated consonant is not a viable word; hence adults segment speech in such a way as to avoid creating isolated consonants. Measuring the time children spent listening to stimuli, Johnson, Jusczyk, Cutler, and Norris (2003) found that 12-month-old children use the same strategy. Hence, from an early age children segment speech so as to avoid creating isolated units that could not be words. In addition, very young infants also seem to be sensitive to the prosody of language. Prosodic information concerns the pitch of the voice, its loudness, and the length of sounds. Neonates prefer to listen to parental rather than non-parental speech. Using the sucking habituation technique, Mehler et al. (1988) showed that infants as young as 4 days old can distinguish languages from one another. Infants prefer to listen to the language spoken by their parents. For example, six babies born to French-speaking mothers preferred to listen to French rather than Russian. The likely explanation for this is that the child learns the prosodic characteristic of the language in the womb. Sensitivity to prosody helps the infant to identify legal syllables of their language (Altmann, 1997). After some months' exposure to a language, infants learn to make use of knowledge of lexical stress in identifying words; for example, children growing up exposed to English adopt a stress initial syllable strategy, enabling them to identify when a new word is starting (Curtin, Mintz, & Christiansen, 2005; Thiessen & Saffran, 2007).

Just because some mechanisms of speech perception are innate, it does not follow that they are necessarily language- or even species-specific. All children need is a general-purpose learning algorithm that helps them detect statistical regularities. Kuhl (1981) showed that chinchillas (a type of South American rodent) display categorical perception of syllables such as "da" and "ta" in the same way as humans do. The cotton-top tamarin, a type of New World monkey, can segment a sequence of sounds based on distributional information, with some sequences being more common than others, just like human infants (Hauser, Newport, & Aslin, 2001). However, even if animals can perform these perceptual distinctions, it does not necessarily follow that the perceptual mechanisms they employ are identical to those of humans, and, furthermore, humans possess language abilities that go far beyond categorical perception and speech-stream segmentation.

Finally, for a while children actually regress in their speech perception abilities (Gerken, 1994): The ability of young children to discriminate sounds is worse than that of infants. In part this regression might be an artifact of using more stringent tasks to test older children: Tests for infants just involve discriminating new sounds from old ones, but tests for older children require them to match particular sounds. It might also occur because of a change in focus of the child's language-perception system. Infants aged 14 months do not attend to fine phonetic detail (e.g., "bih" versus "dih") when learning new words, though children aged 8 months are capable of discriminating these sounds in a perception task (Stager & Werker, 1997). When children know only a few words, it might be possible to represent them in terms of rather gross characteristics; indeed, limiting the amount of detail to which you need to attend might be advantageous. But as children grow older and acquire more words, they are forced to represent words in terms of their detailed sound structure. Hence, early on—perhaps up to a vocabulary size of about 50 words—detailed sound contrasts are not yet needed by the child (Gerken, 1994). Perceptual skills, experience, and the task at hand all interact to determine performance.

Young children quickly become very good at speech recognition. Children aged 18 months can identify a large number of words without having to hear the whole word: the first 300 ms is sufficient, as shown by studies looking at children's eye movements to pictures of objects while listening to speech (Fernald, Swingley, & Pinto, 2001). Once children have made a start on segmentation, "bootstrapping" can come into play: they can use their existing knowledge to facilitate the acquisition of new knowledge (Werker & Yeung, 2005). PRIMIR (Processing

Rich Information from Multidimensional Interactive Representations) is a model that emphasizes the role of bootstrapping in early word learning (Werker & Curtin, 2005). Although children continue to perceive phonetic variations in the speech stream, by 17 months old they have learned a sufficient number of word–object pairings to enable them to focus on the phonological distinctions that are important for distinguishing new words.

Babbling

From about the age of 6 months to 10 months, before infants start speaking, they make speech-like sounds known as babbling. Babbling is clearly more language-like than other early vocalizations such as crying and cooing, and consists of strings of vowels and consonants combined into sometimes lengthy series of syllables, usually with a great deal of repetition, such as "bababa gugugu," sometimes with an apparent intonation contour. There are two types of babbling (Oller, 1980). Reduplicated babble is characterized by repetition of consonant–vowel syllables, often producing the same pair for a long time (e.g., "bababababa"). Non-reduplicated or variegated babble is characterized by strings of non-repeated syllables (e.g., "bamido"). Babbling lasts for 6–9 months, fading out as the child produces the first words. It appears to be universal: deaf infants also babble (Sykes, 1940), although it is now known that they produce slightly different babbling patterns. This suggests that speech perception plays some role in determining what is produced in babbling (Oller, Eilers, Bull, & Carney, 1985). Across many languages, the 12 most frequent consonants constitute 95% of babbled consonants (Locke, 1983), although babbling patterns differ slightly across languages, again suggesting that speech perception determines some aspects of babbling (de Boysson-Bardies, Halle, Sagart, & Durand, 1989; de Boysson-Bardies, Sagart, & Durand, 1984).

What is the relation between babbling and later speech? The continuity hypothesis (Mowrer, 1960) states that babbling is a direct precursor of language—in babbling the child produces all of the sounds that are to be found in all of the world's languages. This range of sounds is then gradually narrowed down, by reinforcement by parents and others of some sounds but not others (and by the lack of exposure to sounds not present within a particular language), to the set of sounds in the relevant language. (The extreme version of this of course is the behaviorist account of language development discussed earlier: Words are acquired by the processes of reinforcement and shaping of random babbling sounds.) For example, a parent might give the infant extra food when he or she makes a "ma" sound, and progressively encourages the child to make increasingly accurate approximations to sounds and words in their language. There are a number of problems with the continuity hypothesis. Many sounds, such as consonant clusters, are not produced at all in babbling, and also parents are not that selective about what they reinforce in babbling: they encourage all vocalization (Clark & Clark, 1977). Nor does there appear to be much of a gradual shift towards the sounds particular to the language to which the child is exposed (Locke, 1983).

The discontinuity hypothesis states that babbling bears no simple relation to later development. Jakobson (1968) postulated two stages in the development of sounds. In the first stage children babble, producing a wide range of sounds that do not emerge in any particular order and that are not obviously related to later development. The second

According to Mowrer (1960), babbling is a direct precursor of language. The range of babbling sounds is gradually narrowed down over time by reinforcement by the carer of some sounds but not others.

stage is marked by the sudden disappearance of many sounds that were previously in their repertoires. Some sounds are dropped temporarily, re-emerging perhaps many months later, whereas some are dropped altogether. Jakobson argued that it is only in this second stage that children are learning the phonological contrasts appropriate to their particular language, and these contrasts are acquired in an invariant order. However, the idea that from the beginning babbling contains the sounds of all the world's languages is not true: the early babbling repertoire is quite limited (Hoff-Ginsberg, 1997). For example, the first consonants tend to be just the velar ones (/k/ and /g/). Furthermore, although Jakobson observed that there was a silent period between babbling and early speech, there is probably some overlap (Menyuk, Menn, & Silber, 1986). Indeed, there seem to be some phonological sequences that are repeated that are neither clearly babbling nor words. These can be thought of as protowords. Early words might be embedded in variegated babble. There are preferences for certain phonetic sequences that are found later in early speech (Oller, Wieman, Doyle, & Ross, 1976). This points to some continuity between babbling and early speech.

Thus there is no clear evidence for either the continuity or the discontinuity hypothesis. What then is the function of babbling? Perhaps babbling has a motor origin, for example, in practice at gaining control over the articulatory tract (Clark & Clark, 1977; MacNeilage & Davis, 2000). Perhaps infants are learning to produce the prosody of their language rather than particular sounds (Crystal, 1986; de Boysson-Bardies et al., 1984). It is worth noting that children exposed to sign language "babble" on their hands, reinforcing the view that there is a strong biological drive to produce babble, and that babbling does more than enable motor control over the mouth and jaw (Petitto & Marentette, 1991). Interestingly, hearing babies who are exposed just to sign language produce a different pattern of sign-babbling from those exposed to sign language and speech (Petitto, Holowka, Sergio, Levy, & Ostry, 2004). This difference suggests that babbling does have some specifically linguistic component to its origin, allowing babies to discover how sounds are related and contrasted to each other.

Later phonological development

Early speech uses fewer sounds compared with the babbling of just a few months before, but it contains some sounds that were only rarely or not all produced then (particularly clusters of consonants, e.g., "str"). Words are also often changed after they have been mastered. Children appear to be hypothesis testing, with each new hypothesis necessitating a change in the pronunciation of words already mastered, either directly as a consequence of trying out a new rule, or indirectly as a result of a shift of attention to other parts of the word.

Jakobson (1968) proposed that the way in which children learn the contrasts between sounds is related to the sound structure of languages. For example, the sounds /p/ and /b/ are contrasted by the time the vocal cords start to vibrate after the lips are closed. He argued that children learn the contrasts in a universal order across languages. He also argued that the order of acquisition of the contrasts is predictable from a comparison of the languages of the world: The phonological contrasts that are most widespread are acquired first, whereas those that are to be found in only a few languages are acquired last.

One weakness of this approach is that because the theory emphasizes the acquisition of contrasts, other features of phonological development are missed or cannot be explained (Clark & Clark, 1977; Kiparsky & Menn, 1977). For example, even when children have acquired the contrast between one pair of voiced and unvoiced consonants (/p/ and /b/) and between a labial and a velar consonant (/p/ and /k/), they are often unable to combine these contrasts to produce the voiced velar consonant (/g/). So just knowing the contrasts does not seem to be enough. There are also exceptions that counter any systematic simplification of a child's phonological structure. Children can often produce a word containing a particular phonological string when all other similar words are simplified or omitted. For example, Hildegard could say the word "pretty" when she simplified all her other words and used no consonant clusters (such as "pr") at all (Clark & Clark, 1977; Leopold, 1939–1949).

Output simplification

Young children simplify the words they produce (see Figure 4.3). Smith (1973) described four ways in which children do this, with a general tendency towards producing shorter strings. Young children often omit the final consonant, they reduce consonant clusters, they omit unstressed syllables, and they repeat syllables. For example, "ball" becomes "ba," "stop" becomes "top," and "tomato" becomes "mado." Younger children often substitute easier sounds (such as those in the babbling repertoire) for more difficult sounds (those not to be found in the babbling repertoire). Simplification is found in all languages.

Why do young children simplify words? There are a number of possible explanations. The memory of young children is not so limited that this degree of simplification is necessary (Clark & Clark, 1977). Children must have some representation of the correct sounds, because they can still correctly perceive the sounds they cannot yet produce (Smith, 1973). Jakobson (1968) argued that one reason why this happens is because the child has not yet learned the appropriate phonological contrasts. For example, a child might sometimes produce "fis" instead of "fish" because he or she has not yet mastered the distinction between alveolar and postalveolar fricatives (which captures the distinction between the /s/ and /sh/ sounds). This explanation cannot be the complete story, because there are too many exceptions, and because children are at least aware of the contrasts even if they cannot always apply them.

A second explanation of output simplification is that children are using phonological rules to change the perceived forms into ones that they can produce (Menn, 1980; Smith, 1973). As children sometimes alternate between different forms of simplification, the rules they use would have to be applied non-deterministically. A third possibility is that simplification is a by-product of the development of the speech production system (Gerken, 1994). It is likely that all of these factors play some role.

LEXICAL AND SEMANTIC DEVELOPMENT

Words are produced from the age of about 1 year. New words are added slowly in the first year, so that by the age of 18–24 months the child has a vocabulary of about 50 words. Around this point the vocabulary explosion occurs. Nelson (1973) examined the first 10 words produced by children and found that the categories most commonly referred to were important person names, animals, food, and toys. However, children differ greatly in their earliest words. Indeed, Nelson was able to divide the children into two broad groups based on the types of early words produced: children in the

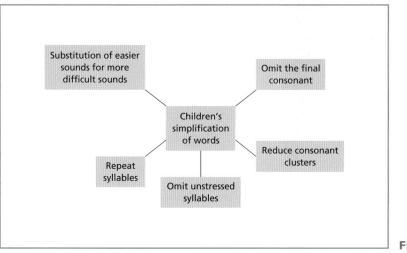

FIGURE 4.3

"expressive style" group emphasize people and feelings, while children in the "referential style" group emphasize objects. These differences probably arise for several reasons. Nelson argued that they arise because of differences in what children think language is for: Children who think language is primarily for labeling objects are likely to be referential, while those who think it is for social interaction are likely to be more expressive. The differences also probably reflect differences in language use by the parents; some parents spend a great deal of time producing object labels for their children, and such children tend to fall in the referential style group (Pine, 1994a). It was once thought that the referential style led to faster language development; however, when you take into account factors such as vocabulary size and the age at which children produce the first word (both types of children reach 50 words at the same age, but as the referential children tend to produce their first word later, they appear to rush faster towards that limit), there is no obvious difference in subsequent development (Bates et al., 1994; Hoff-Ginsberg, 1997).

Some children's first words tend to refer to objects ("referential") whereas some children's are more likely to refer to people and feelings ("expressive").

Greenfield and Smith (1976) found that early words may refer to many different roles, not just objects, and further proposed that the first utterances may always name roles. For example, the early word "mama" might be used to refer to particular actions carried out by the mother, rather than to the mother herself. Generally, the earliest words can be characterized as referring either to things that move (such as people, animals, vehicles) or things that can be moved (such as food, clothes, toys). Moving things tend to be named before movable things. Places and the instruments of actions are very rarely named.

There is some debate as to whether the earliest referential words may differ in their use and representation from later ones (McShane, 1991). In particular, the child's earliest use of reference (what things refer to) appears to be qualitatively different from later use. The youngest children name objects spontaneously or give names of objects in response to questions quite rarely, in marked contrast to their behavior at the end of the second year.

It would be surprising if children got the meanings of words right every time. Consider the size of the task facing very young children. A mother says to a baby sitting in a pram and looking out of the window: "Isn't the moon pretty?" How, from all the things in the environment, does the child pick out the correct referent for "moon"? That is, how does the child know what the word goes with in the world? It is not even immediately obvious that the referent is both an object and an object the infant can see. Even when the child has picked out the appropriate referent, substantial problems remain. He or she has to learn that "moon" refers to the object, not some property such as "being silver colored" or "round." What are the properties of the visual object that are important? The child has to learn that the word "moon" refers to the same thing, even when its shape changes (from crescent to full moon). The task, then, of associating names with objects and actions is an enormous one, and it is surprising that children are as good at acquiring language as they are. Errors are therefore only to be expected. Sentences (6) and (7) are examples of errors in acquiring meaning from Clark and Clark (1977):

(6) Mother pointed out and named a dog "bow-wow."

Child later applies "bow-wow" to dogs, but also to cats, cows, and horses.

(7) Mother says sternly to child: "Young man, you did that on purpose."

When asked later what "on purpose" means, child says: "It means you're looking at me."

What are the features that determine the child's first guess at the meaning of words? How do the first guesses become corrected so that they converge on the way adults use words? The errors that children make turn out to be a rich source of evidence about how they learn word meaning.

Clark and Clark (1977) argued that, in the very earliest stages of development, the child must start with two assumptions about the purpose of language: Language is for communication, and language makes sense in context. From then on they can form hypotheses about what the words mean, and develop strategies for using and refining those meanings.

The emergence of early words

Children's semantic development is dependent on their conceptual development. They can only map meanings into the concepts they have available at that time. In this respect, linguistic development must follow cognitive development. Of course, not all concepts may be marked by simple linguistic distinctions. We don't have different words for brown dogs as opposed to black dogs. There must surely be some innate processes, if only to categorize objects, so the child is born with the ability to form concepts. Quinn and Eimas (1986) suggest that categorization is part of the innate architecture of cognition.

However, children's early vocabularies cannot be predicted just on the basis of the words they hear. Their vocabularies contain many more names for objects than are present in the speech directed towards them (Bloom, 2001a). Clearly

there is some bias in learning, and one of the goals of understanding semantic development is to work out how this bias arises.

The first words emerge out of situations where an exemplar of the category referred to by the word is present in the view of parent and child (see Chapter 3 on the social precursors of language). However, there are well-known philosophical objections to a simple "look and name," or **ostensive** model of learning the first words (Quine, 1960). Ostensive means pointing—this conveys the idea of acquiring simple words by a parent pointing at a dog and saying "dog," and the child then simply attaching the name to the object. The problem is simply that the child does not know which attribute of input is being labeled. For all the child knows, it could be that the word "dog" is supposed to pick out just the dog's feet, or the whole category of animals, or its brown color, or the barking sound it makes, or its smell, or the way it is moving, and so on. This is often called the mapping problem. One thing that makes the task slightly easier is that adults stress the most important words, and children selectively attend to the stressed parts of the speech they hear (Gleitman & Wanner, 1982). Nevertheless, the problem facing the child is an enormous one.

After the first few words, vocabulary development is very fast and very efficient. Young children are able to associate new words with objects after only one exposure, an ability called fast-mapping. How can the child learn so quickly? Researchers have proposed a number of solutions to the mapping problem.

Constraints on learning names for things

Perhaps the cognitive system is constrained in its interpretations? The developing child makes use of a number of lexical principles to help to establish the meaning of a new word (Golinkoff, Hirsh-Pasek, Bailey, & Wenger, 1992; Golinkoff, Mervis, & Hirsh-Pasek, 1994). The idea of lexical principles as general constraints on how children attach names to objects and their properties is an important one. Several main constraints have been proposed.

The taxonomic constraint (Markman, 1989) predicts that when a child hears a word in the presence of an object, they will go on to label all similar things with that same word. Hence, a dog may be called a "cat" and vice versa.

First, the cognitive system may be constrained so that it tends to treat ostensive definitions as labels for whole objects. This is the whole-object assumption (Markman, 1990; Taylor & Gelman, 1988; Waxman & Markow, 1995). There is some evidence that adults are sensitive to this constraint. Ninio (1980) found that adults talking to children almost wholly use ostensive definition to label whole objects rather than parts or attributes. When adults deviate from this, they try to make it clear—for example, by mentioning the name of the whole object as well. Children make errors that suggest that they are using this constraint. They sometimes think that adjectives are labels for objects (e.g., thinking that "pretty" refers to a flower). Where does this important constraint come from? In fact the whole-object bias is not limited to words (Bloom, 2001a). Prelinguistic infants are strongly biased to split the word up into discrete objects (Spelke, 1994).

The taxonomic constraint is that a word refers to a category of similar things. For example, if a child hears the word "cat" in the presence of a cat, they will first assume that the word labels the whole cat (by the whole-object assumption) and then that all similar things will also be called "cat" (Markman, 1989) (see Figure 4.4). Children prefer to use new words to associate things that are taxonomically related rather than thematically related (e.g., a dog with dog food), even though they often prefer to group things thematically in other circumstances (Markman & Hutchinson, 1984). Of course, we still have to solve the problem of how children identify how objects are taxonomically related. Children begin word learning expecting that new words pick out commonalities between objects, and these commonalities are fine-tuned by further experience (Waxman, 1999; Waxman & Booth, 2001). For example, 14-month-old children recognize that nouns and adjectives are different types of word, and pick out different aspects of relations among objects (membership of a category of similar objects or properties of objects; Waxman & Booth, 2001).

FIGURE 4.4 A significant problem for a child when learning a new word is that the thing it refers to can appear in many different forms. For example, the word "building" can be used to name many different types of structure.

A third possible constraint is the mutual exclusivity assumption, whereby each object can only have one label (Markman & Wachtel, 1988): That is, (unilingual) children do not usually like more than one name for things.

As children acquire words, new strategies become available. For example, they may be biased to assign words to objects for which they do not already have names (the novel name–nameless category or N3C principle; Mervis & Bertrand, 1994). There are syntactic cues to meaning; if we talk about "I see Wolf" we are probably talking about a proper noun, but if we say "I see the wolf" we are talking about a common noun (Bloom, 2001a). Later on, when children's vocabulary is larger and their linguistic abilities more sophisticated, explicit definition becomes possible. Hence superordinate and subordinate terms can be explicitly defined by constructions such as "Tables, chairs, and sofas are all types of furniture."

Other solutions to the mapping problem

Other solutions have been proposed to the mapping problem. There might be an innate basis to the hypotheses children make (Fodor, 1981): We might have evolved such that we are more likely to attach the word "dog" to the object "dog," rather than to its color, or some even more abstruse concept such as "the hairy thing I see on Mondays."

It is likely that social factors play an important role in learning the meanings of early words. Joint attention between adult and infant is an important factor in early word learning. Parents usually take care to talk about what their children are interested in at the time. Even at 16 months of age, children are sensitive to what the speaker is attending to and can work out whether novel labels refer to those things (Baldwin, 1991; Woodward & Markman, 1998). Early words may be constrained so that they are only used in particular discourse settings (Levy & Nelson, 1994; Nelson, Hampson, & Shaw, 1993). The social setting is important in learning new words as a supplement or an alternative to innate or lexical constraints. Tomasello

(1992b) argued that social and pragmatic factors could have an important influence on language development. The problem of labeling objects would be greatly simplified if the adult and child establish through any available communicative means that the discourse is focusing on a particular dimension of an object. For example, if it has been established that the domain of discourse is "color," then the word "pink" will not be used to name a pig, but its color. Adults and children interact in determining the focus of early conversation. Tomasello and Kruger (1992) demonstrated the importance of pragmatic and communicative factors. They showed that young children are surprisingly better at learning new verbs when adults are talking about actions that have yet to happen than when the verbs are used ostensively to refer to actions that are ongoing. This must be because the impending action contains a great deal of pragmatic information that the infant can use, and the infant's attention can be drawn to this. In summary, the social setting can serve the same role as innate principles in enabling the child to determine the reference without knowing the language. Joint attention with adults, or intersubjectivity, is an essential component of learning a language, particularly early in development. Variability in experience of joint attention at 9–18 months may be one of the most important determinants of variability in early lexical development. Nevertheless, there is a limit to what social-pragmatic factors and joint attention can achieve, and as the child gets older the availability and nature of the linguistic input become increasingly important (Hoff & Naigles, 2002). In a study of 63 children, Hoff and Naigles found that, at the age of 24 months, variation in the extent to which mother and child mutually engage in conversation has little effect on the richness of the vocabulary of the child; on the other hand, variation in the lexical richness and syntactic complexity of the mother's utterances does have an effect.

Children appear to vary in the importance they assign to different concepts, and this leads to individual differences and preferences for learning words. The first use of "dog" varies from four-legged mammal-shaped objects, to all furry objects (including inanimate objects such as coats and hats), to all moving objects (Clark & Clark, 1977). In each case the same basic principle is operating: a child forms a hypothesis about the meaning of a word and tries it out. The hypotheses formed differ from child to child.

Brown (1958) was among the earliest to suggest that children start using words at what was later known as the basic level (see Chapter 11). The basic level is the default level of usage. For example, "dog" is a more useful label than "animal" or "terrier." The bulk of early words are basic-level terms (Hall, 1993; Hall & Waxman, 1993; Richards, 1979; Rosch, Mervis, Gray, Johnson, & Boyes-Braem, 1976). Superordinate concepts, above the basic level, seem particularly difficult to acquire (Markman, 1989). Taxonomic hierarchies begin to develop only after the constraint biasing children to acquire basic-level terms weakens. Later on, particular cues become important. Mass nouns (which represent substances or classes of things, such as "water" or "furniture") in particular seem to aid children in learning hierarchical taxonomies, as they often flag superordinate category names (Markman, 1985, 1989). As such, they are syntactically restricted, which is apparent when we try to substitute one for another. Hence although we can say "this is a table," it is incorrect to say "this is a furniture"; similarly "this is a ring" but not "this is a jewelry"; and "this is a dollar" but not "this is a money."

The properties of objects themselves might constrain the types of label that are considered appropriate for them. Soja, Carey, and Spelke (1992) argued that the sorts of inferences children make vary according to the type of object being labeled. For example, if the speaker is talking about a solid object, the child assumes the word is the name of the whole object, but if the speaker is talking about a non-solid substance, then the child infers that the word is the name of parts or properties of the substance.

Finally, there are syntactic cues to word meaning. Brown (1958) proposed that children may use part-of-speech as a cue to meaning. For example, 17-month-olds are capable of attending to the difference between noun phrase syntax as in "This is Sib" and count noun syntax as in "This is a sib." This is obviously a useful cue for determining whether the word is a proper name or stands for a category of things. The ability of using syntactic knowledge to learn meaning is called **syntactic bootstrapping** (Gleitman, 1990; Gleitman, Cassidy, Nappa, Papafragou, & Trueswell, 2005; Landau & Gleitman, 1985; Lidz, Gleitman, & Gleitman, 2003). Children use the structure of the sentences they hear in combination with what they perceive in the world to interpret the meanings of new words. For example, they use the syntax to help them infer the meanings of new verbs by working out the types of relation that are permissible between the nouns involved (Naigles, 1990). For instance, suppose a child does not understand the verb "bringing" in the sentence "Are you bringing me the doll?" The syntactic structure of the sentence suggests that "bring" is a verb whose meaning involves transfer, thus ruling out possible contending meanings such as "carrying," "holding," or "playing." Even children as young as 2 years old can use information about transitive and intransitive verbs to infer the meanings of verbs (Naigles, 1996).

There are a number of reasons why some words are easier to learn than others. First, and most obviously, children are exposed to some words more often in the language and in the environment. Second, some concepts might be more accessible. Conceptual structures change as the child develops, and understanding words like "know," "think," and "believe" might depend on the child having a sophisticated conceptual structure and a theory of mind (Gopnik & Meltzoff, 1997; Huttenlocher, Smiley, & Charney, 1983). Third, the information change model says that the type of information available to the child changes and increases over time, and not all words are acquired in the same way (Gleitman et al., 2005). Of course all of these factors might operate, although Gleitman et al. argue that information change is more important than conceptual change; certain words and syntactic structures have to be learned before others can be successfully acquired.

Evaluation of work on how children acquire early names

Approaches that make use of constraints on how children relate words to the world have some problems. First, we are still faced with the problem of where these constraints themselves come from. Are they innate, and part of the language acquisition device? Second, they are biases rather than constraints, as children sometimes go against them (Nelson, 1988, 1990). In particular, very early words (those used before the vocabulary explosion) often violate the constraints (Barrett, 1986). For example, Bloom (1973) noted that a young child used "car" to refer to cars, but only when watched from a certain location. The constraints only appear to come into operation at around 18 months, which is difficult to explain if they are indeed innate or a component of the language acquisition device. (It is of course possible that the attainment of the concept of object permanence interacts with this.) Third, whereas it is relatively easy to think of constraints that apply to concrete objects and substances, it is less easy to do so for abstract objects and actions.

Nelson (1988, 1990) argued that language development is best seen as a process of social convergence between adult and child, emphasizing communicability. The role of social and pragmatic constraints in early acquisition might have been greatly underestimated. In conclusion, it is likely that a number of factors play a role in how children come to name objects.

Errors in representing meaning

One useful way of discovering how children acquire meaning is to examine the errors children make. Children's early meanings overlap with adult meanings in four ways: the early meaning might be exactly the same as the adult meaning; it might overlap but go beyond it; it might be too restricted; or there might be no overlap at all. Words that have no overlap with adult usage get abandoned very quickly: Bloom (1973) observed that in the earliest stages of talking, inappropriate names are sometimes used for objects and actions, but these are soon dropped, because words that have no overlap in meaning with the adult usage are likely to receive no reinforcement in communication.

Over-extensions and under-extensions

E. Clark (1973) was one of the first researchers to look at **over-extensions** (sometimes called over-generalizations) in detail. When children over-extend a word, they use it in a broader way than the adult usage. Table 4.2 gives

TABLE 4.2 Examples of over-extensions (based on Clark & Clark, 1977).

Object	Domain of application
moon	cakes, round marks on window, round postcards, letter "O"
ball	apples, grapes, eggs, anything round
bars of cot	toy abacus, toast rack with parallel bars, picture of columned building
stick	cane, umbrella, ruler, all stick-like objects
horse	cow, calf, pig, all four-legged animals
toy goat on wheels	anything that moves
fly	specks of dirt, dust, all small insects, toes
scissors	all metal objects
sound of train	steaming coffee pot, anything that makes a noise

some examples of early over-extensions. Over-extensions are very common in early language and appear to be found across all languages. Rescorla (1980) found that one third of the first 75 words were over-extended, including some early high-frequency words.

As we can observe from Table 4.2, over-extensions are often based on perceptual attributes of the object. Although shape is particularly important, the examples show that over-extensions are also possible on the basis of the properties of movement, size, texture, and the sound of the objects referred to. Although Nelson (1974) proposed that functional attributes are more important than perceptual ones, Bowerman (1978) and E. Clark (1973) both found that appearance usually takes precedence over function. That is, children over-extend based on a perceptual characteristic such as shape even when the objects in the domain of application clearly have different functions.

McShane and Dockrell (1983) pointed out that many reports of over-extensions failed to distinguish persistent from occasional errors. They argued that occasional errors tell us little about the child's semantic representation, perhaps arising only from filling a transient difficulty in accessing the proper word with the most available one. Such transient over-generalizations are more akin to adult word substitution speech errors (see Chapter 13), and as such would tell us little about normal semantic development. Hence it is important to show that words involved in real over-extensions are permanently over-extended, and also that the same words are over-extended in comprehension. If a word is over-extended because the representation of its meaning is incomplete, the pattern of comprehension of that word by the child should reflect this. To this end, Thomson and Chapman (1977) showed that young children over-extended the meanings of words in comprehension as well as in production. They found that many words that were over-extended in production by a group of 21- to 27-month-old children were also over-extended in comprehension. However, not all words that were over-extended in production were over-extended in comprehension. Most children chose the appropriate adult referent for about half the words they over-extended in production.

There is some controversy surrounding these findings. Fremgen and Fay (1980) argued that the results of Thomson and Chapman (1977) were an experimental artifact. They pointed out that the children were repeatedly tested on the same words, and this might have led to the children changing their response either out of boredom or to please the experimenter. When Fremgen and Fay tested children only once on each word, they failed to find comprehension over-extensions in words over-extended in production. The situation is complex, however, as Chapman and Thomson (1980) showed that in their original sample there was no evidence of an increase in the number of over-extensions across trials, which would have been expected if Fremgen and Fay's hypothesis was correct. Behrend (1988) also found over-extensions in comprehension in children as young as 13 months.

Clark and Clark (1977) hypothesized that over-extensions develop in two stages. In the earliest stage, the child focuses on an attribute, usually perceptual, and then uses the new word to refer to that attribute. However, with more exposure they realize that the word has a more specific meaning, but they do not know the other words that would enable them to be more precise. In this later stage, then, they use the over-extended word rather as shorthand for "like it." Hence the child might know that there is more to being a ball than being round, yet when confronted with an object like the moon, not having the word "moon" they might call it "ball," meaning "the-thing-with-the-same-shape-as-a-ball."

We should also bear in mind that, like adults, children might sometimes just make mistakes. They might be using words as an analogy—the moon is like a ball. Or they might just be being mischievous (Bloom, 2001a).

Under-extensions occur when words are used more specifically than their meaning—such as using the word "round" to refer only to balls. The number of under-extensions might be dramatically under-recorded, because usually the construction will appear to be true. For example, if a child points at the moon and says "round," this utterance is clearly correct, even if the child thinks that this is the name of the moon.

Three types of theory have been proposed to account for these data. The accounts are all based on the idea that over-extensions occur because of a lexical representation that is incomplete compared to that of the adult, whereas under-extensions occur because the developing representation is more specific than that of the adult.

The semantic feature hypothesis (E. Clark, 1973) is based on a decompositional theory of lexical semantics. This approach states that the meaning of a word can be specified in terms of a set of smaller units of meaning, called **semantic feature**s (see Chapter 11). Over- and under-extensions occur as a result of a mismatch between the features of the word as used by the child compared with the complete adult representation. The child samples from the features, primarily on perceptual grounds. Over-extensions occur when the set of features is incomplete; under-extensions occur when additional spurious features are developed (such as the meaning of "round" including something like [silvery white and in the sky]). Semantic development consists primarily of acquiring new features and reducing the mismatch by restructuring the lexical representations until the features used by the adult and child converge. The features are acquired in an order from most to least general.

Atkinson (1982) and Barrett (1978) discussed problems with this approach. Any theory of lexical development based on a semantic feature theory of meaning will inherit the same problems as the original theory, and there are serious problems with the semantic feature theory (see Chapter 11). In particular, we must be able to point to plausible, simple features in all domains, and this is not always easy, even for the kind of concrete objects and actions that young children talk about. Atkinson (1982) in particular pointed to the central problem that the features proposed to account for the data are arbitrary. The developmental theory cannot easily be related to any plausible general semantic theory, or to an independent theory of perceptual development.

In Nelson's (1974) functional core hypothesis, generalization is not restricted to perceptual similarity; instead, functional features are also emphasized. In other respects this is similar to the featural account and suffers from the same problems.

The prototype hypothesis (Bowerman, 1978) states that lexical development consists of acquiring a prototype that corresponds to the adult version.

Box 4.5 Theoretical accounts of over- and under-extensions

Semantic feature hypothesis (E. Clark)

- The meaning of words can be specified in terms of smaller units of meaning ("semantic features")
- When there is a mismatch between features of the word used by the child and the complete representation used by the adult, an over- or under-extension occurs
- Over-extensions occur when a set of features is incomplete
- Under-extensions occur when a set of features is incomplete
- Semantic development involves acquiring new features and reducing mismatch between adult and child features

- Features are acquired from the most general to the least general

Functional core hypothesis (Nelson)

- Generalization is not restricted to perceptual similarity—functional features are also emphasized
- In other ways, similar to the semantic feature hypothesis

Prototype hypothesis (Bowerman)

- A prototype is an average member of a category
- Lexical development consists of acquiring a prototype that corresponds to the adult version

A **prototype** is an average member of a category. Over-extensions may probably be explained better in terms of concept development and basic category use. Kay and Anglin (1982) found prototypicality effects in over- and under-extensions. The more an object was prototypical of a category, the more likely it was that the conceptual prototype name would be extended to include the object. Words are less likely to be extended for more peripheral category members. This suggests that the concepts are not fully developed but clustered around just a few prototypical exemplars. Once again, a significant problem with this approach is that it inherits the problems of the semantic theory on which it is founded (see Chapter 11).

In summary, the strengths and weaknesses of these developmental theories are the same as those of the corresponding adult theories. There is surely scope for connectionist modeling here, which may yet show that a variant of the semantic feature hypothesis is along the right lines.

The contrastive hypothesis

Once children have a few names for things, how do they accommodate the many new words to which they are exposed? Barrett (1978) argued that the key features in learning the meaning of a word are those that differentiate it from related words. For example, the meaning of "dog" is learned by attaining the contrast between dogs and similar animals (such as cats) rather than simply by learning the important features of dogs. In the revised version of this model (Barrett, 1982), although contrasts are still important, they are not what are acquired first. Instead words are initially mapped onto prototypical representations; the most salient prototypical features are used to group the word with words sharing similar features, and contrastive features are then used to distinguish between semantically similar words.

This emphasis on contrast has come to be seen as very important (E. Clark, 1987, 1993, 1995). The contrastive hypothesis is a pragmatic principle that simply says that different words have different meanings. It is very similar to the lexical constraint of mutual exclusivity. However, the child is still faced with significant problems.

When new word meanings are acquired, because features are contrasted with the features of existing word meanings, the meaning should not overlap with that of existing words: the words' meaning should fill a gap. Children do not like two labels for the same thing.

Unfortunately, young children are sometimes happy with two labels for the same object (Gathercole, 1987). Contrast appears to be used later rather than earlier as an organizing principle of semantic development. Neither is it likely to be the only principle driving semantic development. There comes a point when it is no longer useful for semantic development to make a contrast (for example, between black cats and white cats), and the contrastive hypothesis says nothing about this. It seems just as likely that when children hear someone use a new word, they assume it must refer to something new because otherwise the speaker would have used the original word instead (Gathercole, 1989; Hoff-Ginsberg, 1997).

Summary of work on early semantic development

It is unlikely that only one principle is operating in semantic development. On the one hand, children have to learn appropriate contrasts between words, but they must not learn inappropriate or too many contrasts. As this is just the sort of domain where the learning of regularities and the relation between many complex inputs and outputs is important, computational modeling should make a useful contribution here; however, as yet there has been no research on this topic. One obvious problem is that it is most unclear how to model the input to semantic development. How should the salient perceptual and functional attributes of objects and actions be encoded? Finally, we should not underestimate the importance of the social setting of language development.

The later development of meaning

Children largely stop over-extending at around the age of 2½ years. At this point they start asking questions such as "What's the name of that?" and vocabulary develops quickly from then on. From this point, a good guide to the order of acquisition of words is the semantic complexity of the semantic domain under consideration. Words with simpler semantic representations are acquired first. For example, the order of acquisition of dimensional terms used to describe size matches their relative semantic complexity. These terms are acquired in the sequence shown in (8):

(8) big–small
    tall–short, long–short
    high–low
    thick–thin
    wide–narrow, deep–shallow

"Big" and "small" are the most general of these terms, and so these are acquired first. "Wide" and "narrow" are the most specific terms, and are also used to refer to the secondary dimension of size, and hence these are acquired later on. The other terms are intermediate in complexity and are acquired in between (Bierwisch, 1970; Clark & Clark, 1977; Wales & Campbell, 1970).

Nouns are acquired more easily than verbs. One explanation for this might be that verbs are more cognitively complex than nouns, in that whereas nouns label objects, verbs label relations between objects (Gentner, 1978). An alternative although related view is that their acquisition depends on the prior acquisition of some nouns and some information about how syntax operates at the clause level (Gillette, Gleitman, Gleitman, & Lederer, 1999). That is, verb acquisition depends on acquiring knowledge about linguistic context. Gillette et al. presented adults with video clips of adults speaking to children. Some words on the soundtrack were replaced with beeps or made-up words such as "gorp." The adults had to identify the meanings of the beeps and made-up words. The extralinguistic context was surprisingly uninformative: adults found it quite difficult to identify the meanings of words on the basis of environmental information alone. They were particularly poor, however, at identifying verbs relative to nouns, and extremely bad at identifying verbs relating to mental states (e.g., "think," "see"). Performance increased markedly when syntactic cues were available. As an example, the "gorp" in "Vlad is gorping" is more likely to mean "sneeze" than "kick," but in "Vlad is gorping the snaggle" it is more likely to mean "kick" than "sneeze." In summary, environmental context might be less powerful than was once thought, while linguistic context provides powerful cues. Verbs are more difficult to acquire than nouns because of their greater reliance on complex linguistic context. Later semantic development sees much interplay between lexical and syntactic factors.

Does comprehension always precede production?

Comprehension usually precedes production for the obvious reason that the child has to more or less understand (or think they understand) a concept before producing it. Quite often contextual cues are strong enough for the child to get the gist of an utterance without perhaps being able to understand the details. In such cases there is no question of the child being able to produce language immediately after being first exposed to a particular word or structure. Furthermore, as we have seen, even when a child starts producing a word or structure, it might not be used in the same way as an adult would use it (e.g., children over-extend words). There is more to development than a simple lag, however. The order of comprehension and

At around the age of 2½ years, children start to ask questions such as "What's the name of that?" This marks the onset of a period of accelerated vocabulary development.

production is not always preserved: words that are comprehended first are not always those that are produced first (Clark & Hecht, 1983). Early comprehension and production vocabularies may differ quite markedly (Benedict, 1979). There are even cases of words being produced before there is any comprehension of their meaning (Leonard, Newhoff, & Fey, 1980).

SYNTACTIC DEVELOPMENT

We have seen that a stage of single-word speech (called holophrastic speech) precedes a stage of two-word utterances. After this, early speech is telegraphic, in that grammatical morphemes may be omitted. We can broadly distinguish between continuous and discontinuous theories. In continuous theories, children are believed to have knowledge of grammatical categories from the very earliest stages (e.g., Bloom, 1994; Brown & Bellugi, 1964; Menyuk, 1969; Pinker, 1984). The child's goal is to attach particular words to the correct grammatical categories, and then use them with the appropriate syntactic rules. In discontinuous theories, early multiword utterances are not governed by adult-like rules (Bowerman, 1973; Braine, 1963; Maratsos, 1983). Theoretical approaches also vary depending on the extent to which they emphasize the semantic richness of the early utterances.

How do children learn syntactic categories?

One of the most basic requirements of understanding and using language is identifying the major syntactic categories to which words belong. Is a word a noun, a verb, an adverb, or an adjective? How do children learn these categories, and which words belong to them?

Are syntactic categories innate?
How do children begin to work out the meaning of what they hear before they acquire the rules of the grammar? Accounts differ in the extent to which they posit the need for innate knowledge.

One important approach says that knowledge about the basic syntactic categories is innate (Pinker, 1984, 1989). Children know that nouns refer to objects and verbs refer to actions. Pinker argued that the child first learns the meaning of some content words, and uses these to construct semantic representations of some simple input sentences. With the surface structure of a sentence and knowledge about its meaning, the child is in a position to make an inference about its underlying structure. Children start off with their innate knowledge of syntactic categories and a set of innate linking rules that relate them to the semantic categories of **thematic roles**. Thematic roles are a way of labeling who did what in a sentence: For example, in the sentence "Vlad kissed Agnes," Vlad is the **agent** (the person or thing initiating the action) and Agnes the **patient** (the person or thing being acted on by the agent). An innate linking rule relates the syntactic categories of subject and object to the semantic categories of agent and patient, respectively. So on exposure to language, all the child has to do is identify the agents in utterances, and this information then provides knowledge about the syntactic structure. This process is known as **semantic bootstrapping** (see Figure 4.5).

Although nativist accounts have the advantage of providing a simple explanation for many

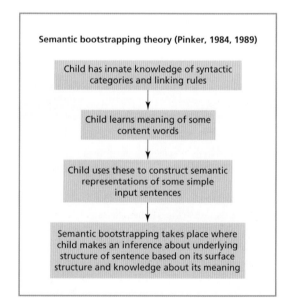

Semantic bootstrapping theory (Pinker, 1984, 1989)

Child has innate knowledge of syntactic categories and linking rules

↓

Child learns meaning of some content words

↓

Child uses these to construct semantic representations of some simple input sentences

↓

Semantic bootstrapping takes place where child makes an inference about underlying structure of sentence based on its surface structure and knowledge about its meaning

FIGURE 4.5

otherwise mysterious phenomena, they have a number of disadvantages. The predictions they make are not always borne out by the data.

First, the theory depends on the child hearing plenty of utterances early on that contain easily identifiable agents and actions relating to what the child is looking at that can be mapped onto nouns and verbs. However, it can sometimes be very difficult to work out the meaning of new words, particularly verbs (Gillette et al., 1999; Gleitman, 1990).

Second, Bowerman (1990) showed that there was little difference in the order of acquisition of verbs that the semantic bootstrapping account predicts should be easiest for children to map onto thematic roles, compared with those that should be more difficult. For example, verbs where the theme maps onto the subject (as is the case with many verbs, such as "fall," "chased") should be easier to acquire than verbs where the location, goal, or source maps onto the subject and the theme onto the object (such as "have," "got," and "lose"). Instead Bowerman, in an analysis of the speech of her two children, Christy and Eva, found that the two types of verb are acquired at the same time. In general, children do not produce sentences corresponding to the basic structure "agent–action–patient" any earlier than other types of structure.

Third, Braine (1988a, 1988b), in detailed reviews of Pinker's theory, questioned the need for semantic bootstrapping, and examined the evidence against the existence of very early phrase-structure rules. He argued that semantic information is sufficient for children to be able to learn syntactic categories.

Finally, postulating the possession of specific innate knowledge is very powerful—perhaps too powerful. After all, the processes of language development are slow and full of errors. There is a fine balance between a developmental system that is innately constrained as Pinker proposed, and yet is unconstrained enough to accommodate all these false starts.

Does semantics come first?

From the constructivist-semantic or meaning-first view, grammatical classes are first constructed on a semantic basis (e.g., Gleitman, 1981;

Macnamara, 1972, 1982), which means that the very earliest stages of language development are asyntactic (Goodluck, 1991). A gross distinction is that nouns correspond to objects, adjectives to attributes, and verbs to actions. But although many nouns do indeed refer to objects, others are used to refer to salient abstract concepts (e.g., "sleep," "truth," "time," "love," "happiness"). So one of the major failings of a semantic approach to early grammar is that semantics alone cannot provide a direct basis for syntax. It is possible, however, that early semantic categories could underlie syntactic categories (McShane, 1991); after all, children learn about objects before they learn about truth and time. Perhaps the category of "noun" is based on a semantic category of objecthood (Gentner, 1982; Slobin, 1981).

According to Schlesinger's (1988) semantic assimilation theory (see Figure 4.6), early semantic categories develop into early syntactic categories without any abrupt transition. At an early age children use an "agent–action" sentence schema. This can be used to analyze new NP–VP sequences. The important point is that it is possible to give an account of early syntactic development without having to assume that syntactic categories are innate.

Macnamara (1972) proposed that the child focuses at first on individual content words so that a small lexicon is acquired. Information pertaining to word order is ignored at this stage. The child combines the meanings of the individual words with the context to determine the speaker's intended meaning. For example, a child who

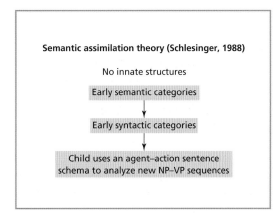

FIGURE 4.6

sees Mommy drop a ball knows the meaning of the words "Mommy," "drop," and "ball," and on hearing the sentence "Mommy dropped the ball" can work out the intended meaning of that utterance. In doing so, the child can also take the first steps towards mapping words onto roles in sentences. One of the earliest observations is that the default sentence order (in English at least, as we have seen) is subject (or agent), action, and object (or person or thing acted on). The nature of child-directed speech (in referring to the here-and-now and using syntactically simplified constructions) facilitates this process.

The acquisition of verbs is more difficult to account for in this way. Although many verbs do describe actions, a large number of important early verbs do not (e.g., "love," "think," "want," "need," "see," "stop"). Many early verbs refer to states, but many adjectives also describe states (e.g., "hungry," "nice"). Hence, if the early syntactic prototype for verbs is based on the semantic notions of actions and states, one might occasionally expect errors where adjectives get used as verbs (e.g., "I hungries"). However, such constructional errors are never found (McShane, 1991). Therefore it seems unlikely that children are inducing the early verb concept from a pure semantic notion.

Maratsos (1982) proposed that early syntactic categories are formed on the basis of shared grammatical properties. For example, in English nouns can occupy first positions in declarative sentences. Once one category has been formed, bootstrapping facilitates the acquisition of subsequent ones: adjectives come before and modify or specify nouns, verbs come between nouns, and so on. Maratsos also proposed that the types of modifications that a word can undergo indicate its syntactic category. For example, if a word can be modified by adding "-ed" and "-ing" to the end, then it must be a verb. Bates and MacWhinney (1982) proposed that abstract nouns later become assimilated to the category because the words behave in the same way as the more typical nouns; for example, they occupy the same sorts of positions in sentences. That is, children might again be making use of distributional information.

Distributional analysis

An alternative view has emerged that children can acquire syntactic categories from a very early age with very little or no semantic information (Bloom, 1994; Levy & Schlesinger, 1988). This approach exemplifies how children might view language as a rule-governed "puzzle" that has to be solved. Children as young as 2 easily acquire gender inflections in languages such as Hebrew, even though these syntactic constructions have very little semantic basis and contribute little to the meaning of the message (Levy, 1983, 1988). Gender may play an important role in marking word boundaries, and may be particularly prominent to children if they are viewing language as a puzzle. Children acquiring Hebrew attend to syntactic regularities before they attend to semantic regularities (Levy, 1988). Syntactic cues are far more effective than semantic cues for acquiring the distinction between count nouns (which can represent single objects, such as "broomstick") and mass nouns (e.g., "water"). It is possible to say "a broomstick," but not "a furniture"; similarly we can say "much furniture," but not "much broomstick." We can form plurals of count nouns ("broomsticks" is acceptable) but not of mass nouns ("furnitures" is not acceptable). Children seem to acquire the distinction not by noting that count and mass nouns can correspond to objects versus substances, but by making use of these syntactic cues (Gathercole, 1985; Gordon, 1985). Children do not miscategorize nouns whose semantic properties are inappropriate, but instead make use of the syntactic information.

This new approach to acquiring syntactic categories claims that children perform a distributional analysis on the input data (Gathercole, 1985; Levy & Schlesinger, 1988; Valian, 1986). This means that children essentially search for syntactic regularities with very little semantic information. Distributional analysis shows that many aspects of children's early utterances, including the errors they make, can be accounted for by the statistical properties of the language they hear, without recourse to innate knowledge.

Connectionist modeling of distributional analysis demonstrates that knowledge about categories can be acquired on a statistical basis alone (Elman, 1990; Finch & Chater, 1992; Mintz, 2003; Redington & Chater, 1998). This approach shows how syntactic categories can be acquired without explicit knowledge of syntactic rules or semantic information. Instead, all that is necessary is statistical information about how words tend to cluster together. This approach also answers the criticism that a distributional analysis of syntactic categories is beyond children's computational abilities (Pinker, 1984). In particular, some words are ambiguous and belong to multiple syntactic categories. A child hearing the first three sentences might conclude on the basis of distributional analysis alone that the fourth sentence is also acceptable:

(9)   Vlad eats fish.
(10) Vlad eats rabbits.
(11) Vlad can fish.
(12) *Vlad can rabbits.

However, computer modeling shows that statistical distributional analysis in fact works very well. MOSAIC is a computer model that has no built-in syntactic knowledge and learns by the distributional analysis of an input of child-directed speech (Freudenthal, Pine, & Gobet, 2005, 2006). It provides input to a range of data in English, Dutch, Italian, and Spanish, fitting the errors that children make and how those errors change in time in the light of further input. Mintz (2003) shows how exposure to words in frequent frames produces extremely accurate categories. To give a very simple example, any word in the X position in "the X laughs" must be a noun.

Researchers currently disagree about how much innate knowledge is necessary before distributional learning can successfully take place. The current trend in research is to show how less knowledge must be innate because the input with which children work is richer than was once realized. For example, Redington and Chater (1998) pointed out that children have access to distributional information in addition to co-occurrence information. For instance, morphology varies regularly with syntactic category and this provides a strong cue to the syntactic function of a word. Words that take the suffixes -s and -ed

are typically verbs, but words that only take the suffix -s are typically nouns (Maratsos, 1988). In English bisyllabic words, nouns tend to have stress on the first syllable, but verbs have stress on the second syllable (Kelly, 1992).

Evaluation of work on learning syntactic categories

In summary, the relation between the development of syntax and the development of semantics is likely to be a complex one. Early work emphasized the importance of semantic information in the acquisition of syntactic categories, but more recent work has shown how these categories can be acquired with little or no semantic information. Children probably learn syntactic categories through a distributional analysis of the language, and connectionist modeling has been very useful in understanding how this occurs. It is unlikely that innate principles are needed to learn syntactic categories.

Two-word grammars

Soon after the vocabulary explosion, the first two-word utterances appear. There is a gradation between one-word and two-word utterances in the form of two single words juxtaposed (Bloom, 1973). Children remain in the two-word phase for some time.

Early research focused on uncovering the grammar that underlies early language. It was hoped that detailed longitudinal studies of a few children would reveal the way in which adult grammar was acquired. Early multiword speech is commonly said to be telegraphic in that it consists primarily of content words, with many of the function words absent (Brown & Bellugi, 1964; Brown & Fraser, 1963).

It would be a mistake to characterize telegraphic speech as consisting only of semantically meaningful content words. Braine (1963) studied three children from when they started to form two-word utterances (at about the age of 20 months). He identified a small number of what he called pivot words. These were words that were used frequently and always occurred in the same fixed position in every sentence. Pivot words were not used alone and were not found in conjunction with other pivot words. Most pivot words (called P1 words) were to be found in the initial position, although a smaller group (the P2 words) were to be found in the second position. There was a larger group of what Braine called open words that used less frequently and that varied in the position in which they were used, but were usually placed second. This idea that sentences are formed from a small number of pivot words is called pivot grammar. Hence most two-word sentences were of the form (P1 + open) words (e.g., "pretty boat," "pretty fan," "other milk," "other bread") with a smaller number of (open + P2) forms (e.g., "push it"). Some (open + open) constructions (e.g., "milk cup") and some utterances consisting only of single open words are also found.

Brown (1973) took a similar longitudinal approach with three children named "Adam," "Eve," and "Sarah." Samples of their speech were recorded over a period of years from when they started to speak until the production of complex multiword utterances. Brown observed that the children appeared to be using different rules from adults, but rules nevertheless. This idea that children learn rules but apply them inappropriately is an important concept. They produced utterances such as "more nut," "a hands," and "two sock." Brown proposed a grammar similar in form to pivot grammar, whereby noun phrases were to be rewritten according to the rule NP → (modifier + noun). The category of "modifier" did not correspond to any single adult syntactic category, containing articles, numbers, and some (demonstrative) adjectives and (possessive) nouns. As the children grew older, however, these distinctions emerged, and the grammar became more complex.

Problems with the early grammar approaches

Bowerman (1973) reviewed language development across a number of cultures, particularly English and Finnish. She concluded that the rules of pivot grammar were far from universal. Indeed, they did not fully capture the speech of American children. She confirmed that young children use a small number of words in relatively fixed positions, but

not the other properties ascribed to pivot words. On closer analysis she found that the open class was not undifferentiated, using instead a number of classes. Harris and Coltheart (1986) suggested that the children in the Bowerman study might have been linguistically more advanced than those of the earlier studies, and therefore more likely to show increased syntactic differentiation.

Bloom (1970) argued that these early grammatical approaches failed to capture the semantic richness of these simple utterances because they placed too much emphasis on their syntactic structure. The alternative approach—that of placing more emphasis on the context and content of children's utterances, rather than just on their form—became known as rich interpretation. It soon became apparent that two-word utterances with the same form could be used in different ways. In one famous example, Bloom noted that the utterance "mommy sock," uttered by a child named Kathryn, was used on one occasion to refer to the mother's sock, and on another to refer to the action of the child having her sock put on by the mother. Bloom argued that it was essential to observe the detailed context of each utterance.

The rich interpretation methodology has its own problems. In particular, the observation of an appropriate context and the attribution of the intended meaning of a child's utterance to a particular utterance in that context is a subjective judgment by the observer. It is difficult to be certain, for example, that the child really did have two different meanings in mind for the "mommy sock" utterance.

In summary, it is difficult to uncover a simple grammar for early development that is based on syntactic factors alone. An additional problem is that the order of words in early utterances is not always consistent.

Semantic approaches to early syntactic development

The apparent failure of pure syntactic approaches to early development, and the emerging emphasis on the semantic richness of early utterances, led to an emphasis on semantic accounts of early grammars (Schlesinger, 1971; Slobin, 1970). Aspects

Box 4.6 Eleven important early semantic relations and examples (based on Brown, 1973)

Attributive	"big house"
Agent–Action	"Daddy hit"
Action–Object	"hit ball"
Agent–Object	"Daddy ball"
Nominative	"that ball"
Demonstrative	"there ball"
Recurrence	"more ball"
Non-existence	"all-gone ball"
Possessive	"Daddy chair"
Entity + Locative	"book table"
Action + Locative	"go store"

of Brown's (1973) grammar were also derived from this: for instance, he observed that 75% of two-word utterances could be described in terms of only 11 semantic relations (see Box 4.6 for examples).

There is some appeal to the semantic approach in the way in which it de-emphasizes syntax and innate structures, and emphasizes mechanisms such as bootstrapping, but it has its problems. First, there is a lack of agreement on which semantic categories are necessary. Second, it is unclear whether children are conceptually able to make these distinctions. Third, this approach does not give any account of the other 25% of Brown's observed utterances. Fourth, the order of acquisition and the emergence of rules differ across children. Finally, Braine (1976) argued that this approach was too general: the evidence is best described by children learning rules about specific words rather than general semantic categories. For example, when children learn the word "more," is this a case of learning that the word "more" specifically combines with entities, or is it more generally the case that they understand that it represents the idea of "recurrence plus entities"? If the latter is the case, then when children learn the word "more" they should be able to use other available recurrence terms (e.g., "another") freely in similar ways; however, they do not. Hence the

child appears to be learning specific instances rather than just semantic categories. Braine gives the example of a child who learned to use "other" mostly only with nouns denoting food and clothing. He concluded that children use a combination of general and specific rules.

The acquisition of verb-argument structure

An important aspect of learning syntax is to learn the appropriate argument structure of verbs. For example, we know that "hits" is a transitive verb that takes an object, that "falls" is an intransitive verb that does not take an object, and that some verbs are more complex in that they can have direct and indirect objects ("Boris gives the ball to Agnes"). How do children learn this important aspect of language?

The acquisition of verb-argument structure follows a U-shaped function: performance is good, then poor, then good again. Young children tend to produce the correct forms; they then go through a period where they produce incorrect forms, particularly making over-generalization errors. For example, they tend to use intransitive verbs in transitive ways ("Adam fall toy"), because they are developing structures where the link between causal actions and transitive verbs is inappropriately generalized to intransitive verbs. Finally, they become adult-like in producing the correct form of complex verbs (Akhtar, 1999; Alishahi & Stevenson, 2005). Clearly this pattern is a clue as to how children are learning verb-argument structure.

Perhaps children come to use semantic information about which sorts of verbs can and cannot participate in certain verb-argument structures (Pinker, 1989). For example, verbs that convey information about motion in a specified direction (fall, climb, ascend, descend) can only occur in intransitive constructions. This idea is called the semantic verb class hypothesis. Children make over-generalization errors when they have not yet learned the precise semantic representations of the verbs.

A second idea is that particular importance is attached to the acquisition of certain key verbs. Children learn some verbs and the particular ways in which they are used. These early verbs that form the basis of utterances are called "verb islands" (Akhtar & Tomasello, 1997; Tomasello, 1992a, 2000, 2003). Tomasello (2000, 2003) questioned the continuity assumption—the idea that a child's grammar is adult-like, using the same sort of grammatical rules as adults and with an adult-like linguistic competence. He argued that young children's syntactic abilities have been greatly overestimated: in particular, they produce far fewer novel utterances than is usually attributed to them. Instead, their language development proceeds in a piecemeal fashion that is based on particular items (mainly verbs), with little evidence of using general structures such as syntactic categories. Lieven, Pine, and Baldwin (1997) found that virtually all their sample of young children (1–3 years old) used verbs in only one type of construction, suggesting that their syntax was built around these particular lexical items. Tomasello emphasizes the importance of syntactic development by analogy-making based on verb islands. The verb-island hypothesis accounts for the data because children are learning some specific high-frequency examples (giving the correct pattern in the first instance) that are then used to form generalizations; however, the application of some of these generalizations sometimes leads to errors. Eventually the child realizes that both rules and exceptions are necessary.

The verb-island hypothesis has generated considerable debate, particularly about whether or not there is a paradox in accounts of early child language. Naigles (2002) argues that at first sight there is a paradox: infants seem to be very good at statistical learning and abstracting general patterns from specific instances, while toddlers are very poor, dealing instead with non-abstract, item-specific information (e.g., the key verb of verb islands). It is though as they get older children actually lose their ability for abstraction. She argues that this difference arises in part from differences in methodologies: Studies on younger children tend to test comprehension, and find more evidence of abstraction, while studies on older children tend to use test production, and find more evidence of the use of specific instances. As we have noted before, production is usually more difficult than comprehension. Furthermore, most of the stimuli that test early comprehension tend to involve nonsense words or artificial languages, whereas later production studies usually involve real language where word meaning is involved. Naigles suggests that the patterns the younger children extract are not yet tied to meaning. Toddlers do not lose these early abstractions, but their specific use of them is very limited until they can integrate them with meaning. As she says, learning form is easy, but learning meaning is hard. She argues that there is no reason to suppose that very young children are not making abstractions across syntactic structures, so she resolves the paradox by saying that toddlers do use abstraction. Young children have difficulty extending meaning, not frames. Tomasello and Akhtar (2003) continued the debate (see Naigles, 2003, for a reply), arguing that there is no paradox. They contended that there is converging evidence that up to the age of 3 young children are unable to abstract across syntactic structures, focusing instead on specific items and expressions, and using a few specific syntactic frames. Tomasello and Akhtar argued that diary studies of spontaneous speech, and the production studies where children are taught novel verbs, produce particularly compelling data that toddlers do not form abstract syntactic representations.

If adults hear a particular syntactic structure, they are more likely to use that structure in production in the immediate future, a phenomenon known as structural priming (see Chapter 13 for details). For example, you are more likely to produce a passive construction if you have just heard a passive sentence than if you have just heard an active one. Children over 4 show this structural priming effect; however, children under 4 do not (Savage, Leiven, Theakston, & Tomasello, 2003). One explanation for this finding is that young children have no general syntactic structures to prime, but the finding might also suggest that imitation plays some role in older children.

A third solution is that repeated instances of a verb in particular constructions cause the child to make a probabilistic inference that the verb is only associated with a particular verb-argument structure. The more often children hear a verb used in a particular construction, the less often they should generalize it to a novel input. This idea is called the entrenchment hypothesis (Braine & Brooks, 1995; Theakston, 2004). The more often children hear a verb being used, the less likely they should be to get it wrong. Therefore verb frequency is particularly important here, with over-generalization errors particularly likely on low-frequency verbs. Hence children are more likely to (incorrectly) say that "She arrived her to the park" is grammatical than the similar construction containing the higher frequency verb in "She came me to the school" (Theakston, 2004).

Of course word frequency and the amount of exposure to semantic information are confounded. An alternative account combines the above accounts. It dispenses with rules and exceptions, and argues that children carry out a type of distributional analysis of verb structures, with semantic information playing an important role (Alishahi & Stevenson, 2005). In this model the acquisition of verb-argument structure is probabilistic. Children learn the argument structures of each specific verb over many specific instances, as well as the more general semantic characteristics of that type of verb. Early on children imitate specific forms, but increasingly rely on generalizations based on general patterns. At first this general information overwhelms the specific information, but as the child encounters more examples of infrequent verbs they come to be able to use those less frequent verbs correctly.

The study of the acquisition of verb-argument structures enables us to make a more general point about how children learn syntax. Clearly an important part of learning is to abstract information out of specific instances. After the age of 3, children are able to combine novel verbs with the appropriate syntactic structures with ease. For example, consider the sentences "Agnes kicked Vlad" and "Agnes kissed Vlad." There are similarities between these sentences—for example, both are transitive sentences involving agents and objects (as opposed, say, to kickers and things being kicked), but to recognize these similarities

requires a level of syntactic abstraction. How early does this abstraction happen? According to late-syntax theories abstraction happens relatively late, suggesting that syntax takes time to be learned and is acquired through abstracted experience, with children early on interpreting sentences with lexical or verb-specific knowledge (Braine, 1992; Lieven, Pine, & Baldwin, 1997; Tomasello, 2003). According to early-syntax theories, abstraction happens relatively early (Fisher, 2002; Naigles, 2002; Pinker, 1984). If abstraction happens early, children must be making use of some additional information, which might be innate (Pinker, 1984), or might arise from the structure of the general cognitive architecture used to learn language (Chang, Dell, & Bock, 2006; Saffran, 2002). Unfortunately different methodologies give different results and support different theories (Chang et al., 2006). Results using elicited production (getting children to speak) support the late-syntax theory, while results examining comprehension support the early-syntax theory. Even different comprehension tasks give different results. Tasks in which comprehension is assessed by children acting out sentences find that children under 3 do not seem to use word order to comprehend who is acting on whom (Akhtar & Tomasello, 1997). On the other hand, tasks using the preferential-looking technique find that children under 3 do use word order information (Fernandes, Marcus, Di Nubila, & Vouloumanos, 2006; Gertner, Fisher, & Eisengart, 2006). Chang et al. show that a connectionist model that learns and predicts sequences from repeated exposure to grammatical strings of words, and which also makes use of information about the meaning of utterances, can account for the data from both sorts of methodology. The model can simulate both the elicited production and preferential-looking data. Children appear to understand complex structures early on with the preferential-looking task because it provides a choice between two interpretations. The system develops partial structural representations before it can produce correct whole structures. In effect, it has enough information to be able to understand when alternatives are provided, but not enough to be able to produce from scratch.

A more general way of phrasing these questions was put by Lidz et al. (2003): Is word learning driven by observation of the outside world, or is it driven by properties already inside the child? Causative verbs make a particularly good arena for testing this question. In English, causativity and transitivity are entwined: Causative verbs (whose meanings contain some notion of causation) are transitive. For example, the causative verb "kill" (meaning "cause to die") is transitive—it can take an object ("Vlad kills Boris"); "swim" is not causative and is an intransitive verb—it cannot take an object. In the Dravidian language Kannada (spoken in the subcontinent of India), however, transitivity is not the best predictor of causativity: There is a causative morpheme which is never present unless the verb is a causative one. How do children come to learn verbs in such a language? The emergentist theory, which says that learning is driven by observation, will mean that for the child the most reliable cue (which will not be transitivity, but the presence of the causative morpheme) will be associated with causativity. The syntactic universalist theory, however, where learning is driven by the properties of the syntax already present in the child, predicts that they should still make most use of transitivity. Lidz et al. found that 3-year-old children largely ignore the causative morphology and make most use of the less useful transitive structures when understanding verbs.

Evaluation of work on early syntactic development

Can early syntactic development be both non-syntactic and non-semantic? The identification of early syntactic categories might occur without much semantic help, and without being based on the acquisition of an explicit grammar. Instead, children seem to learn grammatical categories by distributional analysis. Can this type of approach be extended to account for how children produce two-word and early multiword utterances?

Perhaps children's early productions are much more limited than has frequently been thought (Messer, 2000). Perhaps their early multiword utterances just statistically reflect the most common types of utterance they hear? According to this view, children have a much less formal grammar than is commonly supposed. Evidence for this comes from the observation that early language use is much less flexible than it would be if children were using explicit grammatical rules (Pine & Lieven, 1997).

In general, the idea that there is a syntax module that drives language development is becoming less popular. It is clear that language development must be seen within the context of social development and the way language is used (Messer, 2000). The shift is also mirrored in Chomsky's more recent work (1995), where the importance of grammatical rules is much reduced.

Perhaps there is no straightforward way of separating grammatical and lexical development; the two are intertwined (Bates & Goodman, 1997, 1999). For example, grammatical development is related to vocabulary size: The best predictor of grammatical development at 28 months is vocabulary size at 20 months, suggesting that the two share something important (Bates & Goodman, 1999; Fenson et al., 1994). Furthermore, there is no evidence for a dissociation between grammatical and vocabulary development in either early or late talkers: We cannot identify children with normal grammatical development but with very low or high vocabulary scores for their age. Neither is there any evidence of any clear dissociations between grammatical and lexical development in language in special circumstances (such as Williams syndrome and Down's syndrome). Bates and Goodman (1999) concluded that there is little support for the idea of a separate module for grammar.

In conclusion, recent work tends to downplay the role of an innate grammatical module and the attribution of adult-like grammatical competence to young children.

Later syntactic development

Brown (1973) suggested that the mean length of utterance (MLU) is a useful way of charting the

TABLE 4.3 Mean length of utterance (MLU) and language development. Based on Brown (1973).

Stage I	MLU < 2.25	many omissions, few grammatical words and inflections
Stage II	2.25–2.75	much variation
Stage III	2.75–3.5	(c. 3 years) pluralization, most basic syntactic rules
Stage IV	3.5–4	increasing syntactic sophistication
Stage V	4+	imperatives, negatives, questions, reflexives, passives (5–7 years), in that order

progress of syntactic development. This is the mean length of an utterance measured in morphemes averaged over many words. Brown divided early development into five stages based on MLU. Naturally MLU increases as the child gets older; we find an even better correlation with age if single-word utterances are omitted from the analysis (Klee & Fitzgerald, 1985). This approach is rather descriptive and there is little correlation between MLU and age after the age of 5. Nevertheless, it is a convenient and much-used measure (see Table 4.3).

The rule-based nature of linguistic development is clear from the work of Berko (1958). She argued that if children used rules, their use should be apparent even with words the children had not used before. They should be able to use appropriate word endings even for imaginary words. In a famous study, Berko used nonsense words to name pictures of strange animals and people doing odd actions. For example, she would point to a drawing and say: "This is a wug. This is another one. Now there are two __ " (see Figure 4.7). The children would fill in the gap with the appropriate plural ending "wugs." In fact, they could use rules to generate possessives ("the bik's hat"), past tenses ("he ricked yesterday"), and number agreement in verbs ("he ricks every day").

The development of order of acquisition of grammatical morphemes is relatively constant across children (James & Khan, 1982). The earliest acquired is the present progressive (e.g., "kissing"), followed by spatial prepositions, plurals, possessives, articles, and the past tense in different forms.

Inflecting verbs: Acquiring the past tense

The development of the past tense has come under particular scrutiny. Brown (1973) observed that the youngest children use verbs in uninflected forms ("look," "give"). He argued that children seem to be aware of the meaning of the different syntactic roles before they could use the inflections. That is, the youngest children use the simplest form to convey all of the syntactic roles. They learn to use the appropriate inflections very quickly: past tenses to convey the sense of time (usually marked by adding "-ed"), the use of the "-ing" ending, number modification, and modification by combination with auxiliaries. However, although regular verbs can be modified by applying a simple rule (e.g., form the past tense by adding "-ed"), a large number of verbs are irregular.

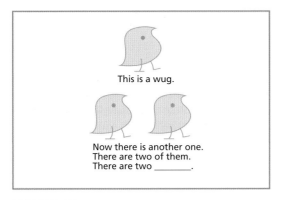

This is a wug.

Now there is another one.
There are two of them.
There are two _____.

FIGURE 4.7

The time course of development of irregular verbs and nouns is an example of U-shaped development. Behavior changes from good performance, to poor performance, before improving again. Early on, children produce both regular and irregular forms. Importantly, in the poor performance phase, children make a large number of over-regularization errors (e.g., Brown, 1973; Cazden, 1968; Kuczaj, 1977). Later on they can produce both the regular and irregular forms once again.

One explanation of this pattern is that the youngest children have just learned specific instances. They then learn a rule by induction (e.g., form the past tense by adding -ed to verbs, form plurals by adding -s to nouns) and apply this in all cases. Only later do they start to learn the exceptions to the rule. Hence children develop a past-tense formation system with two separate routes: a symbolic system that uses a rule to generate regular forms, and a route accessing a separate listing of irregular forms (Pinker, 1994, 1999). Evidence for a dual-route model comes from several dissociations of performance on regular and irregular verbs. Patients with fluent aphasia (see Chapter 13) tend to be worse at reading and producing irregular forms than regular forms, while patients with non-fluent aphasia tend to be relatively worse at processing the regular forms. Imaging data suggest the processing of regular and irregular forms involves different parts of the brain. PET imaging suggests that only Broca's area is activated when processing regular past tenses, but the temporal lobes of the brain are involved in processing irregular past tenses (Jaeger et al., 1996). fMRI data suggest that while the posterior temporal lobes are involved in processing both regular and irregular forms, only regular forms produce activation around the frontal gyrus (Pinker & Ullman, 2002). There is also evidence that regular and irregular plurals are processed in different ways. Clahsen (1999) argued that experimental and neuroimaging work on plural formation in German suggests that the language system is divided into a lexicon and a computational system that, among other things, generates irregular forms. Patients with Alzheimer's disease are relatively worse at irregular forms, while patients with Parkinson's disease are relatively worse at regular forms. More controversially, children with Williams syndrome may fare worse with irregular forms, while children with specific language impairment (SLI) fare worse with regular forms (Pinker, 1994, 1999; see Thomas & Karmiloff-Smith, 2003, for a review). A problem with acquiring the dual-route model is that regular and irregular forms coexist; the proportion of over-regularizations never rose above 46% in 14 children studied by Kuczaj (1977), suggesting that a very general, powerful rule is not learned.

An alternative account, connectionist modeling of the acquisition of the past tense, has generated substantial controversy. The basic idea of these models is that we do not need two distinct routes to produce regular and irregular forms; instead, knowledge of regular forms comes from knowledge about phonological regularities, whereas knowledge of irregular forms comes from lexical-semantic knowledge. fMRI imaging data suggest that it is the phonological characteristics of the past tense forms that are important for determining which brain regions are activated: Irregular forms that sound as if they could be regular forms (e.g., "slept," "sold") produce a pattern of activation similar to regular forms (Joanisse & Seidenberg, 2005). Rumelhart and McClelland (1986) simulated the acquisition of the past tense using back-propagation. The input consisted of the root form of the verb, and the output consisted of the inflected form. The training schedule was particularly important, as it was designed to mimic the type of exposure that children have to verbs. At first the model was trained on 10 of the highest frequency words, 8 of which happened to be irregular. After 10 training cycles, 410 medium-frequency verbs were introduced for another 190 learning trials. Finally 86 low-frequency verbs were introduced. The model behaved as children do: it initially produced the correct output, but then began to over-regularize. Rumelhart and McClelland pointed out that the model behaved in a rule-like way, without explicitly learning or having been taught a rule. Instead, the behavior emerged as a consequence of the statistical properties of the input. If true, this might be an important general point about language development.

What are the problems with this account? Pinker and Prince (1988) made the most substantial criticisms of this work. They noted that irregular verbs are not really totally irregular. It is possible to predict which verbs are likely to be irregular, and the way in which they will be irregular. This is because irregular verbs still obey the general phonological constraints of the language. Hence it is possible that irregular forms are derived by general phonological rules. In addition, the way in which some verbs have both regular and irregular past tenses, and the way in which they are inflected, depends on the semantic context ("hang" and "hanged" and "hung," and "ring" and "ringed" and "rung," for example). The network also made errors of a type that children never produce (e.g., "membled" for the past tense of "mail"). Pinker and Prince also pointed out that there is no explicit representation for a word in Rumelhart and McClelland's (1986) model. Instead, it is represented as a distributed pattern of activation. However, words as explicit units play a vital role in the acquisition process. Pinker and Prince also argued that the simulation's U-shaped development resulted directly from its training schedule. The drop in performance of the model occurred when the number of regular verbs in the training vocabulary was suddenly increased. There is no such discontinuity in the language to which young children are exposed. Obtaining the U-shaped curve also depended on having a disproportionately large number of irregular verbs in the initial training phase. This is not mirrored by what children are actually exposed to. Finally, the way in which the medium-frequency, largely regular verbs are all introduced in one block on trial 11 is quite unlike what happens to children, where exposure is cumulative and gradual (McShane, 1991).

Plunkett and Marchman (1991, 1993) argued that connectionist networks can model the acquisition of verb morphology, but many more factors have to be taken into account. In particular, they proposed that the training set must more realistically reflect what happens with children. Rather than present all the verbs to be learned in one go, or with a sudden discontinuity as in the original Rumelhart and McClelland model, they gradually increased the number of verbs the system must learn, to simulate the gradual increase in children's vocabulary size. They concluded that a network could display U-shaped learning even when there are no discontinuities in the training. MacWhinney and Leinbach (1991) reached similar conclusions. Nevertheless, some problems remain (Clahsen, 1999; Marcus, 1995). Obtaining the U-shaped curve in modeling seems to depend on presenting the training stimuli in a certain way—in particular, it depends on sudden changes in the training regime, in contrast to the smooth changes of input that children are faced with. Furthermore, connectionist models make more irregularization errors than children. It is possible that the single-route mechanism actually fits the child data better than rule-based accounts (Marchman, 1997). In particular, children are more likely to regularize irregular verbs that are similar to other verbs that behave in a regular way. For example, "throw" forms an irregular past tense as "threw." There are other verbs like it, however, that form their past tenses in a regular way (e.g., "flow," "show"). An irregular verb like "hit," however, has no competing enemies. As the connectionist constraint-based model predicts, children are more likely to produce "throwed" than "hitted."

One outcome of the modeling work by Rumelhart and McClelland has been to focus attention on the details of how children acquire skills such as forming the past tense (e.g., Marchman & Bates, 1994; Marcus et al., 1992). We now know much more than we did before. A general problem with the connectionist accounts is that these models need explicit feedback in order to learn. As we have seen, the extent and influence of explicit feedback in real language development is limited. One frequent counter to this objection is that the modeling is merely demonstrating the principle that association and statistical regularities in the language can account for the phenomena without recourse to explicit rules, and the details of the learning mechanisms involved are not important in this respect. Another possibility is that as children listen to speech, they make predictions about what comes next. They can then match the predictions to the actual input. However, there is presently little evidence that this happens (Messer, 2000).

Finally, computational modeling shows how developmental disruption to past-tense acquisition can account for the apparent dissociation between the patterns of acquisition shown in Williams syndrome and SLI (Thomas & Karmiloff-Smith, 2003). Rather than a static model, whereby children come with two routes, one of which is either spared or destroyed, high-level deficits (past-tense formation) can arise from relatively low-level deficits (phonological processing and the lexical-semantic system) in conjunction with the effects of development and compensation.

Individual differences in language development

The way in which adults talk to children appears to have an effect as the child gets older: There are large individual differences in the ability of preschool children to form and understand syntactically complex sentences, and the quality of what children hear correlates highly with these differences (Huttenlocher, Vasilyeva, Cymerman, & Levine, 2002). Children who hear complex structures master them earlier. Even here, it is difficult to be certain about what is causal. The most important source of input for young children is their parents, so we cannot rule out genetic factors: Syntactic complexity in parent and child might reflect parent–child genetic similarity. However, the language of teachers also comes to have an effect: The syntactic abilities of children taught by teachers who use syntactically more complex speech develops faster than those taught by teachers who use simpler constructions (Huttenlocher et al., 2002). Hence language input does play a role.

Cross-linguistic differences in language development

Languages differ in their syntactic complexity. For example, English is relatively constrained in its use of word order, whereas other languages (such as Russian) are more highly inflected and have freer word order. Not surprisingly, these differences lead to differences in the detail of language development.

What is perhaps surprising is the amount of uniformity in language development across languages. For example, stage 1 speech (covering the period with the first multiword utterances, up to MLU of 2.0) seems largely uniform across the world (Dale, 1976; Slobin, 1970). There are of course some differences: Young Finnish children do not produce yes–no questions (Bowerman, 1973). This is because you cannot form questions by rising intonation in Finnish, so speakers must rely on an interrogative inflection. Some differences emerge in later development. Plural marking is an extremely complex process in Arabic, but relatively simple in English. Hence plural marking is acquired early in English-speaking children, but is not entirely mastered until the teenage years for Arabic-speaking children (see McCarthy & Prince, 1990; Prasada & Pinker, 1993). In complex inflectional languages such as Russian, development generally progresses from the most concrete (e.g., plurals) first to the most abstract later (e.g., gender usually has no systematic semantic basis; see Slobin, 1966b).

The development of syntactic comprehension

More complicated syntactic constructions naturally provide the child with a number of challenges. The youngest children have difficulty with passives because they are inappropriately applying the standard canonical order strategy, which simply says that the subject of the sentence is the agent. Older children (around 3 years old) start to map the roles of passives as adults do, but they make mistakes depending on the semantic context of the utterance. Children have particular difficulty with reversible passives, when the subject and object can be reversed and the sentence still makes sense (such as "Vlad was kissed by Agnes").

Here there are no straightforward semantic cues available to assist them. M. Harris (1978) showed that animacy is an important cue in the development of understanding passives. Animate things tend to get placed earlier in the sentence. Hence, in a picture description task, when the object being acted on was animate (such as a boy being run over by a car), a passive construction tended to be used to put the animate object first ("the boy was run over by the car"). The type of verb also matters: Young children find passives with action verbs easier to manipulate than stative verbs such as "remember" (Sudhalter & Braine, 1985).

More recently eye-tracking has been used to investigate how children understand sentences. Trueswell, Sekerina, Hill, and Logrip (1999) used head-mounted eye-trackers to discover where children looked in a scene as they responded to ambiguous spoken instructions to move objects about that scene. As we shall see in Chapters 10 and 14, adults can make use of many sources of information to resolve ambiguous instructions such as "Put the frog on the napkin in the box," and are also very good at

revising their initial interpretations if they turn out to be wrong. Five-year-old children did not use context to resolve ambiguous structures and were unable to revise their initial interpretation. Children always preferred the "destination" interpretation (put the frog on the napkin) rather than the "modifier" interpretation (take the frog that is on the napkin and put it in the box), regardless of the visual context. Young children therefore use different principles to understand sentences; little is known about the way in which these principles turn into their adult equivalent.

The development of comprehension skills is a long and gradual process with no clear-cut end point (Hoff-Ginsberg, 1997). Markman (1979) found that a significant number of 12-year-olds erroneously judged that (13) made sense (I had to read it twice myself to find the problem):

(13) There is absolutely no light at the bottom of the ocean. Some fish that live at the bottom of the ocean know their food by its color. They will only eat red fungus.

An eye-tracker can be used to record and store information about an observer's eye fixations. Trueswell et al. (1999) used this method to discover where children looked in a scene as they responded to instructions to move objects about that scene.

SUMMARY

- Rationalists believed that knowledge was innate, whereas empiricists argued that it arose from experience.
- An analysis of the effects of correcting speech on young children shows that language acquisition cannot be driven just by imitation or reinforcement.
- Because the linguistic input that children hear does not seem to contain sufficient information (it is an impoverished input), Chomsky proposed that they have an innate Language Acquisition Device.
- In particular, he argued that we are born with a fixed set of switches (parameters), the positions of which are set by exposure to particular languages.
- In practice it has proved difficult to identify these parameters, and to explain how bilingual children and children using sign language use them.
- Human languages have a surprising amount in common; this might be because they are all derived from the same universal grammar.
- There are different types of linguistic universals; some show how a particular aspect of language may have implications for other features.
- The drive to use language in general and rules of word order in particular is so great that children develop them even if they are absent from their input.
- Young children move from babbling to one-word or holophrastic speech, through abbreviated or telegraphic speech, before they master the full syntactic complexity of their language.
- Correcting children's errors makes surprisingly little difference to their speech patterns.
- Adults speak to young children in a special way; this child-directed speech (CDS for short; sometimes called "motherese") simplifies the child's task in acquiring language.
- CDS is clear, and what is being talked about is usually obvious from the context.
- As CDS is not used by all cultures it may not be necessary for language development, although it might facilitate it.
- There are specific language impairments (SLIs) that are genetically marked, although the precise nature of the impairment is disputed.
- All young children go through a stage of babbling, but it is not clear how the sounds they make are related to the sounds of the language to which they are exposed.
- Infants are born with rich speech-perception abilities.
- It is likely that babbling serves to enable infants to practice articulatory movements and to learn to produce the prosody of their language.
- There is an explosion in children's vocabulary at around 18 months.
- There have been a number of proposals for how children learn to associate the right word with things in the world, including lexical constraints, innate concepts, syntactic cues, and social-pragmatic cues.
- Young children make errors in the use of words; in particular, they occasionally over-extend them inappropriately.
- A number of models have been proposed to account for over-extensions; one of the most influential has been the idea that the child has not yet acquired the appropriate semantic features for a word.
- Later semantic development depends on conceptual and syntactic factors.
- A number of mechanisms have been proposed for how children learn the syntactic categories of words.
- One view is that knowledge of syntactic categories and how objects and actions are mapped onto nouns and verbs is innate.
- Once children have learned a few correspondences, their progress can be much faster because of bootstrapping.

- According to the constructivist or meaning-first view, there is an early asyntactic phase of development, which is driven only by semantic factors.
- More recent approaches have focused on the idea that children monitor the distribution of words and use co-occurrence information to derive syntactic categories.
- Braine proposed that two-word grammars were founded on a small number of "pivot" words that were also used in the same position in sentences.
- Purely grammatical approaches to early speech have difficulty in explaining all the utterances children make, and ignore the semantic context in which the utterances are made.
- The acquisition of past tenses is best described by a U-shaped pattern, as performance goes from perfect performance on irregular verbs through a phase of incorrectly regularizing them, before using the correct irregular forms again.
- There has been much debate as to whether the learning of the past tense is best explained by the acquisition of specific rules or by constraint-based models based on connectionist modeling.

QUESTIONS TO THINK ABOUT

1. What cognitive processes do you think need to be innate for language development to occur?
2. Throughout this chapter we have talked of "language development" or "language acquisition" rather than (first) language learning. What is the advantage of avoiding the term "language learning"?
3. To what extent are the errors that children make like the errors adult speakers routinely make? (You might need to read Chapter 13 before attempting this question.)
4. Consider the first words made by someone you know. (You might be able to discover your own.) What do you think accounts for them?
5. Produce a detailed summary of the time course of language development.
6. To what extent is the telegraphic speech of young children like the agrammatic speech of some aphasics (see Chapter 13)?
7. In some studies with young infants children pay attention for longer to easy or familiar stimuli, whereas in others they attend longer to unfamiliar material. What might determine when each of these happens?

FURTHER READING

Many texts describe language development in far more detail than can be attempted in a single chapter: see, for example, include Hoff-Ginsberg (1997) and Owens (2004) for an introductory approach. Hoff-Ginsberg includes very good descriptions of language development in special circumstances. Messer (2000) is a very short review of the main themes. See Bloom (1998) for another good review with an emphasis on the effect of the context of development.

(Continued)

(Continued)

See Werker and Yeung (2005) for a review of early speech perception and word learning. Bloom (2001a) reviews work on how children learn the meaning of words; Bloom (2001b) is a summary of the book, with a commentary. See also Hollich, Hirsh-Pasek, and Golinkoff (2000) for word learning. Although we have focused on nouns and verbs, we should not forget that there are other categories of words; see Mintz and Gleitman (2002) for work on how children learn adjectives.

There are several introductions to Chomsky's work that cover his ideas on language, language development, syntax (see Chapter 2), and sometimes his political ideas as well. See Cogswell and Gordon (1996), Lyons (1991), and Maher and Groves (1999). A convincing defense of the position that language has an important innate component is presented in a very approachable way by Pinker (1994); see Pinker (1989) for more on formal approaches to language development. See Leonard (2000) for a review of SLI. For more on language development as parameter setting, see Stevenson (1988). Cook and Newson (2007) provide a great deal of material on Chomsky's work, with particular evidence on language development. In particular, they provide a very clear account of the poverty of the stimulus argument. See McClelland and Seidenberg (2000) and Seidenberg and Elman (1999) for critiques of nativism. For more on early phonological and segmentation skills, see Saffran, Werker, and Werner (2006). See Vihman (1996) for more on phonological development.

MacWhinney (1999) is an edited collection with an emphasis on how language is an emergent property. Elman et al. (1996) discuss how connectionism has changed our view of what it means for something to be innate. Their emphasis is on how behavior arises from the interactions between nature and nurture. Plunkett and Elman (1997) provide practical examples of connectionist modeling relevant to this in a simulation environment called tlearn. See Deacon (1997) for a review of the biological basis of language, how it might have evolved, how humans differ from animals, and how language might constrain language learning.

Broeder and Murre (2000) present a collection of articles that emphasizes computational modeling of language development.

For a review of work on past-tense formation, see Clahsen (1999). Altmann (1997) has a good section on the phonological skills of infants.

CHAPTER 5

BILINGUALISM AND SECOND LANGUAGE ACQUISITION

INTRODUCTION

Oddly enough for someone who has written several books on language, languages were my worst subject at school. My worst exam performance by far was in French, where I could literally hardly understand a word. I of course blame the teaching.

Many people believe that it is more difficult for older children and adults to learn another language. Given the same amount of exposure in the same way in both languages, is this assumption correct? This chapter examines the topic of second language acquisition in more detail. How does second language acquisition differ from first? How do children and adults store the two sets of words in their lexicons? How do the children manage to keep the languages apart? How do they learn to recognize that two distinct languages are involved? By the end of this chapter you should:

- Know how young children can acquire two languages simultaneously.
- Understand how we can learn a second language in adulthood.
- Have some idea about how a second language should best be taught.

BILINGUALISM

If a speaker is fluent in two languages, then they are said to be **bilingual**. The commonly held image of a bilingual person is of someone brought up in a culture where they are exposed to two languages from birth. It is not necessary for them to be equally fluent in both languages, but at least they should be very competent in the second one. Some people are trilingual, or even multilingual. This definition of **bilingualism** is a little vague as it depends on what we mean by "fluent." It is perhaps best to think of proficiency in multiple languages as lying on a continuum, rather than being an either–or idea. Some authorities (e.g., Bialystock, 2001) distinguish between productive bilingualism (speakers can produce and understand both languages) and receptive bilingualism (speakers can understand both languages, but have more limited production abilities).

Bilingualism is common in some parts of the world (to mention just a few examples: North Wales and Welsh–English; Canada and French–English; and places where there are many ethnic minorities within a culture). By convention the language learned first is called **L1** and the language learned second is called **L2**. Sometimes, however, the two languages are learned simultaneously, and sometimes the language that is learned first turns out to be the secondary language of use in later life. We can distinguish between **simultaneous bilingualism** (L1 and L2 learned about the same time), early **sequential bilingualism** (L1 learned first, but L2 learned relatively early, in childhood), and late (in adolescence onwards) bilingualism (Bialystok & Hakuta, 1994). Early sequential bilinguals form the largest group world-wide, and the number is increasing, particularly in countries with large immigration rates.

Box 5.1 Categories of bilingualism

- *Simultaneous bilingualism*: L1 and L2 learned at the same time.
- *Early sequential bilingualism*: L1 learned first, but L2 learned relatively early in childhood.
- *Late bilingualism*: L2 learned later, in adolescence or after.

A number of factors determine which language people use in a bilingual society. Naturally the speaker's home background is very important, as is to whom the person is speaking. Some societies may have a history of attempting to impose one language as being higher in prestige than others. Using a particular language may be a signal of solidarity with or distance from others. For example, in Paraguay, Spanish is the language used in more formal situations, while Guarani is the language of intimacy, signaling solidarity with the other person. Courtship frequently begins in Spanish and ends in Guarani (Crystal, 2010; Rubin, 1968).

What can we learn from the study of bilingualism? First, it is clearly of practical importance to many societies. Second, psycholinguistics should inform us about the best way of teaching people a second language. Third, how do people represent the two languages? Do they have a separate lexicon (mental dictionary) for each one, or just separate entries for each word form but a shared conceptual representation? And how do people translate between the two languages? Finally, the study of bilingualism is a useful tool for examining other cognitive processes: for example, it casts light on the critical period for language (see Chapter 3).

One of the earliest detailed studies of bilingualism was the diary study of Leopold (1939–1949). Leopold was a German linguist, whose daughter Hildegard had an American mother and lived from an early age in the USA. German was used in the home at first, but this soon gave way to English, the environment language. The diary showed that young children can quickly (within 6 months) forget the old language and pick up a new one if they move to another country. Initially the two languages are mixed up, but differentiation quickly emerges (Vihman, 1985). We observe language mixing when words combine, such as an English suffix added to a German root, or English words put into a French syntactic structure, or responding to questions in one language with answers in another (Redlinger & Park, 1980; Swain & Wesche, 1975). Code switching (also called language switching) is the name given to the tendency of bilinguals when speaking to other bilinguals to switch from one language to another, often to more appropriate words or phrases. This process is highly variable between individuals.

What happens if a child has already become moderately proficient in L1 when they start learning L2? Although we saw in our discussion of the critical period in Chapter 3 that the duration of exposure to L2 (which is often the length of residence in the new country) is important, other factors are also vital. These include the personality and cognitive attributes of the person learning L2 (Cummins, 1991). Proficiency in L1 is extremely important: the development of L1 and L2 is interdependent. Children who have attained a high level of skill at L1 are also likely to do so at L2, particularly on relatively academic measures of language performance.

The advantages of being bilingual

Bilingual children suffer no obvious linguistic disadvantages from learning two languages simultaneously (Snow, 1993). There might be some initial delay in learning vocabulary items in one language, but this delay is soon made up, and of course the total bilingual vocabulary of the children is much greater.

Bilingualism also has costs and benefits for other aspects of cognitive processing. Bilingual people tend to have a slight deficit in cognitive processing and working memory for tasks that are carried out in L2. On the other hand, they show clear gains in metalinguistic awareness and cognitive flexibility, and superior verbal fluency (Ben-Zeev, 1977; Bialystock, 2001; Cook, 1997;

Pearl & Lambert, 1962). For example, Lambert, Tucker, and d'Anglejan (1973) found that children in the Canadian immersion program (for learning French) tended to score more highly on tests of creativity than monolinguals. Bilingual children, compared with monolingual children, show an advantage in knowing that a word is an arbitrary name for something (Hakuta & Diaz, 1985).

Although some researchers have argued that there is no obvious processing cost attached to being bilingual (e.g., see Nishimura, 1986), others have found indications of interference between L1 and L2 (see B. Harley & Wang, 1997, for a review). For example, increasing proficiency in L2 by immigrant children is associated with reduced speed of access to L1 (Magiste, 1986). B. Harley and Wang (1997, p. 44) conclude that "monolingual-like attainment in each of a bilingual's two languages is probably a myth (at any age)."

On the other hand, there is now an overwhelming body of research showing that bilingualism confers a general cognitive advantage in the form of enhanced flexibility. There is even evidence that being bilingual protects people to some extent against developing Alzheimer's disease by helping to build up the mind's "cognitive reserve" that slows down cognitive aging (Bialystok, Craik, & Luk, 2012).

Bilingual language processing

How many lexicons does a bilingual speaker possess? Is there a separate store for each language, or just one common store? In separate-store models, there are separate lexicons for each language. These are connected at the semantic level (Potter, So, von Eckardt, & Feldman, 1984). Evidence for the separate-stores model comes from the finding that the amount of facilitation gained by repeating a word (a technique called **repetition priming**) is much greater and longer lasting within than between languages (Kirsner, Smith, Lockhart, King, & Jain, 1984), although repetition priming might not be tapping semantic processes (Scarborough, Gerard, & Cortese, 1984). In common-store models, there is just one lexicon and one semantic memory system, with words from both languages stored in it

and connected directly together (Paivio, Clark, & Lambert, 1988). This model is supported by evidence that semantic priming produces facilitation between languages (e.g., Chen & Ng, 1989; Jin, 1990; Schwanenflugel & Rey, 1986; see Altarriba, 1992, and Altarriba & Mathis, 1997, for a review). Studies that minimize the role of attentional processing and participants' strategies, and that maximize automatic processing (e.g., by masking the stimulus, or by varying the proportion of related pairs—see Chapter 6), suggest that equivalent words share an underlying semantic representation that can mediate priming between the two words (Altarriba, 1992). Most of the evidence now tends to favor the common-store hypothesis. However, early and late learners show different patterns of cross-language priming, with late learners showing much less priming (Silverberg & Samuel, 2004), suggesting once again that age-of-acquisition is critical in how bilinguals represent and access words, with late learners having separate lexicons mediated at the conceptual levels.

Another possibility is that some people use a mixture of common and separate stores (Taylor & Taylor, 1990). For example, concrete words, **cognates** (words in different languages that have the same root and meaning and which look similar), and culturally similar words act as though they are stored in common, whereas abstract and other words act as though they are in separate stores. Also steering between the common- and separate-stores models, Grosjean and Soares (1986) argued that the language system is flexible in a bilingual speaker, and that its behavior depends on the circumstances. In unilingual mode, when the input and output are limited to only one of the available languages, and perhaps when the other speakers involved are unilingual in that language, interaction between the language systems is kept to a minimum; the bilingual tries to switch off the second language. In the bilingual mode, both language systems are active and interact. How speakers have strategic control over their language systems is a topic that largely remains to be explored.

What happens when a bilingual speaker hears or sees a word? How do they prevent the two languages from interfering with one another? Bilingual speakers must have mechanisms in place to prevent interference. In an event-related potential (ERP) study, bilingual Spanish–Catalan speakers were instructed to press a button when they saw a word in one of the languages, and to ignore words in the other (Rodriguez-Fornells, Rotte, Heinze, Nosselt, & Munte, 2002). The brain potentials of the participants showed that they were not sensitive to the frequency of the words in the ignored language, suggesting that the words did not reach a high level of processing. However, fMRI activation had a lot in common with the way in which we process nonwords. This pattern of results suggests that speakers use quite low-level information to block words in the non-target language at a very early stage, such that the meanings of these words do not become activated. Further evidence for this low-level blocking of the non-target language comes from an electrophysiological study of very fluent Italian–Slovenian bilinguals. The pattern of activation while reading suggested that discrimination between the two languages is taking place at a very early stage (Proverbio, Cok, & Zani, 2002).

Bilingual syntactic processing

There has been much less research on how bilingual people process syntax than there has on how they process individual words. The issues are much the same: for languages that use similar sorts of construction, do people store syntactic knowledge separately for each language, or just once, in a shared store? A study of Spanish–English bilingual speakers found that a particular syntactic structure in one language could make it easier to use the same structure in the second language, supporting the "shared syntax" idea (Hartsuiker, Pickering, & Veltkamp, 2004). Similarly, Loebell and Bock (2003) found that production of German datives primed the subsequent use of English datives, and vice versa. Similar results have been found in Dutch–English bilinguals (Salamoura & Williams, 2006).

Translating between languages

How do we translate between two languages? As we might remember from school, or from our last foreign holiday, translating a foreign language can be fraught with difficulties. I remember once complimenting a chef in Spanish on his swimming pool (rather than his fish).

Kroll and Stewart (1994) proposed that translation by second-language novices is an asymmetric process. They argued that we translate words from our first language into the second language (called forward translation) by conceptual mediation. This means that we must access the meaning of a word in order to translate it. In contrast, we translate from the second language into the first (called backward translation) by word association—that is, we use direct links between items in the lexicon (see Figure 5.1). The evidence for this asymmetry is that semantic factors (such as the items to be translated being presented in semantically arranged lists) have a profound effect on forward translation, but little or no effect on backward translation. In addition, backward translation is usually faster than forward translation.

Having said this, there is some evidence that backward translation (from L2 to L1) might also be semantically mediated. De Groot, Dannenburg, and van Hell (1994) found that semantic variables such as imageability affect translation times in backward translation, although to a lesser extent than in forward translation. La Heij, Hooglander, Kerling, and van der Velden (1996) found that backward translation was facilitated by the presence of congruent pictures and hindered by incongruent pictures, suggesting that the translation involves accessing semantics. Hence it is likely that translation in both directions involves going through the semantic representations of the words. It is also probable that the extent of conceptual mediation increases as the speaker becomes more proficient in L2.

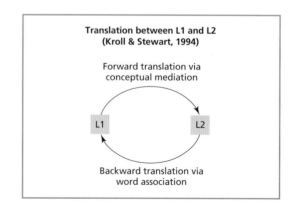

**Translation between L1 and L2
(Kroll & Stewart, 1994)**

Forward translation via
conceptual mediation

L1   L2

Backward translation via
word association

FIGURE 5.1

Picture–word interference studies suggest that in production only words of the target language are ever considered for selection. Many studies have shown that words in different languages interfere with one another (e.g., Ehri & Ryan, 1980). For example, it takes Catalan–Spanish bilinguals longer to name the picture of a table in Catalan if the Spanish word for chair is the distractor rather than an unrelated word. Costa, Miozzo, and Caramazza (1999) presented Catalan–Spanish bilinguals with pictures to name in Catalan. In their experiment, the name of the picture (not the name of a word related in meaning) was printed on top of the picture either in Catalan (same-language pairs) or Spanish (different-language pairs). The critical condition is the different-language pair. If choosing a word is not language-specific, the different-language condition should cause a great deal of interference, as the word written in Spanish and the name of the picture in Catalan will compete with each other. But if choosing a word is language-specific, then the Spanish distractor name should not be able to compete with the Catalan word. Instead, if anything, it should facilitate the production of the Catalan name through the intermediary of its meaning. Costa et al. found the latter: Having the name of the picture printed above the target picture in the non-response language led to facilitation. This finding suggests that only words of the target language are ever considered for output.

A different picture holds for auditory comprehension. Eye-tracking studies suggest that both languages are automatically considered. When bilingual people look at visual scenes searching for particular items in the first language, they also look at items with a name starting the same in the second, irrelevant language (Marian & Spivey, 2003; Spivey & Marian, 1999). For example, when an English–Russian bilingual looks for a "spear" in a visual array, they will also glance at a box of matches, because its name in Russian ("spichki") overlaps substantially with the English word.

Models of bilingualism

The most influential model of bilingualism that attempts to tell a complete story of the psychological processes involved is the Bilingual Interactive Activation Plus (BIA+) model (a development of the original BIA model to include phonological and sublexical levels of processing; see Dijkstra & van Heuven, 2002; Dijkstra, van Heuven, & Grainger, 1998). The model attempts to bring together all types of evidence concerning the orthographic processing of two languages, but makes particular use of how we recognize cognates—words that look the same (or very similar) in the two languages (such as "silence" in English and French, or "animal" in English and Spanish). In the BIA+ model, lexical access is non-language specific in its earliest stages, so words from both languages are activated, whatever the input. The model comprises a network of nodes at each level of representation (e.g., words, phonemes), connected together by facilitatory and inhibitory connections. The model is purely bottom-up in the sense that word recognition cannot be affected by the particular task (e.g., naming, lexical decision) being carried out. The model is characterized by "language" nodes, which tag representations according to the language to which they belong. The "language" nodes can receive activation from words (bottom-up) but can also send top-down inhibition. Recent work has centered on how bilingual processing is localized in the brain (e.g., Moreno & Kutas, 2009).

The neuroscience of bilingualism

There is some evidence that bilinguals with right-hemisphere damage show more aphasia (crossed aphasia) than monolinguals (Albert & Obler, 1978; Hakuta, 1986). Crossed aphasia might arise because the right hemisphere is involved in L2 acquisition, particularly if L2 is acquired relatively late (Martin, 1998; Obler, 1981; Vaid, 1983), or because language is less asymmetrically represented in the two hemispheres in bilingual speakers—although this is highly controversial (Obler & Hannigan, 1996; Paradis, 1997). An ERP study of responses to words in 19–22-month-old English–Spanish bilingual children showed that the more dominant language becomes lateralized before the less dominant one (Conboy & Mills, 2006). In addition to the types of aphasia shown by individuals who speak only one language, brain damage sometimes causes additional disorders in people who speak two languages. For example, we can observe pathological switching and mixing of languages, and difficulties in translating between the languages.

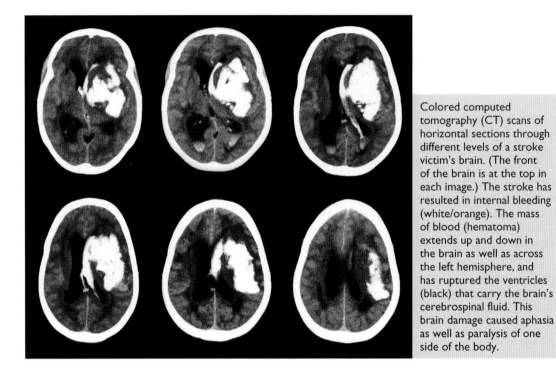

Colored computed tomography (CT) scans of horizontal sections through different levels of a stroke victim's brain. (The front of the brain is at the top in each image.) The stroke has resulted in internal bleeding (white/orange). The mass of blood (hematoma) extends up and down in the brain as well as across the left hemisphere, and has ruptured the ventricles (black) that carry the brain's cerebrospinal fluid. This brain damage caused aphasia as well as paralysis of one side of the body.

The most interesting issue is the extent to which processing of different languages tends to be localized in different parts of the brain. One of the first reports of this was by Scoresby-Jackson, describing the case of an Englishman who, after a blow to the head, selectively lost his knowledge of Greek. Since then there have been a number of reports of the selective impairment of one language following brain damage, and many more of differential recovery of the two languages (see Fabbro, 2001; Obler & Hannigan, 1996; Paradis, 1997). The evidence is consistent with two independent language systems connected at the conceptual level.

Imaging suggests that the time of acquisition most affects the grammatical aspects of language. The lexicons of both early and late bilinguals are organized similarly. However, individuals who acquire the second language after the age of 7 show different organization (Fabbro, 2001). In particular, in early-acquisition bilinguals, closed- and open-class words are stored in different parts of the brain; in late-acquisition bilinguals closed-class words are stored with open-class words. There are other differences in comprehension between monolinguals and bilinguals. Bilinguals are generally slower to respond to linguistic stimuli, regardless of what language the stimuli are in (Green, 1986; Proverbio et al., 2002). Electrophysiological measures show complex differences in reading and comprehension (Proverbio et al., 2002).

SECOND LANGUAGE ACQUISITION

Second language acquisition happens when a child or an adult has already become competent at a language and then attempts to learn another. We should distinguish between learning a second language naturalistically (e.g., when a child or person moves to a new country) and class-based instruction.

There are a number of reasons why a person might find learning a second language difficult. First, we saw in Chapter 3 that some aspects of language learning, particularly involving syntax, are more difficult outside the critical period. Second, older children and adults often have less time and motivation to learn a second language. Third, there will of course be similarities and differences between the first (L1) and second (L2) languages. The contrastive hypothesis (Lado, 1957) says that the learner will experience difficulty when L1 and L2 differ. In general, the more idiosyncratic a feature is in a particular language relative to other languages, the more difficult it will be to acquire (Eckman, 1977). This cannot be the whole story, however, as not all differences between languages cause problems. For example, Duskova (1969) found that many errors made by Czech speakers learning English were made on syntactic constructions in which the two languages do not differ.

There is some evidence that the time course of L2 acquisition follows a U-shaped curve: initial learning is good, but then there is a decline in performance before the learner becomes more skilled (McLaughlin & Heredia, 1996). The decline in performance is associated with the substitution of more complex internal representations for less complex ones. That is, the learner's knowledge becomes restructured. For example, as learners move from learning by rote to using syntactic rules, utterances tend to become shorter.

A number of methods have been used to teach a second language (see Figure 5.2). The traditional method is based on translation from one to another, with lectures in grammar in the primary language. Direct methods (such as the Berlitz

A number of methods can be used to teach a second language. One of these is the audiolingual method, which emphasizes speaking and listening before reading and writing.

method) on the other hand carry out all teaching in L2, with emphasis on conversational skills. The audiolingual method emphasizes speaking and listening before reading and writing. The immersion method teaches a group of learners exclusively through the medium of the foreign language. In the more extreme submersion method, the learner is surrounded exclusively by speakers of L2, usually in the foreign country, and the learner has to "sink or swim."

The work of Krashen (1982) has proved influential, if controversial, in understanding how we might better teach languages. He proposed five hypotheses concerning language acquisition

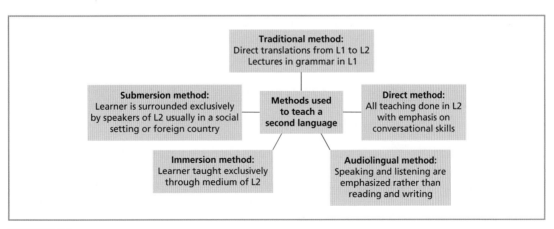

Traditional method:
Direct translations from L1 to L2
Lectures in grammar in L1

Submersion method:
Learner is surrounded exclusively by speakers of L2 usually in a social setting or foreign country

Methods used to teach a second language

Direct method:
All teaching done in L2 with emphasis on conversational skills

Immersion method:
Learner taught exclusively through medium of L2

Audiolingual method:
Speaking and listening are emphasized rather than reading and writing

FIGURE 5.2

that together form the monitor model of second language learning (see Figure 5.3). Central to his approach is a distinction between language learning (which is what traditional methods emphasize) and language acquisition (which is more akin to what children do naturally). Learning emphasizes explicit knowledge of grammatical rules, whereas acquisition emphasizes their unconscious use. Although learning has its role, to be more successful second language acquisition should place more emphasis on acquisition. The first of the five hypotheses is the acquisition and learning distinction hypothesis: children acquire their first language largely unconsciously and automatically—they do not learn it. Earlier views that emphasized the importance of the critical period maintained that adults could only learn a second language consciously and effortfully. Krashen argued that adults could indeed acquire the second language. The second hypothesis is the natural order in acquisition hypothesis. The order of acquisition of syntactic rules, and the types of errors of generalization made, are the same in both languages.

The third and fourth hypotheses are central to Krashen's approach. The third hypothesis is the monitor hypothesis. It states that the acquisition processes create sentences in the second language, but learning enables the development of a monitoring process to check and edit this output. This can only happen if there is sufficient time in the interaction; hence it is difficult to employ the monitor in spontaneous conversation. The monitor uses knowledge of the rules rather than the rules themselves (in a way reminiscent of

Chomsky's distinction between competence and performance). The fourth hypothesis is the comprehensible input hypothesis. In order to move from one stage to the next, the acquirer must understand the meaning and the form of the input. This hypothesis emphasizes the role of comprehension. Krashen argues that production does not need to be explicitly taught: it emerges itself in time, given understanding, and the input at the next highest level need not contain only information from that level. Finally, the active filter hypothesis says that attitude and emotional factors are important in second language acquisition, and that they account for a lot of the apparent difference in the facility with which adults and children can learn a second language.

Krashen's approach provides a useful framework, and has proved to be one of the most influential theoretical approaches to teaching a second language. More recent work has moved away from the idea that acquisition and learning are so very different, emphasizing the practicalities of how learners can best acquire novel material, and exploring the role of attention and covert learning in language learning (see Doughty & Long, 2005).

In addition to teaching method, individual differences between second language learners play some role in how easily people acquire L2 (Robinson, 2001). In a classic study, Carroll (1981) identified four sources of variation in people's ability to learn a new language. These were: phonetic coding ability (the ability to identify new sounds and form associations between them—an aspect of what is called phonological awareness); grammatical sensitivity (the ability to recognize the grammatical functions of words and other syntactic structures); rote-learning ability; and inductive learning ability (the ability to infer rules from data). Working memory plays an important role in foreign language vocabulary learning (Papagno, Valentine, & Baddeley, 1991), and it is possible to recast Carroll's four components of language learning in terms of the size, speed, and efficiency of working memory functions (McLaughlin & Heredia, 1996). Motivation, of course, also plays a significant role; people who want or need to learn will do better (Dörnyei, 1990).

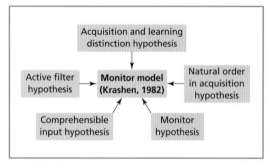

FIGURE 5.3

How can we make second language acquisition easier?

Second language acquisition is often characterized by a phase or phases of silent periods when few productions are offered despite obvious development of comprehension. Classroom teaching methods that force students to speak in these silent periods might be doing more harm than good. Newmark (1966) argued that this has the effect of forcing the speaker back onto the rules of the first language. Hence silent periods should be respected.

Krashen (1982) argued we should make second language acquisition more like first language acquisition by providing sufficient comprehensible input. The immersion method, involving complete exposure to L2, exemplifies these ideas. Whole schools in Montreal, Canada, contain English-speaking children who are taught in French in all subjects from their first year (Bruck, Lambert, & Tucker, 1976). Immersion seems to have no deleterious effects, and if anything might be beneficial for other areas of development (e.g., mathematics). The French acquired is very good but not perfect: there is a slight accent, and syntactic errors are sometimes made.

There might be limits, however, to how much immersion is ideal. Recall the "less-is-more" theory from Chapter 4: that starting small is an advantage to children learning language. Kersten and Earles (2001) found that adults learned an artificial language better when they were initially presented with only small segments of the language than when they were exposed to the full complexity of the language from the beginning. Perhaps children learn the new language in spite of the immersion rather than because of it. Immersion might be particularly counter-productive for adults who, without the cognitive limitations of childhood, will have great difficulty in applying a "less-is-more" strategy.

Sharpe (1992) identified what he called the "four Cs" of successful modern language teaching (see Figure 5.4). These are communication (the main purpose of learning a language is aural communication, and successful teaching emphasizes this); culture (which means learning about the culture of the speakers of the language and de-emphasizing direct translation); context (which is similar to providing comprehensible input); and giving the learners confidence. These points may seem obvious, but they are often neglected in traditional, grammar-based methods of teaching foreign languages.

Finally, some particular methods of learning second languages are of course better than others. Ellis and Beaton (1993) reviewed what facilitates learning foreign language vocabulary. They concluded that simple rote repetition is best for learning to produce the new words, but that using keywords is best for comprehension. Naturally, learners want to be able to do both, so a combination of techniques is the optimum strategy.

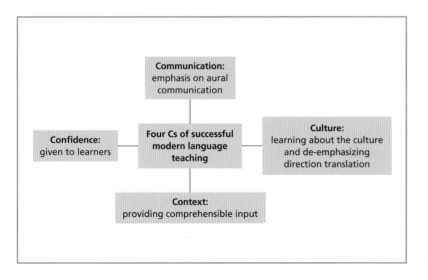

FIGURE 5.4

EVALUATION OF WORK ON BILINGUALISM AND SECOND LANGUAGE ACQUISITION

The study of bilingualism and second language acquisition is an increasingly important topic in psycholinguistics. First, the way in which bilingual people represent and process two languages is of great interest to psycholinguists. Second, it is clearly important that we should be able to teach a second language in the most efficient way. Third, it provides us with an additional tool for investigating language and cognition. For example, Altarriba and Soltano (1996) used knowledge of how bilinguals store language to investigate the phenomenon known as repetition blindness (Kanwisher, 1987). Repetition blindness refers to the observation that people are very poor at recalling repeated words when the words are presented rapidly. For example, when given the sentence "she ate salad and fish even though the fish was raw," participants showed very poor recall of the second presentation of the word "fish." The explanation of repetition blindness is that the repeated word is not recognized as a distinct event and somehow becomes assimilated with the first presentation of the word. It appears to be the visual and phonological (sound) similarity that is important in generating repetition blindness: Words that sound the same (e.g., "won" and "one") produce repetition blindness, whereas words that are similar in meaning (e.g., "autumn" and "fall") do not (Bavelier & Potter, 1992; Kanwisher & Potter, 1990). Altarriba and Soltano confirmed that meaning plays no part in repetition blindness using non-cognate translation equivalents. These are words in different languages that have the same meaning but different physical forms (e.g., "nephew" and "sobrino" in English and Spanish). They found that a sentence such as (1) generated repetition blindness in fluent Spanish–English participants (people had very poor recall for the second instance of "ant") but (2) did not:

(1) I thought we had killed the ants but there were ants in the kitchen.
(2) I thought we had killed the ants pero habian hormigas en la cocina.

Clearly similarity in meaning cannot be responsible for the repetition blindness effect. The results also show that conceptual access in translation is very rapid for bilingual speakers, and also that bilingualism may facilitate some aspects of memory.

Learning and using one language is an impressive achievement; learning and managing several is incredible.

SUMMARY

- Second language acquisition in adulthood and later childhood is difficult because it is not like first language acquisition.
- There are probably both costs and benefits of learning two languages at once. There might be some general cognitive advantages.
- There has been much debate as to how we translate words between languages; in particular, whether or not there are direct links between words in our mental dictionaries, or whether the entries are mediated by semantic links.
- Translation probably does involve conceptual mediation.
- Bilingualism is a useful tool for studying other language processes.

QUESTIONS TO THINK ABOUT

1. How would you suggest teaching a second language based on psycholinguistic principles?
2. How would your answer differ if you were teaching (a) 3-year-olds; (b) 10-year-olds; (c) 20-year-olds?
3. What are the advantages of knowing more than one language? What are the disadvantages?

FURTHER READING

There are many reference works on bilingualism and second language acquisition. Examples of more detailed reviews include Kilborn (1994) and Klein (1986). Books covering the area in greater depth include Bialystok and Hakuta (1994), de Groot and Kroll (1997), Ritchie and Bhatia (1996)—particularly the review chapter by Romaine—and Romaine (1995). For a review of research on code switching, see Grosjean (1997). Altarriba (1992) reviews work on bilingual memory. The book by Fabbro (1999) provides an introduction to the neuropsychology of bilingualism; see also Fabbro (2001). See McLaughlin (1987) for a discussion of Krashen's work. For a cognitive approach to second language learning, see Skehan (1998). Doughty and Long's *Handbook of Second Language Acquisition* (2005) provides a fairly recent review of all the main topics in the area.

SECTION C

WORD RECOGNITION

This section examines how we recognize printed (or written) and spoken words, and how we turn printed words into sound. It also examines disorders of reading, and how children learn to read.

Chapter 6, Recognizing visual words, examines the process that takes place when we recognize a written word. How do we decide on the meaning of a word, or even whether we know the word or not? What methods are available to psycholinguists to study phenomena involved in word recognition, and what models best explain them?

Chapter 7, Reading, looks at how human beings access sound and meaning from a written text. What can studies of people with brain damage tell us about this process?

Chapter 8, Learning to read and spell, looks at how children learn to read. What is the best method of teaching this vital skill? How do children learn to spell? Why do some children find reading difficult to learn?

Chapter 9, Understanding speech, turns to the question of how we recognize the sounds we hear as speech. How do we decide where one word ends and another begins in the stream of sound that is spoken language? How can context help, and what models have been suggested to explain how spoken word recognition operates?

INTRODUCTION

How do we recognize written or printed words? When we see or hear a word, how do we access its representation and meaning within the lexicon? How do we know whether an item is stored there or not? If there are two or more meanings for the same word (e.g., "bank"), how do we know which meaning is intended?

Although recognition involves identifying an item as familiar, we are not only interested in discovering how we decide if a printed string of letters is familiar or not, but also how all the information that relates to a word becomes available. For example, when you see the string of letters "g h o s t," you know more than that they make up a word. You know what the word means, that it is a noun and can therefore occupy certain roles in sentences but not others, and how the word is pronounced. You further know that its plural is formed regularly as "ghosts." In lexical access, we access the representation of an item from its perceptual representation and then this sort of information becomes available.

In this chapter we focus on how lexical access takes place, how we assess a word's familiarity, how we recognize it, and how we access its meaning. In the next chapter, we concentrate on how we pronounce the word, and on the relation between accessing its sound and accessing its meaning.

Is there a gap between recognizing a word and accessing its meaning? Balota (1990) called the point in time when a person recognizes a word and accesses its meaning "the magic moment." In models with a magic moment, a word's meaning can only be accessed after it has been recognized. Johnson-Laird (1975) proposed that the depth of lexical access may vary. He noted that sometimes we retrieve hardly any information for a word. Gerrig (1986) extended this idea, arguing that there are different "modes of lexical access" in different contexts. It is an intuitively appealing idea, fitting with our introspection that sometimes when we read we are getting very little sense from what we are reading.

Although the processing of spoken language has a great deal in common with the processing of visual language, one important difference is that the speech signal is only available for a short

Gerrig (1986) argued that there are different "modes of lexical access." This fits with our feeling that sometimes we get very little sense from what we are reading.

time, whereas under normal conditions a written word is available for as long as the reader needs it. Nevertheless, many of the processes involved in accessing the meaning of words are common to both visual and spoken word recognition. We will look at spoken word recognition in Chapter 9, although many of the findings in the present chapter also apply to the way we understand spoken words. For example, facilitation of recognition by words related in meaning is found in studies of both spoken and visual word recognition. Selecting the appropriate meaning of an ambiguous word is a problem for both spoken and visual word recognition.

While the great majority of human beings have used spoken language for a very long time, literacy is a relatively recent development. There has been a great deal of research on visual word recognition, in part because of convenience. Although written language might not be as fundamental as spoken language, it is exceptionally useful. Literacy is an important feature of modern civilization. The study of word recognition should have many implications for teaching children to read, for the remediation of illiteracy, and for the rehabilitation of people with reading difficulties. By the end of this chapter you should:

- Appreciate how word recognition is related to other cognitive processes.
- Know that recognizing a word occurs when we access its representation in the mental lexicon.
- Know what makes word recognition easier or more difficult.
- Understand the phenomenon of semantic priming and how it occurs.
- Know how the various tasks used to study word recognition might give different results.
- Appreciate that different aspects of a word's meaning are accessed over time.
- Know how we process morphologically complex words.
- Know about the serial search, logogen, and Interactive Activation and Competition (IAC) models of word recognition.
- Understand how we cope with lexical ambiguity, when a word can have two meanings.

BASIC METHODS AND FINDINGS

Six main methods have been used to explore visual word recognition. These are brain imaging (see Chapter 1); examining eye movements; measuring naming, lexical decision, and categorization times; and tachistoscopic identification.

Studying eye movements

The study of eye movements has become important in helping us understand both how we recognize words and how we process larger units of printed language. There are a number of different techniques available for investigating eye movements. One simple technique is called limbus tracking. An infra-red beam is bounced off the eyeball and tracks the boundary between the iris and the white of the eye (the limbus). Although this system is good at tracking horizontal eye movements, it is relatively poor at tracking vertical movements. Therefore one of the most commonly used techniques is the Purkinje system, which is accurate at tracking both horizontal and vertical movements. It takes advantage of the fact that there are several sources of reflection from the eye, such as the cornea and the back of the lens. The system computes the movements of the exact center of the pupil from this information.

When we read, we do not move our eyes smoothly. Instead, the eyes travel in jumps called **saccade**s of about 20 to 60 ms in duration, with intervals of around 200 to 250 ms when the eye is still (Rayner, 1998). These still periods are called fixations (see Figure 6.1). Very little information is taken in while the eye is moving in a saccade. The information that can be taken in within a fixation is limited—15 characters to the right and only 3–4 to the left in English speakers (McConkie & Rayner, 1976; Rayner, Well, & Pollatsek, 1980). This asymmetry is reversed for Hebrew readers, who read from right to left (Pollatsek, Bolozky, Well, & Rayner, 1981). Skilled readers may be able to take in more information in one fixation—that is, they have a larger span—than less skilled readers (Martin, 2004). Information from the more distal regions of the span is used to guide future eye movements.

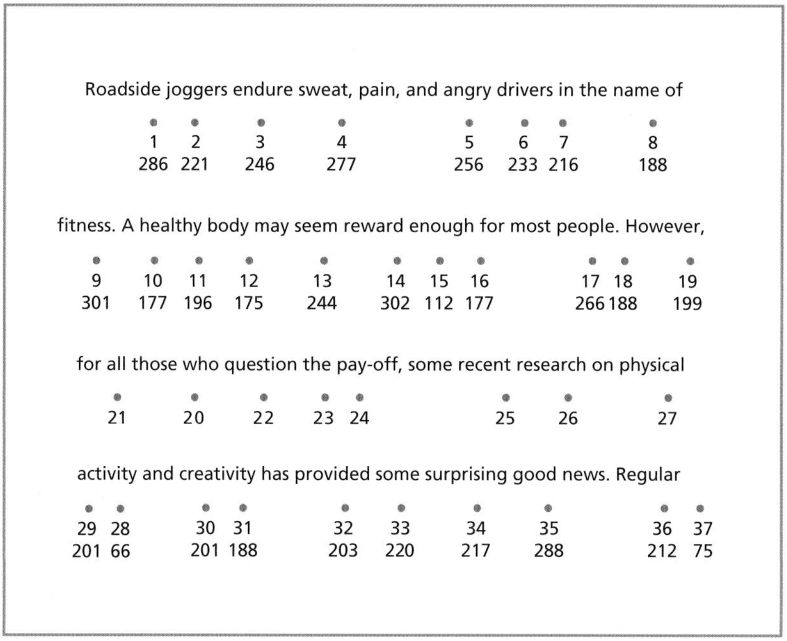

Roadside joggers endure sweat, pain, and angry drivers in the name of

•	•	•	•		•		•	•	•		•
1	2	3	4		5	6	7		8
286	221	246	277		256	233	216		188

fitness. A healthy body may seem reward enough for most people. However,

•	•	•	•		•		•	•	•		•	•		•
9	10	11	12		13		14	15	16		17	18		19
301	177	196	175		244		302	112	177		266	188		199

for all those who question the pay-off, some recent research on physical

| • | | • | | • | | • | • | | | • | | • | | | • |
| 21 | | 20 | | 22 | | 23 | 24 | | | 25 | | 26 | | | 27 |

activity and creativity has provided some surprising good news. Regular

•	•		•	•		•		•		•		•		•	•
29	28		30	31		32		33		34		35		36	37
201	66		201	188		203		220		217		288		212	75

FIGURE 6.1 Diagram showing a typical progression of fixations and variations in saccade length. The dots indicate the place of the fixation; the first number below the dot indicates its position in the sequence (note the "overshoot" phenomenon at fixation 20, in which the first fixation on a new line often falls too far into a sentence and a regression is required). The second number below the dot indicates the duration of each fixation in milliseconds.

The fovea is the most sensitive part of the visual field, and corresponds to the central seven characters or so of average-size text, subtending the central 2° of vision. The fovea is surrounded by the parafovea (extending 5° either side of the fixation point) where visual acuity is poorer; beyond this is the periphery, where visual acuity is even poorer. We extract most of the meaning of what we read from the foveal region. Rayner and Bertera (1979) displayed text to readers with a moving mask that creates a moving blindspot. If the foveal region was masked, reading was possible from the parafoveal region (just outside the fovea), but at a greatly reduced rate (only 12 words a minute). If both the foveal and parafoveal regions were masked, virtually no reading was possible. Participants knew that there were strings of letters outside the masked portion of text, could report the occasional grammatical function word such as "and," and could sometimes obtain information about the starts of words. For example, one participant read "The pretty bracelet attracted much attention" as "The priest brought much ammunition."

Sometimes we make mistakes, or need to check previous material, and have to look backwards. These eye movements back to previous material, called regressions, are sometimes so brief that we are not aware of it. As we will see in Chapter 10, the study of these regressive eye movements provides important information about how we disambiguate ambiguous material.

There has been considerable debate as to which measure from eye movements is the most informative (Inhoff, 1984; Rayner, 1998). Should it be first fixation duration—the amount of time the eye spends looking at a region in the first fixation—or should it be total gaze time—which also includes the time spent looking at a region in any later regression? Most researchers now select regions of the text for detailed analysis and report a number of measures for that region.

How are eye movements controlled when reading—what determines where the eyes look and when? The most influential model of eye-movement control is the E-Z Reader model (Reichle, Rayner, & Pollatsek, 1999, 2003). In the E-Z Reader attention, visual processing, and oculomotor control jointly determine when and where eyes move when we are reading. The central idea of this model is that, when we read, we fixate on a point, and then visual attention progresses across the line of text until a point is reached where the acuity limitations of the visual system then make it difficult to extract more information and recognize new words. Attention then shifts and an eye movement is programmed into the oculomotor system to move to the point of difficulty. A saccade then takes place to the new location, and the process is repeated. Saccades are programmed in two stages: there is an early labile stage when the planned saccade can be canceled if it turns out that it is no longer necessary (e.g., because we have managed to identify the word in the proposed target location); after this initial labile stage saccades cannot be canceled. The central, and the most controversial, assumption of the model is that attention is allocated to one word after another in a strictly serial fashion, shifting only after each word is identified. This assumption ensures that words are processed in the correct order. Word "identification" occurs in two stages: the first stage is a familiarity check (do I know this word? Am I likely to be able to use it?). Completion of the first stage can trigger the programming of a saccade. The second stage is full lexical access, where meaning is retrieved and the representation of the word integrated with the emerging linguistic structure. Completion of the second stage triggers the shift in attention to the next word along. Hence saccades and attention are decoupled in this model, and have different sources of control (familiarity and identification). Linguistic processing can affect eye movements; for example, if an analysis turns out to be wrong, we might return to an earlier location. In the model, higher level processes intervene in the general drive forward only when something goes wrong.

Reaction time measures

In the naming task, participants are visually presented with a word that they then have to name, and the time it takes a participant to start to pronounce the word aloud (the naming latency) is measured. Naming latencies are typically in the order of 500 ms from the onset of the presentation of the word.

In the lexical decision task the participant must decide whether a string of letters is a word or nonword. In the more common visual presentation method, the letter string is displayed on a computer screen (there is also an auditory version of this task). For example, the participant should press one key in response to the word "nurse" and another key in response to the nonword "murse." The experimenter measures reaction times and error rates. One problem with this task is that experimenters must be sensitive to the problem of speed–accuracy trade-offs (the faster participants respond, the more errors they make; Pachella, 1974), and therefore researchers must be careful about the precise instructions the participants are given. Encouraging participants to be accurate tends to make them respond accurately but more slowly; encouraging them to be fast tends to make them respond faster at the cost of making more mistakes. Researchers therefore usually analyze both reaction times and error rates (although usually these show the same pattern of results). Response times vary, depending on many factors, but are typically in the order of 500 ms to 1 second.

In experiments measuring reaction time, the *absolute* time taken to respond is not particularly useful: we are usually concerned with differences between conditions. We assume that our experimental manipulations change only particular aspects of processing, and everything else remains constant and therefore cancels out. For example, we assume that the time participants take to locate the word on the screen and turn their attention to it is constant (unless of course we are deliberately trying to manipulate it).

In tachistoscopic identification, participants are shown words for very short presentation times. Researchers in the past used a piece of equipment called a **tachistoscope**; now computers are used instead, but the name is still used to refer to the general methodology. The experimenter records the thresholds at which participants can no longer confidently identify items. If the presentation is short enough, or if the normal perceptual processes are interfered with by presenting a second stimulus very quickly after the first, we sometimes find what is commonly known as subliminal perception. In this case participants' behavior is affected although they are unaware that anything has been presented.

The semantic categorization task requires the participant to make a decision that taps semantic processes. For example, is the word "apple" a "fruit" or a "vegetable"? Is the object referred to by the word smaller or bigger than a chair?

Different techniques do not always give the same results. They tap different aspects of processing—an important consideration to which we will return.

One of the most important ideas in word recognition is that of priming. This involves presenting material before the word to which a response has to be made. One of the most common paradigms involves presenting one word prior to the target word to which a response (such as naming or lexical decision) has to be made. The first word is called the prime, and the word to which a response has to be made is called the target. The time between when the prime is first presented (its onset) and the start of the target is called the stimulus–onset asynchrony, or **SOA**. We then observe what effect the prime has on subsequent processing. By manipulating the relation between the prime and the target, and by varying the SOA, we can learn a great deal about visual word recognition. The prime does not have to be a single word: it can be a whole sentence, and does not even have to be linguistic (e.g., it could be a picture).

WHAT MAKES WORD RECOGNITION EASIER (OR HARDER)?

Next we will look at some of the main findings on visual word recognition. You should bear in mind that many of these phenomena also apply to spoken word recognition. In particular, frequency effects and semantic priming are found in both spoken and visual word recognition.

Interfering with identification

We can slow down word identification by making it harder to recognize the stimulus. One way of doing this is by degrading its physical appearance. This is called stimulus degradation and can be achieved by breaking up the letters that form the word, by reducing the contrast between the word and the background, or by rotating the word to an unusual angle.

Presenting another stimulus immediately after the target interferes with the recognition process. This is called backwards masking (see Figure 6.2). There are two different ways of doing this. If the masking stimulus is unstructured—for example, if it is just a patch of randomly positioned black dots, or just a burst of light—then we call it energy (or brightness, or random noise) masking. If the masking stimulus is structured (for example, if it comprises letters or random parts of letters) then we call it pattern masking (or feature masking). These two types of mask have very different effects (Turvey, 1973). Energy masks operate on the visual feature detection level by causing a visual feature shortage and making feature identification difficult. Feature masks cause interference at the letter level and limit the time available for processing.

Masking is used in studies of one of the greatest of all psycholinguistic controversies, that of perception without awareness. Perception without awareness is a form of subliminal perception. Researchers such as Allport (1977) and Marcel (1983a, 1983b) found that words that have been masked, to the extent that participants report they are not aware of their presence, can nevertheless produce activation through the word identification system, even to the level of semantic processing. That is, we can access semantic information about an item without any conscious awareness of that item. The techniques involved are notoriously difficult; the results have been questioned by, among others, Ellis and Marshall (1978) and Williams and Parkin (1980). Holender (1986), in critically reviewing this field, pointed out methodological problems with the early experiments. He emphasized ensuring that participants are equally dark-adapted during the preliminary establishing of individual thresholds and the main testing phase of the experiment. Otherwise we cannot be sure that information is not reaching conscious awareness in the testing phase, even though we think we might have set the time for which the target is presented to a sufficiently short interval. The window between presenting a word quickly enough

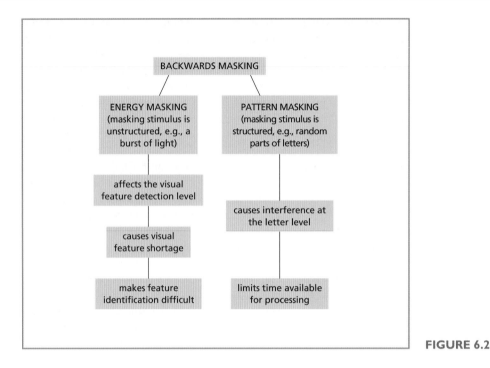

FIGURE 6.2

for it not to be available to consciousness, and so quickly that participants really do see nothing at all, is very small. As yet it is unclear whether we can identify and access meaning-related information about words without conscious awareness, although the balance of evidence is probably that we can. Such a finding does not pose any real problem for our models of lexical access.

Another informative way in which we can interfere with word recognition is to present a word, but delay the presentation of one or two letters at the beginning of the word by backward masking of those letters. What causes most disruption when we do this? In English, after 60 ms it doesn't make much difference, but before that, delaying a consonant disrupts visual word recognition much more than delaying a vowel (Lee, Rayner, & Pollatsek, 2001). Early on, then, consonant identification is particularly important for recognizing a word. In English, consonants have a more regular mapping from visual appearance to sound, whereas vowels do not. In Italian, which has a much more regular mapping for vowels, there is no early advantage for consonants. Hence readers in different languages make differential

early use of information that is most likely to help them identify a word.

Frequency, familiarity, and age-of-acquisition

The frequency of a word is a very important factor in word recognition. Commonly used words are easier to recognize and are responded to more quickly than less commonly used words. The frequency effect was first demonstrated in tachistoscopic recognition (Howes & Solomon, 1951), but has since been demonstrated for a wide range of tasks. Whaley (1978) showed that frequency is the single most important factor in determining the speed of responding in the lexical decision task. Forster and Chambers (1973) found a frequency effect in the naming task.

The effect of frequency is not just a result of differences between frequent and very infrequent words (e.g., "year" versus "heresy"), where you would obviously expect a difference, but also between common and slightly less common words (e.g., "rain" versus "puddle"). It is therefore essential to control for frequency in psycholinguistic experiments, ensuring that different conditions are matched. There are a number of norms of frequency counts available; in the past, Kucera and Francis (1967; see also Francis & Kucera, 1982) was one of the most popular of these, listing the occurrence per million of a large number of words in many samples of printed language. Kucera and Francis is based on written American English. Clearly there are differences between versions of English (e.g., "pavement" and "sidewalk") and between written and spoken word frequency. For example, the pronoun "I" is 10 times more common in the spoken word corpus than the written one (Dahl, 1979; Fromkin et al., 2011). Another popular choice is the CELEX database (Baayen, Piepenbrock, & Gulikers, 1995), which is stored electronically and is therefore easily searchable, making it particularly useful for making up lists of materials with very specific characteristics. The Internet has made possible the collection and analysis of very large samples of text.

Gernsbacher (1984) pointed out that corpora of printed word frequencies are only an approximation to experiential familiarity. This approximation may break down, particularly for low-frequency words. For example, psychologists might be very familiar with a word such as "behaviorism," even though it has quite a low frequency in the general language. People also rate some words with recorded low frequency (such as "mumble," "giggle," and "drowsy") as more familiar than others of similar frequency (such as "cohere," "rend," and "char"). The printed-frequency corpora might not be very accurate for low-frequency words, and language use has changed since many of the corpora were composed. If it is possible to obtain ratings of the individual experiential familiarity of words, they should prove to be a more reliable measure in processing tasks than printed word frequency.

Several other variables correlate with frequency. For example, common words tend to be shorter. If you wish to demonstrate an unambiguous effect of frequency, you must be careful to control for these other factors.

Frequency is particularly entangled with age-of-acquisition (AOA). The age-of-acquisition of a word is the age at which you first learn it (Carroll & White, 1973a; Gilhooly, 1984). On the whole, children learn more common words first, but there are exceptions: for example, "giant" is generally learned early although it is a relatively low-frequency word. Words that are learned early in life are named more quickly and more accurately than ones learned late, across a range of tasks including object naming, word naming, and lexical decision (Barry, Morrison, & Ellis, 1997; Brown & Watson, 1987; Carroll & White, 1973a; Morrison, Ellis, & Quinlan, 1992). The later the age-of-acquisition of a name, the more difficult it will be for someone with brain damage to produce (Hirsh & Ellis, 1994). Frequency and AOA may be correlated, but statistical techniques such as multiple regression enable us to tease them apart. Early-learned items tend to be higher in frequency, although estimates of the size of the correlation have varied from 0.68 (Carroll & White, 1973b) to as low as 0.38 (between an objective measure of AOA, when a word first enters a child's vocabulary, and the logarithm of the spoken word frequency, as in Ellis & Morrison, 1998). It has been suggested that all frequency effects are really AOA effects (e.g., Morrison & Ellis, 1995). On the other hand, it has also been suggested that studies reporting AOA effects have not controlled adequately for frequency; in particular, these studies might not have taken into account cumulative frequency—how often words have been encountered throughout the lifespan (Zevin & Seidenberg, 2002). Measures of frequency such as Kucera and Francis and the CELEX database are quite small (even a million words is small relative to the number we come across in real life), and, as we have seen with familiarity (Gernsbacher, 1984), might not accurately reflect the true occurrence of words in the language. Even then, they just provide a snapshot of adult usage. Importantly, they might particularly underestimate the frequency of words we are exposed to in childhood. However, a large-scale study of French showed that AOA effects persist even when cumulative frequency is controlled for (Bonin, Barry, Méot, & Chalard, 2004). It is probable that both frequency and AOA have effects on word processing (Morrison & Ellis, 2000). Different tasks might differ in their sensitivity to AOA and different measures of frequency; AOA

Generally speaking, children learn more common words first, although some low-frequency words are also learned early on, through storytelling, for example.

particularly affects word reading, while cumulative frequency has an effect in all tasks (Bonin et al., 2004). On the other hand, Zevin and Seidenberg (2002) provide simulations that show that tasks involving redundancy and regularity in the input–output mappings (e.g., reading, where letters map onto sounds in a predictable way) are less prone to AOA effects, and are sensitive only to cumulative frequency, but tasks with less redundancy and regularity (such as learning the names of objects or faces) do show AOA effects.

Age-of-acquisition effects might arise as a consequence of a loss of plasticity in developing systems (Ellis & Lambon Ralph, 2000; Monaghan & Ellis, 2010). Rather than train a connectionist network to learn all items simultaneously, Ellis and Lambon Ralph introduced items into the training regime at different times. Items learned early possess an advantage independently of their frequency of occurrence. As a network learns more items, it becomes less plastic, and late items are not as efficiently or as strongly represented as those learned early, because they are more difficult to differentiate from items that have already been learned. Early-learned items have a head start that enables them to develop stronger representations in the network. Late-learned items can only develop strong representations if they are presented with a very high frequency.

Word length

Gough (1972) argued that during word recognition letters are taken out of a short-term visual buffer one by one at a rate of 15 ms per letter. The transfer rate is slower for poor readers. Therefore it would not be at all surprising if long words were harder to identify than short words. However, a length effect that is independent of frequency has proved surprisingly elusive. One complication is that there are three different ways of measuring word length: how many letters there are in a word, how many syllables, and how long it takes you to say the word (see Figure 6.3).

Although Whaley (1978) found some word length effects on lexical decision, Henderson (1982) did not. However, Chumbley and Balota (1984) found length effects in lexical decision when the words and **nonword**s were matched for length and the regularity of their pronunciation.

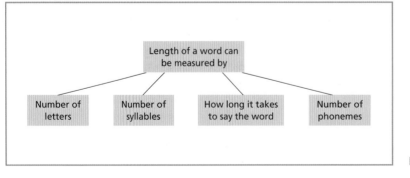

FIGURE 6.3

For some time it was thought that there was clear evidence that longer words take longer to pronounce (Forster & Chambers, 1973). Weekes (1997) found that word length (measured in letters) had little effect on naming words when other properties of words (such as the number of words similar to the target word) were controlled for (although length had some effect on reading nonwords). It seems that the number of letters in a word has little effect for short words, but has some effect on words between 5 and 12 letters long. Furthermore, word length effects in naming words probably reflect the larger number of similar words with similar pronunciations found for shorter words.

Naming time increases as a function of the number of syllables in a word (Eriksen, Pollack, & Montague, 1970). There is at least some contribution from preparing to articulate these syllables in addition to any perceptual effect. We find a similar effect in picture naming. We take longer to name pictures of objects depicted by long words compared with pictures of objects depicted by short words, and longer to read numbers that have more syllables in their pronunciation, such as the number 77 compared with the number 16 (Klapp, 1974; Klapp, Anderson, & Berrian, 1973).

Neighborhood effects

Some words have a large number of other words that look like them (e.g., "mine" has "pine," "line," "mane," among others), whereas other words of similar frequency have few that look like them (e.g., "much"). Coltheart, Davelaar, Jonasson, and Besner (1977) defined the N-statistic as the number of words that can be created by changing one letter of a target word. Hence "mine" has a large N (29): It is said to have many orthographic neighbors (e.g., "pine," "mane," "mire"), but "much" has a low N (5) and few neighbors. The word "bank" has an N-value of 20, but "abhorrence" only has an N-value of 1. (The related word is "abhorrency"—which oddly enough my spell-checker doesn't like!) N is a measure of neighborhood size (or density).

Neighborhood size affects visual word recognition, making words with a high N easy to recognize when other factors have been controlled for, although clear benefits are only found for low-frequency words: Performance on naming and lexical decision tasks is faster for low-frequency words that have many orthographic neighbors (Andrews, 1989; Grainger, 1990; McCann & Besner, 1987). The rime parts of neighbors seem to be particularly important in producing the facilitation (Peereman & Content, 1997).

In addition to neighborhood size, the frequency of the neighbors might also be important, although in a review of the literature Andrews (1997) concluded that neighborhood size has more effect than neighborhood frequency. On the other hand, it is surprising that having many neighbors produces facilitation at all, rather than competition (Andrews, 1997).

Word or nonword?

Words are generally responded to faster than nonwords. Less plausible nonwords are rejected faster than more plausible nonwords (Coltheart et al., 1977). Hence in a lexical decision task we are relatively slow to reject a nonword like "siant" (which might have been a word, and indeed which looks like one, "saint"), but very quick to reject one such as "tnszv." Nonwords that are plausible—that is, that follow the rules of word formation of the language in that they do not contain illegal strings of letters—are sometimes called **pseudoword**s.

Repetition priming

Once you have identified a word, it is easier to identify it the next time you see it. The technique of facilitating recognition by repeating a word is known as **repetition priming**. Repetition facilitates both the accuracy of perceptual identification (Jacoby & Dallas, 1981) and lexical decision response times (Scarborough, Cortese, & Scarborough, 1977). Repetition has a surprisingly long-lasting effect. It is perhaps obvious that having just seen a word will make it easier to recognize straight away, but periods of facilitation caused by repetition have been reported over several hours or even longer.

Repetition interacts with frequency. In a lexical decision task, repetition priming effects are stronger for low-frequency words than for high-frequency ones, an effect known as frequency attenuation (Forster & Davis, 1984). Forster and Davis also pattern-masked the prime in an attempt to wipe out any possible episodic memory of it. They concluded that repetition effects have two components: a very brief lexical access effect, and a long-term episodic effect, with only the latter sensitive to frequency.

There has been considerable debate as to whether repetition priming arises because of the activation of an item's stored representation (e.g., Morton, 1969; Tulving & Schachter, 1990) or because of the creation of a record of the entire processing even in episodic memory (e.g., Jacoby, 1983). An important piece of evidence that supports the episodic view is the finding that we generally obtain facilitation by repetition priming only within a domain (such as the visual or auditory modality), but semantic priming (by meaning or association) also works across domains (see Roediger & Blaxton, 1987).

Form-based priming

We might expect that seeing a word like CONTRAST should make it easier to recognize CONTRACT, because there is overlap between their physical forms. As they share letters, they are said to be orthographically related, and this phenomenon is known as orthographic priming or form-based priming. In fact, form-based priming is very difficult to demonstrate. Humphreys, Besner, and Quinlan (1988) found that form-based priming was only effective with primes masked at short SOAs so that the prime is not consciously perceived. Forster and Veres (1998) further showed that the efficacy of form-based primes depends on the exact make-up of the materials in the task. Form-related primes can even have an inhibitory effect, slowing down the recognition of the target (Colombo, 1986). One explanation for these findings is that visually similar words are in competition during the recognition process, so that in some circumstances similar-looking words inhibit each other. Form-based priming is much

easier to obtain if the prime is masked, perhaps because masked priming is a more "pure" form of priming that has no contribution from conscious processing (Davis & Lupker, 2006; Forster & Davis, 1984; Forster, Davis, Schoknecht, & Carter, 1987).

Semantic priming

For over a century, it has been known that identification of a word can be facilitated by prior exposure to a word related in meaning (Cattell, 1888/1947). Meyer and Schvaneveldt (1971) provided a more recent demonstration of what is one of the most robust and important findings about word recognition. They showed that the identification of a word is made easier if it is immediately preceded by a word related in meaning. They used a lexical decision task, but the effect can be found, with differing magnitudes of effect, across many tasks, and is not limited to visual word recognition (although the lexical decision task shows the largest semantic priming effect; Neely, 1991). For example, we are faster to say that "doctor" is a word if it is preceded by the word "nurse" than if it is preceded by a word unrelated in meaning, such as "butter," or if it is presented in isolation. This phenomenon is known as semantic priming.

The word priming is best reserved for the methodology of investigating what happens when one word precedes another. The first word (the prime) might speed up recognition of the second word (the target), in which case we talk of facilitation. Sometimes the prime slows down the identification of the target, in which case we talk of inhibition.

With very short time intervals, priming can occur if the prime follows the target. Kiger and Glass (1983) placed the primes immediately after the target in a lexical decision task. If the target was presented for 50 ms, followed 80 ms later by the prime, there was no facilitation of the target, but if the target was presented for only 30 ms, and followed only 35 ms later by the prime, there was significant backwards priming of the target. This finding suggests that words are to some extent processed in parallel if the time between them is short enough.

Semantic priming is a type of context effect. One can see that the effect might have some advantages for processing. Words are rarely read (or heard) in isolation, and neither are words randomly juxtaposed. Words related in meaning sometimes co-occur in sentences. Hence processing might be speeded up if words related to the word you are currently reading are somehow made more easily available, as they are more likely to come next than random words. How does this happen? We shall return to this question throughout this chapter.

Other factors that affect word recognition

The ease of visual word recognition is affected by a number of variables (most of which have similar effects on spoken word recognition). There are others that should be mentioned, including the grammatical category to which a word belongs (West & Stanovich, 1986). The imageability, meaningfulness, and concreteness of a word may also have an effect on its identification (see Paivio, Yuille, & Madigan, 1968). In a review of 51 properties of words, Rubin (1980) concluded that frequency, emotionality, and pronunciability were the best predictors of performance on commonly used experimental tasks. Whaley (1978) concluded that frequency, meaningfulness, and the number of syllables had most effect on lexical decision times, although recently age-of-acquisition has come to the fore as an important variable. In a study of a large number of words, Balota, Cortese, Sergent-Marshall, Spieler, and Yap (2004) compared the effects of phonological (e.g., the first sound), lexical (e.g., frequency, length, neighborhood size), and semantic (e.g., imageability) variables on speeded visual word naming and lexical decision. They found that the contribution of the variables was highly task dependent. Semantic variables are especially important, particularly in lexical decision. Finally, the syntactic context affects word recognition. Wright and Garrett (1984) found a strong effect of syntactic environment on lexical decision times. In (1) and (2) the preceding context can be continued with a verb, but not with a noun. In (2) this syntactic constraint is violated:

(1) If your bicycle is stolen, you must [*formulate*]
(2) If your bicycle is stolen, you must [*batteries*]

In both cases the target word (in italics) is semantically unpredictable from the context, yet Wright and Garrett found that syntactic context affected lexical decision times so that people were significantly slower to respond to the noun ("batteries") in this context than the verb ("formulate").

ATTENTIONAL PROCESSES IN VISUAL WORD RECOGNITION

Reading is a mandatory process. When you see a word, you cannot help but read it. Evidence to support this introspection comes from the Stroop task: Naming the color in which a word is written is made more difficult if the color name and the word conflict (e.g., "red" written in green ink) (see Figure 6.4).

How many mechanisms are involved in priming? In a classic experiment, Neely (1977) argued that there were two different attentional modes of priming. His findings relate to a distinction made by Posner and Snyder (1975) and Schneider and Shiffrin (1977) between automatic and attentional (or controlled) processing. **Automatic processing** is fast, parallel, not prone to interference from other tasks, does not demand working memory space, cannot be prevented, and is not directly available to consciousness. **Attentional (or controlled) processing** is slow, serial, sensitive to interference from competing tasks, does

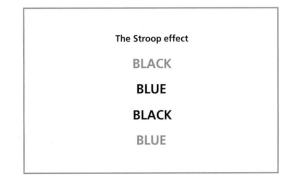

FIGURE 6.4

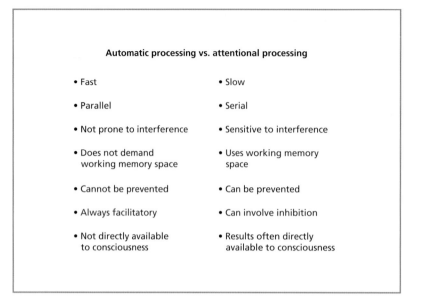

Automatic processing vs. attentional processing

• Fast	• Slow
• Parallel	• Serial
• Not prone to interference	• Sensitive to interference
• Does not demand working memory space	• Uses working memory space
• Cannot be prevented	• Can be prevented
• Always facilitatory	• Can involve inhibition
• Not directly available to consciousness	• Results often directly available to consciousness

FIGURE 6.5

use working memory space, can be prevented or inhibited, and its results are often (but not necessarily) directly available to consciousness (see Figure 6.5).

Neely used the lexical decision task to investigate attentional processes in semantic priming. He manipulated four variables. The first was whether or not there was a semantic relation between the prime and target, so that in the related condition a category name acting as prime preceded the target. Second, he manipulated the participants' conscious expectancies. Third, he varied whether or not participants' attention had to be shifted from one category to another between the presentation of the prime and the presentation of the target. Finally, he varied the stimulus–onset asynchrony, between 250 ms (a very short SOA) and 2,000 ms (a very long SOA).

Importantly, in this experiment there was a discrepancy between what participants were led to expect from the instructions given to them before the experiment started, and what actually happened. Participants were told, for example, that whenever the prime was "BIRD," they should expect that a type of bird would follow, but that whenever the prime was "BODY," a part of a building would follow. Hence their conscious expectancies determined whether they had to

expect to shift or not shift their attention from one category name to members of another category. Examples of stimuli in the key conditions are given in Box 6.1.

Neely found that the pattern of results depended on the SOAs. The crucial condition is what happens after "BODY." At short SOAs, an unexpected but semantically related word such as "HEART" was facilitated relative to the baseline condition, whereas participants took about as long to respond to the expected but unrelated "DOOR" as the baseline. At long SOAs, "HEART" was inhibited—that is, participants were actually slower to respond to it than they were to the baseline condition, whereas "DOOR" was facilitated.

Neely interpreted these results as showing that two different processes are operating at short and long SOAs. At short SOAs, there is fast-acting, short-lived facilitation of semantically related items, which cannot be prevented, irrespective of the participants' expectations. This facilitation is based on semantic relations between words. There is no inhibition of any sort at short SOAs. This is called automatic priming. "BODY" primes "HEART," regardless of what the participants are trying to do. But at long SOAs, there is a slow build-up of facilitation that is dependent on your expectancies. This leads to

Box 6.1 Materials from Neely's (1977) experiment

1.	BIRD	ROBIN	R	E	NS
2.	BODY	DOOR	UR	E	S
3.	BIRD	ARM	UR	UE	NS
4.	BODY	SPARROW	UR	UE	S
5.	BODY	HEART	R	UE	S
6.	CONTROL: to measure the baseline, use XXXX–ROBIN				

R	semantically related
UR	semantically unrelated
E	as expected from instructions
UE	unexpected from instructions
S	shift of attention from one category to another
NS	no shift of attention from one category to another

the inhibition of responses to unexpected items, with the cost that if you do have to respond to them, then responding will be retarded. This is attentional priming. Normally, these two types of priming work together. In a semantic priming task at intermediate SOAs (around 400 ms) both automatic and attentional priming will be cooperating to speed up responding. One can also conclude from this experiment, on the basis of the unexpected–related condition, that the meanings of words are accessed automatically.

Further evidence for a two-process priming model

The details of the way in which two processes are involved in priming have changed a little since Neely's original experiment, although the underlying principle remains the same. Whereas Neely used category–instance associations (e.g., "BODY–ARM"), which are not particularly informative (any part of the body could follow "BODY"), Antos (1979) used instance–category associations (e.g., "ARM–BODY"), which are highly predictive. He then found evidence of inhibition (relative to the baseline) in the unexpected but semantically related condition at shorter SOAs (at 200 ms), suggesting that inhibition

may not just arise from attentional processes, but may also have an automatic component. Antos also showed the importance of the baseline condition, a conclusion supported by de Groot (1984). A row of Xs, as used by Neely, is a conservative baseline, and tends to delay responding; it is as though participants are waiting for the second word before they respond. It may be more appropriate to use a neutral word (such as "BLANK" or "READY") as the neutral condition. When this is done we observe inhibition at much shorter SOAs. Antos also argued that even Neely found evidence of cost at short SOAs, but that this was manifested in an increase in the error rate rather than in a slowing of reaction time. This is evidence of a speed–error trade-off in the data. Generally, in psycholinguistic reaction time experiments, it is always important to check for differences in the error rate as well as reaction times across conditions.

A second source of evidence for attentional effects in priming comes from studies manipulating the predictive validity (sometimes called the cue validity) of the primes. The amount of priming observed increases as the proportion of related words used in the experiment increases (Den Heyer, 1985; Den Heyer, Briand, & Dannenbring, 1983; Tweedy, Lapinski, & Schvaneveldt, 1977).

This is called the proportion effect. If priming were wholly automatic, then the amount found should remain constant across all proportions of associated word pairs. The proportion effect reflects the effect of manipulating the participants' expectancies by varying the proportion of valid primes. If there are a lot of primes that are actually unrelated to the targets, participants quickly learn that they are not of much benefit. This will then attenuate the contribution of attentional priming. Nevertheless, in those cases where primes are related to the target, automatic priming still occurs. The more related primes there are in an experiment, the more participants come to recognize their usefulness, and the contribution of attentional priming increases.

Evaluation of attentional processes in word recognition

There are two attentional processes operating in semantic priming: a short-lived, automatic, facilitatory process that we cannot prevent from happening, and an attentional process that depends on our expectancies and that is much slower to get going. However, the benefits of priming are not without their costs; attentional priming certainly involves inhibition of unexpected alternatives, and if one of these is indeed the target then recognition will be delayed. There is probably also an inhibitory cost associated with automatic priming. Automatic priming probably operates through spreading activation.

We can extend our distinction between automatic and attentional processes to word recognition itself. As we have seen, there must be an automatic component to recognition, because this processing is mandatory. Intuition suggests that there is also an attentional component. If we misread a sentence, we might consciously choose to go back and reread a particular word. To take this further, if we provisionally identify a word that seems incompatible with the context, we might check that we have indeed correctly identified it. These attentional processes operate after we have first contacted the lexicon, and hence we also talk about automatic lexical access and non-automatic post-access effects. Attentional processes are important in word recognition, and may play different roles in the tasks used to study it.

DO DIFFERENT TASKS GIVE CONSISTENT RESULTS?

Experiments on word recognition are difficult to interpret because different experimental tasks sometimes give different results. When we use lexical decision or naming, we are not just studying pure word recognition: we are studying word recognition plus the effects of the measurement task. Worse still, the tasks interact with what is being studied. It is rather like using a telescope to judge the color of stars when the glass of the telescope lens changes color depending on the distance of the star—and we don't realize it.

By far the most controversy surrounds the naming and lexical decision tasks. Which of these better tap the early, automatic processes involved in word recognition?

Lexical decision has been particularly criticized as being too sensitive to post-access effects. In particular, it has been argued that it reflects too much of participants' strategies rather than the automatic processes of lexical access (e.g., Balota & Lorch, 1986; Neely, Keefe, & Ross, 1989; Seidenberg, Waters, Sanders, & Langer, 1984). This is because it measures participant decision-making times in addition to the pure lexical access times (Balota & Chumbley, 1984; Chumbley & Balota, 1984). Participants do not always respond as soon as lexical access occurs; instead, attentional or strategic factors may come into operation, which delay responding. Participants need not be aware of these post-access mechanisms, as not all attentional processes are directly available to consciousness. Participants might use one or both of two types of strategy. First, as we have seen, participants have expectancies that affect processing. In a lexical decision experiment, participants usually notice that some of the prime–target word pairs are related. So when they see the prime, they can generate a set of possible targets. Hence they can make the "word" response faster if the actual target matches one of their generated words than if it does not. The second is a postlexical or post-access checking strategy. Participants might use information subsequent to lexical access to aid their decision. The presence of a semantic relation between the prime and target suggests that the prime must be a word, and hence they respond "word" faster in a lexical decision task, as there can be no semantic relation between a word and nonword. That is, using postlexical checking, participants might respond on the basis of an estimate of the semantic relation between prime and target, and not directly on the results of trying to access the lexicon. Strategic factors might even lead some participants, some of the time, to respond before they have recognized a word (that is, they guess, or respond to stimuli on very superficial characteristics).

What is the evidence that word naming is less likely to engage participant strategies than lexical decision? First, inhibitory effects are small or non-existent in naming (Lorch, Balota, & Stamm, 1986; Neely et al., 1989). As we have seen, inhibition is thought to arise from attentional processes, so its absence in the naming task suggests that naming does not involve attentional processing. Second, **mediated priming** is found much more reliably in the naming task than in lexical decision (Balota & Lorch, 1986; de Groot, 1983; Seidenberg, Waters, Sanders, et al., 1984). Mediated priming is facilitation between pairs of words that are connected only through an intermediary (e.g., "dog" primes "cat," which primes "mouse" for the prime–target pair "dog mouse"). It is much more likely to be automatic than expectancy-driven because participants are unlikely to be able to generate a sufficient number of possible target words from the prime in sufficient time by any other means. Mediated priming is not usually found in lexical decision because normally participants speed up processing by using post-access checking. It is possible to demonstrate mediated priming in lexical decision by manipulating the experimental materials and design so that post-access checking is discouraged (McNamara & Altarriba, 1988). For example, we observe mediated priming if all the related items only are mediated ("dog" and "mouse"), with no directly related semantic pairs

(e.g., "dog" and "cat") mixed in. Nevertheless, lexical decision does seem to routinely involve post-access checking. Third, backwards semantic priming of words that are only associated in one direction but not another (see later) is found in the lexical decision task but is not normally found in naming (Seidenberg, Waters, Sanders, et al., 1984). This type of priming again more plausibly arises through post-access checking than through the automatic spread of activation.

These results suggest that the naming task is less sensitive to postlexical processes. The naming task, however, has a production component in the way that lexical decision does not (Balota & Chumbley, 1985). In particular, naming involves assembling a pronunciation for the word that might bypass the lexicon altogether (using what is known as a sublexical route, discussed in detail in Chapter 7). There are also some possible strategic effects in naming: People are unwilling to utter words that may be incorrect in some way—for example, they may hesitate if they are unsure of the word's pronunciation (O'Seaghdha, 1997).

Clearly both lexical decision and naming have their disadvantages. For this reason, many researchers now prefer to use analysis of eye movements. Fortunately, the results from different methods often converge. Schilling, Rayner, and Chumbley (1998) found that although the lexical decision task is more sensitive to word frequency than naming and gaze duration, there is nevertheless a significant correlation between the frequency effect and response time in all three tasks. We either need to place more stress on results on which the three techniques converge, or have a principled account of why they differ.

The locus of the frequency effect

At what stage does frequency have its effect? Is it inherent in the way that words are stored, or does it merely affect the way in which participants respond in experimental tasks? An experiment by Goldiamond and Hawkins (1958) suggested the latter. The first part of this experiment was a training phase. Participants were exposed to nonwords (such as "lemp" and "stunch"). Frequency was simulated by giving a lot of exposure to some words (mimicking high frequency), and less to others (mimicking low frequency). For example, if you see "lemp" a lot of times relative to "stunch," then it becomes a higher frequency item for you, even though it is a nonword. In the second part of the experiment, participants were tested for tachistoscopic recognition at very short intervals. Although the participants were told to expect the words on which they were trained, only a blurred stimulus that they had not seen before was in fact presented. Nevertheless, participants generated the trained nonwords even though they were not present, but also with the same frequency distribution on which they were trained. That is, they responded with the more frequent words more often, even though nothing was actually present. It can be argued from this that frequency does not have an effect on the perception or recognition of a word, only on the later output processes. That is, frequency creates a response bias. This leads to what is sometimes called a guessing model. This type of experiment only shows that frequency can affect the later, response stages. It does not show that it does not involve the earlier recognition processes as well. Indeed, Morton (1979a) used mathematical modeling to show that sophisticated guessing cannot explain the word frequency effect alone.

A frequency effect could arise in two ways. A word could become more accessible because we see (or hear) frequent words more than we see (or hear) less frequent ones, or because we speak (or write) frequent words more often. Of course, most of the time these two possibilities are entangled; we use much the same words in speaking as we are exposed to as listeners. Another way of putting this is to ask if frequency effects arise through recognition or generation. Morton (1979a) disentangled these two factors. He concluded that the data are best explained by models whereby the advantage of high-frequency words is that they need less evidence to reach some threshold for identification. The effect of repeated exposure to a word is therefore to lower this threshold. The

later recognition of a word is facilitated every time we are exposed to it, whether through speaking, writing, listening, or reading. Hence frequency of experience and frequency of generation are both important.

Most accounts of the frequency effect assume that it arises as a kind of practice—the more often we do something, the better we get at it. This idea has been challenged recently by Murray and Forster (2004), who show that the time it takes to identify words is linearly related to frequency, rather than varying as a logarithmic function, as you would expect if frequency was based on learning that in turn was based on multitudinous repetitions. (Eventually you get diminishing returns from repeating things more times.) They argue that the frequency effect is better accounted for by searching serially through lists of words, where all that matters is relative frequency rather than absolute frequency. We examine the serial search model in more detail below.

There has been considerable debate about whether the naming and lexical decision tasks are differentially sensitive to word frequency (Balota & Chumbley, 1984, 1985, 1990; Monsell, Doyle, & Haggard, 1989). Balota and Chumbley argued that word frequency has no effect on semantic categorization. This is a task that must involve accessing the meaning of the target word. They concluded that when frequency has an effect on word recognition, it does so because of post-access mechanisms, such as checking in lexical decision, and preparing for articulation in naming. They also showed that the magnitude of the frequency effect depended on subtle differences in the stimulus materials in the experiment (such as length differences between words and nonwords). This can be explained if the effect is mediated by participants' strategies. Furthermore, the magnitude of the frequency effect is much greater in lexical decision than naming. The argument is that this is because the frequency effect has a large attentional, strategic component, with any automatic effect being small or non-existent. Lexical decision is more sensitive to strategic factors; therefore lexical decision is more sensitive to frequency.

However, most researchers believe that frequency does have an automatic, lexical effect on word recognition. Monsell et al. (1989) found that frequency effects in naming can be inflated to a similar level to that found in lexical decision by manipulating the regularity of the pronunciation of words; participants must access the lexical representation of irregular words to pronounce them. It is possible that frequency effects are absorbed by other components of the naming task (Bradley & Forster, 1987). Furthermore, delaying participants' responses virtually eliminates the frequency effect (Forster & Chambers, 1973; Savage, Bradley, & Forster, 1990). Delaying responding eliminates preparation and lexical access effects, but not articulation. This casts doubt on the claim that there is a major articulatory component to the effect of frequency on naming, and suggests that the effect must be occurring earlier.

Grainger (1990; see also Grainger & Jacobs, 1996; Grainger, O'Regan, Jacobs, & Segui, 1989) reported experiments that addressed both the locus of the frequency effect and also task differences between lexical decision and naming. He showed that response times to words are also sensitive to the frequency of the neighbors of the target words. The neighbors of a word are those that are similar to it in some way—in the case of visually presented words, it is visual or orthographic similarity that is important. For example, there is much overlap in the letters and visual appearance of "blue" and "blur." Grainger found that when the frequency of the lexical neighborhood of a word is controlled, the magnitude of the effect of frequency in lexical decision is reduced to that of the naming task. Responses to words with a high-frequency neighbor were slowed in the lexical decision task and facilitated in the naming task. He argued that as low-frequency targets necessarily tend to have more high-frequency neighbors, previous studies had confounded target frequency with neighborhood frequency. Furthermore, he argued that the finding that frequency effects are stronger in lexical decision than naming cannot necessarily be attributed to task-specific post-access processes, and that

they arise instead because of this confound with neighborhood frequency. Hence the extent of post-access processes in lexical decision might be less than originally thought.

Evaluation of task differences

Throughout this section we have seen that different variables have different effects on performance, depending on which measure is used. In particular, lexical decision and word naming do not always give the same results. The differences arise because other tasks include aspects of non-automatic processing. Naming times include assembling a phonological code and articulation; lexical decision times include response preparation and post-access checking. Hence the differences in reaction times between the tasks may reflect differing accounts of post-access rather than access processes. Given that the goal of reading is to extract meaning, the extent to which either lexical decision or naming gets at this is questionable.

IS THERE A DEDICATED VISUAL WORD RECOGNITION SYSTEM?

How might our ability to read have come about? Although there has been plenty of time for speech to evolve (see Chapter 1), reading is a much more recent development. It is therefore unlikely that a specific system has had time to evolve for visual word processing. It seems more likely that the word recognition system must be tacked onto other cognitive and perceptual processes. However, words are unusual: We are exposed to them a great deal, they have a largely arbitrary relation with their meaning, and most importantly, in alphabetic writing systems at least, they are composed of units that correspond to sounds.

Is the word-processing system distinct from other recognition systems? This can be examined most simply in the context of naming pictures of objects, the picture-naming task. One important way of looking at this is to examine the extent to which the presentation of printed words affects the processing of other types of material, such as pictures. Pictures facilitate semantically related words in a lexical decision task (Carr, McCauley, Sperber, & Parmalee, 1982; McCauley, Parmalee, Sperber, & Carr, 1980; Sperber, McCauley, Ragain, & Weil, 1979; Vanderwart, 1984). However, the magnitude of the priming effect is substantially less than the size of the within-modality priming effect (pictures priming pictures, or words priming words). These findings suggest that the picture-naming and word recognition systems are distinct, although this is controversial (Glaser, 1992). The results are sensitive to the particulars of the tasks used. Morton (1985) discussed differences in the details of experimental procedures that might account for different findings. For example, in experiments such as those of Durso and Johnson (1979) the pictures were presented very clearly, whereas in those of Warren and Morton (1982) they were presented very briefly. Very brief presentation acts in a similar way to degrading the stimulus, and produces a processing bottleneck not present in other experiments.

Parts of the left ventral visual cortex around the fusiform gyrus respond more to words and

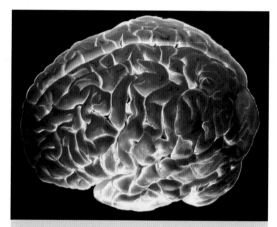

Brain activity during the reading of words. This is a composite of a 3-D magnetic resonance imaging (MRI) scan (blue) of the brain, overlaid with positron emission tomography (PET) scan data (red/green) showing brain activity. The brain is seen from the side, with the front of the brain at left. In this test, words are being read, and the occipital lobe (far right) is active. This is the brain's visual center. Also active is an area of the temporal lobe (lower right), which is associated with comprehension of words.

A man taking part in a word recognition experiment. The speed with which he can name images representing common or rare words is being recorded. Photographed at Newcastle University, England.

pseudowords than strings of consonants. fMRI imaging studies show that this area is sensitive to the orthographic rather than the perceptual properties of words; strings of letters where the case is alternated (cAsE) are perceptually unfamiliar, but still activate this brain region (Cohen & Dehaene, 2004; Polk & Farah, 2002). These imaging data suggest that there is a dedicated brain region, often called the visual word form area, that processes words at an abstract level of representation. Given that the region also responds to pseudowords, but not strings of consonants, the region must be picking something up involving the orthographic regularity of a sequence of abstract letters. The idea of a dedicated visual word form area is disputed, however, because the area does respond to word-like nonwords and to other familiar objects (Price & Devlin, 2003).

Farah (1991) argued that two fundamental visual recognition processes underlie all types of visual processing. These are the holistic processing of non-decomposed perceptual representations and the parallel processing of complex, multiple parts. She proposed that recognizing faces depends just on holistic processing, whereas recognizing words depends on part processing. Recognizing other types of objects involves both sorts of processing to different degrees, depending on the specific object concerned.

Farah's proposal makes specific predictions about the co-occurrence of neuropsychological deficits. Because object recognition depends on both holistic and part processing, you should never find a deficit of object recognition (called **agnosia**) without either a deficit of face recognition (called prosopagnosia) or word recognition (dyslexia). Similarly, if a person has both prosopagnosia and dyslexia, then they should also have agnosia.

Although this is an interesting proposal, it is not clear-cut that face perception is holistic, that object recognition is dependent on both wholes and parts, and that word recognition depends on just parts. Furthermore, Humphreys and Rumiati (1998) described the case of MH, a woman showing signs of general cortical atrophy. MH was very poor at object recognition, yet relatively good at word and face processing. This is the pattern that Farah predicted should never occur. Humphreys and Rumiati concluded that there are some differences between word and object processing: for example, there is much more variation in the spatial positions of parts in objects than letters in words. Words are two-dimensional and objects three-dimensional. Lambon Ralph, Sage, and Ellis (1996) describe a case study of a patient who can recognize words and objects (as familiar or unfamiliar, by a lexical or object decision task), but who is selectively impaired at retrieving the meanings of words. This behavior can be explained if there is a specific visual word form area, but it has become disconnected from the semantic system.

In summary there is considerable evidence that a dedicated brain region processes information about visual words.

MEANING-BASED FACILITATION OF VISUAL WORD RECOGNITION

We have seen that semantic priming is one of the most robust effects on word recognition. It turns out that there are different types of semantic priming, and they have different effects.

Types of "semantic" priming

One obvious question is whether all types of semantic relation are equally successful in inducing priming. The closer the meanings of the two words, the larger the size of the priming effect observed. We can also distinguish between associative priming and non-associative semantic priming.

Two words are said to be associated if participants produce one in response to the other in a word association task. This can be measured by word association norms such as those of Postman and Keppel (1970). Norms such as these list the frequency of responses to a number of words in response to the instruction "Say the first word that comes to mind when I say … doctor." If you try this, you will probably find words such as "nurse" and "hospital" come to mind. It is important to note that not all associations are equal in both directions. "Bell" leads to "hop" but not vice versa: hence "bell" facilitates "hop," but "hop" does not facilitate "bell." Some words are produced as associates of words that are not related in meaning: an example might be "waiting" generated in response to "hospital." Priming by associates is called associative priming; the two associates might or might not also be semantically related.

Non-associative semantically related words are those that still have a relation in terms of meaning to the target, but that are not produced as associates. Consider the words "dance" and "skate." They are clearly related in meaning, but "skate" is rarely produced as an associative of "dance." "Bread" and "cake" are an example of another pair of semantically related but unassociated words. Superordinate category names (e.g., "animal") and category instances (e.g., "fox") are clearly semantically related, but are not always strongly associated. Members of the same category (e.g., "fox" and "camel" are both animals) are clearly related, but are not always associated. Priming by words that are semantically but not associatively related is called non-associative semantic priming.

Most studies of semantic priming have looked at word pairs that are both associatively and semantically related. However, some studies have examined the differential contributions of association and pure semantic relatedness to priming. In particular, to what extent are these types of priming automatic? The evidence for automatic associative priming is fairly clear-cut, and most of the research effort has focused on the question of whether or not we can find automatic non-associative semantic priming.

Many early studies found no evidence of automatic pure semantic facilitation. Lupker (1984) found virtually no semantic priming of non-associated words in a naming task. The word pairs were related in his experiment by virtue of being members of the same semantic category, but were not commonly associated (e.g., "ship" and "car" are related by virtue of both being types of vehicles, but are not associated). Shelton and Martin (1992) showed that automatic priming is obtained only for associatively related word pairs in a lexical decision task, and not for words that are semantically related but not associated. This result suggests that automatic priming appears to occur only within the lexicon by virtue of associative connections between words that frequently co-occur. Moss and Marslen-Wilson (1993) found that semantic associations (e.g., chicken–hen) and semantic properties (e.g., chicken–beak) have different priming effects in a cross-modal priming task. (In a cross-modal task, the prime is presented in one modality—e.g., auditorially—and the target in another—e.g., visually.) Associated targets were primed context-independently, whereas semantic-property targets were affected by the context of the whole surrounding sentence. Moss and Marslen-Wilson concluded that associative priming does not reflect the operation of semantic representations, but is a low-level, intra-lexical automatic process.

On the other hand, Hodgson (1991) found no priming for semantically related pairs in a naming task, but significant priming for the same pairs in a lexical decision task. It is possible that the instructions in his lexical decision task encouraged non-automatic processing (Shelton & Martin, 1992). Both Fischler (1977) and Lupker (1984) found some priming effect of semantic relation without association, also in a lexical decision task. The lexical decision task seems to be a less pure measure of automatic processing than naming, and hence this priming might have arisen through non-automatic means. Although Shelton and Martin (1992) also used a lexical decision task, they designed their experiment to minimize attentional processing. Rather than passively reading a prime and then responding to the target, participants made rapid successive lexical decisions to individual words. On a small proportion of trials two successive words would be related, and the amount of priming to the second word could be recorded. This technique of minimizing non-automatic processing produced priming only for the associated words, and not for the non-associated related words.

These results suggest that automatic priming in low-level visual word recognition tasks that tap the processes of lexical access can be explained by associations between words, rather than by mediation based on word meaning. "Doctor" primes "nurse" because these words frequently co-occur, leading to the strengthening of connections in the lexicon, rather than because of an overlap in their meaning, or the activation of an item at a higher level of representation. Indeed, co-occurrence might not even be necessary for words to become associated: it might be sufficient that two words tend to be used in the same sort of contexts. For example, both "doctor" and "nurse" tend to be used in the context of "hospital," so they might become associated even if they do not directly co-occur (Lund, Burgess, & Atchley, 1995; Lund, Burgess, & Audet, 1996).

McRae and Boisvert (1998) questioned this conclusion. They argued that the studies that failed to find automatic semantic priming without association (most importantly, Shelton & Martin, 1992) failed to do so because the items used in these experiments were not sufficiently closely related (e.g., "duck" and "cow," "nose" and "hand"). McRae and Boisvert used word pairs that were more closely related but still not associated (e.g., "mat" and "carpet," "yacht" and "ship"). With these materials McRae and Boisvert found clear facilitation even at very short (250 ms) SOAs. It now seems likely that at least some aspects of semantic relation can cause automatic facilitation.

The pattern of results observed also depends on the precise nature of the semantic relations involved. Moss, Ostrin, Tyler, and Marslen-Wilson (1995) found that both semantically and associatively related items produced priming of targets in an auditory lexical decision task. Furthermore, semantically related items produced a "boost" in the magnitude of priming if they were associatively related as well. However, a different pattern of results was observed in a visual lexical decision version of the task (which was also probably the version of the task that minimized any involvement of attentional processing). Here, whether or not pure (non-associative) semantic priming was observed depended on the type of semantic relation. Category coordinates (e.g., "pig–horse") did not produce automatic priming without association, whereas instrument relations (e.g., "broom–floor") did. This suggests that information about the use and purpose of an object is immediately and automatically activated.

Moss, McCormick, and Tyler (1997) also showed that some semantic properties of words are available before others. Using a cross-modal priming task, they found significant early priming for information about the function and design of artifacts, but not for information about their physical form. There are grounds to suppose (see Chapter 11 on the neuropsychology of semantics) that a different pattern of results would be obtained with other semantic categories. In particular, information about perceptual attributes might be available early for living things.

Finally, it should be pointed out that semantic priming may have different results in word recognition and word production. For example, Bowles and Poon (1985) showed that semantic priming has an inhibitory effect on retrieving a word given its definition (a production task), whereas we have just seen that in lexical decision (a recognition task) semantic priming has a facilitatory effect.

Does sentence context affect visual word recognition?

Priming from sentence context is the amount of priming contributed over and above that of the associative effects of individual words in the sentence. The beginning of the sentence "It is important to brush your teeth every single __" facilitates the recognition of a word such as "day," which is a highly predictable continuation of the sentence, compared with a word such as "year," which is not. The sentence context facilitates recognition even though there is no semantic relation between "day" and other words in the sentence. Can sentence context cause facilitation?

Schuberth and Eimas (1977) were the first to appear to demonstrate sentence context effects in visual word recognition. They presented incomplete context sentences followed by a word or nonword to which participants had to make a lexical decision. Response times were faster if the target word was congruent with the preceding context. West and Stanovich (1978) demonstrated similar facilitation by congruent contexts on word naming. Later studies have revealed limitations with regard to when and how much contextual facilitation can occur.

Fischler and Bloom (1979) used a paradigm similar to that of Schuberth and Eimas. They showed that facilitation only occurs if the target word is a highly probable continuation of the sentence. For example, consider the sentence "She cleaned the dirt from her __." The word "shoes" is a highly predictable continuation here; the word "hands" is an unlikely but not anomalous continuation; "terms" would clearly be an anomalous ending. (We do not need to rely on our intuitions for this; we can ask a group of other participants to give a word to end the sentence and count up the numbers of different responses.) We find that an appropriate context has a facilitatory effect on the highly predictable congruent words ("shoes") relative to the congruent but unlikely word (e.g., "hands"), and an inhibitory effect to the anomalous words (e.g., "terms"). As there is no direct associative relation between "shoes" and other words in the sentence, this seems to be attributable to priming from sentence context.

Stanovich and West (1979, 1981; see also West & Stanovich, 1982) found that contextual effects are larger for words that are harder to recognize in isolation. Contextual facilitation was much larger when the targets were degraded by reduced contrast. In clear conditions, we find mainly contextual facilitation of likely words; in conditions of target degradation, we find contextual inhibition of anomalous words. Children, who of course are less skilled at reading words in isolation than adults, also display more contextual inhibition. Different tasks yield different results. Naming tasks tend to elicit more facilitation of congruent words, whereas lexical decision tasks tend to elicit more inhibition of incongruent words. The inhibition is most likely to arise because lexical decision is again tapping post-access, attentional processes. It is likely that these processes involve integrating the meanings of the words accessed with a higher level representation of the sentence.

West and Stanovich (1982) argued that the facilitation effects found in the naming task arise through simple associative priming from preceding words in the sentence. It is very difficult to construct test materials that eliminate all associative priming from the other words in the sentence to the target. If this explanation is correct, any facilitation found is simply a result of associative priming from the other words in the sentence. Sentence context operates by the post-access inhibition of words incongruent with the preceding context, and this is most likely to be detected with tasks such as lexical decision that are more sensitive to post-access mechanisms. One problem with this conclusion is that lexical relatedness is not always sufficient in itself to produce facilitation in sentence contexts (O'Seaghdha, 1997; Sharkey & Sharkey, 1992; Williams, 1988). This suggests that the facilitation observed comes from the integration of material into a higher text-level representation. Forster (1981) noted that the use of context may be very demanding of cognitive resources. This suggests that contextual effects

should at least sometimes be non-automatic. Perhaps the potential benefit is too small for it to be worth the language processor routinely using context. Sentence context may only be of practical help in difficult circumstances, such as when the stimulus is degraded.

As naming does not necessitate integration of the target word into the semantic structure, the analysis of eye movements is revealing here. Schustack, Ehrlich, and Rayner (1987) found evidence of the effects of higher level context in the analysis of eye movements, but not of naming times. Inhoff (1984) had participants read short passages of text from *Alice in Wonderland*. A moving visual pattern mask moved in synchrony with the readers' eyes. Ease of lexical access was manipulated by varying word frequency, and ease of conceptual processing was manipulated by varying how predictable the word was in context. Analysis of eye movements suggested that lexical access and context-dependent conceptual processing could not be separated in the earliest stages of word processing. The mask affected frequency and predictability differentially, suggesting that there is an early automatic component to lexical access, and a later non-automatic, effortful processing involving context. So context may have some early effects, but lexical access and conceptual processing later emerge as two separate processes. This experiment is also further support for the idea that early lexical processing is automatic, whereas later effects of context involve an attentional component.

Van Petten (1993) examined event-related potentials (ERPs) to semantically anomalous sentences. One advantage of the ERP technique is that it enables the time course of word recognition to be examined before an overt response (such as uttering a word or pressing a button) is made. The effects of lexical and sentence context were distinguishable in the ERP data, and the effects of sentence context were more prolonged. Van Petten concluded that there was indeed an effect of sentence context that could not be attributed to lexical priming. Furthermore, the priming effects appear to start at the same time, which argues against a strict serial model where lexical priming precedes sentence context priming. Similarly,

Kutas (1993) found that lexical and sentence context had very similar effects on ERPs. Both give rise to N400s (a large negative wave present 400 ms after the stimulus) whose amplitudes vary with the strength of the association or sentence context. Finally, Altarriba, Kroll, Sholl, and Rayner (1996) examined naming times and eye movements in an experiment where fluent English–Spanish bilinguals read mixed-language sentences. They found that sentence context operated both through intra-lexical priming and high-level priming. Contextual constraints still operate across languages, although the results were moderated by a lexical variable, word frequency.

Clearly the results are variable, and seem to be task-dependent. It is possible that processing in discourse is different from the processing of word lists such as are typically used in semantic priming experiments. Hess, Foss, and Carroll (1995) manipulated global and local context in a task where participants heard discourse over headphones, and then had to name the concluding target word, which appeared on a screen in front of them. The most important conditions were where the target word was globally related to the context but locally unrelated to the immediately preceding words (3), and globally unrelated but locally related (4):

(3) The computer science major met a woman who he was very fond of. He had admired her for a while but wasn't sure how to express himself. He always got nervous when trying to express himself verbally so the computer science major wrote the poem.

(4) The English major was taking a computer science class that she was struggling with. There was a big project that was due at the end of the semester which she had put off doing. Finally, last weekend the English major wrote the poem.

Hess et al. found that only global context facilitated naming the target word "poem." This result does not show that automatic semantic priming does not occur: we certainly observe it with isolated items presented rapidly together. The experiment does show that in real discourse the effects of global context may be more important.

Morris and Harris (2002) argue the RSVP (rapid serial visual presentation) technique is particularly suited to investigating the effects of sentence context because it resembles normal reading in that a whole sentence has to be read and processed, in contrast to tasks that involve responding to one particular word in a sentence. In the RSVP task, words are displayed one at a time in the same location, each new word overwriting the previous one. Readers tend to misread the word "rice" in sentences such as "She ran her best time yet in the rice last week" as "race" when the items are presented using RSVP (Potter, Moryadas, Abrams, & Noel, 1993). Clearly here sentence context is causing the misperception, but at what stage? The early, interactive accounts state that sentence context is one factor interacting with all others to determine the activation of a word, and affects recognition; the late, modular accounts state that "rice" is indeed selected, and corrected later as a result of postperceptual processing, or recall. Morris and Harris combined the RSVP task with repetition blindness, whereby people seeing a word repeated very soon after its first instance tend to omit the repetition in the reports of what they have seen—that is, they are blind to the repetition (Kanwisher, 1987). Repetition blindness can be so strong that people might report having seen "When she spilled the ink there was all over," which doesn't make sense, when they actually saw "When she spilled the ink there was ink all over." The preponderance of evidence (e.g., from ERP studies) suggests that repetition blindness has an early, perceptual effect.

What happens if we combine RSVP with corrected words and repetition blindness in a misreading repetition blindness paradigm? Suppose we present participants with "race" very soon after the sentence "She ran her best time yet in the rice last week"? If the perceptual account of the correction is correct, "rice" should be "perceived" like "race," and therefore we should get repetition blindness for the "second" "race." If the postperceptual account is correct, people really do "see" "rice," and therefore this case should not cause repetition blindness. Morris and Harris found that the perceptual account fitted the data better: reconstructions cause repetition blindness.

In summary, sentence context can have either an early perceptual effect or a late postperceptual effect. We can observe early effects, but only in certain tasks, particularly ones that resemble reading of whole sentences and discourse rather than responding to isolated words.

Summary of meaning-based priming studies

We can distinguish between associative semantic priming, associative non-semantic priming, and non-associative semantic priming. All sorts of priming have both automatic and attentional components, although there has been considerable debate as to the status of automatic non-associative semantic priming. Attentional processes include checking that the item accessed is the correct one, using conscious expectancies, and integrating the word with higher level syntactic and semantic representations of the sentence being analyzed. The remaining question is the extent to which sentence context has an automatic component. Researchers are divided on this, but there is a reasonable amount of evidence that it has. Schwanenflugel and LaCount (1988) suggested that sentential constraints determine the semantic representations generated by participants as they read sentences. The more specific the constraints, the more specific the expected semantic representations generated. Connectionist modeling also suggests a mechanism whereby sentence context could have an effect. In an interactive system, sentence context provides yet another constraint that operates on word recognition in the same way as lexical variables, facilitating the recognition of more predictable words.

How does priming occur? The dominant theory says that semantic priming occurs by the spread of activation. Activation is a continuous property, rather like heat, that spreads around a network. Items that are closely related will be close together in the network. Retrieving something from memory corresponds to activating the appropriate items. Items that are close to an item in the network will receive activation by its spread from the source unit. The farther away other items are from the source, the less activation they will receive.

A few researchers argue that activation does not spread, and instead propose a compound-cue theory (e.g., Ratcliff & McKoon, 1981, 1988; see also Hodgson, 1991). The central idea of spreading activation—which Ratcliff and McKoon disputed—is that activation can permeate some distance through a network, and that this permeation takes time. The further activation travels, the more time should pass, and it can be very difficult to detect some of these very small effects. Instead, according to compound-cue theory, priming involves the search of memory with a compound cue that contains both the prime and the target. This theory predicts that priming can only occur if two items are directly linked in memory. It therefore cannot account for mediated priming where two items that are not directly linked can be primed through an intermediary (see McNamara, 1992, 1994). Furthermore, there is now evidence that time elapses while activation spreads, and the more distantly related two things are, the longer the time that elapses (McNamara, 1992; McNamara & Altarriba, 1988).

PROCESSING MORPHOLOGICALLY COMPLEX WORDS

So far we have mainly looked at morphologically simple words. How are morphologically complex words stored in the lexicon? Is there a full listing of all derivations of a word, so that there are entries for "kiss," "kissed," "kisses," and "kissing"? We call this the full-listing hypothesis. Or do we just list the stem ("kiss-"), and produce or decode the inflected items by applying a rule (you add "-ed" to the stem of a word to form the past tense)? As English contains a large number of irregular derivations (e.g., "ran," "ate," "mice," "sheep"), we would then have to list the exceptions separately, so we would store a general rule and a list of exceptions. We call this the obligatory decomposition hypothesis (Smith & Sterling, 1982; Taft, 1981, 2004). There is an intermediate position, called the dual-pathway hypothesis. Although it is uneconomical to list all inflected words, some frequent and common inflected words do have their own listing (Monsell, 1985; Sandra, 1990).

According to the obligatory decomposition hypothesis, to recognize a morphologically complex word we must first strip off its affix, a process known as affix stripping (Taft & Forster, 1975; see also Taft, 1985, 1987). In a lexical decision task, words that look as though they have a prefix, but in fact do not (e.g., "interest," "result"), take longer to recognize than control words (Taft, 1979, 1981). It is as though participants are trying to strip these words of their affixes but are then unable to find a match in the lexicon and have to reanalyze. In a task where participants were asked to judge whether a visually presented word was pronounced identically to another word (i.e., the word was a **homophone**), Taft (1984) observed people have difficulty with words such as "fined" that have a morphological structure different from their homophonic partner (here "find"). Taft argued that the difficulty with such words arises from the fact that inflected words are represented in the lexicon as stems plus their affix. Finally, consider words like "seeming" and "mending"; they have very similar surface frequencies—that is, those particular forms occur with about equal frequency in the language. However, the stems have very different base frequencies: "Seem" and all its variants (seems, seemed) is much more frequent than "mend" and its variants (mends, mended). Which determines the ease of recognition—surface or base frequency? It turns out that on the whole lexical decision is much faster, and there are fewer errors, for words with high base frequencies, again suggesting that complex words are decomposed and recognized by their stem (Taft, 1979, 2004). However, the base frequency effect is not found for all words; for some common words there is no effect of base frequency but there is one of surface frequency (Baayen, Dijkstra, & Schreuder, 1997; Bertram, Schreuder, & Baayen, 2000; Schreuder & Baayen, 1997). This finding is evidence for the dual-pathway hypothesis, although the debate is ongoing, with Taft arguing that base- and surface-frequency effects arise at different stages of processing, so that the lack of a base-frequency effect is not evidence against obligatory decomposition.

Compound words whose meanings are not transparent from their components (e.g., "buttercup") will also be stored separately (Sandra,

1990). Hence neither "milk" nor "spoon" will facilitate the recognition of "buttercup."

Marslen-Wilson, Tyler, Waksler, and Older (1994) examined how we process derivationally complex words in English. Marslen-Wilson et al. used a cross-modal lexicon decision task to examine what we decompose morphologically complex words into, and therefore the sorts of words that they can influence. For example, a participant would hear a spoken prime (e.g., "happiness") and then immediately have to make a lexical decision to a visual probe (e.g., "happy"). The cross-modal nature of the task is important because it obliterates any possible phonological priming between similar words. Instead, any priming that occurs must result from lexical access.

The pattern of results was complicated and showed that the extent of priming found depends on the ideas of phonological transparency and semantic transparency. The relation between two morphologically related words is said to be phonologically transparent if the shared part sounds the same. Hence the relation in "friendly" and "friendship" is phonologically transparent ("friend" sounds the same in each word), but in "sign" and "signal" it is not (the "sign" components have different pronunciations). (Phonological transparency is really a continuum rather than a dichotomy, with some word pairs, such as "pirate" and "piracy," in between the extremes.) A morphologically complex word is semantically transparent if its meaning is obvious from its parts: hence "unhappiness" is semantically transparent, being made up in a predictable fashion from "un-," "happy," and "-ness." A word like "department," even though it contains recognizable morphemes, is not semantically transparent. The meaning of "depart" in "department" is not obviously related to the meaning of "depart" in "departure." It is semantically opaque.

Semantic and phonological transparency affect the way in which words are identified. Semantically transparent forms are morphologically decomposed, regardless of whether or not they are phonologically transparent. Semantically opaque words, however, are not decomposed. Furthermore, suffixed and prefixed words behave differently. Suffixed and prefixed derived words prime each other, but pairs of suffixed words produce interference. This is because when we hear a suffixed word, we hear the stem first. All the suffixed forms then become activated, but as soon as there is evidence for just one of them, the others are suppressed. Therefore, if one of them is subsequently presented, we observe inhibition.

The experiment of Marslen-Wilson et al. shows that in English there is a level of lexical representation that is modality-independent (because we observe cross-modal priming), and that it is morphologically structured for semantically transparent words (because of the pattern of facilitation shown). More recent studies have found that morphological priming effects are independent of meaning similarity; that is, there is no difference in the priming effects for semantically transparent and opaque derivations in several languages, including English (Rastle, Davis, & New, 2004), French (Longtin, Segui, & Halle, 2003), and Hebrew (Frost, Forster, & Deutsch, 1997). These results suggest that morphological priming in general is obtained because of morphological structure rather than because of semantic overlap between similar items.

MODELS OF VISUAL WORD RECOGNITION

In this section, we examine some models of visual lexical access. They all take as input a perceptual representation of the word, and output desired information such as meaning, sound, and familiarity. The important question of how we access a word's phonological form will be examined in the next chapter.

All models of word recognition have to address four main questions. First, is processing autonomous or interactive—in particular, are there top-down effects on word recognition? Second, is lexical access a serial or a parallel process? Third, can activation cascade from one level of processing to a later one, or must processing by the later stage wait until that of the earlier one is complete? Fourth, how do we find items? Do we find them by searching through the lexicon, or can

we locate them because their storage location is defined by their content—a feature called content addressability?

Carr and Pollatsek (1985) use the term lexical instance models for models that have in common that there is simply perceptual access to a memory system, the lexicon, where representations of the attributes of individual words are stored, and they do not have any additional rule-based component that converts individual letters into sounds. We can distinguish two main types of lexical instance model. These differ in whether they employ serial search through a list, or the direct, multiple activation of units. The best known instance of a search model is the serial search model. Direct access, activation-based models include the logogen model, localist connectionist models, as well as the cohort model of spoken word recognition (see Chapter 9). More difficult to fit into this simple scheme are hybrid or verification models (which combine direct access and serial search), and distributed connectionist models (which although very similar to the logogen model do not have simple lexical units at all).

Forster's autonomous serial search model

Imagine how you might try to find a word by searching through a dictionary; you search through the entries, which are arranged to facilitate search on the basis of visual characteristics (that is, they are in alphabetical order), until you find the appropriate entry. The entry in the dictionary gives you all the information you need about the word: its meaning, pronunciation, and its syntactic class. A commonly used analogy here is that of searching through a catalog to find the location of a book in the library. The model is a two-stage one; you can use the catalog to find out where the book is, but you still have to go to the shelf, find the book's actual location, and extract information from it. Forster (1976, 1979) proposed that we identify words by a serial search through the lexicon. In this model the catalog system corresponds to what are called access files, and the shelf full of books to the master file.

In the serial search model, perceptual processing is followed by the sequential search of access

Forster (1976) proposed that we identify words by a serial search through the lexicon. A library is a useful analogous tool, whereby the library's catalog system corresponds to access files, and the shelf full of books to the master file.

files that point to an entry in the lexicon. Access files are modality-specific: there are different ones for orthographic, phonological, and syntactic–semantic (used in speech production) sources. These access files give pointers to a master file in the lexicon that stores all information to do with the word, including its meaning. To speed up processing, these access files are subdivided into separate bins on the basis of the first syllable or the first few letters of a word. Items within these bins are then ordered in terms of frequency, such that the more frequent items are examined first. Hence more frequent items will be accessed before less frequent ones. This frequency-based searching is an important characteristic of the model. Semantic priming arises as the result of cross-references between entries in the master file. The model is shown in Figure 6.6.

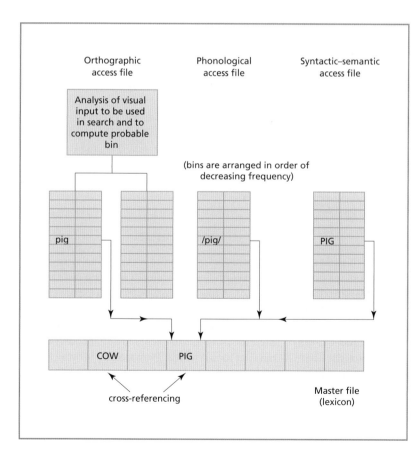

FIGURE 6.6 Forster's serial search model of lexical access (based on Forster, 1976).

Search is not affected by syntactic or semantic information, which is why the search is said to be autonomous. The only type of context that can operate on lexical access is associative priming within the master file. There is no early role for the effect of sentence context; sentence context can only have an effect through post-access mechanisms such as checking the output and integrating it with higher level representations. Repetition can temporarily change the order of items within bins, which is why we observe repetition priming. Illegal nonwords can be rejected early on in the bin selection process, but legal nonwords are only rejected after the exhaustive search of the appropriate bin.

Evaluation of the serial search model

The most significant criticism of the serial search model concerns the plausibility of a serial search mechanism. Although introspection suggests that word recognition is direct rather than involving serial search, we cannot rely on these sorts of data. Making a large number of serial comparisons will take a long time, but word recognition is remarkably fast. The model accounts for the main data in word recognition, and makes a strong prediction that priming effects should be limited to associative priming within the lexicon. There should be no top-down involvement of extra-lexical knowledge in word recognition. Finally, the model does not convincingly account for how we pronounce nonwords.

Forster (1994) addressed some of these problems. In particular, he introduced an element of parallelism by suggesting that all bins are searched simultaneously. The subdivision of the system into bins greatly speeds up the search, and it makes it possible to conclude that a string of letters is a nonword much more quickly than if the whole lexicon has to be searched.

The serial search model also provides an account of the effects of word frequency on lexical access. It was originally thought that the effect of frequency is roughly logarithmic, so that the difference in access times between a common and a slightly less common word is much less than between a rare and a slightly more rare word (Howes & Solomon, 1951; Murray &

Forster, 2004). In the serial search model only the relative frequency of words within a bin has an effect on access time, not the absolute frequency. This idea is called the rank hypothesis (Murray & Forster, 2004). Suppose you have two bins; in one bin the absolute frequency of the first item is 100,000 and of the second item just 10, while in the second bin the frequency of the first item is just 20 and of the second 10. Hence in the first bin there is a big absolute difference in frequency between the two items, and in the second bin a small absolute difference. But in each case the relative frequencies are the same—the first item compared with the second item. Most of the evidence suggests that relative frequency is more important in determining access time than absolute frequency. Detailed experimental analysis of lexical decision times and error rates for words with a wide range of frequencies shows that reaction times fit better to a linear rank function (as predicted by the rank hypothesis where all that matters is relative frequency) than to a logarithmic function (where absolute frequency matters). In particular, the extremes of the distribution do not behave as expected: Both very high frequency and very low frequency words are responded to more slowly and inaccurately than the logarithmic function predicts.

The serial search model has proved very influential and is a standard against which to compare other models. Can we justify using lexical access mechanisms more complex than serial search?

The logogen model

In this model every word we know has its own simple feature counter called a logogen corresponding to it. A logogen accumulates evidence until its individual threshold level is reached. When this happens, the word is recognized. Lexical access is therefore direct, and occurs simultaneously and in parallel for all words. Proposed by Morton (1969, 1970), the logogen model was related to the information processing idea of features and demons, as described in Lindsay and Norman's classic (1977) textbook, where "demons" monitor the perceptual input for specific "features"; the more evidence there is for a particular feature in the perceptual input, the louder the associated demon shouts. The model was originally formulated to explain how context affects word recognition with very brief exposure to the word, but has been extended to account for many word recognition phenomena. The full mathematical model is presented in Morton (1969), but a simplified account can be found in Morton (1979a).

Each logogen unit has a resting level of activation. As it receives corroborating evidence that it corresponds to the stimulus presented, its activation level increases. Hence if a "t" letter is identified in the input, the activation levels of all logogens that correspond to words containing a "t" will increase. If the activation level manages to pass a threshold, the logogen "fires" and the word is "recognized." Both perceptual and contextual evidence will increase the activation level. That is, there is no distinction between evidence for a word from external and internal sources. Context increases a logogen's activation level just as relevant sensory data do. Any use of the logogen will give rise to subsequent facilitation by lowering the threshold of that logogen. More frequent items have lower thresholds. Nonwords will be rejected if no logogen has fired by the time a deadline has passed. Logogens compute phonological codes from auditory and visual word analysis, and also pass input after detection to the cognitive system. The cognitive system does all the other work, such as using semantic information. The connections are bidirectional, as semantic and contextual information from the cognitive system can affect logogens. (See Figure 6.7 for a depiction of the early version of the logogen model.)

Problems with the original logogen model

In the original logogen model, a single logogen carried out all language tasks for a particular word, regardless of modality. That is, the same logogen would be used for recognizing speech and visually presented words, for speaking, and for writing. The model predicts that the modality of the source of activation of a logogen should not matter. For example, visual recognition of a word should be as equally facilitated by a spoken prime

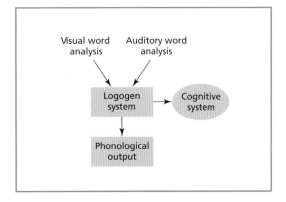

FIGURE 6.7 The original logogen model of lexical access (based on Morton, 1979b).

as by a visual prime. Subsequent experiments contradicted this prediction.

Winnick and Daniel (1970) showed that the prior reading aloud of a printed word facilitated tachistoscopic recognition of that word. However, naming a picture or producing a word in response to a definition produced no subsequent facilitation of tachistoscopic recognition of those words. That is, different modalities produce different amounts of facilitation. Indeed, Morton (1979b) reported replications of these results, clearly indicating that the logogen model needed revision. (For further details of the experiments, see also Clarke & Morton, 1983; Warren & Morton, 1982.) Hence Morton divided the word recognition system into different sets of logogens for different modalities (e.g., input and output). Morton (1979b) also showed that although the modality of response appeared to be immaterial (reading or speaking a word in the training phase), the input modality did matter. The model was revised so that instead of one logogen for each word, there were two modality-specific ones (see Figure 6.8). The consequence of this change ensured that only visual inputs could facilitate subsequent visual identification of words, and that auditorily presented primes would not facilitate visually presented targets in tachistoscopic recognition. Subsequent evidence suggests that four logogen systems are necessary: one for reading, one for writing, one for listening, and one for speaking.

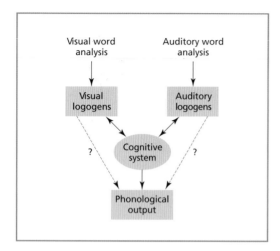

FIGURE 6.8 The revised logogen model of lexical access (based on Morton, 1979b).

Some have argued that Morton was too hasty in giving up the simpler model, arguing that the possible ways in which the primes and targets are represented in the tachistoscopic results mean that no firm conclusion can be drawn (P. Brown, 1991), or that the precise way in which the facilitation effect occurs is unclear (Besner & Swan, 1982). Neuropsychological evidence (see Chapter 15 for details) supports the splitting of the logogen system, and this is currently the dominant view.

Interaction of variables in the logogen model

The effects of context and stimulus quality (whether or not the stimulus is degraded) should interact if the logogen model is correct. Furthermore, frequency and context are handled in the same way in the logogen model, and hence they should show similar patterns of interaction with any other variable (Garnham, 1985). For example, stimulus quality should have the same effects when combined with manipulations of context and frequency. Less perceptual information is required to recognize a high-frequency word than a low-frequency one, and less information is required to recognize a word in context than out of context. The findings are complex and contradictory. Some researchers find an interaction; Meyer, Schvaneveldt, and Ruddy (1974) found

that the less legible the stimuli, the more beneficial the effects of context. Others have found them to be additive (Becker & Killion, 1977; Stanners, Jastrzembski, & Westwood, 1975). Later experiments by Norris (1984) clarified these results. He found that frequency and stimulus quality could interact, but that the interaction between stimulus quality and context is larger and more robust.

In summary, it is very difficult to draw conclusions from this research. The issues involved are complex and the experimental results often contradictory. Morton (1979a) proposed that frequency does not affect the logogen system itself, but rather the cognitive systems to which it outputs at the end of the recognition process. The implications of this revision make the interpretation of these data yet more complex.

The logogen model has been overtaken by connectionist models of word recognition, and in many respects it can be seen as a precursor of them.

Interactive activation models of word recognition

McClelland and Rumelhart (1981) and Rumelhart and McClelland (1982) developed a model called interactive activation and competition (IAC). It is one of the earliest of all connectionist models. (If you haven't studied connectionist models before, I strongly advise you to read the Appendix carefully at this point.)

The original purpose of this model was to account for word context effects on letter identification. Reicher (1969) and Wheeler (1970) showed that, in tachistoscopic recognition, letters are easier to recognize in words than when seen as isolated letters. This is known as the word superiority effect. However, the model can be seen as a component of a general model of word recognition. We will only look at the general principles of the model here.

The IAC model consists of many simple processing units arranged in three levels. There is an input level of visual feature units, a level where units correspond to individual letters, and an output level where each unit corresponds to a word. Each unit is connected to each unit in the level immediately before and after it. Each of these

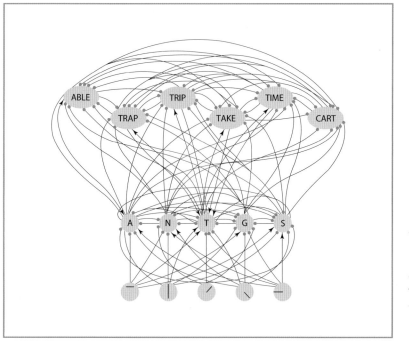

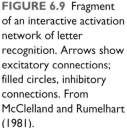

FIGURE 6.9 Fragment of an interactive activation network of letter recognition. Arrows show excitatory connections; filled circles, inhibitory connections. From McClelland and Rumelhart (1981).

connections is either excitatory (that is, positive or facilitatory), if it is an appropriate one, or inhibitory (negative), if it is inappropriate. For example, the letter "T" would excite the word units "TAKE" and "TASK" in the level above it, but would inhibit "CAKE" and "CASK." Excitatory connections make the destination units more active, while inhibitory connections make them less active. Each unit is connected to each other unit within the same level by an inhibitory connection. This introduces the element of competition. The network is shown in Figure 6.9.

When a unit becomes activated, it sends activation in parallel along the connections to all the other units to which it is connected. If it is connected by a facilitatory connection, it will have the effect of increasing activation at the unit at the other end of the connection, whereas if it is connected by an inhibitory connection, it will have the effect of decreasing the activation at the other end. Hence if the unit corresponding to the letter "T" in the initial letter position becomes activated, it will increase the activation level of the word units corresponding to "TAKE" and "TASK," but decrease the activation level of "CAKE." But because units

are connected to all other units at the same level by inhibitory connections, as soon as a unit (e.g., a word) becomes activated, it starts inhibiting all the other units at that level. Hence if the system "sees" a "T," then "TAKE," "TASK," and "TIME" will become activated, and immediately start inhibiting words without a "T" in them, like "CAKE," "COKE," and "CASK." As activation is also sent back down to lower levels, all letters in words beginning with "T" will become a little bit activated and hence "easier" to "see." Furthermore, as letters in the context of a word receive activation from the word units above them, they are easier to see in the context of a word than when presented in isolation, when they receive no supporting top-down activation—hence the word superiority effect. Equations described in the Appendix determine the way in which activation flows between units, is summed by units, and is used to change the activation level of each unit at each time step.

Suppose the next letter to be presented is an "A." This will activate "TAKE" and "TASK" but inhibit "TIME," which will then also be inhibited in turn by within-level inhibition from "TASK" and "TIME." The "A" will of course also activate

"CASK" and "CAKE," but these will already be some way behind the two words starting with "T." If the next letter is a "K," then "TAKE" will be the clear leader. Time is divided into a number of slices called processing cycles. Over time, the pattern of activation settles down or relaxes into a stable configuration so that only "TAKE" remains activated, and hence is the word "seen" or recognized.

The interactive activation model of letter and word recognition has been highly influential. As the name implies, this type of model is heavily interactive; hence any evidence that appears to place a restriction on the role of context is problematic for it. The scope of the model is limited, and gives no account of the roles of meaning and sound in visual word processing. Connection strengths have to be coded by hand. Models where the connection strengths are learned have become more popular. We will examine a connectionist learning model of word recognition and naming in the next chapter.

Hybrid models

Hybrid models combine parallelism (as in the logogen and connectionist models) with serial search (as in Forster's model). In Becker's (1976, 1980) verification model, bottom-up, stimulus-driven perceptual processes cannot recognize a word on their own. A process of top-down checking or verification has the final say. Rough perceptual processing generates a candidate or sensory set of possible lexical items. This sensory set is ordered by frequency. Context generates a contextual or semantic set of candidate items. Both the sensory and the semantic set are compared and verified by detailed analysis against the visual characteristics of the word. The semantic set is verified first; verification is serial. If a match is not found, then the matching process proceeds to the sensory set. This process will generate a clear advantage for words presented in an appropriate context. The less specific the context, the larger the semantic set, and the slower the verification process. As the context precedes the target word, the semantic set is ready before the sensory set is ready. Paap, Newsome, McDonald, and Schvaneveldt (1982) also presented a version of the verification model.

Verification models can be extended to include any model where there is verification or checking that the output of the bottom-up lexical access processes is correct. Norris (1986) argued that a post-access checking mechanism checks the output of lexical access against context and resolves any ambiguity.

Comparison of models

There are two dichotomies that could be used to classify these models. The first is between interactive and autonomous models. The second dichotomy is between whether words are accessed directly or through a process of search. The logogen and interactive activation models are both interactive direct access models; the serial search model is autonomous and obviously search-based. Most researchers agree that the initial stages of lexical access involve parallel direct access, although serial processes might subsequently be involved in checking prepared responses. There is less agreement on the extent to which context affects processing. All these models can explain semantic priming, but the serial search model has no role for sentence context.

COPING WITH LEXICAL AMBIGUITY

Ambiguity in language arises in a number of ways. There are ambiguities associated with the segmentation of speech. Consider the spoken phrases "gray tape" with "great ape," and "ice cream" with "I scream": in normal speech they sound the same. Some sentences have more than one acceptable syntactic interpretation. Although this chapter is primarily about visual word recognition, in this section we will look at lexical ambiguity for both visual and spoken words.

There are a number of types of lexical ambiguity. Homophones are words with different meanings that sound the same. Some examples of pure homophones are "bank" (a place for money, or a place beside a river) and "pen" (a writing instrument or a place to keep animals). **Heterographic homophones** sound the same but are spelled differently (e.g., "knight" and "night," and "weight" and "wait"). **Homographs** are ambiguous when written down, and some of these may be disambiguated when pronounced (such as "lead"—as in "dog lead" and "lead" the metal). Most interesting of all are **polysemous words**, which have multiple meanings. There are many examples of polysemous words in English, such as "bank," "straw," "ball," and "letter." Consider sentences (5) to (8). Some words are also syntactically ambiguous—"bank" can operate as a verb as well as a noun, as in (7) or (8):

(5) The fisherman put his catch on the bank.
(6) The businessman put his money in the bank.
(7) I wouldn't bank on it if I were you.
(8) The plane is going to bank suddenly to one side.

Frazier and Rayner (1990) distinguished between words with multiple meanings, where the meanings are unrelated (e.g., the meanings of "bank" or "ball"), and words with multiple senses, where the senses are related (e.g., a "film" can be the physical reel or the whole thing that is projected on a screen or watched on television, "twist" can be a coil, or to operate something by turning, or to sprain an ankle, or to distort the meaning of something—all the meanings are related). It is not always easy to decide whether a word has multiple meanings or senses.

We are faster to make lexical decisions about ambiguous words compared with matched unambiguous words—this advantage is called the ambiguity advantage (Jastrzembski, 1981). However, the advantage is only found for lexical decision. For other tasks there is no advantage or even a disadvantage (e.g., on eye-movement measures; see Rayner, 1998). Perhaps ambiguous words benefit from having multiple entries in the lexicon. This observation needs qualification: while multiple senses of a word confer an advantage, distinct multiple meanings do not (Rodd, Gaskell, & Marslen-Wilson, 2002).

Most of the time we are probably not even aware of the ambiguity of ambiguous words; we have somehow used the context of the sentence to disambiguate the sentence—that is, to select the appropriate sense. The two main processing questions are: How do we resolve the ambiguity—that is, how do we choose the appropriate meaning or reading? And at what stage is context used?

Early work on lexical ambiguity

Early research on lexical ambiguity used a variety of tasks to examine at what point we select the appropriate meaning of an ambiguous word. Most of these tasks were off-line, in the sense that they used indirect measures that tap processing some time after the ambiguity has been resolved.

Early models of lexical ambiguity

When we come across an ambiguous word, do we immediately select the appropriate sense, or do we access all of the senses and then choose between them, either in some sequence or in parallel? Early researchers worked within the framework of three types of model of resolving lexical ambiguity.

We can call the first model the context-guided single-reading lexical access model (Glucksberg, Kreuz, & Rho, 1986; Schvaneveldt, Meyer, & Becker, 1976; Simpson, 1981). According to this model, the context somehow restricts the access process so that only the relevant meaning is ever accessed. One problem with this model is that it is unclear how context can provide such an immediate constraint.

The second model is called the ordered-access model (Hogaboam & Perfetti, 1975). All of the senses of a word are accessed in order of their individual meaning frequencies. For example, the "writing instrument" sense of "pen" is more frequent than the "agricultural enclosure for animals" sense. Each sense is then checked serially against the context to see if it is appropriate. We check the most common sense against the context first to see if it is consistent. Only if it is not do we try the less common meaning.

The third model is called the multiple-access model (Onifer & Swinney, 1981; Swinney, 1979; Tanenhaus, Leiman, & Seidenberg, 1979). According to this model, when an ambiguous word is encountered, all its senses are activated, and the appropriate one is chosen when the context permits.

Early experiments on processing lexical ambiguity

Early experiments appeared to show that we routinely access all the meanings of ambiguous words. This interpretation is based on the premise that if an ambiguous word is harder to process according to some measure than a control unambiguous word, even in a strongly biasing context, then this suggests that at some level the language-processing system has detected the ambiguity. For example, MacKay (1966) used a sentence-completion task whereby participants have to complete an initial sentence fragment (9 or 10) with an appropriate ending:

(9) After taking the right turn at the intersection, I …

(10) After taking the left turn at the intersection, I …

Participants take longer to complete (9) than (10) because of the ambiguity of the word "right." (It could mean "right" in the sense of "the opposite of left," or "right" in the sense of "correct.") This finding suggests that both senses are being considered, and the delay arises because the participant is making a choice.

In these sentences the ambiguity is unresolved by the context—both senses of "right" are appropriate here. Do we find that ambiguous words are more difficult even when the context biases us to one interpretation? Consider sentences (11) and (12). Here the context of "farmer" is strongly biasing towards the farmyard sense of "straw" rather than the sense of short drinking implement. Foss (1970) used a technique called phoneme monitoring to show that ambiguous words take longer to process even when they are strongly biased by context. In this task, participants have to monitor spoken speech for a particular sound or phoneme, and press a button when they detect it. In these sentences the target is /b/. Participants are slower to detect the /b/ in (11) than in (12), presumably because they are slowed down by disambiguating the preceding word.

(11) The farmer put his straw beside the machine.
(12) The farmer put his hay beside the machine.

One problem is that the phoneme monitoring task is sensitive to other linguistic variables, such as the length of the preceding word. Short words leave us little time to process them, whereas long words are often identified and processed before their end; it is as though processing of short words has to continue into the next word. This processing carry-over delays identification of the phoneme for which participants are monitoring. Mehler, Segui, and Carey (1978) showed that this effect disappears if the ambiguous words are properly controlled for length. It so happens that in English ambiguous words tend to be shorter than non-ambiguous words.

In the dichotic-listening task, different messages are presented to the left and right ears (see Figure 6.10). Participants are told to attend to one ear and ignore the other. In experiments by Lackner and Garrett (1972) and MacKay (1973) the attended message was (13), and the unattended message either (14) or (15):

(13) The spy put out the torch as a signal to attack.
(14) The spy extinguished the torch in the window.
(15) The spy displayed the torch in the window.

Afterwards participants were asked to paraphrase the attended message. Their interpretation was affected by the unattended message that disambiguated the ambiguous phrase "put out."

The experiments discussed so far suggest that all meanings of an ambiguous word are accessed in parallel. Hogaboam and Perfetti (1975) showed that the time taken to access meaning depends on frequency of use. They used an ambiguity detection task, which simply measures the time that participants take to detect the ambiguity. People are slow to detect ambiguity when the word occurs in its most frequent sense (16 rather than 17). This is because in (16) participants access the common reading of "pen" automatically, integrate it with the context, and afterwards have to reanalyze to detect the ambiguity. In (17) participants try the most common sense of the word, fail to integrate it with the context, and then access the second sense. Hence in this case the ambiguity is detected in routine processing.

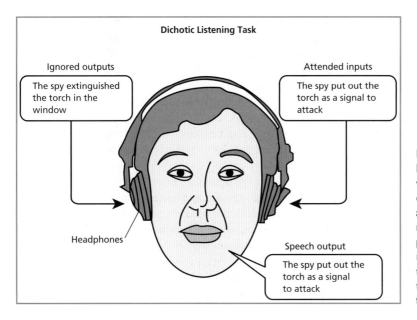

Dichotic Listening Task

Ignored outputs

The spy extinguished the torch in the window

Attended inputs

The spy put out the torch as a signal to attack

Headphones

Speech output

The spy put out the torch as a signal to attack

FIGURE 6.10 Dichotic listening task: different words are presented to each ear. Participants are instructed to ignore material presented to a particular ear (here the right ear), and to shadow the material presented just to the left ear. See text for further information.

(16)   The accountant filled his pen with ink.
(17)   The farmer put the sheep in the pen.

Schvaneveldt et al. (1976) employed a successive lexical decision task, in which participants see individual words presented in a stream, and have to make lexical decisions for each word. In this case participants become far less aware of relations between successive words. The lexical decision time to triads of words such as (18), (19), and (20) is the main experimental concern:

(18)   save   bank money
(19)   river   bank money
(20)   day   bank money

The fastest reaction time to "money" was in (18) where the appropriate meaning of "bank" had been primed by the first word ("save"). Reaction time was intermediate in control condition (20), but slowest in (19) where the incorrect sense had been primed. If all senses of "bank" had been automatically accessed when it was first encountered, then "money" should have been primed by "bank" whatever the first word. This result therefore supports selective access.

Swinney's (1979) experiment

Some of the early evidence supported multiple access, and some selective access. The results we find are very task-dependent. Furthermore, the tasks are either off-line, in the sense that they reflect processing times well after the ambiguity has been processed (such as ambiguity detection, dichotic listening, and sentence completion), or are on-line tasks such as phoneme monitoring that are very sensitive to other variables. We need a task that tells us what is happening immediately when we come across an ambiguous word. Swinney (1979) carried out such an experiment. He used a cross-modal priming technique in which participants have to respond to a visual lexical decision task while listening to correlated auditory material.

(21)   Rumor had it that, for years, the government building had been plagued with problems. The man was not surprised when he found several (spiders, roaches, and other) bugs₁ in the cor₂ner of his room.

In (21) the ambiguous word is "bugs." The phrase "spiders, roaches, and other" is a disambiguating context that strongly biases participants towards the "insect" sense of "bugs" rather than the "electronic" sense. Only half the participants saw this strongly disambiguating phrase. There was a visually presented lexical decision task either immediately after (at point 1) or slightly later (three syllables after the critical word, at point 2). The target in the lexical decision was either "ant" (associated with the biased sense), "spy" (associated with the irrelevant sense), or "sew" (a neutral control). Swinney found facilitation at point 1 for both meanings of "bugs," including the irrelevant meaning, but facilitation only for the relevant meaning at point 2. This suggests that when we first come across an ambiguous word, we automatically access all its meanings. We then use context to make a very fast decision between the alternatives, leaving only the consistent sense active.

Swinney's experiment showed that semantic context cannot restrict initial access. Tanenhaus et al. (1979) performed a similar experiment based on a naming task rather than lexical decision. They used words that were syntactically ambiguous (e.g., "watch," which can be a verb or a noun). Tanenhaus et al. found that both senses of the word were initially activated in sentences such as "Boris began to watch" and "Boris looked at his watch." Again, the context-independent meaning faded after about 200 ms. Hence syntactic context cannot constrain initial access either. Tanenhaus and Lucas (1987) argued that there are good reasons to expect that initial lexical access should not be restricted by syntactic context. Set-membership feedback is of little use in deciding whether or not a word belongs to a particular syntactic category: put another way, the likelihood of correctly guessing what word is presented given just its syntactic category is very low.

In summary, the data so far suggest that when we hear or see an ambiguous word, we unconsciously access all the meanings immediately, but use the context to very quickly reject all inappropriate senses. This process can begin after approximately 200 ms. Less frequent meanings take longer to access because more evidence is needed to cross their threshold for being considered appropriate to the context. This suggests that the processes of lexical access are

autonomous, or informationally encapsulated, in that all senses of the ambiguous word are output, but then semantic information is utilized very quickly to select the appropriate sense. This in turn suggests that the construction of the semantic representation of the sentence is happening more or less on a word-by-word basis.

McClelland (1987) argued that these findings are consistent with interactive theories. He argued that context might have an effect very early on, but the advantage it confers is so small that it does not show up in these experiments. This approach is difficult to falsify, so for now the best interpretation of these experiments is that we access all the meanings.

The effects of meaning frequency and prior context

There is now agreement that when we encounter an ambiguous word, all meanings are activated and context is subsequently used to very quickly select the correct meaning. Recent research has used on-line techniques, primarily cross-modal priming and eye-movement measures, to refine these ideas. Research has focused on three main issues. First, what effect does the relative frequency of the different meanings of the ambiguous word have on processing? Second, what is the effect of presenting strong disambiguating context before the ambiguous word? Third, how does context affect the access of semantic properties of words?

There is controversy about whether the relative frequencies of meanings affect initial access. On the one hand, Onifer and Swinney (1981) replicated Swinney's experiment using materials with an asymmetry in the frequency of the senses of the ambiguous word, so that one meaning was much more frequent than the other meaning. Nevertheless, they still observed that all meanings were initially activated, regardless of the biasing context. However, the dominant meaning may be activated more strongly and perhaps sooner than less frequent ones (Simpson & Burgess, 1985). Extensive use has been made recently of studying eye movements, which are thought to reflect on-line processing. Studies making use of this technique showed that the time participants take gazing at ambiguous words depends on whether the alternative meanings of the ambiguous word are relatively equal or highly discrepant in frequency. Simpson (1994) called the two types of ambiguous words balanced and unbalanced respectively.

In most of the studies we have examined so far, the disambiguating context comes after the ambiguous word. The evidence converges on the idea that all meanings are immediately accessed but that the context is quickly used to select one of them. What happens when the disambiguating context comes before the ambiguous words? Three models have been proposed to account for what happens.

According to the selective access model, prior disambiguating material constrains access so that only the appropriate meaning is accessed.

According to the reordered access model, prior disambiguating material affects the access phase in that the availability of the appropriate meaning of the word is increased (Duffy, Morris, & Rayner, 1988; Rayner, Pacht, & Duffy, 1994). It is a hybrid model between autonomous and **interactive models**, where the influence that context can have is limited. Duffy et al. (1988) examined the effect of prior context on balanced or unbalanced ambiguous words, with the unbalanced words always biased by the context to their less common meaning. Processing times for balanced words and their controls were the same, but participants spent longer looking at unbalanced words than the control words. Duffy et al. argued that the prior disambiguating context increased availability of appropriate meanings for both balanced and unbalanced words. In the case of the balanced words, the meaning indicated by the context was accessed before the other meanings. In the case of the unbalanced words with the biasing context, the two meanings were accessed at the same time, with additional processing time then needed to select the appropriate subordinate meaning. This additional time is called the subordinate bias effect (Rayner et al., 1994). A biasing context can reorder the availability of the meanings so that the subordinate meaning becomes available at the same time as the dominant meaning.

According to the autonomous access model, prior context has no effect on access; meanings are accessed exhaustively. In a version of this called the integration model, the successful integration of one meaning with prior context terminates the search for alternative meanings of that word (Rayner & Frazier, 1989). Hence there is selective (single meaning) access when the integration of the dominant meaning is fast (due to the context) but identification of a subordinate meaning is slow.

Dopkins, Morris, and Rayner (1992) carried out an experiment to distinguish between the reordered access and integration models. In their experiment, an ambiguous word was both preceded and followed by context relevant to the meaning of the word. The context that followed the ambiguous word always conclusively disambiguated it. The main manipulation in this experiment was the extent to which the prior context was consistent with the meanings of the ambiguous word. In the positive condition, the ambiguous word was preceded by material that highlighted an aspect of its subordinate meaning, although the context was also consistent with the dominant meaning (e.g., 22). In the negative condition, the word was preceded by material that was inconsistent with the dominant meaning but did not contain any strong bias to the subordinate meaning (e.g., 23). In the neutral condition, the ambiguous word was preceded by context that provided support for neither of its meanings (e.g., 24).

(22) Having been examined by the king, the page was soon marched off to bed. [positive condition]
(23) Having been hurt by the bee-sting, the page was soon marched off to bed. [negative condition]
(24) Just as Henrietta had feared, the page was soon marched off to bed. [neutral condition]

What do the two models predict? The critical condition is the positive condition. The integration model predicts that context has no effect on the initial access phase. The meanings of ambiguous words will be accessed in a strict temporal sequence that is independent of the context, with the dominant meaning always accessed first. If this meaning can be integrated with the context, it will be selected; if not, the processor will try to integrate the next meaning with the context, and so on. In the positive and neutral conditions, the context will contain no evidence that the dominant meaning is inappropriate, so the processor will succeed in integrating this meaning, halt before the subordinate meaning is accessed, and move on. When the subsequent material is encountered, the processor realizes its mistake and has to backtrack. In the negative condition, the preceding context indicates that the dominant meaning is inappropriate, so the processor will then have to spend time accessing the subordinate meaning. The later context will provide no conflict. The integration model predicts that processing times for the ambiguous word will be longer in the negative condition than in the positive and neutral conditions, but processing time for the later disambiguating context will be longer in the positive and neutral conditions than in the negative.

The reordered access model predicts that the preceding context will have an effect on the initial access of the ambiguous word in the positive condition but not in the negative or neutral conditions. In the positive condition, the context will lead to the subordinate meaning being accessed early. This means that when the context after the word is encountered, the processor will not have to recompute anything, so processing in the disambiguating region will be fast. In the negative and neutral conditions the preceding context contains no evidence for the subordinate meaning and the predictions are similar to the integration model.

The key condition, then, is the positive condition, which favors the subordinate meaning but is also consistent with the dominant meaning. The reordered access model predicts that processing times in the subsequent disambiguation region will be relatively fast, whereas the integration model predicts that they will be relatively slow. The results supported the reordered access model. Dopkins et al. found that reading times for the disambiguating material were indeed relatively fast in the positive condition.

The reordered access model finds further support from an experiment by Folk and Morris (1995). They examined reading fixation times and naming times when reading words that were semantically ambiguous (e.g., "calf") had the same pronunciation but different meanings and orthographies (e.g., "break" and "brake"), or had multiple semantic and phonological codes (e.g., "tear"). They found that semantic, phonological, and orthographic constraints all had an early effect, influencing the order of availability of the meanings.

So far, then, the data support a reordered access model over a strictly autonomous one such as the integration model. Contextual information can be used to restrict the access of meanings. In the reordered access model, however, the role of context is restricted by meaning frequency. In particular, the subordinate-biased context cannot inhibit the dominant meaning from becoming available. Recent research has examined the extent to which this is true. An alternative model is the context-sensitive model (Simpson, 1994; Vu, Kellas, & Paul, 1998), where meaning frequency and biasing context operate together, dependent on contextual strength. This is the degree of constraint that the context places on an ambiguous word. According to this model, the subordinate bias effect that motivated the reordered access model only arises in weakly biasing contexts. If the context is sufficiently strong, the subordinate meaning alone can become available.

If the context-sensitive model is correct, then a sufficiently strong context should abolish the subordinate bias effect whereby we spend longer looking at an ambiguous word when its less frequent meaning is indicated by the context. This idea was tested in an experiment by Martin, Vu, Kellas, and Metcalf (1999). Martin et al. varied the strength of the discourse context: (25) is a weakly biasing context towards the subordinate meaning, but (26) is a strongly biasing context to the subordinate meaning; (27) and (28) show the control contexts for the dominant meanings.

(25) The scout patrolled the area. He reported the mine to the commanding officer. [weak context favoring subordinate meaning]

(26) The gardener dug a hole. She inserted the bulb carefully into the soil. [strong context favoring subordinate meaning]
(27) The farmer saw the entrance. He reported the mine to the survey crew. [weak context favoring dominant meaning]
(28) The custodian fixed the problem. She inserted the bulb into the empty socket. [strong context favoring dominant meaning]

According to the reordered access model, the dominant meaning will always be generated regardless of context, so time will be needed to resolve the competition. Hence there will be a subordinate bias effect, and the reading times on the ambiguous word should be the same, and longer than the reading time for the dominant meanings, regardless of the strength of the context. According to the context-sensitive model, there should only be conflict and therefore a subordinate bias effect in the weak context condition; therefore reading times of the ambiguous word should be faster with the strong biasing context compared with the weak context. The data from a self-paced reading task supported the context-sensitive model. A sufficiently strong context can eliminate the subordinate bias effect so that reading times on a word with either the subordinate or the dominant meaning strongly indicated are the same.

Rayner, Binder, and Duffy (1999) criticized the materials in this experiment. They argued that many of the items were unsuitable. For example, some items appeared to be more balanced than biased, and some contexts were consistent with the same meaning. They also argued that the reordered access model predicts that in very strong contexts the subordinate meaning might be accessed before the dominant meaning. Nevertheless, access is exhaustive: the dominant meaning is still always accessed—unless the context contains a strong associate of the intended meaning, as in Seidenberg, Tanenhaus, Leiman, and Bienkowski (1982). Hence, Rayner et al. (1999) argue, the data from Martin et al. are not contrary to the reordered access model. In reply, Vu and Kellas (1999), while admitting that there were problems with some of their stimuli, claim that these problems could not have led to erroneous results.

Accessing selective properties of words

Tabossi (1988a, 1988b) used a cross-modal priming task to show that sentence context that specifically constrains a property of the prime word leads to selective facilitation. She argued for a modified version of context-dependency: not all aspects of semantic-pragmatic context can constrain the search through the possible meanings, but semantic features constraining specific semantic properties can provide such constraints. For example, the context in (29) clearly suggests the "sour" property of "lemon." Tabossi observed facilitation when the target "sour" was presented visually in a lexical decision task immediately after the prime ("lemon"), relative both to the same context but with a different noun (30) and a different context with the same noun (31).

(29) The little boy shuddered eating the lemon.
(30) The little boy shuddered eating the popsicle.
(31) The little boy rolled on the floor a lemon.

In effect, Tabossi argued that there are large differences in the effectiveness of different types of contextual cues. If the context is weakly constraining, we observe exhaustive access, but if it is very strongly constraining, we observe selective access. However, Moss and Marslen-Wilson (1993) pointed out that the acoustic offset of the prime word might be too late to measure an effect, given that initial lexical access occurs very early, before words are completed. Tabossi used two-syllable-long words, and it is possible that these words were long enough to permit initial exhaustive access with selection occurring before presentation of the target. Tabossi and Zardon (1993) examined this possibility in a cross-modal lexical decision task by presenting the target 100 ms before the end of the ambiguous prime. They still found that only the dominant, relevant meaning was activated when the context was strongly biasing towards that meaning. Tabossi and Zardon also found that if the context strongly biases the interpretation to the less frequent meaning, both the dominant meaning (because of its dominance) and less dominant meaning (because of the effect of context) are active after 100 ms (see also Simpson & Krueger, 1991).

Moss and Marslen-Wilson (1993) also explored the way in which aspects of meaning can be selectively accessed. They measured lexical access very early on, before the presentation of the prime had finished. Semantically associated targets were primed independent of context, whereas access to semantic-property targets was affected by the semantic context. Semantic properties were not automatically accessed whenever heard, but could be modulated by prior context, even at the earliest probe position. Hence this finding again indicates that neither exhaustive nor selective access models may be quite right, in that what we find depends on the detailed relation between the context and the meanings of the word.

Evaluation of work on lexical ambiguity

Early on, there were two basic approaches to how we eventually select the appropriate sense of ambiguous words. According to the autonomous view, we automatically access all the multiple senses of a word, and use the context to select the appropriate reading. Semantic information context is then used to access the appropriate sense of the word. On the interactive view, the context enables selective access of the appropriate sense of the ambiguous word. The experiments used in this area are very sensitive to properties of the target and context length. When we get context-sensitive priming in these cross-modal experiments depends on the details of the semantic relation between the target and prime. Early experiments using off-line tasks found contradictory results for both multiple and context-specific selective access. Later experiments using more sophisticated cross-modal priming indicated multiple access with rapid resolution.

More recent experiments suggest that the pattern of access depends on the relative frequencies of the alternative senses of the ambiguous word and the extent to which the disambiguating context constrains the alternatives. All recent models of disambiguation incorporate an element of interactivity: the question now is the extent to which it is restricted. Can a sufficiently constraining semantic context prevent the activation of the less dominant meaning of a word? Hence the way in which we deal with lexical ambiguity depends on both the characteristics of the ambiguous word and the type of disambiguating context.

A number of questions remain to be answered. In particular, how does context exert its influence in selecting the right meaning? How does semantic integration occur? MacDonald, Pearlmutter, and Seidenberg (1994b) address this issue, and also address the relation between lexical and syntactic ambiguity. They propose that the two are resolved using similar mechanisms based on an enriched lexicon. Kawamoto (1993) constructed a connectionist model of lexical ambiguity resolution. The model showed that, even in an interactive system, multiple candidates become active, even when the context clearly favors one meaning. (This happens because the relation between a word's perceptual form and its meanings is much stronger than the relation between the meaning and the context.) This suggests that multiple access is not necessarily diagnostic of modularity.

Although ambiguous words appear to cause difficulty for the language system, there are some circumstances where ambiguous words have an advantage. We may be quicker to name ambiguous words compared with unambiguous words, and they have an advantage in lexical decision (e.g., Balota, Ferraro, & Conner, 1991; Jastrzembski, 1981; Kellas, Ferraro, & Simpson, 1988; Millis & Button, 1989; but see Borowsky & Masson, 1996). There are a number of explanations for this possible advantage, but they all center around the idea that having multiple target meanings speeds up processing of the word. For example, if each word meaning corresponds to a detector such as a logogen, then a word with two meanings will have two detectors. The probability of an ambiguous word activating one of its multiple detectors will be higher than the probability of an unambiguous word activating its only detector.

SUMMARY

- Word recognition is distinct from object and face recognition.
- Recognizing a word occurs when we uniquely access its representation in the mental lexicon.
- Eyes fixate on material that is being read for 200–250 ms, with movements between fixations called saccades.
- Lexical access is affected by repetition, frequency, age-of-acquisition, word length, the existence of similar words, the physical and semantic similarity of preceding items, and stimulus quality.
- Semantic priming is the facilitation of word recognition by prior presentation of an item related in meaning.
- Semantic priming has a fast, automatic, mandatory, facilitatory component, and a slow, attentional component that inhibits unexpected candidates.
- The lexical decision and naming tasks sometimes give different results, with lexical decision more prone to contamination by post-access processes such as response checking, and naming prone to contamination by the processes involved in assembling a word's pronunciation.
- Semantic priming has an automatic component based on association, and an attentional component involving non-associative semantic relations.
- Some types of non-associative semantic relations may give rise to automatic facilitation; instrumental semantic priming at least is automatic.
- Different aspects of a word's meaning are accessed over time, with functional information about artifacts becoming available before perceptual information.
- Sentence-based contextual priming operates through expectancy-based attentional mechanisms, but may also have an early automatic component.
- In English, morphologically complex words are decomposed into their stems by affix stripping, but morphologically complex high-frequency words may have their own lexical listing.
- There is a level of lexical representation that is modality-independent (because we observe cross-modal priming), and that is morphologically structured for semantically transparent words in English.
- Compound words whose meanings are not transparent from their components (e.g., "buttercup") will also be stored separately.
- Forster's model of word recognition is based on serial search through frequency-ordered bins.
- Morton's logogen model proposes that each word has an individual feature counter—a logogen associated with it that accumulates evidence until a threshold is exceeded.
- IAC (Interactive Activation and Competition) networks are connectionist networks with excitatory connections between letters and words to which the letters belong, and inhibitory connections elsewhere.
- Lexical ambiguity is when a word can have two meanings.
- How we access the meaning of ambiguous words depends on the relative frequencies of the alternative senses of the ambiguous word, and the extent to which the disambiguating context constrains the alternatives.
- When we come across an ambiguous word, all its meanings are activated, but the context is very quickly used to select the appropriate sense.

QUESTIONS TO THINK ABOUT

1.   What might be different about reading in languages such as Hebrew that read from right to left?
2.   Is the lexicon really like a dictionary?
3.   Compare and contrast two models of word recognition.
4.   How many types of priming are there?
5.   What are the differences between naming, recognition, lexical access, and accessing the meaning? What might neuropsychology tell us about these processes?

FURTHER READING

For a collection of papers surveying the field, see Andrews (2006). For reviews of the eye-movement literature, see van Gompel, Fischer, Murray, and Hill (2006), and the collection edited by Henderson and Ferreira (2004). For a detailed discussion of the latest version of the E-Z Reader model (version 7), and a comparison with several other important models of eye-movement control in reading, with peer commentary, see Reichle, Rayner, and Pollatsek (2003). In addition to the E-Z Reader, there are other recent models of eye-movement control in reading. See McDonald, Carpenter, and Shillcock (2005) for the SERIF model. The SERIF model emphasizes the way in which information from each half of the visual field is transmitted to the contralateral visual cortex. See Legge, Klitz, and Tjan (1997) for the Mr. Chips model, and Martin (2004) for the Encoder model.

See Dean and Young (1996) for a review of work on repetition priming, and experimental evidence that is troublesome for the episodic view. Morrison, Chappell, and Ellis (1997) provide age-of-acquisition norms for a large set of object names.

More recent work on perception without awareness can be found in the papers by Doyle and Leach (1988) and Dagenbach, Carr, and Wilhelmsen (1989). Humphreys (1985) reviewed the literature on attentional processes in priming. Neely (1991) provides a wide-ranging review of semantic priming. For discussion of whether associative priming occurs through a mechanism of spreading activation or some more complex process, see McNamara (1992, 1994). Plaut and Booth (2000) present a connectionist model that incorporates both facilitation and inhibition using a single mechanism. See Kinoshita and Lupker (2003) for a review of work on masked priming.

An excellent review of models of word recognition is Carr and Pollatsek (1985); they provide a useful diagram showing the relation of all types of recognition model. See Garnham (1985) for more detail on the interactions between frequency, context, and stimulus quality.

CHAPTER 7

READING

INTRODUCTION

In Chapter 6 we looked at how we recognize words; this chapter is about how we read them. How do we gain access to the sounds and meanings of words? We also examine the effects of brain damage on reading (giving rise to acquired dyslexia), and show how reading disorders can be related to a model of reading. The next chapter looks at how children learn to read.

Reading aloud and reading to oneself are clearly different, but related, tasks. When we read aloud (or name words), we must retrieve the sounds of words. When we read to ourselves, we read to obtain the meaning, but most of us, most of the time, experience the sounds of the words as "inner speech." Is it possible to go to the meaning of a word when reading without also accessing its sounds? By the end of this chapter you should:

- Know how different languages translate words into sounds, and understand the alphabetic principle.
- Understand the motivation for the dual-route model of reading, and know about its strengths and weaknesses.
- Appreciate how different types of dyslexia relate to the dual-route model, and also the problems they pose for it.
- Know about connectionist models of reading and how they account for dyslexia.

THE WRITING SYSTEM

The basic unit of written language is the letter. The name **grapheme** is given to the letter or combination of letters that represents a phoneme. For example, the word "ghost" contains five letters and four graphemes ("gh," "o," "s," and "t"), representing four phonemes. There is much more variability in the structure of written languages than there is in spoken languages. Whereas all spoken languages utilize a basic distinction between consonants and vowels, there is no such common thread to the world's written languages. The sorts of written language most familiar to speakers of English and other European languages are alphabetic scripts. English uses an alphabetic script. In alphabetic scripts, the basic unit represented by a grapheme is essentially a phoneme. However, the nature of this correspondence can vary. In transparent languages such as Serbo-Croat and Italian there is a one-to-one grapheme–phoneme correspondence, so that every grapheme is realized by only one phoneme and every phoneme is realized by only one grapheme. In languages such as English this relation can be one-to-many in both directions. A phoneme can be realized by different graphemes (e.g., compare "to," "too," "two," and "threw"), and a grapheme can be realized by many different phonemes (e.g., the letter "a" in the words "fate," "pat," and "father"). Some languages lie between these extremes. In French, correspondences between graphemes and phonemes are

TABLE 7.1 Types of written languages.

	Examples	Features
Alphabetic script	English Other European languages	The basic unit represented by a grapheme is essentially a phoneme.
Consonantal script	Hebrew Arabic	Not all sounds are represented, as vowels are not written down.
Syllabic script	Cherokee Japanese kana	Written units represent syllables.
Logographic/ideographic script	Chinese Japanese kanji	Each symbol represents a whole word.

quite regular, but a phoneme may have different graphemic realizations (e.g., the graphemes "o," "au," "eau," "aux," and "eaux" all represent the same sounds). In consonantal scripts, such as Hebrew and Arabic, not all sounds are represented, as vowels are not written down at all. In syllabic scripts (such as Cherokee and the Japanese script kana), the written units represent syllables. Finally, some languages do not represent any sounds. In ideographic languages (sometimes also called logographic languages), such as Chinese and the Japanese script kanji, each symbol is equivalent to a morpheme (see Table 7.1).

One consequence of this variation in writing systems is that there must be differences in processing between readers of different languages.

Hence this chapter should be read with the caution in mind that some conclusions may be true of English and many other writing systems, but not necessarily of all of them.

Unlike speech, reading and writing are a relatively recent development. Writing emerged independently in Sumer and Mesoamerica, and perhaps also in Egypt and China. The first writing system was the cuneiform script printed on clay in Sumer, which appeared just before 3000 BC. The emergence of the alphabetic script can be traced to ancient Greece in about 1000 BC. The development of the one-to-many correspondence in English orthography primarily arose between the fifteenth and eighteenth centuries as a consequence of the development of the printing press and the activities of spelling "reformers" who tried to make the Latin and Greek origins of words more apparent in their spellings (see Ellis, 1993, for more detail). Therefore it is perhaps not surprising that reading is actually quite a complex cognitive task. There is a wide variation in reading abilities, and many different types of reading disorder arise as a consequence of brain damage.

A PRELIMINARY MODEL OF READING

Introspection can provide us with a preliminary model of reading. Consider how we might name or pronounce the word "beef." Words like this are said to have a regular spelling-to-sound correspondence. That is, the graphemes map onto

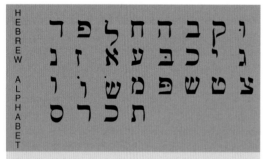

HEBREW ALPHABET

There is much more variability in the structure of written languages than there is in spoken languages. In consonantal scripts, such as Hebrew (above) and Arabic, not all sounds are represented.

phonemes in a totally regular way; you need no special knowledge about the word to know how to pronounce it. If you had never seen the word "beef" before, you could still pronounce it correctly. Some other examples of regular word pronunciations include "hint" and "rave." In these words, there are alternative pronunciations (as in "pint" and "have"), but "hint" and "rave" are pronounced in accordance with the most common pronunciations. These are all regular words, because all the graphemes have the standard pronunciation.

Not all words are regular, however. Some are irregular or exception words. Consider the word "steak." This has an irregular spelling-to-sound (or grapheme-to-phoneme) correspondence: the grapheme "ea" is not pronounced in the usual way, as in "streak," "sneak," "speak," "leak," and "beak." Other exceptions to a rule include "have" (an exception to the rule that leads to the regular pronunciations "gave," "rave," "save," and so forth) and "vase" (in British English, an exception to the rule that leads to the regular pronunciations "base," "case," and so forth). English has many irregular words. Some words are extremely irregular, containing unusual patterns of letters that have no close neighbors, such as "island," "aisle," "ghost," and "yacht." These words are sometimes called lexical hermits.

Finally, we can pronounce strings of letters such as "nate," "smeak," "fot," and "datch," even though we have never seen them before. These letter strings are all pronounceable nonwords or pseudowords. Therefore, even though they are novel, we can still pronounce them, and we all tend to agree on how they should be pronounced. If you hear nonwords like these, you can spell them correctly; you assemble their pronunciations from their constituent graphemes. (Of course, not all nonwords are pronounceable—e.g., "xzhgh.")

Our ability to read nonwords on the one hand and irregular words on the other suggests the possibility of a dual-route model of naming. We can assemble pronunciations for words or nonwords we have never seen before, yet also pronounce correctly irregular words that must need information specific to those words (that is, lexical information). The classic dual-route model (see Figure 7.1) has two routes for turning words into sounds. There is a direct access or lexical route, which is needed for irregular words. This must at least in some way involve a direct link between print and sound. That is, the lexical route takes us directly to a word's entry in the lexicon and we are then able to retrieve the sound of a word. There is also a grapheme-to-phoneme conversion (GPC) route (also called the indirect or non-lexical or **sublexical** route), which is used for reading nonwords. This route carries out what is called phonological recoding. It does not involve lexical access at all. The non-lexical route was first proposed in the early 1970s (e.g., Gough, 1972; Rubenstein, Lewis, & Rubenstein, 1971). Another important justification for a grapheme-to-phoneme conversion route is that it is useful for children learning to read by sounding out words letter by letter.

Given that neither route can in itself adequately explain reading performance, it seems that we must use both. Modern dual-route theorists see reading as a "race" between these routes. When

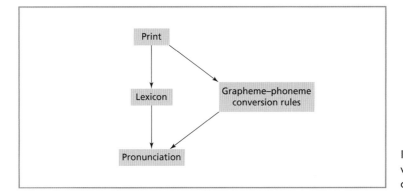

FIGURE 7.1 The simplified version of the dual-route model of reading.

we see a word, both routes start processing it. For skilled readers, most of the time the direct route is much faster, so it will usually win the race and the word will be pronounced the way that it recommends. The indirect route will only be apparent in exceptional circumstances, such as when we see a very unfamiliar word; in that case, if the direct route is slower than normal, then the direct and GPC routes will produce different pronunciations at about the same time, and these words might be harder to pronounce.

In the previous chapter we examined a number of models of word recognition. These can all be seen as theories of how the direct, lexical access reading route operates. The dual-route is the simplest version of a range of possible multi-route or parallel coding models, some of which posit more than two reading routes. Do we really need a non-lexical route at all for routine reading? Although we appear to need it for reading nonwords, it seems a costly procedure. We have a mechanism ready to use for something we rarely do—pronouncing new words or nonwords. Perhaps it is left over from the development of reading, or perhaps it is not as costly as it first appears. We will see later that the non-lexical route is also apparently needed to account for the neuropsychological data. Indeed, whether or not two routes are necessary for reading is a central issue of the topic of reading. Models that propose that we can get away with only one (such as connectionist models) must produce a satisfactory account of how we can pronounce nonwords.

Of course, except for reading aloud, the primary goal of reading is not getting the sound of a word, but getting the meaning. As we shall see in Chapter 8, in the early stages of learning to read children get to the meaning through the sound; that is, they spell out the sound of the words, and then access meaning as they recognize those sounds. Some researchers believe that even skilled adults primarily get to meaning by going from print to phonology and then to meaning, an idea called phonological mediation (discussed in more detail below). Most researchers, however, believe that in skilled adults, most of the time, there is a direct route from print to semantics. Indeed, as we shall see below, most researchers believe that there is a

direct route from print to sound, and a direct route via semantics; what is debated is the role of the indirect route in normal reading (see Taft & van Graan, 1998, for further discussion of these issues).

THE PROCESSES OF NORMAL READING

According to the dual-route model, there are two independent routes when naming a word and accessing the lexicon: a lexical or direct access route and a sublexical or grapheme–phoneme conversion route. This section looks at how we name nonwords and words.

Reading nonwords

It sounds odd to start a section on "normal reading" by talking about how we can read nonwords, but they're very revealing. According to the dual-route model, the pronunciation of all nonwords should be assembled using the GPC route. This means that all pronounceable nonwords should be alike and their similarity to words should not matter. However, pronounceable nonwords are not all alike.

The pseudohomophone effect
Pseudohomophones are pronounceable nonwords that sound like words when pronounced (such as "brane," which sounds like the word "brain" when spoken). The behavior of the pseudohomophone "brane" can be compared with the very similar nonword "brame," which does not sound like a word when it is spoken. Rubenstein et al. (1971) showed that pseudohomophones are more confusable with words than other types of nonwords are. Participants are faster to name them, but slower to reject them as nonwords than control nonwords.

Is the effect caused by the phonological or visual similarity between the nonword and word? Martin (1982) and Taft (1982) argued that it is visual similarity that is important. Pseudohomophones are more confusable with words than other nonwords are because they look more similar to words than non-pseudohomophones, rather than because they sound the same. Pring (1981) alternated the case of letters within versus across graphemes, such as the "AI" in "grait," to produce "GraIT" or "GRaiT." These strings look different but still sound the same. Alternating letter cases within a grapheme or spelling unit (aI) eliminates the pseudohomophone effect; alternating letters elsewhere in the word (aiT) does not. Hence we are sensitive to the visual appearance of spelling units of words.

The pseudohomophone effect suggests that not all nonwords are processed in the same way. The importance of the visual appearance of the nonwords further suggests that something else apart from phonological recoding is involved here. It remains to be seen whether the phonological recoding route is still necessary, but if it is, then it must be more complex than we first thought.

Glushko's (1979) experiment: Lexical effects on nonword reading

Glushko (1979) performed a very important experiment on the effect of the regularity of the word-neighbors of a nonword on its pronunciation. Consider the nonword "taze." Its word-neighbors include "gaze," "laze," and "maze"; these are all themselves regularly pronounced words. Now consider the word-neighbors of the nonword "tave." These also include plenty of regular words (e.g., "rave," "save," and "gave") but there is an exception word-neighbor ("have"). As another example, compare the nonwords "feal" and "fead": both have regular neighbors (e.g., "real," "seal," "deal," and "bead") but the pronunciation of "fead" is influenced by its irregular neighbor "dead." Glushko (1979) showed that naming latencies to nonwords such as "tave" were significantly slower than to ones such as "taze." That is, reaction times to nonwords that have orthographically irregular spelling-to-sound correspondence word-neighbors are slower than to other nonword controls. Also, people make pronunciation "errors" with such nonwords: "pove" might be pronounced to rhyme with "love" rather than "cove"; and "heaf" might be pronounced to rhyme with "deaf" rather than "leaf." In summary, Glushko found that the pronunciation of nonwords is affected by the pronunciation of similar words, and that nonwords are not the same as

each other. Subsequent research has shown that the proportion of regular pronunciations of nonwords increases as the number of orthographic neighbors increases (McCann & Besner, 1987). In summary, there are lexical effects on nonword processing.

More on reading nonwords

The nonword "yead" can be pronounced to rhyme with "bead" or "head." Kay and Marcel (1981) showed that its pronunciation can be affected by the pronunciation of a preceding prime word: "bead" biases a participant to pronounce "yead" to rhyme with it, whereas the prime "head" biases participants to the alternative pronunciation. Rosson (1983) primed the nonword by a semantic relative of a phonologically related word. The task was to pronounce "louch" when preceded either by "feel" (which is associated with "touch") or by "sofa" (which is associated with "couch"). In both cases "louch" tended to be pronounced to rhyme with the appropriate relative.

Finally, nonword effects in complex experiments are sensitive to many factors, such as the pronunciation of the surrounding words in the list. This also suggests that nonword pronunciation involves more than just grapheme-to-phoneme conversion.

Evaluation of research on reading nonwords

These data do not fit the simple version of the dual-route model. The pronunciation of nonwords is affected by the pronunciation of visually similar words. That is, there are lexical effects in nonword processing; the lexical route seems to be affecting the non-lexical route.

Reading words

According to the dual-route model, words are accessed directly by the direct route. This means that all words should be treated the same in respect of the regularity of their spelling-to-sound correspondences. An examination of the data reveals that this prediction does not stand up.

One problem for the simple dual-route model is that pronunciation regularity affects response times, although in a complex way. Baron and Strawson (1976) provided an early demonstration of this problem, finding that a list of regular words was named faster than a list of frequency-matched exception words (e.g., "have"). This task is a simplified version of the naming task, with response time averaged across many items rather than taken from each one individually. There have been many other demonstrations of the influence of regularity on naming time (e.g., Forster & Chambers, 1973; Frederiksen & Kroll, 1976; Stanovich & Bauer, 1978). A well-replicated finding is that of an interaction between regularity and frequency: regularity has little effect on the pronunciation of high-frequency words, but low-frequency regular words are named faster than low-frequency irregular words (e.g., Andrews, 1982; Seidenberg, Waters, Barnes, & Tanenhaus, 1984), even when we control for age-of-acquisition (Monaghan & Ellis, 2002). Jared (1997b) found that high-frequency words can be sensitive to regularity, but the effect of regularity is moderated by the number and frequencies of their "friends" and "enemies" (words with similar or conflicting pronunciations). That is, it is important to control for the neighborhood characteristics of the target words as well as their regularity in order to observe the interaction. On the other hand, it is not clear whether there are regularity effects on lexical decision. They have been obtained by, for example, Stanovich and Bauer (1978), but not by Coltheart et al. (1977), or Seidenberg et al. (1984). In particular, a word such as "yacht" looks unusual, as well as having an irregular pronunciation. The letter pairs "ya" and "ht" are not frequent in English; we say they have a low bigram frequency. Obviously the visual appearance of words is going to affect the time it takes for direct access, so we need to control for this when searching for regularity effects. Once we control for the generally unusual appearance of irregular words, regularity and consistency only seem to affect naming times, not lexical decision times. Age-of-acquisition has a similar effect to frequency, and gives rise to a similar interaction: Consistency has a much bigger impact on naming time for late-acquired than early-acquired words (Monaghan & Ellis, 2002). Why do late-acquired and low-frequency inconsistent words stand out?

One possibility is that late-acquired low-frequency consistent words can make use of the network structure of other consistent words; inconsistent items cannot, and need new associations to be learned between input and output (Monaghan & Ellis, 2002).

In general, regularity effects are more likely to be found when participants have to be more conservative, such as when accuracy rather than speed is emphasized. The finding that regularity affects naming might appear problematic for the dual-route model, but makes sense if there is a race between the direct and indirect routes. Remember that there is an interaction between regularity and frequency. The pronunciation of common words is directly retrieved before the indirect route can construct any conflicting pronunciation. Conflict arises when the lexical route is slow, as when retrieving low-frequency words, and when the pronunciation of a low-frequency word generated by the lexical route conflicts with that generated by the non-lexical route (Norris & Brown, 1985).

Glushko's (1979) experiment: Results from words

Glushko (1979) also found that words behave in a similar way to nonwords, in that the naming times of words are affected by the phonological consistency of neighbors. The naming of a regular word is slowed down relative to that of a control word of similar frequency if the test word has irregular neighbors. For example, the word "gang" is regular, and all its neighbors (such as "bang," "sang," "hang," and "rang") are also regular. Consider on the other hand "base"; this itself has a regular pronunciation (compare it with "case"), but it is inconsistent, in that it has one irregular neighbor, "vase" (in British English pronunciation). We could say that "vase" is an enemy of "base." This leads to a slowing of naming times. In addition, Glushko found true naming errors of over-regularization: for example, "pint" was sometimes given its regular pronunciation—to rhyme with "dint."

Pronunciation neighborhoods

Continuing this line of research, Brown (1987) argued that the number of consistently pronounced neighbors (friends) determines naming times, rather than whether a word has enemies (that is, whether or not it is regular). It is now thought that the number of both friends and enemies affects naming times (Brown & Watson, 1994; Jared, McRae, & Seidenberg, 1990; Kay & Bishop, 1987).

Andrews (1989) found effects of neighborhood size in both the naming and the lexical decision tasks. Responses to words with large neighborhoods were faster than words with small neighborhoods (although this may be moderated by frequency, as suggested by Grainger, 1990). Not all readers produce the same results. Barron (1981) found that good and poor elementary school readers both read regular words more quickly than irregular words. However, once he controlled for neighborhood effects, he found that there was no longer any regularity effect in the good readers, although it persisted in the poor readers.

Parkin (1982) found more of a continuum of ease-of-pronunciation than a simple division between regular and irregular words. All this work suggests that a binary division into words with regular and irregular pronunciations is no longer adequate. Patterson and Morton (1985) provided a more satisfactory but complex categorization rather than a straightforward dichotomy between regular and irregular words (see Table 7.2). This classification reflects two factors: first, the regularity of the pronunciation with reference to spelling-to-sound correspondence rules; second, the agreement with other words that share the same **body**. (This is the end of a monosyllabic word, comprising the central vowel plus final consonant or consonant cluster; e.g., "aint" in "saint" or "us" in "plus.") We need to consider not only whether a word is regular or irregular, but also whether its neighbors are regular or irregular. The same classification scheme can be applied to nonwords.

In summary, just as not all nonwords behave in the same way, neither do all words. The regularity of pronunciation of a word affects the ease with which we can name it. In addition, the pronunciation of a word's neighbors can affect its naming. The number of friends and enemies affects how easy it is to name a word.

The role of sound in accessing meaning: Phonological mediation

There is some experimental evidence suggesting that a word's sound may have some influence on accessing the meaning (Frost, 1998; van Orden,

TABLE 7.2 Classification of word pronunciations depending on regularity and consistency (based on Patterson & Morton, 1985).

Word type	Example	Characteristics
Consistent	gaze	All words receive the same regular pronunciation of the body
Consensus	lint	All words with one exception receive the same regular pronunciation
Heretic	pint	The irregular exception to the consensus
Gang	look	All words with one exception receive the same irregular pronunciation
Hero	spook	The regular exception to the gang
Gang without a hero	cold	All words receive the same irregular pronunciation
Ambiguous: conformist	cove	Regular pronunciation with many irregular exemplars
Ambiguous: independent	love	Irregular pronunciation with many regular exemplars
Hermit	yacht	No other word has this body

1987; van Orden, Johnstone, & Hale, 1988; van Orden, Pennington, & Stone, 1990). In a category decision task, participants have to decide if a visually presented target word is a member of a particular category. For example, given "A type of fruit" you would respond "yes" to "pear," and "no" to "pour." If the "no" word is a homophone of a "yes" word (e.g., "pair"), participants make a lot of false positive errors—that is, they respond "yes" instead of "no." Participants seem confused by the sound of the word, and category decision clearly involves accessing the meaning. The effect is most noticeable when participants have to respond quickly. Lesch and Pollatsek (1998) found evidence of interference between homophones in a semantic relatedness task (e.g., SAND–BEECH). We take longer to respond to homophones in a lexical decision task (e.g., MAID), presumably because the homophones are generating confusion in lexical access, perhaps through feedback from phonology to orthography (Pexman, Lupker, & Jared, 2001; Pexman, Lupker, & Reggin, 2002).

Hence there is considerable evidence that the recognition of a word can be influenced by its phonology. The dominant view is that this influence arises through the indirect route, although word recognition is primarily driven by the direct route (or routes)—a view that has been labeled the weak phonological perspective (Coltheart, Rastle, Perry, Langdon, & Ziegler, 2001; Rastle & Brysbaert, 2006). Most of the models described in this chapter subscribe to the weak phonological view. The alternative, strong phonological view—that we primarily get to the meaning through sound—is called phonological mediation. The most extreme form of this idea is that visual word recognition cannot occur in the absence of computing the sound of the word.

There is a great deal of controversy about the status of phonological mediation. Other experiments support the idea. Folk (1999) examined eye movements as participants read sentences containing either "soul" or "sole." Folk found that the homophones were read with longer gaze duration—that is, they were processed as though they were lexically ambiguous—even though the orthography should have prevented this. This result is only explicable if the phonology is in some way interfering with the semantic access.

On the other hand, Jared and Seidenberg (1991) showed that prior phonological access only happens with low-frequency homophones. In an examination of proof-reading and eye movements, Jared, Levy, and Rayner (1999) also found that phonology only plays a role in accessing the meanings of low-frequency words. In addition, they found that poor readers are more likely to have to access phonology in order to access semantics, whereas good readers primarily activate semantics first. Daneman, Reingold, and Davidson (1995) reported eye fixation data on homophones that suggested the meaning of a word is accessed first whereas the phonological code is accessed later, probably post-access. They found that gaze duration times were longer on an incorrect homophone (e.g., "brake" was in the text when the context demanded "break"), and that the fixation times on the incorrect homophone were about the same as on a spelling control (e.g., "broke"). This means that the appropriate meaning must have been activated before the decision to move the eyes, and that the phonological code is not activated at this time. (If the phonological code had been accessed before meaning then the incorrect homophone would sound all right in the context, and gaze durations should have been about the same.) The phonological code is accessed later, however, and influences the number of regressions (when the eyes look back to earlier material) to the target word. (However, see Rayner, Pollatsek, & Binder, 1998, for different conclusions. It is clear that these experiments are very sensitive to the materials used.)

Taft and van Graan (1998) used a semantic categorization task to examine phonological mediation. Participants had to decide whether or not words belonged to a category of "words with definable meanings" (e.g., "plank," "pint") or the category of "given names" (e.g., "Pam," "Phil"). There was no difference in the decision times between regular definable words (e.g., "plank") and irregular definable words (e.g., "pint"), although a regularity effect was shown in a word naming task. This suggests that the sound of a word does not need to be accessed on the route to accessing its meaning.

A number of studies have tried to decide between the strong and weak phonological views using masked phonological priming. In this technique, targets (e.g., "clip") are preceded by phonologically identical nonword primes (e.g., "klip"). Responses to the targets are faster and more accurate than when the target is preceded by an unrelated word. Several studies have found priming effects occur even when the primes have been masked and presented so briefly that they cannot be consciously observed and reported, suggesting that the phonological stimulus must occur automatically and extremely quickly (e.g., Lukatela & Turvey, 1994a, 1994b; Perfetti, Bell, & Delaney, 1988). While some researchers interpret masked phonological priming as supporting phonological mediation—Why else should early phonological activation happen so early unless it is essential?—other researchers point out that these effects are very sensitive to environmental conditions, and are not always reliably found (see Rastle & Brysbaert, 2006, for a review). In a meta-analysis of the literature, Rastle and Brysbaert (2006) do find small but significant masked phonological priming effects.

These data suggest that the sound of a word is usually accessed at an early stage. However, there is much evidence suggesting that phonological recoding cannot be obligatory in order to access the word's meaning (Ellis, 1993). For example, some dyslexics cannot pronounce nonwords, yet can still read many words. Hanley and McDonnell (1997) described the case of a patient, PS, who understood the meaning of words in reading without being able to pronounce them correctly. Critically, PS did not have a preserved inner phonological code that could be used to access the meaning. Some patients have preserved inner phonology and preserved reading comprehension, but make errors in speaking aloud (Caplan & Waters, 1995b). Hanley and McDonnell argued that PS did not have access to his phonological code because he was unable to access both meanings of a homophone from seeing just one in print. Thus PS could not produce the phonological forms of words aloud correctly, and did not have access to an internal phonological representation of those words, yet he could still understand them when reading them. For example, he

could give perfect definitions of printed words. In general, a review of the neuropsychological literature suggests that people can recognize words in the absence of phonology (Coltheart, 2004). Hence it is unlikely that phonological recoding is an obligatory component of visual word recognition (Rastle & Brysbaert, 2006).

How then can we explain the data showing phonological mediation? There are a number of alternative explanations. First, although phonological recoding prior to accessing meaning may not be obligatory, it might occur in some circumstances. Given there is a race between the lexical and sublexical routes in the dual-route model, if for some reason the lexical route is slow in producing an output, the sublexical route might have time to assemble a conflicting phonological representation. Second, there might be feedback from the speech production system to the semantic system, or the direct access route causes inner speech that interferes with processing. Third, it is possible that lexical decision is based on phonological information (Rastle & Brysbaert, 2006).

Silent reading and inner speech

Although it seems unlikely that we have to access sound before meaning, we do routinely seem to access some sort of phonological code after accessing meaning in silent reading. Subjective evidence for this is the experience of "inner speech" while reading. Tongue-twisters such as (1) take longer to read silently than sentences where there is variation in the initial consonants (Haber & Haber, 1982). This suggests that we are accessing some sort of phonological code as we read.

(1) Boris burned the brown bread badly.

However, this inner speech cannot involve exactly the same processes as overt speech because we can read silently much faster than we can read aloud (Rayner & Pollatsek, 1989), and because overt articulation does not prohibit inner speech while reading. Furthermore, although most people who are profoundly deaf read very poorly, some read quite well (Conrad, 1972). Although this might suggest that eventual phonological coding is optional, it is likely that

The experience of "inner speech" while reading demonstrates that we can access some sort of phonological code after accessing meaning in silent reading.

these deaf able readers are converting printed words into some sign language code (Rayner & Pollatsek, 1989). Evidence for this is that deaf people are troubled by the silent reading of word strings that correspond to hand-twisters (Treiman & Hirsh-Pasek, 1983). (Interestingly, deaf people also have some difficulty with signing phonological tongue-twisters, suggesting that difficulty can arise from lip-reading sounds.)

Hence, when we read we seem to access a phonological code that we experience as inner speech. That is, when we gain access to a word's representation in the lexicon, all its attributes become available. The activation of a phonological code is not confined to alphabetic languages. On-line experimental data using priming and semantic judgment tasks suggest that phonological information about ideographs is automatically activated in both Chinese (Perfetti & Zhang, 1991, 1995) and Japanese kanji (Wydell, Patterson, & Humphreys, 1993).

Inner speech seems to assist comprehension; if it is reduced, comprehension suffers for all but the easiest material (Rayner & Pollatsek, 1989). McCutchen and Perfetti (1982) argued that whichever route is used for lexical access in reading, at least part of the phonological code of each word is automatically accessed—in particular we access the sounds of beginnings of words. Although there is some debate about the precise nature of the phonological code and how much of

it is activated, it does seem that silent reading necessarily generates some sort of phonological code (Rayner & Pollatsek, 1989). This information is used to assist comprehension, primarily by maintaining items in sequence in working memory.

The role of meaning in accessing sound

Phonological mediation means that we might access meaning via sound. Sometimes we need to access the meaning before we can access a word's sound. Words such as "bow," "row," and "tear" have two different pronunciations. This type of word is called a homograph. How do we select the appropriate pronunciation? Consider sentences (2) and (3):

(2)   When his shoelace came loose, Vlad had to tie a bow.
(3)   At the end of the play, Dirk went to the front of the stage to take a bow.

Clearly here we need to access the word's meaning before we can select the appropriate pronunciation. Further evidence that semantics can affect reading is provided by a study by Strain, Patterson, and Seidenberg (1995). They showed that there is an effect of imageability on skilled reading such that there is a three-way interaction between frequency, imageability, and spelling consistency. People are particularly slow and make more errors when reading low-frequency exception words with abstract meanings (e.g., "scarce"). Although a subsequent study by Monaghan and Ellis (2002) suggests that this semantic effect might be at least in part the result of a confound with age-of-acquisition, as abstract low-frequency exception words tend to have late AOA, this interaction is still found when we control for AOA (Strain, Patterson, & Seidenberg, 2002). Hence, at least some of the time, we need to access a word's semantic representation before we can access its phonology.

Does speed reading work?

Occasionally you might notice advertisements in the press for techniques for improving your reading speed. The most famous of these techniques is known as "speed reading." Proponents of speed reading claim that you can increase your reading speed from the average of 200–350 words a minute to 2,000 words a minute or even faster, yet retain the same level of comprehension. Is this possible? Unfortunately, the preponderance of psychological research suggests not. As you increase your reading speed above the normal rate, comprehension declines. Just and Carpenter (1987) compared the understanding of speed readers and normal readers on an easy piece of text (an article from *Reader's Digest*) and a difficult piece of text (an article from *Scientific American*). They found that normal readers scored 15% higher on comprehension measures than the speed readers across both passages. In fact, the speed readers performed only slightly better than a group of people who skimmed through the passages. The speed readers did as well as the normal readers on the general gist of the text, but were worse at details. In particular, speed readers could not answer questions when the answers were located in places where their eyes had not fixated.

Speed reading, then, is not as effective as normal reading. Eye movements are the key to why speed reading confers limited advantages (Rayner & Pollatsek, 1989). For a word to be processed properly, its image has to land close to the fovea and stay there for a sufficient length of time. Speed reading is nothing more than skimming through a piece of writing (Carver, 1972). This is not to say that readers obtain nothing from skimming: if you have sufficient prior information about the material, your level of comprehension can be quite good. If you speed read and then read normally, your overall level of comprehension and retention might be better than if you had just read the text normally. It is also a useful technique for preparing to read a book or article in a structured way (see Chapter 12). Finally, associated techniques such as relaxing before you start to read might well have beneficial effects on comprehension and retention.

Evaluation of experiments on normal reading

There are two major problems with a simple dual-route model. First, we have seen that there are lexical effects on reading nonwords, which should be read by a non-lexical route that is insensitive to lexical information. Second, there are effects of regularity of pronunciation on reading words, which should be read by a direct, lexical route that is insensitive to phonological recoding.

A race model fares better. Regularity effects arise when the direct and indirect routes produce an output at about the same time, so that conflict arises between the irregular pronunciation proposed by the lexical route and the regular pronunciation proposed by the sublexical route. However, it is not clear how a race model where the indirect route uses grapheme–phoneme conversion can explain lexical effects on reading nonwords. Neither is it clear how semantics can guide the operation of the direct route.

Skilled readers have a measure of attentional or strategic control over the lexical and sublexical routes such that they can attend selectively to lexical or sublexical information (Baluch & Besner, 1991; Monsell, Patterson, Graham, Hughes, & Milroy, 1992; Zevin & Balota, 2000). For example, Monsell et al. found that the composition of word lists affected naming performance. High-frequency exception words were pronounced faster when they were in pure blocks than when they were mixed with nonwords. Monsell et al. argued that this was because participants allocated more attention to lexical information when reading the pure blocks. Participants also made fewer regularization errors when the words were presented in pure blocks (when they can rely solely on lexical processing) than in mixed blocks (when the sublexical route has to be involved).

At first sight, then, this experiment suggests that in difficult circumstances people seem able to change their emphasis in reading from using lexical information to sublexical information. However, Jared (1997a) argued that people need not change the extent to which they rely on sublexical information, but instead might be responding at different points in the processing of the stimuli. She argued that the faster pronunciation latencies found in Monsell et al.'s experiment in the exception-only condition could just be the result of a general increase in response speed, rather than a reduction in reliance on the non-lexical route.

However, there is further evidence for strategic effects in the choice of route when reading.

Using a primed naming task, Zevin and Balota (2000) found that nonword primes produce a greater dependence on sublexical processing, but low-frequency exception word primes produce a greater dependence on lexical processing. Coltheart and Rastle (1994) suggested that lexical access is performed so quickly for high-frequency words that there is little scope for sublexical involvement, but with low-frequency words or in difficult conditions people can devote more attention to one route or the other.

THE NEUROSCIENCE OF ADULT READING DISORDERS

What can studies of people with brain damage tell us about reading? This section is concerned with disorders of processing written language. We must distinguish between **acquired disorder**s (which, as a result of head trauma such as stroke, operation, or head injury, lead to disruption of processes that were functioning normally beforehand) and **developmental disorder**s (which do not result from obvious trauma, and which disrupt the development of a particular function). Disorders of reading are called the **dyslexia**s; disorders of writing are called the dysgraphias. Damage to the left hemisphere will generally result in dyslexia, but as the same sites are involved in speaking, dyslexia is often accompanied by impairments to spoken language processing.

We can distinguish central dyslexias, which involve central, high-level reading processes, from peripheral dyslexias, which involve lower level processes. Peripheral dyslexias include visual dyslexia, attentional dyslexia, letter-by-letter reading, and neglect dyslexia, all of which disrupt the extraction of visual information from the page. As our focus is on understanding the central reading process, we will limit discussion here to the central dyslexias. In addition, we will only look at acquired disorders in this section, and defer discussion of developmental dyslexia until our examination of learning to read.

If the dual-route model of reading is correct, then we should expect to find a double dissociation of the two reading routes. That is, we should find some patients have damage to the lexical route but can still read by the non-lexical route only, whereas we should be able to find other patients who have damage to the non-lexical route but can read by the lexical route only. The existence of a double dissociation is a strong prediction of the dual-route model, and a real challenge to any single-route model.

Surface dyslexia

People with surface dyslexia have a selective impairment in the ability to read irregular (exception) words. Hence they would have difficulty with "steak" compared with a similar regular relative word such as "speak." Marshall and Newcombe (1973) and Shallice and Warrington (1980) described some early case histories. Surface dyslexics often make over-regularization errors when trying to read irregular words aloud. For example, they pronounce "broad" as "brode," "steak" as "steek," and "island" as "eyesland." On the other hand, their ability to read regular words and nonwords is intact. In terms of the dual-route model, the most obvious explanation of surface dyslexia is that these patients can only read via the indirect, non-lexical route: that is, it is an impairment of the lexical (direct access) processing route. The comprehension of word meaning is intact in these patients. They still know what an "island" is, even if they cannot read the word, and they can still understand it if you say the word to them.

The effects of brain damage are rarely localized to highly specific systems, and, in practice, patients do not show such clear-cut behavior as the ideal of totally preserved regular word and nonword reading, and the total loss of irregular words. The clearest case yet reported is that of a patient referred to as MP (Bub, Cancelliere, & Kertesz, 1985). She showed completely normal accuracy in reading nonwords, and hence her non-lexical route was totally preserved. She was not the best possible case of surface dyslexia, however, because she could read some irregular words (with an accuracy of 85% on high-frequency items, and 40% on low-frequency exception words). This means that her lexical route must have been partially intact. The pure cases are rarely found. Other patients show considerably less clear-cut reading than this, with even better performance on irregular words, and some deficit in reading regular words.

If patients were reading through a non-lexical route, we would not expect lexical variables to affect the likelihood of reading success. Kremin (1985) found no effect of word frequency, part of speech (noun versus adjective versus verb), or whether or not it is easy to form a mental image of what is referred to (called **imageability**), on the likelihood of reading success. Although patients such as MP, from Bub et al. (1985), show a clear frequency effect in that they make few regularizations of high-frequency words, other patients, such as HTR, from Shallice, Warrington, and McCarthy (1983), do not. Patients also make homophone confusions (such as reading "pane" as "to cause distress").

Surface dyslexia may not be a unitary category. Shallice and McCarthy (1985) distinguished between Type I and Type II surface dyslexia. Patients of both types are poor at reading exception words. The more pure cases, known as Type I patients, are highly accurate at naming regular words and pseudowords. Other patients, known as Type II, also show some impairment at reading regular words and pseudowords. The reading performance of Type II patients may be affected by lexical variables such that they are better at reading high-frequency, high-imageability words, better at reading nouns than adjectives and at reading adjectives than verbs, and better at reading short words than long. Type II patients must have an additional, moderate impairment to the non-lexical route, but the dual-route model can nevertheless still explain this pattern.

Phonological dyslexia

People with **phonological dyslexia** have a selective impairment in the ability to read pronounceable nonwords, called pseudowords (such as "sleeb"), while their ability to read matched words (e.g., "sleep") is preserved. Phonological dyslexia was first described by Shallice and Warrington (1975, 1980), Patterson (1980), and Beauvois and Derouesné (1979). Phonological dyslexics find irregular words no harder to read than regular ones. These symptoms suggest that these patients can only read using the lexical route, and therefore that phonological dyslexia is an impairment of the non-lexical (GPC) processing route. As with surface dyslexia, the "perfect patient," who in this case would be able to read all words but no nonwords, has yet to be discovered. The clearest case yet reported is that of patient WB (Funnell, 1983), who could not read nonwords at all; hence the non-lexical GPC route must have been completely abolished. He was not the most extreme case possible of phonological dyslexia, however, because there was also an impairment to his lexical route; his performance was about 85% correct on words.

For those patients who can pronounce some nonwords, nonword reading is improved if the nonwords are pseudohomophones (such as "nite" for "night," or "brane" for "brain"). Those patients who also have difficulty in reading words have particular difficulty in reading the function words that do the grammatical work of the language. Low-frequency, low-imageability words are also poorly read, although neither frequency nor imageability seems to have any overwhelming role in itself. These patients also have difficulty in reading morphologically complex words—those that have syntactic modifications called inflections. They sometimes make what are called derivational errors on these words, where they read a word as a grammatical relative of the target, such as reading "performing" as "performance." Finally, they also make visual errors, in which a word is read as another with a similar visual appearance, such as reading "perform" as "perfume."

There are different types of phonological dyslexia. Derouesné and Beauvois (1979) suggested that phonological dyslexia can result from disruption of either orthographic or phonological processing. Some patients are worse at reading graphemically complex nonwords (e.g., CAU, where a phoneme is represented by two letters; hence this nonword requires more graphemic parsing) than graphemically simple nonwords (e.g., IKO, where there is a one-to-one mapping between letters and graphemes), but show no advantage for pseudohomophones. These patients suffer from a disruption of graphemic parsing. Another group of patients are better at reading pseudohomophones than non-pseudohomophones, but show no effect of orthographic complexity. These patients suffer from a disruption of phonological processing. Friedman (1995) distinguished between phonological dyslexia arising from an impairment of orthographic-to-phonological processing (characterized by relatively poor function word reading but good nonword repetition) from that arising from an impairment of general phonological processing (characterized by the reverse pattern).

Following this, a three-stage model of sublexical processing has emerged (Beauvois & Derouesné, 1979; Coltheart, 1985; Friedman, 1995). First, a graphemic analysis stage parses the letter string into graphemes. Second, a print-to-sound conversion stage assigns phonemes to graphemes. Third, in the phonemic blending stage the sounds are assembled into a phonological representation. There are patients whose behavior can best be explained in terms of disruption of each of these stages (Lesch & Martin, 1998). MS (Newcombe & Marshall, 1985) suffered from disruption to graphemic analysis. Patients with disrupted graphemic analysis find nonwords in which each grapheme is represented by a single letter easier to read than nonwords with multiple correspondences. WB (Funnell, 1983) suffered from disruption in the print-to-sound conversion stage; here nonword repetition is intact. ML (Lesch & Martin, 1998) was a phonological dyslexic who could carry out tasks of phonological assembly on syllables, but not on sub-syllabic units (onsets, bodies, and phonemes). MV (Bub, Black, Howell, & Kertesz, 1987) suffered from disruption to the phonemic stage.

Why do some people with phonological dyslexia have difficulty reading function words? One possibility is that function words are difficult because they are so abstract (Friedman, 1995). However, patient MC (Druks & Froud, 2002) had great difficulty in reading nonwords, morphologically complex words, and function words in isolation. Crucially, he could read highly abstract content words, so it cannot be the abstractness

of the function words that caused his problems. Nevertheless, he could understand the meaning of function words that he could not read, and his deficit was confined to reading single words. His reading of function words in continuous text was much better. It is likely that MC at least has a problem with syntactic processing such that when producing words in isolation he is unable to access syntactic information.

People with phonological dyslexia show complex phonological problems that have nothing to do with orthography. Indeed, it has been proposed that phonological dyslexia is a consequence of a general problem with phonological processing (Farah, Stowe, & Levinson, 1996; Harm & Seidenberg, 2001; Patterson, Suzuki, & Wydell, 1996). If phonological dyslexia arises solely because of problems with ability to translate orthography into phonology, then there must be brain tissue dedicated to this task. This implies that this brain tissue becomes dedicated by school-age learning, which is an unappealing prospect. The alternative view is that phonological dyslexia is just one aspect of a general impairment of phonological processing. This impairment will normally be manifested in performance on non-reading tasks such as rhyming, nonword writing, phonological short-term memory, nonword repetition, and tasks of phonological synthesis ("what does "c–a–t spell out?") and phonological awareness ("what word is left if you take the "p" sound out of "spoon"?). This proposal also explains why pseudohomophones are read better than non-pseudohomophones. An important piece of evidence in favor of this hypothesis is that phonological dyslexia is never observed in the absence of a more general phonological deficit (but see Coltheart, 1996, for a dissenting view). A general phonological deficit makes it difficult to assemble pronunciations for nonwords. Words are spared much of this difficulty because of support from other words and top-down support from their semantic representations. Repeating words and nonwords is facilitated by support from auditory representations, so some phonological dyslexics can still repeat some nonwords. However, if the repetition task is made more difficult so that patients can no longer gain support from the auditory representations, repetition performance declines markedly (Farah et al., 1996). This idea that phonological dyslexia is caused by a general phonological deficit is central to the connectionist account of dyslexia, discussed later.

Deep dyslexia

At first sight, surface and phonological dyslexia appear to exhaust the possibilities of the consequences of damage to the dual-route model. There is, however, another even more surprising type of dyslexia called **deep dyslexia**. Marshall and Newcombe (1966, 1973) first described deep dyslexia in two patients, GR and KU, although it is now recognized that the syndrome had been observed in patients before this (Marshall & Newcombe, 1980). In many respects deep dyslexia resembles phonological dyslexia. Patients have great difficulty in reading nonwords, and considerable difficulty in reading the grammatical, function words. Like phonological dyslexics, they make visual and derivational errors. However, the defining characteristic of deep dyslexia is the presence of semantic reading errors or **semantic paralexia**s, when people produce a word related in meaning to the target instead of the target, as in examples (4) to (7):

(4) DAUGHTER   "sister"
(5) PRAY   "chapel"
(6) ROSE   "flower"
(7) KILL   "hate"

The imageability of a word is an important determinant of the probability of reading success in deep dyslexia. The easier it is to form a mental image of a word, the easier it is to read. Note that just an imageability effect in reading does not mean that patients with deep dyslexia are better at all tasks involving more concrete words. Indeed, Newton and Barry (1997) described a patient (LW) who was much better at reading high-frequency concrete words than abstract words, but who showed no impairment in comprehending those same abstract words.

Coltheart (1980) listed 12 symptoms commonly shown by deep dyslexics: They make semantic errors, they make visual errors, they substitute incorrect function words for the target, they make derivational errors, they can't pronounce nonwords, they show an imageability effect, they find nouns easier to read than adjectives, they find adjectives easier to read than verbs, they find function words more difficult to read than content words, their writing is impaired, their auditory short-term memory is impaired, and their reading ability depends on the context of a word (e.g., FLY is easier to read when it is a noun in a sentence than a verb).

There has been some debate about the extent to which deep dyslexia is a syndrome (a syndrome is a group of symptoms that cluster together). Coltheart (1980) argued that the clustering of symptoms is meaningful, in that they suggest a single underlying cause. However, although these symptoms tend to occur in many patients, they do not apparently necessarily do so. For example, AR (Warrington & Shallice, 1979) did not show concreteness and content word effects and had intact writing and auditory short-term memory. A few patients make semantic errors but very few visual errors (Caramazza & Hillis, 1990). Such patients suggest that it is unlikely that there is a single underlying deficit. Like phonological dyslexics, deep dyslexics obviously have some difficulty in obtaining non-lexical access to phonology via grapheme–phoneme recoding, but they also have some disorder of the semantic system. We nevertheless have to explain why these symptoms are so often associated. One possibility is that the different symptoms of deep dyslexia arise because of an arbitrary feature of brain anatomy: Different but nearby parts of the brain control processes such as writing and auditory short-term memory, so that damage to one is often associated with damage to another. As we will see, a more satisfying account is provided by connectionist modeling.

Shallice (1988) argued that there are three subtypes of deep dyslexia that vary in the precise impairments involved. Input deep dyslexics have difficulties in reaching the exact semantic representations of words in reading. In these patients, auditory comprehension is superior to reading. Central deep dyslexics have a severe auditory comprehension deficit in addition to their reading difficulties. Output deep dyslexics can process words up to their semantic representations, but then have difficulty producing the appropriate phonological output. In practice it can be difficult to assign particular patients to these subtypes, and it is not clear what precise impairment of the reading systems is necessary to produce each subtype (Newton & Barry, 1997).

The right-hemisphere hypothesis

Does deep dyslexia reflect attempts by a greatly damaged system to read normally, as has been argued by Morton and Patterson (1980), among others? Or does it instead reflect the operation of an otherwise normally suppressed system coming through? Perhaps deep dyslexics do not always use the left hemisphere for reading. Instead, people with deep dyslexia might use a reading system based in the right hemisphere that is normally suppressed (Coltheart, 1980; Saffran, Bogyo, Schwartz, & Marin, 1980; Zaidel & Peters, 1981). This right-hemisphere hypothesis is supported by the observation that the more of the left hemisphere that is damaged, the more severe the deep dyslexia observed (Jones & Martin, 1985; but see Marshall & Patterson, 1985). Furthermore, the reading performance of deep dyslexics resembles that of split-brain patients when words are presented to the left visual field, and therefore to the right hemisphere. Under such conditions they also make semantic paralexias, and have an advantage for concrete words. Finally, Patterson, Vargha-Khadem, and Polkey (1989) described the case of a patient called NI, a 17-year-old girl who had had her left hemisphere removed for the treatment of severe epilepsy. After recovery she retained some reading ability, but her performance resembled that of deep dyslexics.

In spite of these points in its favor, the right-hemisphere reading hypothesis has never won wide acceptance. In part this is because the hypothesis is considered a negative one, in that if it were correct, deep dyslexia would tell us nothing about normal reading. In addition, people with deep dyslexia read much better than split-brain patients who are forced to

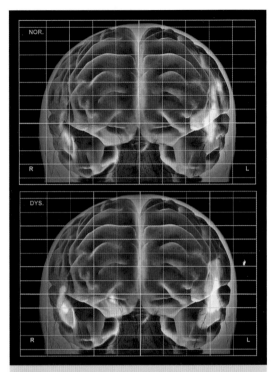

Brain activity during reading aloud in a normal (top) and dyslexic (bottom) subject. These are composites of 3-D magnetic resonance imaging (MRI) scans of the brain, with positron emission tomography (PET) scans overlaid to show active areas (orange). The most active areas are in the left cerebral hemisphere (right), site of the brain's language centers. In the dyslexic, there is an abnormal area of activity in the globus pallidus (just left of center) of the right cerebral hemisphere.

rely on the right hemisphere for reading. The right-hemisphere advantage for concrete words is rarely found, and the imageability of the target words used in these experiments might have been confounded with length (Ellis & Young, 1988; Patterson & Besner, 1984). Finally, Roeltgen (1987) described a patient who suffered from deep dyslexia as a result of a stroke in the left hemisphere. He later suffered from a second left-hemisphere stroke, which had the effect of destroying his residual reading ability. If the deep dyslexia had been a consequence of right-hemisphere reading, it should not have been affected by the second stroke in the left hemisphere.

Summary of research on deep dyslexia
There has been debate as to whether the term "deep dyslexia" is a meaningful label. The crucial issue is whether or not its symptoms must necessarily co-occur because they have the same underlying cause. Are semantic paralexias always found associated with impaired non-word reading? So far they seem to be; in all reported cases semantic paralexias have been associated with all the other symptoms. How then can deep dyslexia be explained by one underlying disorder? In terms of the dual-route model, there would need to be damage to both the semantic system (to explain the semantic paralexias and the imageability effects) and the non-lexical route (to explain the difficulties with nonwords). We would also then have to specify that for some reason damage to the first is always associated with damage to the second (e.g., because of an anatomical accident that the neural tissue supporting both processes is in adjoining parts of the brain). This is inelegant. As we shall see, connectionist models have cast valuable light on this question. A second issue is whether we can make inferences from deep dyslexia about the processes of normal reading, as we can for the other types of acquired dyslexia. We have seen that the dual-route model readily explains surface and phonological dyslexia, and that their occurrence is as expected if we were to lesion that model by removing one of the routes. Hence, it is reasonable to make inferences about normal reading on the basis of data from such patients. There is some doubt, however, as to whether we are entitled to do this in the case of deep dyslexia; if the right-hemisphere hypothesis were correct, deep dyslexia would tell us little about normal reading. The balance of evidence is at present that deep dyslexia does not reflect right-hemisphere reading, but does reflect reading by a greatly damaged left hemisphere. Deep dyslexia suggests that normally we can in some way read through meaning; that is, we use the semantic representation of a word to obtain its phonology. This supports our earlier observation that with homographs (e.g., "bow") we use the meaning to select the appropriate pronunciation.

Non-semantic reading

Schwartz, Marin, and Saffran (1979), and Schwartz, Saffran, and Marin (1980a), described WLP, an elderly patient suffering from progressive dementia. WLP had a greatly impaired ability to retrieve the meaning of written words; for example, she was unable to match written animal names to pictures. She could read those words out loud almost perfectly, getting 18 out of 20 correct and making only minor errors, even on low-frequency words. She could also read irregular words and nonwords. In summary, WLP could read words without any comprehension of their meaning. Coslett (1991) described a patient, WT, who was virtually unable to read nonwords, suggesting an impairment of the indirect route of the dual-route model, but who was able to read irregular words quite proficiently, even though she could not understand those words. These case studies suggest that we must have a direct access route from orthography to phonology that does not go through semantics.

Summary of the interpretation of the acquired dyslexias

We have looked at four main types of adult central dyslexia: surface, phonological, deep, and non-semantic reading. We have seen how a dual-route model explains surface dyslexia as an impairment of the lexical, direct access route, and explains phonological dyslexia as an impairment of the non-lexical, phonological recoding route. The existence of non-semantic reading suggests that the simple dual-route model needs refinement. In particular, the direct route must be split into two. There must be a non-semantic direct access route that retrieves phonology given orthography, but which does not pass through semantics first, and a semantic direct access route that passes through semantics and allows us to select the appropriate sounds of non-homophonic homographs (e.g., "wind"). In non-semantic reading, the semantic direct route has been abolished but the non-semantic direct route is intact. An analysis of acquired dyslexia by Coltheart (1981) is shown in Figure 7.2.

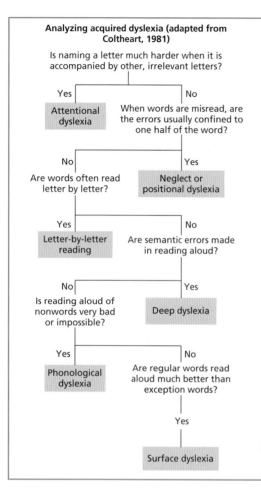

Analyzing acquired dyslexia (adapted from Coltheart, 1981)

Is naming a letter much harder when it is accompanied by other, irrelevant letters?

- **Yes** → Attentional dyslexia
- **No** → When words are misread, are the errors usually confined to one half of the word?
  - **Yes** → Neglect or positional dyslexia
  - **No** → Are words often read letter by letter?
    - **Yes** → Letter-by-letter reading
    - **No** → Are semantic errors made in reading aloud?
      - **Yes** → Deep dyslexia
      - **No** → Is reading aloud of nonwords very bad or impossible?
        - **Yes** → Phonological dyslexia
        - **No** → Are regular words read aloud much better than exception words?
          - **Yes** → Surface dyslexia

FIGURE 7.2

Acquired dyslexia in other languages

Languages such as Italian, Spanish, or Serbo-Croat, which have totally transparent or shallow alphabetic orthographies—that is, where every grapheme is in a one-to-one relation with a phoneme—can show phonological and deep dyslexia, but not surface dyslexia, defined as an inability to read exception words (Patterson, Marshall, & Coltheart, 1985a, 1985b). However, we can find the symptoms that can co-occur with an impairment of exception word reading, such as homophone confusions, in the languages that permit them (Masterson, Coltheart, & Meara, 1985).

Whereas languages such as English have a single, alphabetic script, Japanese has two different scripts, kana and kanji (see Coltheart, 1980; Sasanuma, 1980). Kana is a syllabic script, and kanji is a logographic or ideographic script. Therefore words in kanji convey no information on how a word should be pronounced. While kana allows sublexical processing, kanji must be accessed through a direct, lexical route. The right hemisphere is better at dealing with kanji, and the left hemisphere is better at reading kana (Coltheart, 1980). Reading of briefly presented kana words is more accurate when they are presented to the right visual field (left hemisphere), but reading of kanji words is better when they are presented to the left visual field (right hemisphere). The analog of surface dyslexia is found in patients where there is a selective impairment of reading kanji, but the reading of kana is preserved. The analog of phonological dyslexia is an ability to read both kana and

Chinese (shown here) is a logographic or ideographic script, providing no information on word pronunciation.

kanji, but a difficulty in reading Japanese non-words. The analog of deep dyslexia is a selective impairment of reading kana, while the reading of kanji is preserved. For example, patient TY could read words in both kanji and kana almost perfectly, but she had great difficulty with non-words constructed from kana words (Sasanuma, Ito, Patterson, & Ito, 1996).

Chinese is an ideographic language. Butterworth and Wengang (1991) reported evidence of two routes in reading in Chinese. Ideographs can be read aloud either through a route that associates the symbol with its complete pronunciation, or through one that uses parts of the symbol. (Although Chinese is non-alphabetic, most symbols contain some sublexical information on pronunciation.) Each route can be selectively impaired by brain damage, leading to distinct types of reading disorder.

The study of other languages that have different means of mapping orthography onto phonology is still at a relatively early stage, but it is likely to greatly enhance our understanding of reading mechanisms. The findings suggest that the neuropsychological mechanisms involved in reading are universal, although there are obviously some differences related to the unique features of different orthographies.

MODELS OF WORD NAMING

Both the classic dual-route and the single-route, lexical-instance models face a number of problems. First, there are lexical effects for nonwords and regularity effects for words, and therefore reading cannot be a simple case of automatic grapheme-to-phoneme conversion for nonwords, and automatic direct access for all words. Single-route models, on the other hand, appear to provide no account of nonword pronunciation, and it remains to be demonstrated how neighborhood effects affect a word's pronunciation. Second, any model must also be able to account for the pattern of dissociations found in dyslexia. While surface and phonological dyslexia indicate that two reading mechanisms

are necessary, other disorders suggest that these alone will not suffice. At first sight it is not obvious how a single-route model could explain these dissociations at all.

Theorists have taken two different approaches depending on their starting point. One possibility is to refine the dual-route model. Another is to show how word-neighborhoods can affect pronunciation, and how pseudowords can be pronounced in a single-route model. This led to the development of analogy models. More recently, a connectionist model of reading has been developed that takes the single-route, analogy-based approach to the limit.

The revised dual-route model

We can save the dual-route model by making it more complex. Morton and Patterson (1980) and Patterson and Morton (1985) described a three-route model (see Figure 7.3). First, there is a non-lexical route for assembling pronunciations from sublexical grapheme–phoneme conversion. The non-lexical route now consists of two subsystems. A standard grapheme–phoneme conversion mechanism is supplemented with a body subsystem that makes use of information about correspondences between orthographic and phonological rimes. This is needed to explain lexical effects on nonword pronunciation. Second, the direct route is split into a semantic and a non-semantic direct route.

The three-route model accounts for the data as follows. The lexical effects on nonwords and regularity effects on words are explained by cross-talk between the lexical and non-lexical routes. Two types of interaction are possible: interference during retrieval, and conflict in resolving multiple phonological forms after retrieval. The two subsystems of the non-lexical route also give the model greater power. Surface dyslexia is the loss of the ability to make direct contact with the orthographic lexicon, and phonological dyslexia is the loss of the indirect route. Non-semantic reading is a loss of the lexical-semantic route. Deep dyslexia remains rather mysterious. First, we have to argue that these patients can only read through the lexical-semantic route. While accounting for the symptoms that resemble

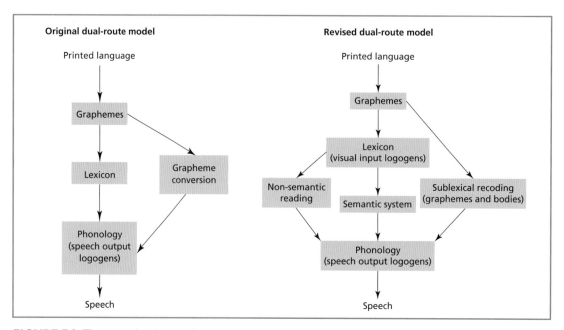

FIGURE 7.3 The original and revised dual-route models of reading.

phonological dyslexia, it still does not explain the semantic paralexias. One possibility is that this route is used normally, but not always success-fully, and that it needs additional information (such as from the non-lexical and non-semantic direct route) to succeed. So when this information is no longer available it functions imperfectly. It gets us to the right semantic area, but not necessarily to the exact item, hence giving paralexias. This additional assumption seems somewhat arbitrary. An alterna-tive idea is that paralexias are the result of addi-tional damage to the semantic system itself. Hence a complex pattern of impairments is still necessary to explain deep dyslexia, and there is no reason to suggest that these are not dissociable.

Multi-route models are becoming increasingly complicated as we find out more about the reading process (for example, see Carr & Pollatsek, 1985). Another idea is that multiple levels of spelling-to-sound correspondences combine in determining the pronunciation of a word. In Norris's (1994a) multiple-levels model, different levels of spelling-to-sound information, including phoneme, rime (the final part of the word giving rise to the words with which it rhymes, e.g., "eak" in "speak"), and word-level correspondences, combine in an interactive

activation network to determine the final pronun-ciation of a word. Such an approach develops ear-lier models that make use of knowledge at multiple levels, such as those of Brown (1987), Patterson and Morton (1985), and Shallice, Warrington, and McCarthy (1983).

The most recent version of the dual-route model is the dual-route cascaded, or DRC, model (Coltheart, Curtis, Atkins, & Haller, 1993; Coltheart & Rastle, 1994; Coltheart, Rastle, Perry, Langdon, & Ziegler, 2001). This is a computational model based on the architecture of the dual-route model—although it is in fact misleadingly so called, as it is really based on the three-route model, with a non-lexical grapheme–phoneme rule system and a lexi-cal system, which in turn is divided into one route that passes through the semantic system and a non-semantic route that does not. The model makes use of cascaded processing, in that as soon as there is any activation at the letter level, activation is passed on to the word level. The computational model can simulate performance on both lexical decision and naming tasks, showing appropriate effects of fre-quency, regularity, pseudohomophones, neighbor-hood, and priming. Regularity is now a central motivation of the model; words are either regular, or they are not. Irregular words take longer to pronounce than regular ones because the lexical and non-lexical routes produce conflicting pronunciations. The model accounts for surface dyslexia by making entries in the orthographic lexicon less available, and for phonological dyslexia by damaging the grapheme–phoneme conversion route.

There is not uniform agreement that it is necessary to divide the direct route into two. In the summation model (Hillis & Caramazza, 1991b; Howard & Franklin, 1988), the only direct route is reading through semantics. How does this model account for non-semantic reading? The idea is that access to the semantic system is not completely obliterated. Activation from the sublexical route combines (or is "summated") with activation trickling down from the damaged direct semantic route to ensure the correct pronunciation.

It is difficult to distinguish between these variants of the original dual-route model, although the three-route version provides the more explicit account of the dissociations observed in dyslexia. There is also some evidence against the summation hypothesis. EP (Funnell, 1996) could read irregular words that she could not name, and priming the name with the initial letter did not help her naming, contrary to the prediction of the summation hypothesis. Many aspects of the dual-route model have been subsumed by the triangle model that serves as the basis of connectionist models of reading. The situation is complicated even more by the apparent co-occurrence of the loss of particular word meanings in dementia and surface dyslexia (see later).

The analogy model

The analogy model arose in the late 1970s when the extent of lexical effects on nonword reading and differences between words became apparent (Glushko, 1979; Henderson, 1982; Kay & Marcel, 1981; Marcel, 1980). It is a form of single-route model that provides an explicit mechanism for how we pronounce nonwords. It proposes that we pronounce nonwords and new words by analogy with other words. When a word (or nonword) is presented, it activates its neighbors, and these all influence its pronunciation. For example, "gang"

activates "hang," "rang," "sang," and "bang"; these are all consistent with the regular pronunciation of "gang," and hence assembling a pronunciation is straightforward. When presented with "base," however, "case" and "vase" are activated; these conflict, and hence the assembly of a pronunciation is slowed down until the conflict is resolved. A nonword such as "taze" is pronounced by analogy with the consistent set of similar words ("maze," "gaze," "daze"). A nonword such as "mave" activates "gave," "rave," and "save," but it also activates the conflicting enemy "have," which hence slows down pronunciation of "mave." In order to name by analogy, you have to find candidate words containing appropriate orthographic segments (like "-ave"); obtain the phonological representation of the segments; and assemble the complete phonology ("m + ave").

Although attractive in the way they deal with regularity and neighborhood effects, early versions of analogy models suffered from a number of problems. First, the models did not make clear how the input is segmented in an appropriate way. Second, the models make incorrect predictions about how some nonwords should be pronounced. Particularly troublesome are nonwords based on gangs; "pook" should be pronounced by analogy with the great preponderance of the gang comprising "book," "hook," "look," and "rook," yet it is given the "hero" pronunciation (see Table 7.2)—which is in accordance with grapheme–phoneme correspondence rules—nearly 75% of the time (Kay, 1985). Analogy theory also appears to make incorrect predictions about how long it takes us to make regularization errors (Patterson & Morton, 1985). Finally, it is not clear how analogy models account for the dissociations found in acquired dyslexia. Nevertheless, in some ways the analogy model was a precursor of connectionist models of reading.

Connectionist models: Seidenberg and McClelland's (1989) model of reading

The original Seidenberg and McClelland (1989) model evolved in response to criticisms that I will examine after describing the original model. The Seidenberg and McClelland (1989) model (often abbreviated to SM) shares many features with the interactive activation model of letter recognition discussed in Chapter 6. The SM model provides an account of how readers recognize letter strings as words and pronounce them. This first model simulated one route of a more general model of lexical processing (see Figure 7.4). Reading and speech involve three types of code: orthographic, meaning, and phonological. These are connected with feedback connections. The shape of the model has given it the name of the triangle model. As in the revised dual-route model, there is a route from orthography to phonology by way of semantics. The key feature of the model is that there is only one other route from orthography to phonology; there is no route involving grapheme–phoneme correspondence rules.

Seidenberg and McClelland (1989) just simulated the orthographic-to-phonology part of the overall triangle model. The model has three levels, each containing many simple units. These are the input, hidden, and output layers (see Figure 7.5). Each of the units in these layers has an activation level, and each unit is connected to all the units in the next level by a weighted connection, which can be either excitatory or inhibitory. An

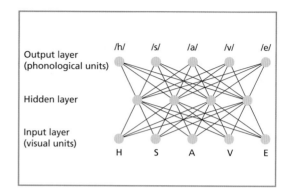

FIGURE 7.5 The layers of Seidenberg and McClelland's (1989) model of word recognition (simplified—see text for details). Based on Seidenberg and McClelland (1989).

important characteristic of this type of model is that the weights on these connections are not set by the modelers, but are learned. This network learns to associate a phonological output with an orthographic input by being given repeated exposure to word-pronunciation pairs. It learns using an algorithm called **back-propagation**. This involves slowly reducing the discrepancy between the desired and actual outputs of the network by changing the weights on the connections. (See the Appendix for more information.)

Seidenberg and McClelland used 400 units to code orthographic information for input and 460 units to code phonological information for output, mediated by 200 hidden units. Phonemes and graphemes were encoded as a set of triples, so that each grapheme or phoneme was specified with its flanking grapheme or phoneme. This is a common trick to represent position-specificity (Wickelgren, 1969). For example, the word "have" was represented by the triples "#ha," "hav," "ave," and "ve#," with "#" representing a blank space. A non-local representation was used: The graphemic representations were encoded as a pattern of activation across the orthographic units rather than corresponding directly to particular graphemes. Each phoneme triple was encoded as a pattern of activation distributed over a set of units representing phonetic features—a representation known as a Wickelfeature. The underlying architecture was not a simple feedforward one, in that the

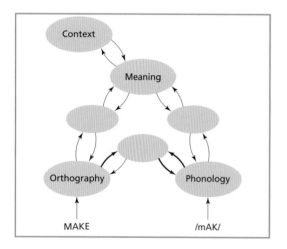

FIGURE 7.4 Seidenberg and McClelland's (1989) "triangle model" of word recognition. Implemented pathways are shown in bold. Reproduced with permission from Harm and Seidenberg (2001).

hidden units fed back to the orthographic units, mimicking top-down word-to-letter connections in the IAC model of word recognition. However, there was no feedback from the phonological to the hidden units, so phonological representations could not directly influence the processing of orthographic-level representations.

The training corpus comprised all 2,897 uninflected monosyllabic words of at least three or more letters in the English language present in the Kucera and Francis (1967) word corpus. Each trial consisted of the presentation of a letter string that was converted into the appropriate pattern of activation over the orthographic units. This in turn fed forward to the phonological units by way of the hidden units. In the training phase, words were presented a number of times with a probability proportional to the logarithm of their frequency. This means that the ease with which a word is learned by the network, and the effect it has on similar words, depends to some extent on its frequency. About 150,000 learning trials were needed to minimize the differences between the desired and actual outputs.

After training, the network was tested by presenting letter strings and computing the orthographic and phonological error scores. The error score is a measure of the average difference between the actual and desired output of each of the output units, across all patterns. Phonological error scores were generated by applying input to the orthographic units, and measured by the output of the phonological units; they were interpreted as reflecting performance on a naming task. Orthographic error scores were generated by comparing the pattern of activation input to the orthographic units with the pattern produced through feedback from the hidden units, and were interpreted as a measure reflecting the performance of the model in a lexical decision task. Orthographic error scores are therefore a measure of orthographic familiarity. Seidenberg and McClelland showed that the model fitted human data on a wide range of inputs. For example, regular words (such as "gave") were pronounced faster than exception words (such as "have").

Note that the Seidenberg and McClelland model uses a single mechanism to read nonwords and exception words. There is only one

set of hidden units, and only one process is used to name regular, exception, and novel items. As the model uses a distributed representation, there is no one-to-one correspondence between hidden units and lexical items; each word is represented by a pattern of activation over the hidden units. According to this model, lexical memory does not consist of entries for individual words. Orthographic neighbors do not influence the pronunciation of a word directly at the time of processing; instead, regularity effects in pronunciation derive from statistical regularities in the words of the training corpus—all the words we have learned—as implemented in the weights of connections in the simulation. Lexical processing therefore involves the activation of information, and is not an all-or-none event.

Evaluation of the original SM model

Coltheart et al. (1993) criticized important aspects of the Seidenberg and McClelland (SM) model. They formulated six questions about reading that any account of reading must answer:

- How do skilled readers read exception words aloud?
- How do skilled readers read nonwords aloud?
- How do participants make visual lexical decision judgments?
- How does surface dyslexia arise?
- How does phonological dyslexia arise?
- How does developmental dyslexia arise?

Coltheart et al. then argued that Seidenberg and McClelland's model only answered the first of these questions.

Besner, Twilley, McCann, and Seergobin (1990) provided a detailed critique of the Seidenberg and McClelland model, although a reply by Seidenberg and McClelland (1990) answered some of these points. First, Besner et al. argued that in a sense the model still possesses a lexicon, where instead of a word corresponding to a unit, it corresponds to a pattern of activation. Second, they pointed out that the model "reads" nonwords rather poorly—certainly much less well than a skilled reader. In particular, it only produced the "correct," regular pronunciation of a nonword under 70% of the time. This contrasts with the model's excellent performance on its original training set. Hence the model's performance on nonwords is impaired from the beginning. In reply, Seidenberg and McClelland (1990) pointed out that their model was trained on only 2,987 words, as opposed to the 30,000 words that people know, and that this may be responsible for the difference. Hence the model simulates the direct lexical route rather better than it simulates the indirect grapheme–phoneme route. Therefore any disruption of the model will give a better account of disruption to the direct route—that is, of surface dyslexia. The model's account of lexical decision is inadequate in that it makes far too many errors—in particular it accepts too many nonwords as words (Besner et al., 1990; Fera & Besner, 1992). The model did not perform as well as people do on nonwords, in particular on nonwords that contain unusual spelling patterns (e.g., JINJE, FAIJE). In addition, the model's account of surface dyslexia was problematic and its account of phonological dyslexia non-existent.

Forster (1994) evaluated the assumptions behind connectionist modeling of visual word recognition. He made the point that showing that a network model can successfully learn to perform a complex task such as reading does not mean that that is the way humans actually do it. Finally, Norris (1994b) argued that a major stumbling block for the Seidenberg and McClelland model was that it could not account for the ability of readers to shift strategically between reliance on lexical and sublexical information.

The revised connectionist model: PMSP

A revised connectionist model performs much better at pronouncing nonwords and at lexical decision than the original (Plaut, 1997; Plaut & McClelland, 1993; Plaut, McClelland, Seidenberg, & Patterson, 1996; Seidenberg, Petersen, MacDonald, & Plaut, 1996; Seidenberg, Plaut, Petersen, McClelland, & McRae, 1994). The model, called PMSP for short, used more realistic input and output representations. Phonological representations were based on phonemes with phonotactic constraints (that constrain which sounds occur together in the language), and orthographic representations were based on graphemes with graphotactic constraints (that constrain which letters occur together in the language). The original SM model performed badly on nonwords because Wickelfeatures disperse spelling–sound regularities. For example, in GAVE, the A is represented in the context of G and V, and has nothing in common with the A in SAVE (represented in the context of S and V). In the revised PMSP model, letters and phonemes activate the same units irrespective of context. A mathematical analysis showed that a response to a letter string input is a function that depends positively on the frequency of exposure to the pattern, positively to the sum of the frequencies of its friends, and negatively to the sum of the frequencies of its enemies. The response to a letter string is non-linear, in that there are diminishing returns: For example, regular words are so good they gain little extra benefit from frequency. This explains the interaction we observe between word consistency and frequency. As we shall see, the revised model also gives a much better account of dyslexia.

Accessing semantics

Of course the goal of reading is to access the meaning of words. The PMSP model simulates the orthography–phonology side of the triangle. Clearly, according to the model, we can access semantics either directly (OS: orthography–semantics) or indirectly (OPS: orthography–phonology–semantics—what we have also called phonological mediation). Hence there is a division of labor between the two routes. Harm and Seidenberg (2004) model the access of semantics. In the full model, all parts of the system operate simultaneously and contribute to the activation of meaning. The Harm and Seidenberg model is a complete implementation of the triangle model. It is trained to produce the correct pattern of activation across a set of semantic features given an orthographic input. In the first phase, the model is trained for a while on the phonology–semantics side of the triangle, to simulate the knowledge of young children who cannot yet read, but who know what words mean. These weights are then frozen. In the second phase, the orthography–phonology and orthography–semantics sides of the triangle are then trained.

How does the trained model perform? Perhaps not surprisingly, in simulations resembling the skilled reader in normal conditions, the OS route is normally faster, with the OPS route lagging somewhat behind. Nevertheless, analysis of how activation of the input determines activation of the output shows that activation of the semantic system is driven by both pathways. Even if the OPS path is slower, it still always contributes to the final output. In addition, because of interactivity in the system, activation of the semantic system activates corresponding phonological representations, which in turn affect the semantic system. Simulations show that the relative contributions of the two pathways (OS and OPS) are modulated by a number of factors, including skill (phonological information is more important early on in training, corresponding to less skilled readers) and word frequency (for high-frequency words the OS pathway is more efficient). The model also simulates the response times of van Orden (1987), where people are slow to say "no" to "Is it a flower? ROWS."

CONNECTIONIST MODELS OF DYSLEXIA

Modeling surface dyslexia

Over the last few years connectionist modeling has contributed to our understanding of deep and surface dyslexia. Patterson, Seidenberg, and McClelland (1989) artificially damaged or "lesioned" the Seidenberg and McClelland (1989) network after the learning phase by destroying hidden units or connection weights, and then observed the behavior of the model. Its performance resembled the reading of a surface dyslexic. Patterson et al. (1989) explored three main types of lesion: damage to the connections between the orthographic input and hidden units (called early weights); damage to the connections between the hidden and output (phonological) units (called late weights); and damage to the hidden units themselves. Damage was inflicted by probabilistically resetting a proportion of the weights or units to zero. The greater the amount of damage being simulated, the higher the proportion of weights that was changed. The consequences were measured in two ways. First, the damage was measured by the phonological error score, which as we have seen reflects the difference between the actual and target activation values of the phonological output units. Obviously, high error scores reflect impaired performance. Second, the damage was measured by the reversal rate. This corresponds to a switch in pronunciation by the model, so that a regular pronunciation is given to an exception item (for example, "have" is pronounced to rhyme with "gave").

Increasing damage at each location produces near-linear increases in the phonological error scores of all types of word. On the whole, though, the lesioned model performed better with regular than with exception words. The reversal rate increased as the degree of damage increased, but nevertheless there were still more reversals occurring on exception words than on regular words. Damage to the hidden units in particular produced a large number of instances where exception words were produced with a regular pronunciation; this is similar to the result whereby surface dyslexics over-regularize their pronunciations. However, the number of regularized pronunciations that were produced by the lesioned model was significantly lower than that produced by surface dyslexic patients. No lesion made the model perform selectively worse on nonwords. Hence the behavior of the lesioned model resembles that of a surface dyslexic.

Patterson et al. also found that word frequency was not a major determinant of whether a pronunciation reversed or not. (It did have some effect, so that high-frequency words were generally more robust to damage.) As we have seen, some surface dyslexics show frequency effects on reading, while others do not. Patterson et al. found that the main determinant of reversals was the number of vowel features by which the regular pronunciation differs from the correct pronunciation, a finding verified from the neuropsychological data.

An additional point of interest is that the lesioned model produced errors that have traditionally been interpreted as "visual" errors. These are mispronunciations that are not over-regularizations and that were traditionally thought to result from an impairment of early graphemic analysis. If this analysis is correct, then Patterson et al. should only have found such errors when there was damage to the orthographic units involved. In contrast, they found them even when the orthographic units were not damaged. This is an example of a particular strength of connectionist modeling; the same mechanism explains what were previously considered to be disparate findings. Here visual errors result from the same lesion that causes other characteristics of surface dyslexia, and it is unnecessary to resort to more complex explanations involving additional damage to the graphemic analysis system.

There are three main problems with this particular account. First, we have already seen that the original Seidenberg and McClelland model was relatively bad at producing non-words before it was lesioned. We might say that the original model is already operating as a phonological dyslexic. Yet surface dyslexics are good at reading nonwords. Second, the model does not really over-regularize, it just changes the vowel sound of words. Third, Behrmann and Bub (1992) reported data that are inconsistent with this model. In particular, they showed that the performance of the surface dyslexic MP on irregular words does vary as a function of word frequency. They interpreted this frequency effect as problematic for connectionist models. Patterson et al. (1989) were quite explicit in simulating only surface dyslexia; their model does not address phonological dyslexia.

Exploring semantic involvement in reading

The revised model, abbreviated to PMSP, provides a better account of dyslexia. The improvements come about because the simulations implement both pathways of the triangle model in order to explain semantic effects on reading.

Surface dyslexia arises in the progressive neurological disease dementia (see Chapter 11 on semantics for details of dementia). Importantly, people with dementia find exception words difficult to pronounce and repeat if they have lost the meaning of those words (Hodges, Patterson, Oxbury, & Funnell, 1992; Patterson & Hodges, 1992; but see Funnell, 1996). Patterson and Hodges proposed that the integrity of lexical representations depends on their interaction with the semantic system: Semantic representations bind phonological representations together with a semantic glue; hence this is called the semantic glue hypothesis. As the semantic system gradually dissolves in dementia, so the semantic glue gradually comes unstuck, and the lexical representations lose their integrity. Patients are therefore forced to rely on a sublexical or grapheme–phoneme correspondence reading route, leading to surface dyslexic errors. Furthermore, they have difficulty in repeating irregular words for which they have lost the meaning, if the system is sufficiently stressed (by repeating lists of words), but they can repeat lists of words for which the meaning is intact (Patterson, Graham, & Hodges, 1994; but see Funnell, 1996, for a patient who does not show this difference).

PMSP showed that a realistic model of surface dyslexia depends on involving semantics in reading. Support from semantics normally relieves the phonological pathway from having to master low-frequency exception words by itself. In surface dyslexia the semantic pathway is damaged, and the isolated phonological pathway reveals itself as surface dyslexia.

Plaut (1997) further examined the involvement of semantics in reading. He noted that some patients have substantial semantic impairments but can read exception words accurately (e.g., DC of Lambon Ralph, Ellis, & Franklin, 1995; DRN of Cipolotti & Warrington, 1995; WLP of Schwartz, Marin, & Saffran, 1979). To explain why some patients with semantic impairments cannot read exception words but some can, Plaut suggested that there are individual differences in the division of labor between semantic and phonological pathways. Although the majority of patients with semantic damage show surface dyslexia (Graham, Hodges, & Patterson, 1994), some exceptions are predicted. He also argued that people use a number of strategies in performing lexical decision, one of which is to use semantic familiarity as a basis for making judgments. The revised model therefore takes into account individual differences between speakers, and shows how small differences in reading strategies can lead to different consequences after brain damage.

Modeling phonological dyslexia

The triangle model provides the best connectionist account of phonological dyslexia. It envisages reading as taking place through the three routes conceptualized in the original SM model. The routes are orthography to phonology, orthography to semantics, and semantics to phonology (Figure 7.4). This approach sees phonological dyslexia as nothing other than a general problem with phonological processing (Farah et al., 1996; Sasanuma et al., 1996). Phonological dyslexia arises through impairments to representations at the phonological level, rather than to grapheme–phoneme conversion. This is called the phonological impairment hypothesis. People with phonological dyslexia can still read words because their weakened phonological representations can be accessed through the semantic level. (Hence this approach is also a development of the semantic glue hypothesis.) We have already noted that the original Seidenberg and McClelland (1989) model performed rather like a phonological dyslexic patient, in that it performed relatively poorly on nonwords. Consistent with the phonological deficit hypothesis, the explanation for this poor performance was that the source of these errors was the impoverished phonological representations used by the model.

An apparent problem with the phonological deficit hypothesis is that it is not clear that it would correctly handle the way in which people with phonological dyslexia read pseudohomophones better than other types of nonwords (Coltheart, 1996). Furthermore, patient LB of Derouesné and Beauvois (1985) showed an advantage for pseudohomophones, but no obvious general phonological impairment. There have also been effects of orthographic complexity and visual similarity, suggesting that there is also an orthographic impairment present in phonological dyslexia (Derouesné & Beauvois, 1985; Howard & Best, 1996). For example, Howard and Best showed that their patient Melanie-Jane read pseudohomophones that were visually similar to the related word (e.g., GERL) better than pseudohomophones that were visually more distant (e.g., PHOCKS). There was no effect of visual similarity for control nonwords. However, Harm and Seidenberg (2001) show how phonological impairment in a connectionist model can give rise to such effects. A phonological impairment magnifies the ease with which different types of stimuli are read.

Modeling deep dyslexia

Hinton and Shallice (1991) lesioned another connectionist model to simulate deep dyslexia. Their model was trained by back-propagation to associate word pronunciations with a representation of the meaning of words. This model is particularly important, because it shows that one type of lesion can give rise to all the symptoms of deep dyslexia, particularly both paralexias and visual errors.

The underlying semantic representation of a word is specified as a pattern of activation across semantic feature units (which Hinton and Shallice called sememes). These correspond to semantic features or primitives such as "main-shape-2D," "has-legs," "brown," and "mammal." These can be thought of as atomic units of meaning (see Chapter 11). The architecture of the Hinton and Shallice (1991) model comprised 28 graphemic input units and 68 semantic output units with an intervening hidden layer containing 40 intermediate units. The model was trained to produce an appropriate output representation given a particular orthographic input using back-propagation. The model was trained on 40 uninflected monosyllabic words.

The structure of the output layer is quite complex. First, there were interconnections between some of the semantic units. The 68 semantic feature units were divided into 19 groups depending on their interpretation, with inhibitory connections between appropriate members of the group. For example, in the group of semantic features that define the size of the object denoted by the word, there are three semantic features: "max-size-less-foot," "max-size-foot-to-two-yards," and "max-size-greater-two-yards." Each of these features inhibits the others in the group, because obviously an object can only have one size. Second, an additional set of hidden units called cleanup units was connected to the semantic units. These permit more complex interdependencies between the semantic units to be learned, and have the effect of producing structure in the output layer. This results in a richer semantic space where there are strong semantic **attractor**s. An attractor can be seen as a point in semantic space to which neighboring states of the network are attracted; it resembles the bottom of a valley or basin, so that objects positioned on the sides of the basin tend to migrate towards the lowest point. This corresponds to the semantic representation ultimately assigned to a word.

As in Patterson et al.'s (1989) simulation of surface dyslexia, different types of lesion were possible. There are two dimensions to remember: one is what is lesioned, the other is how it is lesioned. The connections involved were the grapheme–intermediate, intermediate–sememe, and sememe–cleanup. Three methods of lesioning the network were used. First, each set of connections was taken in turn, and a proportion of their weights was set to zero (effectively disconnecting units). Second, random noise was added to each connection. Third, the hidden units (the intermediate and cleanup units) were ablated by destroying a proportion of them.

The results showed that the closer the lesion was to the semantic system, the more effect it had. The lesion type and site interacted in their effects; for example, the cleanup circuit was more sensitive to added noise than to disconnections. Lesions resulted in four types of error: semantic (where an input gave an output word

that was semantically but not visually close to the target; these resemble the classic semantic paralexias of deep dyslexics); visual (words visually but not semantically similar); mixed (where the output is both semantically and visually close to the target); and others. All lesion sites and types (except for that of disconnecting the semantic and cleanup units) produced the same broad pattern of errors. Finally, on some occasions the lesions were so severe that the network could not generate an explicit response. In these cases, Hinton and Shallice tested the below-threshold information left in the system by simulating a forced-choice procedure. They achieved this by comparing the residual semantic output to a set of possible outputs corresponding to a set of words, one of which was the target semantic output. The model behaved above chance on this forced-choice test, in that its output semantic representation tended to be closer to that of the target than to the alternatives.

Hence the lesioned network behaves like a deep dyslexic patient, in particular in making semantic paralexias. The paralexias occur because semantic attractors cause the accessing of feature clusters close to the meanings of words that are related to the target. A "landscape" metaphor may be useful. Lesions can be thought of as resulting in the destruction of the ridges that separate the different basins of attraction. The occurrence of such errors does not seem to be crucially dependent on the particular lesion type or site under consideration. Furthermore, this account provides an explanation of why different error types, particularly semantic and visual errors, nearly always co-occur in such patients. Two visually similar words can point in the first instance to nearby parts of semantic space, even though their ultimate meanings in the basins may be far apart; if you start off on top of a hill, going downhill in different directions will take you to very different ultimate locations. Lesions modify semantic space so that visually similar words are then attracted to different semantic attractors.

Hinton and Shallice's account is important for cognitive neuropsychologists for a number of reasons. First, it provides an explicit mechanism whereby the characteristics of deep dyslexia can be derived from a model of normal reading. Second, it shows that the actual site of the lesion is not of primary importance. This is mainly because of the "cascade" characteristics of these networks. Each stage of processing is continually activating the next, and is not dependent on the completion of processing by its prior stage (McClelland, 1979). Therefore, effects of lesions at one network site are very quickly passed on to surrounding sites. Third, it shows why symptoms that were previously considered to be conceptually distinct necessarily co-occur. Semantic and visual errors can result from the same lesion. Fourth, it thus revives the importance of syndromes as a neuropsychological concept. If symptoms co-occur as a result of any lesion to a particular system, then it makes sense to look for and study such co-occurrences.

Plaut and Shallice (1993a) extended this work to examine the effect of word abstractness on lesioned reading performance. As we have seen, the reading performance of deep dyslexic patients is significantly better on more imageable than on less imageable words. Plaut and Shallice showed that the richness of the underlying semantic representation of a word is an analog of imageability. They hypothesized that the semantic representations of abstract words contain fewer semantic features than those of concrete words; that is, the more concrete a word is, the richer its semantic representation. Jones (1985) showed that it was possible to account for imageability effects in deep dyslexia by recasting them as ease-of-predication effects. Ease-of-predication is a measure of how easy it is to generate things to say about a word, or predicates, and is obviously closely related to the richness of the underlying semantic representation. It is easier to find more things to say about more imageable words than about less imageable words. Plaut and Shallice (1993a) showed that when an attractor network similar to that of Hinton and Shallice (1991) is lesioned, concrete words are read better than abstract words. One exception was that severe lesions of the cleanup system resulted in better performance on abstract words. Plaut and Shallice argue that this is consistent with patient CAV (Warrington, 1981), who showed such an advantage. Hence this network can account for both the usual better performance of deep dyslexic patients on concrete words, and also the rare exception where the reverse is the case. They also showed that lesions closer to the grapheme units tended to produce more visual errors, whereas lesions closer to the semantic units tended to produce more semantic errors. The model also provides an account of the behavior of normal participants reading degraded words (McLeod, Shallice, & Plaut, 2000). If words are presented very rapidly to people, they make both visual and semantic errors. The data fit the connectionist model well.

Connectionist modeling has advanced our understanding of deep dyslexia in particular, and neuropsychological deficits in general. The finding that apparently unrelated symptoms can necessarily co-occur as a result of a single lesion is of particular importance. It suggests that deep dyslexia may after all be a unitary condition. However, there is one fly in the ointment. The finding that at least some patients show imageability effects in reading but not in comprehension is troublesome for all models that posit a disturbance of semantic representations as the cause of deep dyslexia (Newton & Barry, 1997). Instead, in at least some patients, the primary disturbance may be to the speech production component of reading.

COMPARISON OF MODELS

A simple dual-route model provides an inadequate account of reading, and needs at least an additional lexical route through imageable semantics. The more complex a model becomes, the greater the worry that routes are being introduced on an arbitrary basis to account for particular findings. Analogy models have some attractive features, but their detailed workings are vague and they do not seem able to account for all the data. Connectionist modeling has provided an explicit, single-route model that covers most of the main findings, but has its problems. At the very least it has clarified the issues involved in reading. Its contribution goes beyond this, however. It has set the challenge that only one route is necessary in reading words and nonwords, and that regularity effects in pronunciation arise out of statistical regularities in the words of the language. It may not be a complete or correct account; however, it is certainly a challenging one.

Currently we are faced with two serious alternatives: a connectionist model such as the triangle model, and a variant of the dual-route model such as the dual-route cascaded model. The literature is full of claim and counter-claim, and it would be presumptuous for a text like this to say that one is clearly right and the other wrong. There are many studies providing support for and against one or the other of the models. Many of them focus on how we read nonwords (Besner et al., 1990; Seidenberg et al., 1994), because the division of labor in the DRC model between a lexical route with knowledge of individual words and a non-lexical route with spelling rules is absent in connectionist models, and this difference is the key one between the two sorts of models. The DRC emphasizes regularity (does the word obey the rule?), which is a categorical concept—either the word obeys the spelling–sound rules or it does not, with nonwords having to be pronounced by the rule. The triangle model emphasizes consistency of rimes and other units (how often is -AVE pronounced in a certain way?), which is a statistical concept. According to Zevin and Seidenberg (2006), consistency effects such as those shown in Glushko's (1979) and Jared's (1997b) studies are the critical test between models. Words like PAVE are regular but inconsistent; according to the DRC model they should be as easy to pronounce as regular and consistent words such as PANE; according to the triangle model they should not. Now of course we know from Glushko's study that regular inconsistent words are slower to pronounce than regular consistent ones, but Coltheart et al. (2001) argue that these differences are an artifact arising from several confounding factors (e.g., the presence of exception words in the materials, and

an increase in the number of times it is necessary to reanalyze inconsistent words as we read them from left to right). Zevin and Seidenberg (2006) argued that graded sensitivity to consistency effects in nonwords provides the critical test between the models, with only connectionist models correctly predicting the presence of such effects, and being able to account for individual differences in nonword pronunciation. However, doubtless this debate will run and run.

Perhaps the choice between the triangle and the dual-route cascaded model comes down to which one values most: explaining a wide range of data, or parsimony in design.

Balota (1990) asked if there is a magic moment when we recognize a word but do not yet have access to its meaning. He argued that the tasks most commonly used to study word processing (lexical decision and word naming) are both sensitive to post-access processes. This makes interpretation of data obtained using these tasks difficult (although not, as we have seen, impossible). Furthermore, deep dyslexia (discussed earlier) suggests that it is possible to access meaning without correctly identifying the word, while non-semantic reading suggests that we can recognize words without necessarily accessing their meaning. Whereas unique lexical access is a prerequisite of activating meaning in models such as the logogen and the serial search model, cascading connectionist models permit the gradual activation of semantic information while evidence is still accumulating from perceptual processing. A model such as the triangle model (Patterson et al., 1996; Plaut et al., 1996) seems best able to accommodate all these constraints.

Finally, all of these models—particularly the connectionist ones—are limited in that they have focused on the recognition of morphologically simple, often monosyllabic words. Rastle and Coltheart (2000) have developed a rule-based model of reading bisyllabic words, emphasizing how we produce the correct stress, and Ans, Carbonnel, and Valdois (1998) have developed a connectionist model of reading polysyllabic words.

SUMMARY

- Different languages use different principles to translate words into sounds; languages such as English use the alphabetic principle.
- Regular words have a regular grapheme-to-phoneme correspondence, but exception words do not.
- According to the dual-route model, words can be read through a direct lexical route or a sublexical route; in adult skilled readers the lexical route is usually faster.
- The sublexical route was originally thought to use grapheme–phoneme conversion, but now it is considered to use correspondences across a range of sublexical levels.
- There are effects of lexical similarity in reading certain nonwords (pseudohomophones), while not all words are read with equal facility (the consistency of the regularity of a word's neighbors affects its ease of pronunciation).
- It might be necessary to access the phonological code of a word before we can access its meaning; this process is called phonological mediation.
- Phonological mediation is most likely to be observed with low-frequency words and with poor readers.
- Readers have some attentional control over which route they emphasize in reading.
- Access to some phonological code is mandatory, even in silent reading, but normally does not precede semantic access.
- Increasing reading speed above about 350 words a minute (by speed reading, for example) leads to reduced comprehension.
- Surface dyslexia is difficulty in reading exception words; it corresponds to an impairment of the lexical route in the dual-route model.
- Phonological dyslexia is difficulty in reading nonwords; it corresponds to an impairment of the sublexical route in the dual-route model.
- Deep dyslexic readers display a number of symptoms including making visual errors, but the most important characteristic is the presence of semantic reading errors or paralexias.
- There has been some debate as to whether deep dyslexia is a coherent syndrome.
- Non-semantic readers can pronounce irregular words even though they do not know their meaning.
- The revised dual-route model uses multiple sublexical correspondences and permits direct access through a semantic lexical route and a non-semantic lexical route.
- The dual-route cascaded model allows activation to trickle through levels before processing is necessarily completed at any level.
- Seidenberg and McClelland (SM) produced an important connectionist model of reading; however, it performed poorly on nonwords and pseudohomophones.
- Lesioning the SM network gives rise to behavior resembling surface dyslexia, but its over-regularizations differ from those made by humans.
- The revised version of this model, PMSP, gives a much better account of normal reading and surface dyslexia; it uses a much more realistic representation for input and output than the original model.
- There are clear semantic influences on normal and impaired reading, and recent connectionist models are trying to take these into account.
- The triangle model accounts for phonological dyslexia as an impairment to the phonological representations: this is the phonological impairment hypothesis.
- Deep dyslexia has been modeled by lesioning semantic attractors; the lesioned model shows how the apparently disparate symptoms of deep dyslexia can arise from one type of lesion.

(Continued)

(Continued)

- More imageable words are relatively spared because they have richer semantic representations.
- There has been considerable debate as to whether developmental dyslexia is qualitatively different from very poor normal reading, and whether there are subtypes that correspond to acquired dyslexias; the preponderance of evidence suggests that developmental dyslexia is on a continuum with normal reading.
- Connectionist modeling shows how two distinct types of damage can lead to a continuum of impairment between development surface and phonological dyslexia extremes.

QUESTIONS TO THINK ABOUT

1. Is there a "magic moment" when we recognize a word?
2. Why might reading errors occur? Keep a record of any errors you make and try to relate them to what you have learned in this and the previous chapter.
3. What practical tips could help adult dyslexic readers to read more effectively?
4. Do we make errors in inner speech?

FURTHER READING

Many of the references at the end of Chapter 6 will also be relevant here. There are a number of works that describe the orthography of English, and discuss the rules whereby certain spelling-to-sound correspondences are described as regular and others as irregular. One of the best known of these is Venezky (1970). For an example of work on reading in a different orthographic system, see Kess and Miyamoto (1999).

For a general introduction to reading, writing, spelling, and their disorders, see Ellis (1993). For more discussion of dyslexia, including peripheral dyslexias, see Ellis and Young (1988). Two volumes (entitled *Deep Dyslexia*, 2nd ed., by Coltheart, Patterson, & Marshall, 1987, and *Surface Dyslexia,* by Patterson, Marshall, & Coltheart, 1985b) cover much of the relevant material. A special issue of the journal *Cognitive Neuropsychology* (1996, volume 13, part 6) was devoted to phonological dyslexia.

For recent overviews of reading, see Andrews (2006) and Snowling and Hulme (2007).

CHAPTER 8

LEARNING TO READ AND SPELL

INTRODUCTION

How do we learn to read? Unlike speaking and listening, reading and writing are clearly not easy tasks to learn, as shown by the large number of people who find them difficult, and the amount of explicit tuition apparently necessary. The complexities of English spelling make the task facing the learner a difficult one. Here we will concentrate on the most fundamental aspect of reading development, that of how we learn to read words. Reading development is closely associated with skills such as spelling, and we will also examine this. Finally, disproportionate difficulty in learning to read and spell—developmental dyslexia and dysgraphia—are relatively common, and we will examine these in the context of a model of normal reading development. Developmental dyslexias can be categorized in a similar way to acquired dyslexia, which has been used as further justification for a dual-route model of reading.

By the end of this chapter you should:

- Know the course of normal reading development.
- Understand the importance of the alphabetic principle.
- Understand the importance of phonological awareness in learning to read.
- Know how reading should best be taught.
- Know about developmental reading disorders.
- Know how poor readers can be helped to read better.

NORMAL READING DEVELOPMENT

I remember being taught reading at school: the letters of the alphabet were written in capitals on separate pieces of card, with an appropriate picture accompanying each letter (apple for A, cat for C; I can't remember what X and Z were). Great pride was associated with being able to recite the alphabet backwards.

Nearly all children at some point go through a stage of alphabetic reading where they make use of grapheme–phoneme correspondences, yet skilled readers eventually end up using some sort of direct route to sound and meaning that makes little use of rule-based correspondences. Hence, learning skilled reading involves a developmental shift away from reading by a reliance on phonological recoding to a more direct route from print to meaning. How does this shift occur? There is general agreement that children learn to read alphabetic languages by discovering the principles of phonological recoding (Jorm & Share, 1983; Share, 1995).

Children probably learn to read in a series of stages, although as Rayner and Pollatsek (1989) point out, it is likely that these stages reflect the use of increasingly sophisticated skills and strategies, rather than the biologically and environmentally driven sequence of stages that might underlie cognitive development. A number of broadly similar developmental sequences have been proposed (e.g., Ehri, 1992, 1997a, 1997b; Frith, 1985; Marsh, Desberg, &

Cooper, 1977; Marsh, Friedman, Welch, & Desberg, 1981). Frith (1985) described three stages. First, in the logographic stage, the child recognizes individual words by particular salient characteristics of the word; hence the child cannot read new words or nonwords. Second, in the alphabetic stage, the child learns to read by grapheme–phoneme correspondences. Third, in the orthographic stage, the child has acquired an adult-like reading system, being able to recognize whole words without having to decode each individual grapheme. Nevertheless the child can still use the grapheme–phoneme conversion system for new words and nonwords.

Ehri (1992, 1997a, 1997b) prefers the term "phase" to stage, as it has fewer implications about how discrete the boundary between phases is. Ehri described four phases of reading development (see Figure 8.1). During the pre-alphabetic phase, children know little about letter–sound correspondences, so they read by rote, learning direct links between the visual appearances of words and their meanings. For example, the word "yellow" might be remembered because it "has two tall bits together in the middle." In some cases at least, children are remembering the concept associated with the visual pattern rather than the word: Harste, Burke, and Woodward (1982) describe how one child read "Crest" (the name of a brand of toothpaste) as "toothpaste" on one occasion and "brush teeth" on another. This phase is short, and might not happen with all children. Although this is a version of direct access, it is very different from the direct access of skilled readers. There are no systematic relationships and no detailed processing, with the child relying on arbitrary, salient cues. Knowledge about sounds is important from a very early stage.

In the partial alphabetic reading phase, young readers use their partial knowledge of letter names and sounds to form partial correspondences between spellings and pronunciations. Some letters are associated with sounds. Ehri proposed that the first and final letters are the ones that are often first associated with sounds because they are easiest to pick out. The connections are only partial because children at this stage are unable to segment the word's pronunciation into all of its sounds.

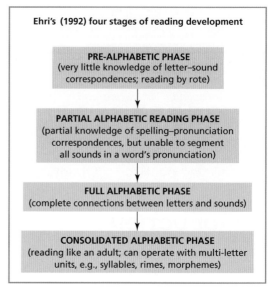

FIGURE 8.1

In the full alphabetic phase, complete connections are made between letters and sounds. At this stage children can read words they have never seen before. Gradually, as children practice reading words often enough, words become known by sight. They can then be read aloud by the direct route without the need for letter–sound conversion. Sight-word reading has the advantage that it is much faster than letter–sound conversion. Finally, in the consolidated alphabetic phase, the child reads like an adult. Letter patterns that recur across words become familiar, so the child can operate with multi-letter units such as syllables, rimes, and morphemes. The rime is the end part of a word that produces the rhyme (e.g., the rime in "rant" is "ant"); it is the VC or VCC (vowel–consonant or vowel–consonant–consonant) part of a word—the phonological equivalent of the orthographic body of a monosyllabic word. As we will see, rimes may play an important part in learning to read.

Poor readers never get far beyond the second stage because they have poor phonological recoding skills. Competent readers have two types of knowledge about spelling: they know about the alphabetic system, and they know about the spellings of specific words (Ehri, 1997a). Words are difficult to spell if they violate the alphabetic principle or if they place a heavy load on memory. Hence words containing graphemes with irregular pronunciations, phonemes with many graphemic options, and graphemes with no phonological correspondences will all be difficult to spell.

In this scheme, then, there is an initial phase of direct access based only on visual cues. Barron and Baron (1977) showed that concurrent articulation had no effect on extracting the meaning of a printed word. However, this initial phase of visual access is very short. There is some evidence that phonetic information is used from a very early stage (Ehri, 1992; Ehri & Wilce, 1985; Rack, Hulme, Snowling, & Wightman, 1994). Early readers set up partial associations between sounds and the letters for which they stand, even though these partial associations are not the same as conscious letter-by-letter decoding. Ehri and Wilce (1985) showed that children who could not yet use phonological decoding still found it easier to learn the simplified spelling cue "jrf," which bears some phonetic resemblance to the target word "giraffe," than "wbc," which is visually very distinctive but bears no phonological relation to the target. Semantic factors also influence very early reading: Laing and Hulme (1999) found that children performed better at associating spelling cues with words when they were clearer about the meanings

of words. They also performed better on more imageable words. So even children in the earliest stages of reading are sensitive to spelling–sound relations, but semantic factors also play a role.

PHONOLOGICAL AWARENESS

Phonological awareness—the awareness of the sounds of a word—is important when learning to read. It is one aspect of more general knowledge of our cognitive abilities (called *metacognitive knowledge*) that is thought to play an essential role in cognitive development (Karmiloff-Smith, 1986). Many tasks have been used to test phonological awareness (see Table 8.1 for some examples). Phonological awareness is just one aspect of our knowledge of language. Gombert (1992) distinguished between epilinguistic knowledge (implicit knowledge about our language processes that is used unconsciously) and metalinguistic knowledge (explicit knowledge about our language processes of which we are aware and can report, and of which we can make deliberate use). This distinction is reflected in the tasks that have been used to test phonological awareness (e.g., those in Table 8.1).

TABLE 8.1 Some tasks used to assess phonological awareness (based on Yopp, 1988).

Task	Example
Sound-to-word matching	Is there a /f/ in "calf"?
Word-to-word matching	Do "pen" and "pipe" begin the same?
Recognition of rhyme	Does "sun" rhyme with "run"?
Isolating sounds	What is the first sound in "rose"?
Phoneme segmentation	What sounds do you hear in "hot"?
Phoneme counting	How many sounds do you hear in "cake"?
Phoneme blending	Combine these sounds: /k/ /a/ /t/
Phoneme deletion	What would be left if you took /t/ out of "stand"?
Specifying deleted phoneme	What sound do you hear in "meat" that's missing in "eat"?
Phoneme reversal	Say "as" with the first sound last and last sound first.

Although it was first thought that these tasks may all measure the same thing, it is now agreed that they do not. In an analysis of 10 commonly used tests of phonological awareness, Yopp (1988) identified two related factors, one to do with manipulating single sounds and another to do with holding sounds in memory while performing operations on them. Muter, Hulme, Snowling, and Taylor (1998) identified distinct factors in tests of phonological awareness, one to do with segmentation skills and one with rhyming skills. The underlying ability to determine that two words have a sound in common (phoneme constancy) might be a particularly important phonological skill for learning to read (Byrne, 1998).

Phonological awareness and literacy are closely related. Illiterate adults (from an agricultural area of south Portugal) performed poorly on phonological awareness tasks, particularly those involving manipulating phonemes (e.g., adding or deleting phonemes to the starts of nonwords). Ex-illiterate adults, who had received some literacy training in adulthood, performed much better (Morais, Bertelson, Cary, & Alegria, 1986; Morais, Carey, Alegria, & Bertelson, 1979). Speakers of Chinese, who use a non-alphabetic writing system where there is no correspondence between written symbols and individual sounds, seem less aware of individual phonemes. Chinese adult speakers who were literate in both an alphabetic and a non-alphabetic system could readily perform tasks such as deleting or adding consonants in spoken Chinese words; speakers who were literate only in the non-alphabetic system found the deletion and addition tasks extremely difficult (Read, Zhang, Nie, & Ding, 1986). These studies show that phonological awareness works in both ways: literacy in alphabetic scripts can lead to phonological awareness.

Where phonological awareness tasks have been applied systematically to all levels of the syllable from small units (phonemes) through intermediate-size units (onsets and rimes) to large units (syllables), researchers have found a sequence of phonological development. Implicit awareness is measured by tasks such as matching sounds (e.g., finding rimes) and detecting oddities; explicit awareness is measured by tasks such as isolating, segmenting, and manipulating sounds as evidenced by production. Implicit awareness follows a large-to-small developmental sequence, as indicated by early performance in matching tasks (Treiman & Zukowski, 1996), but this has little controlling effect on learning to read. Explicit awareness follows a small-to-large unit sequence and reflects the demands of learning to read using letter–sound correspondences. For example, beginning readers' explicit awareness of rimes and onsets can be poor, while implicit knowledge of rhyming can be good (Duncan, Seymour, & Hill, 1997, 2000). Younger children were best at finding the common unit in sounds when the units were small (e.g., initial consonants, as in "face" and "food" rather than "boat" and "goat"). Thus, although they were able to make the implicit judgment that "boat" and "goat" rhymed, they were poor at explicitly identifying the common sound in those words. As children grow older they are more sensitive to the rimes of words and better able to generate word analogies for nonwords (e.g., "door" for "goor").

Early work suggested that rime-level awareness could predict late reading ability in longitudinal studies (Goswami, 1993; Goswami & Bryant, 1990); more recent studies have claimed that phoneme-level segmentation skill and letter-name knowledge are strong predictors of level of reading ability, while rhyming skill is only a weak predictor (Muter et al., 1998), although there is some controversy about the effects of the specific instructions given to children (Bryant, 1998; Hulme, Muter, & Snowling, 1998).

Beginning readers have difficulty with phonological awareness tasks, but their performance improves with age. Developing phonological awareness improves reading skills and, as children learn to read, their phonological awareness increases. Phonological awareness plays a driving role in reading development (Rayner & Pollatsek, 1989). Training on phonological awareness can lead to an improvement in segmenting and reading skills in general (Bradley & Bryant, 1983) if it is linked to reading (Hatcher, Hulme, & Ellis, 1994; see Bus & van Ijzendoorn, 1999, for a review). Laing and Hulme (1999) showed that phonological awareness correlates with the ability of young children to learn to associate phonetic cues with words (e.g., "bfr" for "beaver," as in the Ehri & Wilce, 1985, task described earlier). A recent meta-analysis of studies of learning to read demonstrates the importance of phonological awareness in learning to read, and how an impairment in phonological awareness is associated with reading difficulties (Melby-Lervåg, Lyster, & Hulme, 2012).

As we have noted several times before, different languages map spelling onto sounds in different ways. How do these differences affect the development of phonological awareness? Before children learn to read, we would expect children from different language communities to show broadly the same features of phonological awareness. After they learn to read, however, their knowledge of how letters map onto sounds in their particular language might lead to particularities in their phonological awareness skill that might be different from that of other languages. Experimental results support this idea (Goswami, Ziegler, & Richardson, 2005). English and German are very similar in the sorts of sounds they use, and pre-literate children have very similar phonological awareness. However, German is much more consistent in its spelling–sound correspondences, while as we know English is highly variable. After the first year of reading instruction there are clear differences in the phonological awareness skills of children learning to read these two languages. In particular, English children pay more attention to the rime of a word than do the German children. German children on the other hand develop awareness of the role of individual phonemes relatively more quickly (because small reading units have more regular correspondences in English). These results also show that phonological awareness and reading development have a reciprocal relationship—learning to read changes our phonological awareness.

In summary, phonological awareness is a central concept in reading, and is absent or impoverished in unskilled readers. The ability to manipulate phonemes and knowledge of letter–sound correspondences are particularly important. Phonological awareness and literacy must be interrelated, because impaired phonological awareness leads to difficulty in reading (see later), but the absence of literacy leads to poor performance on tasks of phonological awareness. However, not all researchers accept that it has yet been conclusively shown that phonological awareness skills precede and play a causal role in learning to read, rather than being just correlated with, or a consequence of, reading development. Longitudinal studies reveal correlations, while there are potential difficulties with the training studies that are most likely to reveal causal links between phonological awareness and reading skill (Castles & Coltheart, 2004). For example, several studies that train phonological awareness also trained other skills (e.g., letter names), and virtually all studies have used children who could already read, and for whom therefore the phonological awareness training might have reinforced some pre-existing reading skill. So although it is clear that phonological awareness and reading development are related, there remains controversy as to whether phonological awareness is the cause or consequence of literacy (Castles & Coltheart, 2004; Hulme, Snowling, Caravolas, & Carroll, 2005).

The size of early reading units

Do children have to learn phonological decoding before they can become skilled readers and use processes such as reading by analogy? There has been considerable debate about the progression in reading development. Do beginning readers start with large units and then move to small, or do they start with small units and then move to large? Although Goswami (1993) argued that the correspondences between sounds and the rimes of syllables are probably the first to be acquired, it is now generally agreed that grapheme–phoneme correspondences are learned first.

Goswami (1986, 1988, 1993) argued that young children read words by analogy, before they are able to use phonological recoding. It is harder for beginning readers to sound out and blend phonemes than to sound out and blend larger subunits such as onsets and rimes. Children's ability to detect rhyming words in a sequence is strongly predictive of their later analogical reading performance. Goswami presented children with a clue word (e.g., "beak") and asked them to read several other words and nonwords, some of which were analogs of the clue word (e.g., "bean," "beal," "peak," and "lake"). She found that the children read the analog words better than the control words, suggesting that they are making use of the rime to read by analogy. For Goswami, children start to read by identifying large units (onset and rime) first, and only later identify small units such as phonemes.

Most studies, however, have found that beginning readers need some grapheme–phoneme decoding skill in order to able to read words by analogy (see Brown & Deavers, 1999; Coltheart & Leahy, 1992; Duncan, Seymour, & Hill, 2000; Ehri, 1992; Ehri & Robbins, 1992; Laxon, Masterson, & Coltheart, 1991; Marsh et al., 1981; Savage, 1997). That is, beginning readers start by identifying how letters correspond to sounds. For example, beginning readers are more adept at segmenting words into phonemes than into onsets and rimes (Seymour & Evans, 1994). The differences between these results are probably attributable to the materials and tasks Goswami used. Her control words might have been more difficult to read than the analogs. Muter, Snowling, and Taylor (1994) pointed out that the majority of these tasks involved the simultaneous presentation of clue words and target words, which might have provided additional information that might not be available in normal reading. Along these lines, Savage (1997) showed that there was no privileged role for onsets and rimes in the absence of the concurrent prompts. Ehri and Robbins (1992) showed that children could only read words by analogy in natural reading if they already possessed grapheme–phoneme recoding skills. Brown and Deavers (1999) showed that reading strategy varied depending on the reading age of the child. Although less skilled readers (with a mean reading age of 8 years 8 months) could make use of rime-based correspondences (that is, read by analogy), they preferred to read by grapheme–phoneme correspondences. Children with a higher reading age (11 years 6 months) were more likely to read by analogy, with the rime being particularly important. Using a clue word increased the amount of reading-by-analogy

in all age groups, again suggesting that the child's reading strategy is task-dependent. Hence learning to read involves a process of learning through several different reading routes (Grainger, Lété, Bertand, Dufau, & Ziegler, 2012).

Given that different languages map spelling onto sound in different ways, it is perhaps not surprising that languages differ in the preferred size of the key unit that emerges while learning to read. We have just seen that in English the rime emerges as a key reading unit. In languages such as German, Greek, and Spanish, which are much more regular in the spelling–sound correspondences, it is possible to make systematic use of smaller units and hence older children come to rely on simple grapheme–phoneme conversion without needing to develop reading by analogy based on rimes. Speakers of orthographically regular languages do not need to make use of larger units. The data support this idea. There are many words in English and German that are orthographically identical (sand, zoo). However, as we saw in Chapter 7, the ease of pronunciation of a target word in English depends on the number of words that share the same rime with the target: a word like "start" has many neighbors and is easier to pronounce, while a word such as "storm" has fewer neighbors and is more difficult. In German, this effect in adult speakers is much less pronounced, while the effect of length is stronger (Ziegler, Perry, Jacobs, & Braun, 2001). The idea that different languages make use of different-sized preferred reading units is called the psycholinguistic grain size theory (Ziegler & Goswami, 2005).

In summary, in natural situations younger reading-age children tend to read using grapheme–phoneme correspondences, and older reading-age children tend to read by analogy based mainly on rime. They are sensitive to task demands, however, and younger children can be encouraged to read by analogy by the clue word technique.

There is evidence that once children know something about reading—once they have acquired the basics of phonological recoding—they in part teach themselves to read (Share, 1995). Bowey and Muller (2005) gave third-grade children (about 8 years old) short stories to read silently. The stories contained nonwords, and in a subsequent test the children were asked to read lists of words containing those nonwords. They pronounced these nonwords more quickly than control nonwords.

HOW SHOULD READING BE TAUGHT?

When should reading be taught? The age at which children start to learn to read seems to be relatively unimportant—indeed, even when it is delayed until age 7 there are no serious or permanent side effects (Rayner & Pollatsek, 1989). In fact, older children learn to read more quickly in comparison with younger children (Feitelson, Tehori, & Levinberg-Green, 1982). As a corollary of this, very early tuition does not provide any obvious long-term benefits, as late starters catch up so easily.

The main question then is *how* should reading be taught? There are two traditional approaches to teaching children how to read (see Figure 8.2). These correspond to emphasizing one of the two routes in the dual-route model. In the look-and-say or whole word method, children learn to associate the sound of a word with a particular visual pattern. This corresponds to emphasizing the lexical or direct access route. In the alternative phonic method, children are taught to associate sounds with letters and letter sequences, and use these associations to build up the pronunciations of words. This method therefore emphasizes the non-lexical, grapheme–phoneme conversion route.

It is generally agreed that the phonic method gives much better results (Adams, 1990). A meta-analysis (which is a method of combining the results of two or more, often many, experiments) of the

reading literature showed that systematic training on phonics produced a strong beneficial effect on learning to read (Ehri, Nunes, Stahl, & Willows, 2001). Indeed, many studies show that discovering the alphabetic principle (that letters correspond systematically to sounds) is the key to learning to read (see Backman, 1983; Bradley & Bryant, 1978, 1983; Byrne, 1998; Rayner & Pollatsek, 1989; Share, 1995). Other methods do not work anywhere near as well. Seymour and Elder (1986) examined the reading performance of a class of young children (aged 4½ to 5½ years) who were taught to "sight read" with relatively little emphasis on the alphabetic principle. They found that the children were limited to reading only words that they had been taught. They made many reading errors, and their performance in some ways resembled that of people with deep and phonological dyslexia.

Hence the most efficient way of learning to read in an alphabetic language is to learn what phonemes correspond to. In the absence of tuition, however, children try to assign letters to words rather than sounds, although most children soon realize that this will not work (Byrne, 1998; Ferreiro, 1985). Anything that expedites this realization facilitates reading. Teaching the alphabetic principle explicitly does this, and, as we have seen, training on phonological awareness improves reading skills, presumably by focusing on phonemes and preparing the way to showing how they can be mapped onto letters. As Byrne (1998, p. 144) concludes, "if we want children to know something, we would be advised to teach it explicitly."

There are two types of phonics instruction. Analytic phonics is generally taught after reading

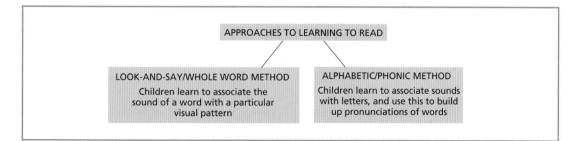

FIGURE 8.2

has begun. Letter sounds are introduced gradually; reading is practiced using sets of words that share common sounds (e.g., dog and dig). Analytic phonics is currently the most common method of teaching reading in the United Kingdom. In synthetic phonics, children are taught all the letters and letter sounds before anything else. Teaching emphasizes word-building activities involving the blending together of constituent sounds. Recent work in Clackmannanshire in Scotland suggests that being taught by synthetic phonics is greatly preferable to being taught by analytic phonics (Johnston & Watson, 2004, 2005). A 7-year longitudinal study showed that children who were taught by synthetic phonics learned to read and spell faster than children who were taught by other methods. The advantages of learning to read by synthetic phonics appear to be long-lasting,

In the phonic method, children are taught to associate sounds with letters in order to build up the pronunciation of whole words.

with children taught by this method showing a reading advantage several years later.

Finally, mere exposure to print has beneficial effects. Stanovich, West, and Harrison (1995) showed that exposure to print was a significant predictor of vocabulary size and declarative knowledge even after other factors such as working memory differences, educational level, and general skill were taken into account. It is particularly important for adults to involve young children actively with print, rather than children just merely being passively exposed to it (Levy, Gong, Hessels, Evans, & Jared, 2006). Hence games and activities that get children to manipulate letters and words and involve them in carrying out some early form of reading are highly desirable. Indeed, lack of exposure to print can lead to a developmental delay in reading, and may even be one factor causing developmental surface dyslexia (Stanovich, Siegel, & Gottardo, 1997).

LEARNING TO SPELL

Spelling is an important skill associated with the emergence of phonological awareness and learning to read. Spelling can be thought of as the reverse of reading: Instead of having to turn letters into sounds, you have to turn sounds into letters. Indeed the classic model of spelling is a dual-route one based on the dual-route model of reading (Brown & Ellis, 1994). In this model, there is a spelling-to-sound, or assembled or non-lexical, route, which can only work for regular words, and a direct, or addressed or lexical, route, which will work for all words. The crucial determinant in spelling development is the acquisition of phonological representations of words (Brown & Ellis, 1994).

Given the similarities between reading and spelling, it is no surprise that the same sorts of issues are found in spelling research as in reading research, and that the two areas are closely connected longitudinally. Spelling errors are a rich source of information about how children spell. In the earliest stages of spelling, around the age of 3, children know that writing is different from drawing, but do not yet understand the alphabetic principle. Young children believe that the written forms of words should reflect their meanings; hence they think that the names of large objects such as "whale" should be spelled with more letters than the names of small objects such as "mosquito" (Lundberg & Tornéus, 1978; Treiman, 1997). Gradually, children's spelling becomes motivated by their realization of the importance of the alphabetic principle—that letters correspond to sounds. At first the application of this principle might be sporadic, but eventually it comes to dominate. Early spelling errors often reflect the over-application of the alphabetic principle. For example, "Trevor" (age 6) spelled "eat" as "et," with two letters, because it only has two sounds (Treiman, 1997). Early errors may also reflect the fact that sometimes children's analyses of words into phonemes do not match those of adults; hence "dragon" becomes "jragin" (Read, 1975). Another source of error is that young children are over-rigorous about applying letter names. This is a particular problem with vowels: because the name of "e" is /i/, children make errors such as spelling "clean" as "clen" and "happy" as "hape" (Treiman, 1994).

Very young children may use groups of sounds that are larger than a phoneme. In particular, they may try to spell with a letter for each syllable (Ferreiro & Teberosky, 1982). For example, 5-year-old "Bobby" spelled monosyllabic words with one letter each: "be" became "b" and "should" became "c." Consonant clusters may be spelled with just one letter: "street" becomes "set" (Treiman, 1993).

Children also soon become sensitive to the distributional information about the orthographic patterns to which they have been exposed. For example, in English the string of letters "ck" can occur in the middle and at the end of words, but not at the beginning. Early spellers seem aware of this: they make few errors such as "ckak" (for "cake") that violate these constraints (Treiman, 1997). Young children do however produce some orthographically illegal strings in error: "hr" for "her" is quite a common error.

As children grow older, they use information in addition to the alphabetic principle. They learn to spell irregular words, and learn that morphemes are spelled in regular ways—for example, that the past tense ending of regular verbs is always spelled "ed," no matter how it is pronounced (Treiman, 1997).

DEVELOPMENTAL DYSLEXIA

Developmental dyslexia is an impairment in developing reading abilities: whereas acquired dyslexia involves damage to reading systems that were known to be functionally normal before the brain trauma, developmental dyslexic children grow up such that the normal acquisition of reading is impaired. In the popular press, the term is often used to refer to difficulties with writing and poor spelling; strictly speaking, these symptoms should be called developmental dysgraphia, although naturally developmental dyslexia and dysgraphia usually occur together. To qualify for developmental dyslexia, the child's reading age must be below what would be expected from their age and IQ, and the child's IQ, home background, and level of education must reach certain levels of attainment (Ellis, 1993). Estimates of the incidence of developmental dyslexia range from 10% to as high as 30% (Freberg, 2006).

There are several important issues in the study of developmental dyslexia. Although developmental dyslexia is a convenient label, there has been considerable debate as to whether it represents one end of a continuum of reading skills, or whether it is a distinct deficit with a single underlying cause (or causes if there is more than one type). Neither is there agreement that there are clear-cut subtypes of developmental dyslexia that

Developmental dysgraphia (difficulty with writing and poor spelling) and developmental dyslexia (an impairment in developing reading abilities) usually occur together.

correspond to the acquired dyslexias. Identifying developmental dyslexic children is complex: By definition, they read less well than age-matched controls, but how much less well do you have to read to be a developmental dyslexic, rather than just a poor reader?

A problem that arises when trying to infer the properties of the reading system from cases of developmental dyslexia is that the developing reading system may be very different from the adult system. For example, grapheme–phoneme conversion might play a larger role in children's reading. Furthermore, the nature of the child's reading system will depend on the way in which the child is being taught to read. The look-and-say method emphasizes the role of the direct access route, and the phonic method emphasizes grapheme–phoneme conversion.

The biology of developmental dyslexia

The relation between developmental dyslexia and other cognitive abilities is complicated (Ellis, 1993). Some developmental dyslexic children have other language problems, such as in speaking or object naming. It is often thought that dyslexic children are clumsier than average, but it is unclear whether this is really the case. Some children with surface developmental dyslexia might similarly have impaired visual memory (Goulandris & Snowling, 1991), although not all do. "Allan" (Hanley, Hastie, & Kay, 1992) performed extremely well on tests of visual short-term and long-term memory. People with developmental dyslexia are slightly more likely to be left-handed or ambidextrous than people without (Eglinton & Annett, 1994). There is some evidence that the oscillatory brain activity of people with developmental dyslexia is abnormal, associated with aberrant lateralization and leading to problems with phonological processing and memory (Kraus, 2012).

Many studies have also found developmental dyslexia to be associated with visual deficits (e.g., Lovegrove, Martin, & Slaghuis, 1986). In particular, the magnocellular visual pathway, involving large cells that respond quickly and are sensitive to contrast and movement, seems to be affected. Deficits in the magnocellular system lead to problems with controlling and fixating the eyes, giving rise to the sensation that letters are moving around the page (Stein, 2003). Deficits in the magnocellular pathway are unlikely to be the sole cause of developmental dyslexia, however, because many individuals without dyslexia have the same visual deficits in this pathway as individuals with dyslexia (Skoyles & Skottun, 2004); indeed, most individuals with this visual deficit do not show dyslexia. Furthermore, not all people with dyslexia have this visual deficit (Lovegrove et al., 1986). We need to look elsewhere for a widespread underlying cause.

Reading disabilities tend to run in families, and recent work shows that dyslexia has a significant genetic component, with a number of chromosomal loci identified (Eckert, Lombardino, & Leonard, 2001; Fisher et al., 1999). There is some uncertainty—and perhaps variation—about how these genetic abnormalities are ultimately manifest at the level of brain structure. Imaging studies suggest that the thalamus, frontal lobes, and cerebellum all play some role, although the left planum temporale, a structure at the heart of Wernicke's area, plays a particularly important role in the origin of developmental dyslexia (see Figure 8.3). The planum temporale is usually larger in the left hemisphere than in the right; the difference in size is much less in individuals with developmental dyslexia (Beaton, 1997). At a processing level, damage to these brain areas seems to be manifest primarily as a disturbance to phonological skills (see below). An autopsy of four men with developmental dyslexia found this abnormal symmetry of the planum temporale, but also found neuronal ectopias (abnormal clusters of neurons) and dysplasias (abnormally oriented neurons)—both conditions associated with abnormalities in the migration phase of brain development in the fetus, when neurons move to their eventual location (Galaburda, Sherman, Rosen, Aboitiz, & Geschwind, 1985). Neurons tend to be smaller in the left medial geniculate nucleus, an important part of the brain for relaying auditory information, than in the right in people with developmental dyslexia

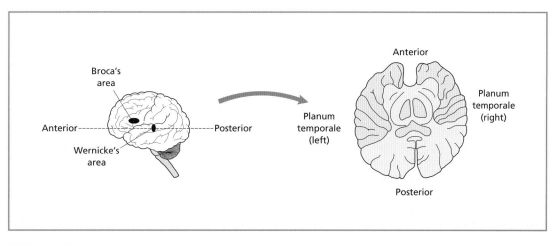

FIGURE 8.3 An axial cross-section of the brain to show the planum temporale. As here, the left planum temporale is usually larger than the right. In an individual with developmental dyslexia the size difference would be much less.

(Galaburda, Menard, & Rosen, 1994). Imaging studies also reveal that the occipital regions of the brain show increased activity—probably because people are using additional visual strategies to cope with their phonological deficits (Casey, Thomas, & McCandliss, 2001).

Clearly genetic and brain abnormalities play an important role in determining a child's reading ability. However, given the variation observed in orthographies and dyslexia, it is unlikely that a single biological factor can account for all types of reading difficulty (Hadzibeganovic et al., 2010; Seidenberg, 2011).

Are there subtypes of developmental dyslexia?

There has been some controversy about whether or not there are different types of developmental dyslexia. Frith (1985) emphasized the importance of progressing from the logographic stage to the alphabetic stage, arguing that classic developmental dyslexics fail to make this progression. Less severely affected are those readers who are arrested at the alphabetic stage and cannot progress to the orthographic stage. Less severe still is what is called type-B spelling disorder, where there is a failure of orthographic access for spelling but not for reading.

Bryant and Impey (1986) reported a comparison of dyslexic and reading-age-matched control children and found that the "normal" children made exactly the same types of reading error as the dyslexic children. If dyslexic and normal children make the same types of error then this weakens the argument that developmental dyslexia arises from the same type of brain damage as acquired dyslexia. In addition, we find large differences in normal young readers. Bryant and Impey suggest that there are many different reading styles, and some children adopt styles that lead them into difficulty. Indeed, Baron and Strawson (1976) found that some adult normal readers were particularly good at phonological skills but relatively poor at orthographic skills (they called these Phoenicians; they correspond to a very mild version of surface dyslexia). Others were particularly good at orthographic skills but relatively poor at phonological skills (Baron and Strawson called these Chinese readers, corresponding to phonological dyslexia). Baron and Strawson proposed that these were the ends of a continuum of individual differences in the normal population. Developmental dyslexics would lie at the extremes of this continuum (but see also Coltheart, 1987, and Temple, 1987, for detailed replies). Olson, Kliegel, Davidson, and Foltz (1984) also found that individual differences in reading skills in their participants fell along a normally distributed continuum rather than into distinct subtypes.

A number of researchers have pointed out that there are similarities between acquired and developmental dyslexia. Jorm (1979) compared developmental dyslexia with deep dyslexia. In both cases grapheme–phoneme conversion is impaired, which leads to a particular difficulty with nonwords. He concluded that the same part of the parietal lobe of the brain was involved in each case; it was damaged in deep dyslexia, and failed to develop normally in developmental dyslexia. However, Baddeley, Ellis, Miles, and Lewis (1982) found that although the phonological encoding of people with developmental dyslexia was greatly impaired, they could do some tasks that necessitate it. For example, they could read nonwords at a much higher level than deep dyslexics, although of course nowhere near as well as age-matched controls.

Most people with developmental dyslexia rarely make semantic paralexias, so perhaps they resemble phonological dyslexics rather more? Campbell and Butterworth (1985), and Butterworth, Campbell, and Howard (1986), describe the case of RE, a successful university student, who resembled a phonological dyslexic. RE could only read a new word once she had heard someone else say it. She could not inspect the phonological form of words, and could not "hear words in the head." Such a skill may be necessary for the development of the phonological recoding route. In addition, she had an abnormally low digit span. A similar case is that of JM, a person of superior intelligence whose reading age was consistently 2 years less than his chronological age (Hulme & Snowling, 1992; Snowling & Hulme, 1989). At the age of 15 his word reading was comparable to that of reading-age-matched controls, but he was completely unable to read two-syllable nonwords. He also had a severely reduced short-term memory span and difficulty with other tests of phonology such as nonword repetition. Howard and Best (1996) described the case of "Melanie-Jane," an 85-year-old person with developmental phonological dyslexia. Melanie-Jane was highly impaired at nonword reading, but read words with normal accuracy and latencies. She reported that she had experienced no difficulties in learning to read or write at school. She never experienced any difficulty in "real-life" reading. Like all these people, Melanie-Jane had difficulty with other tasks involving phonology (e.g., assembly and segmentation). In summary, many developmental dyslexics resemble people with acquired phonological dyslexia.

Castles and Coltheart (1993) examined the reading of 56 developmental dyslexics, and argued that they did not form a homogeneous population, showing instead a clear dissociation between surface and phonological dyslexic reading patterns. They concluded that such a dissociation is the norm in developmental dyslexia. In this interpretation, the types of developmental dyslexia correspond to a failure to "acquire" normally one of the two routes of the dual-route model. One subgroup was relatively skilled at sublexical processing (as they were good at reading nonwords and poor at reading exception words) and another relatively skilled at lexical processing (as they showed the reverse pattern). Hence Castles and Coltheart concluded that there are surface and phonological subtypes of developmental dyslexia. Subsequent work looking at the heritability of developmental dyslexia among twins suggests that although both types are significantly inheritable, the genetic contribution is much larger in developmental phonological dyslexia (Castles, Datta, Gayan, & Olson, 1999).

An important consideration in studying developmental dyslexia is selecting an appropriate control group. Snowling (1983, 2000) urged caution in comparing types of acquired and developmental dyslexia. In particular, she argued that the best comparison in understanding what has gone wrong is not between developmental and acquired dyslexics, but between developmental dyslexics and reading-age-matched controls. That is, if someone with a chronological age of 14 has a reading age of 10, they should be compared with normal readers of 10. The study by Castles and Coltheart did not use appropriate reading-age-matched controls, and did not control for IQ (Snowling, Bryant, & Hulme, 1996; Stanovich, Siegel, Gottardo, Chiappe, & Sidhu, 1997). It is therefore possible that any apparent differences between the two types of developmental dyslexics just reflect individual differences in normal readers of a lower reading age. When compared with children at the same reading age (rather than chronological age), the two groupings disappear, because children at different reading ages differ in the difficulty they have with exception words and nonwords.

The consensus of opinion is that most impairments in developmental dyslexia lie on a continuum, rather than falling into two neat categories, with phonological developmental dyslexics and surface developmental dyslexics at the ends of the continuum (Manis, Seidenberg, Doi, McBride-Chang, & Petersen, 1996; Seymour 1987, 1990; Wilding, 1990). Those developmental dyslexics near the surface dyslexia end are poor at reading irregular words but are not so troubled by nonwords, whereas those at the phonological dyslexia end have severe nonword reading problems and make many phonological errors while reading. Children at the phonological dyslexic end of the continuum are impaired on tasks of phonological awareness, while children at the surface dyslexic end do not differ from age-matched controls on such tasks (Manis et al., 1996).

It seems then that those at the surface dyslexic end of the continuum read and perform very similarly to reading-age-matched controls, suggesting that a general developmental delay is the root of the problem, rather than a deviant reading pattern. Clearly problems with phonology play a central role in the deviant reading pattern shown in developmental phonological dyslexia. Most people with developmental dyslexia are indeed worse at tasks involving both nonword reading and phonological awareness (Bradley & Bryant, 1983; Goswami & Bryant, 1990; Metsala, Stanovich, & Brown, 1998; Rack, Snowling, & Olson, 1992; Siegel, 1998; Snowling, 1987). Bradley and Bryant (1978) showed that people with developmental dyslexia perform less well than reading-age-matched control children at picking out a phonologically distinct word from a group of four (e.g., cat, fat, hat, net). These difficulties with phonological

awareness may be related to difficulties with phonological short-term memory (Campbell & Butterworth, 1985; Hulme & Snowling, 1992; Snowling, Stackhouse, & Rack, 1986). There is also evidence of a speech perception deficit in children at the developmental phonological dyslexia extreme. Manis et al. (1997) showed that dyslexics with low phonological awareness were poor at distinguishing between the sounds "p" and "b."

Harm and Seidenberg (1999) argued that while children at the developmental phonological dyslexia end of the continuum share a core deficit in phonological processing, children at the developmental surface dyslexia end are like beginner readers, who are also much worse at reading exception words than sounding out nonwords. They therefore concluded that surface developmental dyslexics are delayed readers. They showed how both surface and phonological developmental dyslexia can be generated by different types of damage to an attractor connectionist network. This model also shows that it is possible to have a phonological deficit that is severe enough to interfere with reading development but not severe enough to interfere with speech perception and production. Developmental phonological dyslexia arises as a consequence of damage to phonological representations before the model is trained to read. Developmental surface dyslexia can arise in several ways, including less training (corresponding to less experience of reading), making technical changes to the way in which the model learns so that it does not obtain the normal benefits from the same amount of learning, reducing the number of hidden units that mediate between orthography and phonology, and degrading the orthographic input to the model (corresponding to visual-perceptual deficits). Relatively pure examples of phonological and surface dyslexia (corresponding to the extremes of the continuum) were associated with mild forms of impairment; more severe impairments created a mixed pattern of nonword and exception word impairment that lies somewhere along the continuum.

This work therefore shows how two distinct types of damage to a connectionist model can give rise to a continuum of impairments. As we noted above, this phonological deficit arises as a consequence of damage to specific brain areas, and has both biological and environmental causes. Phonological awareness skills can "run in the family." Pennington and Lefly (2001) found that members of one family had a much higher incidence than expected of developmental dyslexia. Children who later developed dyslexia showed deficits on a range of phonological measures from an early age. Furthermore, the scores on phonological tasks were continuous, with some children in the family scoring worse than control children, yet not developing full-blown dyslexia. Snowling, Gallagher, and Frith (2003) similarly found that the risk of developing dyslexia within a high-risk family is continuous, and that good general language skills—particularly good early vocabulary development—can sometimes partly compensate for a specific phonological deficit. Even children classified as normal readers had some difficulties spelling and reading nonwords. Hence, within a family at genetic risk of dyslexia, apparently unaffected members do in fact have subtle reading and phonological deficits. These results also reiterate the conclusion that although developmental dyslexia may have a genetic component, the causes are complex, and environmental factors also play a role.

Although most of the studies reported have examined reading difficulties in English, a phonological processing deficit is present in poor readers of other languages, whether they have more regular grapheme–phoneme correspondences (e.g., French and Portuguese), use a different script (e.g., Arabic and Hebrew), or are non-alphabetic (e.g., Chinese). In each case there is a core phonological deficit (Siegel, 1998). In fact the ability to segment phonemes arising from a deficit in analyzing the rhythmic properties of speech appears to be a universal problem, including at least in children with dyslexia speaking English, Spanish, and Chinese (Goswami et al., 2011).

In summary, there is a consensus that a phonological processing deficit, measured by a deficit in phonological awareness, underlies developmental dyslexia. This account is called the *phonological deficit model* of reading

disabilities. This deficit, measurable on phonological awareness tasks, has a partial genetic basis. The deficit also lies on a continuum, with children at the less severe extreme being able to learn to read relatively normally. However, not all developmental reading disorders can be accounted for in terms of a phonological deficit. Some children show poor comprehension (as measured by semantic tasks such as synonymy judgment—e.g., do "boat" and "ship" have similar meanings?) yet appear unimpaired at tasks involving phonology, such as nonword reading. These children are worst at reading low-frequency irregular words, probably because they are receiving inadequate support from semantics (Nation & Snowling, 1998). Note though that a correlation does not of course imply causality: just because we observe a phonological deficit in every case of dyslexia does not mean that the deficit causes dyslexia; it could be that both are caused by some third factor. Some researchers argue that both dyslexia and phonological awareness deficits arise from an early problem in visual attention (Facoetti et al., 2010; Vidyasagar & Pammer, 2010).

How can we improve the reading of people with developmental dyslexia?

We have seen that a lack of phonological awareness plays an important role in developmental dyslexia. Therefore one obvious technique to improve reading is to improve phonological awareness from as early an age as possible (Snowling, 1987). There is some evidence that training in sound categorization might assist reading and spelling development in developmental dyslexia as well as normal reading development. In an experiment by Bradley and Bryant (1983), a group of children who had previously been shown to be poor at a rhyme judgment task were given training on categorizing words on the basis of the similarity of their sounds. For example, they had to put "hat" with "cat" on the basis of shared rimes, but with "hen" on the basis of shared initial sounds. This training was given individually and weekly for 2 years. After 4 years, the experimental group who had received sound training were much better at reading and spelling than the control groups. The effects of the training were specific to reading and spelling development; it had no carry-over into other educational skills such as mathematics. It has since been shown that training on a range of phonological skills linked to the teaching of reading is the best way of improving the reading of poor readers (Hatcher et al., 1994).

Other techniques focus on training the ability to segment words into onsets and rimes (Snowling, 1987). Related words with the same rime can then be read by analogy (e.g., "rain," "pain," and "stain" are all pronounced in similar ways). In contrast, the Orton–Gillingham–Stillman *multisensory method* emphasizes the systematic and explicit teaching of individual grapheme–phoneme rules. The multisensory aspect of the techniques is probably important in its success: Children see, say, write, and even feel new spelling patterns (Fernald, 1943). There is some evidence that multisensory techniques improve poor reading: Hulme (1981) showed that poor readers remembered strings of letters better if they were allowed to trace them.

Broom and Doctor (1995a, 1995b) suggested that it is possible to provide specific remedial therapy if the locus of the deficit in the model of reading can be located. They described the case of DF, a 10-year-old boy with poor reading skills that resembled surface dyslexia. They argued that DF had become arrested at the alphabetic reading stage, and therefore improved orthographic reading by focusing on low-frequency irregular words. They similarly showed that it was possible to improve the reading skills of SP, an 11-year-old boy with phonological developmental dyslexia, by training on phonological reading skills.

For those for whom visual deficits play an obvious and significant role, improving the performance of the visual magnocellular system by training eye fixations can lead to improvements in reading (Stein, 2003). Using yellow filters might also lead to some improvement for those

A dyslexic girl wearing yellow glasses while reading. These filters might improve the function of the brain cells concerned with visual perception (the magnocellular system) in those with dyslexia, helping them to read.

with visual problems, although there have been very few controlled studies, and much of the evidence of improvement is anecdotal (Stein, 2003; Wilkins & Neary, 1991). Increasing letter spacing might help (Zorzi, Barbierob, Facoettia, & Ziegler, 2012).

Successful techniques for improving poor reading, then, possess two features. First, they provide explicit training on the skills in which the person is deficient. This means improving poor phonological awareness in developmental dyslexia at the phonological dyslexia end of the continuum, and establishing an orthographic lexicon in people at the surface dyslexia end. Second, they use techniques well known from studies of memory and mnemonics to improve memory for spelling patterns.

SUMMARY

- Acquiring the alphabetic principle is an important part of learning to read.
- Phonological awareness is an awareness of the sounds of words; phonological awareness is essential for the development of skilled reading.
- Reading is best taught by the phonic method because this emphasizes grapheme–phoneme correspondences.
- There has been considerable debate as to whether developmental dyslexia is qualitatively different from very poor normal reading, and whether there are subtypes that correspond to acquired dyslexias; the preponderance of evidence suggests that developmental dyslexia is on a continuum with normal reading.
- Developmental dyslexia is associated with impaired phonological awareness.
- Connectionist modeling shows how two distinct types of damage can lead to a continuum of impairment between developmental surface and phonological dyslexia extremes.
- We can produce improvements in the reading skills of people with developmental dyslexia using techniques derived from our theories.

QUESTIONS TO THINK ABOUT

1. What are the differences between good and poor readers?
2. What does psycholinguistics say about the best way of teaching children how to read? Which words are likely to cause children the most difficulty?
3. Find out how you learned to read. Did you face any particular difficulties? Have these affected your subsequent experience of reading?
4. Some authorities recommend that exam questions should be printed on colored paper for people with reading disabilities. How could this make a difference to reading performance?
5. How should students with dyslexia be compensated in assessment?
6. Why do you think dyslexia is so commonly thought to be to do with problems spelling and writing? Is it fair to say that poor memory and concentration skills are part of the dyslexia syndrome?

FURTHER READING

See McBride-Chang (2004) for an introduction to literacy development. Ellis (1993) includes an excellent description of developmental dyslexia. Snowling (2000) is a very approachable review of work on developmental dyslexia, and Olson (1994) provides an up-to-date review. For general overviews of learning to read, with emphasis on individual differences in reading ability, see Goswami and Bryant (1990), McShane (1991), Oakhill (1994), and Perfetti (1994). For a popular account of connectionist models of reading, see Hinton (1992), and Hinton, Plaut, and Shallice (1993). Brown and Ellis (1994) review research on spelling. Harris and Hatano (1999) provide a cross-linguistic perspective on learning to read and write.

For an excellent recent review of the whole area, with emphasis on phonological awareness, see Ziegler and Goswami (2005). For more detail see Snowling and Hulme (2007).

CHAPTER 9

UNDERSTANDING SPEECH

INTRODUCTION

Speech is at the heart of language. This chapter is about how we understand spoken words and continuous speech.

Speech perception is about how we identify or perceive the sounds of language, while spoken word recognition is about the higher level process of recognizing the words that the sounds make up. This convenient distinction is perhaps artificial. It could be that we do not identify all the sounds of a word and then put them together to recognize the word; perhaps knowing the word helps us to identify the constituent sounds. We may not even need to hear all the sounds of a word before we can identify it. The effect of word-level knowledge on sound perception is an important and controversial topic. By the end of this chapter you should:

- Understand how we segment speech.
- Know how context is used in recognizing speech.
- Appreciate that we recognize a word at its recognition point, but that the recognition point does not have to correspond to when the word is first uniquely distinguishable from other, similar-sounding words.
- Know about the cohort and TRACE models of word recognition.
- Understand how brain damage can affect speech recognition.

RECOGNIZING SPEECH

What sort of representations are used to access our mental dictionary, the lexicon? What units

are involved? We can distinguish the prelexical code, which is the sound representation used prior to the identification of a word, from the postlexical code, which is information that is only available after **lexical access**. An important task for understanding speech recognition is to specify the nature of the prelexical code. Among the important topics here are whether or not phonemes are represented explicitly in this representation, and the role of syllables in speech perception.

Why is speech perception difficult?

There are obvious differences between spoken and visual word perception. The most important difference between the tasks is that spoken words are present only very briefly, whereas a written or printed word is there in front of you for however long you want to analyze it. You only get one chance with a spoken word, but you can usually go back and check a visually presented word as many times as you like. Furthermore, there is not such an easy segmentation of words into component sounds as words into letters; sounds and even whole words tend to slur into one another.

In spite of these difficulties, we are rather good at recognizing speech. The process is automatic; when you hear speech, you cannot make yourself not understand it. Most of the time it happens effortlessly and with little apparent difficulty. Speech perception is fast (Liberman, Cooper, Shankweiler, & Studdert-Kennedy, 1967). When people are given sequences of sounds consisting of a buzz, hiss, tone, and vowel, they can only distinguish the order of the sounds if they are presented at

Although spoken words are transient in terms of their availability for analysis, recognizing speech is automatic and usually effortless.

a rate slower than 1.5 sounds per second (Clark & Clark, 1977; Warren, Obusek, Farmer, & Warren, 1969). Yet in 1 second we can understand speech at the rate of 20 phonemes per second, and sometimes much faster. We can identify spoken words in context from about 200 ms after their onset (Marslen-Wilson, 1984). Furthermore, speech sounds seem to be at an advantage over non-speech sounds when heard against background noise. Miller, Heise, and Lichten (1951) found that the more words there are to choose from a predetermined set (as they put it, the greater the information transmitted per word), the louder the signal had to be relative to the noise for the participants to identify them equally well. Bruce (1958) showed that words in a meaningful context are recognized better against background noise than words out of context, and we take nearly twice as long to recognize a word if it is presented in isolation, out of the context of the sentence in which it occurs (Lieberman, 1963).

In summary, there is clearly some advantage to recognizing speech in context compared with speech out of context and non-speech sounds. What is this advantage?

Acoustic signals and phonetic segments: How do we segment speech?

The acoustic properties of phonemes are not fixed. They vary with the context they are in, and they even vary acoustically depending on the speaking

rate (Miller, 1981). The "b" sounds in "ball," "bill," "able," and "rob" are acoustically distinct. This sort of acoustic variability makes phoneme identification a complex task, as it means that they cannot be identified by comparison with a "perfect exemplar" of that phoneme, called a template. There is an analogy with recognizing letters; there are lots of perfectly acceptable ways of writing the same letter. This variation is most clear in the context of different phones that are the same phoneme in a language, such as aspirated and unaspirated /p/ (see Chapter 2). Yet we successfully map these different phones onto one phoneme.

If we look at the physical acoustic signal and the sounds conveyed by the signal, it is apparent the relation between the two is a complex one. In their review of speech perception, Miller and Jusczyk (1989) pointed out that this complexity arises because of two main features that must act as major constraints on theories of speech perception. These features are both facets of the lack of identity or *isomorphism* between the acoustic and phonemic levels of language, and are called the segmentation and invariance problems. The **invariance** problem is that the same phoneme can in fact sound different depending on the context in which it occurs. The **segmentation** problem is that sounds slur together and cannot easily be separated. Let us look at these problems in more detail.

Acoustic invariance arises because the details of the realization of a phoneme vary depending on the context of its surrounding phonemes. This means that phonemes take on some of the acoustic properties of their neighbors, a process known as **assimilation**. Hence the /I/ phoneme is usually produced without any nasal quality, but in words such as "pin" and "sing" the way in which the vocal tract anticipates the shape it needs to adopt for the next phoneme means that /I/ takes on a nasal quality. That is, there are **co-articulation** effects, in that as we produce one sound our vocal apparatus has just moved into position from making another sound, and is preparing to change position again to make the subsequent sound. Co-articulation has advantages for both the speaker and the listener. For the speaker, it means that speech can be produced more quickly than if each phoneme had to be clearly and separately articulated. For the listener, co-articulation has the advantage that information about the identity of phonetic segments may be spread over several acoustic segments. Although this has the apparent disadvantage that phonemes vary slightly depending on the context, it also has the advantage that we do not gather information about only one phoneme at any one time; they provide us with some information about the surrounding sounds (a feature known as parallel transmission). For example, the /b/ phonemes in "bill," "ball," "bull," and "bell" are all slightly different acoustically, and tell us about what is coming next.

The segmentation problem is that it is not easy to separate sounds in speech, as they run together (except for stop consonants and pauses). This problem does not just apply to sounds within words; in normal conditions, words also run into each other. To take a famous example, in normal speech the strings "I scream" and "ice cream" sound indistinguishable. The acoustic segments visible in spectrographic displays do not map in any easy way into phonetic segments. One obvious constraint on segmenting speech is that we prefer to segment speech so that each speech segment is accounted for by a possible word. This is called the possible-word constraint: We do not like to segment speech so that it leaves parts of syllables unattached to words (Norris, McQueen, Cutler, & Butterfield, 1997). Any segmentation of the speech string that results in impossible words (such as isolated consonants) is likely to be rejected. Hence, other things being equal, the segmentation of "fill a green bucket" will be preferred to "filigree n bucket" because the latter results in an unattached "n" sound.

Other strategies that we develop to segment speech depend on our exposure to a particular language. Strong syllables bear stress and are never shortened to unstressed neutral vowel sounds; weak syllables do not bear stress and are often shortened to unstressed neutral vowel sounds. In English, strong syllables are likely to be the initial syllables of main content-bearing words, while weak syllables are either not word-initial, or start a function word (Cutler & Butterfield, 1992; Cutler & Norris, 1988). A strategy that uses this type of information is called the metrical segmentation strategy. It is possible to construct experimental materials that violate these expectations, and these reliably induce mishearings in listeners. For example, Cutler and Butterfield described how one participant, given the unpredictable words "conduct ascents uphill" presented very faintly, reported hearing "The doctor sends the bill," and another "A duck descends some pill." The listeners have erroneously inserted word boundaries before the strong syllables and deleted the boundaries before the weak syllables. This type of segmentation procedure, whereby listeners segment speech by identifying stressed syllables, is called stress-based segmentation. An alternative mechanism, which is based on detecting syllables and is used in languages such as French that have very clear and unambiguous syllables, is called syllable-based segmentation. In stress-based languages such as English, syllable boundaries can be unclear, and identifying the syllables is not reliable. Hence the form of the listener's language determines the precise segmentation strategy used (Cutler, Mehler, Norris, & Segui, 1986).

How do bilingual speakers segment languages? They do not simply mimic the monolingual speakers of the language. Their segmentation strategy is determined by which is their dominant language. Cutler, Mehler, Norris, and Segui (1992) tested English–French bilingual speakers on segmenting English and French materials, using a syllable monitoring task where the participants had to respond as quickly as possible if they heard a particular sequence of sounds. The French words "balance" and "balcon" (meaning "balance" and "balcony") begin with different syllables ("ba" in "balance" and "bal" in "balcon"). Native French speakers find it easy to detect "ba" in "balance" and "bal" in "balcon." On the other hand, they take longer to find the "bal" in "balance" and "ba" in "balcon" because although these sounds are present, they do not correspond to the syllables. The syllable structure of the English word "balance" is far less clear; people are uncertain to which syllable the "l" sound belongs. Hence the time it takes English speakers to detect "ba" and "bal" does not vary with the syllable structure of the word they hear ("balance" or "balcony"). French makes use of syllables, but English does not.

In Cutler et al.'s experiment, the English–French bilingual speakers segmented depending on their primary or dominant language: English-dominant speakers showed stress-based segmentation with English language materials, and never showed syllable-based segmentation, whereas French-dominant speakers showed syllabic segmentation, and only with French materials. It is as though the segmentation strategy is fixed at an early age, and only that strategy is developed further. Hence all bilingual speakers are monolingual at the level of segmentation. This is not as big a disadvantage as it might seem: Efficient bilinguals are able to discard ineffective segmentation processes and use other, more general, analytical processes instead (Cutler et al., 1986, 1992).

Categorical perception

Even though there is all this variation in the way in which phonemes can sound, we rarely, if ever, notice these differences. We classify speech sounds as one phoneme or another; there is no halfway house. This phenomenon is known as the **categorical perception** of phonemes (first demonstrated by Liberman, Harris, Hoffman, & Griffith, 1957). Liberman et al. used a speech synthesizer to create a continuum of artificial syllables that differed in the place of articulation. In spite of the continuum, participants placed these syllables into three quite distinct categories beginning with /b/, /d/, and /g/. Another example of categorical perception is voice onset time (abbreviated to VOT). In the voiced consonants (e.g., /b/ and /d/), the vocal cords start vibrating as soon as the vocal tract is closed, whereas in the unvoiced consonants (e.g., /p/ and /t/), there is a delay of about 60 ms. The pairs /p/ and /b/, and /t/ and /d/, differ only in this minimal feature of voicing. Voicing lies on a continuum; it is possible to create sounds with a VOT of, for example, 30 ms. Although this is midway between the two extremes, we actually categorize such sounds as being either simply voiced or unvoiced—exactly which may differ from time to time and from person to person, and people can actually be biased towards one end of the continuum or the other. It

is possible to fatigue the feature detectors hypothesized to be responsible for categorical perception by repeated exposure to a sound, and to shift perception towards the other end of the continuum (Eimas & Corbit, 1973). This technique is called selective adaptation. For example, repeated presentation of the syllable "ba" makes people less sensitive to the voicing feature of the /b/. This means that immediately afterwards the boundary between /b/ and /p/ shifts towards the /p/ end of the continuum. Hence, even though speech stimuli may be physically continuous, perception is categorical.

The boundaries between categories are not fixed, but are sensitive to contextual factors such as the rate of speech. The perceptual system seems able to adjust to fast rates of speech so that, for example, a sound with a short VOT that should be perceived as /b/ is instead perceived as /p/. In effect, an absolutely short interval can be treated as a relatively long one if the surrounding speech is rapid enough (Summerfield, 1981). This is not necessarily learned, as infants are also sensitive to speech rate. They are able to interpret the relative duration of different frequency components of speech depending on the rate of speech (Eimas & Miller, 1980; Miller & Jusczyk, 1989; see Altmann, 1997, for more detail).

At first, researchers thought that listeners were actually unable to distinguish between slightly different members of a phoneme category. However, this does not appear to be the case. Pisoni and Tash (1974) found that participants were faster to say that two /ba/ syllables were the same if the /b/ sounds in each were acoustically identical, than if the /b/ sounds differed slightly in VOT. Participants are in fact sensitive to differences within a category. Hence the importance of categorical perception has recently come into question. It is possible that many phenomena in speech perception are better described in terms of continuous rather than categorical perception, and although our phenomenal experience of speech identification is that sounds fall into distinct categories, the evidence that early sensory processing is really categorical is much weaker (Massaro, 1987, 1994). Massaro argued that the apparent poor discrimination within categories does not result from early perceptual processing, but instead just arises from a bias of participants to say that items from the same category are identical. Nevertheless, the idea of categorical perception remains popular in psycholinguistics.

What is the nature of the prelexical code?

Do we need to identify phonemes before we identify spoken words? Savin and Bever (1970) asked participants to respond as soon as they heard a particular unit, which was either a single phoneme or a syllable. They found that participants responded more slowly to phoneme targets than to syllable targets, and concluded that phoneme identification is subsequent to the perception of syllables. They proposed that phonemes are not perceptually real in the sense that syllables are: we do not recognize words through perceiving their individual phonemes, but instead can only recognize them through perceiving some more fundamental unit, such as the syllable. Foss and Swinney (1973) queried this conclusion, arguing that the phoneme and syllable monitoring task used by Savin and Bever did not directly tap into the perception process. That is, just because we can become consciously aware of a higher unit first does not mean that it is processed perceptually earlier.

Foss and Blank (1980) proposed a dual-code theory where speech processing employs both a prelexical (or phonetic) code and a postlexical (or phonemic) code. The prelexical code is computed directly from the perceptual analysis of the input acoustic information, whereas the postlexical code is derived from information derived from higher level units such as words. In the phoneme monitoring task, participants have to press a button as soon as they hear a particular sound. Foss and Blank showed that phoneme monitoring times to target phonemes in words and nonwords were approximately the same. In this case, the participants must have been responding to the phonetic code, as nonwords cannot have phonological codes. Foss and Blank also found that the frequency of the target word does not affect phoneme monitoring times. On the other hand, manipulating the semantic context of a word leads to people responding on the basis of the postlexical code.

(For example, people are faster to respond to the word-initial "b" in the predictable word "book" than the less word predictable "bill" in the context of "He sat reading a book/bill until it was time to go home for his tea.") Foss and Blank argued that people respond to the prelexical code when the phoneme monitoring task is made easy, but to the postlexical code when the task is difficult (such as when the target word is contextually less likely). Subsequently Foss and Gernsbacher (1983) failed to find experimental support for the dual-code model. Increasing the processing load of the participants (e.g., by requiring them to monitor for multiple targets) did not shift them towards responding on the basis of the postlexical code. They concluded that people generally respond in the phoneme monitoring task on the basis of the prelexical code, and only in exceptional circumstances make use of a postlexical code. These results suggest that phonemes form part of the prelexical code.

Marslen-Wilson and Warren (1994) provided extensive experimental evidence on a range of tasks that phoneme classification does not have to be finished before lexical activation can begin. Nonwords that are constructed from words are more difficult to reject in an auditory lexical decision task than nonwords constructed from nonwords. In this experiment, you start off with "smog" (a word) and "smod" (a nonword). In each case you then take off the final consonant and splice on a new one, "b," to give you a new nonword, "smob." Although they might initially sound the same, the version made from "smog" is more difficult to reject as a nonword because the co-articulation information from the vowel is consistent with a word. Furthermore, the effects were also found across a number of different tasks. If the phonetic representation of the vowel had been translated into a phoneme before lexical access, then the co-articulation information would have been lost and the two types of nonword would have been equally difficult. Marslen-Wilson and Warren argued that lexical representations are directly accessed from featural information in the sound signal. Co-articulation information from vowels is used early to identify the following consonant and therefore a word.

In summary, there is controversy about whether or not we need to identify phonemes before recognizing a word. Most data suggest that while phonemes might be computed during word recognition, we do not need to complete phoneme identification before word recognition can begin. The research on phonological awareness described in Chapter 8 suggests that we seem to be less aware of phonemes than other phonological constituents of speech, such as syllables. Morais and Kolinsky (1994) proposed that there are two quite distinct representations of phonemes: an unconscious system operating in speech recognition and production, and a conscious system developed in the context of the development of literacy (reading and writing).

What role does context play in identifying sounds?

The effect of context on speech recognition is of central importance, and has been hotly debated. Is speech recognition a purely bottom-up process, or can top-down information influence its outcome? If we can show that the word in which a sound occurs, or indeed the meaning of the whole sentence, can influence the recognition of that particular sound, then we will have shown a top-down influence on sound perception. In this case, we will have shown that speech perception is in part at least an interactive process; knowledge about whole words is influencing our perception of their component sounds. Of course, different types of context could have an effect at every level of phonological processing, and in principle the effects might be different at each level.

The first piece of relevant evidence is based on the categorical perception of sounds varying along a continuum. For example, although /p/ and /b/ typically differ in VOT between 0 and 60 ms, sounds in between will be assigned to one or the other category. Word context affects where the boundary between the two lies. Ganong (1980) varied an ambiguous phoneme along the appropriate continuum (e.g., /k/ to /g/), inserted this in front of a context provided by a word ending (e.g., "-iss"), and found that context affected the perceptual changeover point. That is, participants are

willing to put a sound into a category they would not otherwise choose if the result makes a word: "kiss" is a word, but "giss" is not, and this influences our categorical perception of the ambiguous phoneme. This is known as lexical identification shift. In this respect, word context is influencing our categorization of sounds. Findings using this technique, developed by Connine and Clifton (1987), further strengthen the argument that lexical knowledge (information about words) is available to the categorical perception of ambiguous stimuli. They showed that other processing advantages accrue to the ambiguous stimuli when this lexical knowledge is invoked, but not at the ends of the continuum, where perceptual information alone is sufficient to make a decision. Later studies using a method of analysis known as signal detection also suggest that the lexical identification shift in a categorical perception task is truly perceptual. Signal detection theory provides a means of describing the identification of imperfectly discriminable stimuli. Lexical context is not sensitive to manipulations (primarily the extent to which correct responses are rewarded and incorrect ones punished) known to influence postperceptual processes (Pitt, 1995a, 1995b; but see Massaro & Oden, 1995, for a reply). Connine (1990) found that sentential context (provided by the meaning of the whole sentence) behaves differently from lexical context (the context provided by the word in which the ambiguous phoneme occurs). In particular, sentential context has a similar effect to the obviously postperceptual effect of the amount of monetary payoff, where certain responses lead to greater rewards. She therefore concluded that sentential context has postperceptual effects.

A classic psycholinguistic finding known as the *phoneme restoration effect* appears at first sight to be evidence of contextual involvement in sound identification (Obusek & Warren, 1973; Warren, 1970; Warren & Warren, 1970). Participants were presented with sentences such as "The state governors met with their respective legi*latures convening in the capital city." At the point marked with an asterisk *, a 0.12-second portion of speech corresponding to the /s/ phoneme had been cut out and replaced with a cough. Nevertheless, participants could not detect that a sound was missing from the sample. That is, they appear to restore the /s/ phoneme to the word "legislatures." The effect is quite dramatic. Participants continue to report that the deleted phoneme is perceptually restored even if they know it is missing. Moreover, participants cannot correctly locate the cough in the speech. The effect can still be found if an even larger portion of the word is deleted (as in le***latures). Warren and his colleagues argued that participants are using semantic and syntactic information far beyond the individual phonemes in their processing of speech. The actual sound used is not critical; a buzz or a tone elicits the effect as successfully as a cough. There are limits on what can be restored, however; replacing a deleted phoneme with a short period of silence is easily detectable and does not elicit the effect.

In an even more dramatic example, participants were presented with sentences (1) to (4) (Warren & Warren, 1970):

(1) It was found that the *eel was on the orange.
(2) It was found that the *eel was on the axle.
(3) It was found that the *eel was on the shoe.
(4) It was found that the *eel was on the table.

The participants listened to tapes that had been specially constructed so that the only thing that differed between the four sentences was the last word. In each case, a different final word was spliced onto a physically identical beginning. This is important because it means that there can be no subtle phonological or intonational differences between the sentences that might cue participants. Once again, the phoneme at the beginning of *eel was replaced with a cough. It was found that the phoneme that participants restored depended on the semantic context given by the final word of the sentence. Participants restored a phoneme that would make an appropriate word for that context. These are "peel" in (1), "wheel" in (2), "heel" in (3), and "meal" in (4).

Although at first sight it seems that the perception of speech is constrained by higher level information such as semantic and syntactic constraints, it is unclear in these experiments how the restoration is occurring. Do participants really perceive the missing phoneme? Fodor (1983) asked whether the restoration occurs at the phonological processing level, or at some higher level. Perhaps it is just the case, for example, that participants guess the deleted phoneme. The guessing does not even need to be conscious. Another way of putting this issue is, does the context affect the actual perception or some later process?

There is evidence that in some circumstances phoneme restoration is a true perceptual effect. Samuel (1981, 1987, 1990, 1996) examined the effects of adding noise to the segment instead of just replacing the segment with noise. If phoneme restoration is truly perceptual, participants should not be able to detect any difference between these conditions; in each case they will think they hear a phoneme plus sound. On the other hand, if the effect is postperceptual, there should be good discrimination between the two conditions. Samuel concluded that lexical context does indeed lead to true phoneme restoration and that effect was prelexical. On the other hand he concluded that sentence context does not affect phoneme recognition, and affects only postlexical processing. Consider the sentences in (5) and (6):

(5) The travelers found horrible bats in the cavern/ tavern when they visited it.
(6) The travelers found horrible food in the cavern/ tavern when they visited it.

In (5) the sentential context supports "cavern" more than "tavern"; in (6) the reverse is the case. If sentence context has an effect, we should therefore get stronger phoneme restoration of the deleted initial phoneme for "cavern" than "tavern" in (5), and the opposite way round in (6). This was not the case. In conclusion, only information about particular words affects the identification of words; information about the meaning of the sentence affects a later processing stage.

Samuel (1997) investigated the suggestion that people just guess the phoneme in the restoration task, rather than truly restore it at a perceptual level. He combined the phoneme restoration technique with the selective adaptation technique of Eimas and Corbit (1973). Listeners identified sounds from the /bI/–/dI/ continuum where the sounds that were acting as adaptors were the third syllable of words beginning either with /b/ or /d/ (e.g., "alphabet" and "academic"). After repeated presentation of the adaptor (e.g., /b/, by listening to the word "alphabet" 40 times), participants were less likely to classify a subsequent sound as /b/. Crucially, this adaptation occurred even if the critical phoneme in the adaptor word was replaced with a loud burst of noise (e.g., "alpha*et," with * signifying the noise). The adaptation only occurred when the critical phonemes were replaced with a burst of noise, but not when they were replaced with silence.

At first sight this study suggests that restored phonemes can act like real ones and cause adaptation. Others, however, have argued that these findings can be explained without interaction if the restored phonological code is created by top-down lexical context rather than just provided by the lexical code. The lexical context does not seem to be improving the perceptibility of the phoneme (the sensitivity), but just affects how participants respond (the bias). To this extent top-down information is not really affecting the sensitivity of word recognition. Perhaps listeners come to learn to recognize the noise as an instance of a "b" sound, and hence it causes adaptation in the same way that a "real" "b" would (Norris, McQueen, & Cutler, 2000, 2003).

The balance of the data here, and as discussed later in the description on the TRACE model, suggests that top-down context has at best a limited role in sound identification. In particular, there is little evidence that sentential context affects speech processing.

The time course of spoken word recognition

The terms "word recognition" and "lexical access" are often used in the spoken word recognition literature to refer to different processes (Tanenhaus & Lucas, 1987), and so it is best to be clear in advance about what our terms mean. We can identify three stages of identification: initial contact, lexical selection, and word recognition (Frauenfelder & Tyler, 1987) (see Figure 9.1). These stages might overlap; whether they do or not is an empirical question, and is an aspect of our concern with modularity.

Recognizing a spoken word begins when some representation of the sensory input makes initial contact with the lexicon, called the initial contact phase. Once lexical entries begin to match the contact representation, they change in some way; they become "activated." The activation might be all-or-none (as is the case in the original cohort model described later), or the relative activation levels might depend on properties of the words (such as word frequency), or words may be activated in proportion to the current goodness of fit with the sensory data (as in the more recent cohort model, or in the connectionist TRACE model). In the selection phase, activation accumulates until one lexical entry is selected. Word recognition is the end point of the selection phase.

In the simplest case, the word **recognition point** corresponds to its **uniqueness point**, where the word's initial sequence is common to that word and no other. Often recognition will be delayed until after the uniqueness point, and in principle

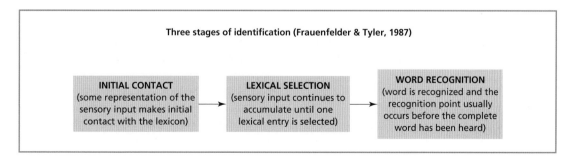

Three stages of identification (Frauenfelder & Tyler, 1987)

INITIAL CONTACT
(some representation of the sensory input makes initial contact with the lexicon) → **LEXICAL SELECTION**
(sensory input continues to accumulate until one lexical entry is selected) → **WORD RECOGNITION**
(word is recognized and the recognition point usually occurs before the complete word has been heard)

FIGURE 9.1

we might recognize a word before its uniqueness point—in strongly biasing contexts, for example. If this happens, the point at which this occurs is called the isolation point. This is the point in a word where a proportion of listeners identify the word correctly, even though they may not be confident about this decision (Grosjean, 1980; Tyler & Wessels, 1983). By the isolation point, the listener has isolated a word candidate; they then continue to monitor the sensory input until some level of confidence is reached; this is the recognition point. Lexical access refers to the point at which all the information about a word—phonological, semantic, syntactic, pragmatic—becomes available following its recognition. The process of integration that then follows is the start of the comprehension process proper, where the semantic and syntactic properties of the word are integrated into the higher level sentence representation.

When does frequency affect spoken word recognition?

Frequency has a very early effect on spoken word recognition. Dahan, Magnuson, and Tanenhaus (2001) examined people's eye movements while looking at pictures on a computer screen. The participants had to follow spoken instructions about which object in the scene they had to click with their mouse. Participants tended to look at objects with the higher frequency name first, compared with a competitor picture with a lower frequency name but the same initial sounds (e.g., the spoken word was "bench," and alongside the picture of a bench were pictures of a bed—a high-frequency competitor—and a bell—low-frequency). Participants also needed to look for less time at targets with higher frequency names. A detailed analysis of how these effects unfolded over time showed that word frequency is important from the very earliest stages of processing, and that these effects persisted for some time.

Context effects on word recognition

Does context affect spoken word recognition? The context is all of the information not in the immediate sensory signal. It includes information available from the previous sensory input (the prior context) and from higher knowledge sources (e.g., lexical, syntactic, semantic, and pragmatic information). The nature of the context being discussed also depends on the level of analysis. For example, we might have word-level context operating on phoneme identification, and sentence-level context operating on word identification. To show that context affects recognition, we need to demonstrate top-down influences on the bottom-up processing of the acoustic signal. We have already examined whether context affects low-level perceptual processing; here we are concerned with the possible effects of context on word identification. The issues involved are complex. Even if there are some contextual effects, we would still need to determine which types of context have an effect, at what stage or stages they have an effect, and how they have this effect.

We have already noted that there are two opposing positions on the role of context in recognition, which can be called the autonomous and interactionist positions. The autonomous position says that context cannot have an effect prior to word recognition. It can only contribute to the evaluation and integration of the output of lexical processing, not its generation. However, the lateral flow of information is permitted in these models. For example, information flow is allowed between words within the lexicon, but not from the lexicon to lower level processes such as phoneme identification. On the other hand, interactive models allow different types of information to interact with one another. In particular, there may be feedback from later levels of processing to earlier ones. For example, information about the meaning of the sentence or the pragmatic context might affect perception.

This description is the simplest way of putting the autonomous–interactive distinction. However, perhaps the autonomous and interactive models should be looked at as the extreme ends of a continuum of possible models rather than as the two poles of a dichotomy. There might be some restrictions on permitted interaction in interactive models. For example, context can propose candidates for what word the stimulus might be before sensory processing has begun (Morton, 1969), or it might be restricted to disposing of candidates and not proposing them (Marslen-Wilson, 1987). Because there are such huge differences between models it can be difficult to test between them. Strong evidence for the interactionist view is if context has an effect before or during the access and selection phases. In an autonomous model, context can only have an influence after a word has emerged as the best fit to the sensory input.

Frauenfelder and Tyler (1987) distinguished between two types of context: non-structural and structural. Non-structural context can be thought of as information from the same level of processing as that which is currently being processed. An example is facilitation in processing arising from intra-lexical context, such as an associative relation between two words like "doctor" and "nurse." It can be explained in terms of relations within a single level of processing, and hence need not violate the principle of autonomy, in terms of the spread of activation within the lexicon. Alternatively, associative facilitation can be thought of as occurring because of hard-wired connections between similar things at the same level. According to autonomy theorists such as Fodor (1983) and Forster (1981), this is the only type of context that affects processes prior to recognition.

Structural context affects the combination of words into higher level units, and it involves higher level information. It is top-down processing. There are a number of possible types of structural context. Word knowledge (lexical context) might be used to help identify phonemes, and sentence-level knowledge (sentence and syntactic context) might be used to help identify individual words. The most interesting types of structural context are those based on meaning. Frauenfelder and Tyler (1987) distinguished two subtypes: semantic and interpretative. Semantic context is based on word meanings. There is much evidence that this affects word processing. Words that are appropriate for the context are responded to faster than those that are not, across a range of tasks which I discuss in more detail later, such as phoneme monitoring, shadowing, naming, and gating (e.g., Marslen-Wilson, 1984; Marslen-Wilson &

Tyler, 1980; Tyler & Wessels, 1983). But it is not clear whether non-structural and semantic structural context effects can be distinguished, or at which stages they operate. Furthermore, these effects must be studied using tasks that minimize the chance of postperceptual factors operating. For this reason the delay between the stimulus and the response cannot be too long; otherwise participants would have a chance to reflect on and maybe alter their decisions, which would obviously reflect late-stage, post-access mechanisms. Interpretative structural context involves more high-level information, such as pragmatic information, discourse information, and knowledge about the world.

There is some evidence that non-linguistic context can have an effect on word recognition. Tanenhaus, Spivey-Knowlton, Eberhard, and Sedivy (1995) studied people's eye movements while they were examining a visual scene while following instructions. They found that visual context can facilitate spoken word recognition. For example, the words "candy" and "candle" sound similar until about halfway through. Following the instruction "pick up the candle," participants were faster to move their eyes to the object mentioned if only a candle was in the scene than if both a candle and candy were present. Indeed, when no confusion object was present participants identified the object before hearing the end of the word. This result suggests that interpretative structural context can affect word recognition.

MODELS OF SPEECH RECOGNITION

Before we can start to access the lexicon, we have to translate the output of the auditory nerves from the ear into an appropriate format. Speech perception is concerned with this early stage of processing. It is obviously an important topic for the machine recognition of speech, as there are many obvious advantages to computers and other machines being able to understand speech.

Early models of speech recognition examined the possibility that word recognition occurred by *template matching*. Target words are stored as templates, and identification occurs when a match is found. A template is an exact description of the sound or the word for which we are searching. However, there is far too much variation in speech for this to be a plausible account except in the most restricted domains. Speakers differ in their dialect, basic pitch, basic speed of talking, and in many other ways. One person can produce the same phoneme in many different ways—you might be speaking loudly, or more quickly than normal, or have a cold, for example. The number of templates that would have to be stored would be prohibitively large. Generally, template models are not considered as plausible accounts in psycholinguistics.

One early model of speech perception was that of *analysis-by-synthesis* (Halle & Stevens, 1962; Liberman et al., 1967; Stevens, 1960). The basis of analysis-by-synthesis is that we recognize speech by reference to the actions necessary to produce a sound. The important idea underlying this model was that when we hear speech, we produce or synthesize a succession of speech sounds until we match what we hear. The synthesizer does not randomly generate candidates for matching against the input; it creates an initial best guess constrained by acoustic cues in the input, and then attempts to minimize the difference between this and the input. This approach had a few advantages. First, it uses our capacity for speech production to cope with speech recognition as well. Second, it copes easily with intra-speaker differences, because the listeners are generating their own candidates. Third, it is easy to show how constraints of all levels might have an effect; the synthesizer only generates candidates that are plausible. It will not, for example, generate sequences of sounds that are illegitimate within that language. One variant of the model, the motor theory, proposes that the speech synthesizer models the articulatory apparatus and motor movements of the speaker. It effectively computes which motor movements would have been necessary to create those sounds. Evidence for this model is that the way sounds are made provides a perfect description of them; for example, all /d/s are made by tapping the tongue against the alveolar ridge. Note that the specification of the motor movements must be quite abstract; mute people can understand speech perfectly well (Lenneberg, 1962), and we can understand speech we cannot ourselves produce (e.g., that of people with stutters, or foreign accents).

Analysis-by-synthesis models suffer from two substantial problems. First, there is no apparent way of translating the articulatory hypothesis generated by the production system into the same format as the heard speech in order for the potential match to be assessed. Second, we are extremely adept at recognizing clearly articulated words that are improbable in their context, which suggests that speech recognition is primarily a data-driven process. In summary, Clark and Clark (1977) argued that this theory is underspecified and has little predictive power. Nevertheless, in recent years motor theories of perception have seen something of a resurgence. They do have the advantage that matching the auditory signal to motor representations for producing our own speech provides a means for categorizing the acoustic signal; indeed, some researchers go so far as to argue that these motor representations have a privileged role in language processing, and that perceiving speech resembles perceiving motor gestures, in the sense that the goal of speech perception is recognizing which vocal tract movements could give rise to the sounds, rather than the more abstract identification of the sounds themselves (Galantucci, Fowler, & Turvey, 2006; Liberman & Whalen, 2000). Imaging data show that the motor areas of the brain become activated during speech perception (Watkins & Paus, 2004), although of course this activation does not mean that the motor areas play a causal role in perception. Although analysis-by-synthesis cannot be the whole story of speech perception, it does seem as though motor processes play some role.

We are left with two basic types of model of word recognition. The cohort model of Marslen-Wilson and colleagues emphasizes the bottom-up nature of word recognition. The connectionist model TRACE emphasizes its interactive nature, and allows feedback between levels of processing. Partly in response to TRACE, Marslen-Wilson modified the cohort model, so we should distinguish between early and late versions of it.

The cohort model

The cohort model of spoken word recognition was proposed by Marslen-Wilson and Welsh (1978; Marslen-Wilson, 1984, 1987) (see Figure 9.2). The central idea of the model is that as we hear speech, we set up a cohort of possible items the word could be. Items are then eliminated from this set until only one is left. This is then taken as the word currently trying to be recognized. We should distinguish an early version of the model (Marslen-Wilson, 1984), which permitted more interaction, from a later version (Marslen-Wilson, 1989, 1990), where processing was more autonomous and the recognition system was better able to recover if the beginnings of words were degraded.

There are three stages of processing in the cohort model. First, in the access stage the perceptual representation is used to activate lexical items, and thereby to generate a candidate set of items. This set of candidates is known as the cohort. The beginning of the word is particularly important in generating the cohort. Second, there is a selection stage when one item only is chosen from this set. Third, there is an integration stage in which the semantic and syntactic properties of the chosen word are utilized—for example, in integrating the word into a complete representation of the whole sentence. The access and selection stages are prelexical, and the integration stage is postlexical. Like Morton's logogen model (see Chapter 6), the original cohort model is based on parallel, interactive, direct access, but whereas logogens passively accumulate positive evidence, words in the cohort actively seek to eliminate themselves. On the presentation of the beginning of a word, a "word-initial cohort" of candidate words is set up. These are then actively eliminated by all possible means, including further phonological evidence, and semantic and syntactic context. In particular, as we hear increasing stretches of the word, candidates are eliminated.

Remember that the uniqueness point is the point at which a word can be distinguished uniquely from all similar words. It is around this point that the most intense processing activity occurs. Consider the following increasing segments of a word (7–11). Obviously when we hear /t/ alone (7) there are many possible words—the cohort will be very large. The next segment (8) reduces the cohort somewhat, but it will still be very large. With more information (9) the cohort of possible items is reduced still further, but there are still a number of items the word might be (e.g., "trespass," "trestle," "trend," "trench"). The next phoneme (in 10) reduces the cohort to only three ("trespass," "tress," and "trestle"), but it is only at (12) that the cohort is reduced to one word (or more properly, one root morpheme)—"trespass." This point is called the uniqueness point.

(7)   /t/
(8)   /tr/
(9)   /tre/
(10) /tress/
(11) /tresp/
(12) /trespass/

It is important to note that the recognition point does not have to coincide with the uniqueness point. Suppose we heard the start of a sentence "The poacher ignored the sign not to tres-." In the early version of this model, at this point the context might be sufficiently strong to eliminate all other words apart from "trespass" from the cohort. Hence it could be recognized before its uniqueness point. The early version of the model

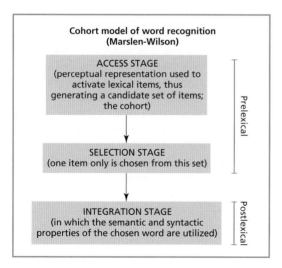

**Cohort model of word recognition
(Marslen-Wilson)**

ACCESS STAGE
(perceptual representation used to activate lexical items, thus generating a candidate set of items; the cohort)

SELECTION STAGE
(one item only is chosen from this set)

INTEGRATION STAGE
(in which the semantic and syntactic properties of the chosen word are utilized)

Prelexical

Postlexical

FIGURE 9.2

was very interactive in this respect; context is clearly affecting the prelexical selection stage. The cost of all this is that sometimes strong contextual bias might lead to error. On the other hand, if the sensory information is poor, the recognition point might not be until well after a word's uniqueness point. Indeed, the uniqueness point and recognition point of a word are only likely to coincide in the case of a very clear, isolated word.

In a revision of the basic model (e.g., Marslen-Wilson, 1989), context only affects the integration stage. The model has bottom-up priority, meaning that context cannot be used to restrict which items form the initial cohort. Bottom-up priority is a feature of both the early and late versions of the cohort model, but in the later version, context cannot be used to eliminate members of the cohort before the uniqueness point. This change was motivated by experimental data (from the gating task to be discussed later) that suggested that the role of context is more limited than was originally thought: Context cannot be used to eliminate candidates at an early stage. Another important modification in the later version of the cohort model is that the elimination of candidates from the cohort no longer becomes all-or-none. This counters one objection to the original model: What happens if the start of a word is distorted or misperceived? This would have prevented the correct item from being in the word-initial cohort, yet we can sometimes overcome distortions even at the start of a word. Suppose we hear a word like "bleasant" (e.g., as in "the dinner was very bleasant"). Although we might be slowed down, we can still recover to identify the word as "pleasant." (For example, a model such as TRACE, described later, will successfully identify "bleasant" as "pleasant" because the degree of overlap is high and there is no better word candidate.) Hence, in the revised model degree of overlap is important, although the beginnings of words are particularly important in generating the cohort. Also in the revised cohort model, in the absence of further positive information, candidates gradually decay back down to their normal resting state. They can be revived again by subsequent positive information. The activation level of contextually inappropriate candidates decays: context disposes, not proposes. Lexical candidates that are contextually appropriate are integrated into the higher level representation of the sentence. Sentential context cannot override perceptual hypotheses, but only has a late effect when one candidate is starting to emerge as the likely winner. The frequency of a word affects the activation level of candidates in the early stages of lexical access. The rate of gain of activation is greater for higher frequency words. There are relative frequency effects within the initial cohort, so that being in the cohort is not all-or-none, but instead items vary along a continuum of activation. The most recent version of the model (Marslen-Wilson & Warren, 1994) emphasizes the direct access of lexical entries on the basis of an acoustic analysis of the incoming speech signal.

Experimental tests of the cohort model

Marslen-Wilson and his colleagues have used a number of experimental tasks to gather evidence for the cohort model. Marslen-Wilson and Welsh (1978) used a technique known as shadowing to examine how syntax and semantics interact in word recognition. In this task, participants have to listen to continuous speech and repeat it back as quickly as possible (typically after a 250 ms delay). The speech samples have deliberate mistakes in them—distorted sounds so that certain words are mispronounced. Participants are not told that there are mispronunciations, but are told they have to repeat back the passage of speech as they hear it. But Marslen-Wilson and Welsh found that participants often (about 50% of the time) repeat these back as they should be rather than as they actually are, and without any audible disruption to the fluency of their speech. That is, we find what are called fluent restorations, such as producing "travedy" as "tragedy." (On a small proportion of trials participants restored words after a hesitation; these non-fluent hesitations, along with errors, were excluded from further analysis.) The more distorted a sound is, the more likely you are to get an exact repetition.

In Marslen-Wilson and Welsh's experiment there were three variables of interest. The first variable was the size of the discrepancy between the target and the erroneous word. This discrepancy was measured in terms of the number of distinctive features changed in the deliberate error (either one feature, as in "trachedy," or three features, as in "travedy"). The second variable was the lexical constraint, which reflected the number of candidates available at different positions in the word by manipulating the syllable position on which the error was located (first or third syllable). The third variable was the context (the word involved was a probable or improbable continuation of the start of the sentence). An example of a high-constraint context was "Still, he wanted to smoke a cigarette," and of a low-constraint case, "It was his misfortune that they were stationary."

Marslen-Wilson and Welsh found that most of the fluent restorations were made when the distortion was slight, when the distortion was in the final syllable, and when the word was highly predictable from its context. On the other hand, most of the exact reproductions occur with greater distortion when the word is relatively unconstrained by context. In a suitable constraining context, listeners make fluent restorations, even when deviations are very prominent. These results were interpreted as demonstrating that the immediate percept is the product of both bottom-up perceptual input and top-down contextual constraints. Shadowing experiments showed that both syntactic and semantic analyses of speech start to happen almost instantaneously, and are not delayed until a whole clause has been heard (Marslen-Wilson, 1973, 1975, 1976).

We do not pay attention equally to all parts of a word. The beginning of the word, particularly the first syllable, is especially salient. This was demonstrated by the listening for mispronunciations task (Cole, 1973; Cole & Jakimik, 1980). In this task participants listen to speech where a sound is distorted (e.g., "boot" is changed to "poot"), and detect these changes. Consistent with the shadowing task, participants are more sensitive to changes to the beginning of the words.

Indeed, word fragments that match a word from the onset are nearly as effective a prime as the word itself. For example, "capt-" is almost as good a prime of the word "ship" as the word "captain" (Marslen-Wilson, 1987; Zwitserlood, 1989).

On the other hand, rhyme fragments of words produce very little priming. For example, neither a word ("cattle") nor a derived nonword ("yattle") prime "battle" (Marslen-Wilson, 1993; Marslen-Wilson & Zwitserlood, 1989). (Marslen-Wilson, 1993, argued on this basis that the cohort model gives a better account than that of the TRACE model described later. According to TRACE, "cattle" should compete with "battle" through the lateral inhibition connections, but as there is no word match for "yattle" it should not compete, and may even facilitate.)

The **gating task** (Grosjean, 1980; Tyler, 1984; Tyler & Wessels, 1983) involves presenting gradually increasing amounts of a word, as in examples (7) to (12) given earlier. This enables the isolation points of words to be found: This is the mean time it takes from the onset of a word for listeners to be able to guess it correctly. This task demonstrates the importance of context: Participants need an average of 333 ms to identify a word in isolation, but only 199 ms in an appropriate context, such as "At the zoo, the kids rode on the" for the word "camel" (Grosjean, 1980). On the other hand, these studies also showed that candidates are generated that are compatible with the perceptual representation up to that point, but that are not compatible with the context. Strong syntactic and semantic constraints do not prevent the accessing, at least early on, of word candidates that are compatible with the sensory input but not with the context. Hence sentential context does not appear to have an early effect.

In a visual equivalent of the gating task, participants looked at a computer screen showing pictures of a clown, cloud, dog, and parrot, and were instructed to "click on the cloud" (Allopenna, Magnuson, & Tanenhaus, 1998). On hearing the onset "cl-" participants were equally likely to look at the picture of the cloud and that of the clown, but then as soon as they heard further disambiguating information they looked at just the target picture.

Although context might not be able to affect the generation of candidates, it might be able to remove them. A technique known as cross-modal priming enables the measurement of contextual effects at different times in recognizing a word

(Zwitserlood, 1989). This technique necessitates participants listening to speech over headphones while simultaneously looking at a computer screen to perform a lexical decision task to visually presented words. The relation between the word on the screen and the speech, and the precise time relation between the two, can be systematically varied. Zwitserlood showed that context can assist in selecting semantically appropriate candidates before the word's recognition point. Consider the word "captain." (Zwitserlood's experiment actually used Dutch materials, where the equivalent item is "kapitein.") Participants heard differing amounts of the word before either a related or a control word appeared on a computer screen. At the point of hearing just "cap," the word is not yet unique. It is consistent with a number of continuations, including the word "captain" but also a competitor, "capital." Zwitserlood found facilitation for the recognition of both relatives of the target (e.g., "ship") and competitors ("money" for "capital"). By the end of the word, however, only relatives of the target could be primed. There was also more priming by the more frequent candidate than by less frequent candidates, as predicted by the cohort model. Importantly, constraining context did not have any effect early on in the word: Even if context strongly favors a word so that its competitors are implausible (e.g., as in "With dampened spirits the men stood around the grave. They mourned the loss of their captain"), they nevertheless still prime their neighbors. After a word's isolation point, however, we do find effects of context. Context then has the effect of boosting the word's activation level relative to its competitors. These results support the ideas that context cannot override perceptual hypotheses, and that sentential context has a late effect, on interpreting a word and integrating it with the syntax and semantics of the sentence. Context speeds up this process of integration.

Recent imaging data support the idea that semantics plays a role in selecting among candidates. In a lexical decision task, high imageability words generated stronger activation than low imageability words, in competitive contexts (Zhuang, Randall, Stamatakis, Marslen-Wilson, & Tyler, 2011). The imaging work now shows that selection is not driven purely by the phonetic properties of the incoming words.

The influence of lexical neighborhoods

In the cohort model, the evaluation of competitors to the target word takes place in parallel, and hence the number of competitors (the cohort size) at any time should not have any effect on the recognition of the target (Marslen-Wilson, 1987). However, data from Goldinger, Luce, and Pisoni (1989) and Luce, Pisoni, and Goldinger (1990) suggest that cohort size does affect the time course of word recognition. Luce et al. found that the structure of a word's neighborhood affects the speed and accuracy of auditory word recognition on a range of tasks, including identifying words and performing an auditory lexical decision task. The number and characteristics of a word's competitors (such as their frequency) are very important. For example, we are less able to identify high-frequency words that have many high-frequency neighbors than words with fewer neighbors or low-frequency neighbors. Luce and his colleagues argue that the number of competitors, what they call the neighborhood density, influences the decision. Words with many neighbors take longer to identify and produce more errors because of competition.

Marslen-Wilson (1990) examined the effect of the frequency of competitors on recognizing words. He found that the time it takes you to recognize a word such as "speech" does not just depend on the relative uniqueness points of competitors (such as "speed" and "specious") in the cohort, but also on the frequency of those words. Hence, you are faster to identify a high-frequency word that only has low-frequency neighbors than vice versa. The rise in activation of a high-frequency word is much greater than for a low-frequency one.

Phonological neighborhood is not the only factor that can affect auditory recognition. Orthographic neighborhood can also affect auditory recognition, but does so in a facilitatory fashion. That is, spoken words with many visually similar neighbors are faster to identify than spoken words with few neighbors (Ziegler, Muneaux, & Grainger, 2003). Somehow the printed word can sometimes affect spoken word recognition, presumably because somewhere in the system sublexical units, or word units, or both, for different modalities are linked.

Evaluation of the cohort model

The cohort model has changed over the years, and in the light of more recent data it places less emphasis on the role of context. In the early version of the model, context cannot affect the access stage, but it can affect the selection and integration stages. In the later version of the model, context cannot affect selection but only affects integration. In the revised version (Marslen-Wilson, 1987), elements are not either "on" or "off," but have an activation level proportional to the goodness-of-fit between the element and the acoustic input, so that a number of candidates may then be analyzed further in parallel. This permits a gradual decay of candidates rather than immediate elimination. The model does not distinguish between provisional and definite identification; there are some probabilistic aspects to word recognition (Grosjean, 1980). The later version, by replacing all-or-none elimination from the cohort with gradual elimination, also better accounts for the ability of the system to recover from errors. A continuing problem for the cohort model is its reliance on knowing when words start without having any explicit mechanism for finding the starts of words.

TRACE and related models

TRACE is a highly interactive model of spoken word recognition (McClelland & Elman, 1986), derived from the McClelland and Rumelhart (1981) interactive activation model of letter and visual word identification (see Chapter 6). Here I will outline only the principal features of the model. (Once again, if you haven't studied connectionist models before, I strongly advise you to read the Appendix carefully at this point if you haven't already done so.) The most important characteristic of TRACE is that it emphasizes the role of top-down processing (context) on word recognition. Hence, lexical context can directly assist acoustic-perceptual processing, and information above the word level can directly influence word processing.

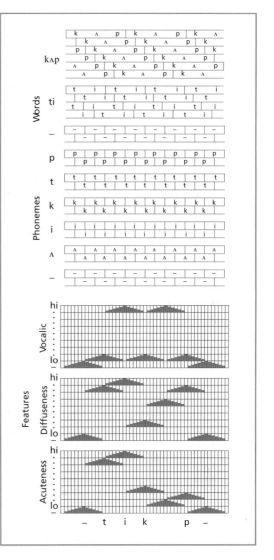

FIGURE 9.3 Architecture of the TRACE model of speech recognition. Each rectangle represents one unit. Units at different levels span different portions of the speech trace. In this example, the phrase "tea cup" has been presented to the model. Its input values on three phonetic features are illustrated by the blackened histograms. From McClelland, Rumelhart, and the PDP Research Group (1986).

TRACE is a connectionist model, and so consists of many simple processing units connected together. These units are arranged in three levels of processing. It assumes some early, fairly sophisticated perceptual processing of the acoustic signal. The level of input units represents phonological features; these are connected to phoneme units, which in turn are connected to the output units that represent words (see Figure 9.3). Input units are provided with energy or "activated," and this energy or activation spreads along the connections in a manner described in the Appendix, with the result that eventually only one output unit is left activated. The winner in this stable configuration is the word that the network "recognizes." Units on different levels that are mutually consistent have excitatory connections. All connections between levels are bidirectional, in that information flows along them in both directions. This means that both bottom-up and top-down processing can occur. There are inhibitory connections between units within each level, which has the effect that once a unit is activated, it tends to inhibit its competitors. This mechanism therefore emphasizes the concept of competition between units at the same level. The model deals with time by simulating it as discrete slices. Units are represented independently in each time-slot. The model is implemented in the form of computer simulations, and runs of the simulations are compared with what happens in normal human speech processing. The model shows how lexical knowledge can aid perception—for example, if an input ambiguous between /p/ and /b/ is given followed by the ending corresponding to -LUG, then /p/ is "recognized" by the model. Categorical

perception arises in the model as a consequence of within-level inhibition between the phoneme units. As activation provided by an ambiguous input cycles through time, mutual inhibition between the phoneme units results in the input being classified as at one or other end of the continuum. TRACE accounts for position effects in word recognition (word-initial sounds play a particularly important role) because input unfolds over time, so that word-initial sounds contribute much more to the activation of word nodes than word-final sounds do (see Figures 9.4 and 9.5).

Evaluation of the TRACE model

TRACE handles context effects in speech perception very well. It can cope with some acoustic variability, and gives an account of findings such as the phoneme restoration effect and co-articulation effects. TRACE gives a very good account of lexical context effects. It is good at finding word boundaries and copes extremely well with noisy input—which is a considerable advantage, given the noise present in natural language. An attractive aspect of TRACE is that features that are a problem for older models, such as co-articulation effects in template models, actually facilitate processing, just as they clearly do in humans, through top-down processing. As with all computer models, TRACE has the advantage of being explicit.

There are several problems with TRACE, however. There are many parameters that can be

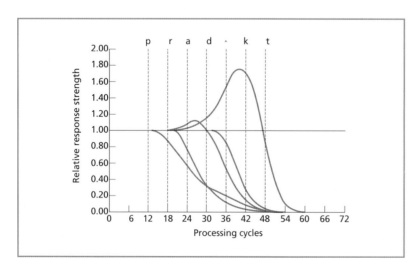

FIGURE 9.4 Response strengths in TRACE of the units for several words relative to the response strength of the unit for product, as a function of time relative to the peak of the first phoneme that fails to match the word. The successive curves coming off the horizontal line representing the normalized response strength of product are for the words trot, possible, priest, progress, and produce, respectively.

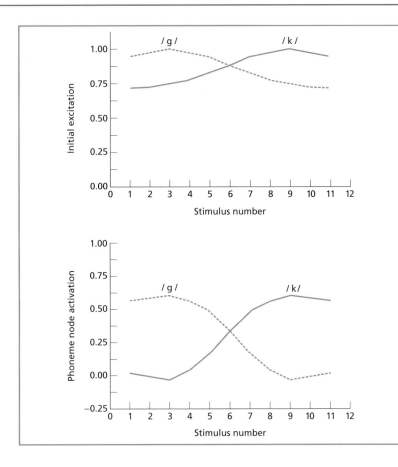

FIGURE 9.5 Categorical phoneme perception in TRACE. The top panel shows the level of bottom-up activation to the phoneme units /g/ and /k/, for each of 12 stimuli (shown on the x-axis). The lower panel shows the activation for the same phoneme units after cycle 60. Stimuli 3 and 9 correspond to canonical /g/ and /k/, respectively. At cycle 60, the boundary between the phonemes is much sharper. From McClelland, Rumelhart, and the PDP Research Group (1986).

manipulated in the model, and it is possible to level the criticism that TRACE is too powerful, in that it can accommodate any result. By adjusting some of the parameters, can the model be made to simulate any data from speech recognition experiments, whatever they show? Moreover, the way in which the model deals with time, simulating it as discrete slices, is implausible.

Massaro (1989) pointed out a number of problems with the TRACE model. He carried out an experiment in which listeners had to make a forced-choice decision about which phoneme they heard, when the sound they heard was on the continuum between /l/ and /r/. The sounds occurred in the contexts of /s_i/, /p_i/, and /t_i/. The first context favors the identification of /l/, as there are a number of English words that begin with /sli-/ but no words that begin /sri-/ The third context favors /r/ because there are words beginning with /tri-/ but not /tli-/. Finally, the second context favors

both phonemes approximately equally, as there are words beginning with both /pli-/ and /pri-/. Massaro found that the context biases performance so that, for example, listeners were more likely to classify an ambiguous phoneme as /l/ in the /s_i/ context and /r/ in the /t_i/ context. The behavior of humans in this task differed from the behavior of the TRACE network. In particular, in TRACE context has the biggest effect when the speech signal is most ambiguous, and has less effect when the signal is less ambiguous. With humans, the effects of context are constant with respect to the ambiguity of the speech signal. Although McClelland's (1991) reply accepted many of Massaro's points, and tried making the model's output probabilistic (or **stochastic**), Massaro and Cohen (1991) found that the problems persisted even after this modification. Massaro's work is important in that it shows that it is possible to make falsifiable predictions about connectionist models such as TRACE. Massaro argues for a model where phonetic recognition uses features that serve as an input to a decision strategy involving variable conjunctions of perceptual features called fuzzy prototypes (see Klatt, 1989, for more detail). Choosing between these models is difficult, and it is not clear that they are addressing precisely the same issues: TRACE is concerned with the time course of lexical access, whereas the fuzzy logic model is more concerned with decision making and output processes (McClelland, 1991).

The main problem with TRACE is that it is based on the idea that top-down context permeates the recognition process. The extent to which top-down context influences speech perception is controversial. In particular, there is also experimental evidence against the types of top-down processing that TRACE predicts occur in speech processing: Context effects are only really observed with perceptually degraded stimuli (Burton, Baum, & Blumstein, 1989; McQueen, 1991; Norris, 1994b). In support of TRACE, Elman and McClelland (1988) reported an experiment showing interactive effects on speech recognition of the sort predicted by TRACE. They argued that they had demonstrated that between-level processes can affect within-level processes at a lower level. In particular, they showed that illusory phonemes created by top-down, lexical knowledge (in a manner analogous to phoneme restoration) can affect co-articulation (the influence of one sound on a neighboring sound) operating at the basic sound perception level in the way predicted by simulations in TRACE. Consider word pairs such as "English dates/gates" or "copious dates/gates," where the initial phoneme of the second word was ambiguous, lying on the continuum between /d/ and /g/. The co-articulatory effects of the final sound of the first word affect the precise way in which we produce the first sound of the second word. Listeners are sensitive to these co-articulation effects in speech: the effect is called compensation for co-articulation. In particular, we are more likely to identify the ambiguous phoneme as a /d/ when it follows a /sh/, as in "English," but more likely to identify it as a /g/ when following /s/, as in "copious." So listeners should tend to report hearing "English dates" but "copious gates." Elman and McClelland showed that this compensation effect was obtained even when the final sounds

of "English" and "copious" were replaced with a sound halfway between /s/ and /sh/.

At first sight then, the data of Elman and McClelland (1988) support an interactive model rather than an autonomous one. The lexicon appears to be influencing a prelexical effect (compensation). There are, however, accounts of the data compatible with the autonomous model. First, it is not necessary after all to invoke lexical knowledge. Connectionist simulations using strictly bottom-up processing can learn the difference between /g/ after /s/ and /sh/, and also that /s/ is more likely to follow one vowel and /sh/ another. That is, there are sequential dependencies between phonemes that mean that we do not need to invoke lexical knowledge: Some sequences of phonemes are just more likely (Cairns, Shillcock, Chater, & Levy, 1995; Norris, 1993). Pitt and McQueen (1998) demonstrated that this sequential information can be used in speech perception. They found compensation for co-articulation effects on the categorization of stop consonants when they were preceded by ambiguous fricative sounds at the end of nonwords. For example, the sequence of phonemes in the nonword "der?" is biased towards an /s/ conclusion, while the sequence in "nai?" is biased towards a /sh/ conclusion. (In both cases the final sound in fact was halfway between /s/ and /sh/.) The nonwords were followed by a word beginning with a stop consonant sound along the /t/ to /k/ continuum, from "tapes" to "capes." The identification of the stop consonant was influenced by the preceding ambiguous fricative differently depending on the nonword context of the fricative. As the preceding item was a nonword, lexical knowledge could not be used. The fact that compensation is still obtained suggests that sequential knowledge about which phonemes co-occur is being used.

TRACE is also poor at detecting mispronunciations. TRACE is a single-outlet model (Cutler, Mehler, Norris, & Segui, 1987): The only way TRACE can identify phonemes is to see which phonemes are identified at the phoneme level. However, suppose a mispronounced word is presented. The phonemes will activate the best match word. This word node will then feed back activation to the phoneme level, so that the phonemes in the best match will become activated: The incorrect phonemes will be corrected. But mispronunciations are not overlooked; they have a distinct adverse effect on performance (Gaskell & Marslen-Wilson, 1998).

Single-outlet models can be contrasted with multiple-outlet models, such as the Race model (Cutler & Norris, 1979), where two sources of information, the stored and maintained prelexical analysis of the word, and a word's lexical entry, compete for output. The decision is made on the basis of which route produces the answer first—hence the race aspect. Because there are two outlets, prelexical and lexical, it should be possible to emphasize one rather than the other by shifting attention. Lexical effects on phoneme processing should be maximized when people pay particular attention to the lexical outlet, and minimized when they pay particular attention to the prelexical outlet. This pattern is exactly what is observed, and is difficult for single-outlet models such as TRACE to account for (Cutler et al., 1987; Norris et al., 2000). For example, the magnitude of the lexical effect in phoneme monitoring tasks depends on the composition of the other filler items used in the experiment.

In their review of the literature on context effects on speech recognition, Norris et al. (2000) argued that feedback is never necessary in speech recognition. Indeed, top-down feedback, they argue, would hinder recognition. Feedback cannot improve accuracy in processing (indeed, it can override the detection of mispronunciations and can actually decrease accuracy); it can only speed up processing. The cost to this increase in speed is a trade-off with accuracy. The crux of the argument is whether or not there is lexical involvement in phonemic decision making—which are all tasks where listeners are required to make decisions about sounds, such as phoneme monitoring, phoneme restoration, and phonetic categorization.

Finally, there is experimental evidence against other assumptions of the model. Frauenfelder, Segui, and Dijkstra (1990) found no evidence of top-down inhibition on phonemes in a task involving phoneme monitoring of unexpected phonemes late in a word compared with control nonwords. TRACE predicts that once a word is accessed, phonemes that are not in it should be subject to top-down inhibition. TRACE also predicts that targets (e.g., t) in nonwords derived from changed words (e.g., vocabutary) should be identified more slowly than targets in control nonwords (e.g., socabutary) because the actual phoneme competes with the phoneme in the real word (l) because of top-down feedback. However, there was no difference between the two nonword conditions. Cutler et al. (1987) found that phoneme monitoring latencies were faster to word-initial phonemes than to phonemes at the start of nonwords. According to the TRACE model there should be no difference for phonemes at the start of words and nonwords as activation will not have had time to build up and feed back to the phoneme level.

TRACE is also unable to account for the findings from subcategorical mismatch experiments (Marslen-Wilson & Warren, 1994). This task involves cross-splicing the initial consonants and consonant clusters from matched pairs of words (e.g., "job" and "smob"). Marslen-Wilson and Warren examined the effect of splicing on lexical decision (is it a word?) and phoneme categorization (what sort of sound did you hear?). The effect of the cross-splice on nonwords was much greater when the spliced material came from a word (e.g., an item like "smob," where the "sm-" component came from the word "smog"), such that performance was poorer when the cross-spliced nonword came from a word, but the splicing made little difference to the processing of words. These data are difficult for many models. They are difficult for independent race models because decisions about nonwords can only be made by the prelexical route, and therefore should be unaffected by the lexical status of the items from which the materials are derived. They are difficult for TRACE because simulations in TRACE show that words should be affected as well as nonwords, and in nonwords the inhibitory effect should be greater than it actually is. TRACE does poorly because it cannot use data about the mismatch between two items.

TRACE is successful in accounting for a number of phenomena in speech recognition, and is particularly good at explaining context effects. Its weakness is that the extent to which its predictions are supported by data is questionable.

Other connectionist models of speech recognition

Recent networks use recurrent connections from the hidden layer to a context to store information about previous states of the network (Elman, 1990) (see Figure 9.6). This modification enables networks to encode information about time. Hence, they give a much more plausible account of the time-based nature of speech processing than does TRACE, which uses fixed time-based units and therefore finds it difficult to cope with variations in speech rate.

Gaskell and Marslen-Wilson (1997, 1998, 2002) extended the cohort model to model the process that maps between phonological and lexical information. They constructed a connectionist model that emphasized the distributed nature of lexical representations (unlike TRACE, which uses local representation) so that information about any one word is distributed across a large number of processing units. The other important way in which it differed from other connectionist models such as TRACE is that low-level speech information, represented by phonetic features, is mapped directly onto lexical forms. There are no additional levels of phonological processing involved (although there is a layer of hidden units mediating between the feature inputs and the semantic and phonological output layers).

Gaskell and Marslen-Wilson's model simulated several important aspects of speech processing. First, it gave a good account of the time course of lexical access. It showed that multiple candidates could become activated in parallel. The target word only becomes strongly differentiated from its competitors close to its uniqueness point. Second, the model successfully simulated the experimental data of Marslen-Wilson and Warren (1994). Third, unlike other connectionist models such as TRACE, and like humans, their model shows very little tolerance. As in Marslen-Wilson and Warren's (1994) experiment, a nonword such as "smob" that matches a word quite closely ("smog") except for the place of articulation of the final segment, and which is constructed so that the vowels are consistent with the proper target, does not in fact activate the lexical representation of the word ("smog") very much. The network requires a great deal of phonetic detail to access words—just like humans. Gaskell and Marslen-Wilson propose that this feature of the model is a consequence of the realistic way in which the inputs are presented (with words embedded in a stream of speech), and the training of the network on a large number of similar phonological forms. These features force the network to be intolerant about the classification of inputs. Fourth, because words are represented in a way such that similar items overlap in their representations, competition between similar items is an essential part of processing. The simultaneous activation of more than one candidate creates conflict. Gaskell and Marslen-Wilson present a series of experiments using cross-modal priming that show that competition reduces the magnitude of the semantic

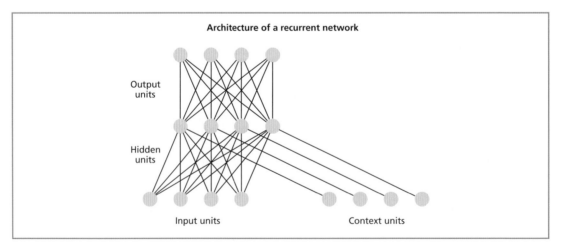

Architecture of a recurrent network

Output units

Hidden units

Input units   Context units

FIGURE 9.6

priming effect. When a word is still ambiguous, for example "capt-," which could be either "captain" or "captive," it is not particularly effective at priming "ship"; it only becomes effective relatively late, after we have reached the word's uniqueness point. Note though that "capt-" still produces some priming; you can access meaning prior to the uniqueness point, which allows some facilitation of semantically related words, but as you cannot get complete access, semantic priming is weaker than after the uniqueness point. Finally, the model accounts for the different pattern of effects found in cross-modal repetition priming and cross-modal semantic priming. Gaskell and Marslen-Wilson argue that the amount of competition between words depends on the coherence of the competing set. The candidates activated by a partial sound input will necessarily sound similar (e.g., captain and captive): the candidate set is coherent. In contrast the semantic properties of the candidate words will be unrelated. Hence repetition priming can make direct use of the set of lexical candidates directly activated by the input (e.g., "capt-" is closely related to "captain" and "captive"). Semantic priming cannot do so, as it generates multiple unrelated candidate items; the candidate words related to the prime "capt-" include "ship" and "prisoner," which are unrelated—this set is incoherent. Furthermore, with incoherent candidate sets, the more candidates there are, the more competition there will be, while with coherent sets, the number of candidates matters much less, and hence priming should be less affected by the cohort set size. Hence competition effects should be much more prominent in cross-modal semantic priming than in repetition priming, and more sensitive to cohort set size—which is just what was found.

Norris (1990) showed that recurrent networks can identify spoken words at their uniqueness points, and can also cope with variations in speech rate. However, he noted that, unlike TRACE, recurrent networks cannot recover if they misidentify parts of words. They have no way of undoing early decisions about parts of words in a way that TRACE manages to do through competition between whole words. Norris's (1994b) SHORTLIST model tries to combine the best of both approaches, with a hybrid architecture where a recurrent network provides input to an interactive activation network (see Figure 9.7).

The SHORTLIST model is entirely bottom-up and is based on a vocabulary of tens of thousands of words. Essentially the model views spoken word recognition as a bottom-up race between similar words. A competition network is created "on the fly" from the output of a bottom-up recognition network in which candidates detected in the incoming speech stream are allowed to compete with each other. Only a few words are active enough to be used in the list (hence the name). The main drawback of this approach concerns the plausibility of creating a new competitive network at each time step (Protopapas, 1999).

Given that they argue there is no top-down feedback in speech recognition, Norris, McQueen, and Cutler (2000) propose a purely data-driven model. They call this model MERGE. MERGE is a competition-activation model similar to SHORTLIST. In the MERGE model, activation flows from the prelexical level to the lexicon and to phoneme-decision nodes. Crucially, there is no feedback between the lexical nodes and the prelexical nodes. However, lexical information can influence the phoneme-decision nodes. Decisions are made on the basis of merging

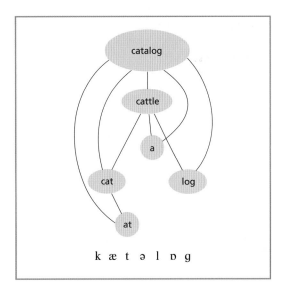

FIGURE 9.7 The pattern of inhibitory connections between candidate words in the SHORTLIST model (Norris, 1994b). Only the subset of candidates that completely match the input are shown. From Norris (1994b).

these two inputs. Norris et al. provide simulations that show that such a model does a good job of accounting for a wide range of experimental data. Critics (see commentary in Norris et al.) argue that merging is a form of interaction, as the phoneme-decision nodes are influenced by lexical information, and the MERGE is a model specifically about phoneme-decision tasks rather than a general model of speech recognition.

Comparison of models of spoken word recognition

Let us look again at the three phases of speech recognition we identified and see what the different models we have examined so far have to say about them. When we hear speech, we have to do two things. We have to segment the speech stream into words, and we have to recognize those words. The amount of speech needed to compute the contact representation determines when initial contact can occur. According to Klatt (1989), contact can be made after the first 10 ms. Models that use syllables to locate possible word onsets, and which need larger units of speech, will obviously take longer before they can access the lexicon. Different models also emphasize how representations make contact with the lexicon. Hence in the cohort model, the beginning of the word (the first 150 ms) is used to make first contact. In other models (e.g., Grosjean & Gee, 1987), the more salient or reliable parts of the word, such as the most stressed syllable, are used. All of these models where initial contact is used to generate a subset of lexical entries have the disadvantage that it is difficult to recover from a mistake (e.g., a mishearing). Models such as TRACE, where there is not a unique contact for each word, do not suffer from these problems. Each identified phoneme—the whole word—contributes to the set of active lexical entries. The cost of this is that these sets may be very large and this might be computationally costly.

The revised cohort model negates the problem of recovering from catastrophic early mistakes by allowing gradual activation of candidates rather than all-or-none activation. Furthermore, we have seen that while the beginnings of words are important in lexical access, the rhyme parts

produce no priming. On the other hand, the evidence for the amount of interaction that TRACE entails is limited.

The Gaskell and Marslen-Wilson model is very similar to the SHORTLIST model of Norris (1994b). Both models differ from TRACE in making less use of top-down inhibition and more use of bottom-up information. SHORTLIST combines the advantages of recurrent nets and TRACE. At present, these types of connectionist model show how models of spoken word recognition are likely to develop, although SHORTLIST currently suffers from the problem that it is not clear how interactive activation networks can be set up quickly "on the fly."

Virtually all models of word recognition view spoken word recognition as incorporating an element of competition between the target word and its neighbors. Therefore priming a word should retard recognition of another sharing the same initial sounds (Monsell & Hirsh, 1998). Unfortunately, the bulk of the research has shown either facilitation or no effect of priming phonologically related items, rather than the expected inhibition. Why might this be? Monsell and Hirsh pointed out that in these studies the lag between the prime and the probe is very brief. It is possible that any inhibitory effects are cancelled out by short-acting facilitatory effects generated by other factors, such as processing shared sublexical constituents (such as phonemes or rimes). If this is the case, then inhibition should be apparent at longer time lags, when the short-lived facilitatory effects have had time to die away. This is what Monsell and Hirsh observed. In an auditory lexical decision task, with time lags of 1–5 minutes between prime and target, the response time for a monosyllabic word preceded by a word sharing its onset and vowel (e.g., "chat" and "chap") increased relative to an unprimed control. Similarly, response time increased for polysyllabic words preceded by another sharing the first syllable (e.g., "beacon" and "beaker"). The effect was limited to word primes—nonword primes (e.g., "chass" and "beacal") did not produce this inhibition. Hence priming phonological competitors does indeed retard the subsequent recognition of items, but the effect is only manifest when other short-term facilitatory effects have died down.

Finally, we make use of other types of information when understanding speech. Even people with normal hearing can make some use of lip-reading. McGurk and MacDonald (1976) showed participants a video of someone saying "ba" repeatedly, but gave them a soundtrack with "ga" repeated. Participants reported hearing "da," apparently blending the visual and auditory information. This effect suggests that speech perception is the result of the best guess of the whole perceptual system, using multiple sources of information, among which speech is usually the most important.

THE NEUROSCIENCE OF SPOKEN WORD RECOGNITION

Some difficulty in speech recognition is quite common in adults with a disturbance of language functions following brain damage. Varney (1984) reported that 18% of such patients had some problem in discriminating speech sounds. Brain damage can affect most levels of the word recognition process, including access to the prelexical and the postlexical codes.

There are many cases of patients who have difficulty in constructing the prelexical code. Caplan (1992) reviews these. For example, brain damage can affect the earliest stages of acoustic-phonetic processing of features such as voice onset time, or the later stages involving the identification of sounds based on these features (Blumstein, Cooper, Zurif, & Caramazza, 1977). Neuropsychological evidence suggests that vowels and consonants are processed by different systems. Caramazza, Chialant, Capasso, and Miceli (2000) describe two Italian-speaking aphasic patients who show selective difficulties in producing vowels and consonants. Patient AS produced mainly errors on vowels, while patient IFA produced mainly errors on consonants. These differences remained even when other possible confounding factors (such as the degree of sonority—essentially the amount of acoustic energy in a sound) were taken into account.

Patients with pure word deafness can speak, read, and write quite normally, but cannot understand speech, even though their hearing is otherwise normal (see Saffran, Marin, & Yeni-Komshian, 1976, for a case history). Patients with pure word deafness cannot repeat speech and have extremely poor auditory comprehension. They are impaired at tasks such as distinguishing stop consonants from each other (e.g., /pa/ from /ba/ and /ga/ from /ka/). On the other hand Saffran et al.'s patient could identify musical instruments and non-speech noises, and could identify the gender and language of a recorded voice. This pattern of performance suggests that these people suffer from disruption to a prelexical, acoustic processing mechanism. A very rare and controversial variant of this is called word meaning deafness. Patients with word meaning deafness show the symptoms of pure word deafness but have intact repetition abilities. The most famous case of this was a patient living in Edinburgh in the 1890s (Bramwell, 1897/1984), although more recent cases have been reported by Franklin, Howard, and Patterson (1994), and Kohn and Friedman (1986). Pure word deafness shows that we can produce words without necessarily being able to understand them.

Only one patient (EDE) clearly showed intact acoustic-phonetic processing (and therefore the ability to construct a prelexical code), but also then had difficulties with lexical access (Berndt & Mitchum, 1990). This patient performed well on all tests of phoneme discrimination and acoustic processing, yet made many errors in deciding whether a string of sounds made up a word or not (e.g., "horse" is a word, but "hort" is not). Nevertheless EDE generally performed well on routine language comprehension tasks, and Berndt and Mitchum interpreted her difficulties with this particular task in terms of a short-term memory deficit rather than of lexical access. As yet there have been no reports of patients who have completely intact phonetic processing but who cannot access the postlexical code. This might be because so far we have not looked hard enough, or perhaps have just been unlucky.

SUMMARY

- We can recognize meaningful speech faster and more efficiently than we can identify non-speech sounds.
- Sounds run together (the segmentation problem), and vary depending on the context in which they occur (the invariance problem).
- The way in which we segment speech depends on the language we speak.
- We use a number of strategies to segment speech; stress-based segmentation is particularly important in English.
- Consonants are classified categorically, but it is unclear how early in perception this effect arises, because listeners are sensitive to differences between sounds within a category.
- The lexicon is our mental dictionary.
- The prelexical code is the sound representation used to access the lexicon.
- There is controversy about whether phonemes are represented directly in the prelexical code, or whether they are constructed after we access the lexicon.
- Studies of co-articulation effects in words and nonwords suggest that a low-level phonetic representation is used to access the lexicon directly.
- The lexical identification shift of ambiguous phonemes varies depending on the lexical context.
- Phonemes masked by noise can be restored by an appropriate context.
- There has been debate about whether the lexical identification shift and phoneme restoration effects are truly perceptual effects or instead reflect later processing.
- Word recognition can be divided into initial contact, lexical selection, and word recognition phases.
- A spoken word's uniqueness point is when the stream of sounds is finally unambiguously distinguishable from all other words.
- We recognize the word at its recognition point; the recognition point does not have to correspond to the uniqueness point.
- Although the extent to which top-down sentential context has an effect on the early stages of word recognition is controversial, the preponderance of evidence suggests that context only has its effects after lexical access.
- Early models of speech recognition included template matching and analysis-by-synthesis.
- According to the cohort model of word recognition, when we hear a word a group of candidates—the cohort—is set up; as further evidence arrives, the cohort is reduced until only one word remains.
- Later revisions of the cohort model introduced the idea of graded activation rather than all-or-none membership of the cohort, and reduced the role of contextual effects.
- Evidence for the cohort model comes from studies of fluent restorations in speech, listening for mispronunciations, and studies using the gating and cross-modal priming techniques.
- The lexical neighborhood comprises all words that sound like a particular word, and can have effects on its recognition.
- TRACE is a highly interactive connectionist model of spoken word recognition.
- The main difficulty with TRACE is that it assumes more interaction than there is evidence for.
- Models such as SHORTLIST show how bottom-up, data-driven connectionist models can account for most of the major findings of speech processing research.
- Vowels and consonants are processed by different systems.
- People with pure word deafness cannot understand speech even though their hearing is otherwise unimpaired and they can read and write quite well.
- People with the rare disorder known as word meaning deafness cannot understand speech even though they can repeat it back.

QUESTIONS TO THINK ABOUT

1. What particular processing problems might people with a different dialect cause a listener?
2. Why might mishearings occur?
3. What sort of special problems might code switching by bilinguals create for speech recognition by their listeners?
4. What are the main differences between the cohort and SHORTLIST models of spoken word recognition?

FURTHER READING

Luce (1993) is an introduction to acoustics, the low-level processes of hearing, and how the ear works. See MacMillan and Creelman (1991) for an introduction to signal detection theory. See Ward (2010, Chapter 10) for a description of the neuroscience of auditory processing. Remez and Pisoni (2005) is an edited collection that covers the whole field of speech perception and spoken word recognition.

The classic textbook by Clark and Clark (1977) has a good description of the earlier models of speech perception, particularly analysis-by-synthesis. The paper by Frauenfelder and Tyler (1987) in a special issue on spoken word recognition in the journal *Cognition* is an introduction to the issues involved in spoken word recognition. Two collections of papers on speech processing are to be found in Altmann (1990) and Altmann and Shillcock (1993). Altmann (1997) provides excellent coverage of speech perception, particularly on the importance of sound perception by infants and other species.

Ellis and Humphreys (1999) review connectionist models of speech processing. Massaro (1989) provides a critique of connectionist models in general and TRACE in particular. Norris (1994b) is a good summary of the problems with TRACE, and see Protopapas (1999) for a review of connectionist models of speech perception. Grosjean and Frauenfelder (1996) review the methods commonly used to study spoken word recognition. For a review of the literature on speech recognition, with the conclusion that speech perception is bottom-up and data-driven, see Norris, McQueen, and Cutler (2000), with commentaries.

SECTION D

MEANING AND USING LANGUAGE

This section examines the processes of comprehension. How do we extract meaning from what we read or hear and make use of word order information? How do we represent and make use of the meaning of words and sentences?

Chapter 10, Understanding the structure of sentences, tackles the complexities of sentence interpretation and parsing. Once we have recognized words, how do we decide between all the different roles the words can take—who is doing what to whom? (You may find it useful to read Chapter 2 again before starting Chapter 10.)

Chapter 11, Word meaning, examines issues involved in the study of semantics, in particular how we represent the meanings of individual words. Categorization, associations between words, use of metaphor and idiom, and connectionist modeling of semantics are among the topics addressed.

Chapter 12, Comprehension, looks at what follows after we have identified words and built the syntactic structure of a sentence. What do we remember of text that we read or hear? How do we know when to draw inferences or move beyond the literal meaning of the text? This chapter also addresses the specific problems inherent in understanding spoken conversation.

CHAPTER 10

UNDERSTANDING THE STRUCTURE OF SENTENCES

INTRODUCTION

I'm going to be honest here; most students find this chapter difficult, and many say they can't see the point of parsing. But how do you tell the difference between "Vlad killed Boris" and "Vlad was killed by Boris"? And when you hear "I saw the Pennines flying to Dundee," why don't you think, "Cor, those Pennines are overhead on their way to Dundee again." And when you come across sentences such as "The cop shot the burglar the gun," how do you know just who had a gun? These are details that give language its fantastic expressive power.

So far we have largely been concerned with the processing of individual words. What happens after we recognize a word? When we access the lexical entry for a word, two major types of information become available: information about the word's meaning, and information about the syntactic and thematic roles that the word can take. The goal of sentence interpretation is to assign thematic roles to words in the sentence being processed—who is doing what to whom (see Box 10.1). One of the most important guides to thematic roles comes from an analysis of the **verb**'s **argument structure** (sometimes called subcategorization frame). For example, the verb "give" has the structure AGENT gives THEME to RECIPIENT (e.g., "Vlad gave the ring to Agnes"). Hence verbs and their argument structures play a central role in **parsing**. Indeed, people are likely to identify sentences as being similar on the basis of the main verb rather than on the basis of the subject of the sentence,

with argument structure being particularly important (Bencini & Goldberg, 2000; Healy & Miller, 1970). To assign thematic roles, at least some of the time we must compute the syntactic structure of the sentence, a process known as parsing. The first step in parsing is to determine the syntactic category to which each word in the sentence belongs (e.g., noun, verb, adjective, adverb, and so on). We then combine those categories to form phrases. An important step in parsing is to determine the subject of the sentence (what the sentence is about). From such information about individual words we start to construct a representation of the meaning of the sentence we are reading or hearing. This chapter is about the process of assembling this representation.

Box 10.1 Thematic roles	
Agent	The instigator of an action (corresponding to the subject, usually animate)
Theme	The thing that has a particular location or change of location
Recipient	The person receiving the theme
Location	Where the theme is
Source	Where the theme is coming from
Goal	Where the theme is moving to
Time	Time of the event
Instrument	The thing used in causing the event

When we hear and understand a sentence, information about the word order is often crucial (at least in languages such as English). This is information about the syntax of the sentence. Sentences (1) and (2) have the same word order structure but different meanings; (1) and (3) have different word order structures but the same meaning:

(1) The ghost chased the vampire.
(2) The vampire chased the ghost.
(3) The vampire was chased by the ghost.

A number of important questions arise about parsing and the human sentence parsing mechanism. How does parsing operate? Why are some sentences more difficult to parse than others? What happens to the syntactic representation after parsing? Why are sentences assigned the structures that they are? How many stages of parsing are there? What principles guide the operation of these stages? What happens if there is a choice of possible structures at any point? At what stage is non-structural (semantic, discourse, and frequency-based) information used? This last question is another manifestation of the issue of whether language processes are modular or not. Is there an enclosed syntactic module that uses only syntactic information to parse a sentence, or can other types of information guide the parsing process? Any account of parsing must be able to specify why sentences are assigned the structure that they are, why we are biased to parse structurally ambiguous sentences in a certain way, and why some sentences are harder to parse than others.

We should distinguish between autonomous and interactive models of parsing, and one-stage and two-stage models. In autonomous models, the initial stages of parsing at least can only use syntactic information to construct a syntactic representation. According to interactive models, other sources of information (e.g., semantic information) can influence the syntactic processor at an early stage.

In one-stage models, syntactic and semantic information are both used to construct the syntactic representation in one go. In two-stage models, the first stage is invariably seen as an autonomous stage of syntactic processing. Semantic information is used only in the second stage. Hence the question about the number of stages is really the same question as whether parsing is modular or interactive.

The goal of understanding is to extract the meaning from what we hear or read. Syntactic processing is only one stage in doing this, but it is nevertheless an important one. Whether it is always an essential one is an important issue. There is, however, another reason why we should study syntax. Fodor (1975) argued that there is a "language of thought" that bears a close resemblance to our surface language. In particular, the syntax that governs the language of thought may be very similar or identical to that of external language. Studying syntax may therefore provide a window onto fundamental cognitive processes.

Different languages use different syntactic rules. English in particular is a strongly configurational language whose interpretation depends heavily on word order. In inflectional languages such as German, word order is less important. It is therefore possible that the predominance of studies that have examined parsing in English may have given a misleading view of how human parsing operates. For this reason, an important recent development has been the study of parsing in languages other than English. Most psycholinguists hope and expect that the important parsing mechanisms will be common to speakers of all languages. By the end of this chapter you should:

- Know that parsing is incremental.
- Understand how we assign syntactic structures to ambiguous sentences.
- Be able to evaluate the extent to which parsing is autonomous or interactive.
- Understand the importance of verbs in parsing.
- Understand how brain damage can disrupt parsing.

DEALING WITH STRUCTURAL AMBIGUITY

My local newspaper, *The Dundee Courier*, recently had a headline that read "Police seek orange attackers." Do you think that the headline meant "Police seek attackers who are orange," "Police seek attackers of an orange," or "Police seek attackers who attacked with an orange"? (It was meant to be the last of these.) Here is another example: "Enraged cow injures farmer with axe." In this example the ambiguity arises because the **prepositional phrase** "with axe" could be attached to either "farmer" or "injures"; that is, there are two possible structures for this sentence. So, as well as being poorly written, these sentences are ambiguous.

It is difficult to discern the operations of the processor when all is working well. For this reason, most research on parsing has involved syntactic ambiguity because ambiguity causes processing difficulty. Studying syntactic ambiguity is an excellent way of discovering how sentence processing works.

There are different types of ambiguity involving more than one word. We have the bracketing ambiguity of example (4), which could be interpreted either in the sense of (5) or in the sense of (6):

(4)   old men and women leave first
(5)   ([old men] and women)
(6)   (old [men and women])

More complex are structural ambiguities associated with parsing, such as in sentence (7). What was done yesterday—Boris saying or Vlad finishing? Although both structures are equally plausible in (7), this is not the case in (8):

(7)   Boris said that Vlad finished it yesterday.
(8)   I saw the Alps flying to Romania.

Many of us would not initially recognize a sentence such as (8) as ambiguous. On consideration, this might be because one of its two meanings is so semantically anomalous (the interpretation that I looked up and saw a mountain range in the sky flying to a country) that it does not appear even to be considered. But psychology has shown us many times that we cannot rely on our intuitions. Recording eye movements has been particularly important in studying parsing. The bulk of evidence shows that we spend no longer

reading the ambiguous regions of sentences than the unambiguous regions of control sentences, but we often spend longer in reading the disambiguation region.

The central issue in parsing is when different types of information are used. In principle there are two alternative parse trees that could be constructed for (8). We could construct one of them on purely syntactic grounds, and then decide using semantic information whether it makes sense or not. If it does, we accept that representation; if it does not, we go back and try again. This is a serial autonomous model. Alternatively, we could construct all possible syntactic representations in parallel, again using solely syntactic information, and then use semantic or other information to choose the most appropriate one (Mitchell, 1994). This would be a parallel autonomous model. Or we could use semantic information from the earliest stages to guide parsing so that we only construct semantically plausible syntactic representations. Or we could activate representations of all possible analyses, with the level of activation affected by the plausibility of each. The final two are versions of an interactive model.

So far we have just looked at examples of permanent (also called global) ambiguity. In these cases, when you get to the end of the sentence it is still syntactically ambiguous. Many sentences are locally (or temporarily, or transiently) ambiguous, but the ambiguity is disambiguated (or resolved) by subsequent material (the disambiguation region). We are sometimes made forcefully aware of temporary ambiguity when we appear to have chosen an incorrect syntactic representation. Consider (9) from Bever (1970). The verb "raced" is ambiguous in that it could be a main verb (the most frequent sense) or a past **participle** (a word derived from a verb acting as an adjective):

(9)   The horse raced past the barn fell.
(10) The log floated past the bridge sank.
(11) The ship sailed round the Cape sank.
(12) The old man the boats.

When you hear or read a sentence like (9), it can be interpreted in a straightforward way until the final unexpected word "fell." When we come across the last word we realize that we have been led up the garden path. We realize that our original analysis was wrong and we have to go back and reanalyze. We have the experience of having to backtrack. We then arrive at the interpretation of "The horse that was raced past the barn was the one that fell." (Some people take some time to work out what the correct interpretation is.) That is, we initially try to parse it as a simple noun phrase followed by a verb phrase. In fact, it contains a **reduced relative** clause. (A **relative clause** is one that modifies the main noun, and it is "reduced" because it lacks the relative pronoun "which" or "that.") Examples (10), (11), and (12) should also lead you up the garden path. **Garden path sentence**s are favorite tools of researchers interested in parsing.

Many people might think that garden path sentences are rather odd: Often there would be pauses in normal speech and commas in written language, which, although strictly optional, are usually there to prevent the ambiguity in the first place. For example, Rayner and Frazier (1987) intentionally omitted punctuation in order to mislead the participants' processors. Deletion of the **complementizer** "that" can also produce misleading results (Trueswell, Tanenhaus, & Kello, 1993). In such cases it might be possible that these sentences are not telling us as much about normal parsing as we think. In fact, reduced relatives are surprisingly common; "that" was omitted in 33% of sentences containing relative

Garden path sentences, such as "The horse raced past the barn fell," are favorite tools of researchers interested in parsing.

clauses in a sample from the *Wall Street Journal* (Elsness, 1984; Garnsey, Pearlmutter, Myers, & Lotocky, 1997; McDavid, 1964; Thompson & Mulac, 1991). There is evidence that appropriate punctuation such as commas can reduce (but not obliterate) the magnitude of the garden path effect by enhancing the reader's awareness of the phrasal structure (Hill & Murray, 2000; Mitchell & Holmes, 1985). In real life, speakers give prosodic cues to provide disambiguating information, and listeners are sensitive to this type of information; for example, speakers tend to emphasize the direct-object nouns, and insert pauses akin to punctuation (Snedeker & Trueswell, 2003). Similarly, disfluencies influence the way in which people interpret garden path sentences. When an interruption (saying "uh") comes before an unambiguous noun phrase, listeners are more likely to think that the noun phrase is the subject of a new clause rather than the object of an old one (Bailey & Ferreira, 2003). Disfluencies can help, but only as long as they are in the right place. They are helpful in (13) where they correctly flag a new subject, but not in (14), where they do not.

(13) Vlad bumped into the ghost and the (um) ghoul told him to be careful.

(14) Vlad bumped into the (um) ghost and the ghoul told him to be careful.

However, just because speakers give prosodic cues, and listeners make use of these cues, does not mean that speakers always mean to give these cues for the express purpose of helping the listener (what has been called the **audience design** hypothesis). Speakers are not always aware that what they are saying is ambiguous, and they tend to produce the same cues even when there is no audience (Kraljic & Brennan, 2005). Prosody and pauses probably reflect both the planning needs of the speaker (see Chapter 13) as well as a deliberate source of information to aid the listener.

Perhaps even more tellingly, McKoon and Ratcliff (2003) showed that sentences with reduced relatives with verbs like "race" (e.g., (9)) occur in natural language with near-zero probability. So, although such sentences might technically be syntactically correct, most people find these sorts of sentence unacceptable. Indeed, McKoon and Ratcliff go so far as to argue that sentences with reduced relatives with verbs similar to "race" are ungrammatical. Hence considerable caution is necessary when drawing conclusions about the syntactic processor from studies of garden path sentences.

At first sight, our experience of garden path sentences is evidence for a serial autonomous processor. But what has led us up the garden path? We could have been taken there by either semantic or syntactic factors. There has been a great deal of research on trying to decide which. According to the serial autonomy model, we experience the garden path effect because the single syntactic representation we are constructing on syntactic grounds turns out to be incorrect. According to the parallel autonomy model, one representation is much more active than the others because of the strength of the syntactic cues, but this turns out to be wrong. According to the interactive model, various sources of information support the analysis more than its alternative. However, later information is inconsistent with these initial activation levels.

EARLY WORK ON PARSING

Early models of parsing were based on Chomsky's theory of generative grammar. In particular, psychologists tested the idea that understanding sentences involved retrieving their deep structure. As it became apparent that this could not provide a complete account of parsing, emphasis shifted to examining strategies based on the surface structure of sentences.

For early psycholinguists still influenced by ideas from transformational grammar such as the autonomy of syntax, the process of language understanding was a simple story (e.g., Fodor, Bever, & Garrett, 1974). First, we identify the words on the basis of perceptual data. Recognition and lexical access give us access to the syntactic category of the words. We can use this information to build a parse tree for each clause. It is only when each clause is completely analyzed that we finally start to build a semantic representation of the sentence. It is often said that "syntax proposes; semantics disposes." The simplest approach treats syntax as an independent or autonomous processing module: Only syntactic information is used to construct the parse tree. Is this true?

What size are the units of parsing?

What are the constituents used in parsing, and how big are they? Jarvella (1971) showed that listeners only begin to purge memory of the details of syntactic constituents after a sentence boundary has been passed (see Chapter 12 for more details). Once a sentence has been processed, verbatim memory for it fades away very quickly. Hence, perhaps not surprisingly, the sentence is a major processing unit. Beneath this, the clause also turns out to be an important unit. A clause is a part of a sentence that has both a subject and predicate. Furthermore, people find material easier to read a line at a time if each line corresponds to a major constituent (Anderson, 2010; Graf & Torrey, 1966). There is a clause boundary effect in recalling words: it is easiest to recall words from within the clause currently being processed, independent of the number of words in the clause (Caplan, 1972). The processing load is highest at the end of the clause, and eye fixations are longer on the final word of a clause (Just & Carpenter, 1980).

One of the first techniques used to explore the size of the syntactic unit in parsing was the click displacement technique (Fodor & Bever, 1965; Garrett, Bever, & Fodor, 1966). The basic idea was that major processing units resist interruption: We finish what we are doing, and then process other material at the first suitable opportunity. Participants heard speech over headphones in one ear, and at certain points in the sentence, extraneous clicks were presented in the other ear. Even if the click falls in the middle of a real constituent, it should be perceived as falling at a constituent boundary. That is, the clicks should appear to migrate according to listeners' reports. This is what was observed:

(15) That he was* happy was evident from the way he smiled.

For example, a click presented at * in (15) migrated to after the end of the word "happy." This is at the end of a major constituent, at the end of the clause. The original study claimed to show that the clause is a major perceptual unit. The same results were found when all non-syntactic perceptual cues, such as intonation and pauses, were removed. This suggests that the clause is a major unit of perceptual and syntactic processing.

However, this interpretation is premature. The participants' task is a complex one: They have to perceive the sentence, parse it, understand it, remember it, and give their response. Click migration could occur at any of these points, not just perception or parsing. Reber and Anderson (1970) carried out a variant of the technique in which participants listened to sentences that actually had no clicks at all. They were told that it was an experiment on subliminal perception, and were asked to say where they thought the clicks occurred. Participants still placed the non-existent clicks at constituent boundaries. This suggested that click migration occurs in the response stage: Participants are intuitively aware of the existence of constituent boundaries and have a response bias to put clicks there. Wingfield and Klein (1971) showed that the size of the migration effect is greatly reduced if participants can point to places in the sentence on a visual display at the same time as they hear them, rather than having to remember them. It was also unclear whether intonation and pausing are as unimportant in determining structural boundaries as was originally claimed.

Hence these early studies probably reflect the operations of memory rather than the operations of syntactic processing. It is now agreed that parsing is largely an incremental process—we try to build structures on a word-by-word basis. That is, we do not sit idly by while we wait for the clause to finish. The experiments of Marslen-Wilson (1973, 1975) and Marslen-Wilson and Welsh (1978; see Chapter 9 for details) demonstrate that we try to integrate each word into a semantic representation as soon as possible. Many studies have shown that syntactic and semantic analysis is incremental (Just & Carpenter, 1980; Tyler & Marslen-Wilson, 1977). For example, Traxler and Pickering (1996) found that readers' processing

was disrupted immediately after they read the word "shot" in (16). The immediate disruption means that they must have processed the sentence syntactically and semantically up to that point. However, syntactic effects are often delayed so that they occur a few words later.

(16)   That is the very small pistol with which the heartless killer shot the hapless man yesterday afternoon.

Not only do people construct the representation incrementally, they try to anticipate what is coming next. In an experiment with Dutch speakers, van Berkum, Brown, Zwitserlood, Kooijman, and Hagoort (2005) examined the ERPs of people listening to stories. The stories led people to expect specific nouns. However, if participants then heard a gender-marked adjective immediately before the expected noun, and the gender was not the right match for the expected noun, the inconsistent adjectives elicited a marked ERP.

Indeed, people even anticipate properties of upcoming words in the sentence, so that, for example, the argument structure of a verb can be used to anticipate the subsequent theme (Altmann & Kamide, 1999). For example, the verb "drink" requires that the direct object is something drinkable; this information is used to predict what is coming next, and people only pay attention to drinkable things thereafter (as measured by their eye movements while looking at a picture). That is, people make anticipatory eye movements towards probable upcoming objects. In a related experiment, Kamide, Altmann, and Haywood (2003) tracked the eye movements of people looking at a visual scene. They found that people anticipated a great deal of information, even with more complex verb structures. For example, given a picture containing a man and a slice of bread, on hearing "The woman will spread the butter –" people make anticipatory eye movements to the bread when they hear butter, but to the man when they hear "The woman will slide the butter –." In general, language processing interacts with the representation of a visual scene so linguistic information can determine where we look next (Altmann & Kamide, 2009). The conclusion is that the processor draws on different sources of information, some of them non-linguistic, at the earliest opportunity, to construct as full an interpretation as possible.

We saw earlier that Chomsky's description of language placed great emphasis on the hierarchical and recursive nature of syntactic structure. There is, however, debate as to which hierarchical structure is actually used in cognitive processing. In line with the incremental models, Frank and Bod (2011) found that reading times are best predicted by purely sequential models; people do not appear to use hierarchical structure information to predict what word is coming next.

In summary, the language processor operates incrementally: It rapidly constructs a syntactical analysis for a sentence fragment, assigns it a semantic interpretation, and relates this interpretation to world knowledge (Pickering, 1999). Any delay in this process is usually very slight. Incremental analysis makes a lot of sense from a processing point of view: Imagine having to wait until the sentence finishes or the other person stops speaking before you can begin analyzing what you have seen or heard.

Parsing strategies based on surface-structure cues

The surface structure of the sentence often provides a number of obvious cues to the underlying syntactic representation. One obvious approach is to use these cues and a number of simple strategies that enable us to compute the syntactic structure. The earliest detailed expositions of this idea were by Bever (1970) and Fodor and Garrett (1967). These researchers detailed a number of parsing strategies that used only syntactic cues. Perhaps the simplest example is that when we see or hear a determiner such as "the" or "a," we know a noun phrase has just started. A second example is based on the observation that although word order is variable in English, and transformations such as passivization can change it, the common structure noun–verb–noun often maps on to what is called the canonical sentence structure SVO (subject–verb–object). That is, in most sentences we hear or read, the first noun is the subject, and

the second one the object. In fact, if we made use of this strategy we could get a long way in comprehension. This is called the canonical sentence strategy. We try the simpler strategies first, and if these do not work, we try other ones. If the battery of surface structure strategies become exhausted by a sentence, we must try something else.

Fodor, Bever, and Garrett (1974) developed this type of approach in one of the most influential works in the history of psycholinguistics. They argued that the goal of parsing was to recover the underlying, deep structure of a sentence. As it had been shown that this was not done by explicitly undoing transformations, it must be done by perceptual heuristics; that is, using our surface structure cues. However, there is little evidence that deep structure is represented mentally independently of meaning (Johnson-Laird, 1983). Nevertheless, the general principle that when we parse we use surface structure cues has remained influential, and has been increasingly formalized.

Two early accounts of parsing

Kimball (1973) also argued that surface structure provides cues that enable us to uncover the underlying syntactic structure. He proposed seven principles of parsing to explain the behavior of the human sentence parsing mechanism. He argued that we initially compute the surface structure of a sentence guided by rules that are based on psychological constraints such as minimizing memory load. He argued that these principles explained why sentences are assigned the structure that they are, why some sentences are harder to parse than others, and why we are biased to parse many structurally ambiguous sentences in a certain way.

The first principle is that parsing is top-down, except when a conjunction (such as "and") is encountered. It means that we start from the sentence node and predict constituents. To avoid an excessive amount of backtracking, the processor employs limited lookahead of one or two words. For example, if you see that the first word of the next constituent is "the," then you know that you are parsing a noun phrase.

The second principle is called right association, which is that new words are preferentially attached to the lowest possible node in the structure constructed so far. This places less of a load on memory. Consider (17):

(17) Vlad figured that Boris wanted to take the pet rat out.

Here we attach "out" to the right-most available constituent, "take" rather than "figured." This means that although this structure is potentially ambiguous, we prefer the interpretation "take out" to "figured out" (see Figure 10.1). Right association gives English its typically right-branching structure, and it also explains why structures that are not right-branching are more difficult to understand (e.g., "the ghost who Vlad expected to leave's ball").

Kimball's third principle was new nodes. Function words signal a new phrase. The fourth principle is that the processor can only cope with nodes associated with two sentence nodes at any one time. For example, center-embedding splits up noun phrases and verb phrases associated with the sentences so that they have to be held in memory. When there are two embedded clauses, three sentence nodes will have to be kept active at once. Hence sentences of this sort, such as (18), will be difficult, but corresponding right-branching paraphrases such as (19) cause no difficulty, because the sentence nodes do not need to be kept open in memory:

(18) The vampire the ghost the witch liked loved died.
(19) The witch liked the ghost that loved the vampire that died.

The fifth principle is that of closure, which says that the processor prefers to close a phrase as soon as possible. The sixth principle is called fixed structure. Having closed a phrase, it is computationally costly to reopen it and reorganize the previously closed constituents, and so this is avoided if possible. This principle explains our difficulty with garden path sentences. The final principle is the principle of processing. When a phrase is closed it exits from short-term memory and is passed on to a second stage of deeper, semantic processing. Short-term memory has limited capacity, and details of the syntactic structure of a sentence are very quickly forgotten.

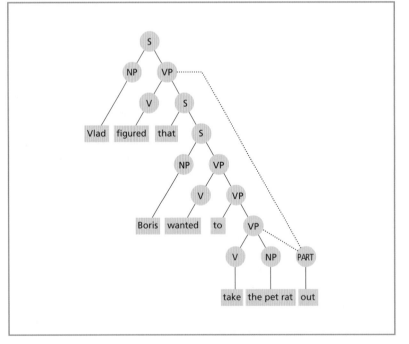

FIGURE 10.1 Alternative structures for the sentence "Vlad figured that Boris wanted to take the pet rat out," showing how right association leads us to attach "out" to the right-most verb phrase node ("take") rather than to the higher verb node ("figured"). S = sentence; NP = noun phrase; VP = verb phrase; V = verb; PART = participle.

Kimball's principles do a good job of explaining a number of properties of the processor. However, given that the principle of processing underlies so many of the others, perhaps the model can be simplified to reflect this? In addition, there are some problems with particular strategies. For example, the role of function words in parsing might not be as essential as Kimball thought. Eye fixation research shows that we may not always gaze directly at some function words: Very short words are frequently skipped (Rayner & McConkie, 1976; although we might be able to process them parafoveally—that is, we could still extract information from them even though they are not centrally located in our visual field; see Kennedy, 2000, and Rayner & Pollatsek, 1989).

Frazier and Fodor (1978) simplified Kimball's account by proposing a model they called the "sausage machine," because it divides the language input into something that looks like a link of sausages. The sausage machine is a two-stage model of parsing. The first stage is called the preliminary phrase packager, or PPP. This is followed by the sentence structure supervisor, or SSS. The PPP has a limited viewing window of about six words, and cannot attach words to structures that reflect dependencies longer than this. The SSS assembles the packets produced by the PPP, but cannot undo the work of the PPP. The idea of the limited length of the PPP, and a second stage of processing that cannot undo the work of the first, operationalizes Kimball's principle of processing. The PPP can only make use of syntactic knowledge and uses syntactic heuristics, such as preferring simpler syntactic structures if there is a choice of structures (known as minimal attachment).

Wanner (1980) pointed out a number of problems with the sausage machine model. For example, there are some six-word sentences that are triply embedded, but because they are so short, should fit easily into the PPP window, such as (20). Nevertheless, we still find them difficult to understand. There are also some six-word sentences where right association operates when minimal attachment is unable to choose between the alternatives, as they are both of equal complexity (21). Here we prefer the interpretation

"cried yesterday" to "said yesterday." The sausage machine cannot account for the preference for right association in some six-word sentences.

(20)   Vampires werewolves rats kiss love sleep.
(21)   Vlad said that Boris cried yesterday.

Fodor and Frazier (1980) conceded that right association does not arise directly from the sausage machine's architecture. They added a new principle that governs the performance of the sausage machine, which says that right association operates when minimal attachment cannot determine where a constituent should go. The sausage machine evolved into one of the most influential models of parsing, the garden path model.

PROCESSING STRUCTURAL AMBIGUITY

One of the major foci of current work on parsing is on trying to understand how we process syntactic ambiguity, because this gives us an important tool in evaluating alternative models of how the syntactic processor operates.

Two models have dominated research on parsing. The garden path model is an autonomous two-stage model, while the constraint-based model is an interactive one-stage model. Choosing between the two depends on how early discourse context, frequency, and other semantic information can be shown to influence parsing choices. Is initial attachment—the way in which syntactic constituents are attached to the growing parse tree—made on the basis of syntactic knowledge alone, or is it influenced by semantic factors?

The garden path model

According to the garden path model (e.g., Frazier, 1987a), parsing takes place in two stages. In the first stage, the processor draws only on syntactic information. If the incoming material is ambiguous, only one structure is created. Initial attachment is determined only by syntactic preferences dictated by the two principles of minimal attachment and late closure. If the results of the first pass turn out to be incompatible with further syntactic, pragmatic, or semantic and thematic information generated by an independent thematic processor, then a second pass is necessary to revise the parse tree. In the garden path model, thematic information about semantic roles can only be used in the second stage of parsing (Rayner, Carlson, & Frazier, 1983).

Two fundamental principles of parsing determine initial attachment, called minimal attachment and late closure. According to minimal attachment, incoming material should be attached to the phrase marker being constructed using the fewest nodes possible. According to late closure, incoming material should be incorporated into the clause or phrase currently being processed. If there is a conflict between these two principles, then minimal attachment takes precedence.

Constraint-based models of parsing

A type of interactive model called the constraint-based approach has become very popular (e.g., Boland, Tanenhaus, & Garnsey, 1990; MacDonald, 1994; MacDonald, Pearlmutter, & Seidenberg, 1994a; Tanenhaus, Carlson, & Trueswell, 1989; Taraban & McClelland, 1988; Trueswell et al., 1993). On this account, the processor uses multiple sources of information, including syntactic, semantic, discourse, and frequency-based, called constraints. The construction that is most strongly supported by these multiple constraints is most activated, although less plausible alternatives might also remain active. Garden paths occur when the correct analysis of a local ambiguity receives little activation.

Evidence for autonomy in syntactic processing

The garden path model says that we resolve ambiguity using minimal attachment and late closure, without semantic assistance. As (22) is consistent with late closure, it does not cause the processor any problem; (23) is not ultimately consistent with late closure, however, and the processor tries in the first instance to attach the NP "a mile and a half" to the

first verb. When we come to "seems" it is apparent that this structure is incorrect—we have been led up a garden path. In an eye-movement study, Frazier and Rayner (1982) found that the reading time was longer for (23) than (22), and in (23) the first fixation in the disambiguating region was longer.

(22)   Since Jay always jogs a mile and a half this seems a short distance to him.
(23)   Since Jay always jogs a mile and a half seems a very short distance to him.

Rayner and Frazier (1987) monitored participants' eye movements while they read sentences such as (24) and (25).

(24)   The criminal confessed his sins harmed many people.
(25)   The criminal confessed that his sins harmed many people.

When we start to read (24), minimal attachment leads to the adoption of the structure that contains the fewest number of nodes. Hence when we get to "his sins" the simplest analysis is that "his sins" is the object of "confessed," rather than the more complex analysis that it is the subject of the complement clause (as later turns out to be the case). Readers should therefore be led up the garden path in (24), and will then be forced to reanalyze when they come to "harmed." However, (25) should not lead to a garden path, because "that" blocks the object analysis of the sentence. Rayner and Frazier found that participants did indeed experience difficulty when they reached "harmed" in (24) but not in (25).

Ferreira and Clifton (1986) described an experiment that suggests that semantic factors cannot prevent us from being garden-pathed. Garden path theory predicts that, because of minimal attachment, when we come across the word "examined" we should take it to be the main verb in (26) and (27) rather than the verb in a reduced relative clause:

(26)   The defendant examined by the lawyer turned out to be unreliable.
(27)   The evidence examined by the lawyer turned out to be unreliable.

Consider what sorts of structure we might have generated by the time we get to the word "examined" in (26) and (27). "Examined" requires an agent. In (26), "the defendant" is animate and can therefore fulfill the role of agent, as in "the defendant examined the evidence"; but of course, "the defendant" can also be what is examined, so the syntactic structure is ambiguous between a reduced relative clause and a main verb analysis. In (27) "the evidence" is inanimate and therefore cannot fulfill the role of the agent; it must be what is examined, and therefore this structure can only be a reduced relative. However, analysis of eye-movement evidence suggested that the semantic evidence available in sentences such as (27) did not prevent participants from getting garden-pathed. Instead, we still appear to construct the initial interpretation to be the syntactically most simple according to minimal attachment. Ferreira and Clifton argued that semantic information does not prevent or cause garden-pathing, but can hasten recovery from it. The difficulty caused by the ambiguity is very short in duration, and is resolved while reading the word following the verb, "by" (Clifton & Ferreira, 1989).

Mitchell (1987), on the basis of data from a self-paced reading task (where participants read a computer display and press a key every time they are ready for a new word or phrase), concluded that the initial stage only makes use of part-of-speech information, and that detailed information from the verb only affects the second, evaluative, stage of processing. Consider sentences (28) and (29). In (28), according to garden path theory, the processor prefers to assign the phrase "the doctor" as direct object of "visited" (to comply with late closure, keeping the first phrase open for as long as possible). As expected, participants were garden-pathed by (28). However, if semantic and thematic information about verbs is available from an early stage, then in (29) thematic information should tell the processor that "sneezed" cannot take a direct object (a process called lexical guidance). Nevertheless, participants are still led up the garden path with (29); hence the initial parse must be ignoring verb information.

(28) After the child had visited the doctor prescribed a course of injections.
(29) After the child had sneezed the doctor prescribed a course of injections.

Van Gompel and Pickering (2001) came to the same conclusion using an eye-movement methodology: readers experience difficulty after "sneezed." These experiments suggest that the first stage of parsing is short-sighted and does not use semantic or thematic information. Similarly, Ferreira and Henderson (1990) examined data from eye movements and word-by-word self-paced reading of ambiguous sentences, concluding that verb information does not affect the initial parse, although it might guide the second stage of reanalysis.

We can manipulate the semantic relatedness of nouns and verbs in contexts where they are either syntactically appropriate or inappropriate. Their different effects can then be teased out in lexical decision and naming tasks (O'Seaghdha, 1997). The results suggest that syntactic analysis precedes semantic analysis and is independent of it. Consider (30) and (31):

(30) The message that was shut.
(31) The message of that shut.

In (30), the target word "shut" is syntactically appropriate but semantically anomalous. In (31), the target is both syntactically and semantically anomalous. In the lexical decision task, in (30) we observe meaning-based inhibition relative to a baseline. In (31), we do not observe any inhibition. In the naming task, there is no sensitivity to semantic anomaly, but there is sensitivity to the syntactic inappropriateness of the target in (31). O'Seaghdha suggested that the inhibition occurs in (30) in the lexical decision task because of a difficulty in integrating the target word into a high-level text representation. We do not get that far in (31) because the failure to construct a syntactic representation blocks any semantic integration. The results look as though they support interactivity because the lexical decision task is sensitive to post-access integration processes. The naming data are less contaminated by post-access processing and suggest that syntactic analysis is prior to semantic integration and independent of it.

Evidence from neuroscience suggests that semantic and syntactic processing are independent. Breedin and Saffran (1999) described a patient, DM, who had a significant and pervasive loss of semantic knowledge as a result of dementia. For example, he found it very difficult to match a picture of an object to another appropriate picture (e.g., knowing that a pyramid is associated with a palm tree rather than a pine tree). Yet his semantic deficit had no apparent effect on his syntactic abilities. He performed extremely well at detecting grammatical violations (e.g., he knew that "what did the exhausted young woman sit?" was ungrammatical). He also had no difficulty in assigning semantic roles in a sentence. For example, he could correctly identify who was being carried in the sentence "The tiger is being carried by the lion," even though he had difficulty in recognizing lions and tigers by name.

Brain-imaging studies are also useful here. A negative event-related potential (ERP) found 400 ms after an event (and hence called the N400) is thought to be particularly sensitive to semantic processing, and is particularly indicative of violations of semantic expectancy (Batterink, Karns, Yamada, & Neville, 2010; Kounios & Holcomb, 1992; Kutas & Hillyard, 1980; Nigram, Hoffman, & Simons, 1992). A sentence such as (32) generates a semantic anomaly:

(32) Boris noticed a puncture and got out to change the wheel on the castle.

The N400 occurs 400 ms after the anomalous word "castle."

There is also a positive wave found 600 ms after a syntactic violation (Hagoort, Brown, & Groothusen, 1993; Osterhout & Holcomb, 1992; Osterhout, Holcomb, & Swinney, 1994). A P600 would be observed with (33):

(33) Boris persuaded to fly.

These anomalies can be used to map the time course of syntactic and semantic processing. These ERP data suggest that syntactic and semantic processing are distinct (Ainsworth-Darnell, Shulman, & Boland, 1998; Friederici, 2002; Neville, Nicol, Barss, Forster, & Garrett, 1991; Ni et al., 2000; Osterhout & Nicol, 1999). For example, Ainsworth-Darnell et al. examined ERPs when people heard sentences that contained a syntactic anomaly, a semantic anomaly, or both. The sentences that contained both types of anomaly still provoked both an N400 and a P600. Ainsworth-Darnell et al. concluded that different parts of the brain automatically become involved when syntactic and semantic anomalies are present, and therefore that these processes are represented separately. Osterhout and Nicol (1999) gave participants sentences with different types of anomaly to read (34)–(37):

(34) The cats won't eat the food that Mary leaves them. (non-anomalous)
(35) The cats won't bake the food that Mary leaves them. (semantic anomaly)
(36) The cats won't eating the food that Mary leaves them. (syntactic anomaly)
(37) The cats won't baking the food that Mary leaves them. (doubly anomalous)

As expected, semantically anomalous sentences, such as (35), elicited the N400, and syntactically anomalous sentences, such as (36), elicited the P600. Doubly anomalous sentences, such as (37), elicited both an N400 and a P600, with the magnitude of each effect being about the same as if each anomaly were present in isolation. The brain responds differently to syntactic and semantic anomalies, and the response to each type of anomaly is unaffected by the presence of the other type. Osterhout and Nicol concluded that syntactic and semantic processes are separable and independent.

There has been some debate as to the strength of this claim. It is useful to distinguish between representational modularity and processing modularity (Pickering, 1999; Trueswell, Tanenhaus, & Garnsey, 1994). Representational modularity says that semantic and syntactic knowledge are represented separately. That is, there are distinct types of linguistic representation, which might be stored or processed in different parts of the brain.

This is relatively uncontroversial. Most of the debate is about processing modularity: Is initial processing restricted to syntactic information, or can all sources of information influence the earliest stages of processing?

Evidence for interaction in syntactic processing

The experiments discussed so far suggest that the first stage of parsing only makes use of syntactic preferences based on minimal attachment and late closure, and does not use semantic or thematic information. On the interactive account, however, semantic factors influence whether or not we get garden-pathed. What is the evidence that semantic factors play an early role in parsing?

Perhaps the syntactic principles of minimal attachment and late closure can be better explained by semantic biases? Taraban and McClelland (1988) compared self-paced reading times for sentences such as (38) and (39) (see Figure 10.2):

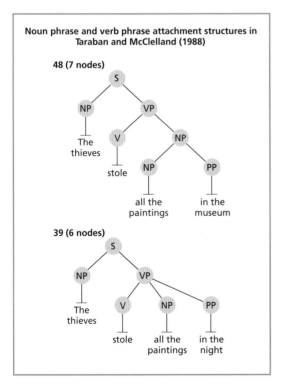

Noun phrase and verb phrase attachment structures in Taraban and McClelland (1988)

48 (7 nodes)

39 (6 nodes)

FIGURE 10.2

(38)   The thieves stole all the paintings in the museum while the guard slept.

(39)   The thieves stole all the paintings in the night while the guard slept.

Sentence (39) is a minimal attachment structure but (38) is not. In (38) the phrase "in the museum" must be formed into a noun phrase with "paintings"; in (39) the phrase "in the night" must be formed into a verb phrase with "stole." The noun phrase attachment in (38) produces a grammatically more complex structure than the verb phrase attachment in (39). Nevertheless, Taraban and McClelland found that (38) is read faster than (39). They argued that this is because all the words up to "museum" and "night" create a semantic bias for the non-minimal interpretation. They concluded that violations of the purely syntactic process of the attachment of words to the developing structural representation do not slow down reading, but violations of the semantic process of assigning words to thematic roles do. Taraban and McClelland also concluded that previous studies that had appeared to support minimal attachment had in fact confounded syntactic simplicity with semantic bias.

Why do we find garden-pathing on some occasions but not others? Milne (1982) was one of the first to argue that semantic factors rather than syntactic factors lead us up the garden path. Consider the three sentences (40)–(42). Only (40) causes difficulty, because it sets up semantic expectancies that are then violated:

(40)   The granite rocks during the earthquake.
(41)   The granite rocks were by the seashore.
(42)   The table rocks during the earthquake.

How can semantic factors explain our difficulty with reduced relatives?

Crain and Steedman (1985) used a speeded grammaticality judgment task to show that an appropriate semantic context can eliminate syntactic garden paths. In this task, participants see a string of words and have to decide as quickly as possible whether the string is grammatical or not. Participants in this task on the whole are more likely to misidentify garden path sentences as non-grammatical than non-garden path sentences. Sentence (43) was incorrectly judged ungrammatical far more often than the structurally identical but semantically more plausible sentence (44):

(43) The teachers taught by the Berlitz method passed the test.
(44) The children taught by the Berlitz method passed the test.

Crain and Steedman argued that there is no such thing as a truly neutral semantic context. Even when semantic context is apparently absent from the sentence, participants bring prior knowledge and expectations to the experiment. They argued that all syntactic parsing preferences can be explained semantically. All syntactic alternatives are considered in parallel, and semantic considerations then rapidly select among them. Semantic difficulty is based on the amount of information that has to be assumed: The more assumptions that have to be made, the harder the sentence is to process. Hence sentences such as (45) are difficult compared with (46), where the existence of only one horse is assumed. This assumption is incompatible with the semantic representation needed to understand (45)—that there are a number of horses but it was the one that was raced past the barn that was the one that fell. That is, if the processor encounters a definite noun phrase in the absence of any context, only one entity (e.g., one horse) is postulated, and therefore no modifier is necessary. If one is present, processing difficulty ensues.

(45) The horse raced past the barn fell.
(46) The horse raced past the barn quickly.

Altmann and Steedman (1988) measured reading times on sentences such as (47) and (48):

(47) The burglar blew open the safe with the dynamite and made off with the loot.
(48) The burglar blew open the safe with the new lock and made off with the loot.

These sentences are ambiguous: the prepositional phrases "with the dynamite" and "with the new lock" can modify either the noun phrase "the safe" or the verb phrase "blew open the safe." Altmann and Steedman presented the participants with prior discourse context that disambiguated the sentences. A prior context sentence referred to either one or two safes. ("Once inside he saw that there was a safe with a new lock and a strongbox with an old lock" versus "Once inside he saw that there was a safe with a new lock and a safe with an old lock.") If the context sentence mentioned only one safe, then the complex noun phrase "the safe with the new lock" is redundant, and causes extra processing difficulty. Hence the prepositional phrase in (48) took relatively longer to read. If the context sentence mentioned two safes, then the simple noun phrase "the safe" in (47) fails to identify a particular safe, so the prepositional phrase "with the dynamite" in (47) took relatively longer to read.

Altmann and Steedman (1988) emphasized that the processor constructs a syntactic representation incrementally, on a word-by-word basis. At each word, alternative syntactic interpretations are generated in parallel, and then a decision is made using context. Altmann and Steedman called this "weak" interaction, as opposed to strong interaction, where context actually guides the parsing process so that only one alternative is generated. This approach is called the referential theory of parsing. The processor constructs analyses in parallel and uses discourse context to disambiguate them immediately. It is the immediate nature of this disambiguation that distinguishes the referential theory from garden path models. As many factors guide parsing, it must be semantic considerations that in this case must lead us up the garden path.

Is it possible to distinguish between the referential and the constraint-based theories? The theories are similar in that each denies that parsing is restricted to using syntactic information. In constraint-based theories, all sources of semantic information, including general world knowledge, are used to disambiguate, but in referential theory only referential complexity within the discourse model is important. Ni, Crain, and Shankweiler (1996) tried to separate the effects of these different types of knowledge by studying reading times and eye movements when reading ambiguous sentences. The results suggested that semantic-referential information is used immediately, but more general world knowledge takes longer to become available. Furthermore, world knowledge was dependent on working memory capacity, whereas use of semantic-referential principles was not. (In general, people with larger working memory spans are better able to maintain multiple syntactic representations and therefore will be more effective at processing ambiguous sentences; see MacDonald, Just, & Carpenter, 1992; Pearlmutter & MacDonald, 1995.) Ni et al. argued that the focus operator "only" presupposes the existence of more than one vampire (in this example), and therefore a modifier is needed to select one of them. Consider (49) and (50):

(49) The vampires loaned money at low interest were told to record their expenses.

(50)   Only vampires loaned money at low interest were told to record their expenses.

Sentence (49) provokes a garden path effect but (50) does not. Analysis suggested that these referential principles were used immediately to resolve ambiguity. Information about semantic plausibility of interpretations was used later. However, as Pickering (1999) noted, referential theory cannot be a complete account of parsing, because it can only be applied to ambiguities involving simple and complex noun phrases. There is also more to context than discourse analysis. Referential theory was an early version of a constraint-based theory, applied to a limited type of syntactic structure. Nevertheless, the idea that discourse information can be used to influence parsing decisions is one essential component of constraint-based theories.

Altmann, Garnham, and Dennis (1992) used eye-movement measures to investigate how context affects garden pathing. Consider sentence (51):

(51)   The fireman told the man that he had risked his life for to install a smoke detector.

Garden path theory predicts that (51) should always lead to a garden path. We always start to parse "the man" as a simple noun phrase because this has a simpler structure than the alternative (which turns out to be the correct analysis), in which the noun is the head of a complex noun phrase. According to referential theory, the resolution of ambiguities in context depends on whether a unique referent can be found. The context can bias the processor towards or away from garden-pathing. The null context induces a garden path in (51). However, some contexts will bias the processor towards a relative clause interpretation and prevent garden-pathing. Such a biasing context can be obtained by preceding the ambiguous relative structure with a relative-supporting referential context. One way of doing this is to provide more than one possible referent for "the man." (For example, "A fireman braved a dangerous fire in a hotel. He rescued one of the guests at great danger to himself. A crowd of men gathered around him.") Eye-movement measurements verified this prediction. Measurements of difficulty associated with garden-pathing were reflected in longer average reading times per character in the ambiguity region, and an increased probability of regressive eye movements. When syntactic information leads to ambiguity and a garden path is possible, then the processor proceeds to construct a syntactic representation on the basis of the best semantic bet.

Further evidence for constraint-based models comes from the finding that thematic information can be used to eliminate the garden path effect in these reduced relative sentences (MacDonald et al., 1994a; Trueswell & Tanenhaus, 1994; Trueswell et al., 1994). For example, consider the ambiguous sentence fragments (52) and (53):

(52)   The fossil examined –
(53)   The archeologist examined –

The fragments are ambiguous because they are consistent with two sentence constructions: the most frequent order, the unreduced structure, where the first NP is the agent (e.g., "The archeologist examined the fossil"), and with a reduced relative clause ("The fossil examined by the archeologist was important"). However, consider the thematic roles associated with the verb "examine." It has the roles of agent, best fitted by an animate entity, and a theme, best fitted by an inanimate object (Trueswell & Tanenhaus, 1994). So semantic considerations associated with thematic roles suggest that (52) is likely to be a reduced relative structure, and (53) a simple sentence structure. Difficulty ensues if subsequent material conflicts with these interpretations, or if the context provided by the nouns is not sufficiently biasing. Trueswell et al. (1994) examined eye movements to investigate how people understood sentences such as (52) and (53). They found that if semantic constraints were sufficiently strong, reduced relative clauses were no more difficult than the unreduced constructions.

Remember that, in contrast, Ferreira and Clifton (1986) found evidence of increased difficulty with very similar materials, (26) and (27). Why is there a discrepancy? Trueswell et al. argued that the semantic bias in Ferreira and Clifton's experiment was too weak. If the semantic constraint is not strong enough, we will be garden-pathed. McRae, Spivey-Knowlton, and Tanenhaus (1998) found that strong plausibility can also overcome garden-pathing. On the other side of the coin, people are reluctant to abandon plausible analyses in favor of implausible ones, even when the plausible analysis is turning out to be wrong (Pickering & Traxler, 1998).

An important idea in constraint-based models is that of verb bias (Garnsey et al., 1997; Trueswell et al., 1993). This is the idea that although some verbs can appear in a number of syntactic structures, some of their syntactic structures are more common than others. The relative frequencies of alternative interpretations of verbs predict whether or not people have difficulty in understanding reduced relatives (MacDonald, 1994; Trueswell, 1996). Hence, although the verb "read" can appear with sentence complements ("the ghost read the book had been burned"), it is most commonly followed by a direct object (as in simply, "the ghost read the book during the plane journey"). Direct-object verbs are those where the most frequent continuation is the direct object; sentence-complement verbs are those where the most frequent continuation is the sentence complement.

According to constraint-based models, verb-bias information becomes available immediately the verb is recognized. Trueswell et al. (1993) found evidence for the immediate availability of verb-bias information across a range of tasks (priming, self-paced reading, and eye movements). They found that verbs with a sentence-complement bias did not cause processing difficulty, whereas verbs with direct-object bias did. Furthermore, the more frequently a sentence complement verb appears in the language without a complementizer ("that"), the less likely it is to lead to processing difficulty in sentence-complement constructions. Using a carefully controlled set of materials combined with eye-movement and self-paced reading analyses, Garnsey et al. (1997) also found that people's prior experience with particular verbs guides their interpretation of temporary ambiguity. Verb bias guides readers to a sentence-complement interpretation with sentence-complement verbs. This information is available very quickly (certainly by the word following the verb). Furthermore, verb-bias information interacts with how plausible the temporarily ambiguous noun is as a direct object. For example, "the decision" is more plausible as a direct object than "the reporter." This result is best explained by constraint-based models, as according to the garden path model there should be no early effect of plausibility and verb bias.

Note though that there is controversy over whether verb-bias effects are real: Some studies have found no effect of verb-frequency information. For example, using an eye-tracking methodology, Pickering, Traxler, and Crocker (2000) found that readers experienced difficulty with temporarily ambiguous sentence-complement clauses even when the verbs were biased towards that analysis. Consider the sentence beginning (54).

(54) The young athlete realized her potential –

There are now two possible analyses: the object analysis (simply, "The young athlete realized her potential"), and the sentence-complement analysis (as in "The young athlete realized her potential might one day make her a world class athlete"). The sentence-complement analysis is the most common for the verb "realized," so readers should adopt that and not the object analysis. However, they do not. People preferred to attach noun phrases as arguments of verbs, regardless of whether or not this analysis was likely to be correct. Kennison (2001) similarly found that ambiguous structures caused difficulty regardless of the verb bias. Pickering and van Gompel (2006) concluded that verb-bias information has some influence on syntactic processing, but often not enough to prevent us having difficulty with temporally ambiguous sentences.

In constraint-based models, syntactic ambiguity is eventually resolved by competition (MacDonald et al., 1994a, 1994b). The constraints activate different analyses to differing degrees; if two or more analyses are highly activated, competition is strong and there are severe processing difficulties. Tabor and Tanenhaus (1999; see also Tabor, Juliano, & Tanenhaus, 1997) proposed that the competition is resolved by settling into a basin of attraction in an attractor network similar to those postulated to account for word recognition (Hinton & Shallice, 1991; see Chapter 7). Along similar lines, McRae et al. (1998) proposed a connectionist-like model of ambiguity resolution called competition-integration. Competition between alternative structures plays a central role in a parsing process that essentially checks its preferred structure after each new word. Evidence for parallel competition models comes from studies that show that the more committed people become to a parsing choice, the more difficult it is for them to recover, an effect called digging-in (Tabor & Hutchins, 2004). For example, increasing the gap between the ambiguity and the disambiguating information causes the comprehenders to "dig in" as they become more committed to the wrong analysis (e.g., (55) is easier than (56); materials from Ferreira & Henderson, 1991). Once they have dug in, alternative interpretations (including the correct one) become less activated.

(55) After the Martians invaded the town was evacuated.
(56) After the Martians invaded the town that the city bordered was evacuated.

Another important aspect of constraint-based models is that syntactic and lexical ambiguity are resolved in similar ways because of the importance of lexical constraints in parsing (MacDonald et al., 1994a, 1994b). Syntactic ambiguities arise because of ambiguities at the lexical level. For example, "raced" is an ambiguous word, with one sense of a past tense, and another of a past participle. In (57), only the past tense sense is consistent with the preceding context. This information eventually constrains the processor to a particular syntactic interpretation. But in (58), both senses are consistent with the context. Although contextual constraints are rarely strong enough to restrict activation to the appropriate alternative, they provide useful information for distinguishing between alternative candidates. In this type of approach, a syntactic representation of a sentence is computed through links between items in a rich lexicon (MacDonald et al., 1994a).

(57) The horse who raced –
(58) The horse raced –

Part of the difficulty in distinguishing between the autonomous and interactive constraint-based theories is in obtaining evidence about what is happening in the earliest stages of comprehension. Tanenhaus et al. (1995) examined the eye movements of participants who were following instructions to manipulate real objects. Analysis of the eye movements suggested that people processed the instructions incrementally, making eye movements to objects immediately after the relevant instruction. People typically made an eye movement to the target object 250 ms after the end of the word that uniquely specified the object. With more complex instructions, participants' eyes moved around the array looking for possible referents.

The best evidence for the independence of parsing comes from reading studies of sentences with brief syntactic ambiguities, where listeners have clear preferences for particular interpretations, even when the preceding linguistic context supports the alternative interpretation. Tanenhaus et al. pointed out that in this sort of experiment the context may not be immediately available because it has to be retrieved from memory. They examined the interpretation of temporarily ambiguous sentences in the context of a visual array so that information is immediately available. They auditorily presented participants with the sentence (59) with one of two visual contexts.

(59) Put the apple on the towel in the box.

In the one-referent condition there was just one apple on a towel and another towel without an apple on it. In the two-referent condition there were two possible referents for the apple, one on a towel and one on a napkin. According to modular theories, "on the towel" should always be initially interpreted as the destination (where the apple should be put, because this is structurally simplest). However, analysis of the eye movements across the scene showed that "on the towel" was initially interpreted as the destination only in the one-referent condition. In the two-referent condition, "on the towel" was interpreted as the modifier of "apple." In the one-referent condition, participants looked at the incorrect destination (the irrelevant towel) 55% of the time; in the two-referent condition, they rarely did so. This experiment is strong evidence that people use contextual information immediately to establish reference and to process temporarily ambiguous sentences.

A similar experiment by Sedivy, Tanenhaus, Chambers, and Carlson (1999) showed that people very quickly take context into account when interpreting adjectives. On the basis of these findings, Sedivy et al. argued that syntactic processing is incremental—that is, a semantic representation is constructed with very little lag following the input. People immediately try to integrate adjectives into a semantic model even when they do not have a stable core meaning (e.g., tall is a scalar object—it is a relative term and depends on the noun it is modifying; tall in "a tall glass" means something different from in "a tall building"). They do this by establishing contrasts between possible referents in the visual array (or memory).

Brain-imaging fMRI studies show that the brain processes ambiguous and unambiguous sentences differently (Mason, Just, Keller, & Carpenter, 2003). Higher levels of brain activation are shown for ambiguous sentences, but also during reading more complex structures and unpreferred

structures (those where the reduced relative reading is the correct one). Furthermore, and contrary to the reading time results, higher activation was shown while reading ambiguous sentences when the ambiguity was resolved in favor of the preferred syntactic construction. The higher workload was spread among the superior temporal gyrus (including Wernicke's area) and the inferior frontal gyrus (including Broca's area), hinting that multiple processes are involved in ambiguity resolution (see Figure 10.3). In particular, Broca's area might be involved in generating abstract syntactic frames, and Wernicke's in interpreting and elaborating them with semantic information. These findings are more consistent with parallel models where multiple parses are kept open at the same time.

There is also recent electrophysiological evidence that shows that people predict what is coming next (DeLong, Urbach, & Kutas, 2005; see also Kutas, DeLong, & Smith, 2011). DeLong et al. examined the phonological regularity in the English indefinite article ("a" before a consonant, "an" before a vowel) using ERP, and concluded that people pre-activate words in a graded fashion.

Cross-linguistic differences in attachment

A final point concerns the extent to which any parsing principles apply to languages other than English. Cuetos and Mitchell (1988) examined the extent to which speakers of English and Spanish used the late-closure strategy to interpret the same

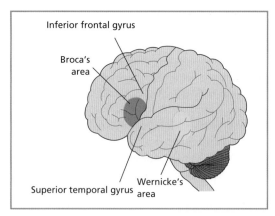

FIGURE 10.3

sorts of sentences. They found that although the interpretations of the English speakers could be accounted for by late closure, this was not true of the Spanish speakers. For example, given (60), English speakers prefer to attach the relative clause ("who had the accident") to "the colonel," because that is the phrase currently being processed. We can find this out simply by asking readers "Who had the accident?"

(60) The journalist interviewed the daughter of the colonel who had the accident.

Spanish speakers, on the other hand, given the equivalent sentence (61), seem to follow a strategy of early closure. That is, they attach the relative clause to the first noun phrase.

(61) El periodista entrevisto a la hija del coronel que tuvo el accidente.

Other languages also show a preference for attaching the relative clause to the first noun phrase, including French (Zagar, Pynte, & Rativeau, 1997) and Dutch (Brysbaert & Mitchell, 1996). These results suggest that late closure may not be a general strategy common to all languages. Instead, the parsing preferences may reflect the frequency of different structures within a language (Mitchell, Cuetos, Corley, & Brysbaert, 1995). These **cross-linguistic** differences question the idea that late closure is a process-generated principle that confers advantages on the comprehender, such as minimizing processing load. Frazier (1987b) proposed that late closure is advantageous because if a constituent is kept open as long as possible, it avoids the processing cost incurred by closing it, opening it, and closing it again.

The results of this study can be explained in one of three ways. First, late closure may not originate because of processing advantages, and the choice of strategy (early versus late closure) is essentially an arbitrary choice in different languages. Second, late closure may have a processing advantage and may be the usual strategy, but in some languages, in some circumstances, other strategies may dominate (Cuetos & Mitchell,

1988). Third, as constraint-based models advocate, parsing does not make use of linguistic principles at all. The results of interpretation depend on the interaction of many constraints that are relevant in sentence processing. Whatever the answer, it is clear that if we limit our studies of parsing to English then we miss out on a great deal of potentially important data.

Constraint-based models contain a probabilistic element in that the most strongly activated analysis can vary depending on the circumstances. Another example of a probabilistic model is the tuning hypothesis (Brysbaert & Mitchell, 1996; Mitchell, 1994; Mitchell et al., 1995). The tuning hypothesis emphasizes the role of exposure to language. Parsing decisions are influenced by the frequency with which alternative analyses are used. Put another way, people resolve ambiguities in a way that has been successful in the past (Sturt, Costa, Lombardo, & Frasconi, 2003). Given the reasonable assumption that people vary in their exposure to different analyses, then their preferred initial attachments will also vary. Attachment preferences may vary from language to language, and from person to person, and indeed might even vary within a person across time. Brysbaert and Mitchell (1996) used a questionnaire to examine attachment preferences in Dutch speakers, and found individual differences in these preferences.

Comparison of garden path and constraint-based theories

When do syntax and semantics interact in parsing? This has proved to be the central question in parsing, as well as one of the most difficult to answer. In serial two-stage models, such as the garden path model, the initial analysis is constrained by using only syntactic information and preferences, and a second stage using semantic information. In parallel constraint-based models, multiple analyses are active from the beginning, and both syntactic and non-syntactic information is used in combination to activate alternative representations. Unfortunately, there is little consensus about which model gives the better account. Different techniques seem to give different answers, and the results are sensitive to the materials used. Proponents of the garden path model argue that the effects that are claimed to support constraint-based models arise because the second stage of parsing begins very quickly, and that many experiments that are supposed to be looking at the first stage are in fact looking at the second stage of parsing. Any interaction observed is occurring at this second stage, which starts very early in processing. They argue that experiments supporting constraint-based models are methodologically flawed, and that constraint-based models fail to account for the full range of data (Frazier, 1995). On the other hand, proponents of the constraint-based models argue that researchers favoring the garden path model use techniques that are not sensitive enough to detect the interactions involved, or that the non-syntactic constraints used are too weak.

Other models of parsing

Is there any way out of this dilemma? Alternative approaches to garden path and constraint-based theories have recently come to the fore.

The first alternative may be called the unrestricted-race model. To understand the basis of this model, we must consider exactly how syntactic ambiguity is resolved. We also need to distinguish between models that always adopt the same analysis of a particular ambiguity and those that do not (van Gompel, Pickering, & Traxler, 2000, 2001).

The garden path model can be described as a fixed-choice two-stage model. It is fixed choice in that it has no probabilistic element in its decision making. Given a particular structure, the same syntactic structure will always be generated on the basis of late closure and minimal attachment. Either the correct analysis is chosen on syntactic grounds from the beginning, or, if the initial syntactic analysis becomes implausible, reanalysis is needed.

Constraint-based models are variable-choice one-stage models. In constraint-based models, syntactic ambiguity is resolved by competition. When there are alternative analyses of similar activation, competition is particularly intense, causing considerable processing difficulty. Competition

might continue for a long time. In the competition-integration model (McRae et al., 1998; Spivey & Tanenhaus, 1998), competition is long-lasting but decreases as the sentence unfolds.

So do we resolve ambiguity by reanalysis or competition? Van Gompel et al. (2001) examined how we resolve ambiguity. They constructed sentences such as (62) to (64):

(62) The hunter killed only the poacher with the rifle not long after sunset.
(63) The hunter killed only the leopard with the rifle not long after sunset.
(64) The hunter killed only the leopard with the scars not long after sunset.

The prepositional phrase ("with the rifle/scars") can be attached either to "killed" (a VP **attachment** analysis: the hunter killed with the rifle/scars) or to "poacher/leopard" (an NP attachment: the poacher/leopard had the rifle/scars). In (63), only the VP attachment is plausible (that the hunter killed with the rifle, rather than that the leopard had the rifle); this is the VP condition. In (64), only the NP attachment is plausible (that the leopard had the scars, as you cannot kill with scars); this is the NP condition. In (62), both the VP and NP attachments are plausible; this is called the ambiguous condition.

What do the different theories predict? The garden path model (an example of a fixed-choice two-stage model where ambiguity is resolved by reanalysis) predicts, on the basis of minimal attachment, that the processor will always initially adopt the VP analysis, because this generates the simpler structure. (It creates a structure with fewer nodes than the NP analysis; see Chapter 2.) The processor only reanalyzes if the VP attachment turns out subsequently to be implausible. Hence (62) should be as difficult as (63), but (64) should cause more difficulty. Constraint-based theories predict little competition in (64), because plausibility supports only the NP interpretation. In (63) there should be little competition, because the semantic plausibility information supports only the VP analysis. Crucially, in this experiment there was no syntactic preference for VP or NP attachment. The ambiguity was balanced (usually

VP/NP ambiguities are biased towards VP attachment). In (62), however, there should be competition because both interpretations are plausible. In summary, garden path theory predicts that (62) and (63) should be equally easy, but (64) should be difficult; constraint-based theory predicts that (63) and (64) should be easy, but (62) should be difficult.

Van Gompel et al. examined readers' eye movements to discover when these sentences caused difficulty. They found that an inspection of reading difficulty favored neither pattern of results. Instead, they found that the ambiguous condition was easier to read than the two disambiguated ones. That is, (64) was easy but (62) and (63) were difficult.

Neither garden path nor constraint-based theories seem able to explain this pattern of results. Van Gompel et al. argue that only a variable-choice two-stage model can account for this pattern of results. The unrestricted race is such a model (Traxler, Pickering, & Clifton, 1998; van Gompel et al., 2000, 2001). As in constraint-based models, all sources of information, both syntactic and semantic, are used to select among alternative syntactic structures (hence it is unrestricted). The alternatives are constructed in parallel and engaged in a race. The winner is the analysis that is constructed fastest, and this is adopted as the syntactic interpretation of the fragment. So in contrast to constraint-based theories, only one analysis is adopted at a time. If this analysis is inconsistent with later information, the processor has to reanalyze, at considerable cost; hence it is also a two-stage model. It is also a variable-choice model, as the initial analysis is affected by the particular characteristics of the sentence fragment (as well as by individual differences resulting from differences in experience).

Let us consider how the unrestricted-race model accounts for these data. Because there is no particular bias for NP or VP in (62)–(64), people will adopt one of these as their initial preference on about half the trials. In (62), people will never have to reanalyze, because either preference turns out to be plausible, but (63) and (64) will both cause difficulty on those occasions when the initial preference turns out to be wrong, and the

processor will be forced to reanalyze. The critical and surprising finding that only a variable-choice two-stage model such as the unrestricted-race model seems able to explain is that sometimes ambiguous sentences cause less difficulty than disambiguated sentences.

Need detailed syntactic processing necessarily precede semantic analysis? In a second alternative approach Bever, Sanz, and Townsend (1998) suggest that semantics comes first. In an extension of the idea that probabilistic, statistical considerations play an important role in comprehension, Bever et al. argue that statistically based strategies are used to propose an initial semantic representation. This then constrains the detailed computation of the syntactic representation. They argued that the frequency with which syntactic representations occur constrains the initial stage of syntactic processing. At any one time, the processor assigns the statistically most likely interpretation to the incoming material. Bever et al. argued that a principle such as minimal attachment cannot explain why we find reduced relatives so very difficult, but the statistical rarity of this sort of construction can (just because they are so rare). On this account, the role of the processor is reduced to checking that everything is accounted for, and that the initial semantic representation indeed corresponds with the detailed syntactic representation.

Do we always construct a complete, idealized syntactic structure? Christianson, Hollingworth, Halliwell, and Ferreira (2001) argue that we do not. They focus on what people understand after they have read garden path sentences such as "While the man hunted the deer ran into the woods." This emphasis on comprehension—for example, asking people what they thought were the subjects, objects, and actions of clauses, and how confident they were about these judgments— is different from that of most of the other studies we have looked at, which emphasize on-line measures of what is happening when we process individual words while looking at garden path sentences. They found that people do not always completely reanalyze sentences, and often retain a mistaken interpretation derived from the initial misanalysis. They concluded that people do not strive towards perfect analyses, but instead are happy with interpretations that seem to work; they settle for "good enough." In a return related to the early idea of surface cues, some researchers now think that people use simple heuristics when processing language, in addition to detailed and complete syntactic processing (Ferreira, 2003). Comprehenders start out with the assumption that a sentence is in canonical, NVN form, and sentences that violate this heuristic (e.g., passives) are more difficult to understand.

A different approach is taken by McKoon and Ratcliff (2002, 2003). They argue that syntactic constructions themselves carry meaning, beyond the meaning of their constituent words. A passive sentence provides a different emphasis from its corresponding active, and therefore has a different meaning. Sentences (65) and (66), although superficially similar, convey different meanings.

(65)   Boris loaded the truck with hay.
(66)   Boris loaded hay onto the truck.

Here, sentence (65) conveys the notion that the truck is completely full of hay, but (66) does not. A difference in syntax conveys a difference in meaning. Reduced relative constructions convey a particular meaning. McKoon and Ratcliff argue that this meaning means that it can only be combined with particular sorts of nouns and verbs. The reduced relative can only be used to talk about particular sorts of things: The main noun participates in an event caused by some force or other entity external to itself. The main verb has to convey this sense of external participation. A sentence such as (67) satisfies this constraint, but a sentence such as (68) does not.

(67)   Cars and trucks abandoned in a terrifying scramble for safety.
(68)   The horse raced past the barn fell.

"Abandoned" conveys this sense of external causation ("something caused cars and trucks to be abandoned"), but "raced" does not (because it is the horse itself that is doing the racing). McKoon and Ratcliff propose that reduced relatives with verbs denoting internally caused events really

are ungrammatical, which is why people have so much difficulty with them. A study of a large corpus of natural speech confirms that people only produce reduced relatives with these external-causation verbs. With verbs where the control is internal, in real life speakers use non-reduced constructions ("the horse that was raced past the barn fell").

McKoon and Ratcliff call this approach, where syntactic constructions convey particular meanings that restrict what sorts of nouns and verbs can be used with them, and particularly what sort of verb-argument structures can be used, meaning through syntax (MTS). They further argue that the MTS conflicts with constraint-based theories. According to constraint-based theories, the language processor knows about statistics of usage, not meanings and rules, whereas according to MTS, the language processor knows about meanings and rules, but not statistics. McKoon and Ratcliff found that statistical information about verbs derived from an actual corpus of speech does not predict reading times of sentences containing those verbs.

The MTS approach is criticized by McRae, Hare, and Tanenhaus (2005), who argue that the difficulty of reduced relatives is best accounted for not by the internal–external distinction, but by temporary processing difficulty resulting from ambiguity. Furthermore, the syntactic constructions can on occasion force, or coerce, a particular interpretation regardless of the meaning of the verb: We can still understand a sentence such as "Boris sneezed the tissue off the table" even though "sneezed" does not normally imply causation. Sentence constructions do carry meaning independently of their constituent verbs. In summary, it is difficult to see how the MTS approach can replace alternative theories of parsing difficulty. Indeed, instead of replacing constraint-based theories, the internal–external causation distinction may be just one more constraint.

Processing syntactic-category ambiguity

One type of lexical ambiguity that is of particular importance for processing syntax is lexical-category ambiguity, where a word can be from more than one syntactic category (e.g., a noun or a verb, as in "trains" or "watches"). This type of ambiguity provides a useful test of the idea that lexical and syntactic ambiguity are aspects of the same thing and are processed in similar ways.

According to serial-stage models such as garden path theory, lexical and syntactic ambiguity are quite distinct, because lexical representations are already computed but syntactic representations must be computed (Frazier & Rayner, 1987). According to Frazier (1989), distinct mechanisms are needed to resolve lexical-semantic, syntactic, and lexical-category ambiguity. Lexical-semantic ambiguity is resolved in the manner described in Chapter 6: The alternative semantic interpretations are generated in parallel, and one meaning is rapidly chosen on the basis of context and meaning frequency. Syntactic ambiguity is dealt with by the garden path model in that only one analysis is constructed at any one time; if this turns out to be incorrect, then reanalysis is necessary. Lexical-category ambiguity is dealt with by a delay mechanism. When we encounter a syntactically ambiguous word, the alternative meanings are accessed in parallel, but no alternative is chosen immediately. Instead, the processor delays selection until definitive disambiguating information is encountered later in the sentence. The advantage of the delay strategy is that it saves extensive computation because usually the word following a lexical-category ambiguity provides sufficient disambiguating information.

Frazier and Rayner (1987) provided some experimental support for the delay strategy. They examined how we process two-word phrases containing lexical-category ambiguities, such as "desert trains." After the word "desert," two interpretations are possible. The first noun can either be a noun to be followed by a verb (in which case "desert" will be the subject of the verb "trains"—this is the NV interpretation), or it can be a modifier noun that precedes a head noun (in which case "desert" will be the modifying noun and "trains" the head noun—this is the NN interpretation). Frazier and Rayner examined eye movements in ambiguous and unambiguous sentences. The ambiguous sentences started with

"the" ("the desert trains"), which permits both NV and NN interpretations, and the unambiguous controls started with "this" (giving "this desert trains" for an unambiguous NV interpretation) or with "these" (giving "these desert trains" for an unambiguous NN interpretation). The rest of the sentence provided disambiguating information, as shown in the full sentences (69) and (70):

(69) I know that the desert trains young people to be especially tough.
(70) I know that the desert trains are especially tough on young people.

Frazier and Rayner found that reading times in the critical, ambiguous region ("desert trains") were shorter in the ambiguous ("the") condition than the unambiguous ("this"/"these") conditions. However, in the ambiguous condition, reading times were longer in the disambiguating material later in the sentence. They proposed that when the processor encounters the initial ambiguity, very little analysis takes place. Instead, processing is delayed until subsequent disambiguating information is reached, when additional work is necessary.

According to constraint-based theories, there is no real difference between lexical-semantic ambiguity and lexical-category ambiguity. In each case, alternatives are activated in parallel depending on the strength of support they receive from multiple sources of information. Hence multiple factors, such as context and the syntactic bias of the ambiguous word (that is, whether it is more frequently encountered as a noun or a verb), immediately affect interpretation.

How can constraint-based theories account for Frazier and Rayner's findings that we seem to delay processing lexical-category ambiguities until the disambiguating region is reached? MacDonald (1993) suggested that the control condition in their experiment provided an unsuitable baseline, in that they introduced an additional factor. The determiners "this" and "these" serve a deictic function, in that they point the comprehender to a previously mentioned discourse entity. When there is no previous entity, they sound quite odd. Hence Frazier and Rayner's control sentences (71) and (72) in isolation read awkwardly:

(71) I know that this desert trains young people to be especially tough.

(72) I know that these desert trains are especially tough on young people.

Therefore, MacDonald suggested, the relatively fast reading times in the ambiguous region of the experimental condition arose because the comparable reading times in the control condition were quite slow, as readers were taken aback by the infelicitous use of "this" and "these." MacDonald therefore used an additional type of control sentence. Rather than using different determiners, she used the unambiguous phrases "deserted trains" and "desert trained." She found that "this" and "these" did indeed slow down processing, even in the unambiguous version ("I know that these deserted trains could resupply the camp" compared with "I know that the deserted trains could resupply the camp").

MacDonald went on to test the effects of the semantic bias of the categorically ambiguous word. The semantic bias is the interpretation that people give to the ambiguity in isolation. It can turn out either to be correct if it is supported by the context, such as in (73), which normally has a noun–verb interpretation, or to be incorrect if it is not, as in (74), where "warehouse fires" normally has a noun–noun interpretation:

(73) The union told reporters that the corporation fires many workers each spring without giving them notice.

(74) The union told reporters that the warehouse fires many workers each spring without giving them notice.

According to the delay model, even a strong semantic bias should not affect initial resolution, because all decisions are delayed until the disambiguation region: Reading times should be the same whether the bias is supported or not. According to the constraint-based model, a strong semantic bias should have an immediate effect. If the interpretation favored by the semantic bias turns out to be correct, ambiguous reading times should not differ from the unambiguous control condition. It is only when the interpretation favored by the semantic bias turns out to be incorrect that reading times of the ambiguous sentence should increase. The pattern of results favored the constraint-based model. Semantic bias has an immediate effect.

(75) She saw her duck –

What happens when we encounter an ambiguous fragment such as (75)? In this situation, the continuation using "duck" in its sense as a verb (e.g., "She saw her duck and run") is statistically more likely than that as a noun (e.g., "She saw her duck and chickens"). It is possible to bias the interpretation with a preceding context sentence (e.g., "As they walked round, Agnes looked at all of Doris's pets"). Boland (1997), using analysis of reading times, showed that whereas probabilistic lexical information is used immediately to influence the generation of syntactic structures, background information is used later to guide the selection of the appropriate structure. These findings support the constraint-based approach: When we identify a word, we do not just access its syntactic category, we activate other knowledge that plays an immediate role in parsing, such as the knowledge about the frequency of alternative syntactic structures. However, the finding that context sometimes has a later effect requires modification of standard constraint-based theories.

GAPS, TRACES, AND UNBOUNDED DEPENDENCIES

Syntactic analysis of sentences suggests that sometimes constituents have been deleted or moved. Compare (76) and (77):

(76) Vlad was selling and Agnes was buying.

(77) Vlad was selling and Agnes_buying.

Sentence (77) is perfectly grammatically well formed. The verb ("was") has been deleted to avoid repetition, but it is still there, implicitly. Its deletion has left a **gap** in the location marked.

Parts of a sentence can be moved elsewhere in the sentence. When they are moved they leave a special type of gap called a trace. There is no trace in (78), but in (79) "sharpen" is a transitive verb demanding an object; the object "sword" has been moved, leaving a trace (indicated by t). This type of structure is called an unbounded dependency, because closely associated constituents are separated from each other (and can, in principle, be infinitely far apart).

(78) Which sword is sharpest?
(79) Which sword did Vlad sharpen [t] yesterday?

Gaps and traces may be important in the syntactic analysis of sentences, but is there any evidence that they affect parsing? If so, the gap has to be located and then filled with an appropriate **filler** (here "the sword").

There is some evidence that we fill gaps when we encounter them. First, traces place a strain on memory: The dislocated constituent has to be held in memory until the trace is reached. Second, processing of the trace can be detected in measurements of the brain's electrical activity (Garnsey, Tanenhaus, & Chapman, 1989; Kluender & Kutas, 1993), although it is difficult to disentangle the additional effects of plausibility and working memory load in these studies. Third, all languages seem to employ a recent filler strategy, whereby in cases of ambiguity a gap is filled with the most recent grammatically plausible filler. For example, Frazier, Clifton, and Randall (1983) noted that sentences of the form of (80) are understood 100 ms faster (as measured by reading times) than sentences such as (81):

(80) This is the girl the teacher wanted [t1] to talk to [t2].
(81) This is the girl the teacher wanted [t] to talk.

One possibility is that when the processor detects a gap it fills it with the most active item, and is prepared to reanalyze if necessary. This is the active-filler strategy (Frazier & Flores d'Arcais, 1989). Another possibility is that the processor detects a gap, and fills it with a filler, that is, the most recent potential dislocated constituent. This

is the recent-filler strategy. This leads to the correct outcome in (80): Here the constituent "the teacher" goes into the gap t1, leaving "the girl" to go into t2. In (81), however, it is "the girl" that should go into the gap t, and not the most recent constituent ("the teacher"). This delays processing, leading to the slower reading times. These two strategies can be quite difficult to distinguish, but in each case trace-detection plays an important role in parsing.

Finally, at first sight some of the strongest evidence for the processing importance of traces is the finding that traces appear able to prime the recognition of the dislocated constituents or antecedents with which they are associated. That is, the filler of the gap becomes semantically reactivated at the point of the gap. There is significant priming of the NP filler at the gap (Nicol, 1993; Nicol & Swinney, 1989). In a sentence such as (82), the NP "astute lawyer" is the antecedent of the trace [t], as the "astute lawyer" is the underlying subject who is going to argue during the trial (Bever & McElree, 1988). In the superficially similar control sentence (83) no constituent has been moved, and therefore there is no trace.

(82) The astute lawyer, who faced the female judge, was certain [t] to argue during the trial.
(83) The astute lawyer, who faced the female judge, hated the long speeches during the trial.

We find that the gap in (82) does indeed facilitate the recognition of a probe word from the antecedent (e.g., "astute"). The control sentence (83) produces no such facilitation. Hence, when we find a trace, we appear to retrieve its associated antecedent—a process known as binding the dislocated constituent to the trace, thereby making it more accessible.

On the other hand, there is other research suggesting that traces are not important in on-line processing. McKoon, Ratcliff, and Ward (1994) failed to replicate the studies that show wh- traces (traces formed by a question formation) can prime their antecedents (e.g., Nicol & Swinney, 1989). Although unable to point to any conclusive theoretical reasons why it should be the case, they found that the choice of control words in the lexical decision was very important; a choice of different words could obliterate the effect. They found no priming when the control words were chosen from the same set of words as the test words, yet priming was reinstated when the control words were from a different set of words than the test words. In addition, when they found priming, they found it for locations both after and before the verb. This should not be expected if the trace is reinstating the antecedent, as the trace is only activated by the verb. Clearly what is happening here is poorly understood.

An alternative view to the idea that we activate fillers when we come to a gap is that interpretation is driven by the verbs rather than the detection of the gaps, so that we postulate expected arguments to a verb as soon as we reach it (Boland, Tanenhaus, Carlson, & Garnsey, 1989). In the earlier sentences where there was evidence of semantic reactivation, the traces were adjacent to the verbs, so the two approaches make the same prediction. What happens if they are separated? Consider sentence (84):

(84) Which bachelor did Boris grant the maternity leave to [t]?

This sentence is semantically anomalous, but when does it become implausible? If the process of gap postulation and filling is driven by the syntactic process of trace analysis, it should only become implausible when people reach the trace at the end of the sentence. The role of "bachelor" can only be assigned after the preposition "to." But if the process is verb-driven, the role of "bachelor" can be determined as soon as "maternity leave" is assigned to the role of the direct object of "grant"; hence "bachelor" is the recipient. So the anomaly will be apparent here. This is what Boland et al. found. Hence the postulation and filling of gaps are immediate and are driven by the verbs (for similar results see Altmann, 1999; Boland, Tanenhaus, Garnsey, & Carlson, 1995; Nicol, 1993; Pickering & Barry, 1991; Tanenhaus, Boland, Mauner, & Carlson, 1993). For example, consider (85) from Traxler and Pickering (1996):

(85) That is the very small pistol in which the heartless killer shot the hapless man [t] yesterday afternoon.

Clearly this sentence is implausible, but when do readers experience difficulty? Here the gap location is after "man" (because in the plausible version the word order should be the heartless killer shot the hapless man with the very small pistol yesterday afternoon), but the readers experience processing difficulty immediately on reading "shot." The unbounded dependency has been formed before the gap location is reached. The parsing mechanism seems to be using all sources of information to construct analyses as soon as possible.

Similarly, Tanenhaus et al. (1989) presented participants with sentences such as (86) and (87):

(86) The businessman knew which customer the secretary called [t] at home.
(87) The businessman knew which article the security called [t] at home.

At what point do people detect the anomaly in (87)? Analysis of reading times showed that participants detect the anomaly before the gap, when they encounter the verb "called." ERP studies confirm that the detection of the anomaly is associated with the verb (Garnsey et al., 1989).

In summary, the preponderance of evidence suggests that fillers are postulated by activating the argument structure of verbs.

THE NEUROSCIENCE OF PARSING

As we would expect of a complex process such as parsing, it can be disrupted as a consequence of brain damage. Deficits in parsing, however, might not always be apparent, because people can often rely on semantic cues to obtain meaning. The deficit becomes apparent when these cues are removed and the patient is forced to rely on syntactic processing.

There is some evidence that syntactic functions take place in specific, dedicated parts of the brain. The evidence includes the differing effects of brain damage to regions of the brain such as Broca's and Wernicke's areas (see Chapters 3 and 13), and studies of brain imaging (e.g., Dogil, Haider, Schaner-Wolles, & Husman, 1995; Friederici, 2002; Neville et al., 1991).

The comprehension abilities of agrammatic aphasics

The disorder of syntactic processing that follows damage to Broca's area is called **agrammatism**. The most obvious feature of agrammatism is impaired speech production (see Chapter 13), but many people with agrammatism also have difficulty in understanding syntactically complex sentences. The ability of people with agrammatism to match sentences to pictures when semantic cues are eliminated is impaired (Caramazza & Berndt, 1978; Caramazza & Zurif, 1976; Saffran, Schwartz, & Marin, 1980). These patients are particularly poor at understanding reversible passive constructions (e.g., "The dog was chased by the cat" compared with "The flowers were watered by the girl") and object relative constructions (e.g., "The cat that the dog chased was black" compared with "The flowers that the girl watered were lovely") in the absence of semantic cues.

One explanation for these people's difficulty is that brain damage has disrupted their parsing ability. One suggestion is that these patients are unable to access grammatical elements correctly (Pulvermüller, 1995). Another idea is that this difficulty arises because syntactic traces are not processed properly, and the terminal nodes in the parse trees that correspond to function words are not properly formed (Grodzinsky, 1989, 1990; Zurif & Grodzinsky, 1983). Grodzinsky (2000) spelled out the trace-deletion hypothesis. This hypothesis states that people with an agrammatic comprehension deficit have difficulty in computing the relation between elements of a sentence that have been moved by a grammatical transformation and their origin (trace), as well as in constructing the higher parts of the parse tree. One problem with this view is that, as we have seen, the evidence for the existence of traces in parsing is questionable.

Some evidence against the idea that people with agrammatism have some impairment in parsing comes from the grammaticality judgment task. This task simply involves asking people whether a string of words forms a proper grammatical sentence or not. Linebarger, Schwartz, and Saffran (1983) showed that the patients are much more sensitive to grammatical violations than one might expect from their performance on sentence comprehension tasks. They performed poorly in a few conditions containing structures that involve making comparisons across positions in the sentence (such as being insensitive to violations like "*the man dressed herself" and "*the people will arrive at eight o'clock didn't they?"). It appears, then, that these patients can compute the constituent structure of a sentence, but have difficulty using that information, both for the purposes of detecting certain kinds of violation as well as for thematic role assignment. Schwartz, Linebarger, Saffran, and Pate (1987) showed that agrammatic patients could isolate the arguments of the main verb in sentences that were padded with extraneous material, but had difficulty using the syntax for the purpose of thematic role assignment. These studies suggest that these patients have not necessarily lost syntactic knowledge, but are unable to use it properly. Instead, the mapping hypothesis is the idea that the comprehension impairment arises because although low-level parsing processes are intact, agrammatics are limited by what they can do with the results of these processes. In particular, they have difficulty with thematic role assignment (Linebarger, 1995; Linebarger et al., 1983). They compensate, at least in part, by making use of semantic constraints, although Saffran, Schwartz, and Linebarger (1998) have shown that reliance on these constraints may sometimes lead them astray. Thus these patients failed to detect anomalies such as "*The cheese ate the mouse" and "*The children were watched by the movie" approximately 50% of the time.

Some types of patient that we might expect to find have so far never been observed. In particular, no one has (yet) described a case of a person who knows the meaning of words but who is unable to assign them to thematic roles (Caplan, 1992; although Schwartz, Saffran, & Marin, 1980b, describe a patient who comes close).

A completely different approach emerged that postulated that the syntactic comprehension deficit results from an impairment of general memory. According to this idea, the pattern of impairment observed depends on the degree of reduction of language capacity, and the structural complexity of the sentence being processed (Miyake, Carpenter, & Just, 1994). (Somewhat confusingly, although Miyake et al. talk of a reduction in working memory capacity, they mean a reduction in the capacity of a component of the central executive of Baddeley's 1990 conception of working memory that serves language comprehension; see Just & Carpenter, 1992.) In particular, these limited computational resources mean that people with a syntactic comprehension deficit suffer from restricted availability of the materials. Miyake et al. simulated agrammatism in normal comprehenders with varying memory capacities by increasing computational demands using very rapid presentation of words (120 ms a word). Along similar lines, Blackwell and Bates (1995) created an agrammatic performance profile in normal participants who had to make grammaticality judgments about sentences while carrying a memory load. In other words, people with a syntactic comprehension deficit are just at one end of a continuum of central executive capacity compared with the normal population. Syntactic knowledge is still intact, but cannot be used properly because of this working memory impairment. Grammatical elements are not processed in dedicated parts of the brain, but are particularly vulnerable to a global reduction in computational resources. Further evidence for this idea comes from self-reports from aphasic patients suggesting that they have limited computational resources ("other people talk too fast"—Rolnick & Hoops, 1969) and conversely that slower speech facilitates syntactic comprehension in some aphasic patients (e.g., Blumstein, Katz, Goodglass, Shrier, & Dworetzky, 1985). Increased time provides more opportunity for using the limited resources of the central executive. Indeed, time

shortage or the rapid decay of the results of syntactic processing might play a causal role in the syntactic comprehension deficit and in agrammatic production (Kolk, 1995).

This is an interesting idea that has provoked a good deal of debate. The extent to which the comprehension deficit is related to limited computational resources is debatable. For example, giving these patients unlimited time to process sentences does not lead to an improvement in processing (Martin, 1995; Martin & Feher, 1990). The degree to which Miyake et al. simulated aphasic performance has also been questioned (Caplan & Waters, 1995a). In particular, the performance of even their lowest-span participants was much better than that of the aphasic comprehenders. Caplan and Waters pointed out that rapid presentation might interfere with the perception of words rather than syntactic processing. Furthermore, patients with **Alzheimer's disease (AD)** with restricted working memory capacity show little effect of syntactic complexity, but do show large effects of semantic complexity (Rochon, Waters, & Caplan, 1994). Addressing these concerns, Dick et al. (2001) compared the syntactic comprehension abilities of agrammatic patients with college students working under a variety of stressful conditions (e.g., with the speech masked by noise, or by compressing the speech). The two groups then performed similarly.

Finally, if there is a reduction in processing capacity involved in syntactic comprehension deficits, it might be a reduction specifically in syntactic processing ability, rather than a reduction in general verbal memory capacity (Caplan, Baker, & Dehaut, 1985; Caplan & Hildebrandt, 1988; Caplan & Waters, 1999). The extent to which this is the case, or whether general verbal working memory is used in syntactic processing (the capacity theory), is still a hotly debated topic with few signs of settling on any agreement (Caplan & Waters, 1996, 1999; Just & Carpenter, 1992; Just, Carpenter, & Keller, 1996; Waters & Caplan, 1996; see also Chapter 15). On balance it looks as though a general reduction in working memory capacity cannot cause the syntactic deficit in agrammatism.

Are content and function words processed differently?

Remember that content words do the semantic work of the language and include nouns, verbs, adjectives, and most adverbs, while function words, which are normally short, common words, do the grammatical work of the language. Are content and function words processed in different parts of the brain?

Content words are sensitive to frequency in a lexical decision task, but function words are not. For a while it was thought that this pattern is not observed in patients with agrammatism (Bradley, Garrett, & Zurif, 1980). Instead, agrammatic patients are sensitive to the frequency of function words, as well as to the frequency of content words. This is because the brain damage means that function words can no longer be accessed by the special set of processes and have to be accessed as other content words. Perhaps the comprehension difficulties of these patients arise from difficulty in activating function words? Unfortunately, the exact interpretation of these results has proved very controversial, and the original studies have not been replicated (see, for example, Gordon & Caramazza, 1982; Swinney, Zurif, & Cutler, 1980). Caplan (1992) concluded that there is no clear neuropsychological evidence that function words are treated specially in parsing.

Is automatic or attentional processing impaired in agrammatism?

Most of the tasks used in the studies described so far (e.g., sentence–picture matching tasks, anomaly detection, and grammaticality judgment) are off-line, in that they do not tap parsing processes as they actually happen. Therefore, the results obtained might reflect the involvement of some later variable (such as memory). So do these impairments reflect deficits of automatic parsing processes, or deficits of some subsequent attentional process?

Tyler (1985) provided an indication that at least some deficits in some patients arise from a deficit of attentional processing. She examined aphasic comprehension of syntactic and semantic anomalies, comparing performance on an on-line measure (monitoring for a particular word) with that on an off-line measure (detecting an anomaly at the end of the sentence). She found patients who performed normally on the on-line task but very poorly on the off-line task. This suggests that the automatic parsing processes were intact, but the attentional processes were impaired.

This is a complex issue that has spawned a great deal of research (e.g., Friederici & Kilborn, 1989; Haarmann & Kolk, 1991; Martin, Wetzel, Blossom-Stach, & Feher, 1989; Milberg, Blumstein, & Dworetzky, 1987; Tyler, Ostrin, Cooke, & Moss, 1995). Clearly at least some of the deficits we observe arise from attentional factors: the question remaining is, how many?

Evaluation of work on the neuroscience of parsing

Although there has been a considerable amount of work on the neuropsychology of parsing, it is much more difficult to relate to the psychological processes involved in parsing. Much of the work is technical in nature and relates to linguistic theories of syntactic representation. It is also unlikely that there is a single cause for the range of deficits observed (Tyler et al., 1995).

Friederici (2002) describes a model of sentence processing where the left temporal regions identify sounds and words; the left frontal cortex is involved in sequencing and the formation of structural and semantic relations; and the right hemisphere is involved in identifying prosody (see Figure 10.4). She argues that imaging and electrophysiological data suggest that sentence processing takes place in three phases. In Phase 1 (100–300 ms) the initial syntactic structure is formed on the basis of information about word category. In Phase 2 (300–500 ms) lexical-syntactic processes take place, resulting in thematic role assignment. In Phase 3 (500–1,000 ms) the different types of information are integrated. She argues that syntactic and semantic processes only interact in Phase 3.

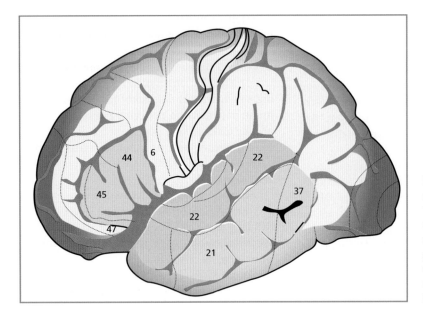

FIGURE 10.4 Brodmann areas in the left hemisphere. The inferior frontal gyrus (IFG) is shown in green, the superior temporal gyrus (STG) in red, and the middle temporal gyrus (MTG) in blue. From Friederici (2002).

SUMMARY

- The clause is an important unit of syntactic processing.
- In autonomous models, only syntactic information is used to construct and select among alternative syntactic structures; in interactive models non-syntactic information is used in the selection process.
- Psycholinguists have particularly studied how we understand ambiguous sentences, such as garden path constructions.
- One of the most studied types of garden path sentence is the reduced relative, as in the well-known sentence "The horse raced past the barn fell."
- Early models of parsing focused on parsing strategies using syntactic cues.
- Kimball proposed seven surface structure parsing strategies.
- The sausage machine of Frazier and Fodor comprised a limited window preliminary phrase packager (PPP) and a sentence structure supervisor (SSS).
- The principle of minimal attachment says that we prefer the simplest construction, where simple means the structure that creates the minimum number of syntactic nodes.
- The principle of late closure says that we prefer to attach incoming material to the clause or phrase currently being processed.
- Languages may differ in their attachment preferences.
- The garden path model of parsing is still a two-stage model, where only syntactic information can affect the first stage.
- The referential model of parsing explains the garden path effect in terms of discourse factors such as the number of entities presupposed by the alternative constructions.
- In constraint-based models, all types of information (e.g., thematic information about verbs) are used to select among alternative structures.

- The experimental evidence for and against the autonomous garden path and interactive constraint-based models is conflicting.
- In constraint-based models, lexical and syntactic ambiguity are considered to be fundamentally the same thing, and resolved by similar mechanisms.
- Statistical preferences may have some role in parsing.
- Some recent models have questioned whether syntax needs to precede semantic analysis.
- Gaps are filled by the semantic reactivation of their fillers.
- Gaps may be postulated as soon as we encounter particular verb forms.
- Verbs play a central role in parsing.
- ERP studies show that people try and predict what is coming next.
- Some aphasics show difficulties in parsing when they cannot rely on semantic information.
- There is no clear neuropsychological evidence that content and function words are processed differently in parsing.
- Some off-line techniques might be telling us more about memory limitations or semantic integration than about what is actually happening at the time of parsing.
- Electrophysiological and imaging data suggest that sentence comprehension takes place in three phases, and different components of processing are identifiable with distinct regions of the brain.

QUESTIONS TO THINK ABOUT

1. What does the evidence from the study of language development tell us about the relation between syntax and other language processes? (You may need to look at Chapters 2 and 3 again in order to be able to answer this question.)
2. What do studies of parsing tell us about some of the differences between good and poor readers?
3. Is the following statement true: "Syntax proposes, semantics disposes"?
4. How does the notion of "interaction" in parsing relate to the notion of "interaction" in word recognition?
5. Which experimental techniques discussed in this chapter are likely to give the best insight into what is happening at the time of parsing? How would you define "best"?

FURTHER READING

Fodor, Bever, and Garrett (1974) is the classic work on much of the early research on the possible application of Chomsky's research to psycholinguistics, including deep structure and the derivational theory of complexity. Greene (1972) covers the early versions of Chomsky's theory, and detailed coverage of early psycholinguistic experiments relating to it. See Clark and Clark (1977) for a detailed description of surface structure parsing cues. Johnson-Laird (1983) discusses different types of parsing systems with special reference to garden path sentences.

(Continued)

(Continued)

For reviews on parsing work see Pickering and van Gompel (2006) and van Gompel and Pickering (2007). For a model based on a rational analysis of what parsing involves, see Hale (2010).

As Mitchell (1994) pointed out, most of the work in parsing has examined a single language. There are exceptions, including work on Dutch (Frazier, 1987b; Frazier, Flores d'Arcais, & Coolen, 1993; Mitchell, Brysbaert, Grondelaers, & Swanepoel, 2000), French (Holmes & O'Reagan, 1981), East Asian languages (Special Issue of *Language and Cognitive Processes*, 1999, volume 14, parts 5 and 6), German (Bach, Brown, & Marslen-Wilson, 1986; Hemforth & Konieczny, 1999), Hungarian (MacWhinney & Pleh, 1988), Japanese (Mazuka, 1991), and Spanish (Cuetos & Mitchell, 1988), but the great preponderance of the work has been on English alone. It is possible that this is giving us at best a restricted view of parsing, and at worst a misleading view.

See Caplan (1992; the paperback edition is 1996) for a detailed review of work on the neuro-psychology of parsing. See Haarmann, Just, and Carpenter (1997) for a computer simulation of the resource-deficit model of syntactic comprehension deficits.

CHAPTER ⬛⬛ 11

WORD MEANING

INTRODUCTION

How do we represent the meaning of words? How do we organize our knowledge of the world? These are questions about the study of meaning, or **semantics**. In Chapter 10 we saw how the sentence-processing mechanism constructs a representation of the syntactic relations between words. Important as this stage might be, it is only an intermediate step towards the final goal of comprehension, which is constructing a representation of the meaning of the sentence that can be used for the appropriate purpose. Derivation of meaning is hence the ultimate goal of language processing—and meaning is the start of the production process. Having some effective means of being able to represent meaning is practically important, too: effective translation between languages depends on meaning, as does effective information storage and retrieval (as in intelligent search engines). In this chapter, I examine how the meanings of individual words are represented. In Chapter 12, we will see how we combine these meanings to form a representation of the meaning of the sentence and beyond.

The discussion of non-semantic reading in Chapter 7 showed that the phonological and orthographic representations of words can be dissociated from their meanings. There is further intuitive evidence to support this dissociation (Hirsh-Pasek, Reeves, & Golinkoff, 1993). First, we can translate words from one language to another, even though not every word meaning is represented by a simple, single word in every language. Second, there is an imperfect mapping between words and their meanings such that some words have more than one meaning (ambiguity), while some words have the same meaning as each other (synonymy). Third, the meaning of words depends to some extent on the context. Hence a big ant is very different in size from a big elephant, and the red in "the red sunset" is a different color from "she blushed and turned red."

Tulving (1972) distinguished between episodic and semantic memory. **Episodic memory** is our memory for events and particular episodes; **semantic memory** is, in simple terms, our general knowledge. Hence my knowledge that the capital of France is Paris is stored in semantic memory, while my memory of a trip to Paris is an instance of an episodic memory. Semantic memory develops from or is abstracted from episodes that may be repeated many times. I cannot now recall when I learned the name of the capital of France, but clearly I must have been exposed to it at least once. We have seen that our mental dictionary is called the **lexicon**, and similarly our store of semantic knowledge is called our mental encyclopedia. Clearly there is a close relation between the two, both in developing and developed systems. Neuropsychology reveals important dissociations in this respect. We have seen that words and their meanings can be dissociated; but we must be wary of confusing a loss of semantic information with the inability to access or use that information. This problem is particularly important when we consider semantic neuropsychological deficits. Although the distinction between semantic and episodic memory is a useful one, the extent to which they involve different memory processes is less clear (McKoon, Ratcliff, & Dell, 1986).

The notion of meaning is closely bound to that of categorization. A concept determines how things are related or categorized. It is a mental representation of a category. It enables us to group things together, so that instances of a category all have something in common. Thus concepts somehow specify category membership. All words have an underlying concept, but not all concepts are labeled by a word. For example, we do not have a special word for brown dogs. In English we have a word "dog" that we can use about certain things in the world, but not about others. There are two fundamental questions here. The philosophical question is how does the concept of "dog" relate to the members of the category dog? The psychological question is how is the meaning of "dog" represented and how do we pick out instances of dogs in the environment?

In principle we could have a word, say "brog," to refer to brown dogs. We do not have such a term, probably because it is not a particularly useful one. Rosch (1978) pointed out that the way in which we categorize the world is not arbitrary, but determined by two important features of our cognitive system. First, the categories we form are determined in part by the way in which we perceive the structure of the world. Perceptual features are tied together because they form objects and have a shared function. How the categories we form are determined by biological factors is an important topic, about which little is known, although we know how color names relate to perceptual constraints (see Chapter 3). Second, the structure of categories might be determined by cognitive economy. This means that semantic memory is organized so as to avoid excessive duplication. There is a trade-off between economy and informativeness: A memory system organized with just the categories "animal," "plant," and "everything else" would be economical but not very informative (Eysenck & Keane, 2010). We may also need to make distinctions between members of some categories more often than others. Another disadvantage of cognitive economy might be increased retrieval time, as we need to search our memories for where the appropriate facts are stored.

It should be obvious that the study of meaning therefore necessitates capturing the way in which words refer to things that are all members of the same category and have something in common, yet are different from non-members. (Of course something can belong to two categories at once: We can have a category labeled by the word "ghost," and another by the word "invisible," and indeed we can join the two to form the category of invisible ghosts labeled by the words "invisible ghosts.") There are two issues here. What distinguishes items of one category from items of another? And how are hierarchical relations between categories to be captured? There are category relations between words. For example, the basic-level category "dog" has a large number of category superordinate levels above it (such as "mammal," "animal," "animate thing," and "object") and subordinates (such as "terrier," "Rottweiler," and "German shepherd"—these are said to be category coordinates of each other).

Hierarchical relations between categories are one clear way in which words can be related in meaning, but there are other ways that are equally important. Some words refer to associates of a thing (e.g., "dog" and "lead"). Some words (antonyms) are opposites in meaning (e.g., "hot" and "cold"). We can attempt to define many words: for example, we might offer the definition "unmarried man" for "bachelor." A fundamental issue for semantics concerns how we should capture all these relations.

Semantics concerns more than associations (see Chapter 6). Words can be related in meaning without being associated (e.g., "yacht" and "ship"), so any theory of word meaning cannot rely simply on word association. Words with similar meanings tend to occur in similar contexts. Lund, Burgess, and Atchley (1995) showed that semantically similar words (e.g., "bed" and "table") are interchangeable within a sentence; the resulting sentence, while maybe pragmatically implausible, nevertheless makes sense. Consider (1) and (2). If "table" is substituted for the semantically related word "bed" the sentence still makes sense. Word pairs that are only associated (e.g., "baby" and "cradle") result in meaningless sentences. If we substitute "baby" for its associate "cradle" in (3), we end up with the anomalous sentence (4).

(1) The child slept on the bed.
(2) The child slept on the table.
(3) The child slept in the cradle.
(4) *The child slept in the baby.

Associations arise from words regularly occurring together, while semantic relations arise from shared contexts and higher level relations. One task of research in semantics is to capture how contexts can be shared and how these higher level relations should be specified.

Semantics is also the interface between language and the rest of perception and cognition. This relation is made explicit in the work of Jackendoff (1983), who proposed a theory of the connection between semantics and other cognitive, perceptual, and motor processes. He proposed two constraints on a general theory of semantics. The grammatical constraint says that we should prefer a semantic theory that explains otherwise arbitrary generalizations about syntax and the lexicon. Some aspects of syntax will be determined by semantics. Some AI theories and theories based on logic (in particular, a form of logic known as predicate calculus) fail this constraint. In order to work, they have to make up entities that do not correspond to anything involved in cognitive processing, and they break up the semantic representation of single words across several constituents. This constraint says that syntax and semantics should be related in a sensible way. The cognitive constraint says that there is a level of representation where semantics must interface with other psychological representations, such as those derived from perception. There is some level of representation where linguistic, motor, and sensory information are compatible. Connectionist models in particular show how this constraint can be satisfied.

This chapter focuses on a number of related topics. How do we represent the meaning of words? In particular, how does a model of meaning deal with the issues we have just raised? Is a word decomposed into more elemental units of meaning or not? How are words related to each other by their meanings? This deals with issues such as priming, and how word meanings are related. What does the neuropsychology of meaning tell us about its representation and its relation with the encyclopedia? In the next chapter, we will examine how word meanings are combined to form representations of the meaning of sentences and large units of language. By the end of this chapter you should:

* Understand the difference between sense and reference.
* Know how semantic networks might represent meaning.
* Know about the strengths and weaknesses of representing word meaning in terms of smaller units of meaning.
* Understand how we store information about categories.
* Appreciate how brain damage can affect how meaning is represented.
* Know whether we have one or more semantic memory systems.
* Understand the importance of the difference between perceptual and functional information.
* Know how semantic information breaks down in dementia.
* Be able to evaluate the importance of connectionist modeling of semantic memory.

CLASSIC APPROACHES TO SEMANTICS

It is useful to distinguish immediately between a word's denotation and its connotation. The denotation of a word is its core, essential meaning. The connotations of a word are all of its secondary implications, or emotional or evaluative associations. For example, the denotation of the word "dog" is its core meaning: it is the relation between the word and the class of objects to which it can refer. The connotations of "dog" might be "nice," "frightening," or "smelly." Put another way, people agree on the denotation, but the connotations differ from person to person. In this chapter I am primarily concerned with the denotational aspect of meaning, although the distinction can become quite hazy.

Ask a person on the street what the meaning of "dog" is, and they might well point to one. This theory of meaning, that words mean what they refer to, is one of the oldest, and is called the referential theory of meaning. There are two major problems with this lay theory, however. First, it is not at all clear how such a theory treats abstract concepts. How can you point to "justice" or "truth," let alone point to the meaning of a word such as "whomsoever"? Second, there is a dissociation between a word and the things to which it can refer. Consider the words "Hesperus" (Greek for "The Evening Star") and "Phosphorus" (Greek for "The Morning Star"). They have the same referent in our universe, namely the planet Venus, but they have different senses. The ancients did not know that Hesperus and Phosphorus were the same thing, so even though the words actually refer to the same thing (the planet Venus), the words have different senses (Johnson-Laird, 1983). The sense of "Hesperus" is the planet you can see in the evening sky, but the sense of "Phosphorus" is the one in the morning sky. This distinction was made explicit in the work of Frege (1892/1952), who distinguished between the sense (often called the intension) of a word and its reference (often called its extension). The intension is a word's sense: It is its abstract specification that determines how it is related in meaning to other words. It specifies the properties an object must have to be a member of the class. The extension is what the word stands for in the world; that is, the objects picked out by that intension. These notions can be extended from words or descriptive phrases to expressions or sentences. Frege stated that the reference of a sentence was its truth value (which is simply whether it is true or not), while its sense was derived by combining the intensions of the component words, and specified the conditions that must hold for the sentence to be true.

Logicians have developed this formal semantics approach of building logical models of meaning into complex systems of meaning known as model-theoretic semantics. (Because

Referential theory (which proposes that words mean what they refer to) can be problematic. "Hesperus" (Greek for "The Evening Star") and "Phosphorus" (Greek for "The Morning Star") both refer to the planet Venus, but they have altogether different senses.

of the importance of truth in these theories, they are sometimes known as truth-theoretic semantics.) Although the original idea was to provide an account of logic, mathematics, and computing languages, logicians have tried to apply it to natural language. But, although formal approaches to semantics help refine what meaning might be, they appear to say little about how we actually represent or compute it (Johnson-Laird, 1983).

SEMANTIC NETWORKS

One of the most influential of all processing approaches to meaning is based on the idea that the meaning of a word is given by how it is embedded within a network of other meanings. Some of the earliest theories of meaning, from those of Aristotle to those of the behaviorists, viewed meaning as deriving from a word's association. From infancy, we are exposed to many episodes involving the word "dog." For the behaviorists, the meaning of the word "dog" was simply the sum of all our associations to the word: It obtains its meaning by its place in a network of associations. The meaning of "dog" might involve an association with "barks," "four legs," "furry," and so on. It soon became apparent that association in itself was insufficiently powerful to be able to capture all aspects of meaning. There is no structure in an associative network, with no relation between words, no hierarchy of information, and no cognitive economy. In a semantic network, this additional power is obtained by making the connections between items do something—they are not merely associations representing frequent co-occurrence, but themselves have a semantic value. That is, in a semantic network the links between concepts themselves have meaning.

The Collins and Quillian semantic network model

Perhaps the best-known example of a semantic network is that of Collins and Quillian (1969). This work arose from an attempt to develop a "teachable language comprehender" to assist machine translation between languages.

A semantic network is particularly useful for representing information about **natural kind** terms. These are words that denote naturally occurring categories and their members—such as types of animal, or metal, or precious stone. The scheme attributes fundamental importance to their inherently hierarchical nature: For example, a bald eagle is a type of eagle, an eagle is a type of bird of prey, a bird of prey is a bird, and a bird is a type of animal. This is a very economical method of storing information. If you store the information that birds have wings at the level of bird, you do not need to repeat it at the level of particular instances (e.g., eagles, bald eagles, and robins). An example of a fragment of such a network is shown in Figure 11.1. In the network, nodes are connected by links that specify the relation between the linked nodes; the most common link is an ISA link which means that the lower level node "is a" type of the higher level node. Attributes are stored at the lowest possible node at which they are true of all lower nodes in the network. For example, not all animals have wings, but all birds do—so "has wings" is stored at the level of birds.

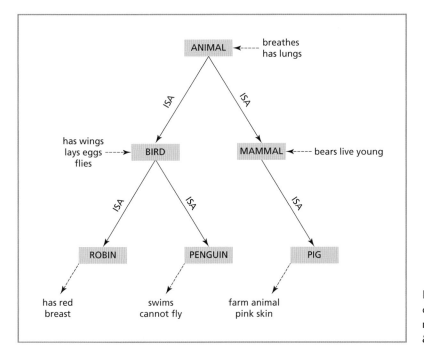

FIGURE 11.1 Example of a hierarchical semantic network (based on Collins & Quillian, 1969).

The sentence verification task

One of the most commonly used tasks in early semantic memory research was sentence verification. Participants are presented with simple "facts" and have to press one button if the sentence is true, another if it is false. The reaction time is an index of how difficult the decision was. Collins and Quillian (1969) presented participants with sentences such as (5) to (8):

(5) A robin is a robin.
(6) A robin is a bird.
(7) A robin is an animal.
(8) A robin is a fish.

Sentence (5) is trivially true, but it obviously still takes participants some time to respond "yes"; clearly they have to read the sentence and initiate a response. This sentence therefore provides a baseline measure. The response time to (5) is less than that to (6), which in turn is less than that to (7). Furthermore, the difference between the reaction times is about the same—that is, there is a linear relation. Sentence (8) is of course false.

Why do we get these results? According to this model, participants produce responses by starting off from the node in the network that is the subject in the sentence (here "robin"), and traveling through the network until they find the necessary information. As this traveling takes a fixed amount of time for each link, the farther away the information is, the slower the response time. To get from "robin" to "bird" involves traveling along only one link, but to get from "robin" to "animal" necessitates traveling along two links. That is, the semantic distance between "robin" and "animal" is greater than that between "robin" and "bird." If the information is not found, the "no" response is made.

The characteristic of property inheritance also shows the same pattern of response times, as we have to travel along links to retrieve the property from the appropriate level. Hence reaction times are fastest to (9), as the "red-breasted" attribute is stored at the "robin" node, slower to (10), as "has wings" is stored at the "bird" level above "robin," and slowest to (11), as this information is stored two levels above "robin" at the "animal" level.

(9)   A robin has a red breast.
(10) A robin has wings.
(11) A robin has lungs.

These data from early sentence verification experiments therefore supported the Collins and Quillian model.

Problems with the Collins and Quillian model

A number of problems with this model soon emerged. First, clearly not all information is easily represented in hierarchical form. What is the relation between "truth," "justice," and "law," for example? A second problem is that the materials in the sentence verification task that appear to support the hierarchical model confound semantic distance with what is called conjoint frequency. This is exemplified by the words "bird" and "robin"; these words appear together in the language—for example, they are used in the same sentence—far more often than "bird" and "animal" occur together. Conjoint frequency is a measure of how frequently two words co-occur. When you control for conjoint frequency, the linear relation between semantic distance and time is weakened (Conrad, 1972; Wilkins, 1971). In particular, hierarchical effects can no longer be found for verifying statements about attributes ("a canary has lungs"), although they persist for class inclusion ("a canary is an animal"). These findings suggest that an alternative interpretation of the sentence verification results is that the sentences that give the faster verification times contain words that are more closely associated. Another possible confound in the original sentence verification experiments is with category size. The class of "animals" is by definition bigger than the class of "birds," so perhaps it takes longer to search (Landauer & Freedman, 1968).

Third, the hierarchical model makes some incorrect predictions. We find that a sentence such as (12) is verified much faster than (13), even though "animal" is higher in the hierarchy than "mammal" (Rips, Shoben, & Smith, 1973). This suggests that memory structure does not always reflect logical category structure.

(12)   A cow is an animal.
(13)   A cow is a mammal.

We do not reject all untrue statements equally slowly. Sentence (14) is rejected faster than (15), even though both are equally untrue (Schaeffer & Wallace, 1969, 1970; Wilkins, 1971). This is called the relatedness effect: The more related two things are, the harder it is to disentangle them, even if they are not ultimately from the same class.

(14)   A pine is a church.
(15)   A pine is a flower.

Neither are all true statements involving the same semantic distance responded to equally quickly. Sentence (16) is verified faster than (17), even though both involve only one semantic link (Rips et al., 1973), and a "robin" is judged to be a more typical bird than a "penguin" or an "ostrich" (Rosch, 1973). This advantage for more typical items is called the prototypicality effect.

(16)   A robin is a bird.
(17)   A penguin is a bird.

A related observation is that non-necessary features are involved in classification. When people are asked to list features of a concept, they include properties that are not possessed by all instances of the concept (e.g., "flies" is not true of all birds). Feature listings correlate with categorization times: We are faster to categorize instances the more features they share with a concept (Hampton, 1979).

In summary there are too many problematical findings from sentence verification experiments to accept the hierarchical network model in its original form. We shall see that of these troublesome findings, the prototypicality and relatedness effects are particularly important. Semantic networks do not capture the graded nature of semantic knowledge (Anderson, 2010).

Revisions to the semantic network model

Collins and Loftus (1975) proposed a revision of the model based on the idea of spreading activation. The structure of the network became more

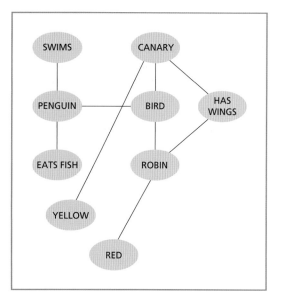

FIGURE 11.2 Example of a spreading activation semantic network. It should be noted that two dimensions cannot do justice to the necessary complexity of the network. Based on Collins and Loftus (1975).

complex, with the links between nodes varying in strength or distance (see Figure 11.2). Hence "penguin" is more distant from "bird" than is "robin." The structure is no longer primarily hierarchical, although hierarchical relations still form parts of the network. Access and priming in the network occur through a mechanism of spreading activation. The concepts of activation traveling along links of different strengths, and of many simple units connected together in complex ways, are of course important concepts in connectionist models. The problem with this model is that it is very difficult to test: It is hard to see what sorts of experiments could falsify it. Nevertheless, the idea of activation spreading around a network has proved influential in more recent models of meaning (e.g., connectionist models).

SEMANTIC FEATURES

Another approach to semantic memory views the meaning of a word as determined not by the position of the word in a network of meaning, but by its decomposition into smaller units of meaning. These smaller units of meaning are called semantic features (or sometimes semantic attributes, or semantic markers). Theories that make use of semantic features are often called decompositional theories. The alternative is that each word is represented by its own concept that is not decomposed further.

Semantic features work very well in some simple domains where there is a clear relation between the terms. One such domain, much studied by anthropologists, is that of kinship terms. A simple example is shown in Table 11.1. Here the meanings of the four words, "mother," "father," "son," and "daughter," are captured by combinations of the three features "human," "male" or "female," and "older" or "younger." We could provide a hierarchical arrangement of these features (e.g., human → young and old; young → male or female; and old → male or female), but it would either be totally unprincipled (there is no reason why adult/young should come before male/female, or vice versa), or would involve duplication (if we store both hierarchical forms). Instead, we can list the meaning in terms of a list of features, so that father is (+ human, − female, + older).

We can take the idea of semantic features further, and represent the meanings of all words in terms of combinations of as few semantic features as possible. When we use features in this way it is as though they become "atoms of meaning," and are called semantic primitives. This approach has been particularly influential in AI. For example, Schank (1972, 1975) argued that the meaning of sentences could be represented by the conceptual dependencies between the semantic primitives underlying the words in the sentence. All common verbs can be analyzed in terms of 12 primitive

actions that concern the movement of objects, ideas, and abstract relations. For example, there are five physical actions (called "expel," "grasp," "ingest," "move," and "propel"), and two abstract ones ("attend" and "speak"). Their names are fairly self-explanatory, and it is not necessary to go into detail of their meanings here. Wilks (1976) described a semantic system where the meaning of 600 words in the simulation can be reduced to combinations of only 80 primitives. In this system the action sense of "beat" is denoted by ("strike" [subject—human] [object—animate] [instrument—thing]). The semantic representation and syntactic roles in which the word can partake are intimately linked. In a similar vein, Wierzbicka (2004) argues that in spite of their apparent diversity, all natural languages share a common core of about 60 conceptual primitives present in all languages. Other word meanings can be built up by combining these primitives (e.g., a plant is a living thing that cannot feel or do). Of course, just because we can reduce the meaning of all words to a relatively small number of primitives does not mean that is how we do actually represent them.

One possibility is that all words are represented in terms of combinations of only semantic primitives. In addition to these AI models, the model of Katz and Fodor (1963), described later, is of this type. Another possibility is that words are represented as combinations of features not all of which need be primitives. These non-primitive features might eventually be represented elsewhere in semantic memory as combinations of primitives. For example, the meaning of "woman" might include "human" but not "object," because the meaning of "human" might include "animal," and eventually the meaning of "animal" includes "object" (McNamara & Miller, 1989). This idea is similar to the principle of economy incorporated into hierarchical semantic networks. Jackendoff (1983) and Johnson-Laird (1983) described models of this type.

Early decompositional theories

One of the earliest decompositional theories was that of Katz and Fodor (1963). This theory

TABLE 11.1 Decomposition of kinship terms.

Feature	Father	Mother	Daughter	Son
Human	+	+	+	+
Older	+	+	−	−
Female	−	+	+	−

showed how the meanings of sentences could be derived by combining the semantic features of each individual word in the sentence. It emphasized how we understand ambiguous words. Consider examples (18) and (19). A different sense of "ball" is used in each sentence. Then consider (20), which is semantically anomalous:

(18) The witches played around on the beach and kicked the ball.

(19) The witches put on their party frocks and went to the ball.

(20) ? The rock kicked the ball.

There are no syntactic cues to be made use of here, so how do the meanings of the words in the sentence combine to resolve the ambiguity in (18) and (19) and identify the anomaly in (20)? First, Katz and Fodor postulated a decompositional theory of meaning so that the meanings of individual words in the sentence are broken down into their component semantic features (called semantic markers by Katz and Fodor). Second, the combination of features across words is governed by particular constraints called selection restrictions. There is a selection restriction on the meaning of "kick" such that it must take an animate subject and an optional object, but if there is an object then it must be a physical object. An ambiguous word such as "ball" has two sets of semantic features, one of which will be specified as something like (sphere, small, used in games, physical object ...), the other as (dance, event ...). Only one of these contains the "physical object" feature, so "kick" picks out that sense. Similarly there is a selection restriction on the verb "went" such that it picks out locations and events, which contradicts the "physical object" sense of "ball." Finally, the selection restriction on "kick" that specifies an animate subject is incompatible with the underlying semantic features of "rock." As there are no other possible subjects in this sentence, we consider it anomalous. As we shall see, one of the problems with this type of approach is that for most words it is impossible to provide an exhaustive listing of all of its features.

Feature-list theories and sentence verification

We have seen that decompositional theories of meaning enable us to list the meanings of words as lists of semantic features. What account does such a model give of performance on the sentence verification task, and in particular what account does it give of the problems to which hierarchical network models fall prey? Rips et al. (1973) proposed that there are two types of semantic feature. Defining features are essential to the underlying meaning of a word, and relate to properties that things must have to be a member of that category (for example, a bird is living, it is feathered, lays eggs, and so forth). Characteristic features are usually true of instances of a category, but are not necessarily true (for example, most birds can fly, but penguins and ostriches cannot).

According to Rips et al., sentence verification involves making comparisons of the feature lists representing the meaning of the words involved in two stages. For this reason this particular approach is called the feature-comparison theory. In the first stage, the overall featural similarity of the two words is compared, including both the defining and characteristic features. If there is very high overlap, we respond "true"; if there is very low overlap, we respond "false." If we compare "robin" and "bird," there is much overlap and no conflict in the complete list of features, so we can respond "true" very easily. With "robin"

Characteristic features are not necessarily relevant to all members of a given category; most birds can fly, for example, but penguins cannot.

and "pig," there is very little overlap and a great deal of conflict, so we can respond "false" very quickly. However, if the amount of overlap is neither very high nor very low, we then have to go on to a second stage of comparison, where we consider only the defining features. This obviously takes additional time. An exact match on these is then necessary to respond "true." For example, when we compare "penguin" and "bird," there is a moderate amount of overlap and some conflict (on flying, for example). An examination of the defining features of "penguin" then reveals that it is, after all, a type of bird. The advantage of the first stage is that although the comparison is not detailed, it is very quick. We do not always need to make detailed comparisons.

One problem with the feature-list model is that it is very closely tied to the sentence verification paradigm. A more general problem is that many words do not have obvious defining features. Smith and Medin (1981) extended and modernized the feature theory with the probabilistic feature model. In this approach there is an important distinction between the core description and the identification procedures of a concept (see Figure 11.3). The core description comprises the essential defining features of the concept and captures the relations between concepts, while the identification procedures concern those aspects of meaning that are related to identifying instances of the concept. For physical objects, perceptual features form an important part of the identification procedure. Semantic features are weighted according to a combination of how salient they are and the probability of their being true of a category. For example, the feature "has four limbs" has a large weighting because it relates to something that is perceptually salient and is true of all mammals. "Bears live young" has a lower weighting because although true of almost all mammals it is less salient, while "eats meat" is even lower because it is not even true of most mammals. In a sentence verification task, a candidate instance is accepted as an instance of the category if it exceeds some critical weighted sum of features. For example, "a robin is a bird" is accepted quickly because the features of "robin" that correspond to "bird" easily exceed "bird's" threshold.

The revised model has the advantage of emphasizing the relation between meaning and identification, and can account for all the verification time data. Because identifying an exemplar of a category only involves passing a threshold rather than examining the possession of defining features, categories that have "fuzzy" or unclear boundaries are no longer problematic. At this point it becomes difficult to distinguish empirically between this model and the prototype model described later.

Evaluation of decompositional theories

There is evidence for and against decompositional theories. It is a difficult area in which to carry out experiments. Indeed, Hollan (1975)

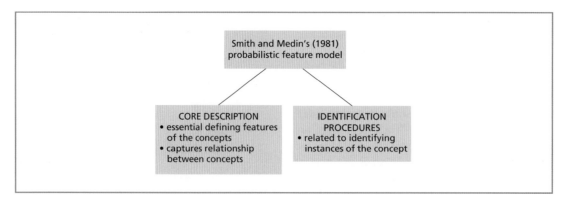

FIGURE 11.3

argued that it is impossible to devise an experiment to distinguish between feature-list and semantic network theories because they are formally equivalent, in that it is impossible to find a prediction that will distinguish between them (but see Rips, Smith, & Shoben, 1975, for a reply). Hence for all intents and purposes we can consider network models to be a type of decompositional model.

On the one hand, decompositional theories have an intuitive appeal, and they make explicit how we make inferences based on the meaning of words in the sentence verification task. In reducing meaning to a small number of primitives, they are very economical. On the other hand, it is difficult to construct decompositional representations for even some of the most common words. Some categories do not have any obvious defining features that are common to all their members. The most famous example of this was provided by Wittgenstein (1953), who asked what all games have in common, and therefore how "game" should be defined—that is, how it should be decomposed into its semantic primitives. There is no clear complete definition; instead, it is as though there are many different "games," which have in common a family resemblance. If you consider some examples of games (e.g., boxing, chess, football, ring-a-ring-a-roses, solitaire), all have some of the important features (competition, recreation, teams, winners and losers), but none has all. So if we cannot define an apparently simple concept such as this, how are we going to cope with more complex examples? A glance at the examples we mentioned earlier should reveal another problem: Even when we can apparently define words, the features we come up with are not particularly appealing or intuitively obvious; one suspects that an alternative set could be generated with equal facility. It is not even clear that our definitions are complete: Often it is as though we have to anticipate all possible important aspects of meaning in advance. Bolinger (1965) criticized Katz and Fodor's theory because of its inability to provide an explanation of the way in which we understand examples such as (21):

(21) He became a bachelor.

The word "bachelor" is ambiguous between the senses of "unmarried man who has never been married" and "a person with a university degree." Why do we select the second interpretation in the case of (21)? You might say that it is because we know that you cannot become an unmarried man who has never been married. So does that mean that "impossible to become" is part of the underlying meaning of this sense of bachelor—that this is one of its semantic features? This seems very implausible. Generally, the interpretation of word meaning is very sensitive to world knowledge. Is it part of the meaning of "pig" that it does not have a trunk? This also seems most unlikely. We could suggest that these problems are solved by making inferences rather than just accessing semantic memory, but then the problem becomes much more complex. Finally, we have more knowledge about word meaning than can be represented as a list of features. We also know relationships between features. For example, if something flies and builds a nest, it usually lays eggs; if a living thing has four legs, it gives birth (with a few exceptions) to live young. We say that features are intercorrelated.

The feature-comparison theory has additional problems. First, it is very specific to the sentence verification task. Second, there are some methodological problems with the Smith, Shoben, and Rips (1974) experiments. Semantic relatedness and stimulus familiarity were confounded in the original experimental materials (McCloskey, 1980). Moreover, Loftus (1973) showed that if you reverse the order of the nouns in the sentences used in sentence verification, you find effects not predicted by the theory. If we only compare lists of features for the instance and class nouns, their order should not matter. Hence (22) should be verified in the same time as (23):

(22) Is a robin a bird?
(23) Is a bird a robin?

Loftus found that noun order is important. For sentences such as (22), the verification times were a function of how often the category was mentioned given a particular instance, but for sentences such as (23) the times were a function of how often the instance was given for the category. However, the task involved in verifying sentences such as (23) seems unnatural compared with that of (22). Third, Holyoak and Glass (1975) showed that people may have specific strategies for disconfirming sentences, such as thinking of a specific counter-example, rather than carrying out extensive computation. Finally, and most tellingly, it is not easy to distinguish empirically between defining and characteristic features. Hampton (1979) showed that in practice defining features do not always define category membership. The model still cannot easily account for the finding that some categories have unclear or fuzzy boundaries. For example, for many people it is unclear whether a tomato is a fruit or a vegetable, or both. McCloskey and Glucksberg (1978) showed that although participants agree on many items as members of categories, they also disagree on many. For example, although all participants agree that "cancer" is a disease and "happiness" is not, half think that "stroke" is a disease and about half think that it is not. Similarly, about 50% of participants think that "pumpkin" is a type of fruit and 50% do not. Labov (1973) showed that there is no clear boundary between membership and non-membership of a category for a simple physical object like a "cup": "cup" and "bowl" vary along a continuum, and different participants put the cut-off point in different places. Furthermore, asking participants to focus on different aspects of the object can alter this point. If they are asked to imagine an object that is otherwise half-way between a cup and a bowl as containing mashed potato, participants are more likely to think of it as a bowl.

Finally, it is important to remember that semantic features or primitives need not have ready linguistic counterparts. We obviously use examples that are easy to put into words. Some semantic features might be perceptual, or at least non-verbal. We will return to this important point when we examine connectionist models of meaning.

Is semantic decomposition obligatory?

From a psychological perspective, there are two important issues (McNamara & Miller, 1989).

Fruit or vegetable? In practice, defining features do not always define category membership. Some categories have unclear or fuzzy boundaries.

The first is whether we represent the meanings of words in terms of features. The other is whether we make use of those features in comprehension.

So is the decomposition of a word into its component semantic features obligatory? That is, when we see a word like "bachelor," is the retrieval of its features an automatic process? In featural terms, the meaning of the unmarried man sense of "bachelor" must clearly contain features that correspond to (+unmarried, +man), although these in turn might summarize decomposition into yet more primitive features, or there might also be others (see earlier). In any case, on the decompositional account, when you see or hear or think the word "bachelor," you automatically have to decompose it. Therefore you will automatically draw all the valid inferences that are implied by its featural representation—for example, the feature (+unmarried) automatically becomes available in all circumstances.

Obligatory automatic decomposition is a very difficult theory to test experimentally. However, Fodor, Fodor, and Garrett (1975) observed that some words have a negative implicit in their definition. They called these pure definitional negatives (PDNs for short). For example, the word "bachelor" has such an implicit negative in (+unmarried), which is equivalent to (not married). It is well known that double negatives, two negatives together, are harder to process than one alone. Fodor et al. compared sentences (24), (25), and (26):

(24)   The bachelor married Sybil.
(25)   The bachelor did not marry Sybil.
(26)   The widow did not marry Sybil.

According to decompositional theories, (24) contains an implicit negative in the form of the PDN in "bachelor." If this is correct, and such features are accessed automatically, then (25) is implicitly a double negative and should be harder to understand than a control sentence such as (26), which contains only an explicit negative and no PDN. Fodor et al. could find no processing difference between sentences of the types (25) and (26). They concluded that features are not accessed automatically, and instead proposed a non-decompositional account in which the meaning of words is represented as a whole. (Hence Fodor had completely changed his view of decomposition from the earlier Katz and Fodor work.) They argued that to draw an inference such

as "a bachelor is unmarried," you have to make a special type of inference (called a meaning postulate). We do this only when required. A problem with this study is that it is difficult to make up good controls (for example, sentences matched for length and syntactic complexity) for this type of experiment (see Katz, 1977).

Fodor, Garrett, Walker, and Parkes (1980) examined the representation of words called lexical causatives. These are verbs that bring about or cause new states of affairs. In a decompositional analysis such verbs would contain this feature in their semantic representation. For example, "kill" would be represented as something like (cause to die), although this is obviously a far from perfect decomposition. In Figure 11.4, (a) shows the surface structure for the two sentences with the apparently similar verbs "kiss" and "kill." For the control verb "kiss," the deep structure analysis is the same, but if "kill" is indeed decomposed into "cause to

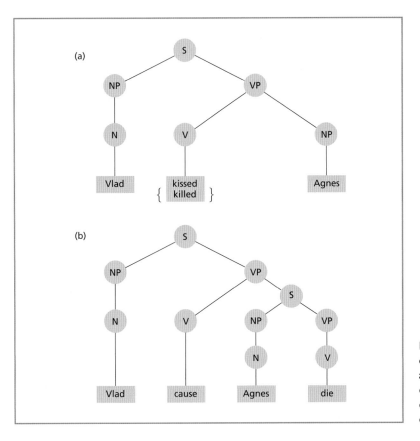

FIGURE 11.4 Examples of analysis of semantics of a causative verb showing different deep structure distances. Based on Fodor et al. (1980).

die," its deep structure should be like that of (b). Fodor et al. asked participants to rate the perceived relatedness between words in these sentences. In (b), "Vlad" and "Agnes" are farther apart than they are in the deep structure of "kissed," as there are more intervening nodes. Therefore "Vlad" and "Agnes" should be rated as less related in the sentence with the causative verb "Vlad killed Agnes" than with a non-causative verb as in "Vlad kissed Agnes." However, Fodor et al. found no difference in the perceived relatedness ratings in these sentences, and therefore no evidence that participants decompose lexical causatives.

Gergely and Bever (1986) questioned this finding. In particular, they questioned whether perceived relatedness between words truly is a function of their structural distance. They provided experimental evidence to support their contention, concluding that the technique of intuitions about the relatedness of words cannot be used to test the relative underlying complexity of semantic representations. The conclusion also depends on a failure to show a difference rather than on obtaining a difference, which is always less satisfactory.

Some studies have concluded that complex sentences that are hypothesized to contain more semantic primitives are no less memorable or harder to process than simpler sentences that presumably contain fewer primitives (Carpenter & Just, 1977; Kintsch, 1974; Thorndyke, 1975). On the other hand, these experiments confounded the number of primitives with other factors (Gentner, 1981), particularly syntactic complexity (as pointed out by Gentner, 1981, and McNamara & Miller, 1989).

Although Fodor et al. (1980) argued that semantic complexity should slow processing down, it is more likely that it speeds processing up. In Hinton and Shallice's (1991) model of deep dyslexia, highly imageable words have rich featural representations that make them more robust (see Chapter 7). Features also provide scope for interconnections. Sentences that contain features that facilitate interconnections between their elements are recalled better than those that do not (Gentner, 1981). For example, "give" decomposes into the notion of transferring the ownership

of objects between participants in the sentence, while "sold" decomposes into the notion of transferring the ownership of objects plus an exchange of money between participants. Hence sentences of the type "Vlad sold the wand to Agnes" are remembered more accurately than sentences of the type "Vlad gave the wand to Agnes" because the verb has a more complex underlying structure (Gentner, 1981; see also Coleman & Kay, 1981).

Although memory tasks do not always provide an accurate reflection of what is happening at the time of processing, there is further evidence in favor of semantic decomposition. People with aphasia tend to be more successful at retrieving verbs with rich semantic representations compared with verbs with less rich representations (Breedin, Saffran, & Schwartz, 1998). For example, the verb "hurry" has a richer representation than "go" because it includes the meaning of "go" with the additional features representing "quickly." Semantically related word substitution speech errors (see Chapter 13) always show a featural relation between the target and occurring words. Finally, much of the work on semantic development (see Chapter 4) is best explained in terms of some sort of featural representation.

In summary, it is likely that we represent the meanings of words as combinations of semantic features, although these ideas are fiendishly difficult to test. McNamara and Miller (1989) suggested that young children automatically decompose early words into semantic primitives, but as they get older, they mainly decompose them into non-primitive features. Eventually words themselves might act as features in the semantic system. There has recently been a resurgence of interest in semantic features. This has come from the interplay between connectionist modeling and neuropsychological studies of semantic memory. Vigliocco, Vinson, Lewis, and Garrett (2004) describe an updated feature-based model called the Featural and Unitary Semantic Space hypothesis. They argue that object and action words at least are represented by combinations of features grounded in perception and organized according to modality. These ideas of grounding and modality-specific organization are important ones to which we will return later.

FAMILY RESEMBLANCE MODELS

We have seen that one of the major problems with the decompositional theory of semantics is that it is surprisingly difficult to come up with an intuitively appealing list of semantic features for many words. Many categories seem to be defined by a family resemblance between their members rather than the specification of defining features that all members must possess. How can we account for the wooliness of concepts?

Prototype theories

A **prototype** is an average family member (Rosch, 1978). Potential members of the category are identified by how closely they resemble the prototype or category average. Some instances of a category are judged to be better exemplars than other instances. The prototype is the "best example" of a concept, and is often a non-existent, composite example. For example, a blackbird (or alternatively, American robin) is very close to being a prototypical bird; it is of average size, has wings and feathers, can fly, and has average features in every respect. A penguin is a long way from being a prototypical bird, and hence we take longer to verify that it is indeed a member of the bird category.

The idea of a prototype arose from many different areas of psychology. Posner and Keele (1968) showed participants abstract patterns of dots. Unknown to the participants, the patterns were distortions of just one underlying pattern of dots that the participants did not actually see. The underlying pattern of dots corresponds to the category prototype. Even though participants never saw this pattern, they later treated it as the best example, responding to it better than the patterns they did see. I considered the related work of Rosch on prototypes and color naming earlier, in Chapter 3.

A prototype is a special type of **schema**. A schema is a frame for organizing knowledge that can be structured as a series of slots plus fillers (see Chapter 12). A prototype is a schema with all the slots filled in with average values. For example, the schema for "bird" comprises a series of slots such as "can fly?" ("yes" for blackbird and robin, "no" for penguin and emu), "bill length" ("short" for robin, "long" for curlew), and "leg length" ("short" for robin, "long" for stork). The bird prototype will have the most common or average values for all these slots (can fly, short bill, short legs). Hence a robin will be closer to the prototype than an emu. Category boundaries are unclear or "fuzzy." For some items, it is not clear which category they should belong in; and in some extreme cases, some instances may be in two categories (for example, a tomato may be categorized as both a vegetable and a fruit).

There is a wealth of evidence supporting prototype theory over feature theory. Rosch and Mervis (1975) measured family resemblance among instances of concepts such as fruit, furniture, and vehicles by asking participants to list their features. Although some features were given by all participants for particular concepts, these were not technically defining features, as they did not distinguish the concept from other concepts. For example, all participants might say of "birds" that "they're alive," but then so are all other animals. The more specific features that were listed were not shared by all instances of a concept—for example, not all birds fly.

A number of results demonstrate the processing advantage of a prototype over particular instances (see for example Mervis, Catlin, & Rosch, 1975). Sentence verification time is faster for prototypical members of a category. Prototypical members can substitute for category names in sentences, whereas non-prototypical members cannot. Words for typical objects are learned before words for atypical ones. In a free recall task, adults retrieve typical members before atypical ones (Kail & Nippold, 1984). Prototypes share more features with other instances of the category, but minimize the featural overlap with related categories (Rosch & Mervis, 1975). Hence, for most people, "apple" is very close to the prototype of "fruit" (Battig & Montague, 1969), and is similar to other fruit and dissimilar to "vegetables," but "tomato" is a peripheral member and indeed overlaps with "vegetable." There are prototypes that possess an advantage over other members of the category even when they are all formally identical. Participants consider the number "13" to be a better "odd number" than "23" or "501" (Armstrong, Gleitman, & Gleitman, 1983), and "mother" is a better example of "female" than "waitress." We have already seen that these typicality effects can also be found in sentence verification times. Generally, the closer an item is to the prototype, the easier we process it.

Prototype theories are not necessarily inconsistent with feature theories. According to prototype theories, word meaning is not only represented by essential features; non-essential features also play a role. Theories based on features have the additional attractive property that they can explain how we acquire new concepts, such as "liberty" or "hypocrisy": we merely combine existing features. Network models can also form new concepts, by adding new nodes to the network with appropriate connections to existing nodes. As we have seen, it is unclear whether this is a meaningful distinction in practice. On the other hand, new concepts are problematical for non-decompositional theories. One suggestion is that all concepts, including complex ones, are innate (Fodor, 1981).

Basic levels
Rosch (1978) argued that a compromise between cognitive economy and maximum informativeness results in a **basic level** of categorization that tends to be the default level at which we categorize and think, unless there is particular reason to do otherwise. In general, we use the basic level of "chairs," rather than the lower level of "armchairs" or the higher level of "furniture." That is, there is a basic level of categorization that is particularly psychologically salient (Rosch et al., 1976). The basic level is the level that has the most distinctive attributes and provides the most economical arrangement of semantic memory. There is a large gain in distinctiveness from the basic level to levels above, but only a small one to levels below. For example, there seems to be a large jump from "chairs" to "furniture" and to other types of furniture such as "tables," but a less obvious difference between different types of chair. Objects at the basic level are readily distinguished from each other, but objects in levels beneath the basic level

are not so easily distinguished from each other. Nevertheless, objects at the same basic level share perceptual contours; they resemble each other more than they resemble members of other similar categories. It is the level at which we think, in the sense that those are the labels we choose in the absence of any particular need to do otherwise. The basic level is the most general category for which a concrete image of the whole category can be formed (Rosch et al., 1976).

Rosch et al. (1976) showed that basic levels have a number of advantages over other categories. Participants can easily list most of the attributes of the basic level; it is the level of description most likely to be spontaneously used by adults; sentence verification time is faster for basic-level terms; and children typically acquire the basic level first. We can also name objects at the basic level faster than at the superordinate or subordinate levels (Jolicoeur, Gluck, & Kosslyn, 1984).

Problems with the prototype model
Hampton (1981) pointed out that not all types of concepts appear to have prototypes: Abstract concepts in particular are difficult to fit into this scheme. What does it mean, for example, to talk about the prototype for "truth"? The prototype model does not explain why categories cohere. Lakoff (1987) points to some examples of very complex concepts for which it is far from obvious how there could be a prototype—the Australian Aboriginal language Dyirbal has a coherent category of "women, fire, and dangerous things" marked by the word "balan." Furthermore, the prototype model cannot explain why typicality judgments vary systematically depending on the context (Barsalou, 1985). Any theory of categorization that relies on similarity risks being circular: Items are in the same category because they are similar to each other, and they are similar to each other because they are in the same category (Murphy & Medin, 1985; Quine, 1977). It is necessary to explain how items are similar, and prototype theories do not do a good job of this. Finally, the characterization of the basic level as the most psychologically fundamental is not as clear-cut as at first sight (Komatsu, 1992). The amount of information we can retrieve about subordinate

levels varies with our expertise (Tanaka & Taylor, 1991). Birdwatchers, for example, know nearly as much about subordinate members such as blackbirds, jays, and olivaceous warblers, as they do about the basic level. Nevertheless, although expertise increases the knowledge available at other levels, the original basic level retains a privileged status (Johnson & Mervis, 1997).

Instance theories

Is abstraction an essential component of conceptual representation? An alternative view is that of representing exemplars without abstraction: Each concept is representing a particular, previously encountered instance. We make semantic judgments by comparison with specific stored instances. This is the instance approach (Komatsu, 1992), also called the exemplar theory. There are different varieties of the instance approach, depending on how many instances are stored, and on the quality of these instances. The instance approach provides greater informational richness at the expense of cognitive economy.

It is quite difficult to distinguish between prototype and instance-based theories. Many of the phenomena explained by prototype theories can also be accounted for by instance-based theories. Both theories predict that people process central members of the category better than peripheral members (Anderson, 2010). Prototype theories predict this because central members are closer to the abstract prototype, while instance-based theories predict this because central instances are more similar to other instances of the category. Instance-based theories predict that specific instances should affect the processing of other instances regardless of whether or not they are close to the central tendency, and this has been observed (Medin & Schaffer, 1978; Nosofsky, 1991). For example, although the average dog barks, if we experience an odd-looking one that does not, we will expect similar-looking ones not to (Anderson, 2010). On the other hand, abstraction theories correctly predict that people infer tendencies that are not found in any specific instance (Elio & Anderson, 1981). The predictive power of instance-based models increases

as the number of instances considered increases (Storms, De Boeck, & Ruts, 2000). Both abstraction-based theories (Gluck & Bower, 1988) and instance-based theories (in the Jets and Sharks model of McClelland, 1981; see also Kruschke, 1992) have been implemented in connectionist models. Across a range of tasks involving natural language categories, instance-based models give a slightly better account than prototype models (Storms et al., 2000). The instantiation principle might be one possible resolution to this conflict (Heit & Barsalou, 1996). According to this principle, a category includes detailed information about its range of instances. Although it is clearly implemented in instance-based theories, it is possible to incorporate it into prototype theories. This idea represents a shift from emphasizing cognitive economy in our theories. This might not be as disadvantageous as it first seems. Nosofsky and Palmeri (1997) suggested that category membership decisions are made by retrieving instances one at a time from semantic memory until a decision can be made. In this case, the more instances you have stored, the faster you can respond.

Theory theories

A final theory of classification and concept representation has emerged from work on how children represent natural kind categories (e.g., Carey, 1985; Markman, 1989), on judgments of similarity (Rips & Collins, 1993), and on how categories cohere (Murphy & Medin, 1985). According to theory theories, people represent categories as miniature theories (mini-theories) that describe facts about those categories and why the members cohere (Murphy & Medin, 1985; Rips, 1995). A theory underlying a concept is thought to be very similar to the type of theory a scientist uses, say to decide what sort of insect a particular specimen might be. Mini-theories are sets of beliefs about what makes instances members of categories, and an idea about what the normal properties of an instance of a category should possess. They look rather like encyclopedia entries. Concept development throughout childhood is a case of the child evolving theories of categories that become increasingly like those used by adults.

Evaluation of work on classification

The current battleground on how we classify objects is between instance-based theories and theory theories. Other accounts can be seen as special cases of these. For example, schema theories are just a version of theory theory, and as we have seen, prototypes can be difficult to distinguish from instance-based theories, but also can be thought of as theory-like entities (Rips, 1995). Instance-based theories have particular difficulty in accounting for how we understand novel concepts formed by combining words, whereas theory theories do rather better.

COMBINING CONCEPTS

So far we have largely been concerned with how we represent the meanings of individual words. How do we combine concepts and understand novel phrases such as "green house"?

Rips (1995) points out that instance-based theories run into obvious difficulties in providing an account of how we combine concepts. We can still understand novel phrases even though we might have no instances of them. We would still be able to decide whether a particular house is an instance of "green house" or not. Novel phrases and sentences enable us to express an infinite number of novel concepts whose comprehension is beyond the reach of a finite number of already encountered specific instances.

Theory theories have less difficulty in accounting for concept combination, but still face some difficulties (Rips, 1995). How do mini-theories actually get combined? What is the relation between the new mini-theory and past mini-theories when they become revised in the light of new information? Rips (1995) argued that mini-theories alone cannot account for how we combine concepts. They must be combined with some other mechanism. He proposes a dual approach combining mini-theories with a fixed atomic symbol for each category. He calls this a "word-like entity in the language of thought." A dual approach enables us to keep track of changes

to mini-theories and provides the power to be able to recognize when some of our beliefs conflict with each other.

How do we understand noun–noun combinations (e.g., "boar burger," "robin hawk")? How do we know that "corn oil" means "oil made from corn" but that "baby oil" means "oil rubbed on babies" (Wisniewski, 1997)? People's interpretations of a novel phrase like "robin hawk" fall into three categories. In one there is a thematic relation between the two entities: "a hawk that preys on robins." In another there is a property link between the two: "a hawk with a red breast like a robin." A third, less frequent category is hybridization, where the compound is a combination or conjunction of the constituents (e.g., a "robin canary" is a cross between the two, and a "musician painter" refers to someone who is both).

Most of the research has been carried out on thematic and property interpretations. There is a general assumption in the research literature that people try the thematic relation first, and only if this fails to generate a plausible combination do they attempt a property interpretation. Property interpretations appear to be rare in natural, communicative contexts (Downing, 1977). One reason for this bias is that relation interpretations preserve the meaning of each noun in the combination, whereas property interpretations use just one property of the noun that is acting as a modifier (e.g., the red breast of the robin). People prefer to assume that combinations involve the usual meanings of their constituents, so they prefer to use this strategy first. This is called the last resort strategy.

However, Wisniewski and Love (1998) showed that in certain circumstances people prefer to comprehend noun combinations on the basis of property relations. High similarity between the constituents of a combination facilitates the production of property relations. People then look for a critical difference between them that can act as the basis of the interpretation. For example, consider "zebra horse." "Zebra" and "horse" are close in meaning, and the critical difference "has stripes" can easily be used to generate the property relation "a horse with stripes." However, no such relation exists for "tree zebra,"

Wisniewski and Love (1998) showed that people often prefer noun combinations based on property relations. For example, a "zebra horse" is easily interpreted as a horse with stripes.

so we might generate a thematic relation like "a zebra that lives in trees." In a survey of familiar noun–noun combinations, 71% of combinations had thematic relation meanings and 29% property meanings.

People are also influenced by what might be called a noun's combinatorial history—the way in which a particular word has combined with other words before. For example, when "mountain" is used in compound nouns, it usually indicates a location relation (e.g., "mountain stream," "mountain goat," and "mountain resort"). Hence when we come across a new combination involving "mountain" (e.g., "mountain fish") we tend to interpret it in the same way. The modifying (first) noun of the pair is the most important in determining this (Shoben & Gagne, 1997; Wisniewski, 1997). Further evidence that experience matters is that exposure to a word pair related in a similar way makes it easier to understand a new word pair. For example, prior exposure to the word pair "glass eye" makes people faster to understand "copper horse," when the same conceptual relation (second word is made of the first) is instantiated (Estes & Jones, 2006).

Hence the interpretation of compound nouns depends on a number of factors, including past experience, similarity, and whether plausible relations between the stimuli exist. Although there might be some bias towards understanding them on the basis of thematic relations, property relations are by no means rare, and in some circumstances form the strategy of preference.

Combining categories presents formidable difficulties for the way we understand language, which have yet to be resolved.

FIGURATIVE LANGUAGE

So far we have been concerned with how we process literal language—that is, where the intended meaning corresponds exactly to the meanings of the words. Humans make extensive use of non-literal or **figurative** language. In this we go beyond the literal meanings of the words involved, for humor, effect, politeness, to play, to be creative—and for a mixture of these and other reasons. There are three main types of figurative language.

First, we use what can broadly be called **metaphor**. This involves making a comparison, or drawing a resemblance. A metaphor is a special type of conceptual combination, where we combine two concepts that are not normally thought of as being related for some special effect. There are many types of metaphor, depending on the relation between the words actually used and the intended meaning. Here are a few examples:

(27) Vlad fought like a tiger. (Simile)
(28) Vlad exploded with fury. (Strict metaphor)
(29) All hands on deck. (Synecdoche)

Cacciari and Glucksberg (1994) argued that there is no dichotomy between literal and metaphoric usage: rather, there is a continuum. How do we process metaphorical utterances? The standard theory is that we process non-literal language in three stages (Clark & Lucy, 1975; Searle, 1979). First, we derive the literal meaning of what we hear. Second, we test the literal meaning against the context to see if it is consistent with it. Third, if the literal meaning does not make sense with the context, we seek an alternative, metaphorical meaning (see Figure 11.5). fMRI imaging data suggests that in processing metaphors people activate regions of the brain involved in general reasoning and thinking, involving working memory and executive processing, to understand more abstract metaphors (Prat, Mason, & Just, 2012).

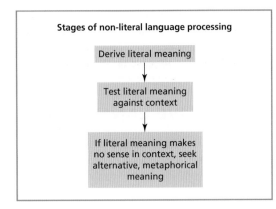

Stages of non-literal language processing

Derive literal meaning

↓

Test literal meaning against context

↓

If literal meaning makes no sense in context, seek alternative, metaphorical meaning

FIGURE 11.5

One prediction of this three-stage model is that people should ignore the non-literal meanings of statements whenever the literal meaning makes sense, because they never need to proceed to the third stage. There is some evidence that people are unable to ignore non-literal meanings. Glucksberg, Gildea, and Bookin (1982) found that when good metaphoric interpretations of literally false sentences were available (e.g., "Some jobs are jails"), people take longer to decide that such sentences are literally false. That is, the metaphoric meaning seems to be processed at the same time as the literal meaning.

Is additional processing always brought into play whenever we recognize the falsity of what we read or hear (Glucksberg, 1991)? For example, in (28) we recognize that Vlad did not actually explode. The problem with this view is that not all metaphors are literally false (e.g., "no man is an island," "my husband's an animal"). Cacciari and Glucksberg (1994) concluded that metaphors are interpreted through a pragmatic analysis in the same way that we process conversational implicatures (see Chapter 14): We assume that what we read is maximally informative. The class-inclusion model claims that metaphors are meant to be taken literally as assertions of category membership. For example, in the metaphor "That desk is a junkyard," the topic (desk) is intended to be interpreted as a member of the vehicle for the metaphor, in this case "junkyard" (Glucksberg & Keysar, 1990). When we are faced with a metaphor such as this, we use the vehicle (junkyard) to create the category "all things that are cluttered"; we then include the topic (desk) in this category to generate an interpretation of the metaphor (Jones & Estes, 2005). Jones and Estes confirmed this idea by showing that priming with a metaphor (e.g., "that lie is a boomerang") increases the probability that a person will judge the topic (lie) to be an actual member of the vehicle category (boomerang), compared with a similar but literal prime ("that lie was about a boomerang").

Second, **idioms** can be thought of as frozen metaphors. Whereas we make metaphors up as we go along, idioms have a fixed form and are in general use. The meaning of an idiom is usually quite unrelated to the meaning of its component words. Examples include "to kick the bucket" and "fly off the handle." Gibbs (1980), using reading times, found that participants take less time to comprehend conventional uses of idioms than unconventional, literal uses, suggesting that people analyze the idiomatic senses of expressions before deriving the literal, unconventional interpretation. Swinney and Cutler (1979) also found that people are as fast to understand familiar idioms as they are comparable phrases used non-idiomatically. They suggested that people store idioms like single lexical items.

The meaning we intend to convey goes beyond what we actually say. When Vlad says (30), he isn't really asking if the listener has the ability to get a glass of milk:

(30)   Can you get me a glass of milk?

Instead, he is making an indirect request, asking for a glass of milk. Indirect requests are seen as more polite than the corresponding direct request (31):

(31)   Get me a glass of milk!

In addition to indirect requests, we frequently expect listeners to draw inferences that go well beyond what we say. Indirect requests and inferences in conversation are discussed in more detail in Chapter 12.

How do we construct new metaphors? There is obviously an essential creative component to this; we must be able to see new connections.

Nevertheless, there are constraints. The meaning of the words cannot be either too similar or too dissimilar. Neither (32) nor (33), examples given by Aitchison (1994), is memorable:

(32)   Jam is honey.
(33)   Her cheeks were typewriters.

Clearly we have to generate just the right amount of overlap: the words must share an appropriate but minor characteristic overlap. Little is known about how we can generate just the right amount of overlap. Producing metaphors and jokes is an aspect of our metalinguistic ability—our ability to reflect on and manipulate language, of which phonological awareness (see Chapter 7) is just one component.

THE NEUROSCIENCE OF SEMANTICS

What can we learn about the representation of meaning from examining the effects of brain damage? Obviously, just because a person cannot name a word or object does not mean that the semantic representation of that word has been lost or damaged. People can fail to access the phonology of a word while they still have access to its semantic representation. There are a number of reasons why this must be the case. Some people who are having difficulty accessing the whole phonological form might be able to access part of it. These people might be able to comprehend the word in speech. They might be able to produce the word in spontaneous speech. Importantly, they know how to use the objects, and they can group pictures together appropriately. In these cases we can conclude that the word meanings are intact, and that such people are having difficulty with later stages of processing. Nevertheless there are some instances where the semantic representation is clearly disrupted.

Can we distinguish between a "central" semantic deficit, when a concept is truly lost (or at least when its representation is degraded), and an "access" semantic impairment (sometimes called a refractory semantic deficit), when there is difficulty in gaining access to the concept? Shallice (1988; see also Warrington & Cipolotti, 1996, and Warrington & Shallice, 1979) discussed five

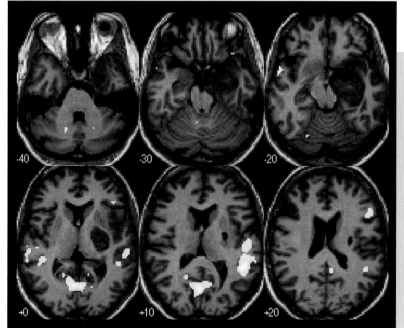

Magnetic resonance imaging (MRI) scans of the brain of a woman with a tumor (center right of scans) in the left temporal lobe. (Front of the brain is at top.) Six views are seen showing transverse sections through different levels of the brain. Language areas within the brain are seen to be active (colored areas) during sentence generation from a list of verbs. The temporal lobe is important for the processing of language meaning (semantics). Damage in this region can create problems with language processes.

criteria that could distinguish problems associated with the loss of a representation from problems of accessing it. First, performance should be consistent across trials. If an item is permanently lost, it should never be possible to access it. If an item is available on some trials rather than on others, the difficulty must be one of access. Second, for both degraded stores and access disorders, it should be easier to obtain the superordinate category than to name the item, because that information is very strongly represented; but once the superordinate is obtained, it will be very difficult to obtain any further information in a degraded store. Warrington (1975) found that superordinate information (e.g., that a lion is an animal) may be preserved when more specific information is lost. She proposed that the destruction of semantic memory occurs hierarchically, with lower levels storing specific information being lost before higher levels storing more general information. Hence, information about superordinates tends to be better preserved than information about specific instances. Impaired access should affect all levels equally. Third, low-frequency items should be lost first. Low-frequency items should be more susceptible to loss, whereas problems of access should affect all levels equally. Fourth, priming should no longer be effective, as an item that is lost obviously cannot be primed. Fifth, if the knowledge is lost then performance should be independent of the presentation rate, whereas disturbances of access should be sensitive to the rate of presentation of the material.

There has been considerable debate about how reliably these criteria distinguish access disorders from loss disorders, and how many patients show all of these features (Rapp & Caramazza, 1993). To be confident that items have been lost from semantic memory we need to observe at least consistent failure to access items across tasks. However, a number of semantic-access deficit patients have now been clearly identified (Warrington & Cipolotti, 1996; Warrington & Crutch, 2004), and other patients show elements of semantic-access deficit (e.g., Forde & Humphreys, 1995, 1997). Gotts and Plaut (2002) present a connectionist model that suggests that central and access deficits result from different types of underlying neurological damage. One type involves damage to a neuromodulatory system that normally functions to maintain and enhance neuronal signals, while the second involves damage to the neuronal system that encodes semantic information. Hence the idea is that "refractoriness," a reduction in the ability to use the semantic system in the same way for a period of time following the initial response, builds up abnormally. (The idea is similar to that of the **refractory period** in neuronal firing.)

Studies of the neuropsychology of semantics cast light on a number of important issues. In particular, how many semantic memory systems are there, and how is semantic memory organized?

How many semantic systems are there?

Do we have separate semantic memory systems for each input modality? So far we have discussed semantic information as though there is only one semantic store. This is called the unimodal store hypothesis. It is the idea, perhaps held by most people, that we have one central store of meaning that we can access from different modalities (vision, taste, sound, touch, and smell). However, perhaps each modality has its own store of information? In practice, we are most concerned with a distinction between a store of visual semantic information and a store of verbal semantic information. Paivio (1971) proposed a dual-code hypothesis of semantic representation, with a perceptual code encoding the perceptual characteristics of a concept, and a verbal code encoding the abstract, non-sensory aspects of a concept. Experimental tests of this hypothesis produced mixed results (Snodgrass, 1984). For example, participants are often faster to access abstract information from pictures than from words (see for example Banks & Flora, 1977). Some support for the dual-code hypothesis is that brain-imaging studies show that concrete and abstract words are processed differently (Kounios & Holcomb, 1994).

The idea of multiple or modality-specific semantic stores, whereby verbal material (words) and non-verbal material (pictures) are separated, has enjoyed something of a resurgence owing to data from brain-damaged participants. There are three main reasons for this (Caplan, 1992). First, priming effects have been discovered that have been found to be limited to verbal material. Second, some case studies show impairments limited to one sensory modality. For example, patient TOB (McCarthy & Warrington, 1988) had difficulty in understanding living things, but only when they were presented as spoken names. He could name their pictures without difficulty. Patient EM (Warrington, 1975) was generally much more impaired at verbal tasks than at visual tasks. Third, patients with semantic deficits are not always equally impaired for verbal and visual material (e.g., Warrington, 1975). Warrington and Shallice's (1979) patient AR showed a much larger benefit from cuing when reading a written word than when naming the corresponding picture. They interpreted this finding as evidence for separate verbal and visual conceptual systems.

Coltheart, Inglis, Cupples, Michle, Bates, and Budd (1998) described the case of AC, who was unable to access visual semantic attributes, but could access other sensory semantic attributes as well as non-sensory attributes. This was observed independently of the modality of testing and of the semantic category tested. Coltheart et al. proposed that semantic memory is organized into subsystems. There is a subsystem for each sensory modality, and a subsystem for non-sensory semantic knowledge. This non-sensory subsystem is in turn divided into subsystems for semantic categories such as living and non-living things. This approach takes the fractionation of semantic memory to the extreme.

Evaluation of multiple-stores models

Alternative explanations have been offered for these studies. Riddoch, Humphreys, Coltheart, and Funnell (1988) argued that patients who perform better on verbal material might have a subtle impairment of complex visual processing. This idea is supported by the finding that the disturbance in processing pictures is greater for categories with many visually similar members (e.g., fruit and vegetables). The reverse dissociation of better performance on visual material may arise because of the abundance of indirect visual cues

in pictures. For example, the presence of a large gaping mouth and heavy paws in the picture of a lion is an excellent indirect cue to how to answer a comprehension question such as "is it dangerous?," even if you do not know it is a picture of a lion (Caplan, 1992).

Nevertheless, some research is more difficult to explain away. Bub, Black, Hampson, and Kertesz (1988) describe the case of MP, who showed very poor comprehension of verbal material, did not show automatic semantic priming, but did show much better comprehension of the meaning of pictures. The nature of the detailed information MP was able to provide about the objects in the pictures, such as the color of a banana from a black-and-white line drawing, could not easily be inferred from perceptual cues without access to semantic information about the object. Warrington and Shallice (1984) found high item consistency in naming performance as long as the modality was held constant, again suggesting different semantic systems were involved. Lauro-Grotto, Piccini, and Shallice (1997) described a patient with semantic dementia (a type of degenerative dementia where semantic memory is lost while episodic memory is relatively well preserved) who was much better at tasks involving visual input than verbal input.

Finally, supportive evidence comes from modality-specific anomia, in which the naming disorder is confined to one modality. For example, in the disorder known as optic aphasia (Beauvois, 1982; Coslett & Saffran, 1989), patients are impaired at the naming of visually presented stimuli, but without general visual anomia or agnosia. They are unable to name objects presented visually, but can name them if they are exposed to them through other modalities (e.g., patients cannot name a cat by sight, but can if they hear it mew, or if they are given one to touch), or if they are given a definition of the word. Hence the names of objects must still be intact, showing there is no general anomia. Patients can also mime the use of objects, or sort pictures into appropriate categories, showing there is no general agnosia.

The interpretation of these data is controversial. The most obvious interpretation of optic aphasia, for example, is that we can access different modality-specific stores, with one of the stores being wiped out. Riddoch and Humphreys (1987) argued that optic aphasia is a disorder of accessing a unitary semantic system through the visual system, rather than disruption to a visual modality-specific semantic system. Much hangs on the interpretation of gestures made by the patient. Do they indeed reflect preserved visual semantics—so that patients understand the objects they see—with disruption of verbal semantics, or are they merely inferences made from the perceptual attributes of objects? Riddoch and Humphreys' patient JV produced only the most general of gestures to objects, and other experiments indicated a profound disturbance of comprehension of visual objects. Of course, we must remember the caveat that different patients display different behaviors, and one must be wary of drawing too general a conclusion from a single patient.

Caramazza, Hillis, Rapp, and Romani (1990) argued that there is some confusion about what the terms "semantics" and "semantic stores" mean when used in neuropsychological contexts. Is semantic information general knowledge about objects and events, or just something that mediates between input and output? They distinguished four versions of the multiple-stores hypothesis. In the input account, the same semantic system, containing everything (both visual and verbal), is duplicated for each modality of input. There is little evidence for this idea. In the modality-specific content hypothesis, there is a semantic store for each input modality. Each store contains information relevant to that modality, but in an abstract or modality-neutral format. The modality-specific format hypothesis is similar to this, but the store is in the format of the input (e.g., visual information for vision, verbal for verbal). In the modality-specific context hypothesis, visual and verbal semantics refer to the information acquired in the context of visually presented objects or words. For example, if you acquired "tigers have stripes" through verbal exposure, that information is stored verbally rather than visually. These hypotheses are difficult to distinguish, but appear to make three predictions. First, they predict that access from a particular modality always activates

the appropriate semantic store first. Second, they predict that activation of phonological and orthographic representations is mediated by verbal semantics. Third, they predict that information can only be accessed directly through the appropriate input modality. Caramazza et al. argued that the data do not really support these predictions. All the data really motivate is that there is a relation between input modality and semantic content type; it does not have to be in a modality-specific format. They proposed an alternative model of the semantic system that they called OUCH (short for organized unitary content hypothesis). In this model, pictures of objects have privileged access to a unimodal store. This is because a picture of an object has a more direct relationship to the object itself than a word denoting the object. A fork is a fork because you can eat with it, and you can eat with it because it has tines and a handle. Some semantic connections are more important than others. This idea is attractively simple, but OUCH cannot explain patients who have more trouble with pictures than words (e.g., FRA of McCarthy & Warrington, 1986). Finally, it is not clear that a distinction between a semantic system and subsystem is a meaningful one. Perhaps they amount to the same thing (Shallice, 1993).

How can we explain optic aphasia? There are several accounts (Sitton, Mozer, & Farah, 2000). Optic aphasia shows that the simple canonical model of meaning, where we go from sensory input to semantics, and then to name, cannot be correct, because in optic aphasia people have accessed the semantics and therefore should always be able to access the name. The modality-specific multiple-stores models accounts for optic aphasia by positing a disconnection between verbal semantics and visual semantics, with producing the correct name depending on access to verbal semantics. According to OUCH (Hillis & Caramazza, 1995), we observe optic aphasia when the semantic representation that is computed from visual input is enough to support action patterns (mimes), but not naming. Shallice (1993) pointed out that this would make optic aphasia indistinguishable from visual associative agnosia. In a similar vein Riddoch and Humphreys (1987) also hypothesize an impairment from vision to semantics, but argue that a direct pathway from vision to gesture is preserved. Both ideas note that visual objects have affordances (Gibson, 1979); the shape of a chair encourages or creates the idea of sitting in it. Finally, Sitton et al. (2000) argue that instead of optic aphasia arising from damage to multiple semantic systems or multiple pathways, it arises from damage at multiple sites in a unitary model. They argue that lesions to the pathways mapping visual input to semantics, and also semantics to naming, can account for optic aphasia if those lesions are what they call super-additive. Super-additive means that a task requiring both pathways (naming a visually presented object) gives a much higher failure rate than would be expected on the basis of the error rates on tasks involving just one of the paths (e.g., gesturing from semantics). They present a connectionist model that shows that super-additivity can occur and that damage to a system with a single semantic store and with visual and auditory inputs and name and gesture outputs (see Figure 11.6) gives rise to a pattern of performance similar to optic aphasia. Essentially brain damage in two parts of the brain is particularly damaging for some tasks, while leaving performance on tasks that involve just one part close to normal.

Caplan (1992) proposed a compromise between the multiple-stores and unitary store theories in which only a subset of semantic information is dedicated to specific modalities. This has become known as the identification semantics hypothesis (Chertkow, Bub, & Caplan, 1992).

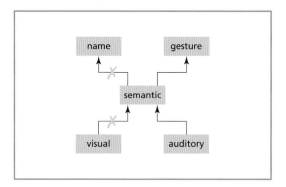

FIGURE 11.6 A schematic depiction of the super-additive impairment account of optic aphasia (Farah, 1990). From Sitton, Mozer, and Farah (2000).

The perceptual information necessary to identify and name an object is only a subset of the meaning of a concept. If this information is intact and the amodal associative store is impaired, a person will still be able to name an object, but will not be able to access the other verbal semantic information about the object. One argument against this hypothesis is that patient RM of Lauro-Grotto et al. (1997) had much better preserved semantic abilities than we would expect, given that she was impaired at tasks involving verbal semantics. In particular, she still had knowledge about visual contextual contiguity (knowing what items tend to occur together visually, such as a windshield wiper and a car tax disc, which in the UK is displayed in the corner of the windshield) and even functional contextual contiguity (the way objects tend to be used in the same function, such as a screwdriver and a screw). Lauro-Grotto et al. argue that these types of information are stored in visual semantics rather than being an amodal component of semantic memory.

In summary, most researchers currently believe that there are multiple semantic systems. Most importantly, there are distinct systems for verbal and visual semantics. However, it is important to note that the representations and mechanisms used by these systems need to be spelled out, and it can be quite difficult to distinguish between different theories.

Category-specific semantic disorders

Perhaps the most intriguing and hotly debated phenomena in this area are category-specific disorders. Sometimes brain damage disrupts knowledge about particular semantic categories, leaving other related ones intact. For example, Warrington and Shallice's (1984) patient JBR performed much better at naming inanimate objects than animate objects. He also had a relative comprehension deficit for living things. At first sight this suggests that semantic memory is divided into animate and inanimate categories. JBR's brain damage caused the loss of the animate category. The picture is more complicated, however. JBR was good at naming parts of the body, even though these are parts of living things. He was also poor at naming musical instruments, foodstuffs, types of cloth, and precious stones, even though these are clearly all inanimate things. Difficulties with a particular semantic category are not restricted to naming pictures of its members. They arise across a range of tasks, including picture naming, picture–name matching, answering questions, and carrying out gestures appropriate to the object (Warrington & Shallice, 1984).

Even more specific semantic disorders have been observed. Hart, Berndt, and Caramazza (1985) reported a patient, MD, who also had specific difficulties in naming fruit and vegetables; PC (Semenza & Zettin, 1988) had selective difficulty with proper names; BC (Crosson, Moberg, Boone, Rothi, & Raymer, 1997) just had difficulty with medical instruments. Knowledge about nouns and verbs seems to be processed by different parts of the brain (Caramazza & Hillis, 1991; Hillis, Tuffiash, & Caramazza, 2002; Shapiro & Caramazza, 2003). It is unlikely that this dissociation can be reduced to the effects of semantic variables because of the report of a patient by Rapp and Caramazza (2002) who has greater difficulty speaking nouns than verbs, but greater difficulty writing verbs than nouns.

Methodological issues in investigating category-specific deficits

There are a number of methodological problems in studying category-specific semantic disorders. Funnell and Sheridan (1992) reported an apparent category-specific effect whereby their patient, SL, appeared to show a selective deficit in naming pictures and defining words for living versus non-living things. When they controlled for the familiarity of the stimulus, this effect disappeared. They made a general observation about the materials used for these types of experiment. Most experiments use as stimulus materials a set of black-and-white line drawings from Snodgrass and Vanderwart (1980). Some examples are given in Figure 11.7. Funnell and Sheridan (1992) showed that within this set there were more pictures of low-frequency animate objects than there were of low-frequency inanimate objects. There were few low-familiarity non-living things and few high-familiarity living things. That is, randomly selected pictures of animate things are likely to be less familiar than a random sample of inanimate objects. Hence, if frequency is important in brain-damaged naming, an artifactual effect will show up unless care is taken to control for frequency across the categories. Furthermore, there were two anomalous subcategories. SL was poor at naming human body parts (high familiarity but a subcategory of living things) and musical instruments (low frequency but inanimate). These were the two anomalous categories mentioned by Warrington and Shallice (1984) in their description of JBR.

Stewart, Parkin, and Hunkin (1992) also argued that there had been a lack of control of word name frequency, but pointed out in addition that the complexity and familiarity of the pictures used in these experiments varied between categories. Gaffan and Heywood (1993) showed that pictures of living things are visually more similar to each other than pictures of non-living things. With very brief presentation times, normal participants make more errors on living things. In reply to these criticisms, Sartori, Miozzo, and Job (1993) concluded that their patient "Michelangelo" had a real category-specific deficit for living things, even when these factors were controlled for. The

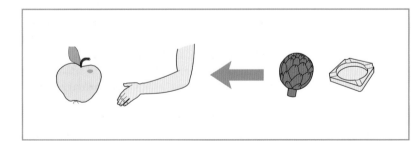

FIGURE 11.7 Examples of line drawings from the Snodgrass and Vanderwart (1980) set.

debate was continued by Parkin and Stewart (1993), and Job, Miozzo, and Sartori (1993). One conclusion is that it is important to measure and control the familiarity, visual featural complexity, and visual similarity of pictures.

On the other hand, we cannot explain all category-specific effects by these methodological problems. Now studies are careful to control for the potential confounding variables, yet category-specific deficits persist. Some patients are poor at tasks involving living things that do not involve picture naming, such as comprehension and definition (e.g., Warrington & Shallice, 1984). Most importantly, we observe a double dissociation between the categories of living and non-living things. Warrington and McCarthy (1983, 1987) describe patients who are the reverse of JBR in that they perform better on living objects than on inanimate objects. Their patient YOT, for example, who generally had an impairment in naming inanimate objects relative to animate ones, on closer examination could identify large outdoor objects such as buildings and vehicles. There also appears to be a distinction between small and large artifacts. CW also found non-living things and body parts harder to name than living things (Sacchett & Humphreys, 1992). Hillis and Caramazza (1991a) examined two patients, JJ and PS, who exemplified this double dissociation when tested on the same stimuli. Although there are fewer patients who show selective difficulties with non-living things, there are enough of them to be very convincing. The performance of these patients cannot be explained away as experimental artifacts, as they are having difficulty with members of the category that should prove easiest to process if all that matters is visual complexity and familiarity.

What explains the living–non-living dissociation?

There are three possible explanations for category-specific disorders. The first is that different types of semantic information are located at different sites in the brain, so that brain damage destroys some types and not others. On this view, information about fruit and vegetables is stored specifically in one part of the brain. If this explanation is correct then category-specific disorders are important because they reveal the structure of the categories as represented by the brain. Hence the distinction between living and non-living things would be a fundamental organizing principle in semantic memory. Farah (1994) argued that this approach would go against what we know about the organization of the brain. More importantly, this idea does not explain why deficits to particular categories tend to co-occur. Why are impairments on naming living things associated with impairments on naming gems, cloths, foodstuffs, and musical instruments, and why are impairments on naming non-living things associated with impairments on naming body parts? It is also difficult to reconcile with the observation that patients impaired at naming animals perform worse on tasks involving perceptual properties (Saffran & Schwartz, 1994; Sartori & Job, 1988; Silveri & Gainotti, 1988). The second possible explanation is that the categories that are disrupted share some incidental property that makes them susceptible to loss. Riddoch et al. (1988) proposed that categories that tend to be lost also tend to include many similar and confusable items. However, it is not clear that these patients have any perceptual disorder (Caplan, 1992). The third possible explanation is that the differences between the categories are mediated by some other variable so that the items that are lost share some more abstract property. We will look at this idea in detail.

The sensory–functional theory

Non-living things are distinguished from one another primarily in terms of their functional properties, whereas living things tend to be differentiated primarily in terms of their perceptual properties (Warrington & McCarthy, 1987; Warrington & Shallice, 1984). That is, the representation of living things depends on what they look like, but the representation of most non-living things depends on what they are used for. Hence JBR, who generally showed a deficit for living things, also performed poorly on naming musical instruments, precious stones, and fabrics. What these things all have in common is that, like living things, they are recognized primarily in terms of their perceptual characteristics, rather than being distinguished from each other on largely functional terms. This distinction is also consistent with the organization of the brain, which has distinct processing pathways for perceptual and motor information (Farah, 1994).

Farah, Hammond, Mehta, and Ratcliff (1989) showed that control participants were poor at answering questions on the perceptual features of both living and non-living objects (e.g., "Are the hind legs of kangaroos larger than their front legs?"). If visual attributes are more difficult to process than functional ones, then categories that depend more on them would be more susceptible to loss. This explains why we observe loss of information about living things more frequently than loss of information about non-living things.

There is some support from neuroimaging work for this hypothesis. There is no obvious difference in the blood flow in the temporal lobes with responses to living and non-living things, but there is with a difference with the processing of perceptual and functional information (Lee, Graham, Simons, & Hodges, 2002), with more activation of the posterior regions of the left temporal cortex when we are dealing with perceptual information, and more activation of the middle regions when dealing with functional information.

Modality-specific and category-specific effects

Is there any relation between the findings of modality-specific and category-specific effects? Farah and McClelland (1991) argued that there is. They constructed a connectionist model and showed that damage to a modality-specific semantic memory system can lead to category-specific deficits. The architecture of their model comprised three "pools" of units: verbal input and output units (corresponding to name units), visual input and output units (picture units), and semantic memory units (divided into visual and functional units). Farah and McClelland asked students to rate dictionary definitions of living and non-living things according to the number of sensory and functional elements each definition contained. The meaning of each word in the model was based on these findings. For living things, the ratio of perceptual to functional features active

for each word was 7.7:1. For non-living things, it was only 1.4:1. The network was then taught to associate the correct semantic and name pattern when presented with each picture pattern, and to produce the correct semantic and picture pattern when presented with each name pattern. Farah and McClelland then lesioned the network. They found that damage to visual semantic units primarily impaired knowledge of living things, whereas damage to functional semantic units primarily impaired knowledge about non-living things. Furthermore, when a category was impaired, knowledge of both types of attribute was lost. This is because of the distributed nature of the semantic representations. Lesioning the model results in a loss of support between parts of the representation. The elements of the representation remaining after damage do not have sufficient critical mass to become activated.

In summary, the sensory–functional theory says knowledge of animate objects is derived primarily from visual information, whereas knowledge of inanimate objects is derived primarily from functional information. Non-living things do not necessarily have more functional attributes than perceptual attributes, but they have relatively more than living things.

Challenges to the sensory–functional theory

Caramazza and Shelton (1998) challenged the prevalent view that the living–non-living distinction merely reflects an underlying differential dependence on sensory and functional information. They focused on the pattern of associated categories in category-specific disorders. They argued that if the sensory–functional theory is correct, then a patient with an impairment on living things should be impaired at tasks involving all types of living things, and also always impaired on the associated categories of musical instruments, fabrics, foodstuffs, and gemstones. They pointed out that this is not the case. Some patients are impaired at tasks involving animals but not foodstuffs (e.g., KR of Hart & Gordon, 1992; JJ of Hillis & Caramazza, 1991a), whereas others are impaired at tasks involving food but not animals (e.g., PS of Hillis & Caramazza, 1991a). Some patients impaired at tasks involving animals are good at musical instruments (e.g., Felicia of De Renzi & Lucchelli, 1994). Animals can be spared or damaged independently of plants (Hillis & Caramazza, 1991a), and the category of plants can be damaged independently of animals (e.g., TU of Farah & Wallace, 1992). It is of course possible that some types of perceptual feature are more important for some categories than for others. For example, animals might depend on shape, while foodstuffs might depend on color (Warrington & McCarthy, 1987). These further dissociations would then reflect selective loss of particular types of sensory feature, rather than of all of them. Caramazza and Shelton argue that there is no independent evidence for this approach.

The sensory–functional hypothesis also appears to predict that people with a selective impairment for living things should show a disproportionate difficulty with visual properties. Although this has been observed sometimes, studies that have carefully controlled for the level of difficulty of the different types of question have not always found it to be the case (Funnell & de Mornay Davies, 1996; Laiacona, Barbarotto, & Capitani, 1993; Sheridan & Humphreys, 1993).

However, Farah and McClelland's (1991) simulations showed that when a category was impaired, knowledge of both types of attribute was lost. This is because of the distributed nature of the semantic representations.

In addition PET and fMRI imaging suggests that knowledge about animals and tools is indeed stored in separate, identifiable parts of the brain (Caramazza & Shelton, 1998; Vigliocco et al., 2004). To summarize, knowledge about animals is stored in occipital-temporal areas, while knowledge about tools is stored in lateral temporal-parietal-occipital areas (see Figure 11.8).

Caramazza and Shelton also argued that the concept of functional information is poorly defined. In the dictionary rating experiment of Farah and McClelland, participants were told that "it was what things are for." But it is possible that much other non-sensory verbal information is really involved (for example, a lion is a carnivore and it lives in a jungle). Biological function information (such as animals breathe and can see) is preserved in RC, even though other types of functional information (what an animal eats or where it lives) are impaired (Tyler & Moss, 1997, 2001).

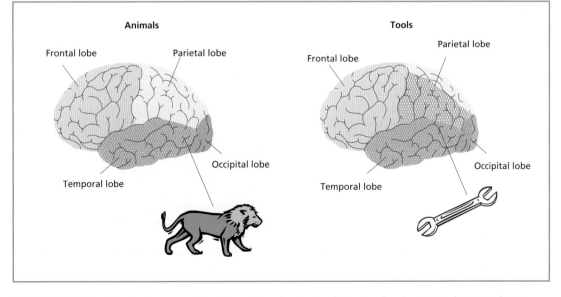

FIGURE 11.8 Imaging studies suggest that knowledge about animals is stored in the occipital-temporal areas, whereas knowledge about tools is stored in lateral temporal-parietal-occipital areas.

Caramazza and Shelton proposed an alternative explanation of the data, which they called the domain-specific knowledge hypothesis (DSKH). They argued that specific, innate neural mechanisms for distinguishing between living and non-living things have evolved because of the importance of this distinction. They cite two lines of evidence for this. First, very young children (within the first few months) can distinguish between living and non-living things (Bertenthal, 1993; Quinn & Eimas, 1996). The presence of this ability so soon after birth suggests that it is innate. Second, studies of lesion sites and recent studies using brain imaging both suggest that different parts of the brain might, after all, be dedicated to processing living and non-living things. Living things are generally associated with the temporal lobe, while artifacts tend to be more associated with the dorsal region of the temporal, parietal, and frontal lobes.

It is too early to evaluate these alternative approaches. Currently most researchers in the field subscribe to the sensory–functional hypothesis. Time will tell whether the domain-specific knowledge hypothesis will be preferred. Imaging data suggest that while knowledge about animals and tools might be stored in different parts of the brain, this might be because of an underlying dependence on some other factor. While animals are associated with activation of the lateral fusiform gyrus, and tools with activation of the medial fusiform gyrus, some non-living things (e.g., chairs) cause activation of areas outside that associated with tools (Chao, Haxby, & Martin, 1999; Vigliocco et al., 2004).

The structure of semantic memory: Evidence from studies of dementia

Dementia is a general label for the widespread decay of cognitive functioning, generally found in old age. The ultimate causes of dementia are unknown, although it is likely that both genetic and environmental factors play some role, and it is clear that there are several subtypes, the most common of which is **Alzheimer's disease** (AD). In dementia, memory and semantic information are particularly prone to disruption. A subtype of dementia called semantic dementia is particularly interesting: In semantic dementia, the loss of semantic information is disproportionately great relative to the loss of other cognitive functions, such as episodic memory (Hodges et al., 1992; Mayberry, Sage, & Lambon Ralph, 2011; Snowden, Goulding, & Neary, 1989; Warrington, 1975). This selective disturbance of semantic information makes it particularly useful for studying how we represent meaning. Alzheimer's disease and semantic dementia reflect damage (at least initially) to different brain regions: Neuroimaging studies show that Alzheimer's disease typically begins with medial temporal lobe atrophy, including the hippocampus, with more advanced cases showing global atrophy. Semantic dementia on the other hand is marked by atrophy beginning particularly in the left anterior temporal region of the brain, with much less early damage to the hippocampus. Patients with semantic dementia show impaired word naming and a loss of word meaning, but preserved syntax. Imaging results suggest that the left middle and inferior temporal cortex of the brain play a particularly important role in accessing and representing meaning (Chan et al., 2001; Garrard & Hodges, 2000).

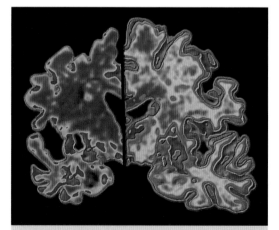

An Alzheimer brain scan (left) compared with a normal brain (right). The Alzheimer's diseased brain is considerably atrophied, due to the degeneration and death of nerve cells. Apart from a decrease in brain volume, the surface of the brain is often more deeply folded.

Semantic memory disturbances in dementia

There is a huge body of work indicating problems with semantic processing in dementia (see Nebes, 1989, and Harley, 1998, for reviews). Here are just a few examples of these findings. People with dementia are often impaired on the category fluency task, where they have to list as many members as possible of a particular category (e.g., Martin & Fedio, 1983). They have difficulty listing attributes that are shared by all members of a category (Martin & Fedio, 1983; Warrington, 1975). They have difficulty in differentiating between items from the same semantic category (Martin & Fedio, 1983). They tend to classify items as being similar to different items more than controls do (Chan et al., 1993a, 1993b). They are also poor at judging the semantic coherence of simple statements: For example, they are more likely to judge "The door is asleep" to be a sensible statement than controls (Grossman, Mickanin, Robinson, & d'Esposito, 1996).

Difficulties with picture naming

People with dementia often have difficulty in naming things. There is evidence that the semantic deficit is involved in picture naming. Most of the naming errors in dementia involve the production of semantic relatives of the target (e.g., Hodges, Salmon, & Butters, 1991). The extent of the naming impairment is correlated with the extent of the more general semantic difficulties (Diesfeldt, 1989). Naming performance in dementia is sometimes affected by the semantic variable of imageability. With other types of neuropsychological damage, patients usually find high-imageable items easier than low-imageable items (e.g., Coltheart, Patterson, & Marshall, 1987; Nickels & Howard, 1994; Plaut & Shallice, 1993b; for an exception, see Warrington, 1981). On the other hand, Warrington (1975) described how AB was worse at defining concrete words than abstract words, while EM, with the same diagnosis, showed the reverse and more typical pattern. Breedin, Saffran, and Coslett (1994) described a patient, DM, who showed a relative sparing of abstract nouns relative to concrete nouns.

Clearly problems with semantic processing are implicated in the naming difficulty of people with dementia, but might other levels of processing also be disrupted?

There is some evidence that visual processing is impaired in dementia, and that sufferers have difficulty in recognizing objects. (See Figure 11.9 for a model of object naming.) Rochford (1971) found a high proportion of perceptual errors in a naming task (e.g., calling an anchor a "hammer"). Kirshner, Webb, and Kelly (1984) manipulated the perceptual difficulty of the target stimuli, by presenting them either as a masked line drawing, a line drawing, a black and white photograph, or the object. They found that the perceptual clarity of the stimuli affected naming performance. It is unlikely that difficulties with visual processing of stimuli can account for all the naming problems, because people with dementia clearly have many other deficits that do not involve visual processing. In particular, they show a clear deficit on tasks involving the same materials presented in the auditory modality.

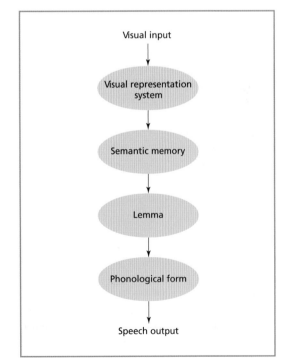

FIGURE 11.9 An outline of a model of object naming. (See Chapter 13 for more detail.)

Two main lines of evidence suggest that people with dementia also have a deficit at the phonological level. First, they have particular difficulty in naming low-frequency objects (e.g., Barker & Lawson, 1968). Jescheniak and Levelt (1994) argued that the word frequency effect in speech production arises from differences in the thresholds of phonological forms. Second, phonological priming of the target improves their naming (Martin & Fedio, 1983).

There are three possible explanations of these findings (Tippett & Farah, 1994). First, there might be heterogeneity among patients. If dementia affects each patient in a different way, then each patient might have a different locus of impairment, depending on the precise effects of their dementia. Each type of impairment might result in a naming deficit. Second, there might be multiple loci of impairments within each patient, such that dementia leads to disruption of the perceptual, semantic, and lexical systems. Third, a single locus of impairment might give rise to all the impairments observed. According to this hypothesis, damage to the semantic system in some way results in additional perceptual and lexical deficits.

Connectionist modeling supports the single locus hypothesis. Tippett and Farah (1994) described a computational model of important aspects of naming in dementia. In particular, they showed how apparent visual and lexical deficits can arise solely from damage to semantic memory. In their model, bidirectional links connect visual input units to visual hidden units, which connect to semantic units, which connect to name hidden units, which in turn connect to name input units (see Figure 11.10). The meaning of a word is encoded as a distributed pattern of activation across the semantic units, such that each unit corresponds to a semantic feature. The bidirectional links, together with the cascading activation, mean that the model is highly interactive. The model was first trained so that the application of a pattern to one of the input layers produced correct outputs at the two layers. Dementia was simulated by removing random subsets of the semantic units.

The main finding was that damage to the semantic units alone rendered the network more

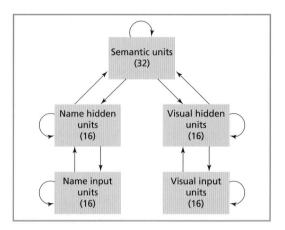

FIGURE 11.10 Functional architecture of Tippett and Farah's model of naming in Alzheimer's disease. The numbers refer to the number of units.

sensitive to manipulations at the visual and name levels. The bidirectional links mean that damage to one level has consequences at other levels too. Lesioning the semantic level meant that the network became more sensitive to visual degradation of the visual input units. Visual degradation was simulated by reducing the overall strength of the visual inputs. The lesioned network also had more difficulty in producing low-frequency names than high-frequency names. Lexical frequency was simulated by giving more training to some pairs than others. Finally, naming after damage was improved by phonological priming. This was simulated by presenting part of the target phonological output pattern at the start of the test phase.

In summary, the Tippett and Farah model shows that damage to the semantic system alone can account for the range of semantic, visual, and lexical impairments shown in dementia. This is because, in a highly interactive network, damage at one level may have consequences at all the others.

Evaluation of research on the neuroscience of semantic memory

In the last few years the study of the neuroscience of semantics has contributed greatly to our understanding of the area. Although there is still considerable disagreement in the field, it has indicated what the important questions in the psychology of meaning are. What are the types of feature that underlie word meaning? How are categories organized by the brain? How does our semantic system relate to input and output systems?

CONNECTIONIST APPROACHES TO SEMANTICS

Connectionism has made an impact on semantic memory, just as it did in earlier years on lower level processes such as word recognition. We saw in Chapter 7 how Hinton and Shallice (1991) and Plaut and Shallice (1993a) incorporated the semantic representation of words into a model of the semantic route of word recognition. This approach gives rise to the idea that semantic memory depends on semantic microfeatures.

Note that this approach is not necessarily a competitor to other theories such as prototypes; one instance of a category might cause one pattern of activation across the semantic units, another instance will cause another similar pattern, and so on. We can talk of the prototype that defines a category as the average pattern of activation of all the instances.

Semantic microfeatures

In the connectionist models we have examined, a semantic representation does not correspond to a particular semantic unit, but to a pattern of activation across all of the semantic units. For example, in Tippett and Farah's model the meaning of each word or object was represented as a pattern of activation over 32 semantic units, each representing a semantic microfeature. A microfeature is an individual, active unit; the prefix "micro" emphasizes that these units are involved in low-level processes rather than explicit symbolic processing (Hinton, 1989), but there really isn't much difference between a feature and a microfeature. Connectionist models suppose that human semantic memory is based on microfeatures. A semantic microfeature is really just a semantic feature, but the prefix "micro" is added in computational modeling to emphasize their

low-level nature. They mediate between perception, action, and language, and do not necessarily have any straightforward linguistic counterparts. While semantic microfeatures might correspond to simple semantic features, they might correspond to something far more abstract. There is no reason to assume that the semantic microfeatures that we develop will correspond to any straightforward linguistic equivalent (such as a word or an attribute), in much the same way that hidden units in a connectionist network do not always acquire an easily identifiable, specific function. In support of this idea, there is evidence that the loss of specific semantic information can affect a set of related concepts (Gainotti, di Betta, & Silveri, 1996). Hence semantic microfeatures might encode knowledge at a very low level of semantic representation, or in a very abstract way that has no straightforward linguistic correspondence (Harley, 1998; Jackendoff, 1983; McNamara & Miller, 1989). The encoding of visual information by at least some of the semantic microfeatures is yet another reason to expect lesions to the semantic system to result in visual errors and perceptual processing difficulty in naming with dementia.

In Hinton and Shallice's (1991) model of deep dyslexia, meaning was represented as a pattern of activation across a number of semantic feature units, or sememes, such as "hard," "soft," "maximum-size-less-foot," "made-of-metal," and "used-for-recreation." No one claims that such semantic features are necessarily those that humans use, but there is some evidence for this sort of approach from data on word naming by Masson (1995). In Hinton and Shallice's model the semantic features are grouped together so that features that are mutually excluded inhibit each other, and only one can be active at any one time. For example, an object cannot be both "hard" and "soft," or "maximum-size-less-foot" and "maximum-size-greater-two-yards," at the same time. In addition, another set of units called "cleanup" units modulate the activation of the semantic units. These features allow combinations of semantic units to influence each other. We saw in Chapter 7 that semantic memory can be thought of as a landscape with many hills and valleys. The bottom of each valley corresponds to a particular word meaning. Words that are similar in meaning will be in valleys that are close together. The initial pattern of activation produced by a word when it first activates the network might be very different from its ultimate semantic representation, but as long as you start somewhere along the sides of the right valley, you will eventually find its bottom. The valley bottoms, which correspond to particular word meanings, are called attractors. This type of network is called an attractor network.

If meanings are represented as a pattern of activation distributed over many microfeatures, then it makes less sense to talk about loss of individual items in the model. Instead, the loss of units will result in the loss of microfeatures. This will result in a general degradation in performance.

Explaining language loss in people with Alzheimer's disease: The semantic microfeature loss hypothesis

What happens if a disease such as dementia results in the loss of semantic microfeatures? The effect will be to distort semantic space so that some semantic attractors might be lost altogether, while others might become inaccessible on some tasks because of the erosion of the boundaries of the attractor basins. Damage to a subset of microfeatures will lead to a probabilistic decline in performance. Depending on the importance of the microfeature lost to a particular item in a particular patient, the pattern of performance observed will vary from patient to patient and from task to task. Different tasks will give different results because they will provide differing amounts of residual activation to the damaged system. Thus, although microfeatures are permanently lost in dementia, when tested experimentally this loss will sometimes look like loss of information, but will at other times look like difficulty in accessing information.

Consider response consistency, usually taken as the clearest indication of item loss. If a unit corresponding to the meaning of the word "vampire" is lost, the meaning of that word is always going to be unavailable. Similarly, if the unit corresponding to the attribute "bites" is lost, then that attribute will always be unavailable. If, however, a unit corresponding to more abstract information that is not easily linguistically encoded is lost, then the consequences might be less apparent in any linguistic task. The loss of a feature may mean that the higher level, linguistically encoded units become permanently unavailable, but alternatively it might just mean that the higher level units become more difficult to access. Hence there is a probabilistic aspect to whether a word or an attribute will be consistently unavailable. So an increasing number of linguistically encoded units should become permanently unavailable as the severity of dementia increases and more microfeatures are lost, as is observed (e.g., Schwartz & Chawluk, 1990).

Tippett and Farah (1994) pointed out that experimental tasks differ in the degree of constraint provided on possible responses. Connectionist models are sensitive to multiple constraints: If one sort of constraint is lost, other consistent ones might still be able to facilitate the correct output. For example, in Tippett and Farah's model, phonological priming provided an additional constraint. Hence the availability of items will depend on the degree to which tasks provide constraints. Patients with Alzheimer's disease perform relatively well in highly constrained tasks.

Modeling category-specific disorders in dementia

Connectionist models of category-specific disorders in dementia are also interesting because they tell us both about the progress of the disease and about the structure of semantic memory. Dementia generally causes more global damage to the brain than the very specific lesioning effects of herpes simplex that typically cause category-specific disorders. Therefore category-specific deficits are more elusive in dementia. There is also the question of which semantic categories are more prone to disruption in dementia. Gonnerman, Andersen, Devlin, Kempler, and Seidenberg (1997) found that sufferers show selective impairments on tasks involving both living things and artifacts, depending on the level of severity of the disease. Early on there is a slight relative deficit of naming artifacts, followed later by a deficit on naming living things, followed by poor naming performance across all categories.

What explains the way in which category-specificity varies with severity? To understand this, we need to look more closely at semantic features. In an important study, McRae, de Sa, and Seidenberg (1997) argued that there are different types of semantic feature, depending on the extent to which each feature is related to other ones (see Figure 11.11). Intercorrelated features tend to occur together: For example, most things that have beaks can also fly, and most things that have fur often have tails and claws. Living things tend to be represented by many intercorrelated features. Semantic features also differ in the extent to which they enable us to distinguish among things. Some features are more important than others. Distinctive (sometimes called distinguishing) features enable members of a category to be distinguished: For example, a leopard can be distinguished from other large cats because it has spots. Many members of a natural kind category will share intercorrelated features, but distinguishing features are exclusive to single items within the category. Artifacts tend not to be represented by many intercorrelated features, but rather by many distinguishing features. Using a primed semantic verification task (e.g., "is an apple used to make cider?"), Cree, McNorgan, and McRae (2006) showed that distinctive features hold a privileged status in semantic memory; they are activated more strongly than shared, non-distinctive features.

As intercorrelated features are particularly common in the category of living things, a small amount of damage to the semantic network, characteristic of early dementia, will have little effect on living things. This is because the richly interconnected intercorrelated features support each other (Devlin, Gonnerman, Andersen, & Seidenberg, 1998). Hence, early on in the progression of dementia, tasks involving living things will appear not to be affected. Beyond a critical amount of damage, however, this support will no longer be available. When a critical mass of distinguishing features is lost, there will be catastrophic failure of the memory system. Then, whole categories will suddenly become unavailable. Artifacts, however, tend not to be represented by many intercorrelated features, but by relatively many informative distinguishing features. The loss of just a few of these features might result in the loss of a specific item. Increasing damage then results in the gradual loss of an increasing number of items across categories, rather than the catastrophic loss observed with living things.

It is important to emphasize the probabilistic nature of this loss. If a distinguishing feature for an animal happens to be lost early on, then that animal will be confused with other animals from that point on (Gonnerman et al., 1997). However, there are more intercorrelated than non-correlated distinguishing features within the living things category. Hence an intercorrelated feature is more likely to be affected, but usually with no obvious consequence, than a distinguishing feature. This type of approach is promising, but we must be wary about the relatively limited amount of data on which this sort of

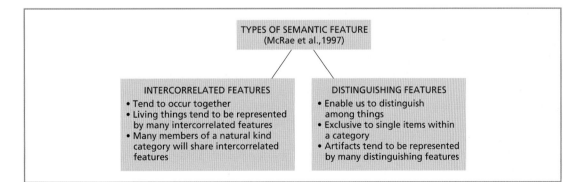

FIGURE 11.11

model is based. For example, Garrard, Patterson, Watson, and Hodges (1998) failed to find any interaction between disease severity and the direction of dissociation. Instead, they found a group advantage for artifacts, with a few individuals showing an advantage for living things.

Latent semantic analysis

We have seen that connectionism represents meaning by a pattern of activation distributed over many simple semantic features. In these models, the features are hand-coded; they are not learned, but are built into the simulations. How do humans learn these features? Connectionist models suggest one means: connectionist models are particularly good at picking out statistical regularities in data, so it is possible that we abstract them from many exposures to words. A closely related approach makes explicit the role of co-occurrence information in acquiring knowledge. This technique is called latent semantic analysis (**LSA**) (Landauer & Dumais, 1997; Landauer, Foltz, & Laham, 1998; see Burgess & Lund, 1997, for the similar HAL—hyperspace analog to language—model). Latent semantic analysis needs no prior linguistic knowledge. Instead, a mathematical procedure abstracts dimensions of similarity from a large corpus of items based on analysis of the context in which words occur. We saw earlier how Lund et al. (1995) showed that semantically similar words are interchangeable within a sentence. This means that the context in which words can (and cannot) occur provides a powerful constraint on how word meanings are represented. Latent semantic analysis makes use of this context to acquire knowledge about words. At first sight these constraints might not seem particularly strong, there are a huge number of them, and we are exposed to them many times. Constraints on the co-occurrence of words provide a vast number of interrelations that facilitate semantic development. LSA learns about these interrelations through a mechanism of induction. The mathematical techniques involved are too complex to describe here, but essentially the algorithm tries to minimize the number of dimensions necessary to represent all the co-occurrence information. Indeed, this type of model is often called the HDM (high-dimensional memory) approach.

Landauer and Dumais examined how latent semantic analysis might account for aspects of vocabulary acquisition. After exposure to a large amount of text, the model generated performed well at a multiple-choice test of selecting the appropriate synonym of a target word. It also acquired vocabulary at the same rate as children. (To give some idea of the complexity of the task, and to provide another demonstration of the importance of computers in modern psycholinguistics, 300 dimensions were necessary to represent relations among 4.6 million words of text taken from an encyclopedia.) This statistical sort of approach is very good at accounting for later vocabulary learning, where direct instruction is very rare. Instead, we infer the meanings of new words from the context. LSA also shows how we can reach agreement on the usage of words without any external referent. This observation is particularly useful in explaining how we acquire words describing private mental experiences. How do you know that I mean the same thing by "I'm sad today" as you do? The answer is in the context in which these words repeatedly do and do not occur.

One criticism of the HDM models is that they are overly concerned with the context in which words occur, so that words are related to other words, rather than to the world, and therefore these models find it difficult to cope with novel situations (Glenberg & Robertson, 2000; see Burgess, 2000, for a reply). For example, we know that it makes sense to use a newspaper to protect our head from the wind, but not a matchbox. We will return to how meaning is connected to perception at the end of this chapter.

Evaluation of connectionist models of semantic memory

Throughout this chapter we have seen how connectionist modeling has indicated how apparently disparate theories and phenomena—here the time course of dementia, modality-specific stores, functional versus perceptual attributes, and category-specific memory—may be subsumed under one model. Connectionist modeling of neuropsychological deficits is particularly promising. The data and modeling work suggest that the language deficits shown in diseases such as dementia result from the gradual loss of semantic microfeatures.

Grounding: Connecting language to the world

Language and meaning are not a closed system. Meaning is a way of mapping language onto the external world. At some point the semantic system has to interface with the perceptual systems; this interfacing is sometimes called *grounding* (see Jackendoff, 1987, 2002, 2003; Roy, 2005; Vigliocco et al., 2004). How does grounding occur? Rogers et al. (2004) describe a connectionist model of semantic memory that provides an account of how language and perception are connected. They constructed a model that maps between modality-specific representations of objects and their verbal descriptions (see Figure 11.12). Semantic representations mediate between these two output representations. In their model, a semantic level mediates between visual features (e.g., is round) and verbal descriptors, which in turn comprise names (e.g., bird), perceptual descriptors (e.g., has wings), functional descriptors (e.g., can fly), and encyclopedic descriptors (e.g., lives in Africa). The model learns to associate inputs with outputs. The internal semantic structure is constrained by both visual and verbal outputs; hence visually similar inputs give rise to similarly structured internal representations. As noted above, the semantic representations do not necessarily encode semantic features (e.g., has eyes) directly; they just have to be "good enough" to do the job (e.g., giving a name to an object, answering a question such as "does a chair have eyes?").

As Rogers et al. note, such a computational approach, although broadly similar to the feature-based model, has several advantages. First, we no longer have to be worried about what features we should use and whether they are arbitrary; features emerge to do the job. We no longer have to worry about whether a dog's bark and a cow's moo are the same or different features. Second, the computational model forces us to be explicit about how every semantic or perceptual task is carried out. Third, the model provides an account of semantic dementia. Semantic dementia was simulated by removing a proportion of the weights; increasing severity is modeled by removing a larger proportion of the weights. The lesioned model resembles the behavior of patients with semantic dementia. For example, in both the model and the patients, as severity increases so does the proportion of omission and superordinate errors, while the production of semantic substitutions initially increases but then declines. With a little damage, the model first confuses similar items, but with increasing damage it becomes unable to generate any information that distinguishes one item from another, and whole categories merge together. Hence, although individual names may not be accessible, superordinate categories remain so. With yet more damage, even broad categories may become indistinguishable. The model gives a similarly good account of other semantic tasks, such as sorting words and pictures, drawing, copying after a delay, and matching words to pictures. The model makes some specific predictions: Because fruits share some properties with animals (e.g., they are living, or at least not man-made), they have many visual attributes in common with man-made objects. And patients do indeed treat fruit differently, sorting them with

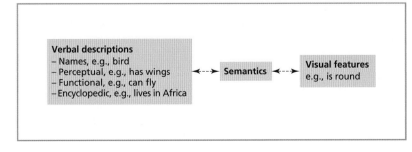

FIGURE 11.12 Rogers et al.'s (2004) connectionist model of semantic memory. Adapted from Rogers et al. (2004).

artifacts. The simulations also predicted that more omission errors should be made when naming artifacts and more substitution errors when naming living things, because of the greater structure in the domain of living things, a prediction verified by the data from patients with semantic dementia.

This kind of computational approach does not contradict the HAL (hyperspace analog to language) model of Burgess and Lund (1997) or the LSA (latent semantic analysis) model of Landauer and Dumais (1997). Indeed, all these approaches show that we extract and abstract semantic information from large bodies of information. However, while HAL and LSA are reliant on verbal input, this computational approach links verbal and perceptual information. The computational model also links semantic processing to neuropsychology.

The semantic representation is unitary and amodal, although different modalities will provide different inputs to the mediating semantic representation. In that respect the model resembles OUCH. Indeed, semantic memory might better be seen as a system that mediates different perceptual systems, rather than a store of propositional facts. The anterior regions of the temporal lobes play a particularly important role in this process.

The idea that our internal representations are grounded in our perceptions, actions, and feelings is an important one: put another way, our cognition is *embedded* in the world. Concepts have very direct links to the world (Barsalou, 2003, 2008; Glenberg, 2007). Our minds don't work in isolation—they are situated within the world. According to this view, concepts and meaning aren't just abstract things: thinking about real-world objects, for example, involves the visual perceptual system. Furthermore, according to the situated cognition idea, concepts are less stable than has usually been thought, varying depending on the context and situation. Barsalou (2003) had people perform two tasks simultaneously: using their hands to imagine performing some manual operations, and identifying the properties of concepts. Sometimes the actions being performed were relevant to the concepts being described, in which case the participants were more likely to mention related aspects of the concepts. For

example, if they were performing the action of opening a drawer, they were more likely to mention clothes likely to be found inside a clothes dresser than otherwise.

There is evidence that our mental situation in the world takes a very concrete form, in that there are direct links between representations of perceptions and actions. What happens in the brain when we hear the word "kick"? Using brain imaging, we see Wernicke's region, the part of the left temporal lobe of the brain that we know plays a vital role in accessing word meanings, become highly activated. We also see some activation in Broca's area, a region towards the front of the left hemisphere that we know to be involved in producing speech. What is even more surprising is the fMRI scans show that there is activation in the parts of the brain that deal with motor control, and particularly the motor control of the leg (Glenberg, 2007; Hauk, Johnsrude, & Pulvermüller, 2004). It's as though when we hear "kick," we give a mental kick. Similarly, if we hear a word such as "catch," we see activation in the parts of the brain that control the movements of the hand, and if you hear "I eat an apple," you get activation of the parts that control the mouth (Tettamanti et al., 2005). This motor activity peaks extremely quickly: within 20 ms of the peak activation in the parts of the brain traditionally thought to be involved in recognizing words and processing meaning (Pulvermüller, Shtyrov, & Illmoniemi, 2003), which is so fast that it rules out the explanation that people are just consciously reflecting on or rehearsing what they've just heard. This idea that thinking or understanding language causes activation in the parts of the brain to do with how the body deals with these concepts is called *embodiment*. Language is grounded to the world, and grounding happens in the parts of the brain that deal with perception and action (Willems & Casasanto, 2011).

Brain imaging studies reinforce the view that wide areas of the brain are involved in processing meaning at many different levels, initially involving modality-specific sensory and motor systems, and then increasingly abstract representations that tap into a variety of other cognitive, emotional, and social processes carried out by the brain (Binder & Desai, 2011).

SUMMARY

- Semantics is the study of meaning.
- Episodic memory is memory for events, and semantic memory is memory for general knowledge.
- Association alone cannot explain how semantic memory is organized.
- Semantics is the interface between language processing and the rest of cognition.
- The denotation of a word is its core meaning, and its connotations are its associations.
- The reference (extension) of a word is what it refers to in the world, and its sense (intension) is the underlying concept that specifies how it is related to its referents.
- Semantic networks encode semantic information in the form of networks of linked nodes.
- The Collins and Quillian network emphasizes hierarchical relations and cognitive economy; it attempted to give an account of sentence verification times.
- Hierarchical networks could not explain similarity and relatedness effects.
- Spreading activation networks can account for similarity and relatedness effects, but the theory is difficult to falsify.
- The meaning of words can be decomposed into smaller units of meaning called semantic features.
- The idea that word meanings can be split up into smaller units is called semantic decomposition.
- Katz and Fodor showed how sentence meanings could be derived from the combination of semantic features for each word in the sentence, and in particular how this information could be used to select the appropriate sense of ambiguous words.
- Feature-list theories account for sentence verification times by postulating that we compare lists of defining and characteristic features.
- A major problem for early decompositional features is that it is not always possible to specify the features necessary to encode word meaning; that is, not all words are easily defined.
- A number of experiments have been carried out on whether semantic decomposition is obligatory; on balance, the results suggest that it is.
- A prototype is an abstraction that represents the average member of a category.
- The basic level of a category is the one that is maximally informative and which we prefer to use unless there are good reasons to use more general or specific levels.
- In contrast to abstraction theories, in instance-based theories each instance is represented individually, and comparisons are made with specific instances rather than with an abstract central tendency.
- We probably have different memory systems for visual and verbal semantics.
- Semantic categories can be selectively impaired by brain damage; in particular, performance on tasks involving living and non-living things can be selectively disrupted.
- These impairments cannot be explained away in terms of methodological artifacts because we observe a double dissociation.
- According to the sensory–functional theory, category-specific semantic impairments for living and non-living things arise because living things are represented primarily in terms of perceptual knowledge, but non-living things are represented primarily in terms of functional knowledge.
- According to the domain-specific knowledge hypothesis, category-specific semantic impairments for living and non-living things arise because knowledge about living and non-living things is stored in different parts of the brain.
- Dementia is a progressive degeneration of the brain resulting in deteriorating performance across a range of tasks; in semantic dementia, semantic knowledge is disproportionately impaired.

(Continued)

(Continued)

- People with probable Alzheimer's disease have difficulty with picture naming; this can be explained in terms of their underlying semantic deficit.
- In connectionist modeling, word meaning is represented as a pattern of activation distributed across many semantic features; this pattern corresponds to a semantic attractor.
- Semantic features (called microfeatures in computational modeling) do not necessarily have straightforward perceptual or linguistic correspondences.
- Semantic dementia can be explained as the progressive loss of semantic features.
- Living things tend to be represented by many shared intercorrelated features, whereas non-living things are represented primarily by distinctive features.
- The pattern of category-specificity displayed in dementia depends on the level of severity of the disease.
- Connectionist modeling shows how the differential dependence of living and non-living things on intercorrelated and distinctive features explains the interaction between performance on different semantic categories and severity of dementia.
- Latent semantic analysis shows how co-occurrence information is used to acquire knowledge.
- Grounding is how symbols are connected to perceptual representations.

QUESTIONS TO THINK ABOUT

1. Can introspection tell us anything about how we represent meaning?
2. To what extent are feature-based theories of meaning concerned with a level of representation beneath prototype and instance-based theories of concepts?
3. How would you explain case studies showing the loss of knowledge about very specific semantic categories (e.g., medical terms)?
4. What sort of categories might a cat or dog possess?

FURTHER READING

A recent review of the psychology of semantics is Vigliocco and Vinson (2009). The classic linguistics work on semantics is Lyons (1977a, 1977b). Johnson-Laird (1983) provides an excellent review of a number of approaches to semantics, including the relevance of the more philosophical approaches.

General problems with network models are discussed by Johnson-Laird, Herrman, and Chaffin (1984). Chang (1986) and Smith (1988) review the experimental support for psychological models of semantic memory. Kintsch (1980) is a good review of the early experimental work on semantic memory, particularly on the sentence verification task.

For more on definitional versus non-definitional theories of meaning, see the debate between J. A. Fodor (1978, 1979) and Johnson-Laird (1978; Miller & Johnson-Laird, 1976). For more on instance-based theories, see Hintzman (1986), Murphy and Medin (1985), Nosofsky (1991), Smith and Medin (1981), and Whittlesea (1987). For an important overview of connectionist approaches to semantics, see Rogers and McClelland (2004).

Aitchison (1994) is a good introduction to processing figurative language.

For an excellent brief review of the neuropsychology of semantics, see Saffran and Schwartz (1994). Caplan (1992) also provides an extensive review of the neuropsychology of semantic memory. For a review of optic aphasia see Sitton et al. (2000). See Vinson (1999) for an introductory review of language in dementia; Harley (1998) for a review of work about naming and dementia; and Schwartz (1990) for an edited volume of work on dementia with a cognitive bias.

HAL is another latent semantic analysis model (Lund et al., 1995, 1996); it produces an account of semantic priming that is similar to McRae and Boisvert (1998; see Chapter 6).

CHAPTER 12

COMPREHENSION

INTRODUCTION

This chapter is about the higher level processes of comprehension. What happens after we have identified the words and built the syntactic structure of a sentence? How do we build up a representation of the meaning of the whole sentence, given the meanings of the individual words? How do we combine sentences to construct a representation of the whole conversation or text? And how do we use the meaning of what we have processed?

Comprehension is the stage of processing that follows word recognition and parsing. As a result of identifying words (Chapters 6, 7, and 9) and parsing the sentence, we have identified their thematic roles (Chapter 10) and accessed their individual meanings (Chapter 11). The task now facing the reader or listener is to integrate these different aspects into a representation of the sentence, to integrate it with what has gone on before, and to decide what to do with this representation.

One of the central themes in the study of comprehension is whether it is a constructive process or a minimal process. How far do we go beyond the literal meaning of the sentence? Do we construct a complex model of what is being communicated, or do we do as little work as possible—just enough so as to be able to make out the sense? We go beyond the literal material when we make inferences. When and how do we make them? In comprehension, we construct a model of what we think is being communicated. How do we work out what the words in the incoming sentences refer to in this model? We use the model that we are constructing to help us make sense of the material. We shall see that it is possible to take this idea of comprehension as construction too far: We do not do more work than is necessary during comprehension. If comprehension for meaning is like building a house to live in, we do not build an extravagant mansion.

Text is printed or written material, usually longer than a sentence. A story is a particular, self-contained type of text, although a story in a psycholinguistic experiment might only be two sentences long. **Discourse** is the spoken equivalent of text. Conversations are spoken interchanges where the topic may change as the conversation unfolds. Conversations have their own particular mechanisms for controlling who is talking at any time. It should be noted that most of the research has been carried out on text comprehension rather than discourse comprehension. Of course there may be many things in common in representing and understanding spoken and written language, but there are also important differences. Time is less of a constraint on processing written language, and we also have the advantage with written language that the text is there for us to reread if we should so wish. Comprehending spoken language is affected by the transience of the speech signal and the time constraints this imposes. However, apart from the final section on conversation, most of what will be discussed in this chapter applies to both written and spoken language.

Conversations are spoken interchanges which have a clearly defined structure, even though the topic may change as the conversation unfolds.

It is useful to distinguish between semantic and referential processing (Garnham & Oakhill, 1992). Semantic processing concerns working out what words and sentences mean, whereas referential processing concerns working out their role in the model—what must the world be like for a sentence to be true? In general, semantic processing precedes referential processing. In incremental parsing models (such as Altmann & Steedman, 1988), semantic and referential processing occur on a word-by-word basis. So not only have we got to work out the meaning of what we hear or read, we also have to relate this information to a model of the world. Everything new changes or adds to this model in some way. What is the nature of this model?

An important characteristic of text and discourse is that it is coherent. The material has a topic and forms a semantically integrated whole. Gernsbacher (1990) proposed four sources of coherence. Referential coherence refers to consistency in who or what is being talked about. Temporal coherence refers to consistency in when the events occur. Locational coherence refers to consistency in where the events occur. Causal coherence refers to consistency in why events happen. Text is also cohesive, in that the same

entities are referred to in successive sentences (Bishop, 1997). When we read or listen, we strive to maintain coherence and cohesion. We generally assume that what we are processing is coherent and makes sense. We assume that **pronouns** are referring to things that have previously been introduced. These are powerful constraints on processing, and we will see that we maintain coherence in a number of ways.

Throughout this chapter we will come across a number of findings that point to factors that can make comprehension easier or more difficult. Some of them are perhaps not surprising: For example, it is difficult to remember material if the sense of a story is jumbled. Thorndyke and Hayes-Roth (1979) showed that the structure of individual sentences could affect the recall of the whole story. In particular, they showed that repetition of the same sentence structure improves recall when the content of the sentences changes, as long as not too much information is presented using the same sentence structure—that is, if it is not repeated too many times with different content. Throughout this chapter, measures of how much we remember of a story are often used to tell us how difficult the material is. It is assumed that good memory equals good comprehension. This is rather different from the other measures we have considered in previous chapters, which have tended to be on-line in the sense that they measure processing at the time of presentation. Memory may reflect processing subsequent to initial comprehension.

The organization of this chapter is as follows. First, I look at what makes comprehension easy or difficult. Then I examine what determines what we remember of text. Next, I examine the process of inference-making in comprehension in detail, with particular emphasis on the problems of deciding what words refer to in our model. Then I review some influential theories of text comprehension. By the end of this chapter you should:

- Know how we integrate new material with previous information.
- Understand how reliable our memory really is for what we have read or heard.

- Appreciate how we make inferences about what we read or hear.
- Know how we make inferences as we process language.
- Know how we represent text.
- Understand about the story grammar, schema, propositional network, mental model, and construction–integration models of text comprehension.
- Know what differentiates skilled from less able comprehenders.
- Know the best way to try to understand difficult material.

When testifying to the Watergate Committee in June 1973, John Dean's recall of the specific conversations in Nixon's office was inaccurate.

MEMORY FOR TEXT AND INFERENCES

Like eyewitness testimony, literal, verbatim memory is notoriously unreliable. If we needed to be reminded of this, Neisser (1981) discussed the case study of the memory of John Dean, who was an aide of President Richard Nixon at the time of the Watergate cover-up and scandal in the early 1970s. Unknown to Dean, the conversations in Nixon's office were tape-recorded, so his recall of them when testifying to the Watergate Committee in June 1973 could be checked against the tape-recordings, 9 months after the original events. His recall was highly inaccurate. Nixon did not say many of the things that Dean attributed to him, and much was omitted. Dean's recall was only really accurate at a very general thematic level: The people involved did discuss the cover-up, but not in the precise way Dean said that they had. It seems that Dean's attitudes influenced what he remembered. For example, Dean said that he wanted to warn the President the cover-up might fall apart, but in fact he did not; at the hearings, he said that he thought he had uttered this warning. Assuming that Dean was being truthful about his recall of the events, we see that in spite of their belief to the contrary, speakers only remember the gist of previous conversations. We see a tendency to abstract information, and to "remember" things that never actually happen. These findings have been replicated many times, so abstraction is clearly an important feature of memory. It is also well known

that eyewitness testimony is often unreliable, and can easily be influenced by many factors, and that our memory can easily be led astray by misleading questions (Loftus, 1996). So what determines what we remember and what we forget, and can we ever remember material verbatim?

People generally forget the details of word order very quickly. We remember only the meaning of what we read or hear, not the details of the syntax. Sachs (1967) presented participants with a sentence such as (1) embedded in a story. She later tested their ability to distinguish it from possible confusion sentences (2) to (4):

(1) He sent a letter about it to Galileo, the great Italian scientist. (original)
(2) He sent Galileo, the great Italian scientist, a letter about it. (formal word order change)
(3) A letter about it was sent to Galileo, the great Italian scientist. (syntactic change)
(4) Galileo, the great Italian scientist, sent him a letter about it. (semantic change)

Sachs tested recognition after 0, 80, or 160 intervening syllables (which are equal to approximately 0, 25, or 50 second delays respectively), and found that the participants' ability to detect changes to word order and syntax decreased very quickly. Participants could not tell the difference between the original and the changed sentences (2) and (3). They were however sensitive to changes in meaning (such as (4)). Generally, we remember the gist of text, and very quickly dump the details of word order.

We start to purge our memory of the details of what we hear after sentence boundaries. Jarvella (1971) presented participants with sentences such as (5) and (6) embedded in a story:

(5) The tone of the document was threatening. Having failed to disprove the charges, Taylor was later fired by the President.

(6) The document had also blamed him for having failed to disprove the charges. Taylor was later fired by the President.

The participants were then tested on what they remembered. They remembered the clause "having failed to disprove the charges" more accurately in (5) than (6), presumably because in (5) it was part of the final sentence before the interruption.

The way in which we describe what we recall from immediate memory can be influenced by the syntactic structure of what we have just read or heard. Potter and Lombardi (1998) found that the tendency to use the same syntactic structure in material recalled from immediate memory results from syntactic priming by the target material (see Chapter 13 for more details). That is, we tend to reuse the same words and sentence structures in the material we recall because they were there in the original material. Potter and Lombardi showed that it was possible to change the way people phrased the material they recalled by priming them with an alternative sentence structure. This is consistent with the idea that immediate recall involves generation from a meaning-level representation, rather than true verbatim memory (Potter & Lombardi, 1990, 1998).

The details of surface syntactic form are not always lost. Yekovich and Thorndyke (1981) showed that we can sometimes recognize exact wording up to at least 1 hour after presentation. Bates, Masling, and Kintsch (1978) tested participants' recognition memory for conversations in television soap operas. As expected, memory for meaning straight after the program was nearly perfect, but participants could also remember the detailed surface form when it had some significance.

Kintsch and Bates (1977) studied students' memory of lectures. They found that verbatim memory was good after 2 days but was greatly reduced after 5 days. Extraneous remarks were remembered best: We remember the precise wording of jokes and announcements particularly well. Perhaps surprisingly, there were no differences in literal memory for sentences that were centrally related to the topic compared with those concerned with detail. A depressing result for teachers is that memory was worst for central topic statements and overall conclusions. These studies show that there are differences between coherent naturalistic conversation, and isolated artificial sentences and other materials constructed just for psycholinguistic experiments. In real conversation (counting soap operas as examples of real conversation), quite often what might be considered surface detail serves a particular function. For example, the way in which we use pronouns or names depends in part on factors like how much attention we want to draw to what is being referred to. This result accords with our intuitions: Although we often remember only the gist of what is said to us, on occasion we can remember the exact wording, particularly if it is important or emotionally salient.

Items and properties that become incorporated into our model of what we hear are more memorable than those that do not. Consider these two sentences, (7) and (8):

(7) Vlad was relieved that Agnes was wearing her pink dress.

(8) Vlad was relieved that Agnes was not wearing her pink dress.

Both sentences mention the word "pink," but while in the first sentence there is a pink dress in our representation of the sentence, in the second there is not. We are explicitly told that there is no pink dress present. How does this affect the memorability of the word "pink"? Suppose we present the word "pink" after hearing these two sentences, and ask participants whether or not the word was present. What we find depends on the delay between the sentence and presenting the probe word ("pink"). After 500 ms, "pink" is equally accessible in both sentences, but after 1,500 ms, participants respond faster if the item is present (7) compared with when it is not present (8). That is, immediately after hearing a sentence, linguistic structure and content determines memory; after a longer delay, linguistic structure is less important than discourse structure (Kaup & Zwaan, 2003).

Exactly why we sometimes remember the exact surface form is not currently known. Is a decision taken to store it permanently, and if so when? Neither is the relation between our memory for surface form and the structure of the parser well understood. Clearly we can routinely remember more than one clause, even if there has been subsequent interfering material, so it cannot be simply that we always immediately discard surface form. Clearly the parser can process one sentence while we are storing details of another.

Importance

Not surprisingly, people are more likely to remember what they consider to be the more important aspects of text. Johnson (1970) showed that participants were more likely to recall ideas from a story that had been rated as important by another group of participants. Keenan, MacWhinney, and Mayhew (1977) examined memory for a linguistics seminar, and compared sentences that were considered to be HIC (high interactional content—which is material having personal significance) and sentences with LIC (low interactional content—which is material having little personal significance).

(9) I think you've made a fundamental error in this study.
(10) I think there are two fundamental tasks in this study.

Sentences with high interactional content, such as (9), were more likely to be recalled by the appropriate participants in the seminar than sentences with low interactional content, such as (10).

Although it may not be surprising that more important information is recalled better, there are a number of reasons why it might be so. We might spend longer reading more important parts

of the text; indeed, eye-movement research suggests this is in part the case. In this case the better memory would simply reflect more processing time. However, Britton, Muth, and Glynn (1986) restricted the time participants could spend reading parts of the text so they spent equal amounts of time reading the more and the less important parts of a story, and found that they still remembered the important parts better. Hence there is a real effect of the role the material plays in the meaning of the story. Important material must be flagged in comprehension and memory in some way.

The importance of an idea relative to the rest of the story also affects its memorability (Bower, Black, & Turner, 1979; Kintsch & van Dijk, 1978; Thorndyke, 1977). As you would expect, the more important a proposition is, the more likely it is to be remembered. Text processing theories should predict why some ideas are more "important" than others. One suggestion is that important ideas are those that receive more processing because themes in the text are more often related to important ideas than less important ones are.

What effect does prior knowledge have?

The effect of prior knowledge on what we remember and on the processes of comprehension was explored in an important series of experiments by Bransford and his colleagues. For example, Bransford and Johnson (1973, p. 392) read participants the following story (11):

(11) "If the balloons popped, the sound wouldn't be able to carry far, since everything would be too far away from the correct floor. A closed window would also prevent the sound from carrying, since most buildings tend to be well insulated. Since the whole operation depends upon a steady flow of electricity, a break in the middle of the wire would also cause problems. Of course, the fellow could shout, but the human voice is not loud enough to carry that far. An additional problem is that a string could break on the instrument. Then there could be no accompaniment to the message. It is clear

that the best situation would involve less distance. Then there would be fewer potential problems. With face-to-face contact, the least number of things could go wrong."

This story was specially designed to be abstract and unfamiliar. Bransford and Johnson measured participants' ratings of the comprehensibility of the story and also the number of ideas recalled. Participants were divided into three groups, called "no context," "context before," and "context after." The context here was provided in the form of a picture that makes sense of the story (see Figure 12.1). Bransford and Johnson found that this context was only useful if it was presented before the story: the "no context" group recalled an average of 3.6 ideas out of a maximum of 14, the "context after" group also recalled 3.6 ideas, but the "context before" group recalled an average of 8.0 ideas. Hence context must provide more than just retrieval cues; it must also improve our comprehension, and this improvement in comprehension then leads to an improvement in recall. Context provides a frame for understanding text. The role of context and background information is a recurring theme in addressing how we understand and remember text, and its importance cannot be overestimated.

In this experiment, the story and the context were novel. Bransford and Johnson (1973, p. 400) also showed that a familiar context could facilitate comprehension. They presented participants with the following story (12):

(12) "The procedure is actually quite simple. First you arrange things into two different groups. Of course, one pile may be sufficient depending on how much there is to do. If you have to go somewhere else due to lack of facilities, that is the next step; otherwise you are pretty well set. It is important not to overdo things. That is, it is better to do fewer things at once than too many. In the short run this might not seem important, but complications can easily arise. A mistake can be expensive as well. At first the whole procedure will seem complicated. Soon, however, it will become just another facet of life. It is difficult to foresee any end

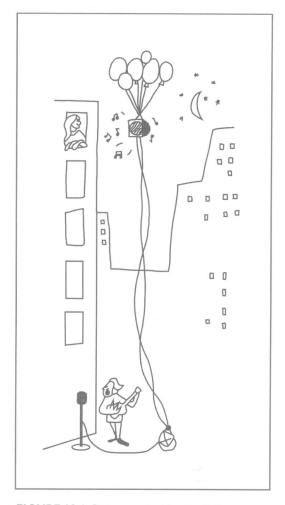

FIGURE 12.1 Picture context for the "balloon story" (11). Figure from Bransford and Johnson (1973).

to the necessity for this task in the immediate future, but then one can never tell. After the procedure is completed, one arranges the material into different groups again. Then they can be put into their appropriate places. Eventually they will be used once more, and the whole cycle will then have to be repeated. However, that is part of life."

When you know that this is called the "clothes washing" story, it probably all makes sense. Those who read the passage without this context later recalled an average of only 2.8 out of a maximum of 18 ideas; those who had the context after reading it also only recalled on average 2.7 ideas. However, those participants given the context before the story recalled an average of 5.8 ideas. These experiments suggest that background knowledge by itself is not sufficient: you must recognize when it is applicable.

Appropriate context may be as little as the title of a story. Dooling and Lachman (1971, p. 218) showed the effect of providing participants with a title that helped them make sense of what was read, but once again it had to be given before reading the story (13):

(13)   "With hocked gems financing him, our hero bravely defied all scornful laughter that tried to prevent his scheme. 'Your eyes deceive,' he had said. 'An egg, not a table, correctly typifies this unexplored planet.' Now three sturdy sisters sought proof. Forging along, sometimes through vast calmness, yet more often over turbulent peaks and valleys, days became weeks as doubters spread fearful rumours about the edge. At last, from nowhere, welcome winged creatures appeared signifying monumental success."

Without the title of "Christopher Columbus's discovery of America," the story makes little sense. In fact, "three sturdy sisters" refers to the three ships, the "turbulent peaks and valleys" to the waves, and "the edge" refers to the supposed edge of a flat earth.

It might reasonably be objected that all these stories so far have been designed to be obscure, without a title or context, and are not representative of normal texts. What happens with less obtuse stories?

This can be seen in an experiment by Anderson and Pichert (1978), who showed how a shift in perspective provides different retrieval cues. Participants read a story summarized in (14)—a more colloquial British term for "playing hooky" is "playing truant," or "skiving":

(14)   Two boys play hooky from school. They go to the home of one of the boys because his mother is never there on a Thursday. The family is well off. They have a fine old home which is set back from the road and which has attractive grounds. But since it is an old house it has some defects: for example, it has a leaky roof, and a damp and musty cellar. Because the family is wealthy, they have a lot of valuable possessions—such as ten-speed bike, a color television, and a rare coin collection.

The story was 373 words long and identified by the experimenters as containing 72 main ideas. Other participants had previously rated the main ideas of the story according to their relevance to a potential house buyer or a potential burglar. For example, a leaky roof and a damp basement are important features of a house to house buyers but not to burglars, whereas valuable possessions and the fact that no one is in on Thursday are more relevant to burglars. The participants in the experiment read the story from either a "house buying" or a "burglar" perspective in advance. Not surprisingly, the perspective influenced the ideas the participants recalled. Half the participants were then told the other perspective, while a control group of the other half of the participants just had the first repeated. The shift in perspective improved recall: participants could recall things they had previously forgotten. This is because the new perspective provides a plan for searching memory.

At first sight the findings of this experiment appear to contradict those of Bransford and Johnson. Bransford and Johnson showed that context has little effect when it is presented after a story, but Anderson and Pichert showed that changing the perspective after the story—which of course is a form of context—can improve recall. The difference is that, unlike the Bransford and Johnson experiments, the Anderson and Pichert story was easy to understand. It is hard to encode difficult material in the first place, let alone recall it later. With easier material the problem is in recalling it, not encoding it. People encode information from both perspectives, but the perspective biases what people recall. In an extension of this study, Baillet and Keenan (1986) looked at what happens if perspective is shifted after reading but before recall. Participants who recalled the material immediately depended on the retrieval perspective; however, participants who recalled it after a much longer interval (1 week) were not affected by the retrieval perspective—only the perspective given at encoding mattered.

There is a huge amount of potentially relevant background knowledge. Almost anything we know can be brought to bear on understanding text. (Indeed, one way to improve our memory for text is to construct as many connections as possible between new and old material.) Culture-specific information also influences comprehension (Altarriba, 1993; Altarriba & Forsythe, 1993). For example, in an experiment by Steffensen, Joag-dev, and Anderson (1979), groups of American and Indian participants read two passages, one describing a typical American wedding and the other a typical Indian wedding. Participants read the passage appropriate to their native culture more rapidly and remembered more of it, and distorted more information from the culturally inappropriate passage. Culture does not mean just nationality: religious affiliation can affect reading comprehension. Lipson (1983) showed that children from strongly Catholic or strongly Jewish backgrounds showed faster comprehension of and better recall for text that was appropriate to their affiliation.

In summary, prior knowledge has a large effect on our ability to understand and remember language. The more we know about a topic, the better we can comprehend and recall new material. The disadvantage of this is that sometimes prior knowledge can lead us astray.

Inferences

We make an **inference** when we go beyond the literal meaning of the text. An inference is the derivation of additional knowledge from facts already known; this might involve going beyond the text to maintain coherence, or to elaborate on what was actually presented. Inferences do not always lead to the correct conclusion, however. Prior knowledge and context are mixed blessings. Although they can help us to remember material that we would otherwise have forgotten, they can also make us think we have "remembered" material that was never presented in the first place!

For example, Sulin and Dooling (1974, p. 256) showed that background knowledge could also be a source of errors if it is applied inappropriately. Consider the following story (15):

(15) "Gerald Martin strove to undermine the existing government to satisfy his political ambitions. Many of the people of his country supported his efforts. Current political problems made it relatively easy for Martin to take over. Certain groups remained loyal to the old government and caused Martin trouble. He confronted these groups directly and so silenced them. He became a ruthless, uncontrollable dictator. The ultimate effect of his rule was the downfall of his country."

Half of the participants in their experiment read this story as given here, with the main actor in the story called "Gerald Martin." The other half read it with the name "Adolf Hitler" instead. Participants in the "Hitler" condition afterwards were more likely to believe incorrectly that they had read a sentence "He hated the Jews particularly and so persecuted them," than a neutral control sentence such as "He was an intelligent man but had no sense of human kindness." That is, they made inferences from their background world knowledge that influenced their memory of the story. Here the prior knowledge was a source of errors. Participants in the fictitious character condition were of course unable to use this background information.

There are three main types of inference, called logical, bridging, and elaborative inferences. Logical inferences follow from the meanings of words. For example, hearing "Vlad is a bachelor" enables us to infer that Vlad is male. Bridging inferences (sometimes called backward inferences) help us relate new to previous information (Clark, 1977a, 1977b). Another way of putting this is that texts have coherence in a way that randomly jumbled sentences do not have. We strive to maintain this coherence, and make inferences to do so. One of the major tasks in comprehension is sorting out what pronouns refer to. Sometimes even more cognitive work is necessary to make sense of what we read or hear. How can we make sense of (16)? We can if we assume that the moat refers to a moat around the castle mentioned in the first sentence. This is an example of how we maintain coherence: We comprehend on the basis that there is continuity in the material that we are processing, and that it is not just a jumble of disconnected ideas. Bridging inferences provide links among ideas to maintain coherence.

(16)   Vlad looked around the castle. The moat was dry.

We make elaborative inferences when we extend what is in the text with world knowledge. The Gerald Martin example is an (unwarranted) elaborative inference. This type of inference proves to be very difficult for AI simulations of text comprehension, and is known as the frame problem. Our store of world general knowledge is enormous, and potentially any of it can be brought to bear on a piece of text, to make both bridging and elaborative inferences. How does text elicit relevant world knowledge? This is a significant problem for all theories of text processing. Bridging and elaborative inferences have sometimes been called backward and forward inferences respectively, as backward inferences require us to go back from the current text to previous information, whereas forward inferences allow us to predict the future. As we shall see, there are reasons to think that different mechanisms are responsible for these two types of inference. Taken together, all inferences that are not logical are sometimes called pragmatic inferences.

As we have seen, people make inferences on the basis of their world knowledge. We have also seen that we only remember the gist of what we read or hear, not the detailed form. Taken together, these suggest that we should find it very difficult to distinguish the inferences we make from what we actually hear. Bransford, Barclay, and Franks (1972) demonstrated this experimentally. They showed that after a short delay the target sentence (17) could not be distinguished from the valid inference (18):

(17)   Three turtles rested on a floating log and a fish swam beneath them.

(18)   Three turtles rested on a floating log and a fish swam beneath it.

If you swim beneath a log with a turtle on it, then you must swim beneath the turtle. If you change "on" to "beside," then participants are very good at detecting this change, because the inference is no longer true and therefore not one likely to be made.

When are inferences made?

In the past, most researchers subscribed to a constructionist view that inferences are involved in constructing a representation of the text. Comprehenders are more likely to make inferences related to the important components of a story and not incidental details (Seifert, Robertson, & Black, 1985). The important components are the main characters and their goals, and actions relating to the main plan of the story. According to constructionists, text processing is driven on a "need to know" basis. The comprehender forms goals when processing text or discourse, and these goals determine the inferences that are made, what is understood and what is remembered about the material, and the type of model constructed.

The alternative view is the minimalist hypothesis (McKoon & Ratcliff, 1992). According to the minimalist hypothesis, we automatically make bridging inferences, but we keep the number of elaborative inferences to a minimum. Those that are made are kept as simple as possible and use only information that is readily available. Most elaborative inferences are made at the time of recall. According to the minimalist approach, text processing is data-driven. Comprehension is enabled by the automatic activation of what is in memory: it is therefore said to be memory-based. In part the issue comes down to when the inferences are made. Is a particular inference made automatically at the time of comprehension, or is it made with prompting during recall?

The studies that show that we make elaborative inferences look at our memory for text. Memory measures are indirect measures of comprehension, and may give a distorting picture of the comprehension process. In particular, this may have led us to overestimate the role of construction in comprehension. The most commonly used on-line measure is reading time, assuming that making an automatic inference takes time, necessitating us to look at the guilty material for longer. For an inference to be made automatically, appropriate supporting associative semantic information must be present in the text. For example, McKoon and Ratcliff (1986, 1989) showed that in a lexical decision task, the recognition of a word that is likely to be inferred in a "strong association predicting context," for example the word "sew" in (19), is facilitated much more than the word that might be inferred in a "weak association context," the word "dead" in (20).

(19)   The housewife was learning to be a seamstress and needed practice so she got out the skirt she was making and threaded her needle.
(20)   The director and cameraman were ready to shoot close-ups when suddenly the actress fell from the 14th floor.

In both cases the target word is part of a valid inference from the original sentence, but whereas "sew" is a semantic associate of the words "seamstress," "threaded," and "needle" in (19), the word "dead" needs an inference to be made in (20). The actress does not have to die as a result of this accident, and this conclusion is not supported by a strong associative link between the words of the sentence (as would be the case if the material said, "the actress was murdered"). Such inferences do not therefore have to be drawn automatically, and indeed may not ever be made. (This is why this viewpoint is known as minimalist.)

Singer (1994) also provided evidence that bridging inferences are made automatically, but elaborative inferences are not. He presented sentences (21), (22), and (23), and then asked participants to verify whether "A dentist pulled a tooth."

(21)   The dentist pulled the tooth painlessly. The patient liked the method.
(22)   The tooth was pulled painlessly. The dentist used a new method.

(23)   The tooth was pulled painlessly. The patient liked the new method.

In (21) the statement to be verified is explicitly stated, so people are fast to verify the probe statement. In (22) a bridging inference that the dentist is pulling the tooth is necessary to maintain coherence; people are as fast to verify the probe as they are when it is explicitly stated in (21). This suggests that the bridging inference has been made automatically in the comprehension process. But in (23) people are about 250 ms slower to verify the statement; this suggests that the elaborative inference has not been drawn automatically.

It now seems likely that only bridging or reference-related inferences necessary to maintain the coherence of the text are made automatically during comprehension, and elaborative inferences are generally only made later, during recall. Evidence supporting this is that people make more intrusion inferences (the sort of elaborative inference where people think that something was in the study material when it was not) the longer the delay between study and test (Dooling & Christiaansen, 1977; Spiro, 1977). This is because people's memory for the original material deteriorates with time, and they have to do more reconstruction. Corbett and Dosher (1978) found that the word "scissors" was an equally good cue for recalling each of the sentences (24)–(26):

(24)   The athlete cut out an article with scissors for his friend.
(25)   The athlete cut out an article for his friend.
(26)   The athlete cut out an article with a razor blade for his friend.

The mention of a "razor blade" in sentence (26) blocks any inference being drawn then about the use of scissors. One explanation of the finding that "scissors" is just as effective a cue is that participants are working backwards at recall from the cue to an action, and then retrieving the sentence. A problem with this sort of experiment, however, is that subsequent recall might not give an accurate reflection of what happens when people first read the material.

Dooling and Christiaansen (1977) carried out an experiment similar to the Sulin and Dooling (1974) study with the "Gerald Martin" text. They tested the participants after 1 week, telling them that Gerald Martin was really Adolf Hitler. People still made intrusion errors that in this case could not have been made at the time of study. These results suggest that elaborative and reconstructive inferences are made at the time of test and recall, and when readers are reflecting about material they have just read (Anderson, 2010).

Garrod and Terras (2000) distinguished between two types of information that might assist in making a bridging inference. Consider the story in (27):

(27)   Vlad drove to Memphis yesterday. The car kept overheating.

To maintain coherence, we make the inference that "the car" must be the one that Vlad drove to Memphis—even though the car has not yet been mentioned. "The car" is said to fill an open discourse role, and is linked to previous material by a bridging inference that maintains coherence. There are two types of information to do this that might be used here. First, there are lexical-semantic factors: "drive" implies using a vehicle of some sort. Second, there might be more general background contextual information. Garrod and Terras tried to tease apart the influence of these two factors in a study where they examined eye movements of participants reading stories such as (28) and (29):

(28)   The teacher was busy writing a letter of complaint to a parent.
(29)   The teacher was busy writing an exercise on the blackboard.

The discourse context in (28) is consistent with the instrumental filler "pen," but in (29) it is consistent with "chalk." In both cases, however, the lexical-semantic context of "write" is much more strongly associated with "pen" than with "chalk." Now consider what happens when (28) and (29) are followed by the continuation (30):

(30)   However, she was disturbed by a loud scream from the back of the class and the chalk/pen dropped on the floor.

What happens when the reader comes to the word "chalk" or "pen"? The analysis of eye movements indicates when readers are experiencing difficulty by telling us how long they are looking at particular items and whether they are looking back to re-examine earlier information. If role resolution is dominated by lexical-semantic context, then "pen" will be suggested by the lexical-semantic context of "write," regardless of the discourse context it is in. This is what Garrod and Terras observed. People spent no longer looking at "pen" in either the appropriate or the inappropriate context, although the first-pass reading time of "chalk," which is not so lexically constrained as "pen," was affected by the context. That is, "writing on a blackboard" is just as good as "writing a letter." The appropriateness of the discourse context does have a subsequent effect, however, in that inappropriate context has a delayed effect that makes people re-examine earlier material in both cases.

To account for these data, Garrod and Terras propose a two-stage model of how people resolve open discourse roles. The first stage is called bonding. In this stage, items that are suggested by the lexical context (e.g., "pen") are automatically activated and bound with the verb. In the second stage of resolution the link between proposed filler and verb is tested against the discourse context. A non-dominant filler, such as "chalk," cannot be automatically bound to the verb in the first stage, and causes some initial processing difficulty. The resolution process is a combination of automatic, bottom-up processing and non-automatic, contextual processing. Inference-making in comprehension involves both types of process.

Practical implications of research on inferences

Of course, there are some obvious implications for everyday life if we are continually making inferences on the basis of what we read and hear. Much social interaction is based on making inferences from other people's conversation—and we have seen that these inferences are not always drawn correctly. There are two main applied areas where elaborative inferences are particularly important, and those are eyewitness testimony and methods of advertising.

The work of Loftus (1975, 1996) on eyewitness testimony is very well known. She showed how unreliable eyewitness testimony actually is, and how inferences based on the wording of questions could prejudice people's answers. For example, the choice of either an indefinite article ("a") or a definite article ("the") influences comprehension. The first time something is mentioned, we usually use an indefinite article; after that, we can use the definite article. Sentence (31) is straightforward, but (32) is distinctly odd:

(31) A pig chased a cow. They went into a river. The pig got very wet.
(32) ? The pig chased a cow. They went into a river. A pig got very wet.

When we come across a definite article we make an inference that we already know something about what follows. Sometimes this can lead to memory errors. Loftus and Zanni (1975) showed participants a film of a car crash. Some participants were asked (33), while others were asked (34):

(33) Did you see a broken headlight?
(34) Did you see the broken headlight?

In fact, there was no broken headlight. Participants were more likely to respond "yes" incorrectly to question (34) than to question (33), because the definite article presupposes that a broken headlight exists. Loftus and Palmer (1974) also showed participants a film of a car crash. They asked some of the participants (35) and others (36) (see Figure 12.2):

(35) About how fast were the cars going when they hit each other?
(36) About how fast were the cars going when they smashed into each other?

Participants asked (36) reliably estimated the speed of the cars to be higher than those asked (35). A week later the participants that had been asked (36) were much more likely to think that they had seen broken glass than those asked (35), although broken glass had not been mentioned. The way a question is phrased can influence the inferences people make and therefore the answers that they give.

R. Harris (1978) simulated a jury listening to courtroom witnesses, and found that although participants were more likely to accept directly asserted statements as true than only implied statements for which they had to make an inference, there was still a strong tendency to accept the implied statements. Instructions to participants telling them to be careful to distinguish between asserted and implied information did not help either. Furthermore, this test took place only 5 minutes after hearing the statements, whereas in a real courtroom the delays can be weeks, and the potential problem much worse. Harris (1977) similarly found that people find it difficult

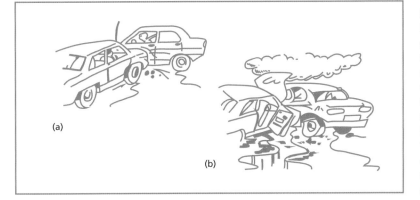

FIGURE 12.2 Loftus and Palmer (1974) found that assessment of speed of a videotaped car crash and recollection of whether there was broken glass present were affected by the verb used to ask the question. Use of the verbs "hit" and "smash" have different connotations as shown in (a) and (b). Adapted from Loftus and Palmer (1974).

Harris' (1978) jury demonstrated a strong tendency to accept the implied statements, despite instructions to be careful to distinguish between asserted and implied information.

to distinguish between assertions and implications in advertising claims. Participants are best at distinguishing assertions from implications if they have been warned to do so before hearing the claim, and are asked about it immediately afterwards. Deviation from this pattern leads to a rapid impairment of our ability to distinguish fact from implication.

REFERENCE AND AMBIGUITY

An important part of comprehension is working out what things refer to: this is called **reference**. In (37) both "Vlad" and "he" refer to the same thing—Vlad the vampire, or at least our mental representation of him. We call the case when two linguistic expressions refer to the same thing (e.g., "Vlad" and "he") **co-reference**. A common example of co-reference involves the use of pronouns such as "she," "her," "he," "him," and "it," such as in (38). Often we find that we cannot determine the reference of a linguistic expression without referring to another linguistic expression, called the **antecedent**; this case, and the material that we cannot identify in isolation, is called **anaphor**. In (38) "Vlad" and "knife" are the antecedents of the anaphors "he" and "it," respectively. Co-reference does not have to involve pronouns; it can also involve other nouns referring to the same thing—"the

vampire" in (39), an example of definite noun phrase anaphor—or verbs—"does" in (40).

(37) Vlad put the knife on the table. Then he forgot where it was.
(38) After he had finished with the knife, Vlad put it on the table.
(39) Vlad went to the cinema. The vampire really enjoyed the film.
(40) Vlad loves Boris and so does Dirk.

Comprehenders must work out what anaphors refer to—what their antecedents are. This process is called resolution. Anaphor resolution is a backward inference that we carry out to maintain a coherent representation of the text.

How do we resolve anaphoric ambiguity?

In many cases anaphor resolution can be straightforward. In a story such as (41) there is only one possible antecedent:

(41) Vlad was happy. He laughed.

What makes anaphor resolution difficult is that often it is not obvious what the antecedent of the anaphor is. The anaphor is ambiguous when there is more than one possible antecedent, such as in (42):

(42) Vlad stuck a dagger in the corpse. It was made out of silver. It oozed blood.

In this case we have no apparent difficulty in understanding what each "it" refers to. How do we do this? In more complex cases there might be a number of alternatives, or background or world knowledge is necessary to disambiguate.

We cope with anaphoric ambiguity by using a number of coping strategies. Whether or not these strategies are used to guide an explicit search process, or to exclude items from a search set, or both, or even to avoid an explicit search altogether, is at present unclear.

One strategy for anaphor resolution is called parallel function (Sheldon, 1974). We prefer to match anaphors to antecedents in the same relevant position. Anaphor resolution is more difficult when the expectations generated by this strategy are flouted. In (43) and (44) the appropriate order of antecedents and pronouns differs. In (43) "he" refers to "Vlad," which comes first in "Vlad sold Dirk," but in (44) "he" refers to "Dirk," which comes second. Therefore (44) is harder to understand than (43).

(43) Vlad sold Dirk his broomstick because he hated it.
(44) Vlad sold Dirk his broomstick because he needed it.

We can distinguish two groups of further strategies: those dependent on the meaning of the actual words used, or their role in the sentence; and those dependent on the emergent discourse model.

Of the strategies dependent on the words used, one of the most obvious is the use of **gender** (Corbett & Chang, 1983):

(45) Agnes won and Vlad lost. He was sad and she was glad.

In (45) it is clear that "he" must refer to Vlad, and "she" to Agnes. Most of the evidence suggests that gender information is used automatically. Other experiments show that the effects of gender are more complicated and depend on what other referents are accessible at the time of reading. Arnold, Eisenband, Brown-Schmidt, and Trueswell (2000) examined eye movements to investigate how gender information is used. Participants examined pictures of familiar cartoon characters while listening to text. Arnold et al. found that gender information about the pronoun was accessed very rapidly (within 200 ms after the pronoun). If the picture contained both a female and a male character (e.g., Minnie Mouse and Donald Duck), participants were able to use the gender cue ("she" or "he") very quickly to look at the appropriate picture. If the pictures were of same-sex characters (e.g., Micky Mouse and Donald Duck), gender was no longer a cue, and participants took longer to converge on the picture that

referred to the pronoun. However, Arnold et al. also manipulated order of mention, and this interacted with gender so that there was only evidence of an effect of gender on pronoun resolution for the less-accessible second-mentioned character. For the first-mentioned character, people looked quickly at the target no matter whether the gender was ambiguous or not. In summary, the effects of gender can only really be observed when we take into account what other information influences pronoun resolution. Rigalleau and Caplan (2000) found that people are slower to say the pronoun "he" when it is inconsistent with the only noun in the discourse (46) compared with when it is consistent (47):

(46) Agnes paid without being asked; he had a sense of honor.
(47) Boris cried in front of the grave; he had a tissue.

Rigalleau and Caplan suggest that pronouns become immediately and automatically related to possible antecedents. The resolution process that ultimately determines which of the possible antecedents is finally attached to the pronoun might depend on other factors. Resolution only involves attentional processing if the initial automatic processes fail to converge on a single noun as the antecedent, or if pragmatic information makes the selected noun an unlikely antecedent. Some techniques are better at establishing the time course of anaphor resolution than others. In particular, the use of probes, as used in the earlier studies, might disrupt the comprehension process, giving a misleading picture of what is happening.

Different verbs carry different implications about how the actors involved should be assigned to roles. If participants are asked to complete the sentences (48) and (49), they usually produce continuations in which "he" refers to the subject (Vlad) in (48), and the object (Boris) in (49). Verbs such as "sell" are called NP1 verbs, because causality is usually attributed to the first, subject, noun phrase; verbs such as "blame" are called NP2 verbs, because causality is usually attributed to the second, object, noun phrase (Grober, Beardsley, & Caramazza, 1978).

(48) Vlad sold his broomstick to Boris because he . . .

(49) Vlad blamed Boris because he . . .

When does implicit causality have its effect? Is it early, enabling us to focus on the appropriate antecedent, or late, facilitating the integration of material? The difference between the two possible time courses is whether or not causality information affects the initial processing of the "he" in (48) and (49). An experiment by Stewart, Pickering, and Sanford (2000) suggests that implicit causality only has a late effect. Stewart et al. manipulated information about the cause of an action, and about the type of anaphor used. They manipulated the implicit cause (through verb bias) and the explicit cause, which is derived from the whole sentence. The two types of cause could be either congruent or in conflict, a condition they called incongruent. They also manipulated whether the anaphor was a pronoun or a proper name. They measured ease of processing using self-paced reading. Sentence (50) is an example of a congruent condition with names, and (51) is an incongruent condition with pronouns—note that "apologize" is usually a NP1-bias verb.

(50) Daniel apologized to Arnold because Daniel had been behaving selfishly.

(51) Daniel apologized to Arnold because he didn't deserve the criticism.

The pronoun "he" is ambiguous, whereas the name is not. The early-focus account predicts that we should determine the antecedent of the pronoun on the basis of the implicit causality bias of the verb. In incongruent sentences with pronouns, therefore, the early-focus account predicts conflict and therefore reading difficulty; this difficulty should not be present in the sentences with the unambiguous names instead of pronouns. So, if the early-focus account is correct, there should be an interaction between congruence and type of anaphor. Stewart et al. found no such interaction, a result that supports the late-integration account. Indeed, they found congruence mattered for just repeated names, suggesting that implicit bias has a late effect.

The second group of anaphor resolution strategies are those dependent on the perceived prominence of possible referents in the emergent text model. We might be biased, for example, to select the referent in the model that is most frequently mentioned. Antecedents are generally easier to locate when they are close to their referents than when they are farther away, in terms of the number of intervening words (Murphy, 1985; O'Brien, 1987). In more complicated examples alternatives can sometimes be eliminated using background knowledge and elaborative inferences, as in (52). Exactly how this background knowledge is used is unclear. In this case we infer that becoming a vegetarian would not make someone want to buy piglets, but more likely to sell them, as they would be less likely to have any future use for them.

(52) Vlad sold his piglets to Dirk because he had become a vegetarian.

Pronouns are read more quickly when the referent of the antecedent is still in the focus of the situation being discussed than when the situation has changed so that it is no longer in focus (Garrod & Sanford, 1977; Sanford & Garrod, 1981). Items in explicit focus are said to be foregrounded and have been explicitly mentioned in the preceding text. Such items can be referred to pronominally. Items in implicit focus are only implied by what is in explicit focus. For example, in (53) Vlad is in explicit focus, but the car is in implicit focus. It sounds natural to continue with "he was thirsty," but not with "it broke down." Instead, we would need to bring the car into explicit focus with a sentence like "his car broke down."

(53) Vlad was driving to Philadelphia.

Experiments on reading time suggest that implicit focus items are harder to process. Items are likely to stay in the foreground if it is an important theme in the discourse, and these items are likely to be maintained in working memory. Pronouns with antecedents in the foreground, or topic antecedents, are read quickly, regardless of the distance between the pronoun and referent (Clifton & Ferreira, 1987). In conversation, we do not normally start using pronouns for referents that we have not mentioned for some time. In general, unstressed pronouns are used to refer to the most salient discourse entity—the one at the center of focus—while definite noun phrase anaphors (e.g., "the intransigent vampire") are used to refer to non-salient discourse entities—those out of focus.

In general, then, the more salient an entity is in discourse, the less information is contained in the anaphoric expression that refers to it. Almor (1999) proposed that NP anaphor processing is determined by informational load: this is the amount of information an anaphor contains. The informational load of an anaphor with respect to its antecedent should either aid the identification of the antecedent, or add new information about it, or both. The processing of anaphors is a balance between the benefits of maximum informativeness and the cost of minimizing working memory load. This idea that anaphor processing is a balance between informativeness and processing cost leads to several predictions. For example, anaphors with a high informational load with respect to their antecedent, but which do not add new information about them, will be difficult to process when the antecedent is in focus. Hence repetitive NP anaphors such as (54) will be difficult:

(54) It was the bird that ate the fruit. The bird seemed very satisfied.
(55) What the bird ate was the fruit. The bird seemed very satisfied.

Here the antecedent ("a bird") is in focus and the default antecedent, so a pronoun ("it") will do. The NP anaphor ("the bird") has a high informational load, so it is not justified. It is only justified when the antecedent is out of focus (55), because then it aids the identification of the antecedent. Almor verified this prediction in a self-paced reading task. "The bird" was read slower when the antecedent was in focus (54) than when it was out of it (55). Hence the use and processing of pronominal and NP anaphors is a complex trade-off between informativeness, focus, and working memory load.

Given that there are a number of strategies for interpreting anaphors, how do we choose the best one? Badecker and Straub (2002) argue that all potential cues contribute to the selection of the appropriate antecedent. They propose an interactive parallel constraint model, where the multiple constraints influence the activation of the candidate entities. The more conflict there is, the more candidates there are, and the more plausible they are, the more difficult choosing an antecedent will be.

Accessibility

Some items are more accessible than others. We are faster at retrieving the referent of more accessible antecedents. At this stage some caution is necessary to avoid a circular definition of accessibility. Accessibility is a concept related both to anaphora and to the work on sentence memory. It can be measured by recording how long it takes participants to detect whether a word presented while participants are reading sentences is present in the sentence.

Common ground is shared information between participants in a conversation (Clark, 1996; Clark & Carlson, 1982). A piece of information is in the common ground if it is mutually believed by the speakers, and if all the speakers believe that all the others believe it to be shared. Information that is in the common ground should have particular importance in determining reference. The restricted search hypothesis states that the initial search for referents is restricted to entities in the common ground, whereas the unrestricted search hypothesis places no such restriction. That is, according to the restricted search hypothesis, things in the common ground should be more accessible than things that are not. The evidence currently favors the unrestricted search hypothesis (Keysar, Barr, Balin, & Paek, 1998). Consider (56) (Keysar et al., 1998, p. 5):

(56) "It is evening, and Boris' young daughter is playing in the other room. Boris, who lives in Chicago, is thinking of calling his lover in Europe. He decides not to call because she is probably asleep given the transatlantic time difference. At that moment his wife returns home and asks, 'Is she asleep?'"

How does Boris search for the referent of "she"? If the restricted search hypothesis were correct, and search is restricted to possible referents in the common ground, the lover should not be considered, as the wife is not informed about the lover. However, entities that are not in the common ground still interfere with reference resolution, as measured by error rates, verification times, and eye-movement measures. Although common ground might not restrict which possible referents are initially checked, it almost certainly plays an important later role in checking, monitoring, and correcting the results of the initial search. Conversants take into account what each other knows when establishing common ground (Knutsen & Le Bigot, 2012).

Generally we are biased to referring back to the subject of a sentence; there is also an advantage to first mention. This means that participants that are mentioned first in a sentence are more accessible than those mentioned second. Gernsbacher and Hargreaves (1988) showed that there was an advantage for first mention, independent of other factors such as whether the words involved were subject or object. Gernsbacher, Hargreaves, and Beeman (1989) explored the apparent contradiction between first mention and recency, in that items that are more recent should also be more accessible. Gernsbacher and Hargreaves explained this with a constructionist, structure-building account: The goal of comprehension is to build a coherent model of what is being comprehended. Comprehenders represent each clause of a multi-clause sentence with a separate substructure, and have easiest access to the substructure they are currently working on. However, at some point the earlier information becomes more accessible because it serves as a foundation for the whole sentence-level representation. So it is only as the representation is being developed that recency is important. Recency is detectable only when accessibility is measured immediately after the second clause; elsewhere first mention is important, and has the more long-lasting effect. This explanation is reminiscent of Kintsch's propositional model, discussed later, and shows how it is possible to account for anaphor resolution in terms of the details of the emergent comprehension model.

The given–new contract

One of the most important factors that determines comprehensibility and coherence is the order in which new information is presented relative to what we know already. Clearly this affects the ease with which we can integrate the new information into the old. It has been argued that there is a "contract" between the writer and the reader, or participants in a conversation, to present new information so that it can easily be assimilated with what people already know. This is called the given–new contract (Clark & Haviland, 1977; Haviland & Clark, 1974). It takes less time to understand a new sentence when it explicitly contains some of the same ideas as an earlier sentence than when the relation between the content of the sentences has to be inferred.

Utterances are linked together in discourse so that they link back to previous material and forward to material that can potentially be the focus of future utterances. Centering theory, developed in AI models of text processing, provides a means of describing these links (Gordon, Grosz, & Gilliom, 1993; Grosz, Joshi, & Weinstein, 1995). According to centering theory, each utterance in coherent discourse has a single backward-looking center that links to the previous utterance, and one or more forward-looking centers that offer potential links to the next utterance. People prefer to realize the backward-looking center as a pronoun. The forward-looking centers are ranked in order of prominence, according to factors such as the position in the sentence and the stress. The reading times of sentences increase if these rules are violated. For example, people actually take longer to read stories where proper names are repeated compared with sentences where appropriate pronouns are used.

Summary of work on memory, inferences, and anaphora

Any model of comprehension must be able to explain the following characteristics. We read for gist, and very quickly forget details of surface form. Comprehension is to some extent a constructive process: We build a model of what we are processing, although the level of detail involved is controversial. At the very least, we make inferences to maintain coherence. One of the most important mechanisms involved in this is anaphor resolution. Inferences soon become integrated into our model as we go along, and we are very soon unable to distinguish our inferences from what we originally heard. There is a foreground area of the model containing important and recent items, so that they are more accessible.

MODELS OF TEXT PROCESSING

We now examine some models of how we represent and process text. AI has heavily influenced models of comprehension. Although the ideas thus generated are interesting and explicit, there is a disadvantage that the specific mechanisms we use are unlikely to be exactly the same as the explicit mechanisms used to implement the AI concepts.

Propositional network models of representing text

The meaning of sentences and text can be represented by a network where the intersections (or nodes) represent the meaning of words, and the connections represent the relations between words. This approach is related to Fillmore's (1968) theory of case grammar, which in turn was derived from generative semantics, a grammatical theory that emphasized the importance of semantics. Case grammar emphasizes the roles, or cases, played by what the words refer to in the sentence. It emphasizes the relation between verbs and the words associated with them. (Cases are more or less the same as thematic roles; see Box 10.1 for some examples.) One disadvantage of case grammar is that there is little agreement over exactly what the cases that describe the language should be, or even how many cases there are. This lack of agreement about the basic units involved is a common problem with models of comprehension.

In network models, sentences are first analyzed into **proposition**s. A proposition is the smallest unit of meaning that can be put in

predicate-argument form (with a verb operating on a noun). A proposition has a truth value— that is, we can say whether it is true or false. For example, the words "witch" and "cackle" are not propositions: They are unitary and have no internal structure, and it is meaningless to talk of individual words being true or false. On the other hand, "the witch cackles" contains a proposition. This can be put in the predicate-argument form "cackle(witch)," which does have a truth value: the witch is either cackling or she isn't.

Propositions are connected together in propositional networks, as in Figure 12.3. The model of Anderson and Bower (1973) was particularly influential. Originally known as HAM (short for Human Associative Memory), the model evolved first into ACT (short for Adaptive Control of Thought; see Anderson, 1976) and later ACT* (pronounced "ACT-star"; Anderson, 1983). These models include a spreading activation model of semantic memory, combined later with a production system for executing higher level operations. A production system is a series of if–then rules: if x happens, then do y. ACT* gives a good account of fact retrieval from short stories. For example, the more facts there are associated with a concept, the slower the retrieval of any one of those facts.

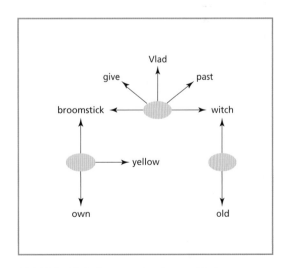

FIGURE 12.3 An example of a simplified propositional network underlying the sentence "Vlad gave his yellow broomstick to the old witch."

This is known as the fan effect (Anderson, 1974, 2010). When you are presented with a stimulus, activation spreads to all its associates. There is a limit to the total amount of activation, however, so the more items it spreads to, the less each individual item can receive.

Another influential network model has been the conceptual dependency theory of Schank (1975). This starts off with the idea that meaning can be decomposed into small, atomic units. Text is represented by decomposing the incoming material into these atomic units, and by building a network that relates them. An important intermediate step is that the atomic units of meaning are combined into conceptualizations that specify the actors involved in the discourse and the actions that relate them. Once again, this approach has the advantage that as it has been implemented (in part) as a computer simulation: its assumptions and limitations are therefore very clear.

Evaluation of propositional network models

Just as there is little agreement on the cases to use, so there is little agreement on the precise types of roles and connections to use. If we measure propositional networks against the requirements listed for memory, inferences, and anaphora, we can see that they satisfy some of the requirements, but leave a lot to be desired as models of discourse processing. Most propositional network models show how knowledge might be represented, but they have little to say about when or how we make inferences, or how some items are maintained in the foreground, or how we extract the gist from text (Johnson-Laird et al., 1984; Woods, 1975). Propositional networks by themselves are inadequate as a model of comprehension, but form the basis of more complex models. Kintsch's construction–integration model (see later) is based on a propositional model, but includes explicit mechanisms for dealing with the foreground and making inferences.

Story grammars

Stories possess a structure: they have a beginning, a middle, and an end. The structure present in stories is the basis of story grammars, which are analogous with sentence grammar. Stories have an underlying structure, and the purpose of comprehension is to reconstruct this underlying structure. This structure includes settings, themes, plots, and how the story turns out (see Mandler, 1978; Mandler & Johnson, 1977; Rumelhart, 1975, 1977; and Thorndyke, 1977, for examples).

Like sentence grammars, story grammars are made out of phrase-structure rules (see the example in Box 12.1). The nature of the syntactic rules in Box 12.1 is expanded by a corresponding semantic rule: for example, once you have a setting then an episode is possible. You can draw tree structures just as with sentences, hence emphasizing their hierarchical structure. The basic units, corresponding to individual words in sentence grammars, are propositions, which are eventually assigned the lowest-level slots.

In the recall, paraphrasing, and summarizing of stories, the less important details are omitted. According to story grammars, humans compute the importance of a sentence or a fact by its height in the hierarchy. Cirilo and Foss (1980) showed that participants spend more time reading sentences high in the structure than those low down in the structure. However, any sensible theory of text processing should predict that we pay more attention to the important elements of a story.

Thorndyke (1977) presented participants with one of two simple stories. The story "Circle

---

Box 12.1 Example of a fragment of a story grammar (based on Rumelhart, 1975)

Story	→	Setting + theme + plot + resolution
Setting	→	Characters + location + time
Theme	→	(Event)* + goal
Plot	→	Episode*
Episode	→	Subgoals + attempt* + outcome

Asterisks show the element can be repeated.

Island" was about building a canal on an island, and the second story was about an old farmer trying to put his donkey into a shed. One group of participants heard these stories in their normal straightforward form. A second group heard a modified version of the stories where the story structure had been tampered with. The modifications included putting the theme at the end of the story (rather than before its plot, where it is most effective), deleting the goal of the story, or, in its most extreme version, presenting the component sentences in random order. Thorndyke found that the more the story structure was tampered with, the less of the story participants could subsequently recall. Hence jumbled stories are harder to understand and remember than originals. According to story grammar theory, this is because jumbling a story destroys its structure. However, jumbling also destroys referential continuity. Garnham, Oakhill, and Johnson-Laird (1982) restored referential continuity in jumbled stories; this greatly reduced the difficulty participants had with them (as measured by memory for the stories, and the readers' ratings of comprehensibility). For example, (57) is the original story, and (58) the same story with the sentences unchanged but in a random order, but in (59) some of the noun phrases have been changed so as to re-establish referential continuity:

(57) David was playing with his big, colored ball in the garden. He bounced it so hard that it went right over the fence. The people next door were out so he climbed over to get it. He found his ball and threw it back. David carried on with his game.

(58) He found his ball and threw it back. The people next door were out so he climbed over to get it. David carried on with his game. He bounced it so hard that it went right over the fence. David was playing with his big, colored ball in the garden.

(59) David found his big, colored ball and threw it back. The people next door were out so he climbed over to get it. He carried on with his game. He bounced his ball so hard that it went right over the fence. David was playing with it in the garden.

Stories have a structure which includes settings, themes, plots, and conclusion. Thorndyke (1977) found that the more this story structure was tampered with, the less of the story participants could subsequently recall.

Evaluation of story grammars

A major problem with story grammars is in getting agreement on what their elements, rules, and terminal elements should be. In a sentence grammar, the meaning of non-terminal elements such as "noun" and "verb" is independent of their content, and well defined. This is not true of story grammars. Neither are there formally agreed criteria for specifying a finite, well-specified set of terminal elements—there are a finite number of words, but an infinite number of propositions. We therefore cannot (as we can with words) make a list of propositions and the categories to which they belong. Furthermore, propositions might belong to different categories, depending on the context. There is no agreement on story structure: virtually every story grammatician has proposed a different grammar. Story grammars only provide a limited account of a subset of all possible stories. Furthermore, the analogy of story categories, with formal syntactic grammars such as NP, VP, and their rules of combination, is very weak. There is much variation with stories, and, unlike sentences, the analysis of stories is content-dependent. Story grammars fail to provide an account of how stories are actually produced or understood. (See Black & Wilensky, 1979; Garnham, 1983b; Johnson-Laird, 1983; and Wilensky, 1983, for details of these criticisms.) Given the fundamental nature of some of these difficulties, story grammars are no longer influential in comprehension research.

Schema-based theories

The idea of a **schema** (the plural can be either schemata or schemas) was originally introduced by Bartlett (1932). Bartlett argued that memory is determined not only by what is presented, but also by the prior knowledge a person brings to the story. He presented people with stories that conflicted with prior knowledge, and observed that over time people's memory for the story became increasingly distorted in the direction of fitting in with their prior knowledge.

A schema is an organized packet of knowledge that enables us to make sense of new knowledge. It is related to ideas in both AI on visual object recognition (Minsky, 1975) and experimental psychology (Posner & Keele, 1968). The schema gives knowledge-organizing activation that means that the whole is greater than the sum of its parts. It can be conceptualized as a series of slots that can be filled with particular values. Anderson (2010) gives the following example (60) of a possible schema for a house.

(60) House schema:
      Isa: building
      Parts: rooms
      Materials: bricks, stone, wood
      Function: human dwelling
      Shape: rectilinear, triangular
      Size: 100–10,000 square feet

There are four central processes involved in schema formation. First, the appropriate aspects of the incoming stimuli must be selected. Second, the meaning must be abstracted, and syntactic and lexical details dispensed with. Third, appropriate prior knowledge must be activated to interpret

this meaning. Finally, the information must be integrated to form a single holistic representation.

The idea of a schema cannot in itself account for text processing, but it is a central concept in many theories. Although it provides a means of organization of knowledge, and explains why we remember the gist of text, it does not explain how we make inferences, how material is foregrounded, or why we sometimes remember the literal meaning. To solve these problems the notion must be supplemented in some way.

Scripts

A **script** is a special type of schema (Schank & Abelson, 1977). Scripts represent our knowledge of routine actions and familiar repeated sequences. Scripts include information about the usual roles, objects, and the sequence of events to be found in an action; they enable plans to be made and allow us to draw inferences about what is not explicitly mentioned. Two famous examples are the "restaurant script" and the "attending a lecture script" (see Table 12.1).

Psychological evidence for the existence of scripts comes from an experiment by Bower et al. (1979). Bower et al. asked participants to list about 20 events in activities such as visiting a restaurant, attending a lecture, getting up in the morning, visiting the doctor, or going shopping. Some examples are shown in Table 12.1. Items labeled (1) were mentioned by the most participants and are considered the most important actions in a script; items labeled (2) were mentioned by fewer participants; and items labeled (3) were mentioned by the fewest participants. These are considered the least important parts of the script. The events are shown in the order in which they were usually mentioned. All of these events were mentioned by at least 25% of the participants. Hence participants agree about the central features that constitute a script, and their relative importance.

Scripts are useful in explaining some results of experiments on anaphoric reference. Walker and Yekovich (1987) showed that a central concept of a script (such as a "table" in the restaurant script) was comprehended faster (regardless of whether it was explicitly mentioned in the story)

TABLE 12.1 Examples of scripts (based on Bower et al., 1979).

Visiting a restaurant script		Attending a lecture script	
Open door	3	Enter room	1
Enter	2	Look for friends	2
Give reservation name	2	Find seat	1
Wait to be seated	3	Sit down	1
Go to table	3	Settle belongings	3
Be seated	1	Take out notebook	1
Order drinks	2	Look at other students	2
Put napkins on lap	3	Talk	2
Look at menu	1	Look at lecturer	3
Discuss menu	2	Listen to lecturer	1
Order meal	1	Take notes	1
Talk	2	Check time	1
Drink water	3	Ask questions	3
Eat salad or soup	2	Change position in seat	3
Meal arrives	3	Daydream	3
Eat food	1	Look at other students	3
Finish meal	3	Take more notes	3
Order dessert	2	Close notebook	2
Eat dessert	2	Gather belongings	2
Ask for bill	3	Stand up	3
Bill arrives	3	Talk	3
Pay bill	1	Leave	1
Leave tip	2		
Get coats	3		
Leave	1		

Items labeled (1) are considered most important, (3) least important.

than a peripheral concept. Peripheral concepts of scripts were dealt with particularly slowly when their antecedents were only implied. That is, we find it easier to assign referents to the important elements of scripts.

Occasionally events happen that are not in the script: for example, the waiter might spill the soup on you. Schank and Abelson (1977) referred to such interruptions as obstacles or distractions, because they get in the way of the main purpose of the script (here, eating). Bower et al. made predictions about two types of event in stories relating to scripts. First, distractions that interrupt the purpose of the script should be more salient than the routine events, and should therefore be more likely to be remembered. Second, events that are irrelevant to the purpose of the script (such as the color of the waiter's shoes) should be poorly remembered. Both of these predictions were verified.

Schank (1982) pointed out that most of life is not governed by predetermined, over-learned sequences such as those encapsulated by a script. Knowledge structures need to be flexible. Dissatisfied with this limitation of scripts, Schank focused on the role of reminding in memory. He argued that memory is a dynamic structure driven by its failures. Memory is organized into different levels, starting at the lower end with scenes. Examples of these in what would earlier have been called a "going to the doctor script" include "reception room scene," "waiting scene," and "surgery scene." Scenes are organized into memory organization packets or MOPs, which are all linked by being related to a particular goal. In any enterprise, more than one MOP might be active at once. MOPs are themselves organized into meta-MOPs if a number of MOPs have something in common (for example, all MOPs involving going on a trip). At a higher level than MOPs and meta-MOPs are thematic organization points or TOPs, which deal with abstract information independent of particular physical or social contexts.

There is some support for MOPs from a series of experiments by McKoon, Ratcliff, and Seifert (1989) and Seifert, McKoon, Abelson, and Ratcliff (1986). They showed that elements of MOPs could prime the retrieval of other elements from the same MOP. Participants read a number of stories, some of which shared the same MOPs, as construed by the experimenters. They then had to make "old" or "new" recognition judgments about a number of test sentences, some of which had been in the original stories, and some of which had not. A priming phrase from the same story as the test sentence always produced facilitation for the subsequent test sentence. However, a priming phrase that had originally been in a different story from the test sentence also produced facilitation if it was in the same MOP as the test sentence. The amount of facilitation found was the same whether the original phrase was from a different story or from the same story. There was no facilitation if the priming phrase was from a different story and a different MOP to the test sentence.

Evaluation of schema and script-based approaches

The primary accusation against schema and script-based approaches is that they are nothing more than redescriptions of the data. This is quite difficult to rebuff. Ross and Bower (1981) suggested that schemas have an organizing ability beyond their constituents, but this has yet to be demonstrated of scripts, although the data from McKoon et al. could be interpreted in this way. It is also unclear how particular scripts get activated. It cannot just be by word association. For example, the phrase "the five-hour journey from London to New York" should activate the "plane flight script," yet no single word in this utterance is capable of doing so (Garnham, 1985).

Although there are some experimental findings that support the idea that knowledge is organized around schema-like structures, they cannot as yet provide a complete account of text processing. They can only give an account of stereotyped knowledge. They show how such knowledge might be organized, and what kinds of inference we can make, but at present they have little to say about how these inferences are made, how anaphors are resolved, or which items are foregrounded. To do this we must consider not only how knowledge is represented in memory, but also the processes that operate on that knowledge, and relate it to incoming information.

Mental models

Comprehenders construct a model as they go along to represent what they hear and read. If the information is represented in a form analogous to what is being represented, this type of representation is called a mental model (Johnson-Laird, 1983; see also Garnham, 1985, 1987). If the information is represented propositionally, this type of representation is called a situation model (van Dijk & Kintsch, 1983), although many researchers do not distinguish between the two terms. A mental model directly represents the situation in the text. Its structure is not arbitrary in the way that a propositional representation is, but directly mirrors what is represented. We form mental models of specific things, and these models can give rise to mental images. Whereas schemas contain general information abstracted over many instances, in the mental models approach a specific model is constructed to represent new information from general information of space, time, causality, and human intentionality (Brewer, 1987). Mental models are not just used in the short term in working memory to interpret text—people have long-term memory for the models they construct, as well as some memory for the surface text (Baguley & Payne, 2000).

The application of mental models is most apparent in representing spatial information. There is some evidence that the spatial layout of what is represented in the text affects processing. For example, Morrow, Bower, and Greenspan (1989) argued that readers construct a mental model representing the actors involved and their relative spatial locations. They showed that the accessibility of objects mentioned in the text depended on the relative spatial location of the objects and the actors, rather than on the accessibility of the hypothesized propositions that might be used to represent those locations. Ehrlich and Johnson-Laird (1982) examined how we might form a mental model of a text describing spatial information. The "turtles story" of Bransford et al. (1972), given earlier in (17) and (18), also suggests that we construct a spatial layout of some text. The accessibility of referents also depends on the spatial distance from the focus of attention in the model (Glenberg, Meyer, & Lindem, 1987; Rinck & Bower, 1995). In Rinck and Bower's experiment, participants memorized a diagram of a building and then read a story describing characters' activities in the building. The reading times of sentences increased with the number of rooms between the room containing an object mentioned in the sentence and the room where the protagonist of the story was currently located.

Mental models represent more than spatial information, however. There is agreement that they are multidimensional and represent five kinds of information: spatial, causal, and temporal information about people's goals, and information about the characteristics of people and objects (Zwaan & Radvansky, 1998). There is some evidence that different aspects of the mental model are maintained independently in working memory. Friedman and Miyake (2000) had people read short stories while responding to spatial and causal probe questions. They found that the spatial measures were influenced by the spatial demands of the texts, but not the causal demands, whereas the causal measures were only influenced by the causal demands. Spatial aspects of the text become encoded in spatial memory, but the causal aspects become encoded in verbal memory.

The mental models approach is an extreme version of a constructionist approach. Indeed, Brewer (1987) distinguished mental models from other approaches by saying that rather than accessing pre-existing structures, mental models are specific knowledge structures constructed to represent each new situation, using general information such as knowledge of spatial relations and general knowledge. Exactly how this construction takes place, and the precise nature of the representations involved, is sometimes unclear.

Updating the model

Text processing is dynamic. As people comprehend text, and new material becomes available, they have to update their mental representations. Zwaan and Madden (2004) distinguish two approaches to how updating occurs. According to the here-and-now model, information that is currently relevant to the protagonist of the text is more available than less relevant material (Morrow,

Greenspan, & Bower, 1987; Morrow et al., 1989; Zwaan & Radvansky, 1998). According to the resonance model, new information resonates with all information in memory, even with information that is not apparently immediately relevant or up-to-date (Myers & O'Brien, 1998). Importantly, passive reactivation of old material cannot be prevented: all immediately irrelevant information will become active as long as it is related. Zwaan and Madden show that comprehenders can update situation models with new information that is consistent with the current situation, but inconsistent with the prior situation, as easily as material that was never inconsistent with the prior situation. This finding suggests that the most important determinant of updating is what is currently available, and new information does not resonate with all information in memory. However, the findings in this sort of experiment are very sensitive to the details of the materials used, and this conclusion is controversial (e.g., see O'Brien, Cook, & Peracchi, 2004; O'Brien, Rizzella, Albrect, & Halleran, 1998).

Time is clearly an important determinant of how we construct models. In addition to the absolute time—the time at which information becomes available in real time—relative time in a story is also important. A story unfolds in time, with the focus continually shifting. As a consequence, some events are immediate, some are in the recent past, and some are perhaps quite a long time away. Relative time can affect the accessibility of entities in a model. Entities are less accessible when the temporal distance between the "now" point and the past is long rather than short: readers need to take more time to access entities remote in time. However, the effect of relative time only applies to consecutive events (Kelter, Kaup, & Claus, 2004). The critical comparison is the difference between sentences such as (61) and (62).

(61) She then goes to the hairdresser and buys hairspray.
(62) She then goes to the hairdresser and gets a perm.

There is no difference in utterance length here, but more time is likely to elapse in (62) than in (61). Entities mentioned before these critical sentences take longer to access after (62) than after (61).

Given the importance of relative time in the model, people pay particular attention to words and phrases that indicate relative time, particularly those that indicate a shift of time in the narrative. Words and phrases such as "later" or "two days later" are called segmentation markers—they tell the reader that there is a temporal discontinuity and a potential shift of topic. People take longer to read the first sentence after a shift of topic (an effect called the boundary effect), but this penalty is lessened if the shift is flagged by a segmentation maker (Bestgen & Vonk, 2000).

Kintsch's construction–integration model

Kintsch (1988) described a detailed and plausible model of spoken and written text comprehension known as the construction–integration model. This model emphasizes how texts are represented in memory and understanding, and how they are integrated into the comprehender's general knowledge base. The construction–integration model combines aspects of the network, schema-based, and mental model approaches. Text is represented at a number of levels and processed cyclically in two phases. A text base is created from the linguistic input and from the comprehender's knowledge base in the form of a propositional network. The text base is used to form the situation model (which can also be represented propositionally), where the individuality of the text has been lost, and the text has been integrated with other information to form a model of the whole situation described in the text.

The early version of the model (Kintsch, 1979; Kintsch & van Dijk, 1978) is a sophisticated propositional network. The input is dealt with in processing cycles. Short-term memory acts as a buffer to store incoming material. We build up a representation of a story given two inputs: the story itself, and the goals of the reader. The goals and knowledge of the reader are represented by the goal schema, which does things such as stating what is relevant, setting expectations, and

demanding that certain inferences be drawn if needed facts are not explicitly stated.

Text is represented in the form of a network of connected propositions or facts called a coherence graph. The coherence graph is built up hierarchically. This text base has both a microstructure and a macrostructure. The microstructure is this network of connected propositions. In processing text, we work through it in input cycles that usually correspond to a sentence, with an average size of seven propositions. In each cycle the overlap of the proposition arguments is noted; propositions are semantically related when they share arguments. If there is no overlap between the incoming propositions and the propositions currently in working memory, then there must be a time-consuming process of inference involving a reinstatement search (search of long-term memory). If there is overlap, then the new propositions are connected to the active part of the coherence graph by coherence rules. The macrostructure concerns the higher level of description and the processes operating on that. Relevant schemas are retrieved in parallel from long-term memory. The knowledge base in long-term memory is stored in an associative network. Rules called macrorules provide operations that delete propositions from microstructure, summarize propositions, and construct inferences (e.g., to fill gaps in the text). Script-like information would be retrieved at this stage. The final situation model represents the text, but in it the individuality of the text has been lost, and the text has been integrated with other information into a larger structure. Temporality, causality, and spatiality are particularly important in the situation model (Gernsbacher, 1990). Reading time studies suggest that comprehenders pay particular attention to these aspects of text (Zwaan, Magliano, & Graesser, 1995).

As the text is being processed, certain propositions will be stored in working memory. As this has a limited capacity, what determines what goes into this buffer? First, recency is important. Second, the level at which a proposition is stored is important, with propositions higher in the coherence graph more likely to receive more processing cycles in working memory.

The construction–integration model itself (Kintsch, 1988) keeps most of the features of the earlier model (see Figure 12.4). In the construction phase of processing, word meanings are activated, propositions formed, and inferences made, by the mechanisms described earlier. The initial stages of processing are bottom-up. In the integration phase, the network of interrelated items is integrated into a coherent structure. The text base constructed in the construction phase may contain contradictions or may be incorrect, but any contradictions are resolved in the integration phase by a process of spreading activation around the network until a stable, consistent structure is attained. Information is represented at four levels: the microstructure of the text; the local structure (sentence-by-sentence information integrated with information retrieved from long-term memory); the macrostructure (the hierarchically ordered set of propositions derived from the microstructure); and the situation model (the integration of the text base—microstructure and macrostructure together—with the results of inferences).

Evaluation of the construction–integration model

The construction–integration model explains many experimental findings. First, the more propositions there are in a passage, the longer it takes to read per word (Kintsch & Keenan, 1973). Second, as we have seen, there is a levels effect in the importance of a proposition owing to the multiple processing of high-level propositions. They are held in working memory longer, and elaborated more. Whenever a proposition is selected from working memory, its probability of being reproduced increases. Kintsch and van Dijk (1978) found that the higher the level of a proposition, the more likely it is to be recalled in a free recall task.

Inferences are confused with original material because the propositions created as a result of the inferences are stored along with explicitly presented propositions. The two sorts of proposition are indistinguishable in the representation. That this depends on the operation of goal and other schemas also explains why material can be hard to understand and remember if we do not know what it is about. We remember different things if we change perspective because different goal schemas become active.

The model also explains readability effects and the difficulty of the text. Kintsch and van Dijk (1978) defined the readability of a story as the number of propositions in the story divided by the time it takes to read it. The best predictors of readability turned out to be the frequency of words in the text and the number of reinstatement searches that have to be made, as predicted from the model. Kintsch and Vipond (1979) confirmed that readability is not determined solely by the text, but is an interaction between the text and the readers. The most obvious example is that reinstatement searches are only necessary when a proposition is not in working memory, and obviously the greater the capacity of an individual's working memory, the less likely such a reader is to need to make reinstatement searches. Daneman and Carpenter (1980) found that individual differences in working memory size can affect reading performance. So if you want to write easily readable text, you should use short words, and try to write so as to avoid the reader having to retrieve a lot of material from long-term memory.

The model can explain some differences between good and poor readers. Vipond (1980)

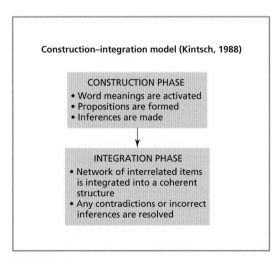

Construction–integration model (Kintsch, 1988)

CONSTRUCTION PHASE
• Word meanings are activated
• Propositions are formed
• Inferences are made

INTEGRATION PHASE
• Network of interrelated items is integrated into a coherent structure
• Any contradictions or incorrect inferences are resolved

FIGURE 12.4

presented readers with passages containing technical material. Comprehension ease could be predicted from the number of times a reader must make a reinstatement, by the number of propositions reinstated, by the number of inferences and reorganizations required to keep the network coherent, and by the number of levels in the network required to represent the text. Vipond examined how these variables operate at the microlevel (to do with sentences) and the macrolevel (to do with paragraphs). He found that involvement of microprocesses predicts the reading performance of less skilled readers, whereas the involvement of macroprocesses predicts the reading performance of better readers. He argued that microprocesses have greater influence in question answering, recognition, and locating information in text, whereas macroprocesses have greater influence in integration and long-term retention.

Fletcher (1986) examined eight strategies that participants might use to keep propositions in the short-term buffer. Four were local strategies ("most recent proposition"; "most recent topical"—the first agent or object mentioned in a story; "most recent containing the most frequent argument"; and "leading edge"—a combination of the most recent and the most important proposition) and four were global strategies ("follow a script"; "correspond to the major categories of a story grammar"; "indicate a character's goal or plan"; "are part of the most recent discourse topic"). These were tested against 20 texts in a recall task and a "think-aloud protocol" task, where participants had to read the story and elaborate out loud. There was no clear preference for local versus global strategies, although the "plan/goal" strategy was top in both tasks, and story structure was also important. There were large task differences: for example, frequency was bottom in recall but third most used in the protocol task.

Finally, the model also predicts how good memory is for text and how prior knowledge affects the way in which people answer questions (Kintsch, Welsch, Schmalhofer, & Zimny, 1990). The more background knowledge comprehenders have, the more likely they are to answer questions based on their situation model. Comprehenders with less prior knowledge rely more on the surface detail in the text base to answer questions.

Comparison of models

Story grammars suffer from a number of problems: In particular, it is difficult to agree on what the terminal and non-terminal categories and rules of the grammar should be. Propositional networks and schema models, while providing useful constructs, are not in themselves sufficient to account for all the phenomena of text processing. Of these models, Kintsch's is the most detailed and promising, and as a consequence has received the most attention. It combines the best of schema-based and network-based approaches to form a well-specified mental model theory.

INDIVIDUAL DIFFERENCES IN COMPREHENSION SKILLS

Throughout this book, we have seen that there are individual differences in reading skills, and the same is true of text processing: people differ in their ability to process text effectively. There are a number of ways in which people differ in comprehension abilities, and a number of reasons for these differences. For example, less skilled comprehenders draw fewer inferences when processing text or discourse, and are also less well able to integrate meaning across utterances (Oakhill, 1994; Yuill & Oakhill, 1991). Working memory plays a role in these difficulties, but is unlikely to be the sole reason.

Working or short-term memory is used for storing currently active ideas, and for the short-term storage of mental computations (Baddeley, 1990). Differences in working memory span have a number of consequences for the ability to understand text (Singer, 1994). For example, a high span will enable an antecedent to be kept active in memory for longer, and will enable more elaborative inferences to be drawn. A useful measure of working memory capacity for test processing is reading span as defined by Daneman and Carpenter (1980). People hear or read sets of unrelated sentences, and after each set attempt to recall the last word of each sentence. Reading span is the largest size set for which a participant can correctly recall all the last words. Reading span correlates with the ability to answer questions about texts, with pronoun resolution accuracy, and even with general measures of verbal intelligence such as SAT scores (a standardized test of academic and intellectual achievement in the USA, standing for Scholastic Assessment Test). Daneman and Carpenter argued that reading span gives a much better measure of comprehension ability than traditional word span scores. On the other hand, it has proved much harder to find effects of memory capacity on elaborative inferences, perhaps because optional elaborations are not always reliably inferred by readers (Singer, 1994). Less able readers are also more prone to mind wandering when reading (McVay & Kane, 2012), suggesting that attentional control and executive processing also play an important role in skilled reading, in addition to working memory capacity.

We saw earlier that prior knowledge influences comprehension. Possessing prior knowledge can be advantageous. In general, the more you know about a subject, the easier it is to understand and remember related text. (You can easily verify this for yourself by picking up a book or an article on a topic you know nothing about.) Prior knowledge provides a framework for understanding new material, activates appropriate concepts more easily, and affects the processing of inferences. It helps us to decide what is important and relevant in material and what is less so. The effects of prior knowledge can be quite specific (Singer, 1994). Although experts are more accurate and faster than novices at making judgments about statements related to their expertise, this advantage does not carry over to material in the same text that is not related to their expertise, and does not help in making complicated elaborative inferences.

Skilled comprehenders are also better able to suppress irrelevant and inappropriate material (Gernsbacher, 1997). **Suppression** can be distinguished from the related attentional process of inhibition that is important in attentional expectancy-based priming (see Chapter 6). Suppression is the attenuating of activation, whereas inhibition is the blocking of activation (Gernsbacher, 1997). Suppression requires that

material becomes activated before it can be suppressed. Reading activates a great deal of material, and skilled comprehenders are better able to suppress that material that is less relevant to the task at hand. It reduces interference. Less skilled comprehenders are less efficient at suppressing the inappropriate meaning of homonyms such as SPADE (Gernsbacher, Varner, & Faust, 1990). When presented with the test word "ace" 850 ms after the sentence "He dug with a spade," skilled comprehenders showed no interference, but less skilled comprehenders took longer to reject the test word. Less skilled comprehenders are also less efficient at suppressing the activation of related pictures when reading words. They are even less good at processing puns—this is because they are less able to quickly suppress the contextually appropriate meaning of a pun (Gernsbacher, 1997).

Finally, although there has been considerable debate as to the exact mechanisms involved, some cognitive abilities decline with normal aging (Woodruff-Pak, 1997). There is experimental evidence that young people are more effective at relating ideas in text (Cohen, 1979; Singer, 1994). Healthy elderly people are less efficient at suppressing irrelevant material than young people.

How to become a better reader

We saw in Chapter 7 that increases in reading speed are at the cost of impaired comprehension. However, psycholinguistics has suggested a number of tips about how one's level of comprehension of text can be improved.

You can improve your reading ability by providing yourself with a framework. One of the best known methods for studying is called the PQ4R method (Anderson, 2010; Thomas & Robinson, 1972) (see Figure 12.5). This method emphasizes identifying the key points of what you are reading, and adopting an active approach to the material. In terms of Kintsch's model, this enables appropriate goal schema to be activated right from the start. It also enables you to process the material more deeply, and think about its implications. Material should also be related to prior knowledge. The technique also maximizes memory retention. Making up questions and answering them is known to improve memory, with question-making the more effective of the two (Anderson, 2010). Finally, elaborative processing of material is highly beneficial; we saw earlier that we tend to remember our inferences. The PQ4R method makes incidental use of all of these insights. The method goes like this. It can be applied either to a whole book or to just one chapter in a book:

- Preview. Survey the material to determine what is discussed in it. Examine the contents list. If the book or chapter has an introduction or summary, read it. Read the conclusions. Look at the figures and tables to get a feel for what the material is about. Identify the sections to be read as single units. Apply the next four steps to each section.
- Questions. Make up questions for each section. Try to make your questions related to your goals in reading the material. You can sometimes turn section headings into questions. (I've already tried to do this where possible in this book.)
- Read. Read the material carefully, trying to answer the questions you made up.

- Reflect. Reflect on the material as you read it. Try to think of examples, and try to relate the material to prior knowledge. Try to understand it. If you don't understand it all the first time, don't worry. Some difficult material takes several readings.
- Recite. After finishing a section, try to recall the information that was in it. Try answering the questions you made up earlier. If you cannot, reread the difficult material and the parts relevant to the questions you could not answer.
- Review. After you have finished, go through it mentally, recalling the main points. Again try answering the questions you made up. A few minutes after you have finished this process, flick through the material once more. If possible, repeat this an hour or so later.

You might need to repeat the whole process if you want to approach the material with a different emphasis. This method is not always appropriate, of course. I wouldn't like to read a novel by the PQ4R method, for example. But if you have to study material for some purpose—such as this textbook for an exam—it is much better to rely on psycholinguistic principles than to read it like a novel.

THE NEUROSCIENCE OF TEXT PROCESSING

Much less is known about the neuropsychology of text processing than about the neuropsychology of many other language processes. This is because text processing and semantic integration really comprise many processes, at least some of which are not specific to language, and involve much of the cortex. It is much more straightforward to track down the effects of brain damage on modular processes. Many types of brain damage will lead to some impairment of comprehension ability. For example, people with **receptive aphasia** have difficulty in understanding the meaning of words; this obviously impairs their ability to follow coherent text and conversation. People with syntactic processing impairments have difficulty in parsing sentences (see also Chapter 10). However, it has proved much more difficult to find deficits that are

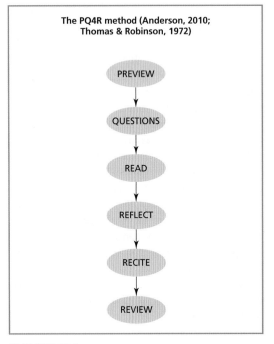

The PQ4R method (Anderson, 2010; Thomas & Robinson, 1972)

PREVIEW

QUESTIONS

READ

REFLECT

RECITE

REVIEW

FIGURE 12.5

restricted to text processing. Some patients with Wernicke's aphasia have difficulty in maintaining the coherence of discourse; they might repeat ideas or introduce irrelevant ones (Christiansen, 1995). Children with SLI (specific language impairment) are poor at story comprehension and making inferences. The source of their comprehension difficulty is uncertain: Limited working memory span might play a role, and it is also possible that ability to suppress information is impaired. It may also be that the difficulties arise because these children spend so much time processing individual words and parsing sentences, as they have a host of other difficulties (Bishop, 1997). Of course, all of these factors might play a part.

In spite of this difficulty, there are reports of people with an impaired ability to understand discourse, but without other language impairments. Most of these reports involve (right-handed) people with right-hemisphere damage (Caplan, 1992). For example, such patients have some difficulty in understanding jokes (Brownell & Gardner, 1988; Brownell, Michel, Powelson, & Gardner, 1983). Consider the following joke (63) with three possible punchlines (from Brownell et al., 1983, selected by Caplan, 1992):

(63) The quack was selling a potion which he claimed would make men live to a great age. He claimed he himself was hale and hearty and over 300 years old.
"Is he really as old as that?" asked a listener of the youthful assistant.
"I can't say," said the assistant,
"X."
Which best fits X?
A. Correct punchline: "I've only worked with him for 100 years."
B. Coherent non-humorous ending: "I don't know how old he is."
C. Incoherent ending: "There are over 300 days in a year."

Brownell et al. found that right-hemisphere patients were not very good at picking the correct punchline. They often chose the incoherent ending. They knew that the ending of a joke should be surprising, but were unable to maintain coherence.

Right-hemisphere patients also find some discourse inferences difficult to make (Brownell, Potter, Bihrle, & Gardner, 1986). In particular, while they are able to draw straightforward inferences from discourse, they are unable to revise them in the light of new information that should make them inappropriate (Caplan, 1992).

We saw in Chapter 3 that children with semantic-pragmatic disorder have difficulty in conversations where they have to draw inferences (Bishop, 1997). They give very literal answers to questions, and fail to take the preceding conversational and social context into account. Semantic-pragmatic disorder is best explained in terms of these children having difficulty in representing other people's mental states.

Many people with short-term memory impairments show comprehension impairments. We saw earlier that reading span tends to be lower in people with poor comprehension skills. Brain damage can dramatically reduce short-term memory span (to just one or two digits). Patient BO had particular difficulty understanding sentences with three or more noun phrases (Caplan, 1992). McCarthy and Warrington (1987b) described a patient who had difficulty in translating commands into actions. People with dementia have difficulty in keeping track of the referents of pronouns; this is likely to be because of their impaired working memory (Almor, Kempler, MacDonald, Andersen, & Tyler, 1999). Vallar and Baddeley (1987) described a patient with impaired short-term memory who could not detect anomalies involving reference. Although short-term memory seems to play little role in parsing (Chapter 10), it is important in integration and maintaining a discourse representation.

We saw earlier that one aspect of being a skilled comprehender is to suppress irrelevant material. People with dementia are very inefficient at suppressing irrelevant material (Faust, Balota, Duchek, Gernsbacher, & Smith, 1997). This leads to a reduced ability to understand text and conversation. Furthermore, the more severe the dementia, the less efficient the suppression. People with dementia also seem to change the topic of conversation more often and more unexpectedly than people without dementia, and are generally less able to maintain coherence in conversation (Garcia & Joanette, 1997).

SUMMARY

- In comprehension, we go beyond word meaning and syntactic structure to integrate the semantic roles into a larger representation that integrates the text or discourse with previous material and with background information.
- Text has a structure and coherence that makes it easy to understand.
- People try to make new information as easy to assimilate as possible for the listener.
- Literal memory is normally very unreliable.
- People generally forget the syntactic and lexical details of what they hear or read, and just remember the gist.
- We can remember some of the literal form, particularly where the wording matters, and for incidental material such as jokes.
- We have better memory for what we consider to be important material.
- Prior knowledge is important; it helps us to understand and remember material.
- Changing perspective can help you remember additional information if the story was easy to understand in the first place.
- As we read or listen, we make inferences.
- Eyewitness testimony can be quite unreliable, as people confuse inference with what originally happened, and can be misled by the wording of questions.
- Bridging inferences enable us to maintain the coherence of text, elaborative inferences to go beyond the text.
- We find it difficult to distinguish our inferences from the original material.
- According to the constructionist viewpoint, we construct a detailed model of the discourse, using many elaborative inferences; according to the minimalist viewpoint, we make only those inferences we need to maintain the coherence of the representation.
- The number of inferences we make at the time of comprehension might be quite minimal; we make only those necessary to make sense of the text and keep it coherent.
- Many elaborative inferences are made at the time of recall.
- Resolving anaphoric reference involves working out who or what (the antecedent) should be associated with pronouns and referring phrases.
- Gender is an important cue for resolving anaphoric ambiguity.
- Some topics are more accessible than others; they are said to be in the foreground.
- Common ground refers to items that are mutually known by participants in conversations, when the participants know that the others know about these things too.
- Factors such as common ground cannot restrict the initial search for possible referents, but may be an important constraint in selecting among alternatives.
- Propositions are units of meaning relating two things.
- Propositional networks form a useful basis for representing text, but cannot be sufficient in themselves, because they do not show how we make inferences, or how some items are kept in the foreground.
- According to story grammars, stories have a structure analogous to that of a sentence; however, unlike sentence grammars, there is no agreement on how stories should be analyzed, or on what the appropriate units should be.
- Schemas are organized packets of knowledge that have been abstracted from many instances; they are particularly useful for representing stereotypical sequences (such as going to a restaurant).
- A mental model is a structure that represents what the text is about, particularly preserving spatial information.

- The construction–integration model combines propositional networks, schema theory, and mental models to provide a detailed account of how we understand text.
- Working memory span is an important constraint on comprehension ability.
- Skilled comprehenders are better able to suppress irrelevant material.
- The PQ4R method is a powerful method for approaching difficult material.
- People with right-hemisphere brain damage have difficulty in understanding jokes and drawing appropriate inferences.
- Children with semantic-pragmatic disorder have difficulty following conversations because they cannot represent other people's mental states.
- Impaired short-term memory disrupts the ability to comprehend text and discourse.
- Dementia reduces the ability to comprehend text and discourse and to maintain a coherent conversation.

QUESTIONS TO THINK ABOUT

1. What makes some stories easier to follow than others?
2. How is watching a film like reading a book? In what ways does it differ?
3. Many of the experiments on parsing involved analyses of reaction times. In contrast, experiments such as those of Bransford and Johnson (1973; see Figure 12.1) necessitate a more qualitative analysis that involves dividing a story up into "ideas." How easy is it to identify an idea?
4. What determines how easy it is to assign an antecedent to an anaphoric expression?
5. What has psychology told us about how comprehension skills should be taught?
6. To what extent are the same sorts of processes considered to be automatic in word recognition, parsing, and comprehension?

FURTHER READING

Fletcher (1994) reviews the classic literature on text memory. See Altarriba (1993) for a review of cultural effects in comprehension.

There are many references on the debate between minimalism and constructionism (e.g., Graesser, Singer, & Trabasso, 1994; McKoon, Gerrig, & Greene, 1996; Potts, Keenan, & Golding, 1988; Singer, 1994; Singer & Ferreira, 1983; Singer, Graesser, & Trabasso, 1994).

Kintsch (1994) reviews models of text processing. Another early influential propositional network model was that of Norman and Rumelhart (1975). Brewer (1987) compares the mental model and schema approaches to memory. See Mandler and Johnson (1980) and Rumelhart (1980) for replies to critics of story grammars. See Eysenck and Keane (2010) for more on schemas. Wilkes (1997) describes how knowledge is represented.

See Bishop (1997) for a review of developmental discourse disorders, including semantic-pragmatic disorder.

SECTION E

PRODUCTION AND OTHER ASPECTS OF LANGUAGE

This section looks at how we produce language. It also examines the structure of the language system, with emphasis on how we repeat words and the role of memory in language processing. It ends with a brief look at the main themes outlined in Chapter 1, and some possible future issues.

Chapter 13, Language production, looks at the process involved in deciding what we want to say, and how we turn these words into sounds. Where does comprehension end and production begin? Writing is another way of producing language that is examined here.

Chapter 14, How do we use language?, looks at how we use language. The chapter examines conversation and pragmatics, and the relation between language and the visual world.

Chapter 15, The structure of the language system, draws together issues from the rest of the book, looking at how the components of the system interrelate, particularly with reference to memory.

Chapter 16, New directions, evaluates the present status of psycholinguistics and the ways in which the themes introduced in Chapter 1 may be developed in the future.

CHAPTER 13

LANGUAGE PRODUCTION

INTRODUCTION

This chapter examines how we produce language. There has been less research on language production than on language comprehension. Consider the amount of space devoted to these topics in this book: several chapters on input and only one on output. Clearly we do not spend disproportionately more time listening or reading than we do speaking, so why is there this imbalance of research? The investigation of production is perceived to be more difficult than the investigation of comprehension, primarily because it is difficult to control the input in experiments on production. It is relatively easy

to control the frequency, imageability, and visual appearance (or any other aspect that is considered important) of the materials of word recognition experiments, but our thoughts are much harder to control experimentally.

The processes of speech production fall into three broad areas called conceptualization, formulation, and execution (Levelt, 1989). At the highest level, the processes of conceptualization involve determining what to say. These are sometimes also called message-level processes. The processes of formulation involve translating this conceptual representation into a linguistic form. Finally, the processes of articulation involve

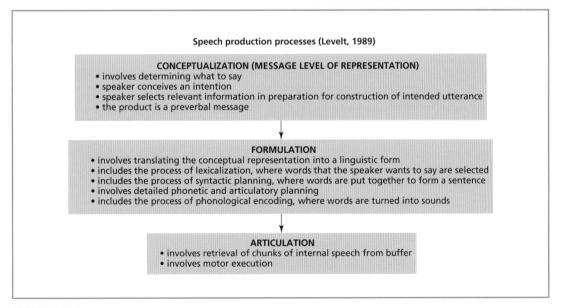

Speech production processes (Levelt, 1989)

CONCEPTUALIZATION (MESSAGE LEVEL OF REPRESENTATION)
- involves determining what to say
- speaker conceives an intention
- speaker selects relevant information in preparation for construction of intended utterance
- the product is a preverbal message

FORMULATION
- involves translating the conceptual representation into a linguistic form
- includes the process of lexicalization, where words that the speaker wants to say are selected
- includes the process of syntactic planning, where words are put together to form a sentence
- involves detailed phonetic and articulatory planning
- includes the process of phonological encoding, where words are turned into sounds

ARTICULATION
- involves retrieval of chunks of internal speech from buffer
- involves motor execution

FIGURE 13.1

detailed phonetic and articulatory planning (see Figure 13.1).

During conceptualization, speakers conceive an intention and select relevant information from memory or the environment in preparation for the construction of the intended utterance. The product of conceptualization is a preverbal message. This is called the message level of representation. To some extent, the message level is the forgotten level of speech production. A problem with talking about intention and meaning, as Wittgenstein (1958) observed, is that they induce "a mental cramp." Very little is known about the processes of conceptualization and the format of the message level. Obviously the message level involves interfacing with the world (particularly with other speakers), and with semantic memory. The start of the production process must have a great deal in common with the end point of the comprehension process. When we talk, we have an intention to achieve something with our language. How do we decide on the illocutionary force of what we want to say? Levelt (1989) distinguished between macroplanning and microplanning conceptualization processes. Macroplanning involves the elaboration of a communicative goal into a series of subgoals and the retrieval of appropriate information. Microplanning involves assigning the right propositional shape to these chunks of information, and deciding on matters such as what the topic or focus of the utterance will be.

There are two major components of formulation: We have to select the individual words that we want to say (**lexicalization**), and we have to put them together to form a sentence (syntactic planning). It might not always be necessary to construct a syntactic representation of a sentence in order to derive its meaning. Clearly this is not an option when speaking. Given this, it is perhaps surprising that more attention has not been paid to syntactic encoding in production, but the difficulties of controlling the input are substantial.

Finally, the processes of phonological encoding involve turning words into sounds in the right order, spoken at the correct speed, with the appropriate prosody (intonation, pitch, loudness, and rhythm). The sounds must be produced in the correct sequence and specify how the muscles of the articulatory system should be moved.

What types of evidence have been used to study production? First, researchers have analyzed transcripts of how speakers choose what to say and how to say it (Beattie, 1983). For example, Brennan and Clark (1996) found that speakers cooperate in conversation so that they come to agree on the same names for objects. Computer simulations and connectionist modeling, as in other areas of psycholinguistics, have become very influential. Much has been learned by the analysis of the distribution of hesitations or pauses in speech. Until fairly recently the most influential data were spontaneously occurring speech errors, or slips of the tongue, but in recent years experimental studies, often based on picture naming, have become important. By the end of this chapter you should:

- Know about the different types of speech error and why we make them.
- Know the difference between conceptualization, formulation, and execution.
- Understand how we plan the syntax of what we say.
- Appreciate how we retrieve words when we speak.
- Know about Garrett's model and the interactive activation models of speech production.
- Know why we pause when we speak.
- Understand how brain damage affects language production.
- Know how we plan what we write.

SLIPS OF THE TONGUE

Until fairly recently, models of speech production were primarily based on analyses of spontaneously occurring speech errors. Casual examination of our speech will reveal (in the unlikely event that you do not know this already) that it is far from perfect, and rife with errors. Analysis of these errors is one of the oldest research topics in psycholinguistics. Speech errors are frequently commented on in everyday life. The case of the Reverend Dr. Spooner is quite commonly known; indeed, he gave his name to a particular type of error involving the exchange of initial consonants between words, the spoonerism. Some of Reverend Spooner's alleged **spoonerisms** are shown in examples (1) to (3). (See Potter, 1980, for a discussion of whether Reverend Spooner's errors were in fact so frequent as to suggest an underlying pathology.)

(1) Utterance: You have hissed all my mystery lectures.
Target: ... missed all my history lectures.
(2) Utterance: In fact, you have tasted the whole worm.
Target: ... wasted the whole term.
(3) Utterance: The Lord is a shoving leopard to his flock.
Target: ... a loving shepherd.

Most people have heard of the Freudian slip. In part of a general treatise on action slips or errors of action called parapraxes, Freud (1901/1975) noted the occurrence of slips of the tongue, and proposed that they revealed our repressed thoughts. In one example he gives, a professor said in a lecture, "In the case of female genitals, in spite of many Versuchungen (temptations)—I beg your pardon, Versuche (experiments) ..."

Not all Freudian slips need arise from a repressed sexual thought. In another example he gives, the President of the Lower House of the Austrian Parliament opened a meeting with "Gentlemen, I take notice that a full quorum of members is present and herewith declare the sitting closed!" (instead of open). Freud interpreted this as revealing the President's true thoughts, that he secretly wished a potentially troublesome meeting closed. However, Freud was not the first to study speech errors; a few years before, Meringer and Mayer (1895) provided what is now considered to be a more traditional analysis. Ellis (1980) reanalyzed Freud's collection of speech errors in terms of a modern process-oriented account of speech production.

The most common method of analyzing speech errors is to collect a large corpus of errors by recording as many as possible. Usually the researcher will interrupt the speaker when he or she detects the error, and ask the speaker what was the intended target, why they thought the error was made, and so on. Although this method introduces the possibility of observer bias, this appears to be surprisingly weak, if present at all. A comparison of error corpora against a smaller sample taken from a rigorous transcription of a

Freud (1901) proposed that slips of the tongue revealed our repressed thoughts.

sample of tape-recorded conversation (Garnham, Shillcock, Brown, Mill, & Cutler, 1982) suggests that the types and proportion of errors are very similar. For example, word substitution errors and sound anticipation and substitution errors are particularly common. Furthermore, it is possible to induce slips of the tongue artificially by, for example, getting participants to read words out at speed (Baars, Motley, & MacKay, 1975). The findings from such studies corroborate the naturalistic data.

There are many different types of speech error. We can categorize them by considering the linguistic units involved in the error (for example, at the phonological feature, phoneme, syllable, morpheme, word, phrase, or sentence levels) and the error mechanism involved (such as the blend, substitution, addition, or deletion of units). Fromkin (1971/1973) argued that the existence of errors involving a particular unit shows that these units are psychologically real. Table 13.1 gives some examples of speech errors from my own corpus to illustrate these points. In any error there was the target that the speaker had in mind, and the erroneous utterance as actually produced; the erroneous part of the utterance is in italics.

What can speech errors tell us?

Let us now analyze a speech error in more detail to see what can be learned from them. Consider the famous example of (4) from Fromkin (1971/1973):

(4) *a weekend* for MANIACS—*a maniac* for WEEKENDS

The capital letters indicate the primary stress and the italics secondary stress. The first thing to notice is that the sentence stress was left unchanged by the error, suggesting that stress is generated independently of the particular words involved. Even more strikingly, the plural morpheme "-s" was left at the end of the second word where it was originally intended to be in the first place: it did not move with "maniac." We say it was stranded. Furthermore, this plural morpheme was realized in sound as /z/ not as /s/. That is, the plural ending sounds consistent with the word that actually came before it, not with the word that was originally intended to come before it. (Plural endings are voiced "/z/" if the final consonant of the word to which it is attached is voiced, as in "weekend," but are unvoiced "/s/" if

TABLE 13.1 Examples of speech errors classified by unit and mechanism.

Type	Utterance	Target
Feature perseveration	Turn the kno*p*	knob
Phoneme anticipation	The *m*irst of May	first
Phoneme perseveration	God rest *r*e merry gentlemen	ye
Phoneme exchange	Do you *r*eel *f*eally bad?	feel really bad
Affix deletion	The chimney cat*ch* fire	catches fire
Phoneme deletion	Back*g*ound lighting	background
Word blend	The *chung* of today	children + young
Word exchange	Guess whose *mind* came to *name*?	whose name came to mind
Morpheme exchange	I *random*ed some *sampl*y	I sampled some randomly
Word substitution	Get me a *fork*	spoon
Phrase blend	Miss you *a very much*	very much + a great deal

the final consonant is unvoiced, as in "maniac.") This is an example of accommodation to the phonological environment.

Such examples tell us a great deal about speech production. Garrett's model, described next, is based on a detailed analysis of such examples. On the other hand, Levelt et al. (1991a) argued that too much emphasis has been placed on errors, and that error analysis needs to be supported by experimental data. If these two approaches give conflicting results, we should place more emphasis on the experimental data, as the error data are only telling us about aberrant processing. There are three points that can be made in response to this. First, a complete model should be able to account for both experimental and speech error data. Second, the lines of evidence converge rather than giving conflicting results (Harley, 1993a). Third, it is possible to simulate spontaneously occurring speech errors experimentally, and these experimental simulations lead to the same conclusion as the natural errors. Using a technique they called SLIP, Baars et al. (1975) required participants to rapidly read pairs of words such as "big dog," "blocked drain," and then "dart board." If participants have to read these pairs from right to left, the priming effect of the preceding pairs leads them to make many spoonerisms on "dart board." Furthermore, the participants are more likely to produce "barn door" (two real words) than they are the corresponding "bart doard"—an instance of the bias towards lexical outcomes also displayed in the naturalistic data. On the other hand, using the same technique, speakers are less likely to make exchanges that result in taboo words (e.g., from "hit shed"; work it out) than ones that do not. Furthermore, galvanic skin responses were elevated on these taboo trials, suggesting that speakers generated the spoonerism internally, but are in some way monitoring their output (Motley, Camden, & Baars, 1982).

We should note that we sometimes correct our speech errors, which shows that we are monitoring our speech. Sometimes we notice the error before we speak it and can prevent it from being made; sometimes we notice the error as we are

speaking and can correct, or repair, it; sometimes we notice it only after we have finished speaking. Often we never notice we have made an error. The idea of a monitor plays an important role in the WEAVER++ model of speech production, discussed below.

Naming errors probably do not arise from people rushing their preparation, or, in the case of naming, from insufficient word preparation, or a failure to check names against objects. Griffin (2004) examined people's eye movements while they described a visual scene. People tend to gaze at objects while they are preparing their names. If errors arise from rushed preparation, they should spend less time looking at an object just before naming it incorrectly (e.g., saying "hammer" when looking at an axe); however, they do not. Instead they spend just as long gazing at a referent before uttering errors as they do before uttering correct names. Indeed, if they corrected their utterance ("ham – axe"), they spent longer looking at the object after making their error, presumably because they were preparing their repair.

Garrett's model of speech production

In an important series of papers based primarily on speech error analysis, Garrett (1975, 1976, 1980a, 1980b, 1982, 1988, 1992) argued that we produce speech through a series of discrete levels of processing. In Garrett's model, processing is serial, in that at any one stage of processing only one thing is happening. Of course, more than one thing is happening at different processing levels, because obviously even as we speak we might be planning what we are going to say next. However, these levels of processing do not interact with one another. The model distinguishes two major stages of syntactic planning (see Figure 13.2). At the functional level, word order is not yet explicitly represented. The semantic content of words is specified and assigned to syntactic roles such as subject and object. At the positional level, words are explicitly ordered. There is a dissociation between syntactic planning and lexical retrieval. Garrett argued that content and function words play very different roles in language production.

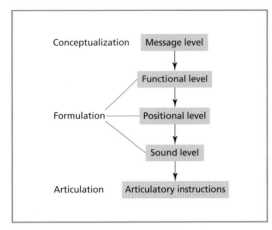

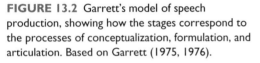

FIGURE 13.2 Garrett's model of speech production, showing how the stages correspond to the processes of conceptualization, formulation, and articulation. Based on Garrett (1975, 1976).

(Remember that content words are nouns, verbs, adjectives, and adverbs, and do the semantic work of the language, while function words are a small number of words that do most of the syntactic work.) Content words are selected at the functional level, whereas function words are not selected until the positional level.

Box 13.1 provides an example of how we generate a sentence. We start with an intention to say a particular message; here, for example, about someone doing the washing up. This happens at the message level (A). As we saw earlier, there has been surprisingly little research on the message level; often it is just shown as a cartoon-like "thoughts" bubble. We choose what we are going to say and the general way in which we are going to say it. The task of speech production is then to produce these parallel ideas one at a time: that is, they must be linearized. We go on to form an abstract semantic specification where functional relations are specified. These are then mapped onto syntactic functions. This is the functional level (B). Word exchanges occur at this stage. As only the functional roles of the words, and not their absolute positions, have been specified at this point, word exchanges are constrained by syntactic category, but much less so by the distance between the exchanging words. Next we generate a syntactic frame for

the planned sentence (C). Function words are said to be immanent in this frame; they are an inherent part of it, fully implied by its description. The phonological representations of content words are then accessed from the lexicon using the semantic representation (D). These are then inserted into the syntactic planning frame where final positions are specified. This is the positional level (E). The function words and other grammatical elements are then phonologically specified to give the sound-level representation (F). Sound exchanges occur at this stage and, as their absolute position is now specified, are constrained by distance. Other tidying up might then occur, as this is translated into a series of phonological features that then drive the articulatory apparatus (G).

Evidence for Garrett's model of speech production

In morpheme exchanges such as (4), it is clear that the root or stem morpheme ("maniac") has been accessed independently of its plural affix—in this

> **Box 13.1 An example of how we produce an utterance based on Garrett's (1975, 1976) model of speech production**
>
> (A) Message level—intention to convey particular meaning activates appropriate propositions
> (B) SUBJECT = "mother concept," VERB = "wipe concept," OBJECT = "plate concept"
>   TIME = past
>   NUMBER OF OBJECTS = MANY
> (C) (DETERMINER) N_1 V [+PAST]
>   (DETERMINER) N_2 [+PLURAL]
> (D) /mother/ /wipe/ /plate/
> (E) (DETERMINER) /mother/ /wipe/ + [PAST]
>   (DETERMINER) /plate/ + [PLURAL]
> (F) /the/ /mother/ /wiped/ /the/ /plates/
> (G) Low-level phonological processing and articulation

case the plural ending "-s." (In English, **affix**es are either **prefix**es, which come before a word, or suffixes, which come after, and are always **bound morphemes**, in that they cannot occur without a stem; morphemes that can be found as words by themselves are called free morphemes. Bound morphemes can be either derivational or inflectional—see Chapter 1.) Because the bound morpheme has been left in its original place while the free morpheme has moved, this type of exchange is called morpheme stranding. Content words behave differently from the grammatical elements, which include inflectional bound morphemes and function words. This suggests that they are involved in different processing stages.

In (4) the plural suffix was produced correctly for the sentence as it was actually uttered, not as it was planned. This accommodation to the phonological environment suggests that the phonological specification of grammatical elements occurs rather late in speech production, at least after the phonological forms of content words have been retrieved. This **dissociation** between specifying the sounds of content words and specifying the grammatical elements is of fundamental importance in the theory of speech production, and is an issue that will recur in our discussions of its pathology. Furthermore, in word exchange errors, the sentence stress is left unchanged, suggesting that this is specified independently of the content words.

Error analysis suggests that when we speak we specify a syntactic plan or frame for a sentence that consists of a series of slots into which content words are inserted. Word exchanges occur when content words are put into the wrong slot. Grammatical elements are part of the syntactic frame, but their detailed phonological forms must be specified late.

This model predicts that when parts of a sentence interact to produce a speech error, they must be elements of the same processing vocabulary. That is, things only exchange if they are involved in the same processing level. Therefore certain types of error should never be found. Garrett observed that content words almost always only exchange with other content words, and that function words exchange with other function words.

This is an extraordinarily robust finding: In my corpus of several thousand speech errors, there is not a single instance of a content word exchanging with a function word. This supports the idea that content and function words are from computationally distinct vocabularies that are processed at different levels.

There are also different constraints on word and sound exchange errors. Sounds only exchange across small distances, whereas words can exchange across phrases; words that exchange tend to come from the same syntactic class, whereas this is not a consideration in sound errors, which swap with words regardless of their syntactic class. In summary, word exchange errors involve content words and are constrained by syntactic factors; sound errors are constrained by distance.

Evaluation of Garrett's model

Garrett's model accounts for a great deal of the speech error evidence, but a number of findings subsequently have suggested that some aspects of it might not be correct. First, it is not at all clear that speech production is a serial process. There is clearly some evidence for at least local parallel processing in that we find word blend errors, which must be explained by two (or more) words being simultaneously retrieved from the lexicon, as in (5) for example. More problematically, we find blends of phrases and sentences, such as in (6). Furthermore, the locus of these blends is determined phonologically (Butterworth, 1982), so that the two phrases cross over where they sound most alike. This suggests that two alternative messages are processed in parallel from the message to the phonological levels.

We also observe two types of cognitive intrusion errors where material extraneous to the utterance being produced intrudes into it. The message level can intrude into the utterance and lower levels of processing, producing errors called non-plan-internal errors, such as in (7). These errors are often phonologically facilitated. Phonological facilitation means that errors are more likely to occur if the target word and intrusion sound alike.

We find that targets and intrusions in non-plan-internal errors sound more alike than would be expected by chance alone, although special care is necessary to determine what the intended utterance was (Harley, 1984).

(5) Utterance: It's difficult to valify. (Targets: validate + verify)
(6) Target 1: I'm making some tea.
    Target 2: I'm putting the kettle on.
    Utterance: I'm making the kettle on.
(7) Target: I've read all my library books.
    Utterance: I've eaten all my library books.
    Context: The speaker reported that he was hungry and was thinking of getting something to eat.

The names of objects or words in the outside environment can also intrude into speech, producing environmental contamination. Consider (8) from Harley (1984). The intruding item ("Clark's") sounds similar to the target. Again, we find that phonological facilitation of these intrusions occurs more often than one would expect on a chance basis (although to a lesser degree than with other cognitive intrusions).

(8) Target: Get out of the car.
    Utterance: Get out of the clark.
    Context: The speaker was looking at a shopfront in the background that had the name "Clark's" printed on it. The speaker reported that he was not aware of this at the time of speaking.

These cognitive intrusions clearly have a high-level or message-level source. Hence speech production can involve parallel processing, with high-level processes constrained by low-level processes such as phonological similarity.

Word substitution speech errors are also constrained by the similarity of the target and the intrusion, and tend to result in familiar outcomes; the results are discussed in more detail later. Bock (1982; see later) found that the availability of words affects syntactic planning, further suggesting that levels of processing interact in syntactic planning. These findings all suggest that the levels of processing cannot be independent of one another but must interact. These data drive the interactive models of lexicalization described later.

A final problem, about which little can be done, is that the distinction between content and function words is confounded with frequency (Stemberger, 1985), in that function words include some of the most common words of the language (for example, "the," "a"). Processing differences may reflect this, rather than their being processed by different systems. However, the observation that bound morphemes behave like function words supports Garrett's hypothesis, as does neuropsychological data, discussed later.

SYNTACTIC PLANNING

Garrett's model tells us a great deal about the relative stages of syntactic planning, but says little about the syntactic processes themselves. Bock and her colleagues examined these in an elegant series of experiments based on a technique of seeing whether participants can be biased to produce particular constructions. An important finding is that word order in speech is determined by a number of factors that interact (Bock, 1982). For example, animate nouns tend to be the subjects of transitive sentences (McDonald, Bock, & Kelly, 1993), and conceptually more accessible items (e.g., as measured by concreteness) tend to be placed early in sentences (Bock, 1987; Bock & Warren, 1985; Kelly, Bock, & Keil, 1986). In general, these experiments show that the grammatical role assignment component of syntactic planning is controlled by semantic-conceptual factors rather than by properties of words such as word lengths. Speakers also construct sentences so that they provide "given" before "new" information (Bock & Irwin, 1980). Generally, ease of lexical access can affect syntactic planning.

Studies of eye movements in the visual world paradigm (see also Chapters 10 and 14) tell us something about how people formulate descriptions of visual scenes. Speakers gaze at referents in the visual scene as they prepare words to refer to them (Griffin, 2001; Meyer,

Sleiderink, & Levelt, 1998). They also gaze at the referents of direct-object nouns while producing the subject; if they are uncertain which argument to produce immediately after the verb, their gaze moves between the alternative referents (Griffin & Bock, 2000). Gaze is a reliable indicator of what and when people are thinking and planning. Indeed, as is often said, the eyes can give us away; speakers will look at the intended referent of an object even if they are preparing to "lie" by giving an intentionally inaccurate label for it (Griffin & Oppenheimer, 2006).

Syntactic priming

We reuse words and sentence structures within conversation (Schenkein, 1980). The repetition of syntactic structure is called structural priming or syntactic persistence (Bock, 1986). Structural priming suggests that we can separate meaning and form, because we can prime sentence structures independently of sentence meaning.

Syntactic persistence is one aspect of the more general phenomenon of syntactic priming, whereby processing of a particular syntactic structure influences processing of subsequently presented sentences. Syntactic priming is wholly facilitatory, and has been observed in comprehension, in production, and bidirectionally between comprehension and production (Branigan, Pickering, Liversedge, Stewart, & Urbach, 1995). One common method used to study syntactic priming is to get participants to repeat a prime sentence that contains the syntactic structure of interest, and then to describe a picture. Syntactic priming studies show that speakers use a particular word order if the prime sentence used that order (Bock, 1986, 1989; Bock & Loebell, 1990; Branigan et al., 1995; Hartsuiker, Kolk, & Huiskamp, 1999). Suppose we have to describe a picture of a vampire handing a hat to a ghost. A preceding prepositional-object structure prime, such as (9), steers us towards producing a prepositional-object construction in our description: for example, we might say (11); while a double-object prime, such as (10), steers us towards producing a double-object construction such as (12):

(9) The ghoul sold a vacuum cleaner to a werewolf.
(10) The ghoul sold a werewolf a vacuum cleaner.
(11) The vampire handed a hat to the ghost.
(12) The vampire handed the ghost a hat.

Importantly, syntactic priming does not depend on superficial similarities between the prime and utterance. It does not depend on reusing words (lexical priming) or on repeating thematic roles, but instead reflects the more general construction of syntactic constituent structures. Similarly, the magnitude of the priming effect shown by verbs does not depend on the **tense**, **number**, or **aspect** of the verb (Pickering & Branigan, 1998). For example, a prime sentence such as (13) was just as effective as the prime sentence (14) in eliciting a prepositional-object construction involving the word "to" (Bock, 1989). Put more generally, prepositional-object sentences prime descriptions to use prepositional-object constructions regardless of the preposition (e.g., "to" and "for") used in the prime sentences. However, repeating the verb (regardless of tense, aspect, or number) does enhance priming, an effect Pickering and Branigan call the *lexical boost*. The lexical boost is important because it suggests that the verb has a special role in production. Priming is also enhanced by the repetition of word order between prime and target (Hartsuiker & Westenberg, 2000; Pickering, Branigan, & McLean, 2002). In summary, we can prime abstract syntactic structures, but the magnitude of the priming effect is greater if we repeat word order and the verb. Indeed, a verb prime alone may be sufficient to bias speakers' subsequent productions (Melinger & Dobel, 2005).

(13) The werewolf baked a cake for the witch.
(14) The werewolf took a cake to the witch.

Along similar lines, Bock and Loebell (1990) showed that only sentences like (15) produce priming of the prepositional-object description (17). A construction such as (16) does not, even though it is superficially very similar to (15). It has similar words (most noticeably, it contains the word "to") and has a similar stress pattern. However, it has a very different syntactic structure ("a book to study" is a noun phrase, not a prepositional-object phrase). Hence it is the underlying syntactic structure that is important in obtaining syntactic priming, not the surface form of the words. Syntactic priming has been demonstrated for a variety of syntactic structures.

(15)   Vlad brought a book to Boris.
(16)   Vlad brought a book to study.
(17)   The witch is handing a paintbrush to the ghost.

Syntactic persistence can continue for quite some time. Bock and Griffin (2000) found that the structural priming could persist over as long as 10 intervening sentences (although the priming effect can be short-lived—Levelt & Kelter, 1982). Such persistence suggests that the priming is due to more than short-term memory, and may have some long-term learning component.

Speakers also tend to reuse the syntactic constructions of other speakers (Branigan, Pickering, & Cleland, 2000). For example, speakers will use a complex noun phrase (e.g., "the square that's red") more often after hearing a syntactically similar noun phrase than a simple one ("the red square"), and are particularly likely to do so if the main noun ("square") is repeated (Cleland & Pickering, 2003). We find this priming effect on noun-phrase structure if the prime and target noun are semantically related ("sheep" and "goat"), but not if they are phonologically related (e.g., "sheep" and "ship"), suggesting that while syntactic encoding is unsurprisingly affected by the semantic representation, it is not affected by feedback from the phonological representation (Cleland & Pickering, 2003).

Syntactic priming does more than just influence descriptions. Potter and Lombardi (1998) showed that immediate recall can be affected by syntactic persistence. In their experiment, participants silently read words presented one at a time and at a fast rate on a computer screen. They then performed another distractor task before being asked to repeat the sentence out aloud. This task is quite difficult, and speakers sometimes changed the syntactic structure of what they had just read. In particular, people tend to reuse previous syntactic structures: that is, they recalled the sentence just presented with the syntactic structure of a previous item. So syntactic priming influences our memory, too. It can also lead us to produce ungrammatical utterances, when we are erroneously influenced by a structure we have just heard (Ivanova, Pickering, McLean, Costa, & Branigan, 2012).

It is also possible to prime the productions of patients who have an impairment of syntactic planning in speech production, although not all types of sentence structure are primed as easily as others (Hartsuiker & Kolk, 1998; Saffran & Martin, 1997). The number of passives (e.g., "the cat was chased by the dog") was increased by passive primes, but the production of dative constructions (e.g., "give the food to the dog") showed no immediate increase after the primes. Some of the newly generated constructions were morphologically deviant, suggesting that although phrase structure and closed-class elements are normally closely linked in production (as in Garrett's model), they can be separated.

At first sight, the way in which syntactic frames can be primed independently of meaning points to a separation of meaning and form. Greater overlap in meaning does not generally lead to a larger amount of priming; in most cases all that matters is the overlap in surface syntax. This finding suggests that sentence frames are independent syntactic representations, and in particular that they have some existence independent of the meaning of what they encode. It also points to a probabilistic element in syntactic planning, where the precise form of the words we choose is affected by environmental factors such as what we have just heard. Chang, Dell, and Bock (2006) describe a connectionist model of sentence production that can account for the structural priming data. In their model, sequencing in production makes use of two types of information. A sequencing system uses a recurrent connectionist model that uses statistical information to predict what is coming next. However, the model also makes use of semantic information about events and the message to be produced.

The model has two advantages. First, there are some recent data that suggest that meaning can have some effect on priming. Chang, Bock, and Goldberg (2003) found that similar thematic roles can cause priming even when the surface syntax is held constant (e.g., "The man sprayed water on the wall" has the theme (water) before the location (wall), and "The man sprayed the wall with water" has the location before the theme; but both sentences have the same surface structure of NP–V–NP–PP). Chang et al.'s model can account for this result because of the meaning-based route.

Syntactic priming probably serves two main functions. First, it enables speakers in a conversation to coordinate or align information. Using the same words and syntax helps conversants to collaborate more efficiently. Second, it results from implicit learning of how people use syntax to convey meaning—people unconsciously adjust how they convey information on the basis of experience. The finding that syntactic priming can be persistent over surprisingly long periods of time is consistent with the idea that it results from learning rather than just reflecting transient activation of syntactic structures.

Coping with dependencies

How do we cope with dependencies between words? One particular problem facing speakers is ensuring number agreement between subjects and verbs. For instance, we must ensure that we say "the woman does" and "the men do," and not "the woman do" or "the men does." We do not always get agreement right; number agreement errors are fairly common in speech. We particularly have a tendency to make attraction errors such as (18), where we make the verb (here "were" instead of "was") agree with a noun ("unions") that is closer to the verb than the subject ("membership") with which it should agree (Bock & Eberhard, 1993).

(18)   Membership in these unions were voluntary.

In an important series of experiments, Bock and her colleagues used a sentence-completion task designed to elicit agreement errors (e.g., Bock & Cutting, 1992; Bock & Eberhard, 1993;

Bock & Miller, 1991). These experiments look at what type of factors cause number agreement errors. Consider the sentence fragments (19)–(21) from Bock and Eberhard (1993):

(19)   The player on the court –
(20)   The player on the courts –
(21)   The player on the course –

A suitable continuation for this might be "was very good." A continuation containing an agreement error might be "were very good." Which of these fragments causes agreement errors? Sentence (19) is very straightforward; both nouns are singular. As we might expect, this type of fragment produces no agreement errors. In (20) the noun closest to the verb is plural, while the noun that should determine number ("player") is singular. In this condition we observe many errors. What about (21)? Although the local noun ("course") is singular, it is a pseudoplural, because the end of the word is an /s/ sound. (Remember that regular plurals in English are formed by adding an -s to the end of the singular form of the noun.) So if the plural sound alone were important in determining agreement, we would expect sentences like (21) to generate many agreement errors. In fact, they generate none. Hence agreement cannot be determined by the sound of surrounding words (in particular, whether they sound as though they have plural endings) but by something more fundamental. Further evidence for this is that regular ("boys") and irregular ("men") versions of nouns cause equal numbers of agreement errors, as do individual ("ship") and collective (e.g., "audience," "fleet," and "herd"). At first sight what seems to be important in determining number agreement is only the syntactic number of the nouns, suggesting that syntactic planning is modular.

More recent work has challenged this idea that syntactic processing is feedforward and modular. Distributive noun phrases, such as "the label on the bottles," where the semantics of the phrase implies the existence of multiple labels, leads speakers in several languages to produce plural verbs (Eberhard, 1999; Vigliocco, Butterworth, & Garrett, 1996). It now seems likely that whether or not we find semantic effects on verb agreement depends on subtle factors such as the precise materials we use in the experiments. Haskell and MacDonald (2003) showed that number agreement can be accounted for in terms of constraint satisfaction. This approach is similar to that in language comprehension, and makes use of the constraint-satisfaction idea that several sources of information interact to determine output. If the different sources of information conflict, then processing time increases. If one of the sources strongly predicts singular or plural, then additional weak factors have little additional cost, but if the sources of information are approximately equal, then competition is maximal and the cost to processing time greatest (Haskell & MacDonald, 2003). For example, ordinary singular nouns (e.g., horse, ship) are very good predictors that a singular verb is necessary, and produce little competition. Collective nouns (e.g., family, fleet, team) share characteristics of both singulars and plurals. Although they should strictly generate singular verbs, their plural characteristics induce some competition between plural and singular verb forms, leading to longer processing times and more variability in output.

Similar experimental methods also show that number agreement takes place within the clause (Bock & Cutting, 1992). Analysis of number agreement also provides further evidence that syntactic structure is generated before words are assigned to their final positions. Vigliocco and Nicol (1998) note that grammatical encoding has three functions: assigning grammatical functions (e.g., assigning the agent of an action to the subject of the sentence), building syntactic hierarchical constituent structures to reflect this (e.g., turning the subject into a NP), and arranging the constituents in linear order. We have seen that speech error data clearly separate the first and third functions (that is, the functional and positional stages of Garrett's model), but can we distinguish building abstract hierarchical structures from the final serial ordering of words? Vigliocco and Nicol argued that we can. They showed that number agreement errors do not so much depend on the surface or linear proximity

of the local noun to the verb, as on its proximity in the underlying syntactic structure. In one experiment participants had to generate sentences from a sentence beginning and an adjective, e.g., (22). A correct continuation would be (23), and one with an agreement error (24):

(22) The helicopter for the flights + safe.
(23) The helicopter for the flights is safe.
(24) The helicopter for the flights are safe.

In a second experiment participants had to generate questions from (22), such as (25):

(25) Is the helicopter for the flights safe?
(26) Are the helicopter for the flights safe?

Participants made about the same number of agreement errors as in the first experiment, e.g., (26), even though here the "local noun" ("flights") is much farther away in terms of the number of intervening words. This is because, according to linguistic theory, the declarative sentence (23) and the question (25) have the same underlying syntactic structure.

According to Bock, Eberhard, and Cutting (2004) we need two processes to ensure that number agreement proceeds smoothly. First, we need a specification that takes into account the number of things we are talking about in the message. Bock et al. call this processing marking. For example, if we are talking about one helicopter, then the verb is marked as singular. Now suppose we are talking about one pair of scissors. With regard to the message content, the verb will be marked as singular. But we treat "scissors" as a plural noun, even if we are only talking about one of them. We say "the scissors are," never "the scissor is." Hence we need to override the syntactic process of marking with a process that takes account of the morphology of the subject. This second process is called morphing. This overriding process can lead to attraction errors, where the verb erroneously comes to agree with the number of a neighboring noun phrase that is not in fact that verb's controller, as in (27). Pronouns are more vulnerable to the number of their controllers, leading to agreement errors such as (28). This difference suggests that number agreement might involve different processes for pronouns and verbs (Eberhard, Cutting, & Bock, 2005). Verbs are particularly controlled by the grammatical number—a syntactic process, while pronouns are controlled by what is called notional number—the speaker's initial, fleeting perspective on the number of things involved, and which involves lexical processes (e.g., our first impression of the word "fleet" is that it is plural). Eberhard et al. provide a detailed model of marking and morphing in number agreement that accounts for a wide range of data.

(27) The time to find the scissors are now.
(28) The key to the cabinets disappeared. They were never found again.

Is syntactic planning incremental?

Word exchange speech errors suggest that the broad syntactic content is sketched out in clause-sized chunks. This idea is supported by picture–word interference studies that suggest that before we start uttering phrases and short sentences containing two names, we select the nouns (technically, we select the lemma—see later) and the sound form of the first noun. Meyer (1996) presented participants with pictures of pairs of objects that they then had to name ("the arrow and the bag"), or place in short sentences ("the arrow is next to the bag"). At the same time, the participants heard an auditory distractor that could be related in meaning or sound to the first or second noun, or to both. She found that the time it took participants to initiate speaking was longer when the distractor was semantically related to either the first or the second noun, but the phonological distractor only had an effect (by facilitating initiation) when it was related to the first noun. This pattern of results suggests that we prepare the meaning of short phrases and select the appropriate words before we start speaking, but only retrieve the sound of the first word. (This finding is also evidence that lexical access takes place in speech production in two stages; see later.)

Schriefers, Teruel, and Meinshausen (1998) used a picture–word interference technique to show that the detailed selection of a verb is not an obligatory component of advance planning—even

though the verb clearly must play a central role in syntactic planning. They showed that semantic interference between the verb and a distractor was only obtained for verbs at the very beginning of German sentences. Therefore, in sentence-final positions it could not have been retrieved by the time the participants started speaking.

Smith and Wheeldon (1999) had participants describe moving pictures. They found longer onset latencies for single clause sentences beginning with a complex noun phrase (e.g., "the dog and the kite move above the house") than for similar sentences beginning with a simple phrase (e.g., "the dog moves above the kite and the house"). Participants also take longer to initiate double clause sentences (e.g., "the dog and the foot move up and the kite moves down") than single clause sentences. These results suggest that people do not plan the entire syntactic structure of complex sentences in advance. They suggest that when people start speaking they have completed lemma access for the first phrase of an utterance, and started but not completed processing the remainder.

Schnur, Costa, and Caramazza (2006) used a picture–word interference design to examine how far we plan ahead. Participants produced sentences while ignoring words that were phonologically related or unrelated to the verb of the sentence. Schnur et al. found that the time to begin producing the sentence was faster in the presence of the phonologically related distractor, even if the sentence the speaker was producing was relatively long. These results suggest that phonological planning extends some way ahead, and can in some circumstances (if the verb is primed) cross phrase boundaries.

On the other hand, there is a great deal of evidence that suggests that syntactic planning is incremental—that is, we make it up as we go along. Ferreira (1996) found that speakers find production easier when they have more syntactic options available to continue what they are saying, presumably because they can be flexible and pick the most suitable or available continuation one at any time. If we make up a detailed plan before we start speaking, the number of options shouldn't matter, or might even get in the way, as we choose between them.

Ferreira and Swets (2002) also found evidence for incremental planning. They had speakers answer arithmetic sums of differing difficulty in different sorts of syntactic construction (e.g., complete "the answer to 49 plus 73 is . . ."). When speakers were encouraged to speak and plan simultaneously—that is, incrementally—by trying to beat a deadline, both latency to begin speaking and utterance duration were affected by the difficulty of the problem. The more difficult the problem, the longer people took to produce the sentence, suggesting that they did not know the answer—and therefore what they were going to say—before they started speaking.

Why the discrepancy in results? One explanation is that evidence of detailed advance planning comes from the study of either phrases or very short, simple sentences. Perhaps these are dealt with differently from more complex constructions. Another explanation is that the verb in the experiments suggesting that there is considerable advance planning is a simple linking verb ("is"). Or perhaps the demands of the task affect how much participants plan in detail before they start speaking. Speech production probably involves both preparation and planning ahead and incremental planning; which wins the day depends on the particular circumstances of the utterance.

How does this incremental planning relate to semantic and syntactic processing? Solomon and Pearlmutter (2004) contrast two approaches to planning production and coordinating multiple phrases, serial and parallel. They argue that serial systems must rely on memory to shift representations in and out of memory. Memory-shifting should be easier for phrases where the constituents are tightly integrated, with the consequence that there should be fewer errors in such phrases. Parallel systems rely on the parallel activation of multiple representations simultaneously maintained in memory. Parallel activation means that more integrated phrases will be processed together and will be active simultaneously, leading to interference, with the consequence that there should be more errors in tightly integrated phrases. Solomon and Pearlmutter used a sentence-completion task comparing sentences such as "The drawing of the flower" (where the two nouns are tightly integrated) with sentences such as "The drawing with the flower" (where the two nouns are less closely integrated semantically). More errors were made in the completions in the "of" condition, where the components were tightly integrated, supporting the parallel model. Hence when we speak we maintain multiple components of the sentence in memory; we plan and speak simultaneously; and we make it up as we go along, rather than planning one chunk at a time and only producing it when planning is complete.

Producing morphologically complex words

You will remember from Chapter 2 that words can be morphologically modified in two ways: We can derive new words from existing ones (e.g., forming "entertainment" from "entertain"), and we can inflect words to change noun number or verb tense (e.g., "mouse/mice," "run/ran"). The new part of the word (e.g., "-ment") is called an affix. Speech errors cast some light on how affixes are represented in speech production. We find errors where stems of lexical items can become separated from their affixes (e.g., the morpheme stranding errors discussed earlier). Affixes are also sometimes added incorrectly, anticipated, or deleted. Indeed, Garrett's speech production model rests on a dissociation between content words and grammatical elements that are accessed at different times. The neuropsychological evidence from affix loss in Broca's-type disorders, and affix addition to neologisms in jargon aphasia (described later), also suggests that affixes are added to stems. But how?

You will remember that while most inflections are regular (we form the plural by adding "s" to the end of the noun, and the past tense by adding -ed to the verb), some (usually common) words are formed in an irregular way (e.g., mice, sheep, ran, did). How do we produce these irregular forms? One plausible model is that we know a rule for producing the regular versions, and learn by rote a list of exceptions for dealing with the irregular ones, stored in our lexicon. Evidence for this dual-mechanism model comes from the observation that while we are happy to form English compound nouns with either singular or plural irregular modifying nouns (both "mouse-eating" and "mice-eating" sound acceptable to us), we only form compound nouns with singular regular nouns (hence "a rat-eating man" sounds acceptable, but "a rats-eating man" does not). It seems that inflected forms generated by a rule cannot be used as a modifier in a compound noun. How do we come to know what is acceptable and what is not? One possibility is that the child has some innate knowledge of grammar (Pinker, 1999).

There is also neuropsychological evidence for a dual-mechanism model. Ullman et al. (1997) reported a double dissociation between performance on sentence completion and reading on words with regular and irregular past tenses. Patients with what is called fluent aphasia (described in more detail below, but arising from damage to the rear of the left hemisphere) were better at producing the past tense of regular verbs, whereas patients with non-fluent aphasia (arising from damage to the more frontal regions of the left hemisphere) were better at producing irregular past tenses. One explanation for this result is that we make use of a rule-based mechanism for generating regular forms, and this mechanism is located in the front of the left hemisphere (and left intact in fluent aphasia), and a lexicon for storing irregular verbs, located in more posterior regions (and left intact in non-fluent aphasia).

There is an alternative explanation for this double dissociation, which is that regular and irregular verbs are processed by the same system, but the processing of regular verbs depends more on phonological information, while the processing of irregular verbs depends more on semantics (McClelland & Patterson, 2002). Regular past verbs tend to be more phonologically complicated and less distinct than irregular ones—they tend to be longer, for example, and sound and look more like their associated stems. When we control for phonological complexity, the relative disadvantage shown by non-fluent aphasic patients on regular past tenses disappears (Bird, Lambon Ralph, Seidenberg, McClelland, & Patterson, 2003). The access of regular words, because of their greater phonological complexity, is more affected in non-fluent patients (with damage in Broca's area), who have a central phonological deficit (see Chapter 7). These non-fluent patients also showed deficits on other phonological tasks, such as making judgments about whether words rhyme, and segmenting words. On the other hand, damage to the semantic system leads to more difficulty with irregular verbs, where phonology receives support from the semantic system (Joanisse & Seidenberg, 1999). Patient AW is problematic for this account. While having a selective deficit in producing irregular forms of verbs, he performed perfectly on a range of tasks involving semantics (Miozzo, 2003).

Haskell, MacDonald, and Seidenberg (2003) tackled the observations on the acceptability of noun modifiers. One problem for the dual-mechanism account is that there are many exceptions to the central observation (we have "awards ceremony" and "sports announcer"). Why should some exceptions be acceptable? Haskell et al. proposed that acceptability is decided by a multiple-constraint satisfaction process, where semantic, phonological, and other factors come together to decide acceptability. These processes are acquired by children through general-purpose learning algorithms. There is no need, they argued, for two different innately specified mechanisms.

Evaluation of work on syntactic planning

In recent years there has been a notable increase in the amount of research examining syntactic planning. This has largely been due to the evolution of new experimental techniques, particularly syntactic priming, scene description, and sentence completion. Although much remains to be done, we now know a considerable amount about how we translate thoughts into sentences. In particular, it is clear that there is a syntactic module used in production that generates syntactic structures that are, to some extent at least, independent of the meaning of what they convey. It is also clear that there is a probabilistic aspect to production. Syntactic planning is quite inertial, and tends to reuse whatever is easily available.

LEXICALIZATION

Lexicalization is the process in speech production whereby we turn the thoughts underlying words into sounds: We translate a semantic representation (the meaning) of a content word into its phonological representation of form (its sound). There are three main questions to answer here. First, how many steps or stages are involved? Second, what is the time course of the processes involved? Third, are these stages independent, or do they interact with one another?

How many stages are there in lexicalization?

There is widespread agreement that lexicalization is a two-stage process, with the first stage being meaning-based, and the second phonologically based. When we produce a word, we first go from the semantic level to an intermediate level of individual words. Choosing the word is called lexical selection. We then retrieve the phonological forms of these words in a stage of phonological encoding.

Although there is consensus about these two stages, there is disagreement about what happens at the level of lexical representation (Rapp & Goldrick, 2000). All theories assume there is at least one stage of lexical representation in production where there are units that correspond to words, but there is disagreement about the nature and functions of this representation. According to the best known lemma theory (e.g., Levelt, 1989), each word is represented by a **lemma**. Lemmas are specified syntactically and semantically but not phonologically. The stage of specifying in a pre-phonological, abstract way the word that we are just about to say is called lemma selection; the second stage of specifying the actual concrete phonological form of the word is called **lexeme** or phonological form selection (see Figure 13.3). Hence in the lemma account there are two layers of lexical representation. Lemmas are amodal— that is, the level of representation mediating semantics and phonology takes no account of modality. A consequence of their syntactic specification is that access to lexical syntax must occur before access to the phonological form.

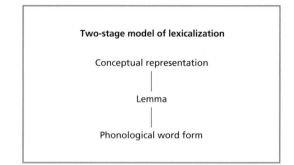

Two-stage model of lexicalization

Conceptual representation

|

Lemma

|

Phonological word form

FIGURE 13.3

While there is a great deal of evidence supporting the general two-stage hypothesis, the evidence for the existence of lemmas is more debatable.

Evidence from speech errors

Fay and Cutler (1977) presented one of the earliest models of how we produce words and why we make word substitutions. They observed that there were two distinct types of whole word substitution speech error: semantic substitutions, such as examples (29) and (30), and form-based substitutions, such as examples (31) and (32). Form-based word substitutions are sometimes called phonologically related word substitution errors or **malapropisms**. (The word "malapropism" originally came from a character called Mrs. Malaprop in Sheridan's play *The Rivals*, who was always using words incorrectly, such as saying "reprehend" for "apprehend" and "epitaphs" for "epithets." Note that while Mrs. Malaprop produced these substitutions out of ignorance, the term is used slightly confusingly in psycholinguistics to refer to errors where the speaker knows perfectly well what the target should be.)

(29) fingers → toes
(30) husband → wife
(31) equivalent → equivocal
(32) historical → hysterical

Fay and Cutler argued that the occurrence of these two types of word substitution suggests that the processes of word production and comprehension use the same lexicon, but in opposite directions. Items in the lexicon are arranged phonologically for recognition, so that words that sound similar are close together. The lexicon is accessed in production by traversing a semantic network or decision tree (see Figure 13.4). Semantic errors occur when traversing the decision tree, and phonological errors occur when the final phonological form is selected. As we shall see in Chapter 15, the argument that there is a single lexicon for comprehension and production is very controversial. If this is not the case, then some other mechanism will be necessary to account for the existence of malapropisms. The important idea of Fay and Cutler's model is that phonological and semantic word substitutions happen as a result of mistakes in different parts of the word retrieval process.

Butterworth (1982) formulated word retrieval explicitly in terms of a two-stage process. In Butterworth's model an entry in a semantic lexicon is first selected, which gives a pointer to an entry in a separate phonological lexicon. In general, in the two-stage model semantic and phonological substitutions occur at different levels. The Fay and Cutler (1977) model predicts that semantic and phonological processes should be independent.

Word substitution errors, while supporting the two-stage model in general, say nothing about the existence of amodal, syntactically specified lemmas.

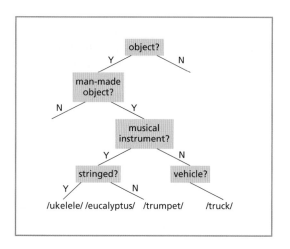

FIGURE 13.4 An example of a search-based single lexicon model. Based on Fay and Cutler (1977).

Experimental evidence

The earliest experimental evidence for the division of lexical access into two stages came from studies of the description of simple scenes (Kempen & Huijbers, 1983). They analyzed the time people take before they start speaking when describing these scenes, and argued that people do not start speaking until the content to be expressed has been fully identified. The selection of several lemmas for a multiword sentence can take place simultaneously. We cannot produce the first word of an utterance until we have accessed all the lemmas (at least for these short utterances) and at least the first phonological word form. Individual word difficulty affects only word form retrieval times.

Further experimental evidence for two stages in lexicalization comes from Wheeldon and Monsell's (1992) investigation of repetition priming in lexicalization. Like repetition priming in visual word recognition, this effect lasts a long time, spanning over 100 intervening naming trials. Wheeldon and Monsell showed that naming a picture is facilitated by recently having produced the name in giving a definition or reading aloud. Prior production of a homophone (e.g., "weight" for "wait") is not an effective prime, so the source of the facilitation cannot be phonologically mediated. Instead, it must be semantic or lemma-based. Evidence from speeded picture naming suggests that repetition priming arises from residual activation in the connections between semantics and lemmas (Vitkovitch & Humphreys, 1991).

Monsell, Matthews, and Miller (1992) looked at this effect in Welsh–English bilinguals. There was facilitation within a language, but not across (as long as the phonological forms of the words differed). Taken together the experiments show that both the meaning and the phonological forms have to be activated for repetition priming in production to occur. Repetition priming occurs as a result of the strengthening of the connections between the lemmas and phonological forms.

Evidence for a phase of early semantic activation in lexical selection and a later phase of phonological activation in phonological encoding comes from picture–word interference studies (Levelt et al., 1991a; Schriefers, Meyer, & Levelt, 1990). These experiments, discussed in more detail later in the section on the time course of lexicalization, used a picture–word interference paradigm in which participants see pictures that they have to name as quickly as possible. At about the same time they are given an auditorily presented word for which they have to make a lexical decision. Words prime semantic neighbors early on, whereas late on they prime phonological neighbors. This suggests that there is an early stage when semantic candidates are active (this is the lemma stage), and a late stage when phonological forms are active.

The semantic-interference paradigm provides evidence for two stages, and furthermore, that the lexical items activated by the first stage compete against each other (Starreveld & La Heij, 1995, 1996). In semantic-interference studies, participants have to name pictures which have superimposed distractor words that they have to ignore; naming times are longer when the picture and the word are related. The distractors lead to the activation of semantic competitors that slow down the selection of the lexical target. In the related word translation task, semantically related words induce semantic interference; however, related pictures produce facilitation (Bloem & La Heij, 2003). The SOA is, however, critical; if the interfering words are presented 200 ms after the target, we observe semantic interference, but if they are presented 400 ms before the target, we observe semantic facilitation (Bloem, van den Boogaard, & La Heij, 2004). Bloem and La Heij proposed a model of lexical access in which semantic facilitation is localized at the conceptual level, semantic interference is localized at the lexical level, and only one concept is selected for lexicalization. They called this the Conceptual Selection Model (CSM). They account for the effects of SOA with the assumption that lexical representations decay faster than conceptual representations.

Whether or not we observe facilitation or inhibition in the picture–word interference paradigm depends on the details of the experimental set-up. In the most famous example of picture–word interference, the Stroop task (naming the color in which a word is printed when the word spells out a color name), there is striking inhibition. Usually we find interference with semantically related pairs from the same category, and facilitation with phonologically related pairs. Schriefers et al. (1990) found that inhibition disappears if participants have to press buttons instead of naming pictures, suggesting that the interference reflects competition among lexical items at the stage of lemma selection. The details of the task and the timings involved are also critical (Bloem & La Heij, 2003; Bloem et al., 2004).

Evidence from neuroscience

Different regions of the brain become activated in sequence as we produce words (Indefrey & Levelt, 2000, 2004). Conceptual selection of a word in picture naming is associated with activation of the mid-part of the left middle temporal gyrus; accessing a word's phonological code is associated with activation of Wernicke's area; and phonological encoding, in terms of the preparation of syllables, sounds, and the prosody of the word, is associated with activation around Broca's area. As we shall see, lesions to these areas lead to different types of impairment to word naming, with damage to more posterior regions of the brain resulting in difficulty in accessing the meanings of words, and damage to more frontal regions resulting in difficulty in accessing the sounds of words. A survey of the imaging literature also reveals the timings of word retrieval in naming an object (Indefrey & Levelt, 2004): Visual and conceptual processing take on average 175 ms; the best-fitting lexical item, or lemma, is retrieved between 150 and 225 ms; the phonological representations are retrieved between 250 and 330 ms; and the details of the sounds of the word at around 450 ms (see Figure 13.5).

Electrophysiological evidence also supports the two-stage model (van Turenout, Hagoort, & Brown, 1998). Dutch-speaking participants were shown colored pictures and had to name them with a simple noun phrase (e.g., "red table"). At the same time the participants had to push buttons depending on the grammatical gender of the noun, and

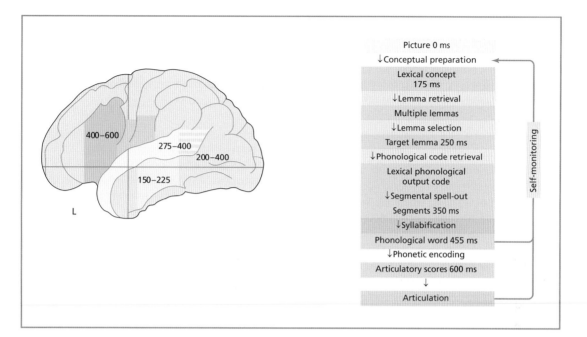

Picture 0 ms
↓ Conceptual preparation
Lexical concept
175 ms
↓ Lemma retrieval
Multiple lemmas
↓ Lemma selection
Target lemma 250 ms
↓ Phonological code retrieval
Lexical phonological
output code
↓ Segmental spell-out
Segments 350 ms
↓ Syllabification
Phonological word 455 ms
↓ Phonetic encoding
Articulatory scores 600 ms
↓
Articulation

Self-monitoring

400–600
275–400
200–400
150–225
L

FIGURE 13.5 Time taken (in ms) for different processes to occur in picture naming. The specific processes are shown on the right and the relevant brain regions are shown on the left. Reprinted from Indefrey and Levelt (2004).

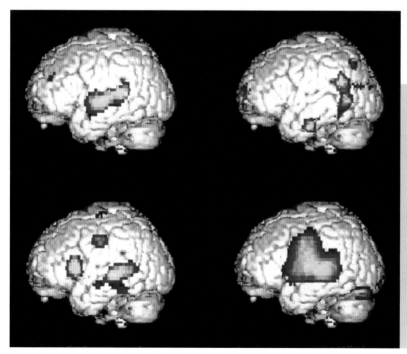

PET scans of human brain areas which are active while speaking and listening. Top left—monitoring imagined speech lights up the auditory cortex. Top right—working out the meaning of heard words activates other areas of the temporal lobe. Bottom left—repeating words activates Wernicke's area for language comprehension (right), Broca's area for speech generation (left), and a motor region producing speech. Bottom right—monitoring speech activates the auditory cortex.

on whether or not it began with a particular sound. The electrophysiological data for the preparation of the motor movements suggested that the syntactic properties were accessed before the phonological information. However, the time delay between the two was very short—in the order of 40 ms.

Evidence from the tip-of-the-tongue phenomenon

The **tip-of-the-tongue (TOT)** state is a noticeable temporary difficulty in lexical access. It is an extreme form of a pause, where the word takes a noticeable time to come out (sometimes several weeks!). You are almost certainly familiar with this phenomenon: You know that you know what the word is, yet you are unable to get the sounds out. TOTs are accompanied by strong "feelings of knowing" what the word is. They appear to be universal; they have even been observed in children as young as 2 (Elbers, 1985). The incidence of TOTs increases with old age (Burke, MacKay, Worthley, & Wade, 1991), and TOTS are more common in bilingual speakers (Gollan & Acenas, 2004; Gollan & Brown, 2006). They appear to be universal; deaf speakers experience "tip-of-the-finger" states (Thompson, Emmorey, & Gollan, 2005).

Brown and McNeill (1966) were the first to examine the TOT state experimentally. They induced TOTs in participants by reading them definitions of low-frequency words, such as (33):

The tip-of-the-tongue (TOT) state is an extreme form of a pause, where the word takes a noticeable time to come out.

(33) "A navigational instrument used in measuring angular distances, especially the altitude of the sun, moon, and stars at sea."

Stop and try to name the item defined by (33). You may experience a TOT.

Example (33) defines the word "sextant." Brown and McNeill found that a proportion of the participants will be placed in a TOT state by this task. Furthermore, they found that lexical retrieval is not an all-or-none affair. Partial information, such as the number of syllables, the initial letter or sound, and the stress pattern, can be retrieved. Participants also often output near phonological neighbors like "secant," "sextet," and "sexton." These other words that come to mind are called interlopers. TOTs show us that we can be aware of the meaning of a word without being aware of its component sounds; and furthermore, that phonological representations are not unitary entities.

There are two theories of the origin of TOTs. These are called the partial activation and blocking (or interference) hypotheses. Brown (1970) first proposed the partial activation hypothesis. This says that the target items are inaccessible because they are only weakly represented in the system. Burke et al. (1991) provided evidence in favor of this model from both an experimental and a diary study involving a group of young and old participants. They argued that the retrieval deficit involves weak links between the semantic and the phonological systems: there is a transmission deficit in getting between the two. A broadly similar approach by Harley and MacAndrew (1992) localized the deficit within a two-stage model of lexical access, between the abstract lexical units and the phonological forms. At first sight Kohn et al. (1987) provided evidence contrary to the partial activation hypothesis in the form of a free association task. They showed that the partial information provided by participants does not in time narrow or converge on the target. However, A. S. Brown (1991) pointed out that participants might not say out loud the interlopers in the order in which they came to mind. Furthermore, in a noisy system there is no reason why each attempt at retrieval should give the same incorrect answer.

The blocking hypothesis, first suggested by Woodworth (1938), states that the target item is actively suppressed by a stronger competitor. Jones and Langford (1987) used a variant of the Brown and McNeill task known as phonological blocking to test this idea. They presented a phonological neighbor of the target word and showed that this increases the chance of a TOT state occurring, whereas presenting a semantic neighbor does not. They interpreted this as showing that TOTs primarily arise as a result of competition. Jones (1989) further showed that the blocker is only effective if it is presented at the time of retrieval rather than just before. However, Perfect and Hanley (1992) and Meyer and Bock (1992) discussed methodological problems with these experiments. Exactly the same results are found with these materials when the blockers are not presented, suggesting that the original results were an artifact of the materials. In fact, prior processing of phonologically related words actually decreases the chance of being in a tip-of-the-tongue state, and increases the probability of retrieving the target word (James & Burke, 2000), a finding consistent with the insufficient activation hypothesis—TOTs arise because there is a deficit in transmitting activation from the semantic to the phonological level. The finding that bilingual speakers are more prone to TOTs is also best explained by the insufficient activation idea—presumably the semantic–phonological links are weaker in bilingual speakers because they speak each language only some of the time (Gollan & Acenas, 2004).

Harley and Bown (1998) showed that TOTs are more likely to arise on low-frequency words that have few close phonological neighbors. For example, the words "ball" and "growth" are approximately equal in their frequency of occurrence. There are a lot of other words that sound like "ball" (e.g., "call," "fall," "bore"), but few that are close to "growth." These data fit a partial activation model of the origin of TOTs rather than an interference model. Indeed, phonological neighbors appear to play a supporting rather than a blocking role in lexical access.

Additional evidence for this claim comes from the finding that pictures with names in sparse phonological neighborhoods are named more slowly than words with dense neighborhoods where there are many similar sounding words (Vitevitch, 2002).

The TOT data best support the partial activation hypothesis. They also suggest that the levels of semantic and phonological processing in lexical retrieval are distinct. The tip-of-the-tongue state is readily explained as success of the first stage of lexicalization but failure of the second. There is some evidence that supports this idea. Vigliocco, Antonini, and Garrett (1997) showed that grammatical gender can be preserved in tip-of-the-tongue states in Italian. That is, even though speakers cannot retrieve the phonological form of a word, they can retrieve some syntactic information about it.

There is also evidence from preservation of gender in an Italian person, called Dante, who suffered from word-finding difficulties or anomia (Badecker, Miozzo, & Zanuttini, 1995). Dante could give details about the grammatical gender of words that he could not produce. Information about grammatical gender is part of the lexical-semantic and syntactic information encoded by lemmas, such as knowing that a word is a noun. Hence Dante had access to the lemmas, but was then unable to access the associated phonological forms. It is important to note that for many Italian words grammatical gender is not predictable from semantics. Furthermore, Dante could retrieve the gender for both regular and exception words, which suggests that Dante could not just have used partial phonological information to predict grammatical gender. However, while Dante's performance is entirely compatible with the two-stage account, it is also compatible with an account where such information is stored elsewhere. Gender can be put with other syntactic information in the lexicon, such that it is stored with words. In that case, how could gender be preferentially lost? We have a choice of only three genders, but of many more phonological forms. It is possible that in an interactive activation network we would be able to retrieve the correct gender without the network being able to settle down enough to select the appropriate one of many phonological forms.

Further evidence that TOTs are associated with a difficulty in retrieving the phonological forms of words comes from brain imaging. Shafto, Burke, Stamatakis, Tam, and Tyler (2007) had people aged 19–88 name pictures of famous people. The number of TOTs increased with age and with atrophy of the left insula, a region of the brain known to be involved (among other things) in phonological production.

Problems with the lemma model

Although most researchers favor the two-stage model of lexicalization, there is less agreement on the need for lemmas as a level of amodal, syntactically specified representations mediating between concepts and phonological forms (Caramazza, 1997; Caramazza & Miozzo, 1997, 1998; Miozzo & Caramazza, 1997).

One point is that it is not clear that the need for lemmas is strongly motivated by the data. Most of the evidence really only demands a distinction between the semantic and the phonological levels. The strongest evidence for lemmas comes from the finding that gender can be retrieved when in the tip-of-the-tongue state, although this interpretation has been disputed. It should not be possible to retrieve phonological information for a word without retrieving the syntactic information for that word such as gender, as the phonological stage can only be reached through the lemma stage. Tip-of-the-tongue data suggest, however, that syntactic

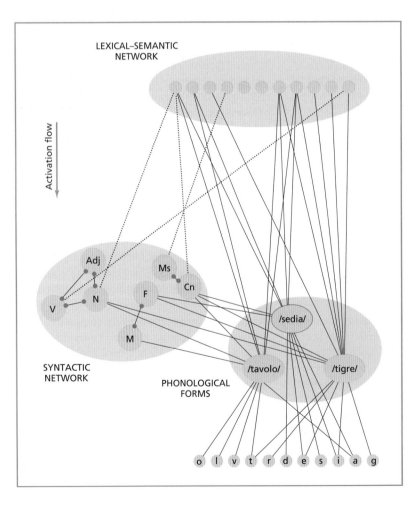

FIGURE 13.6 A detailed representation of Caramazza's (1997) model. The flow of information is from semantic to lexeme and syntactic networks and then on to segmental information. N = noun; V = verb; Adj = adjective; M = masculine; F = feminine; Cn = count noun; Ms = mass noun. Dotted lines indicate weak activation. Links within a network are inhibitory. Reproduced with permission from Caramazza (1997).

and phonological information are independent (Caramazza & Miozzo, 1997, 1998; Miozzo & Caramazza, 1997): Italian speakers can sometimes retrieve partial phonological information when they cannot retrieve the gender of the word, and vice versa. Importantly, there was no correlation between the retrieval of gender and phonological information; people are no better at recalling gender when they correctly recall the initial phoneme of the target in a TOT state than when they fail to do so. Hence, phonological retrieval does not necessarily depend on syntactic retrieval, and therefore these results do not support the idea of syntactic mediation. Arguing that lemmas are unnecessary complications, Caramazza (1997) dispenses with them. He proposes that lexical access in production involves the interaction of a semantic network, a syntactic network, and phonological forms (see Figure 13.6). Semantic representations activate both appropriate nodes in the syntactic network and the phonological network.

If lemmas exist, given they are amodal and are syntactically specified, then grammatical impairments involving words should not be modality-specific. However, we find patients who are selectively impaired in producing words of one grammatical class in only one output modality (Caramazza, 1997; Caramazza & Miozzo, 1998). For example, patient SJD has difficulty in producing verbs in writing but not in speaking; she can produce nouns equally well in writing and speaking (Caramazza & Hillis, 1991). Although her errors include semantic substitutions, SJD does not have a central semantic impairment because she has no difficulty with comprehending these words, and because her difficulties are restricted to one output modality. It is difficult to account for this pattern of results with the lemma model (but see Roelofs, Meyer, & Levelt, 1998, for an attempt).

Another way of distinguishing between the two accounts is to examine how we produce homophones. Consider the words "none" and "nun." According to the lemma model, these two words have shared lexeme representations but separate lemma representations. The alternative is that they just have two distinct lexeme representations. If homophones share

a representation, the frequency of the lexeme representation will be the sum of the two homophones. Hence a less frequent word like "nun" will behave like a more frequent word, assuming that frequency operates at the lexeme level. Some studies find that frequency effects appear to reflect total-homophone frequency rather than word-specific frequency (Levelt, Roelofs, & Meyer, 1999). For example, Jescheniak and Levelt (1994) found that the translation speeds of a word like "nun" by Dutch–English bilinguals depended on total-homophone frequency (the rather large "none" plus "nun") rather than word-specific frequency (the rather low frequency of just "nun") compared with control words. In contrast Caramazza, Costa, Miozzo, and Bi (2001) found that naming latencies in a range of experimental tasks were determined just by word-specific frequency (i.e., "nun" behaves like a low-frequency word rather than a high-frequency word).

Clearly there is conflict in the data here, and it is unclear how this conflict is best resolved (Bonin & Fayol, 2002; Caramazza, Bi, Costa, & Miozzo, 2004; Jescheniak, Meyer, & Levelt, 2003). Whether we find word-specific or total-homophone frequency effects depends on the number and type of materials, the controls used, and where frequency effects operate. There is now, for example, a considerable amount of evidence that frequency affects lexical selection (the retrieval of lemmas), rather than just the retrieval of phonological forms. For example, Navarrete, Basagni, Alario, and Costa (2006) found effects of frequency (in the form of faster response times for high-frequency items) on tasks in Spanish that require the retrieval of gender but not phonological properties. For example, they found frequency effects in a gender decision task, and in a task where participants had to describe pictures using pronouns rather than the name of the object.

Perhaps the best conclusion is that no firm conclusion can be drawn from these translation tasks, although picture-naming data suggest that specific-word frequency best predicts naming times (Caramazza et al., 2004). So in spite of initial optimism, homophone production does not provide clear evidence for the two-stage model.

In summary, although there is some dissent about the nature of the two stages, and the extent to which there are amodal, syntactically specified lemmas, there is consensus that lexical retrieval takes place in two stages, with a semantic-lexical stage followed by a lexical-phonological stage.

Is lexicalization interactive?

Given that there are two stages involved in lexicalization, how do they relate to each other? Interaction involves the influence of one level of processing on the operation of another. It comprises two ideas. First, there is the notion of temporal discreteness. Are the processing stages temporally discrete or do they overlap, as they would if information or activation is allowed to cascade from one level to the following one before it has completed its processing? The case when processing levels overlap, in that one level can pass on information to the next before it has completed its processing, is known as processing in cascade (McClelland, 1979). If the stages overlap, then multiple candidates will be activated at the second stage. For example, many lemmas will become partially activated while activation is accruing at the target. Activation will then cascade down to the phonological level. The result is that on the overlap hypothesis we get leakage between levels so that non-target lemmas become phonologically activated. We can examine this by looking at the time course of lexicalization. Second, there is the notion of the reverse flow of information. In this case, information from a lower level feeds back to the prior level. For example, phonological activation might feed back from the phonological forms to the lemmas. Overlap and reverse flow of information are logically distinct aspects of interaction. We could have overlap without reverse flow (but reverse flow without overlap would not make much sense).

The time course of lexicalization: Discrete or cascaded processing?

How do the two stages of lexicalization relate to one another in time? Are they independent, or do they overlap? That is, does the second stage of phonological specification only begin when the first stage of lemma retrieval is complete, or does it begin while the first stage is still going on? The speech error evidence of the existence of mixed whole word substitutions indicates overlap or interaction between the two stages. To make the distinction between independent and overlapping models concrete, suppose that you want to say the word "sheep." According to the two-stage hypothesis, you formulate the semantic representation underlying sheep, and use this to activate a number of competing abstract lexical items. Obviously in the first instance these will all be semantic relatives (like "sheep," "goat," "cow," etc.). The independence issue is this: Before you start choosing the phonological form of the target word, how many of these competing units are left? According to the independence (modular) theory, only one item is left active before we start accessing phonological forms. This is of course the target word, "sheep." According to the interactive theory, any number of them might be. So according to the interactive theory, when you intend to say "sheep," you might also be thinking of the phonological form /gout/, and this will in turn have an effect on the selection of "sheep." Another way of putting this is that according to the discrete models, the semantic-lexical and lexical-phonological stages cannot overlap, but according to the interactive model, they can. The issues involved are exactly the same as those discussed in word recognition.

Levelt et al. (1991a) performed an elegant experiment to test between these two hypotheses. They looked for what is called a mediated priming effect: When you say "sheep," it facilitates the recognition of the word "goat" (which obviously is a semantic relative of "sheep"); but does "goat" then go on to facilitate in turn one of its phonological neighbors, such as "goal"? Levelt et al. argue that the interactive model suggests that this mediated priming effect should occur, whereas the independence model states that it should not. The participants' task was this: They were shown simple pictures of objects (such as a sheep) and had to name these objects as quickly as possible. This typically takes most people approximately 500 to 800 ms to do. When we see a picture or an object, we typically spend the first 150 ms doing visual processing and activating the appropriate concept. We then spend another 125 ms or so selecting the lemma. Phonological

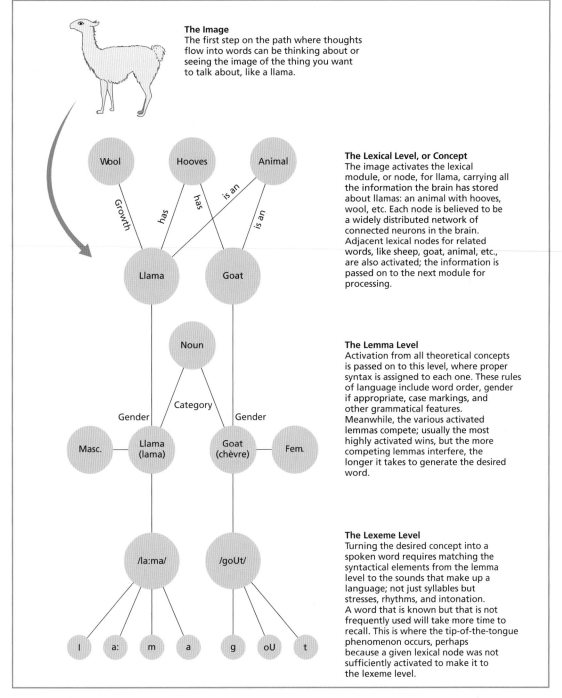

The Image
The first step on the path where thoughts flow into words can be thinking about or seeing the image of the thing you want to talk about, like a llama.

The Lexical Level, or Concept
The image activates the lexical module, or node, for llama, carrying all the information the brain has stored about llamas: an animal with hooves, wool, etc. Each node is believed to be a widely distributed network of connected neurons in the brain. Adjacent lexical nodes for related words, like sheep, goat, animal, etc., are also activated; the information is passed on to the next module for processing.

The Lemma Level
Activation from all theoretical concepts is passed on to this level, where proper syntax is assigned to each one. These rules of language include word order, gender if appropriate, case markings, and other grammatical features. Meanwhile, the various activated lemmas compete; usually the most highly activated wins, but the more competing lemmas interfere, the longer it takes to generate the desired word.

The Lexeme Level
Turning the desired concept into a spoken word requires matching the syntactical elements from the lemma level to the sounds that make up a language; not just syllables but stresses, rhythms, and intonation. A word that is known but that is not frequently used will take more time to recall. This is where the tip-of-the-tongue phenomenon occurs, perhaps because a given lexical node was not sufficiently activated to make it to the lexeme level.

FIGURE 13.7 Processes involved in naming an object in a picture, according to the two-stage model of lexicalization. From Levelt et al. (1991).

encoding starts around 275 ms and we usually start uttering the name from 600 ms.

In the interval between presentation and naming, subjects were given a word in an acoustic form through headphones (e.g., "goal"). The participants had to press a button as soon as they decided whether this second item was a word or not. That is, it was an auditory lexical decision task. There were two critical results. First, Levelt et al. found that "sheep" did not facilitate "goal": "sheep" affected the subsequent processing of "goat," but not of "goal." That is, there was no mediated priming. Hence they argued that no interaction occurred. Second, in a separate experiment, they showed that "sheep" only affects the access of semantic neighbors (e.g., "goat") early on, whereas late on it only affects the access of phonological neighbors (e.g., "sheet"). That is, there was no late semantic priming. The priming effects were inhibitory: that is, related items slowed down processing through interference. Levelt et al. concluded that, in picture naming and lexicalization, there is an early stage when semantic candidates are active (this is the lemma selection stage), and a late stage when phonological forms are active (see Figure 13.7). Furthermore, these two stages are temporally discrete and do not overlap or interact.

Dell and O'Seaghdha (1991) showed with simulations that a model that incorporated local interaction (between adjacent stages) could appear to be globally modular. This is because, in these types of model, different types of information need not spread very far (but see Levelt et al., 1991b). Only very weak mediated priming would be predicted here—insufficient to be detected by this task. Harley (1993a) showed that a model based on interactive activation could indeed produce exactly this time course while permitting interaction between levels.

Levelt et al.'s findings have also been questioned by the results of an experiment by Peterson and Savoy (1998). They did find mediated priming. They showed that "soda" is activated when we retrieve "couch," as the word "couch" primes the word "sofa" through mediated priming. The difference between their experiment and that of Levelt et al. is that

whereas Levelt et al. used categorical associates ("sheep" and "goat"), Peterson and Savoy used near synonyms ("couch" and "sofa"). It is likely that categorical associates are too weakly activated to produce measurable activation of their corresponding phonological forms. Near synonyms, though, are very closely semantically related and therefore highly activated.

Whereas Peterson and Savoy used targets and distractors that had a very strong semantic relation, Cutting and Ferreira (1999) used distractors that had a very strong phonological relation to the target picture. Participants had to name pictures that had homophonic names (e.g., "ball"). Auditory distractor words were presented 150 ms before the picture onset. Homophones have the strongest phonological relation possible, because by definition the sound of the two meanings (round toy and formal dance) is identical. If the discrete stage model is correct, at such an early SOA only an appropriate-meaning semantic distractor (e.g., "game") should have an effect. But if the cascade model is correct, then the phonological form of the inappropriate-meaning distractor (e.g., "dance") should also have an effect. The results supported the cascade model. The appropriate-meaning distractor produced inhibition relative to an unrelated control ("hammer"), but the inappropriate-meaning distractor produced significant facilitation. The phonologically related distractor affects picture naming at the same early stage as a semantically related distractor. Similarly, Morsella and Miozzo (2002) presented participants with two superimposed pictures, and asked them to name one but ignore the other. They found that naming was faster when the two pictures were phonologically related (e.g., a picture of a bed and a bell, compared with a bed and a pin). This finding again suggests that activation from the unselected lexical node still trickles down to the phonological level.

Further support for cascade models of lexicalization comes from a study by Griffin and Bock (1998). They examined how long it took participants to name pictures embedded in sentences. They varied the degree of constraint of the sentences and the frequency of the picture names. For example, (34) highly constrains the following target picture name, whereas (35) produces very little constraint.

(34) Boris taught his son to drive a –
(35) Boris drew his son a picture of a –

Griffin and Bock found that the effects of constraint and frequency interacted in determining naming times. High-constraint sentences show reduced frequency effects compared with low-constraint sentences. In discrete stage models there is no means for the constraint present in the lemma selection stage to influence the effect of word frequency in the separate and subsequent stage of phonological encoding. However, this finding is exactly what cascade models predict.

Data from bilingual speakers also support the cascade model. Costa, Caramazza, and Sebastian-Galles (2000) examined the naming times of pictures whose names are cognates in Catalan and Spanish (words that sound and look similar in both language—e.g., "gat" in Catalan and "gato" in Spanish, both meaning "cat"). For bilingual speakers, if activation does indeed cascade from unselected lexical nodes, then the activation levels of the phonemes /g/ /a/ /t/ should be very high because they are receiving activation from two lexical nodes—the selected Spanish target word and the non-selected Catalan node. Costa et al. indeed found that the naming times for cognate words was shorter in bilingual speakers (but not for monolingual speakers).

In summary, these experiments show that word selection precedes phonological encoding. There is much evidence that the two stages of lexicalization overlap, and little unambiguous evidence against this idea. They found that naming times were shorter for cognate words in bilingual (but not monolingual) speakers. Only the cascaded-processing model clearly predicts this result. In the cascade model, activation cascades down from non-selected lexical nodes (the cognates) to their phonological segments, as well as from the target nodes. The result of this additional activation of the phonological segments is to speed up naming.

Is there feedback in lexicalization?

Is there reverse information flow when we choose words? Models based primarily on speech error data see speech production as primarily an interactive process involving feedback, mainly because speech errors show evidence of multiple constraints such as a lexical bias and similarity effects (Dell, 1986; Dell & Reich, 1981; Harley, 1984; Stemberger, 1985).

A familiarity bias is the tendency for errors to produce familiar sequences of phonemes. In particular, lexical bias is the tendency for sound-level speech errors such as spoonerisms to result in a word rather than a nonword (e.g., "barn door" being produced as "darn bore") more often than chance would predict. Of course, we would expect some sound errors to form words sometimes by chance, but Dell and Reich showed that word outcomes happen far more often than is expected by chance. This, then, is evidence of an interaction between lexical and phonological processes. This bias has been shown both for naturally occurring speech errors (Dell, 1985, 1986; Dell & Reich, 1981) and in artificially induced spoonerisms (Baars et al., 1975), and in languages other than English (e.g., in Spanish; Hartsuiker, Anton-Méndez, Roelstraete, & Costa, 2006). Some aphasic speakers show clear lexical bias in their errors (Blanken, 1998).

Similarity effects arise when the error is more similar to the target according to some criterion than would be expected by chance. In mixed substitutions the intrusion is both semantically and phonologically related to the target, such as in (36) and (37). Obviously we will find some mixed errors by chance, but we find them far more often than would be expected by chance alone (Dell & Reich, 1981; Harley, 1984; Shallice & McGill, 1978). Obviously we need a formal definition of phonological similarity; here both the target and the intrusion start with the same consonant, and contain the same number of syllables. We also find similar results in artificially induced speech errors (e.g., Baars et al., 1975; Motley & Baars, 1976) and in errors arising in complex naming tasks (Martin, Weisberg, & Saffran, 1989). Laine and Martin (1996) discuss the effect of task training on a severely anomic patient, IL. They found a strong phonological relatedness effect.

(36)   comma → colon
(37)   calendar → catalogue

Similarity effects are problematical for serial models such as Fay and Cutler's. At the very least, then, the basic model must be modified, and this can be done in two ways. Butterworth (1982) proposed that a filter or editor checks the output to see that it is plausible; it is less likely to detect an error if the word output sounds like the target should have been, or is related in meaning. Such a mechanism, although it might be related to comprehension processes, is not parsimonious (see Stemberger, 1983).

Horizontal information flow

We can call the type of information flow while speaking we have discussed so far "vertical information"; we have been concerned with how information flows from the conceptual level to the sound level for individual words. We have seen that the evidence favors a cascade model; words are simultaneously active at multiple levels of information. We have also seen that speech production is an incremental process; we plan as we speak. And we have seen that information about lexical items can affect the syntax of the sentence—for example, we construct sentences such that more accessible items are placed earlier in the sentence.

Given all this, it would not be surprising if words affect other words in the sentence—what is called horizontal information flow. Smith and Wheeldon (2004) used a picture–word interference task to demonstrate that information does indeed flow horizontally as well as vertically in speech production. They used a modified version of the picture–word interference task where participants produced sentences describing a moving scene on a computer screen. For example, they might see a picture of a saw moving above the printed word "axe," and would have to say "The saw moves above the axe." They found that two semantically related nouns produced interference even if they were different phrases of a sentence (as in "the saw moves above the axe"). As we might expect from the differences in scope of word and sound exchange errors, two phonologically

related nouns produced facilitation, but only if they were in the same phrase (as in "the watch and the wand move down"). Rapp and Samuel (2000) asked participants to complete sentence fragments, finding a missing word in a sentence such as (38) or (39):

(38)   The neighbors were shocked to hear Vlad had killed her. He had an argument with his wife and had returned with a –.
(39)   The neighbors were shocked to hear Vlad had killed her. He had an argument with his spouse and had returned with a –.

Participants were much more likely to complete (38) with the word "knife" than (39). The completions reflected both the semantic and phonological prior context. Taken further, horizontal flow enables us to write humorously or lyrically: puns and poetry depend on horizontal flow.

The interactive activation model of lexicalization

There is an emerging consensus among speech production theorists that lexicalization can be described by spreading activation in a model similar to the interactive activation model of context effects in letter identification proposed by McClelland and Rumelhart (1981). Different versions of the same basic model have been described by Dell (1986), Dell and O'Seaghdha (1991), Harley (1993a), and Stemberger (1985). For example, in Harley's model lexicalization proceeds in two stages. The meaning of a word is represented as a set of semantic features (see discussion of the Hinton & Shallice, 1991, and Plaut & Shallice, 1993a, model of deep dyslexia in Chapter 7, and the discussion of semantic representation in Chapter 11). These feed into a level of representation where abstract lexical representations equivalent to the lemmas are stored, and these in turn activate the phonological representations equivalent to lexemes. The basic architecture of the model is shown in Figure 13.8; the rules that govern the behavior of the network are similar to those in the McClelland and Rumelhart model of word recognition and the TRACE model

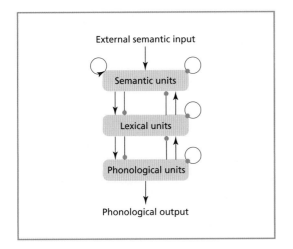

External semantic input

Semantic units

Lexical units

Phonological units

Phonological output

FIGURE 13.8 Architecture of an interactive activation model of lexicalization. Arrows show excitatory connections; filled circles show inhibitory connections. The semantic within-level connections are more complex, with partial connectivity, as indicated by the unfilled circle.

of speech perception. As we have just noted, computer simulations based on this model can also explain the picture-naming data of Levelt et al. (1991a).

Dell's (1986) interactive model of speech production

Dell (1986) proposed an interactive model of lexicalization based on the mechanism of spreading activation. Items are slotted into frames at each level of processing. Processing units specify the syntactic, morphological, and phonological properties of words. Activation spreads down from the sentence level, where items are coded for syntactic properties, through a morphological level, to a phonological level. At each level, the most highly activated item is inserted into the currently active slot in the frame. For example, the sentence frame might be quantifier–noun–verb. The morphological frame might be stem plus affix. The phonological frame might be onset–nucleus–coda. The final output is a series of phonemes coded for position (e.g., /s/ in word-onset position). The flow of activation throughout the network is time-dependent, so that the first noun in a sentence is activated before the second noun.

The model (see Figure 13.9) gives a good account of speech errors. Several units may be active at each level of representation at any one time. If there is sufficient random noise an item might be substituted for another one. As items are coded for syntactic category and position in a word, the other units that are active at any one time tend to be similar to the target in these respects. There is feedback between levels. The feedback between the phonological and lexical levels gives rise to lexical bias and similarity constraints.

A related issue that has recently arisen is the degree to which there is competition within a level between similar units. Recall that in the IAC model of letter recognition there are within-level inhibitory links leading to competition between similar units. The key issue therefore is whether the time to produce a word is affected by the activation of similar words. This issue is currently unresolved, with some researchers arguing for competition, others against it, while yet others claim that the data can be accounted for by an internal monitor checking planned productions against internal goals (Dhooge & Hartsuiker, 2012; Melinger & Rahman, 2013).

Evaluation of work on lexicalization

There is consensus (although by no means universal) that lexicalization in speech production occurs in two stages. There is certainly plenty of evidence that information cascades between levels. Strict serial models can only account for the data by introducing additional assumptions (e.g., a non-serial component of the comprehension process interacting with speech production in the picture–word interference task; allowing multiple selection of lemmas in limited special circumstances). There is less consensus on whether the stages are discrete, and on whether they interact.

It is possible to construct cascade models that re-create the pattern of performance shown by the mediated priming experiments of Levelt and his colleagues. One possible weakness of the interactive models is that they have many free parameters, and hence could potentially explain

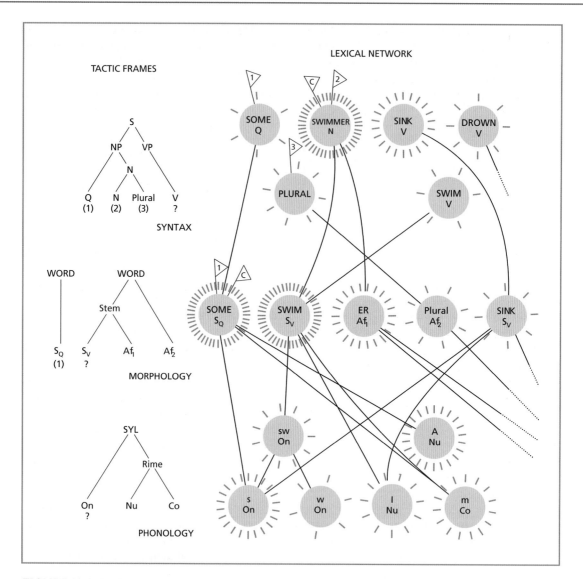

FIGURE 13.9 Dell's (1986) connectionist model of speech production. This figure depicts the momentary activation present in the production of the sentence "Some swimmers sink." On the left there are tree structures analogous to the representation at each level of the model. The numbered slots have already been filled in and the "flag" indicates each node in the network that stands for an item filling a slot (the number indicates the order and the c flag indicates the current node on each level). The ? indicates the slot in each linguistic frame that is currently being filled. The highlighting on each unit indicates the current activation level. Each node is labeled for membership of some category. Syntactic categories are: Q for quantifier; N for noun; V for verb; plural marker. Morphological categories are: S for stem; Af for affix. Phonological categories are: On for onset; Nu for nucleus; Co for coda. Many nodes have been left out to simplify the network, including nodes for syllables, syllabic constituents, and features. From Dell (1986).

any pattern of results. It has become difficult to distinguish empirically between the cascade and discrete models.

Hence all the data are consistent with non-discrete, cascading models. Levelt et al. (1991a) argued that real-time picture-naming experiments present a more accurate view of the normal lexicalization process. Nevertheless, any complete model of lexicalization should also provide an account of the speech error data. Feedback explains similarity and lexical biases, but it is of course most unlikely that feedback connections should exist just to give phonological facilitation in speech errors (Levelt, 1989). One reason feedback links might exist is that the system is used in speech production and comprehension, but this is implausible given experimental and neuropsychological evidence for a separation (see Chapter 15). Hence models with feedback are in some respects problematic.

One possibility is to explain the speech error data away. Given that the main evidence for interaction is facilitation and lexical bias, perhaps these phenomena can be explained by other mechanisms. An alternative explanation is the use of monitors (Baars et al., 1975; Butterworth, 1982; Levelt, 1989; Postma, 2000). Of course we monitor our speech; we sometimes detect errors and correct them. The idea that we make use of a comprehension system to monitor what we say is called the *perceptual-loop* hypothesis. Postma (2000) discusses three ways in which a monitor might operate: It might be completely perceptual, having access only to our speech output; it might have access to levels of processing prior to output, comparing intermediate levels of representation against the conceptual message; or it might make use of relative information about activation levels (e.g., if two lemmas are simultaneously very highly activated, a warning light might flash). It is, however, difficult to distinguish between these alternatives, and indeed all might well be true.

The use of a monitor to edit some slips adds complexity to the system (Stemberger, 1985). We also observe aphasic speakers with error patterns that contradict the editor hypothesis. For example, Blanken (1998) describes a patient who makes errors that come from different syntactic categories on some occasions, but not on others. The editor should be very good at detecting syntactic category violations and should be consistent. So, although the monitor might sometimes prevent some types of error

more than others, it is unlikely to be able to do so to the extent that can account for the number of mixed errors actually found. Generally the dissociation between aphasic speakers with comprehension deficits who show good error detection is a problem for the perceptual-loop hypothesis. Instead, it might be that speech error detection arises from the ability of the speech production system to detect conflicts between planned output and intention, using mechanisms located in the anterior cingulate cortex of the brain (Nozari, Dell, & Schwartz, 2011).

What role does feedback serve? Feedback is unlikely to be the same mechanism that is used in comprehension: speech production is not just comprehension in reverse. (For detailed justification of this statement, see Chapter 12.) Any increase in processing speed that feedback provides is likely to be marginal, and feedback is most unlikely to exist just to ensure that errors are words. One possibility is that it plays a role in monitoring speech and detecting and preventing errors.

Connectionist modeling provides an alternative explanation to feedback. In Chapter 7 we saw how mixed errors can arise in a feedforward architecture, as one of the properties of an attractor network (Hinton & Shallice, 1991). Perhaps in a similar way we can talk about phonological attractors. More work is necessary on this topic.

Rapp and Goldrick (2000) reviewed the literature on discreteness and interactivity, paying particular attention to the pattern of errors made by normal and brain-damaged people. This review provoked a lively debate (Rapp & Goldrick, 2004; Roelofs, 2004a, 2004b). Rapp and Goldrick (2000) argued that the degree of bias towards mixed errors and the lexical bias in errors made by normal individuals can only plausibly be accounted for by the presence of feedback in the system. Furthermore, brain damage can disrupt language production at either the semantic or the post-semantic level, and yet lead to only semantic errors. However, individuals with brain damage show the mixed-error effect only if the locus of damage is post-semantic—a semantic locus of impairment leads to semantic errors but no larger number of mixed errors than would be expected by chance. For example, patient KE has a semantic deficit, as indicated by a profound difficulty in understanding the meaning of words, and made only pure semantic errors and no mixed errors (or no more than chance). In contrast, patient PW had a post-semantic deficit, as indicated by his excellent comprehension, and made semantic and mixed errors (but no form-related errors). Using computer simulations of different types of production architecture, Rapp and Goldrick conclude that there is cascading activation and feedback between semantic and phonological processing levels, but that it is restricted. Modeling shows that too much feedback actually makes production more difficult and does not fit the range of data. They argue in particular that the pattern of data from brain-damaged people shows that the amount of feedback from the lexical to the semantic level must be minimal or zero.

Given that some feedback is necessary, the key question is, whereabouts in the production system does it occur? Is it production-internal, in the form of feedback connections between phonology and lemmas, as Rapp and Goldrick argue, or is it comprehension-based, in the form of a monitor checking the output of a pure feedforward system, as Roelofs argues? In Rapp and Goldrick's RIA (restricted interaction account) model, there is a limited amount of feedback within the production network. In Roelofs' WEAVER++ model, a purely feedforward production network generates an output that then acts as an input for a purely feedforward comprehension network. There is unfortunately no critical evidence that enables us to distinguish between these two alternative accounts, so at present the debate continues. However, it would be difficult to argue with the conclusion reached by Vigliocco and Hartsuiker (2002), who, in their review of the literature on speech production, conclude that the traditional serial model, where information is encapsulated within levels and where information flow between levels is limited, needs revision. Vigliocco and Hartsuiker argue for a maximalist approach, where there is feedback (a bidirectional flow of information) and maximal input (each level of information receives as much input as early as possible—cascading activation—from as many sources as possible).

PHONOLOGICAL ENCODING

The main problem in phonological encoding is ensuring that the sounds of words come out in the appropriate order, with the appropriate prosody. Four solutions to this problem have been proposed.

The first account of phonological encoding is based on a distinction between structure and content. This approach is the most simple and commonly used method for ensuring correct sequencing. Linguistic structures create frames with slots, and we then retrieve linguistic content to fill these slots. A frame is stored for each word we know. One of the best known versions of this approach is the scan-copier mechanism (Shattuck-Hufnagel, 1979). The sound segments are retrieved separately from this frame and inserted into the appropriate slots in a syllabic frame. When we speak, we produce an abstract frame for the up-coming phrase that is copied into a buffer. The frame specifies the syllabic structure of the phrase (in terms of onset, nucleus, and coda). A scan-copier device works through a syllabic frame in left-to-right serial order selecting phonemes to insert into each position of the frame. As a phoneme is selected, it is checked off. Disruption of this mechanism leads to difficulty in sequencing sounds in words (Buckingham, 1986). For example, if the scan-copier selects an incorrect phoneme but incorrectly marks off that phoneme as used, we will end up with a phoneme exchange speech error. If the scan-copier selects an incorrect phoneme but fails to mark that phoneme as used, we get a perseveration or exchange error. Garrett's model of syntactic planning uses the same idea. Frame-based models are very good at accounting for sound-level speech errors. For example, a sophisticated frame-based model can account for how the proportions of anticipatory (e.g., "heft hemisphere") and persevatory (e.g., "left lemisphere") sound-level speech errors vary with age and speech rate (Dell, Burger, & Svec, 1997). Schwartz, Saffran, Bloch, and Dell (1994) distinguished between "good" and "bad" error patterns. The good pattern is that found in normal speech: Errors are relatively rare, they tend to create words, and the majority of them are anticipations. The bad pattern is when there are many errors and the proportion of perseverations is high. The bad pattern is found with some types of aphasia, in childhood when the material is less familiar, and with a faster speech rate. Frame-based models are very good at accounting for these sorts of data. Decreasing the available time and weakening connection strengths in the model both lead to an increase in the bad error pattern.

The second account, competitive queuing (Hartley & Houghton, 1996), is a connectionist model that also uses a frame, but which provides an explicit mechanism for inserting segments into slots. The segments to be inserted form an ordered queue controlled by processes of activation and inhibition. There are two control units, an initiation and an end unit. Sounds that belong at the start of a word have strong connections to a unit that controls the initiation of speech, while sounds at the ends of words have strong connections to a unit that controls the end of the sequence. The strength of connections of other sounds in a word to these control units varies as a function of their position in a word. After a sound is selected, it is temporarily suppressed. Failure to do this properly leads to perseveration errors. Although this model was originally formulated to account for serial order effects in remembering lists, it can be extended to account for all of speech production. It has the advantage of being able to learn how to order items.

Connectionist models suggest that the frame–filler distinction does not have to be represented explicitly, but that it can emerge from the phonological structure of the language (Dell, Juliano, & Govindjee, 1993). Dell et al. used a type of connectionist network called a **recurrent network** to associate words with their phonological representations in sequence, without any explicit representation of the structure–content distinction. Recurrent networks are very good at learning sequences of patterns. Dell et al.'s model incorporated two kinds of feedback. External feedback copied the output of the most recent segment, and therefore provided the model with memory of the past phonological states of the model. Internal feedback copied the past state of the hidden units of the network, and therefore provided the model with memory of its past internal structure. When the model made errors, it exhibited four properties observed in human sound speech errors. First, it obeyed the phonotactic constraint: errors result in sound sequences that occur in the language spoken. Second, consonants exchanged with other consonants, and vowels exchanged with other vowels. Third, the syllabic constituent effect is that vowel–consonant errors are less common than consonant–vowel errors. Finally, initial consonants are more likely to slip than non-initial ones.

Phonological encoding in the lemma model

The final account of phonological encoding is provided by the WEAVER++ model of Levelt, Roelofs, and colleagues (e.g., Levelt, 2001; Levelt, Roelofs, & Meyer, 1999; Roelofs, 1992, 1997a, 1997b, 2002, 2004a, 2004b; see Figure 13.10). WEAVER++ is a discrete two-stage model without any interaction between levels. Concepts select lemmas by enhancing the activation level of the concept dominating the lemma. Activation spreads through the network, with the important restriction that cascaded processing is not permitted, so that activation of the corresponding word form can only begin after a unique lemma has been selected. A phonological code is retrieved for each lemma; for multimorphemic words the phonological code is retrieved for each of the morphemes (e.g., if the target is "horses," we retrieve "horse" and "-z"). The phonological codes are spelled out as ordered sets of phonemes. The phonological code is retrieved for the word as a whole; in picture–word interference studies, priming by parts of words facilitates the naming of the target (e.g., naming a hammer is facilitated by presenting "mer" as a distractor), suggesting that all the parts of the word have been retrieved in one go (Levelt, 2001; Roelofs, 1997a, 1997b). These ordered sets of phonemes are then incrementally strung together to form syllables, a process known as syllabification. Syllables are not stored in the lexicon; rather, we create them as

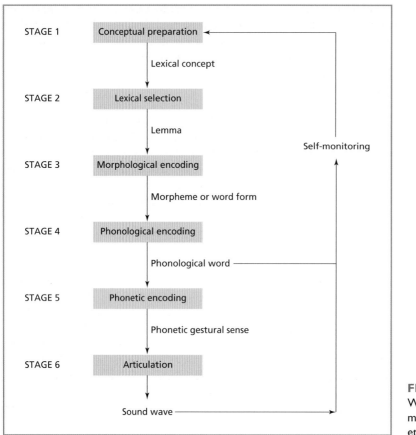

STAGE 1   Conceptual preparation

Lexical concept

STAGE 2   Lexical selection

Lemma

Self-monitoring

STAGE 3   Morphological encoding

Morpheme or word form

STAGE 4   Phonological encoding

Phonological word

STAGE 5   Phonetic encoding

Phonetic gestural sense

STAGE 6   Articulation

Sound wave

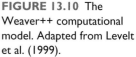

FIGURE 13.10 The Weaver++ computational model. Adapted from Levelt et al. (1999).

we go along, depending on the context. As syllables are composed, they form the input to the final step of encoding, that of phonetic encoding, which forms the details of the sounds and acts as an input to the articulatory apparatus.

An important concept in phonetic encoding is the mental syllabary. The syllabary is a store of highly practiced syllabic "gestures" that can drive articulation; as syllabification proceeds, the corresponding syllabic patterns are retrieved from the syllabary for execution (Levelt, 2001; Levelt et al., 1999). Evidence for the existence of the syllabary comes from the finding that, when word frequency is controlled for, syllable frequency affects naming times (Cholin, Levelt, & Schiller, 2006; Levelt & Wheeldon, 1994). Although English has more than 10,000 different syllables, 80% of the time we use just 500 (Levelt, 2001). It makes sense to make use of

these highly overlearned motor patterns to speed up production.

These models are perhaps not as mutually exclusive as they might first appear. They represent evolution in theorizing, and also emphasize different aspects of phonological encoding. The main difference is once again the extent to which information has to be explicitly encoded in the model, or whether it emerges as a consequence of the statistical regularities of the language. At present, frame-based models are better able to account for how we can produce novel sequences of sounds (Dell, Schwartz, Martin, Saffran, & Gagnon, 1997).

The role of syllables in phonological encoding

One major difference between many of the connectionist and WEAVER++ models concerns the role of the syllable. Most connectionist models make use of metrical frames that specify the number, order, and structure of syllables and their stress pattern; syllables are then inserted into this metrical frame. In contrast, in the WEAVER++ model the metrical frame specifies only the stress pattern, and does not contain syllable information.

We can test this distinction, although the experiments are complex. Roelofs and Meyer (1998) examined whether we store the structure of syllables in the metrical frame. They used an implicit priming paradigm. Participants had to produce one word out of a small set of words as quickly as possible. The sets of words were either homogeneous, when all the words in the set had the same word-initial segments, or heterogeneous, when they did not. They found that priming depended on the words having the same number of syllables and the same stress pattern, but not the same syllable structure (the same number of consonants and vowels). Roelofs and Meyer concluded that the lack of priming suggests that syllable structure is not stored in the metrical frame. Cholin, Schiller, and Levelt (2004) used the same paradigm, and concluded that syllable frames are not stored with a word and retrieved during encoding, but instead are generated "on the fly." The general idea with these studies is that if syllables are not explicitly stored in the lexicon, there should be no syllable-specific priming effect, which is what these studies find. Hence they support the view that syllables are made up only when necessary, as in the WEAVER++ model.

Other studies come to a different conclusion. Costa and Sebastian-Gallés (1998) used a picture–word interference paradigm: Participants had to name a picture while a word was presented 150 ms later. The results showed that participants were faster to name the picture when the target and the distractor shared the same abstract structure. For example, "cuña" (meaning "wedge") has a CV.CV (consonant–vowel consonant–vowel) structure. "Cuña" primes the target word "mono" (monkey), which has the same syllabic structure (CV.CV), but no overlap in actual sounds (segmental content), relative to a control item (e.g., "culpa," meaning fault, which is structurally and segmentally unrelated). This result suggests that abstract syllabic structures are used in phonological encoding.

It is difficult to come to any firm conclusion about the existence of pre-stored, abstract syllabic structures on the basis of the current contradictory findings (see Cholin et al., 2006, for a summary).

How far do we plan ahead?

What is the main unit of planning at the phonological level? According to Levelt (1989), we have to prepare the phonological word before we can start speaking. The phonological word is the smallest prosodic unit of speech: it is a stressed (strong) syllable and any associated unstressed (weak) syllables (Levelt, 1989; Sternberg, Knoll, Monsell, & Wright, 1988; Wheeldon & Lahiri, 1997). For example, "the vampire" is one phonological word; "the bad vampire" is two. The phonological word is prepared prior to rapid execution. Wheeldon and Lahiri showed that when all other factors are controlled for (e.g., syntactic structure, number of lexical items, and number of syllables), the time it takes us to prepare a sentence (as measured by the time it takes us to begin speaking the prepared material) is a function of the number of phonological words in it.

In addition to content words, phonological words can contain function words, although in some circumstances function words can form phonological words in themselves if we decide to stress them (e.g., "you CAN do that"). Further evidence for the importance of phonological words in phonological planning is that resyllabification occurs within phonological words, but not across them. This means that sounds from the end of one syllable can migrate to form the beginning of the next syllable. Consider (40) from Wheeldon and Lahiri (1997):

(40)   Get me a beer, if the beer is cold.

A final /r/ sound has been added explicitly to the end of the second "beer," and this has then resyllabified to become the onset of the following "is," so that it is pronounced "beea-riz." No such resyllabification can occur with the first "beer," however, because the following /I/ is in a different phonological word.

On the other hand, some more recent work suggests that we do plan farther ahead than one phonological word. For example, Costa and Caramazza (2002) used a picture–word interference design to examine how we produce noun phrases in English and Spanish. They asked speakers to produce simple (determiner noun) and complex (determiner adjective noun) constructions while ignoring phonological distractors. They found that the distractors phonologically related to the noun produced faster naming latencies, regardless of the type of construction and the position of the noun. This result shows that the level of activation of the phonological forms of the lexical nodes outside the first phonological form affect naming latency, meaning that the second phonological word of the noun phrase (the noun, in the complex construction) is activated before articulation begins (because it is facilitated by the prime). Hence, in at least some circumstances, phonological encoding extends beyond a phonological word (see also Alario, Costa, & Caramazza, 2002a, 2002b; Levelt, 2002).

One possible resolution of these apparently discrepant findings is that the phonological representations of words are activated in a graded way as we speak; the closer to output an item is, the more it is activated (Jescheniak, Schriefers, & Hantsch, 2003).

THE ANALYSIS OF HESITATIONS

Hesitation analysis is concerned with the distribution of pauses and other dysfluencies in speech (see Figure 13.11). An unfilled pause is simply a moment of silence. A filled hesitation can be a filled pause (where a gap in the flow of words is filled with a sound such as "uh" or "um"), a repetition, a false start, or a parenthetical remark (such as "well" or "I mean"). People often start what they are saying, hesitate when they discover that they haven't really worked out what to say or how to say it, and repeat their start when they have (Clark & Wasow, 1998). Unfilled pauses are easier to detect mechanically by the equipment used to measure pause duration, so analysis has focused on them. It has been argued that pauses represent two types of difficulty: one in what might be called microplanning (due to retrieving particularly difficult words), and a second in macroplanning (due to planning the syntax and content of a sentence). The theoretical emphasis in the past has been that pauses predominantly reflect semantic planning.

Pauses and lexicalization

Goldman-Eisler (1958, 1968) examined the distribution of unfilled pauses (defined variously as longer than 200 or 250 ms) across time, using a device nicknamed the "pauseometer." Obviously there are gaps between speakers' "turns" in conversation, known as switching pauses, but there are many pauses within a single conversational turn. They tend to occur every five to eight words.

Goldman-Eisler (1958, 1968) showed that pauses are more likely to occur, and to be of

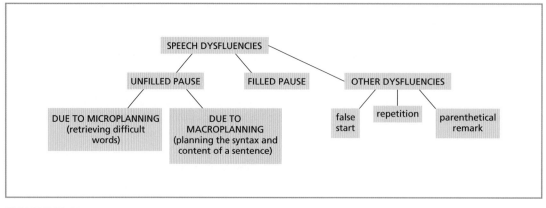

FIGURE 13.11

longer duration, before words that are less predictable in the context of the preceding speech. Predictability reflects a number of notions, including word frequency and familiarity, and the preceding semantic and syntactic context. Pauses before less predictable words are hypothesized to reflect microplanning and to correspond to a transient difficulty in lexical access. We know the meaning of the word we want to say but we cannot immediately retrieve its sound. Of course, not all hesitations precede less predictable words, and not all less predictable words are preceded by pauses. Sections of repeated speech behave differently from pauses, tending to follow unpredictable words rather than preceding them, as though they are used to check that the speaker has selected the correct word (Tannenbaum, Williams, & Hillier, 1965).

Beattie and Butterworth (1979) attempted to disentangle the effects of word frequency from contextual probability. They showed that the relation between pausing and predictability did not appear to be attributable simply to word frequency, and concluded that the main component of predictability that determined hesitations was difficulty in semantic planning. However, their study did not rule out possible contributions from syntactic difficulty (Petrie, 1987).

People often use appropriate gestures during these hesitations (Butterworth & Beattie, 1978). Suppose you are having difficulty in retrieving the word "telephone." You pause just before you say it, and in that pause make a gesture appropriate to a telephone (such as holding your fist to the side of your head, with thumb and little finger extended). This suggests that you know the meaning of what you want to say—that is, that the difficulty lies elsewhere than in semantic planning. It suggests a two-stage model of lexical access in production. We first formulate a semantic specification of what we want to say, and phonological retrieval follows this. On this account the pause reflects a successful first stage but a delay in the second stage, that of retrieving the particular phonological form of the word. This account ties in with the evidence from tip-of-the-tongue states, which can be seen as extreme examples of microplanning pauses.

Pauses and sentence planning

Goldman-Eisler (1958, 1968) argued that in some pauses we plan the content of what we are about to say. She found that the difficulty of the speaking task affected the number of pauses a speaker makes, with more difficult tasks (for example, interpreting a cartoon rather than simply describing a cartoon) leading to more pauses in speech. She argued that speakers were using these additional pauses to carry out additional planning.

Pauses cast some light on the size of planning units in speech. Maclay and Osgood (1959) argued that the planning units must be larger than a single word because false starts involve corrections of the grammatical words associated with the unintended content-bearing words. We tend to produce corrections such as "The dog— the cat was …" Boomer (1965) argued on the basis of hesitations that an appropriate unit of analysis corresponds to a phonemic clause that essentially has only one major stressed element within it, and which corresponds to a clause of the surface structure. He argued that the clause is planned in the hesitation at the start of the clause. Ford and Holmes (1978) used dual-task performance to monitor cognitive load during speech production, whereby the participant had to speak while monitoring for a tone over headphones. They argued that planning does not span sentences because reaction times to the tone were no longer at the ends of sentences, suggesting that people are not planning the next sentence at the end of the previous one. On the other hand, Holmes (1988) asked participants to read several sentences that began a story, and then produce a one-sentence continuation. She found that, contrary to instructions, some speakers produced more than one sentence, and when they did so a pause was more likely at the start of their speech than when they produced only one sentence. Different tasks seem to indicate that different units are the fundamental unit. Nevertheless, the clause does seem to be an important unit of planning.

What exactly is planned in the pauses? In particular, is the planning syntactic or semantic in nature, or both? Goldman-Eisler (1968) claimed that pause time was not affected by the syntactic complexity of the utterances being produced, and concluded that planning is primarily semantic rather than syntactic. This conclusion is now considered controversial (see Petrie, 1987). One problem concerns what measure should be taken of syntactic complexity. At this stage it would be premature to rule out the possibility that macroplanning pauses represent planning both the semantic and the syntactic content of a clause.

Henderson, Goldman-Eisler, and Skarbek (1966) proposed that there were cognitive cycles in the planning of speech. In particular, phases of highly hesitant speech alternate with phases of more fluent speech. The hesitant phases also contain more filled pauses, and more false starts, than the fluent phases. It is thought that most of the planning takes part in the hesitant phase, and in the fluent phase we merely say what we have just planned in the preceding hesitant phase (see Figure 13.12). Butterworth (1975, 1980) argued that a cycle corresponds to an idea. He asked independent judges to divide other speakers' descriptions of their routes home into semantic units, and compared these with hesitation cycles. An idea lasts for several clauses. Roberts and Kirsner (2000) found that new cycles are associated with topic shifts in conversation.

One problem with this work is the way in which the units were identified by inspection of plots of unfilled pauses against articulation time. Jaffe, Breskin, and Gerstman (1972) showed that apparently cyclic patterns could be generated completely randomly. However, other phenomena (such as filled hesitations) also cluster within the planning phase of a cognitive cycle. For example, speakers tend to gaze less at their listeners during the planning phase, maintaining more eye contact during the execution phase (Beattie, 1980; Kendon, 1967). The use of gestures also depends on the phase of speech (Beattie, 1983). Speakers tend to use more batonic gestures (gestures used only for emphasis) in the hesitant phases, and more iconic gestures (gestures that in some way resemble the associated object, such as the one described earlier when about to say "telephone") in the fluent phase (particularly before less predictable words). The observation that several features cluster together in hesitant phases suggests that these cycles are indeed psychologically real. Finally, Roberts and Kirsner (2000) used the statistical technique of time series analysis to find further support for the existence of temporal cycles.

Evaluation of research on dysfluencies

Some dysfluencies might do more than just indicate temporary processing difficulty. Sometimes speakers deliberately (though perhaps usually unconsciously) put pauses into their speech to make the listener's job easier, perhaps aiding them to segment speech, or to give them time to parse the speech (see also Chapter 14, on audience design). Lounsbury (1954) distinguished between hesitation pauses, which reflect planning by the speaker, and juncture pauses, which are put in by the speaker to mark major syntactic boundaries, perhaps for the convenience of the listener. Good and Butterworth (1980) provided experimental evidence that hesitations might be used to achieve some interactional goal, as well as reflecting the speaker's cognitive load. They found that speakers paused more when giving descriptions of their route into work when the experimenter asked them to appear to be more thoughtful. Listeners do make use of

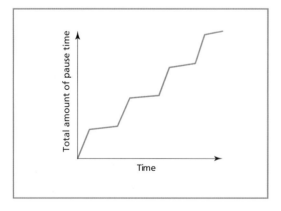

FIGURE 13.12 Planning and execution phases: Cognitive cycles in speech production.

dysfluencies when parsing the input (Ferreira & Bailey, 2004). For example, filled pauses and repetitions are more common at the start than at the end of clauses—the parser could therefore make use of this information to decide on clause boundaries when there are alternative constructions (e.g., in garden path sentences). The use of "oh" indicates to the speaker that the following utterance is not connected to the immediately preceding information, but to something earlier in the conversation (Fox Tree & Schrock, 1999). "Uh" and "um" may serve different functions in speech, with "uh" signaling a short delay, and "um" a longer delay, in speaking (Clark & Fox Tree, 2002). Hence dysfluencies do more than just reflect processing difficulty; they convey information to the listener. Of course, it is quite possible that any one particular dysfluency might serve more than one function.

Different types of pause might have different causes. Goldman-Eisler (1958) argued that micropauses (those shorter than 250 ms) merely reflect articulation difficulties rather than planning time; however, this view has been challenged (see, for example, Hieke, Kowal, & O'Connell, 1983). There is some measure of interchangeability between different types of hesitations. Beattie and Bradbury (1979) showed that if speakers were dissuaded from making many lengthy pauses (by being "punished" by the appearance of a red light every time they paused for longer than 600 ms), their

pause rate did indeed go down, but the number of repeats they made went up instead.

Although the early work was originally interpreted as showing that pausing reflected semantic planning, this is far from clear. It is likely that microplanning difficulties arise in retrieving the phonological forms and planning propositions, whereas macroplanning pauses reflect both semantic and syntactic planning of larger chunks of language. It is possible that macroplanning and microplanning may conflict (Levelt, 1989); if we spend too much time on macroplanning, there will be fewer resources available for microplanning, leading to an increase in pausing and decreased fluency as we struggle for particular words.

THE NEUROSCIENCE OF SPEECH PRODUCTION

What else does neuroscience tell us about speech production?

Aphasia

In the past, researchers placed a great deal of emphasis on the distinction between Broca's and Wernicke's aphasias. These terms refer to what were once considered to be syndromes, or symptoms that cluster together, resulting from damage to different parts of the left hemisphere. Broca's area is toward the front

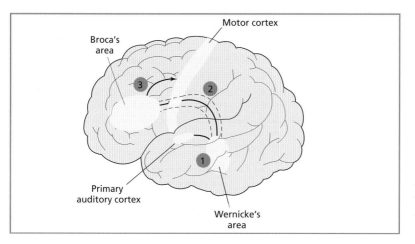

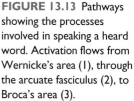

FIGURE 13.13 Pathways showing the processes involved in speaking a heard word. Activation flows from Wernicke's area (1), through the arcuate fasciculus (2), to Broca's area (3).

of the brain, in the frontal lobe, and Wernicke's area is toward the rear, in the posterior temporal lobe (see Figure 13.13). These terms are also still meaningful for clinicians and neurologists, and they are still acceptable terms in those literatures.

Broca's aphasia

Broca's aphasics have non-fluent speech, characterized by slow, laborious, hesitant speech, with little intonation (called **dysprosody**), and with obvious articulation difficulties (called speech **apraxia**). There is also an obvious impairment in the ability to order words. At the most general level, Broca's-type patients have difficulty with sequencing units of the language. An example of Broca's aphasia is given in (41) (from Goodglass, 1976, p. 238), where the dots indicate long pauses. Although all Broca's patients suffer from different degrees of speech apraxia, not all obviously have a syntactic disorder.

(41)   "Ah … Monday … ah Dad and Paul … and Dad … hospital. Two … ah … doctors … and ah … thirty minutes … and yes … ah … hospital. And er Wednesday … nine o'clock. And er Thursday, ten o'clock … doctors. Two doctors … and ah … teeth."

Wernicke's aphasia

Damage to Wernicke's area, which is in the left temporal-parietal cortex, results in the production of fluent but often meaningless speech. This is called Wernicke's (sometimes sensory) aphasia. As far as one can tell, patients speak in well-formed sentences, with copious grammatical elements and with normal prosody. Comprehension is noticeably poor, and there are obvious major content word-finding difficulties, with many word substitutions and made-up words. Zurif, Caramazza, Myerson, and Galvin (1974) found that patients were unable to pick the two most similar words from triads as "shark, mother, husband." An example of the speech of someone with Wernicke's aphasia is given in (42) (from Goodglass & Geschwind, 1976, p. 410):

(42)   "Well this is … mother is away here working her work out o'here to get her better, but when she's looking, the two boys looking in the other part. One their small tile into her time here. She's working another time because she's getting, too …"

For Wernicke, this type of aphasia resulted from the disruption of the "sensory images" of words. Clearly aspects of word meaning processing are disrupted in this type of aphasia, while syntactic processing is left relatively intact.

Comparison of Broca's and Wernicke's aphasias

Broca's and Wernicke's aphasias are not really mirror images. They are distinguished on two dimensions: intact versus impaired comprehension, and the availability or unavailability of the syntactic components of language (see Figure 13.14). This categorization relates more to the links between the characteristics of the impaired speech and anatomical regions of the brain, while currently the emphasis is on developing more functional descriptions relating to psycholinguistic models of the impairments. It is now considered more useful to distinguish between fluent aphasia, which is characterized by fluent (though sometimes meaningless) speech, and non-fluent aphasia. At the same time we can also distinguish between those patients who can comprehend language and those who have a comprehension deficit. Traditional Broca's-type aphasics are non-fluent with no obvious comprehension deficit, whereas traditional Wernicke's-type aphasics are fluent with an obvious comprehension deficit. Bear in mind that no classification scheme for neuropsychological disorders of language is perfect: there are always exceptions and patients who appear to cut across categories (see Schwartz, 1984). Furthermore, all patients have some degree of anomia (word-finding difficulties, discussed in more detail below)—even agrammatic Broca's aphasics (Dick et al., 2001).

Agrammatism

The syntactic disorder of non-fluent patients tells us a great deal about the processes involved in speech production. In traditional neuropsychology terms, such patients suffer from what has been labeled **agrammatism**.

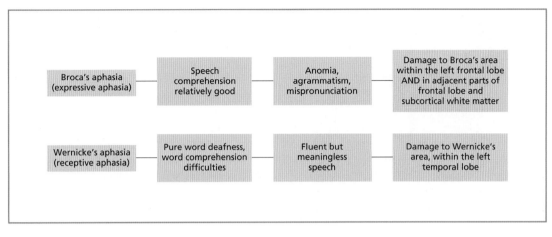

FIGURE 13.14 Comparison between Broca's and Wernicke's aphasias.

Agrammatism has three components. First, there is a sentence construction deficit, such that patients have an impaired ability to output correctly ordered words. The words do not always form sentences, but look as though they are being output one at a time. In some cases, simple sentences can be generated (e.g., a patient might repeat "the old man is washing the window" as "the man is washing window. The man is old"; Ostrin & Schwartz, 1986). The disorder extends to sentence repetition, where complex phrases are simplified. Second, some parts of speech are better preserved than others. In particular, there is a selective impairment of grammatical elements, such that content words are best preserved, and function words and word endings (bound inflectional morphemes) are least well preserved. Third, although for some time it was thought that their comprehension was spared, some people with agrammatism also have difficulty in understanding syntactically complex sentences (see Chapter 10). It is also possible that certain differences between agrammatic speakers reflect different adaptations to the deficit. For example, some people show better retention of bound morphemes, and others of free grammatical morphemes.

Whether or not these components are dissociable is an important question. There has been considerable debate as to whether terms such as Broca's aphasia and agrammatism have any place in modern neuropsychology. The debate centers on whether agrammatism is a coherent deficit: Do people with agrammatism show symptoms that consistently cluster together, and hence, is there a single underlying deficit that can account for them? If it is a meaningful syndrome, we should find that the sentence construction deficit, grammatical element loss, and a syntactic comprehension deficit should always co-occur. A number of single-case studies have found dissociations between these impairments (Caplan et al., 1985; Goodglass & Menn, 1985; Miceli, Mazzucci, Menn, & Goodglass, 1983; Nespoulous et al., 1988; Saffran et al., 1980; Schwartz et al., 1987).

These dissociations suggest that there is a syntax module in the brain, but that the module itself has neurologically distinct components. This idea is supported by recent neuroimaging data (Grodzinsky & Friederici, 2006). Grodzinsky and Friederici identify different sorts of syntactic processing, and indicate where they might take place in the brain (see Figure 13.15). Broca's area is particularly important for identifying how different constituents in the sentence are related to each other, with regions in the superior temporal gyrus (including Wernicke's area) more involved in syntactic integration. Imaging suggests that even parts of the right hemisphere play some role in syntactic processing.

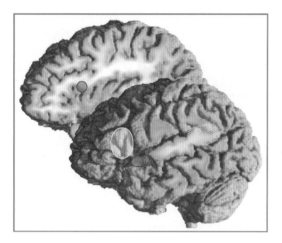

FIGURE 13.15 The main brain areas involved in syntactic processing. Pink areas (frontal operculum and anterior superior temporal gyrus) are involved in the build-up of local phrase structures; the yellow area (BA33/45) is involved in the computation of dependency relations between sentence components; the striped area (posterior superior temporal gyrus and sulcus) is involved in integration processes. Reprinted from Grodzinsky and Friederici (2006).

More recently it has been observed that agrammatism can be observed in a wide range of aphasic patients, and is not restricted to non-fluent aphasics (Dick et al., 2001). Agrammatism can even be observed in neurologically intact people under stress.

If there is no such syndrome as agrammatism, it is meaningless to perform group experiments on what is in fact a functionally disparate group of patients. Instead, one should only perform single-case studies (Badecker & Caramazza, 1985). In reply Caplan (1986) argued that at the very least agrammatism is a convenient label. Although there might be subtypes, there is still a meaningful underlying deficit. This issue sparked considerable debate, both on the status of agrammatism (see Badecker & Caramazza, 1986, for a reply to Caplan) and on the methodology of single-case studies (see Bates et al., 1991; Caramazza, 1991; McCloskey & Caramazza, 1988).

Explanations of agrammatism

One explanation of agrammatism is that the patients' articulation difficulties play a causal role. It might be that patients find articulation so difficult that they drop function words in an attempt to conserve resources. But agrammatism is much more than a loss of grammatical morphemes, as there is also a sentence construction and, in most cases, a syntactic comprehension deficit.

Other theories attempt to find a single underlying cause for the three components. One obvious suggestion is that Broca's area is responsible for processing function words and other grammatical elements (see also Chapter 10). We saw earlier that content and function words suffer very different constraints in normal speech production: for example, they never exchange with each other in word exchange speech errors. There is also some neuropsychological evidence that content and function words are served by different processing routines. French-speaking agrammatic patients made more phonological errors on reading function words than matched content words (Biassou, Obler, Nespoulous, Dordain, & Harris, 1997), a finding often observed in deep dyslexia, which often co-occurs with agrammatism. Probabilistic difficulty in accessing grammatical elements will lead to difficulty in understanding complex syntactic constructions, and deficits in syntactic production (Pulvermüller, 1995). Along these lines, Kean (1977) proposed a single phonological deficit hypothesis, later revised by Lapointe (1983), based on the assignment of stress to a syntactic frame. Kean argued that agrammatic patients omit items that are unstressed components of phonological words (see earlier). Hence content words tend to be preserved, and affixes and function words are lost. This hypothesis sparked considerable debate (see Caplan, 1992; Grodzinsky, 1984, 1990; Kolk, 1978). The main problem is that although it explains grammatical element loss, it does not account so well for the other components of the disorder (particularly the sentence construction deficit), nor for the patterns of dissociation that we can observe, in particular the patients' ability to make judgments about the grammaticality of sentences. Furthermore, as we saw in Chapter 10, the conclusion that function and content words are processed differently is questionable.

Stemberger (1984) compared agrammatic errors with normal speech errors. He proposed that in agrammatic patients there is an increase in random noise, and an increase in the threshold that it is necessary to exceed for access to occur. In these conditions substitutions and omissions, particularly of low-frequency items, occur. He argued that agrammatism is a differential exacerbation of problems found in normal speech; this idea, that aphasic behavior is just an extreme version of normal speech errors, is one frequently mentioned. Harley (1990) made a similar proposal for the origin of paragrammatisms. These are errors involving misconstructed grammatical frames, and can be explained in terms of excessive substitutions. Again, however, these approaches do not explain all the characteristics of agrammatism. Although uninflected words are more common than inflected forms, the high-frequency function words are more likely to be lost than content words, which are of lower frequency, on average. Stemberger argued that the syntactic structures that involve function words are less frequent than structures that do not.

Schwartz (1987) related agrammatism to Garrett's model. Consider what would happen in this model if there were a problem translating from the functional level to the positional level. No sentence frame would be constructed, and no grammatical elements would be retrieved. This is what is observed. This does not provide an account of the comprehension deficit, which would arise from damage to other systems. The dissociation between the sentence construction deficit and grammatical element loss suggests that different processes must be responsible in Garrett's model for constructing the sentence frame and retrieving grammatical elements. Although lacking detail, this line of thought both supports and extends Garrett's model, and shows how neuropsychological impairments can be related to a model of normal processing.

We saw that reduced computational resources might play some role in the syntactic comprehension deficit. Similarly, limited memory might play some role in agrammatic production. However, any role is a complicated one, as severely reduced

short-term memory (STM) does not necessarily lead to agrammatism (Kolk & van Grunsven, 1985; Shallice & Butterworth, 1977). Hence any impairment would have to be to some component of memory other than the phonological loop. This could be to a specialist store for syntactic planning, or perhaps to a special part of the central executive component of working memory. Nevertheless, reduced computational resources may play some role in the production deficits in agrammatism (Blackwell & Bates, 1995; Kolk, 1995). If this is so, one possibility is that grammatical elements are particularly susceptible to loss when computational resources are greatly reduced.

Jargon aphasia

Jargon aphasia is an extreme type of fluent aphasia in which syntax is primarily intact, but speech is marked by gross word-finding difficulties. People with jargon aphasia often have difficulty in recognizing that their speech is aberrant, and may become irritated when people fail to understand them, indicating a problem with self-monitoring (Marshall, Robson, Pring, & Chiat, 1998).

The word-finding difficulties in jargon aphasia are marked by content-word substitutions (**paraphasia**s) and made-up words (**neologism**s). Paraphasias include unrelated verbal paraphasias, such as (43), semantic paraphasias (44), form-based or formal paraphasias (45) (all from Martin & Saffran, 1992, and Martin, Dell, Saffran, & Schwartz, 1994), and phonemic paraphasias (46) (from Ellis, 1985). Of particular interest are neologisms, which are made-up words not to be found in a dictionary. There are a number of types of neologisms, including distortions of real words, for example (47) and (48) (from Ellis, 1985), and abstruse paraphasias with no discernible relatives, where it is often difficult to discern the intended word (49) (from Butterworth, 1979). As an example, consider the description (50) of connected speech. This is a description by patient CB (from Buckingham, 1981, p. 54) of the famous Boston "cookie theft" picture, which depicts a mother washing plates while the sink overfills, while in the background a little boy and girl steal the cookies.

(43)   thermometer   → typewriter
(44)   scroll   → letters
(45)   pencil   → pepper
(46)   swan   → swom
(47)   octopus   → opupkus
(48)   whistle   → swizl
(49)   ?   → kwailai
(50)   "You mean like this boy? I mean [noy], and this, uh, [neoy]. This is a [kaynit], [kahken]. I don't say it, I'm not getting anything from it. I'm getting, I'm [dime] from it, but I'm getting from it. These were [eksprehsez], [ahgrashenz] and with the type of [mah-kanic] is standing like this … and then the … I don't know what she [goin] other than. And this is [deli] this one is the one and this one and this one and … I don't know."

Butterworth (1985) noted that jargon aphasia changes over time as patients recover some of their abilities. A typical progression is from undifferentiated strings of phonemes, to neologistic speech, to word paraphasias, and then perhaps to circumlocutory phrases.

Butterworth (1979) examined hesitations before neologisms in the speech of patient KC, and found that they resembled those made by normal speakers before less predictable words. KC was more likely to hesitate before a neologism or a paraphasia than before a real word. The presence of pauses before neologisms argues against any account of neologisms relying on disinhibition— that the lexical retrieval system is overactive. Butterworth instead argued that such errors arise when the patient is unable to activate any phonological form, and instead uses a random phoneme generation device to produce a pseudoword. Butterworth, Swallow, and Grimston (1981) examined the gestures in the pauses preceding the neologisms. They found that KC's use of gestures was generally the same as that of normal speakers, and they therefore concluded that the semantic system was intact in this patient. However, many gestures produced just before neologisms were incomplete. Iconic gestures are thought to be generated at the semantic level. Butterworth (1985) argued that the first stage of lexical access (what we have called lemma retrieval) functions correctly, but the retrieval of the phonological forms fails. He also suggested that aphasic errors are accentuated normal slips of the tongue, and pointed to a large number of instances of word blend errors in KC's speech, combined with or perhaps caused by a failure in the mechanisms that normally check speech output. Ellis, Miller, and Sin (1983) found that the main determinant of probability of successful retrieval in jargon is word frequency. We would expect to have particular difficulty in retrieving low-frequency items.

Buckingham (1986) provided an account of jargon aphasia in terms of the traditional Garrett model of speech production. Buckingham posited disruption of the functioning of the device known as a scan-copier that is responsible for outputting the phonemes of a word into the syntactic frame in the correct order (Shattuck-Hufnagel, 1979). Buckingham (1981) pointed out that neologisms may actually have many different sources, but also invoked the notion of a random syllable generator.

Neologisms display appropriate syntactic accommodation, and their affixes appear correct for their syntactic environment (Butterworth, 1985). This is further support for the Garrett model, as content words are retrieved independently from their syntactic frames and inflections, and jargon is a disorder of lexical retrieval. All Wernicke's-type deficits can be seen as problems with the semantic-phonological access system. It is as yet unclear whether there are two subtypes, one involving a semantic impairment and one involving only a problem in the retrieval of phonological forms, although given the two-stage model, such a division would be expected.

Anomia

Anomia is an impairment of retrieving the names of objects and pictures of objects, and can be found in isolation, or accompanying other disorders such as Wernicke's-type or Broca's aphasia. In fact virtually all types of aphasia are marked by some degree of anomia. The two-stage model of lexicalization suggests that there are two things that could go wrong in naming. We can have difficulty in retrieving the lemma from the semantic specification, or we could have difficulty in retrieving the phonological

Anomia is an impairment of retrieving the names of objects and pictures of objects.

form of a word after we have accessed its lemma. Therefore we observe two types of anomia.

Lexical-semantic anomia

Perhaps the most striking evidence for involvement of the semantic level in naming disorders is when patients can name members of one semantic category (such as inanimate objects) better than another (such as animate objects). We examined these category-specific semantic disorders in detail in Chapter 11. In many of these patients, however, the deficit is a central one: The central semantic store (or stores) is disrupted, as performance is poor in comprehension as well as production (Warrington & Shallice, 1984).

Lexical-semantic anomia is an inability to use the semantic representation to select the correct lemma. Howard and Orchard-Lisle (1984) described patient JCU, who had a general semantic disorder. Her naming of all types of object was

substantially impaired (she could correctly name only 3% of pictures without help), and she made many semantic errors. Her naming performance could be improved if she was given a phonological cue to the target, such as its initial phoneme. However, these phonological cues could lead her astray; if she was given a cue to a close semantic relative of the target she would produce that. For example, the cue "l" would lead her to say "lion" in response to a picture of a tiger. Howard and Orchard-Lisle concluded that her processes of object recognition were normal. JCU scored highly on the pyramids and palm trees test. In this task the participant has to match a picture of an object to an associate. In the eponymous trial, the participant must match a picture of a pyramid to a picture of a palm tree rather than to one of a deciduous tree. This pattern of performance suggests that in JCU both object recognition processes and the underlying conceptual representation were intact. JCU performed less well on a picture categorization task where there were close semantic distractors (such as matching an onion to a peapod rather than to an apple), although performance was still above chance. Howard and Orchard-Lisle concluded that JCU suffered from a semantic impairment such that there was interference between close semantic relatives. She was led to the approximate semantic domain so the target word was distinguishable from semantically unrelated words, but the semantic representation was too impoverished to enable her to home in any more precisely. JCU could only access incomplete semantic information.

Some patients make semantic errors yet have apparently intact semantic processing. Howard and Franklin (1988) described the case of a patient known as MK who had a moderate comprehension deficit. MK was poor at naming, producing semantic relatives of the target, yet performed well at the pyramid and palm trees task. For example, MK named a caterpillar as "slug," yet had no difficulty in associating a picture of a caterpillar with a picture of a butterfly rather than with a picture of a dragonfly. Hence, although the semantics were intact, MK still made semantic paraphasias. MK probably had problems getting from an intact semantic system to the lemma.

Phonological anomia

Kay and Ellis (1987) described the case of EST. (See Laine & Martin, 1996, for a description of a similar sort of patient, IL.) This patient knew the precise meaning of words and was good at all semantic tasks, but was very poor at retrieving any phonological information about the target. For example, he performed normally on the pyramids and palm trees test, and often offered detailed semantic information about the word that he could not retrieve. He was not prone to interference from close semantic distractors. He was much better at retrieving high-frequency words than low-frequency ones. He had full and clear understanding of the items he was trying to name, but he still could not retrieve targets, although he sometimes had partial phonological information, and could produce associated semantic information such as the superordinate category of the word and a functional description of the associated object. Phonological cuing of the target helped only a little, and unlike JCU, EST could not be misled into producing a category coordinate. This type of anomia is reminiscent of the tip-of-the-tongue state. EST's problems appeared to arise at the phonological level rather than at the semantic level.

Evaluation of anomia research

The existence of two types of anomia supports a distinction between semantic and phonological processing in speech production. Although it is usually adduced as evidence for the two-stage model of lexicalization, it might also be consistent with a one-stage model. In the two-stage account, lexical-semantic anomia can be explained as difficulty in retrieving the lemma, whereas non-semantic impairment can be explained as difficulty in retrieving the phonological representation after the lemma has been successfully accessed. In the one-stage model, lexical-semantic anomia could arise from the failure of the semantic system, while phonological anomia could arise from failures of accessing the word forms (as do jargon and neologisms). As we saw earlier, the best evidence for two stages in lexicalization comes from the study of anomic patients in languages with gender.

Another complication is that the effects of phonological priming are more complex than described above. Wilshire and Saffran (2005) gave two fluent aphasic patients with anomia auditory primes just before naming a picture. They found that patient IG, who made many semantic and phonological substitutions, was helped only by word-initial phonological priming (e.g., ferry–feather). Patient GL, who made phonological errors and substitutions, only benefited from word-final primes (e.g., brother–feather). It is likely that word-initial and word-final primes have effects at different stages, with word-initial information becoming available very early, while the lemma is being selected, whereas word-final information is only available later, after the lemma has been selected and the detailed phonological form of the word is being retrieved.

Connectionist modeling of aphasia

Connectionist modeling of aphasia has focused on difficulties with lexical retrieval.

Harley and MacAndrew (1992) lesioned a model of normal lexicalization with the aim of producing some of the characteristics of aphasic paraphasias. They tested four hypotheses. First, Martin and Saffran (1992) proposed that a pathological increase in the rate of decay leads to increased paraphasias and neologisms. Second, Harley (1993b) argued that the loss of within-level inhibitory connections would lead to impaired processing; if lexical units were involved, neologisms and paraphasias would result, whereas if connections between syntactic units were lost, paragrammatisms (Butterworth & Howard, 1987) would result. Third, Stemberger (1985) argued that normal speech errors result from noise in an interactive activation network; perhaps aphasic errors result from excessive random noise. Finally, Miller and Ellis (1987) argued that neologisms result from the weakening of the connections between the semantic and lexical units. Harley and MacAndrew concluded that weakened semantic–lexical connections best fit the error data: Weakening the value of the parameter that governs the rate of spread of activation from semantic to lexical units often results in target and competing lexical items having similar high activation levels.

Currently the most comprehensive computational model of aphasia is based on Dell's (1986) model of speech production. Martin and Saffran (1992) reported the case of patient NC, a young man who suffered a left hemisphere **aneurysm** that resulted in a pathological short-term memory span and a disorder known as **deep dysphasia**. This is an aphasic analog of deep dyslexia; it is a relatively rare disorder marked by an inability to repeat non-words and the production of semantic errors in the repetition of single words (see Howard & Franklin, 1988). Additionally, in word naming NC produced a relatively high rate of **formal paraphasia**s (sound-related word substitutions, such as producing "schools" for "skeleton") (see Figure 13.16). Martin and Saffran argued that the semantic errors in word repetition and the formal paraphasias in production arise because of a pathological increase in the rate at which the activation of units decays. In naming, formal paraphasias arise because when the lexical unit corresponding to the target is activated,

activation spreads to the appropriate phonological units. Feedback connections from the phonological to the lexical level ensure that lexical units corresponding to words that are phonologically similar to the target word become activated. Martin and Saffran argued that if the activation of lexical units decays pathologically quickly, then the target lexical unit (as well as semantically related lexical units primed by earlier feedforward activation) will be no more highly activated than other phonologically related lexical units that have been activated later by phonological–lexical feedback. Repetition errors are accounted for by a similar, but reversed, mechanism. The target and phonologically related lexical units are primed early by feedforward activation from auditory input, and suffer more from decay. This activation feeds forward to semantic feature units that in turn feed back to the lexical network to refresh the activation of the decaying target unit. At the same time, this feedback primes semantically related units. Because they are primed

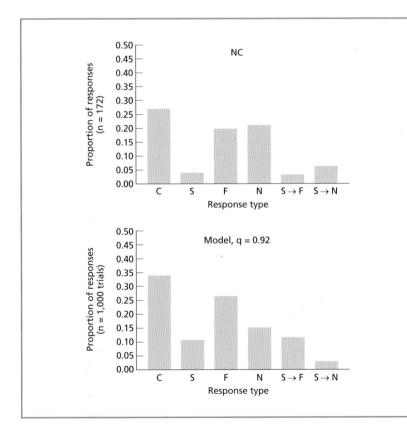

FIGURE 13.16 Proportion of naming errors by deep dysphasic patient, NC, and the lesioned version of Dell's (1986) model of speech production (where the lesion led to abnormal decay of activation). The response categories are: C = correct; S = semantic error; F = formal paraphasia; N = neologism (nonsense word); S → F = formal paraphasia on a semantic error; S → N = neologism on a semantic error. q is decay rate. Figure from Martin et al. (1994).

later, the semantic competitors suffer less from the cumulative effects of the decay impairment, and thus the likelihood increases that they will be selected instead of the target and phonologically related words. It is difficult to sustain the activation of the target lexical unit given rapid decay, particularly when it is hindered in other ways (such as when the target is low frequency, or is supported by impoverished semantic representations).

The idea that a pathological rate of decay and impaired activation processes play a central role in word retrieval deficits has been developed further. Dell, Schwartz, Martin, Saffran, and Gagnon (1997) simulated these deficits with Dell's computational model of speech production. The basic model (called the DSMSG model after the authors) is the interactive two-stage model described earlier: Activation flows from the semantic level through the lemma level to the phoneme level. There are feedback connections between levels. Dell et al. impaired the functioning of the network by reducing the connection weights or increasing the decay rate of the model (or both). These changes were made globally: the same parameter determines processing at each level. Decreasing the connection strength produces a large increase in the number of nonword errors, and a small increase in the number of semantic and phonological word substitutions. Increasing the decay rate at first increases the number of semantic and phonological word substitutions, although eventually more nonword errors are created. The most important dimension determining performance is the severity of damage: Aphasic naming performance lies on a continuum between normal performance and a completely random pattern. As damage becomes severe, the error pattern becomes more random. The model also accounts for the pattern of recovery shown by aphasic speakers with time by gradually resetting the decay variable to its normal value. The model described the naming errors of 21 fluent aphasic patients. It can also account for the pattern of performance shown by two brothers with a degenerative brain disease called progressive aphasia (Croot, Patterson, & Hodges, 1999). The language of one brother (RB) can best be explained by reduced connection strength, while the language of the other (CB) is best explained by an abnormally high decay rate.

Modeling work suggests that the performance of patients with impaired lexical access is better accounted for by impairments to two parameters, semantic weight and phonological weight, rather than by one weight-decay parameter (Foygel & Dell, 2000). These two parameters are measures of the weights, or connection strengths, between the semantic and the lexical (lemma) units, and between the lemma and the phonological units. Damage in the model occurs by varying these weights. The new model fits the patient data slightly better than the weight-decay model. For example, some patients (e.g., PW of Rapp & Caramazza, 1998; DP of Cuetos, Aguado, & Caramazza, 2000) make exclusively semantic errors, and some patients (e.g., JBN of Hillis, Boatman, Hart, & Gordon, 1999; DM of Caramazza, Papagno, & Ruml, 2000) make exclusively phonological errors. These types of patients were not present in the sample modeled by the original DSMSG model, but can be modeled by the Foygel and Dell model. The new model provides an extremely good fit to the naming and repetition performance of a large (94 participant) group of aphasic patients (Dell, Martin, & Schwartz, 2007; Schwartz, Dell, Martin, Gahl, & Sobel, 2006). Finally, the new model fits in very simply with the two-stage model of lexicalization: We can account for the pattern of all types of lexical access failure in terms of the structure of the two-stage model without introducing new parameters (such as decay). Hence the model is more parsimonious than its predecessor.

Although these two models are based on sound psycholinguistic principles, there has been considerable debate about how well their outputs fit a wide range of patient data, and about the extent to which aphasic errors can all result from global damage to all levels of a system, as is the case with pathological delay, an idea called the globality assumption (Ruml & Caramazza, 2000; Ruml, Caramazza, Shelton, & Chialant, 2000). One reason why it is difficult to draw any firm conclusions from this controversy is that there is no agreement on how well a computational model has to fit the data for it to be a good model (Dell, Schwartz, Martin, Saffran, & Gagnon, 2000; Ruml & Caramazza, 2000).

Other types of aphasia

We have concentrated on three major categories of aphasia because of what they tell us about normal speech production. However, there are other types. In global aphasia, spontaneous speech, naming, and repetition are all severely affected. In crossed aphasia, disorders of language arise from damage to the right hemisphere, even in right-handed people.

In conduction aphasia, repetition is relatively impaired, while production and comprehension are relatively good. This dissociation is clear evidence that the processes of repetition can be distinguished from the processes of production and comprehension. There are two subtypes of conduction aphasia. In reproduction conduction aphasia, repetition is poor because of poor phonological encoding. People with reproduction conduction aphasia show impairments in all language production tasks, including speaking, repetition, reading, and writing (Kohn, 1984). Repetition of longer and less familiar words is particularly poor. When reproduction conduction aphasics attempt to correct their errors, they make repeated attempts to produce a word that progressively approximates to the target, a phenomenon known as conduit d'approche (Martin, 2001). In particular, an output phonological buffer is thought to be impaired in reproduction conduction aphasia (Caramazza, Miceli, & Villa, 1986; Shallice, Rumiati, & Zadini, 2000). In STM conduction aphasia, repetition is poor because of an impairment of input auditory short-term memory; these patients make few errors in spontaneous speech production, but repetition of strings of short familiar words is poor (Shallice & Warrington, 1977; Warrington & Shallice, 1969).

On the other hand, people with **transcortical aphasia** can repeat words relatively well. There are two types of transcortical aphasia, depending on the precise site of the lesion. In transcortical sensory aphasia, comprehension is impaired, output is fluent and may even include jargon, but repetition is relatively good. There are two subtypes of transcortical sensory aphasia (Coslett, Roeltgen, Rothi, & Heilman, 1987): one type where both lexical and non-lexical repetition are preserved, and another where only repetition through a non-lexical route is intact. Patients differ in the types of error they

make in naming and spontaneous speech, and on the types of reading error they make. Impairment of the lexical route leads to many word substitutions in speech and surface dyslexia. In transcortical motor aphasia, comprehension and repetition are very good, but there is very little spontaneous speech output.

These disorders can be related to a more detailed model of normal production, but a full account of this depends on an understanding of the relation between language and short-term memory. This topic is covered in Chapter 15.

Evaluation of the contribution of aphasia research to understanding normal processing

At first sight then there is a double dissociation between word-finding and the production of grammatical forms, with these processes located in different brain regions. Broca's patients have difficulty producing grammatical forms, yet have relatively well-preserved word-finding. Wernicke's patients have severe word-finding difficulties, yet have relatively well-preserved syntax. Just as we would expect from Garrett's model, there is a double dissociation between syntactic planning and grammatical element retrieval on the one hand and content word retrieval on the other. This apparent double dissociation supports the main principles of the model.

The types of disorder observed support dissociations between the production of syntax and the retrieval of lexical forms, between the generation of syntax and the access of grammatical morphemes, and the retrieval of the phonology of content words. Garrett argued that content and function words are from different computational vocabularies, and this is confirmed by the neuropsychological work. Schwartz (1987) interpreted agrammatism and jargon aphasia within the framework of Garrett's model. At present, this approach identifies the broad modules found in production rather than the detailed mechanisms involved.

Although syntactic production and comprehension deficits tend to co-occur, the dissociation of grammatical impairments in comprehension and production suggests that at some level there are distinct syntactic processes in production and comprehension. That is, some agrammatic patients have no comprehension impairments, and some people with comprehension deficits do not have any production impairments. Furthermore, there is no correlation between the severity of the production and comprehension syntactic deficits that patients exhibit (Caplan, 1992). The parser and the syntactic planner are to a large degree separable.

There is a problem with this double dissociation: it might be an artifact of considering just people who speak English. Cross-linguistic studies of speakers of languages that are much more richly inflected show different types of break-down (Dick et al., 2001). In particular, patients with damage to Wernicke's area make many more grammatical errors, making many grammatical substitutions (something for which there is little scope in English). Dick et al. argue that Broca's aphasics tend to omit things and Wernicke's aphasics tend to substitute things, not because of underlying grammatical reasons, but simply because of the differing speech rates of the two groups. When speech is very slow, many items fail to reach a critical level of activation, meaning that weakly represented elements are omitted. Substitution errors increase with speech rate, but in English there is little scope for grammatical substitution. Hence it looks as though people with Broca's aphasia are making grammatical errors, and those with Wernicke's aphasia lexical errors, but really the two disorders lie on a continuum of omission and substitution errors, with the nature of English limiting the sort of errors that can occur. Dick et al. argue that their results show that grammar is not localized in one specific brain region (such as Broca's area), but instead makes use of many regions. Damage to Broca's area has serious consequences for grammatical processing, but in a more distributed account it does not necessarily mean that grammar is located there.

WRITING AND AGRAPHIA

There has been even less work on writing than there has been on speaking. Obviously writing and speaking are similar, but there are also significant differences. In Chapter 15 I will show that the neuropsychological evidence suggests that speaking and writing use different lexical systems. We have much more time available when writing compared with when speaking. We also (usually) speak to another person, but write alone (even if for an audience). This leads to two major differences between spoken and written language (Chafe, 1985). Written language is more integrated and syntactically complex than spoken language. We take more time to write, and can plan and edit our output more easily. Second, writing involves little interaction with other people, and as a result shows less personal involvement than speech. This has important consequences for teaching writing skills (Czerniewska, 1992).

Hayes and Flower (1980, 1986) identified three stages of writing. The first is the planning stage. Here goals are set, ideas are generated, and information is retrieved from long-term memory and organized into a plan for what to write. The second is the translation stage. Here written language is produced from the representation in memory. The plan has to be turned into sentences. In the third stage, reviewing, the writer reads and edits what has been written.

Collins and Gentner (1980) described the planning stage in some detail. They distinguished between the initial generation of ideas, and their subsequent manipulation into a form suitable for translation into the final text. They suggested several means of generating ideas: Writing down all the ideas you have on a topic, keeping a journal of interesting ideas, brainstorming in a group, looking in books and journals, getting suggestions from other people, and trying to explain your ideas to somebody. Although these ideas must be put down in tangible form, at this stage it is important not to get too carried away with translation into text. Collins and Gentner identified several methods of manipulating ideas into a form suitable for translation. These include identifying dependent variables, generating critical cases, comparing similar cases, contrasting dissimilar cases, simulating, categorizing, and imposing structure.

A number of factors are known to distinguish good from less able writers. Differences at the planning stage are particularly important (Eysenck & Keane, 2010). Better writers can manipulate the knowledge they have, rather than just telling it (Bereiter & Scardamalia, 1987). Better writers are more able to construct suitable plans than less able writers. They are more flexible about their plans, changing them as new information becomes available or as it becomes apparent that the original plan is unsatisfactory (Hayes & Flower, 1986). Indeed, one of the most serious errors that novice writers can commit is to confuse idea generation and planning with translation into text, so that text constraints enter at too early a stage (Collins & Gentner, 1980). If this happens the writer loses track of the desired content and spends too much time editing text that is then often discarded. Text that is undesirable may be kept in just because the writer is reluctant to discard it given all the effort that has been put into it.

Although the planning stage is particularly important, there are also differences at the other two levels. Good writers can generate longer sentence parts: They seem to think in larger "writing chunks" (Kaufer, Hayes, & Flower, 1986). Good writers can also readily produce appealing text: They know that good text must be enticing, comprehensible, memorable, and persuasive (Collins & Gentner, 1980). When they revise their material, good writers are more likely than less skilled writers to change the meaning of what they have written (Faigley & Witte, 1983).

Finally, although producing outlines improves the quality of the final work, perhaps surprisingly, producing more detailed rough drafts does not (Eysenck & Keane, 2010; Kellogg, 1988). This is because planning is the most important and difficult part of writing, and producing an outline assists this stage. Producing a rough draft confers very little additional advantage to this (Eysenck & Keane, 2010).

Where should you begin when writing? Quite often the beginning might not be the best place. Some people recommend starting with the section that you think will be easiest to write (e.g., Rosnow & Rosnow, 1992). It probably doesn't matter too much; the important thing is to have constructed a plan of what you need to write before you start.

The neuroscience of writing

The phonic mediation theory says that, when we write, we first retrieve the spoken sounds of words and then produce the written word (Luria, 1970). Neuropsychological data show that the phonic mediation theory is almost certainly wrong (Ellis & Young, 1988/1996). There are patients who can spell words that they cannot speak (e.g., Bub & Kertesz, 1982b; Caramazza, Berndt, & Basili, 1983; Ellis et al., 1983; Levine, Calvanio, & Popovics, 1982). That is, inner speech is not necessary for writing.

Brain damage can affect writing to produce **dysgraphia**. There are types of dysgraphia similar to the types of dyslexia. Shallice (1981) described the case of PR, who was a patient with phonological dysgraphia. This patient could spell many familiar words, but could not generate spellings from sounds. That is, he could spell words but not nonwords. (This is also further evidence against the phonological mediation theory.) Beauvois and Derouesné (1981) reported RG, who could spell nonwords but who would regularize irregular words, a condition called *surface dysgraphia*. Finally, there are examples of people with deep dysgraphia who make semantic errors in writing (e.g., writing "star" as "moon"; see Bub & Kertesz, 1982a; Newcombe & Marshall, 1980; Saffran, Schwartz, & Marin, 1976).

Degenerative diseases such as Alzheimer's (see Chapter 11) can affect the high-level processes involved in writing. It is possible to detect very early changes in writing style as a consequence of the disease. The acclaimed British writer Iris Murdoch won the Booker Prize in 1978 with her novel *The Sea, the Sea*. Her final novel, *Jackson's Dilemma* (published in 1995), met with an unenthusiastic response from literary critics. She originally attributed her writing difficulties to "writer's block," but showed a general cognitive decline around this time, and was diagnosed with Alzheimer's disease in 1996. She died in 1999. A detailed analysis of her early and midperiod novels compared with her final novel shows that although there were few differences in syntax, there were large differences in the choice of words (Garrard, Maloney, Hodges, & Patterson, 2005). Words in the final novel tended to be much higher in frequency, and chosen from a much more restricted vocabulary.

SUMMARY

- Speech production has been studied less than language comprehension because of the difficulty in controlling the input (our thoughts).
- Speech production can be divided into conceptualization, formulation, and execution.
- Formulation comprises syntactic planning and lexicalization.
- Lexicalization is the process of retrieving the sound of a word given its meaning.
- Speech errors are an important source of data in speech production, and can be described in terms of the units and mechanisms involved.
- One of the best known models of formulation is Garrett's; Garrett argues that speech error evidence suggests there is a distinction between a functional level of planning and a positional level of planning.
- Explicit serial order information is not encoded at the functional level of Garrett's model.
- The distinction between function and content words is central in speech production, as they never exchange with each other in speech errors.
- Syntactic persistence is the phenomenon whereby we tend to reuse syntactic structures; hence we can facilitate and direct production with appropriate prime sentences.
- Number agreement is determined by the underlying number of the subject noun.
- Production and syntactic planning has an incremental component to it.
- The strong version of Garrett's model, in which the stages are discrete and do not interact, is undermined by phonologically facilitated cognitive intrusions, blends of phrases merging at the point of maximum phonological similarity, and similarity and familiarity biases in speech errors.
- In the two-stage model of lexicalization, a meaning-based stage is followed by a phonologically based stage.
- Tip-of-the-tongue (TOT) states are noticeable pauses in retrieving a word; they arise because of insufficient activation of the words in the lexicon.
- Evidence for two stages comes from an analysis of speech errors and TOTs, and of anomia in languages that have gender.
- Lemmas are syntactically and semantically specified, amodal lexical representations.
- The amodal nature and syntactic mediation function of lemmas are debatable.
- Experimental studies of picture naming do not always find mediated semantic-phonological priming. Although this result suggests that the two stages of processing are discrete, simulations show that it is not inconsistent with a cascade model, and other evidence suggests that the two stages are accessed in cascade.
- Speech errors show lexical (familiarity) and similarity biases; these findings suggest that lexicalization is interactive.
- Models such as that of Dell provide an interactive account of lexicalization.
- It is not clear why feedback connections exist, but connectionist models based on phonological attractors can in principle still account for the data.
- The main problem for phonological encoding is ensuring that we produce the sounds in the correct sequence.
- One important method of ensuring correct sequencing is to make a distinction between frames and content.
- The phonological word is the basic unit of phonological planning.
- Hesitations reflect planning by the speaker, although they may also serve social and segmentation functions.
- Microplanning pauses indicate transient difficulty in retrieving the phonological forms of less predictable words, whereas macroplanning pauses indicate both semantic and syntactic planning.

- We sometimes hesitate before less predictable words, suggesting that we are having a temporary difficulty in retrieving them.
- We tend to pause between major syntactic units of speech, and in these pauses we plan the content of what we want to say.
- Speech falls in planning cycles, with fluent execution phases following hesitant planning phases in which we do a relatively large amount of planning, each cycle corresponding to an idea.
- Aphasia is an impairment of language processing following brain damage.
- Broca's aphasia patients are not fluent, often with some deficit in syntactic comprehension, whereas Wernicke's aphasics are fluent, usually with very poor comprehension.
- Agrammatism is a controversial label covering a number of aspects of impaired syntactic processing, including a sentence construction deficit, the loss of grammatical elements of speech, and impaired syntactic comprehension.
- Jargon aphasia is a disorder of lexical retrieval characterized by paraphasias and neologisms.
- Lexical-semantic anomia arises because of an impairment of semantic processing, whereas phonological anomia arises because of difficulty in accessing phonological word forms.
- Naming errors can be modeled by manipulating connection strengths and the rate of decay of activation.
- Writing is less constrained by time than speech production, and is less cooperative than speech.
- Writing involves planning, translation, and reviewing; of these, planning is the most difficult.
- There are types of dysgraphia analogous to the types of dyslexia.

QUESTIONS TO THINK ABOUT

1. How does writing differ from reading?
2. How similar are speech errors to other sorts of action slip (e.g., intending to switch a light off when it has already been switched off)?
3. Collect your own speech errors for 2 weeks. How well can they be accounted for by models of speech production?
4. Observe when you pause and hesitate when speaking. Relate these observations to what you have learned in this chapter.
5. Models of speech production have largely used connectionist architectures based on interactive activation networks, whereas models of word recognition have largely used feedforward networks trained with back-propagation. Can you think of any reason for this difference in emphasis?

FURTHER READING

See Wheeldon (2000) and Alario, Costa, Pickering, and Ferreira (2006) for collections of papers covering all aspects of language production. A classic reference is Levelt (1989). Levelt discusses what might happen at the message level. Dennett (1991) speculates about how the conceptualizer might work.

(Continued)

(Continued)

In addition to number agreement, in many languages it is important that gender is matched between adjectives, articles, and nouns. For work in this area, see Alario and Caramazza (2002); Costa, Kovacic, Fedorenko, and Caramazza (2003); Schiller and Caramazza (2003); Schiller and Costa (2006); Schriefers, Jescheniak, and Hantsch (2005); and Schriefers and Teruel (2000).

For more on hesitations and pauses, see Beattie (1983) for a sympathetic review and Petrie (1987) for a critical review. For a review of the role of interaction in lexicalization and syntactic planning, see Vigliocco and Hartsuiker (2002).

See Meyer (2004) for a review of work on the visual world and speech production.

For further information on the neuropsychology of language, see Kolb and Whishaw (2009). For more on what cognitive neuropsychology tells us about normal speech production, see Caplan (1992, with a paperback edition in 1996). See Roelofs, Meyer, and Levelt (1998) for a response to Caramazza on the necessity of lemmas. See Rapp and Goldrick (2005) for a review of the literature on the neuropsychology of word production.

See Vinson (1999) for an introductory review of language in aphasia. The methodological issues involved in cognitive neuropsychology have spawned a large literature of their own. Indeed, a special issue of the journal *Cognitive Neuropsychology* (1988, volume 5, issue 5) is completely devoted to this topic. Much of the emphasis in this area has been on the status of agrammatism. For a more detailed discussion, see also Shallice (1988). The nature of agrammatism has always been central in this debate. See Hale (2002) for an account of what it must be like to lose language after a stroke, and how the loss affects the family of the person.

See Emmorey (2001) for a review of the production of sign language. Sign language breaks down after brain damage in interesting ways. Ellis and Young (1988) review the literature on the neuropsychology of sign languages and gestures.

For more on the dual versus single route models of how we generate regular and irregular verbs, see the debate in *Trends in Cognitive Science* (Marslen-Wilson & Tyler, 2003; McClelland & Patterson, 2002, 2003; Pinker & Ullman, 2002).

For excellent overviews of research on writing, see Ellis (1993) and Eysenck and Keane (2010). The latter covers the Hayes and Flower model in detail. Flower and Hayes (1980) discuss the planning process in more detail. Ellis (1993) also has a section on disorders of writing, the dysgraphias. Ellis and Young (1988) also cover peripheral dysgraphias, which affect the lower levels of writing. See Czerniewska (1992) for information on learning how to write, and how writing should best be taught.

CHAPTER 14

HOW DO WE USE LANGUAGE?

INTRODUCTION

There is more to being a skilled language user than just understanding and producing language. The study of **pragmatics** looks at how we deal with those aspects of language that go beyond the simple meaning of what we hear and say. One obvious way of doing this is by making **inference**s. Pragmatics is concerned with how we get things done with language and how we work out what the purpose is behind the speaker's utterance.

Furthermore, much of what we have been concerned with so far is either how a comprehender understands language, or how a speaker produces language. But usually we use language in a social setting: we engage in dialog. It is possible that the sorts of theory we have considered so far offer limited theories of language processing (Pickering & Garrod, 2004).

This chapter is about how we use language. The study of pragmatics can be divided into two interrelated topics. The first is how we as hearers and speakers go beyond the literal meaning of what we hear to make and draw inferences. (Of course, not all inferences are always intended!) For example, if I say "Can you pass the salt?" I am usually not really asking you whether you have the ability to pass the salt; it is an indirect, polite way of saying, "Please pass the salt." Except perhaps in psycholinguistics experiments, we do not produce random utterances; we are trying to achieve particular goals when speaking. So how do we get things done with language? Clark (1996) calls this type of behavior layering. In practice, language has multiple layers of meaning.

The second topic is how we maintain conversations. To get things done, we have to collaborate. For example, we clearly do not want to talk all at the same time. How do we avoid this? Do conversations have a structure that helps us to prevent this? And can we draw any inferences from apparent transgressions of conversational structure?

Language use is a huge topic with many textbooks devoted to it, and I can only consider the most important ideas here. A central theme here is that people are always making inferences at all levels on the basis of what they hear. Our utterances interact with the context in which they are uttered to give them their full meaning.

By the end of this chapter you should:

- Understand how we use language.
- Understand how we go beyond literal meaning.
- Understand how we manage conversations.
- Know how researchers use the visual world to investigate language processing.

MAKING INFERENCES IN CONVERSATION

We have seen that inferences play an important part in understanding text, and are just as important in conversation. We make inferences not just from what people say, but also from how they say it, and even from what they do not say. In conversation, though, we have an additional resource: we can ask the other person. Conversation is a cooperative act.

Speech acts

When we speak, we have goals, and it is the listener's task to discover those goals. According to Austin (1962/1976) and Searle (1969), every time we speak we perform a **speech act**. That is, we are trying to get things done with our utterances.

Austin (1976) began with the goal of exploring sentences containing performative verbs. These verbs perform an act in their very utterance, such as "I hereby pronounce you man and wife" (as long as the circumstances are appropriate—such as that I have the authority to do so; such circumstances are called the felicity conditions). Austin concluded that all sentences are performative, though mostly in an indirect way. That is, all sentences are doing something—if only stating a fact. For example, the statement "My house is terraced" can be analyzed as "I hereby assert that my house is terraced." Austin distinguished three effects or forces that each sentence possesses (see Figure 14.1). The locutionary force of an utterance is its literal meaning. The illocutionary force is what the speaker is trying to get done with the utterance. The perlocutionary force is the effect the utterance actually has on the actions and beliefs of the listener. For example, if I say (1) the literal meaning is that I am asking you whether you have the ability to pass the gin. The illocutionary force is that I hereby request you to pass the gin. The utterance might have the perlocutionary force of making you think that I drink too much.

(1) Can you pass the gin?

"Top me up!" This directive speech act may be interpreted beyond its literal meaning and have the perlocutionary effect of making fellow diners think that she has had quite enough wine to drink already!

According to Searle (1969, 1975), when we speak we make speech acts. Every speech act falls into one of five categories (see Figure 14.2):

- *Representatives.* The speaker is asserting a fact and conveying his or her belief that a statement is true. ("Boris rides a bicycle.")
- *Directives.* The speaker is trying to get the listener to do something. (In asking the question "Does Boris ride a bicycle?" the speaker is trying to get the hearer to give information.)
- *Commissives.* The speaker commits him or herself to some future course of action. ("If Boris doesn't ride a bicycle, I will give you a present.")
- *Expressives.* The speaker wishes to reveal his or her psychological state. ("I'm sorry to hear that Boris only rides a bicycle.")

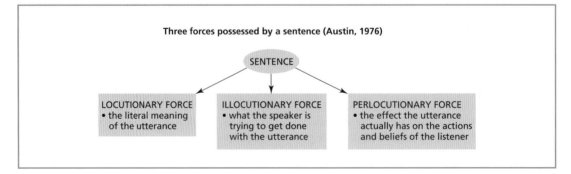

Three forces possessed by a sentence (Austin, 1976)

SENTENCE

LOCUTIONARY FORCE	ILLOCUTIONARY FORCE	PERLOCUTIONARY FORCE
• the literal meaning of the utterance	• what the speaker is trying to get done with the utterance	• the effect the utterance actually has on the actions and beliefs of the listener

FIGURE 14.1

- *Declaratives.* The speaker brings about a new state of affairs. ("Boris—you're fired for riding a bicycle!")

Different theorists specify different categories of speech acts. For example, D'Andrade and Wish (1985) described seven types. They distinguished between assertions and reactions (such as "I agree") as different types of representatives, and they distinguished requests for information from other request directives. The lack of agreement and the lack of detailed criteria of what constitutes any type of speech act are obvious problems here. Furthermore, some utterances might be ambiguous, and if so, how do we select the appropriate speech act analysis? A further challenge is that it needs to be made explicit how the listener uses the context to assign the utterance to the appropriate speech act type.

Direct speech acts are straightforward utterances where the intention of the speaker is revealed in the words. Indirect speech acts require some work on the part of the listener. The most famous example is "Can you pass the salt?," as analyzed earlier. Speech acts can become increasingly indirect ("Is the salt at your end of the table?" to "This food is a bit bland"), often with

increasing politeness. The less conventional they are, the more computational work is required by the listener. Over 90% of requests are indirect in English (Gibbs, 1986b). Indirectness serves a function: it is an important mechanism for conveying politeness in conversation (Brown & Levinson, 1987). It also enables the speaker to be *strategic* in their language: for example, if you are offering someone a bribe, you might want to do so indirectly, so you can fall back on the direct meaning should they turn out to be more honest than you—"I never meant it that way!" (Lee & Pinker, 2010).

The meanings of indirect speech acts are not always immediately apparent. Searle (1979) proposed a two-stage mechanism for computing the intended meaning. First, the listener tries the literal meaning to see if it makes sense in context, and it is only if it does not that he or she will do the additional work of finding a non-literal meaning. There is an opposing one-stage model where people derive the non-literal meaning either instead of or as well as the literal one (Keysar, 1989). The evidence is conflicting, but certainly the non-literal meaning is understood as fast as or faster than the literal meaning, which favors a one-stage model. For example, Gibbs (1986a) found that in an appropriate context

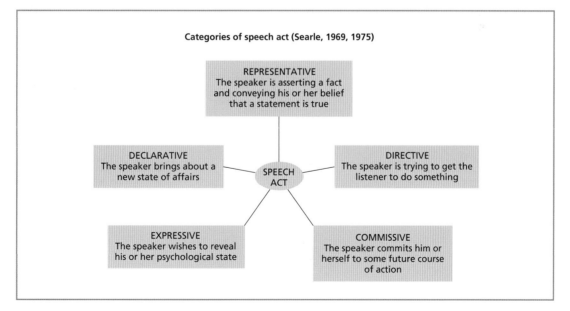

Categories of speech act (Searle, 1969, 1975)

REPRESENTATIVE
The speaker is asserting a fact and conveying his or her belief that a statement is true

DECLARATIVE
The speaker brings about a new state of affairs

SPEECH ACT

DIRECTIVE
The speaker is trying to get the listener to do something

EXPRESSIVE
The speaker wishes to reveal his or her psychological state

COMMISSIVE
The speaker commits him or herself to some future course of action

FIGURE 14.2

participants took no longer to understand the sarcastic sense of "You're a fine friend!" than the literal sense in a context where that was appropriate.

Clark (1994) detailed examples of many kinds of layering that can occur in conversation. We can be ironic, sarcastic, or humorous, we can tease, we can ask rhetorical questions that do not demand answers, and so on. Although we probably understand these types of utterance using similar sorts of mechanisms as with indirect speech acts, much work remains to be done in this area.

How to run a conversation: Grice's maxims

Grice (1975) proposed that in conversations speakers and listeners cooperate to make the conversation meaningful and purposeful. That is, we adhere to a cooperative principle. To comply with this, according to Grice, you must make your conversational contribution such as is required, when it is required. This is achieved by use of four **conversational maxim**s (see Figure 14.3):

- Maxim of quantity. Make your contributions as informative as is required, but no more.
- Maxim of quality. Make your contribution true. Do not say anything that you believe to be false, or for which you lack sufficient evidence.

- Maxim of relevance. Make your contribution relevant to the aims of the conversation.
- Maxim of manner. Be clear: Avoid obscurity, ambiguity, wordiness, and disorder in your language.

Subsequently there has been some debate on whether there is any redundancy in these maxims. Sperber and Wilson (1986) argued that relevance is primary among them and that the others can be deduced from it.

Conversations quickly break down when we deviate from these maxims without purpose. However, we usually try to make sense of conversations that appear to deviate from them. We assume that overall the speaker is following the cooperative principle. To do this, we make a particular type of inference known as a conversational **implicature**. Consider the following conversational exchange (2).

(2) Vlad: Do you think my nice new expensive gold fillings suit me?
     Boris: Gee, it's hot in here.

Boris's utterance clearly violates the maxim of relevance. How can we explain this? Most of us would make the conversational implicature that in refusing to answer the question, Boris is

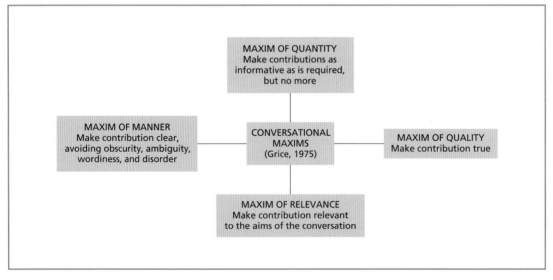

FIGURE 14.3

implying that he dislikes Vlad's new fillings and doesn't think they suit him at all, but for some reason doesn't want to say so to his face. Indeed, face management is a common reason for violating the maxim of relevance (Goffman, 1967; Holtgraves, 1998): People do not want to hurt or be hurt. The listeners' recognition of this plays an important role in how they make inferences that make sense of remarks that apparently violate relevance (Holtgraves, 1998).

There are other ways in which speakers cooperate in conversations. Garrod and Anderson (1987) observed people cooperating in an attempt to solve a computer-generated maze game. The pairs of speakers very quickly adopted similar forms of description—a phenomenon called lexical entrainment. For example, we could call a picture of a dog "a dog," "a poodle," "a white poodle," or even "an animal." The frequency and recency of name selection can override other factors that influence lexical choice, such as informativeness, accessibility, and being at the basic level. Brennan and Clark (1996) proposed that in conversations speakers jointly make conceptual pacts about which names to use. Conceptual pacts are dynamic: They evolve over time, can be simplified, and even abandoned for new conceptualizations.

Of course, sometimes we don't want to cooperate in conversations. Some people sometimes want to lie; frequently we want to keep things to ourselves. This privacy can sometimes be very difficult to maintain. Readers of a certain age might remember an episode of the UK television program "Dad's Army," where Captain Mainwaring, desperate to keep Corporal Pike's name from the invaders, says "Don't tell him (your name), Pike." (Here is another example: DON'T think of a pink elephant.) Often it seems that the harder we try to keep something private, the more likely it is to pop out. An experiment carried out by Wardlow Lane, Groisman, and Ferreira (2006) showed that this impression is correct. Speakers described simple objects (e.g., triangles) to other people. Some information was known only to the speakers (e.g., that there was also another, larger triangle in the scene concealed from the listeners). Wardlow Lane et al. call this type of information

privileged information. They found that if speakers were told to keep this privileged information secret, they were in fact more likely to refer to the concealed objects. Wardlow Lane et al. explain the results in terms of our monitoring speech; monitoring can bring things that we are trying to avoid into awareness, increasing the chance that they are in fact produced. Freud (1975) would talk in terms of repression; the two explanations are not a million miles apart.

The right hemisphere of the brain plays an important role in processing some pragmatic aspects of language (see Lindell, 2006, for a review). We saw in Chapter 12 that patients with right-hemisphere damage have difficulty in understanding jokes; more generally, the right hemisphere is involved in non-literal processing. Patients with right-hemisphere damage have difficulty in understanding jokes, idioms, metaphors, and proverbs. Imagine the sort of literal image provoked by the phrase "crying your eyes out" (Lindell, 2006; Winner & Gardner, 1977).

THE STRUCTURE OF CONVERSATION

There are two different approaches to analyzing the way in which conversations are structured (Levinson, 1983). Discourse analysis uses the general methods of linguistics. It aims to discover the basic units of discourse and the rules that relate them. The most extreme version of this is the attempt to find a grammar for conversation in the same way as there are sentence and story grammars. Labov and Fanshel (1977), in one of the most famous examples of the analysis of discourse, looked at the structure of psychotherapy episodes. Utterances are segmented into units such as speech acts, and conversational sequences are regulated by a set of sequencing rules that operate over these units. Conversation analysis is much more empirical, aiming to uncover general properties of the organization of conversation without applying rules. Conversation analysis was pioneered by ethnomethodologists, who examine social behavior in its natural setting. The data consist of tape-recordings and more latterly videos of transcripts of naturally occurring conversations.

In a conversation, speaker A says something, speaker B has a turn, speaker A then has another turn, and so on; we call this aspect of conversation turn-taking. A turn varies in length, and might contain more than one idea. Other speakers might speak during a turn in the form of back-channel communication, making sounds ("hmm hmm"), words ("yep"), or gestures (e.g., nodding) to show that the listener is still listening, is understanding, agrees, or whatever (Duncan & Niederehe, 1974; Yngve, 1970). Turn structure is made explicit by the example of adjacency pairs (such as question–answer pairs, or greeting–greeting pairs, or offer–acceptance pairs). The exact nature of the turns and their length depend on the social settings: seminars are different from spontaneous drunken conversation. Nevertheless speakers manage to control conversations remarkably accurately. Less than 5% of conversation consists of the overlap of two speakers talking at once, and the average gap between turns is just a few tenths of a second (Ervin-Tripp, 1979).

Speakers must use quite a sophisticated mechanism for ensuring that turn-taking proceeds smoothly. Sacks, Schegloff, and Jefferson (1974) proposed that the minimal turn-constructional unit from which a turn is constructed is determined by syntactic and semantic structure, and by the intonational contour of the utterance (over which the speaker has a great deal of control). A speaker is initially assigned just one of these minimal units, and then a transition relevance place where a change of speaker might arise. Sacks et al. discussed a number of rules that govern whether or not speakers actually do change at this point. Gaze is important: We tend to look at our listeners when we are coming to the end of a turn. Hand gestures might be used to indicate that the speaker wishes to continue. As important as visual cues might be, they cannot be the whole story, as we have no difficulty in ensuring smooth turn transitions in telephone conversations. Filled pauses indicate a wish to continue speaking. Speakers might deliberately invite a change of speakers by asking a question; otherwise

Visual cues, such as gaze and hand gestures, are important in ensuring smooth turn-taking. However, they play only a small part in the complex sequence of social rules that govern conversation.

a complex sequence of social rules comes into play. The advantage of the system discussed by Sacks et al. is that it can predict other characteristics of conversation, such as when overlaps (competing starts of turns, or where transitional relevance places have been misidentified) or gaps do occur.

Wilson and Wilson (2005) propose a more biological model of the control of turn-taking. They argue that during conversation endogenous oscillators in the brains of speaker and listener become synchronized, or entrained. Endogenous oscillators are groups of neurons that fire together in a periodic way and hence act like clocks in the brain. The driving force of this synchronization is the speaker's rate of syllable production. A cyclic pattern develops, with the probability of one of the conversants initiating speech at any time being out of phase with the other, so minimizing the likelihood that the two people will start speaking at the same time. The two key ideas of this proposal are that biological clocks ensure we do not speak simultaneously, and these clocks obtain their timing from the speech stream.

COLLABORATION IN DIALOG

Conversation is a collaborative enterprise, and speakers collaborate with listeners to ensure that their utterances are understood (Clark & Wilkes-Gibbs, 1986; Schober & Clark, 1989). People go to considerable lengths to take the other person's point of view in dialog, sometimes regardless of the cognitive load necessitated (Duran, Dale, & Kreuz, 2011). The idea that speakers tailor their utterances to the particular needs of the addressees is called **audience design** (Clark, 1996).

In Chapter 12 we saw how readers and listeners construct representations of incoming language. Conversation is a process of communicating these representations, of trying to make the representation of the speaker and the listener the same—almost of filling in gaps. (Of course, there are exceptions; when someone is lying, or deliberately withholding information, they are trying to make sure that the gaps are not filled in.) Pickering and Garrod (2004) call this process of trying to make the language representations of speakers and listeners coincide alignment. In their interactive alignment model, during dialog the linguistic representations of the participants become aligned at many levels (including the overall mental model of what is going on, the syntactic level, and the lexical level). They argue alignment occurs by means of four types of largely automatic mechanism: priming, inference, the use of routine expressions, and the monitoring and repair of language output. Such alignment of linguistic representations leads to the alignment of the speaker's and the listener's situation models (Zwaan & Radvansky, 1998). Perhaps the most important of these alignment mechanisms is priming. We have examined priming in several contexts (e.g., lexical priming in Chapter 6, syntactic priming in Chapter 13). Priming of words and syntactic structures ensures that linguistic representations become aligned at a number of levels. This account assumes much less explicit reasoning about one's interlocutor than alternative views such as that of Clark (1996). Pickering and Garrod (2006) further emphasize the way in which listeners make predictions in conversations, and that these predictions are made by the speech production system: Comprehension draws on production, particularly in difficult circumstances.

There are other reasons for supposing that audience design is an emergent, interactive process. Horton and Gerrig (2005) found that the memory requirements of a task influence speakers. They used a task in which "Directors" gave instructions about manipulating an array of cards to "Matchers." They found that the Directors were much better able to take the needs of the Matchers into account when their own memory demands produced by the task were lower. If speakers have a lot to remember, they find it difficult to take the needs of the listeners and the detailed past history of their conversational interaction into account.

Audience design

The idea that speakers tailor their productions to address the specific needs of their listeners is called *audience design*. An example of audience design is child-directed speech (see Chapter 4), when adults modify their utterances when speaking to infants and children.

We also saw in Chapter 10 that speakers sometimes use prosody and pausing to help listeners disambiguate what they say. Speakers also seem to monitor what they say with the goal of reducing ambiguity. While speakers sometimes avoid linguistic ambiguity (e.g., ambiguous words, as of the type we examined in Chapter 6, or temporarily ambiguous structures, of the sort we examined in Chapter 10), they go out of their way to avoid non-linguistic ambiguity (Ferreira, Slevc, & Rogers, 2005). Non-linguistic ambiguity arises when there are multiple instances of similar meanings—for example, if there are several instances of the same object in the visual scene, or several instances that could be described by the same word. If there are two apples in front of us, one red and one green, we are unlikely to say just "give me the apple." In their experiment, speakers described target objects (e.g., the flying mammal "bat") in contexts where there were other objects that could cause linguistic (a baseball) or non-linguistic (a larger flying mammal) ambiguity (see Figure 14.4). Ferreira et al.'s results found that speakers monitor their speech and can sometimes detect and avoid linguistic ambiguity before producing it, but almost always avoid non-linguistic ambiguity. Speakers are much better at dealing with non-linguistic ambiguity than with linguistic ambiguity. A related study looking at dialog between two speakers engaged in moving objects on a grid found that when the visual context was potentially ambiguous, speakers tried to disambiguate their utterances (Haywood, Pickering, & Branigan, 2005). Hence speakers do pay some attention to the needs of the listener.

There are, however, limits to how far a speaker will go to make the listener's life easier. Ferreira and Dell (2000) examined the extent to which speakers used optional complementizers (e.g., "that," which is optional in "the vampire knew [that] you hated blood," a structure that is ambiguous up until the word "hated"). If speakers are trying to produce structures that are as easy to understand and as unambiguous as possible, they should frequently include these optional words in sentences that would otherwise be ambiguous. However, they do not. Instead they choose structures that are easy to produce and that enable them to produce the main content words as early as possible. Speech production proceeds with quickly selected lemmas being produced as soon as possible. In addition, while speakers produce prosodic cues (such as lengthening words and inserting pauses) to syntactic boundaries, and listeners do pay attention to these cues, speakers tend to do so regardless of whether or not the listener really needs it. For example, the speakers provide disambiguating cues to the syntactic structure of instructions such as "Put the dog in the basket on the star" regardless of whether or not the referential situation is actually ambiguous (Kraljic & Brennan, 2005). This finding suggests that there are limitations to audience design. What is more, speakers overestimate how good they are at conveying information (Keysar & Henly, 2002). Keysar and Henly looked at 40 speakers producing syntactically ambiguous sentences such as "Boris shot the man with the gun" and lexically ambiguous sentences such as "The typist tried to read the letter without her glasses." Nearly half (46%) of the time the speaker thought the listeners had correctly understood the sentence; in fact they had not. So not only are there limits to how much speakers tailor their productions to their listeners, they do not always do so correctly even when they try.

SOUND AND VISION

We saw in Chapter 3 that human language is so powerful because we can talk about anything—we can talk about things remote in time and space, and about very abstract notions. However, just because we can do these things, it doesn't mean we do them all the time. In fact a great deal of the time we talk literally about what is in front of our eyes. For much of everyday life we converse about the "here-and-now." Not surprisingly, therefore, the study of how language interacts with the visual world has become of considerable importance over the last few years. Perhaps the only surprise is why it has taken so long

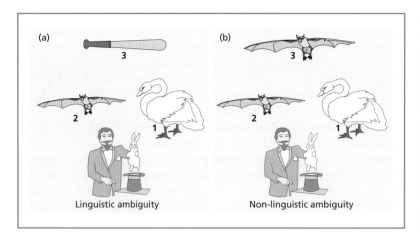

FIGURE 14.4 Sample displays used by Ferreira et al., in which the object labeled 3 had to be named so as to discriminate it from the other objects. In (a), there is linguistic ambiguity (baseball bat vs. mammal bat); in (b), there is non-linguistic ambiguity (large vs. small bat). Performance was much worse with linguistic than with non-linguistic ambiguity. Adapted from Ferreira et al. (2005).

for this topic to become so prominent. The answer to this question is that the study of how we interact with the visual world requires sophisticated eye-movement technology, and such technology has only recently become available.

A second reason why the study of the visual world has become so important is that it provides us with a new tool for studying how we understand language and speech. We can now see in real time how people make use of external, visual information when processing language. The visual world paradigm has recently proved very popular for investigating sentence processing (see many studies in Chapter 10) and speech production (see Chapter 13).

While adults make considerable use of the visual world, similar studies show that children do so to a much lesser extent (Snedeker & Trueswell, 2004; Trueswell, Sekerina, Hill, & Logrip, 1999). Five-year-old children rely exclusively on verb-bias information. Highly reliable cues, such as lexical bias, emerge first in development, with referential information gradually being used as the child gets older. Furthermore, although referential information may not determine which structures young children construct, it may reduce the time it takes to construct them (Snedeker & Trueswell, 2004).

Using visual information in comprehension

We saw in Chapter 10 that many sources of information are used to help us construct a syntactic representation and to resolve syntactic ambiguity. While adult readers rely mostly on lexical information to generate alternative syntactic structures, adult listeners make a great deal of use of the visual world in front of them. In particular, people can use referential information from the visual scene at which they are looking to override very strong lexical biases (Tanenhaus et al., 1995).

The role of the visual world in comprehension has since been demonstrated in several experiments. For example, Spivey, Tanenhaus, Eberhard, and Sedivy (2002) monitored the eye movements of participants following spoken instructions about picking up moving objects in a visual workspace. The eye movements were closely linked to the associated referential expressions (phrases describing objects) in the instructions. What happens when people are given temporarily ambiguous sentences, such as (3), which contains a temporarily ambiguous prepositional phrase?

(3) Put the apple on the towel in the box.

The normally preferred initial interpretation is the goal-argument analysis (put the apple on the towel); the less usual initial interpretation is the noun-phrase modifier (the apple that is already on the towel should be put somewhere else). The answer depends on the visual context. If there was just one apple in the visual scene, people would go with the usual preferred

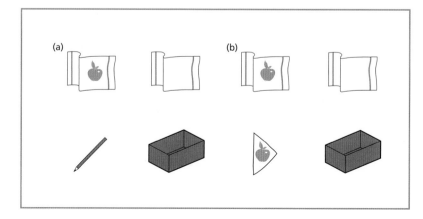

FIGURE 14.5 Examples of the display conditions used by Spivey et al. (2002). In scene (a) participants spent time looking at the target destination (the empty towel), whereas in scene (b) they spent less time looking at the empty towel. Based on Spivey et al. (2002).

analysis, and spend time looking at the supposed (but incorrect) target destination (an empty towel). If there was more than one apple, however, participants assumed the less usual modification analysis, and did not spend much time looking at the empty towel (see Figure 14.5). Eye movements showed that the initial interpretation was the one consistent with the visual context.

Using a similar sort of design, Chambers, Tanenhaus, and Magnuson (2004) showed that properties of objects in the visual world can influence parsing. They gave participants temporarily ambiguous sentences such as "Pour the egg in the bowl over the flour." The eggs in the scene could be in a liquid form, or whole. You cannot pour whole eggs, so people spend little time looking at them given the start of this instruction. Listeners restrict their attention to objects that are physically compatible with what they hear. If all you can see is one egg, in a bowl, in liquid form, you will analyze the sentence from the beginning with the structure of "pour the egg that's in the bowl"—and your eyes will give you away. Hence real-world properties of objects constrain the referential domain, and this

information in turn is used from a very early stage to influence parsing.

The results show that language processing immediately takes into account relevant non-linguistic context, and argues against models where initial syntactic decisions are guided solely by syntactic information.

One particular sort of visual information is information from the speaker themselves. We have seen in Chapter 9 that people's recognition of speech can be influenced by the lip movements of the speaker (the McGurk effect). Lip-readers clearly make extensive use of this sort of information. The eye movements of the speaker (see also Chapter 13) provide another rich source of information for listeners. We tend to look at what the speaker is looking at; indeed, eye movements can be used to flag attention or a particular referent. When a speaker is describing a scene to a listener, the speaker naturally looks over the scene, and their eye movements relate to what they are describing. The eye movements of the listener come to match the eye movements of the speaker; they move over the scene in the same way, but with a delay of 2 seconds (Richardson & Dale, 2005).

SUMMARY

- Pragmatics is concerned with what people do with meaning.
- When we speak we do things with language; we make speech acts.
- In an indirect speech act, the intended meaning has to be inferred from the literal meaning.
- Indirectness is an important mechanism for maintaining politeness.
- Grice proposed that conversations are maintained by the four maxims of quantity, quality, relevance, and manner; of these, relevance is the most important.
- If an utterance appears to flout one of these maxims, we make a conversational implicature to make sense of it.
- Conversations have a structure; we take turns to speak, and use many cues (such as gaze) to ensure smooth transitions between turns.
- Audience design is the process of speakers modifying their utterances to take the needs of listeners into account.
- In conversation speakers come to align their internal representations at all levels.
- Language processing takes relevant non-linguistic context into account.

QUESTIONS TO THINK ABOUT

1.   Keep a record for a few days of what you talk about. How much is to do with the here-and-now?
2.   When do people interrupt others?
3.   When you talk, what do you look at? Why?
4.   When you talk to someone, how much attention do you pay to whether or not they are following you?
5.   How would you modify your speech if a tourist who is obviously a poor speaker of your native language stops you in the street and asks you for directions? What does this example tell us about audience design?

FURTHER READING

Sperber and Wilson (1987) is a summary of their book on relevance, with a peer commentary. Clark (1996) is a classic work on using language. See Henderson and Ferreira (2004) for an edited collection on language and the visual world.

CHAPTER 15

THE STRUCTURE OF THE LANGUAGE SYSTEM

INTRODUCTION

This penultimate chapter draws together many issues from the rest of the book. The architecture of a building indicates what it looks like, how its parts are arranged, its style, and how to get from one room to another. What is the architecture of the language system? How are its modules arranged, and how do they interact with one another? How many lexicons are there? This chapter examines how the components of the language system relate to one another. In particular, it will look at how different types of word recognition and production interrelate. A final question is the extent to which language processes depend on other cognitive processes. Although this issue was also considered in Chapter 3, we focus here on the relation between language processing and memory.

Caplan (1992) described four main characteristics of the language-processing system, based on Fodor's (1983) classic account of the modularity of mind. First, the language system is not a unitary structure, but is divided into a number of modules. Fodor (1983) said that modules are informationally encapsulated: Each module takes only one particular representation as input, and delivers only one type of output. For example, the syntactic processor only takes a word-level representation and does not accept input directly from the acoustic level. We would have to revise this assumption if we found evidence for interaction or leakage between modules. Many researchers believe that a completely modular system is the most economical one, and it is parsimonious to

believe that the language system comprises encapsulated modules unless there is good evidence to the contrary. We have seen throughout this book that language is highly modular, and these modules can be located in distinct brain regions, but the extent to which the modules are encapsulated is often highly controversial.

Second, processes within a module are mandatory and automatic in that if there is an input to the module, subsequent processing is obligatory. For example, normally we cannot help but read a word and access its meaning, even when it is to our advantage not to do so (as in the Stroop task, where we cannot ignore the meaning of the word whose ink color we are trying to name). Nevertheless, our views on what is automatic do change. Imaging studies show that when the attentional system is overloaded, the brain cannot distinguish between random letters and meaningful words—that is, in situations of extreme overload, reading a word is not mandatory (Rees, Russell, Frith, & Driver, 1999).

Third, language processes generally operate unconsciously. Indeed, the detailed lower level processes are not even amenable to conscious introspection. Finally, Caplan observed that most language processing takes place very quickly and with great accuracy. Taking these final points together, much of language processing is characteristic of automatic processing (Posner & Snyder, 1975; Shiffrin & Schneider, 1977). Obviously most real-life language tasks involve a number of modules, and trying to coordinate them might be slow and error-prone, as is the case with speech production.

Throughout the book, it has become obvious that the extent to which language processes interact is very controversial. As a very general conclusion, we have observed that the earlier in processing a process is, the more likely it is to be autonomous. By the end of this chapter and book you should:

- Know about the components of the language system and how they relate to each other.
- Understand the extent to which language processes are interactive.
- Appreciate some differences between reading and listening.
- Understand how we repeat words, and how repetition can be affected by brain damage.
- Understand the role that working memory plays in language processing.

WHAT ARE THE MODULES OF LANGUAGE?

What modules of the language system can we identify? When we see, hear, or produce a sentence, we have to recognize or produce the words (Chapters 6, 7, 9, and 13), and decode or encode the syntax of the sentence (Chapters 10 and 13). All of these tasks involve specific language modules. Little is known at present about the relation between the syntactic encoder and decoder, although the evidence described in Chapter 13 suggests that they are distinct. But does semantic information direct syntactic modules to do particular analyses (strong interaction), or just to reject implausible analyses and cause reanalysis? We looked at this in the chapter on parsing and syntactic ambiguity (Chapter 10).

The semantic-conceptual system is responsible for organizing and accessing our world knowledge and for interacting with the perceptual system. We discussed the way in which word meanings might be represented in Chapter 11. Most researchers currently think that they are decomposed into semantic features, some of which might be fairly abstract. Initial contact with the conceptual system is probably made through modality-specific stores. The meanings of words can be connected together to form a propositional network that is operated on by schemata (in comprehension—see Chapter 12) and the conceptualizer (in production—see Chapter 13).

Throughout this book we have seen how neuropsychological case studies show us that brain damage can affect some components of language while leaving others intact. We have seen dissociations in reading and speech production. Some patients have preserved lexical access but impaired syntactic processing, while others show the reverse pattern. The pattern of performance of people with Parkinson's disease and Alzheimer's disease is quite different, leading some researchers to conclude that specific instances are stored in the mental lexicon in one part of the brain, while general grammatical rules are processed elsewhere, although again this is controversial (see Chapters 3 and 13).

There are obviously enormous differences between language processing in the visual and the auditory modalities, given the very different natures of the inputs. Even if there is phonological recoding in reading, it is unlikely to be obligatory to gain access to meaning in languages with deep orthography that have many irregular words, such as English. In addition, the temporal demands of spoken and visual word recognition are very different. In normal circumstances, we have access to a visual stimulus for much longer than an acoustic stimulus. We can backtrack while reading, but we are unable to do this when listening. It is even possible that fundamental variables have different effects in the two modalities. It is more difficult to find frequency effects in spoken language recognition than in visual word recognition (Bradley & Forster, 1987). Nevertheless, in normal circumstances the reading and listening systems develop closely in tandem: Except for very young children, there is a very high correlation between auditory and visual comprehension skills (Palmer, MacLeod, Hunt, & Davidson, 1985). Differences between the modalities may extend beyond word recognition. Kennedy, Murray, Jennings, and Reid (1989) argued that parsing differs in the two modalities. With written language, we have the opportunity to go back to it, but access to spoken language is more transient.

We saw in Chapter 9 that the data strongly suggest that speech recognition is a data-driven, purely bottom-up process. In contrast, we saw in Chapter 13 that the data suggest that speech production is a non-modular process involving feedback. Is there a contradiction here? Why should recognition involve no feedback, but production a great deal of it? The tasks are very different: In speech recognition, the goal is to extract the correct meaning as quickly as possible; the speech signal fades rapidly; and there is some redundancy in the input. And while we need to get at the meaning and truth of what we are hearing, we do not need to construct detailed representations of everything. In production, however, we need to be accurate. We do need to produce every word in full and construct every syntactic representation in detail. We need to make sure that one part of the sentence agrees with all the others. Traditionally, language production and language comprehension have been treated as distinct modules; however, recent thinking is that they are much more intertwined (Pickering & Garrod, 2013).

Inner speech

What about inner speech, that little voice we often hear in our head telling us what to do? Clearly inner speech is produced by the speech production system, but it stops short of full articulation. How short? Vigliocco and Hartsuiker (2002) argue that inner speech is in a phonetic code—that is, it is relatively late. There are two main pieces of relevant evidence. The first is that articulatory suppression (speaking out aloud) stops the inner voice, and articulatory suppression interferes with the phonetic code. Second, levels of representation are not accessible to consciousness prior to the phonetic code (we have no sense of knowing what a lemma or a phonological code is), but clearly inner speech is accessible to consciousness. Recent research on getting people to mentally recite tongue twisters has shown that people make speech errors in inner speech showing phonological effects resembling those made in overt speech, such as the lexical bias effect. However, opinion is divided as to whether the errors show that inner speech is specified as far as the sound featural

level, or whether it is only specified at some more abstract level, as there is uncertainty about the degree of phonological similarity effects found in these internal errors (Corley, Brocklehurst, & Moat, 2011; Oppenheim, 2012; Oppenheim & Dell, 2008). Finally, we saw in Chapter 7 that reading often results in inner speech.

HOW MANY LEXICONS ARE THERE?

We have seen how some researchers believe that there are multiple semantic memory systems, one for each input modality. How many lexicons are there? When we recognize a word, do we make contact with the same lexicon regardless of whether we are listening to speech or reading written language? Do we have just one mental dictionary, or is it fractionated, with a separate one for each modality? Clearly the peripheral features of lexical processing—letters versus sounds, for example—must differ depending on the modality, so the question should be rephrased as: Is there one lexicon of lemmas (abstract lexical units; see Chapter 13), or multiple systems of lemmas, one for each modality? In Levelt's original conception of lemmas they are modality neutral, but is that actually the case? In fact lemmas, although an important idea in speech production, are rarely mentioned in the word recognition literature.

The most parsimonious arrangement is that there is only one lexicon, used for the four tasks of reading, listening, writing, and speaking. Alternatively, we may have four lexicons, one each for the tasks of writing, reading, speaking, and listening. It is also plausible that there are two lexicons: One possibility is that there are separate lexicons for written (visual) language and spoken (verbal) language (each covering input and output tasks—that is, recognition and production), and another is that there are separate lexicons for input and output (each covering written and spoken language).

Note that to some extent the answers to these questions depend on how we define our terms. If by "lexicon" we just mean "the complete mental dictionary," there can be only one lexicon, but perhaps with a number of subsystems and peripheral stores. If on the other hand we mean a discrete system used to access semantics, we could have a number of them. Differences in the use of terminology like this make lexical architecture a difficult and confusing topic.

Experimental data

Fay and Cutler (1977) interpreted form-based word substitution speech errors as evidence that a single lexicon was accessed in two different directions for speech production and comprehension (Chapter 13). We saw, however, that malapropisms can readily be explained without recourse to a common lexicon in an interactive two-stage model of lexicalization. In fact, most of the data argue against a single lexicon used for both recognition and production.

Winnick and Daniel (1970) showed that tachistoscopic recognition of a printed word was facilitated by the prior reading aloud of that word, whereas naming a picture or producing a word in response to a definition did not facilitate subsequent tachistoscopic recognition of those words (Chapter 6). Furthermore, priming in the visual modality produces much more facilitation on a test in the visual modality than auditory priming does, and vice versa (Morton, 1979b). In response, Morton (1979b) revised the logogen model, so that instead of one logogen for each word, logogen stores were modality-specific. He further distinguished between input and output systems. In support of this fractionation, Shallice, McLeod, and Lewis (1985) found that having to monitor a list of auditorily presented words for a target created little interference on reading words aloud. Furthermore, listening to a word does not activate the same areas of the brain that are activated by reading a word aloud and word repetition, as shown by PET (positron emission tomography) brain imaging (Petersen, Fox, Posner, Mintun, & Raichle, 1989). These pieces of evidence suggest that the speech input and output pathways are different.

Dell (1988) suggested that the feedback connections in his interactive model of lexicalization

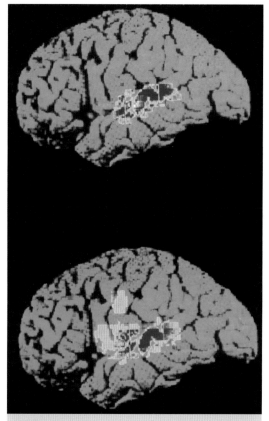

Listening to and repeating words. Color positron emission tomography (PET) scan showing areas of the human brain involved in word recognition. The active areas are highlighted in red and yellow. At top, the subject is listening to words only. The part of the brain activated is the auditory region as word sounds are heard. At bottom, the subject is both listening to words, and repeating them. The auditory (hearing) region is activated as well as a small motor control area (yellow, above the auditory region) involved in speech. Active areas show cerebral blood flow detected by PET, superimposed onto an image of the brain.

may be necessary for word recognition. Hence interactions in speech production arise through leakage along the comprehension route. As we have seen, evidence favors the view that the production and comprehension lexicons are distinct. Perhaps the role of feedback is limited or nonexistent in both production and recognition, but both involve attractor networks, giving rise to the observed interactions.

As we saw in Chapter 11, it can be difficult to distinguish between problems of access and problems of storage. Allport and Funnell (1981) argued that perhaps we do not need separate lexicons, just distinct access pathways to one lexicon. On the other hand, we have seen that semantic memory is split into multiple, modality-specific stores. It seems uneconomical to have four access pathways (for reading, writing, speaking, and listening) going to and from one lexicon, and then to four semantic systems. Indeed, the most plausible arrangement is that there are distinct lexical systems. Language processes split early in processing, and do not converge again until quite late.

Monsell (1987) examined whether the same set of lexical units is used in both production and recognition. He compared the effects of priming word recognition in an auditory lexical decision task by perceiving a word or generating a word. He found that generating a word facilitated its recognition, suggesting that producing a word activates some representation that is also accessed in recognition. This suggests that production and recognition use the same lexicon or separate networks that are connected in some way. Further evidence that the input and output phonological pathways cannot be completely separate is that there are sublexical influences of speech production on speech perception. For example, Gordon and Meyer (1984) found that preparing to speak influences speech perception, so there must be some sharing of common mechanisms. Monsell tentatively argued that the interconnection between the speech production and recognition systems happens at a sublexical level such as the phonological buffer used in memory-span tasks.

In summary, experimental data from people without brain damage suggest that spoken and visual word recognition make use of different mechanisms. There are distinct input and output stores, perhaps sharing some sublexical mechanisms.

Neuropsychological data and lexical architecture

There are very many neuropsychological dissociations found between reading, writing, and visual and spoken word recognition. In this section I examine data from patients whose behavior is consistent with damage to some routes of a model of lexical processing while other routes are intact. Several theorists, drawing on many sources, have tried to bring all this material together to form some idea of the overall structure of the language system (e.g., Ellis & Young, 1988; Kay, Lesser, & Coltheart, 1992; Patterson & Shewell, 1987). One such arrangement is shown in Figure 15.1. The neuropsychological data strongly suggest that there are four different lexicons, one each for speaking, writing, and spoken and visual word recognition, although these systems must clearly communicate in normal circumstances. This conclusion is consistent with the data from experiments on people without brain damage.

At the heart of the model is a system where word meanings are stored and that interfaces with the other cognitive processes. This is the semantic system (or systems, with the multiple-semantics view). The four most important language behaviors are speaking, listening, reading, and writing.

Speaking involves going from the semantic system to a store of the sounds of words. This is the phonological output store. Understanding speech necessitates the auditory analysis of incoming speech in order to access a representation of stored spoken word forms. This is the phonological input store.

People with anomia have difficulty in retrieving the names for objects, yet can show perfect comprehension of those words. EE was consistently unable to name particular words, yet he had no impairment of the auditory recognition or comprehension of the words that he could not name (Howard, 1995). This finding suggests that the input and output phonological lexicons are distinct.

Some patients show a disorder called pure word deafness. People with pure word deafness can speak, read, and write quite normally, but cannot understand speech (Chapter 9). These patients also cannot repeat speech back. However, there are a few patients with word deafness who still have intact repetition, a condition called word meaning deafness. Word meaning deafness is rare, but has been reported by Bramwell (1897/1984)

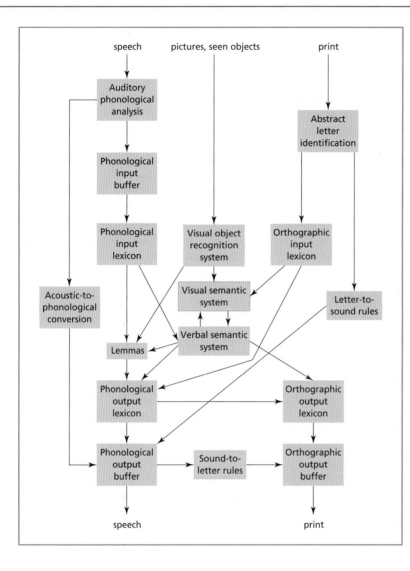

FIGURE 15.1 The overall structure of the language system. It is possible that the speech lemma system is unnecessary, or that other links to lemmas need to be introduced.

and Kohn and Friedman (1986). This shows that word repetition need not depend on lexical access. Indeed, if Figure 15.1 is correct, then we should be able to repeat speech using three routes (in a manner analogous to the three-route model of reading). First, there is a repetition route through semantics. Second, there is a lexical repetition route from the input phonological lexicon to the output phonological lexicon. Third, there is a sublexical repetition route from the input phonological buffer to the output phonological buffer that bypasses lexical systems altogether. Disentangling precisely which is impaired depends on the pattern

of word and nonword repetition performance, along with the effect of semantic variables such as imageability. Obviously (assuming that they can be distinguished), if either the input or output buffer is disrupted, repetition should be impaired; I examine this idea later. We should also be able to see disruptions resulting from selective damage to and preservation of our three repetition routes.

If both the sublexical and the lexical routes are destroyed, then the person will be forced to rely on repetition through the semantic route. If the semantic route is intact, there will be an imageability effect in repetition, with more imageable words repeated more readily. If there is also some damage to the semantic route, patients will make semantic errors in repetition (for example, repeating "reflection" as "mirror"). This is called **deep dysphasia**. Howard and Franklin (1988) described the case of MK, who was good at speech production. He was severely impaired at single-word and nonword repetition, but was good at the matching span task. He made semantic errors in repetition. Howard and Franklin concluded that MK had preserved input and output phonological systems, total loss of the sublexical repetition route, partial impairment of the lexical repetition route, and partial impairment of the semantic repetition route.

If only the lexical repetition route is left intact, then patients will be able to repeat words but not nonwords (as nonwords do not have a lexical entry). They will not be able to comprehend the words they repeat (as there is no link with semantics), and they will probably have difficulty in understanding and producing speech (because of the disruption to semantics). Nor should they show the effects of semantic variables such as imageability in repetition. They might also make lexicalization errors (repeating nonwords as close words—e.g., repeating "sleeb" as "sleep"). Dr. O (Franklin, Turner, Lambon Ralph, Morris, & Bailey, 1996) was close to this pattern. He could understand written words, but could not understand spoken words. He could, however, repeat spoken words quite well (80%) but was very poor at nonword repetition (7%).

If only the sublexical repetition route is left intact, patients will be able to repeat both words and nonwords, but will have no comprehension of the meaning of the words. Transcortical sensory aphasia fits this pattern (Chapter 13).

There are other possible combinations, of course. Patients might have damage to only one of the routes, leaving two intact. Damage to the sublexical route alone would lead to an impairment of repetition, with particularly poor repetition of nonwords, as they cannot be repeated through the direct and semantic repetition routes. This is the pattern observed in conduction aphasia (Martin, 2001). As damage to the lexical route alone should result in relatively good repetition of both words

and nonwords (through the sublexical repetition route) and good comprehension (through the semantic route), a deficit of this type will be difficult to detect. The important conclusion, however, is that the patterns of repetition impairment found can be explained by this sort of model.

Different lexical systems are involved in reading and writing. Bramwell's patient could not comprehend spoken words, but could still write even irregular words to dictation. This is incompatible with any general system mediating lexical stores, and with obligatory phonological mediation of orthographic-to-cognitive codes. We also saw in Chapter 7 that phonological mediation does not appear to be necessary for writing single words.

There is a great deal of neuropsychological evidence that there are distinct phonological and orthographic output stores. Beauvois and Derouesné (1981) reported a patient showing impaired spelling yet intact lexical reading. MH was severely anomic in speech but had much less severe written word-finding difficulties (Bub & Kertesz, 1982b). Patient WMA produced inconsistent oral and written naming responses. When given a picture of peppers, he wrote "tomato" but said "artichoke" (Miceli, Benvegnu, Capasso, & Caramazza, 1997). If a single lexicon were used for both speaking and writing, WMA would have given the same (erroneous) response in both cases. Some patients are better at written picture naming than spoken picture naming (Rapp, Benzing, & Caramazza, 1997; Shelton & Weinrich, 1997). The existence of patients such as PW who can write the names of words that they can neither define nor name aloud is evidence for the independence of these systems, and argues against obligatory phonological mediation in writing (Rapp et al., 1997). Rapp and Caramazza (2002) describe a patient who has more difficulty speaking nouns than verbs but greater difficulty writing verbs than nouns. This evidence suggests that different output stores are involved in speaking and writing, and that writing does not require the generation of a phonological representation of the word. Although there are some dissenting voices (e.g., Behrmann & Bub, 1992), most studies suggest that multiple lexical systems are involved.

However, it is likely that they interact, as damage to word meaning usually leads to comparable difficulties in both written and spoken output (Miceli & Capasso, 1997).

Sketch of a model

As we saw in Chapter 7, reading makes use of a number of routes. The exact number is controversial, as connectionist models suggest that the direct and indirect lexical routes should be combined. Figure 15.1 shows the traditional model incorporating an indirect reading route; the figure shows the maximum sophistication necessary in a model of lexical architecture. The direct route goes from abstract letter identification to an orthographic input store and then to the semantic system. The direct lexical reading route then goes straight on to the phonological output store. The indirect or sublexical route (which as we saw in Chapter 7 might in turn be quite complex) bypasses the orthographic input store and the semantic system, giving us a direct link between letter identification and speech. We saw that non-semantic reading means that the semantic system can sometimes be bypassed. We can also read out aloud a language with a regular orthography (e.g., Italian) without being able to understand it. Allport and Funnell (1981) argued that we cannot have a separate amodal lexicon mediating between systems. They reviewed evidence from word meaning deafness, phonological dyslexia, and deep dyslexia. They described a number of studies of patients that argue for a dissociation of cognitive and lexical functions. The semantic paraphasias of deep dyslexics rule out any model where translation to a phonological code is a necessary condition to be able to access a semantic code (as these patients can access meaning without retrieving sound).

Writing and speaking produce output across time. It makes sense to retrieve a word in one go rather than having to access the lexicon afresh each time we need to produce a letter or sound. This means that we have to store the word while we speak out its constituent sounds, or write out its constituent letters in order. This in turn means that we also need phonological and orthographic

buffers. Writing involves going from the semantic system to print through the orthographic output store. We can also write nonwords to dictation, so there must be an additional connection between the phonological output buffer and the orthographic output buffer that provides sound-to-letter rules.

Of course, we can do other things as well. We can name objects. Most people think that we access the names of objects through the semantic system from a system of visual object recognition. We saw in Chapter 11 that some people think that different semantic systems are used for words and objects, so we might have to split the semantic system in two. There is also some controversial evidence from the study of dementia that at least one patient (DT) can name objects and faces without going through semantics (Brennen, David, Fluchaire, & Pellat, 1996; but see Hodges & Greene, 1998, and Brennen, 1999, for a reply). In this case, we need to add an additional route from the visual object recognition system that bypasses semantics to get to the phonological output store.

Note that there is no direct connection between the orthographic input store and the orthographic output store. Are there patients who can copy words (but not nonwords) without understanding them? Finding such patients would suggest that such a link will be necessary. We would need to find these sorts of patient to be certain about these links. There is also some question about whether we need distinct input and output phonological buffers, or whether one will suffice. We examine these issues in more detail later.

By the time we add lemmas and a non-semantic object-naming route, we end up with a model that is even more complicated than Figure 15.1, just to produce single words! Remember that this is the most complex model necessary. Connectionist modeling may show how routes (in addition to the lexical and sublexical reading routes) may be combined without loss of explanatory adequacy.

A final point on lexical organization is that it is not too important for the architecture of this model whether words are represented in the lexicon in a local or a distributed representation. In a distributed representation, words correspond to patterns of activation over units rather than to individual units (see the discussion of the Seidenberg & McClelland, 1989, model in Chapter 7). Hence the visual input store corresponds to the hidden units in their model. In practice, it is very difficult, perhaps impossible, to distinguish between these possibilities. Given that individual words clearly do not correspond to individual neurons, they must be distributed to some extent. The important issue is the extent to which these distributed representations overlap. Of course, this is not to say that the processes that happen in the boxes in Figure 15.1 are not important; they are crucial. But we can nevertheless identify the general components of the language system and the way that information flows through it.

There are two complications with this type of neuropsychological data. The first is distinguishing between having two separate stores and having one store with two separate input and output pathways. This is a fundamental problem, first raised in Chapter 11 and earlier in this chapter. It is not always straightforward to address. The second complication is distinguishing between impairments to connections between input and output stores, and input and output phonological buffers.

LANGUAGE AND SHORT-TERM MEMORY

What is the relation between language processes and **short-term memory** (STM)? The role short-term memory plays in processes as diverse as speech perception, word repetition, parsing, comprehension, and learning to speak and read has inspired much research on both impaired and unimpaired speakers. Language plays an important role in short-term memory, and the contents of short-term memory are often linguistic.

Psychological research on short-term memory suggests that it is not a unitary structure. Baddeley and Hitch (1974) called the set of structures involved **working memory**. Working memory comprises a central executive (which is

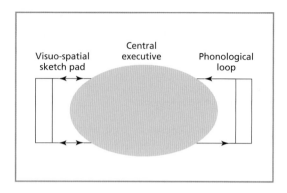

FIGURE 15.2 A simplified representation of the working memory model (based on Baddeley & Hitch, 1974).

an attentional system), a visuo-spatial sketch pad (for short-term storage of spatial information), and a phonological loop (see Figure 15.2). Both the central executive and the phonological loop are important in language processing. The central executive plays an important role in semantic integration and comprehension, while the phonological loop plays a role in phonological processes in language. It is debatable, however, whether any component of general verbal memory plays a role in parsing.

We saw in Chapter 12 that reading **span** predicts performance on a range of reading and comprehension measures (Daneman & Carpenter, 1980). People hear or read sets of unrelated sentences, and after each set attempt to recall the last word of each sentence. Reading span is the largest size set for which a participant can correctly recall all the last words. This measure of reading span correlates with the ability to answer questions about texts, with pronoun resolution accuracy, and even with general measures of verbal intelligence such as SAT scores. Poor comprehenders often have a reduced reading span. Reading span is determined by the size or efficacy of working memory capacity. (Daneman & Carpenter have a different notion of working memory from Baddeley: Their "working memory" is most equivalent to the language-related components of the central executive in Baddeley's scheme.) Low skills on a range of complex working memory tasks are associated with language disabilities in childhood, particularly difficulty in learning to read (Gathercole, Alloway, Willis, & Adams, 2006).

Short-term verbal memory and lexical processing

In Baddeley's (1990) conception of working memory, the phonological loop comprises a passive phonological store that is linked with speech perception, and an articulatory control process linked with speech production, which can maintain and operate on the contents of the phonological store. The effectiveness of the phonological loop is measured by **auditory short-term memory (ASTM)** tasks. These tasks measure our memory for digits and words in a number of ways. In the single-word repetition task, a person has to repeat single words (or digits) back aloud. In the two-word repetition task, the person has to repeat pairs of words back. In the pointing span task, the person hears a sequence of words or digits and then has to point in sequence to pictures corresponding to those items. In the matching span task, the person just has to say whether two lists are the same or different. No overt repetition is needed in the matching span tasks, but items have to be maintained in the input phonological buffer. Note that differing ways of measuring span size might give different results; for example, the pointing span task requires activation of semantic information in a way that repetition does not (Martin & Ayala, 2004).

One plausible idea is that the passive phonological store of the working memory system is the phonological buffer of the system we described earlier. A reduction in the size of the phonological store as a consequence of brain damage therefore should have consequences for language processing, but the consequences are less dramatic than you might at first suppose. Reduced ASTM capacity should hinder language comprehension, because material cannot be stored in the phonological buffer for very long. However, very often this does not matter because we can access the syntactic and semantic properties of words very quickly. We can then maintain

lexical representations (e.g., by support from semantics) without the support of the phonological loop (Martin, 1993). However, impairment of the phonological loop does hinder the ability to repeat words, and particularly nonwords. Patients with impaired ASTM show an effect of word length in repetition. Patients with a repetition disorder (Shallice & Warrington, 1977) show very little impairment in language production and comprehension, but are still impaired at repeating words (Saffran, 1990).

The extent to which phonological short-term memory impairments are accompanied by speech perception impairments is controversial. Some studies (e.g., Campbell & Butterworth, 1985; Vallar & Baddeley, 1984) report patients with very reduced ASTM span, yet with apparently normal phonological processing, whereas others (e.g., Allport, 1984) argued that many patients have a subtle phonological processing deficit that can only be detected by difficult tests. One resolution of this conflict may be that phonological short-term memory impairments may involve damage to either the input or the output phonological buffer, but not to phonological processing.

The degree of ASTM impairment influences language function. A span reduced to just one or two items can have profound consequences for language processing, including single-word processing. At spans of two or three, single-word processing is usually intact, but performance on longer sequences of words can be impaired (Martin, Saffran, & Dell, 1996). Even when naming and word repetition are relatively spared, performance on nonword repetition tasks might still be impaired, because nonwords cannot receive support from semantic representations.

Can lexical processing be damaged leaving ASTM intact? Martin, Lesch, and Bartha (1999) argued that it cannot. They proposed that memory buffers for phonological, lexical, and semantic processing contain those items in long-term memory structures that have been recently activated. Damage to semantic representations will have consequences for maintaining the integrity of lexical representations.

Some patients with mild speech perception deficits do not show impairments of ASTM (Martin & Breedin, 1992). In cases of mild speech perception impairment, lexical items will still be able to become activated.

Martin and Saffran (1990) examined the repetition abilities of a patient (ST) with transcortical sensory aphasia. They showed that their patient could not repeat more than two words without losing information about the earlier items in the input (here the first word of two words). People with a semantic impairment cannot maintain items at the beginning of a sequence. Word repetition is supported by phonological processes, but these processes are of short duration without the feedback support of semantic processes. Items at the beginning of the sequence get lost because their maintenance depends on activation spreading to semantics. Items at the end of the sequence benefit from the recency of phonological activation, and are not dependent on that semantic feedback at the time of recall. So, although good repetition is characteristic of transcortical sensory aphasia, even that ability is limited. Martin and Saffran (1997) found similar associations between the occurrence of semantic and phonological deficits and serial position effects in single-word repetition. Semantic deficits are associated with errors on the initial portion of the word, while phonological deficits are associated with errors on the final part of the word. This again points to the integrity of the language and memory systems.

Are there separate input and output phonological buffers?

Can we distinguish between the input and output phonological buffers? If Figure 15.1 is correct then we should be able to do so, and there is some neuropsychological evidence that we can. Shallice and Butterworth (1977) described the case of JB. On tasks probing memory span, JB performed poorly, suggesting an impaired input phonological buffer, but she had normal speech production, suggesting a preserved output phonological buffer. Nickels and Howard (1995) found no correlation between the number of

phonological errors made in production by their sample of aphasic speakers and three measures of input phonological buffer processing (phoneme discrimination, lexical decision, and synonym judgments). However, Martin and Saffran (1998) found a negative relation between the proportion of target-related nonword errors in a naming task and the patient's ability to discriminate phonemes. One possible resolution of this disagreement is that the two buffers are interconnected.

Other evidence also supports the existence of separate input and output phonological buffers. Romani (1992) described a patient with poor sentence and word repetition but good performance on immediate probe recognition, suggesting an impaired output buffer but an intact input buffer. Similarly, R. C. Martin et al. (1999) describe the case of an anomic patient, MS, who showed a different pattern of performance on tasks involving the input and output phonological buffers. In particular, his performance was poor on STM tasks that required verbal output, but normal on STM tasks that did not require verbal output but required the retention of verbal input. The pattern of performance suggests that separate input and output phonological buffers are involved. Shallice et al. (2000) described a patient (LT) with reproduction conduction aphasia. LT was impaired across a range of language output tasks; remember that the best explanation for such a pattern of performance is an impairment to the phonological buffer. Yet LT had an intact short-term memory span, suggesting that the input phonological buffer was spared but the output phonological buffer was damaged. Finally, patients with impaired ASTM fall into clusters in performance on visual homophone judgment, pseudohomophone judgment, and auditory and visual rhyme decision tasks in a way that can best be accounted for by separate input and output phonological buffers (Nickels, Howard, & Best, 1997). In particular, some patients showed evidence of damage to the input buffer, in being impaired on all tasks apart from homophone judgment. Other patients showed evidence of damage to the output buffer, in that they were impaired on all tasks other than auditory rhyme judgments.

Furthermore, some patients showed evidence of a lesion to the link between the output and the input buffers, in that they could perform homophone and auditory rhyme judgments well, but were poor at pseudohomophone detection and visual rhyme detection.

The phonological loop and vocabulary learning

We have seen that because we can access the meaning of words so quickly, damage to the phonological loop has surprisingly few consequences for language processing. The main role for the phonological loop is now thought to be limited to learning new words (Baddeley, Gathercole, & Papagno, 1998). Verbal short-term memory also plays a role in vocabulary acquisition in children (Gathercole & Baddeley, 1989, 1990, 1993; Gupta & MacWhinney, 1997). The size of verbal STM and vocabulary size are strongly correlated, and early nonword-repetition ability predicts later vocabulary size. Nonword repetition skills also predict success at foreign language vocabulary acquisition (Papagno et al., 1991). Patients with impaired short-term phonological memory (e.g., PV of Baddeley et al., 1998) find it difficult to learn a new language. Phonological memory is used to sustain novel phonological forms so that they can be built into more permanent representations.

Working memory and parsing

Although short-term memory plays some role in integration and maintaining a discourse representation, the extent to which an impairment of STM affects parsing is controversial. Early models of parsing considered the minimization of STM demands to be a primary constraint on parsing (e.g., Kimball, 1973). With a conception of working memory as a phonological loop and central executive, the phonological representations of words are stored in the phonological buffer of the loop, and the semantic representations of focal components of the discourse are handled by the central executive. The central executive might play a role in parsing, in computing parsing processes, and in manipulating the intermediate results of computations.

The idea that a central memory capacity is used in language comprehension is known as the capacity theory of comprehension (Just & Carpenter, 1992). Just and Carpenter argued that working memory constrains language comprehension. Individual differences between linguistic working memory capacity lead to differences in reading ability, and reduction of working memory capacity through aging or brain damage leads to language comprehension deficits. As we saw in Chapter 10, some researchers have put forward the controversial view that the deficits observed in syntactic comprehension are best explained by a reduction in central executive capacity (Blackwell & Bates, 1995; Miyake et al., 1994). Waters and Caplan (1996) criticized the capacity theory, arguing that language processing makes use of two distinct working memory systems, one dedicated to controlled, verbally mediated tasks, and one dedicated to automatic, obligatory "routine" language processing. They call this the domain-specific view of working memory (Caplan & Waters, 1999).

There is some evidence against the domain-specific view suggesting that working memory is involved in parsing. Gibson (1998) examined the relation between working memory and sentence processing. He argued that comprehension has two sorts of demands on available computational resources: a cost associated with integrating components, and a cost associated with keeping track of syntactic structures. The costs increase the longer a unit must be kept in memory before it can be integrated into the developing representation of the sentence. Gibson argued that the human parsing mechanism prefers the structure that incurs the least memory load. More recent dual-task studies show that parsing is impaired if people have to remember additional related material; the more syntactically complex the material, the greater the cost of remembering additional words. The key to observing interference is that the additional items that must be kept active in memory must be related to the material participants are trying to understand, rather than being unrelated digits, for example (Fedorenko, Gibson, & Rohde, 2006; Gordon, Hendrick, and Levine, 2002). As noted in Chapter 10, the debate about whether or not language comprehension uses general working memory or a dedicated store is important, but is unresolved and ongoing.

Does parsing involve the phonological loop in particular? On the one hand, some researchers argue that the phonological loop maintains some words in short-term memory to assist in parsing, particularly when parsing is difficult (e.g., Baddeley, Vallar, & Wilson, 1987; Vallar & Baddeley, 1984, 1987). Although some patients with STM deficits have impaired syntactic comprehension abilities (e.g., Vallar & Baddeley, 1987), others crucially do not (e.g., Butterworth, Campbell, & Howard, 1986; Howard & Butterworth, 1989; Waters, Caplan, & Hildebrandt, 1991). For example, TB (a patient with a digit span of only two) showed increasing problems with comprehension as sentence length increased (Baddeley & Wilson, 1988). On the other hand, other researchers have argued that the phonological loop plays no role in parsing, but is involved in later processing after the sentence has been interpreted syntactically and semantically (e.g., McCarthy & Warrington, 1987a, 1987b; Warrington & Shallice, 1969). This later processing includes checking the meaning against the pragmatic context, making some inferences, and aspects of semantic integration. For example, patient BO had a memory span of only two or three items, yet had excellent comprehension of syntactically complex sentences, including those with dependencies spanning more than three words (Caplan, 1992; Waters et al., 1991). RE was a highly literate young woman with a greatly reduced digit span. Although she displayed phonological dyslexia and impaired sentence repetition, her syntactic analysis and comprehension abilities appeared to be intact (Butterworth et al., 1986; Campbell & Butterworth, 1985; but see Vallar & Baddeley, 1989). McCarthy and Warrington (1987a) observed a double dissociation, with some patients showing an impairment to a passive phonological store involved in unrelated word list repetition, but who were good at repeating sentences, and others showing an impairment to a memory system involving meaningful sentence repetition, but who could repeat lists of unrelated words. Rochon et al. (1994) examined syntactic processing in a group of patients with Alzheimer's-type dementia. Although the participants' working memory capacity was reduced, there was little effect of syntactic complexity, although semantic complexity was affected. Such results suggest that STM is not involved directly in parsing. Such patients can still display a variety of comprehension difficulties (such as turning commands into actions, or detecting discourse anomalies), suggesting that limited STM can affect later integrative processing.

Hence it seems likely that if there is a reduction in processing capacity involved in syntactic comprehension deficits, it is a reduction specifically in syntactic processing ability, rather than a reduction in general verbal memory capacity (Caplan et al., 1985; Caplan & Hildebrandt, 1988; Caplan & Waters, 1996, 1999). Parsing uses a specific mechanism that does not draw on verbal working memory. However, these more general processes may become involved later in the comprehension process. This topic is hotly debated (Caplan & Waters, 1996, 1999; Just & Carpenter, 1992; Just et al., 1996; Waters & Caplan, 1996). The conclusions to be drawn from all this depend on exactly how syntactic complexity is to be defined, and on the range of sentence types, tasks, patient categories, and language examined (Bates, Dick, & Wulfeck, 1999).

MacDonald and Christiansen (2002) take a totally different approach to the idea of working memory as a separate store. They adopt a connectionist perspective, arguing that the capacity limitations arise from the architecture of the language system, and from individual differences in reading experience. In particular, there is no separate working memory in the sense that there is a box into which the results of linguistic computations are put. Capacity and knowledge are inseparable. Instead, capacity limitations arise from the behavior of the whole system, rather than from one component of it. MacDonald and Christiansen provided a connectionist model to simulate individual differences in language comprehension, showing how these differences can arise from differences in the amount of training the networks receive. This alternative approach has generated considerable controversy (Caplan & Waters, 2002; Just & Varma, 2002). Nevertheless the idea is pleasingly simple and parsimonious.

Evaluation of work on language and memory

Experimental and neuropsychological research points to the integrity of the language and memory systems: The phonological loop is the phonological buffer of language processing. Hence disruptions to language and short-term memory are intimately related. Auditory short-term memory is therefore involved in many linguistic tasks. Nevertheless, because we access the syntactic and semantic properties of words so quickly, damage to the phonological loop has surprisingly few consequences for language processing, apart from impairments in repetition ability and vocabulary acquisition. So all aphasics have span impairments, but not everyone with span impairments is aphasic.

The contents of the phonological stores are those items in long-term representations that have become highly activated. Indeed, all levels of linguistic processing may correspond to components of working memory. This is the multiple components idea. Evidence supporting it comes from neuropsychological studies that show that some span-reduced patients are worse at tasks involving semantic information than those involving phonological information, whereas other patients show the reverse pattern (Hanten & Martin, 2000; Martin, Shelton, & Yaffee, 1994). The components of lexical processing are the components of the memory system (see Martin & Saffran, 1992; R. C. Martin & Lesch, 1996). Phonological STM deficits are linked with damage to the temporal-parietal region of the brain, while semantic STM deficits are linked with damage to frontal regions (Romani & Martin, 1999).

Language research is revealing about the structure of working memory. In particular, it suggests that there are two phonological stores involved in the phonological loop—an input and an output buffer, each of which can be selectively disrupted.

SUMMARY

- Most language processes are fast, mandatory, and mostly automatic.
- Language processing involves a number of modules; the extent to which these modules are independent of each other is hotly debated.
- The lack of permanence of the auditory input in listening leads to a number of differences between reading and listening.
- Experimental data from people without brain damage suggest that there are different lexical systems for language production and language comprehension; this conclusion is supported by brain-imaging studies.
- The neuropsychological data suggest that there are distinct lexical systems for reading, writing, listening, and speaking.
- It is possible to create a model of the architecture of word processing (see Figure 15.1).
- There are three routes that can be used for word repetition, and these routes can be selectively lost or spared.
- Working memory has a number of components; the most important for language is the phonological loop, comprising a passive phonological store and an articulatory control process.
- It is likely that there are separate input and output phonological stores (buffers).
- Impairment to auditory short-term memory (ASTM) has significant consequences for language processing.
- Working memory is involved in language comprehension and integration, but the extent to which it is involved in parsing is very questionable.
- The phonological loop is important in first- and second-language vocabulary acquisition.

QUESTIONS TO THINK ABOUT

1. Do you think that a language system with multiple semantic stores is more plausibly combined with separate or unitary lexical systems?
2. Are there kinds of patients that we should not observe, if Figure 15.1 is correct?
3. What role does the central executive play in language?
4. How do we decide whether or not two words rhyme?
5. What is a lexicon?
6. How does the content of what we know about the structure of the language system relate to what we have learnt about the brain in earlier chapters?

FURTHER READING

For reviews of picture naming, see Glaser (1992) and Morton (1985). Allport and Funnell (1981) review many of the issues concerning lexical fractionation; they argue for the reparability of cognitive and lexical codes. Monsell (1987) is a comprehensive review of the literature on the fractionation of the lexicon. Ellis and Young (1988, Ch. 8) provide a detailed discussion of the neuropsychological evidence for their proposed architecture of the language system. See also the PALPA test battery (Kay, Lesser, & Coltheart, 1992). See Shelton and Caramazza (1999) for a review and discussion of how lexical architecture relates to semantic memory. Bradley and Forster (1987) review the differences between spoken and visual word recognition.

See Baddeley (2007) and Eysenck and Keane (2010) for more on working memory. Howard and Franklin (1988) give a detailed single-case study of a patient (MK) with a repetition disorder, and Martin (2001) is an excellent review of repetition disorders in aphasia. For more on the role of the phonological loop in vocabulary learning, see the debate between Bowey (1996, 1997) and Gathercole and Baddeley (1997). See Meyer, Wheeldon, and Krott (2006) for a collection that examines which language processes might be automatic and which might require resources.

CHAPTER 16

NEW DIRECTIONS

INTRODUCTION

In this chapter we re-examine the themes raised in the first chapter. I also summarize the present status of the psychology of language, and indicate where it might go in the future.

By now I hope you have been convinced that psycholinguists have made great progress in understanding the processes involved in language. Since the birth of modern psycholinguistics, sometime around Chomsky's (1959) review of Skinner's book *Verbal Behavior*, it has achieved independence from linguistics and has flourished on all fronts. I also hope you have been convinced that the cognitive approach to psycholinguistics in particular has taught us a very great deal indeed. Many questions remain, and in some respects the more we learn, the more questions are raised.

THEMES IN PSYCHOLINGUISTICS REVISITED

I raised ten main themes in Chapter 1. Let's look at them all again.

The first theme was to discover the processes involved in producing and understanding language. Modern psycholinguistics is founded on data. Careful behavioral and neuroscience experiments have clearly told us a great deal about the processes involved in language. However, as in all science, there are two main ways of doing things. These can be called the bottom-up and the top-down approaches to science. In the bottom-up mode, psycholinguists are driven by empirical findings. Perhaps there is a novel finding, or a prediction from a theory that does not come out as predicted. A model is then constructed to account for these findings. Alternatively, a theory might be bolstered by having its predictions verified. Either way, experimental results drive theoretical advances. A top-down approach does not necessarily worry too much about the data in the first instance (although it obviously cannot afford to avoid them), but instead tries to develop a theoretical framework that can then be used to make sense of the data. Predictions are derived from these frameworks and then tested. In the past, examples of top-down approaches have included linguistics and symbolic AI, and currently the most influential top-down approach is connectionism. Of course these modes of thought are not exclusive. We know a great deal about language processes from both experiments and modeling. Progress is a process of interaction between the bottom-up and top-down approaches.

The second theme is the question of whether apparently different language processes are related to one another. For example, to what extent are the processes involved in reading also involved in speaking? We have seen that while there is some overlap, there is also a great deal of separation (e.g., see Figure 15.1).

The third theme is whether or not processes in language operate independently of one another, or whether they interact. In modular models, the boxes of the diagrams used to represent the structure of language systems carry out their computations independently of the others, and other boxes only get access to the final output. Interactive models allow boxes to fiddle around with the contents of other boxes while they are still processing, or they are allowed to start processing on the basis of an early input rather than having to wait for the preceding stage to complete its processing. This issue has recurred through every chapter on adult psycholinguistics. Although there is a great deal of disagreement among psycholinguists, the preponderance of evidence—in my opinion—suggests that language processing is strongly interactive, although there are constraints. There may be modules, but they are leaky ones: modules need not be informationally encapsulated. The debate has now largely moved on from simply whether language processes are modular or interactive, to examining the detailed time course of processing. When does interaction occur? What types of information interact? Can interactions be prevented? Psycholinguists have started to dispense with broad, general considerations, and to focus on the details of what happens. Context can have different effects at different levels of processing.

Fourth, what is innate about language? We have seen that there is still disagreement about whether the developing child needs innate, language-specific content in order to acquire language. Connectionist modeling has shown how language might be an emergent process, the development of which depends on general constraints, although this remains controversial.

Fifth, do we need to refer to explicit rules when considering language processing? There is currently little agreement on this, with researchers in the connectionist camp against much explicit rule-based processing, and traditionalists in favor of it (e.g., see the debates on past tense acquisition in Chapter 4 and on dual-route models of reading in Chapter 7). There is considerable evidence that children make much use of statistical learning of distributional information when acquiring language. A recent study, for example, has found a correlation between children's statistical learning skills and reading ability (Arciuli & Simpson, 2012).

The sixth theme is the extent to which language processes are specific to language. We have seen how this issue has proved very controversial,

particularly in language development. There is a divide between those who argue that children need language-specific information (which is usually thought to have some innate origin) to acquire language, and those who argue that acquisition needs no more than general learning principles, such as the ability to make use of distributional information.

Seventh, how sensitive are the results of our experiments to the particular techniques employed? Our results are sometimes very sensitive to the techniques used, and this means that in addition to having a theory about the principal object of study, we need to have a theory about the tools themselves. Perhaps this is most clearly exemplified by the debate about lexical decision and naming, and whether they measure the same thing.

Eighth, a great deal can be learned by examining the language of people with damage to the parts of the brain that control language. In recent years, cognitive neuroscience imaging data has provided some of the most interesting and important contributions to psycholinguistics.

Ninth, language is cross-cultural. Studies of processing in different languages have told us a great deal about topics such as language development, reading, parsing, language production, and neuropsychology. The results suggest that while the same basic architecture is used to process different languages, it is exploited in different ways. That is, we all share the same hard-wired

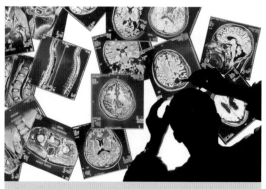

Cognitive neuropsychology has provided some interesting and important contributions to the study of language.

modules, but they vary slightly in what they do. Hence there are some important cross-linguistic differences, and these differences are of theoretical interest.

Finally, we should be able to apply psycholinguistic research to everyday problems. We can discern five key applications: First, we now know a great deal about reading and comprehension, and this can be applied to improving methods of teaching reading (Chapters 8 and 12). Second, these techniques should also be of use in helping children with language disabilities; for example, the study of developmental dyslexia has aroused much interest (Chapter 8). Third, psycholinguistics helps us to improve the way in which foreign languages can be acquired by children and adults (Chapter 5). Fourth, we have greatly increased our understanding of how language can be disrupted by brain damage. This has had consequences for the treatment and rehabilitation of brain-damaged patients (e.g., see Howard & Hatfield, 1987). Fifth, there are obvious advantages if we can develop computers that can understand and produce language. This is a complex task, but an examination of how humans perform these tasks has been revealing. Generally, computers are better at lower level tasks such as word recognition. Higher level, integrative processes involve a great deal of context (Chapters 12 and 13), and this has proved a major stumbling block for work in the area.

In addition to these ten themes, we noted in Chapter 1 that modern psycholinguistics is eclectic. In particular, we have made use of data from cognitive neuropsychology and techniques of connectionist modeling.

We have seen that the study of impairments to the language system has cast light on virtually every aspect of psycholinguistics. For example, it has provided a major motivation for the dual-route model of reading (Chapter 7); it has enhanced our understanding of the development of reading and spelling (Chapter 8); it has provided interesting if complex data that any theory of semantics must explain (Chapter 11); it has bolstered the two-stage model of lexicalization (Chapter 13); and it has been revealing about the nature of parsing and syntactic planning (Chapters 10 and 13).

Connectionism has made many important contributions to psycholinguistics over the last 30 years. What are its virtues that have made it so attractive? First, as we have seen, unlike traditional AI it is more brain-like, in that processing takes place in lots of simple, massively interconnected neuron-like units. It is important not to get too carried away with this metaphor, but at least we have the feeling that we are starting off with the right sort of models. Second, just like traditional AI, connectionism has the virtue that modeling forces us to be totally explicit about our theories. This explicitness has had three major consequences. First, recall that many psycholinguistic models are specified as box-and-arrow diagrams (e.g., Figure 15.1). This approach is sometimes called, rather derogatorily, "boxology." It is certainly not unique to psycholinguistics, and such an approach is not as bad as is sometimes hinted. It at least gives rise to an understanding of the architecture of the language system—what the modules of the language system are, and how they are related to others. However, connectionism has meant that we have had to focus on the processes that take place inside the boxes of our models. In some cases (such as the acquisition of past tense), this has led to a detailed re-examination of the evidence. Second, connectionism has forced us to consider in detail the representations used by the language system. This has led to a healthy debate, even if the first representations used by connectionist modelers turned out later not to be the correct ones (e.g., see Chapter 7 and the debate on using Wickelfeatures as a representation of phonology in the input to the reading system). Third, the emphasis on learning in many connectionist models focuses on the developmental aspect that is hopefully leading to an integration of adult and developmental psycholinguistics.

SOME GROWTH AREAS?

Students of any subject are obviously interested primarily in where a subject has been, whereas researchers naturally focus on where a subject is going—and on helping it to get there. The study of the psychology of language has traveled an enormous distance since its beginning. It came into its own with the realization that there are psychological processes to be studied that are independent of linguistic knowledge. The proliferation of research in the area is enormous. Even in the years since the first edition of this book, the subject has been transformed, mostly by the influence of computational modeling and cognitive neuroscience. So, where is it going? Unfortunately, as Einstein once remarked, "it is difficult to predict, especially the future." In every edition I have tried to predict where psycholinguistics will be in five years' time; and every time I have been wrong.

There is no particular reason to expect a revolution in the way we examine or understand language. To some extent, the next five years are likely to see progress in solving the same sorts of problems using the same sorts of techniques. Of course, our models will be more sophisticated, and our experimental techniques more refined. My list of likely developments is rather arbitrary and perhaps personal, and some of these points have been covered in greater detail in earlier chapters. Nevertheless, this selection gives some flavor of global trends in the subject. Generally, the trend is towards more inclusive models covering more complex phenomena. For example, now our processing of morphologically simple words is relatively well understood, interest is growing in words that are morphologically more complex.

First, new techniques in neuroscience have become more accurate and more accessible, and will continue to do so. Imaging might tell us a great deal about the time course of processes, and when we make use of different sources of information (see Chapter 1). Brain scans are being increasingly presented in the case study literature. The continued increased use of imaging is perhaps the single most likely thing we can predict for the next five years.

Second, we will develop new computational models of language. The use of straightforward connectionist models has more or less been exhausted, but there are other types of

Techniques in brain imaging are becoming more accurate. This photo shows a child in a magnetoencephalographic scanner. This detects the magnetic fields generated by neural activity in different parts of the brain when stimulated by auditory signals received through the tubes to the ears and by visual information shown on a screen. The reactions within his brain are recorded by the scanner, and the eye-tracking device in front of the subject gives data on the gaze related to the brain activity.

mathematical and computational models being used. Bayesian models are becoming increasingly popular in cognitive psychology in general, and will probably expand into areas of language processing.

Third, we can expect the more widespread use of developmental data to help resolve adult questions. For example, the study of how children learn and represent word meanings might be revealing with regard to adult semantic representation. There is also much more scope for computational modeling in this area. Developmental models will become more process orientated, and we will form a clearer understanding of how processing changes throughout childhood before settling on the adult form.

Fourth, a full understanding of psycholinguistics would entail an understanding of the nature of all the components of the language processor, and how they are related to each other. We saw in Chapter 15 (Figure 15.1) how a start has been made on the word recognition system. One important goal of any integrative theory is to specify how the language system interfaces with other cognitive systems. That is, what is the final output of comprehension and the initial input to production? It is likely these are the same. In Chapter 12 we saw how currently the most likely proposal about the form of the output is a propositional representation associated with the activation of goals and other schemata (see the description of Kintsch's model in that chapter). In Chapter 13, we saw that the conceptualizer that creates the input to the production system has been much neglected. In Chapter 11, we saw that the work of people like Jackendoff (1983) puts restrictions on the interface between the semantic and cognitive systems. There is a move to integrating research across areas. For example, the connectionist model of Chang, Dell, and Bock (2006) accounts for data from adult speech production (structural priming) and language acquisition (verb-argument structures). The Chang et al. model shows how language acquisition and adult speech production make use of the same mechanisms. A related question is how production and comprehension are related (e.g., Ferreira & Bailey, 2004; Pickering & Garrod, 2013). Clearly much remains to be done in this important area.

Fifth, the Internet and social networking make possible the use of very large corpora of language. We have seen in the study of semantics how HAL makes use of the co-occurrence information of a very large sample of text. Watts (2012) explores what we can learn about behavior and communication using Twitter and Facebook. For the first time we have readily available millions of samples of language in actual use. So, for example, rather than estimating things such as word frequency, we can specify it for a very large corpus of actual usage. The Internet also makes it relatively easy through crowdsourcing to collect large-scale norms. We can also carry out "mega-studies" using a huge number of participants and items. The challenge is developing new tools that will enable us to extract meaningful conclusions from these very large samples (see for example Bestgen & Vincze, 2012).

Finally, psycholinguistics will explore other participant groups and more naturalistic settings in greater detail. Recent years have seen an enormous diversification in who is being studied. We saw in the first chapter that many experiments have been on the visual processing of language by healthy monolingual college-aged participants. That is changing. One particularly important aspect of this is the cross-linguistic study of language. Most of the experiments described in this book have been on speakers of the English language. This does not just reflect my bias, because most of the work carried out has been on English. Research is also driven by the assumption that the underlying processing architecture is shared by languages, although there may be some important differences. There is likely to be more emphasis on how we process natural speech in more natural settings, away from the single word presented on a computer screen. The "visual world" paradigm (discussed particularly in Chapters 10, 13, and 14) has become particularly important in this respect, and is likely to become even more so.

Chomsky's ideas have been very influential in this respect. You will remember that according to his position language is an innate faculty specified by the language acquisition device (LAD). All languages, because they are governed by the form of the LAD, are similar at some deep level. Variation between languages boils down to differences in vocabulary, and the parameters set by the exposure to a particular language. An alternative view is the connectionist one that similar constraints from general development and inherent in the data lead to similarities in development and processing across languages. In general, cross-linguistic comparisons help us to constrain the nature of this architecture and to explain the important differences. What are the consequences of these differences? Much research remains to be done on this.

There are many areas where it is useful to compare languages. First, the observation that there are similar constraints on syntactic rules has been used to motivate the concept of universal grammar (Chapters 2, 3, and 4). To what extent can the connectionist view that language is an emergent process give an account of these findings? Second, we also saw in Chapter 10 that examining a single language (English) might have given us a distorted view of the parsing process. Third, similarities and differences in languages have consequences for language development (Chapter 4). For example, the cross-linguistic analysis of the development of gender argues against a semantic basis for the development of syntactic categories. Finally, what can analysis of different languages that map orthography onto phonology in different ways tell us about reading (Chapter 7)? And do different languages break down in different ways after brain damage?

Related to cross-linguistic studies, much remains to be learned about bilingualism, which is still receiving increasing attention in the research literature, both as a subject in its own right, and as a means to investigate underlying language processes.

CONCLUSION

The eventual goal of psycholinguistics is a detailed and unified theory of language and how it relates to other cognitive processes. The more we know, in some ways the harder it is to carry out psycholinguistics experiments. Cutler (1981) observed that the list of variables that had to be controlled in psycholinguistics experiments was large and growing, and there were many that were rarely considered. Here is Cutler's (adapted) list for experiments on single words: syntactic class, ambiguity, frequency, frequency of related morphological and phonological forms, length, associations, age of acquisition, autobiographical associations, categorizability, concreteness, bigram frequency, imagery, letter frequency, number of meanings, orthographic regularity, meaningfulness, emotionality, recognition threshold, regularity, position of recognition point, and morphological complexity. Since then we have discovered that not only are the neighbors of words important, but also the properties of the neighbors are important. And this is before we have begun to consider constraints on processing units larger than a word. Cutler, writing in 1981, asked, "will we be able to run any psycholinguistic experiments at all in 1990?" The year 1990 has passed and we are still doing experiments in 2012, so the answer is obviously "yes," but it is getting more difficult, and we have to make a number of carefully justified assumptions. It is apparent that we have to be particularly careful about how we choose our materials. Controlling variables we know about might not be enough. Forster (2000) showed that skilled psycholinguists have a great deal of implicit knowledge about language. When asked to make predictions about which word would be responded to fastest on a lexical decision task from word pairs controlled for known predictor variables, skilled researchers performed above chance. Hence it is always possible that researchers are unconsciously constructing their materials in a particular way. The remedy for this problem is making more use of random sampling of materials.

There still remains a great deal to do in psycholinguistics. It should be clear from reading this book that there is much we don't know, and many occasions when there are competing interpretations of the data. If this book has inspired any reader to investigate further and even actually contribute to the subject, it has more than served its purpose.

QUESTIONS TO THINK ABOUT

1. How will this book be different in 2025?
2. Will the psychology of language (contrasted with the neuroscience of language) still be taught in universities in 2050?

This appendix provides a more formal and detailed description of connectionism than is given in the main text. I hope it is comprehensible to anyone with some knowledge of basic algebra. If you find the mathematics daunting, it is worth persevering, as many of the most important models in current psycholinguistics are types of connectionist models. See the suggestions for further reading for more detailed and comprehensive coverage.

Connectionism has become the preferred term to describe a class of models that all have in common the principle that processing occurs through the action of many simple, interconnected units; parallel distributed processing (PDP) and neural networks are other commonly used terms that are almost synonymous. There are three very important concepts underpinning all connectionist models. The first basic idea of connectionism is that there are many simple processing units connected together. These units don't do very much other than modify and pass on activation (one number). The second basic idea is that energy or activation spreads around the network in a way determined by the strengths of the connections between units. Strong positive weights magnify the output of units; strong negative weights produce a large negative, inhibitory value. Units have activation levels that are modified by the amount of activation they receive from other units. The third idea is that high-level, complex "intelligent" behavior emerges from the interaction and cooperation of these many simple "dumb" units.

There are many types of connectionist model. One important distinction is between models that do not learn and models that do. In psychology the most important examples of the models that

do not learn are those based on interactive activation and competition (IAC), and of models that do learn, those trained using back-propagation. We should distinguish the architecture of a network, which describes the layout of the network (how many units there are and how they are connected to each other), the algorithm that determines how activation spreads around the network, and the learning rule, if appropriate, that specifies how the network learns.

We look here at two approaches that have been the most influential in psycholinguistics. Other important learning algorithms that have been used include Hebbian learning and the Boltzmann machine (Hinton & Sejnowski, 1986); see the suggestions for further reading for details of these.

INTERACTIVE ACTIVATION MODELS

I'll start with the interactive activation model because historically it was the first connectionist type model to have an impact on psychology, and because it's relatively easy to understand. McClelland and Rumelhart (1981) and Rumelhart and McClelland (1982) presented the interactive activation and competition (IAC) model to account for word context effects on letter identification. The TRACE model of spoken word recognition (McClelland & Elman, 1986) is an IAC model.

The model consists of many simple processing units arranged in three levels. There is an input level of visual feature units, a level where units correspond to individual letters, and an output level where each unit corresponds to a word. Each unit is connected to each unit in the level immediately before and after it. Each of these connections is either excitatory (that is, positive or facilitatory) or inhibitory (negative). Excitatory connections make the units at the end of the connection more active, whereas inhibitory connections make the connections at the end less active. Each unit is connected to each other unit within the same level by an inhibitory connection. See Figure 6.9 for a graphical representation of this architecture.

When a unit becomes activated, it sends off energy, or activation, simultaneously along the connections to all the other units to which it is connected. If it is connected by a facilitatory connection, it will increase the activation of the unit at the other end of the connection, whereas if it is connected by an inhibitory connection, it will decrease the activation at the other end. Consider the IAC model of Figure 6.9. If the unit corresponding to the letter "T" in the initial letter position becomes activated, it will increase the activation level of the word units corresponding to "TAKE" and "TASK," because they start with a "T," but will decrease the activation level of "CAKE," because it does not. Because units are connected to all other units within the same level by inhibitory connections, as soon as a unit becomes activated, it starts inhibiting all the other units at that level. The equations summarized in the next section determine the way in which activation flows between units, is summed by units, and is used to change the activation level of each unit at each time step. Over time, the pattern of activation settles down or relaxes into a stable configuration so that only one word remains active.

Basic equations of the interactive activation model

As we have seen, in the IAC model activation spreads from each unit to neighboring units along excitatory or inhibitory connections. Connections have numbers or weights that determine how much activation spreads along that connection,

and hence how quickly activation builds up at the unit at the end of the connection. The total activation, called net_i, arriving at each unit i from j connections is shown in equation (A.1). Put in words, this equation means that the activation arriving at a unit is the sum (S) of the products of the output activation (a_j) of all the j units that input to it and the weights (w) on the connection between the input and receiving unit (w_{ji}). You just multiply all the output of connecting units by the strength of the appropriate weight and add them up.

$$net_i = \sum_j a_j . w_{ji} \qquad (A.1)$$

An example should make this clear. Figure A.1 shows part of a very simple network. There are four input units to one destination unit. We say that the input vector is [1 0 1 1]. (Here we are assuming that the input units are either simply "on" [with a value of 1] or "off" [with a value of 0]. That is, we are restricting them to binary values. In principle, we could let the input units be "on" to different extents, e.g., 0.3.) The total amount of activation arriving at the destination unit will be the sum of all the products of the outputs of the units that input to it with the appropriate weights on the connections: that is, $((1 \times +0.2) + (0 \times -0.5) + (1 \times +0.7) + (1 \times -0.1)) = +0.8$. The underlying idea is that this equation is a simplified model of a neuron: Neurons become excited or inhibited by all the other neurons that contact them. Found that bit

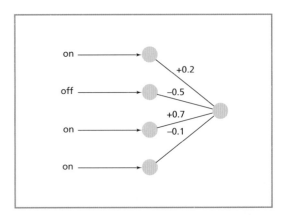

FIGURE A.1 A simplified connectionist unit or "neuron." This unit takes multiple inputs (derived from the weighted output of other units) and converts them to a single output.

of arithmetic tedious? Imagine doing it hundreds or thousands, or more, times. No wonder connectionism relies on computers to do the computation.

Finally, a further equation is needed to determine what happens to a unit in each processing cycle after it receives an input. In the IAC model, each unit changes its activation level depending on how much or how little input it receives, and whether that input is overall positive (excitatory) or negative (inhibitory). In each cycle the new activation level of a unit i, Δa_i, is given by equations (A.2) and (A.3):

$$\Delta a_i = (max - a_i)net_i - decay(a_i - rest)$$
$$\text{if } net_i > 0 \quad (A.2)$$

$$\Delta a_i = (a_i - min)net_i - decay(a_i - rest)$$
$$\text{otherwise} \quad (A.3)$$

where *rest* is the unit's resting level, *decay* is a parameter that makes the unit tend to decay back to its resting level in the absence of new input, *max* is the unit's maximum permitted level of activation, and *min* is the unit's minimum permitted level of activation. So if absolutely nothing happens, eventually the activation of the unit will decay back to its resting level.

Processing takes place in cycles to represent the passage of time. At the end of each cycle, the activation levels of all the units in the network are updated. In the next cycle the process is repeated using the new activation levels. Processing continues until some criterion (e.g., a certain number of processing cycles or a certain level of stability) is attained.

BACK-PROPAGATION

Back-propagation is the most widely used connectionist learning rule. It enables networks to learn to associate input patterns with output patterns. It is called an error-reduction learning method because it is an algorithm that enables networks to be trained to reduce the error between what the network actually outputs given a particular input, and what it should output given that input.

The simplest type of network architecture that can be trained by back-propagation has three layers or levels. Again, each typically contains many simple units. These are called the input, hidden, and output levels (see Figure 7.5 for an example). As in the IAC model, each of the units in these layers has an activation level, and each unit is connected to all the units in the next level by a weighted connection, which can be either excitatory or inhibitory. These networks learn to associate an input pattern with an output pattern using a learning rule called back-propagation. The most important difference between IAC and back-propagation networks is that in the case of the latter the weights on connections are learned rather than hand-coded at the start.

How does the network learn? The connections in the network all start off with random weights. Suppose we want the model to learn to pronounce the printed word "DOG"; that is, we want to train the network to associate the input pattern of graphemes D O G with the output pattern of sounds or phonemes /d/ /o/ /g/. One pattern of activation over the input units corresponds to "DOG." In Figure 7.5 I have for simplicity made the representation a local one—that is, for example, one unit corresponds to "D," one to "O," one to "G," and so on. In more realistic models these patterns are usually distributed so that DOG is represented by a pattern of activation over the input units with no one single unit corresponding to any one single letter. Hence DOG might be represented by input unit 1 on, input unit 2 off, input unit 3 on, and so on. These units then pass activation on to the **hidden units** according to the values of the connections between the input and the hidden units. Activation is then summed by each unit in the hidden unit layer in just the same way as in the interactive activation model. In models that learn using back-propagation, the output of a unit is a complex function of its input: For reasons that we can skip, there must be a non-linear relation between the two, given by a special type of function called the logistic function. The output o_u of a unit u is related to its input by equation (A.4). Here $netinput_u$ is the total input to the unit u from all the other units that input to it, and e is the exponential constant (the base of natural logarithms, with a value of about 2.718).

$$o_u = 1/(1 + e - netinput_u) \qquad (A.4)$$

As an example, let us take the unit shown in Figure A.1 once again. The total input to that unit, *netinput_u*, is $[(1 \times +0.2) + (0 \times -0.5) + (1 \times +0.7) + (1 \times -0.1)] = 0.8$. Hence the output *ou* for this unit is $1/(1 + e - 0.8) = 0.69$.

Each unit has an individual threshold level or bias. (This is usually implemented by attaching an additional unit, the bias unit, which is always on, to each principal unit. The value of the weights between the bias and other units can be learned like any other weights.)

Activation is then passed on from the hidden to the output units, and so eventually the output units end up with activation values. But as we started off with totally random values, they are extremely unlikely to be the correct ones. As the target output, we wanted the most activated output units to correspond to the phonemes /d/ /o/ /g/, but the actual output is going to be totally random, maybe something close to /k/ /i/ /j/. What the learning rule does then is to modify the connections in the network so that the output will be a bit less like what it actually produced, and a bit more like what it should be. It does this in a way that is very like what happens in calculating the mean squared error in an analysis of variance. The difference between the actual and the target outputs is computed, and the values of all the weights from the hidden to the output units are adjusted slightly to try to make this difference smaller. This process is then "back-propagated" to change the weights on the connections between the input and the hidden units. The whole process can then be repeated for a different input–output (e.g., grapheme–phoneme) pair. Eventually, the weights of the network converge on values that give the best output (that is, the least difference between desired and actual output) averaged across all input–output pairs.

The back-propagation learning rule is based on the generalized delta rule. The rule for changing the weights following the presentation of a particular pattern *p* is given by equation (A.5), where *j* and *i* index adjacent upper and lower layers in the network, t_{pj} is the *j*th component of the desired target pattern, o_{pj} is the corresponding *j*th component of the actual output pattern *p*, and i_{pi} is the *i*th component of the input pattern.

$$\Delta_p w_{ij} = (t_{pj} - o_{pj}) \cdot i_{pi} \qquad (A.5)$$

The error for the output units is given by equation (A.6), and that for the hidden units by equation (A.7), where *l* and *m* are connecting layers. The weight change is given by equation (A.8).

$$\delta_{pj} = (t_{pj} - o_{pj}) \cdot o_{pj} \cdot (1 - o_{pj}) \qquad (A.6)$$

$$\delta_{pl} = o_{pl} \cdot (1 - o_{pl}) \cdot \Sigma \, \delta_{pm} \cdot w_{lm} \qquad (A.7)$$

$$\Delta w_{ij(n+1)} = \eta \cdot (\delta_{pj} \cdot o_{pi}) + \alpha \cdot \Delta w_{ij(n)} \qquad (A.8)$$

There are two new constants in equation (A.8): η is the learning rate, which determines how quickly the network learns, and α is the momentum term, which stops the network changing too much and hence overshooting on any learning cycle. (The dots "·" mean the same as "multiply," but make the equations easier to read.) Needless to say, this training process cannot be completed in a single step. It has to be repeated many times, but gradually the values of actual and desired outputs converge. You can modify the training set in a number of ways to make the task more realistic. For example, if you are interested in word frequency, you have to encode it in the training in some way, perhaps by presenting more input–output pairings of frequent words more often.

Networks trained by back-propagation show some interesting properties. Most interestingly, if you present a trained network with an item that it has not seen before, it can often manage to produce the appropriate output quite well. For example, in the case of the model learning to read, although the network has not been taught any explicit rules of pronunciation, it behaves as though it has learned them, and can generalize appropriately.

One of the most important and commonly used modifications to the simple feedforward architecture is to introduce recurrent connections from one layer (usually the hidden layer) to another layer (called the context layer). For example, if the context layer stores the past state of the hidden unit layer, then the network can learn to encode sequential information—what follows what in a sequence (Elman, 1990).

You should bear in mind that this description is a simplification. Why you need hidden units in such a model, what happens if you do not have them, and how you select how many units to have are all important issues. Furthermore, there are other learning algorithms that are sometimes used—of these, Hebbian learning and Boltzmann machines are those that you are most likely to come across in psycholinguistics. The general principles involved are much the same, and furthermore, the end result is generally the same. We are usually most interested in the behavior of the trained network, and how it is trained is usually not relevant.

FURTHER READING

Bechtel and Abrahamsen (2001) is an excellent textbook on connectionism. Ellis and Humphreys (1999) is a text that emphasizes the role of connectionism in cognitive psychology. The two-volume set *Parallel Distributed Processing* (Rumelhart, McClelland, & the PDP Research Group, 1986; McClelland, Rumelhart, & the PDP Research Group, 1986) is a classic. Caudill and Butler (1992), Dawson (2005), McClelland and Rumelhart (1988), Orchard and Phillips (1991), and Plunkett and Elman (1997) provide exercises and simulation environments. Plunkett and Elman is a companion volume to Elman et al. (1996) and includes a simulation environment called tlearn that runs on both Macintosh and Windows platforms.

There are a number of popular books about emergent systems, attractors, chaos, and complexity, including Gleick (1987), Stewart (1989), and Waldrop (1992).

GLOSSARY

Acoustics: the study of the physical properties of sounds.

Acquired disorder: a disorder caused by brain damage is acquired if it affects an ability that was previously intact (contrasted with **developmental disorder**).

Activation: can be thought of as the amount of energy possessed by something. The more highly activated something is, the more likely it is to be output.

Adjective: a describing word (e.g., "red").

Adverb: a type of word that modifies a verb (e.g., "quickly").

Affix: a **bound morpheme** that cannot exist on its own, but that must be attached to a stem (e.g., re-, -ing). It can come before the main word, when it is a **prefix**, or after, when it is a **suffix**.

Agent: the **thematic role** describing the entity that instigates an action.

Agnosia: disorder of object recognition.

Agrammatism: literally, "without grammar"; a type of **aphasia** distinguished by an impairment of syntactic processing (e.g., difficulties in sentence formation, inflection formation, and parsing). There has been considerable debate about the extent to which agrammatism forms a **syndrome**.

Allophones: phonetic variants of **phonemes**. For example, in English the phoneme /p/ has two variants, an aspirated (breathy) and unaspirated (non-breathy) form. You can feel the difference if you say the words "pit" and "spit" with your hand a few inches from your mouth.

Alzheimer's disease (AD): Alzheimer's disease or dementia—often there is some uncertainty about the diagnosis, so this is really shorthand for "probable Alzheimer's disease" or "dementia of the Alzheimer's type."

American Sign Language (ASL): American Sign Language (sometimes called AMESLAN).

Anaphor: a linguistic expression for which the **referent** can only be determined by taking another linguistic expression into account—namely the anaphor's **antecedent** (e.g., "Vlad was happy; *he* loved the vampire"—here *he* is the anaphor and *Vlad* is the antecedent).

Aneurysm: dilation of blood vessel (e.g., in the brain), where a sac in the blood vessel is formed and presses on surrounding tissue.

Anomia: difficulty in naming objects.

Antecedent: the linguistic expression that must be taken into account in order to determine the **referent** of an **anaphor** ("*Vlad* was happy; *he* loved the vampire"—here *he* is the anaphor and *Vlad* the antecedent). Often the antecedent is the thing for which a pronoun is being substituted.

Aphasia: a disorder of language, including a defect or loss of **expressive** (production) or **receptive** (comprehension) aspects of written or spoken language as a result of brain damage.

Apraxia: an inability to plan movements, in the absence of paralysis. Of particular relevance is speech apraxia, an inability to carry out properly controlled movements of the **articulatory apparatus**. Compare with **dysarthria**.

Articulatory apparatus: the parts of the body responsible for making speech sounds, such as the larynx, tongue, teeth, and lips.

Aspect: the use of verb forms to show whether something is finished, continuing, or repeated. English has two aspects: progressive (e.g., "we are cooking dinner") versus non-progressive (e.g., "we cook dinner"), and perfect, involving forms of the auxiliary "have" (e.g., "we have cooked dinner"), versus non-perfect (without the auxiliary).

Aspirated: a sound that is produced with an audible breath (e.g., at the start of "pin").

Assimilation: the influence of one sound on the articulation of another, so that the two sounds become slightly more alike.

Attachment: attachment concerns how phrases are connected together to form syntactic structures. In "the vampire saw the ghost with the binoculars" the **prepositional phrase** ("with the binoculars") can be attached to either the first noun phrase ("the vampire") or the second ("the ghost").

Attentional (or controlled) processing: processing requiring central resources. It is non-obligatory, generally uses working memory space, is prone to dual-task interference, is relatively slow, and may be accessible to consciousness. (The opposite is **automatic processing**.)

Attractor: a point in the connectionist attractor network to which related states are attracted.

Audience design: the idea that speakers tailor their productions to address the specific needs of their listeners.

Auditory short-term memory (ASTM): a short-term store for spoken material.

Automatic processing: processing that is unconscious, fast, obligatory, facilitatory, does not involve working memory space, and is generally not susceptible to dual-task interference. (The opposite is **attentional processing**.)

Auxiliary verb: a linking verb used with other verbs (e.g., in "You *must have* done that," "must" and "have" are auxiliaries).

Babbling: an early stage of language, starting at the age of about 5 or 6 months, where the child babbles, repetitively combining consonants and vowels into syllable-like sequences (e.g., "bababababa").

Back-propagation: an algorithm for learning input–output pairs in connectionist networks. It works by alternately reducing the error between the actual output and the desired output of the network.

Basic level: the level of representation in a hierarchy that is the default level (e.g., "dog" rather than "terrier" or "animal").

Bilingual: speaking two languages.

Bilingualism: having the ability to speak two languages. There are three types depending on when **L2** (the second

language) is learned relative to **L1**: simultaneous (L1 and L2 learned about the same time), early sequential (L1 learned first but L2 learned relatively early, in childhood), and late (in adolescence onwards).

Body: the same as a **rime**—the final vowel and terminal consonants.

Bootstrapping: the way in which children can increase their knowledge when they have some—such as inferring syntax when they have semantics.

Bottom-up: processing that is purely data-driven.

Bound morphemes: a morpheme that cannot exist on its own (e.g., un, ent).

Brain imaging: techniques for looking at what the brain is doing when we carry out some activity.

Broca's aphasia: a type of aphasia that follows from damage to Broca's region of the brain, characterized by many dysfluencies, slow, laborious speech, difficulties in articulation, and by **agrammatism**.

Cascade model: a type of processing where information can flow from one level of processing to the next before the first has finished processing; contrast with **discrete stage model**.

Categorical perception: perceiving things that lie along a continuum as belonging to one distinct category or another.

Child-directed speech (CDS): the speech of carers to young children that is modified to make it easier to understand (sometimes called "*motherese*").

Class: the grammatical class of a word is the major grammatical category to which a **word** belongs—e.g., noun, adjective, verb, adverb, determiner, preposition, pronoun.

Clause: a group of related words containing a **subject** and a **verb**.

Closed-class item: same as **function word**.

Co-articulation: the way in which the articulatory apparatus takes account of the surrounding sounds when a sound is articulated; as a result, a sound conveys information about its neighbors.

Cognates: words in different languages that have developed from the same root (e.g., many English and French words have developed from the same Latin root: "horn" [and "cornet"] and "corne" are derived from the Latin "cornu"); occasionally used for words that have the same form in two languages (e.g., "oblige" in English and French).

Competence: our knowledge of our language, as distinct from our linguistic performance.

Complementizer: a category of words (e.g., "that") used to introduce a subordinate clause.

Conjunction: a part of speech that connects words within a sentence (e.g., "and," "because").

Connectionism: an approach to cognition that involves computer simulations with many simple processing units, and where knowledge comes from learning statistical regularities rather than explicitly presented rules.

Connectionist: a computational model involving many simple, neuron-like units connected together by weighted links.

Consonant: a sound produced with some constriction of the airstream, unlike a **vowel**.

Constituent: a linguistic unit that is part of a larger linguistic unit.

Content word: one of the enormous number of words that convey most of the meaning of a sentence—nouns, verbs, adjectives, adverbs. Content words are the same as **open-class words**. Contrasted with **function word**.

Conversational maxim: a rule that helps us to make sense of conversation.

Co-reference: two or more **noun phrases** with the same **reference**. For example, in "There was a vampire in the kitchen; Boris was scared to death when he saw him," the co-referential noun phrases are *vampire* and *him*.

Creole: a pidgin that has become the language of a community through an evolutionary process known as "creolization."

Cross-linguistic: involving a comparison across languages.

Deep dyslexia: disorder of reading characterized by semantic reading errors.

Deep dysphasia: disorder of repetition characterized by **semantic** repetition errors.

Derivational morphology: the study of derivational inflections.

Determiner: a grammatical word that determines the number of a noun (e.g., "the," "a," "an," "some").

Developmental disorder: a disorder where the normal development or acquisition of a process (e.g., reading) is affected.

Diphthong: a type of vowel that combines two vowel sounds (e.g., in "boy," "cow," and "my").

Discourse: linguistic units composed of several sentences.

Discrete stage model: a processing model where information can only be passed to the next stage when the current one has completed its processing (contrast with **cascade model**).

Dissociation: a process is dissociable from other processes if brain damage can disrupt it, while leaving the others intact.

Distributional information: information about what tends to co-occur with what; for example, the knowledge that the letter "q" is almost always followed by the letter "u," or that the word "the" is always followed by a noun, are instances of distributional information.

Double dissociation: a pattern of dissociations whereby one patient can do one task but not another, whereas another patient shows the reverse pattern.

Dysarthria: difficulty with executing motor movements. In addition to difficulties with executing speech plans, there are problems with automatic activities such as eating. Compare with **apraxia**, which is a deficit limited to motor planning.

Dysgraphia: disorder of writing.

Dyslexia: disorder of reading.

Dysprosody: a disturbance of **prosody**.

EEG: electroencephalography—a means of measuring electrical potentials in the brain by placing electrodes across the scalp.

Episodic memory: knowledge of specific episodes (e.g., what I had for breakfast this morning, or what happened in the library yesterday).

ERP: event-related potential—electrical activity in the brain after a particular event. An ERP is a complex electrical waveform related in time to a specific event, measured by EEG.

Expressive: a form of aphasia to do with producing language, primarily speaking.

Facilitation: making processing faster, usually as a result of priming. It is the opposite of inhibition.

Figurative speech: speech that contains non-literal material, such as metaphors and similes (e.g., "he ran like a leopard").

Filler: what fills a **gap**.

fMRI: functional magnetic resonance imaging—a modern method of mapping the brain's activity by recording blood flow in real time.

Formal paraphasia: substitution in speech of a word that sounds like another word (e.g., "caterpillar" for "catapult"). Sometimes called a form-related paraphasia.

Formant: a concentration of acoustic energy in a sound.

Function word: one of the limited numbers of words that do the grammatical work of the language (e.g., **determiners**, **prepositions**, **conjunctions**—such as "the," "a," "to," "in," "and," "because"). Contrasted with **content word**.

Gap: an empty part of the syntactic construction that is associated with a **filler**.

Garden path sentence: a type of sentence where the syntactic structure leads you to expect a different conclusion from that which it actually has (e.g., "the horse raced past the barn fell").

Gating task: a task that involves presenting increasing amounts of a word.

Gender: some languages (e.g., French and Italian) distinguish different cases depending on their gender—male, female, or neuter.

Generative grammar: a finite set of rules that will produce or generate all the sentences of a language (but no non-sentences).

Glottal stop: a sound produced by closing and opening the glottis (the opening between the vocal folds); an example is the sound that replaces the /t/ sound in the middle of "bottle" in some dialects of English (e.g., in parts of London).

Grammar: the set of syntactic rules of a language.

Grammatical element: a difficulty in physically producing the sounds of language, usually due to brain damage affecting control of the muscles involved in moving the articulatory apparatus.

Grapheme: a unit of written language that corresponds to a **phoneme** (e.g., "steak" contains four graphemes, s t ea k, corresponding to the four component sounds).

Hemidecortication: complete removal of the cortex of one side of the brain.

Heterographic homophones: two words with different spellings that sound the same (e.g., "soul" and "sole"; "night" and "knight").

Hidden units: a unit from the hidden layer of a connectionist network that enables the network to learn complex input–output pairs by the **back-propagation** algorithm. The hidden layer forms a layer between the input and output layers.

Homographs: different words that are spelled the same; they may or may not be pronounced differently, e.g., "lead" (as in what you use to take a dog for a walk) and "lead" (as in the metal).

Homophone: two words that sound the same.

Idioms: an expression particular to a language, whose meaning cannot be derived from its parts (e.g., "kick the bucket").

Imageability: a semantic variable concerning how easy it is to form a mental image of a word: "rose" is more imageable than "truth."

Implicature: an inference that we make in conversations to maintain the sense and relevance of the conversation.

Independent models: models in which processing occurs without reference to any external processes or information (e.g., purely **bottom-up**).

Inference: the derivation of additional knowledge from facts already known; this might involve going beyond the text to maintain coherence or to elaborate on what was actually presented.

Inflection: a grammatical change to a verb (changing its tense, e.g., -ed) or noun (changing its number, e.g., -s, or "mice").

Inflectional morphology: the study of **inflections**.

Inhibition: this has two uses. In terms of processing it means slowing processing down. In this sense priming may lead to inhibition. Inhibition is the opposite of **facilitation**. In comprehension it is closely related to the idea of **suppression**. In terms of networks it refers to how some connections decrease the amount of activation of the target unit.

Inner speech: that voice we hear in our head; speech that is not overtly articulated.

Interactive models: models where different sorts of information are allowed to influence current processing (e.g., a mixture of **bottom-up** and **top-down**).

Intransitive verb: a verb that does not take an object (e.g., "The man laughs").

Invariance: the same phoneme can in fact sound different depending on the context in which it occurs.

L1: the language learned first by bilingual people.

L2: the language learned second by bilingual people.

Language acquisition device (LAD): Chomsky argued that children hear an impoverished language input and therefore need the assistance of an innate language acquisition device in order to acquire language.

Lemma: a level of representation of a word between its semantic and phonological representations; it is syntactically specified, but does not yet contain sound-level information; it is the intermediate stage of two-stage models of **lexicalization**.

Lesion: damage to a particular part of the brain.

Lexeme: the phonological word form, in a format where phonology is represented.

Lexical access: accessing a word's entry in the **lexicon**.

Lexicalization: in speech production, going from semantics to sound.

Lexicon: our mental dictionary.

LSA: latent semantic analysis—a means of acquiring knowledge from the co-occurrence of information.

Malapropisms: a type of speech error where a similar-sounding word is substituted for the target (e.g., saying "restaurant" instead of "rhapsody").

Manner of articulation: the way in which the airstream is constricted in speaking (e.g., stop).

Maturation: the sequential unfolding of characteristics, usually governed by instructions in the genetic code.

Mediated priming: (facilitatory) priming through a semantic intermediary (e.g., "lion" to "tiger" to "stripes").

MEG: magnetoencephalography—a technique for mapping the brain's electrical activity by recording the magnetic field produced by the brain.

Metaphor: a figure of speech that works by association, comparison, or resemblance (e.g., "he's a tiger in a fight," "the leaves swam around the lake").

Minimal pair: a pair of words that differ in meaning when only one sound is changed (e.g., "pear" and "bear").

Model: an account of the data that provides an explanation of why the data are as they are and that makes novel, testable predictions.

Modifier: a part of speech that is dependent on another, which it modifies or qualifies in some way (e.g., adjectives modify nouns).

Modularity: the idea that the mind is built up from discrete modules; its resurgence is associated with the American philosopher Jerry Fodor, who said that modules cannot tinker around with the insides of other modules. A further step is to say that the modules of the mind correspond to identifiable neural structures in the brain.

Monosyllabic: a word having just one syllable.

Morpheme: the smallest unit of meaning (e.g., "dogs" contains two, dog + plural s).

Morphology: the study of how words are built up from **morphemes**.

Nativist: the idea that knowledge is innate.

Natural kind: a category of naturally occurring things (e.g., animals, trees).

Neologism: a "made-up word" that is not in the dictionary. Neologisms are usually common in the speech of people with jargon aphasia.

Nonword: a string of letters that does not form a **word**. Although most of the time nonwords mentioned in psycholinguistics refer to pronounceable nonwords (**pseudowords**), not all nonwords need be pronounceable.

Noun: the syntactic category of **words** that can act as names and can all be **subjects** or **objects** of a **clause**; all things are nouns.

Noun phrase: a grammatical **phrase** based on a **noun** (e.g., "the red house"), abbreviated to NP.

Number: the number of a verb is whether one or more subjects are doing the action (e.g., "the ghost was" but "the ghosts were").

Object: the person, thing, or idea that is acted on by the verb. In the sentence "The cat chased the dog," "cat" is the subject, "chased" the verb, and "dog" is the object. Objects can be either direct or indirect—in the sentence "She gave the dog to the man," "dog" is the direct object and "the man" is the indirect object.

Onset: the beginning of something. It has two meanings. The onset of a stimulus is when it is first presented. The onset of a printed word is its initial consonant cluster (e.g., "sp" in "speak").

Open-class word: same as **content word**.

Ostensive: you can define an **object** ostensively by pointing to it.

Over-extension: when a child uses a word to refer to things in a way that is based on particular attributes of the word, so that many things can be named using that word (e.g., using "moon" to refer to all round things, or "stick" to all long things, such as an umbrella).

Parameter: a component of Chomsky's theory that governs aspects of language, and that is set in childhood by exposure to a particular language.

Paraphasia: a spoken word substitution.

Parsing: analyzing the grammatical structure of a sentence.

Participle: a type of verbal phrase where a **verb** is turned into an **adjective** by adding -ed or -ing to the verb: "we live in an *exciting* age."

Patient: the **thematic role** of a person or thing acted on by the **agent**.

Performance: our actual language ability, limited by our cognitive capacity, distinct from our **competence**.

Phoneme: a sound of the language; changing a phoneme changes the meaning of a word.

Phonetics: the acoustic detail of speech sounds and how they are articulated.

Phonological awareness: awareness of sounds, measured by tasks such as naming the common sound in words (e.g., "bat" and "ball"), and deleting a sound from a word (e.g., "take the second sound of bland"); thought to be important for reading development but probably other **aspects** of language too.

Phonological dyslexia: a type of dyslexia where people can read words quite well but are poor at reading nonwords.

Phonology: the study of sounds and how they relate to languages; phonology describes the sound categories each language uses to divide up the space of possible sounds.

Phrase: a group of **words** forming a grammatical unit beneath the level of a **clause** (e.g., "up a tree"). A phrase does not contain both a **subject** and a **predicate**. In general, if you can replace a sequence of words in a sentence with a single word without changing the overall structure of the sentence, then that sequence of words is a phrase.

Pidgin: a type of language, with reduced structure and form, without any native speakers of its own, and which is created by the contact of two peoples who do not speak each other's native languages.

Place of articulation: where the airstream in the articulatory apparatus is constricted.

Polysemous words: words that have more than one meaning.

Pragmatics: the aspects of meaning that do not affect the literal truth of what is being said; these concern things such as choice from words with the same meaning, implications in conversation, and maintaining coherence in conversation.

Predicate: the part of the clause that gives information about the subject (e.g., in "The ghost is laughing," "the ghost" is the subject and "is laughing" is the predicate).

Prefix: an **affix** that comes before the **stem** (e.g., dis-interested). Contrast with **suffix** which comes after the stem.

Preposition: a grammatical word expressing a relation (e.g., "to," "with," "from").

Prepositional phrase: a phrase beginning with a preposition (e.g., "with the telescope," "up the chimney").

Priming: affecting a response to a target by presenting a related item prior to it; priming can have either facilitatory or inhibitory effects.

Pronouns: a grammatical **class** of words that can stand for **nouns** or **noun phrases** (e.g., "she," "he," "it").

Proposition: the smallest unit of knowledge that can stand alone: it has a truth value—that is, a proposition can be either true or false.

Prosody: the way in which speech is stressed and intoned to give it a rhythm.

Prototype: an abstraction that is the best example of a category.

Pseudohomophone: a **nonword** that sounds like a word when pronounced (e.g., "nite").

Pseudoword: a string of letters that form a pronounceable **nonword** (e.g., "smeak").

Psycholinguist: someone who does **psycholinguistics**.

Psycholinguistics: the psychology of language.

Receptive aphasia: a form of aphasia to do with understanding language.

Recognition point: the point at which we recognize a word.

Recurrent network: a type of **connectionist** network that is designed to learn sequences. It does this by means of an additional layer of units called context units that stores information about past states of the network.

Reduced relative: a relative **clause** that has been reduced by removing the relative pronoun and "was" ("The horse raced past the barn fell").

Reference: what things refer to.

Referent: the object or concept to which a pronoun refers.

Refractory period: after firing, a unit, cell, or organ is much less likely to fire again during the refractory period, until it has recovered.

Relative clause: a clause normally introduced by a relative **pronoun** that modifies the main **noun** ("The horse that was raced past the barn fell"— here the relative clause is "that was raced past the barn").

Repetition priming: (facilitatory) priming by repeating a stimulus.

Rime: the end part of a word that produces the rhyme (e.g., the rime constituent in "rant" is "ant," or "eak" in "speak"): more formally, it is the VC or VCC (vowel–consonant or vowel–consonant–consonant) part of a word.

Saccade: a fast movement of the eye, for example to change the fixation point when reading.

Schema: a means for organizing knowledge.

Script: a script for procedural information (e.g., going to the doctor's).

Segmentation: splitting speech up into constituent **phonemes**.

Semantic bootstrapping: the idea that the meaning of a word provides a cue as to the syntactic category to which that word belongs.

Semantic feature: a unit that represents part of the meaning of a word.

Semantic memory: a memory system for the long-term storage of facts (e.g., a robin is a bird; Paris is the capital of France).

Semantic paralexia: a reading error based on a word's meaning.

Semantic priming: priming, usually facilitatory, obtained by the prior presentation of a stimulus related in meaning (e.g., "doctor" – "nurse").

Semantics: the study of meaning.

Sentence: a group of words that expresses a complete thought, indicated in writing by the capitalization of the first letter, and ending with a period (full stop). Sentences contain a **subject** and a **predicate** (apart from a very few exceptions, notably one-word sentences such as "Stop!").

Sequential bilingualism: L2 acquired after L1— this can be either early in childhood or later.

Short-term memory: a limited capacity memory store that holds incoming information for short periods of time only.

Simultaneous bilingualism: L1 and L2 acquired simultaneously.

SOA: short for stimulus–onset asynchrony—the time between the onset (beginning) of the presentation of one stimulus and the onset of another. The time between the offset (end) of the presentation of the first stimulus and the onset of the second is known as stimulus offset–onset asynchrony.

Span: the number of items (e.g., digits) that a person can keep in short-term memory.

Specific language impairment: a developmental disorder affecting just language.

Speech act: an utterance defined in terms of the intentions of the speaker and the effect that it has on the listener.

Spoonerism: a type of speech error where the initial sounds of two words get swapped (named after the Reverend William A. Spooner, who is reported as saying things such as "you have tasted the whole worm" instead of "you have wasted the whole term").

Stem: the root **morpheme** to which other **bound morphemes** can be added.

Stochastic: probabilistic.

Subject: the word or phrase that the sentence is about—the **clause** about which something is predicated (stated). The subject of the **verb**: who or what is doing something. More formally it is the grammatical category of the **noun phrase** that is immediately beneath the sentence node in the phrase-structure tree; the thing about which something is stated.

Sublexical: correspondences in spelling and sound beneath the level of the whole word.

Sucking habituation paradigm: a method for examining whether or not very young infants can discriminate between two stimuli. The child sucks on a special piece of apparatus; as the child habituates to the stimulus, their sucking rate drops, but if a new stimulus is presented, the sucking rate increases again, but only if the child can detect that the stimulus is different from the first.

Suffix: a morpheme added to the end of a word to form a derivative (e.g. -ed, -ing, -s).

Suppression: in comprehension, suppression is closely related to **inhibition**. Suppression is the attenuation of **activation**, while inhibition is the blocking of activation. Material must be activated before it can be suppressed.

Syllable: a rhythmic unit of speech (e.g., po-lo contains two syllables); it can be analyzed in terms of **onset** and **rime** (or rhyme), with the rime further being analyzable into nucleus and coda. Hence in "speaks," "sp" is the onset, "ea" the nucleus, and "ks" the coda; together "eaks" forms the rime.

Syndrome: a medical term for a cluster of symptoms that cohere as a result of a single underlying cause.

Syntactic bootstrapping: the idea that the syntactic frame associated with a verb provides a cue as to the word's meaning.

Syntax: the rules of word order of a language.

Tachistoscope: a device for presenting materials (e.g., words) for extremely short durations; tachistoscopic presentation therefore means an item that is presented very briefly.

Telegraphic speech: a type of speech used by young children, marked by syntactic simplification, particularly in the omission of **function words**.

Tense: the tense of a **verb** is whether it is in the past, present, or future (e.g., "she gave," "she gives," and "she will give").

Thematic roles: the set of **semantic** roles in a sentence that conveys information about who is doing what to whom, as distinct from the syntactic roles of subject and object. Examples include agent and theme.

Theme: the thing that is being acted on or being moved.

Tip-of-the-tongue (TOT): when you know that you know a word, but you cannot immediately retrieve it (although you might know its first sound, or how many syllables it has).

TMS: transcranial magnetic stimulation—producing activity in certain brain regions using locally applied magnetic fields.

Top-down: processing that involves knowledge coming from higher levels (such as predicting a word from the context).

Transcortical aphasia: a type of language disturbance following brain damage characterized by relatively good repetition but poor performance in other aspects of language.

Transformation: a grammatical rule for transforming one syntactic structure into another (e.g., turning an active sentence into a passive one).

Transformational grammar: a system of grammar based on transformations, introduced by Chomsky.

Transitive verb: a verb that takes an **object** (e.g., "The cat hit the dog").

Unaspirated: a sound that is produced without an audible breath (e.g., the /p/ in "spin").

Uniqueness point: the point at which a word is unique and differs from all its neighbors.

Universal grammar: the core of the grammar that is universal to all languages, and which specifies and restricts the form that individual languages can take.

Unvoiced: a sound that is produced without vibration of the vocal cords, such as /p/ and /t/—the same as *voiceless* and *without voice*.

Verb: a syntactic class of words expressing actions, events, and states, and which have tenses.

Verb-argument structure: the set of possible themes associated with a verb (e.g., a person gives something to someone—or agent–theme–goal).

Voice onset time (VOT): the time between the release of the constriction of the airstream when we produce a **consonant**, and when the vocal cords start to vibrate.

Voicing: consonants produced with vibration of the vocal cords.

Vowel: a speech sound produced with very little constriction of the airstream, unlike a consonant.

Wernicke's aphasia: a type of **aphasia** resulting from damage to Wernicke's area of the brain, characterized by poor comprehension and fluent, often meaningless speech with clear word-finding difficulties.

Word: the smallest unit of grammar that can stand alone.

Working memory: in the USA, often used as a general term for short-term memory. According to the British psychologist Alan Baddeley, working memory has a particular structure comprising a central executive, a short-term visual store, and a phonological loop.

EXAMPLE OF SENTENCE ANALYSIS

The vampire chased the ghost from the cupboard to the big cave.

Syntactic analysis

Determiner noun verb determiner noun preposition determiner noun preposition determiner adjective noun

Subject, verb, direct object, indirect object 1, indirect object 2

Verb-argument structure

Chase Agent CHASE Theme Source Goal

Thematic role assignment

Agent	the vampire
Theme	the ghost
Source	the cupboard
Goal	the big cave

REFERENCES

Adams, M. J. (1990). *Beginning to read: Thinking and learning about print*. Cambridge, MA: MIT Press.

Ainsworth-Darnell, K., Shulman, H. G., & Boland, J. E. (1998). Dissociating brain responses to syntactic and semantic anomalies: Evidence from event-related potentials. *Journal of Memory and Language, 38*, 112–130.

Aitchison, J. (1994). *Words in the mind: An introduction to the mental lexicon* (2nd ed.). Oxford: Blackwell.

Aitchison, J. (1996). *The seeds of speech: Language origin and evolution*. Cambridge: Cambridge University Press.

Aitchison, J. (1998). *The articulate mammal* (4th ed.). London: Routledge.

Akhtar, N. (1999). Acquiring basic word order: Evidence for data-driven learning of syntactic structure. *Journal of Child Language, 26*, 339–356.

Akhtar, N., & Tomasello, M. (1997). Young children's productivity with word order and verb morphology. *Developmental Psychology, 33*, 952–965.

Alario, F.-X., & Caramazza, A. (2002). The production of determiners: Evidence from French. *Cognition, 82*, 179–223.

Alario, F.-X., Costa, A., & Caramazza, A. (2002a). Frequency effects in noun phrase production: Implications for models of lexical access. *Language and Cognitive Processes, 17*, 299–319.

Alario, F.-X., Costa, A., & Caramazza, A. (2002b). Hedging one's bets too much? A reply to Levelt (2002). *Language and Cognitive Processes, 17*, 673–682.

Alario, F.-X., Costa, A., Pickering, M., & Ferreira, V. (2006). *Language production*. Hove, UK: Psychology Press.

Albert, M. L., & Obler, L. K. (1978). *The bilingual brain: Neuropsychological and neurolinguistic aspects of bilingualism*. New York: Academic Press.

Alishahi, A., & Stevenson, S. (2005). A probabilistic model of early argument structure acquisition. *Proceedings of the 27th Annual Conference of the Cognitive Science Society*, Stresa, Italy.

Allopenna, P. D., Magnuson, J. S., & Tanenhaus, M. K. (1998). Tracking the time course of spoken word recognition: Evidence for continuous mapping models. *Journal of Memory and Language, 38*, 419–439.

Allport, D. A. (1977). On knowing the meaning of words we are unable to report: The effects of visual masking. In S. Dornic (Ed.), *Attention and performance VI* (pp. 505–534). Hillsdale, NJ: Lawrence Erlbaum Associates, Inc.

Allport, D. A. (1984). Auditory short-term memory and conduction aphasia. In H. Bouma & D. Bouwhis (Eds.), *Attention and performance X* (pp. 313–326). Hillsdale, NJ: Lawrence Erlbaum Associates, Inc.

Allport, D. A., & Funnell, E. (1981). Components of the mental lexicon. *Philosophical Transactions of the Royal Society of London, Series B, 295*, 397–410.

Almor, A. (1999). Noun-phrase anaphora and focus: The informational load hypothesis. *Psychological Review, 106*, 748–765.

Almor, A., Kempler, D., MacDonald, M. C., Andersen, E. S., & Tyler, L. K. (1999). Why do Alzheimer patients have difficulty with pronouns? Working memory, semantics, and reference in comprehension and production in Alzheimer's disease. *Brain and Language, 67*, 202–227.

Altarriba, J. (1992). The representation of translation equivalents in bilingual memory. In R. J. Harris (Ed.), *Cognitive processing in bilinguals* (pp. 157–174). Amsterdam: North-Holland.

Altarriba, J. (Ed.). (1993). *Cognition and culture: A cross-cultural approach to psychology*. Amsterdam: North-Holland.

Altarriba, J., & Forsythe, W. J. (1993). The role of cultural schemata in reading comprehension. In J. Altarriba (Ed.), *Cognition and culture: A cross-cultural approach to psychology* (pp. 145–155). Amsterdam: North-Holland.

Altarriba, J., Kroll, J. F., Sholl, A., & Rayner, K. (1996). The influence of lexical and conceptual constraints on reading mixed-language sentences: Evidence from eye fixations and naming times. *Memory and Cognition, 24*, 477–492.

Altarriba, J., & Mathis, K. E. (1997). Conceptual and lexical development in second language acquisition. *Journal of Memory and Language, 36*, 550–568.

Altarriba, J., & Soltano, E. G. (1996). Repetition blindness and bilingual memory: Token individuation for translation equivalents. *Memory and Cognition, 24,* 700–711.

Altmann, G. T. M. (Ed.). (1990). *Cognitive models of speech processing.* Cambridge, MA: MIT Press.

Altmann, G. T. M. (1997). *The ascent of Babel: An exploration of language, mind, and understanding.* Oxford: Oxford University Press.

Altmann, G. T. M. (1999). Thematic role assignment in context. *Journal of Memory and Language, 41,* 124–145.

Altmann, G. T. M., Garnham, A., & Dennis, Y. (1992). Avoiding the garden path: Eye movements in context. *Journal of Memory and Language, 31,* 685–712.

Altmann, G. T. M., & Kamide, Y. (1999). Incremental interpretation at verbs: Restricting the domain of subsequent reference. *Cognition, 73,* 247–264.

Altmann, G. T. M., & Kamide, Y. (2009). Discourse-mediation of the mapping between language and the visual world: Eye movements and mental representation. *Cognition, 111,* 55–71.

Altmann, G. T. M., & Shillcock, R. C. (Eds.). (1993). *Cognitive models of speech processing.* Hove, UK: Lawrence Erlbaum Associates.

Altmann, G. T. M., & Steedman, M. J. (1988). Interaction with context during human sentence processing. *Cognition, 30,* 191–238.

Anderson, J. R. (1974). Retrieval of propositional information from long-term memory. *Cognitive Psychology, 6,* 451–474.

Anderson, J. R. (1976). *Language, memory, and thought.* Hillsdale, NJ: Lawrence Erlbaum Associates, Inc.

Anderson, J. R. (1983). *The architecture of cognition.* Cambridge, MA: Harvard University Press.

Anderson, J. R. (2010). *Cognitive psychology and its implications* (7th ed.). New York: Worth.

Anderson, J. R., & Bower, G. H. (1973). *Human associative memory.* Washington, DC: Winston & Sons.

Anderson, K. J., & Leaper, C. (1998). Meta-analyses of gender effects on conversational interruption: Who, what, when, where, and how. *Sex Roles, 39,* 225–252.

Anderson, R. C., & Pichert, J. W. (1978). Recall of previously unrecallable information following a shift in perspective. *Journal of Verbal Learning and Verbal Behavior, 12,* 1–12.

Andrewes, D. (2001). *Neuropsychology: From theory to practice.* Hove, UK: Psychology Press.

Andrews, S. (1982). Phonological recoding: Is the regularity effect consistent? *Memory and Cognition, 10,* 565–575.

Andrews, S. (1989). Frequency and neighborhood effects on lexical access: Activation or search? *Journal of Experimental Psychology: Learning, Memory, and Cognition, 15,* 802–814.

Andrews, S. (1997). The effect of orthographic similarity on lexical retrieval: Resolving neighborhood conflicts. *Psychonomic Bulletin and Review, 4,* 439–461.

Andrews, S. (2006). *From inkmarks to ideas.* Hove, UK: Psychology Press.

Ans, B., Carbonnel, S., & Valdois, S. (1998). A connectionist multiple-trace memory model for polysyllabic word reading. *Psychological Review, 105,* 678–723.

Antos, S. J. (1979). Processing facilitation in a lexical decision task. *Journal of Experimental Psychology: Human Perception and Performance, 5,* 527–545.

Arbib, M. A. (2005). From monkey-like action recognition to human language: An evolutionary framework for neurolinguistics. *Behavioral and Brain Sciences, 28,* 105–167.

Arciuli, J., & Simpson, I. C. (2012). Statistical learning is related to reading ability in children and adults. *Cognitive Science, 36,* 286–304.

Armstrong, S., Gleitman, L. R., & Gleitman, H. (1983). What some concepts might not be. *Cognition, 13,* 263–274.

Arnold, J. E., Eisenband, J. G., Brown-Schmidt, S., & Trueswell, J. C. (2000). The rapid use of gender information: Evidence of the time course of pronoun resolution from eyetracking. *Cognition, 76,* B13–B36.

Atkinson, M. (1982). *Explanations in the study of child language development.* Cambridge: Cambridge University Press.

Au, T. K. (1983). Chinese and English counterfactuals: The Sapir Whorf hypothesis revisited. *Cognition, 15,* 155–187.

Au, T. K. (1984). Counterfactuals: In reply to Alfred Bloom. *Cognition, 17,* 289–302.

Austin, J. L. (1976). *How to do things with words* (2nd ed.). Oxford: Oxford University Press. [First edition published 1962.]

Baars, B. J., Motley, M. T., & MacKay, D. G. (1975). Output editing for lexical status from artificially elicited slips of the tongue. *Journal of Verbal Learning and Verbal Behavior, 14,* 382–391.

Baayen, R. H., Dijkstra, T., & Schreuder, R. (1997). Singulars and plurals in Dutch: Evidence for a parallel dual route model. *Journal of Memory and Language, 37,* 94–117.

Baayen, R. H., Piepenbrock, R., & Gulikers, L. (1995). The CELEX lexical database [CD-ROM]. Philadelphia: Linguistic Data Consortium, University of Pennsylvania.

Bach, E., Brown, C., & Marslen-Wilson, W. (1986). Crossed and nested dependencies in German and Dutch: A psycholinguistic study. *Language and Cognitive Processes, 1–4,* 249–262.

Backman, J. E. (1983). Psycholinguistic skills and reading acquisition: A look at early readers. *Reading Research Quarterly, 18,* 466–479.

Baddeley, A. D. (1990). *Human memory: Theory and practice*. Hove, UK: Lawrence Erlbaum Associates.

Baddeley, A. D. (2007). *Working memory, thought, and action*. Oxford: Oxford University Press.

Baddeley, A. D., Ellis, N. C., Miles, T. R., & Lewis, V. J. (1982). Developmental and acquired dyslexia: A comparison. *Cognition, 11*, 185–199.

Baddeley, A. D., Gathercole, S., & Papagno, C. (1998). The phonological loop as a language learning device. *Psychological Review, 105*, 158–173.

Baddeley, A. D., & Hitch, G. J. (1974). Working memory. In G. H. Bower (Ed.), *The psychology of learning and motivation* (Vol. 8, pp. 47–90). London: Academic Press.

Baddeley, A. D., Vallar, G., & Wilson, B. (1987). Comprehension and the articulatory loop: Some neuropsychological evidence. In M. Coltheart (Ed.), *Attention and performance XII* (pp. 509–530). Hillsdale, NJ: Lawrence Erlbaum Associates, Inc.

Baddeley, A. D., & Wilson, B. (1988). Comprehension and working memory: A single case neuropsychological study. *Journal of Memory and Language, 27*, 479–498.

Badecker, W., & Caramazza, A. (1985). On considerations of method and theory governing the use of clinical categories in neurolinguistics and cognitive neuropsychology: The case against agrammatism. *Cognition, 20*, 97–125.

Badecker, W., & Caramazza, A. (1986). A final brief in the case against agrammatism: The role of theory in the selection of data. *Cognition, 24*, 277–282.

Badecker, W., Miozzo, M., & Zanuttini, R. (1995). The two-stage model of lexical retrieval: Evidence from a case of anomia with selective preservation of gender. *Cognition, 57*, 193–216.

Badecker, W., & Straub, K. (2002). The processing role of structural constraints on the interpretation of pronouns and anaphors. *Journal of Experimental Psychology: Learning, Memory, and Cognition, 28*, 748–769.

Baguley, T., & Payne, S. J. (2000). Long-term memory for spatial and temporal mental models includes construction processes and model structure. *Quarterly Journal of Experimental Psychology, 53A*, 479–512.

Bailey, K. G. D., & Ferreira, F. (2003). Disfluencies affect the parsing of garden-path sentences. *Journal of Memory and Language, 49*, 183–200.

Baillet, S. D., & Keenan, J. M. (1986). The role of encoding and retrieval processes in the recall of text. *Discourse Processes, 9*, 247–268.

Baldwin, D. A. (1991). Infants' contributions to the achievement of joint reference. *Child Development, 62*, 875–890.

Balota, D. A. (1990). The role of meaning in word recognition. In D. A. Balota, G. B. Flores d'Arcais,

& K. Rayner (Eds.), *Comprehension processes in reading* (pp. 9–32). Hillsdale, NJ: Lawrence Erlbaum Associates, Inc.

Balota, D. A., & Chumbley, J. I. (1984). Are lexical decisions a good measure of lexical access? The role of word frequency in the neglected decision stage. *Journal of Experimental Psychology: Human Perception and Performance, 10*, 340–357.

Balota, D. A., & Chumbley, J. I. (1985). The locus of word-frequency effects in the pronunciation task: Lexical access and/or production? *Journal of Memory and Language, 24*, 89–106.

Balota, D. A., & Chumbley, J. I. (1990). Where are the effects of frequency on visual word recognition tasks? Right where we said they were! Comment on Monsell, Doyle, and Haggard (1989). *Journal of Experimental Psychology: General, 119*, 231–237.

Balota, D. A., Cortese, M. J., Sergent-Marshall, S. D., Spieler, D. H., & Yap, M. J. (2004). Visual word recognition of single-syllable words. *Journal of Experimental Psychology: General, 133*, 283–316.

Balota, D. A., Ferraro, F. R., & Conner, L. T. (1991). On the early influence of meaning in word recognition: A review of the literature. In P. J. Schwanenflugel (Ed.), *The psychology of word meanings* (pp. 187–222). Hillsdale, NJ: Lawrence Erlbaum Associates, Inc.

Balota, D. A., & Lorch, R. F. (1986). Depth of automatic spreading activation: Mediated priming effects in pronunciation but not in lexical decision. *Journal of Experimental Psychology: Learning, Memory, and Cognition, 12*, 336–345.

Baluch, B., & Besner, D. (1991). Visual word recognition: Evidence for strategic control of lexical and nonlexical routines in oral reading. *Journal of Experimental Psychology: Learning, Memory, and Cognition, 17*, 644–652.

Banich, M. T. (2004). *Cognitive neuroscience and neuropsychology*. Boston, MA: Houghton Mifflin.

Banks, W. P., & Flora, J. (1977). Semantic and perceptual processing in symbolic comparison. *Journal of Experimental Psychology: Human Perception and Performance, 3*, 278–290.

Barisnikov, K., van der Linden, M., & Poncelet, M. (1996). Acquisition of new words and phonological working memory in Williams syndrome: A case study. *Neurocase, 2*, 395–404.

Barker, M. G., & Lawson, J. S. (1968). Nominal aphasia in dementia. *British Journal of Psychiatry, 114*, 1351–1356.

Baron, J., & Strawson, C. (1976). Use of orthographic and word-specific knowledge in reading words aloud. *Journal of Experimental Psychology: Human Perception and Performance, 2*, 386–393.

Baron-Cohen, S. (2003). *The essential difference*. Harmondsworth, UK: Penguin.

Barrett, M. D. (1978). Lexical development and overextension in child language. *Journal of Child Language, 5*, 205–219.

Barrett, M. D. (1982). Distinguishing between prototypes: The early acquisition of the meaning of object names. In S. A. Kuczaj (Ed.), *Language development: Vol. 1. Syntax and semantics* (pp. 313–334). New York: Springer-Verlag.

Barrett, M. D. (1986). Early semantic representations and early word-usage. In S. A. Kuczaj & M. D. Barrett (Eds.), *The development of word meaning: Progress in cognitive development research* (pp. 39–67). New York: Springer-Verlag.

Barron, R. W. (1981). Reading skills and reading strategies. In C. A. Perfetti & A. M. Lesgold (Eds.), *Interactive processes in reading* (pp. 299–328). Hillsdale, NJ: Lawrence Erlbaum Associates, Inc.

Barron, R. W., & Baron, J. (1977). How children get meaning from printed words. *Child Development, 48*, 587–594.

Barry, C., Morrison, C. M., & Ellis, A. W. (1997). Naming the Snodgrass and Vanderwart pictures: Effects of age of acquisition, frequency, and name agreement. *Quarterly Journal of Experimental Psychology, 50A*, 560–585.

Barsalou, L. W. (1985). Ideals, central tendency, and frequency of instantiation as determinants of graded structure in categories. *Journal of Experimental Psychology: Learning, Memory, and Cognition, 11*, 629–654.

Barsalou, L. W. (2003). Situated simulation in the human conceptual system. *Language and Cognitive Processes, 18*, 513–562.

Barsalou, L. W. (2008). Grounded cognition. *Annual Review of Psychology, 59*, 617–645.

Bartlett, F. C. (1932). *Remembering: A study in experimental and social psychology*. Cambridge: Cambridge University Press.

Batchelder, E. O. (2002). Bootstrapping the lexicon: A computational model of infant speech segmentation. *Cognition, 83*, 167–206.

Bates, E., Bretherton, I., & Snyder, L. (1988). *From first words to grammar: Individual differences and dissociable mechanisms*. Cambridge: Cambridge University Press.

Bates, E., Dick, F., & Wulfeck, B. (1999). Not so fast: Domain-general factors can account for selective deficits in grammatical processing. *Behavioral and Brain Sciences, 22*, 96–97.

Bates, E., & Goodman, J. C. (1997). On the inseparability of grammar and the lexicon: Evidence from acquisition, aphasia and real-time processing. *Language and Cognitive Processes, 12*, 507–586.

Bates, E., & Goodman, J. C. (1999). On the emergence of grammar from the lexicon. In B. MacWhinney (Ed.), *The emergence of language* (pp. 29–79). Mahwah, NJ: Lawrence Erlbaum Associates, Inc.

Bates, E., & MacWhinney, B. (1982). Functionalist approaches to grammar. In E. Wanner & L. R. Gleitman (Eds.), *Language acquisition: The state of the art* (pp. 173–218). Cambridge: Cambridge University Press.

Bates, E., Marchman, V., Thal, D., Fenson, L., Dale, P. S., Reznick, J. S., et al. (1994). Developmental and stylistic variation in the composition of early vocabulary. *Journal of Child Language, 21*, 85–123.

Bates, E., Masling, M., & Kintsch, W. (1978). Recognition memory for aspects of dialog. *Journal of Experimental Psychology: Human Learning and Memory, 4*, 187–197.

Bates, E., McDonald, J., MacWhinney, B., & Applebaum, M. (1991). A maximum likelihood procedure for the analysis of group and individual data in aphasia research. *Brain and Language, 40*, 231–265.

Bates, E., & Roe, K. (2001). Language development in children with unilateral brain damage. In C. A. Nelson & M. Luciana (Eds.), *Handbook of developmental cognitive neuroscience* (pp. 309–318). Cambridge, MA: MIT Press.

Batterink, L., Karns, C. M., Yamada, Y., & Neville, H. (2010). The role of awareness in semantic and syntactic processing: An ERP attentional blink study. *Journal of Cognitive Neuroscience, 22*, 2514–2529.

Battig, W. F., & Montague, W. E. (1969). Category norms for verbal items in 56 categories: A replication and extension of the Connecticut category norms. *Journal of Experimental Psychology Monograph, 80*, 1–46.

Bavelier, D., & Potter, M. C. (1992). Visual and phonological codes in repetition blindness. *Journal of Experimental Psychology: Human Perception and Performance, 18*, 134–147.

Beaton, A. A. (1997). The relation of planum temporale asymmetry and morphology of the corpus callosum to handedness, gender, and dyslexia: A review of the evidence. *Brain and Language, 60*, 252–322.

Beattie, G. W. (1980). The role of language production processes in the organisation of behaviour in face-to-face interaction. In B. Butterworth (Ed.), *Language production: Vol. 1. Speech and talk* (pp. 69–107). London: Academic Press.

Beattie, G. W. (1983). *Talk: An analysis of speech and non-verbal behaviour in conversation*. Milton Keynes, UK: Open University Press.

Beattie, G. W., & Bradbury, R. J. (1979). An experimental investigation of the modifiability of the temporal structure of spontaneous speech. *Journal of Psycholinguistic Research, 8*, 225–247.

Beattie, G. W., & Butterworth, B. (1979). Contextual probability and word frequency as determinants of pauses and errors in spontaneous speech. *Language and Speech, 22*, 201–211.

Beauvois, M.-F. (1982). Optic aphasia: A process of interaction between vision and language. *Philosophical Transactions of the Royal Society of London, Series B, 298*, 35–47.

Beauvois, M.-F., & Derouesné, J. (1979). Phonological alexia: Three dissociations. *Journal of Neurology, Neurosurgery and Psychiatry, 42*, 1115–1124.

Beauvois, M.-F., & Derouesné, J. (1981). Lexical or orthographic agraphia. *Brain, 104*, 21–49.

Bechtel, W., & Abrahamsen, A. (2001). *Connectionism and the mind: Parallel processing, dynamics and evolution in networks*. Oxford: Blackwell.

Becker, C. A. (1976). Allocation of attention during visual word recognition. *Journal of Experimental Psychology: Human Perception and Performance, 2*, 556–566.

Becker, C. A. (1980). Semantic context effects in visual word recognition: An analysis of semantic strategies. *Memory and Cognition, 8*, 439–512.

Becker, C. A., & Killion, T. H. (1977). Interaction of visual and cognitive effects in word recognition. *Journal of Experimental Psychology: Human Perception and Performance, 3*, 389–407.

Begley, S. (2007). *Train your mind, change your brain*. New York: Ballantine Books.

Behrend, D. A. (1988). Overextensions in early language comprehension: Evidence from a signal detection approach. *Journal of Child Language, 15*, 63–75.

Behrmann, M., & Bub, D. (1992). Surface dyslexia and dysgraphia: Dual routes, single lexicon. *Cognitive Neuropsychology, 9*, 209–251.

Bellugi, U., Bihrle, A., Jernigan, T., Trauner, D., & Doherty, S. (1991). Neuropsychological, neurological, and neuroanatomical profile of Williams syndrome. *American Journal of Medical Genetics Supplement, 6*, 115–125.

Bencini, G. L., & Goldberg, A. E. (2000). The contribution of argument structure constructions to sentence meaning. *Journal of Memory and Language, 43*, 640–651.

Benedict, H. (1979). Early lexical development: Comprehension and production. *Journal of Child Language, 6*, 183–200.

Ben-Zeev, S. (1977). The influence of bilingualism on cognitive strategy and cognitive development. *Child Development, 48*, 1009–1018.

Bereiter, C., & Scardamalia, M. (1987). *The psychology of written composition*. Hillsdale, NJ: Lawrence Erlbaum Associates, Inc.

Berko, J. (1958). The child's learning of English morphology. *Word, 14*, 150–177.

Berlin, B., & Kay, P. (1969). *Basic color terms: Their universality and evolution*. Berkeley: University of California Press.

Berndt, R. S., & Mitchum, C. C. (1990). Auditory and lexical information sources in immediate recall: Evidence from a patient with a deficit to the phonological short-term store. In G. Vallar & T. Shallice (Eds.), *Neuropsychological implications of short-term memory* (pp. 115–144). Cambridge: Cambridge University Press.

Bertenthal, B. I. (1993). Infants' perceptions of biomechanical motions: Intrinsic image and knowledge-based constraints. In C. Granrud (Ed.), *Visual perception and cognition in infancy* (pp. 175–214). Hillsdale, NJ: Lawrence Erlbaum Associates, Inc.

Bertram, R., Schreuder, R., & Baayen, R. H. (2000). The balance of storage and computation in morphological processing: The role of word formation type, affixal homophony, and productivity. *Journal of Experimental Psychology: Learning, Memory, and Cognition, 26*, 489–511.

Berwick, R. C., Pietroski, P., Yankama, B., & Chomsky, N. (2011). Poverty of the stimulus revisited. *Cognitive Science, 35*, 1207–1242.

Berwick, R. C., & Weinberg, A. S. (1983a). The role of grammars in models of language use. *Cognition, 13*, 1–61.

Berwick, R. C., & Weinberg, A. S. (1983b). Reply to Garnham. *Cognition, 15*, 271–276.

Besner, D., & Swan, M. (1982). Models of lexical access in visual word recognition. *Quarterly Journal of Experimental Psychology, 34A*, 313–325.

Besner, D., Twilley, L., McCann, R. S., & Seergobin, K. (1990). On the connection between connectionism and data: Are a few words necessary? *Psychological Review, 97*, 432–446.

Best, B. J. (1973). Classificatory development in deaf children: Research on language and cognitive development. *Occasional Paper No. 15*, Research, Development and Demonstration Center in Education of Handicapped Children, University of Minnesota.

Bestgen, Y., & Vincze, N. (2012). Checking and bootstrapping lexical norms by means of word similarity indexes. *Behavior Research Methods, 44*, 998–1006.

Bestgen, Y., & Vonk, W. (2000). Temporal adverbials as segmentation markers in discourse comprehension. *Journal of Memory and Language, 42*, 74–87.

Bever, T. G. (1970). The cognitive basis for linguistic structures. In J. R. Hayes (Ed.), *Cognition and the development of language* (pp. 279–362). New York: Wiley.

Bever, T. G. (1981). Normal acquisition processes explain the critical period for language learning. In K. C. Diller (Ed.), *Individual differences and universals in language aptitude* (pp. 176–198). Rowley, MA: Newbury House.

Bever, T. G., & McElree, B. (1988). Empty categories access their antecedents during comprehension. *Linguistic Inquiry, 19*, 35–45.

Bever, T. G., Sanz, M., & Townsend, D. J. (1998). The emperor's psycholinguistics. *Journal of Psycholinguistic Research, 27*, 261–284.

Bialystock, E. (2001). Metalinguistic aspects of bilingual processing. *Annual Review of Applied Linguistics, 21*, 169–181.

Bialystok, E., Craik, F. I. M., & Luk, G. (2012). Bilingualism: Consequences for mind and brain. *Trends in Cognitive Sciences, 16*, 240–250.

Bialystok, E., & Hakuta, K. (1994). *In other words: The science and psychology of second-language acquisition*. New York: Basic Books.

Biassou, N., Obler, L. K., Nespoulous, J.-L., Dordain, M., & Harris, K. S. (1997). Dual processing of open- and closed-class words. *Brain and Language, 57*, 360–373.

Bickerton, D. (1981). *Roots of language*. Ann Arbor, MI: Karoma.

Bickerton, D. (1984). The language bioprogram hypothesis. *Behavioral and Brain Sciences, 7*, 173–221.

Bickerton, D. (1986). More than nature needs? A reply to Premack. *Cognition, 23*, 73–79.

Bickerton, D. (1990). *Language and species*. Chicago: University of Chicago Press.

Bickerton, D. (2003). Symbol and structure: A comprehensive framework for language evolution. In M. H. Christiansen & S. Kirby (Eds.), *Language evolution* (pp. 77–93). Oxford: Oxford University Press.

Bierwisch, M. (1970). Semantics. In J. Lyons (Ed.), *New horizons in linguistics* (Vol. 1, pp. 166–185). Harmondsworth, UK: Penguin.

Bigelow, A. (1987). Early words of blind children. *Journal of Child Language, 14*, 47–56.

Binder, J. R., & Desai, R. H. (2011). The neurobiology of semantic memory. *Trends in Cognitive Sciences, 15*, 527–536.

Bird, H., Lambon Ralph, M. A., Seidenberg, M. S., McClelland, J. L., & Patterson, K. E. (2003). Deficits in phonology and past-tense morphology: What's the connection? *Journal of Memory and Language, 48*, 502–526.

Birdsong, D., & Molis, M. (2001). On the evidence for maturational constraints in second-language acquisition. *Journal of Memory and Language, 44*, 235–249.

Bishop, D. (1983). Linguistic impairment after left hemidecortication for infantile hemiplegia? A reappraisal. *Quarterly Journal of Experimental Psychology, 35A*, 199–207.

Bishop, D. (1989). Autism, Asperger's syndrome and semantic-pragmatic disorder: Where are the boundaries? *British Journal of Disorders of Communication, 24*, 107–121.

Bishop, D. (1997). *Uncommon understanding: Development and disorders of language comprehension in children*. Hove, UK: Psychology Press.

Bishop, D., & Mogford, K. (Eds.). (1993). *Language development in exceptional circumstances*. Hove, UK: Lawrence Erlbaum Associates.

Black, J. B., & Wilensky, R. (1979). An evaluation of story grammars. *Cognitive Science, 3*, 213–229.

Blackwell, A., & Bates, E. (1995). Inducing agrammatic profiles in normals: Evidence for the selective vulnerability of morphology under cognitive resource limitation. *Journal of Cognitive Neuroscience, 7*, 228–257.

Blanken, G. (1998). Lexicalisation in speech production: Evidence from form-related word substitutions in aphasia. *Cognitive Neuropsychology, 15*, 321–360.

Bloem, I., & La Heij, W. (2003). Semantic facilitation and semantic interference in word translation: Implications for models of lexical access in language production. *Journal of Memory and Language, 48*, 468–488.

Bloem, I., van den Boogaard, S., & La Heij, W. (2004). Semantic facilitation and semantic interference in language production: Further evidence for the conceptual selection model of lexical access. *Journal of Memory and Language, 51*, 307–323.

Bloom, A. H. (1981). *The linguistic shaping of thought: A study in the impact of thinking in China and the West*. Hillsdale, NJ: Lawrence Erlbaum Associates, Inc.

Bloom, A. H. (1984). Caution—the words you use may affect what you say: A response to Au. *Cognition, 17*, 275–287.

Bloom, L. (1970). *Language development: Form and function in emerging grammars*. Cambridge, MA: MIT Press.

Bloom, L. (1973). *One word at a time: The use of single word utterances before syntax*. The Hague: Mouton.

Bloom, L. (1998). Language acquisition in its developmental context. In W. Damon, D. Kuhn, & R. S. Siegler (Eds.), *Handbook of child psychology* (Vol. 2, 5th ed., pp. 309–370). New York: Wiley.

Bloom, P. (1994). Recent controversies in the study of language acquisition. In M. A. Gernsbacher (Ed.), *Handbook of psycholinguistics* (pp. 741–780). San Diego, CA: Academic Press.

Bloom, P. (2001a). *How children learn the meanings of words*. Cambridge, MA: MIT Press.

Bloom, P. (2001b). Précis of *How children learn the meanings of words*. *Behavioral and Brain Sciences, 24*, 1095–1103.

Bloom, P. (2004). Children think before they speak. *Nature, 430*, 411–412.

Blumstein, S. E., Cooper, W. E., Zurif, E. B., & Caramazza, A. (1977). The perception and production of voice-onset time in aphasia. *Neuropsychologia, 15*, 19–30.

Blumstein, S. E., Katz, B., Goodglass, H., Shrier, R., & Dworetzky, B. (1985). The effects of slowed speech on auditory comprehension in aphasia. *Brain and Language, 24*, 246–265.

Boas, F. (1911). Introduction to *The Handbook of North American Indians (Vol. 1). Bureau of American Ethnology Bulletin, 40* (Part 1).

Bock, J. K. (1982). Toward a cognitive psychology of syntax: Information processing contributions to sentence formulation. *Psychological Review, 89*, 1–47.

Bock, J. K. (1986). Syntactic persistence in language production. *Cognitive Psychology, 18*, 355–387.

Bock, J. K. (1987). An effect of accessibility of word forms on sentence structure. *Journal of Memory and Language, 26*, 119–137.

Bock, J. K. (1989). Closed-class immanence in sentence production. *Cognition, 31*, 163–186.

Bock, J. K., & Cutting, J. C. (1992). Regulating mental energy: Performance units in language production. *Journal of Memory and Language, 31*, 99–127.

Bock, J. K., & Eberhard, K. M. (1993). Meaning, sound and syntax in English number agreement. *Language and Cognitive Processes, 8*, 57–99.

Bock, J. K., Eberhard, K. M., & Cutting, J. C. (2004). Producing number agreement: How pronouns equal verbs. *Journal of Memory and Language, 51*, 251–278.

Bock, J. K., & Griffin, Z. M. (2000). The persistence of structural priming: Transient activation or implicit learning. *Journal of Experimental Psychology: General, 129*, 177–192.

Bock, J. K., & Irwin, D. E. (1980). Syntactic effects of information availability in sentence production. *Journal of Verbal Learning and Verbal Behavior, 19*, 467–484.

Bock, J. K., & Loebell, H. (1990). Framing sentences. *Cognition, 35*, 1–39.

Bock, J. K., & Miller, C. A. (1991). Broken agreement. *Cognition, 23*, 45–93.

Bock, J. K., & Warren, R. K. (1985). Conceptual accessibility and syntactic structure in sentence formulation. *Cognition, 21*, 47–67.

Bohannon, J. N., MacWhinney, B., & Snow, C. E. (1990). No negative evidence revisited: Beyond learnability or who has to prove what to whom. *Developmental Psychology, 26*, 221–226.

Bohannon, J. N., & Stanowicz, L. (1988). The issue of negative evidence: Adult responses to children's language errors. *Developmental Psychology, 24*, 684–689.

Boland, J. E. (1997). Resolving syntactic category ambiguities in discourse context: Probabilistic and discourse constraints. *Journal of Memory and Language, 36*, 588–615.

Boland, J. E., Tanenhaus, M. K., Carlson, G. N., & Garnsey, S. M. (1989). Lexical projection and the interaction of syntax and semantics in parsing. *Journal of Psycholinguistic Research, 18*, 563–576.

Boland, J. E., Tanenhaus, M. K., & Garnsey, S. M. (1990). Evidence for the immediate use of verb control information in sentence processing. *Journal of Memory and Language, 29*, 413–432.

Boland, J. E., Tanenhaus, M. K., Garnsey, S. M., & Carlson, G. N. (1995). Verb argument structure in parsing and interpretation: Evidence from wh-questions. *Journal of Memory and Language, 34*, 774–806.

Bolinger, D. L. (1965). The atomization of meaning. *Language, 41*, 555–573.

Bonin, P., Barry, C., Méot, A., & Chalard, M. (2004). The influence of age of acquisition in word reading and other tasks: A never ending story? *Journal of Memory and Language, 50*, 456–476.

Bonin, P., & Fayol, M. (2002). Frequency effects in the written and spoken production of homophonic picture names. *European Journal of Cognitive Psychology, 14*, 289–313.

Boomer, D. S. (1965). Hesitations and grammatical encoding. *Language and Speech, 8*, 148–158.

Bornkessel-Schlesewsky, I., Schlesewsky, M., & von Cramon, D. Y. (2009). Word order and Broca's region: Evidence for a supra-syntactic perspective. *Brain and Language, 111*, 125–139.

Bornstein, M. H. (1973). Color vision and color naming: A psychophysiological hypothesis of cultural difference. *Psychological Bulletin, 80*, 257–285.

Bornstein, S. (1985). On the development of colour naming in young children: Data and theory. *Brain and Language, 26*, 72–93.

Boroditsky, L. (2001). Does language shape thought? Mandarin and English speakers' conceptions of time. *Cognitive Psychology, 43*, 1–22.

Boroditsky, L. (2003). Linguistic relativity. In L. Nadel (Ed.), *Encyclopedia of cognitive science* (Vol. 2, pp. 917–921). London: Nature Publishing Group.

Borowsky, R., & Masson, M. E. J. (1996). Semantic ambiguity effects in word identification. *Journal of Experimental Psychology: Learning, Memory, and Cognition, 22*, 63–85.

Borsley, R. D. (1991). *Syntactic theory: A unified approach*. London: Edward Arnold.

Bouckaert, R., Lemey, P., Dunn, M., Greenhill, S. J., Alekseyenko, A. V., Drummond, A. J., et al. (2012). Mapping the origins and expansion of the Indo-European language family. *Science, 337*, 957–960.

Bower, G. H., Black, J. B., & Turner, T. J. (1979). Scripts in memory for text. *Cognitive Psychology, 11*, 177–220.

Bowerman, M. (1973). *Learning to talk: A cross linguistic study of early syntactic development, with special reference to Finnish*. Cambridge: Cambridge University Press.

Bowerman, M. (1978). The acquisition of word meanings: An investigation into some current conflicts. In N. Waterson & C. E. Snow (Eds.), *The development of communication* (pp. 263–287). Chichester, UK: Wiley.

Bowerman, M. (1990). Mapping thematic roles onto syntactic functions: Are children helped by innate linking rules? *Linguistics*, *28*, 1253–1289.

Bowey, J. A. (1996). On the association between phonological memory and receptive vocabulary in five-year-olds. *Journal of Experimental Child Psychology*, *63*, 44–78.

Bowey, J. A. (1997). What does nonword repetition measure? A reply to Gathercole and Baddeley. *Journal of Experimental Child Psychology*, *67*, 295–301.

Bowey, J. A., & Muller, D. (2005). Phonological recoding and rapid orthographic learning in third-graders' silent reading: A critical test of the self-teaching hypothesis. *Journal of Experimental Child Psychology*, *92*, 203–219.

Bowles, N. L., & Poon, L. W. (1985). Effects of priming in word retrieval. *Journal of Experimental Psychology: Learning, Memory, and Cognition*, *11*, 272–283.

Bradley, D. C., & Forster, K. I. (1987). A reader's view of listening. *Cognition*, *25*, 103–134.

Bradley, D. C., Garrett, M. F., & Zurif, E. B. (1980). Syntactic deficits in Broca's aphasia. In D. Caplan (Ed.), *Biological studies of mental processes* (pp. 269–286). Cambridge, MA: MIT Press.

Bradley, L., & Bryant, P. (1978). Difficulties in auditory organization as a possible cause of reading backwardness. *Nature*, *271*, 746–747.

Bradley, L., & Bryant, P. (1983). Categorizing sounds and learning to read—A causal connection. *Nature*, *301*, 419–421.

Braine, M. D. S. (1963). The ontogeny of English phrase structure: The first phase. *Language*, *39*, 1–13.

Braine, M. D. S. (1976). Children's first word combinations. *Monographs of the Society for Research in Child Development*, *41* (Serial No. 164).

Braine, M. D. S. (1988a). Review of *Language learnability and language development* by S. Pinker. *Journal of Child Language*, *15*, 189–219.

Braine, M. D. S. (1988b). Modeling the acquisition of linguistic structure. In Y. Levy, I. M. Schlesinger, & M. D. S. Braine (Eds.), *Categories and processes in language acquisition* (pp. 217–259). Hillsdale, NJ: Lawrence Erlbaum Associates, Inc.

Braine, M. D. S. (1992). What sort of innate structure is needed to "bootstrap" into syntax? *Cognition*, *45*, 77–100.

Braine, M. D. S., & Brooks, P. J. (1995). Verb argument structure and the problem of avoiding an overgeneral grammar. In M. Tomasello & W. E. Merriman (Eds.), *Beyond names for things:*

Young children's acquisition of verbs (pp. 352–376). Hillsdale, NJ: Lawrence Erlbaum Associates, Inc.

Bramwell, B. (1897). Illustrative cases of aphasia. *Lancet*, *1*, 1256–1259. [Reprinted in *Cognitive Neuropsychology* (1984), *1*, 249–258.]

Branigan, H. P., Pickering, M. J., & Cleland, A. A. (2000). Syntactic co-ordination in dialogue. *Cognition*, *75*, B13–B25.

Branigan, H. P., Pickering, M. J., Liversedge, S. P., Stewart, A. J., & Urbach, T. P. (1995). Syntactic priming: Investigating the mental representation of language. *Journal of Psycholinguistic Research*, *24*, 489–506.

Bransford, J. D., Barclay, J. R., & Franks, J. J. (1972). Sentence memory: A constructive versus interpretive approach. *Cognitive Psychology*, *3*, 193–209.

Bransford, J. D., & Johnson, M. K. (1973). Consideration of some problems of comprehension. In W. G. Chase (Ed.), *Visual information processing* (pp. 383–438). New York: Academic Press.

Breedin, S. D., & Saffran, E. M. (1999). Sentence processing in the face of semantic loss: A case study. *Journal of Experimental Psychology: General*, *128*, 547–562.

Breedin, S. D., Saffran, E. M., & Coslett, H. B. (1994). Reversal of the concreteness effect in a patient with semantic dementia. *Cognitive Neuropsychology*, *11*, 617–660.

Breedin, S. D., Saffran, E. M., & Schwartz, M. (1998). Semantic factors in verb retrieval: An effect of complexity. *Brain and Language*, *63*, 1–35.

Brennan, S. E., & Clark, H. H. (1996). Conceptual pacts and lexical choice in conversation. *Journal of Experimental Psychology: Learning, Memory, and Cognition*, *22*, 1482–1493.

Brennen, T. (1999). Face naming in dementia: A reply to Hodges and Greene (1998). *Quarterly Journal of Experimental Psychology*, *52A*, 535–541.

Brennen, T., David, D., Fluchaire, I., & Pellat, J. (1996). Naming faces and objects without comprehension: A case study. *Cognitive Neuropsychology*, *13*, 93–110.

Brewer, W. F. (1987). Schemas versus mental models in human memory. In P. Morris (Ed.), *Modelling cognition* (pp. 187–197). Chichester, UK: J. Wiley & Sons.

Britton, B. K., Muth, K. D., & Glynn, S. M. (1986). Effects of text organization on memory: Test of a cognitive effect hypothesis with limited exposure time. *Discourse Processes*, *9*, 475–487.

Broeder, P., & Murre, J. (Eds.). (2000). *Models of language acquisition: Inductive and deductive approaches*. Oxford: Oxford University Press.

Bronowski, J., & Bellugi, U. (1970). Language, name, and concept. *Science*, *168*, 669–673.

Broom, Y. M., & Doctor, E. A. (1995a). Developmental phonological dyslexia: A case study of the efficacy of a remediation programme. *Cognitive Neuropsychology, 12*, 725–766.

Broom, Y. M., & Doctor, E. A. (1995b). Developmental surface dyslexia: A case study of the efficacy of a remediation programme. *Cognitive Neuropsychology, 12*, 69–110.

Brown, A. S. (1991). A review of the tip-of-the-tongue experience. *Psychological Bulletin, 109*, 204–223.

Brown, G. D. A. (1987). Resolving inconsistency: A computational model of word naming. *Journal of Memory and Language, 26*, 1–23.

Brown, G. D. A., & Deavers, R. P. (1999). Units of analysis in nonword reading: Evidence from children and adults. *Journal of Experimental Child Psychology, 73*, 208–242.

Brown, G. D. A., & Ellis, N. C. (1994). Issues in spelling research: An overview. In G. D. A. Brown & N. C. Ellis (Eds.), *Handbook of spelling: Theory, process and intervention* (pp. 3–25). London: John Wiley & Sons.

Brown, G. D. A., & Watson, F. L. (1987). First in, first out: Word learning age and spoken word frequency as predictors of word familiarity and word naming latency. *Memory and Cognition, 15*, 208–216.

Brown, G. D. A., & Watson, F. L. (1994). Spelling-to-sound effects in single-word reading. *British Journal of Psychology, 85*, 181–202.

Brown, P. (1991). DEREK: The direct encoding routine for evolving knowledge. In D. Besner & G. W. Humphreys (Eds.), *Basic processes in reading: Visual word recognition* (pp. 104–147). Hillsdale, NJ: Lawrence Erlbaum Associates, Inc.

Brown, P., & Levinson, S. (1987). *Politeness: Some universals in language usage*. Cambridge: Cambridge University Press.

Brown, R. (1958). *Words and things*. New York: Free Press.

Brown, R. (1970). Psychology and reading: Commentary on chapters 5 to 10. In H. Levin & J. P. Williams (Eds.), *Basic studies on reading* (pp. 164–187). New York: Basic Books.

Brown, R. (1973). *A first language: The early stages*. London: George Allen & Unwin.

Brown, R. (1976). In memorial tribute to Eric Lenneberg. *Cognition, 4*, 125–154.

Brown, R., & Bellugi, U. (1964). Three processes in the acquisition of syntax. *Harvard Educational Review, 34*, 133–151.

Brown, R., & Fraser, C. (1963). The acquisition of syntax. In C. Cofer & B. Musgrave (Eds.), *Verbal behavior and learning: Problems and processes* (pp. 158–209). New York: McGraw-Hill.

Brown, R., & Hanlon, C. (1970). Derivational complexity and order of acquisition in child speech. In J. R. Hayes (Ed.), *Cognition and the development of language* (pp. 11–53). New York: John Wiley & Sons.

Brown, R., & Lenneberg, E. H. (1954). A study in language and cognition. *Journal of Abnormal and Social Psychology, 49*, 454–462.

Brown, R., & McNeill, D. (1966). The "tip of the tongue" phenomenon. *Journal of Verbal Learning and Verbal Behavior, 5*, 325–337.

Brownell, H. H., & Gardner, H. (1988). Neuropsychological insights into humour. In J. Durant & J. Miller (Eds.), *Laughing matters* (pp. 17–34). Harlow, UK: Longman.

Brownell, H. H., Michel, D., Powelson, J. A., & Gardner, H. (1983). Surprise but not coherence: Sensitivity to verbal humor in right hemisphere patients. *Brain and Language, 18*, 20–27.

Brownell, H. H., Potter, H. H., Bihrle, A. M., & Gardner, H. (1986). Interference deficits in right brain-damaged patients. *Brain and Language, 27*, 310–321.

Bruce, D. J. (1958). The effects of listeners' anticipations in the intelligibility of heard speech. *Language and Speech, 1*, 79–97.

Bruck, M., Lambert, W. E., & Tucker, G. R. (1976). Cognitive and attitudinal consequences of bilingual schooling: The St. Lambert project through grade six. *International Journal of Psycholinguistics, 6*, 13–33.

Bruner, J. S. (1964). The course of cognitive growth. *American Psychologist, 19*, 1–15.

Bruner, J. S. (1975). From communication to language—a psychological perspective. *Cognition, 3*, 255–287.

Bruner, J. S. (1983). *Child's talk: Learning to use language*. New York: W. W. Norton.

Bryant, P. (1998). Sensitivity to onset and rhyme does predict young children's reading: A comment on Muter, Hulme, Snowling, and Taylor (1997). *Journal of Experimental Child Psychology, 71*, 29–37.

Bryant, P., & Impey, L. (1986). The similarity between normal readers and developmental and acquired dyslexics. *Cognition, 24*, 121–137.

Brysbaert, M., & Mitchell, D. C. (1996). Modifier attachment in sentence parsing: Evidence from Dutch. *Quarterly Journal of Experimental Psychology, 49A*, 664–695.

Bryson, B. (1990). *Mother tongue*. Harmondsworth, UK: Penguin Books.

Bub, D. (2000). Methodological issues confronting PET and fMRI studies of cognitive function. *Cognitive Neuropsychology, 17*, 467–484.

Bub, D., Black, S., Hampson, E., & Kertesz, A. (1988). Semantic encoding of pictures and words: Some neuropsychological observations. *Cognitive Neuropsychology, 5*, 27–66.

Bub, D., Black, S., Howell, J., & Kertesz, A. (1987). Speech output processes and reading. In M. Coltheart, G. Sartori, & R. Job (Eds.), *The cognitive neuropsychology of language* (pp. 79–110). Hove, UK: Lawrence Erlbaum Associates.

Bub, D., Cancelliere, A., & Kertesz, A. (1985). Whole-word and analytic translation of spelling to sound in a non-semantic reader. In K. E. Patterson, J. C. Marshall, & M. Coltheart (Eds.), *Surface dyslexia: Neuropsychological and cognitive studies of phonological reading* (pp. 15–34). Hove, UK: Lawrence Erlbaum Associates.

Bub, D., & Kertesz, A. (1982a). Deep agraphia. *Brain and Language, 17*, 146–165.

Bub, D., & Kertesz, A. (1982b). Evidence for logographic processing in a patient with preserved written over oral single word naming. *Brain, 105*, 697–717.

Buckingham, H. W. (1981). Where do neologisms come from? In J. W. Brown (Ed.), *Jargon-aphasia* (pp. 39–62). New York: Academic Press.

Buckingham, H. W. (1986). The scan-copier mechanism and the positional level of language production: Evidence from phonemic paraphasia. *Cognitive Science, 10*, 195–217.

Burgess, C. (2000). Theory and operational definitions in computational memory models: A response to Glenberg and Robertson. *Journal of Memory and Language, 43*, 402–408.

Burgess, C., & Lund, K. (1997). Representing abstract words and emotional connotation in high-dimensional memory space. In *Proceedings of the Cognitive Science Society* (pp. 61–66). Hillsdale, NJ: Lawrence Erlbaum Associates, Inc.

Burke, D., MacKay, D. G., Worthley, J. S., & Wade, E. (1991). On the tip of the tongue: What causes word finding failures in young and older adults? *Journal of Memory and Language, 30*, 237–246.

Burton, M. W., Baum, S. R., & Blumstein, S. E. (1989). Lexical effects on the phonetic categorization of speech: The role of acoustic structure. *Journal of Experimental Psychology: Human Perception and Performance, 15*, 567–575.

Burton-Roberts, N. (1997). *Analysing sentences: An introduction to English syntax* (2nd ed.). London: Longman.

Bus, A. G., & van Ijzendoorn, M. H. (1999). Phonological awareness and early reading: A meta-analysis of experimental training studies. *Journal of Educational Psychology, 91*, 403–414.

Butterworth, B. (1975). Hesitation and semantic planning in speech. *Journal of Psycholinguistic Research, 4*, 75–87.

Butterworth, B. (1979). Hesitation and the production of neologisms in jargon aphasia. *Brain and Language, 8*, 133–161.

Butterworth, B. (1980). Evidence from pauses in speech. In B. Butterworth (Ed.), *Language production: Vol. 1. Speech and talk* (pp. 155–176). London: Academic Press.

Butterworth, B. (1982). Speech errors: Old data in search of new theories. In A. Cutler (Ed.), *Slips of the tongue and language production* (pp. 73–108). Amsterdam: Mouton.

Butterworth, B. (1985). Jargon aphasia: Processes and strategies. In S. Newman & R. Epstein (Eds.), *Current perspectives in dysphasia* (pp. 61–96). Edinburgh: Churchill Livingstone.

Butterworth, B., & Beattie, G. W. (1978). Gesture and silence as indicators of planning in speech. In R. N. Campbell & P. T. Smith (Eds.), *Recent advances in the psychology of language: Vol. 4. Formal and experimental approaches* (pp. 347–360). London: Plenum Press.

Butterworth, B., Campbell, R., & Howard, D. (1986). The uses of short-term memory: A case study. *Quarterly Journal of Experimental Psychology, 38A*, 705–737.

Butterworth, B., & Howard, D. (1987). Paragrammatisms. *Cognition, 26*, 1–37.

Butterworth, B., Swallow, J., & Grimston, M. (1981). Gestures and lexical processes in jargonaphasia. In J. Brown (Ed.), *Jargonaphasia* (pp. 113–124). New York: Academic Press.

Butterworth, B., & Wengang, Y. (1991). The universality of two routines for reading: Evidence from Chinese dyslexia. *Proceedings of the Royal Society of London, Series B, 245*, 91–95.

Byrne, B. (1998). *The foundation of literacy: The child's acquisition of the alphabetic principle*. Hove, UK: Psychology Press.

Cacciari, C., & Glucksberg, S. (1994). Understanding figurative language. In M. A. Gernsbacher (Ed.), *Handbook of psycholinguistics* (pp. 447–477). San Diego, CA: Academic Press.

Cairns, P., Shillcock, R., Chater, N., & Levy, J. (1995). Bottom-up connectionist modelling of speech. In J. P. Levy, D. Bairaktaris, J. A. Bullinaria, & P. Cairns (Eds.), *Connectionist models of memory and language* (pp. 289–310). London: UCL Press.

Cairns, P., Shillcock, R., Chater, N., & Levy, J. (1997). Bootstrapping word boundaries: A bottom-up corpus-based approach to segmentation. *Cognitive Psychology, 33*, 111–153.

Campbell, R., & Butterworth, B. (1985). Phonological dyslexia and dysgraphia: A developmental case with associated deficits of phonemic processing and awareness. *Quarterly Journal of Experimental Psychology, 37A*, 435–475.

Cantalupo, C., & Hopkins, W. D. (2001). Asymmetric Broca's area in great apes. *Nature, 414*, 505.

Caplan, D. (1972). Clause boundaries and recognition latencies. *Perception and Psychophysics, 12*, 73–76.

Caplan, D. (1986). In defense of agrammatism. *Cognition, 24*, 263–276.

Caplan, D. (1992). *Language: Structure, processing, and disorders*. Cambridge, MA: MIT Press.

Caplan, D., Baker, C., & Dehaut, F. (1985). Syntactic determinants of sentence comprehension in aphasia. *Cognition, 21,* 117–175.

Caplan, D., & Hildebrandt, N. (1988). *Disorders of syntactic comprehension.* Cambridge, MA: Bradford Books.

Caplan, D., & Waters, G. S. (1995a). Aphasic disorders of syntactic comprehension and working memory capacity. *Cognitive Neuropsychology, 12,* 637–649.

Caplan, D., & Waters, G. S. (1995b). On the nature of the phonological output planning processes involved in verbal rehearsal: Evidence from aphasia. *Brain and Language, 48,* 191–220.

Caplan, D., & Waters, G. S. (1996). Syntactic processing in sentence comprehension under dual-task conditions in aphasic patients. *Language and Cognitive Processes, 22,* 525–551.

Caplan, D., & Waters, G. S. (1999). Verbal working memory and sentence comprehension. *Behavioral and Brain Sciences, 22,* 77–126.

Caplan, D., & Waters, G. S. (2002). Working memory and connectionist models of parsing: Reply to MacDonald and Christiansen. *Psychological Review, 109,* 66–74.

Caramazza, A. (1986). On drawing inferences about the structure of normal cognitive systems from the analysis of patterns of impaired performance. *Brain and Cognition, 5,* 41–66.

Caramazza, A. (1991). Data, statistics, and theory: A comment on Bates, McDonald, MacWhinney, and Applebaum's "A maximum likelihood procedure for the analysis of group and individual data in aphasia research." *Brain and Language, 41,* 43–51.

Caramazza, A. (1997). How many levels of processing are there in lexical access? *Cognitive Neuropsychology, 14,* 177–208.

Caramazza, A., & Berndt, R. S. (1978). Semantic and syntactic processes in aphasia: A review of the literature. *Psychological Bulletin, 85,* 898–918.

Caramazza, A., Berndt, R. S., & Basili, A. G. (1983). The selective impairment of phonological processing: A case study. *Brain and Language, 18,* 128–174.

Caramazza, A., Bi, Y., Costa, A., & Miozzo, M. (2004). What determines the speed of lexical access: Homophone or specific-word frequency? A reply to Jescheniak et al. (2003). *Journal of Experimental Psychology: Learning, Memory, and Cognition, 30,* 278–282.

Caramazza, A., Chialant, D., Capasso, R., & Miceli, G. (2000). Separable processing of consonants and vowels. *Nature, 403,* 428–430.

Caramazza, A., Costa, A., Miozzo, M., & Bi, Y. (2001). The specific-word frequency effect: Implications for the representation of homophones. *Journal of Experimental Psychology: Learning, Memory, and Cognition, 27,* 1430–1450.

Caramazza, A., & Hillis, A. E. (1990). Where do semantic errors come from? *Cortex, 26,* 95–122.

Caramazza, A., & Hillis, A. E. (1991). Lexical organization of nouns and verbs in the brain. *Nature, 349,* 788–790.

Caramazza, A., Hillis, A. E., Rapp, B. C., & Romani, C. (1990). The multiple semantics hypothesis: Multiple confusions? *Cognitive Neuropsychology, 7,* 61–189.

Caramazza, A., Miceli, G., & Villa, G. (1986). The role of the (output) phonological buffer in reading, writing, and repetition. *Cognitive Neuropsychology, 3,* 37–76.

Caramazza, A., & Miozzo, M. (1997). The relation between syntactic and phonological knowledge in lexical access: Evidence from the "tip-of-the-tongue" phenomenon. *Cognition, 64,* 309–343.

Caramazza, A., & Miozzo, M. (1998). More is not always better: A response to Roelofs, Meyer, and Levelt. *Cognition, 69,* 231–241.

Caramazza, A., Papagno, C., & Ruml, W. (2000). The selective impairment of phonological processing in speech production. *Brain and Language, 75,* 428–450.

Caramazza, A., & Shelton, J. R. (1998). Domain-specific knowledge systems in the brain: The animate–inanimate distinction. *Journal of Cognitive Neuroscience, 10,* 1–34.

Caramazza, A., & Zurif, E. B. (1976). Dissociation of algorithmic and heuristic processes in language comprehension: Evidence from aphasia. *Brain and Language, 3,* 572–582.

Carey, S. (1985). *Conceptual change in childhood.* Cambridge, MA: MIT Press.

Carmichael, L., Hogan, H. P., & Walter, A. A. (1932). An experimental study of the effect of language on the reproduction of visually presented forms. *Journal of Experimental Psychology, 15,* 73–86.

Carpenter, P. A., & Just, M. A. (1977). Reading comprehension as eyes see it. In M. A. Just & P. A. Carpenter (Eds.), *Cognitive processes in comprehension* (pp. 109–140). Hillsdale, NJ: Lawrence Erlbaum Associates, Inc.

Carr, T. H., McCauley, C., Sperber, R. D., & Parmalee, C. M. (1982). Words, pictures and priming: On semantic activation, conscious identification and the automaticity of information processing. *Journal of Experimental Psychology: Human Perception and Performance, 8,* 757–777.

Carr, T. H., & Pollatsek, A. (1985). Recognizing printed words: A look at current models. In D. Besner, T. J. Waller, & C. E. MacKinnon (Eds.), *Reading research: Advances in theory and practice* (Vol. 5, pp. 1–82). New York: Academic Press.

Carroll, J. B. (1981). Twenty-five years of research on foreign language aptitude. In K. C. Diller (Ed.),

Individual differences and universals in language learning aptitude (pp. 83–118). Rowley, MA: Newbury House.

Carroll, J. B., & Casagrande, J. B. (1958). The function of language classifications in behavior. In E. E. Maccoby, T. M. Newcomb, & E. L. Hartley (Eds.), *Readings in social psychology* (3rd ed., pp. 18–31). New York: Holt, Rinehart & Winston.

Carroll, J. B., & White, M. N. (1973a). Word frequency and age-of-acquisition as determiners of picture-naming latency. *Quarterly Journal of Experimental Psychology, 25,* 85–95.

Carroll, J. B., & White, M. N. (1973b). Age-of-acquisition norms for 220 picturable nouns. *Journal of Verbal Learning and Verbal Behavior, 12,* 563–576.

Carruthers, P. (2002). The cognitive functions of language. *Behavioral and Brain Sciences, 25,* 657–726.

Carston, R. (1987). Review of Gavagai! or the future history of the animal language controversy, by David Premack. *Mind and Language, 2,* 332–349.

Carver, R. P. (1972). Speed readers don't read: They skim. *Psychology Today,* 22–30.

Casey, B. J., Thomas, K. M., & McCandliss, B. (2001). Applications of magnetic resonance imaging to the study of development. In C. A. Nelson & M. Luciano (Eds.), *Handbook of developmental cognitive neuroscience* (pp. 137–147). Cambridge, MA: MIT Press.

Castles, A., & Coltheart, M. (1993). Varieties of developmental dyslexia. *Cognition, 47,* 149–180.

Castles, A., & Coltheart, M. (2004). Is there a causal link from phonological awareness to success in learning to read? *Cognition, 91,* 77–111.

Castles, A., Datta, H., Gayan, J., & Olson, R. K. (1999). Varieties of developmental reading disorder: Genetic and environmental influences. *Journal of Experimental Child Psychology, 72,* 73–94.

Cattell, J. M. (1947). On the time required for recognizing and naming letters and words, pictures and colors. In *James McKeen Cattell, Man of science* (Vol. 1, pp. 13–25). Lancaster, PA: Science Press. [Originally published 1888.]

Caudill, M., & Butler, C. (1992). *Understanding neural networks: Computer explorations* (Vols. 1 & 2). Cambridge, MA: MIT Press.

Cazden, C. B. (1968). The acquisition of noun and verb inflections. *Child Development, 39,* 433–448.

Cazden, C. B. (1972). *Child language and education.* New York: Holt, Rinehart & Winston.

Chafe, W. L. (1985). Linguistic differences produced by differences between speaking and writing. In D. R. Olson, N. Torrance, & A. Hildyard (Eds.), *Literacy, language and learning: The nature and consequences of reading and writing* (pp. 105–123). Cambridge: Cambridge University Press.

Chalmers, A. F. (1999). *What is this thing called science?* (3rd ed.). Milton Keynes, UK: Open University Press.

Chambers Twentieth Century Dictionary. (1998). Edinburgh: Chambers Harrap.

Chambers, C. G., Tanenhaus, M. K., & Magnuson, J. S. (2004). Actions and affordances in syntactic ambiguity resolution. *Journal of Experimental Psychology: Learning, Memory, and Cognition, 30,* 687–696.

Chan, A. S., Butters, N., Paulsen, J. S., Salmon, D. P., Swenson, M. R., & Maloney, L. T. (1993a). An assessment of the semantic network in patients with Alzheimer's disease. *Journal of Cognitive Neuroscience, 5,* 254–261.

Chan, A. S., Butters, N., Salmon, D. P., & McGuire, K. A. (1993b). Dimensionality and clustering in the semantic network of patients with Alzheimer's disease. *Psychology and Aging, 8,* 411–419.

Chang, F., Bock, K., & Goldberg, A. E. (2003). Can thematic roles leave traces of their places? *Cognition, 90,* 29–49.

Chang, F., Dell, G. S., & Bock, K. (2006). Becoming syntactic. *Psychological Review, 113,* 234–272.

Chang, T. M. (1986). Semantic memory: Facts and models. *Psychological Bulletin, 99,* 199–220.

Chao, L. L., Haxby, J. V., & Martin, A. (1999). Attribute-based neural substrates in temporal cortex for perceiving and knowing about objects. *Nature Neuroscience, 2,* 913–919.

Chapman, R. S., & Thomson, J. (1980). What is the source of overextension errors in comprehension testing of two-year-olds? A reply to Fremgen and Fay. *Journal of Child Language, 7,* 575–578.

Chater, N., & Manning, C. D. (2006). Probabilistic models of language processing and acquisition. *Trends in Cognitive Sciences, 10,* 335–344.

Chen, H.-C., & Ng, M.-L. (1989). Semantic facilitation and translation priming effects in Chinese–English bilinguals. *Memory and Cognition, 17,* 454–462.

Chertkow, H., Bub, D., & Caplan, D. (1992). Constraining theories of semantic memory processing: Evidence from dementia. *Cognitive Neuropsychology, 9,* 327–365.

Cholin, J., Levelt, W. J. M., & Schiller, N. O. (2006). Effects of syllable frequency in speech production. *Cognition, 99,* 205–235.

Cholin, J., Schiller, N. O., & Levelt, W. J. M. (2004). The preparation of syllables in speech production. *Journal of Memory and Language, 50,* 47–61.

Chomsky, N. (1957). *Syntactic structures.* The Hague: Mouton.

Chomsky, N. (1959). Review of "Verbal behavior" by B. F. Skinner. *Language, 35,* 26–58.

Chomsky, N. (1965). *Aspects of the theory of syntax.* Cambridge, MA: MIT Press.

Chomsky, N. (1968). *Language and mind.* New York: Harcourt Brace.

Chomsky, N. (1975). *Reflections on language.* New York: Pantheon.

Chomsky, N. (1981). *Lectures on government and binding.* Dordrecht: Foris.

Chomsky, N. (1986). *Knowledge of language.* New York: Praeger Special Studies.

Chomsky, N. (1988). *Language and problems of knowledge: The Managua lectures.* Cambridge, MA: MIT Press.

Chomsky, N. (1991). Linguistics and cognitive science: Problems and mysteries. In A. Kasher (Ed.), *The Chomskyan turn* (pp. 26–53). Oxford: Blackwell.

Chomsky, N. (1995). Bare phrase structure. In G. Webelhuth (Ed.), *Government and binding theory and the minimalist programme* (pp. 383–400). Oxford: Blackwell.

Christiansen, J. A. (1995). Coherence violations and propositional usage in the narratives of fluent aphasics. *Brain and Language, 51,* 291–317.

Christiansen, M. H., Allen, J., & Seidenberg, M. S. (1998). Learning to segment speech using multiple cues: A connectionist model. *Language and Cognitive Processes, 13,* 221–268.

Christiansen, M. H., & Chater, N. (2008). Language as shaped by the brain. *Behavioral and Brain Sciences, 31,* 489–509.

Christiansen, M. H., & Curtin, S. (1999). Transfer of learning: Rule acquisition of statistical learning? *Trends in Cognitive Sciences, 3,* 289–290.

Christiansen, M. H., & Kirby, S. (Eds.). (2003). *Language evolution.* Oxford: Oxford University Press.

Christianson, K., Hollingworth, A., Halliwell, J. F., & Ferreira, F. (2001). Thematic roles assigned along the garden path linger. *Cognitive Psychology, 42,* 368–407.

Chumbley, J. I., & Balota, D. A., (1984). A word's meaning affects the decision in lexical decision. *Memory and Cognition, 12,* 590–606.

Cipolotti, L., & Warrington, E. K. (1995). Semantic memory and reading abilities: A case report. *Journal of the International Neuropsychological Society, 1,* 104–110.

Cirilo, R. K., & Foss, D. J. (1980). Text structure and reading time for sentences. *Journal of Verbal Learning and Verbal Behavior, 19,* 96–109.

Clahsen, H. (1992). Learnability theory and the problem of development in language acquisition. In J. Weissenborn, H. Goodluck, & T. Roeper (Eds.), *Theoretical issues in language acquisition* (pp. 53–76). Hillsdale, NJ: Lawrence Erlbaum Associates, Inc.

Clahsen, H. (1999). Lexical entries and rules of language: A multidisciplinary study of German and inflection. *Behavioral and Brain Sciences, 22,* 991–1060.

Clark, E. V. (1973). What's in a word? On the child's acquisition of semantics in his first language. In T. E. Moore (Ed.), *Cognitive development and the acquisition of language* (pp. 65–110). New York: Academic Press.

Clark, E. V. (1987). The principle of contrast: A constraint on language acquisition. In B. MacWhinney (Ed.), *Mechanisms of language acquisition* (pp. 1–33). Hillsdale, NJ: Lawrence Erlbaum Associates, Inc.

Clark, E. V. (1993). *The lexicon in acquisition.* Cambridge: Cambridge University Press.

Clark, E. V. (1995). Later lexical development and word formation. In P. Fletcher & B. MacWhinney (Eds.), *The handbook of child language* (pp. 393–412). Oxford: Blackwell.

Clark, E. V., & Hecht, B. F. (1983). Comprehension and production. *Annual Review of Psychology, 34,* 325–247.

Clark, H. H. (1977a). Bridging. In P. N. Johnson-Laird & P. C. Wason (Ed.), *Thinking: Readings in cognitive science* (pp. 411–420). Cambridge: Cambridge University Press.

Clark, H. H. (1977b). Inferences in comprehension. In D. LaBerge & S. J. Samuels (Eds.), *Basic processes in reading: Perception and comprehension* (pp. 243–263). Hillsdale, NJ: Lawrence Erlbaum Associates, Inc.

Clark, H. H. (1994). Discourse in production. In M. A. Gernsbacher (Ed.), *Handbook of psycholinguistics* (pp. 985–1022). San Diego, CA: Academic Press.

Clark, H. H. (1996). *Using language.* Cambridge: Cambridge University Press.

Clark, H. H., & Carlson, T. (1982). Speech acts and hearers' beliefs. In N. V. Smith (Ed.), *Mutual knowledge* (pp. 1–59). London: Academic Press.

Clark, H. H., & Clark, E. V. (1977). *Psychology and language: An introduction to psycholinguistics.* New York: Harcourt Brace Jovanovich.

Clark, H. H., & Fox Tree, J. E. (2002). Using uh and um in spontaneous speaking. *Cognition, 84,* 73–111.

Clark, H. H., & Haviland, S. E. (1977). Comprehension and the given-new contract. In R. O. Freedle (Ed.), *Discourse production and comprehension* (pp. 1–40). Norwood, NJ: Ablex.

Clark, H. H., & Lucy, P. (1975). Understanding what is meant from what is said: A study in conversationally conveyed requests. *Journal of Verbal Learning and Verbal Behavior, 14,* 56–72.

Clark, H. H., & Wasow, T. (1998). Repeating words in spontaneous speech. *Cognitive Psychology, 37,* 201–242.

Clark, H. H., & Wilkes-Gibbs, D. (1986). Referring as a collaborative process. *Cognition, 22,* 1–39.

Clarke, R., & Morton, J. (1983). Cross modality facilitation in tachistoscopic word recognition. *Quarterly Journal of Experimental Psychology, 35A,* 79–96.

Clarke-Stewart, K., Vanderstoep, L., & Killian, G. (1979). Analysis and replication of mother–child relations at 2 years of age. *Child Development, 50,* 777–793.

Cleland, A. A., & Pickering, M. J. (2003). The use of lexical and syntactic information in language production: Evidence from the priming of noun-phrase structure. *Journal of Memory and Language, 49,* 214–230.

Clifton, C., & Ferreira, F. (1987). Discourse structure and anaphora: Some experimental results. In M. Coltheart (Ed.), *Attention and performance XII: The psychology of reading* (pp. 635–654). Hove, UK: Lawrence Erlbaum Associates.

Clifton, C., & Ferreira, F. (1989). Ambiguity in context. *Language and Cognitive Processes, 4,* 77–103.

Cogswell, D., & Gordon, P. (1996). *Chomsky for beginners*. London: Readers & Writers Ltd.

Cohen, G. (1979). Language comprehension in old age. *Cognitive Psychology, 11,* 412–429.

Cohen, L., & Dehaene, S. (2004). Specialization within the ventral stream: The case for the visual word form area. *NeuroImage, 22,* 466–476.

Colby, K. M. (1975). *Artificial paranoia*. New York: Pergamon Press.

Cole, R. A. (1973). Listening for mispronunciations: A measure of what we hear during speech. *Perception and Psychophysics, 13,* 153–156.

Cole, R. A., & Jakimik, J. (1980). A model of speech perception. In R. A. Cole (Ed.), *Perception and production of fluent speech* (pp. 133–163). Hillsdale, NJ: Lawrence Erlbaum Associates, Inc.

Coleman, L., & Kay, P. (1981). Prototype semantics. *Language, 57,* 26–44.

Collins, A., & Gentner, D. (1980). A framework for a cognitive theory of writing. In L. W. Gregg & E. R. Sternberg (Eds.), *Cognitive processes in writing* (pp. 51–72). Hillsdale, NJ: Lawrence Erlbaum Associates, Inc.

Collins, A. M., & Loftus, E. F. (1975). A spreading-activation theory of semantic processing. *Psychological Review, 82,* 407–428.

Collins, A. M., & Quillian, M. R. (1969). Retrieval time from semantic memory. *Journal of Verbal Learning and Verbal Behavior, 8,* 240–247.

Colombo, L. (1986). Activation and inhibition with orthographically similar words. *Journal of Experimental Psychology: Human Perception and Performance, 12,* 226–234.

Coltheart, M. (1980). Deep dyslexia: A right hemisphere hypothesis. In M. Coltheart, K. E. Patterson, & J. C. Marshall (Eds.), *Deep dyslexia* (pp. 326–380). London: Routledge & Kegan Paul. [2nd ed., 1987.]

Coltheart, M. (1981). Disorders of reading and their implications for models of normal reading. *Visible Language, 15,* 245–286.

Coltheart, M. (1985). Cognitive neuropsychology and the study of reading. In M. I. Posner & O. S. M. Marin (Eds.), *Attention and performance XI* (pp. 3–37). Hillsdale, NJ: Lawrence Erlbaum Associates, Inc.

Coltheart, M. (1987). Varieties of developmental dyslexia: A comment on Bryant and Impey. *Cognition, 27,* 97–101.

Coltheart, M. (1996). Phonological dyslexia: Past and future issues. *Cognitive Neuropsychology, 13,* 749–762.

Coltheart, M. (2004) Are there lexicons? *Quarterly Journal of Experimental Psychology, 57A,* 1153–1171.

Coltheart, M., Curtis, B., Atkins, P., & Haller, M. (1993). Models of reading aloud: Dual-route and parallel-distributed-processing approaches. *Psychological Review, 100,* 589–608.

Coltheart, M., Davelaar, E., Jonasson, J. T., & Besner, D. (1977). Access to the internal lexicon. In S. Dornic (Ed.), *Attention and performance VI* (pp. 535–555). London: Academic Press.

Coltheart, M., Inglis, L., Cupples, L., Michle, P., Bates, A., & Budd, B. (1998). A semantic subsystem of visual attributes. *Neurocase, 4,* 353–370.

Coltheart, M., Patterson, K. E., & Marshall, J. C. (Eds.). (1987). *Deep dyslexia* (2nd ed.). London: Routledge & Kegan Paul. [1st ed., 1980.]

Coltheart, M., & Rastle, K. (1994). Serial processing in reading aloud: Evidence for dual-route models of reading. *Journal of Experimental Psychology: Human Perception and Performance, 20,* 1197–1211.

Coltheart, M., Rastle, K., Perry, C., Langdon, R., & Ziegler, J. (2001). DRC: A dual route cascaded model of visual word recognition and reading aloud. *Psychological Review, 108,* 204–256.

Coltheart, V., & Leahy, J. (1992). Children's and adults' reading of nonwords: Effects of regularity and consistency. *Journal of Experimental Psychology: Learning, Memory, and Cognition, 18,* 718–729.

Conboy, B. T., & Mills, D. L. (2006). Two languages, one developing brain: Event-related potentials to words in bilingual toddlers. *Developmental Science, 9,* F1–F12.

Connine, C. M. (1990). Effects of sentence context and lexical knowledge in speech processing. In G. T. M. Altmann (Ed.), *Cognitive models of speech processing* (pp. 281–294). Cambridge, MA: MIT Press.

Connine, C. M., & Clifton, C. (1987). Interactive use of lexical information in speech perception. *Journal of Experimental Psychology: Human Perception and Performance, 13,* 291–319.

Conrad, C. (1972). Cognitive economy in semantic memory. *Journal of Experimental Psychology, 92,* 149–154.

Conrad, R. (1979). *The deaf school child: Language and cognitive function*. London: Harper & Row.

Conrad, R., & Rush, M. L. (1965). On the nature of short-term memory encoding by the deaf. *Journal of Speech and Hearing Disorders, 30,* 336–343.

Cook, V. (1997). The consequences of bilingualism for cognitive processing. In A. M. B. de Groot & J. F. Kroll (Eds.), *Tutorials in bilingualism: Psycholinguistic perspectives* (pp. 279–299). Mahwah, NJ: Lawrence Erlbaum Associates, Inc.

Cook, V. J., & Newson, M. (2007). *Chomsky's universal grammar: An introduction* (3rd ed.). Oxford: Blackwell.

Corballis, M. C. (1992). On the evolution of language and generativity. *Cognition*, *44*, 197–226.

Corballis, M. C. (2003). From mouth to hand: Gesture, speech, and the evolution of right-handedness. *Behavioral and Brain Sciences*, *26*, 199–260.

Corballis, M. C. (2004). On the origins of modernity: Was autonomous speech the critical factor? *Psychological Review*, *111*, 543–552.

Corbett, A. T., & Chang, F. (1983). Pronoun disambiguation: Accessing potential antecedents. *Memory and Cognition*, *11*, 383–394.

Corbett, A. T., & Dosher, B. A. (1978). Instrument inferences in sentence encoding. *Journal of Verbal Learning and Verbal Behavior*, *17*, 479–492.

Corina, D. P., Jose-Robertson, L., Guillermin, A., High, J., & Braun, A. R. (2003). Language lateralization in a bimanual language. *Journal of Cognitive Neuroscience*, *15*, 718–730.

Corley, M., Brocklehurst, P. H., & Moat, H. S. (2011). Error biases in inner and overt speech: Evidence from tongue twisters. *Journal of Experimental Psychology: Learning, Memory, and Cognition*, *37*, 162–175.

Corrigan, R. (1978). Language development as related to stage 6 object permanence development. *Journal of Child Language*, *5*, 173–189.

Coslett, H. B. (1991). Read but not write "idea": Evidence for a third reading mechanism. *Brain and Language*, *40*, 425–443.

Coslett, H. B., Roeltgen, D. P., Rothi, L. G., & Heilman, K. M. (1987). Transcortical sensory aphasia: Evidence for subtypes. *Brain and Language*, *32*, 362–378.

Coslett, H. B., & Saffran, E. M. (1989). Preserved object recognition and reading comprehension in optic aphasia. *Brain*, *112*, 1091–1100.

Costa, A., & Caramazza, A. (2002). The production of noun phrases in English and Spanish: Implications for the scope of phonological encoding in speech production. *Journal of Memory and Language*, *46*, 178–198.

Costa, A., Caramazza, A., & Sebastian-Galles, N. (2000). The cognate facilitation effect: Implications for models of lexical access. *Journal of Experimental Psychology: Learning, Memory, and Cognition*, *26*, 1283–1296.

Costa, A., Kovacic, D., Fedorenko, E., & Caramazza, A. (2003). The gender-congruency effect and the selection of freestanding and bound morphemes: Evidence from Croatian. *Journal of Experimental Psychology: Learning, Memory, and Cognition*, *29*, 1270–1282.

Costa, A., Miozzo, M., & Caramazza, A. (1999). Lexical selection in bilinguals: Do words in the bilingual's two lexicons compete for selection? *Journal of Memory and Language*, *41*, 365–397.

Costa, A., & Sebastian-Gallés, N. (1998). Abstract phonological structure in language production: Evidence from Spanish. *Journal of Experimental Psychology: Learning, Memory, and Cognition*, *24*, 886–903.

Cottingham, J. (1984). *Rationalism*. London: Paladin.

Crain, S., & Steedman, M. J. (1985). On not being led up the garden path: The use of context by the psychological parser. In D. Dowty, L. Karttunen, & A. Zwicky (Eds.), *Natural language parsing* (pp. 320–358). Cambridge: Cambridge University Press.

Cree, G. S., McNorgan, C., & McRae, K. (2006). Distinctive features hold a privileged status in the computation of word meaning: Implications for theories of semantic memory. *Journal of Experimental Psychology: Learning, Memory, and Cognition*, *32*, 643–658.

Crocker, M. W. (1999). Mechanisms for sentence processing. In S. Garrod & M. J. Pickering (Eds.), *Language processing* (pp. 191–232). Hove, UK: Psychology Press.

Cromer, R. F. (1991). *Language and thought in normal and handicapped children*. Oxford: Blackwell.

Croot, K., Patterson, K. E., & Hodges, J. R. (1999). Familial progressive aphasia: Insights into the nature and deterioration of single word processing. *Cognitive Neuropsychology*, *16*, 705–747.

Cross, T. G. (1977). Mothers' speech adjustments: The contribution of selected child listener variables. In C. E. Snow & C. A. Ferguson (Eds.), *Talking to children: Language input and acquisition* (pp. 151–188). Cambridge: Cambridge University Press.

Cross, T. G. (1978). Mother's speech and its association with rate of linguistic development in young children. In N. Waterson & C. E. Snow (Eds.), *The development of communication* (pp. 199–216). Chichester, UK: Wiley.

Cross, T. G., Johnson-Morris, J. E., & Nienhuys, T. G. (1980). Linguistic feedback and maternal speech: Comparisons of mothers addressing hearing and hearing-impaired children. *First Language*, *1*, 163–189.

Crosson, B., Moberg, P. J., Boone, J. R., Rothi, L. J. G., & Raymer, A. (1997). Category-specific naming deficit for medical terms after dominant thalamic/capsular hemorrhage. *Brain and Language*, *60*, 407–442.

Crystal, D. (1986). Prosodic development. In P. Fletcher & M. Garman (Eds.), *Language acquisition* (2nd ed., pp. 174–197). Cambridge: Cambridge University Press.

Crystal, D. (1998). *Language play*. Harmondsworth, UK: Penguin Books.

Crystal, D. (2010). *The Cambridge encyclopedia of language* (3rd ed.). Cambridge: Cambridge University Press.

Cuetos, F., Aguado, G., & Caramazza, A. (2000). Dissociation of semantic and phonological errors in naming. *Brain and Language*, *75*, 451–460.

Cuetos, F., & Mitchell, D. C. (1988). Cross-linguistic differences in parsing: Restrictions on the use of the late closure strategy in Spanish. *Cognition*, *30*, 73–105.

Cummins, J. (1991). Interdependence of first- and second-language proficiency in bilingual children. In E. Bialystok (Ed.), *Language processing in bilingual children* (pp. 70–89). Cambridge: Cambridge University Press.

Curtin, S., Mintz, T. H., & Christiansen, M. H. (2005). Stress changes the representational landscape: Evidence from word segmentation. *Cognition*, *96*, 233–262.

Curtiss, S. (1977). *Genie: A psycholinguistic study of a modern-day "wild child."* London: Academic Press.

Curtiss, S. (1989). The independence and task-specificity of language. In M. H. Bornstein & J. Bruner (Eds.), *Interaction in human development* (pp. 105–137). Hillsdale, NJ: Lawrence Erlbaum Associates, Inc.

Cutler, A. (1981). Making up materials is a confounded nuisance, or: Will we be able to run any psycholinguistic experiments at all in 1990? *Cognition*, *10*, 65–70.

Cutler, A., & Butterfield, S. (1992). Rhythmic cues to speech segmentation: Evidence from juncture misperception. *Journal of Memory and Language*, *31*, 218–236.

Cutler, A., Mehler, J., Norris, D., & Segui, J. (1986). The syllable's differing role in the segmentation of French and English. *Journal of Memory and Language*, *25*, 385–400.

Cutler, A., Mehler, J., Norris, D., & Segui, J. (1987). Phoneme identification and the lexicon. *Cognitive Psychology*, *19*, 141–177.

Cutler, A., Mehler, J., Norris, D., & Segui, J. (1992). The monolingual nature of speech segmentation by bilinguals. *Cognitive Psychology*, *24*, 381–410.

Cutler, A., & Norris, D. (1979). Monitoring sentence comprehension. In W. E. Cooper & E. C. T. Walker (Eds.), *Sentence processing: Psycholinguistic studies presented to Merrill Garrett* (pp. 113–134). Hillsdale, NJ: Lawrence Erlbaum Associates, Inc.

Cutler, A., & Norris, D. (1988). The role of strong syllables in segmentation for lexical access. *Journal of Experimental Psychology: Human Perception and Performance*, *14*, 113–121.

Cutsford, T. D. (1951). *The blind in school and society*. New York: American Foundation for the Blind.

Cutting, J. C., & Ferreira, V. (1999). Semantic and phonological information flow in the production lexicon. *Journal of Experimental Psychology: Learning, Memory, and Cognition*, *25*, 318–344.

Czerniewska, P. (1992). *Learning about writing*. Oxford: Blackwell.

D'Andrade, R. G., & Wish, M. (1985). Speech act theory in quantitative research on interpersonal behavior. *Discourse Processes*, *8*, 229–259.

Dagenbach, D., Carr, T. H., & Wilhelmsen, A. (1989). Task-induced strategies and near-threshold priming: Conscious influences on unconscious perception. *Journal of Memory and Language*, *28*, 412–443.

Dahan, D., Magnuson, J. S., & Tanenhaus, M. K. (2001). Time course of frequency effects in spoken-word recognition: Evidence from eye movements. *Cognitive Psychology*, *42*, 317–367.

Dahl, H. (1979). *Word frequencies of spoken American English*. Essex, CT: Verbatim.

Dale, P. S. (1976). *Language development: Structure and function* (2nd ed.). New York: Holt, Rinehart & Winston.

Daneman, M., & Carpenter, P. A. (1980). Individual differences in working memory and reading. *Journal of Verbal Learning and Verbal Behavior*, *19*, 450–466.

Daneman, M., Reingold, E. M., & Davidson, M. (1995). Time course of phonological-activation during reading: Evidence from eye fixations. *Journal of Experimental Psychology: Learning, Memory, and Cognition*, *21*, 884–898.

Davidoff, J., Davies, I., & Roberson, D. (1999a). Colour categories in a stone-age tribe. *Nature*, *398*, 203–204.

Davidoff, J., Davies, I., & Roberson, D. (1999b). Addendum: Colour categories in a stone-age tribe. *Nature*, *402*, 604.

Davies, I., Corbett, G., Laws, G., McGurk, H., Moss, A., & Smith, M. W. (1991). Linguistic basicness and colour information processing. *International Journal of Psychology*, *26*, 311–327.

Davis, C. J., & Lupker, S. J. (2006). Masked inhibitory priming in English: Evidence for lexical inhibition. *Journal of Experimental Psychology: Human Perception and Performance*, *32*, 668–687.

Davis, K. (1947). Final note on a case of extreme social isolation. *American Journal of Sociology*, *52*, 432–437.

Dawson, M. (2005). *Connectionism: A hands-on approach*. Oxford: Blackwell.

de Boysson-Bardies, B., Halle, P., Sagart, L., & Durand, C. (1989). A cross-linguistic investigation of vowel formants in babbling. *Journal of Child Language*, *16*, 1–17.

de Boysson-Bardies, B., Sagart, L., & Durand, C. (1984). Discernible differences in the babbling of infants according to target language. *Journal of Child Language*, *11*, 1–15.

de Groot, A. M. B. (1983). The range of automatic spreading activation in word priming. *Journal of Verbal Learning and Verbal Behavior, 22*, 417–436.

de Groot, A. M. B. (1984). Primed lexical decision: Combined effects of the proportion of related prime–target pairs and the stimulus onset asynchrony of prime and target. *Quarterly Journal of Experimental Psychology, 36A*, 253–280.

de Groot, A. M. B., Dannenburg, L., & van Hell, J. G. (1994). Forward and backward translation by bilinguals. *Journal of Memory and Language, 33*, 600–629.

de Groot, A. M. B., & Kroll, J. F. (Eds.). (1997). *Tutorials in bilingualism: Psycholinguistic perspectives*. Mahwah, NJ: Lawrence Erlbaum Associates, Inc.

de Renzi, E., & Lucchelli, F. (1994). Are semantic systems separately represented in the brain? The case of living category impairment. *Cortex, 30*, 3–25.

de Villiers, J. G., & de Villiers, P. A. (2000). Linguistic determination and the understanding of false beliefs. In P. Mitchell & K. J. Riggs (Eds.), *Children's reasoning and the mind* (pp. 191–228). Hove, UK: Psychology Press.

de Villiers, P. A., & de Villiers, J. G. (1979). *Early language*. London: Fontana/Open Books.

Deacon, T. (1997). *The symbolic species*. Harmondsworth, UK: Penguin Books.

Dean, M. P., & Young, A. W. (1996). An item-specific locus of repetition priming. *Quarterly Journal of Experimental Psychology, 49A*, 269–294.

DeCasper, A. J., & Fifer, W. P. (1980). Of human bonding: Newborns prefer their mothers' voices. *Science, 208*, 1174–1176.

DeCasper, A. J., Lecanuet, J. P., Maugais, R., Granier-Deferre, C., & Busnel, M. C. (1994). Fetal reactions to recurrent maternal speech. *Infant Behavior and Development, 17*, 159–164.

DeCasper, A. J., & Spence, M. J. (1986). Prenatal maternal speech influences newborns' perception of speech sounds. *Infant Behavior and Development, 9*, 133–150.

Dell, G. S. (1985). Positive feedback in hierarchical connectionist models: Applications to language production. *Cognitive Science, 9*, 3–23.

Dell, G. S. (1986). A spreading-activation theory of retrieval in sentence production. *Psychological Review, 93*, 283–321.

Dell, G. S. (1988). The retrieval of phonological forms in production: Tests of predictions from a connectionist model. *Journal of Memory and Language, 27*, 124–142.

Dell, G. S., Burger, L. K., & Svec, W. R. (1997). Language production and serial order: A functional analysis and a model. *Psychological Review, 104*, 123–147.

Dell, G. S., Juliano, C., & Govindjee, A. (1993). Structure and content in language production: A theory of frame constraints in phonological speech errors. *Cognitive Science, 17*, 149–195.

Dell, G. S., Martin, N., & Schwartz, M. F. (2007). A case-series test of the interactive two-step model of lexical access: Predicting word repetition from picture naming. *Journal of Memory and Language, 56*, 490–520.

Dell, G. S., & O'Seaghdha, P. G. (1991). Mediated and convergent lexical priming in language production: A comment on Levelt et al. (1991). *Psychological Review, 98*, 604–614.

Dell, G. S., & Reich, P. A. (1981). Stages in sentence production: An analysis of speech error data. *Journal of Verbal Learning and Verbal Behavior, 20*, 611–629.

Dell, G. S., Schwartz, M. F., Martin, N., Saffran, E. M., & Gagnon, D. A. (1997). Lexical access in aphasic and nonaphasic speakers. *Psychological Review, 104*, 801–838.

Dell, G. S., Schwartz, M. F., Martin, N., Saffran, E. M., & Gagnon, D. A. (2000). The role of computational models in the cognitive neuropsychology of language: A reply to Ruml and Caramazza. *Psychological Review, 107*, 635–645.

DeLong, K. A., Urbach, T. P., & Kutas, M. (2005). Probabilistic word pre-activation during language comprehension inferred from electrical brain activity. *Nature Neuroscience, 8*, 1117–1121.

Demers, R. A. (1988). Linguistics and animal communication. In F. J. Newmeyer (Ed.), *Linguistics: The Cambridge survey: Vol. 3. Language: Psychological and biological aspects* (pp. 314–335). Cambridge: Cambridge University Press.

Demetras, M. J., Post, K. N., & Snow, C. E. (1986). Feedback to first language learners: The role of repetitions and clarification questions. *Journal of Child Language, 13*, 275–292.

Den Heyer, K. (1985). On the nature of the proportion effect in semantic priming. *Acta Psychologica, 60*, 25–38.

Den Heyer, K., Briand, K., & Dannenbring, G. L. (1983). Strategic factors in a lexical decision task: Evidence for automatic and attention driven processes. *Memory and Cognition, 10*, 358–370.

Dennett, D. C. (1991). *Consciousness explained*. Harmondsworth, UK: Penguin.

Dennis, M., & Whitaker, H. A. (1976). Language acquisition following hemidecortication: Linguistic superiority of the left over the right hemisphere. *Brain and Language, 3*, 404–433.

Dennis, M., & Whitaker, H. A. (1977). Hemispheric equipotentiality and language acquisition. In S. J. Segalowitz & F. A. Gruber (Eds.), *Language development and neurological theory* (pp. 93–106). New York: Academic Press.

Derouesné, J., & Beauvois, M.-F. (1979). Phonological processing in reading: Data from dyslexia. *Journal of Neurology, Neurosurgery and Psychiatry, 42*, 1125–1132.

Derouesné, J., & Beauvois, M.-F. (1985). The "phonemic" stage in the non-lexical reading process: Evidence from a case of phonological alexia. In K. Patterson, M. Coltheart, & J. C. Marshall (Eds.), *Surface dyslexia* (pp. 399–457). Hove, UK: Lawrence Erlbaum Associates.

Devlin, J. T., Gonnerman, L. M., Andersen, E. S., & Seidenberg, M. S. (1998). Category specific semantic deficits in focal and widespread brain damage: A computational account. *Journal of Cognitive Neuroscience, 10,* 77–94.

Dhooge, E., & Hartsuiker, R. J. (2012). Lexical selection and verbal self-monitoring: Effects of lexicality, context, and time pressure in picture-word interference. *Journal of Memory and Language, 66,* 163–176.

Dick, F., Bates, E., Wulfeck, B., Utman, J. A., Dronkers, N., & Gernsbacher, M. A. (2001). Language deficits, localization, and grammar: Evidence for a distributive model of language breakdown in aphasic patients and neurologically intact individuals. *Psychological Review, 108,* 759–788.

Diesfeldt, H. F. A. (1989). Semantic impairment in senile dementia of the Alzheimer type. *Aphasiology, 3,* 41–54.

Dijkstra, A., & van Heuven, W. J. B. (2002). The architecture of the bilingual word recognition system: From identification to decision. *Bilingualism: Language and Cognition, 5,* 175–197.

Dijkstra, T., van Heuven, W. J. B., & Grainger, J. (1998). Simulating cross-language competition with the bilingual interactive activation model. *Psychologica Belgica, 38,* 177–196.

Dionne, G., Dale, P. S., Boivin, M., & Plomin, R. (2003). Genetic evidence for bidirectional effects of early lexical and grammatical development. *Child Development, 74,* 394–412.

Dockrell, J., & Messer, D. J. (1999). *Children's language and communication difficulties: Understanding, identification, and intervention.* London: Cassell.

Dogil, G., Haider, H., Schaner-Wolles, C., & Husman, R. (1995). Radical autonomy of syntax: Evidence from transcortical sensory aphasia. *Aphasiology, 9,* 577–602.

Dooling, D. J., & Christiaansen, R. E. (1977). Episodic and semantic aspects of memory for prose. *Journal of Experimental Psychology: Human Learning and Memory, 3,* 428–436.

Dooling, D. J., & Lachman, R. (1971). Effects of comprehension on retention of prose. *Journal of Experimental Psychology, 88,* 216–222.

Dopkins, S., Morris, R. K., & Rayner, K. (1992). Lexical ambiguity and eye fixations in reading: A test of competing models of lexical ambiguity resolution. *Journal of Memory and Language, 31,* 461–476.

Dörnyei, Z. (1990). Conceptualizing motivation in foreign language learning. *Language Learning, 40,* 45–78.

Doughty, C. J., & Long, M. H. (Eds.). (2005). *The handbook of second language acquisition.* Oxford: Blackwell.

Downing, P. (1977). On the creation and use of English compound nouns. *Language, 53,* 810–842.

Doyle, J. R., & Leach, C. (1988). Word superiority in signal detection: Barely a glimpse, yet reading nonetheless. *Cognitive Psychology, 20,* 283–318.

Dronkers, N. F., Wilkins, D. P., van Valin, R. D., Redfern, B. B., & Jaeger, J. J. (2004). Lesion analysis of the brain areas involved in language comprehension. *Cognition, 95,* 145–177.

Druks, J., & Froud, K. (2002). The syntax of single words: Evidence from a patient with a selective function word reading deficit. *Cognitive Neuropsychology, 19,* 207–244.

Duffy, S. A., Morris, R. K., & Rayner, K. (1988). Lexical ambiguity and fixation times in reading. *Journal of Memory and Language, 27,* 429–446.

Duncan, L. G., Seymour, P. H. K., & Hill, S. (1997). How important are rhyme and analogy in beginning reading? *Cognition, 63,* 171–208.

Duncan, L. G., Seymour, P. H. K., & Hill, S. (2000). A small-to-large unit progression in metaphonological awareness and reading? *Quarterly Journal of Experimental Psychology, 53A,* 1081–1104.

Duncan, S. E., & Niederehe, G. (1974). On signaling that it's your turn to speak. *Journal of Experimental Social Psychology, 10,* 234–247.

Duncker, K. (1945). On problem-solving. *Psychological Monographs, 58* (5, Whole No. 270).

Dunlea, A. (1984). The relation between concept formation and semantic roles: Some evidence from the blind. In L. Feagans, C. Garvery, & R. M. Golinkoff (Eds.), *The origins and growth of communication* (pp. 224–243). Norwood, NJ: Ablex.

Dunlea, A. (1989). *Vision and the emergence of meaning: Blind and sighted children's early language.* Cambridge: Cambridge University Press.

Duran, N. D., Dale, R., & Kreuz, R. J. (2011). Listeners invest in an assumed other's perspective despite cognitive cost. *Cognition, 121,* 22–40.

Durkin, K. (1987). Minds and language: Social cognition, social interaction and the acquisition of language. *Mind and Language, 2,* 105–140.

Durso, F. T., & Johnson, M. K. (1979). Facilitation in naming and categorizing repeated pictures and words. *Journal of Experimental Psychology: Human Learning and Memory, 5,* 449–459.

Duskova, L. (1969). On sources of errors in foreign language learning. *International Review of Applied Linguistics, 7,* 11–36.

Eberhard, K. M. (1999). The accessibility of conceptual number to the processes of subject–verb agreement in English. *Journal of Memory and Language, 30,* 210–233.

Eberhard, K. M., Cutting, J. C., & Bock, J. K. (2005). Making syntax of sense: Number agreement in sentence production. *Psychological Review, 112,* 531–559.

Eckert, M. A., Lombardino, L. J., & Leonard, C. M. (2001). Planar asymmetry tips the phonological playground and environment raises the bar. *Child Development, 72,* 988–1002.

Eckman, F. (1977). Markedness and the contrastive analysis hypothesis. *Language Learning, 27,* 315–330.

Eglinton, E., & Annett, M. (1994). Handedness and dyslexia: A meta-analysis. *Perceptual Motor Skills, 79,* 1611–1616.

Ehri, L. C. (1992). Reconceptualizing the development of sight word reading and its relationship to recoding. In P. Gough, L. Ehri, & R. Treiman (Eds.), *Reading acquisition* (pp. 107–143). Hillsdale, NJ: Lawrence Erlbaum Associates, Inc.

Ehri, L. C. (1997a). Sight word learning in normal readers and dyslexics. In B. A. Blachman (Ed.), *Foundations of reading acquisition and dyslexia: Implications for early intervention* (pp. 163–189). Mahwah, NJ: Lawrence Erlbaum Associates, Inc.

Ehri, L. C. (1997b). Learning to read and learning to spell are one and the same, almost. In C. A. Perfetti, L. Rieben, & M. Fayol (Eds.), *Learning to spell: Research, theory, and practice across languages* (pp. 237–269). Mahwah, NJ: Lawrence Erlbaum Associates, Inc.

Ehri, L. C., Nunes, S. R., Stahl, S. A., & Willows, D. M. (2001). Systematic phonics instruction helps students learn to read: Evidence from the National Reading Panel's meta-analysis. *Review of Educational Research, 71,* 393–447.

Ehri, L. C., & Robbins, C. (1992). Beginners need some decoding skill to read words by analogy. *Reading Research Quarterly, 27,* 13–26.

Ehri, L. C., & Ryan, E. B. (1980). Performance of bilinguals in a picture–word interference task. *Journal of Psycholinguistic Research, 9,* 285–302.

Ehri, L. C., & Wilce, L. S. (1985). Movement into reading: Is the first stage of printed word learning visual or phonetic? *Reading Research Quarterly, 20,* 163–179.

Ehrlich, K., & Johnson-Laird, P. N. (1982). Spatial descriptions and referential continuity. *Journal of Verbal Learning and Verbal Behavior, 21,* 296–306.

Eimas, P. D., & Corbit, L. (1973). Selective adaptation of linguistic feature detectors. *Cognitive Psychology, 4,* 99–109.

Eimas, P. D., & Miller, J. L. (1980). Contextual effects in infant speech perception. *Science, 209,* 1140–1141.

Eimas, P. D., Miller, J. L., & Jusczyk, P. W. (1987). On infant speech perception and the acquisition of language. In S. Harnad (Ed.), *Categorical perception* (pp. 161–195). New York: Cambridge University Press.

Eimas, P. D., Siqueland, E. R., Jusczyk, P. W., & Vigorito, J. (1971). Speech perception in infants. *Science, 171,* 303–306.

Elbers, L. (1985). A tip-of-the-tongue experience at age two? *Journal of Child Language, 12,* 353–365.

Elio, R., & Anderson, J. R. (1981). The effects of category generalizations and instance similarity on schema abstraction. *Journal of Experimental Psychology: Human Learning and Memory, 7,* 397–417.

Ellis, A. W. (1980). On the Freudian theory of speech errors. In V. A. Fromkin (Ed.), *Errors in linguistic performance* (pp. 123–132). New York: Academic Press.

Ellis, A. W. (1985). The production of spoken words: A cognitive neuropsychological perspective. In A. W. Ellis (Ed.), *Progress in the psychology of language* (Vol. 2, pp. 107–145). Hove, UK: Lawrence Erlbaum Associates.

Ellis, A. W. (1993). *Reading, writing and dyslexia: A cognitive analysis* (2nd ed.). Hove, UK: Lawrence Erlbaum Associates.

Ellis, A. W., & Lambon Ralph, M. A. (2000). Age of acquisition effects in adult lexical processing reflect loss of plasticity in maturing systems: Insights from connectionist networks. *Journal of Experimental Psychology: Learning, Memory, and Cognition, 26,* 1103–1123.

Ellis, A. W., & Marshall, J. C. (1978). Semantic errors or statistical flukes: A note on Allport's "On knowing the meaning of words we are unable to report." *Quarterly Journal of Experimental Psychology, 30,* 569–575.

Ellis, A. W., Miller, D., & Sin, G. (1983). Wernicke's aphasia and normal language processing: A case study in cognitive neuropsychology. *Cognition, 15,* 111–144.

Ellis, A. W., & Morrison, C. M. (1998). Real age-of-acquisition effects in lexical retrieval. *Journal of Experimental Psychology: Learning, Memory, and Cognition, 24,* 515–523.

Ellis, A. W., & Young, A. W. (1988). *Human cognitive neuropsychology*. Hove, UK: Lawrence Erlbaum Associates. [Augmented edition with readings, 1996.]

Ellis, N. C., & Beaton, A. (1993). Factors affecting the learning of foreign language vocabulary: Imagery keyword mediators and phonological short-term memory. *Quarterly Journal of Experimental Psychology, 46A,* 533–558.

Ellis, N. C., & Hennelly, R. A. (1980). A bilingual word-length effect: Implications for intelligence testing and the relative ease of mental calculations in Welsh and English. *British Journal of Psychology, 71,* 43–52.

Ellis, R., & Humphreys, G. W. (1999). *Connectionist psychology: A text with readings*. Hove, UK: Psychology Press.

Ellis, R., & Wells, G. (1980). Enabling factors in adult–child discourse. *First Language, 1*, 46–62.

Elman, J. L. (1990). Finding structure in time. *Cognitive Science, 14*, 179–211.

Elman, J. L. (1993). Learning and development in neural networks: The importance of starting small. *Cognition, 48*, 71–99.

Elman, J. L. (1999). The emergence of language: A conspiracy theory. In B. MacWhinney (Ed.), *The emergence of language* (pp. 1–27). Mahwah, NJ: Lawrence Erlbaum Associates, Inc.

Elman, J. L., Bates, E. A., Johnson, M. H., Karmiloff-Smith, A., Parisi, D., & Plunkett, K. (1996). *Rethinking innateness: A connectionist perspective on development*. Cambridge, MA: Bradford Books.

Elman, J. L., & McClelland, J. L. (1988). Cognitive penetration of the mechanisms of perception: Compensation for coarticulation of lexically restored phonemes. *Journal of Memory and Language, 27*, 143–165.

Elsness, J. (1984). That or zero? A look at the choice of object relative clause connective in a corpus of American English. *English Studies, 65*, 519–533.

Emmorey, K. (2001). *Language, cognition, and the brain: Insights from sign language research*. Hillsdale, NJ: Lawrence Erlbaum Associates, Inc.

Entus, A. K. (1977). Hemispheric asymmetry in processing of dichotically presented speech sounds. In S. J. Segalowitz & F. A. Gruber (Eds.), *Language development and neurological theory* (pp. 63–73). New York: Academic Press.

Eriksen, C. W., Pollack, M. D., & Montague, W. E. (1970). Implicit speech: Mechanisms in perceptual encoding? *Journal of Experimental Psychology, 84*, 502–507.

Ervin-Tripp, S. (1979). Children's verbal turntaking. In E. Ochs & B. B. Schieffelin (Eds.), *Developmental pragmatics* (pp. 391–414). New York: Academic Press.

Estes, Z., & Jones, L. L. (2006). Priming via relational similarity: A COPPER HORSE is faster when seen through a GLASS EYE. *Journal of Memory and Language, 55*, 89–101.

Evans, N., & Levinson, S. C. (2009). The myth of language universals: Language diversity and its importance for cognitive science. *Behavioral and Brain Sciences, 32*, 429–448.

Evans, W. E., & Bastian, J. (1969). Marine mammal communication: Social and ecological factors. In H. T. Andersen (Ed.), *The biology of marine mammals* (pp. 425–475). New York: Academic Press.

Everett, C., & Madora, K. (2011). Quantity recognition among speakers of an anumeric language. *Cognitive Science, 36*, 130–141.

Everett, D. L. (2005). Cultural constraints on grammar and cognition in Piraha. *Current Anthropology, 46*, 521–646.

Eysenck, M. W., & Keane, M. T. (2010). *Cognitive psychology: A student's handbook* (6th ed.). Hove, UK: Psychology Press.

Fabb, N. (1994). *Sentence structure*. London: Routledge & Kegan Paul.

Fabbro, F. (1999). *The neurolinguistics of bilingualism: An introduction*. Hove, UK: Psychology Press.

Fabbro, F. (2001). The bilingual brain: Cerebral representation of languages. *Brain and Language, 79*, 211–222.

Facoetti, A., Trussardi, A. N., Ruffino, M., Lorusso, M. L., Cattaneo, C., Galli, R., et al. (2010). Multisensory spatial attention deficits are predictive of phonological decoding skills in developmental dyslexia. *Journal of Cognitive Neuroscience, 22*, 1011–1025.

Faigley, L., & Witte, S. (1983). Analysing revision. *College Composition and Communication, 32*, 400–414.

Farah, M. J. (1990). *Visual agnosia: Disorders of object recognition and what they tell us about normal vision*. Cambridge, MA: MIT Press.

Farah, M. J. (1991). Patterns of co-occurrence among the associative agnosias: Implications for visual object recognition. *Cognitive Neuropsychology, 8*, 1–19.

Farah, M. J. (1994). Neuropsychological inference with an interactive brain: A critique of the "locality" assumption [with commentaries]. *Behavioral and Brain Sciences, 17*, 43–104.

Farah, M. J., Hammond, K. M., Mehta, Z., & Ratcliff, G. (1989). Category-specificity and modality-specificity in semantic memory. *Neuropsychologia, 27*, 193–200.

Farah, M. J., & McClelland, J. L. (1991). A computational model of semantic memory impairment: Modality-specificity and emergent category-specificity. *Journal of Experimental Psychology: General, 120*, 339–357.

Farah, M. J., Stowe, R. M., & Levinson, K. L. (1996). Phonological dyslexia: Loss of a reading-specific component of the cognitive architecture? *Cognitive Neuropsychology, 13*, 849–868.

Farah, M. J., & Wallace, M. A. (1992). Semantically-bounded anomia: Implications for the neural implementation of naming. *Neuropsychologia, 30*, 609–621.

Farrar, M. J. (1990). Discourse and the acquisition of grammatical morphemes. *Journal of Child Language, 17*, 607–624.

Farrar, M. J. (1992). Negative evidence and grammatical morpheme acquisition. *Developmental Psychology, 28*, 90–98.

Fauconnier, G., & Turner, M. (2003). *The way we think*. New York: Basic Books.

Faust, M. E., Balota, D. A., Duchek, J. A., Gernsbacher, M. A., & Smith, S. D. (1997). Inhibitory control during sentence processing in individuals with dementia of the Alzheimer type. *Brain and Language*, 57, 225–253.

Fay, D., & Cutler, A. (1977). Malapropisms and the structure of the mental lexicon. *Linguistic Inquiry*, 8, 505–520.

Fedorenko, E., Gibson, E., & Rohde, D. (2006). The nature of working memory capacity in sentence comprehension: Evidence against domain-specific working memory resources. *Journal of Memory and Language*, 54, 541–553.

Fedorenko, E., & Kanwisher, N. (2011). Some regions within Broca's area do respond more strongly to sentences than to linguistically degraded stimuli: A comment on Rogalsky and Hickok (2011). *Journal of Cognitive Neuroscience*, 23, 2632–2635.

Feitelson, D., Tehori, B. Z., & Levinberg-Green, D. (1982). How effective is early instruction in reading? Experimental evidence. *Merrill-Palmer Quarterly*, 28, 458–494.

Felix, S. (1992). Language acquisition as a maturational process. In J. Weissenborn, H. Goodluck, & T. Roeper (Eds.), *Theoretical issues in language acquisition* (pp. 25–51). Hillsdale, NJ: Lawrence Erlbaum Associates, Inc.

Fenson, L., Dale, P., Reznick, J., Bates, E., Thal, D., & Pethick, S. (1994). Variability in early communicative development. *Monographs of the Society for Research in Child Development*, 59 (5, Serial No. 242).

Fera, P., & Besner, D. (1992). The process of lexical decision: More words about a parallel distributed processing model. *Journal of Experimental Psychology: Learning, Memory, and Cognition*, 18, 749–764.

Fernald, A. (1991). Prosody and focus in speech to infants and adults. *Annals of Child Development*, 8, 43–80.

Fernald, A., Swingley, D., & Pinto, J. P. (2001). When half a word is enough: Infants can recognize spoken words using partial phonetic information. *Child Development*, 72, 1003–1015.

Fernald, G. M. (1943). *Remedial techniques in basic school subjects*. New York: McGraw-Hill.

Fernandes, K. J., Marcus, G. F., Di Nubila, J. A., & Vouloumanos, A. (2006). From semantics to syntax and back again: Argument structure in the third year of life. *Cognition*, 100, B10–B20.

Ferreira, F. (2003). The misinterpretation of noncanonical sentences. *Cognitive Psychology*, 47, 164–203.

Ferreira, F., & Bailey, K. G. D. (2004). Disfluencies and human language comprehension. *Trends in Cognitive Sciences*, 8, 231–237.

Ferreira, F., & Clifton, C. (1986). The independence of syntactic processing. *Journal of Memory and Language*, 25, 348–368.

Ferreira, F., & Henderson, J. M. (1990). Use of verb information in syntactic parsing: Evidence from eye movements and word-by-word self-paced reading. *Journal of Experimental Psychology: Learning, Memory, and Cognition*, 16, 555–568.

Ferreira, F., & Henderson, J. M. (1991). Recovery from misanalyses of garden-path sentences. *Journal of Memory and Language*, 30, 725–745.

Ferreira, V. S. (1996). Is it better to give than to donate? Syntactic flexibility in language production. *Journal of Memory and Language*, 35, 724–755.

Ferreira, V. S., & Dell, G. S. (2000). Effect of ambiguity and lexical availability on syntactic and lexical production. *Cognitive Psychology*, 40, 296–340.

Ferreira, V. S., Slevc, L. R., & Rogers, E. S. (2005). How do speakers avoid ambiguous linguistic expressions? *Cognition*, 96, 263–284.

Ferreira, V. S., & Swets, B. (2002). How incremental is language production? Evidence from the production of utterances requiring the computation of arithmetic sums. *Journal of Memory and Language*, 46, 57–84.

Ferreiro, E. (1985). Literacy development: A psychogenetic perspective. In D. R. Olson, N. Torrance, & A. Hildyard (Eds.), *Literacy, language, and learning: The nature and consequences of reading and writing* (pp. 217–228). Cambridge: Cambridge University Press.

Ferreiro, E., & Teberosky, A. (1982). *Literacy before schooling*. New York: Heinemann.

Fillmore, C. J. (1968). The case for case. In E. Bach & R. T. Harms (Eds.), *Universals of linguistic theory* (pp. 1–90). New York: Holt, Rinehart & Winston.

Finch, S., & Chater, N. (1992). Bootstrapping syntactic categories. In *Proceedings of the 14th Annual Conference of the Cognitive Science Society* (pp. 820–825). Hillsdale, NJ: Lawrence Erlbaum Associates, Inc.

Fischler, I. (1977). Semantic facilitation without association in a lexical decision task. *Memory and Cognition*, 5, 335–339.

Fischler, I., & Bloom, P. A. (1979). Automatic and attentional processes in the effects of sentence contexts on word recognition. *Journal of Verbal Learning and Verbal Behavior*, 18, 1–20.

Fisher, C. (2002). The role of abstract syntactic knowledge in language acquisition: A reply to Tomasello (2000). *Cognition*, 82, 259–278.

Fisher, S. E., & Marcus, G. F. (2006). The eloquent ape: Genes, brains and the evolution of language. *Nature Reviews Genetics*, 7, 9–20.

Fisher, S. E., Marlow, A. J., Lamb, J., Maestrini, E., Williams, D. F., Richardson, A. J., et al. (1999). A quantitative-trait locus on chromosome 6p influences different aspects of developmental dyslexia. *American Journal of Human Genetics*, 64, 146–156.

Fisher, S. E., Vargha-Khadem, F., Watkins, K. E., Monaco, A. P., & Pembrey, M. E. (1998). Localisation of a gene implicated in a severe speech and language disorder. *Nature Genetics*, 18, 168–170.

Fitch, W. T., & Hauser, M. D. (2004). Computational constraints on syntactic processing in a nonhuman primate. *Science, 303*, 377–380.

Fitch, W. T., Hauser, M. D., & Chomsky, N. (2005). The evolution of the language faculty: Clarifications and implications. *Cognition, 97*, 179–210.

Flavell, J. H., Miller, P. H., & Miller, S. (1993). *Cognitive development* (3rd ed.). Englewood Cliffs, NJ: Prentice Hall.

Flege, J. E., & Hillenbrand, J. (1984). Limits on phonetic accuracy in foreign language speech production. *Journal of the Acoustical Society of America, 76*, 708–721.

Fletcher, C. R. (1986). Strategies for the allocation of short-term memory during comprehension. *Journal of Memory and Language, 25*, 43–58.

Fletcher, C. R. (1994). Levels of representation in memory for discourse. In M. A. Gernsbacher (Ed.), *Handbook of psycholinguistics* (pp. 589–608). San Diego, CA: Academic Press.

Flower, L. S., & Hayes, J. R. (1980). The dynamics of composing: Making plans and juggling constraints. In L. W. Gregg & E. R. Sternberg (Eds.), *Cognitive processes in writing* (pp. 31–50). Hillsdale, NJ: Lawrence Erlbaum Associates, Inc.

Fodor, J. A. (1972). Some reflections on L. S. Vygotsky's thought and language. *Cognition, 1*, 83–95.

Fodor, J. A. (1975). *The language of thought.* Hassocks, UK: Harvester Press.

Fodor, J. A. (1978). Tom Swift and his procedural grandmother. *Cognition, 6*, 229–247.

Fodor, J. A. (1979). In reply to Philip Johnson-Laird. *Cognition, 7*, 93–95.

Fodor, J. A. (1981). The present status of the innateness controversy. In J. A. Fodor, *Representations* (pp. 257–316). Brighton, UK: Harvester Press.

Fodor, J. A. (1983). *The modularity of mind.* Cambridge, MA: MIT Press.

Fodor, J. A. (1985). Précis and multiple book review of the *Modularity of mind. Behavioral and Brain Sciences, 8*, 1–42.

Fodor, J. A., & Bever, T. G. (1965). The psychological reality of linguistic segments. *Journal of Verbal Learning and Verbal Behavior, 4*, 414–420.

Fodor, J. A., Bever, T. G., & Garrett, M. F. (1974). *The psychology of language.* New York: McGraw-Hill.

Fodor, J. A., & Garrett, M. F. (1967). Some syntactic determinants of sentential complexity. *Perception and Psychophysics, 2*, 289–296.

Fodor, J. A., Garrett, M. F., Walker, E. C. T., & Parkes, C. H. (1980). Against definitions. *Cognition, 8*, 263–367.

Fodor, J. D., Fodor, J. A., & Garrett, M. F. (1975). The psychological unreality of semantic representations. *Linguistic Inquiry, 6*, 515–531.

Fodor, J. D., & Frazier, L. (1980). Is the human sentence parsing mechanism an ATN? *Cognition, 8*, 418–459.

Folk, J. R. (1999). Phonological codes are used to access the lexicon during silent reading. *Journal of Experimental Psychology: Learning, Memory, and Cognition, 25*, 892–906.

Folk, J. R., & Morris, R. K. (1995). Multiple lexical codes in reading: Evidence from eye movements, naming time, and oral reading. *Journal of Experimental Psychology: Learning, Memory, and Cognition, 21*, 1412–1429.

Ford, M., & Holmes, V. M. (1978). Planning units and syntax in sentence production. *Cognition, 6*, 35–53.

Forde, E. M. E., & Humphreys, G. W. (1995). Refractory semantics in global aphasia: On semantic organization and the access–storage distinction in neuropsychology. *Memory, 3*, 265–308.

Forde, E. M. E., & Humphreys, G. W. (1997). A semantic locus for refractory behaviour: Implications for access–storage distinctions and the nature of semantic memory. *Cognitive Neuropsychology, 14*, 367–402.

Forster, K. I. (1976). Accessing the mental lexicon. In R. J. Wales & E. C. T. Walker (Eds.), *New approaches to language mechanisms* (pp. 257–287). Amsterdam: North Holland.

Forster, K. I. (1979). Levels of processing and the structure of the language processor. In W. E. Cooper & E. C. T. Walker (Eds.), *Sentence processing: Psycholinguistic studies presented to Merrill Garrett* (pp. 27–85). Hillsdale, NJ: Lawrence Erlbaum Associates, Inc.

Forster, K. I. (1981). Priming and effects of sentence and lexical contexts on naming time: Evidence of autonomous lexical processing. *Quarterly Journal of Experimental Psychology, 33A*, 465–495.

Forster, K. I. (1994). Computational modeling and elementary process analysis in visual word recognition. *Journal of Experimental Psychology: Human Perception and Performance, 20*, 1292–1310.

Forster, K. I. (2000). The potential for experimenter bias effects in word recognition experiments. *Memory and Cognition, 28*, 1109–1115.

Forster, K. I., & Chambers, S. M. (1973). Lexical access and naming time. *Journal of Verbal Learning and Verbal Behavior, 12*, 627–635.

Forster, K. I., & Davis, C. (1984). Repetition priming and frequency attenuation in lexical access. *Journal of Experimental Psychology: Learning, Memory, and Cognition, 10*, 680–698.

Forster, K. I., Davis, C., Schoknecht, C., & Carter, R. (1987). Masked priming with graphemically related forms: Repetition or partial activation? *Quarterly Journal of Experimental Psychology, 39*, 211–251.

Forster, K. I., & Olbrei, I. (1973). Semantic heuristics and syntactic analysis. *Cognition, 2*, 319–347.

Forster, K. I., & Veres, C. (1998). The prime lexicality effect: Form-priming as a function of prime awareness, lexical status, and discrimination difficulty. *Journal of Experimental Psychology: Learning, Memory, and Cognition, 24,* 498–514.

Foss, D. J. (1970). Some effects of ambiguity upon sentence comprehension. *Journal of Verbal Learning and Verbal Behavior, 9,* 699–706.

Foss, D. J., & Blank, M. A. (1980). Identifying the speech codes. *Cognitive Psychology, 12,* 1–31.

Foss, D. J., & Gernsbacher, M. A. (1983). Cracking the dual code: Toward a unitary model of phoneme identification. *Journal of Verbal Learning and Verbal Behavior, 22,* 609–632.

Foss, D. J., & Swinney, D. A. (1973). On the psychological reality of the phoneme: Perception, identification, and consciousness. *Journal of Verbal Learning and Verbal Behavior, 12,* 246–257.

Fouts, R. S., Fouts, D. H., & van Cantfort, T. E. (1989). The infant Loulis learns signs from cross-fostered chimpanzees. In R. A. Gardner, B. T. Gardner, & T. E. van Cantford (Eds.), *Teaching sign language to chimpanzees* (pp. 280–292). Albany, NY: Suny Press.

Fouts, R. S., Hirsch, A. D., & Fouts, D. H. (1982). Cultural transmission of a human language in a chimpanzee mother–infant relationship. In H. E. Fitzgerald, J. A. Mullins, & P. Gage (Eds.), *Child nurturance* (Vol. 3, pp. 159–193). New York: Plenum.

Fouts, R. S., Shapiro, G., & O'Neil, C. (1978). Studies of linguistic behaviour in apes and children. In P. Siple (Ed.), *Understanding language through sign language research* (pp. 163–185). London: Academic Press.

Fowler, A. E., Gelman, R., & Gleitman, L. R. (1994). The course of language learning in children with Down syndrome: Longitudinal and language level comparisons with young normally developing children. In H. Tager-Flusberg (Ed.), *Constraints on language acquisition: Studies of atypical children* (pp. 91–140). Hillsdale, NJ: Lawrence Erlbaum Associates, Inc.

Fox Tree, J. E., & Schrock, J. C. (1999). Discourse markers in spontaneous speech: Oh what a difference an oh makes. *Journal of Memory and Language, 40,* 280–295.

Foygel, D., & Dell, G. S. (2000). Models of impaired lexical access in speech production. *Journal of Memory and Language, 43,* 182–216.

Francis, W. N., & Kucera, H. (1982). *Frequency analysis of English usage.* Boston, MA: Houghton Mifflin.

Frank, S. L., & Bod, R. (2011). Insensitivity of the human sentence-processing system to hierarchical structure. *Psychological Science, 22,* 829–834.

Franklin, S., Howard, D., & Patterson, K. E. (1994). Abstract word deafness. *Cognitive Neuropsychology, 11,* 1–34.

Franklin, S., Turner, J., Lambon Ralph, M. A., Morris, J., & Bailey, P. J. (1996). A distinctive case of word meaning deafness? *Cognitive Neuropsychology, 13,* 1139–1162.

Frauenfelder, U., Segui, J., & Dijkstra, T. (1990). Lexical effects in phonemic processing: Facilitatory or inhibitory? *Journal of Experimental Psychology: Human Perception and Performance, 16,* 77–91.

Frauenfelder, U. H., & Tyler, L. K. (1987). The process of spoken word recognition: An introduction. *Cognition, 25,* 1–20.

Frazier, L. (1987a). Sentence processing: A tutorial review. In M. Coltheart (Ed.), *Attention and performance XII: The psychology of reading* (pp. 559–586). Hove, UK: Lawrence Erlbaum Associates.

Frazier, L. (1987b). Syntactic processing: Evidence from Dutch. *Natural Language and Linguistic Theory, 5,* 519–560.

Frazier, L. (1989). Against lexical generation of syntax. In W. Marslen-Wilson (Ed.), *Lexical representation and process* (pp. 505–258). Cambridge, MA: MIT Press.

Frazier, L. (1995). Constraint satisfaction as a theory of sentence processing. *Journal of Psycholinguistic Research, 24,* 437–468.

Frazier, L., Clifton, C., & Randall, J. (1983). Filling gaps: Decision principles and structure in sentence comprehension. *Cognition, 13,* 187–222.

Frazier, L., & Flores d'Arcais, G. B. (1989). Filler driven parsing: A study of gap filling in Dutch. *Journal of Memory and Language, 28,* 331–344.

Frazier, L., Flores d'Arcais, G. B., & Coolen, R. (1993). Processing discontinuous words: On the interface between lexical and syntactic processing. *Cognition, 47,* 219–249.

Frazier, L., & Fodor, J. D. (1978). The sausage machine: A new two-stage parsing model. *Cognition, 6,* 291–325.

Frazier, L., & Rayner, K. (1982). Making and correcting errors during sentence comprehension: Eye movements in the analysis of structurally ambiguous sentences. *Cognitive Psychology, 14,* 178–210.

Frazier, L., & Rayner, K. (1987). Resolution of syntactic category ambiguities: Eye movements in parsing lexically ambiguous sentences. *Journal of Memory and Language, 26,* 505–526.

Frazier, L., & Rayner, K. (1990). Taking on semantic commitments: Processing multiple meanings versus multiple senses. *Journal of Memory and Language, 29,* 181–200.

Freberg, L. A. (2006). *Discovering biological psychology.* Boston, MA: Houghton Mifflin.

Frederiksen, J. R., & Kroll, J. F. (1976). Spelling and sound: Approaches to the internal lexicon. *Journal of Experimental Psychology: Human Perception and Performance, 2,* 361–379.

Frege, G. (1892). Über Sinn und Bedeutung. *Zeitschrifte für Philosophie und Philosophische Kritik, 100,* 25–50. [Translated in P. T. Geach &

M. Black (Eds.), *Philosophical writings of Gottlob Frege* (1952). Oxford: Blackwell.]

Fremgen, A., & Fay, D. (1980). Overextensions in production and comprehension: A methodological clarification. *Journal of Child Language, 7,* 205–211.

Freud, S. (1975). *The psychopathology of everyday life* (Trans. A. Tyson). Harmondsworth, UK: Penguin. [Originally published 1901.]

Freudenthal, D., Pine, J., & Gobet, F. (2005). Simulating the cross-linguistic development of optional infinitive errors in MOSAIC. In B. G. Bara, L. Barsalou, & M. Buchiarelli (Eds.), *Proceedings of the 27th Annual Meeting of the Cognitive Science Society* (pp. 702–707). Mahwah, NJ: Lawrence Erlbaum Associates, Inc.

Freudenthal, D., Pine, J. M., & Gobet, F. (2006). Modelling the development of children's use of optional infinitives in English and Dutch using MOSAIC. *Cognitive Science, 30,* 277–310.

Friederici, A. D. (2002). Towards a neural basis of auditory sentence processing. *Trends in Cognitive Sciences, 6,* 78–84.

Friederici, A. D. (2012). The cortical language circuit: From auditory perception to sentence comprehension. *Trends in Cognitive Sciences, 16,* 262–268.

Friederici, A. D., Bahlmann, J., Heim, S., Schubotz, R. I., & Anwander, A. (2006). The brain differentiates human and non-human grammars: Functional localization and structural connectivity. *Proceedings of the National Academy of Sciences of the United States of America, 103,* 2458–2463.

Friederici, A. D., & Kilborn, K. (1989). Temporal constraints on language processing: Syntactic priming in Broca's aphasia. *Journal of Cognitive Neuroscience, 1,* 262–272.

Friedman, N. P., & Miyake, A. (2000). Differential roles for visuospatial and verbal working memory in situation model construction. *Journal of Experimental Psychology: General, 129,* 61–83.

Friedman, R. B. (1995). Two types of phonological alexia. *Cortex, 31,* 397–403.

Frith, U. (1985). Beneath the surface of developmental dyslexia. In K. E. Patterson, J. C. Marshall, & M. Coltheart (Eds.), *Surface dyslexia* (pp. 301–330). Hove, UK: Lawrence Erlbaum Associates.

Fromkin, V. A. (1971/1973). The non-anomalous nature of anomalous utterances. *Language, 51,* 696–719. [Reprinted in V. A. Fromkin (Ed.) (1973), *Speech errors as linguistic evidence* (pp. 215–242). The Hague: Mouton.]

Fromkin, V. A., Krashen, S., Curtiss, S., Rigler, D., & Rigler, M. (1974). The development of language in Genie: A case of language acquisition beyond the "Critical Period." *Brain and Language, 1,* 81–107.

Fromkin, V. A., Rodman, R., & Hyams, N. (2011). *An introduction to language* (9th ed.). Boston, MA: Thomson Heinle.

Frost, R. (1998). Toward a strong phonological theory of visual word recognition: True issues and false trails. *Psychological Bulletin, 123,* 71–99.

Frost, R., Forster, K. I., & Deutsch, A. (1997). What can we learn from the morphology of Hebrew? A masked priming investigation of morphological representation. *Journal of Experimental Psychology: Learning, Memory, and Cognition, 23,* 829–856.

Funnell, E. (1983). Phonological processes in reading: New evidence from acquired dyslexia. *British Journal of Psychology, 74,* 159–180.

Funnell, E. (1996). Response biases in oral reading: An account of the co-occurrence of surface dyslexia and semantic dementia. *Quarterly Journal of Experimental Psychology, 49A,* 417–446.

Funnell, E., & de Mornay Davies, P. (1996). JBR: A reassessment of concept familiarity and a category-specific disorder for living things. *Neurocase, 2,* 461–474.

Funnell, E., & Sheridan, J. (1992). Categories of knowledge? Unfamiliar aspects of living and non-living things. *Cognitive Neuropsychology, 9,* 135–153.

Furth, H. (1966). *Thinking without language.* London: Macmillan.

Furth, H. (1971). Linguistic deficiency and thinking: Research with deaf subjects 1964–69. *Psychological Bulletin, 75,* 58–72.

Furth, H. (1973). *Deafness and learning: A psychosocial approach.* Belmont, CA: Wadsworth.

Gaffan, D., & Heywood, C. A. (1993). A spurious category-specific visual agnosia for living things in normal human and nonhuman primates. *Journal of Cognitive Neuroscience, 5,* 118–128.

Gainotti, G., di Betta, A. M., & Silveri, M. C. (1996). The production of specific and generic associates of living and nonliving, high- and low-familiarity stimuli in Alzheimer's disease. *Brain and Language, 54,* 262–274.

Galaburda, A. M., Menard, M. T., & Rosen, G. D. (1994). Evidence for aberrant auditory anatomy in developmental dyslexia. *Proceedings of the National Academy of Sciences, 91,* 8010–8013.

Galaburda, A. M., Sherman, G. F., Rosen, G. D., Aboitiz, F., & Geschwind, N. (1985). Developmental dyslexia: Four consecutive patients with cortical anomalies. *Annals of Neurology, 18,* 222–233.

Galantucci, B., Fowler, C. A., & Turvey, M. T. (2006). The motor theory of speech perception reviewed. *Psychonomic Bulletin and Review, 13,* 361–377.

Gallaway, C., & Richards, B. J. (Eds.). (1994). *Input and interaction in language acquisition.* Cambridge: Cambridge University Press.

Galton, F. (1879). Psychometric experiments. *Brain, 2,* 149–162.

Ganong, W. F. (1980). Phonetic categorization in auditory word perception. *Journal of Experimental*

Psychology: Human Perception and Performance, 6, 110–125.

Garcia, L. J., & Joanette, Y. (1997). Analysis of conversational topic shifts: A multiple case study. *Brain and Language, 58,* 92–114.

Gardner, M. (1990). *Science: Good, bad, and bogus.* Loughton, UK: Prometheus Books.

Gardner, R. A., & Gardner, B. T. (1969). Teaching sign language to a chimpanzee. *Science, 165,* 664–672.

Gardner, R. A., & Gardner, B. T. (1975). Evidence for sentence constituents in the early utterances of child chimpanzee. *Journal of Experimental Psychology: General, 104,* 244–267.

Gardner, R. A., van Cantfort, T. E., & Gardner, B. T. (1992). Categorical replies to categorical questions by cross-fostered chimpanzees. *American Journal of Psychology, 105,* 27–57.

Garnham, A. (1983a). Why psycholinguists don't care about DTC: A reply to Berwick and Weinberg. *Cognition, 15,* 263–270.

Garnham, A. (1983b). What's wrong with story grammars. *Cognition, 15,* 145–154.

Garnham, A. (1985). *Psycholinguistics: Central topics.* London: Methuen.

Garnham, A. (1987). *Mental models as representation of discourse and text.* Chichester, UK: Horwood.

Garnham, A., & Oakhill, J. (1992). Discourse processing and text representation from a "mental models" perspective. *Language and Cognitive Processes, 7,* 193–204.

Garnham, A., Oakhill, J., & Johnson-Laird, P. N. (1982). Referential continuity and the coherence of discourse. *Cognition, 11,* 29–46.

Garnham, A., Shillcock, R. C., Brown, G. D. A., Mill, A. I. D., & Cutler, A. (1982). Slips of the tongue in the London–Lund corpus of spontaneous conversation. In A. Cutler (Ed.), *Slips of the tongue and language production* (pp. 251–263). Amsterdam: Mouton.

Garnica, O. (1977). Some prosodic and paralinguistic features of speech to young children. In C. E. Snow & C. A. Ferguson (Eds.), *Talking to children: Language input and acquisition* (pp. 63–88). Cambridge: Cambridge University Press.

Garnsey, S. M., Pearlmutter, N. J., Myers, E., & Lotocky, M. A. (1997). The contributions of verb bias and plausibility to the comprehension of temporarily ambiguous sentences. *Journal of Memory and Language, 37,* 58–93.

Garnsey, S. M., Tanenhaus, M. K., & Chapman, R. M. (1989). Evoked potentials and the study of sentence comprehension. *Journal of Psycholinguistic Research, 18,* 51–60.

Garrard, P., & Hodges, J. R. (2000). Semantic dementia: Clinical, radiological and pathological perspectives. *Journal of Neurology, 247,* 409–422.

Garrard, P., Maloney, L. M., Hodges, J. R., & Patterson, K. E. (2005). The effects of very early

Alzheimer's disease on the characteristics of writing by a renowned author. *Brain, 128,* 250–260.

Garrard, P., Patterson, K., Watson, P. C., & Hodges, J. R. (1998). Category specific semantic loss in dementia of Alzheimer's type: Functional–anatomical correlations from cross-sectional analyses. *Brain, 121,* 633–646.

Garrett, M. F. (1975). The analysis of sentence production. In G. Bower (Ed.), *The psychology of learning and motivation* (Vol. 9, pp. 133–177). New York: Academic Press.

Garrett, M. F. (1976). Syntactic processes in sentence production. In R. J. Wales & E. C. T. Walker (Eds.), *New approaches to language mechanisms* (pp. 231–255). Amsterdam: North Holland.

Garrett, M. F. (1980a). Levels of processing in sentence production. In B. Butterworth (Ed.), *Language production: Vol. 1. Speech and talk* (pp. 177–220). London: Academic Press.

Garrett, M. F. (1980b). The limits of accommodation. In V. Fromkin (Ed.), *Errors in linguistic performance: Slips of the tongue, ear, pen, and hand* (pp. 263–271). New York: Academic Press.

Garrett, M. F. (1982). Production of speech: Observations from normal and pathological language use. In A. W. Ellis (Ed.), *Normality and pathology in cognitive functions* (pp. 19–76). London: Academic Press.

Garrett, M. F. (1988). Processes in language production. In F. J. Newmeyer (Ed.), *Linguistics: The Cambridge survey: Vol. 3. Language: Psychological and biological aspects* (pp. 69–96). Cambridge: Cambridge University Press.

Garrett, M. F. (1992). Disorders of lexical selection. *Cognition, 42,* 143–180.

Garrett, M. F., Bever, T. G., & Fodor, J. A. (1966). The active use of grammar in speech perception. *Perception and Psychophysics, 1,* 30–32.

Garrod, S., & Anderson, A. (1987). Saying what you mean in dialogue: A study in conceptual and semantic co-ordination. *Cognition, 27,* 181–218.

Garrod, S. C., & Sanford, A. J. (1977). Interpreting anaphoric relations: The integration of semantic information while reading. *Journal of Verbal Learning and Verbal Behavior, 16,* 77–90.

Garrod, S. C., & Terras, M. (2000). The contribution of lexical and situational knowledge to resolving discourse roles: Bonding and resolution. *Journal of Memory and Language, 42,* 526–544.

Gaskell, G. (Ed.). (2007). *Oxford handbook of psycholinguistics.* Oxford: Oxford University Press.

Gaskell, M. G., & Marslen-Wilson, W. D. (1997). Integrating form and meaning: A distributed model of speech perception. *Language and Cognitive Processes, 12,* 613–656.

Gaskell, M. G., & Marslen-Wilson, W. D. (1998). Mechanisms of phonological inference in speech perception. *Journal of Experimental Psychology: Human Perception and Performance, 24,* 280–396.

Gaskell, M. G., & Marslen-Wilson, W. D. (2002). Representation and competition in the perception of spoken words. *Cognitive Psychology, 45,* 220–266.

Gathercole, S. E., Alloway, T. P., Willis, C., & Adams, A. (2006). Working memory in children with reading disabilities. *Journal of Experimental Child Psychology, 93,* 265–281.

Gathercole, S. E., & Baddeley, A. D. (1989). Evaluation of the role of phonological STM in the development of vocabulary in children: A longitudinal study. *Journal of Memory and Language, 28,* 200–213.

Gathercole, S. E., & Baddeley, A. D. (1990). Phonological memory deficits in language disordered children: Is there a causal connection? *Journal of Memory and Language, 29,* 336–360.

Gathercole, S. E., & Baddeley, A. D. (1993). *Working memory and language.* Hove, UK: Lawrence Erlbaum Associates.

Gathercole, S. E., & Baddeley, A. D. (1997). Sense and sensitivity in phonological memory and vocabulary development: A reply to Bowey (1996). *Journal of Experimental Child Psychology, 67,* 290–294.

Gathercole, V. C. (1985). "He has too much hard questions": The acquisition of the linguistic mass-count distinction in much and many. *Journal of Child Language, 12,* 395–415.

Gathercole, V. C. (1987). The contrastive hypothesis for the acquisition of word meaning: A reconsideration of the theory. *Journal of Child Language, 14,* 493–531.

Gathercole, V. C. (1989). Contrast: A semantic constraint? *Journal of Child Language, 16,* 685–702.

Gazdar, G., Klein, E., Pullum, G. K., & Sag, I. A. (1985). *Generalized phrase structure grammar.* Oxford: Blackwell.

Gazzaniga, M. S., Ivry, R. B., & Mangun, G. R. (2008). *Cognitive neuroscience: The biology of the mind* (3rd ed.). New York: Norton.

Gentner, D. (1978). On relational meaning: The acquisition of verb meaning. *Child Development, 49,* 988–998.

Gentner, D. (1981). Verb structures in memory for sentences: Evidence for componential representation. *Cognitive Psychology, 13,* 56–83.

Gentner, D. (1982). Why nouns are learned before verbs: Linguistic relativity vs. natural partitioning. In S. A. Kuczaj (Ed.), *Language development: Vol. 2. Language, thought, and culture* (pp. 301–334). Hillsdale, NJ: Lawrence Erlbaum Associates, Inc.

Gergely, G., & Bever, T. G. (1986). Related intuitions and the mental representation of causative verbs in adults and children. *Cognition, 23,* 211–277.

Gerken, L. (1994). Child phonology: Past research, present questions, future direction. In M. A. Gernsbacher

(Ed.), *Handbook of psycholinguistics* (pp. 781–820). San Diego, CA: Academic Press.

Gernsbacher, M. A. (1984). Resolving 20 years of inconsistent interactions between lexical familiarity and orthography, concreteness, and polysemy. *Journal of Experimental Psychology: General, 113,* 256–281.

Gernsbacher, M. A. (1990). *Language comprehension as structure building.* Hillsdale, NJ: Lawrence Erlbaum Associates, Inc.

Gernsbacher, M. A. (1997). Group differences in suppression skill. *Aging, Neuropsychology, and Cognition, 4,* 175–184.

Gernsbacher, M. A., & Hargreaves, D. J. (1988). Accessing sentence participants: The advantage of first mention. *Journal of Memory and Language, 27,* 699–717.

Gernsbacher, M. A., Hargreaves, D. J., & Beeman, M. (1989). Building and accessing clausal representations: The advantage of first mention versus the advantage of clause recency. *Journal of Memory and Language, 28,* 735–755.

Gernsbacher, M. A., Varner, K. R., & Faust, M. (1990). Investigating differences in general comprehension skill. *Journal of Experimental Psychology: Learning, Memory, and Cognition, 16,* 430–445.

Gerrig, R. (1986). Processes and products of lexical access. *Language and Cognitive Processes, 1,* 187–196.

Gertner, Y., Fisher, C., & Eisengart, J. (2006). Learning words and rules: Abstract knowledge of word order in early sentence comprehension. *Psychological Science, 17,* 684–691.

Geschwind, N. (1972). Language and the brain. *Scientific American, 226,* 76–83.

Gibbs, R. W. (1980). Spilling the beans on understanding and memory for idioms in conversation. *Memory and Cognition, 8,* 149–156.

Gibbs, R. W. (1986a). On the psycholinguistics of sarcasm. *Journal of Experimental Psychology: General, 115,* 3–15.

Gibbs, R. W. (1986b). What makes some indirect speech acts conventional? *Journal of Memory and Language, 25,* 181–196.

Gibson, E. (1998). Linguistic complexity: Locality of syntactic dependencies. *Cognition, 68,* 1–76.

Gibson, E., & Thomas, J. (1999). Memory limitations and structural forgetting: The perception of complex ungrammatical sentences as grammatical. *Language and Cognitive Processes, 14,* 225–248.

Gibson, J. J. (1979). *The ecological approach to perception.* Boston, MA: Houghton Mifflin.

Gilhooly, K. J. (1984). Word age-of-acquisition and residence time in lexical memory as factors in word naming. *Current Psychological Research, 3,* 24–31.

Gillette, J., Gleitman, H., Gleitman, L., & Lederer, A. (1999). Human simulations of vocabulary learning. *Cognition, 73,* 135–176.

Glaser, W. R. (1992). Picture naming. *Cognition, 42,* 61–105.

Gleason, H. A. (1961). *An introduction to descriptive linguistics.* New York: Holt, Rinehart & Winston.

Gleason, J. B., Hay, D., & Crain, L. (1989). The social and affective determinants of language development. In M. Rice & R. Schiefelbusch (Eds.), *The teachability of language* (pp. 171–186). Baltimore, MD: Paul Brookes.

Gleason, J. B., & Ratner, N. B. (1993). Language development in children. In J. B. Gleason & N. B. Ratner (Eds.), *Psycholinguistics* (pp. 301–350). Fort Worth, TX: Harcourt Brace Jovanovich.

Gleick, J. (1987). *Chaos.* London: Sphere Books.

Gleitman, L. R. (1981). Maturational determinants of language growth. *Cognition, 10,* 105–113.

Gleitman, L. R. (1990). The structural sources of word meaning. *Language Acquisition, 1,* 3–55.

Gleitman, L. R., Cassidy, K., Nappa, R., Papafragou, A., & Trueswell, J. C. (2005). Hard words. *Language Learning and Development, 1,* 23–64.

Gleitman, L. R., & Papafragou, A. (2005). Language and thought. In K. J. Holyoak & R. Morrison (Eds.), *The Cambridge handbook of thinking and reasoning.* Cambridge: Cambridge University Press.

Gleitman, L. R., & Wanner, E. (1982). Language acquisition: The state of the state of the art. In E. Wanner & L. R. Gleitman (Eds.), *Language acquisition: The state of the art* (pp. 3–48). Cambridge: Cambridge University Press.

Glenberg, A. (2007). Language and action: Creating sensible combinations of ideas. In M. G. Gaskell (Ed.), *Oxford handbook of psycholinguistics* (pp. 362–370). Oxford: Oxford University Press.

Glenberg, A. M., Meyer, M., & Lindem, K. (1987). Mental models contribute to foregrounding during text comprehension. *Journal of Memory and Language, 26,* 69–83.

Glenberg, A. M., & Robertson, D. A. (2000). Symbol grounding and meaning: A comparison of high-dimensional and embodied theories of meaning. *Journal of Memory and Language, 43,* 379–401.

Gluck, M. A., & Bower, G. H. (1988). From conditioning to category learning: An adaptive network model. *Journal of Experimental Psychology: General, 8,* 37–50.

Glucksberg, S. (1991). Beyond literal meanings: The psychology of allusion. *Psychological Science, 2,* 146–152.

Glucksberg, S., Gildea, P., & Bookin, H. B. (1982). On understanding nonliteral speech: Can people ignore metaphors? *Journal of Verbal Learning and Verbal Behavior, 21,* 85–98.

Glucksberg, S., & Keysar, B. (1990). Understanding metaphorical comparisons: Beyond similarity. *Psychological Review, 97,* 3–18.

Glucksberg, S., Kreuz, R. J., & Rho, S. H. (1986). Context can constrain lexical access: Implications for models of language comprehension. *Journal of Experimental Psychology: Learning, Memory, and Cognition, 12,* 323–335.

Glucksberg, S., & Weisberg, R. W. (1966). Verbal behavior and problem solving: Some effects of labeling in a functional fixedness problem. *Journal of Experimental Psychology, 71,* 659–664.

Glushko, R. J. (1979). The organization and activation of orthographic knowledge in reading aloud. *Journal of Experimental Psychology: Human Perception and Performance, 5,* 674–691.

Goffman, E. (1967). *Interaction ritual: Essays on face to face behavior.* Garden City, NY: Anchor Books.

Gold, E. M. (1967). Language identification in the limit. *Information and Control, 16,* 447–474.

Goldberg, E., & Costa, L. D. (1981). Hemisphere differences in the acquisition and use of descriptive systems. *Brain and Language, 14,* 144–173.

Goldfield, B. A. (1993). Noun bias in maternal speech to one-year-olds. *Journal of Child Language, 20,* 85–99.

Goldiamond, I., & Hawkins, W. F. (1958). Vexierversuch: The logarithmic relationship between word-frequency and recognition obtained in the absence of stimulus words. *Journal of Experimental Psychology, 56,* 457–463.

Goldin-Meadow, S., Butcher, C., Mylander, C., & Dodge, M. (1994). Nouns and verbs in a self-styled gesture system: What's in a name? *Cognitive Psychology, 27,* 259–319.

Goldin-Meadow, S., Mylander, C., & Butcher, C. (1995). The resilience of combinatorial structure at the word level: Morphology in self-styled gesture systems. *Cognition, 56,* 195–262.

Goldinger, S. D., Luce, P. A., & Pisoni, D. B. (1989). Priming lexical neighbours of spoken words: Effects of competition and inhibition. *Journal of Memory and Language, 28,* 501–518.

Goldman-Eisler, F. (1958). Speech production and the predictability of words in context. *Quarterly Journal of Experimental Psychology, 10,* 96–106.

Goldman-Eisler, F. (1968). *Psycholinguistics: Experiments in spontaneous speech.* London: Academic Press.

Golinkoff, R. M., Hirsh-Pasek, K., Bailey, L. M., & Wenger, N. R. (1992). Young children and adults use lexical principles to learn new nouns. *Developmental Psychology, 28,* 99–108.

Golinkoff, R. M., Mervis, C. B., & Hirsh-Pasek, K. (1994). Early object labels: The case for lexical principles. *Journal of Child Language, 21,* 125–155.

Gollan, T. H., & Acenas, L. R. (2004). What is a TOT? Cognate and translation effects on tip-of-the-tongue states in Spanish–English and Tagalog–English bilinguals. *Journal of Experimental Psychology: Learning, Memory, and Cognition, 30,* 246–269.

Gollan, T. H., & Brown, A. S. (2006). From tip-of-the-tongue (TOT) data to theoretical implications in two steps: When more TOTs means better retrieval. *Journal of Experimental Psychology: General, 135*, 462–483.

Gombert, J. E. (1992). *Metalinguistic development* (Trans. T. Pownall, originally published 1990). London: Harvester Wheatsheaf.

Gomez, R. L., & Gerken, L. (2000). Infant artificial language learning and language acquisition. *Trends in Cognitive Sciences, 4*, 178–186.

Gonnerman, L. M., Andersen, E. S., Devlin, J. T., Kempler, D., & Seidenberg, M. S. (1997). Double dissociation of semantic categories in Alzheimer's disease. *Brain and Language, 57*, 254–279.

Good, D. A., & Butterworth, B. (1980). Hesitancy as a conversational resource: Some methodological implications. In H. W. Dechert & M. Raupach (Eds.), *Temporal variables in speech* (pp. 145–152). The Hague: Mouton.

Goodglass, H. (1976). Agrammatism. In H. Whitaker & H. A. Whitaker (Eds.), *Studies in neurolinguistics* (Vol. 1, pp. 237–260). New York: Academic Press.

Goodglass, H., & Geschwind, N. (1976). Language disorders (aphasia). In E. C. Carterette & M. P. Friedman (Eds.), *Handbook of perception: Vol. VII. Language and speech* (pp. 389–428). New York: Academic Press.

Goodglass, H., & Menn, L. (1985). Is agrammatism a unitary phenomenon? In M.-L. Kean (Ed.), *Agrammatism* (pp. 1–26). New York: Academic Press.

Goodluck, H. (1991). *Language acquisition: A linguistic introduction*. Oxford: Blackwell.

Gopnik, M. (1990a). Dysphasia in an extended family. *Nature, 344*, 715.

Gopnik, M. (1990b). Feature blindness: A case study. *Language Acquisition, 1*, 139–164.

Gopnik, M. (1992). A model module? *Cognitive Neuropsychology, 9*, 253–258.

Gopnik, M., & Crago, M. B. (1991) Familial aggregation of a developmental language disorder. *Cognition, 29*, 1–50.

Gopnik, M., & Meltzoff, A. N. (1997). *Words, thoughts, and theories*. Cambridge, MA: MIT Press.

Gordon, B., & Caramazza, A. (1982). Lexical decision for open and closed-class words: Failure to replicate differential frequency sensitivity. *Brain and Language, 15*, 143–160.

Gordon, P. (1985). Evaluating the semantic categories hypothesis: The case of the count/mass distinction. *Cognition, 20*, 209–242.

Gordon, P. (2004). Numerical cognition without words: Evidence from Amazonia. *Science, 306*, 496–499.

Gordon, P. C., Grosz, B. J., & Gilliom, L. A. (1993). Pronouns, names, and the centering of attention in discourse. *Cognitive Science, 17*, 311–347.

Gordon, P. C., Hendrick, R., & Levine, W. H. (2002). Memory-load interference in syntactic processing. *Psychological Science, 13*, 425–430.

Gordon, P. C., & Meyer, D. E. (1984). Perceptual-motor processing of phonetic features. *Journal of Experimental Psychology: Human Perception and Performance, 10*, 153–178.

Goswami, U. (1986). Children's use of analogy in learning to read: A developmental study. *Journal of Experimental Child Psychology, 42*, 73–83.

Goswami, U. (1988). Orthographic analogies and reading development. *Quarterly Journal of Experimental Psychology, 40A*, 239–268.

Goswami, U. (1993). Towards an interactive analogy model of reading development: Decoding vowel graphemes in beginning reading. *Journal of Experimental Child Psychology, 56*, 443–475.

Goswami, U., & Bryant, P. (1990). *Phonological skills and learning to read*. Hove, UK: Lawrence Erlbaum Associates.

Goswami, U., Wang, H., Cruz, A., Fosker, T., Mead, N., & Huss, M. (2011). Language-universal sensory deficits in developmental dyslexia: English, Spanish, and Chinese. *Journal of Cognitive Neuroscience, 23*, 325–337.

Goswami, U., Ziegler, J. C., & Richardson, U. (2005). The effects of spelling consistency on phonological awareness: A comparison of English and German. *Journal of Experimental Child Psychology, 92*, 345–365.

Gotts, S. J., & Plaut, D. C. (2002). The impact of synaptic depression following brain damage: A connectionist account of "access/refractory" and "degraded-store" semantic impairments. *Cognitive, Affective, and Behavioral Neuroscience, 2*, 187–213.

Gough, P. B. (1972). One second of reading. In J. F. Kavanaugh & I. G. Mattingly (Eds.), *Language by ear and by eye* (pp. 331–358). Cambridge, MA: MIT Press.

Goulandris, A., & Snowling, M. (1991). Visual memory deficits: A plausible case of developmental dyslexia? Evidence from a single case study. *Cognitive Neuropsychology, 8*, 127–154.

Graesser, A. C., Singer, M., & Trabasso, T. (1994). Constructing inferences during narrative text comprehension. *Psychological Review, 101*, 371–395.

Graf, P., & Torrey, J. W. (1966). Perception of phrase structure in written language. *American Psychological Association Convention Proceedings*, 83–88.

Graham, K. S., Hodges, J. R., & Patterson, K. (1994). The relationship between comprehension and oral reading in progressive fluent aphasia. *Neuropsychologia, 32*, 299–316.

Grainger, J. (1990). Word frequency and neighborhood frequency effects in lexical decision and naming. *Journal of Memory and Language, 29*, 228–244.

Grainger, J., & Jacobs, A. M. (1996). Orthographic processing in visual word recognition: A multiple read-out model. *Psychological Review, 103*, 518–565.

Grainger, J., Lété, B., Bertand, D., Dufau, S., & Ziegler, J. C. (2012). Evidence for multiple routes in learning to read. *Cognition, 123*, 280–292.

Grainger, J., O'Regan, K., Jacobs, A. M., & Segui, J. (1989). On the role of competing word units in visual word recognition: The neighbourhood frequency effect. *Perception and Psychophysics, 45*, 189–195.

Green, D. W. (1986). Control, activation, and resource: A framework and a model for the control of speech in bilinguals. *Brain and Language, 27*, 210–223.

Greenberg, J. H. (1963). Some universals of grammar with particular reference to the order of meaningful elements. In J. H. Greenberg (Ed.), *Universals of language* (pp. 58–90). Cambridge, MA: MIT Press.

Greene, J. (1972). *Psycholinguistics*. Harmondsworth, UK: Penguin.

Greenfield, P. M., & Savage-Rumbaugh, E. S. (1990). Grammatical combinations in *Pan paniscus*: Processes of learning and invention in the evolution and development of language. In S. T. Parker & K. R. Gibson (Eds.), *"Language" and intelligence in monkeys and apes: Comparative developmental perspectives* (pp. 540–578). New York: Cambridge University Press.

Greenfield, P. M., & Smith, J. H. (1976). *The structure of communication in early language development*. New York: Academic Press.

Gregory, R. L. (1961). The brain as an engineering problem. In W. H. Thorpe & O. L. Zangwill (Eds.), *Current problems in animal behaviour* (pp. 547–565). London: Methuen.

Grice, H. P. (1975). Logic and conversation. In P. Cole & J. Morgan (Eds.), *Syntax and semantics: Vol. 3. Speech acts* (pp. 41–58). New York: Academic Press.

Griffin, Z. M. (2001). Gaze durations during speech reflect word selection and phonological encoding. *Cognition, 82*, B1–B14.

Griffin, Z. M. (2004). The eyes are right when the mouth is wrong. *Psychological Science, 15*, 814–821.

Griffin, Z. M., & Bock, K. (1998). Constraint, word frequency, and the relationship between lexical processing levels in spoken word production. *Journal of Memory and Language, 38*, 313–338.

Griffin, Z. M., & Bock, K. (2000). What the eyes say about speaking. *Psychological Science, 11*, 274–279.

Griffin, Z. M., & Oppenheimer, D. M. (2006). Speakers gaze at objects while preparing intentionally inaccurate labels for them. *Journal of Experimental Psychology: Learning, Memory, and Cognition, 32*, 943–948.

Grober, E. H., Beardsley, W., & Caramazza, A. (1978). Parallel function in pronoun assignment. *Cognition, 6*, 117–133.

Grodzinsky, Y. (1984). The syntactic characterization of agrammatism. *Cognition, 16*, 88–120.

Grodzinsky, Y. (1989). Agrammatic comprehension of relative clauses. *Brain and Language, 37*, 480–499.

Grodzinsky, Y. (1990). *Theoretical perspectives on language deficits*. Cambridge, MA: MIT Press.

Grodzinsky, Y. (2000). The neurology of syntax: Language use without Broca's area. *Behavioral and Brain Sciences, 23*, 1–71.

Grodzinsky, Y., & Friederici, A. D. (2006). Neuroimaging of syntax and syntactic processing. *Current Opinion in Neurobiology, 16*, 240–246.

Grosjean, F. (1980). Spoken word recognition processes and the gating paradigm. *Perception and Psychophysics, 28*, 267–283.

Grosjean, F. (1997). Processing mixed languages: Issues, findings, and models. In A. de Groot & J. Kroll (Eds.), *Tutorials in bilingualism: Psycholinguistic perspectives* (pp. 225–254). Mahwah, NJ: Lawrence Erlbaum Associates, Inc.

Grosjean, F., & Frauenfelder, U. H. (1996). A guide to spoken word recognition paradigms: Introduction. *Language and Cognitive Processes, 11*, 553–558.

Grosjean, F., & Gee, J. P. (1987). Prosodic structure and spoken word recognition. *Cognition, 25*, 135–155.

Grosjean, F., & Soares, C. (1986). Processing mixed language: Some preliminary findings. In J. Vaid (Ed.), *Linguistics processing in bilinguals: Psycholinguistic and neuropsychological perspectives* (pp. 145–179). Hillsdale, NJ: Lawrence Erlbaum Associates, Inc.

Grossman, M., Mickanin, J., Robinson, K. M., & d'Esposito, M. (1996). Anomaly judgements of subject–predicate relations in Alzheimer's disease. *Brain and Language, 54*, 216–232.

Grosz, B. J., Joshi, A. K., & Weinstein, S. (1995). Centering: A framework for modeling the local coherence of discourse. *Computational Linguistics, 21*, 203–225.

Gumperz, J. J., & Levinson, S. C. (1996). *Rethinking linguistic relativity*. Cambridge: Cambridge University Press.

Gupta, P., & MacWhinney, B. (1997). Vocabulary acquisition and verbal short-term memory: Computational and neural bases. *Brain and Language, 59*, 267–333.

Haarmann, H. J., Just, M. A., & Carpenter, P. A. (1997). Aphasic sentence comprehension as a resource deficit: A computational approach. *Brain and Language, 59*, 76–120.

Haarmann, H. J., & Kolk, H. H. J. (1991). Syntactic priming in Broca's aphasics: Evidence for slow activation. *Aphasiology, 5*, 247–263.

Haber, R. N., & Haber, L. R. (1982). Does silent reading involve articulation? Evidence from tongue-twisters. *American Journal of Psychology, 95*, 409–419.

Hadzibeganovic, T., van den Noort, M., Bosch, P., Perc, M., van Kralingen, R., Mondt, K., &

Coltheart, M. (2010). Cross-linguistic neuroimaging and dyslexia: A critical view. *Cortex, 46,* 1312–1316.

Hagoort, P. (2008). Should psychology ignore the language of the brain? *Current Directions in Psychological Science, 17,* 96–101.

Hagoort, P., Brown, C. M., & Groothusen, J. (1993). The syntactic positive shift as an ERP-measure of syntactic processing. *Language and Cognitive Processes, 8,* 439–483.

Hakuta, K. (1986). *Mirror of language.* New York: Basic Books.

Hakuta, K., & Diaz, R. (1985). The relationship between degree of bilingualism and cognitive ability: A critical discussion and some new longitudinal data. In K. E. Nelson (Ed.), *Children's language* (Vol. 5, pp. 319–344). Hillsdale, NJ: Lawrence Erlbaum Associates, Inc.

Haldane, J. B. S. (1927). A mathematic theory of natural and artificial selection, Part V: Selection and mutation. *Proceedings of the Cambridge Philosophical Society, 23,* 838–844.

Hale, J. T. (2010). What a rational parser would do. *Cognitive Science, 35,* 399–443.

Hale, S. (2002). *The man who lost his language.* Harmondsworth, UK: Penguin Books.

Hall, D. G. (1993). Basic-level individuals. *Cognition, 48,* 199–221.

Hall, D. G. (1994). How mothers teach basic-level and situation-restricted count nouns. *Journal of Child Language, 21,* 391–414.

Hall, D. G., & Waxman, S. R. (1993). Assumptions about word meaning: Individuation and basic-level kinds. *Child Development, 64,* 1550–1570.

Halle, M., & Stevens, K. N. (1962). Speech recognition: A model and a program for research. *IRE Transactions of the Professional Group on Information Theory, 8,* 155–159.

Hampton, J. A. (1979). Polymorphous concepts in semantic memory. *Journal of Verbal Learning and Verbal Behavior, 18,* 441–461.

Hampton, J. A. (1981). An investigation of the nature of abstract concepts. *Memory and Cognition, 9,* 149–156.

Hanley, J. R., Hastie, K., & Kay, J. (1992). Developmental surface dyslexia and dysgraphia: An orthographic processing impairment. *Quarterly Journal of Experimental Psychology, 44A,* 285–320.

Hanley, J. R., & McDonnell, V. (1997). Are reading and spelling phonologically mediated? Evidence from a patient with a speech production impairment. *Cognitive Neuropsychology, 14,* 3–33.

Hanten, G., & Martin, R. C. (2000). Contributions of phonological and semantic short-term memory to sentence processing: Evidence from two cases of close head injury in children. *Journal of Memory and Language, 43,* 335–361.

Harley, B., & Wang, W. (1997). The critical period hypothesis: Where are we now? In A. M. B. de Groot & J. F. Kroll (Eds.), *Tutorials in bilingualism: Psycholinguistic perspectives* (pp. 19–51). Mahwah, NJ: Lawrence Erlbaum Associates, Inc.

Harley, T. A. (1984). A critique of top-down independent levels models of speech production: Evidence from non-plan-internal speech production. *Cognitive Science, 8,* 191–219.

Harley, T. A. (1990). Paragrammatisms: Syntactic disturbance or failure of control? *Cognition, 34,* 85–91.

Harley, T. A. (1993a). Phonological activation of semantic competitors during lexical access in speech production. *Language and Cognitive Processes, 8,* 291–309.

Harley, T. A. (1993b). Connectionist approaches to language disorders. *Aphasiology, 7,* 221–249.

Harley, T. A. (1998). The semantic deficit in dementia: Connectionist approaches to what goes wrong in picture naming. *Aphasiology, 12,* 299–318.

Harley, T. A. (2004a). Does cognitive neuropsychology have a future? *Cognitive Neuropsychology, 21* (Special Issue; Lead article), 3–16.

Harley, T. A. (2004b). Promises, promises. *Cognitive Neuropsychology, 21* (Special Issue; Reply to commentators), 51–56.

Harley, T. A. (2010). *Talking the talk: Language, psychology and science.* Hove, UK: Psychology Press.

Harley, T. A., & Bown, H. E. (1998). What causes a tip-of-the-tongue state? Evidence for lexical neighbourhood effects in speech production. *British Journal of Psychology, 89,* 151–174.

Harley, T. A., & MacAndrew, S. B. G. (1992). Modelling paraphasias in normal and aphasic speech. In *Proceedings of the 14th Annual Conference of the Cognitive Science Society* (pp. 378–383). Hillsdale, NJ: Lawrence Erlbaum Associates, Inc.

Harm, M. W., & Seidenberg, M. S. (1999). Phonology, reading acquisition, and dyslexia: Insights from connectionist models. *Psychological Review, 106,* 491–528.

Harm, M. W., & Seidenberg, M. S. (2001). Are there orthographic impairments in phonological dyslexia? *Cognitive Neuropsychology, 18,* 71–92.

Harm, M. W., & Seidenberg, M. S. (2004). Computing the meanings of words in reading: Cooperative division of labor between visual words and phonological processes. *Psychological Review, 111,* 662–720.

Harris, M. (1978). Noun animacy and the passive voice: A developmental approach. *Quarterly Journal of Experimental Psychology, 30,* 495–504.

Harris, M., & Coltheart, M. (1986). *Language processing in children and adults.* London: Routledge & Kegan Paul.

Harris, M., & Hatano, G. (Eds.). (1999). *Learning to read and write: A cross-linguistic perspective.* Cambridge: Cambridge University Press.

Harris, P. L. (1982). Cognitive prerequisites to language? *British Journal of Psychology, 73,* 187–195.

Harris, R. J. (1977). Comprehension of pragmatic implications in advertising. *Journal of Applied Psychology, 63,* 603–608.

Harris, R. J. (1978). The effect of jury size and judge's instructions on memory for pragmatic implications from courtroom testimony. *Bulletin of the Psychonomic Society, 11,* 129–132.

Harris, Z. S. (1951). *Methods in structural linguistics.* Chicago: University of Chicago Press.

Harste, J., Burke, C., & Woodward, V. (1982). Children's language and world: Initial encounters with print. In J. Langer & M. Smith-Burke (Eds.), *Bridging the gap: Reader meets author* (pp. 105–131). Newark, DE: International Reading Association.

Hart, J., Berndt, R. S., & Caramazza, A. (1985). Category-specific naming deficit following cerebral infarction. *Nature, 316,* 439–440.

Hart, J., & Gordon, B. (1992). Neural subsystems for object knowledge. *Nature, 359,* 60–64.

Hartley, T., & Houghton, G. (1996). A linguistically constrained model of short-term memory for nonwords. *Journal of Memory and Language, 35,* 1–31.

Hartsuiker, R. J., Anton-Méndez, I., Roelstraete, B., & Costa, A. (2006). Spoonish Spanerisms: A lexical bias effect in Spanish. *Journal of Experimental Psychology: Learning, Memory, and Cognition, 32,* 949–953.

Hartsuiker, R. J., & Kolk, H. H. J. (1998). Syntactic facilitation in agrammatic sentence production. *Brain and Language, 62,* 221–254.

Hartsuiker, R. J., Kolk, H. H. J., & Huiskamp, P. (1999). Priming word order in sentence production. *Quarterly Journal of Experimental Psychology, 52A,* 129–147.

Hartsuiker, R. J., Pickering, M. J., & Veltkamp, E. (2004). Is syntax separate or shared between languages? Cross-linguistic syntactic priming in Spanish/English bilinguals. *Psychological Science, 15,* 409–414.

Hartsuiker, R. J., & Westenberg, C. (2000). Word order priming in written and spoken sentence production. *Cognition, 75,* B27–B39.

Haskell, T. R., & MacDonald, M. C. (2003). Conflicting cues and competition in subject–verb agreement. *Journal of Memory and Language, 48,* 760–778.

Haskell, T. R., MacDonald, M. C., & Seidenberg, M. S. (2003). Language learning and innateness: Some implications of compounds research. *Cognitive Psychology, 47,* 119–163.

Hatcher, P. J., Hulme, C., & Ellis, A. W. (1994). Ameliorating early reading failure by integrating the teaching of reading and phonological skills: The phonological linkage hypothesis. *Child Development, 65,* 41–57.

Hauk, O., Johnsrude, I., & Pulvermuller, F. (2004). Somatotopic representation of action words in human motor and premotor cortex. *Neuron, 41,* 301–307.

Hauser, M. D., Chomsky, N., & Fitch, W. T. (2002). The faculty of language: What is it, who has it, and how did it evolve? *Science, 298,* 1569–1579.

Hauser, M. D., Newport, E. L., & Aslin, R. N. (2001). Segmentation of the speech stream in a non-human primate: Statistical learning in cotton-top tamarins. *Cognition, 78,* B53–B64.

Haviland, S. E., & Clark, H. H. (1974). What's new? Acquiring new information as a process of comprehension. *Journal of Verbal Learning and Verbal Behavior, 13,* 515–521.

Hawkins, J. A. (1990). A parsing theory of word order universals. *Linguistic Inquiry, 21,* 223–261.

Hayes, C. (1951). *The ape in our house.* New York: Harper.

Hayes, J. R., & Flower, L. S. (1980). Identifying the organisation of writing processes. In L. W. Gregg & E. R. Sternberg (Eds.), *Cognitive processes in writing* (pp. 3–30). Hillsdale, NJ: Lawrence Erlbaum Associates, Inc.

Hayes, J. R., & Flower, L. S. (1986). Writing research and the writer. *American Psychologist, 41,* 1106–1113.

Hayes, K. J., & Nissen, C. H. (1971). Higher mental functions of a home-raised chimpanzee. In A. M. Schrier & F. Stollnitz (Eds.), *Behaviour of nonhuman primates* (Vol. 4, pp. 60–115). New York: Academic Press.

Haywood, S. L., Pickering, M. J., & Branigan, H. P. (2005). Do speakers avoid ambiguities during dialogue? *Psychological Science, 16,* 362–366.

Healy, A., & Miller, G. (1970). The verb as the main determinant of sentence meaning. *Psychonomic Science, 20,* 372.

Heath, S. B. (1983). *Ways with words.* Cambridge: Cambridge University Press.

Hebb, D. O. (1949). *The organization of behavior.* New York: Wiley.

Heider, E. R. (1971). "Focal" color areas and the development of color names. *Developmental Psychology, 4,* 447–455.

Heider, E. R. (1972). Universals in colour naming and memory. *Journal of Experimental Psychology, 93,* 10–20.

Heit, E., & Barsalou, L. W. (1996). The instantiation principle in natural categories. *Memory, 4,* 413–451.

Hemforth, B., & Konieczny, L. (1999). *German sentence processing.* Dordrecht: Kluwer Academic Publishers.

Henderson, A., Goldman-Eisler, F., & Skarbek, A. (1966). Sequential temporal patterns in speech. *Language and Speech, 8,* 236–242.

Henderson, J. M., & Ferreira, F. (Eds.). (2004). *The interface of language, vision, and action:*

Eye movements and the visual word. New York: Psychology Press.

Henderson, L. (1982). *Orthography and word recognition in reading*. London: Academic Press.

Herman, L. M., Richards, D. G., & Wolz, J. P. (1984). Comprehension of sentences by bottlenosed dolphins. *Cognition, 16*, 129–219.

Herrnstein, R., Loveland, D., & Cable, C. (1977). Natural concepts in pigeons. *Journal of Experimental Psychology: Animal Learning and Memory, 2*, 285–302.

Hespos, S. J., & Spelke, E. (2004). Conceptual precursors to language. *Nature, 430*, 453–456.

Hess, D. J., Foss, D. J., & Carroll, P. (1995). Effects of global and local context on lexical processing during language comprehension. *Journal of Experimental Psychology: General, 124*, 62–82.

Hickerson, N. P. (1971). Review of "Basic Color Terms." *International Journal of American Linguistics, 37*, 257–270.

Hickok, G., & Poeppel, D. (2004). Dorsal and ventral streams: A framework for understanding aspects of the functional anatomy of language. *Cognition, 92*, 67–99.

Hieke, A. E., Kowal, S. H., & O'Connell, D. C. (1983). The trouble with "articulatory" pauses. *Language and Speech, 26*, 203–214.

Hill, R. L., & Murray, W. S. (2000). Commas and spaces: Effects of punctuation on eye movements and sentence parsing. In A. Kennedy, R. Radach, D. Heller, & J. Pynte (Eds.), *Reading as a perceptual process* (pp. 565–589). Oxford: Elsevier.

Hillis, A. (2002). *Handbook of adult language disorders*. Hove, UK: Psychology Press.

Hillis, A. E., Boatman, D., Hart, J., & Gordon, B. (1999). Making sense out of jargon: A neurolinguistic and computational account of jargon aphasia. *Neurology, 53*, 1813–1824.

Hillis, A. E., & Caramazza, A. (1991a). Category-specific naming and comprehension impairment: A double dissociation. *Brain, 114*, 2081–2094.

Hillis, A. E., & Caramazza, A. (1991b). Mechanisms for accessing lexical representations for output: Evidence from a category-specific semantic deficit. *Brain and Language, 40*, 106–144.

Hillis, A. E., & Caramazza, A. (1995). Representation of grammatical categories of words in the brain. *Journal of Cognitive Neuroscience, 7*, 396–407.

Hillis, A. E., Tuffiash, E., & Caramazza, A. (2002). Modality-specific deterioration in naming verbs in nonfluent primary progressive aphasia. *Journal of Cognitive Neuroscience, 14*, 1099–1108.

Hinton, G. E. (1989). Deterministic Boltzmann learning performs steepest descent in weight-space. *Neural Computation, 1*, 143–150.

Hinton, G. E. (1992). How neural networks learn from experience. *Scientific American, 267*, 105–109.

Hinton, G. E., Plaut, D. C., & Shallice, T. (1993). Simulating brain damage. *Scientific American, 269*, 58–65.

Hinton, G. E., & Sejnowski, T. J. (1986). Learning and relearning in Boltzmann machines. In D. E. Rumelhart, J. L. McClelland, & the PDP Research Group, *Parallel distributed processing: Explorations in the microstructure of cognition: Vol. 1. Foundations* (pp. 282–317). Cambridge, MA: MIT Press.

Hinton, G. E., & Shallice, T. (1991). Lesioning an attractor network: Investigations of acquired dyslexia. *Psychological Review, 98*, 74–95.

Hintzman, D. L. (1986). "Schemata abstraction" in a multiple-trace memory model. *Psychological Review, 93*, 411–428.

Hirsh, K. W., & Ellis, A. W. (1994). Age of acquisition and lexical processing in aphasia: A case study. *Cognitive Neuropsychology, 11*, 435–458.

Hirsh-Pasek, K., Kemler-Nelson, D. G., Jusczyk, P. W., Cassidy, K. W., Druss, B., & Kennedy, L. (1987). Clauses are perceptual units for young infants. *Cognition, 26*, 269–286.

Hirsh-Pasek, K., Reeves, L. M., & Golinkoff, R. M. (1993). Words and meaning: From primitives to complex organisation. In J. Berko Gleason & N. B. Ratner (Eds.), *Psycholinguistics* (pp. 134–199). Fort Worth, TX: Harcourt Brace.

Hirsh-Pasek, K., Treiman, R., & Schneiderman, M. (1984). Brown and Hanlon revisited: Mothers' sensitivity to ungrammatical forms. *Journal of Child Language, 11*, 81–88.

Hladik, E. G., & Edwards, H. T. (1984). A comparative analysis of mother–father speech in the naturalistic home environment. *Journal of Psycholinguistic Research, 13*, 321–332.

Hockett, C. F. (1960). The origin of speech. *Scientific American, 203*, 89–96.

Hodges, J. R., & Greene, J. D. W. (1998). Knowing about people and naming them: Can Alzheimer's disease patients do one without the other? *Quarterly Journal of Experimental Psychology, 51A*, 121–134.

Hodges, J. R., Patterson, K. E., Oxbury, S., & Funnell, E. (1992). Semantic dementia: Progressive fluent aphasia with temporal lobe atrophy. *Brain, 115*, 1783–1806.

Hodges, J. R., Salmon, D. P., & Butters, N. (1991). The nature of the naming deficit in Alzheimer's and Huntington's disease. *Brain, 114*, 1547–1558.

Hodgson, J. M. (1991). Informational constraints on pre-lexical priming. *Language and Cognitive Processes, 6*, 169–205.

Hoff, E. (2003). The specificity of environmental influence: Socioeconomic status affects early vocabulary development via maternal speech. *Child Development, 74*, 1368–1378.

Hoff, E., & Naigles, L. (2002). How children use input to acquire a lexicon. *Child Development, 73*, 418–433.

Hoff-Ginsberg, E. (1997). *Language development.* Pacific Grove, CA: Brooks/Cole.

Hoffman, C., Lau, I., & Johnson, D. R. (1986). The linguistic relativity of person cognition. *Journal of Personality and Social Psychology, 51*, 1097–1105.

Hogaboam, T. W., & Perfetti, C. A. (1975). Lexical ambiguity and sentence comprehension: The common sense effect. *Journal of Verbal Learning and Verbal Behavior, 14*, 265–275.

Holender, D. (1986). Semantic activation without conscious identification in dichotic listening, parafoveal vision, and visual masking: A survey and appraisal. *Behavioral and Brain Sciences, 9*, 1–23.

Hollan, J. D. (1975). Features and semantic memory: Set-theoretic or network model? *Psychological Review, 82*, 154–155.

Hollich, G., Hirsh-Pasek, K., & Golinkoff, R. (2000). *Breaking the language barrier: An emergentist coalition of word learning.* Oxford: Blackwell.

Holmes, V. M. (1988). Hesitations and sentence planning. *Language and Cognitive Processes, 3*, 323–361.

Holmes, V. M., & O'Reagan, J. K. (1981). Eye fixation patterns during the reading of relative clause sentences. *Journal of Verbal Learning and Verbal Behavior, 20*, 417–430.

Holtgraves, T. (1998). Interpreting indirect replies. *Cognitive Psychology, 37*, 1–27.

Holyoak, K. J., & Glass, A. L. (1975). The role of contradictions and counter-examples in the rejection of false sentences. *Journal of Verbal Learning and Verbal Behavior, 14*, 215–239.

Horton, W. S., & Gerrig, R. J. (2005). The impact of memory demands on audience design during language production. *Cognition, 96*, 127–142.

Howard, D. (1995). Lexical anomia: Or the case of the missing lexical entries. *Quarterly Journal of Experimental Psychology, 48A*, 999–1023.

Howard, D. (1997). Language in the brain. In M. D. Rugg (Ed.), *Cognitive neuroscience* (pp. 277–304). Hove, UK: Psychology Press.

Howard, D., & Best, W. (1996). Developmental phonological dyslexia: Real word reading can be completely normal. *Cognitive Neuropsychology, 13*, 887–934.

Howard, D., & Butterworth, B. (1989). Short-term memory and sentence comprehension: A reply to Vallar and Baddeley, 1987. *Cognitive Neuropsychology, 6*, 455–463.

Howard, D., & Franklin, S. (1988). *Missing the meaning?* Cambridge, MA: MIT Press.

Howard, D., & Hatfield, F. M. (1987). *Aphasia therapy: Historical and contemporary issues.* Hove, UK: Lawrence Erlbaum Associates.

Howard, D., & Orchard-Lisle, V. (1984). On the origin of semantic errors in naming: Evidence from the case of a global aphasic. *Cognitive Neuropsychology, 1*, 163–190.

Howe, C. (1980). Language learning from mothers' replies. *First Language, 1*, 83–97.

Howes, D. H., & Solomon, R. L. (1951). Visual duration threshold as a function of word probability. *Journal of Experimental Psychology, 41*, 401–410.

Hulme, C. (1981). *Reading retardation and multisensory learning.* London: Routledge & Kegan Paul.

Hulme, C., Muter, V., & Snowling, M. (1998). Segmentation does predict early progress in learning to read better than rhyme: A reply to Bryant. *Journal of Experimental Child Psychology, 71*, 39–44.

Hulme, C., & Snowling, M. (1992). Deficits in output phonology: An explanation of reading failure. *Cognitive Neuropsychology, 9*, 47–72.

Hulme, C., Snowling, M., Caravolas, M., & Carroll, J. (2005). Phonological skills are (probably) one cause of success in learning to read. *Scientific Studies of Reading, 9*, 351–366.

Humphreys, G. W. (1985). Attention, automaticity, and autonomy in visual word processing. In D. Besner, T. G. Waller, & G. E. MacKinnon (Eds.), *Reading research: Advances in theory and practice* (Vol. 5, pp. 253–310). New York: Academic Press.

Humphreys, G. W., Besner, D., & Quinlan, P. T. (1988). Event perception and the word repetition effect. *Journal of Experimental Psychology: General, 117*, 51–67.

Humphreys, G. W., & Rumiati, R. I. (1998). Agnosia without prosopagnosia or alexia: Evidence for stored visual memories specific to objects. *Cognitive Neuropsychology, 15*, 243–277.

Hunt, E., & Agnoli, F. (1991). The Whorfian hypothesis: A cognitive psychology perspective. *Psychological Review, 99*, 377–389.

Hurford, J. R. (2003). The neural basis of predicate-argument structure. *Behavioral and Brain Sciences, 26*, 261–316.

Hurst, J. A., Baraitser, M., Auger, E., Graham, F., & Norell, S. (1990). An extended family with a dominantly inherited speech disorder. *Developmental Medicine and Child Neurology, 32*, 347–355.

Huttenlocher, J., Smiley, P., & Charney, R. (1983). The emergence of action categories in the child: Evidence from verb meanings. *Psychological Review, 90*, 72–93.

Huttenlocher, J., Vasilyeva, M., Cymerman, E., & Levine, S. (2002). Language input and child syntax. *Cognitive Psychology, 45*, 337–374.

Huttenlocher, J., Waterfall, H., Vasilyeva, M., Vevea, J., & Hedges, L. V. (2010). Sources of variability in children's language growth. *Cognitive Psychology, 61*, 343–365.

Indefrey, P., & Levelt, W. J. M. (2000). The neural correlates of language production. In M. Gazzaniga

(Ed.), *The new cognitive neurosciences* (2nd ed., pp. 845–865). Cambridge, MA: MIT Press.

Indefrey, P., & Levelt, W. J. M. (2004). The spatial and temporal signatures of word production components. *Cognition, 92,* 101–144.

Inhoff, A. W. (1984). Two stages of word processing during eye fixations in the reading of prose. *Journal of Verbal Learning and Verbal Behavior, 23,* 612–624.

Ivanova, I., Pickering, M. J., McLean, J. F., Costa, A., & Branigan, H. P. (2012). How do people produce ungrammatical utterances? *Journal of Memory and Language, 67,* 355–370.

Jackendoff, R. (1977). *X-bar syntax: A study of phrase structure.* Cambridge, MA: MIT Press.

Jackendoff, R. (1983). *Semantics and cognition.* Cambridge, MA: MIT Press.

Jackendoff, R. (1987). On beyond zebra: The relation of linguistic and visual information. *Cognition, 26,* 89–114.

Jackendoff, R. (1999). Possible stages in the evolution of the language capacity. *Trends in Cognitive Sciences, 3,* 272–279.

Jackendoff, R. (2002). *Foundations of language.* Oxford: Oxford University Press.

Jackendoff, R. (2003). Précis of *Foundations of language: Brain, meaning, grammar, evolution. Behavioral and Brain Sciences, 26,* 651–707.

Jackendoff, R., & Pinker, S. (2005). The nature of the language faculty and its implications for evolution of language (Reply to Fitch, Hauser, and Chomsky). *Cognition, 97,* 211–225.

Jacobsen, E. (1932). The electrophysiology of mental activities. *American Journal of Psychology, 44,* 677–694.

Jacoby, L. L. (1983). Perceptual enhancement: Persistent effects of an experience. *Journal of Experimental Psychology: Learning, Memory, and Cognition, 15,* 930–940.

Jacoby, L. L., & Dallas, M. (1981). On the relationship between autobiographical memory and perceptual learning. *Journal of Experimental Psychology: General, 110,* 306–340.

Jaeger, J. J., Lockwood, A. H., Kemmerer, D., van Valin, R. D., Murphy, B. W., & Khalak, H. G. (1996). A positron emission tomographic study of regular and irregular verb morphology in English. *Language, 72,* 451–497.

Jaffe, J., Breskin, S., & Gerstman, L. J. (1972). Random generation of apparent speech rhythms. *Language and Speech, 15,* 68–71.

Jakobson, R. (1968). *Child language, aphasia and phonological universals.* The Hague: Mouton.

James, L. E., & Burke, D. M. (2000). Phonological priming effects on word retrieval and tip-of-the-tongue experiences in young and older adults. *Journal of Experimental Psychology: Learning, Memory, and Cognition, 26,* 1378–1391.

James, S. L., & Khan, L. M. L. (1982). Grammatical morpheme acquisition: An approximately invariant order? *Journal of Psycholinguistic Research, 11,* 381–388.

Jared, D. (1997a). Evidence that strategy effects in word naming reflect changes in output timing rather than changes in processing route. *Journal of Experimental Psychology: Learning, Memory, and Cognition, 23,* 1424–1438.

Jared, D. (1997b). Spelling–sound consistency affects the naming of high-frequency words. *Journal of Memory and Language, 36,* 505–529.

Jared, D., Levy, B. A., & Rayner, K. (1999). The role of phonology in the activation of word meanings during reading: Evidence from proofreading and eye movements. *Journal of Experimental Psychology: General, 128,* 219–264.

Jared, D., McRae, K., & Seidenberg, M. S. (1990). The basis of consistency effects in word naming. *Journal of Memory and Language, 29,* 687–715.

Jared, D., & Seidenberg, M. S. (1991). Does word identification proceed from spelling to sound to meaning? *Journal of Experimental Psychology: General, 120,* 358–394.

Jarvella, R. J. (1971). Syntactic processing of connected speech. *Journal of Verbal Learning and Verbal Behavior, 10,* 409–416.

Jastrzembski, J. E. (1981). Multiple meanings, number of related meanings, frequency of occurrence, and the lexicon. *Cognitive Psychology, 13,* 278–305.

Jescheniak, J. D., & Levelt, W. J. M. (1994). Word frequency effects in speech production: Retrieval of syntactic information and of phonological form. *Journal of Experimental Psychology: Learning, Memory, and Cognition, 20,* 824–843.

Jescheniak, J. D., Meyer, A. S., & Levelt, W. J. M. (2003). Specific-word frequency is not all that counts in speech production: Comments on Caramazza, Costa, et al. (2001) and new experimental data. *Journal of Experimental Psychology: Learning, Memory, and Cognition, 29,* 432–438.

Jescheniak, J. D., Schriefers, H., & Hantsch, A. (2003). Utterance format affects phonological priming in the picture–word task: Implications for models of phonological encoding in speech production. *Journal of Experimental Psychology: Human Perception and Performance, 29,* 441–454.

Jin, Y.-S. (1990). Effects of concreteness on cross-language priming in lexical decisions. *Perceptual and Motor Skills, 70,* 1139–1154.

Joanisse, M. F., & Seidenberg, M. S. (1998). Specific language impairment: A deficit in grammar or processing? *Trends in Cognitive Sciences, 2,* 240–247.

Joanisse, M. F., & Seidenberg, M. S. (1999). Impairments in verb morphology after brain injury: A connectionist model. *Proceedings of the National Academy of Sciences USA, 96,* 7592–7597.

Joanisse, M. F., & Seidenberg, M. S. (2005). Imaging the past: Neural activation in frontal and temporal regions during regular and irregular past tense processing. *Cognitive, Affective and Behavioral Neuroscience, 5*, 282–296.

Job, R., Miozzo, M., & Sartori, G. (1993). On the existence of category-specific impairments: A reply to Parkin and Stewart. *Quarterly Journal of Experimental Psychology, 46A*, 511–516.

Johnson, E. K., & Jusczyk, P. W. (2001). Word segmentation by 8-month-olds: When speech cues count more than statistics. *Journal of Memory and Language, 44*, 548–567.

Johnson, E. K., Jusczyk, P. W., Cutler, A., & Norris, D. (2003). Lexical viability constraints on speech segmentation by infants. *Cognitive Psychology, 46*, 65–97.

Johnson, J. S., & Newport, E. L. (1989). Critical period effects in second language learning: The influence of maturational state on the acquisition of English as a second language. *Cognitive Psychology, 21*, 60–99.

Johnson, K. E., & Mervis, C. B. (1997). Effects of varying levels of expertise on the basic level of categorization. *Journal of Experimental Psychology: General, 126*, 248–277.

Johnson, R. E. (1970). Recall of prose as a function of the structural importance of the linguistic units. *Journal of Verbal Learning and Verbal Behavior, 9*, 12–90.

Johnson-Laird, P. N. (1975). Meaning and the mental lexicon. In A. Kennedy & A. Wilkes (Eds.), *Studies in long-term memory* (pp. 123–142). London: John Wiley.

Johnson-Laird, P. N. (1978). What's wrong with Grandma's guide to procedural semantics: A reply to Jerry Fodor. *Cognition, 6*, 249–261.

Johnson-Laird, P. N. (1983). *Mental models*. Cambridge: Cambridge University Press.

Johnson-Laird, P. N., Herrman, D. J., & Chaffin, R. (1984). Only connections: A critique of semantic networks. *Psychological Bulletin, 96*, 292–315.

Johnston, R. S., & Watson, J. E. (2004). Accelerating the development of reading, spelling and phonemic awareness skills in initial readers. *Reading and Writing, 17*, 327–357.

Johnston, R. S., & Watson, J. E. (2005). *The effects of synthetic phonics teaching on reading and spelling attainment: A seven year longitudinal study*. The Scottish Executive, available at http://www.scotland.gov.uk/Publications/2005/02/20688/52449.

Jolicoeur, P., Gluck, M. A., & Kosslyn, S. M. (1984). Pictures and names: Making the connection. *Cognitive Psychology, 16*, 243–275.

Jones, G. V. (1985). Deep dyslexia, imageability, and ease of predication. *Brain and Language, 24*, 1–19.

Jones, G. V. (1989). Back to Woodworth: Role of interlopers in the tip-of-the-tongue phenomenon. *Memory and Cognition, 17*, 69–76.

Jones, G. V., & Langford, S. (1987). Phonological blocking in the tip of the tongue state. *Cognition, 26*, 115–122.

Jones, G. V., & Martin, M. (1985). Deep dyslexia and the right-hemisphere hypothesis for semantic paralexia: A reply to Marshall and Patterson. *Neuropsychologia, 23*, 685–688.

Jones, L. L., & Estes, Z. (2005). Metaphor comprehension as attributive categorization. *Journal of Memory and Language, 53*, 110–124.

Jorm, A. F. (1979). The cognitive and neurological basis of developmental dyslexia: A theoretical framework and review. *Cognition, 7*, 19–32.

Jorm, A. F., & Share, D. L. (1983). Phonological recoding and reading acquisition. *Applied Psycholinguistics, 4*, 103–147.

Jusczyk, P. W. (1982). Auditory versus phonetic coding of speech signals during infancy. In J. Mehler, E. C. T. Walker, & M. Garrett (Eds.), *Perspectives on mental representation* (pp. 361–387). Hillsdale, NJ: Lawrence Erlbaum Associates, Inc.

Just, M. A., & Carpenter, P. A. (1980). A theory of reading: From eye fixations to comprehension. *Psychological Review, 87*, 329–354.

Just, M. A., & Carpenter, P. A. (1987). *The psychology of reading and language comprehension*. Newton, MA: Allyn & Bacon.

Just, M. A., & Carpenter, P. A. (1992). A capacity theory of comprehension: Individual differences in working memory. *Psychological Review, 99*, 122–149.

Just, M. A., Carpenter, P. A., & Keller, T. A. (1996). The capacity theory of comprehension: New frontiers of evidence and arguments. *Psychological Review, 103*, 773–780.

Just, M. A., & Varma, S. (2002). A hybrid architecture for working memory: Reply to MacDonald and Christiansen. *Psychological Review, 109*, 55–65.

Kail, R., & Nippold, M. A. (1984). Unconstrained retrieval from semantic memory. *Child Development, 55*, 944–951.

Kako, E. (1999a). Elements of syntax in the systems of three language-trained animals. *Animal Learning and Behavior, 27*, 1–14.

Kako, E. (1999b). Response to Pepperberg; Herman and Uyeyama; and Shanker, Savage-Rumbaugh, and Taylor. *Animal Learning and Behavior, 27*, 26–27.

Kamide, Y., Altmann, G. T. M., & Haywood, S. L. (2003). The time-course of prediction in incremental sentence processing: Evidence from anticipatory eye movements. *Journal of Memory and Language, 49*, 133–156.

Kaminski, J., Call, J., & Fischer, J. (2004). Word learning in a domestic dog: Evidence for "fast mapping." *Science, 304*, 1682–1683.

Kanwisher, N. (1987). Repetition blindness: Type recognition without token individuation. *Cognition, 27*, 117–143.

Kanwisher, N., & Potter, M. C. (1990). Repetition blindness: Levels of processing. *Journal of Experimental Psychology: Human Perception and Performance, 16*, 30–47.

Karmiloff-Smith, A. (1986). From meta-process to conscious access: Evidence from metalinguistic and repair data. *Cognition, 23*, 95–147.

Katz, J. J. (1977). The real status of semantic representations. *Linguistic Inquiry, 8*, 559–584.

Katz, J. J., & Fodor, J. A. (1963). The structure of a semantic theory. *Language, 39*, 170–210.

Kaufer, D., Hayes, J. R., & Flower, L. S. (1986). Composing written sentences. *Research in the Teaching of English, 20*, 121–140.

Kaup, B., & Zwaan, R. A. (2003). Effects of negational and situational presence on the accessibility of text information. *Journal of Experimental Psychology: Learning, Memory, and Cognition, 29*, 439–446.

Kawamoto, A. (1993). Nonlinear dynamics in the resolution of lexical ambiguity: A parallel distributed processing account. *Journal of Memory and Language, 32*, 474–516.

Kay, D. A., & Anglin, J. M. (1982). Overextension and underextension in the child's expressive and receptive speech. *Journal of Child Language, 9*, 83–98.

Kay, J. (1985). Mechanisms of oral reading: A critical appraisal of cognitive models. In A. W. Ellis (Ed.), *Progress in the psychology of language* (Vol. 2, pp. 73–105). Hove, UK: Lawrence Erlbaum Associates.

Kay, J., & Bishop, D. (1987). Anatomical differences between nose, palm, foot. Or, the body in question: Further dissection of the processes of sub-lexical spelling–sound translation. In M. Coltheart (Ed.), *Attention and performance XII: The psychology of reading* (pp. 449–469). Hove, UK: Lawrence Erlbaum Associates.

Kay, J., & Ellis, A. W. (1987). A cognitive neuropsychological case study of anomia: Implications for psychological models of word retrieval. *Brain, 110*, 613–629.

Kay, J., Lesser, R., & Coltheart, M. (1992). *Psycholinguistic assessments of language processing in aphasia (PALPA): An introduction*. Hove, UK: Lawrence Erlbaum Associates.

Kay, J., & Marcel, A. J. (1981). One process, not two in reading aloud: Lexical analogies do the work of nonlexical rules. *Quarterly Journal of Experimental Psychology, 33A*, 397–414.

Kay, P., & Kempton, W. (1984). What is the Sapir–Whorf hypothesis? *American Anthropologist, 86*, 65–79.

Kean, M.-L. (1977). The linguistic interpretation of aphasic syndromes: Agrammatism in Broca's aphasia, an example. *Cognition, 5*, 9–46.

Keenan, J. M., MacWhinney, B., & Mayhew, D. (1977). Pragmatics in memory: A study of natural conversation. *Journal of Verbal Learning and Verbal Behavior, 16*, 549–560.

Kegl, J., Senghas, A., & Coppola, M. (1999). Creations through contact: Sign language emergence and sign language change in Nicaragua. In M. DeGraff (Ed.), *Comparative grammatical change: The intersection of language acquisition, Creole genesis, and diachronic syntax* (pp. 179–237). Cambridge, MA: MIT Press.

Kellas, G., Ferraro, F. R., & Simpson, G. B. (1988). Lexical ambiguity and the time-course of attentional allocation in word recognition. *Journal of Experimental Psychology: Human Perception and Performance, 14*, 601–609.

Kellogg, R. T. (1988). Attentional overload and writing performance. *Journal of Experimental Psychology: Learning, Memory, and Cognition, 14*, 355–365.

Kellogg, W. N., & Kellogg, L. A. (1933). *The ape and the child*. New York: McGraw-Hill.

Kelly, M. H. (1992). Using sound to solve syntactic problems: The role of phonology in grammatical category assignments. *Psychological Review, 99*, 349–364.

Kelly, M. H., Bock, J. K., & Keil, F. C. (1986). Prototypicality in a linguistic context: Effects on sentence structure. *Journal of Memory and Language, 25*, 59–74.

Kelter, S., Kaup, B., & Claus, B. (2004). Representing a described sequence of events: A dynamic view of narrative comprehension. *Journal of Experimental Psychology: Learning, Memory, and Cognition, 30*, 451–464.

Kempen, G., & Huijbers, P. (1983). The lexicalization process in sentence production and naming: Indirect election of words. *Cognition, 14*, 185–209.

Kendon, A. (1967). Some functions of gaze direction in social interaction. *Acta Psychologica, 26*, 22–63.

Kennedy, A. (2000). Parafoveal processing in word recognition. *Quarterly Journal of Experimental Psychology, 53A*, 429–455.

Kennedy, A., Murray, W. S., Jennings, F., & Reid, C. (1989). Parsing complements: Comments on the generality of the principle of minimal attachment. *Language and Cognitive Processes, 4*, 51–76.

Kennison, S. M. (2001). Limitations on the use of verb information during sentence comprehension. *Psychonomic Bulletin and Review, 8*, 132–138.

Kennison, S. M., & Trofe, J. L. (2004). Comprehending pronouns: A role for word-specific gender stereotype information. *Journal of Psycholinguistic Research, 32*, 355–378.

Kersten, A. W., & Earles, J. L. (2001). Less really is more for adults learning a miniature artificial language. *Journal of Memory and Language, 44,* 250–273.

Kess, J. F., & Miyamoto, T. (1999). *The Japanese mental lexicon: Psycholinguistic studies of Kana and Kanji processing.* Amsterdam: John Benjamins.

Keysar, B. (1989). On the functional equivalence of literal and metaphorical interpretations of discourse. *Journal of Memory and Language, 28,* 375–385.

Keysar, B., Barr, D. J., Balin, J. A., & Paek, T. S. (1998). Definite reference and mutual knowledge: Process models of common ground in comprehension. *Journal of Memory and Language, 39,* 1–20.

Keysar, B., & Henly, A. S. (2002). Speakers' overestimation of their effectiveness. *Psychological Science, 13,* 207–212.

Kiger, J. I., & Glass, A. L. (1983). The facilitation of lexical decisions by a prime occurring after the target. *Memory and Cognition, 11,* 356–365.

Kilborn, K. (1994). Learning language late: Second language acquisition in adults. In M. A. Gernsbacher (Ed.), *Handbook of psycholinguistics* (pp. 917–944). San Diego, CA: Academic Press.

Kim, H. S. (2002). We talk, therefore we think? A cultural analysis of the effect of talking on thinking. *Journal of Personality and Social Psychology, 83,* 828–842.

Kimball, J. (1973). Seven principles of surface structure parsing in natural language. *Cognition, 2,* 15–47.

Kinoshita, S., & Lupker, S. J. (2003). *Masked priming: State of the art.* New York: Psychology Press.

Kintsch, W. (1974). *The representation of meaning in memory.* Hillsdale, NJ: Lawrence Erlbaum Associates, Inc.

Kintsch, W. (1979). On modelling comprehension. *Educational Psychologist, 14,* 3–14.

Kintsch, W. (1980). Semantic memory: A tutorial. In R. S. Nickerson (Ed.), *Attention and performance XIII* (pp. 595–620). Hillsdale, NJ: Lawrence Erlbaum Associates, Inc.

Kintsch, W. (1988). The use of knowledge in discourse processing: A construction-integration model. *Psychological Review, 95,* 163–182.

Kintsch, W. (1994). The psychology of discourse processing. In M. A. Gernsbacher (Ed.), *Handbook of psycholinguistics* (pp. 721–740). San Diego, CA: Academic Press.

Kintsch, W., & Bates, E. (1977). Recognition memory for statements from a classroom lecture. *Journal of Experimental Psychology: Human Learning and Memory, 3,* 187–197.

Kintsch, W., & Keenan, J. M. (1973). Reading rate and retention as a function of the number of propositions in the base structure of sentences. *Cognitive Psychology, 5,* 257–274.

Kintsch, W., & van Dijk, T. A. (1978). Toward a model of text comprehension and production. *Psychological Review, 85,* 363–394.

Kintsch, W., & Vipond, D. (1979). Reading comprehension and readability in educational practice and psychological theory. In L. G. Nilsson (Ed.), *Perspectives in memory research* (pp. 329–366). Hillsdale, NJ: Lawrence Erlbaum Associates, Inc.

Kintsch, W., Welsch, D., Schmalhofer, F., & Zimny, S. (1990). Sentence memory: A theoretical analysis. *Journal of Memory and Language, 29,* 133–159.

Kiparsky, P., & Menn, L. (1977). On the acquisition of phonology. In J. Macnamara (Ed.), *Language learning and thought* (pp. 47–78). New York: Academic Press.

Kirshner, H. S., Webb, W. G., & Kelly, M. P. (1984). The naming order of dementia. *Neuropsychologia, 22,* 23–30.

Kirsner, K., Smith, M., Lockhart, R. S., King, M. L., & Jain, M. (1984). The bilingual lexicon: Language-specific units in an integrated network. *Journal of Verbal Learning and Verbal Behavior, 23,* 519–539.

Klapp, S. T. (1974). Syllable-dependent pronunciation latencies in number naming, a replication. *Journal of Experimental Psychology, 102,* 1138–1140.

Klapp, S. T., Anderson, W. G., & Berrian, R. (1973). Implicit speech in reading considered. *Journal of Experimental Psychology, 100,* 368–374.

Klatt, D. H. (1989). Review of selected models of speech perception. In W. Marslen-Wilson (Ed.), *Lexical representation and process* (pp. 169–226). Cambridge, MA: MIT Press.

Klee, T., & Fitzgerald, M. D. (1985). The relation between grammatical development and mean length of utterance in morphemes. *Journal of Child Language, 12,* 251–269.

Klein, W. (1986). *Second language acquisition.* Cambridge: Cambridge University Press.

Klima, E. S., & Bellugi, U. (1979). *The signs of language.* Cambridge, MA: Harvard University Press.

Kluender, R., & Kutas, M. (1993). Bridging the gap: Evidence from ERPs on the processing of unbounded dependencies. *Journal of Cognitive Neuroscience, 5,* 196–214.

Knutsen, D., & Le Bigot, L. (2012). Managing dialogue: How information availability affects collaborative reference production. *Journal of Memory and Language, 67,* 326–341.

Kohn, S. E. (1984). The nature of the phonological disorder in conduction aphasia. *Brain and Language, 23,* 97–115.

Kohn, S. E., & Friedman, R. B. (1986). Word-meaning deafness: A phonological–semantic dissociation. *Cognitive Neuropsychology, 3,* 291–308.

Kohn, S. E., Wingfield, A., Menn, L., Goodglass, H., Gleason, J. B., & Hyde, M. (1987). Lexical retrieval: The tip-of-the-tongue phenomenon. *Applied Psycholinguistics, 8,* 245–266.

Kolb, B., & Whishaw, I. Q. (2009). *Fundamentals of human neuropsychology* (6th ed.). New York: W. H. Freeman & Co.

Kolk, H. H. J. (1978). The linguistic interpretation of Broca's aphasia: A reply to M.-L. Kean. *Cognition, 6,* 353–361.

Kolk, H. H. J. (1995). A time-based approach to agrammatic production. *Brain and Language, 50,* 282–303.

Kolk, H. H. J., & van Grunsven, M. (1985). Agrammatism as a variable phenomenon. *Cognitive Neuropsychology, 2,* 347–384.

Komatsu, L. K. (1992). Recent views of conceptual structure. *Psychological Bulletin, 112,* 500–526.

Kornai, A., & Pullum, G. K. (1990). The X-bar theory of phrase structure. *Language, 66,* 24–50.

Kounios, J., & Holcomb, P. J. (1992). Structure and process in semantic memory: Evidence from event-related brain potentials and reaction times. *Journal of Experimental Psychology: General, 121,* 459–479.

Kounios, J., & Holcomb, P. J. (1994). Concreteness effects in semantic processing: ERP evidence supporting dual-coding theory. *Journal of Experimental Psychology: Learning, Memory, and Cognition, 20,* 804–823.

Kraljic, T., & Brennan, S. E. (2005). Prosodic disambiguation of syntactic structure: For the speaker or for the addressee? *Cognitive Psychology, 50,* 194–231.

Krashen, S. D. (1982). *Principles and practices in second language acquisition.* Oxford: Pergamon.

Krashen, S. D., Long, M., & Scarcella, R. (1982). Age, rate, and eventual attainment in second language acquisition. In S. D. Krashen, R. Scarcella, & M. Long (Eds.), *Child–adult differences in second language acquisition* (pp. 161–172). Rowley, MA: Newbury House.

Kraus, N. (2012). Atypical brain oscillations: A biological basis for dyslexia? *Trends in Cognitive Sciences, 16,* 12–13.

Kremin, H. (1985). Routes and strategies in surface dyslexia and dysgraphia. In K. E. Patterson, J. C. Marshall, & M. Coltheart (Eds.), *Surface dyslexia: Neuropsychological and cognitive studies of phonological reading* (pp. 105–137). Hove, UK: Lawrence Erlbaum Associates.

Kroll, J. F., & Stewart, E. (1994). Category interference in translation and picture naming: Evidence for asymmetric connections between bilingual memory representations. *Journal of Memory and Language, 33,* 149–174.

Kruschke, J. K. (1992). ALCOVE: An exemplar-based connectionist model of category learning. *Psychological Review, 99,* 22–44.

Kucera, H., & Francis, W. N. (1967). *Computational analysis of present-day American English.* Providence, RI: Brown University Press.

Kuczaj, S. A. (1977). The acquisition of regular and irregular past tense forms. *Journal of Verbal Learning and Verbal Behavior, 16,* 589–600.

Kuhl, P. K. (1981). Discrimination of speech by non-human animals: Basic auditory sensitivities conducive to the perception of speech-sound categories. *Journal of the Acoustical Society of America, 70,* 340–349.

Kursaal Flyers (1976). *Little does she know/Drinking socially.* CBS 4689. Producer: Mike Batt.

Kutas, M. (1993). In the company of other words: Electrophysiological evidence for single-word and sentence context effects. *Language and Cognitive Processes, 8,* 533–572.

Kutas, M., DeLong, K. A., & Smith, N. J. (2011). A look around at what lies ahead: Prediction and predictability in language processing. In M. Bar (Ed.), *Predictions in the brain: Using our past to generate a future* (pp. 190–207). Oxford: Oxford University Press.

Kutas, M., & Hillyard, S. A. (1980). Reading senseless sentences: Brain potentials reflect semantic incongruity. *Science, 207,* 203–205.

Kutas, M., & van Petten, C. (1994). Psycholinguistics electrified: Event-related brain potential investigations. In M. A. Gernsbacher (Ed.), *Handbook of psycholinguistics* (pp. 83–143). San Diego, CA: Academic Press.

Kyle, J. G., & Woll, B. (1985). *Sign language: The study of deaf people and their language.* Cambridge: Cambridge University Press.

La Heij, W., Hooglander, A., Kerling, R., & van der Velden, E. (1996). Nonverbal context effects in forward and backward translation: Evidence for concept mediation. *Journal of Memory and Language, 35,* 648–665.

Labov, W. (1973). The boundaries of words and their meanings. In C.-J. Bailey & R. W. Shuy (Eds.), *New ways of analyzing variations in English* (pp. 340–373). Washington, DC: Georgetown University Press.

Labov, W., & Fanshel, D. (1977). *Therapeutic discourse: Psychotherapy as conversation.* New York: Academic Press.

Lackner, J. R., & Garrett, M. F. (1972). Resolving ambiguity: Effects of biasing context in the unattended ear. *Cognition, 1,* 359–372.

Lado, R. (1957). *Linguistics across cultures.* Ann Arbor: University of Michigan Press.

Lai, C. S. L., Fisher, S. E., Hurst, J. A., Vargha-Khadem, F., & Monaco, A. P. (2001). A forkhead-domain gene is mutated in a severe speech and language disorder. *Nature, 413,* 519–523.

Laiacona, M., Barbarotto, R., & Capitani, E. (1993). Perceptual and associative knowledge in category specific impairment of semantic memory: A study of two cases. *Cortex, 29,* 727–740.

Laine, M., & Martin, N. (1996). Lexical retrieval deficit in picture naming: Implications for word production models. *Brain and Language, 53,* 283–314.

Laing, E., & Hulme, C. (1999). Phonological and semantic processes influence beginning readers' ability to learn to read words. *Journal of Experimental Child Psychology, 73*, 183–207.

Lakatos, I. (1970). Falsification and the methodology of scientific research programmes. In I. Lakatos & A. Musgrave (Eds.), *Criticism and the growth of knowledge* (pp. 91–196). Cambridge: Cambridge University Press.

Lakoff, G. (1987). *Women, fire, and dangerous things*. Chicago: University of Chicago Press.

Lambert, W. E., Tucker, G. R., & d'Anglejan, A. (1973). Cognitive and attitudinal consequences of bilingual schooling. *Journal of Educational Psychology, 85*, 141–159.

Lambon Ralph, M. A., Ellis, A. W., & Franklin, S. (1995). Semantic loss without surface dyslexia. *Neurocase, 1*, 363–369.

Lambon Ralph, M. A., Sage, K., & Ellis, A. W. (1996). Word meaning blindness: A new form of acquired dyslexia. *Cognitive Neuropsychology, 13*, 617–639.

Landau, B., & Gleitman, L. R. (1985). *Language and experience: Evidence from the blind child*. Cambridge, MA: Harvard University Press.

Landauer, T. K., & Dumais, S. T. (1997). A solution to Plato's problem: The latent semantic analysis theory of acquisition, induction, and representation of knowledge. *Psychological Review, 104*, 211–240.

Landauer, T. K., Foltz, P. W., & Laham, D. (1998). An introduction to latent semantic analysis. *Discourse Processes, 25*, 259–284.

Landauer, T. K., & Freedman, J. L. (1968). Information retrieval from long-term memory: Category size and recognition time. *Journal of Verbal Learning and Verbal Behavior, 7*, 291–295.

Lane, H., & Pillard, R. (1978). *The wild boy of Burundi*. New York: Random House.

Lantz, D., & Stefflre, V. (1964). Language and cognition revisited. *Journal of Abnormal Psychology, 69*, 472–481.

Lapointe, S. (1983). Some issues in the linguistic description of agrammatism. *Cognition, 14*, 1–39.

Lauro-Grotto, R., Piccini, C., & Shallice, T. (1997). Modality-specific operations in semantic dementia. *Cortex, 33*, 593–622.

Laws, G., Davies, I., & Andrews, C. (1995). Linguistic structure and non-linguistic cognition: English and Russian blues compared. *Language and Cognitive Processes, 10*, 59–94.

Laxon, V., Masterson, J., & Coltheart, V. (1991). Some bodies are easier to read: The effect of consistency and regularity on children's reading. *Quarterly Journal of Experimental Psychology, 43A*, 793–824.

Lee, A. C. H., Graham, K. S., Simons, J. S., & Hodges, J. (2002). Regional brain activations differ for semantic features but not categories. *Neuroreport, 13*, 1497–1501.

Lee, H., Rayner, K., & Pollatsek, A. (2001). The relative contribution of consonants and vowels to word identification during reading. *Journal of Memory and Language, 44*, 189–205.

Lee, J. J., & Pinker, S. (2010). Rationales for indirect speech: The theory of the strategic speaker. *Psychological Review, 117*, 785–807.

Legge, G. E., Klitz, T. S., & Tjan, B. S. (1997). Mr Chips: An ideal-observer model of reading. *Psychological Review, 104*, 524–553.

Lenneberg, E. H. (1962). Understanding language without ability to speak: A case report. *Journal of Abnormal and Social Psychology, 65*, 419–425.

Lenneberg, E. H. (1967). *The biological foundations of language*. New York: Wiley.

Lenneberg, E. H., & Roberts, J. M. (1956). *The language of experience*. Memoir 13, Indiana University Publications in Anthropology and Linguistics.

Leonard, L. B. (1989). Language learnability and specific language impairment in children. *Applied Psycholinguistics, 10*, 179–202.

Leonard, L. B. (2000). *Children with specific language impairment*. Cambridge, MA: MIT Press.

Leonard, L. B., Newhoff, M., & Fey, M. E. (1980). Some instances of word usage without comprehension. *Journal of Child Language, 7*, 186–196.

Leopold, W. F. (1939–1949). *Speech development of a bilingual child: A linguist's record* (5 vols.). Evanston, IL: Northwestern University Press.

Lesch, M. F., & Martin, R. C. (1998). The representation of sublexical orthographic–phonological correspondences: Evidence from phonological dyslexia. *Quarterly Journal of Experimental Psychology, 51*, 905–938.

Lesch, M. F., & Pollatsek, A. (1998). Evidence for the use of assembled phonology in accessing the meaning of words. *Journal of Experimental Psychology: Learning, Memory, and Cognition, 24*, 573–592.

Levelt, W. J. M. (1989). *Speaking: From intention to articulation*. Cambridge, MA: MIT Press.

Levelt, W. J. M. (2001). Spoken word production: A theory of lexical access. *Proceedings of the National Academy of Sciences, 98*, 13464–13471.

Levelt, W. J. M. (2002). Picture naming and word frequency. *Language and Cognitive Processes, 17*, 663–671.

Levelt, W. J. M., & Kelter, S. (1982). Surface form and memory in question answering. *Cognitive Psychology, 14*, 78–106.

Levelt, W. J. M., Roelofs, A., & Meyer, A. S. (1999). A theory of lexical access in speech production. *Behavioral and Brain Sciences, 22*, 1–75.

Levelt, W. J. M., Schriefers, H., Vorberg, D., Meyer, A. S., Pechmann, T., & Havinga, J. (1991a). The time course of lexical access in speech production: A study of picture naming. *Psychological Review, 98,* 122–142.

Levelt, W. J. M., Schriefers, H., Vorberg, D., Meyer, A. S., Pechmann, T., & Havinga, J. (1991b). Normal and deviant lexical processing: Reply to Dell and O'Seaghdha (1991). *Psychological Review, 98,* 615–618.

Levelt, W. J. M., & Wheeldon, L. (1994). Do speakers have access to a mental syllabary? *Cognition, 50,* 239–269.

Levine, D. N., Calvanio, R., & Popovics, A. (1982). Language in the absence of inner speech. *Neuropsychologia, 20,* 391–409.

Levinson, S. (1983). *Pragmatics.* Cambridge: Cambridge University Press.

Levinson, S. (1996a). Frames of reference and Molyneux's question: Crosslinguistic evidence. In P. Bloom & M. Peterson (Eds.), *Language and space* (pp. 109–169). Cambridge, MA: MIT Press.

Levinson, S. (1996b). Language and space. *Annual Review of Anthropology, 25,* 353–382.

Levinson, S. C., Kita, S., Haun, D. B. M., & Rasch, B. H. (2002). Returning the tables: Language affects spatial reasoning. *Cognition, 84,* 155–188.

Levy, B. A., Gong, Z., Hessels, S., Evans, M. A., & Jared, D. (2006). Understanding print: Early reading development and the contributions of home literacy experiences. *Journal of Child Experimental Psychology, 93,* 63–93.

Levy, E., & Nelson, K. (1994). Words in discourse: A dialectical approach to the acquisition of meaning and use. *Journal of Child Language, 21,* 367–389.

Levy, Y. (1983). It's frogs all the way down. *Cognition, 15,* 75–93.

Levy, Y. (1988). The nature of early language: Evidence from the development of Hebrew morphology. In Y. Levy, I. M. Schlesinger, & M. D. S. Braine (Eds.), *Categories and processes in language acquisition* (pp. 73–98). Hillsdale, NJ: Lawrence Erlbaum Associates, Inc.

Levy, Y., & Schlesinger, I. M. (1988). The child's early categories: Approaches to language acquisition theory. In Y. Levy, I. M. Schlesinger, & M. D. S. Braine (Eds.), *Categories and processes in language acquisition* (pp. 261–276). Hillsdale, NJ: Lawrence Erlbaum Associates, Inc.

Lewis, V. (1987). *Development and handicap.* Oxford: Blackwell.

Li, P., & Gleitman, L. (2002). Turning the tables: Language and spatial reasoning. *Cognition, 83,* 265–294.

Liberman, A. M., Cooper, F. S., Shankweiler, D. P., & Studdert-Kennedy, M. (1967). Perception of the speech code. *Psychological Review, 74,* 431–461.

Liberman, A. M., Harris, K. S., Hoffman, H. S., & Griffith, B. C. (1957). The discrimination of speech sounds within and across phoneme boundaries. *Journal of Experimental Psychology, 53,* 358–368.

Liberman, A. M., & Whalen, D. H. (2000). On the relation of speech to language. *Trends in Cognitive Sciences, 4,* 187–196.

Lidz, J., Gleitman, H., & Gleitman, L. (2003). Understanding how input matters: Verb learning and the footprint of universal grammar. *Cognition, 87,* 151–178.

Lidzha, K., & Krageloh-Mann, I. (2005). Development and lateralization of language in the presence of early brain lesions. *Developmental Medicine and Child Neurology, 47,* 724.

Lieberman, P. (1963). Some effects of semantic and grammatical context on the production and perception of speech. *Language and Speech, 6,* 172–187.

Lieberman, P. (1975). *On the origins of language.* New York: Macmillan.

Lieven, E. (1994). Crosslinguistic and crosscultural aspects of language addressed to children. In C. Gallaway & B. J. Richards (Eds.), *Input and interaction in language acquisition* (pp. 56–73). Cambridge: Cambridge University Press.

Lieven, E., Pine, J., & Baldwin, G. (1997). Lexically-based learning and early grammatical development. *Journal of Child Language, 24,* 187–220.

Lightfoot, D. (1982). *The language lottery: Toward a biology of grammars.* Cambridge, MA: MIT Press.

Lindell, A. K. (2006). In your right mind: Right hemisphere contributions to language processing and production. *Neuropsychology Review, 16,* 131–148.

Lindsay, P. H., & Norman, D. A. (1977). *Human information processing* (2nd ed.). New York: Academic Press.

Linebarger, M. C. (1995). Agrammatism as evidence about grammar. *Brain and Language, 50,* 52–91.

Linebarger, M. C., Schwartz, M. F., & Saffran, E. M. (1983). Sensitivity to grammatical structure in so-called agrammatic aphasics. *Cognition, 13,* 361–392.

Lipson, M. Y. (1983). The influence of religious affiliation on children's memory for text information. *Reading Research Quarterly, 18,* 448–457.

Liu, L. G. (1985). Reasoning counter-factually in Chinese: Are there any obstacles? *Cognition, 21,* 239–270.

Locke, J. (1690). *Essay concerning human understanding* (Ed. P. M. Nidditch, 1975). Oxford: Clarendon.

Locke, J. L. (1983). *Phonological acquisition and change.* New York: Academic Press.

Locke, J. L. (1997). A theory of neurolinguistic development. *Brain and Language, 58,* 265–326.

Loebell, H., & Bock, K. (2003). Structural priming across languages. *Linguistics, 41,* 791–824.

Loftus, E. F. (1973). Category, dominance, instance dominance, and categorization time. *Journal of Experimental Psychology, 97,* 70–74.

Loftus, E. F. (1975). Leading questions and the eyewitness report. *Cognitive Psychology*, *7*, 560–572.

Loftus, E. F. (1996). *Eyewitness testimony* (reprint edition with new preface). Cambridge, MA: Harvard University Press.

Loftus, E. F., & Palmer, J. C. (1974). Reconstruction of automobile destruction: An example of the interaction between language and memory. *Journal of Verbal Learning and Verbal Behavior*, *13*, 585–589.

Loftus, E. F., & Zanni, G. (1975). Eyewitness testimony: The influence of the wording of a question. *Bulletin of the Psychonomic Society*, *5*, 86–88.

Longtin, C. M., Segui, J., & Halle, P. A. (2003). Morphological priming without morphological relationship. *Language and Cognitive Processes*, *18*, 313–334.

Loosemore, R., & Harley, T. A. (2010). Brains and minds. In S. J. Hanson & M. Bunzl (Eds.), *Foundational issues in human brain mapping* (pp. 217–240). Cambridge, MA: MIT Press.

Lorch, R. F., Balota, D. A., & Stamm, E. G. (1986). Locus of inhibition effects in the priming of lexical decisions: Pre- or post-lexical access. *Memory and Cognition*, *9*, 587–598.

Lounsbury, F. G. (1954). Transitional probability, linguistic structure and systems of habit-family hierarchies. In C. E. Osgood & T. A. Sebeok (Eds.), *Psycholinguistics: A survey of theory and research problems* (pp. 93–101). Bloomington: Indiana University Press. [Reprinted 1965.]

Lovegrove, W., Martin, F., & Slaghuis, W. (1986). A theoretical and experimental case for a visual deficit in specific reading disability. *Cognitive Neuropsychology*, *3*, 225–267.

Lowenfeld, B. (1948). Effects of blindness on the cognitive functions of children. *Nervous Child*, *7*, 45–54.

Luce, P. A., Pisoni, D. B., & Goldinger, S. D. (1990). Similarity neighbourhoods of spoken words. In G. T. M. Altmann (Ed.), *Cognitive models of speech processing* (pp. 122–147). Cambridge, MA: MIT Press.

Luce, R. D. (1993). *Sound and hearing: A conceptual introduction*. Hillsdale, NJ: Lawrence Erlbaum Associates, Inc.

Lucy, J. A. (1992). *Language diversity and thought*. Cambridge: Cambridge University Press.

Lucy, J. A. (1996). The scope of linguistic relativity: An analysis and review of empirical research. In J. J. Gumperz & S. C. Levinson (Eds.), *Rethinking linguistic relativity* (pp. 37–69). Cambridge: Cambridge University Press.

Lucy, J. A., & Shweder, R. A. (1979). Whorf and his critics: Linguistic and nonlinguistic influences on colour memory. *American Anthropologist*, *81*, 581–615.

Lukatela, G., & Turvey, M. T. (1994a). Visual lexical access is initially phonological: 1. Evidence from associative priming by words, homophones, and pseudohomophones. *Journal of Experimental Psychology: General*, *123*, 107–128.

Lukatela, G., & Turvey, M. T. (1994b). Visual lexical access is initially phonological: 2. Evidence from phonological priming by homophones and pseudohomophones. *Journal of Experimental Psychology: General*, *123*, 331–353.

Lund, K., Burgess, C., & Atchley, R. A. (1995). Semantic and associative priming in high-dimensional semantic space. *Proceedings of the 17th Annual Conference of the Cognitive Science Society*, 660–665.

Lund, K., Burgess, C., & Audet, C. (1996). Dissociating semantic and associative word relationships using high-dimensional semantic space. *Proceedings of the 18th Annual Conference of the Cognitive Science Society*, 603–608.

Lundberg, I., & Tornéus, M. (1978). Nonreaders' awareness of the basic relationship between spoken and written words. *Journal of Experimental Child Psychology*, *25*, 404–412.

Lupker, S. J. (1984). Semantic priming without association: A second look. *Journal of Verbal Learning and Verbal Behavior*, *23*, 709–733.

Luria, A. R. (1970). *Traumatic aphasia*. The Hague: Mouton.

Lyn, H., & Savage-Rumbaugh, E. S. (2000). Observational word learning in two bonobos (*Pan Paniscus*): Ostensive and non-ostensive contexts. *Language and Communication*, *20*, 255–273.

Lyons, J. (1977a). *Semantics* (Vol. 1). Cambridge: Cambridge University Press.

Lyons, J. (1977b). *Semantics* (Vol. 2). Cambridge: Cambridge University Press.

Lyons, J. (1991). *Chomsky* (3rd ed.). London: Fontana. [First edition 1970.]

Maccoby, E., & Jacklin, C. (1974). *The psychology of sex differences*. Stanford, CA: Stanford University Press.

MacDonald, M. C. (1993). The interaction of lexical and syntactic ambiguity. *Journal of Memory and Language*, *32*, 692–715.

MacDonald, M. C. (1994). Probabilistic constraints and syntactic ambiguity resolution. *Language and Cognitive Processes*, *9*, 157–201.

MacDonald, M. C., & Christiansen, M. H. (2002). Reassessing working memory: Comment on Just and Carpenter (1992) and Waters and Caplan (1996). *Psychological Review*, *109*, 35–54.

MacDonald, M. C., Just, M. A., & Carpenter, P. A. (1992). Working memory constraints on the processing of syntactic ambiguity. *Cognitive Psychology*, *24*, 56–98.

MacDonald, M. C., Pearlmutter, N. J., & Seidenberg, M. S. (1994a). Syntactic ambiguity resolution as lexical ambiguity resolution. In C. Clifton, L. Frazier, & K. Rayner (Eds.), *Perspectives on sentence processing* (pp. 123–153). Hillsdale, NJ: Lawrence Erlbaum Associates, Inc.

MacDonald, M. C., Pearlmutter, N. J., & Seidenberg, M. S. (1994b). The lexical nature of syntactic ambiguity resolution. *Psychological Review*, 101, 676–703.

MacKain, C. (1982). Assessing the role of experience in infant speech discrimination. *Journal of Child Language*, 9, 323–350.

MacKay, D. G. (1966). To end ambiguous sentences. *Perception and Psychophysics*, 1, 426–436.

MacKay, D. G. (1973). Aspects of the theory of comprehension, memory and attention. *Quarterly Journal of Experimental Psychology*, 25, 22–40.

Maclay, H., & Osgood, C. E. (1959). Hesitation phenomena in spontaneous English speech. *Word*, 15, 19–44.

Macmillan, N. A., & Creelman, C. D. (1991). *Detection theory: A user's guide*. Cambridge: Cambridge University Press.

Macnamara, J. (1972). Cognitive basis of language learning in infants. *Psychological Review*, 79, 1–13.

Macnamara, J. (1982). *Names for things: A study of human learning*. Cambridge, MA: MIT Press.

MacNeilage, P. F., & Davis, B. L. (2000). On the origin of internal structure of word forms. *Science*, 288, 527–531.

MacWhinney, B. (Ed.). (1999). *The emergence of language*. Mahwah, NJ: Lawrence Erlbaum Associates, Inc.

MacWhinney, B., & Leinbach, J. (1991). Implementations are not conceptualizations: Revising the verb learning model. *Cognition*, 40, 121–157.

MacWhinney, B., & Pleh, C. (1988). The processing of restrictive relative clauses in Hungarian. *Cognition*, 29, 95–141.

Magiste, E. (1986). Selected issues in second and third language learning. In J. Vaid (Ed.), *Language processing in bilinguals: Psycholinguistic and neuropsychological perspectives* (pp. 97–121). Hillsdale, NJ: Lawrence Erlbaum Associates, Inc.

Maher, J., & Groves, J. (1999). *Introducing Chomsky*. Cambridge: Icon Books. [Originally published as *Chomsky for beginners*, 1996.]

Majid, A., Bowerman, M., Kita, S., Haun, D. B. M., & Levinson, S. C. (2004). Can language restructure cognition? The case for space. *Trends in Cognitive Sciences*, 8, 108–113.

Malotki, E. (1983). *Hopi time: A linguistic analysis of temporal concepts in the Hopi language*. Berlin: Mouton.

Mandler, J. M. (1978). A code in the node: The cue of a story schema in retrieval. *Discourse Processes*, 1, 14–35.

Mandler, J. M., & Johnson, N. S. (1977). Remembrance of things parsed: Story structure and recall. *Cognitive Psychology*, 9, 111–151.

Mandler, J. M., & Johnson, N. S. (1980). On throwing out the baby with the bathwater: A reply to Black and Wilensky's evaluation of story grammars. *Cognitive Science*, 4, 305–312.

Manis, F. R., McBride-Chang, C., Seidenberg, M. S., Keating, P., Doi, L. M., Munson, B., et al. (1997). Are speech perception deficits asociated with developmental dyslexia? *Journal of Experimental Child Psychology*, 66, 211–235.

Manis, F. R., Seidenberg, M. S., Doi, L. M., McBride-Chang, C., & Petersen, A. (1996). On the bases of two subtypes of developmental dyslexia. *Cognition*, 58, 157–195.

Maratsos, M. (1982). The child's construction of grammatical categories. In E. Wanner & L. R. Gleitman (Eds.), *Language acquisition: The state of the art* (pp. 240–266). Cambridge: Cambridge University Press.

Maratsos, M. (1983). Some current issues in the study of the acquisition of grammar. In J. H. Flavell & E. M. Markman (Eds.), *Handbook of child psychology: Vol. 3. Cognitive development* (pp. 707–786) (P. H. Mussen, Series Editor). New York: Wiley.

Maratsos, M. (1988). The acquisition of formal word classes. In Y. Levy, I. M. Schlesinger, & M. D. S. Braine (Eds.), *Categories and processes in language acquisition*. Hillsdale, NJ: Lawrence Erlbaum Associates, Inc.

Maratsos, M. (1998). The acquisition of grammar. In W. Damon, D. Kuhn, & R. S. Siegler (Eds.), *Handbook of child psychology* (Vol. 2, 5th ed., pp. 421–466). New York: Wiley.

Marcel, A. J. (1980). Surface dyslexia and beginning reading: A revised hypothesis of the pronunciation of print and its impairments. In M. Coltheart, K. E. Patterson, & J. C. Marshall (Eds.), *Deep dyslexia* (pp. 227–258). London: Routledge & Kegan Paul. [2nd ed., 1987.]

Marcel, A. J. (1983a). Conscious and unconscious perception: Experiments on visual making and word recognition. *Cognitive Psychology*, 15, 197–237.

Marcel, A. J. (1983b). Conscious and unconscious perception: An approach to the relations between phenomenal experience and perceptual processes. *Cognitive Psychology*, 15, 238–300.

Marchman, V. (1993). Constraints on plasticity in a connectionist model of the English past tense. *Journal of Cognitive Neuroscience*, 5, 215–234.

Marchman, V. (1997). Children's productivity in the English past tense: The role of frequency, phonology, and neighborhood structure. *Cognitive Science*, 21, 283–304.

Marchman, V., & Bates, E. (1994). Continuity in lexical and morphological development: A test of the critical mass hypothesis. *Journal of Child Language*, 21, 339–366.

Marcus, G. F. (1993). Negative evidence in language acquisition. *Cognition*, 46, 53–85.

Marcus, G. F. (1995). The acquisition of English past tense in children and multilayered connectionist networks. *Cognition, 56*, 271–279.

Marcus, G. F. (1999). Reply to Seidenberg and Elman. *Trends in Cognitive Sciences, 3*, 289.

Marcus, G. F., Ullman, M., Pinker, S., Hollander, M., Rosen, T. J., & Xu, F. (1992). Overregularization in language acquisition. *Monographs of the Society for Research in Child Development, 57* (Serial No. 228).

Marcus, G. F., Vijayan, S., Rao, S. B., & Vishton, P. M. (1999). Rule learning by seven-month-old infants. *Science, 283*, 77–80.

Marian, V., & Spivey, M. (2003). Bilingual and monolingual processing of competing lexical items. *Applied Psycholinguistics, 24*, 173–193.

Marien, P., Enggelborghs, S., Fabbro, F., & De Deyn, P. P. (2001). The lateralized linguistic cerebellum: A review and a new hypothesis. *Brain and Language, 79*, 580–600.

Markman, E. M. (1979). Realizing that you don't understand: Elementary school children's awareness of inconsistencies. *Child Development, 50*, 643–655.

Markman, E. M. (1985). Why superordinate category terms can be mass nouns. *Cognition, 19*, 311–353.

Markman, E. M. (1989). *Categorization and naming in children*. Cambridge, MA: MIT Press.

Markman, E. M. (1990). Constraints children place on word meanings. *Cognitive Science, 14*, 57–77.

Markman, E. M., & Hutchinson, J. E. (1984). Children's sensitivity to constraints on word meaning: Taxonomic vs. thematic relations. *Cognitive Psychology, 16*, 1–27.

Markman, E. M., & Wachtel, G. F. (1988). Children's use of mutual exclusivity to constrain the meaning of words. *Cognitive Psychology, 20*, 121–157.

Marr, D. (1982). *Vision: A computational investigation into the human representation and processing of visual information*. San Francisco: W. H. Freeman.

Marsh, G., Desberg, P., & Cooper, J. (1977). Developmental changes in strategies of reading. *Journal of Reading Behaviour, 9*, 391–394.

Marsh, G., Friedman, M. P., Welch, V., & Desberg, P. (1981). A cognitive-developmental theory of reading acquisition. In T. G. Waller & G. E. Mackinnon (Eds.), *Reading research: Advances in theory and practice* (Vol. 3, pp. 199–221). New York: Academic Press.

Marshall, J., Robson, J., Pring, T., & Chiat, S. (1998). Why does monitoring fail in jargon aphasia? Comprehension, judgement, and therapy evidence. *Brain and Language, 63*, 79–107.

Marshall, J. C. (1970). The biology of communication in man and animals. In J. Lyons (Ed.), *New horizons in linguistics* (Vol. 1, pp. 229–242). Harmondsworth, UK: Penguin.

Marshall, J. C., & Newcombe, F. (1966). Syntactic and semantic errors in paralexia. *Neuropsychologia, 4*, 169–176.

Marshall, J. C., & Newcombe, F. (1973). Patterns of paralexia: A psycholinguistic approach. *Journal of Psycholinguistic Research, 2*, 175–199.

Marshall, J. C., & Newcombe, F. (1980). The conceptual status of deep dyslexia: An historical perspective. In M. Coltheart, K. E. Patterson, & J. C. Marshall (Eds.), *Deep dyslexia* (pp. 1–21). London: Routledge & Kegan Paul. [2nd ed., 1987.]

Marshall, J. C., & Patterson, K. E. (1985). Left is still left for semantic paralexias: A reply to Jones and Martin. *Neuropsychologia, 23*, 689–690.

Marslen-Wilson, W. D. (1973). Linguistic structure and speech shadowing at very short latencies. *Nature, 244*, 522–523.

Marslen-Wilson, W. D. (1975). Sentence perception as an interactive parallel process. *Science, 189*, 226–228.

Marslen-Wilson, W. D. (1976). Linguistic descriptions and psychological assumptions in the study of sentence perception. In R. J. Wales & E. C. T. Walker (Eds.), *New approaches to language mechanisms* (pp. 203–230). Amsterdam: North Holland.

Marslen-Wilson, W. D. (1984). Spoken word recognition: A tutorial review. In H. Bouma & D. G. Bouwhis (Eds.), *Attention and performance X: Control of language processes* (pp. 125–150). Hove, UK: Lawrence Erlbaum Associates.

Marslen-Wilson, W. D. (1987). Functional parallelism in spoken word recognition. *Cognition, 25*, 71–102.

Marslen-Wilson, W. D. (Ed.). (1989). *Lexical representation and process*. Cambridge, MA: MIT Press.

Marslen-Wilson, W. D. (1990). Activation, competition, and frequency in lexical access. In G. T. M. Altmann (Ed.), *Cognitive models of speech processing* (pp. 148–172). Cambridge, MA: MIT Press.

Marslen-Wilson, W. D. (1993). Issues of process and representation in lexical access. In G. Altmann & R. Shillcock (Eds.), *Cognitive models of speech processing* (pp. 187–210). Hove, UK: Lawrence Erlbaum Associates.

Marslen-Wilson, W. D., & Tyler, L. K. (1980). The temporal structure of spoken language understanding. *Cognition, 8*, 1–71.

Marslen-Wilson, W. D., & Tyler, L. K. (2003). Capturing underlying differentiation in the human language system. *Trends in Cognitive Science, 7*, 62–63.

Marslen-Wilson, W. D., Tyler, L. K., Waksler, R., & Older, L. (1994). Morphology and meaning in the English mental lexicon. *Psychological Review, 101*, 3–33.

Marslen-Wilson, W. D., & Warren, P. (1994). Levels of perceptual representation and process in lexical access: Words, phonemes, and features. *Psychological Review, 101*, 653–675.

Marslen-Wilson, W. D., & Welsh, A. (1978). Processing interactions and lexical access during word recognition in continuous speech. *Cognitive Psychology, 10*, 29–63.

Marslen-Wilson, W. D., & Zwitserlood, P. (1989). Accessing spoken words: The importance of word onsets. *Journal of Experimental Psychology: Human Perception and Performance, 15*, 576–585.

Martin, A., & Fedio, P. (1983). Word production and comprehension in Alzheimer's disease: The breakdown of semantic knowledge. *Brain and Language, 19*, 124–141.

Martin, C., Vu, H., Kellas, G., & Metcalf, K. (1999). Strength of discourse context as a determinant of the subordinate bias effect. *Quarterly Journal of Experimental Psychology, 52A*, 813–839.

Martin, G. L. (2004). Encoder: A connectionist model of how learning to visually encode fixated text images improves reading fluency. *Psychological Review, 111*, 617–639.

Martin, G. N. (1998). *Human neuropsychology.* London: Prentice Hall.

Martin, N. (2001). Repetition disorders in aphasia: Theoretical and clinical implications. In R. S. Berndt (Ed.), *Handbook of neuropsychology* (Vol. 3, 2nd ed., pp. 137–155). Amsterdam: Elsevier Science.

Martin, N., & Ayala, J. (2004). Measurements of auditory-verbal STM in aphasia: Effects of task, item and word processing impairment. *Brain and Language, 89*, 464–483.

Martin, N., Dell, G. S., Saffran, E. M., & Schwartz, M. F. (1994). Origins of paraphasia in deep dysphasia: Testing the consequences of a decay impairment to an interactive spreading activation mode of lexical retrieval. *Brain and Language, 47*, 609–660.

Martin, N., & Saffran, E. M. (1990). Repetition and verbal STM in transcortical sensory aphasia: A case study. *Brain and Language, 39*, 254–288.

Martin, N., & Saffran, E. M. (1992). A computational account of deep dysphasia: Evidence from a single case study. *Brain and Language, 43*, 240–274.

Martin, N., & Saffran, E. M. (1997). Language and auditory-verbal short-term memory impairments: Evidence for common underlying processes. *Cognitive Neuropsychology, 14*, 641–682.

Martin, N., & Saffran, E. M. (1998). The relationship between input and output phonology: Evidence from aphasia. *Brain and Language, 65*, 225–228.

Martin, N., Saffran, E. M., & Dell, G. S. (1996). Recovery in deep dysphasia: Evidence for a relation between auditory-verbal STM and lexical errors in repetition. *Brain and Language, 52*, 83–113.

Martin, N., Weisberg, R. W., & Saffran, E. M. (1989). Variables influencing the occurrence of naming errors: Implications for models of lexical retrieval. *Journal of Memory and Language, 28*, 462–485.

Martin, R. C. (1982). The pseudohomophone effect: The role of visual similarity in non-word decisions. *Quarterly Journal of Experimental Psychology, 34A*, 395–410.

Martin, R. C. (1993). Short-term memory and sentence processing: Evidence from neuropsychology. *Memory and Cognition, 21*, 176–183.

Martin, R. C. (1995). Working memory doesn't work: A critique of Miyake et al.'s capacity theory of aphasic comprehension deficits. *Cognitive Neuropsychology, 12*, 623–636.

Martin, R. C., & Breedin, S. D. (1992). Dissociations between speech perception and phonological short-term memory deficits. *Cognitive Neuropsychology, 9*, 509–534.

Martin, R. C., & Feher, E. (1990). The consequences of reduced memory span for the comprehension of semantic versus syntactic information. *Brain and Language, 38*, 1–20.

Martin, R. C., & Lesch, M. F. (1996). Associations and dissociations between language impairment and list recall: Implications for models of STM. In S. E. Gathercole (Ed.), *Models of short-term memory* (pp. 149–178). Hove, UK: Psychology Press.

Martin, R. C., Lesch, M. F., & Bartha, M. C. (1999). Independence of input and output phonology in word processing and short-term memory. *Journal of Memory and Language, 41*, 3–29.

Martin, R. C., Shelton, J. R., & Yaffee, L. S. (1994). Language processing and working memory: Neuropsychological evidence for separate phonological and semantic capacities. *Journal of Memory and Language, 33*, 83–111.

Martin, R. C., Wetzel, W. F., Blossom-Stach, C., & Feher, E. (1989). Syntactic loss versus processing deficit: An assessment of two theories of agrammatism and syntactic comprehension deficits. *Cognition, 32*, 157–191.

Masataka, N. (1996). Perception of motherese in a signed language by 6-month-old deaf infants. *Developmental Psychology, 32*, 874–879.

Mason, M. K. (1942). Learning to speak after six and one half years silence. *Journal of Speech and Hearing Disorders, 7*, 295–304.

Mason, R. A., Just, M. A., Keller, T. A., & Carpenter, P. A. (2003). Ambiguity in the brain: What brain imaging reveals about the processing of syntactically ambiguous sentences. *Journal of Experimental Psychology: Learning, Memory, and Cognition, 29*, 1319–1338.

Massaro, D. W. (1987). *Speech perception by ear and eye: A paradigm for psychological enquiry.* Hillsdale, NJ: Lawrence Erlbaum Associates, Inc.

Massaro, D. W. (1989). Testing between the TRACE model and the fuzzy logical model of speech perception. *Cognitive Psychology, 21*, 398–421.

Massaro, D. W. (1994). Psychological aspects of speech perception: Implications for research and theory. In M. A. Gernsbacher (Ed.), *Handbook of psycholinguistics* (pp. 219–264). San Diego, CA: Academic Press.

Massaro, D. W., & Cohen, M. M. (1991). Integration versus interactive activation: The joint influence of stimulus and context in perception. *Cognitive Psychology, 23*, 558–614.

Massaro, D. W., & Oden, G. C. (1995). Independence of lexical context and phonological information in speech perception. *Journal of Experimental Psychology: Learning, Memory, and Cognition, 21*, 1053–1064.

Masson, M. E. J. (1995). A distributed memory model of semantic priming. *Journal of Experimental Psychology: Learning, Memory, and Cognition, 21*, 3–23.

Masterson, J., Coltheart, M., & Meara, P. (1985). Surface dyslexia in a language without irregularly spelled words. In K. E. Patterson, J. C. Marshall, & M. Coltheart (Eds.), *Surface dyslexia: Neuropsychological and cognitive studies of phonological reading* (pp. 215–223). Hove, UK: Lawrence Erlbaum Associates.

Masur, E. F. (1997). Maternal labelling of novel and familiar objects: Implications for children's development of lexical constraints. *Journal of Child Language, 24*, 427–439.

Mattys, S. L., & Jusczyk, P. W. (2001). Phonotactic cues for segmentation of fluent speech by infants. *Cognition, 78*, 91–121.

Mayberry, E. J., Sage, K., & Lambon Ralph, M. A. (2011). At the edge of semantic space: The breakdown of coherent concepts in semantic dementia is constrained by typicality and severity but not modality. *Journal of Cognitive Neuroscience, 23*, 2240–2251.

Mazuka, R. (1991). Processing of empty categories in Japanese. *Journal of Psycholinguistic Research, 20*, 215–232.

McBride-Chang, C. (2004). *Children's literacy development*. London: Arnold.

McCann, R. S., & Besner, D. (1987). Reading pseudohomophones: Implications for models of pronunciation assembly and the locus of word frequency effects in naming. *Journal of Experimental Psychology: Human Perception and Performance, 13*, 14–24.

McCarthy, J. J. (2001). *A thematic guide to optimality theory*. Cambridge: Cambridge University Press.

McCarthy, J. J., & Prince, A. (1990). Foot and word in prosodic morphology: The Arabic broken plural. *Natural Language and Linguistic Theory, 8*, 209–283.

McCarthy, R. A., & Warrington, E. K. (1986). Visual associative agnosia: A clinico-anatomical study of a single case. *Journal of Neurology, Neurosurgery, and Psychiatry, 49*, 1233–1240.

McCarthy, R. A., & Warrington, E. K. (1987a). The double dissociation of short-term memory for lists and sentences: Evidence from aphasia. *Brain, 110*, 1545–1563.

McCarthy, R. A., & Warrington, E. K. (1987b). Understanding: A function of short-term memory? *Brain, 110*, 1565–1578.

McCarthy, R. A., & Warrington, E. K. (1988). Evidence for modality-specific meaning systems in the brain. *Nature, 334*, 428–430.

McCauley, C., Parmalee, C. M., Sperber, R. D., & Carr, T. H. (1980). Early extraction of meaning from pictures and its relation to conscious identification. *Journal of Experimental Psychology: Human Perception and Performance, 6*, 265–276.

McClelland, J. L. (1979). On the time relations of mental processes: An examination of systems of processes in cascade. *Psychological Review, 86*, 287–330.

McClelland, J. L. (1981). Retrieving general and specific information from stored knowledge of specifics. *Proceedings of the 3rd Annual Conference of the Cognitive Science Society*, 170–172.

McClelland, J. L. (1987). The case for interactions in language processing. In M. Coltheart (Ed.), *Attention and performance XII: The psychology of reading* (pp. 3–36). Hove, UK: Lawrence Erlbaum Associates.

McClelland, J. L. (1991). Stochastic interactive processes and the effect of context on perception. *Cognitive Psychology, 23*, 1–44.

McClelland, J. L., & Elman, J. L. (1986). The TRACE model of speech perception. *Cognitive Psychology, 18*, 1–86.

McClelland, J. L., & Patterson, K. E. (2002). Rules or connections in past-tense inflections: What does the evidence rule out? *Trends in Cognitive Science, 6*, 465–472.

McClelland, J. L., & Patterson, K. E. (2003). Differentiation and integration in human language. *Trends in Cognitive Science, 7*, 63–64.

McClelland, J. L., & Rumelhart, D. E. (1981). An interactive activation model of context effects in letter perception: Part 1. An account of the basic findings. *Psychological Review, 88*, 375–407.

McClelland, J. L., & Rumelhart, D. E. (1988). *Explorations in parallel distributed processing*. Cambridge, MA: MIT Press.

McClelland, J. L., Rumelhart, D. E., & the PDP Research Group. (1986). *Parallel distributed processing: Vol. 2. Psychological and biological models*. Cambridge, MA: MIT Press.

McClelland, J. L., & Seidenberg, M. S. (2000). Words and rules—the ingredients of language by Pinker, S. *Science, 287*, 47–48.

McCloskey, M. (1980). The stimulus familiarity problem in semantic memory research. *Journal of Verbal Learning and Verbal Behavior, 19*, 485–504.

McCloskey, M., & Caramazza, A. (1988). Theory and methodology in cognitive neuropsychology: A response to our critics. *Cognitive Neuropsychology*, 5, 583–623.

McCloskey, M., & Glucksberg, S. (1978). Natural categories: Well-defined or fuzzy sets? *Memory and Cognition*, 6, 462–472.

McConkie, G. W., & Rayner, K. (1976). Asymmetry of the perceptual span in reading. *Bulletin of the Psychonomic Society*, 8, 365–368.

McCune-Nicolich, L. (1981). The cognitive bases of relational words in the single word period. *Journal of Child Language*, 8, 15–34.

McCutchen, D., & Perfetti, C. A. (1982). The visual tongue-twister effect: Phonological activation in silent reading. *Journal of Verbal Learning and Verbal Behavior*, 21, 672–687.

McDavid, V. (1964). The alternation of that and zero in noun clauses. *American Speech*, 39, 102–113.

McDonald, J. L., Bock, J. K., & Kelly, M. H. (1993). Word order and world order: Semantic, phonological, and metrical determinants of serial position. *Cognitive Psychology*, 25, 188–230.

McDonald, S. A., Carpenter, R. H. S., & Shillcock, R. C. (2005). An anatomically constrained, stochastic model of eye movement control in reading. *Psychological Review*, 112, 814–840.

McGurk, H., & MacDonald, J. (1976). Hearing lips and seeing voices. *Nature*, 264, 746–748.

McKoon, G., Gerrig, R. J., & Greene, S. B. (1996). Pronoun resolution without pronouns: Some consequences of memory-based text processing. *Journal of Experimental Psychology: Learning, Memory, and Cognition*, 22, 919–932.

McKoon, G., & Ratcliff, R. (1986). Inferences about predictable events. *Journal of Experimental Psychology: Learning, Memory, and Cognition*, 12, 82–91.

McKoon, G., & Ratcliff, R. (1989). Semantic associations and elaborative inference. *Journal of Experimental Psychology: Learning, Memory, and Cognition*, 15, 326–338.

McKoon, G., & Ratcliff, R. (1992). Inference during reading. *Psychological Review*, 99, 440–466.

McKoon, G., & Ratcliff, R. (2002). Event templates in the lexical representations of verbs. *Cognitive Psychology*, 45, 1–44.

McKoon, G., & Ratcliff, R. (2003). Meaning through syntax: Language comprehension and the reduced relative clause construction. *Psychological Review*, 110, 490–525.

McKoon, G., Ratcliff, R., & Dell, G. S. (1986). A critical evaluation of the semantic–episodic distinction. *Journal of Experimental Psychology: Learning, Memory, and Cognition*, 12, 295–306.

McKoon, G., Ratcliff, R., & Seifert, C. M. (1989). Making the connection: Generalized knowledge structures in story understanding. *Journal of Memory and Language*, 28, 711–734.

McKoon, G., Ratcliff, R., & Ward, G. (1994). Testing theories of language processing: An empirical investigation of the on-line lexical decision task. *Journal of Experimental Psychology: Learning, Memory, and Cognition*, 20, 1219–1228.

McLaughlin, B. (1984). *Second language acquisition in childhood* (2nd ed.). Hillsdale, NJ: Lawrence Erlbaum Associates, Inc.

McLaughlin, B. (1987). *Theories of second-language learning*. London: Arnold.

McLaughlin, B., & Heredia, R. (1996). Information-processing approaches to research on second language acquisition and use. In W. C. Ritchie & T. K. Bhatia (Eds.), *Handbook of second language acquisition* (pp. 213–228). London: Academic Press.

McLeod, P., Shallice, T., & Plaut, D. C. (2000). Attractor dynamics in word recognition: Converging evidence from errors by normal subjects, dyslexic patients and a connectionist model. *Cognition*, 74, 91–113.

McNamara, T. P. (1992). Theories of priming: I. Associative distance and lag. *Journal of Experimental Psychology: Learning, Memory, and Cognition*, 18, 1173–1190.

McNamara, T. P. (1994). Theories of priming: II. Types of prime. *Journal of Experimental Psychology: Learning, Memory, and Cognition*, 20, 507–520.

McNamara, T. P., & Altarriba, J. (1988). Depth of spreading activation revisited: Semantic mediated priming occurs in lexical decisions. *Journal of Memory and Language*, 27, 545–559.

McNamara, T. P., & Miller, D. L. (1989). Attributes of theories of meaning. *Psychological Bulletin*, 106, 355–376.

McQueen, J. (1991). The influence of the lexicon on phonetic categorisation: Stimulus quality and word-final ambiguity. *Journal of Experimental Psychology: Human Perception and Performance*, 17, 433–443.

McRae, K., & Boisvert, S. (1998). Automatic semantic similarity priming. *Journal of Experimental Psychology: Learning, Memory, and Cognition*, 24, 558–572.

McRae, K., de Sa, V. R., & Seidenberg, M. S. (1997). On the nature and scope of featural representations of word meaning. *Journal of Experimental Psychology: General*, 126, 99–130.

McRae, K., Hare, M., & Tanenhaus, M. K. (2005). Meaning through syntax is insufficient to explain comprehension of sentences with reduced relative clauses: Comment on McKoon and Ratcliff (2003). *Psychological Review*, 112, 1022–1031.

McRae, K., Spivey-Knowlton, M. J., & Tanenhaus, M. K. (1998). Modeling the influence of thematic fit (and other constraints) in on-line sentence comprehension. *Journal of Memory and Language*, 38, 283–312.

McShane, J. (1991). *Cognitive development*. Oxford: Blackwell.

McShane, J., & Dockrell, J. (1983). Lexical and grammatical development. In B. Butterworth (Ed.), *Speech production: Vol. 2. Development, writing, and other language processes* (pp. 51–99). London: Academic Press.

McVay, J. C., & Kane, M. J. (2012). Why does working memory capacity predict variation in reading comprehension? On the influence of mind wandering and executive attention. *Journal of Experimental Psychology: General, 141*, 302–320.

Medin, D. L., & Schaffer, M. M. (1978). A context theory of classification learning. *Psychological Review, 85*, 207–238.

Mehler, J. (1963). Some effects of grammatical transformations on the recall of English sentences. *Journal of Verbal Learning and Verbal Behavior, 2*, 346–351.

Mehler, J., Jusczyk, P. W., Lambertz, G., Halsted, N., Bertoncini, J., & Amiel-Tison, C. (1988). A precursor of language acquisition in young infants. *Cognition, 29*, 143–178.

Mehler, J., Segui, J., & Carey, P. W. (1978). Tails of words: Monitoring ambiguity. *Journal of Verbal Learning and Verbal Behavior, 17*, 29–35.

Meier, R. P. (1991). Language acquisition by deaf children. *American Scientist, 79*, 60–70.

Melby-Lervåg, M., Lyster, S.-A. H., & Hulme, C. (2012). Phonological skills and their role in learning to read: A meta-analytic review. *Psychological Bulletin, 138*, 322–352.

Melinger, A., & Dobel, C. (2005). Lexically-driven syntactic priming. *Cognition, 98*, B11–B20.

Melinger, A., & Rahman, R. A. (2013). Lexical selection is competitive: Evidence from indirectly activated semantic associates during picture naming. *Journal of Experimental Psychology: Learning, Memory, and Cognition, 39*, 348–364.

Menn, L. (1980). Phonological theory and child phonology. In G. H. Yeni-Komshian, J. F. Kavanagh, & C. A. Ferguson (Eds.), *Child phonology* (Vol. 1, pp. 23–41). New York: Academic Press.

Menyuk, P. (1969). *Sentences children use*. Cambridge, MA: MIT Press.

Menyuk, P., Menn, L., & Silber, R. (1986). Early strategies for the perception and production of words and sounds. In P. Fletcher & M. Garman (Eds.), *Language acquisition* (2nd ed., pp. 198–222). Cambridge: Cambridge University Press.

Meringer, R., & Mayer, K. (1895). *Versprechen und Verlesen: Eine Psychologisch-Linguistische Studie*. Stuttgart: Gössen.

Mervis, C. B., & Bertrand, J. (1994). Young children and adults use lexical principles to learn new nouns. *Child Development, 65*, 1646–1662.

Mervis, C. B., Catlin, J., & Rosch, E. (1975). Relationships among goodness-of-example, category norms, and word frequency. *Bulletin of the Psychonomic Society, 7*, 283–284.

Messer, D. (1980). The episodic structure of maternal speech to young children. *Journal of Child Language, 7*, 29–40.

Messer, D. (2000). State of the art: Language acquisition. *The Psychologist, 13*, 138–143.

Metsala, J. L., Stanovich, K. E., & Brown, G. D. A. (1998). Regularity effects and the phonological deficit model of reading disabilities: A meta-analytic review. *Journal of Educational Psychology, 90*, 279–293.

Meyer, A. S. (1996). Lexical access in phrase and sentence production: Results from picture–word interference experiments. *Journal of Memory and Language, 35*, 477–496.

Meyer, A. S. (2004). The use of eye tracking in studies of sentence generation. In J. M. Henderson & F. Ferreira (Eds.), *The interface of language, vision, and action: Eye movements and the visual world* (pp. 191–211). Hove, UK: Psychology Press.

Meyer, A. S., & Bock, K. (1992). The tip-of-the-tongue phenomenon: Blocking or partial activation? *Memory and Cognition, 20*, 715–726.

Meyer, A. S., Sleiderink, A., & Levelt, W. J. M. (1998). Viewing and naming objects: Eye movements during noun phrase production. *Cognition, 66*, B25–B33.

Meyer, A. S., Wheeldon, L., & Krott, A. (Eds.). (2006). *Automaticity and control in language processing*. Hove, UK: Psychology Press.

Meyer, D. E., & Schvaneveldt, R. W. (1971). Facilitation in recognizing pairs of words: Evidence of a dependence between retrieval operations. *Journal of Experimental Psychology, 90*, 227–235.

Meyer, D. E., Schvaneveldt, R. W., & Ruddy, M. G. (1974). Loci of contextual effects on visual word recognition. In P. M. A. Rabbitt & S. Dornic (Eds.), *Attention and performance V* (pp. 98–118). New York: Academic Press.

Miceli, G., Benvegnu, B., Capasso, R., & Caramazza, A. (1997). The independence of phonological and orthographic lexical forms: Evidence from aphasia. *Cognitive Neuropsychology, 14*, 35–69.

Miceli, G., & Capasso, R. (1997). Semantic errors as neuropsychological evidence for the independence and the interaction of orthographic and phonological word forms. *Language and Cognitive Processes, 12*, 733–764.

Miceli, G., Mazzucci, A., Menn, L., & Goodglass, H. (1983). Contrasting cases of Italian agrammatic aphasia without comprehension disorder. *Brain and Language, 19*, 65–97.

Michaels, D. (1977). Linguistic relativity and color terminology. *Language and Speech, 20*, 333–343.

Milberg, W., Blumstein, S. E., & Dworetzky, B. (1987). Processing of lexical ambiguities in aphasia. *Brain and Language, 31*, 138–150.

Miller, D., & Ellis, A. W. (1987). Speech and writing errors in "neologistic jargonaphasia": A lexical activation hypothesis. In M. Coltheart, G. Sartori, & R. Job (Eds.), *The cognitive neuropsychology of language* (pp. 235–271). Hove, UK: Lawrence Erlbaum Associates.

Miller, G. A., Heise, G. A., & Lichten, W. (1951). The intelligibility of speech as a function of the text of the test materials. *Journal of Experimental Psychology*, *41*, 329–355.

Miller, G. A., & Johnson-Laird, P. N. (1976). *Language and perception*. Cambridge: Cambridge University Press.

Miller, G. A., & McKean, K. E. (1964). A chronometric study of some relations between sentences. *Quarterly Journal of Experimental Psychology*, *16*, 297–308.

Miller, G. A., & McNeill, D. (1969). Psycholinguistics. In G. Lindzey & E. Aronson (Eds.), *The handbook of social psychology* (Vol. 3, pp. 666–794). Reading, MA: Addison-Wesley.

Miller, J. L. (1981). Effects of speaking rate on segmental distinctions. In P. D. Eimas & J. L. Miller (Eds.), *Perspectives on the study of speech* (pp. 39–74). Hillsdale, NJ: Lawrence Erlbaum Associates, Inc.

Miller, J. L., & Jusczyk, P. W. (1989). Seeking the neurobiological bases of speech perception. *Cognition*, *33*, 111–137.

Miller, K. F., & Stigler, J. (1987). Counting in Chinese: Cultural variations in a basic cognitive skill. *Cognitive Development*, *2*, 279–305.

Millis, M. L., & Button, S. B. (1989). The effect of polysemy on lexical decision time: Now you see it, now you don't. *Memory and Cognition*, *17*, 141–147.

Mills, A. E. (Ed.). (1983). *Language acquisition in the blind child: Normal and deficient*. London: Croom Helm.

Mills, A. E. (1987). The development of phonology in the blind child. In B. Dodd & R. Campbell (Eds.), *Hearing by eye: The psychology of lip-reading* (pp. 145–162). Hove, UK: Lawrence Erlbaum Associates.

Mills, D. L., Coffrey-Corina, S. A., & Neville, H. J. (1993). Language acquisition and cerebral specialization in 20-month-old infants. *Journal of Cognitive Neuroscience*, *5*, 317–334.

Mills, D. L., Coffrey-Corina, S. A., & Neville, H. J. (1997). Language comprehension and cerebral specialization from 13 to 20 months. *Developmental Neuropsychology*, *13*, 397–445.

Milne, R. W. (1982). Predicting garden path sentences. *Cognitive Science*, *6*, 349–373.

Minsky, M. (1975). A framework for representing knowledge. In P. H. Winston (Ed.), *The psychology of computer vision* (pp. 211–277). New York: McGraw-Hill.

Mintz, T. H. (2003). Frequent frames as a cue for grammatical categories in child directed speech. *Cognition*, *90*, 91–117.

Mintz, T. H., & Gleitman, L. R. (2002). Adjectives really do modify nouns: The incremental and restricted nature of early adjective acquisition. *Cognition*, *84*, 267–293.

Miozzo, M. (2003). On the processing of regular and irregular forms of verbs and nouns: Evidence from neuropsychology. *Cognition*, *87*, 101–127.

Miozzo, M., & Caramazza, A. (1997). Retrieval of lexical-syntactic features in tip-of-the-tongue states. *Journal of Experimental Psychology: Learning, Memory, and Cognition*, *23*, 1410–1423.

Mitchell, D. C. (1987). Reading and syntactic analysis. In J. R. Beech & A. M. Colley (Eds.), *Cognitive approaches to reading* (pp. 87–112). Chichester, UK: John Wiley & Sons Ltd.

Mitchell, D. C. (1994). Sentence parsing. In M. A. Gernsbacher (Ed.), *Handbook of psycholinguistic research* (pp. 375–410). San Diego, CA: Academic Press.

Mitchell, D. C., Brysbaert, M., Grondelaers, S., & Swanepoel, P. (2000). Modifier attachment in Dutch: Testing aspects of construal theory. In A. Kennedy, R. Radach, D. Heller, & J. Pynte (Eds.), *Reading as a perceptual process* (pp. 493–516). Oxford: Elsevier.

Mitchell, D. C., Cuetos, F., Corley, M. M. B., & Brysbaert, M. (1995). Exposure-based models of human parsing: Evidence for the use of coarse-grained (nonlexical) statistical records. *Journal of Psycholinguistic Research*, *24*, 469–488.

Mitchell, D. C., & Holmes, V. M. (1985). The role of specific information about the verb in parsing sentences with local structural ambiguity. *Journal of Memory and Language*, *24*, 542–559.

Miyake, A., Carpenter, P. A., & Just, M. A. (1994). A capacity approach to syntactic comprehension disorders: Making normal adults perform like aphasic patients. *Cognitive Neuropsychology*, *11*, 671–717.

Moerk, E. (1991). Positive evidence for negative evidence. *First Language*, *11*, 219–251.

Mohay, H. (1982). A preliminary description of the communication systems evolved by two deaf children in the absence of a sign language model. *Sign Language Studies*, *34*, 73–90.

Molfese, D. L. (1977). Infant cerebral asymmetry. In S. J. Segalowitz & F. A. Gruber (Eds.), *Language development and neurological theory* (pp. 21–35). New York: Academic Press.

Molfese, D. L., & Molfese, V. J. (1994). Short-term and long-term developmental outcomes: The use of behavioral and electrophysiological measures in early infancy as predictors. In G. Dawson & K. W. Fischer (Eds.), *Human behavior and the developing brain* (pp. 493–517). New York: Guilford Press.

Monaghan, J., & Ellis, A. W. (2002). What exactly interacts with spelling–sound consistency in word naming? *Journal of Experimental Psychology: Learning, Memory, and Cognition*, *28*, 183–206.

Monaghan, P., & Ellis, A. W. (2010). Modeling reading development: Cumulative, incremental learning in a computational model of word naming. *Journal of Memory and Language, 63,* 506–525.

Monsell, S. (1985). Repetition and the lexicon. In A. W. Ellis (Ed.), *Progress in psychology of language* (Vol. 2, pp. 147–195). Hove, UK: Lawrence Erlbaum Associates.

Monsell, S. (1987). On the relation between lexical input and output pathways for speech. In A. Allport, D. Mackay, W. Prinz, & E. Sheerer (Eds.), *Language perception and production: Shared mechanisms in listening, speaking, reading, and writing* (pp. 273–311). London: Academic Press.

Monsell, S., Doyle, M. C., & Haggard, P. N. (1989). Effects of frequency on visual word recognition tasks: Where are they? *Journal of Experimental Psychology: General, 118,* 43–71.

Monsell, S., & Hirsh, K. W. (1998). Competitor priming in spoken word recognition. *Journal of Experimental Psychology: Learning, Memory, and Cognition, 24,* 1495–1520.

Monsell, S., Matthews, G. H., & Miller, D. C. (1992). Repetition of lexicalization across languages: A further test of the locus of priming. *Quarterly Journal of Experimental Psychology, 44A,* 763–783.

Monsell, S., Patterson, K. E., Graham, A., Hughes, C. H., & Milroy, R. (1992). Lexical and sublexical translations of spelling to sound: Strategic anticipation of lexical status. *Journal of Experimental Psychology: Learning, Memory, and Cognition, 18,* 452–467.

Morais, J., Bertelson, P., Cary, L., & Alegria, J. (1986). Literacy training and speech segmentation. *Cognition, 24,* 45–64.

Morais, J., Cary, L., Alegria, J., & Bertelson, P. (1979). Does awareness of speech as a sequence of phones arise spontaneously? *Cognition, 7,* 323–331.

Morais, J., & Kolinsky, R. (1994). Perception and awareness in phonological processing: The case of the phoneme. *Cognition, 50,* 287–297.

Moreno, E. M., & Kutas, M. (2009). Processing semantic anomaly in two languages: An electrophysiological exploration in both languages, of Spanish–English bilinguals. *Cognitive Brain Research, 22,* 205–220.

Morgan, J. L., & Travis, L. L. (1989). Limits on negative information in language input. *Journal of Child Language, 16,* 531–552.

Morris, A. L., & Harris, C. L. (2002). Sentence context, word recognition, and repetition blindness. *Journal of Experimental Psychology: Learning, Memory, and Cognition, 28,* 962–982.

Morrison, C. M., Chappell, T. D., & Ellis, A. W. (1997). Age of acquisition norms for a large set of object names and their relation to adult estimates and other variables. *Quarterly Journal of Experimental Psychology, 50A,* 528–559.

Morrison, C. M., & Ellis, A. W. (1995). Roles of word frequency and age of acquisition in word naming and lexical decision. *Journal of Experimental Psychology: Learning, Memory, and Cognition, 21,* 116–133.

Morrison, C. M., & Ellis, A. W. (2000). Real age of acquisition effects in word naming. *British Journal of Psychology, 91,* 167–180.

Morrison, C. M., Ellis, A. W., & Quinlan, P. T. (1992). Age of acquisition, not word frequency, affects object naming, not object recognition. *Memory and Cognition, 20,* 705–714.

Morrow, D. G., Bower, G. H., & Greenspan, S. L. (1989). Updating situation models during narrative comprehension. *Journal of Memory and Language, 28,* 292–312.

Morrow, D. G., Greenspan, S. L., & Bower, G. H. (1987). Accessibility and situation models in narrative comprehension. *Journal of Memory and Language, 26,* 165–187.

Morsella, E., & Miozzo, M. (2002). Evidence for a cascade model of lexical access in speech production. *Journal of Experimental Psychology: Learning, Memory, and Cognition, 28,* 555–563.

Morton, J. (1969). Interaction of information in word recognition. *Psychological Review, 76,* 165–178.

Morton, J. (1970). A functional model for human memory. In D. A. Norman (Ed.), *Models of human memory* (pp. 203–260). New York: Academic Press.

Morton, J. (1979a). Word recognition. In J. Morton & J. C. Marshall (Eds.), *Psycholinguistics series: Vol. 2. Structures and processes* (pp. 107–156). London: Paul Elek.

Morton, J. (1979b). Facilitation in word recognition: Experiments causing change in the logogen model. In P. A. Kolers, M. E. Wrolstad, & M. Bouma (Eds.), *Processing of visible language* (pp. 259–268). New York: Plenum.

Morton, J. (1984). Brain-based and non-brain-based models of language. In D. Caplan, A. R. Lecours, & A. Smith (Eds.), *Biological perspectives in language* (pp. 40–64). Cambridge, MA: MIT Press.

Morton, J. (1985). Naming. In S. Newman & R. Epstein (Eds.), *Current perspectives in dysphasia* (pp. 217–230). Edinburgh: Churchill Livingstone.

Morton, J., & Patterson, K. E. (1980). A new attempt at an interpretation, or, an attempt at a new interpretation. In M. Coltheart, K. E. Patterson, & J. C. Marshall (Eds.), *Deep dyslexia* (pp. 91–118). London: Routledge & Kegan Paul. [2nd ed., 1987.]

Moss, H. E., & Marslen-Wilson, W. D. (1993). Access to word meanings during spoken language comprehension: Effects of sentential semantic context. *Journal of Experimental Psychology: Learning, Memory, and Cognition, 19,* 1254–1276.

Moss, H. E., McCormick, S. F., & Tyler, L. K. (1997). The time course of activation of spoken information during spoken word recognition. *Language and Cognitive Processes, 12,* 695–731.

Moss, H. E., Ostrin, R. K., Tyler, L. K., & Marslen-Wilson, W. D. (1995). Accessing different types of lexical semantic information: Evidence from priming. *Journal of Experimental Psychology: Learning, Memory, and Cognition, 21,* 863–883.

Motley, M. T., & Baars, B. J. (1976). Semantic bias effects on the outcomes of verbal slips. *Cognition, 4,* 177–187.

Motley, M. T., Camden, C. T., & Baars, B. J. (1982). Covert formulation and editing of anomalies in speech production: Evidence from experimentally elicited slips of the tongue. *Journal of Verbal Learning and Verbal Behavior, 21,* 578–594.

Mowrer, O. H. (1960). *Learning theory and symbolic processes.* New York: John Wiley & Sons.

Mulford, R. (1988). First words of the blind child. In M. D. Smith & J. L. Locke (Eds.), *The emergent lexicon: The child's development of a linguistic vocabulary* (pp. 293–338). New York: Academic Press.

Muller, R.-A. (1997). Innateness, autonomy, universality? Neurobiological approaches to language. *Behavioral and Brain Sciences, 19,* 611–675.

Murphy, G. L. (1985). Processes of understanding anaphora. *Journal of Memory and Language, 24,* 290–303.

Murphy, G. L., & Medin, D. L. (1985). The role of theories in conceptual coherence. *Psychological Review, 92,* 289–316.

Murray, W. S., & Forster, K. I. (2004). Serial mechanisms in lexical access: The rank hypothesis. *Psychological Review, 111,* 721–756.

Muter, V., Hulme, C., Snowling, M., & Taylor, S. (1998). Segmentation, not rhyming, predicts early progress in learning to read. *Journal of Experimental Child Psychology, 71,* 3–27.

Muter, V., Snowling, M. J., & Taylor, S. (1994). Orthographic analogies and phonological awareness: Their role and significance in early reading development. *Journal of Child Psychology and Psychiatry, 35,* 293–310.

Myers, J. L., & O'Brien, E. J. (1998). Accessing the discourse representation during reading. *Discourse Processes, 26,* 131–157.

Nagy, W., & Anderson, R. (1984). The number of words in printed school English. *Reading Research Quarterly, 19,* 304–330.

Naigles, L. R. (1990). Children use syntax to learn verb meanings. *Journal of Child Language, 17,* 357–374.

Naigles, L. R. (1996). The use of multiple frames in verb learning via syntactic bootstrapping. *Cognition, 58,* 221–251.

Naigles, L. R. (2002). Form is easy, meaning is hard: Resolving a paradox in early child language. *Cognition, 86,* 157–199.

Naigles, L. R. (2003). Paradox lost? No, paradox found! Reply to Tomasello and Akhtar (2003). *Cognition, 88,* 325–329.

Nation, K., & Snowling, M. J. (1998). Semantic processing and the development of word-recognition skills: Evidence from children with reading comprehension difficulties. *Journal of Memory and Language, 39,* 85–101.

Navarette, E., Basagni, B., Alario, F.-X., & Costa, A. (2006). Does word frequency affect lexical selection in speech production? *Quarterly Journal of Experimental Psychology, 59,* 1681–1690.

Nazzi, T., Bertoncini, J., & Mehler, J. (1998). Language discrimination by newborns: Towards an understanding of the role of rhythm. *Journal of Experimental Psychology: Human Perception and Performance, 24,* 756–766.

Nebes, R. D. (1989). Semantic memory in Alzheimer's disease. *Psychological Bulletin, 106,* 377–394.

Neely, J. H. (1977). Semantic priming and retrieval from lexical memory: Roles of inhibitionless spreading activation and limited capacity attention. *Journal of Experimental Psychology: General, 106,* 226–254.

Neely, J. H. (1991). Semantic priming effects in visual word recognition: A selective review of current findings and theories. In D. Besner & G. W. Humphreys (Eds.), *Basic processes in reading: Visual word recognition* (pp. 264–336). Hillsdale, NJ: Lawrence Erlbaum Associates, Inc.

Neely, J. H., Keefe, D. E., & Ross, K. (1989). Semantic priming in the lexical decision task: Roles of prospective prime-generated expectancies and retrospective relation-checking. *Journal of Experimental Psychology: Learning, Memory, and Cognition, 15,* 1003–1019.

Negnevitsky, M. (2004). *Artificial intelligence: A guide to intelligent systems.* Reading, MA: Addison-Wesley.

Neisser, U. (1981). John Dean's memory: A case study. *Cognition, 9,* 1–22.

Nelson, K. (1973). Structure and strategy in learning to talk. *Monographs of the Society for Research in Child Development, 38* (Serial No. 149).

Nelson, K. (1974). Concept, word, and sentence: Inter-relations in acquisition and development. *Psychological Review, 81,* 267–285.

Nelson, K. (1987). What's in a name? Reply to Seidenberg and Petitto. *Journal of Experimental Psychology: General, 116,* 293–296.

Nelson, K. (1988). Constraints on word meaning? *Cognitive Development, 3,* 221–246.

Nelson, K. (1990). Comment on Behrend's "Constraints and development." *Cognitive Development, 5,* 331–339.

Nelson, K., Hampson, J., & Shaw, L. K. (1993). Nouns in early lexicons: Evidence, explanations and implications. *Journal of Child Language, 20,* 61–84.

Nespoulous, J.-L., Dordain, M., Perron, C., Ska, B., Bub, D., Caplan, D., et al. (1988). Agrammatism in sentence production without comprehension deficits: Reduced availability of syntactic structures and/or of grammatical morphemes? A case study. *Brain and Language, 33*, 273–295.

Neville, H., Nicol, J. L., Barss, A., Forster, K. I., & Garrett, M. F. (1991). Syntactically based sentence processing classes: Evidence from event-related brain potentials. *Journal of Cognitive Neuroscience, 3*, 151–165.

Newcombe, F., & Marshall, J. C. (1980). Transcoding and lexical stabilization in deep dyslexia. In M. Coltheart, K. E. Patterson, & J. C. Marshall (Eds.), *Deep dyslexia* (pp. 176–188). London: Routledge & Kegan Paul. [2nd ed., 1987.]

Newcombe, F., & Marshall, J. C. (1985). Reading and writing by letter sounds. In K. E. Patterson, J. V. Marshall, & M. Coltheart (Eds.), *Surface dyslexia* (pp. 34–51). Hove, UK: Lawrence Erlbaum Associates.

Newman, F., & Holzman, L. (Eds.). (1993). *Lev Vygotsky: Revolutionary scientist.* London: Routledge.

Newmark, L. (1966). How not to interfere with language learning. *International Journal of American Linguistics, 32*, 77–83.

Newport, E. L. (1990). Maturational constraints on language learning. *Cognitive Science, 14*, 11–28.

Newport, E. L., & Meier, R. P. (1985). The acquisition of American Sign Language. In D. I. Slobin (Ed.), *The cross-linguistic study of language acquisition: Vol. 1. The data* (pp. 882–938). Hillsdale, NJ: Lawrence Erlbaum Associates, Inc.

Newton, P. K., & Barry, C. (1997). Concreteness effects in word production but not word comprehension in deep dyslexia. *Cognitive Neuropsychology, 14*, 481–509.

Ni, W., Constable, R. T., Menci, W. E., Pugh, K. R., Fulbright, R. K., Shaywitz, S. E., et al. (2000). An event-related neuroimaging study distinguishing form and content in sentence processing. *Journal of Cognitive Neuroscience, 12*, 120–133.

Ni, W., Crain, S., & Shankweiler, D. (1996). Sidestepping garden paths: Assessing the contributions of syntax, semantics, and plausibility in resolving ambiguities. *Language and Cognitive Processes, 11*, 283–334.

Nickels, L., & Howard, D. (1994). A frequent occurrence? Factors affecting the production of semantic errors in aphasic naming. *Cognitive Neuropsychology, 11*, 289–320.

Nickels, L., & Howard, D. (1995). Phonological errors in aphasic naming: Comprehension monitoring and lexicality. *Cortex, 31*, 209–237.

Nickels, L., Howard, D., & Best, W. (1997). Fractionating the articulatory loop: Dissociations and associations in phonological recoding in aphasia. *Brain and Language, 56*, 161–182.

Nicol, J. (1993). Reconsidering reactivation. In G. Altmann & R. Shillcock (Eds.), *Cognitive models of speech processing* (pp. 321–347). Hove, UK: Lawrence Erlbaum Associates.

Nicol, J., & Swinney, D. (1989). The role of structure in coreference assignment during sentence comprehension. *Journal of Psycholinguistic Research, 18*, 5–9.

Nigram, A., Hoffman, J. E., & Simons, R. F. (1992). N400 to semantically anomalous pictures and words. *Journal of Cognitive Neuroscience, 4*, 15–22.

Ninio, A. (1980). Ostensive definition in vocabulary teaching. *Journal of Child Language, 7*, 565–573.

Nisbett, R. E. (2003). *The geography of thought.* London: Nicholas Brealey.

Nishimura, M. (1986). Intrasentential codeswitching: The case of language assignment. In J. Vaid (Ed.), *Language processing in bilinguals* (pp. 123–143). Hillsdale, NJ: Lawrence Erlbaum Associates, Inc.

Noppeny, U., & Price, C. J. (2002). A PET study of stimulus- and task-induced semantic processing. *NeuroImage, 15*, 927–935.

Norman, D. A., & Rumelhart, D. E. (1975). Memory and knowledge. In D. A. Norman, D. E. Rumelhart, & the LNR Research Group (Eds.), *Explorations in cognition* (pp. 3–32). San Francisco: Freeman.

Norris, D. (1984). The effects of frequency, repetition, and stimulus quality in visual word recognition. *Quarterly Journal of Experimental Psychology, 36A*, 507–518.

Norris, D. (1986). Word recognition: Context effects without priming. *Cognition, 22*, 93–136.

Norris, D. (1990). A dynamic-net model of human speech recognition. In G. T. M. Altmann (Ed.), *Cognitive models of speech processing* (pp. 87–104). Cambridge, MA: MIT Press.

Norris, D. (1993). Bottom-up connectionist models of "interaction." In G. Altmann & R. Shillcock (Eds.), *Cognitive models of speech processing* (pp. 211–234). Hillsdale, NJ: Lawrence Erlbaum Associates, Inc.

Norris, D. (1994a). A quantitative multiple-levels model of reading aloud. *Journal of Experimental Psychology: Human Perception and Performance, 20*, 1212–1232.

Norris, D. (1994b). Shortlist: A connectionist model of continuous speech recognition. *Cognition, 52*, 189–234.

Norris, D., & Brown, G. D. A. (1985). Race models and analogy theories: A dead heat? Reply to Seidenberg. *Cognition, 20*, 155–168.

Norris, D., McQueen, J. M., & Cutler, A. (2000). Merging information in speech recognition: Feedback is never necessary. *Behavioral and Brain Sciences, 23*, 299–370.

Norris, D., McQueen, J. M., & Cutler, A. (2003). Perceptual learning in speech. *Cognitive Psychology, 47*, 204–238.

Norris, D., McQueen, J. M., Cutler, A., & Butterfield, S. (1997). The possible-word constraint in the segmentation of continuous speech. *Cognitive Psychology*, *34*, 191–243.

Nosofsky, R. M. (1991). Tests of an exemplar model for relating perceptual classification and recognition memory. *Journal of Experimental Psychology: Human Perception and Performance*, *17*, 3–27.

Nosofky, R. M., & Palmeri, T. J. (1997). An exemplar-based random walk model of speeded classification. *Psychological Review*, *104*, 266–300.

Nowak, M. A. (2006). *Evolutionary dynamics*. Cambridge, MA: Harvard University Press.

Nozari, N., Dell, G. S., & Schwartz, M. F. (2011). Is comprehension necessary for error detection? A conflict-based account of monitoring in speech production. *Cognitive Psychology*, *63*, 1–33.

Oakhill, J. (1994). Individual differences in children's text comprehension. In M. A. Gernsbacher (Ed.), *Handbook of psycholinguistics* (pp. 821–848). San Diego, CA: Academic Press.

Obler, L. (1981). Right hemisphere participation in second language acquisition. In K. C. Diller (Ed.), *Individual differences and universals in language learning aptitude* (pp. 53–64). Rowley, MA: Newbury House.

Obler, L. K., & Hannigan, S. (1996). Neurolinguistics of second language acquisition and use. In W. C. Ritchie & T. K. Bhatia (Eds.), *Handbook of second language acquisition* (pp. 509–523). London: Academic Press.

O'Brien, E. J. (1987). Antecedent search processes and the structure of text. *Journal of Experimental Psychology: Learning, Memory, and Cognition*, *13*, 278–290.

O'Brien, E. J., Cook, A. E., & Peracchi, K. A. (2004). Updating situation models: Reply to Zwaan and Madden (2004). *Journal of Experimental Psychology: Learning, Memory, and Cognition*, *30*, 289–291.

O'Brien, E. J., Rizzella, M. L., Albrect, J. E., & Halleran, J. G. (1998). Updating a situation model: A memory-based text processing view. *Journal of Experimental Psychology: Learning, Memory, and Cognition*, *24*, 1200–1210.

Obusek, C. J., & Warren, R. M. (1973). Relation of the verbal transformation and the phonemic restoration effects. *Cognitive Psychology*, *5*, 97–107.

Ochs, E., & Schieffelin, B. (1995). The impact of language socialization on grammatical development. In P. Fletcher & B. MacWhinney (Eds.), *Handbook of child language* (pp. 73–94). Oxford: Blackwell.

Oller, D. K. (1980). The emergence of sounds of speech in infancy. In G. H. Yeni-Komshian, J. F. Kavanagh, & C. A. Ferguson (Eds.), *Child phonology* (Vol. 1, pp. 93–112). New York: Academic Press.

Oller, D. K., Eilers, R. E., Bull, D. H., & Carney, A. E. (1985). Prespeech vocalizations of a deaf infant: A comparison with normal metaphonological processes. *Journal of Speech and Hearing Research*, *28*, 47–63.

Oller, D. K., Wieman, L. A., Doyle, W. J., & Ross, C. (1976). Infant babbling and speech. *Journal of Child Language*, *3*, 1–11.

Olsen, T. S., Bruhn, P., & Öberg, R. (1986). Cortical hypoperfusion as a possible cause of "subcortical aphasia." *Brain*, *109*, 393–410.

Olson, R. K. (1994). Language deficits in "specific" reading ability. In M. A. Gernsbacher (Ed.), *Handbook of psycholinguistics* (pp. 895–916). San Diego, CA: Academic Press.

Olson, R. K., Kliegel, R., Davidson, B. J., & Foltz, G. (1984). Individual and developmental differences in reading disability. In G. E. MacKinnon & T. G. Waller (Eds.), *Reading research: Advances in theory and practice* (Vol. 4, pp. 1–64). New York: Academic Press.

Onifer, W., & Swinney, D. A. (1981). Accessing lexical ambiguities during sentence comprehension: Effects of frequency of meaning and contextual bias. *Memory and Cognition*, *9*, 225–236.

Oppenheim, G. M. (2012). The case for subphonemic attenuation in inner speech: Comment on Corley, Brocklehurst, and Moat (2011). *Journal of Experimental Psychology: Learning, Memory, and Cognition*, *38*, 502–512.

Oppenheim, G. M., & Dell, G. S. (2008). Inner speech slips exhibit lexical bias, but not the phonemic similarity effect. *Cognition*, *106*, 528–537.

Orchard, G. A., & Phillips, W. A. (1991). *Neural computation: A beginner's guide*. Hove, UK: Lawrence Erlbaum Associates.

Orwell, G. (1949). *Nineteen eighty-four*. Harmondsworth, UK: Penguin.

O'Seaghdha, P. G. (1997). Conjoint and dissociable effects of syntactic and semantic context. *Journal of Experimental Psychology: Learning, Memory, and Cognition*, *23*, 807–828.

Osgood, C. E., & Sebeok, T. A. (Eds.). (1954). *Psycholinguistics: A survey of theory and research problems* (pp. 93–101). Bloomington: Indiana University Press. [Reprinted 1965.]

Osterhout, L., & Holcomb, P. J. (1992). Event-related potentials elicited by syntactic anomaly. *Journal of Memory and Language*, *31*, 785–806.

Osterhout, L., Holcomb, P. J., & Swinney, D. A. (1994). Brain potentials elicited by garden-path sentences: Evidence of the application of verb information during parsing. *Journal of Experimental Psychology: Learning, Memory, and Cognition*, *20*, 786–803.

Osterhout, L., & Nicol, J. (1999). On the distinctiveness, independence, and time course of the brain responses to syntactic and semantic anomalies. *Language and Cognitive Processes*, *14*, 283–317.

Ostrin, R. K., & Schwartz, M. F. (1986). Reconstructing from a degraded trace—a study of sentence repetition in agrammatism. *Brain and Language, 28,* 328–345.

O'Sullivan, C., & Yeager, C. P. (1989). Communicative context and linguistic competence: The effects of social setting on a chimpanzee's conversational skills. In R. A. Gardner & T. E. van Cantford (Eds.), *Teaching sign language to chimpanzees* (pp. 269–279). Albany, NY: Suny Press.

Owens, R. E., Jr. (2004). *Language development: An introduction* (6th ed.). Columbus, OH: Merrill.

Paap, K. R., Newsome, S., McDonald, J. E., & Schvaneveldt, R. W. (1982). An activation-verification model for letter and word recognition: The word superiority effect. *Psychological Review, 89,* 573–594.

Pachella, R. G. (1974). The interpretation of reaction time in information processing research. In B. H. Kantowitz (Ed.), *Human information processing: Tutorials in performance and cognition* (pp. 41–82). Hillsdale, NJ: Lawrence Erlbaum Associates, Inc.

Paget, R. (1930). *Human speech.* New York: Harcourt Brace.

Paivio, A. (1971). *Imagery and verbal processes.* London: Holt, Rinehart & Winston.

Paivio, A., Clark, J. M., & Lambert, W. E. (1988). Bilingual dual-coding theory and semantic-repetition effects. *Journal of Experimental Psychology: Learning, Memory, and Cognition, 14,* 163–172.

Paivio, A., Yuille, J. C., & Madigan, S. (1968). Concreteness, imagery, and meaningfulness values of 925 nouns. *Journal of Experimental Psychology Monographs, 76,* 1–25.

Palmer, J., MacLeod, C. M., Hunt, E., & Davidson, J. E. (1985). Information processing correlates of reading. *Journal of Verbal Learning and Verbal Behavior, 24,* 59–88.

Papafragou, A., Massey, C., & Gleitman, L. (2002). Shake, rattle, 'n' roll: The representation of motion in language and cognition. *Cognition, 84,* 189–219.

Papagno, C., Valentine, T., & Baddeley, A. (1991). Phonological short-term memory and foreign-language vocabulary learning. *Journal of Memory and Language, 30,* 331–347.

Paquier, P. F., & Marien, P. (2005). A synthesis of the role of the cerebellum in cognition. *Aphasiology, 19,* 3–19.

Paradis, M. (1997). The cognitive neuropsychology of bilingualism. In A. M. B. de Groot & J. F. Kroll (Eds.), *Tutorials in bilingualism: Psycholinguistic perspectives* (pp. 331–354). Mahwah, NJ: Lawrence Erlbaum Associates, Inc.

Parkin, A. J. (1982). Phonological recoding in lexical decision: Effects of spelling-to-sound regularity depend on how regularity is defined. *Memory and Cognition, 10,* 43–53.

Parkin, A. J., & Stewart, F. (1993). Category-specific impairments? No. A critique of Sartori et al. *Quarterly Journal of Experimental Psychology, 46A,* 505–509.

Patterson, F. (1981). *The education of Koko.* New York: Holt, Rinehart & Winston.

Patterson, K. E. (1980). Derivational errors. In M. Coltheart, K. E. Patterson, & J. C. Marshall (Eds.), *Deep dyslexia* (pp. 286–306). London: Routledge & Kegan Paul. [2nd ed., 1987.]

Patterson, K. E., & Besner, D. (1984). Is the right hemisphere literate? *Cognitive Neuropsychology, 3,* 341–367.

Patterson, K. E., Graham, N., & Hodges, J. R. (1994). The impact of semantic memory loss on phonological representations. *Journal of Cognitive Neuroscience, 6,* 57–69.

Patterson, K. E., & Hodges, J. R. (1992). Deterioration of word meaning: Implications for reading. *Neuropsychologia, 30,* 1025–1040.

Patterson, K. E., Marshall, J. C., & Coltheart, M. (1985a). Surface dyslexia in various orthographies: Introduction. In K. E. Patterson, J. C. Marshall, & M. Coltheart (Eds.), *Surface dyslexia: Neuropsychological and cognitive studies of phonological reading* (pp. 209–214). Hove, UK: Lawrence Erlbaum Associates.

Patterson, K. E., Marshall, J. C., & Coltheart, M. (Eds.). (1985b). *Surface dyslexia: Neuropsychological and cognitive studies of phonological reading.* Hove, UK: Lawrence Erlbaum Associates.

Patterson, K. E., & Morton, J. (1985). From orthography to phonology: An attempt at an old interpretation. In K. E. Patterson, J. C. Marshall, & M. Coltheart (Eds.), *Surface dyslexia: Neuropsychological and cognitive studies of phonological reading* (pp. 335–359). Hove, UK: Lawrence Erlbaum Associates.

Patterson, K. E., Seidenberg, M. S., & McClelland, J. L. (1989). Connections and disconnections: Acquired dyslexia in a computational model of reading processes. In R. G. M. Morris (Ed.), *Parallel distributed processing: Implications for psychology and neurobiology* (pp. 131–181). Oxford: Clarendon Press.

Patterson, K. E., & Shewell, C. (1987). Speak and spell: Dissociations and word-class effects. In M. Coltheart, G. Sartori, & R. Job (Eds.), *The cognitive neuropsychology of language* (pp. 273–294). Hove, UK: Lawrence Erlbaum Associates.

Patterson, K. E., Suzuki, T., & Wydell, T. N. (1996). Interpreting a case of Japanese phonological alexia: The key is phonology. *Cognitive Neuropsychology, 13,* 803–822.

Patterson, K. E., Vargha-Khadem, F., & Polkey, C. E. (1989). Reading with one hemisphere. *Brain, 112,* 39–63.

Pearce, J. M. (2008). *Animal learning and cognition* (3rd ed.). Hove, UK: Lawrence Erlbaum Associates.

Pearl, E., & Lambert, W. E. (1962). The relation of bilingualism to intelligence. *Psychological Monographs, 76* (27, Whole No. 546).

Pearlmutter, N. J., & MacDonald, M. C. (1995). Individual differences and probabilistic constraints in syntactic ambiguity resolution. *Journal of Memory and Language, 34,* 521–542.

Peereman, R., & Content, A. (1997). Orthographic and phonological neighbours in naming: Not all neighbours are equally influential in orthographic space. *Journal of Memory and Language, 37,* 382–410.

Penfield, W., & Roberts, L. (1959). *Speech and brain mechanisms.* Princeton, NJ: Princeton University Press.

Pennington, B. F., & Lefly, D. L. (2001). Early reading development in children at family risk for dyslexia. *Child Development, 72,* 816–833.

Pepperberg, I. M. (1981). Functional vocalizations by an African grey parrot (*Psittacus erithacus*). *Zeitschrift für Tierpsychologie, 55,* 139–160.

Pepperberg, I. M. (1983). Cognition in the African grey parrot: Preliminary evidence for auditory/vocal comprehension of the class concept. *Animal Learning and Behavior, 11,* 179–185.

Pepperberg, I. M. (1987). Acquisition of the same/different concept by an African grey parrot (*Psittacus erithacus*): Learning with respect to categories of color, shape, and material. *Animal Learning and Behavior, 15,* 423–432.

Pepperberg, I. M. (1999). Rethinking syntax: A commentary on E. Kako's "Elements of syntax in the systems of three language-trained animals." *Animal Learning and Behavior, 27,* 15–17.

Pepperberg, I. M. (2009). *Alex & me: How a scientist and a parrot discovered a hidden world of animal intelligence—and formed a deep bond in the process.* New York: Harper Perennial.

Pérez-Pereira, M. (1999). Deixis, personal reference, and the use of pronouns by blind children. *Journal of Child Language, 26,* 655–680.

Pérez-Pereira, M., & Conti-Ramsden, G. (1999). *Language development and social interaction in blind children.* Hove, UK: Psychology Press.

Perfect, T. J., & Hanley, J. R. (1992). The tip-of-the-tongue phenomenon: Do experimenter-presented interlopers have any effect? *Cognition, 45,* 55–75.

Perfetti, C. A. (1994). Psycholinguistics and reading ability. In M. A. Gernsbacher (Ed.), *Handbook of psycholinguistics* (pp. 849–886). San Diego, CA: Academic Press.

Perfetti, C. A., Bell, L. C., & Delaney, S. M. (1988). Automatic (prelexical) phonetic activation in silent word reading: Evidence from backward masking. *Journal of Memory and Language, 27,* 59–70.

Perfetti, C. A., & Zhang, S. (1991). Phonological processes in reading Chinese characters. *Journal of Experimental Psychology: Learning, Memory, and Cognition, 17,* 633–643.

Perfetti, C. A., & Zhang, S. (1995). Very early phonological activation in Chinese reading. *Journal of Experimental Psychology: Learning, Memory, and Cognition, 21,* 24–33.

Peters, P. S., & Ritchie, R. W. (1973). Context-sensitive immediate constituent analysis: Context-free language revisited. *Mathematical Systems Theory, 6,* 324–333.

Petersen, S. E., Fox, P. T., Posner, M. I., Mintun, M. E., & Raichle, J. (1989). Positron emission tomographic studies of the processing of single words. *Journal of Cognitive Neuroscience, 1,* 153–170.

Petersen, S. E., van Mier, H., Fiez, J. A., & Raichle, M. E. (1998). The effects of practice on the functional anatomy of task performance. *Proceedings of the National Academy of Science USA, 95,* 853–860.

Peterson, R. R., & Savoy, P. (1998). Lexical selection and phonological encoding during language production: Evidence for cascaded processing. *Journal of Experimental Psychology: Learning, Memory, and Cognition, 24,* 539–557.

Petitto, L. (1987). On the autonomy of language and gesture: Evidence from the acquisition of personal pronouns in American Sign Language. *Cognition, 27,* 1–52.

Petitto, L. (1988). "Language" in the prelinguistic child. In F. S. Kessel (Ed.), *The development of language and language disorders* (pp. 187–222). Hillsdale, NJ: Lawrence Erlbaum Associates, Inc.

Petitto, L. A., Holowka, S., Sergio, L. E., Levy, B., & Ostry, D. J. (2004). Baby hands that move to the rhythm of language: Hearing babies acquiring sign languages babble silently on the hands. *Cognition, 93,* 43–73.

Petitto, L. A., & Marentette, P. F. (1991). Babbling in the manual mode: Evidence for the ontogeny of language. *Science, 251,* 1483–1496.

Petrie, H. (1987). The psycholinguistics of speaking. In J. Lyons, R. Coates, M. Deuchar, & G. Gazdar (Eds.), *New horizons in linguistics* (Vol. 2, pp. 336–366). Harmondsworth, UK: Penguin.

Pexman, P. M., Lupker, S. J., & Jared, D. (2001). Homophone effects in lexical decision. *Journal of Experimental Psychology: Learning, Memory, and Cognition, 27,* 139–156.

Pexman, P. M., Lupker, S. J., & Reggin, L. D. (2002). Phonological effects in visual word recognition: Investigating the impact of feedback activation. *Journal of Experimental Psychology: Learning, Memory, and Cognition, 28,* 572–584.

Piaget, J. (1923). *The language and thought of the child* (Trans. M. Gabain, 1955). Cleveland, OH: Meridian.

Piattelli-Palmarini, M. (Ed.). (1980). *Language and learning: The debate between Jean Piaget and Noam Chomsky.* London: Routledge & Kegan Paul.

Piattelli-Palmarini, M. (1989). Evolution, selection, and cognition: From "learning" to parameter setting in biology and the study of language. *Cognition, 31,* 1–44.

Piattelli-Palmarini, M. (1994). Ever since language and learning: Afterthoughts on the Piaget–Chomsky debate. *Cognition, 50,* 315–346.

Pickering, M. J. (1999). Sentence comprehension. In S. Garrod & M. J. Pickering (Eds.), *Language processing* (pp. 123–153). Hove, UK: Psychology Press.

Pickering, M. J., & Barry, G. (1991). Sentence processing without empty categories. *Language and Cognitive Processes, 6,* 229–259.

Pickering, M. J., & Branigan, H. P. (1998). The representation of verbs: Evidence from syntactic priming in language production. *Journal of Memory and Language, 39,* 633–651.

Pickering, M. J., Branigan, H. P., & McLean, J. F. (2002). Constituent structure is formulated in one stage. *Journal of Memory and Language, 46,* 586–605.

Pickering, M. J., & Garrod, S. (2004). Toward a mechanistic psychology of dialogue. *Behavioral and Brain Sciences, 27,* 169–226.

Pickering, M. J., & Garrod, S. (2006). Do people use language production to make predictions during comprehension? *Trends in Cognitive Sciences, 11,* 105–110.

Pickering, M. J., & Garrod, S. (2013). An integrated theory of language production and comprehension. *Behavioral and Brain Sciences, 36,* 329–347.

Pickering, M. J., & Traxler, M. J. (1998). Plausibility and recovery from garden paths: An eye-tracking study. *Journal of Experimental Psychology: Learning, Memory, and Cognition, 24,* 940–961.

Pickering, M. J., Traxler, M. J., & Crocker, M. W. (2000). Ambiguity resolution in sentence processing: Evidence against frequency-based accounts. *Journal of Memory and Language, 43,* 447–475.

Pickering, M. J., & van Gompel, R. P. G. (2006). Syntactic parsing. In M. J. Traxler & M. A. Gernsbacher (Eds.), *The handbook of psycholinguistics* (2nd ed., pp. 455–503). San Diego, CA: Elsevier.

Pine, J. M. (1994a). Environmental correlates of variation in lexical style: Interactional style and the structure of the input. *Applied Psycholinguistics, 15,* 355–370.

Pine, J. M. (1994b). The language of primary caregivers. In C. Gallaway & B. J. Richards (Eds.), *Input and interaction in language acquisition* (pp. 15–37). Cambridge: Cambridge University Press.

Pine, J. M., & Lieven, E. (1997). Lexically-based learning and early grammatical development. *Journal of Child Language, 24,* 187–219.

Pinker, S. (1984). *Language learnability and language development.* Cambridge, MA: MIT Press.

Pinker, S. (1989). *Learnability and cognition.* Cambridge, MA: MIT Press.

Pinker, S. (1994). *The language instinct.* Harmondsworth, UK: Allen Lane.

Pinker, S. (1999). *Words and rules.* London: Weidenfeld & Nicolson.

Pinker, S. (2001). Talk of genetics and vice versa. *Nature, 413,* 465–466.

Pinker, S. (2002). *The blank state.* Harmondsworth: Penguin.

Pinker, S. (2003). Language as an adaptation to the cognitive niche. In M. H. Christiansen & S. Kirby (Eds.), *Language evolution* (pp. 16–37). Oxford: Oxford University Press.

Pinker, S., & Bloom, P. (1990). Natural language and natural selection. *Behavioral and Brain Sciences, 13,* 707–784.

Pinker, S., & Jackendoff, R. (2005). The faculty of language: What's special about it? *Cognition, 95,* 201–236.

Pinker, S., & Prince, A. (1988). On language and connectionism: Analysis of a parallel distributed processing model of language acquisition. *Cognition, 28,* 59–108.

Pinker, S., & Ullman, M. T. (2002). The past and future of the past tense. *Trends in Cognitive Science, 6,* 456–463, and Reply, 472–474.

Pisoni, D. B., & Tash, J. (1974). Reaction times to comparisons within and across phonetic categories. *Perception and Psychophysics, 15,* 285–290.

Pitchford, N., & Mullen, K. (2005). The role of perception, language, and preference in the developmental acquisition of basic colour terms. *Journal of Experimental Child Psychology, 90,* 275–302.

Pitt, M. A. (1995a). The locus of the lexical shift in phoneme identification. *Journal of Experimental Psychology: Learning, Memory, and Cognition, 21,* 1037–1052.

Pitt, M. A. (1995b). Data fitting and detection theory: Reply to Massaro and Oden. *Journal of Experimental Psychology: Learning, Memory, and Cognition, 21,* 1065–1067.

Pitt, M. A., & McQueen, J. M. (1998). Is compensation for coarticulation mediated by the lexicon? *Journal of Memory and Language, 39,* 347–370.

Plaut, D. C. (1997). Structure and function in the lexical system: Insights from distributed models of word reading and lexical decision. *Language and Cognitive Processes, 12,* 765–805.

Plaut, D. C., & Booth, J. R. (2000). Individual and developmental differences in semantic priming: Empirical and computational support for a single-mechanism account of lexical processing. *Psychological Review, 107,* 786–823.

Plaut, D. C., & McClelland, J. L. (1993). Generalizing with componential attractors: Word and nonword reading in an attractor network. In W. Kintsch (Ed.), *Proceedings of the 15th Annual Conference of the Cognitive Science Society* (pp. 824–829). Hillsdale, NJ: Lawrence Erlbaum Associates, Inc.

Plaut, D. C., McClelland, J. L., Seidenberg, M. S., & Patterson, K. E. (1996). Understanding normal and impaired word reading: Computational principles in quasi-regular domains. *Psychological Review, 103*, 56–115.

Plaut, D. C., & Shallice, T. (1993a). Deep dyslexia: A case study of connectionist neuropsychology. *Cognitive Neuropsychology, 10*, 377–500.

Plaut, D. C., & Shallice, T. (1993b). Perseverative and semantic influences on visual object naming errors in optic aphasia: A connectionist account. *Journal of Cognitive Neuroscience, 5*, 89–117.

Plunkett, K., & Elman, J. L. (1997). *Exercises in rethinking innateness: A handbook for connectionist simulations.* Cambridge, MA: Bradford Books.

Plunkett, K., & Marchman, V. (1991). U-shaped learning and frequency effects in a multilayered perceptron: Implications for child language acquisition. *Cognition, 38*, 43–102.

Plunkett, K., & Marchman, V. (1993). From rote learning to system building: Acquiring verb morphology in children and connectionist nets. *Cognition, 48*, 21–69.

Poeppel, D. (1996). A critical review of PET studies of phonological processing. *Brain and Language, 55*, 317–351.

Poeppel, D., & Hickok, G. (2004). Towards a new functional anatomy of language. *Cognition, 92*, 1–12.

Polk, T. A., & Farah, M. J. (2002). Functional MRI evidence for an abstract, not perceptual, word-form area. *Journal of Experimental Psychology: General, 131*, 65–72.

Pollatsek, A., Bolozky, S., Well, A. D., & Rayner, K. (1981). Asymmetries in the perceptual span for Israeli readers. *Brain and Language, 14*, 174–180.

Posner, M. I., & Keele, S. W. (1968). On the genesis of abstract ideas. *Journal of Experimental Psychology, 77*, 353–363.

Posner, M. I., & Snyder, C. R. R. (1975). Facilitation and inhibition in the processing of signals. In P. M. A. Rabbitt & S. Dornic (Eds.), *Attention and performance V* (pp. 669–682). New York: Academic Press.

Postal, P. (1964). *Constituent structure: A study of contemporary models of syntactic description.* Bloomington, IN: Research Center for the Language Sciences.

Postma, A. (2000). Detection of errors during speech production: A review of speech monitoring models. *Cognition, 77*, 97–131.

Postman, L., & Keppel, G. (1970). *Norms of word associations.* New York: Academic Press.

Potter, J. M. (1980). What was the matter with Dr. Spooner? In V. A. Fromkin (Ed.), *Errors in linguistic performance* (pp. 13–34). New York: Academic Press.

Potter, M. C., & Lombardi, L. (1990). Regeneration in the short-term recall of sentences. *Journal of Memory and Language, 29*, 633–654.

Potter, M. C., & Lombardi, L. (1998). Syntactic priming in immediate recall of sentences. *Journal of Memory and Language, 38*, 265–282.

Potter, M. C., Moryadas, A., Abrams, I., & Noel, A. (1993). Word perception and misperception in context. *Journal of Experimental Psychology: Learning, Memory, and Cognition, 19*, 3–22.

Potter, M. C., So, K. F., von Eckardt, B., & Feldman, L. B. (1984). Lexical and conceptual representation in beginning and proficient bilinguals. *Journal of Verbal Learning and Verbal Behavior, 23*, 23–38.

Potts, G. R., Keenan, J. M., & Golding, J. M. (1988). Assessing the occurrence of elaborative inferences: Lexical decision versus naming. *Journal of Memory and Language, 27*, 399–415.

Prasada, S., & Pinker, S. (1993). Generalisation of regular and irregular morphological patterns. *Language and Cognitive Processes, 8*, 1–56.

Prat, C. S., Mason, R. A., & Just, M. A. (2012). An fMRI investigation of analogical mapping in metaphor comprehension: The influence of context and individual cognitive capacities on processing demands. *Journal of Experimental Psychology: Learning, Memory, and Cognition, 38*, 282–294.

Premack, D. (1971). Language in chimpanzee? *Science, 172*, 808–822.

Premack, D. (1976a). *Intelligence in ape and man.* Hillsdale, NJ: Lawrence Erlbaum Associates, Inc.

Premack, D. (1976b). Language and intelligence in ape and man. *American Scientist, 64*, 674–683.

Premack, D. (1985). "Gavagai!" or the future history of the animal language controversy. *Cognition, 19*, 207–296.

Premack, D. (1986a). *Gavagai! or the future history of the animal language controversy.* Cambridge, MA: MIT Press.

Premack, D. (1986b). Pangloss to Cyrano de Bergerac: "Nonsense, it's perfect!" A reply to Bickerton. *Cognition, 23*, 81–88.

Premack, D. (1990). Words: What are they, and do animals have them? *Cognition, 37*, 197–212.

Price, C. J., & Devlin, J. T. (2003). The myth of the visual word form area. *NeuroImage, 19*, 473–481.

Pring, L. (1981). Phonological codes and functional spelling units: Reality and implications. *Perception and Psychophysics, 30*, 573–578.

Protopapas, A. (1999). Connectionist modeling of speech perception. *Psychological Bulletin, 125*, 410–436.

Proverbio, A. M., Cok, B., & Zani, A. (2002). Electrophysiological measures of language processing in bilinguals. *Journal of Cognitive Neuroscience, 14*, 994–1017.

Pullum, G. K. (1981). Languages with object before subject: A comment and a catalogue. *Linguistics, 19*, 147–155.

Pullum, G. K. (1989). The great Eskimo vocabulary hoax. *Natural Language and Linguistic Theory, 7,* 275–281.

Pulvermüller, F. (1995). Agrammatism: Behavioral description and neurobiological explanation. *Journal of Cognitive Neuroscience, 7,* 165–181.

Pulvermüller, F., Shtyrov, Y., & Illmoniemi, R. J. (2003). Spatio-temporal patterns of neural language processing: An MEG study using minimum-norm current estimates. *NeuroImage, 20,* 1020–1025.

Pye, C. (1986). Quiché Mayan speech to children. *Journal of Child Language, 13,* 85–100.

Quine, W. V. O. (1960). *Word and object.* Cambridge, MA: MIT Press.

Quine, W. V. O. (1977). Natural kinds. In S. P. Schwartz (Ed.), *Naming, necessity, and natural kinds* (pp. 155–175). Ithaca, NY: Cornell University Press.

Quinlan, P. T. (1992). *The Oxford psycholinguistic database.* Oxford: Oxford University Press.

Quinlan, P. T., & Dyson, B. (2008). *Cognitive psychology.* Harlow, Essex: Pearson Education.

Quinn, P. C., & Eimas, P. D. (1986). On categorization in early infancy. *Merrill-Palmer Quarterly, 32,* 331–363.

Quinn, P. C., & Eimas, P. D. (1996). Perceptual organization and categorization in young infants. In C. Rovee-Collier & L. P. Lipsitt (Eds.), *Advances in infancy research* (Vol. 10, pp. 2–36). Norwood, NJ: Ablex.

Rack, J. P., Hulme, C., Snowling, M. J., & Wightman, J. (1994). The role of phonology in young children learning to read words: The direct-mapping hypothesis. *Journal of Experimental Child Psychology, 57,* 42–71.

Rack, J. P., Snowling, M. J., & Olson, R. K. (1992). The nonword reading deficit in developmental dyslexia: A review. *Reading Research Quarterly, 27,* 29–43.

Radford, A. (1981). *Transformational syntax: A student's guide to Chomsky's extended standard theory.* Cambridge: Cambridge University Press.

Radford, A. (1997). *Syntax: A minimalist introduction.* Cambridge: Cambridge University Press.

Radford, A., Atkinson, M. A., Britain, D., Clahsen, H., & Spencer, A. (1999). *Linguistics.* Cambridge: Cambridge University Press.

Rapp, B., Benzing, L., & Caramazza, A. (1997). The autonomy of lexical orthography. *Cognitive Neuropsychology, 14,* 71–104.

Rapp, B., & Caramazza, A. (1993). On the distinction between deficits of access and deficits of storage: A question of theory. *Cognitive Neuropsychology, 10,* 113–141.

Rapp, B., & Caramazza, A. (1998). A case of selective difficulty in writing verbs. *Neurocase, 4,* 127–140.

Rapp, B., & Caramazza, A. (2002). Selective difficulties with spoken nouns and written verbs: A single case study. *Journal of Neurolinguistics, 15,* 373–402.

Rapp, B., & Goldrick, M. (2000). Discreteness and interactivity in spoken word production. *Psychological Review, 107,* 460–499.

Rapp, B., & Goldrick, M. (2004). Feedback by any other name is still interactivity: A reply to Roelofs (2004). *Psychological Review, 111,* 573–578.

Rapp, B., & Goldrick, M. (2005). Speaking words: Contributions of cognitive neuropsychological research. *Cognitive Neuropsychology, 22,* 1–34.

Rapp, D. N., & Samuel, A. G. (2000). A reason to rhyme: Phonological and semantic influences on lexical access. *Journal of Experimental Psychology: Learning, Memory, and Cognition, 28,* 564–571.

Rasmussen, T., & Milner, B. (1975). Clinical and surgical studies of the cerebral speech areas in man. In K. J. Zulch, O. Creutzfeldt, & G. C. Galbraith (Eds.), *Cerebral localization* (pp. 238–257). New York: Springer-Verlag.

Rasmussen, T., & Milner, B. (1977). The role of early left brain injury in determining lateralization of cerebral speech functions. *Annals of the New York Academy of Sciences, 299,* 355–369.

Rastle, K., & Brysbaert, M. (2006). Masked phonological priming effects in English: Are they real? Do they matter? *Cognitive Psychology, 53,* 97–145.

Rastle, K., & Coltheart, M. (2000). Lexical and nonlexical print-to-sound translation of disyllabic words and nonwords. *Journal of Memory and Language, 42,* 342–364.

Rastle, K., Davis, M. H., & New, B. (2004). The broth in my brother's brothel: Morpho-orthographic segmentation in visual word recognition. *Psychonomic Bulletin and Review, 11,* 1090–1098.

Ratcliff, J. E., & McKoon, G. (1981). Does activation really spread? *Psychological Review, 88,* 454–462.

Ratcliff, J. E., & McKoon, G. (1988). A retrieval theory of priming in memory. *Psychological Review, 95,* 385–408.

Rayner, K. (1998). Eye movements in reading and information processing: 20 years of research. *Psychological Bulletin, 124,* 372–422.

Rayner, K., & Bertera, J. H. (1979). Reading without a fovea. *Science, 206,* 468–469.

Rayner, K., Binder, K. S., & Duffy, S. A. (1999). Contextual strength and the subordinate bias effect: Comment on Martin, Vu, Kellas, and Metcalf. *Quarterly Journal of Experimental Psychology, 52A,* 841–852.

Rayner, K., Carlson, M., & Frazier, L. (1983). The interaction of syntax and semantics during sentence processing: Eye movements in the analysis of semantically biased sentences. *Journal of Verbal Learning and Verbal Behavior, 22,* 358–374.

Rayner, K., & Frazier, L. (1987). Parsing temporarily ambiguous complements. *Quarterly Journal of Experiment Psychology, 39A,* 657–673.

Rayner, K., & Frazier, L. (1989). Selection mechanisms in reading lexically ambiguous words. *Journal of Experimental Psychology: Learning, Memory, and Cognition, 15,* 779–790.

Rayner, K., & McConkie, G. W. (1976). What governs a reader's eye movements? *Vision Research, 16,* 829–837.

Rayner, K., Pacht, J. M., & Duffy, S. A. (1994). Effects of prior encounter and global discourse bias on the processing of lexically ambiguous words. *Journal of Memory and Language, 33,* 527–544.

Rayner, K., & Pollatsek, A. (1989). *The psychology of reading.* Englewood Cliffs, NJ: Prentice Hall.

Rayner, K., Pollatsek, A., & Binder, K. S. (1998). Phonological codes and eye movements in reading. *Journal of Experimental Psychology: Learning, Memory, and Cognition, 24,* 476–497.

Rayner, K., Well, A. D., & Pollatsek, A. (1980). Asymmetry of the effective visual field in reading. *Perception and Psychophysics, 27,* 537–544.

Read, C. (1975). *Children's categorization of speech sounds in English.* Urbana, IL: National Council of Teachers of English.

Read, C., Zhang, Y., Nie, H., & Ding, B. (1986). The ability to manipulate speech sounds depends on knowing alphabetic writing. *Cognition, 24,* 31–44.

Reber, A. S., & Anderson, J. R. (1970). The perception of clicks in linguistic and nonlinguistic messages. *Perception and Psychophysics, 8,* 81–89.

Redington, M., & Chater, N. (1998). Connectionist and statistical approaches to language acquisition: A distributional perspective. *Language and Cognitive Processes, 13,* 129–191.

Redlinger, W., & Park, T. Z. (1980). Language mixing in young bilinguals. *Journal of Child Language, 7,* 337–352.

Rees, G., Russell, C., Frith, C. D., & Driver, J. (1999). Inattentional blindness versus inattentional amnesia for fixated but ignored words. *Science, 286,* 2504–2507.

Reicher, G. M. (1969). Perceptual recognition as a function of meaningfulness of stimulus materials. *Journal of Experimental Psychology, 81,* 274–280.

Reichle, E. D., Rayner, K., & Pollatsek, A. (1999). Eye movement control in reading: Accounting for initial fixation locations and refixations within the E-Z Reader model. *Vision Research, 39,* 4403–4411.

Reichle, E. D., Rayner, K., & Pollatsek, A. (2003). The E-Z Reader model of eye-movement control in reading: Comparisons to other models. *Behavioral and Brain Sciences, 26,* 445–526.

Remez, R., & Pisoni, D. (Eds.). (2005). *Handbook of speech perception.* Oxford: Blackwell.

Rescorla, L. (1980). Overextension in early language development. *Journal of Child Language, 7,* 321–335.

Richards, B. J., & Gallaway, C. (1994). Conclusions and directions. In C. Gallaway & B. J. Richards (Eds.), *Input and interaction in language acquisition* (pp. 253–269). Cambridge: Cambridge University Press.

Richards, M. M. (1979). Sorting out what's in a word from what's not: Evaluating Clark's semantic features acquisition theory. *Journal of Experimental Child Psychology, 27,* 1–47.

Richardson, D. C., & Dale, R. (2005). Looking to understand: The coupling between speakers' and listeners' eye movements and its relationship to discourse comprehension. *Cognitive Science, 2005,* 1045–1060.

Riddoch, M. J., & Humphreys, G. W. (1987). Visual object processing in optic aphasia: A case of semantic access agnosia. *Cognitive Neuropsychology, 4,* 131–185.

Riddoch, M. J., Humphreys, G. W., Coltheart, M., & Funnell, E. (1988). Semantic systems or system? Neuropsychological evidence re-examined. *Cognitive Neuropsychology, 5,* 3–25.

Rigalleau, F., & Caplan, D. (2000). Effects of gender marking in pronominal coindexation. *Quarterly Journal of Experimental Psychology, 53A,* 23–52.

Rinck, M., & Bower, G. H. (1995). Anaphora resolution and the focus of attention in situation models. *Journal of Memory and Language, 34,* 110–131.

Rips, L. J. (1995). The current status of research on concept combination. *Mind and Language, 10,* 72–104.

Rips, L. J., & Collins, A. (1993). Categories and resemblance. *Journal of Experimental Psychology: General, 122,* 468–486.

Rips, L. J., Shoben, E. J., & Smith, E. E. (1973). Semantic distance and the verification of semantic relations. *Journal of Verbal Learning and Verbal Behavior, 12,* 1–20.

Rips, L. J., Smith, E. E., & Shoben, E. J. (1975). Set-theoretic and network models reconsidered: A comment on Hollan's "Features and semantic memory." *Psychological Review, 82,* 156–157.

Ritchie, W. C., & Bhatia, T. K. (Eds.). (1996). *Handbook of second language acquisition.* London: Academic Press.

Rivas, E. (2005). Recent use of signs by chimpanzees. *Journal of Comparative Psychology, 119,* 404–417.

Rizzolatti, G., Fadiga, L., Fogassi, L., & Gallese, V. (1996). Premotor cortex and the recognition of motor actions. *Cognitive Brain Research, 3,* 1131–1141.

Roberson, D., Davies, I., & Davidoff, J. (2000). Color categories are not universal: Replications and new evidence from a stone-age culture. *Journal of Experimental Psychology, 129,* 369–398.

Roberts, B., & Kirsner, K. (2000). Temporal cycles in speech production. *Language and Cognitive Processes, 15,* 129–157.

Robinson, P. (2001). Individual differences, cognitive abilities and aptitude complexes. *Second Language Research, 17,* 368–392.

Rochford, G. (1971). Study of naming errors in dysphasic and in demented patients. *Neuropsychologia, 9*, 437–443.

Rochon, E., Waters, G. S., & Caplan, D. (1994). Sentence comprehension in patients with Alzheimer's disease. *Brain and Language, 46*, 329–349.

Rodd, J., Gaskell, G., & Marslen-Wilson, W. (2002). Making sense of semantic ambiguity: Semantic competition in lexical access. *Journal of Memory and Language, 46*, 245–266.

Rodriguez-Fornells, A., Rotte, M., Heinze, H. J., Nosselt, T., & Munte, T. (2002). Brain potential and functional MRI evidence for how to handle two languages with one brain. *Nature, 415*, 1026–1029.

Roediger, H. L., & Blaxton, T. A. (1987). Retrieval modes produce dissociations in memory for surface information. In D. S. Gorfein & R. R. Hoffman (Eds.), *Memory and cognitive processes* (pp. 349–377). Hillsdale, NJ: Lawrence Erlbaum Associates, Inc.

Roelofs, A. (1992). A spreading-activation theory of lemma retrieval in speaking. *Cognition, 42*, 107–142.

Roelofs, A. (1997a). Syllabification in speech production: Evaluation of WEAVER. *Language and Cognitive Processes, 12*, 657–693.

Roelofs, A. (1997b). The WEAVER model of word-form encoding in speech production. *Cognition, 64*, 249–284.

Roelofs, A. (2002). Spoken language planning and the initiation of articulation. *Quarterly Journal of Experimental Psychology, 55A*, 465–483.

Roelofs, A. (2004a). Error biases in spoken word planning and monitoring by aphasic and nonaphasic speakers: Comment on Rapp and Goldrick (2000). *Psychological Review, 111*, 561–572.

Roelofs, A. (2004b). Comprehension-based versus production-internal feedback in planning spoken words: A rejoinder to Rapp and Goldrick (2000). *Psychological Review, 111*, 579–580.

Roelofs, A., & Meyer, A. S. (1998). Metrical structure in planning the production of spoken words. *Journal of Experimental Psychology: Learning, Memory, and Cognition, 24*, 922–939.

Roelofs, A., Meyer, A. S., & Levelt, W. J. M. (1998). A case for the lemma/lexeme distinction in models of speaking: Comment on Caramazza and Miozzo (1997). *Cognition, 69*, 219–230.

Roeltgen, D. P. (1987). Loss of deep dyslexic reading ability from a second left-hemisphere lesion. *Archives of Neurology, 44*, 346–348.

Rogalsky, C., & Hickok, G. (2011). The role of Broca's area in sentence comprehension. *Journal of Cognitive Neuroscience, 23*, 1664–1680.

Rogers, T. T., Lambon Ralph, M. A., Garrard, P., Bozeat, S., McClelland, J. L., Hodges, J. R., et al. (2004). Structure and deterioration of semantic memory: A neuropsychological and computational investigation. *Psychological Review, 111*, 205–235.

Rogers, T. T., & McClelland, J. L. (2004). *Semantic cognition: A parallel distributed processing approach.* Cambridge, MA: MIT Press.

Rohde, D. L. T., & Plaut, D. C. (1999). Language acquisition in the absence of explicit negative evidence: How important is starting small? *Cognition, 72*, 67–109.

Rolnick, M., & Hoops, H. R. (1969). Aphasia as seen by the aphasic. *Journal of Speech and Hearing Disorders, 34*, 48–53.

Romaine, S. (1995). *Bilingualism* (2nd ed.). Oxford: Blackwell.

Romani, C. (1992). Are there distinct input and output buffers? Evidence from an aphasic patient with an impaired output buffer. *Language and Cognitive Processes, 7*, 131–162.

Romani, C., & Martin, R. C. (1999). A deficit in the short-term retention of lexical-semantic information: Forgetting words but remembering a story. *Journal of Experimental Psychology: General, 128*, 56–77.

Rosch, E. (1973). Natural categories. *Cognitive Psychology, 4*, 328–350.

Rosch, E. (1978). Principles of categorization. In E. Rosch & B. Lloyd (Eds.), *Cognition and categorization* (pp. 27–48). Hillsdale, NJ: Lawrence Erlbaum Associates, Inc.

Rosch, E., & Mervis, C. B. (1975). Family resemblances: Studies in the internal structure of categories. *Cognitive Psychology, 7*, 573–605.

Rosch, E., Mervis, C. B., Gray, W., Johnson, D., & Boyes-Braem, P. (1976). Basic objects in natural categories. *Cognitive Psychology, 8*, 382–439.

Rosnow, R. L., & Rosnow, M. (1992). *Writing papers in psychology* (2nd ed.). New York: Wiley.

Ross, B. H., & Bower, G. H. (1981). Comparisons of models of associative recall. *Memory and Cognition, 9*, 1–16.

Rosson, M. B. (1983). From SOFA to LOUCH: Lexical contributions to pseudoword pronunciation. *Memory and Cognition, 11*, 152–160.

Roy, D. (2005). Grounding words in perception and action: Computational insights. *Trends in Cognitive Sciences, 9*, 389–395.

Rubenstein, H., Lewis, S. S., & Rubenstein, M. A. (1971). Evidence for phonemic recoding in visual word recognition. *Journal of Verbal Learning and Verbal Behavior, 10*, 645–658.

Rubin, D. C. (1980). 51 properties of 125 words: A unit analysis of verbal behavior. *Journal of Verbal Learning and Verbal Behavior, 19*, 736–755.

Rubin, J. (1968). *National bilingualism in Paraguay.* The Hague: Mouton.

Rumelhart, D. E. (1975). Notes on a schema for stories. In D. G. Bobrow & A. M. Collins (Eds.), *Representation and understanding: Studies in cognitive science* (pp. 211–236). New York: Academic Press.

Rumelhart, D. E. (1977). Understanding and summarizing brief stories. In D. LaBerge & S. J. Samuels (Eds.), *Basic processes in reading: Perception and comprehension* (pp. 265–303). Hillsdale, NJ: Lawrence Erlbaum Associates, Inc.

Rumelhart, D. E. (1980). On evaluating story grammars. *Cognitive Science, 4*, 313–316.

Rumelhart, D. E., & McClelland, J. L. (1982). An interactive activation model of context effects in letter perception: Part 2. The contextual enhancement effect and some tests and extensions of the model. *Psychological Review, 89*, 60–94.

Rumelhart, D. E., & McClelland, J. L. (1986). On learning the past tense of English verbs. In D. E. Rumelhart, J. L. McClelland, & the PDP Research Group, *Parallel distributed processing: Vol. 2. Psychological and biological models* (pp. 216–271). Cambridge, MA: MIT Press.

Rumelhart, D. E., McClelland, J. L., & the PDP Research Group. (1986). *Parallel distributed processing: Vol. 1. Foundations.* Cambridge, MA: MIT Press.

Ruml, W., & Caramazza, A. (2000). An evaluation of a computational model of lexical access: Comment on Dell et al. (1997). *Psychological Review, 107*, 609–634.

Ruml, W., Caramazza, A., Shelton, J. R., & Chialant, D. (2000). Testing assumptions in computational theories of aphasia. *Journal of Memory and Language, 43*, 217–248.

Rymer, R. (1993). *Genie*. London: Joseph.

Sacchett, C., & Humphreys, G. W. (1992). Calling a squirrel a squirrel but a canoe a wigwam: A category-specific deficit for artefactual objects and body parts. *Cognitive Neuropsychology, 9*, 73–86.

Sachs, J., Bard, B., & Johnson, M. L. (1981). Language learning with restricted input: Case studies of two hearing children of deaf parents. *Applied Psycholinguistics, 2*, 33–54.

Sachs, J. S. (1967). Recognition memory for syntactic and semantic aspects of connected discourse. *Perception and Psychophysics, 2*, 437–442.

Sacks, H., Schegloff, E. A., & Jefferson, G. (1974). A simplest systematics for the organization of turn-taking in conversation. *Language, 50*, 696–735.

Saffran, E. M. (1990). Short-term memory impairments and language processing. In A. Caramazza (Ed.), *Cognitive neuropsychology and neurolinguistics* (pp. 137–168). Hillsdale, NJ: Lawrence Erlbaum Associates, Inc.

Saffran, E. M., Bogyo, L. C., Schwartz, M. F., & Marin, O. S. M. (1980). Does deep dyslexia reflect right hemisphere reading? In M. Coltheart, K. E. Patterson, & J. C. Marshall (Eds.), *Deep dyslexia* (pp. 381–406). London: Routledge & Kegan Paul. [2nd ed., 1987.]

Saffran, E. M., Marin, O. S. M., & Yeni-Komshian, G. H. (1976). An analysis of speech perception in word deafness. *Brain and Language, 3*, 209–228.

Saffran, E. M., & Martin, N. (1997). Effects of structural priming on sentence production in aphasia. *Language and Cognitive Processes, 12*, 877–882.

Saffran, E. M., & Schwartz, M. (1994). Of cabbages and things: Semantic memory from a neuropsychological perspective—a tutorial review. In C. Umilta & M. Moscovitch (Eds.), *Attention and performance XV: Conscious and nonconscious information processing* (pp. 507–536). Cambridge, MA: MIT Press.

Saffran, E. M., Schwartz, M. F., & Linebarger, M. C. (1998). Semantic influences on thematic role assignment: Evidence from normals and aphasics. *Brain and Language, 62*, 255–297.

Saffran, E. M., Schwartz, M. F., & Marin, O. S. M. (1976). Semantic mechanisms in paralexia. *Brain and Language, 3*, 255–265.

Saffran, E. M., Schwartz, M. F., & Marin, O. S. M. (1980). Evidence from aphasia: Isolating the components of a production model. In B. Butterworth (Ed.), *Language production: Vol. 1. Speech and talk* (pp. 221–241). London: Academic Press.

Saffran, J. R. (2001). The use of predictive dependencies in language learning. *Journal of Memory and Language, 44*, 493–515.

Saffran, J. R. (2002). Constraints on statistical language learning. *Journal of Memory and Language, 47*, 172–196.

Saffran, J. R., Aslin, R. N., & Newport, E. L. (1996). Statistical learning by 8-month-old infants. *Science, 274*, 1926–1928.

Saffran, J. R., Werker, J. F., & Werner, L. A. (2006). The infant's auditory world: Hearing, speech, and the beginnings of language. In R. Siegler & D. Kuhn (Eds.), *Handbook of child development* (6th ed., pp. 58–108). New York: Wiley.

Salamoura, A., & Williams, J. N. (2006). Lexical activation of cross-language syntactic priming. *Bilingualism: Language and Cognition, 9*, 299–307.

Samuel, A. G. (1981). Phonemic restoration: Insights from a new methodology. *Journal of Experimental Psychology: General, 110*, 474–494.

Samuel, A. G. (1987). The effect of lexical uniqueness on phonemic restoration. *Journal of Memory and Language, 26*, 36–56.

Samuel, A. G. (1990). Using perceptual-restoration effects to explore the architecture of perception. In G. T. M. Altmann (Ed.), *Cognitive models of speech processing* (pp. 295–314). Cambridge, MA: MIT Press.

Samuel, A. G. (1996). Does lexical information influence the perceptual restoration of phonemes? *Journal of Experimental Psychology: General, 125*, 28–51.

Samuel, A. G. (1997). Lexical activation produces potent phonemic percepts. *Cognitive Psychology, 32*, 97–127.

Sandra, D. (1990). On the representation and processing of compound words: Automatic access to constituent morphemes does not occur. *Quarterly Journal of Experimental Psychology, 42A*, 529–567.

Sanford, A. J. (1985). *Cognition and cognitive psychology*. London: Weidenfeld & Nicolson.

Sanford, A. J., & Garrod, S. C. (1981). *Understanding written language*. Chichester, UK: John Wiley.

Santa, J. L., & Ranken, H. B. (1972). Effects of verbal coding on recognition memory. *Journal of Experimental Psychology, 93*, 268–278.

Sartori, G., & Job, R. (1988). The oyster with four legs: A neuropsychological study on the interaction of visual and semantic information. *Cognitive Neuropsychology, 5*, 105–132.

Sartori, G., Miozzo, M., & Job, R. (1993). Category-specific impairments? Yes. *Quarterly Journal of Experimental Psychology, 46A*, 489–504.

Sasanuma, S. (1980). Acquired dyslexia in Japanese: Clinical features and underlying mechanisms. In M. Coltheart, K. E. Patterson, & J. C. Marshall (Eds.), *Deep dyslexia* (pp. 48–90). London: Routledge & Kegan Paul. [2nd ed., 1987.]

Sasanuma, S., Ito, H., Patterson, K., & Ito, T. (1996). Phonological alexia in Japanese: A case study. *Cognitive Neuropsychology, 13*, 823–848.

Savage, C., Lieven, E., Theakston, A., & Tomasello, M. (2003). Testing the abstractness of young children's linguistic representations: Lexical and structural priming of syntactic constructions. *Developmental Science, 6*, 557–567.

Savage, G. R., Bradley, D. C., & Forster, K. I. (1990). Word frequency and the pronunciation task: The contribution of articulatory fluency. *Language and Cognitive Processes, 5*, 203–236.

Savage, R. S. (1997). Do children need concurrent prompts in order to use lexical analogies in reading? *Journal of Child Psychology and Psychiatry, 38*, 235–246.

Savage-Rumbaugh, E. S. (1987). Communication, symbolic communication, and language: A reply to Seidenberg and Petitto. *Journal of Experimental Psychology: General, 116*, 288–292.

Savage-Rumbaugh, E. S., & Lewin, R. (1994). *Kanzi: At the brink of the human mind*. New York: Wiley.

Savage-Rumbaugh, E. S., McDonald, K., Sevcik, R. A., Hopkins, W. D., & Rupert, E. (1986). Spontaneous symbol acquisition and communicative use by pygmy chimpanzees (*Pan paniscus*). *Journal of Experimental Psychology: General, 115*, 211–235.

Savage-Rumbaugh, E. S., Murphy, J., Sevcik, R. A., Brakke, K. E., Williams, S. L., & Rumbaugh, D. M. (1993). Language comprehension in ape and child. *Monographs of the Society for Research in Child Development, 58* (Whole Nos. 3–4).

Savage-Rumbaugh, E. S., Pate, J. L., Lawson, J., Smith, T., & Rosenbaum, S. (1983). Can a chimpanzee make a statement? *Journal of Experimental Psychology: General, 112*, 457–492.

Savage-Rumbaugh, E. S., Rumbaugh, D. M., & Boysen, S. (1978). Linguistically mediated tool use and exchange by chimpanzees. *Behavioral and Brain Sciences, 1*, 539–554.

Savin, H. B., & Bever, T. G. (1970). The non-perceptual reality of the phoneme. *Journal of Verbal Learning and Verbal Behavior, 9*, 295–302.

Savin, H. B., & Perchonock, E. (1965). Grammatical structure and the immediate recall of English sentences. *Journal of Verbal Learning and Verbal Behavior, 4*, 348–353.

Saxton, M. (1997). The contrast theory of negative input. *Journal of Child Language, 24*, 139–161.

Scarborough, D. L., Cortese, C., & Scarborough, H. S. (1977). Frequency and repetition effects in lexical memory. *Journal of Experimental Psychology: Human Perception and Performance, 3*, 1–17.

Scarborough, D. L., Gerard, L., & Cortese, C. (1984). Independence of lexical access in bilingual word recognition. *Journal of Verbal Learning and Verbal Behavior, 23*, 84–99.

Schaeffer, B., & Wallace, R. (1969). Semantic similarity and the comprehension of word meanings. *Journal of Experimental Psychology, 82*, 343–346.

Schaeffer, B., & Wallace, R. (1970). The comparison of word meanings. *Journal of Experimental Psychology, 86*, 144–152.

Schaeffer, H. R. (1975). Social development in infancy. In R. Lewin (Ed.), *Child alive* (pp. 32–39). London: Temple Smith.

Schank, R. C. (1972). Conceptual dependency: A theory of natural language understanding. *Cognitive Psychology, 3*, 552–631.

Schank, R. C. (1975). *Conceptual information processing*. Amsterdam: North Holland.

Schank, R. C. (1982). *Dynamic memory*. Cambridge: Cambridge University Press.

Schank, R. C., & Abelson, R. (1977). *Scripts, plans, goals and understanding*. Hillsdale, NJ: Lawrence Erlbaum Associates, Inc.

Schenkein, J. (1980). A taxonomy for repeating action sequences in natural conversation. In B. Butterworth (Ed.), *Language production: Vol. 1. Speech and talk* (pp. 21–48). London: Academic Press.

Schiff-Myers, N. (1993). Hearing children of deaf parents. In D. Bishop & K. Mogford (Eds.), *Language development in exceptional circumstances* (pp. 47–61). Hove, UK: Lawrence Erlbaum Associates.

Schiller, N. O., & Caramazza, A. (2003). Grammatical feature selection in noun phrase production: Evidence from German and Dutch. *Journal of Memory and Language, 48*, 169–194.

Schiller, N. O., & Costa, A. (2006). Different selection principles of free-standing and bound morphemes in language production. *Journal of Experimental Psychology: Learning, Memory, and Cognition, 32,* 1201–1207.

Schilling, H. E. H., Rayner, K., & Chumbley, J. I. (1998). Comparing naming, lexical decision, and eye fixation times: Word frequency effects and individual differences. *Memory and Cognition, 26,* 1270–1281.

Schlesinger, H. S., & Meadow, K. P. (1972). *Sound and sign: Childhood deafness and mental health.* Berkeley: University of California Press.

Schlesinger, I. M. (1971). Production of utterances and language acquisition. In D. I. Slobin (Ed.), *The ontogenesis of grammar* (pp. 63–102). New York: Academic Press.

Schlesinger, I. M. (1988). The origin of relational categories. In Y. Levy, I. M. Schlesinger, & M. D. S. Braine (Eds.), *Categories and processes in language acquisition* (pp. 121–178). Hillsdale, NJ: Lawrence Erlbaum Associates, Inc.

Schneider, W., & Shiffrin, R. M. (1977). Controlled and automatic human information processing: I. Detection, search and attention. *Psychological Review, 84,* 1–66.

Schnur, T. T., Costa, A., & Caramazza, A. (2006). Planning at the phonological level during sentence production. *Journal of Psycholinguistic Research, 35,* 189–213.

Schober, M. F., & Clark, H. H. (1989). Understanding by addressees and overhearers. *Cognitive Psychology, 21,* 211–232.

Schreuder, R., & Baayen, R. H. (1997). How complex simplex words can be. *Journal of Memory and Language, 37,* 118–139.

Schriefers, H., Jescheniak, J. D., & Hantsch, A. (2005). Selection of gender-marked morphemes in speech production. *Journal of Experimental Psychology: Learning, Memory, and Cognition, 31,* 159–168.

Schriefers, H., Meyer, A. S., & Levelt, W. J. M. (1990). Exploring the time course of lexical access in language production: Picture–word interference studies. *Journal of Memory and Language, 29,* 86–102.

Schriefers, H., & Teruel, E. (2000). Grammatical gender in noun phrase production: The gender interference effect in German. *Journal of Experimental Psychology: Learning, Memory, and Cognition, 26,* 1368–1377.

Schriefers, H., Teruel, E., & Meinshausen, R. M. (1998). Producing simple sentences: Results from picture–word interference experiments. *Journal of Memory and Language, 39,* 609–632.

Schuberth, R. E., & Eimas, P. D. (1977). Effects of context on the classification of words and non-words. *Journal of Experimental Psychology: Human Perception and Performance, 3,* 27–36.

Schustack, M. W., Ehrlich, S. F., & Rayner, K. (1987). The complexity of contextual facilitation in reading: Local and global influences. *Journal of Memory and Language, 26,* 322–340.

Schvaneveldt, R. W., Meyer, D. E., & Becker, C. A. (1976). Lexical ambiguity, semantic context, and visual word recognition. *Journal of Experimental Psychology: Human Perception and Performance, 2,* 243–256.

Schwanenflugel, P. J., & LaCount, K. L. (1988). Semantic relatedness and the scope of facilitation for upcoming words in sentences. *Journal of Experimental Psychology: Learning, Memory, and Cognition, 14,* 344–354.

Schwanenflugel, P. J., & Rey, M. (1986). Interlingual semantic facilitation: Evidence for a common representational system in the bilingual lexicon. *Journal of Memory and Language, 25,* 605–618.

Schwartz, M. F. (1984). What the classical aphasia categories can't do for us, and why. *Brain and Language, 21,* 3–8.

Schwartz, M. F. (1987). Patterns of speech production deficit within and across aphasia syndromes: Application of a psycholinguistic model. In M. Coltheart, G. Sartori, & R. Job (Eds.), *The cognitive neuropsychology of language* (pp. 163–199). Hove, UK: Lawrence Erlbaum Associates.

Schwartz, M. F. (Ed.). (1990). *Modular deficits in Alzheimer-type dementia.* Cambridge, MA: MIT Press.

Schwartz, M. F., & Chawluk, J. B. (1990). Deterioration of language in progressive aphasia: A case study. In M. F. Schwartz (Ed.), *Modular deficits in Alzheimer-type dementia* (pp. 245–296). Cambridge, MA: MIT Press.

Schwartz, M. F., Dell, G. S., Martin, N., Gahl, S., & Sobel, P. (2006). A case-series test of the interactive two-step model of lexical access: Evidence from picture naming. *Journal of Memory and Language, 54,* 228–264.

Schwartz, M. F., Linebarger, M., Saffran, E., & Pate, D. (1987). Syntactic transparency and sentence interpretation in aphasia. *Language and Cognitive Processes, 2,* 85–113.

Schwartz, M. F., Marin, O. S. M., & Saffran, E. M. (1979). Dissociations of language function in dementia: A case study. *Brain and Language, 7,* 277–306.

Schwartz, M. F., Saffran, E. M., Bloch, D. E., & Dell, G. S. (1994). Disordered speech production in aphasic and normal speakers. *Brain and Language, 47,* 52–88.

Schwartz, M. F., Saffran, E. M., & Marin, O. S. M. (1980a). Fractionating the reading process in dementia: Evidence for word-specific print-to-sound associations. In M. Coltheart, K. E. Patterson, & J. C. Marshall (Eds.), *Deep dyslexia* (pp. 259–269). London: Routledge & Kegan Paul.

Schwartz, M. F., Saffran, E. M., & Marin, O. S. M. (1980b). The word order problem in agrammatism I: Comprehension. *Brain and Language*, *10*, 249–262.

Scoresby-Jackson, R. E. (1867). Case of aphasia with right hemiplegia. *Edinburgh Medical Journal*, *12*, 696–706.

Schyns, P. G., Goldstone, R. L., & Thibaut, J.-P. (1998). The development of features in object concepts. *Behavioral and Brain Sciences*, *21*, 1–53.

Searle, J. R. (1969). *Speech acts*. Cambridge: Cambridge University Press.

Searle, J. R. (1975). Indirect speech acts. In P. Cole & J. L. Morgan (Eds.), *Syntax and semantics: Vol. 3. Speech acts* (pp. 59–82). New York: Academic Press.

Searle, J. R. (1979). Metaphor. In A. Ortony (Ed.), *Metaphor and thought* (pp. 92–123). Cambridge: Cambridge University Press.

Sedivy, J. C., Tanenhaus, M. K., Chambers, C. G., & Carlson, G. N. (1999). Achieving incremental semantic interpretation through contextual representation. *Cognition*, *71*, 109–147.

Seidenberg, M. S. (1988). Cognitive neuropsychology and language: The state of the art. *Cognitive Neuropsychology*, *5*, 403–426.

Seidenberg, M. S. (2011). What causes dyslexia? Comment on Goswami. *Trends in Cognitive Sciences*, *15*, 2.

Seidenberg, M. S., & Elman, J. L. (1999). Networks are not "hidden rules." *Trends in Cognitive Sciences*, *3*, 288–289.

Seidenberg, M. S., & McClelland, J. L. (1989). A distributed developmental model of word recognition. *Psychological Review*, *96*, 523–568.

Seidenberg, M. S., & McClelland, J. L. (1990). More words but still no lexicon. Reply to Besner et al. (1990). *Psychological Review*, *97*, 447–452.

Seidenberg, M. S., Petersen, A., MacDonald, M. C., & Plaut, D. C. (1996). Pseudohomophone effects and models of word recognition. *Journal of Experimental Psychology: Learning, Memory, and Cognition*, *22*, 48–62.

Seidenberg, M. S., & Petitto, L. A. (1979). Signing behavior in apes: A critical review. *Cognition*, *7*, 177–215.

Seidenberg, M. S., & Petitto, L. A. (1987). Communication, symbolic communication, and language: Comment on Savage-Rumbaugh, McDonald, Sevcik, Hopkins, and Rupert (1986). *Journal of Experimental Psychology: General*, *116*, 279–287.

Seidenberg, M. S., Plaut, D. C., Petersen, A., McClelland, J. L., & McRae, K. (1994). Nonword pronunciation and models of word recognition. *Journal of Experimental Psychology: Human Perception and Performance*, *20*, 1177–1196.

Seidenberg, M. S., Tanenhaus, M. K., Leiman, J. M., & Bienkowski, M. (1982). Automatic access of the meanings of ambiguous words in context: Some limitations of knowledge-based processing. *Cognitive Psychology*, *14*, 489–537.

Seidenberg, M. S., Waters, G. S., Barnes, M. A., & Tanenhaus, M. K. (1984). When does irregular spelling or pronunciation influence word recognition? *Journal of Verbal Learning and Verbal Behavior*, *23*, 383–404.

Seidenberg, M. S., Waters, G. S., Sanders, M., & Langer, P. (1984). Pre- and post-lexical loci of contextual effects on word recognition. *Memory and Cognition*, *12*, 315–328.

Seifert, C. M., McKoon, G., Abelson, R. P., & Ratcliff, R. (1986). Memory connections between thematically similar episodes. *Journal of Experimental Psychology: Learning, Memory, and Cognition*, *12*, 220–231.

Seifert, C. M., Robertson, S. P., & Black, J. B. (1985). Types of inference generated during reading. *Journal of Memory and Language*, *24*, 405–422.

Semenza, C., & Zettin, M. (1988). Generating proper names: A case of selective inability. *Cognitive Neuropsychology*, *5*, 711–721.

Seymour, P. H. K. (1987). Individual cognitive analysis of competent and impaired reading. *British Journal of Psychology*, *78*, 483–506.

Seymour, P. H. K. (1990). Developmental dyslexia. In M. W. Eysenck (Ed.), *Cognitive psychology: An international review* (pp. 135–196). Chichester, UK: John Wiley.

Seymour, P. H. K., & Elder, L. (1986). Beginning reading without phonology. *Cognitive Neuropsychology*, *3*, 1–36.

Seymour, P. H. K., & Evans, H. M. (1994). Levels of phonological awareness and learning to read. *Reading and Writing*, *6*, 221–250.

Shafto, M., Burke, D., Stamatakis, E., Tam, P., & Tyler, L. (2007). On the tip-of-the-tongue: Neural correlates of increased word-finding failures in normal aging. *Journal of Cognitive Neuroscience*, *19*, 2060–2070.

Shallice, T. (1981). Phonological agraphia and the lexical route in writing. *Brain*, *104*, 413–429.

Shallice, T. (1988). *From neuropsychology to mental structure*. Cambridge: Cambridge University Press.

Shallice, T. (1993). Multiple semantics: Whose confusions? *Cognitive Neuropsychology*, *10*, 251–261.

Shallice, T., & Butterworth, B. (1977). Short-term memory impairment and spontaneous speech. *Neuropsychologia*, *15*, 729–735.

Shallice, T., & McCarthy, R. (1985). Phonological reading: From patterns of impairment to possible procedure. In K. E. Patterson, J. C. Marshall, & M. Coltheart (Eds.), *Surface dyslexia: Neuropsychological and cognitive studies of phonological reading* (pp. 361–397). Hove, UK: Lawrence Erlbaum Associates.

Shallice, T., & McGill, J. (1978). The origins of mixed errors. In J. Requin (Ed.), *Attention and performance VII* (pp. 193–208). Hillsdale, NJ: Lawrence Erlbaum Associates, Inc.

Shallice, T., McLeod, P., & Lewis, K. (1985). Isolating cognitive modules with the dual task paradigm: Are speech perception and production separate processes? *Quarterly Journal of Experimental Psychology, 37A*, 507–532.

Shallice, T., Rumiati, R. I., & Zadini, A. (2000). The selective impairment of the phonological output buffer. *Cognitive Neuropsychology, 17*, 517–546.

Shallice, T., & Warrington, E. K. (1975). Word recognition in a phonemic dyslexic patient. *Quarterly Journal of Experimental Psychology, 27*, 187–199.

Shallice, T., & Warrington, E. K. (1977). Auditory-verbal short-term memory impairment and conduction aphasia. *Brain and Language, 4*, 479–491.

Shallice, T., & Warrington, E. K. (1980). Single and multiple component central deep dyslexic syndromes. In M. Coltheart, K. E. Patterson, & J. C. Marshall (Eds.), *Deep dyslexia* (pp. 199–245). London: Routledge & Kegan Paul. [2nd ed., 1987.]

Shallice, T., Warrington, E. K., & McCarthy, R. (1983). Reading without semantics. *Quarterly Journal of Experimental Psychology, 35A*, 111–138.

Shanker, S. G., Savage-Rumbaugh, E. S., & Taylor, T. J. (1999). Kanzi: A new beginning. *Animal Learning and Behavior, 27*, 24–25.

Shannon, C. E., & Weaver, W. (1949). *The mathematical theory of communication*. Urbana: University of Illinois Press.

Shapiro, K., & Caramazza, A. (2003). The representation of grammatical categories in the brain. *Trends in Cognitive Sciences, 7*, 201–206.

Share, D. L. (1995). Phonological recoding and self-teaching: Sine qua non of reading acquisition. *Cognition, 55*, 151–218.

Sharkey, A. J. C., & Sharkey, N. E. (1992). Weak contextual constraints in text and word priming. *Journal of Memory and Language, 31*, 543–572.

Sharpe, K. (1992). Communication, culture, context, confidence: The four Cs of primary modern language teaching. *Language Learning Journal, 6*, 13–14.

Shattuck, R. (1980). *The forbidden experiment*. New York: Kodansha International.

Shattuck-Hufnagel, S. (1979). Speech errors as evidence for a serial ordering mechanism in speech production. In W. E. Cooper & E. C. T. Walker (Eds.), *Sentence processing: Psycholinguistic studies presented to Merrill Garrett* (pp. 295–342). Hillsdale, NJ: Lawrence Erlbaum Associates, Inc.

Shatz, M., Diesendruck, G., Martinez-Beck, I., & Akar, D. (2003). The influence of language and socioeconomic status on children's understanding of false belief. *Developmental Psychology, 39*, 717–729.

Shatz, M., & Gelman, R. (1973). The development of communication skills: Modifications in the speech of young children as a function of the listener. *Monograph of the Society for Research in Child Development, 152*.

Shaywitz, B. A., Shaywitz, S. E., Pugh, K. R., Constable, R. T., Skudlarski, P., Fulbright, R. K., et al. (1995). Sex differences in the functional organization of the brain for language. *Nature, 373*, 607–609.

Sheldon, A. (1974). The role of parallel function in the acquisition of relative clauses in English. *Journal of Verbal Learning and Verbal Behavior, 13*, 272–281.

Shelton, J. R., & Caramazza, A. (1999). Deficits in lexical and semantic processing: Implications for models of normal language. *Psychonomic Bulletin and Review, 6*, 5–27.

Shelton, J. R., & Martin, R. C. (1992). How semantic is automatic semantic priming? *Journal of Experimental Psychology: Learning, Memory, and Cognition, 18*, 1191–1209.

Shelton, J. R., & Weinrich, M. (1997). Further evidence of a dissociation between output phonological and orthographic lexicons: A case study. *Cognitive Neuropsychology, 14*, 105–129.

Sheridan, J., & Humphreys, G. W. (1993). A verbal-semantic category-specific recognition impairment. *Cognitive Neuropsychology, 10*, 143–184.

Shiffrin, R. M., & Schneider, W. (1977). Controlled and automatic human information processing: II. Perceptual learning, automatic attending, and a general theory. *Psychological Review, 84*, 127–190.

Shoben, E. J., & Gagne, C. L. (1997). Thematic relations and the creation of combined concepts. In T. B. Ward, S. M. Smith, & J. Vaid (Eds.), *Creative thought: An investigation of creative structures and processes* (pp. 31–50). Washington, DC: American Psychological Association.

Siegel, L. S. (1998). Phonological processing deficits and reading disabilities. In J. L. Metsala & L. C. Ehri (Eds.), *Word recognition and beginning literacy* (pp. 141–160). Mahwah, NJ: Lawrence Erlbaum Associates, Inc.

Silverberg, S., & Samuel, A. G. (2004). The effect of age of second language acquisition on the representation and processing of second language words. *Journal of Memory and Language, 51*, 381–398.

Silveri, M. C., & Gainotti, G. (1988). Interaction between vision and language in category-specific semantic impairment. *Cognitive Neuropsychology, 5*, 677–709.

Simpson, G. B. (1981). Meaning dominance and semantic context in the processing of lexical ambiguity. *Journal of Verbal Learning and Verbal Behavior, 20*, 120–136.

Simpson, G. B. (1994). Context and the processing of ambiguous words. In M. A. Gernsbacher (Ed.), *Handbook of psycholinguistic research* (pp. 359–374). San Diego, CA: Academic Press.

Simpson, G. B., & Burgess, C. (1985). Activation and solution processes in the recognition of ambiguous words. *Journal of Experimental Psychology: Human Perception and Performance, 11*, 28–39.

Simpson, G. B., & Krueger, M. A. (1991). Selective access of homograph meanings in sentence context. *Journal of Memory and Language, 30*, 627–643.

Sinclair-de-Zwart, H. (1969). Developmental psycholinguistics. In D. Elkind & J. H. Flavell (Eds.), *Studies in cognitive development* (pp. 315–366). Oxford: Oxford University Press.

Sinclair-de-Zwart, H. (1973). Language acquisition and cognitive development. In T. E. Moore (Ed.), *Cognitive development and the acquisition of language* (pp. 9–26). New York: Academic Press.

Singer, M. (1994). Discourse inference processes. In M. A. Gernsbacher (Ed.), *Handbook of psycholinguistics* (pp. 479–516). San Diego, CA: Academic Press.

Singer, M., & Ferreira, F. (1983). Inferring consequences in story comprehension. *Journal of Verbal Learning and Verbal Behavior, 22*, 437–448.

Singer, M., Graesser, A. C., & Trabasso, T. (1994). Minimal or global inference in comprehension. *Journal of Memory and Language, 33*, 421–441.

Singh, J. A. L., & Zingg, R. M. (1942). *Wolf children and feral man*. Hamden, CT: Shoe String Press. [Reprinted 1966, New York: Harper & Row.]

Sitton, M., Mozer, M. C., & Farah, M. J. (2000). Superadditive effects of multiple lesions in connectionist architecture: Implications for the neuropsychology of optic aphasia. *Psychological Review, 107*, 709–734.

Skehan, P. (1998). *A cognitive approach to language learning*. Oxford: Oxford University Press.

Skinner, B. F. (1957). *Verbal behavior*. New York: Appleton-Century-Crofts.

Skoyles, J., & Skottun, B. C. (2004). On the prevalence of magnocellular deficits in the visual system of non-dyslexic individuals. *Brain and Language, 88*, 79–82.

Skuse, D. H. (1993). Extreme deprivation in early childhood. In D. Bishop & K. Mogford (Eds.), *Language development in exceptional circumstances* (pp. 29–46). Hove, UK: Lawrence Erlbaum Associates.

Slobin, D. I. (1966a). Grammatical transformations and sentence comprehension in childhood and adulthood. *Journal of Verbal Learning and Verbal Behavior, 5*, 219–227.

Slobin, D. I. (1966b). The acquisition of Russian as a native language. In F. Smith & G. A. Miller (Eds.), *The genesis of a language: A psycholinguistic approach* (pp. 129–248). Cambridge, MA: MIT Press.

Slobin, D. I. (1970). Universals of grammatical development in children. In G. Flores d'Arcais & W. J. M. Levelt (Eds.), *Advances in psycholinguistics* (pp. 174–186). Amsterdam: North Holland.

Slobin, D. I. (1973). Cognitive prerequisites for the development of grammar. In C. A. Ferguson &

D. I. Slobin (Eds.), *Studies of child language development* (pp. 175–208). New York: Holt, Rhinehart & Winston.

Slobin, D. I. (1981). The origins of grammatical encoding of events. In W. Deutsch (Ed.), *The child's construction of language* (pp. 185–199). London: Academic Press.

Slobin, D. I. (1985). Crosslinguistic evidence for the language-making capacity. In D. I. Slobin (Ed.), *The crosslinguistic study of language acquisitions: Vol. 2. Theoretical issues* (pp. 1157–1249). Hillsdale, NJ: Lawrence Erlbaum Associates, Inc.

Smith, E. E. (1988). Concepts and thought. In R. J. Sternberg (Ed.), *The psychology of human thought* (pp. 19–49). Cambridge: Cambridge University Press.

Smith, E. E., & Medin, D. L. (1981). *Categories and concepts*. Cambridge, MA: Harvard University Press.

Smith, E. E., Shoben, E. J., & Rips, L. J. (1974). Structure and process in semantic memory: A featural model for semantic decisions. *Psychological Review, 81*, 214–241.

Smith, M., & Wheeldon, L. (1999). High level processing scope in spoken sentence production. *Cognition, 73*, 205–246.

Smith, M., & Wheeldon, L. (2004). Horizontal information flow in spoken sentence production. *Journal of Experimental Psychology: Learning, Memory, and Cognition, 30*, 675–686.

Smith, N., & Tsimpli, I.-M. (1995). *The mind of a savant: Language learning and modularity*. Oxford: Blackwell.

Smith, N. V. (1973). *The acquisition of phonology: A case study*. Cambridge: Cambridge University Press.

Smith, P. T., & Sterling, C. M. (1982). Factors affecting the perceived morphophonemic structure of written words. *Journal of Verbal Learning and Verbal Behavior, 21*, 704–721.

Smith, S. M., Brown, H. O., Thomas, J. E. P., & Goodman, L. S. (1947). The lack of cerebral effects of d-tubocurarine. *Anesthesiology, 8*, 1–14.

Snedeker, J., & Trueswell, J. C. (2003). Using prosody to avoid ambiguity: Effects of speaker awareness and referential context. *Journal of Memory and Language, 48*, 103–130.

Snedeker, J., & Trueswell, J. C. (2004). The developing constraints on parsing decisions: The role of lexical biases and referential scenes in child and adult sentence processing. *Cognitive Psychology, 49*, 238–299.

Snodgrass, J. G. (1984). Concepts and their surface representation. *Journal of Verbal Learning and Verbal Behavior, 23*, 3–22.

Snodgrass, J. G., & Vanderwart, M. (1980). A standardised set of 260 pictures: Norms for name agreement, image agreement, familiarity, and visual complexity. *Journal of Experimental Psychology: Human Learning and Memory, 6*, 174–215.

Snow, C. E. (1972). Mothers' speech to children learning language. *Child Development, 43*, 549–565.

Snow, C. E. (1977). The development of conversation between mothers and babies. *Journal of Child Language*, *4*, 1–22.

Snow, C. E. (1983). Age differences in second language acquisition: Research findings and folk psychology. In K. Bailey, M. Long, & S. Peck (Eds.), *Second language acquisition studies* (pp. 141–150). Rowley, MA: Newbury House.

Snow, C. E. (1993). Bilingualism and second language acquisition. In J. B. Gleason & N. B. Ratner (Eds.), *Psycholinguistics* (pp. 391–416). Fort Worth, TX: Harcourt Brace Jovanovich.

Snow, C. E. (1994). Beginning from baby talk: Twenty years of research on input and interaction. In C. Gallaway & B. J. Richards (Eds.), *Input and interaction in language acquisition* (pp. 3–12). Cambridge: Cambridge University Press.

Snow, C. E. (1995). Issues in the study of input: Finetuning, universality, individual and developmental differences, and necessary causes. In P. Fletcher & B. MacWhinney (Eds.), *The handbook of child language* (pp. 180–193). Oxford: Blackwell.

Snow, C. E., & Hoefnagel-Hohle, M. (1978). The critical period for language acquisition: Evidence from second language learning. *Child Development*, *49*, 1114–1128.

Snowden, J. S., Goulding, P. J., & Neary, D. (1989). Semantic dementia: A form of circumscribed cerebral atrophy. *Behavioural Neurology*, *2*, 167–182.

Snowling, M. J. (1983). The comparison of acquired and developmental disorders of reading. *Cognition*, *14*, 105–118.

Snowling, M. J. (1987). *Dyslexia: A cognitive development perspective*. Oxford: Blackwell.

Snowling, M. J. (2000). *Dyslexia* (2nd ed.). Oxford: Blackwell.

Snowling, M. J., Bryant, P. E., & Hulme, C. (1996). Theoretical and methodological pitfalls in making comparisons between developmental and acquired dyslexia: Some comments on A. Castles and M. Coltheart (1993). *Reading and Writing*, *8*, 443–451.

Snowling, M. J., Gallagher, A., & Frith, U. (2003). Family risk of dyslexia is continuous: Individual differences in the precursors of reading skill. *Child Development*, *74*, 358–373.

Snowling, M. J., & Hulme, C. (1989). A longitudinal case study of developmental phonological dyslexia. *Cognitive Neuropsychology*, *6*, 379–401.

Snowling, M. J., & Hulme, C. (Eds.). (2007). *The science of reading: A handbook*. Oxford: Blackwell.

Snowling, M. J., Stackhouse, J., & Rack, J. (1986). Phonological dyslexia and dysgraphia: A developmental analysis. *Cognitive Neuropsychology*, *3*, 309–339.

Soja, N. N., Carey, S., & Spelke, E. S. (1992). Perception, ontology, and word meaning. *Cognition*, *45*, 101–107.

Sokolov, J. L., & Snow, C. E. (1994). The changing role of negative evidence in theories of language development. In C. Gallaway & B. J. Richards (Eds.), *Input and interaction in language acquisition* (pp. 38–55). Cambridge: Cambridge University Press.

Solomon, E. S., & Pearlmutter, N. J. (2004). Semantic integration and syntactic planning in language production. *Cognitive Psychology*, *49*, 1–46.

Spelke, E. S. (1994). Initial knowledge: Six suggestions. *Cognition*, *50*, 443–447.

Spender, D. (1980). *Man made language*. London: Routledge & Kegan Paul.

Sperber, D., & Wilson, D. (1986). *Relevance: Communication and cognition*. Oxford: Blackwell.

Sperber, D., & Wilson, D. (1987). Précis of *Relevance: Communication and cognition*. *Behavioral and Brain Sciences*, *10*, 697–754.

Sperber, R. D., McCauley, C., Ragain, R. D., & Weil, C. M. (1979). Semantic priming effects on picture and word processing. *Memory and Cognition*, *7*, 339–345.

Spiro, R. J. (1977). Constructing a theory of reconstructive memory: The state of the schema approach. In R. C. Anderson, R. J. Spiro, & W. E. Montague (Eds.), *Schooling and the acquisition of knowledge* (pp. 137–177). Hillsdale, NJ: Lawrence Erlbaum Associates, Inc.

Spivey, M. J., & Marian, V. (1999). Crosstalk between native and second languages: Partial activation of an irrelevant lexicon. *Psychological Science*, *10*, 281–284.

Spivey, M. J., McRae, K., & Joanisse, M. F. (2012). *The Cambridge handbook of psycholinguistics*. Cambridge: Cambridge University Press.

Spivey, M. J., & Tanenhaus, M. K. (1998). Syntactic ambiguity resolution in discourse: Modeling the effects of referential context and lexical frequency. *Journal of Experimental Psychology: Learning, Memory, and Cognition*, *24*, 1521–1543.

Spivey, M. J., Tanenhaus, M. K., Eberhard, K. M., & Sedivy, J. C. (2002). Eye movements and spoken language comprehension: Effects of visual context on syntactic ambiguity resolution. *Cognitive Psychology*, *45*, 447–481.

Stabler, E. P. (1983). How are grammars represented? *Behavioral and Brain Sciences*, *6*, 391–421.

Stager, C. L., & Werker, J. F. (1997). Infants listen for more phonetic detail in speech perception than in word-learning tasks. *Nature*, *388*, 381–382.

Stamenov, M. I., & Gallese, V. (Eds.). (2002). *Mirror neurons and the evolution of brain and language* (Advances in consciousness research 42). Amsterdam: John Benjamins.

Stanners, R. F., Jastrzembski, J. E., & Westwood, A. (1975). Frequency and visual quality in a word–nonword classification task. *Journal of Verbal Learning and Verbal Behavior*, *14*, 259–264.

Stanovich, K. E., & Bauer, D. W. (1978). Experiments on the spelling-to-sound regularity effect in word recognition. *Memory and Cognition, 6,* 410–415.

Stanovich, K. E., Siegel, L. S., & Gottardo, A. (1997). Converging evidence for phonological and surface subtypes of reading disability. *Journal of Educational Psychology, 89,* 114–127.

Stanovich, K. E., Siegel, L. S., Gottardo, A., Chiappe, P., & Sidhu, R. (1997). Subtypes of developmental dyslexia: Differences in phonological and orthographic coding. In B. A. Blachman (Ed.), *Foundations of reading acquisition and dyslexia: Implications for early intervention* (pp. 115–141). Mahwah, NJ: Lawrence Erlbaum Associates, Inc.

Stanovich, K. E., & West, R. F. (1979). Mechanisms of sentence context effects in reading: Automatic activation and conscious attention. *Memory and Cognition, 6,* 115–123.

Stanovich, K. E., & West, R. F. (1981). The effect of sentence context on ongoing word recognition: Tests of a two-process theory. *Journal of Experimental Psychology: Human Perception and Performance, 7,* 658–672.

Stanovich, K. E., West, R. F., & Harrison, M. R. (1995). Knowledge growth and maintenance across the life span: The role of print exposure. *Developmental Psychology, 31,* 811–826.

Stark, R. E. (1986). Prespeech segmental feature development. In P. Fletcher & M. Garman (Eds.), *Language acquisition* (2nd ed., pp. 149–173). Cambridge: Cambridge University Press.

Starreveld, P. A., & La Heij, W. (1995). Semantic interference, orthographic facilitation, and their interaction in naming tasks. *Journal of Experimental Psychology: Learning, Memory, and Cognition, 21,* 686–698.

Starreveld, P. A., & La Heij, W. (1996). Time course analysis of semantic and orthographic context effects in picture naming. *Journal of Experimental Psychology: Learning, Memory, and Cognition, 22,* 896–918.

Steffensen, M. S., Joag-dev, C., & Anderson, R. C. (1979). A cross-cultural perspective on reading comprehension. *Reading Research Quarterly, 15,* 10–29.

Stein, J. (2003). Visual motion sensitivity and reading. *Neuropsychologia, 41,* 1785–1793.

Stemberger, J. P. (1983). Distant context effects in language production: A reply to Motley et al. *Journal of Psycholinguistic Research, 12,* 555–560.

Stemberger, J. P. (1984). Structural errors in normal and agrammatic speech. *Cognitive Neuropsychology, 1,* 281–313.

Stemberger, J. P. (1985). An interactive activation model of language production. In A. W. Ellis (Ed.), *Progress in the psychology of language* (Vol. 1, pp. 143–186). Hove, UK: Lawrence Erlbaum Associates.

Sternberg, S., Knoll, R. L., Monsell, S., & Wright, C. E. (1988). Motor programs and hierarchical organization in the control of rapid speech. *Phonetica, 45,* 175–197.

Stevens, K. N. (1960). Toward a model for speech recognition. *Journal of the Acoustical Society of America, 32,* 47–55.

Stevenson, R. (1988). *Models of language development.* Milton Keynes, UK: Open University Press.

Stewart, A. J., Pickering, M. F., & Sanford, A. J. (2000). The time course of the influence of implicit causality information: Focusing versus integration account. *Journal of Memory and Language, 42,* 423–443.

Stewart, F., Parkin, A. J., & Hunkin, N. M. (1992). Naming impairments following recovery from herpes simplex encephalitis: Category-specific? *Quarterly Journal of Experimental Psychology, 44A,* 261–284.

Stewart, I. (1989). *Does God play dice? The new mathematics of chaos.* Harmondsworth, UK: Penguin.

Stirling, J. (2002). *Introducing neuropsychology.* Hove, UK: Psychology Press.

Storms, G., De Boeck, P., & Ruts, W. (2000). Prototype and exemplar-based information in natural language categories. *Journal of Memory and Language, 42,* 51–73.

Strain, E., Patterson, K., & Seidenberg, M. S. (1995). Semantic effects in single-word naming. *Journal of Experimental Psychology: Learning, Memory, and Cognition, 21,* 1140–1154.

Strain, E., Patterson, K., & Seidenberg, M. S. (2002). Theories of word naming interact with spelling–sound consistency. *Journal of Experimental Psychology: Learning, Memory, and Cognition, 28,* 207–214.

Sturt, P., Costa, F., Lombardo, V., & Frasconi, P. (2003). Learning first-pass structural attachment preferences with dynamic grammars and recursive neural networks. *Cognition, 88,* 133–169.

Sudhalter, V., & Braine, M. D. S. (1985). How does comprehension of passives develop? *Journal of Child Language, 12,* 455–470.

Sulin, R. A., & Dooling, D. J. (1974). Intrusion of a thematic idea in retention of prose. *Journal of Experimental Psychology, 103,* 255–262.

Summerfield, Q. (1981). Articulatory rate and perceptual constancy in phonetic perception. *Journal of Experimental Psychology: Human Perception and Performance, 7,* 1074–1095.

Swain, M., & Wesche, M. (1975). Linguistic interaction: Case study of a bilingual child. *Language Sciences, 17,* 17–22.

Swinney, D. A. (1979). Lexical access during sentence comprehension: (Re)consideration of context effects. *Journal of Verbal Learning and Verbal Behavior, 18,* 545–569.

Swinney, D. A., & Cutler, A. (1979). The access and processing of idiomatic expressions. *Journal of Verbal Learning and Verbal Behavior, 18*, 523–534.

Swinney, D. A., Zurif, E. B., & Cutler, A. (1980). Effects of sentential stress and word class upon comprehension in Broca's aphasics. *Brain and Language, 10*, 132–144.

Sykes, J. L. (1940). A study of the spontaneous vocalizations of young deaf children. *Psychological Monograph, 52*, 104–123.

Tabor, W., & Hutchins, S. (2004). Evidence for self-organised sentence processing: Digging-in effects. *Journal of Experimental Psychology: Learning, Memory, and Cognition, 30*, 431–450.

Tabor, W., Juliano, C., & Tanenhaus, M. K. (1997). Parsing in a dynamical system: An attractor-based account of the interaction of lexical and structural constraints in sentence processing. *Language and Cognitive Processes, 12*, 211–271.

Tabor, W., & Tanenhaus, M. K. (1999). Dynamical models of sentence processing. *Cognitive Science, 23*, 491–515.

Tabossi, P. (1988a). Accessing lexical ambiguity in different types of sentential context. *Journal of Memory and Language, 27*, 324–340.

Tabossi, P. (1988b). Effects of context on the immediate interpretation of unambiguous words. *Journal of Experimental Psychology: Learning, Memory, and Cognition, 14*, 153–162.

Tabossi, P., & Zardon, F. (1993). Processing ambiguous words in context. *Journal of Memory and Language, 32*, 359–372.

Taft, M. (1979). Recognition of affixed words and the word frequency effect. *Memory and Cognition, 7*, 263–272.

Taft, M. (1981). Prefix stripping revisited. *Journal of Verbal Learning and Verbal Behavior, 20*, 289–297.

Taft, M. (1982). An alternative to grapheme–phoneme conversion rules? *Memory and Cognition, 10*, 465–474.

Taft, M. (1984). Evidence for abstract lexical representation of word structure. *Memory and Cognition, 12*, 264–269.

Taft, M. (1985). The decoding of words in lexical access: A review of the morphographic approach. In D. Besner, T. G. Waller, & G. E. MacKinnon (Eds.), *Reading research: Advances in theory and practice* (Vol. 5, pp. 83–123). Orlando, FL: Academic Press.

Taft, M. (1987). Morphographic processing: The BOSS re-emerges. In M. Coltheart (Ed.), *Attention and performance XII: The psychology of reading* (pp. 265–279). Hove, UK: Lawrence Erlbaum Associates.

Taft, M. (2004). Morphological decomposition and the reverse base frequency effect. *Quarterly Journal of Experimental Psychology, 57A*, 745–765.

Taft, M., & Forster, K. I. (1975). Lexical storage and retrieval of prefixed words. *Journal of Verbal Learning and Verbal Behavior, 14*, 638–647.

Taft, M., & van Graan, F. (1998). Lack of phonological mediation in a semantic categorization task. *Journal of Memory and Language, 38*, 203–224.

Tager-Flusberg, H. (1999). Language development in atypical children. In M. Barrett (Ed.), *The development of language* (pp. 311–348). Hove, UK: Psychology Press.

Tallal, P., Townsend, J., Curtiss, S., & Wulfeck, B. (1991). Phenotypic profiles of language-impaired children based on genetic/family history. *Brain and Language, 41*, 81–95.

Tanaka, J. W., & Taylor, M. (1991). Object categories and expertise: Is the basic level in the eye of the beholder? *Cognitive Psychology, 23*, 457–482.

Tanenhaus, M. K., Boland, J. E., Mauner, G. A., & Carlson, G. N. (1993). More on combinatory lexical information: Thematic structure in parsing and interpretation. In G. Altmann & R. Shillcock (Eds.), *Cognitive models of speech processing* (pp. 297–319). Hove, UK: Lawrence Erlbaum Associates.

Tanenhaus, M. K., Carlson, G. N., & Trueswell, J. C. (1989). The role of thematic structure in interpretation and parsing. *Language and Cognitive Processes, 4*, 211–234.

Tanenhaus, M. K., Leiman, J. M., & Seidenberg, M. S. (1979). Evidence for multiple stages in the processing of ambiguous words in syntactic contexts. *Journal of Verbal Learning and Verbal Behavior, 18*, 427–440.

Tanenhaus, M. K., & Lucas, M. (1987). Context effects in lexical processing. *Cognition, 25*, 213–234.

Tanenhaus, M. K., Spivey-Knowlton, M. J., Eberhard, K. M., & Sedivy, J. C. (1995). Integration of visual and linguistic information in spoken language comprehension. *Science, 268*, 1632–1634.

Tannenbaum, P. H., Williams, F., & Hillier, C. S. (1965). Word predictability in the environments of hesitations. *Journal of Verbal Learning and Verbal Behavior, 4*, 134–140.

Taraban, R., & McClelland, J. L. (1988). Constituent attachment and thematic role assignment in sentence processing: Influences of content-based expectations. *Journal of Memory and Language, 27*, 597–632.

Tarshis, B. (1992). *Grammar for smart people*. New York: Pocket Books.

Taylor, I., & Taylor, M. M. (1990). *Psycholinguistics: Learning and using language*. Englewood Cliffs, NJ: Prentice Hall International.

Taylor, M., & Gelman, S. A. (1988). Adjectives and nouns: Children's strategies for learning new words. *Child Development, 59*, 411–419.

Temple, C. M. (1987). The nature of normality, the deviance of dyslexia and the recognition of rhyme: A reply to Bryant and Impey (1986). *Cognition, 27*, 103–108.

Terrace, H. S., Petitto, L. A., Sanders, R. J., & Bever, T. G. (1979). Can an ape create a sentence? *Science, 206*, 891–902.

Tettamanti, M., Buccino, G., Saccuman, M. C., Gallese, V., Danna, M., Scifo, P., et al. (2005). Listening to action-related sentences activates fronto-parietal motor circuits. *Journal of Cognitive Neuroscience, 17*, 273–281.

Thagard, P. (2005). *Mind: An introduction to cognitive science* (2nd ed.). Cambridge, MA: MIT Press.

Thal, D., Marchman, V. A., Stiles, J., Aram, D., Trauner, D., Nass, R., et al. (1991). Early lexical development in children with focal brain injury. *Brain and Language, 40*, 491–527.

Theakston, A. L. (2004). The role of entrenchment in children's and adults' performance of grammaticality-judgement tasks. *Cognitive Development, 19*, 15–34.

Thiessen, E. D., & Saffran, J. R. (2007). Learning to learn: Infants' acquisition of stress-based strategies for word segmentation. *Language Learning and Development, 3*, 73–100.

Thomas, E. L., & Robinson, H. A. (1972). *Improving reading in every class: A sourcebook for teachers.* Boston, MA: Allyn & Bacon.

Thomas, M. S. C. (2003). Limits on plasticity. *Journal of Cognition and Development, 4*, 95–121.

Thomas, M. S. C., & Karmiloff-Smith, A. (2003). Modeling language acquisition in atypical phenotypes. *Psychological Review, 110*, 647–682.

Thompson, C. R., & Church, R. M. (1980). An explanation of the language of a chimpanzee. *Science, 208*, 313–314.

Thompson, R., Emmorey, K., & Gollan, T. H. (2005). "Tip of the fingers" experiences by deaf signers. *Psychological Science, 16*, 856–860.

Thompson, S., & Mulac, A. (1991). The discourse conditions for the use of the complementizer that in conversational English. *Journal of Pragmatics, 15*, 237–251.

Thomson, J., & Chapman, R. S. (1977). Who is "Daddy" revisited: The status of two-year-olds' overextended words in use and comprehension. *Journal of Child Language, 4*, 359–375.

Thorndyke, P. W. (1975). Conceptual complexity and imagery in comprehension. *Journal of Verbal Learning and Verbal Behavior, 14*, 359–369.

Thorndyke, P. W. (1977). Cognitive structures in comprehension and memory of narrative discourse. *Cognitive Psychology, 9*, 77–110.

Thorndyke, P. W., & Hayes-Roth, B. (1979). The use of schemata in the acquisition and transfer of knowledge. *Cognitive Psychology, 11*, 82–106.

Tincoff, R., & Jusczyk, P. W. (1999). Some beginnings of word comprehension in 6-month-olds. *Psychological Science, 10*, 172–175.

Tippett, L. J., & Farah, M. J. (1994). A computational model of naming in Alzheimer's disease: Unitary or multiple impairments? *Neuropsychology, 8*, 1–11.

Tomasello, M. (1992a). *First verbs: A case study of early grammatical development.* Cambridge: Cambridge University Press.

Tomasello, M. (1992b). The social bases of language acquisition. *Social Development, 1*, 67–87.

Tomasello, M. (2000). Do young children have adult syntactic competence? *Cognition, 74*, 209–253.

Tomasello, M. (2003). *Constructing a language: A usage-based theory of language acquisition.* Cambridge, MA: Harvard University Press.

Tomasello, M., & Akhtar, N. (2003). What paradox? A response to Naigles. *Cognition, 88*, 317–323.

Tomasello, M., & Farrar, M. J. (1984). Cognitive bases of lexical development: Object permanence and relational words. *Journal of Child Language, 11*, 477–493.

Tomasello, M., & Farrar, M. J. (1986). Object permanence and relational words: A lexical training study. *Journal of Child Language, 13*, 495–505.

Tomasello, M., & Kruger, A. (1992). Joint attention on actions: Acquiring verbs in ostensive and non-ostensive contexts. *Journal of Child Language, 19*, 311–333.

Traxler, M., & Gernsbacher, M. A. (Eds.). (2006). *Handbook of psycholinguistics* (2nd ed.). Burlington, MA: Academic Press.

Traxler, M. J., & Pickering, M. J. (1996). Plausibility and the processing of unbounded dependencies: An eye-tracking study. *Journal of Memory and Language, 35*, 454–475.

Traxler, M. J., Pickering, M. J., & Clifton, C. (1998). Adjunct attachment is not a form of lexical ambiguity resolution. *Journal of Memory and Language, 39*, 558–592.

Treiman, R. (1993). *Beginning to spell: A study of first-grade children.* New York: Oxford University Press.

Treiman, R. (1994). Sources of information used by beginning spellers. In G. D. A. Brown & N. C. Ellis (Eds.), *Handbook of spelling: Theory, process and intervention* (pp. 75–91). London: John Wiley & Sons Ltd.

Treiman, R. (1997). Spelling in normal children and dyslexics. In B. A. Blachman (Ed.), *Foundations of reading acquisition and dyslexia: Implications for early intervention* (pp. 191–218). Mahwah, NJ: Lawrence Erlbaum Associates, Inc.

Treiman, R., & Hirsh-Pasek, K. (1983). Silent reading: Insights from second-generation deaf readers. *Cognitive Psychology, 15*, 39–65.

Treiman, R., & Zukowski, A. (1996). Children's sensitivity to syllables, onsets, rimes, and phonemes. *Journal of Experimental Child Psychology, 61*, 193–215.

Trevarthen, C. (1975). Early attempts at speech. In R. Lewin (Ed.), *Child alive* (pp. 62–80). London: Temple Smith.

Trueswell, J. C. (1996). The role of lexical frequency in syntactic ambiguity resolution. *Journal of Memory and Language, 35,* 566–585.

Trueswell, J. C., Sekerina, I., Hill, N., & Logrip, M. (1999). The kindergarten-path effect: Studying online sentence processing in young children. *Cognition, 73,* 89–134.

Trueswell, J. C., & Tanenhaus, M. K. (1994). Toward a lexicalist framework for constraint-based syntactic ambiguity resolution. In C. Clifton, L. Frazier, & K. Rayner (Eds.), *Perspectives on sentence processing* (pp. 155–179). Hillsdale, NJ: Lawrence Erlbaum Associates, Inc.

Trueswell, J. C., Tanenhaus, M. K., & Garnsey, S. M. (1994). Semantic influences on parsing: Use of thematic role information in syntactic disambiguation. *Journal of Memory and Language, 33,* 285–318.

Trueswell, J. C., Tanenhaus, M. K., & Kello, C. (1993). Verb-specific constraints in sentence processing: Separating effects of lexical preference from garden paths. *Journal of Experimental Psychology: Learning, Memory, and Cognition, 19,* 528–553.

Tulving, E. (1972). Episodic and semantic memory. In E. Tulving & W. Donaldson (Eds.), *Organization of memory* (pp. 381–403). New York: Academic Press.

Tulving, E., & Schachter, D. L. (1990). Priming and human memory systems. *Science, 247,* 301–306.

Turvey, M. T. (1973). On peripheral and central processes in vision. *Psychological Review, 80,* 1–52.

Tweedy, J. R., Lapinski, R. H., & Schvaneveldt, R. W. (1977). Semantic-context effects on word recognition: Influence of varying the proportion of items presented in an appropriate context. *Memory and Cognition, 5,* 84–89.

Tyler, L. K. (1984). The structure of the initial cohort. *Perception and Psychophysics, 36,* 415–427.

Tyler, L. K. (1985). Real-time comprehension processes in agrammatism: A case study. *Brain and Language, 26,* 259–275.

Tyler, L. K., & Marslen-Wilson, W. D. (1977). The on-line effects of semantic context on syntactic processing. *Journal of Verbal Learning and Verbal Behavior, 16,* 683–692.

Tyler, L. K., & Moss, H. E. (1997). Functional properties of concepts: Studies of normal and brain-damaged patients. *Cognitive Neuropsychology, 14,* 511–545.

Tyler, L. K., & Moss, H. E. (2001). Towards a distributed account of conceptual knowledge. *Trends in Cognitive Science, 5,* 244–252.

Tyler, L. K., Ostrin, R. K., Cooke, M., & Moss, H. E. (1995). Automatic access of lexical information in Broca's aphasics: Against the automaticity hypothesis. *Brain and Language, 48,* 131–162.

Tyler, L. K., & Wessels, J. (1983). Quantifying contextual contributions to word-recognition processes. *Perception and Psychophysics, 34,* 409–420.

Ullman, M. T. (2004). Contributions to memory circuits to language: The declarative/procedural model. *Cognition, 92,* 231–270.

Ullman, M. T., Corkin, S., Coppola, M., Hickok, G., Growdon, J. H., Koroshetz, W. J., et al. (1997). A neural dissociation within language: Evidence that the mental dictionary is part of declarative memory, and that grammatical rules are processed by the procedural system. *Journal of Cognitive Neuroscience, 9,* 266–276.

Vaid, J. (1983). Bilingualism and brain lateralization. In S. Segalowitz (Ed.), *Language functions and brain organization* (pp. 315–339). New York: Academic Press.

Valian, V. (1986). Syntactic categories in the speech of young children. *Developmental Psychology, 22,* 562–579.

Vallar, G., & Baddeley, A. D. (1984). Phonological short-term store, phonological processing and sentence comprehension: A neuropsychological case study. *Cognitive Neuropsychology, 1,* 121–142.

Vallar, G., & Baddeley, A. D. (1987). Phonological short-term store and sentence processing. *Cognitive Neuropsychology, 4,* 417–438.

Vallar, G., & Baddeley, A. D. (1989). Developmental disorders of verbal short-term memory and their relation to sentence comprehension: A reply to Howard and Butterworth. *Cognitive Neuropsychology, 6,* 465–473.

van Berkum, J. J. A., Brown, C., Zwitserlood, P., Kooijman, V., & Hagoort, P. (2005). Anticipating upcoming words in discourse: Evidence from ERPs and reading times. *Journal of Experimental Psychology: Learning, Memory, and Cognition, 31,* 443–467.

van Dijk, T. A., & Kintsch, W. (1983). *Strategies of discourse representation.* New York: Academic Press.

van Gompel, R. P. G., Fischer, M. H., Murray, W. S., & Hill, R. L. (2006). Eye-movement research: An overview of current and past developments. In R. P. G. van Gompel, M. H. Fischer, W. S. Murray, & R. L. Hill (Eds.), *Eye movements: A window on mind and brain.* Oxford: Elsevier Science.

van Gompel, R. P. G., & Pickering, M. J. (2001). Lexical guidance in sentence processing: A note on Adams, Clifton, and Mitchell (1998). *Psychonomic Bulletin and Review, 8,* 851–857.

van Gompel, R. P. G., & Pickering, M. J. (2007). Syntactic parsing. In G. Gaskell (Ed.), *The Oxford handbook of psycholinguistics.* Oxford: Oxford University Press.

van Gompel, R. P. G., Pickering, M. J., & Traxler, M. J. (2000). Unrestricted race: A new model of syntactic ambiguity resolution. In A. Kennedy, R. Radach, D. Heller, & J. Pynte (Eds.), *Reading as a perceptual process* (pp. 621–648). Oxford: Elsevier.

van Gompel, R. P. G., Pickering, M. J., & Traxler, M. J. (2001). Reanalysis in sentence processing: Evidence against constraint-based and two-stage models. *Journal of Memory and Language, 45*, 225–258.

van Orden, G. C. (1987). A rows is a rose: Spelling, sound and reading. *Memory and Cognition, 15*, 181–198.

van Orden, G. C., Johnston, J. C., & Hale, B. L. (1988). Word identification in reading proceeds from spelling to sound to meaning. *Journal of Experimental Psychology: Learning, Memory, and Cognition, 14*, 371–386.

van Orden, G. C., Pennington, B. F., & Stone, G. O. (1990). Word identification in reading and the promise of subsymbolic psycholinguistics. *Psychological Review, 97*, 488–522.

van Petten, C. (1993). A comparison of lexical and sentence-level context effects in event-related potentials. *Language and Cognitive Processes, 8*, 485–531.

van Turenout, M., Hagoort, P., & Brown, C. M. (1998). Brain activity during speaking: From syntax to phonology in 40 milliseconds. *Science, 280*, 572–574.

Vanderwart, M. (1984). Priming by pictures in lexical decision. *Journal of Verbal Learning and Verbal Behavior, 23*, 67–83.

Vargha-Khadem, F., & Passingham, R. (1990). Speech and language defects. *Nature, 346*, 226.

Vargha-Khadem, F., Watkins, K., Alcock, K., Fletcher, P., & Passingham, R. (1995). Praxic and nonverbal cognitive deficits in a large family with a genetically transmitted speech and language disorder. *Proceedings of the National Academy of Science, 92*, 930–933.

Varney, N. L. (1984). Phonemic imperception in aphasia. *Brain and Language, 21*, 85–94.

Venezky, R. L. (1970). *The structure of English orthography*. The Hague: Mouton.

Vidyasagar, T. R., & Pammer, K. (2010). Dyslexia: A deficit in visuo-spatial attention, not in phonological processing. *Trends in Cognitive Sciences, 14*, 57–63.

Vigliocco, G., Antonini, T., & Garrett, M. F. (1997). Grammatical gender is on the tip of Italian tongues. *Psychological Science, 8*, 314–317.

Vigliocco, G., Butterworth, B., & Garrett, M. F. (1996). Subject–verb agreement in Spanish and English: Differences in the role of conceptual constraints. *Cognition, 61*, 261–298.

Vigliocco, G., & Hartsuiker, R. J. (2002). The interplay of meaning, sound, and syntax in sentence production. *Psychological Bulletin, 128*, 442–472.

Vigliocco, G., & Nicol, J. (1998). Separating hierarchical relations and word order in language production: Is proximity concord syntactic or linear? *Cognition, 68*, B13–B29.

Vigliocco, G., & Vinson, D. P. (2009). Semantic representation. In G. Gaskell (Ed.), *The Oxford handbook of psycholinguistics* (pp. 195–216). Oxford: Oxford University Press.

Vigliocco, G., Vinson, D. P., Lewis, W., & Garrett, M. F. (2004). Representing the meanings of object and action words: The featural and unitary semantic space hypothesis. *Cognitive Psychology, 48*, 422–488.

Vigliocco, G., Vinson, D. P., Paganelli, F., & Dworzynski, K. (2005). Grammatical gender effects on cognition: Implications for language learning and language use. *Journal of Experimental Psychology: General, 134*, 501–520.

Vihman, M. M. (1985). Language differentiation by the bilingual infant. *Journal of Child Language, 12*, 297–324.

Vihman, M. M. (1996). *Phonological development*. Oxford: Blackwell.

Vinson, B. P. (1999). *Language disorders across the lifespan: An introduction*. San Diego, CA: Singular Publishing Group.

Vipond, D. (1980). Micro and macroprocesses in text comprehension. *Journal of Verbal Learning and Verbal Behavior, 19*, 276–296.

Vitevitch, M. S. (2002). The influence of phonological similarity neighborhoods on speech production. *Journal of Experimental Psychology: Learning, Memory, and Cognition, 28*, 735–747.

Vitkovitch, M., & Humphreys, G. W. (1991). Perseverant responding in speeded naming of pictures: It's in the links. *Journal of Experimental Psychology: Learning, Memory, and Cognition, 17*, 664–680.

Von Frisch, K. (1950). *Bees, their vision, chemical senses, and language*. Ithaca, NY: Cornell University Press.

Von Frisch, K. (1974). Decoding the language of bees. *Science, 185*, 663–668.

Vu, H., & Kellas, G. (1999). Contextual strength modulates the subordinate bias effect: Reply to Rayner, Binder, and Duffy. *Quarterly Journal of Experimental Psychology, 52A*, 853–855.

Vu, H., Kellas, G., & Paul, S. T. (1998). Sources of sentence constraint on lexical ambiguity resolution. *Memory and Cognition, 26*, 979–1001.

Vygotsky, L. (1934). *Thought and language* (Trans. E. Hanfman & G. Vakar, 1962). Cambridge, MA: MIT Press.

Waldrop, M. M. (1992). *Complexity: The emerging science at the edge of order and chaos*. London: Penguin Books.

Wales, R. J., & Campbell, R. (1970). On the development of comparison and the comparison of development. In G. B. Flores d'Arcais & W. J. M. Levelt (Eds.), *Advances in psycholinguistics* (pp. 373–396). Amsterdam: North Holland.

Walker, C. H., & Yekovich, F. R. (1987). Activation and use of script-based antecedents in anaphoric reference. *Journal of Memory and Language, 26*, 673–691.

Walker, S. (1987). Review of Gavagai! or the future history of the animal language controversy, by David Premack. *Mind and Language, 2*, 326–332.

Wall, R. (1972). *Introduction to mathematical linguistics.* Englewood Cliffs, NJ: Prentice Hall.

Wanner, E. (1980). The ATN and the sausage machine: Which one is baloney? *Cognition, 8*, 209–225.

Ward, J. (2010). *The student's guide to cognitive neuroscience* (2nd ed.). Hove, UK: Psychology Press.

Wardlow Lane, L., Groisman, M., & Ferreira, V. S. (2006). Don't talk about pink elephants! *Psychological Science, 17*, 273–277.

Warren, C., & Morton, J. (1982). The effects of priming on picture recognition. *British Journal of Psychology, 73*, 117–129.

Warren, R. M. (1970). Perceptual restoration of missing speech sounds. *Science, 167*, 392–393.

Warren, R. M., Obusek, C. J., Farmer, R. M., & Warren, R. P. (1969). Auditory sequence: Confusion of patterns other than speech or music. *Science, 164*, 586–587.

Warren, R. M., & Warren, R. P. (1970). Auditory illusions and confusions. *Scientific American, 223*, 30–36.

Warrington, E. K. (1975). The selective impairment of semantic memory. *Quarterly Journal of Experimental Psychology, 27*, 635–657.

Warrington, E. K. (1981). Concrete word dyslexia. *British Journal of Psychology, 72*, 175–196.

Warrington, E. K., & Cipolotti, L. (1996). Word comprehension: The distinction between refractory and storage impairments. *Brain, 119*, 611–625.

Warrington, E. K., & Crutch, S. J. (2004). A circumscribed refractory access disorder: A verbal semantic impairment sparing visual semantics. *Cognitive Neuropsychology, 21*, 299–315.

Warrington, E. K., & McCarthy, R. (1983). Category specific access dysphasia. *Brain, 106*, 859–878.

Warrington, E. K., & McCarthy, R. (1987). Categories of knowledge: Further fractionation and an attempted integration. *Brain, 110*, 1273–1296.

Warrington, E. K., & Shallice, T. (1969). The selective impairment of auditory verbal short-term memory. *Brain, 92*, 885–896.

Warrington, E. K., & Shallice, T. (1979). Semantic access dyslexia. *Brain, 102*, 43–63.

Warrington, E. K., & Shallice, T. (1984). Category-specific semantic impairments. *Brain, 107*, 829–854.

Wason, P. C. (1965). The contexts of plausible denial. *Journal of Verbal Learning and Verbal Behavior, 4*, 7–11.

Waters, G. S., & Caplan, D. (1996). The capacity theory of sentence comprehension: Critique of Just and Carpenter (1992). *Psychological Review, 103*, 761–772.

Waters, G. S., Caplan, D., & Hildebrandt, N. (1991). On the structure of verbal short-term memory and its functional role in sentence comprehension: Evidence from neuropsychology. *Cognitive Neuropsychology, 8*, 81–126.

Watkins, K. E., Dronkers, N. F., & Vargha-Khadem, F. (2002). Behavioural analysis of an inherited speech and language disorder: Comparison with acquired aphasia. *Brain, 125*, 452–464.

Watkins, K. E., & Paus, T. (2004). Modulation of motor excitability during speech perception: The role of Broca's area. *Journal of Cognitive Neuroscience, 16*, 978–987.

Watson, J. B. (1913). Psychology as the behaviorist views it. *Psychological Review, 20*, 158–177.

Watts, D. (2012). *Why everything is obvious (once you know the answer).* New York: Atlantic Books.

Waxman, S. R. (1999). Specifying the scope of 13-month-olds' expectations for novel words. *Cognition, 70*, B35–B50.

Waxman, S. R., & Booth, A. E. (2001). Seeing pink elephants: Fourteen-month-olds' interpretations of novel nouns and adjectives. *Cognitive Psychology, 43*, 217–242.

Waxman, S. R., & Markow, D. B. (1995). Words as invitations to form categories: Evidence from 12- to 13-month-old infants. *Cognitive Psychology, 29*, 257–303.

Weekes, B. S. (1997). Differential effects of number of letters on word and nonword naming latency. *Quarterly Journal of Experimental Psychology, 50A*, 439–456.

Weizenbaum, J. (1966). ELIZA: A computer program for the study of natural language communication between man and machine. *Communications of the Association for Computing Machinery, 9*, 36–45.

Werker, J., & Curtin, S. (2005). PRIMIR: A developmental framework of infant speech processing. *Language Learning and Development, 1*, 197–234.

Werker, J. F., & Tees, R. C. (1983). Developmental changes across childhood in the perception of non-native speech sounds. *Canadian Journal of Psychology, 37*, 278–286.

Werker, J. F., & Tees, R. C. (1984). Crosslanguage speech development: Evidence for perceptual reorganization during the first year of life. *Infant Behavior and Development, 7*, 49–63.

Werker, J. F., & Yeung, H. H. (2005). Infant speech perception bootstraps word learning. *Trends in Cognitive Sciences, 9*, 519–527.

West, R. F., & Stanovich, K. E. (1978). Automatic contextual facilitation in readers of three ages. *Child Development, 49*, 717–727.

West, R. F., & Stanovich, K. E. (1982). Source of inhibition in experiments on the effect of sentence context on word recognition. *Journal of Experimental Psychology: Learning, Memory, and Cognition, 8*, 385–399.

West, R. F., & Stanovich, K. E. (1986). Robust effects of syntactic structure on visual word processing. *Memory and Cognition, 14*, 104–112.

Wexler, K. (1998). Very early parameter setting and the unique checking constraint: A new explanation of the optional infinitive stage. *Lingua, 106*, 23–79.

Whaley, C. P. (1978). Word–nonword classification time. *Journal of Verbal Learning and Verbal Behavior, 17*, 143–154.

Wheeldon, L. (Ed.). (2000). *Aspects of language production*. Hove, UK: Psychology Press.

Wheeldon, L., & Lahiri, A. (1997). Prosodic units in speech production. *Journal of Memory and Language, 37*, 356–381.

Wheeldon, L. R., & Monsell, S. (1992). The locus of repetition priming of spoken word production. *Quarterly Journal of Experimental Psychology, 44A*, 723–761.

Wheeler, D. (1970). Processes in word recognition. *Cognitive Psychology, 1*, 59–85.

Whittlesea, B. W. A. (1987). Preservation of specific experiences in the representation of general knowledge. *Journal of Experimental Psychology: Learning, Memory, and Cognition, 13*, 3–17.

Whorf, B. L. (1956a). *Language, thought, and reality: Selected writings of Benjamin Lee Whorf*. New York: Wiley.

Whorf, B. L. (1956b). Science and linguistics. In J. B. Carroll (Ed.), *Language, thought and reality: Selected writings of Benjamin Lee Whorf* (pp. 207–219). Cambridge, MA: MIT Press. [Originally published 1940.]

Wickelgren, W. A. (1969). Context-sensitive coding, associative memory, and serial order in (speech) behavior. *Psychological Review, 76*, 1–15.

Wierzbicka, A. (2004). Conceptual primes in human languages and their analogues in animal communication and cognition. *Language Sciences, 26*, 413–441.

Wilding, J. (1990). Developmental dyslexics do not fit in boxes: Evidence from the case studies. *European Journal of Cognitive Psychology, 2*, 97–131.

Wilensky, R. (1983). Story grammars versus story points. *Behavioral and Brain Sciences, 6*, 579–623.

Wilkes, A. L. (1997). *Knowledge in minds: Individual and collective processes in cognition*. Hove, UK: Psychology Press.

Wilkins, A. J. (1971). Conjoint frequency, category size, and categorization time. *Journal of Verbal Learning and Verbal Behavior, 10*, 382–385.

Wilkins, A. J., & Neary, G. (1991). Some visual, optometric and perceptual effects of coloured glasses. *Ophthalmic and Physiological Optics, 11*, 163–171.

Wilks, Y. (1976). Parsing English II. In E. Charniak & Y. Wilks (Eds.), *Computational semantics* (pp. 155–184). Amsterdam: North Holland.

Willems, R. M., & Casasanto, D. (2011). Flexibility in embodied language understanding. *Frontiers in Psychology, 2*, 1–11.

Williams, J. N. (1988). Constraints upon semantic activation during sentence comprehension. *Language and Cognitive Processes, 3*, 165–206.

Williams, P. C., & Parkin, A. J. (1980). On knowing the meaning of words we are unable to report—confirmation of a guessing explanation. *Quarterly Journal of Experimental Psychology, 32*, 101–107.

Wilshire, C. E., & Saffran, E. M. (2005). Contrasting effects of phonological priming in aphasic word production. *Cognition, 95*, 31–71.

Wilson, M., & Wilson, T. P. (2005). An oscillator model of the timing of turn-taking. *Psychonomic Bulletin and Review, 12*, 957–968.

Wingfield, A., & Klein, J. F. (1971). Syntactic structure and acoustic pattern in speech perception. *Perception and Psychophysics, 9*, 23–25.

Winner, E., & Gardner, H. (1977). The comprehension of metaphor in brain-damaged patients. *Brain, 100*, 717–729.

Winnick, W. A., & Daniel, S. A. (1970). Two kinds of response priming in tachistoscopic recognition. *Journal of Experimental Psychology, 84*, 74–81.

Winograd, T. A. (1972). *Understanding natural language*. New York: Academic Press.

Wisniewski, E. J. (1997). When concepts combine. *Psychonomic Bulletin and Review, 4*, 167–183.

Wisniewski, E. J., & Love, B. C. (1998). Relations versus properties in conceptual combination. *Journal of Memory and Language, 38*, 177–202.

Wittgenstein, L. (1953). *Philosophical investigations* (Trans. G. E. M. Anscombe). Oxford: Blackwell.

Wittgenstein, L. (1958). *The blue and brown books*. Oxford: Blackwell.

Woodruff-Pak, D. S. (1997). *The neuropsychology of aging*. Oxford: Blackwell.

Woods, B. T., & Carey, S. (1979). Language deficits after apparent clinical recovery from childhood aphasia. *Annals of Neurology, 6*, 405–409.

Woods, B. T., & Teuber, H.-L. (1973). Early onset of complementary specialization of cerebral hemispheres in man. *Transactions of the American Neurological Association, 98*, 113–117.

Woods, W. A. (1975). What's in a link? Foundations for semantic networks. In D. G. Bobrow & A. M. Collins (Eds.), *Representation and understanding: Studies in cognitive science* (pp. 35–82). New York: Academic Press.

Woodward, A. L., & Markman, E. M. (1998). Early word learning. In W. Damon, D. Kuhn, & R. S. Siegler (Eds.), *Handbook of child psychology* (Vol. 2, 5th ed., pp. 371–420). New York: Wiley.

Woodworth, R. S. (1938). *Experimental psychology*. New York: Holt.

Wright, B., & Garrett, M. (1984). Lexical decision in sentences: Effects of syntactic structure. *Memory and Cognition, 12*, 31–45.

Wydell, T. K., Patterson, K. E., & Humphreys, G. W. (1993). Phonologically mediated access to meaning for kanji: Is rows still a rose in Japanese kanji? *Journal of Experimental Psychology: Learning, Memory, and Cognition, 19*, 1082–1093.

Xu, F. (2002). The role of language in acquiring object kind concepts in infancy. *Cognition, 85*, 223–250.

Yamada, J. E. (1990). *Laura: A case for the modularity of language*. Cambridge, MA: MIT Press.

Yekovich, F. R., & Thorndyke, P. W. (1981). An evaluation of alternative models of narrative schema. *Journal of Verbal Learning and Verbal Behavior, 20*, 454–469.

Yngve, V. (1970). On getting a word in edgewise. *Papers from the Sixth Regional Meeting of the Chicago Linguistic Society, 6*, 567–577.

Yopp, H. K. (1988). The validity and reliability of phonemic awareness tests. *Reading Research Quarterly, 23*, 159–177.

Yuill, N., & Oakhill, J. (1991). *Children's problems in text comprehension*. Cambridge: Cambridge University Press.

Zagar, D., Pynte, J., & Rativeau, S. (1997). Evidence for early closure attachment on first-pass reading times in French. *Quarterly Journal of Experimental Psychology, 50A*, 421–438.

Zaidel, E., & Peters, A. M. (1981). Phonological encoding and ideographic reading by the disconnected right hemisphere. *Brain and Language, 14*, 205–234.

Zevin, J. D., & Balota, D. A. (2000). Priming and attentional control of lexical and sublexical pathways during naming. *Journal of Experimental Psychology: Learning, Memory, and Cognition, 26*, 121–135.

Zevin, J. D., & Seidenberg, M. S. (2002). Age of acquisition effects in word reading and other tasks. *Journal of Memory and Language, 47*, 1–29.

Zevin, J. D., & Seidenberg, M. S. (2006). Simulating consistency effects and individual difference in nonword naming: A comparison of current models. *Journal of Memory and Language, 54*, 145–160.

Zhuang, J., Randall, B., Stamatakis, E. A., Marslen-Wilson, W. D., & Tyler, L. K. (2011). The interaction of lexical semantics and cohort competition in spoken word recognition: An fMRI study. *Journal of Cognitive Neuroscience, 23*, 3778–3790.

Ziegler, J. C., & Goswami, U. (2005). Reading acquisition, developmental dyslexia, and skilled reading across languages: A psycholinguistic grain size theory. *Psychological Bulletin, 131*, 3–29.

Ziegler, J. C., Muneaux, M., & Grainger, J. (2003). Neighborhood effects in auditory word recognition: Phonological competition and orthographic facilitation. *Journal of Memory and Language, 48*, 779–793.

Ziegler, J. C., Perry, C., Jacobs, A. M., & Braun, M. (2001). Identical words are read differently in different languages. *Psychological Science, 12*, 379–384.

Zorzi, M., Barbierob, A., Facoettia, C., & Ziegler, J. C. (2012). Extra-large letter spacing improves reading in dyslexia. *Proceedings of the National Academy of Science USA, 109*, 11455–11459.

Zurif, E. B., Caramazza, A., Myerson, P., & Galvin, J. (1974). Semantic feature representations for normal and aphasic language. *Brain and Language, 1*, 167–187.

Zurif, E. B., & Grodzinsky, Y. (1983). Sensitivity to grammatical structure in agrammatic aphasics: A reply to Linebarger, Schwartz, & Saffran. *Cognition, 15*, 207–214.

Zwaan, R. A., & Madden, C. J. (2004). Updating situation models. *Journal of Experimental Psychology: Learning, Memory, and Cognition, 30*, 283–288.

Zwaan, R. A., Magliano, J. P., & Graesser, A. C. (1995). Dimensions of situation model construction in narrative comprehension. *Journal of Experimental Psychology: Learning, Memory, and Cognition, 21*, 386–397.

Zwaan, R. A., & Radvansky, G. A. (1998). Situation models in language comprehension and memory. *Psychological Bulletin, 123*, 162–185.

Zwitserlood, P. (1989). The locus of the effects of sentential-semantic context in spoken-word processing. *Cognition, 32*, 25–64.

AUTHOR INDEX

SUBJECT INDEX

Italic page numbers indicate tables; **bold** numbers indicate figures, pictures and text boxes.